RAND McNALLY

Cleveland
street guide

TELL US WHAT YOU THINK
comment card on last page

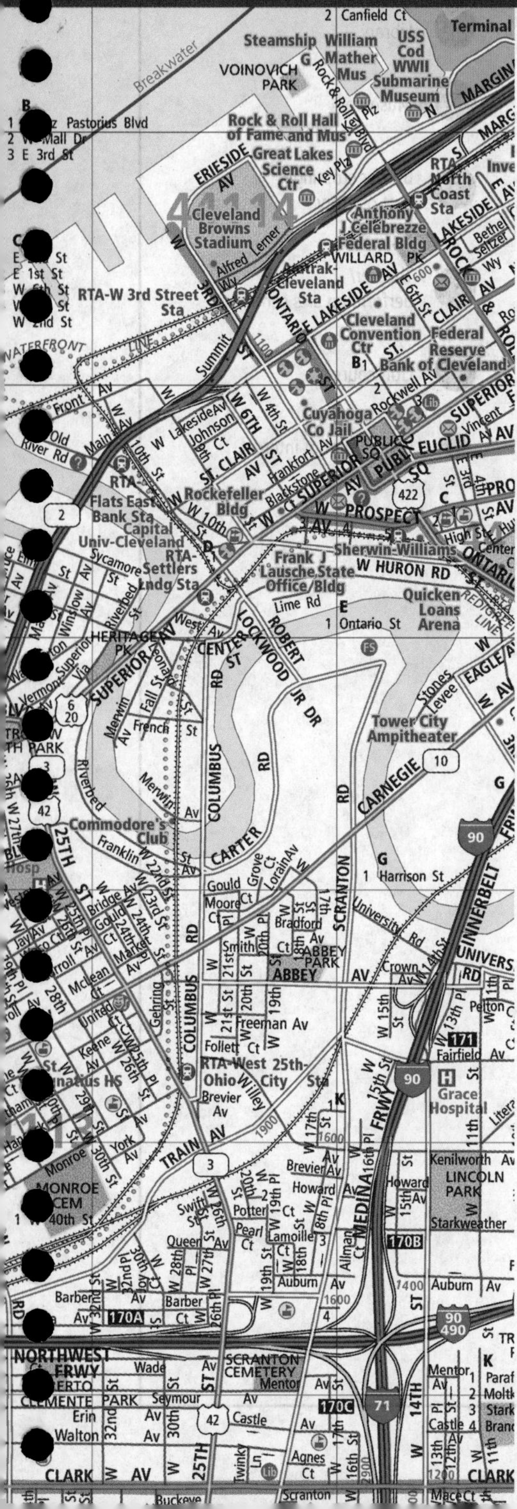

Steamship William G Mather Mus
USS Cod WWII Submarine Museum
VOINOVICH PARK
Rock & Roll Hall of Fame and Mus
Great Lakes Science Ctr
Cleveland Browns Stadium
Anthony J. Celebrezze Federal Bldg
Amtrak-Cleveland Sta
Cleveland Convention Ctr
Federal Reserve Bank of Cleveland
RTA-W 3rd Street Sta
Cuyahoga Co Jail
PUBLIC SQ
EUCLID AV
SUPERIOR AV
PROSPECT AV
Rockefeller Bldg
Flats East Bank Sta
Sherwin-Williams Center
Frank J Lausche State Office Bldg
W HURON RD
Quicken Loans Arena
Tower City Ampitheater
CARNEGIE AV
Commodore's Club
Grace Hospital
LINCOLN PARK
MONROE CEM
SCRANTON CEMETERY
CLARK AV

Contents

Introduction

Using Your Street Guide	A
PageFinder™ Map	B
Legend	D
We've Got You Covered	E

Maps

Downtown Map	F
Street Guide Detail Maps	1842-3161
Vicinity Map	Inside back cover

Lists and Indexes

Cities & Communities Index	1
List of Abbreviations	2
Street Index and Points of Interest Index	3
Comment Card	Last page

PageFinder™ Map U.S. Patent No. 5,419,586
Canadian Patent No. 2,116,425
Patente Mexicana No. 188186

RAND McNALLY
Rand McNally Consumer Affairs
P.O. Box 7600
Chicago, IL 60680-9915
randmcnally.com
For comments or suggestions, please call (800) 777-MAPS (-6277)
or email us at:
consumeraffairs@randmcnally.com

NAVTEQ ON BOARD™

Legend

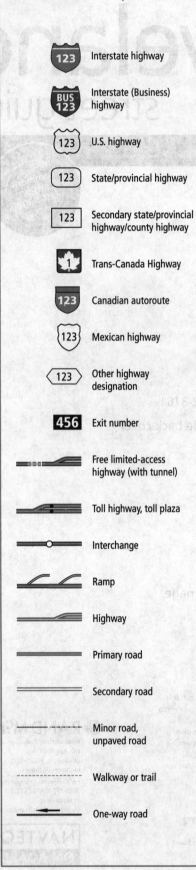

- 123 Interstate highway
- BUS 123 Interstate (Business) highway
- 123 U.S. highway
- 123 State/provincial highway
- 123 Secondary state/provincial highway/county highway
- 1 Trans-Canada Highway
- 123 Canadian autoroute
- 123 Mexican highway
- 123 Other highway designation
- 456 Exit number
- Free limited-access highway (with tunnel)
- Toll highway, toll plaza
- Interchange
- Ramp
- Highway
- Primary road
- Secondary road
- Minor road, unpaved road
- Walkway or trail
- One-way road
- Ferry, waterway
- Levee
- Trolley
- Railroad, station, mass transit line
- Bus station
- Park and ride
- Rest area, service area
- Airport
- 1200 Block number
- International boundary, state boundary
- County boundary
- Township/range boundary, section corner
- 12345 ZIP code boundary, ZIP code
- 45°33'30" 90°33'30" Latitude, longitude
- Hospital
- School
- University or college
- Information/visitor center/welcome center
- Police/sheriff, etc.
- Fire station
- City/town/village hall and other government buildings
- Courthouse
- Post office
- Library
- Museum
- Border crossing/Port of entry
- Theater/performing arts center
- Golf course
- Other point of interest

we've got you COVERED

Rand McNally's broad selection of products is perfect for your every need. Whether you're looking for the convenience of write-on wipe-off laminated maps, extra maps for every car, or a Road Atlas to plan your next vacation or to use as a reference, Rand McNally has you covered.

Street Guides

Ohio Road Atlas
Cincinnati
Cleveland
Columbus
Dayton
Toledo/ Bowling Green

Road Atlases

Road Atlas
Road Atlas & Travel Guide
Large Scale Road Atlas
Midsize Road Atlas
Deluxe Midsize Road Atlas
Pocket Road Atlas

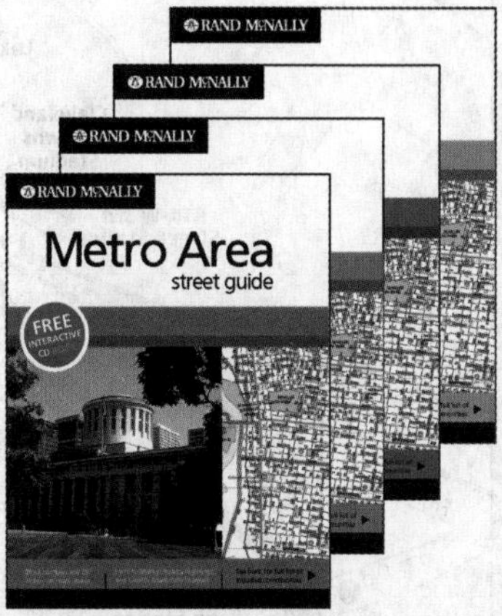
RAND MCNALLY
RAND MCNALLY
RAND MCNALLY
RAND MCNALLY
Metro Area
street guide
FREE

Folded Maps

EasyFinder® Laminated Maps

Ohio
Akron
Canton
Cincinnati/ Dayton Regional
Cleveland
Columbus
Columbus & Vicinity Regional
Dayton
Toledo
Youngstown

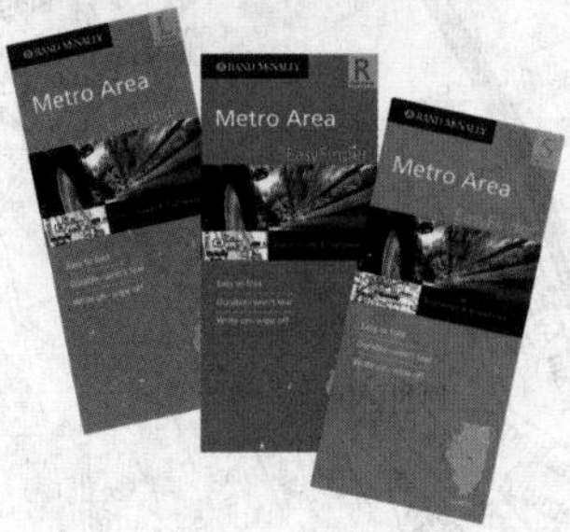
Metro Area
Metro Area
Metro Area

Paper Maps

Ohio
Akron
Butler County
Canton/ Massillon
Clermont County
Cleveland/ Cuyahoga County
Columbus
Dayton
Greater Cincinnati
Hamilton/ Middletown/ Fairfield/ Mason
Lima/ Findlay/ Marion/ Mansfield
Northeast Ohio Regional
Sandusky
Toledo
Vermillion/ Lorain/ Elyria/ Avon
Youngstown/ Warren

Wherever Rand McNally products are sold or at
www.randmcnally.com

Downtown Cleveland

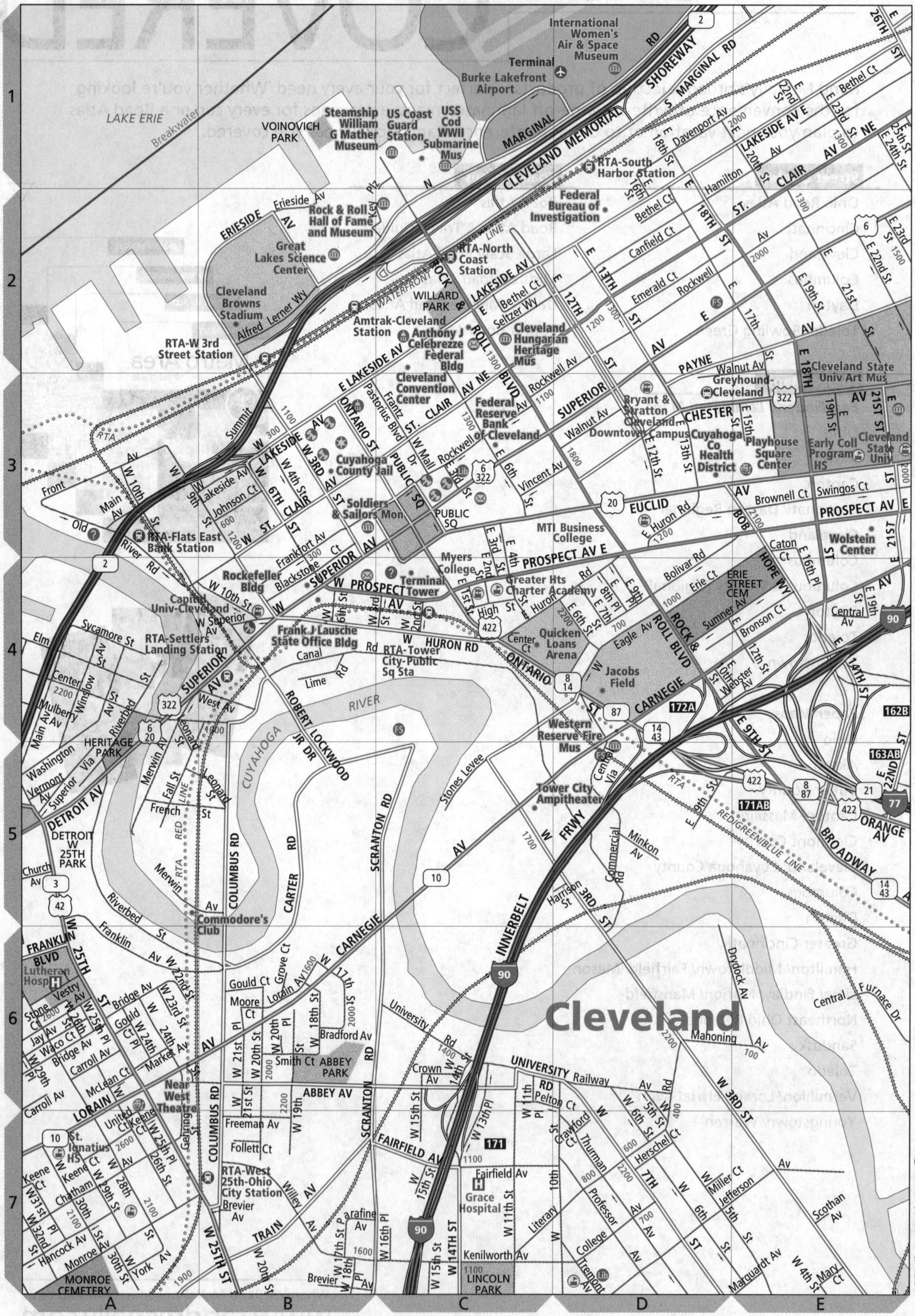
LAKE ERIE
Breakwater
International Women's Air & Space Museum
Terminal
Burke Lakefront Airport
VOINOVICH PARK
Steamship William G Mather Museum
US Coast Guard Station
USS Cod WWII Submarine Mus
SHOREWAY
CLEVELAND MEMORIAL
S MARGINAL RD
MARGINAL
RTA-South Harbor Station
Federal Bureau of Investigation
ERIESIDE AV
Erieside Av
Rock & Roll Hall of Fame and Museum
Great Lakes Science Center
RTA-North Coast Station
Cleveland Browns Stadium
Alfred Lerner Wy
WILLARD PARK
Amtrak-Cleveland Station
Anthony J Celebrezze Federal Bldg
Cleveland Hungarian Heritage Mus
RTA-W 3rd Street Station
Cleveland Convention Center
Federal Reserve Bank of Cleveland
Bryant & Stratton Cleveland Downtown Campus
Greyhound-Cleveland
PAYNE
CHESTER
SUPERIOR
Cuyahoga Co Health District
Playhouse Square Center
Cleveland State Univ Art Mus
Early Coll Program HS
Cleveland State Univ
Cuyahoga County Jail
Soldiers & Sailors Mon
PUBLIC SQ
EUCLID
PROSPECT AV
MTI Business College
Wolstein Center
RTA-Flats East Bank Station
Rockefeller Bldg
Myers College
Terminal Tower
Greater Hts Charter Academy
ERIE STREET CEM
Capital Univ-Cleveland
RTA-Settlers Landing Station
Frank J Lausche State Office Bldg
RTA-Tower City-Public Sq Sta
HURON RD
Quicken Loans Arena
Jacobs Field
CARNEGIE
ROCK & ROLL BLVD
HOPE WY
ONTARIO
HERITAGE PARK
CUYAHOGA
RIVER
ROBERT LOCKWOOD JR DR
Western Reserve Fire Mus
Tower City Ampitheater
DETROIT AV
DETROIT W 25TH PARK
Commodore's Club
COLUMBUS RD
CARTER RD
SCRANTON RD
INNERBELT FRWY
BROADWAY
ORANGE AV
REDGREENBLUE LINE
FRANKLIN BLVD
Lutheran Hosp
W 25TH ST
LORAIN AV
Near West Theatre
ABBEY PARK
ABBEY AV
UNIVERSITY
Cleveland
St. Ignatius HS
RTA-West 25th-Ohio City Station
FAIRFIELD AV
Grace Hospital
TRAIN AV
W 14TH ST
Kenilworth Av
LINCOLN PARK
MONROE CEMETERY
W 3RD ST
Central
Furnace Dr
Mahoning Av
Scothan Av
A
B
C
D
E
1
2
3
4
5
6
7
RAND McNALLY

Note: This grid references this map only

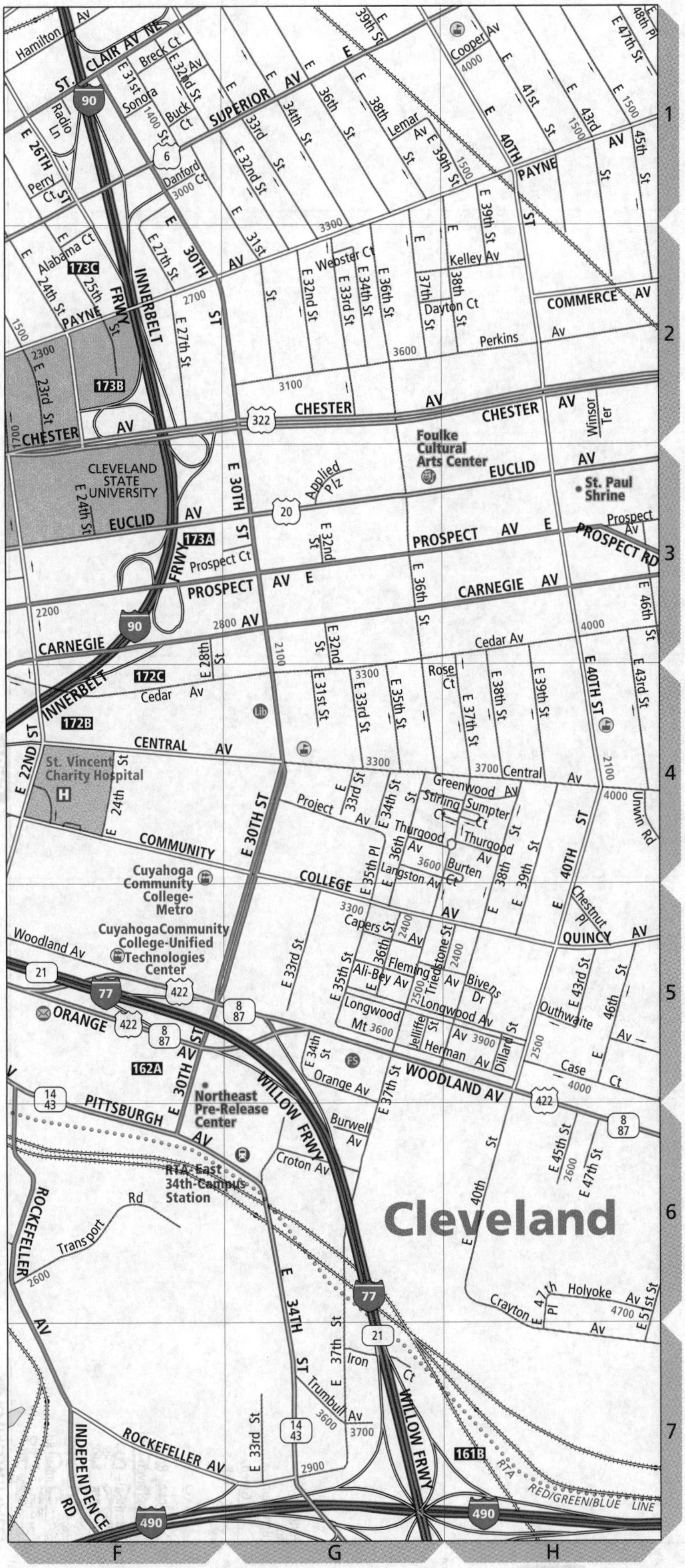

Cleveland
ST. CLAIR AV NE
SUPERIOR AV
PAYNE AV
COMMERCE AV
Perkins Av
CHESTER AV
EUCLID AV
PROSPECT AV
CARNEGIE AV
Cedar Av
CENTRAL AV
COMMUNITY COLLEGE AV
QUINCY AV
Woodland Av
ORANGE AV
WOODLAND AV
PITTSBURGH AV
ROCKEFELLER AV
INDEPENDENCE RD
INNERBELT FRWY
WILLOW FRWY
E 30TH ST
E 40TH ST
E 34TH ST
E 22ND ST
Foulke Cultural Arts Center
St. Paul Shrine
CLEVELAND STATE UNIVERSITY
St. Vincent Charity Hospital
Cuyahoga Community College-Metro
CuyahogaCommunity College-Unified Technologies Center
Northeast Pre-Release Center
RTA-East 34th-Campus Station
RTA RED/GREEN/BLUE LINE
173C
173B
173A
172C
172B
162A
161B
1
2
3
4
5
6
7
F
G
H

Points of Interest

Abbey Park	B6
Anthony J Celebrezze Federal Building	C2
Bryant & Stratton Cleveland Downtown Campus	D3
Burke Lakefront Airport	C1
Capital University-Cleveland	A4
Carl B Stokes United States Court House	B4
Cleveland Browns Stadium	B2
Cleveland City Hall	C2
Cleveland Convention Center	C3
Cleveland Hungarian Heritage Museum	C2
Cleveland Municipal Court	B3
Cleveland Police	B3
Cleveland Post Office	F5
Cleveland Public Library-Main	C3
Cleveland Public Library-Sterling	G4
Cleveland State University	E3
Cleveland State University Art Museum	E2
Commodore's Club	B5
Cuyahoga Community College-Metro	F4
Cuyahoga Community College-Unified Technologies Center	F5
Cuyahoga County Administration Building	B3
Cuyahoga County Court House	B3
Cuyahoga County Health District	D3
Cuyahoga County Jail	B3
Detroit W 25th Park	A5
Erie St Cemetery	D4
Erieview Station Post Office	C2
Federal Bureau of Investigation	D2
Federal Reserve Bank of Cleveland	C3
Foulke Cultural Arts Center	G2
Frank J Lausche State Office Building	B4
Grace Hospital	C7
Great Lakes Science Center	B2
Heritage Park	A5
Howard M Metzenbaum US Courthouse	C3
International Women's Air & Space Museum	D1
Jacobs Field	D4
Jefferson Branch Library	D7
Lincoln Park	C7
Lutheran Hospital	A6
Monroe Cemetery	A7
MTI Business College	C3
Myers College	C4
Near West Theatre	A6
Northeast Pre-Release Center	F5
Playhouse Square Center	E3
Probate Court of Cuyahoga County	B3
Public Square	C3
Public Square Station Post Office	C3
Quicken Loans Arena	C4
Rock & Roll Hall of Fame and Museum	B2
Rockefeller Building	B4
Soldiers & Sailors Monument	B3
St. Paul Shrine	H3
St. Vincent Charity Hospital	F4
Steamship William G Mather Museum	B1
Terminal Tower	C4
Tower City Ampitheater	C5
Tower City Retail Post Office	B4
United States Bankruptcy Court	C3
United States Court of Appeals	C3
US Coast Guard Station	C1
USS Cod WWII Submarine Museum	C1
Visitor Center	A3
Voinovich Park	B1
Western Reserve Fire Museum	D4
Willard Park	C2
Wolstein Center	E3

1 in. = 1400 ft.

0 0.25 0.5

miles

1:24,000
1 in. = 2000 ft.
0 0.25 0.5
miles

SEE B MAP

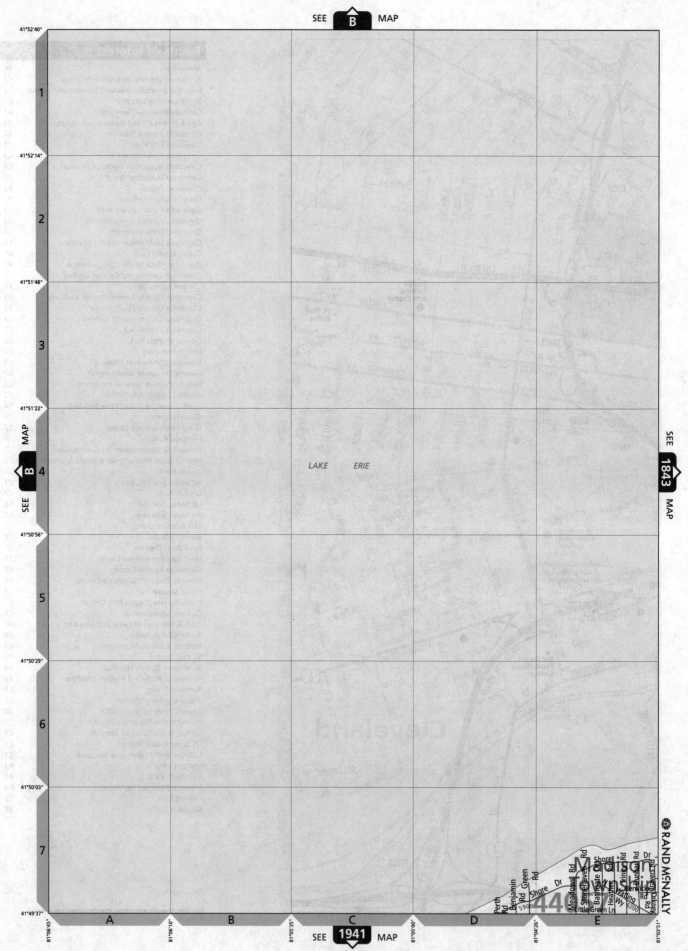
41°52'40"
41°52'14"
41°51'48"
41°51'22"
41°50'56"
41°50'29"
41°50'03"
41°49'37"
1
2
3
4
5
6
7
A
B
C
D
E
81°06'45"
81°06'10"
81°05'35"
81°05'00"
81°04'26"
81°03'51"
LAKE ERIE
Madison Township
44057
Perth Rd
Benjamin Rd
Green Rd
Shore Dr
5900
Meadows Rd
Stonehaven Rd
Bathgate Dr
Wy
Heather Wy
Little Green Ln
Rd
Trinity Rd
Watling
6200
Dunbar Rd
Berwick Rd
Dr
Travers Rd
Orkney Rd

SEE B MAP

SEE 1843 MAP

SEE 1941 MAP

1:24,000
1 in. = 2000 ft.
0 0.25 0.5
miles

SEE B MAP

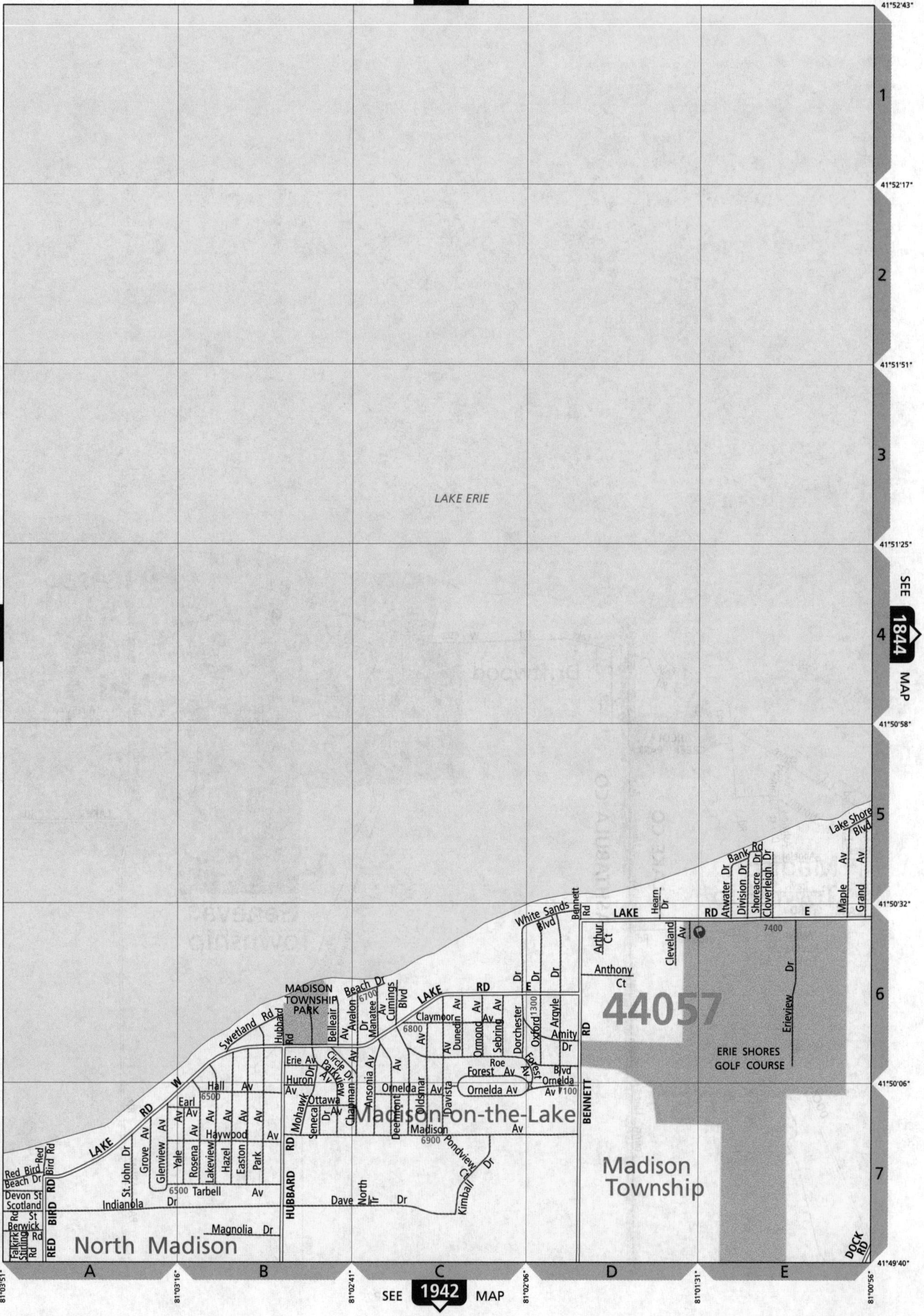
LAKE ERIE
MADISON TOWNSHIP PARK
Madison-on-the-Lake
North Madison
Madison Township
44057
ERIE SHORES GOLF COURSE
LAKE RD W
LAKE RD
LAKE RD E
BENNETT RD
HUBBARD RD
RED BIRD RD
DOCK RD
Swetland Rd
Hubbard Rd
Beach Dr
White Sands Blvd
Bennett Rd
Hearn Dr
Atwater Dr
Bank Rd
Division Dr
Shoreacre Dr
Cloverleigh Dr
Maple Av
Grand Av
Lake Shore Blvd
Arthur Ct
Cleveland Av
Anthony Ct
Erieview Dr
7400
Red Bird Rd
Beach Dr
Devon St
Scotland Rd
Berwick St
Stirling Rd
Falkirk Rd
St. John Dr
Grove Av
Glenview Av
Yale Av
Rosena Av
Lakeview Av
Hazel Av
Easton Av
Park Av
Earl Av
Hall Av
Haywood Av
Tarbell Av
6500
Indianola Dr
Magnolia Dr
Dave Dr
North Tr
Kimball Ct
Pondview Dr
Madison Av
6900
Mohawk Dr
Seneca Dr
Ottawa Dr
Huron Dr
Erie Av
Circle Dr
Parkview Dr
Chapman Av
Ansonia Av
Belleair Av
Avalon Dr
Manatee Av
Cumings Blvd
6700
6800
Claymoor Av
Deermont Av
Oldsmar Av
Davista Av
Ornelda Av
Dunedin Av
Ormond Av
Sebring Av
Dorchester Dr
Oxford Dr
1300
Argyle Dr
Amity Dr
Roe Forest Av
Forest Blvd
Ornelda Av
7100
A
B
C
D
E
1
2
3
4
5
6
7
41°52'43"
41°52'17"
41°51'51"
41°51'25"
41°50'58"
41°50'32"
41°50'06"
41°49'40"
81°03'51"
81°03'16"
81°02'41"
81°02'06"
81°01'31"
81°00'56"

SEE 1842 MAP

SEE 1844 MAP

SEE 1942 MAP

1:24,000
1 in. = 2000 ft.
0 0.25 0.5
miles

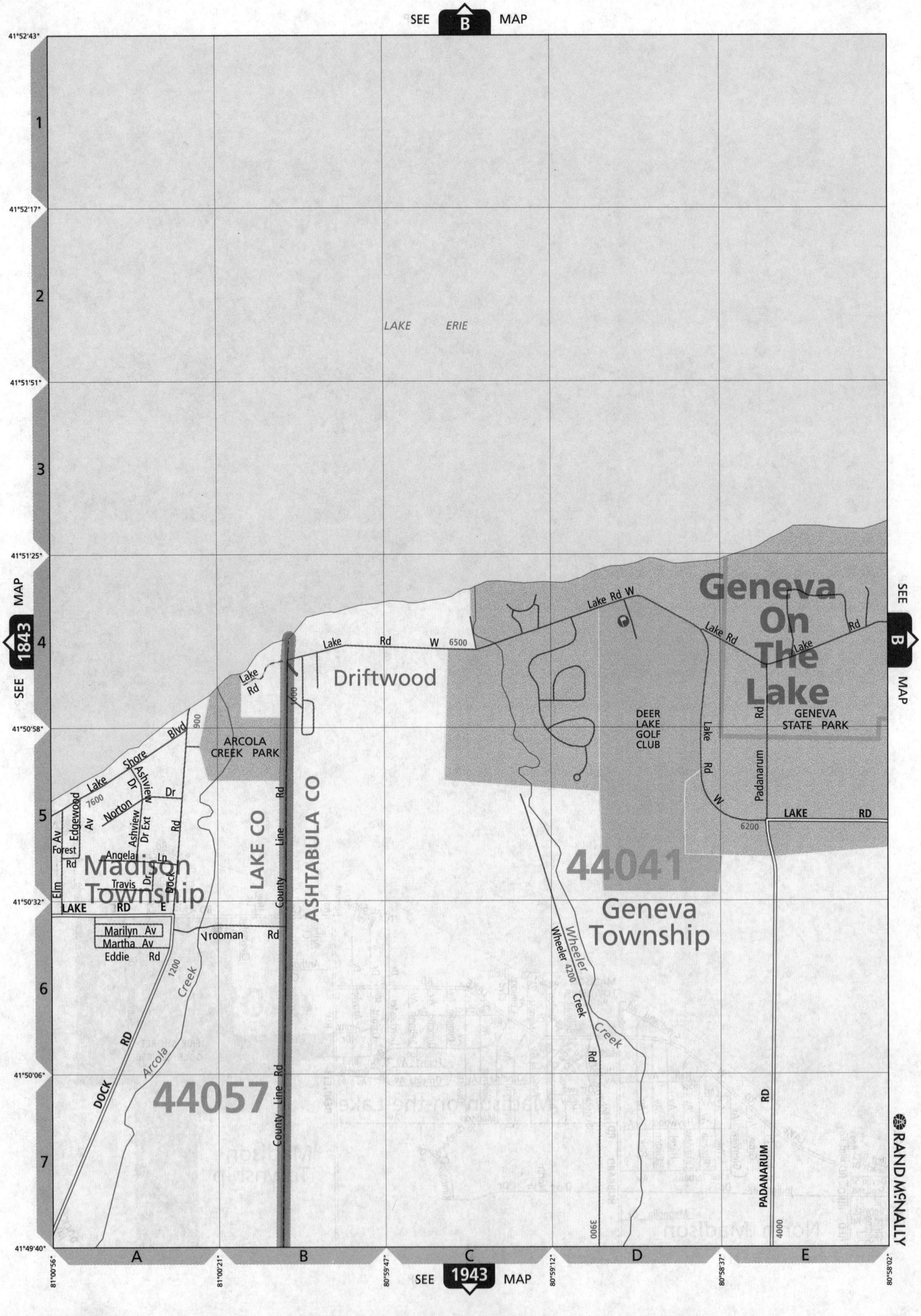
SEE B MAP
SEE 1843 MAP
SEE B MAP
SEE 1943 MAP
LAKE ERIE
Geneva On The Lake
GENEVA STATE PARK
DEER LAKE GOLF CLUB
Driftwood
ARCOLA CREEK PARK
Madison Township
Geneva Township
LAKE CO
ASHTABULA CO
44041
44057
Lake Rd W
Lake Rd W 6500
Lake Rd
Lake Rd W
Padanarum Rd
LAKE RD
6200
Lake Shore Blvd
7600
900
1000
Edgewood Av
Forest Rd
Elm
Norton Dr
Ashview Dr
Ashview Dr Ext
Dock Rd
Angela Ln
Travis Dr
LAKE RD E
Marilyn Av
Martha Av
Eddie Rd
Vrooman Rd
County Line Rd
1200
DOCK RD
Arcola Creek
Wheeler Creek
Wheeler Creek Rd
4200
3900
PADANARUM RD
4000
1
2
3
4
5
6
7
A
B
C
D
E
41°52'43"
41°52'17"
41°51'51"
41°51'25"
41°50'58"
41°50'32"
41°50'06"
41°49'40"
81°00'56"
81°00'21"
80°59'47"
80°59'12"
80°58'37"
80°58'02"
RAND McNALLY

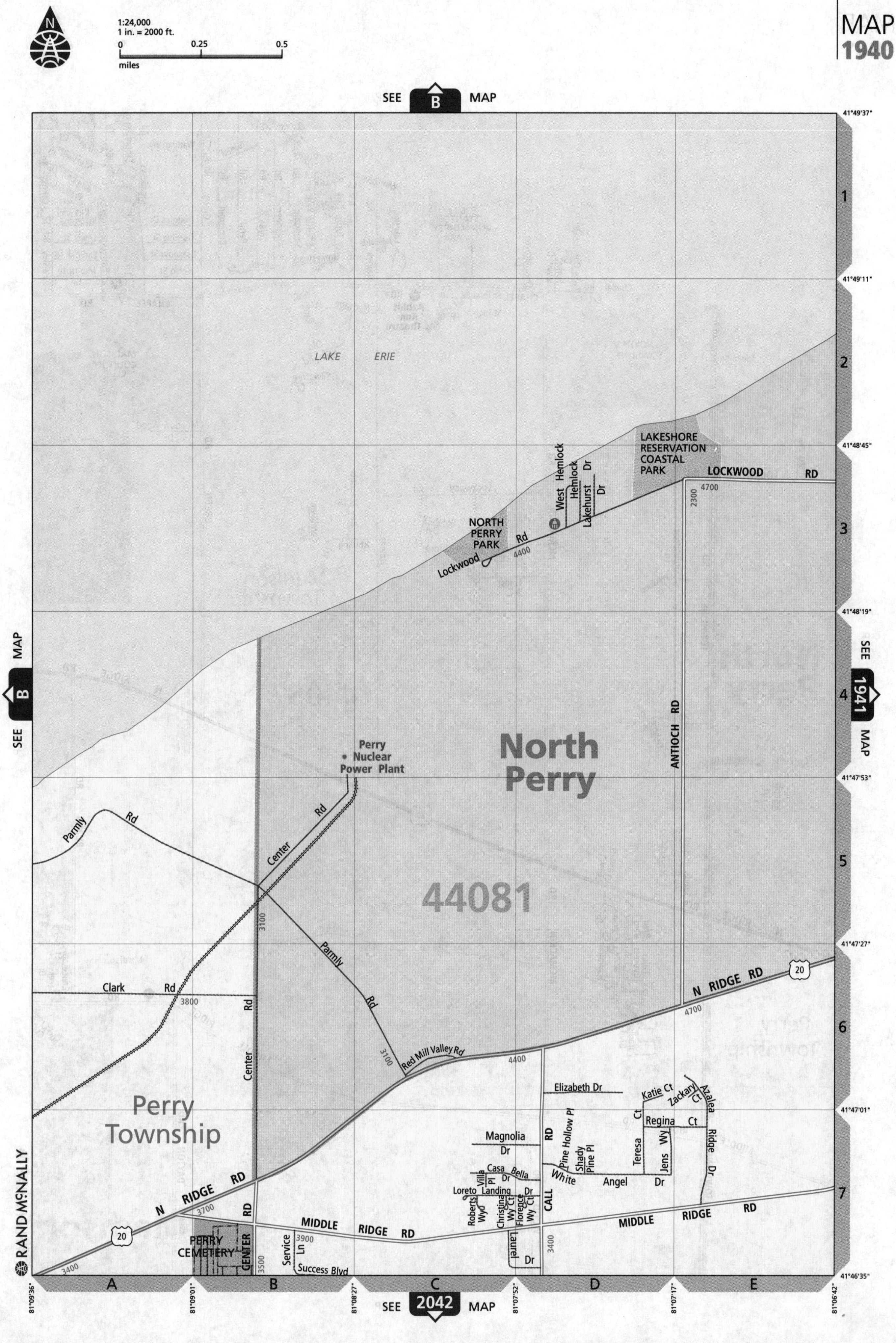
1:24,000
1 in. = 2000 ft.
0 0.25 0.5
miles
SEE B MAP
SEE B MAP
SEE 1941 MAP
SEE 2042 MAP
LAKE ERIE
LAKESHORE RESERVATION COASTAL PARK
LOCKWOOD RD
4700
2300
West Hemlock
Hemlock Dr
Lakehurst Dr
NORTH PERRY PARK
Lockwood Rd
4400
North Perry
44081
ANTIOCH RD
Perry Nuclear Power Plant
Parmly Rd
Center Rd
3100
Clark Rd
3800
N RIDGE RD
20
Red Mill Valley Rd
Elizabeth Dr
Katie Ct
Zackary Ct
Azalea Ridge Dr
Regina Ct
Magnolia Dr
Pine Hollow Pl
Shady Pine Pl
Teresa Ct
Jens Wy
White Angel Dr
Villa Pl
Casa Bella Dr
Loreto Landing Dr
Roberts Wyd
Christina Wy Ct
Florence Wy Ct
CALL RD
3400
Perry Township
N RIDGE RD
3700
3400
MIDDLE RIDGE RD
PERRY CEMETERY
CENTER RD
3500
Service Ln
3900
Success Blvd
Laurel Dr
RAND McNALLY
A B C D E
1 2 3 4 5 6 7
41°49'37"
41°49'11"
41°48'45"
41°48'19"
41°47'53"
41°47'27"
41°47'01"
41°46'35"
81°09'36"
81°09'01"
81°08'27"
81°07'52"
81°07'17"
81°06'42"

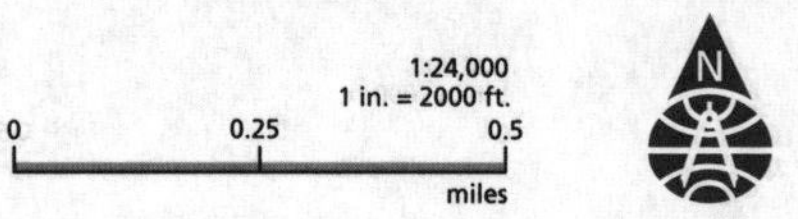
1:24,000
1 in. = 2000 ft.
0
0.25
0.5
miles
N

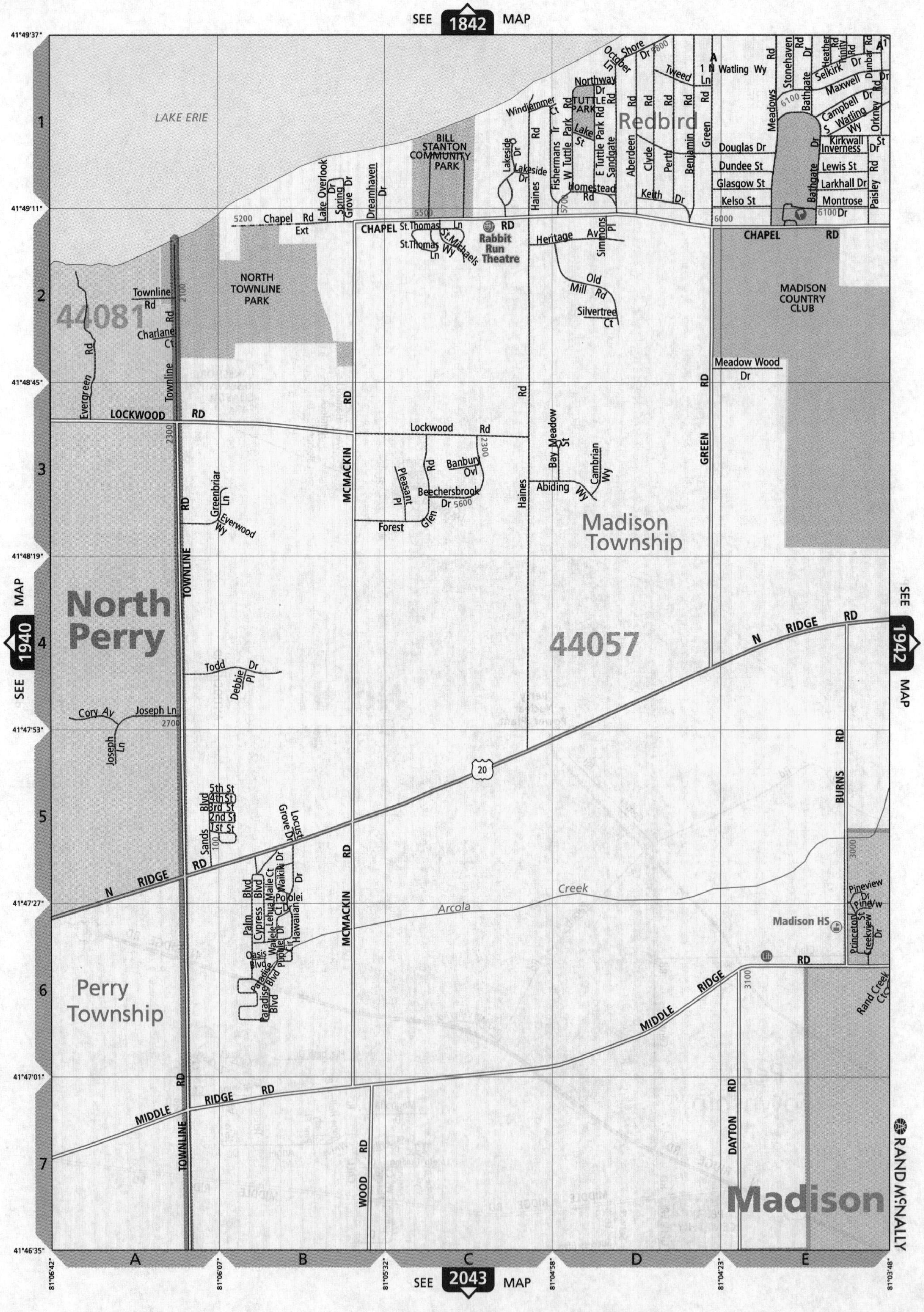
SEE 1842 MAP
SEE 1940 MAP
SEE 1942 MAP
SEE 2043 MAP
LAKE ERIE
BILL STANTON COMMUNITY PARK
NORTH TOWNLINE PARK
TUTTLE PARK
MADISON COUNTRY CLUB
Rabbit Run Theatre
Redbird
44081
44057
North Perry
Madison Township
Perry Township
Madison
Madison HS
CHAPEL RD
LOCKWOOD RD
N RIDGE RD
MIDDLE RIDGE RD
TOWNLINE RD
MCMACKIN RD
GREEN RD
Haines Rd
BURNS RD
DAYTON RD
WOOD RD
20
Chapel Rd Ext
Lake Overlook Dr
Spring Grove Dr
Dreamhaven Dr
St.Thomas Ln
St.Michaels Wy
Heritage Av
Simmons Pl
Old Mill Rd
Silvertree Ct
Windjammer Ct
Lakeside Dr
Fishermans Tr
W Tuttle Park
E Tuttle Park Rd
Lake St
Sandgate Rd
Homestead Rd
Northway Dr
October Ln
Shore Dr
Tweed Ln
N Watling Wy
Aberdeen Rd
Clyde Rd
Perth Rd
Benjamin Rd
Keith Dr
Douglas Dr
Dundee St
Glasgow St
Kelso St
Meadows Rd
Stonehaven Rd
Bathgate Dr
Heather Rd
Selkirk Dr
Dunbar Rd
Maxwell Dr
Campbell Dr
S Watling Wy
Orkney Rd
Kirkwall St
Inverness Dr
Lewis St
Larkhall Dr
Montrose Dr
Paisley Rd
Meadow Wood Dr
Townline Rd
Charlane Ct
Evergreen Rd
Greenbriar Ln
Everwood Wy
Todd Dr
Debbie Pl
Cory Av
Joseph Ln
Lockwood Rd
Banbury Ovl
Pleasant Pl
Beechersbrook Dr
Forest Glen
Bay Meadow St
Cambrian Wy
Abiding Wy
Sands Blvd
5th St
4th St
3rd St
2nd St
1st St
Locust Grove Dr
Palm Blvd
Cypress Blvd
Lehua Ct
Maile Ct
Waikiki Dr
Pololei Dr
Hawaiian Dr
Oasis Blvd
Paradise Blvd
Arcola Creek
Pineview Dr
Pine Vw
Princeton St
Creekview Dr
Rand Creek Ct
RAND McNALLY

1:24,000
1 in. = 2000 ft.
0 0.25 0.5
miles

SEE 1843 MAP

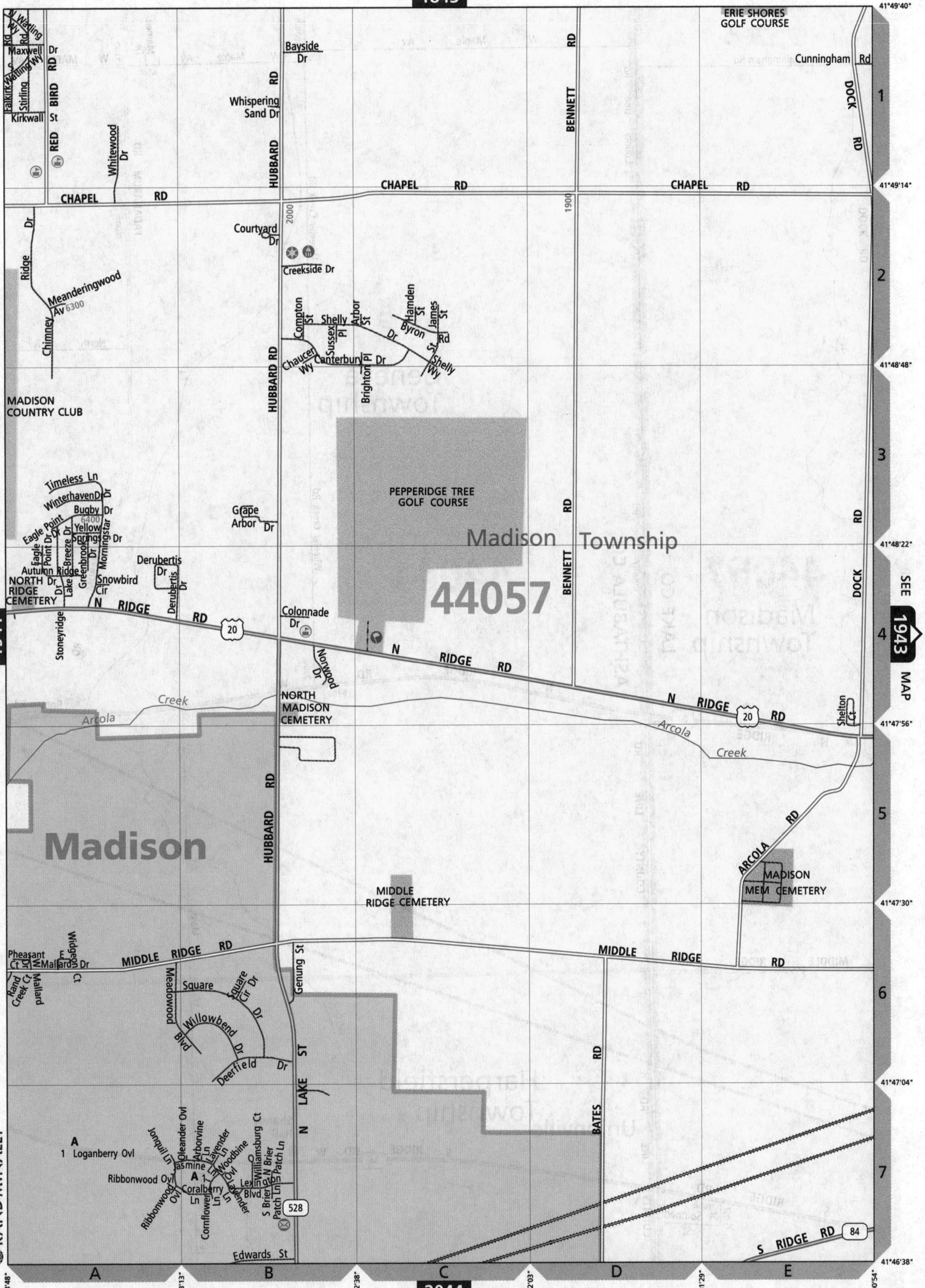
ERIE SHORES GOLF COURSE
Cunningham Rd
Wadling Wy
Maxwell Dr
Watling Wy
Falkirk Rd
Stirling
Kirkwall St
RED BIRD RD
Whitewood Dr
Bayside Dr
Whispering Sand Dr
HUBBARD RD
BENNETT RD
DOCK RD
CHAPEL RD
CHAPEL RD
Courtyard Dr
Creekside Dr
Ridge Dr
Meanderingwood Av
Chimney
Compton St
Shelly Arbor St
Sussex Pl
Hamden St
Byron
James St
Rd
Chaucer Wy
Canterbury Dr
Brighton Pl
Shelly Wy
MADISON COUNTRY CLUB
PEPPERIDGE TREE GOLF COURSE
Madison Township
44057
Timeless Ln
Winterhaven Dr
Bugby Dr
Eagle Point Dr
Yellow Springs Dr
Morningstar Dr
Grape Arbor Dr
Derubertis Dr
Breeze Dr
Greenbrook Dr
Autumn Ridge
Snowbird Cir
NORTH RIDGE CEMETERY
Stoneyridge
N RIDGE RD
20
Colonnade Dr
Norwood Dr
N RIDGE RD
Shelton Ct
Arcola Creek
NORTH MADISON CEMETERY
Arcola Creek
ARCOLA RD
Madison
MIDDLE RIDGE CEMETERY
MADISON MEM CEMETERY
Pheasant Ct
Widgeon Ct
Mallard Dr
Rand Creek Ct
MIDDLE RIDGE RD
Genung St
MIDDLE RIDGE RD
Meadowood
Square Cir Dr
Willowbend Blvd
Deerfield Dr
N LAKE ST
BATES RD
A
1 Loganberry Ovl
Jonquil Ln
Oleander Ovl
Arborvine Ln
Lavender Ln
Jasmine Ln
Woodbine Ovl
Williamsburg Ct
Ribbonwood Ovl
Coralberry Ln
Cornflower Ln
Lexington Blvd
S Brier Patch Ln
N Brier Patch Ln
528
Edwards St
S RIDGE RD
84
A B C D E
1 2 3 4 5 6 7
41°49'40" 41°49'14" 41°48'48" 41°48'22" 41°47'56" 41°47'30" 41°47'04" 41°46'38"
81°03'48" 81°03'13" 81°02'38" 81°02'03" 81°01'29" 81°00'54"

SEE 1941 MAP

SEE 1943 MAP

SEE 2044 MAP

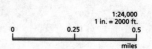

1:24,000
1 in. = 2000 ft.
0 0.25 0.5
miles

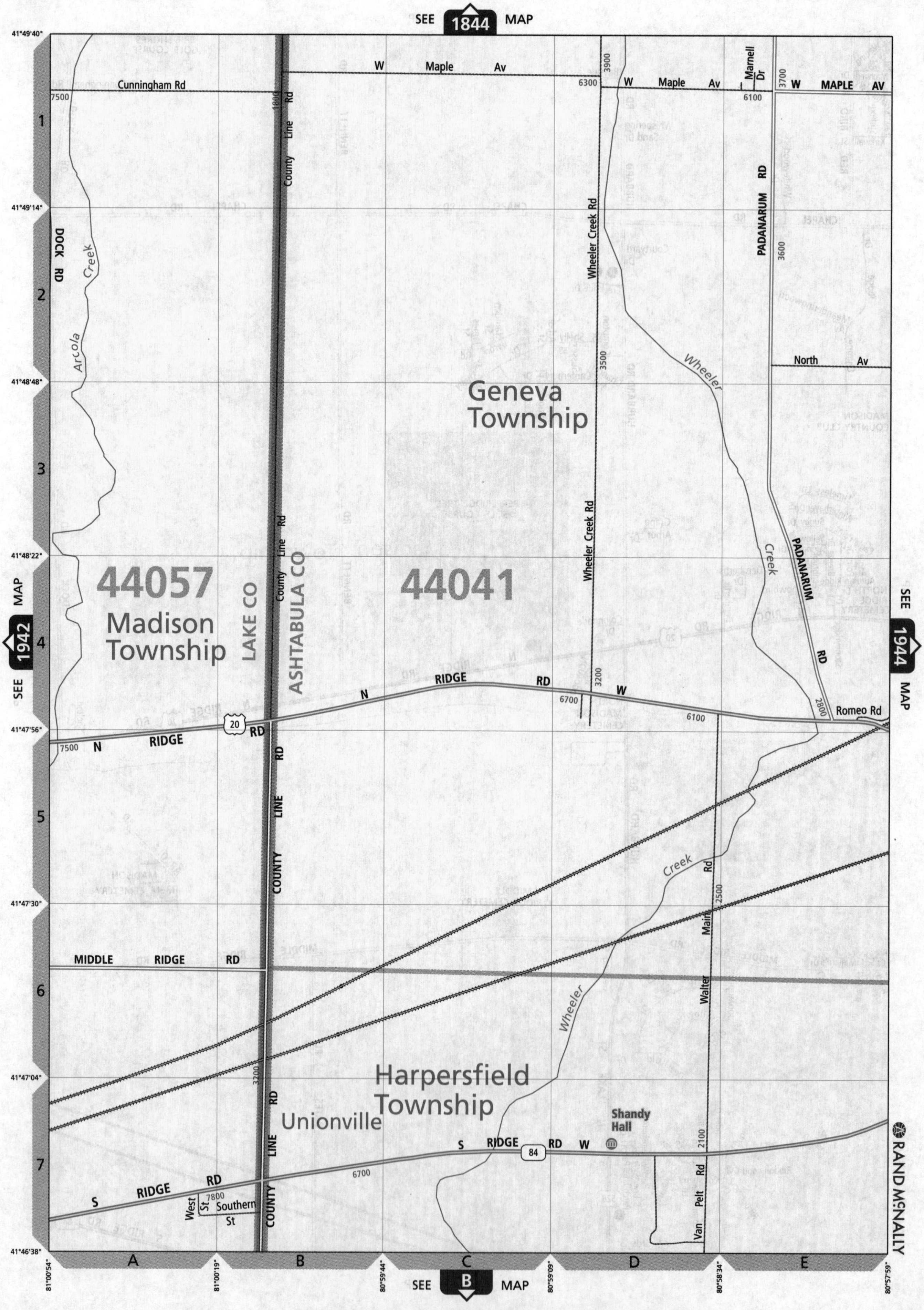
SEE 1844 MAP
SEE 1942 MAP
SEE 1944 MAP
SEE B MAP
44057
Madison Township
44041
Geneva Township
Harpersfield Township
Unionville
LAKE CO
ASHTABULA CO
Cunningham Rd
W Maple Av
W MAPLE AV
Marnell Dr
County Line Rd
COUNTY LINE RD
DOCK RD
Arcola Creek
Wheeler Creek Rd
Wheeler Creek
PADANARUM RD
North Av
N RIDGE RD
W
Romeo Rd
MIDDLE RIDGE RD
Walter Main Rd
Van Pelt Rd
S RIDGE RD W
Shandy Hall
West St
Southern St
20
84
7500
1800
6300
3900
6100
3700
3600
3500
3200
6700
2800
2500
3200
2100
7800
1
2
3
4
5
6
7
A
B
C
D
E
41°49'40"
41°49'14"
41°48'48"
41°48'22"
41°47'56"
41°47'30"
41°47'04"
41°46'38"
81°00'54"
81°00'19"
80°59'44"
80°59'09"
80°58'34"
80°57'59"
RAND McNALLY

1:24,000
1 in. = 2000 ft.
0 0.25 0.5
miles

SEE B MAP

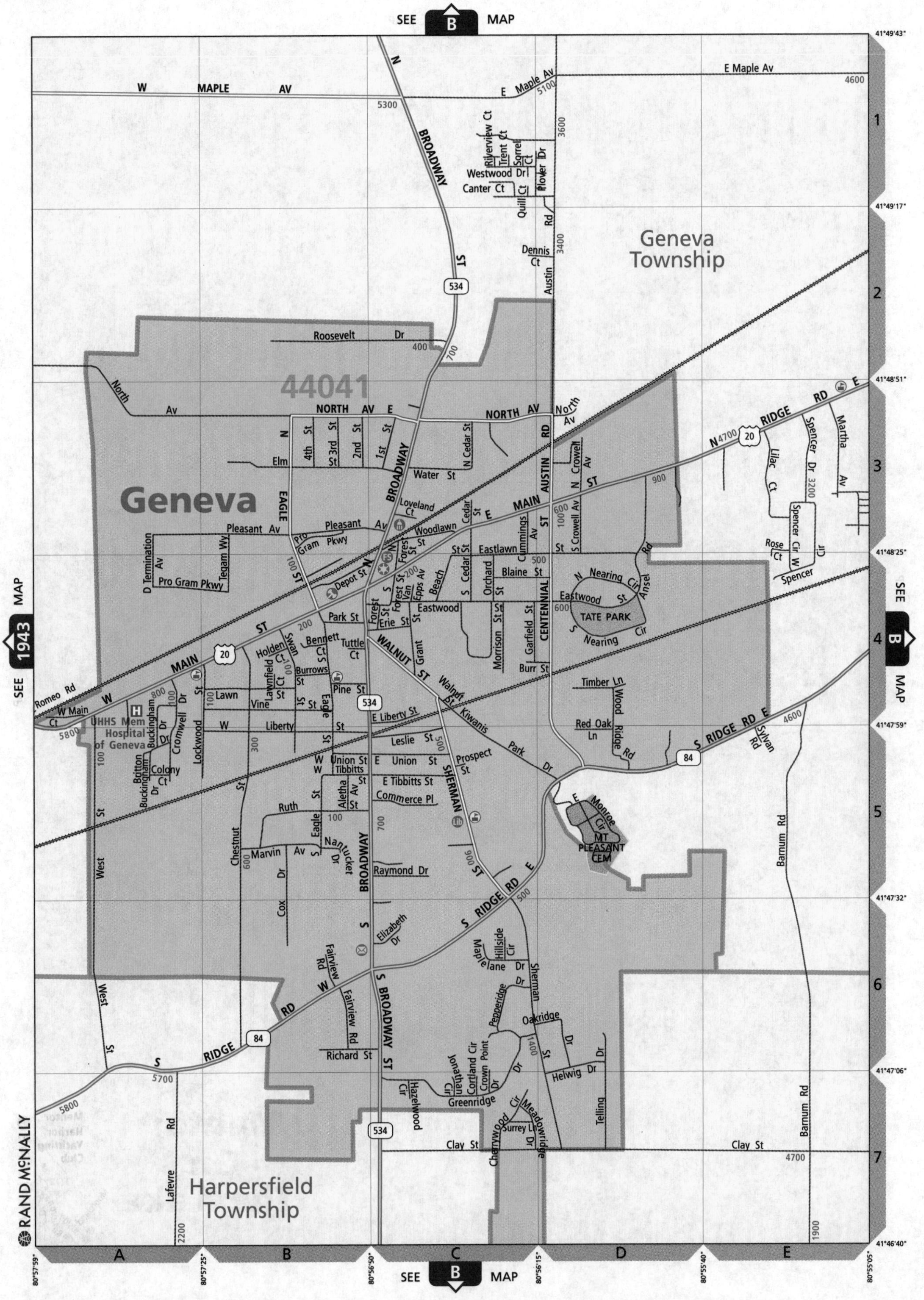
Geneva
Geneva Township
Harpersfield Township
44041
W MAPLE AV
E Maple Av
N BROADWAY ST
S BROADWAY ST
534
20
84
NORTH AV E
N RIDGE RD E
S RIDGE RD E
S RIDGE RD W
W MAIN ST
E MAIN ST
N EAGLE ST
AUSTIN RD
CENTENNIAL
WALNUT ST
SHERMAN ST
TATE PARK
MT PLEASANT CEM
UHHS Mem Hospital of Geneva
Roosevelt Dr
Westwood Dr
Canter Ct
Dennis Ct
Pleasant Av
Pro Gram Pkwy
Water St
Woodlawn
Eastlawn
Eastwood
Blaine St
Nearing Cir
Park St
Tuttle Ct
Burrows St
Pine St
Lawn
Vine St
Liberty
E Liberty St
Leslie St
Union St
E Tibbitts St
Commerce Pl
Ruth
Marvin Av
Raymond Dr
Elizabeth Dr
Kiwanis Park Dr
Timber Ln
Red Oak Ln
Wood Ridge Rd
Sylvan Rd
Barnum Rd
Clay St
Helwig Dr
Greenridge
Oakridge
Richard St
Fairview Rd
Lafevre Rd
West St
Chestnut St
Spencer Dr
Martha Av
Lilac Ct
Rose Ct
Spencer Cir
SEE 1943 MAP
SEE B MAP
A
B
C
D
E
1
2
3
4
5
6
7
RAND McNALLY

SEE B MAP

1:24,000
1 in. = 2000 ft.
0 0.25 0.5
miles

SEE B MAP

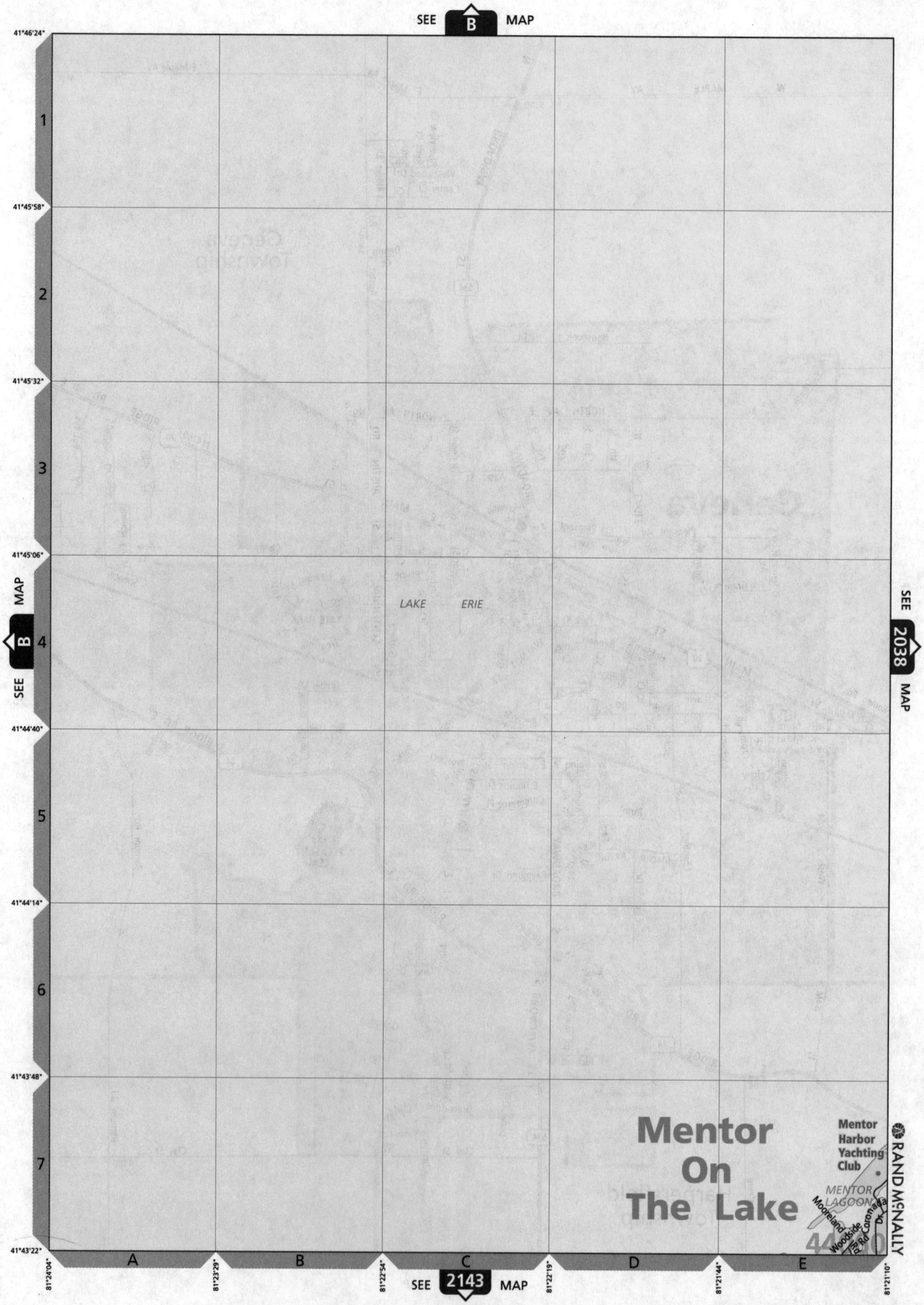
41°46'24"
41°45'58"
41°45'32"
41°45'06"
41°44'40"
41°44'14"
41°43'48"
41°43'22"
1
2
3
4
5
6
7
A
B
C
D
E
81°24'04"
81°23'29"
81°22'54"
81°22'19"
81°21'44"
81°21'10"
LAKE
ERIE
Mentor
On
The Lake
Mentor
Harbor
Yachting
Club
MENTOR
LAGOON
Mooreland
Woodside
Rd
Coronada
Dr

SEE B MAP

SEE 2038 MAP

SEE 2143 MAP

1:24,000
1 in. = 2000 ft.
0 0.25 0.5
miles

SEE B MAP

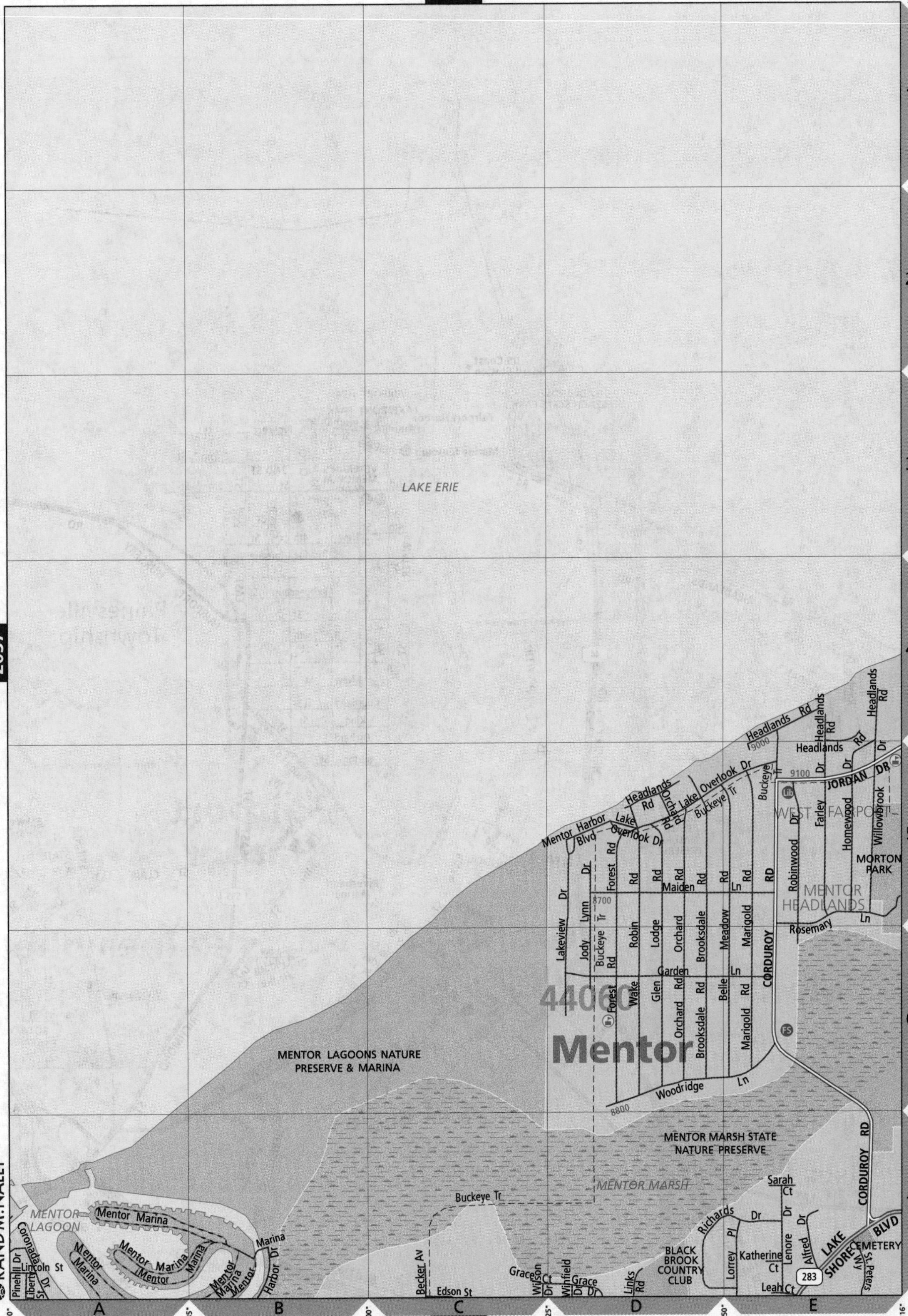
41°46'28"
41°46'02"
41°45'36"
41°45'10"
41°44'44"
41°44'18"
41°43'52"
41°43'25"
1
2
3
4
5
6
7
A
B
C
D
E
81°21'10"
81°20'35"
81°20'00"
81°19'25"
81°18'50"
81°18'16"
LAKE ERIE
Headlands Rd
Headlands Rd
Headlands Rd
Headlands Dr
Headlands Rd
Overlook Dr
Buckeye Tr
Buckeye
Lake
Mentor Harbor Blvd
Lake Overlook Dr
Orchard
9000
9100
JORDAN DR
Lib
WEST FARPORT
Robinwood Dr
Farley
Homewood
Willowbrook
Dr
MORTON PARK
MENTOR HEADLANDS
Rosemary Ln
Lakeview Dr
Jody
Lynn Dr
Forest Rd
Buckeye Tr
Rd
8700
Maiden
Robin
Lodge
Orchard
Brooksdale
Meadow
Marigold
Ln
CORDUROY RD
Garden
Wake
Glen
Orchard Rd
Brooksdale Rd
Belle
Marigold Rd
Forest
44060
Mentor
FS
Woodridge Ln
8800
MENTOR LAGOONS NATURE PRESERVE & MARINA
MENTOR MARSH STATE NATURE PRESERVE
MENTOR MARSH
CORDUROY RD
Sarah Ct
Richards Dr
Dr
Alfred Dr
Lorrey Pl
Katherine Ct
Lenore
Leah Ct
283
LAKE SHORE BLVD
CEMETERY
St. Peters Wy
BLACK BROOK COUNTRY CLUB
Links Rd
Grace Dr
Winfield Dr
Wilson Dr
Grace Ct
Buckeye Tr
Becker Av
Edson St
MENTOR LAGOON
Mentor Marina
Mentor Marina
Mentor Marina
Mentor Marina
Mentor Marina
Harbor Dr
Pinehill Dr
Coronada Dr
Liberty St
Lincoln St
RAND McNALLY

SEE 2037 MAP

SEE 2039 MAP

SEE 2144 MAP

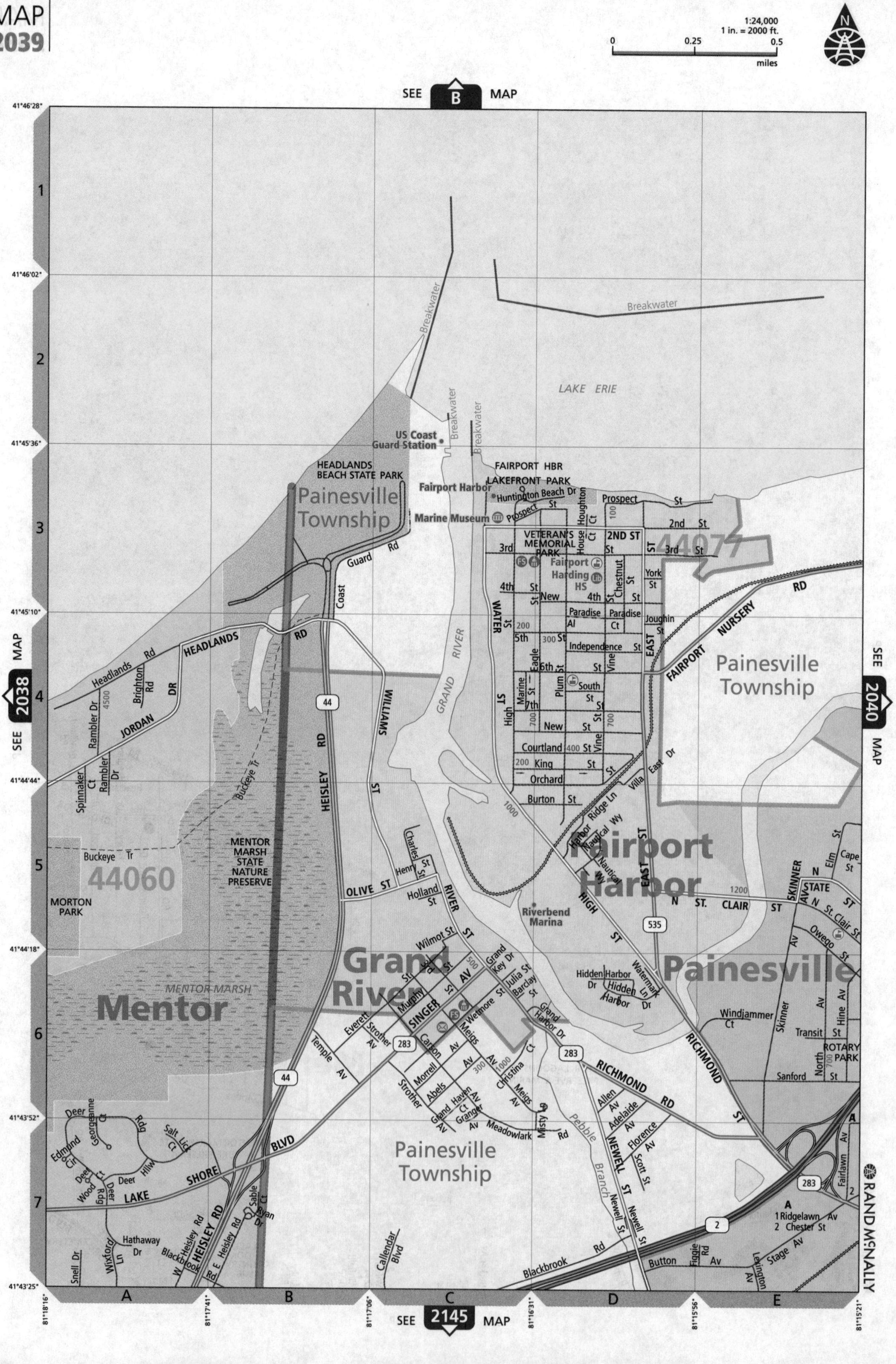
1:24,000
1 in. = 2000 ft.
0
0.25
0.5
miles
N
SEE B MAP
SEE 2038 MAP
SEE 2040 MAP
SEE 2145 MAP
41°46'28"
41°46'02"
41°45'36"
41°45'10"
41°44'44"
41°44'18"
41°43'52"
41°43'25"
81°18'16"
81°17'41"
81°17'06"
81°16'31"
81°15'56"
81°15'21"
1
2
3
4
5
6
7
A
B
C
D
E
LAKE ERIE
Breakwater
Breakwater
Breakwater
Breakwater
US Coast Guard Station
HEADLANDS BEACH STATE PARK
FAIRPORT HBR LAKEFRONT PARK
Fairport Harbor
Huntington Beach Dr
Marine Museum
Painesville Township
Guard Rd
Coast
Prospect St
Prospect St
2nd St
2ND ST
3rd St
3rd
VETERAN'S MEMORIAL PARK
Fairport Harding HS
Houghton Ct
House St
Chestnut St
York St
4th St
New
4th St
Paradise Al
Paradise Ct
Joughin St
WATER ST
5th
300 St
Independence St
EAST ST
6th St
Vine St
Eagle St
Marine St
7th
Plum St
South St
High St
New St
Courtland 400 St
Vine St
200 King St
Orchard
Burton St
Villa St
East Dr
FAIRPORT NURSERY RD
4407
Painesville Township
GRAND RIVER
Headlands Rd
HEADLANDS RD
Brighton Rd
JORDAN DR
Rambler Dr
Rambler Dr
Spinnaker Ct
Buckeye Tr
Buckeye Tr
44
HEISLEY RD
WILLIAMS ST
MENTOR MARSH STATE NATURE PRESERVE
44060
MORTON PARK
Charles St
Henry St
OLIVE ST
Holland St
RIVER ST
Harbor Ridge Ln
Nautical Wy
Nautical Wy
Fairport Harbor
HIGH ST
535
Riverbend Marina
N ST. CLAIR ST
1200
SKINNER AV
N STATE ST
Elm St
Cape St
N St. Clair St
Owego St
Wilmot St
Grand River
Grand Key Dr
Julia St
Barclay St
AV
Murphy
SINGER
Wetmore St
Hidden Harbor Dr
Hidden Harbor Dr
Watermark Ln
Painesville
Windjammer Ct
Skinner Av
Hine Av
MENTOR MARSH
Mentor
Everett
Strother Av
283
Carlson
Meigs
Grand Harbor Dr
Christina Ct
283
RICHMOND RD
RICHMOND ST
Transit St
ROTARY PARK
North St
Sanford St
Temple Av
44
Morrell
Strother
Abels
Grand Haven Av
Granger Av
Meigs Av
Meadowlark Rd
Misty Ln
Pebble Branch
Allen Av
Adelaide Av
Florence Av
Scott St
NEWELL ST
Painesville Township
Deer Rdg
Georgeanne Ct
Salt Lick Ct
Edmund Cir
Deer Hllw
Deer Ct
Wood Rdg
Deer
LAKE SHORE BLVD
Sable Ct
Ryan Dr
HEISLEY RD
W Heisley Rd
E Heisley Rd
Hathaway Dr
Wixford Ln
Blackbrook
Snell Dr
Callendar Blvd
Newell St
Newell St
Blackbrook Rd
Button Av
Figgie Rd
Stage Av
Lexington Av
283
2
A
1 Ridgelawn Av
2 Chester St
Fairlawn Av
A
RAND McNALLY

1:24,000
1 in. = 2000 ft.
0 0.25 0.5
miles

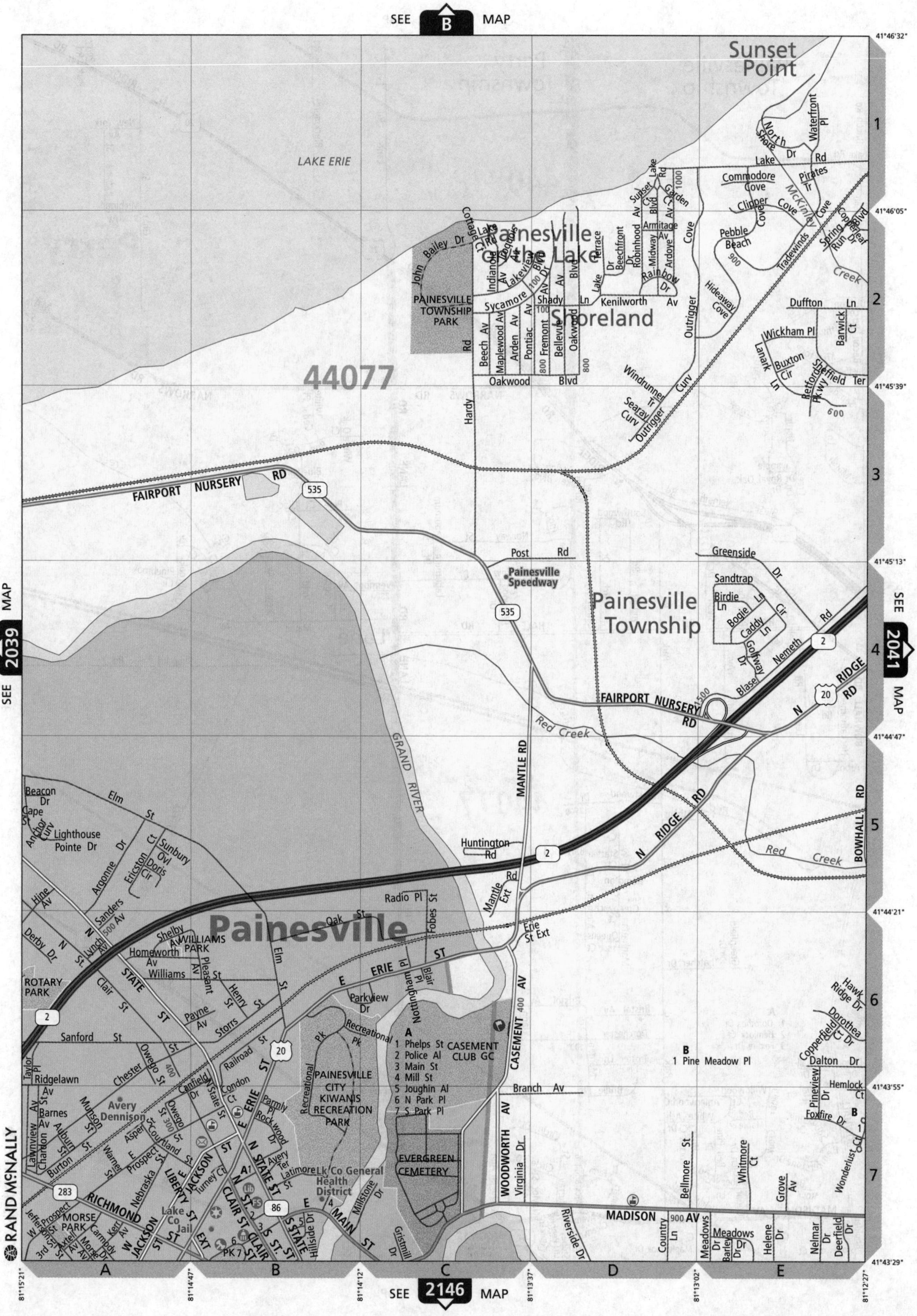
SEE B MAP
SEE 2146 MAP
SEE 2039 MAP
SEE 2041 MAP
LAKE ERIE
Sunset Point
Painesville on the Lake
Shoreland
PAINESVILLE TOWNSHIP PARK
44077
Painesville Township
Painesville Speedway
Painesville
GRAND RIVER
Red Creek
FAIRPORT NURSERY RD
MANTLE RD
N RIDGE RD
BOWHALL RD
CASEMENT AV
WOODWORTH AV
MADISON AV
RICHMOND ST
N STATE ST
E ERIE ST
E MAIN ST
CASEMENT CLUB GC
EVERGREEN CEMETERY
PAINESVILLE CITY KIWANIS RECREATION PARK
ROTARY PARK
WILLIAMS PARK
MORSE PARK
Avery Dennison
Lake Co Jail
Lk Co General Health District
A
1 Phelps St
2 Police Al
3 Main St
4 Mill St
5 Joughin Al
6 N Park Pl
7 S Park Pl
B
1 Pine Meadow Pl
41°46'32"
41°46'05"
41°45'39"
41°45'13"
41°44'47"
41°44'21"
41°43'55"
41°43'29"
81°15'21"
81°14'47"
81°14'12"
81°13'37"
81°13'02"
81°12'27"
A B C D E
1 2 3 4 5 6 7
RAND McNALLY

1:24,000
1 in. = 2000 ft.
0 0.25 0.5 miles

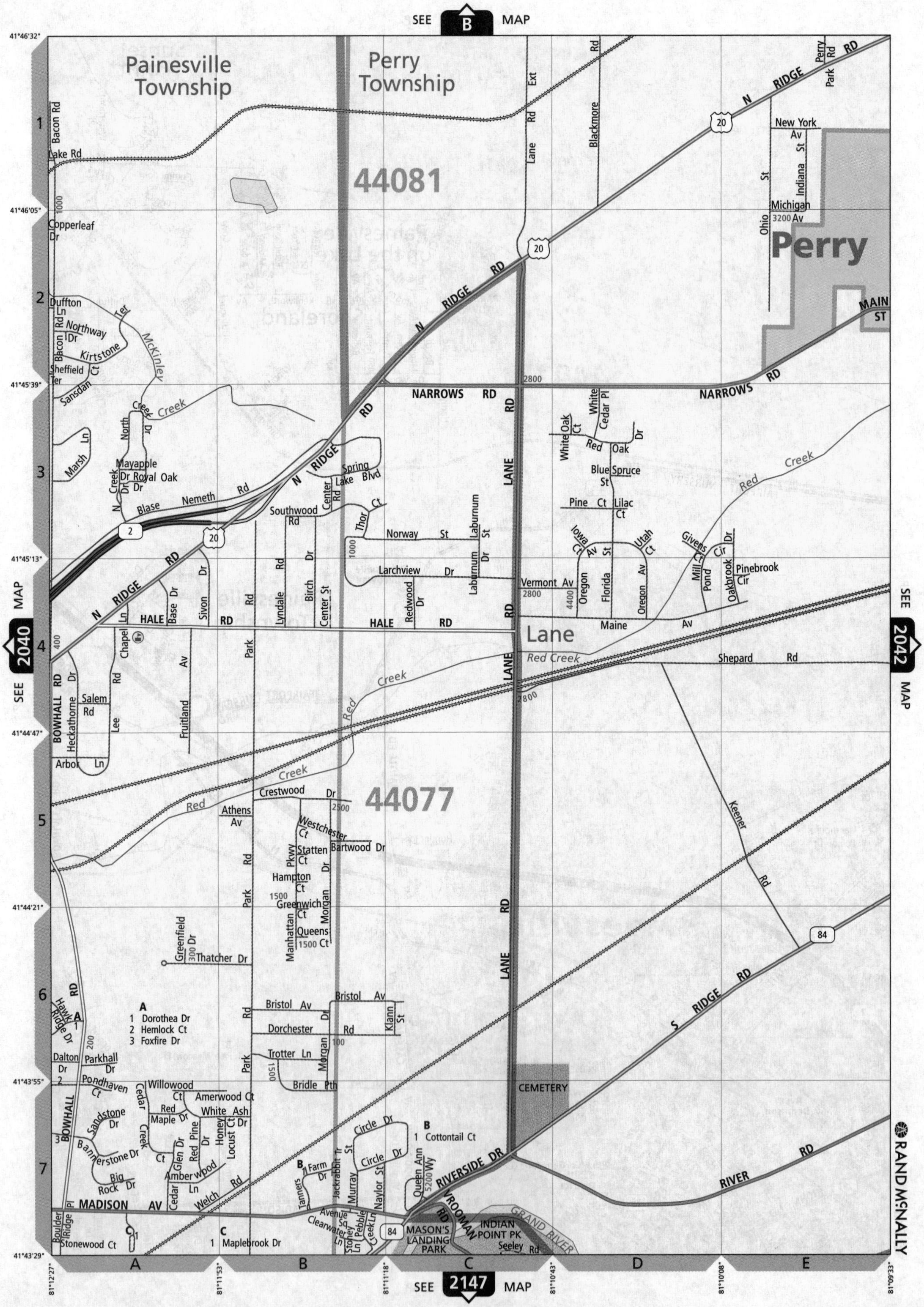
SEE B MAP
SEE 2040 MAP
SEE 2042 MAP
SEE 2147 MAP
Painesville Township
Perry Township
44081
44077
Perry
Lane
N RIDGE RD
NARROWS RD
LANE RD
HALE RD
Lane Rd Ext
Blackmore Rd
Perry Park Rd
New York Av
Indiana St
Ohio St
Michigan Av
MAIN ST
Bacon Rd
Lake Rd
Copperleaf Dr
Duffton Ln
Northway Dr
Kirtstone Ter
Sheffield Ter
Sansdan Ct
McKinley Creek Dr
North Creek Dr
Marsh Ln
Mayapple Dr
Royal Oak Dr
Blase Nemeth Rd
Southwood Rd
Center Rd
Spring Lake Blvd
Thor Ct
Norway St
Laburnum Dr
Larchview Dr
Vermont Av
White Oak Ct
White Cedar Pl
Red Oak Dr
Blue Spruce St
Pine Ct
Lilac Ct
Iowa Ct
Oregon Av
Florida St
Utah Ct
Givens Dr
Mill Ct
Pond Cir
Oakbrook Dr
Pinebrook Cir
Maine Av
Red Creek
Shepard Rd
Base Dr
Sivon Dr
Lyndale Rd
Birch Dr
Center St
Redwood Dr
Chapel Ln
Salem Rd
Heckathorne Dr
Lee Rd
Fruitland Av
Park Rd
BOWHALL RD
Arbor Ln
Crestwood Dr
Athens Av
Westchester Ct
Statten Ct
Bartwood Dr
Manhattan Pkwy
Hampton Ct
Greenwich Ct
Morgan Dr
Queens Ct
Greenfield Dr
Thatcher Dr
Keener Rd
S RIDGE RD
Bristol Av
Klann St
Dorchester Rd
Trotter Ln
Bridle Pth
Hawk Ridge Dr
A
1 Dorothea Dr
2 Hemlock Ct
3 Foxfire Dr
Dalton Dr
Parkhall Dr
Pondhaven Ct
Willowood Ct
Amerwood Ct
Cedar Creek Ct
Red Maple Dr
White Ash Dr
Sandstone Dr
Bannerstone Dr
Glen Dr
Red Pine Dr
Honey Locust Ct
Big Rock Dr
Amberwood Ln
Welch Rd
MADISON AV
Cedar Ln
Circle Dr
B
1 Cottontail Ct
Farm Dr
Jackrabbit Tr
Murray St
Naylor St
Queen Ann Wy
Tanners Ln
Avenue Sq
Clearwater Ln
Stoney Ln
Pebble Creek Ln
RIVERSIDE DR
VROOMAN RD
CEMETERY
MASON'S LANDING PARK
INDIAN POINT PK
GRAND RIVER
Seeley Rd
RIVER RD
Boulder Ridge Pl
Stonewood Ct
C
1 Maplebrook Dr
A B C D E

1:24,000
1 in. = 2000 ft.
0 0.25 0.5
miles

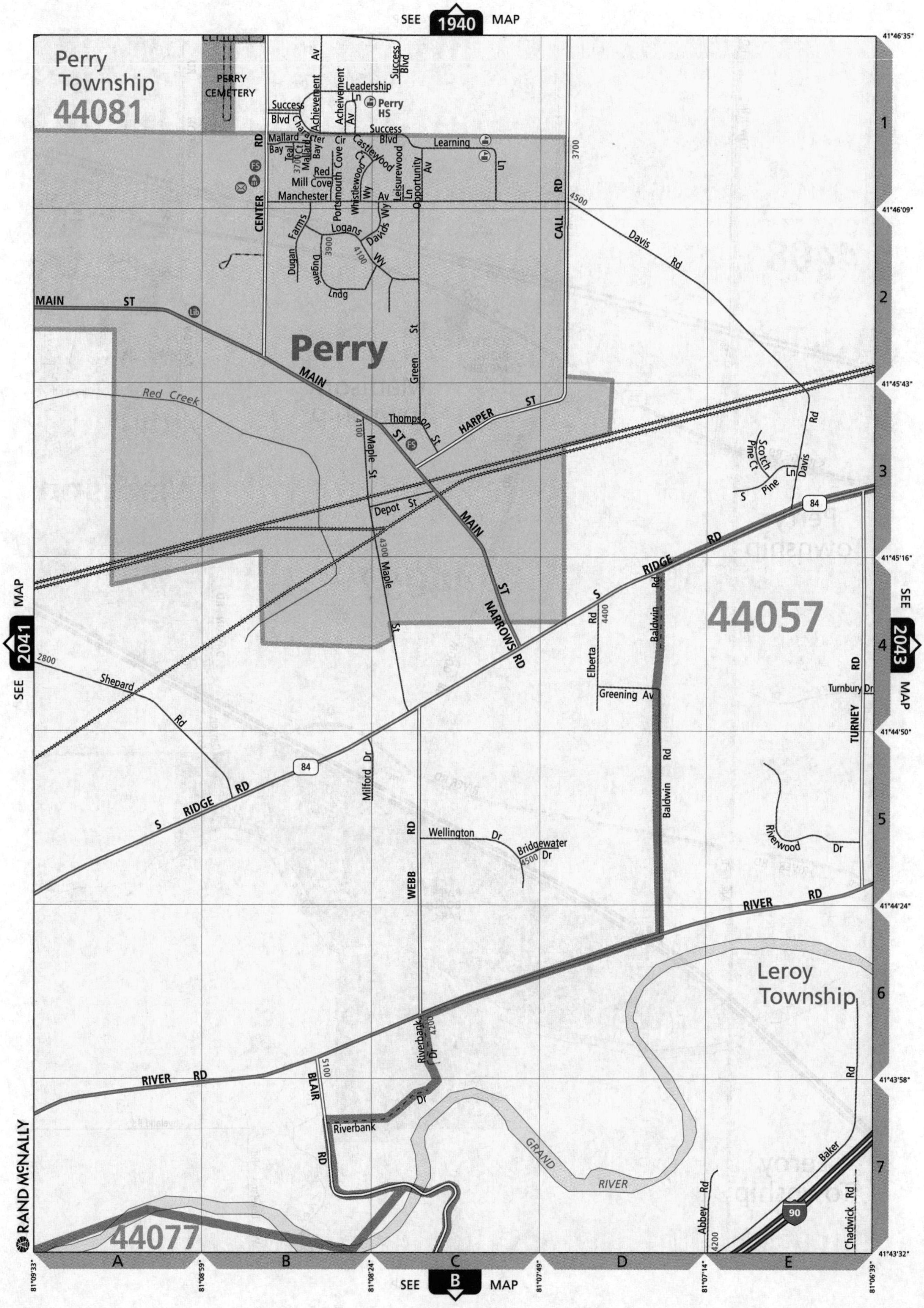
SEE 1940 MAP
SEE B MAP
SEE 2041 MAP
SEE 2043 MAP
Perry Township
44081
PERRY CEMETERY
Perry
Perry HS
44057
44077
Leroy Township
MAIN ST
CENTER RD
CALL RD
3700
4500
Davis Rd
Success Blvd
Leadership
Achievement Av
Achievement Ln
Character
Mallard Bay
Teal Ct
Mallard Bay
Cir
Castlewood
Portsmouth Cove
Red Mill Cove
Whistlewood Wy
Leisurewood Ln
Opportunity Av
Learning Ln
Manchester Av
Dugan Farms
Dugans Lndg
Logans
Davids Wy
3900
4100
Green St
Thompson St
HARPER ST
Red Creek
Maple St
Depot St
4300
NARROWS RD
S RIDGE RD
84
Scotch Pine Ct
S Pine Ln
Elberta Rd
4400
Baldwin Rd
Greening Av
2800
Shepard Rd
Milford Dr
WEBB RD
Wellington Dr
Bridgewater Dr
4500
TURNEY RD
Turnbury Dr
Riverwood Dr
RIVER RD
Riverbank Dr
4200
5100
BLAIR RD
Riverbank
GRAND RIVER
Abbey Rd
4200
Baker Rd
Chadwick Rd
90
A B C D E
1 2 3 4 5 6 7
41°46'35"
41°46'09"
41°45'43"
41°45'16"
41°44'50"
41°44'24"
41°43'58"
41°43'32"
81°09'33"
81°08'59"
81°08'24"
81°07'49"
81°07'14"
81°06'39"
RAND McNALLY

1:24,000
1 in. = 2000 ft.
0 0.25 0.5
miles

SEE 1941 MAP

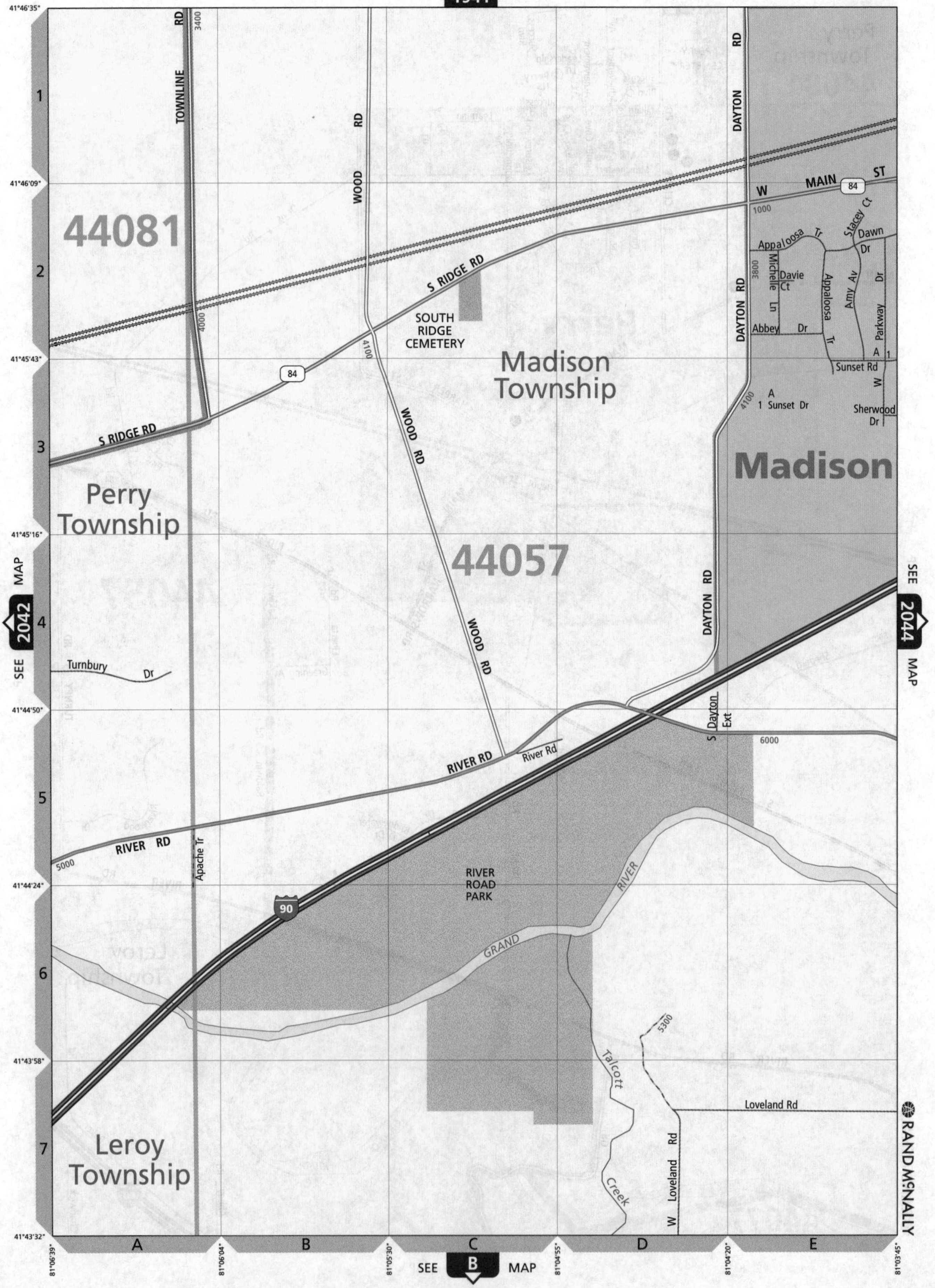
44081
44057
Madison Township
Madison
Perry Township
Leroy Township
TOWNLINE RD
3400
4000
WOOD RD
4100
DAYTON RD
W MAIN ST
84
1000
S RIDGE RD
SOUTH RIDGE CEMETERY
Appaloosa Tr
Stacey Ct
Dawn Dr
Michelle Ln
3800
Davie Ct
Amy Av
Abbey Dr
Parkway
Sunset Rd
A 1 Sunset Dr
Sherwood Dr
Turnbury Dr
RIVER RD
River Rd
5000
6000
S Dayton Ext
Apache Tr
90
RIVER ROAD PARK
GRAND RIVER
Talcott Creek
5300
Loveland Rd
W Loveland Rd
41°46'35"
41°46'09"
41°45'43"
41°45'16"
41°44'50"
41°44'24"
41°43'58"
41°43'32"
81°06'39"
81°06'04"
81°05'30"
81°04'55"
81°04'20"
81°03'45"
A B C D E
1 2 3 4 5 6 7
SEE 2042 MAP
SEE 2044 MAP
SEE B MAP

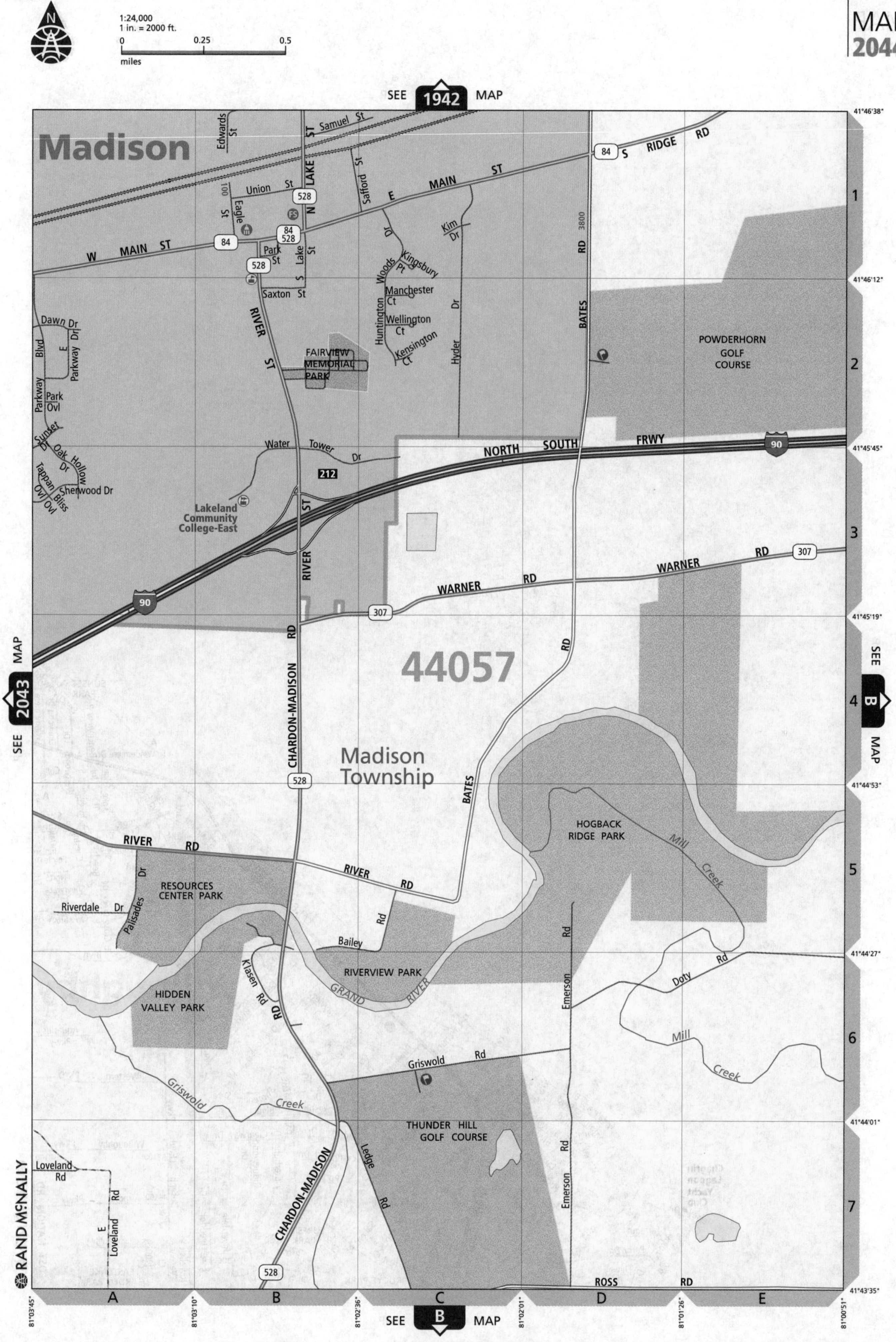
N
1:24,000
1 in. = 2000 ft.
0
0.25
0.5
miles
SEE 1942 MAP
SEE 2043 MAP
SEE B MAP
SEE B MAP
Madison
44057
Madison Township
W MAIN ST
E MAIN ST
S RIDGE RD
Edwards St
Samuel St
N LAKE ST
Union St
Eagle St
Safford St
Park St
S Lake St
Saxton St
Kim Dr
Woods Dr
Kingsbury Pt
Manchester Ct
Wellington Ct
Kensington Ct
Huntington Dr
Hyder Dr
BATES RD
3800
Dawn Dr
E Parkway Dr
Parkway Blvd
Park Ovl
Sunset Dr
Oak Hollow Dr
Tappan Ovl
Bliss Ovl
Sherwood Dr
RIVER ST
FAIRVIEW MEMORIAL PARK
Water Tower Dr
NORTH SOUTH FRWY
Lakeland Community College-East
POWDERHORN GOLF COURSE
WARNER RD
CHARDON-MADISON RD
HOGBACK RIDGE PARK
Mill Creek
RIVER RD
RESOURCES CENTER PARK
Palisades Dr
Riverdale Dr
Bailey Rd
RIVERVIEW PARK
GRAND RIVER
HIDDEN VALLEY PARK
Klasen Rd
Emerson Rd
Doty Rd
Griswold Rd
Griswold Creek
THUNDER HILL GOLF COURSE
Ledge Rd
Loveland Rd
E Loveland Rd
ROSS RD
84
528
90
212
307
1
2
3
4
5
6
7
A
B
C
D
E
41°46'38"
41°46'12"
41°45'45"
41°45'19"
41°44'53"
41°44'27"
41°44'01"
41°43'35"
81°03'45"
81°03'10"
81°02'36"
81°02'01"
81°01'26"
81°00'51"
RAND McNALLY

1:24,000
1 in. = 2000 ft.
0 0.25 0.5
miles

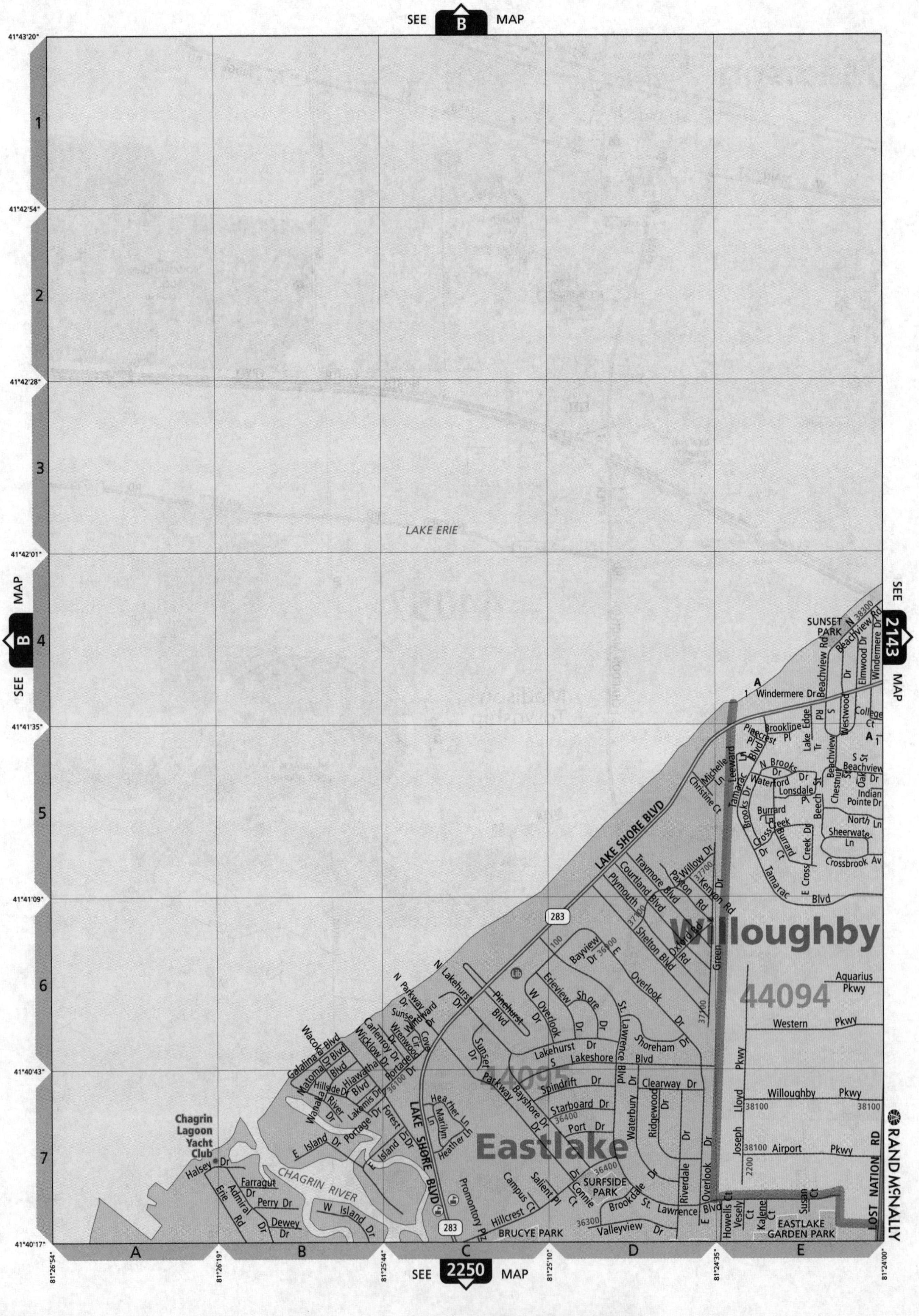
SEE B MAP
SEE 2143 MAP
SEE 2250 MAP
41°43'20"
41°42'54"
41°42'28"
41°42'01"
41°41'35"
41°41'09"
41°40'43"
41°40'17"
81°26'54"
81°26'19"
81°25'44"
81°25'10"
81°24'35"
81°24'00"
A
B
C
D
E
1
2
3
4
5
6
7
LAKE ERIE
SUNSET PARK
Willoughby
44094
44095
Eastlake
Chagrin Lagoon Yacht Club
CHAGRIN RIVER
SURFSIDE PARK
BRUCYE PARK
EASTLAKE GARDEN PARK
LAKE SHORE BLVD
283
Windermere Dr
Beachview Rd
Brookline Pl
Pinecrest Pl
Lake Edge Tr
Westwood
Elmwood Dr
College Ct
N Brooks Dr
Waterford Dr
Lonsdale Pl
Burrard Ln
Cross Creek Dr
Crossbrook Av
Sheerwater Ln
Indian Pointe Dr
North Ln
Tamarac Blvd
Michelle Ln
Christine Ct
Leeward Ln
Traymore Blvd
Courtland Blvd
Plymouth Blvd
Paxton Rd
Willow Dr
Kenyon Rd
Shelton Blvd
Oxford Rd
Green
Aquarius Pkwy
Western Pkwy
Willoughby Pkwy
Airport Pkwy
Joseph Lloyd Pkwy
LOST NATION RD
Bayview Dr
E Overlook Dr
Erieview Dr
Shore Dr
W Overlook Dr
St. Lawrence Blvd
Shoreham Dr
Lakehurst Dr
S Lakeshore Blvd
Clearway Dr
Spindrift Dr
Starboard Dr
Port Dr
Waterbury Dr
Ridgewood Dr
Riverdale Dr
Overlook Dr
Brookdale Dr
St. Lawrence Blvd
Valleyview Dr
Connie Ct
Salient Pl
Campus Ct
Hillcrest Dr
Promontory Pl
Bayshore Dr
Sunset Parkway
Pinehurst Blvd
N Lakehurst Dr
N Parkway Dr
Windward Dr
Sunset Cove
Heather Ln
Marilyn Ln
Galalina Blvd
Wacoka Dr
Hiawatha Blvd
Wicklow Dr
Portage Dr
E Island Dr
W Island Dr
Halsey Dr
Farragut Dr
Admiral Dr
Perry Dr
Dewey Dr
Erie Rd
Howells Ct
Vesely Ct
Kalene Ct
Susan Ct
RAND McNALLY

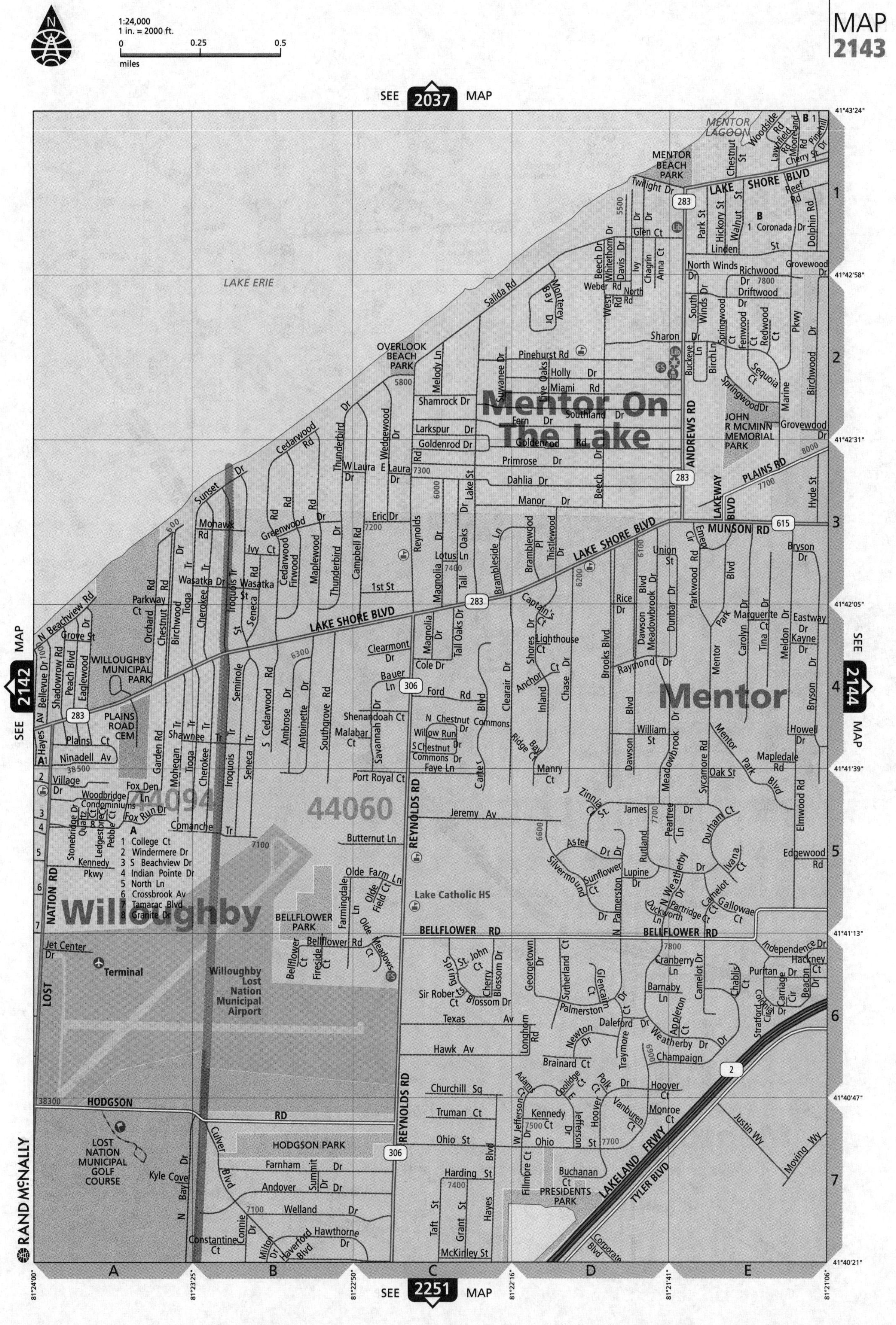
1:24,000
1 in. = 2000 ft.
0 0.25 0.5
miles
SEE 2037 MAP
SEE 2142 MAP
SEE 2144 MAP
SEE 2251 MAP
LAKE ERIE
Mentor On The Lake
Mentor
Willoughby
44094
44060
MENTOR LAGOON
MENTOR BEACH PARK
OVERLOOK BEACH PARK
WILLOUGHBY MUNICIPAL PARK
PLAINS ROAD CEM
JOHN R MCMINN MEMORIAL PARK
BELLFLOWER PARK
Willoughby Lost Nation Municipal Airport
Terminal
Lake Catholic HS
HODGSON PARK
LOST NATION MUNICIPAL GOLF COURSE
PRESIDENTS PARK
LAKE SHORE BLVD
MUNSON RD
PLAINS RD
ANDREWS RD
REYNOLDS RD
BELLFLOWER RD
HODGSON RD
LOST NATION RD
LAKELAND FRWY
TYLER BLVD
LAKEWAY BLVD
A
1 College Ct
2 Windermere Dr
3 S Beachview Dr
4 Indian Pointe Dr
5 North Ln
6 Crossbrook Av
7 Tamarac Blvd
8 Granite Dr
B
1 Coronada Dr
RAND McNALLY

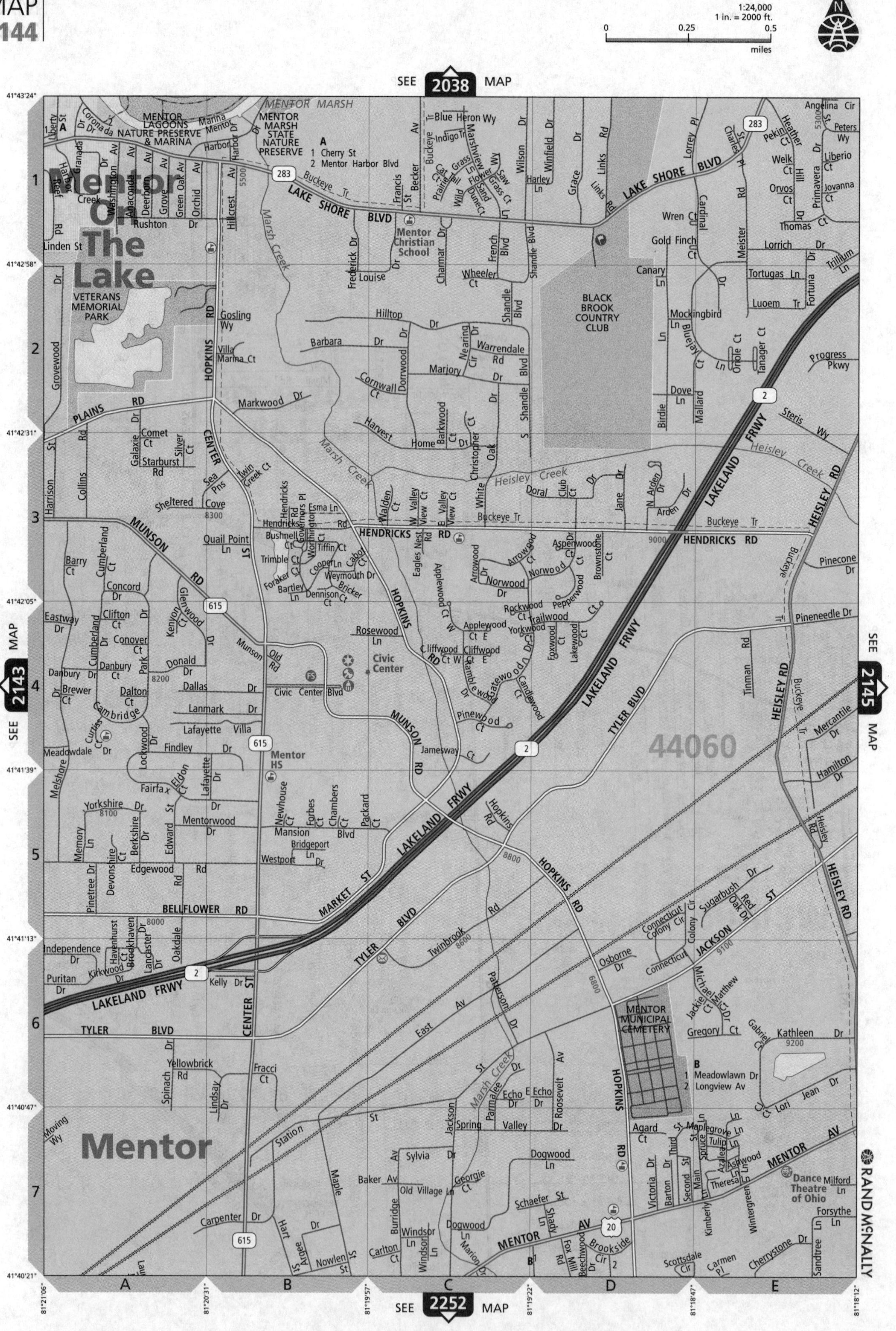
1:24,000
1 in. = 2000 ft.
0
0.25
0.5
miles
SEE 2038 MAP
SEE 2252 MAP
SEE 2143 MAP
SEE 2145 MAP
41°43'24"
41°42'58"
41°42'31"
41°42'05"
41°41'39"
41°41'13"
41°40'47"
41°40'21"
81°21'06"
81°20'31"
81°19'57"
81°19'22"
81°18'47"
81°18'12"
A
B
C
D
E
1
2
3
4
5
6
7
Mentor On The Lake
Mentor
44060
MENTOR MARSH
MENTOR LAGOONS NATURE PRESERVE & MARINA
MENTOR MARSH STATE NATURE PRESERVE
A
1 Cherry St
2 Mentor Harbor Blvd
B
1 Meadowlawn Dr
2 Longview Av
VETERANS MEMORIAL PARK
BLACK BROOK COUNTRY CLUB
Mentor Christian School
Civic Center
Mentor HS
MENTOR MUNICIPAL CEMETERY
Dance Theatre of Ohio
LAKE SHORE BLVD
LAKELAND FRWY
HOPKINS RD
CENTER ST
MUNSON RD
HENDRICKS RD
PLAINS RD
MARKET ST
TYLER BLVD
BELLFLOWER RD
JACKSON ST
MENTOR AV
HEISLEY RD
Marsh Creek
Heisley Creek
Buckeye Tr
East Av
Station St
283
2
615
20
RAND McNALLY

1:24,000
1 in. = 2000 ft.
0 0.25 0.5
miles

SEE 2039 MAP

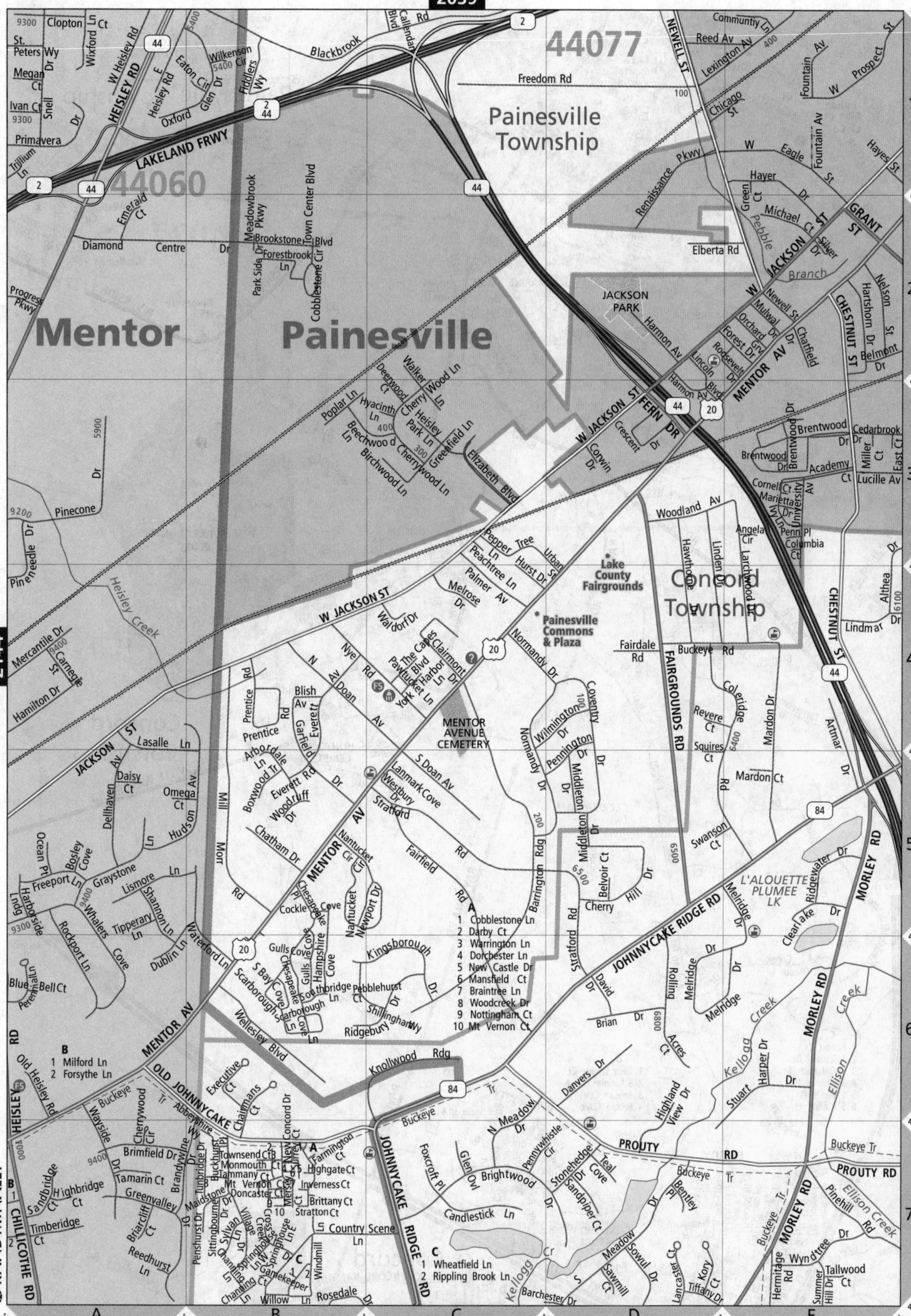
Mentor
Painesville
Painesville Township
Concord Township
44077
44060
LAKELAND FRWY
W JACKSON ST
MENTOR AV
JACKSON PARK
Lake County Fairgrounds
Painesville Commons & Plaza
MENTOR AVENUE CEMETERY
FAIRGROUNDS RD
JOHNNYCAKE RIDGE RD
OLD JOHNNYCAKE
PROUTY RD
MORLEY RD
CHESTNUT ST
HEISLEY RD
CHILLICOTHE RD
L'ALOUETTE PLUMEE LK
Heisley Creek
Kellogg Creek
Ellison Creek
A
1 Cobblestone Ln
2 Darby Ct
3 Warrington Ln
4 Dorchester Ln
5 New Castle Dr
6 Mansfield Ct
7 Braintree Ln
8 Woodcreek Dr
9 Nottingham Ct
10 Mt Vernon Ct
B
1 Milford Ln
2 Forsythe Ln
C
1 Wheatfield Ln
2 Rippling Brook Ln

SEE 2144 MAP

SEE 2146 MAP

SEE 2253 MAP

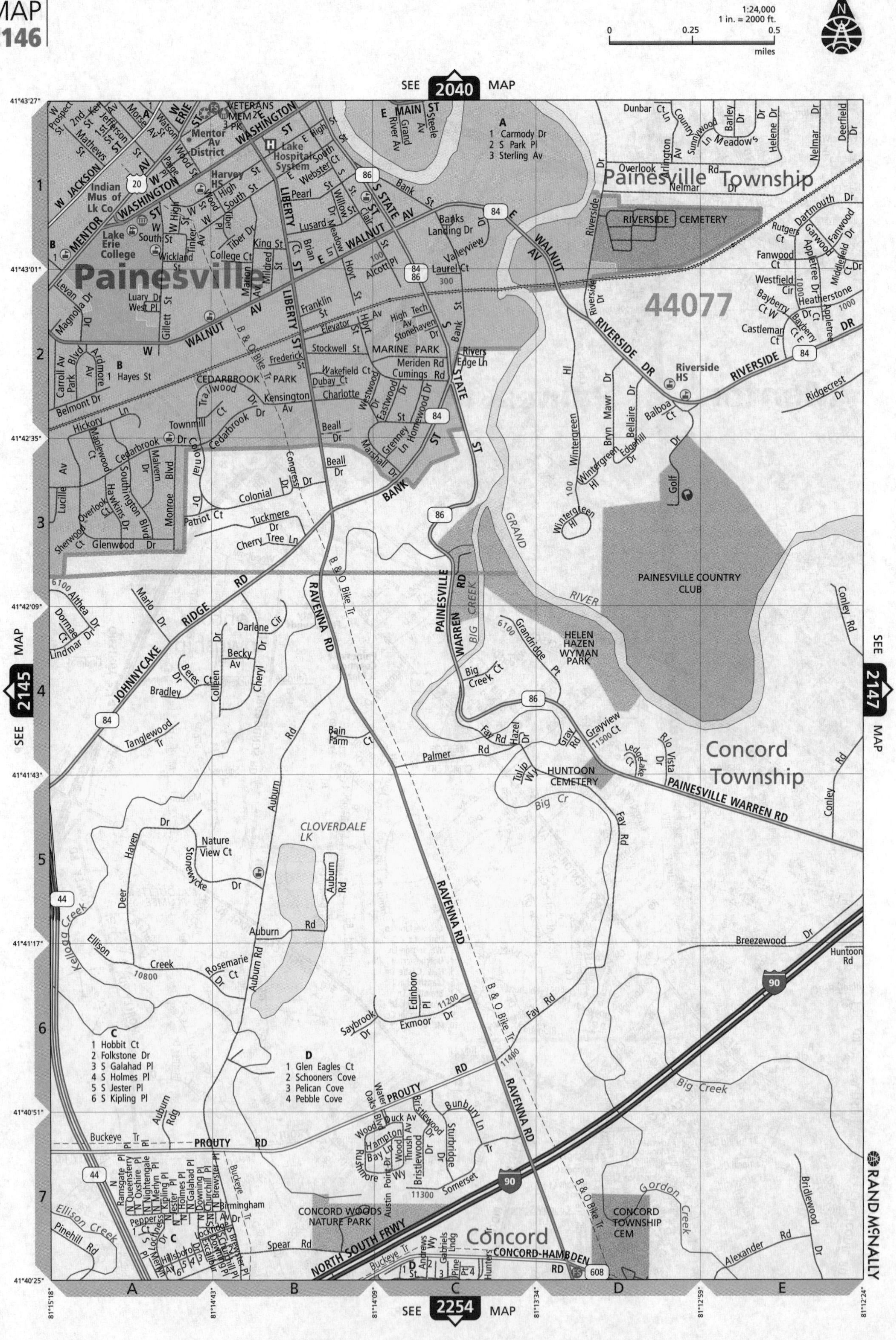
1:24,000
1 in. = 2000 ft.
0 0.25 0.5
miles
SEE 2040 MAP
SEE 2145 MAP
SEE 2147 MAP
SEE 2254 MAP
Painesville
Painesville Township
Concord Township
Concord
44077
Lake Erie College
Indian Mus of Lk Co
Mentor Av District
Lake Hospital System
Harvey HS
Riverside HS
RIVERSIDE CEMETERY
PAINESVILLE COUNTRY CLUB
HELEN HAZEN WYMAN PARK
HUNTOON CEMETERY
CONCORD WOODS NATURE PARK
CONCORD TOWNSHIP CEM
CLOVERDALE LK
GRAND RIVER
Big Creek
Kellogg Creek
Ellison Creek
Gordon Creek
MARINE PARK
CEDARBROOK PARK
VETERANS MEM
W JACKSON ST
W WASHINGTON ST
MENTOR AV
W WALNUT AV
E WALNUT AV
LIBERTY ST
S STATE ST
RIVERSIDE DR
JOHNNYCAKE RIDGE RD
RAVENNA RD
PAINESVILLE WARREN RD
PROUTY RD
NORTH SOUTH FRWY
CONCORD-HAMBDEN RD
B & O Bike Tr
Spear Rd
Palmer Rd
Fay Rd
Auburn Rd
A
1 Carmody Dr
2 S Park Pl
3 Sterling Av
B
1 Hayes St
C
1 Hobbit Ct
2 Folkstone Dr
3 S Galahad Pl
4 S Holmes Pl
5 S Jester Pl
6 S Kipling Pl
D
1 Glen Eagles Ct
2 Schooners Cove
3 Pelican Cove
4 Pebble Cove
20
84
86
44
90
608
41°43'27"
41°43'01"
41°42'35"
41°42'09"
41°41'43"
41°41'17"
41°40'51"
41°40'25"
81°15'18"
81°14'43"
81°14'09"
81°13'34"
81°12'59"
81°12'24"
A B C D E
1 2 3 4 5 6 7
RAND McNALLY

1:24,000
1 in. = 2000 ft.
0 0.25 0.5
miles

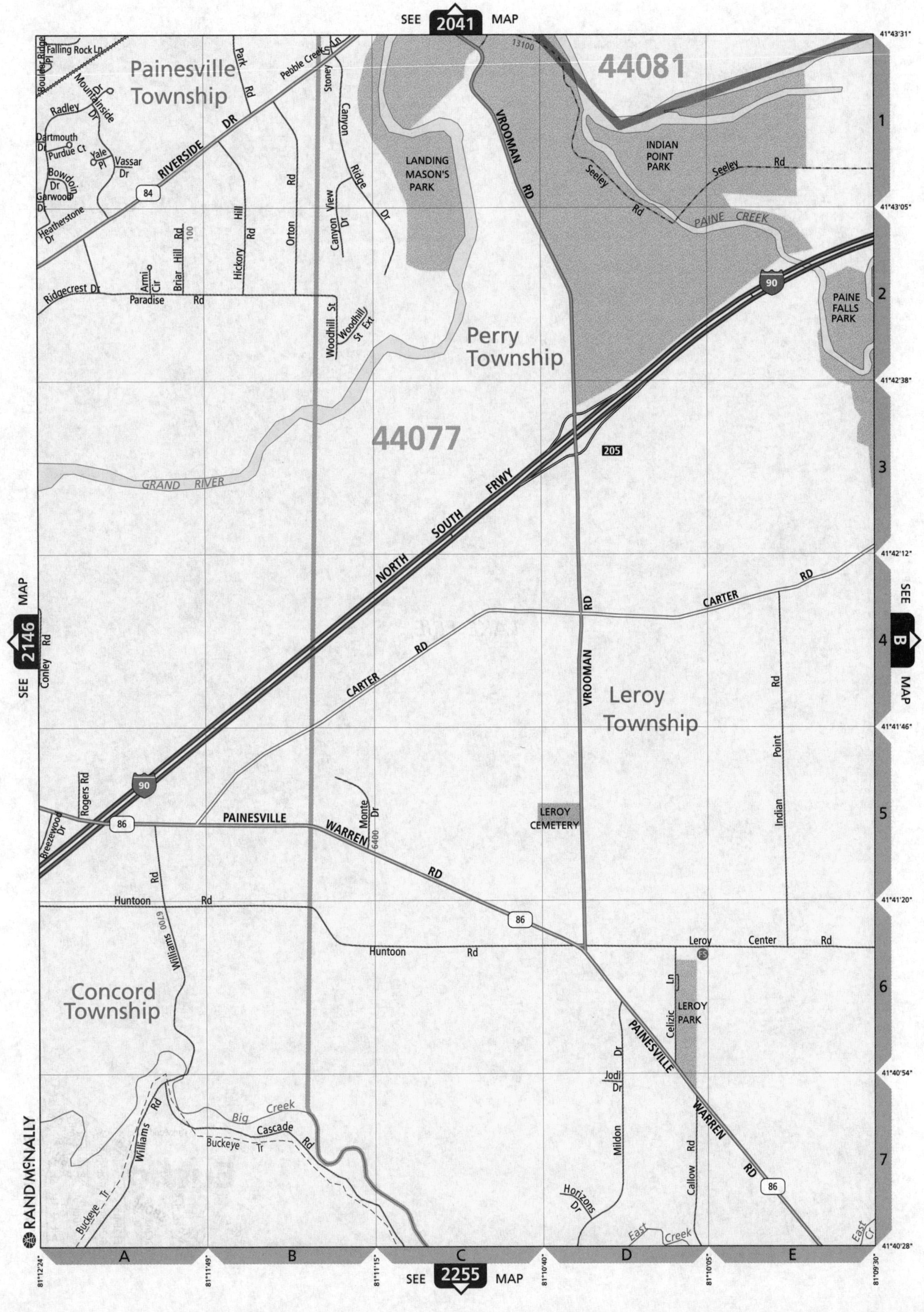
SEE 2041 MAP
SEE 2146 MAP
SEE B MAP
SEE 2255 MAP
Painesville Township
Perry Township
Leroy Township
Concord Township
44081
44077
LANDING MASON'S PARK
INDIAN POINT PARK
PAINE FALLS PARK
LEROY CEMETERY
LEROY PARK
GRAND RIVER
PAINE CREEK
Big Creek
East Creek
East Cr
RIVERSIDE DR
NORTH SOUTH FRWY
VROOMAN RD
CARTER RD
PAINESVILLE WARREN RD
Seeley Rd
Huntoon Rd
Leroy Center Rd
Indian Point Rd
Williams Rd
Cascade Rd
Buckeye Tr
Mildon Dr
Callow Rd
Celizic Ln
Jodi Dr
Horizons Dr
Monte Dr
Rogers Rd
Breezewood Dr
Conley Rd
Paradise Rd
Ridgecrest Dr
Briar Hill Rd
Armi Cir
Hickory Hill Rd
Orton Rd
Park Rd
Pebble Creek Ln
Stoney Canyon Ridge Dr
Canyon View Dr
Woodhill St
Woodhill St Ext
Falling Rock Ln
Boulder Ridge Pl
Mountainside Dr
Radley Dr
Dartmouth Dr
Purdue Ct
Yale Pl
Vassar Dr
Bowdoin Dr
Garwood Dr
Heatherstone Dr
84
86
90
205
A B C D E
1 2 3 4 5 6 7
RAND McNALLY

1:24,000
1 in. = 2000 ft.
0 0.25 0.5
miles

SEE B MAP

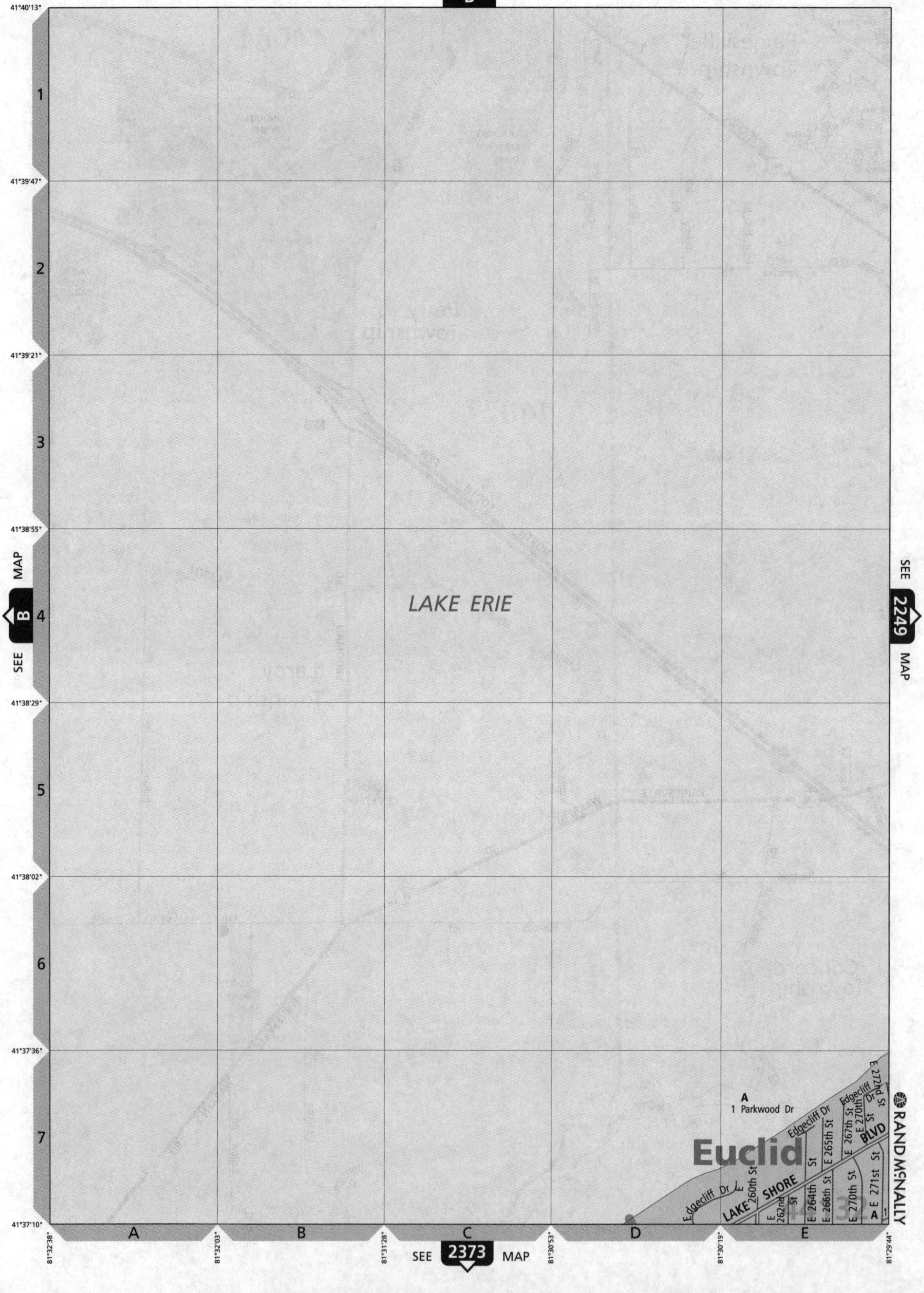
LAKE ERIE
A
1 Parkwood Dr
Euclid
Edgecliff Dr
E 260th St
262nd St
E 264th St
E 265th St
E 266th St
E 267th St
E 270th St
E 271st St
E 272nd St
LAKE SHORE BLVD
A
1
2
3
4
5
6
7
A
B
C
D
E
41°40'13"
41°39'47"
41°39'21"
41°38'55"
41°38'29"
41°38'02"
41°37'36"
41°37'10"
81°32'38"
81°32'03"
81°31'28"
81°30'53"
81°30'19"
81°29'44"

SEE B MAP

SEE 2249 MAP

SEE 2373 MAP

1:24,000
1 in. = 2000 ft.
0 0.25 0.5
miles

SEE B MAP

SEE 2248 MAP

SEE 2250 MAP

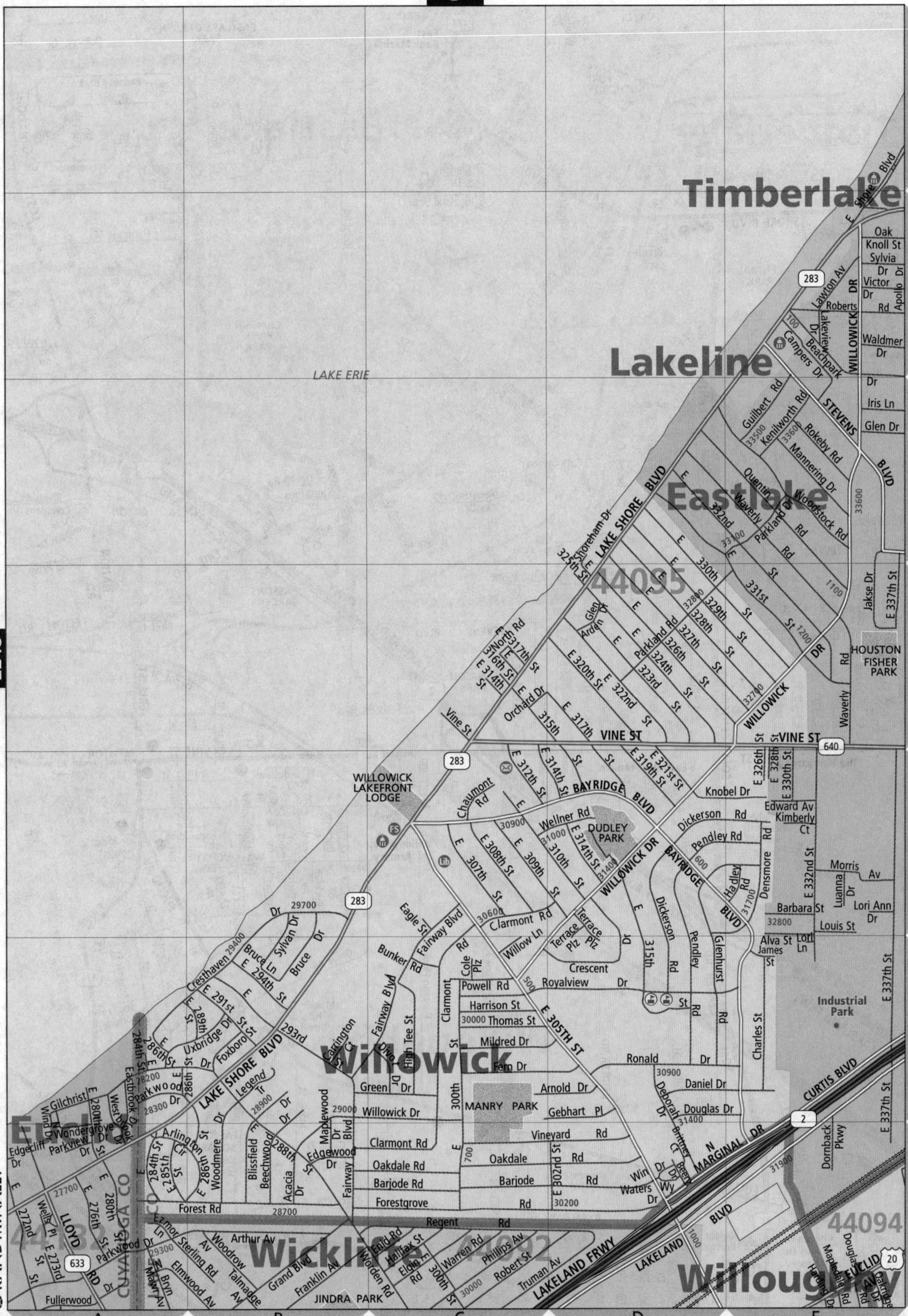
LAKE ERIE
Timberlake
Lakeline
Eastlake
44095
Willowick
Wickliffe
44092
Willoughby
44094
Euclid
WILLOWICK LAKEFRONT LODGE
DUDLEY PARK
MANRY PARK
HOUSTON FISHER PARK
JINDRA PARK
Industrial Park
LAKE SHORE BLVD
E Shore Blvd
WILLOWICK DR
STEVENS BLVD
BAYRIDGE BLVD
VINE ST
E 305TH ST
CURTIS BLVD
N MARGINAL DR
LAKELAND FRWY
LAKELAND BLVD
LLOYD RD
EUCLID AV
CUYAHOGA CO
Regent Rd
Forest Rd
Forestgrove Rd
Barjode Rd
Oakdale Rd
Clarmont Rd
Willowick Dr
Vineyard Rd
Gebhart Pl
Arnold Dr
Fern Dr
Mildred Dr
Thomas St
Harrison St
Powell Rd
Royalview Dr
Crescent Dr
Ronald Dr
Daniel Dr
Douglas Dr
Knobel Dr
Dickerson Rd
Pendley Rd
Glenhurst Rd
Charles St
Densmore Rd
Hadley Rd
Kimberly Ct
Edward Av
Morris Av
Luanna Dr
Lori Ann Dr
Barbara St
Louis St
Alva St
James St
Lori Ln
E 332nd St
E 337th St
Dornback Pkwy
Jakse Dr
Waverly Rd
Guilbert Rd
Kenilworth Rd
Rokeby Rd
Mannering Dr
Woodstock Rd
Quentin Rd
Waverly Rd
Parkland Dr
Shoreham Dr
Glen Arden Dr
Orchard Dr
Vine St
Chaumont Rd
Wellner Rd
Clarmont Rd
Willow Ln
Terrace Plz
Fairway Blvd
Eagle St
Bunker Rd
Cole Plz
Carrington Ct
Divot Dr
High Tee St
Green Dr
Maplewood Dr
Edgewood Dr
Acacia Dr
Beechwood
Blissfield
Woodmere
Arlington Cir
Legend Tr
Parkwood Dr
Uxbridge Dr
Foxboro St
Cresthaven Dr
Sylvan Dr
Bruce Ln
Bruce Dr
Gilchrist
Wondergrove
Parkview
Westbrook Dr
Eastbrook Dr
Edgecliff Dr
Wind Dr
Fullerwood Dr
Ezmor Ln
Sterling Rd
Woodrow Av
Talmadge Av
Arthur Av
Elmwood Av
Grand Blvd
Franklin Av
Worden Rd
Enid Rd
Halifax St
Elgin Rd
Warren Rd
Phillips Av
Robert St
Truman Av
Oak
Knoll St
Sylvia
Victor Dr
Apollo Dr
Roberts Rd
Lawton Av
Lakeview Dr
Beachpark
Campers Dr
Waldmer Dr
Iris Ln
Glen Dr
Win Dr
Waters Dr
Deborah Dr
Brittney Ct
Manhattan Rd
Douglas Rd
283
640
2
20
633

SEE 2374 MAP

RAND McNALLY

1:24,000
1 in. = 2000 ft.
0 0.25 0.5
miles

SEE 2142 MAP

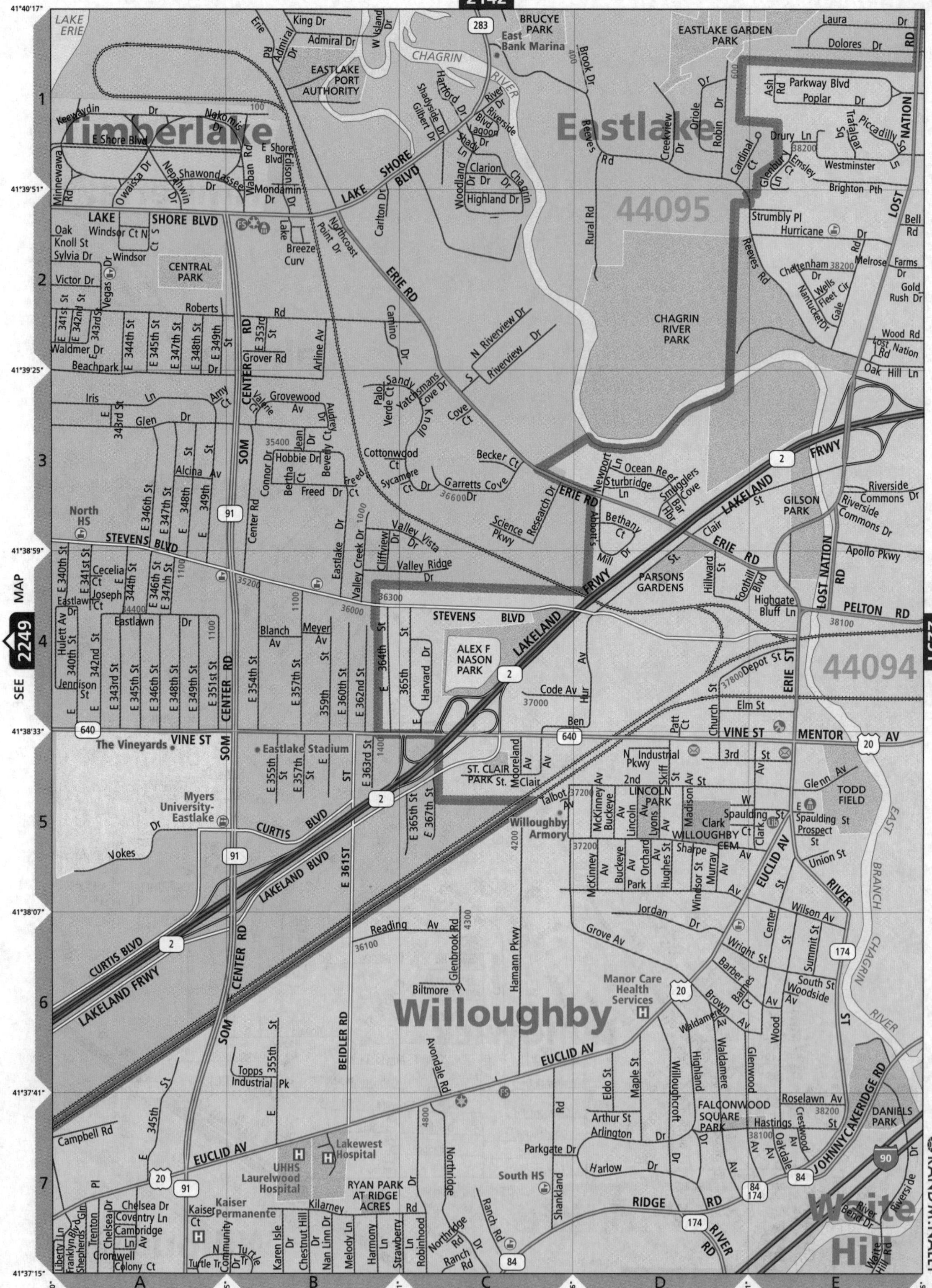
LAKE ERIE
Timberlake
Eastlake
Willoughby
Waite Hill
44095
44094
EASTLAKE GARDEN PARK
BRUCYE PARK
East Bank Marina
EASTLAKE PORT AUTHORITY
CHAGRIN RIVER
CHAGRIN RIVER PARK
CENTRAL PARK
GILSON PARK
PARSONS GARDENS
ALEX F NASON PARK
ST. CLAIR PARK
LINCOLN PARK
WILLOUGHBY CEM
TODD FIELD
FALCONWOOD SQUARE PARK
DANIELS PARK
RYAN PARK AT RIDGE ACRES
North HS
South HS
The Vineyards
Eastlake Stadium
Myers University-Eastlake
Willoughby Armory
Manor Care Health Services
UHHS Laurelwood Hospital
Lakewest Hospital
Kaiser Permanente
LAKE SHORE BLVD
ERIE RD
STEVENS BLVD
VINE ST
MENTOR AV
PELTON RD
LOST NATION RD
LAKELAND FRWY
LAKELAND BLVD
CURTIS BLVD
SOM CENTER RD
BEIDLER RD
E 361ST
EUCLID AV
ERIE ST
RIVER ST
EAST BRANCH CHAGRIN RIVER
JOHNNYCAKERIDGE RD
RIDGE RD
RIVER RD
Hamann Pkwy
Reading Av
Grove Av
Jordan Dr
Wilson Av
Depot St
Elm St
Church St
3rd St
2nd St
Glenn Av
Spaulding St
Union St
Roselawn Av
Hastings St
Harlow Dr
Parkgate Dr
Arlington
Campbell Rd
Vokes Dr
Topps Industrial Pk
Biltmore Pl
Glenbrook Rd
Avondale Rd
Northridge Dr
Robinhood Ln
Kilarney
Science Pkwy
Research Dr
Valley Ridge Dr
Valley Vista Dr
Garretts Cove Dr
Cottonwood Ct
Riverview Dr
N Riverview Dr
Camino Dr
Highland Dr
Clarion Dr
Reeves Rd
Rural Rd
Brook Dr
Creekview Dr
Oriole Dr
Robin Dr
Cardinal Ct
Parkway Blvd
Poplar Dr
Drury Ln
Westminster Ln
Brighton Pth
Hurricane Dr
Chettenham Dr
Melrose Dr
Farms Dr
Gold Rush Dr
Wood Rd
Oak Hill Ln
Laura Dr
Dolores Dr
Riverside Commons Dr
Apollo Pkwy
Highgate Bluff Ln
Admiral Dr
King Dr
E Shore Blvd
Shawondassee Dr
Mondamin Dr
Roberts Rd
Grover Rd
Glen Dr
Iris Ln
Grovewood Av
Stevens Blvd
Eastlawn Dr
Code Av
Blanch Av
Meyer Av
Freed Dr
Alcina Av
Hobbie Dr
A B C D E
1 2 3 4 5 6 7
41°40'17"
41°39'51"
41°39'25"
41°38'59"
41°38'33"
41°38'07"
41°37'41"
41°37'15"
81°26'50"
81°26'15"
81°25'41"
81°25'06"
81°24'31"
81°23'56"

SEE 2249 MAP

SEE 2251 MAP

SEE 2375 MAP

1:24,000
1 in. = 2000 ft.
0 0.25 0.5
miles

SEE 2143 MAP

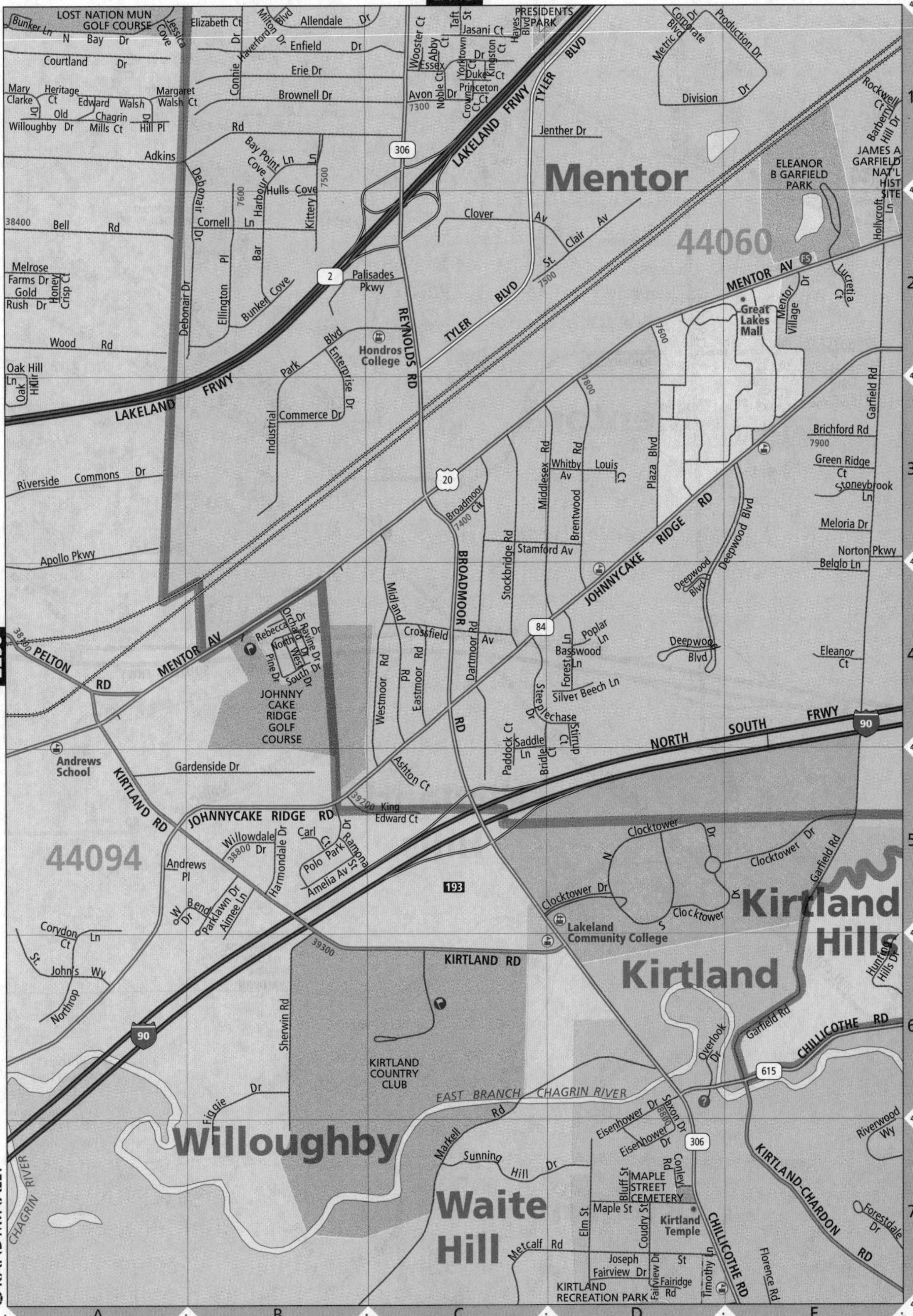
Mentor
44060
44094
Kirtland Hills
Kirtland
Willoughby
Waite Hill
LOST NATION MUN GOLF COURSE
PRESIDENTS PARK
ELEANOR B GARFIELD PARK
JAMES A GARFIELD NAT'L HIST SITE
Great Lakes Mall
Mentor Village
Hondros College
JOHNNY CAKE RIDGE GOLF COURSE
Andrews School
Lakeland Community College
KIRTLAND COUNTRY CLUB
MAPLE STREET CEMETERY
Kirtland Temple
KIRTLAND RECREATION PARK
EAST BRANCH CHAGRIN RIVER
CHAGRIN RIVER
LAKELAND FRWY
TYLER BLVD
REYNOLDS RD
MENTOR AV
JOHNNYCAKE RIDGE RD
BROADMOOR RD
NORTH SOUTH FRWY
KIRTLAND RD
PELTON RD
CHILLICOTHE RD
KIRTLAND-CHARDON RD
Garfield Rd
Clocktower Dr
Industrial Pkwy
Commerce Dr
Riverside Commons Dr
Apollo Pkwy
Gardenside Dr
Bell Rd
Wood Rd
Adkins Rd
Debonair Dr
Clover Av
St. Clair Av
Palisades Pkwy
Division Dr
Production Dr
Corporate Blvd
Metric Dr
Rockwell Ct
Barberry Hill Dr
Hollycroft Ln
Lucretia Ct
Brichford Rd
Green Ridge Ct
Stoneybrook Ln
Meloria Dr
Norton Pkwy
Belglo Ln
Eleanor Ct
Deepwood Blvd
Plaza Blvd
Middlesex Rd
Brentwood Rd
Whitby Av
Louis Ct
Stockbridge Rd
Stamford Av
Midland
Crossfield Av
Westmoor Rd
Eastmoor Rd
Dartmoor Rd
Ashton Ct
Poplar Ln
Basswood Ln
Forest Ln
Silver Beech Ln
Steeplechase Dr
Stirrup Ct
Saddle Ln
Bridle Ct
Paddock Ct
King Edward Ct
Willowdale Dr
Harmondale Dr
Carl Ct
Polo Park Dr
Ramona Dr
Amelia Av
Andrews Pl
W. Bend Dr
Parklawn Dr
Aimee Ln
Corydon Ct
St. John's Wy
Northrop
Sherwin Rd
Fingie Dr
Markell Rd
Sunning Hill Dr
Eisenhower Dr
Saxon Dr
Conley Rd
Maple St
Elm St
Coudry St
Bluff St
Metcalf Rd
Joseph St
Fairview Dr
Fairidge Rd
Timothy Ln
Florence Rd
Overlook Dr
Riverwood Wy
Forestdale Dr
Huntington Hills Dr
Elizabeth Ct
Allendale Dr
Enfield Dr
Erie Dr
Brownell Dr
Bay Dr
Courtland Dr
Bunker Ln
Jessica Cove
Wooster Ct
Avon Dr
Jasani Ct
Jenther Dr
Kittery Dr
Hulls Cove
Bay Point Cove
Cornell Ln
Ellington Pl
Bunker Cove
Melrose Farms Dr
Gold Rush Dr
Honey Crisp Ct
Oak Hill Ln
Willoughby Dr
Chagrin Mills Ct
Margaret Walsh Ct
Rebecca Dr
Pine Dr
South Dr
306
2
20
84
90
193
615
A B C D E
1 2 3 4 5 6 7

SEE 2250 MAP

SEE 2252 MAP

SEE 2376 MAP

1:24,000
1 in. = 2000 ft.
0 0.25 0.5
miles

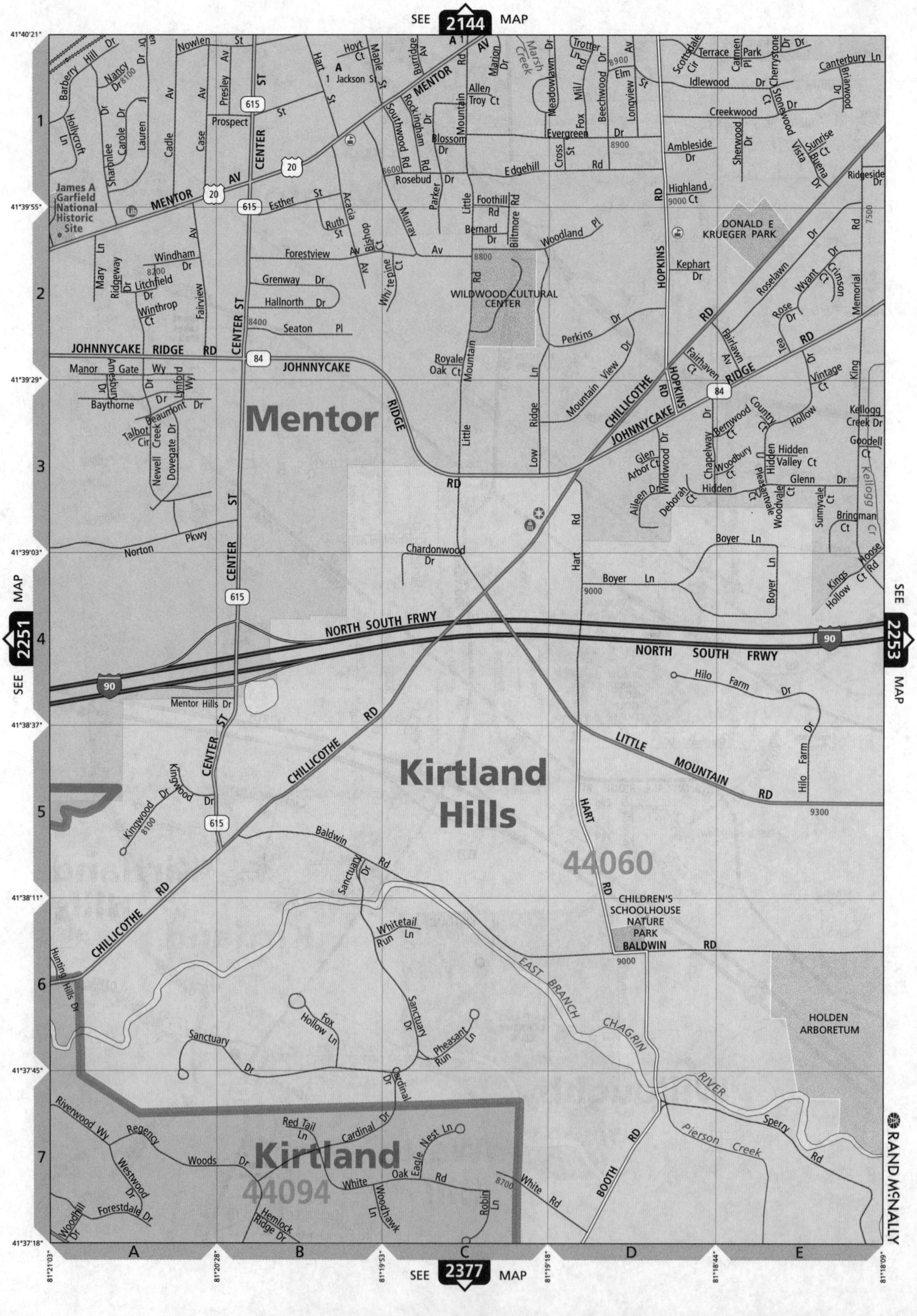
SEE 2144 MAP
SEE 2251 MAP
SEE 2253 MAP
SEE 2377 MAP
Mentor
Kirtland Hills
Kirtland
44060
44094
MENTOR AV
CENTER ST
JOHNNYCAKE RIDGE RD
CHILLICOTHE RD
HOPKINS RD
NORTH SOUTH FRWY
LITTLE MOUNTAIN RD
HART RD
BALDWIN RD
BOOTH RD
EAST BRANCH CHAGRIN RIVER
Pierson Creek
Marsh Creek
Kellogg Cr
James A Garfield National Historic Site
DONALD E KRUEGER PARK
WILDWOOD CULTURAL CENTER
CHILDREN'S SCHOOLHOUSE NATURE PARK
HOLDEN ARBORETUM
Norton Pkwy
Mentor Hills Dr
Baldwin Rd
Sanctuary Dr
Whitetail Run Ln
Fox Hollow Ln
Pheasant Run Ln
Cardinal Dr
Red Tail Ln
Eagle Nest Ln
White Oak Rd
Woodhawk Ln
Robin Ln
Hemlock Ridge Dr
Riverwood Wy
Regency Woods Dr
Westwood Dr
Forestdale Dr
Woodhill Dr
Hunting Hills Dr
Kingwood Dr
Sperry Rd
White Rd
Hilo Farm Dr
Boyer Ln
Chardonwood Dr
Kings Hollow Ct
Hoose Rd
Bringman Ct
Memorial
Canterbury Ln
Idlewood Dr
Creekwood
Edgehill Rd
Evergreen Dr
Rosebud Dr
Foothill Rd
Woodland Pl
Forestview Av
Grenway Dr
Hallnorth Dr
Seaton Pl
Perkins Dr
Mountain View Dr
Low Ridge Ln
Little Mountain Rd
Royale Oak Ct
Windham Dr
Litchfield Dr
Winthrop Ct
Manor Gate Wy
Baythorne Dr
Beaumont Dr
Talbot Cir
Newell Creek Dr
Dovegate Dr
Esther St
Prospect St
Nowlen St
Hidden Valley Ct
Glenn Dr
Vintage Ct
Hollow
Kellogg Creek Dr
Goodell Ct
Roselawn Dr
Crimson
Fairhaven Ct
Fairlawn Av
9000
9300
8700
8900
8800
8400
8200
8100
A B C D E
1 2 3 4 5 6 7
41°40'21"
41°39'55"
41°39'29"
41°39'03"
41°38'37"
41°38'11"
41°37'45"
41°37'18"
81°21'03"
81°20'28"
81°19'53"
81°19'18"
81°18'44"
81°18'09"

1:24,000
1 in. = 2000 ft.
0 0.25 0.5
miles

SEE 2145 MAP

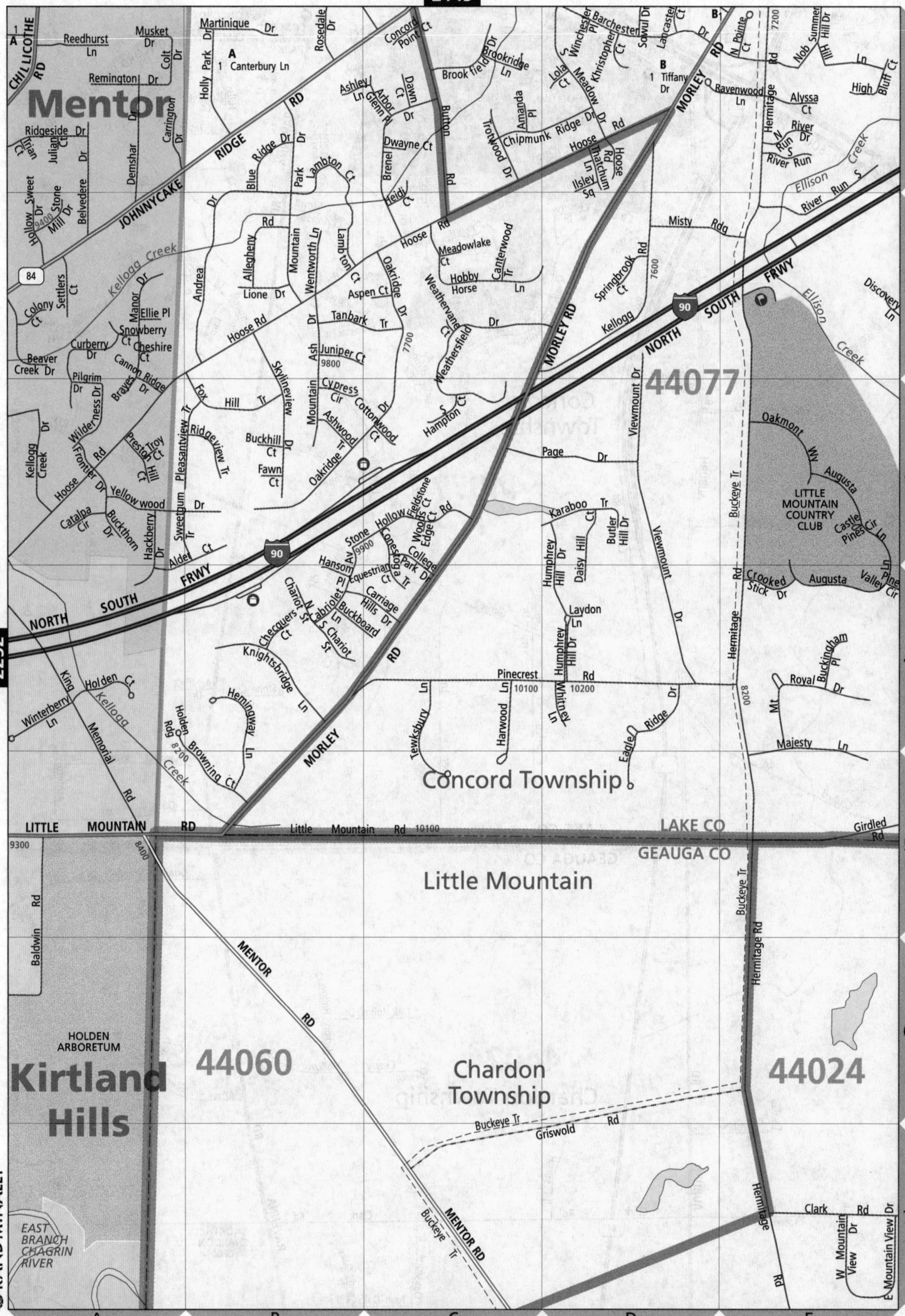
Mentor
Kirtland Hills
Concord Township
Little Mountain
Chardon Township
44077
44060
44024
LAKE CO
GEAUGA CO
HOLDEN ARBORETUM
LITTLE MOUNTAIN COUNTRY CLUB
EAST BRANCH CHAGRIN RIVER
NORTH SOUTH FRWY
90
84
MORLEY RD
JOHNNYCAKE RIDGE RD
CHILLICOTHE RD
LITTLE MOUNTAIN RD
Little Mountain Rd
MENTOR RD
Hermitage Rd
Buckeye Tr
Pinecrest Rd
Viewmount Dr
Hoose Rd
Kellogg Creek
Ellison Creek
Griswold Rd
Clark Rd
Girdled Rd
Baldwin Rd
Memorial Rd
King Memorial Rd
Button Rd
Chipmunk Ridge Dr
Page Dr
Misty Rdg
Springbrook Rd
Oakmont Wy
Augusta
Crooked Stick Dr
Pine Valley Cir
Castle Pines Cir
Royal Dr
Majesty Ln
Mt Royal
Buckingham Pl
Karaboo Tr
Humphrey Hill Dr
Daisy Hill
Butler Hill Dr
Laydon Ln
Whitney Ln
Eagle Ridge Dr
Harwood Ln
Tewksbury Ln
Knightsbridge Ln
Hemingway Ln
Browning Ct
Holden Rdg
Winterberry Ln
Holden Ct
Mountain View Dr
W Mountain View Dr
Reedhurst Ln
Musket Dr
Colt Dr
Remington Dr
Martinique Dr
Holly Park Dr
Rosedale Dr
1 Canterbury Ln
1 Tiffany Dr
Concord Point Ct
Brookfield Dr
Brookridge Ln
Ashley Ln
Arbor Ct
Dawn Ct
Glenn Pl
Dwayne Ct
Brenel Dr
Heidi Ct
Amanda Pl
Trotwood Dr
Lola Ct
Meadow Dr
Winchester Pl
Barchester Dr
Christopher Ct
Sowul Dr
Lancaster Ct
N Pointe Ct
Ravenwood Ln
Alyssa Ct
River Run Dr
Nob Hill Dr
Summer Ln
High Bluff Ct
Thatchum Rd
Isley Ln
Sq
Discovery Ln
Ridgeside Dr
Julian Dr
Demshar Dr
Carrington Dr
Belvedere Dr
Hollow Sweet Dr
Stone Mill Dr
Colony Ct
Settlers Ct
Manor Dr
Ellie Pl
Snowberry Ct
Cheshire Ct
Curberry Dr
Beaver Creek Dr
Pilgrim Dr
Cannon Ridge Dr
Braves Dr
Wilderness Dr
Frontier Rd
Preston Hill Ct
Troy Ct
Kellogg Creek Dr
Yellowwood Dr
Catalpa Cir
Buckthorn Dr
Hackberry Dr
Sweetgum Tr
Alder Ct
Pleasantview Tr
Ridgeview Tr
Fox Hill Tr
Blue Ridge Dr
Park Dr
Lambton Ct
Allegheny Rd
Lione Dr
Andrea Dr
Mountain Dr
Wentworth Ln
Aspen Ct
Oakridge Dr
Tanbark Tr
Juniper Ct
Ash Dr
Skylineview Dr
Cypress Cir
Mountain Dr
Ashwood Tr
Cottonwood Ct
Buckhill Ct
Fawn Ct
Meadowlake Ct
Canterwood Tr
Hobby Horse Ln
Weathervane Ct
Weathersfield Dr
Hampton Ct
Kellogg
Fieldstone Ct
Stone Hollow Av
Woods Edge Ct
Conestoga Tr
College Park Dr
Hanson Pl
Equestrian Ct
Carriage Hills Dr
Chariot St
Cabriolet Ln
Buckboard Ln
Chequers Ct
N Chariot St
S Chariot St
1 2 3 4 5 6 7
A B C D E

SEE 2252 MAP
SEE 2254 MAP
SEE 2378 MAP

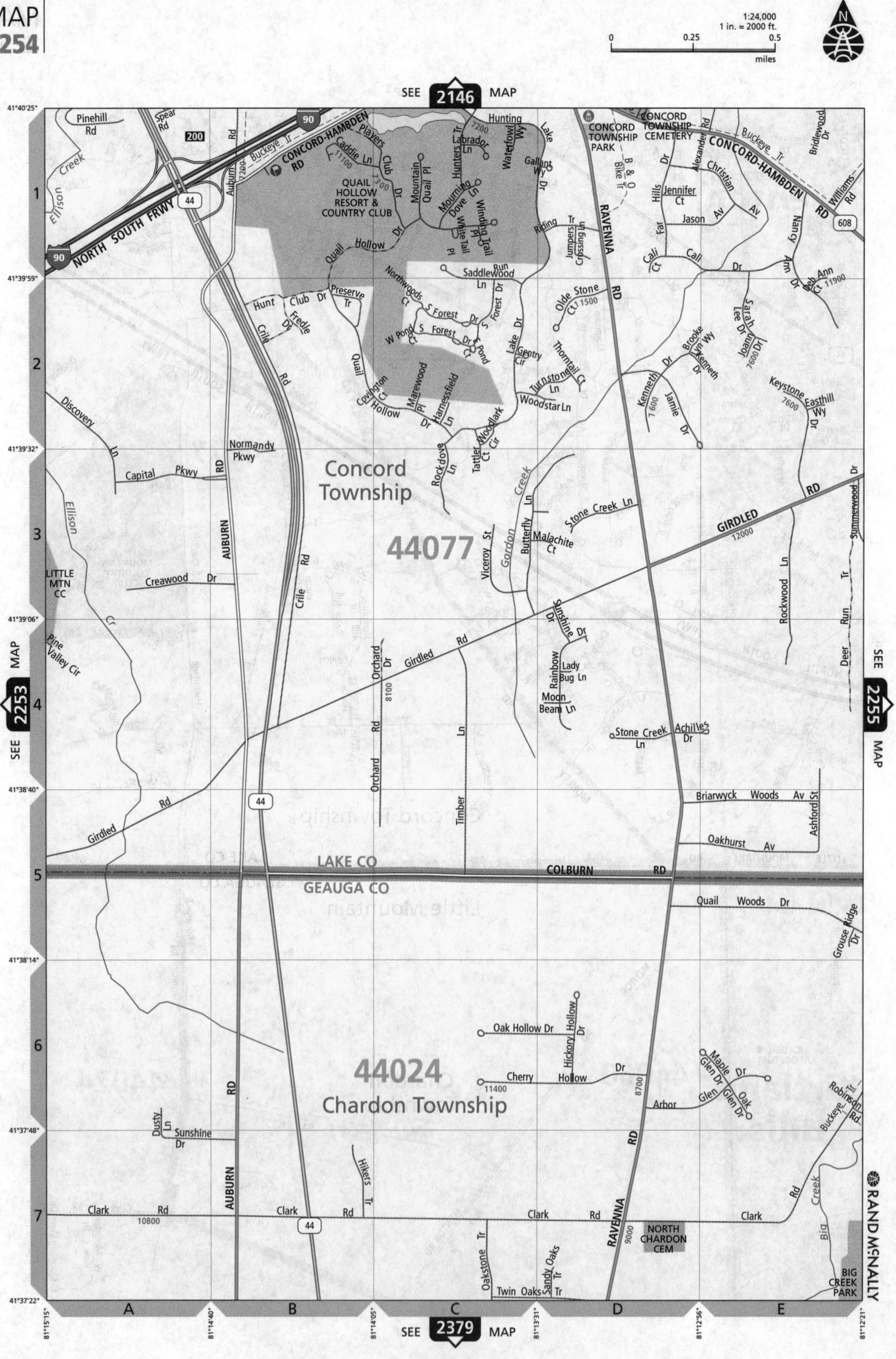
1:24,000
1 in. = 2000 ft.
0
0.25
0.5
miles
N
SEE 2146 MAP
SEE 2379 MAP
SEE 2253 MAP
SEE 2255 MAP
41°40'25"
41°39'59"
41°39'32"
41°39'06"
41°38'40"
41°38'14"
41°37'48"
41°37'22"
81°15'15"
81°14'40"
81°14'05"
81°13'31"
81°12'56"
81°12'21"
A
B
C
D
E
1
2
3
4
5
6
7
Concord Township
44077
44024
Chardon Township
LAKE CO
GEAUGA CO
NORTH SOUTH FRWY
CONCORD-HAMBDEN RD
QUAIL HOLLOW RESORT & COUNTRY CLUB
CONCORD TOWNSHIP PARK
CONCORD TOWNSHIP CEMETERY
LITTLE MTN CC
NORTH CHARDON CEM
BIG CREEK PARK
Pinehill Rd
Spear Rd
Auburn Rd
AUBURN RD
Buckeye Tr
Ellison Creek
Caddie Ln
Players Club Dr
Mountain Quail Pl
Hunters Tr
Labrador Ln
Hunting Lake
Waterfowl Wy
Gallant Wy Dr
Mourning Dove Ln
White Tail Pl
Winding Trail Pl
Quail Hollow Dr
Riding Tr
Jumpers Crossing Ln
RAVENNA RD
B & O Bike Tr
Alexander Rd
Jennifer Ct
Christian Av
Jason Av
Far Hills Dr
Cali Ct
Cali Dr
Bridlewood Dr
Williams Rd
Nancy Ann Dr
Deb Ann Ct
Saddlewood Ln
Run Dr
Olde Stone Ct
Northwoods Ct
S Forest Dr
Forest Dr
W Pond Ct
S Pond Ct
Hunt Club Dr
Preserve Tr
Fredle Dr
Crile Rd
Quail Hollow
Covington Ct
Marewood Pl
Harnessfield Ln
Lake Dr
Gentry Cir
Thorntail Ct
Turnstone Ln
Woodstar Ln
Kenneth Dr
Brooke Lyn Wy
Kenneth Dr
Jamie Dr
Sarah Lee Dr
Joann Dr
Keystone
Easthill Wy Dr
Discovery Ln
Normandy Pkwy
Capital Pkwy RD
Rockdove Ln
Tattler Ct
Woodlark Cir
Gordon Creek
Butterfly Ln
Stone Creek Ln
Malachite Ct
Viceroy St
GIRDLED RD
Summerwood Dr
Rockwood Ln
Deer Run Tr
Creawood Dr
Pine Valley Cir
Orchard Dr
Orchard Rd
Girdled Rd
Timber Ln
Sunshine Dr
Lady Bug Ln
Rainbow Dr
Moon Beam Ln
Stone Creek Ln
Achilles Dr
Briarwyck Woods Av
Ashford St
Oakhurst Av
COLBURN RD
Quail Woods Dr
Grouse Ridge Dr
Oak Hollow Dr
Hickory Hollow Dr
Cherry Hollow Dr
Maple Glen Dr
Oak Glen Dr
Arbor Glen Dr
Robinson Rd
Buckeye Tr
Dusty Ln
Sunshine Dr
Hikers Tr
Clark Rd
Big Creek
Oakstone Tr
Sandy Oaks Tr
Twin Oaks Tr
90
44
200
608
RAND McNALLY

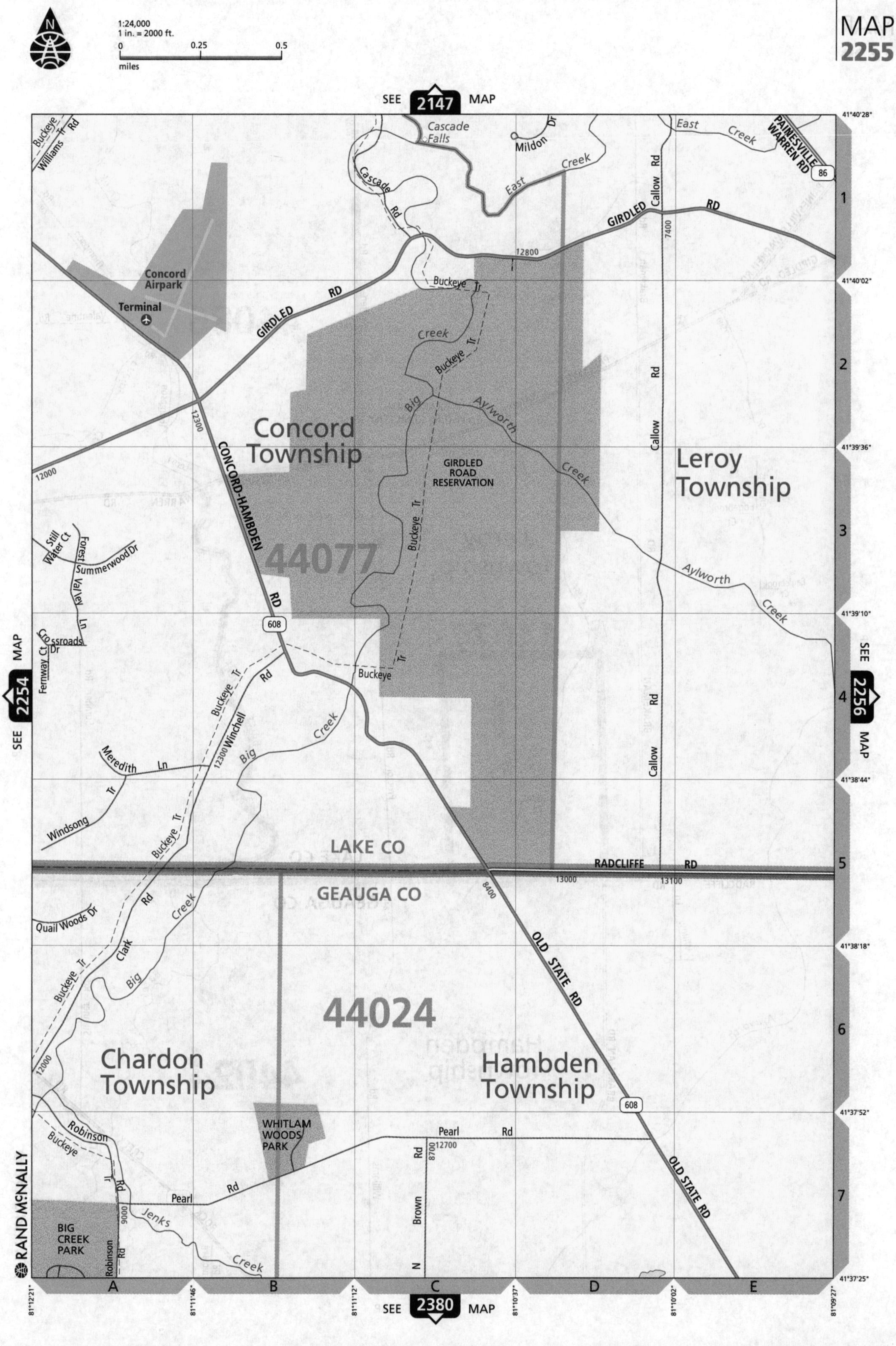
1:24,000
1 in. = 2000 ft.
0 0.25 0.5
miles
SEE 2147 MAP
SEE 2254 MAP
SEE 2256 MAP
SEE 2380 MAP
Concord Township
Leroy Township
Chardon Township
Hambden Township
44077
44024
LAKE CO
GEAUGA CO
Concord Airpark
Terminal
GIRDLED ROAD RESERVATION
WHITLAM WOODS PARK
BIG CREEK PARK
Cascade Falls
GIRDLED RD
CONCORD-HAMBDEN RD
OLD STATE RD
RADCLIFFE RD
PAINESVILLE WARREN RD
Callow Rd
Cascade Rd
Buckeye Tr
Big Creek
Aylworth Creek
East Creek
Jenks Creek
Mildon Dr
Williams Tr Rd
Still Water Ct
Forest Valley Ln
Summerwood Dr
Crossroads Dr
Fernway Ct
Meredith Ln
Winchell Rd
Windsong Tr
Quail Woods Dr
Clark Rd
Robinson Rd
Pearl Rd
Brown Rd
86
608
12000
12300
12800
7400
13000
13100
8400
12700
8700
9000
1 2 3 4 5 6 7
A B C D E
41°40'28"
41°40'02"
41°39'36"
41°39'10"
41°38'44"
41°38'18"
41°37'52"
41°37'25"
81°12'21"
81°11'46"
81°11'12"
81°10'37"
81°10'02"
81°09'27"
RAND McNALLY

1:24,000
1 in. = 2000 ft.
0 0.25 0.5
miles

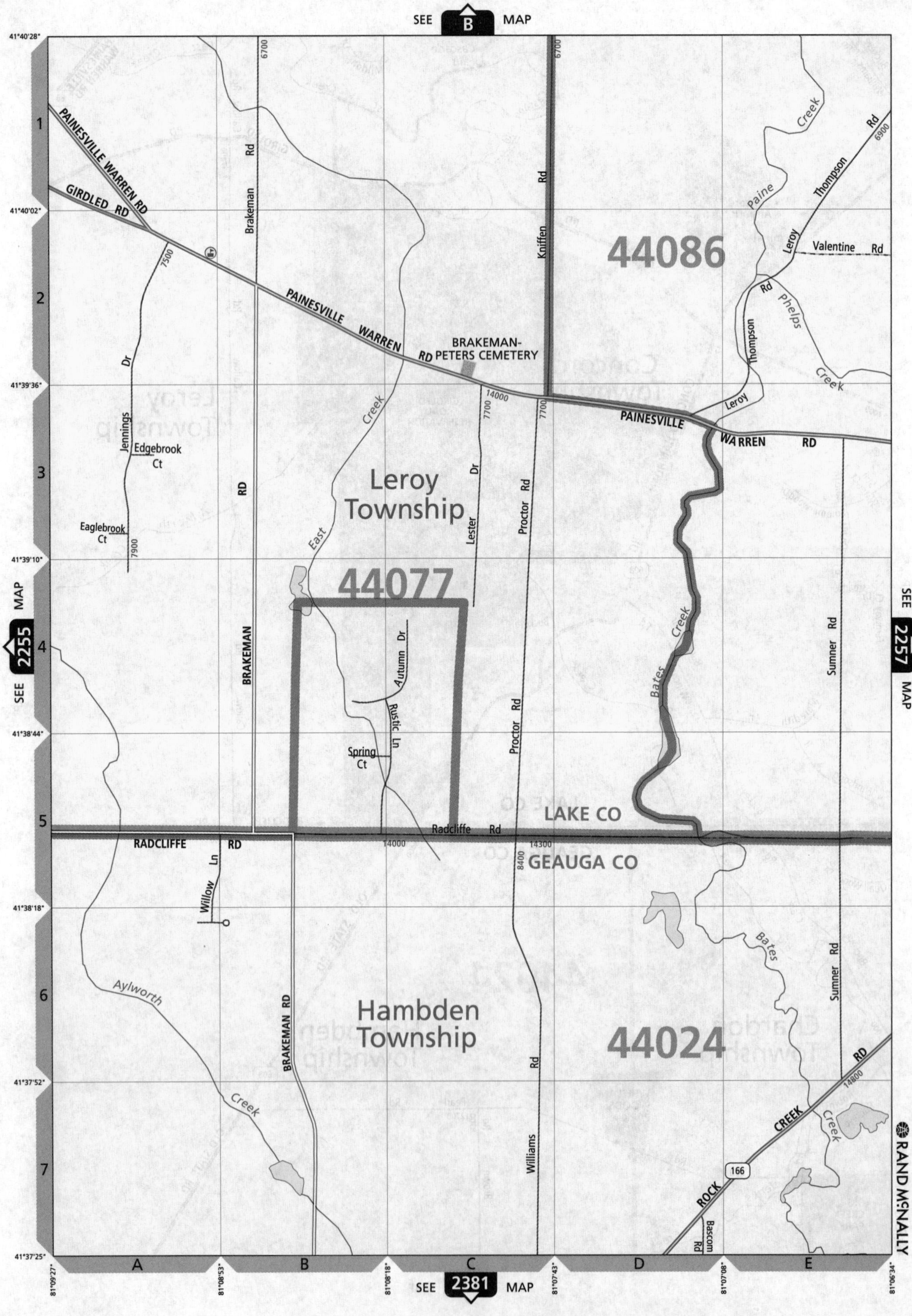
SEE B MAP
SEE 2255 MAP
SEE 2257 MAP
SEE 2381 MAP
41°40'28"
41°40'02"
41°39'36"
41°39'10"
41°38'44"
41°38'18"
41°37'52"
41°37'25"
81°09'27"
81°08'53"
81°08'18"
81°07'43"
81°07'08"
A
B
C
D
E
1
2
3
4
5
6
7
PAINESVILLE WARREN RD
GIRDLED RD
Brakeman Rd
6700
7500
Jennings Dr
Edgebrook Ct
Eaglebrook Ct
7900
PAINESVILLE WARREN RD
BRAKEMAN-PETERS CEMETERY
14000
Kniffen Rd
6700
7700
7700
Lester Dr
Proctor Rd
44086
Paine Creek
Thompson Rd
6900
Leroy
Valentine Rd
Rd
Thompson
Phelps Creek
Leroy
PAINESVILLE
WARREN RD
RD
East Creek
Leroy Township
44077
BRAKEMAN RD
Autumn Dr
Rustic Ln
Spring Ct
Bates Creek
Sumner Rd
LAKE CO
Radcliffe Rd
14000
14300
RADCLIFFE RD
GEAUGA CO
8400
Willow Ln
Bates
Aylworth Creek
BRAKEMAN RD
Hambden Township
Williams Rd
44024
Sumner Rd
ROCK CREEK RD
14800
166
Creek
Bascom Rd
RAND McNALLY

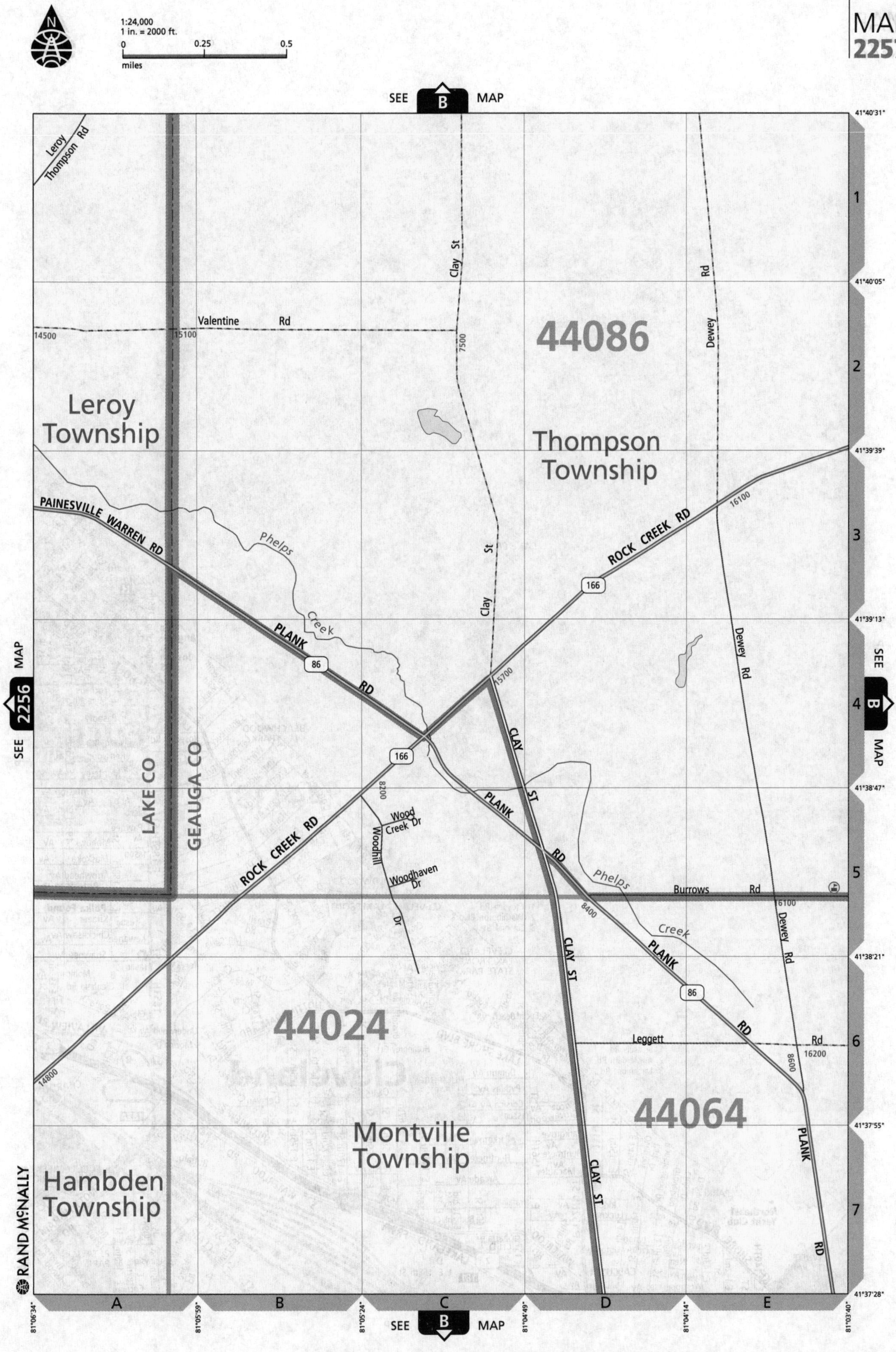
1:24,000
1 in. = 2000 ft.
0
0.25
0.5
miles
SEE B MAP
SEE 2256 MAP
SEE B MAP
SEE B MAP
Leroy Thompson Rd
Valentine Rd
14500
15100
Clay St
7500
Dewey Rd
44086
Leroy Township
Thompson Township
PAINESVILLE WARREN RD
Phelps Creek
ROCK CREEK RD
16100
166
PLANK RD
86
15700
CLAY ST
LAKE CO
GEAUGA CO
8200
Wood Creek Dr
Woodhill Dr
Woodhaven Dr
Burrows Rd
8400
16100
Leggett Rd
16200
8600
44024
44064
Montville Township
Hambden Township
14800
1
2
3
4
5
6
7
A
B
C
D
E
41°40'31"
41°40'05"
41°39'39"
41°39'13"
41°38'47"
41°38'21"
41°37'55"
41°37'28"
81°06'34"
81°05'59"
81°05'24"
81°04'49"
81°04'14"
81°03'40"
RAND McNALLY

1:24,000
1 in. = 2000 ft.
0 0.25 0.5 miles

SEE B MAP

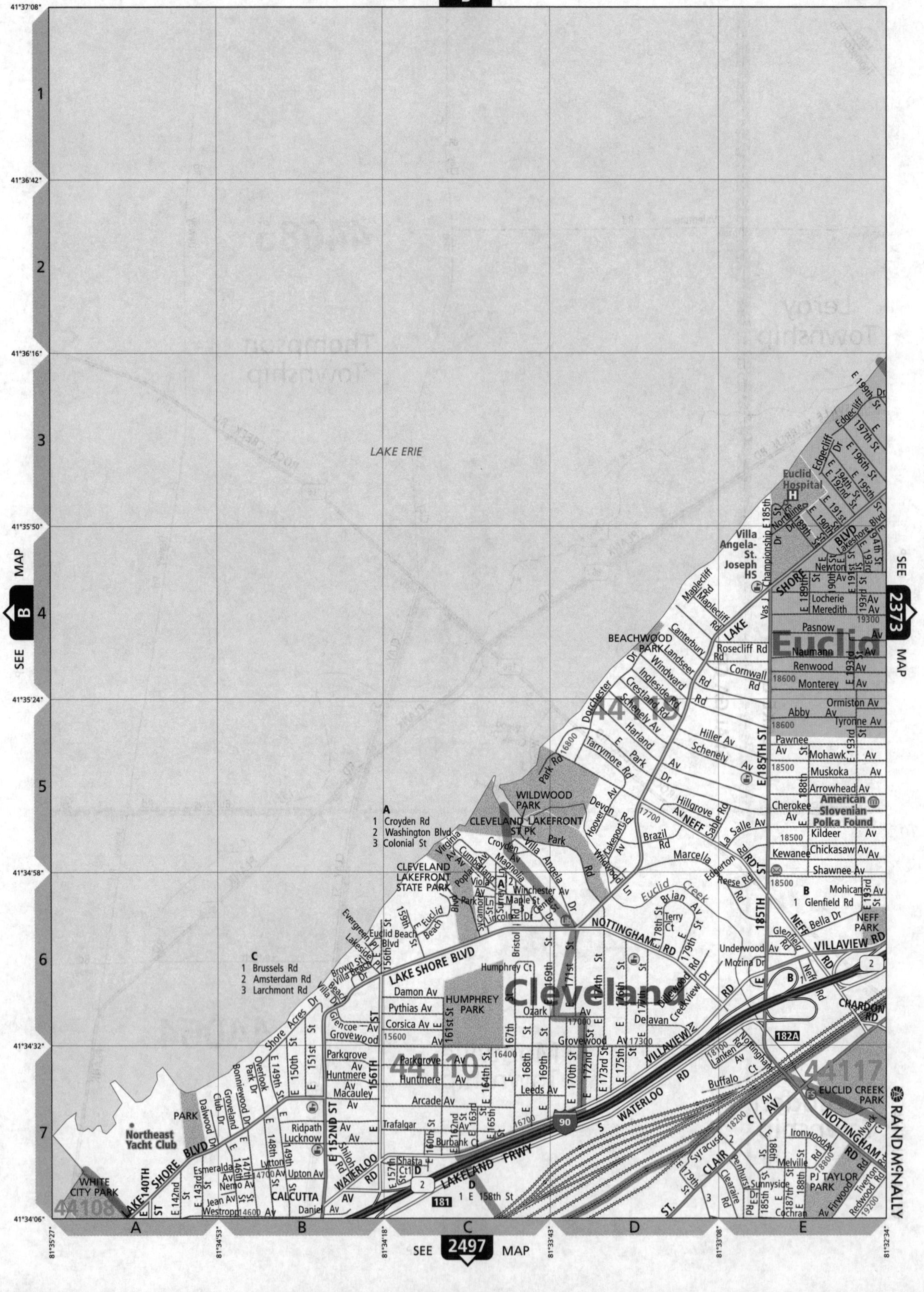
LAKE ERIE
Thompson Township
Leroy Township
Euclid
Cleveland
44110
44117
44119
44108
Euclid Hospital
Villa Angela-St. Joseph HS
BEACHWOOD PARK
WILDWOOD PARK
CLEVELAND LAKEFRONT ST PK
CLEVELAND LAKEFRONT STATE PARK
HUMPHREY PARK
NEFF PARK
EUCLID CREEK PARK
PJ TAYLOR PARK
WHITE CITY PARK
Northeast Yacht Club
American Slovenian Polka Found
LAKE SHORE BLVD
NOTTINGHAM RD
E 185TH ST
VILLAVIEW RD
WATERLOO RD
LAKELAND FRWY
CHARDON RD
CLAIR AV
E 152ND ST
E 156TH ST
E 140TH ST
Euclid Creek
A
1 Croyden Rd
2 Washington Blvd
3 Colonial St
B
1 Glenfield Rd
C
1 Brussels Rd
2 Amsterdam Rd
3 Larchmont Rd
D
1 E 158th St
41°37'08"
41°36'42"
41°36'16"
41°35'50"
41°35'24"
41°34'58"
41°34'32"
41°34'06"
81°35'27"
81°34'53"
81°34'18"
81°33'43"
81°33'08"
81°32'34"

SEE B MAP
SEE 2373 MAP
SEE 2497 MAP

1:24,000
1 in. = 2000 ft.
0 0.25 0.5
miles

SEE 2248 MAP

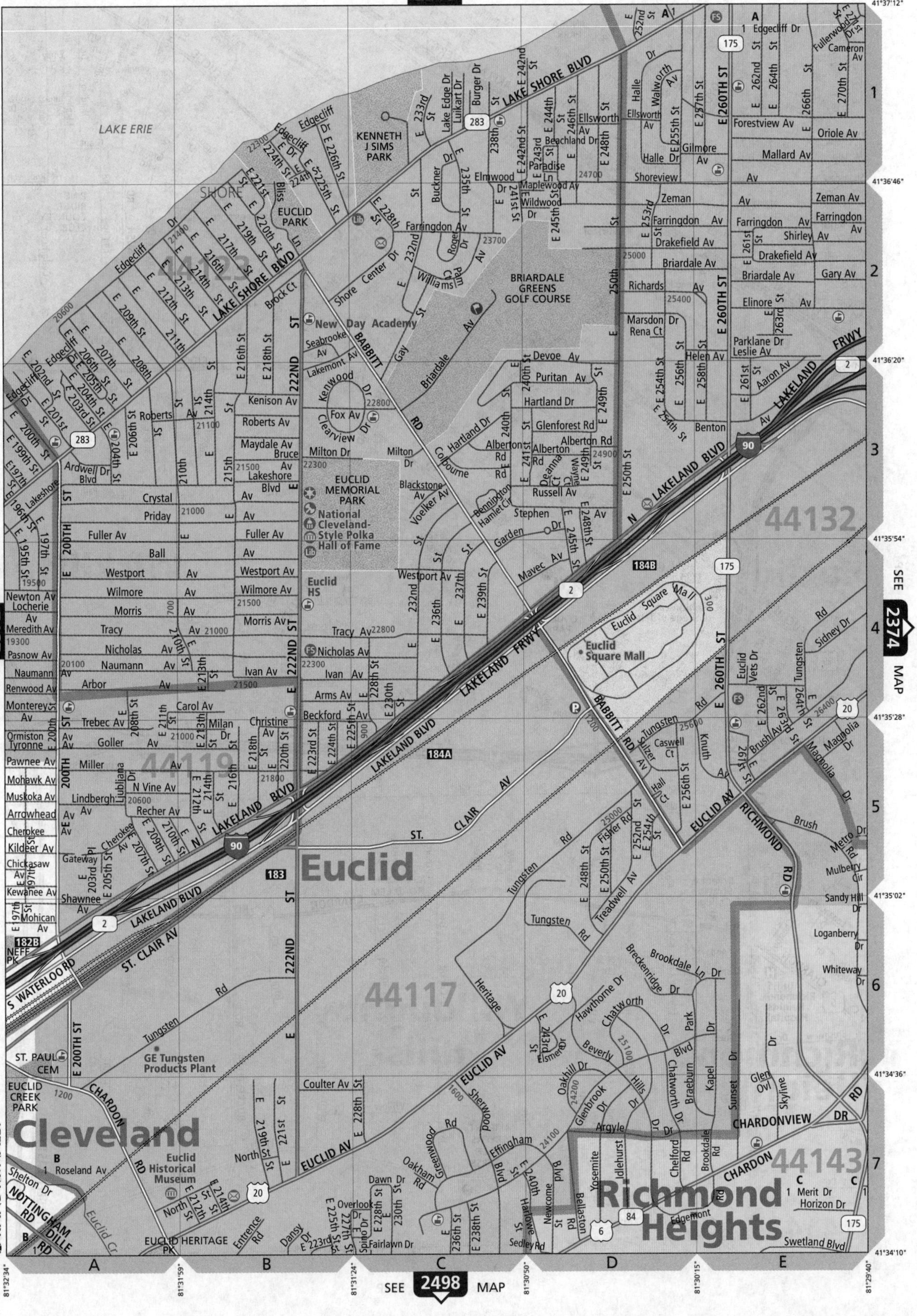
LAKE ERIE
Euclid
Cleveland
Richmond Heights
44123
44119
44117
44132
44143
LAKE SHORE BLVD
LAKELAND FRWY
N LAKELAND BLVD
LAKELAND BLVD
ST. CLAIR AV
EUCLID AV
BABBITT RD
E 222ND ST
E 200TH ST
E 260TH ST
CHARDON RD
CHARDONVIEW DR
RICHMOND RD
KENNETH J SIMS PARK
EUCLID PARK
BRIARDALE GREENS GOLF COURSE
New Day Academy
EUCLID MEMORIAL PARK
National Cleveland-Style Polka Hall of Fame
Euclid HS
Euclid Square Mall
GE Tungsten Products Plant
ST. PAUL CEM
EUCLID CREEK PARK
Euclid Historical Museum
EUCLID HERITAGE PK
S WATERLOO RD
NOTTINGHAM RD
DILLE RD
Tungsten Rd
Heritage
Sherwood
Effingham Blvd
Brookdale Ln
Chatworth
Beverly Hills Dr
Glenbrook Dr
Argyle
Sunset Dr
Skyline
Loganberry Dr
Whiteway Dr
Sandy Hill Dr
Metro Dr
Magnolia Dr
Brush Av
Swetland Blvd
Horizon Dr
Merit Dr
Edgemont
Shelton Dr
Roseland Av
Coulter Av
North St
Dawn Dr
Fairlawn Dr
Sedley Rd
Hallowe St
Newcome Blvd
Bellaston Rd
Yosemite
Idlehurst Dr
Chelford Rd
Brookdale Rd
90
2
20
6
84
175
283
183
184A
184B
182B
41°37'12"
41°36'46"
41°36'20"
41°35'54"
41°35'28"
41°35'02"
41°34'36"
41°34'10"
81°32'34"
81°31'59"
81°31'24"
81°30'50"
81°30'15"
81°29'40"
A B C D E
1 2 3 4 5 6 7

SEE 2372 MAP

SEE 2374 MAP

SEE 2498 MAP

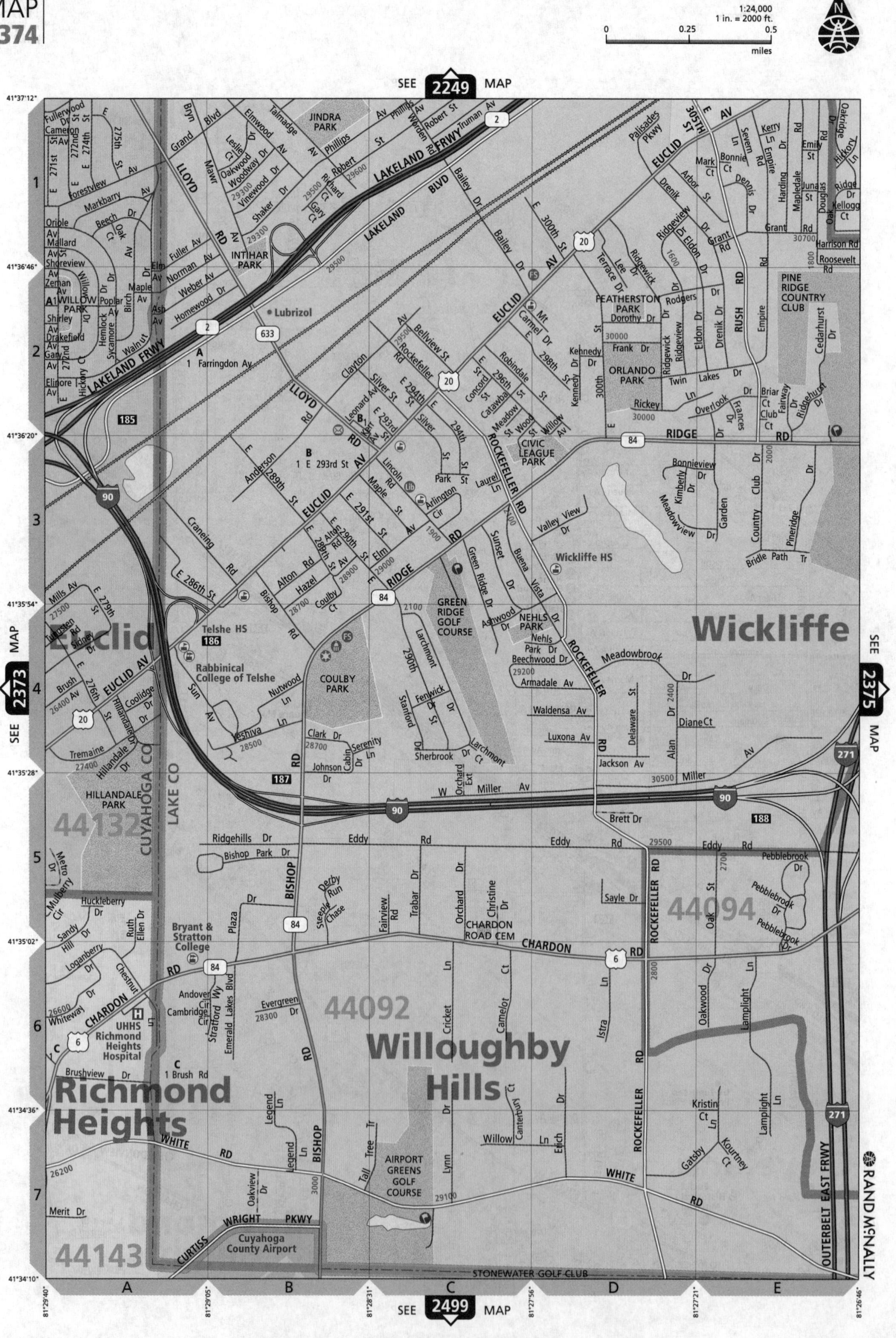
1:24,000
1 in. = 2000 ft.
0
0.25
0.5
miles
SEE 2249 MAP
SEE 2373 MAP
SEE 2375 MAP
SEE 2499 MAP
Euclid
Wickliffe
Richmond Heights
Willoughby Hills
44132
44094
44092
44143
CUYAHOGA CO
LAKE CO
LAKELAND FRWY
LAKELAND BLVD
EUCLID AV
LLOYD RD
ROCKEFELLER RD
RIDGE RD
BISHOP RD
CHARDON RD
WHITE RD
RUSH RD
Eddy Rd
Miller Av
OUTERBELT EAST FRWY
JINDRA PARK
INTIHAR PARK
WILLOW PARK
Lubrizol
A 1 Farringdon Av
B 1 E 293rd St
C 1 Brush Rd
CIVIC LEAGUE PARK
FEATHERSTON PARK
ORLANDO PARK
PINE RIDGE COUNTRY CLUB
Wickliffe HS
GREEN RIDGE GOLF COURSE
NEHLS PARK
Telshe HS
Rabbinical College of Telshe
COULBY PARK
HILLANDALE PARK
Bryant & Stratton College
CHARDON ROAD CEM
UHHS Richmond Heights Hospital
AIRPORT GREENS GOLF COURSE
Cuyahoga County Airport
CURTISS WRIGHT PKWY
STONEWATER GOLF CLUB
RAND McNALLY

1:24,000
1 in. = 2000 ft.
0 0.25 0.5
miles

SEE 2250 MAP

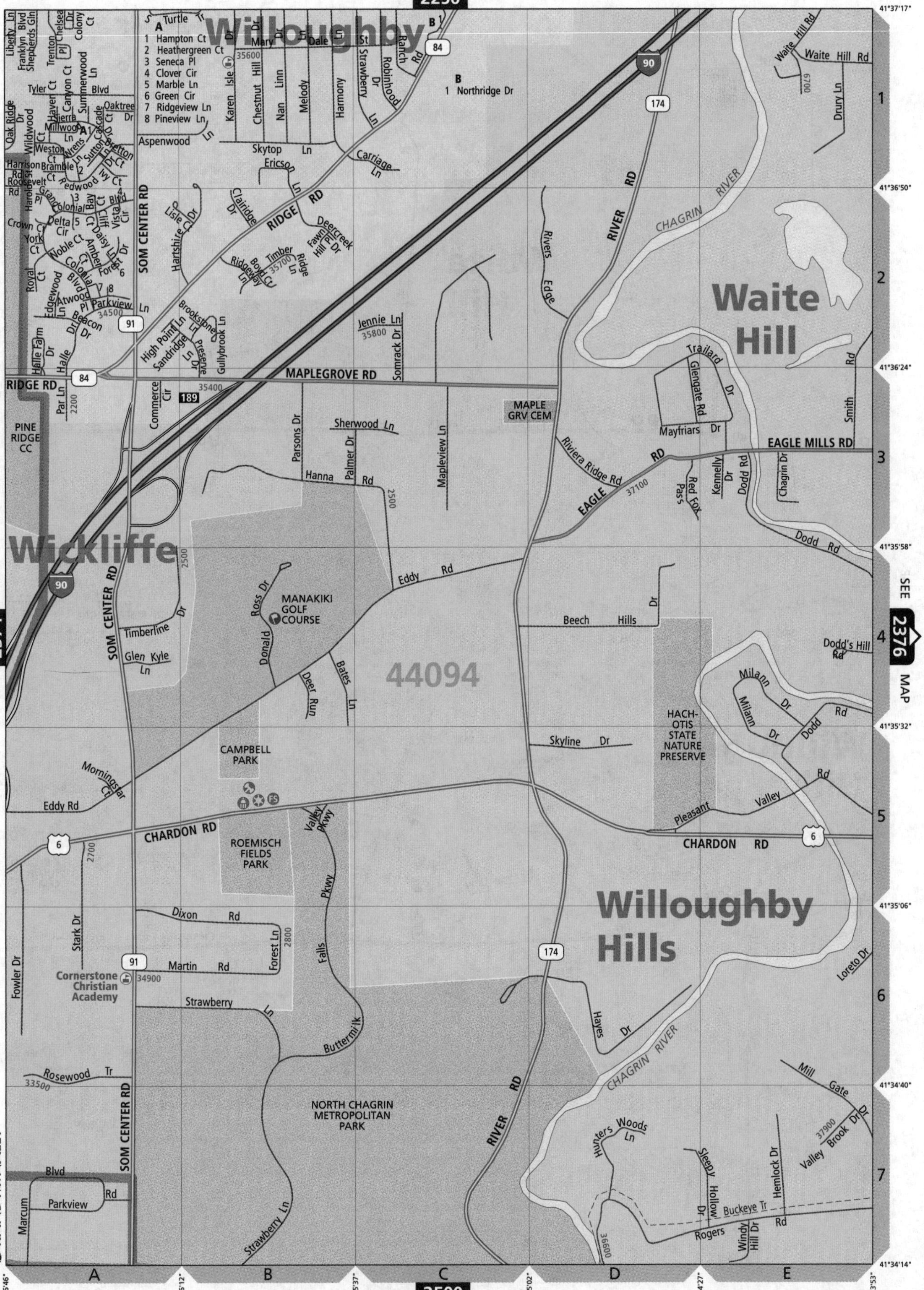
Willoughby
Waite Hill
Wickliffe
Willoughby Hills
44094
A
1 Hampton Ct
2 Heathergreen Ct
3 Seneca Pl
4 Clover Cir
5 Marble Ln
6 Green Cir
7 Ridgeview Ln
8 Pineview Ln
B
1 Northridge Dr
RIDGE RD
MAPLEGROVE RD
EAGLE MILLS RD
EAGLE RD
CHARDON RD
SOM CENTER RD
RIVER RD
CHAGRIN RIVER
Eddy Rd
Hanna Rd
Skytop Ln
Beech Hills Dr
Skyline Dr
Pleasant Valley Rd
Dodd Rd
Waite Hill Rd
Dixon Rd
Martin Rd
Strawberry Ln
Buttermilk Falls Pkwy
Rosewood Tr
Mill Gate Dr
Valley Brook Dr
Hunters Woods Ln
Buckeye Tr
Rogers Rd
PINE RIDGE CC
MAPLE GRV CEM
MANAKIKI GOLF COURSE
CAMPBELL PARK
ROEMISCH FIELDS PARK
HACH-OTIS STATE NATURE PRESERVE
NORTH CHAGRIN METROPOLITAN PARK
Cornerstone Christian Academy
SEE 2374 MAP
SEE 2376 MAP
1
2
3
4
5
6
7
A
B
C
D
E
41°37'17"
41°36'50"
41°36'24"
41°35'58"
41°35'32"
41°35'06"
41°34'40"
41°34'14"
81°26'46"
81°26'12"
81°25'37"
81°25'02"
81°24'27"
81°23'53"

RAND McNALLY

SEE 2500 MAP

SEE 2251 MAP

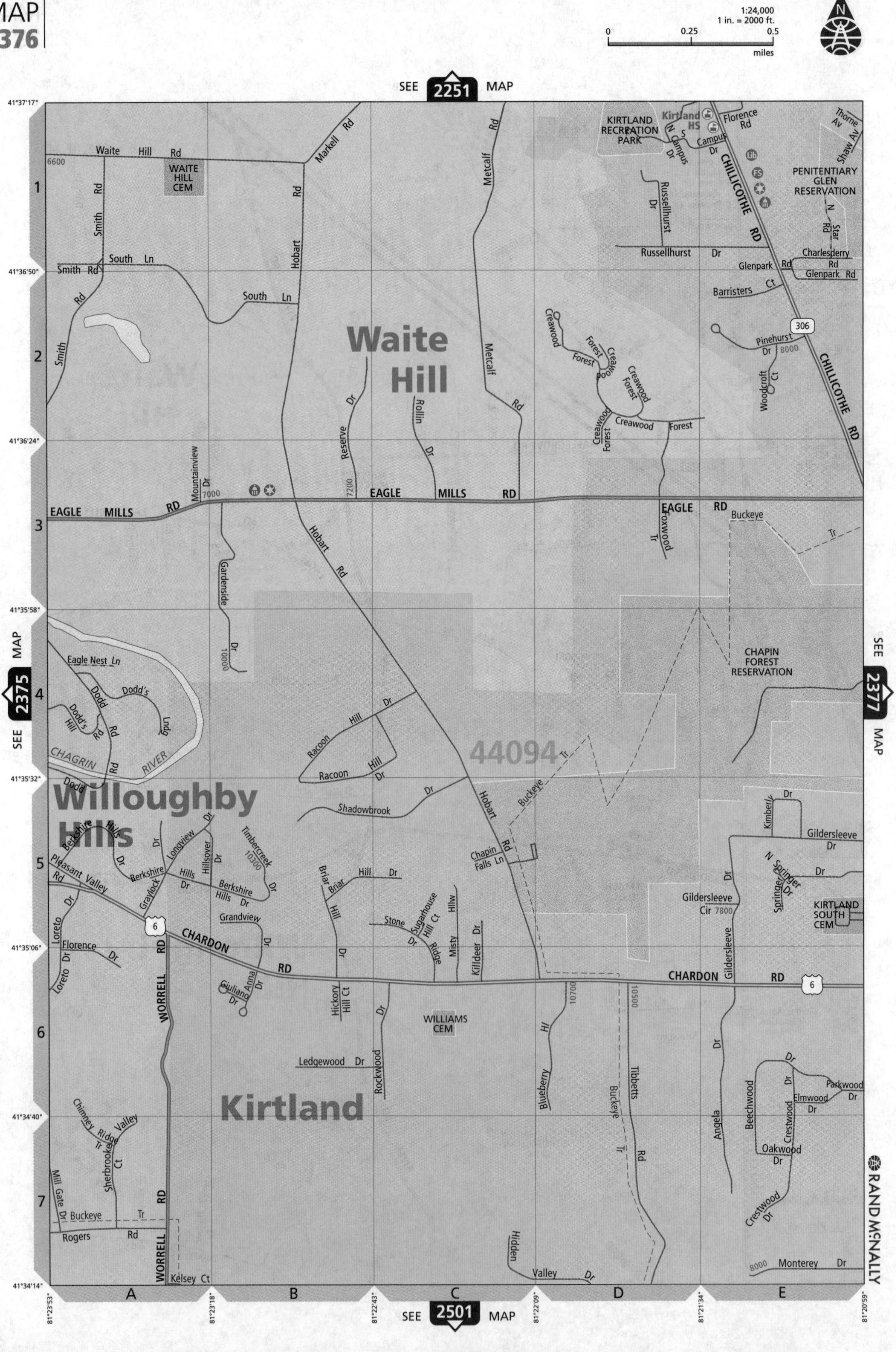
1:24,000
1 in. = 2000 ft.
0
0.25
0.5
miles
N
Waite Hill
Willoughby Hills
Kirtland
44094
WAITE HILL CEM
KIRTLAND RECREATION PARK
Kirtland HS
PENITENTIARY GLEN RESERVATION
CHAPIN FOREST RESERVATION
KIRTLAND SOUTH CEM
WILLIAMS CEM
CHAGRIN RIVER
Waite Hill Rd
Markell Rd
Metcalf Rd
Hobart Rd
Smith Rd
South Ln
Florence Rd
Campus Dr
N Campus Dr
S Campus Dr
Russellhurst Dr
CHILLICOTHE RD
Thorne Av
Shaw Av
N Star Rd
Charlesderry Rd
Glenpark Rd
Barristers Ct
306
Pinehurst Dr
Woodcroft Ct
Creawood Forest
Forest
Reserve Dr
Rollin Dr
Mountainview Dr
EAGLE MILLS RD
EAGLE RD
Foxwood Tr
Buckeye Tr
Gardenside Dr
Eagle Nest Ln
Dodd Rd
Dodd's Lndg
Dodd's Hill Rd
Racoon Hill Dr
Shadowbrook Dr
Chapin Falls Ln
Kimberly Dr
Gildersleeve Dr
N Springer Dr
Springer Dr
Gildersleeve Cir
Berkshire Hills Dr
Longview Dr
Hillsover Dr
Timbercreek Dr
Pleasant Valley Rd
Graylock Dr
Briar Hill Dr
Stone Sugarhouse Hill Ct
Ridge Dr
Misty Hllw
Killdeer Dr
Grandview Dr
Loreto Dr
Florence Dr
6
CHARDON RD
Giuliano Dr
Anna Dr
Hickory Hill Ct
Rockwood Dr
Ledgewood Dr
Blueberry Hl
Tibbetts Rd
Angela Dr
Beechwood Dr
Crestwood Dr
Parkwood Dr
Elmwood Dr
Oakwood Dr
WORRELL RD
Chimney Ridge Tr
Valley
Sherbrooke Ct
Mill Gate Dr
Rogers Rd
Kelsey Ct
Hidden Valley Dr
Monterey Dr
A
B
C
D
E
1
2
3
4
5
6
7
SEE 2375 MAP
SEE 2377 MAP
RAND McNALLY

SEE 2501 MAP

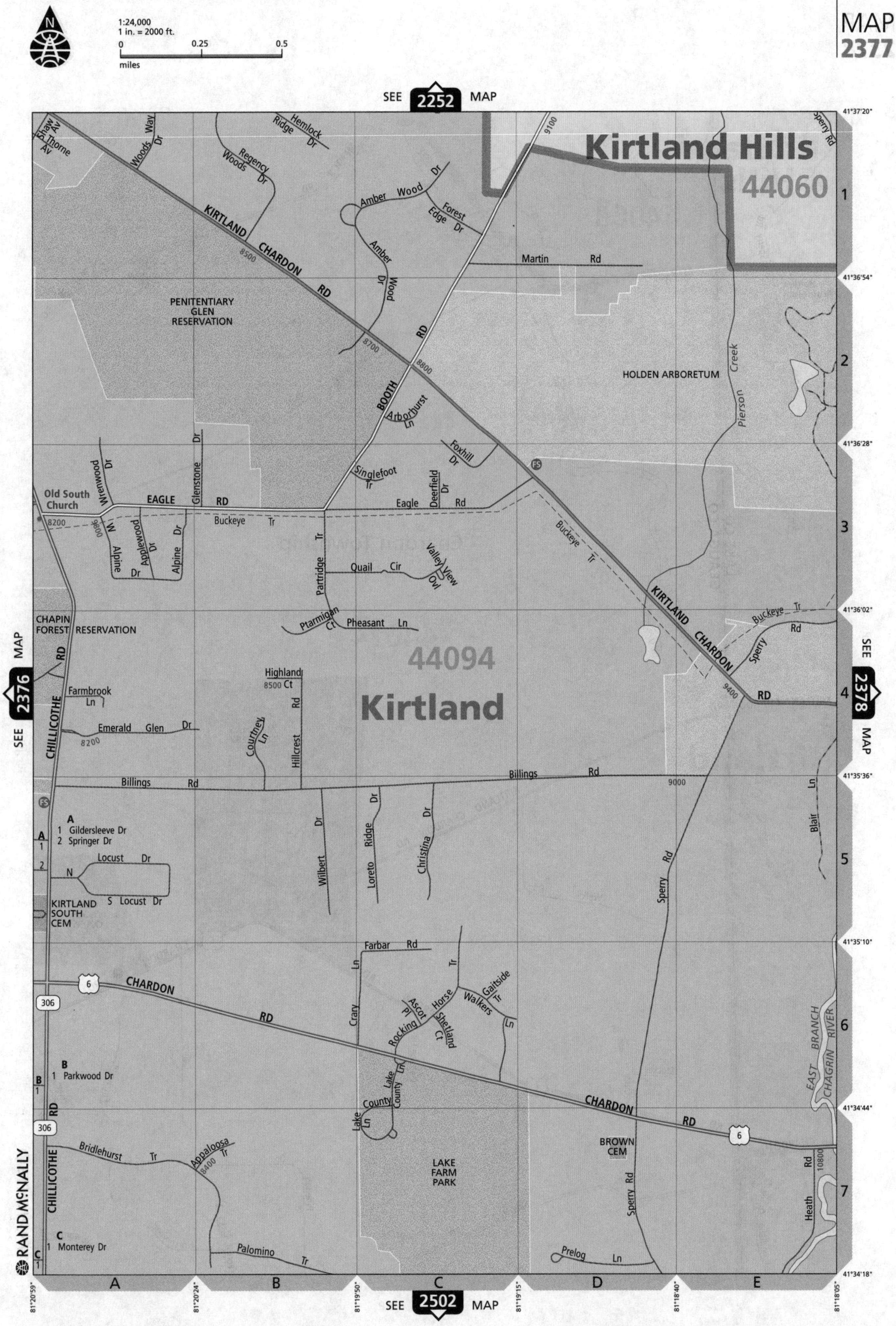
1:24,000
1 in. = 2000 ft.
0 0.25 0.5
miles
SEE 2252 MAP
SEE 2502 MAP
SEE 2376 MAP
SEE 2378 MAP
Kirtland Hills
44060
Kirtland
44094
Shaw Av
Thorne Av
Woods Way Dr
Hemlock Ridge Dr
Regency Woods Dr
Amber Wood Dr
Forest Edge Dr
Amber Wood Dr
Martin Rd
KIRTLAND CHARDON RD
8500
8700
8800
9100
9400
9000
8200
8400
10800
BOOTH RD
PENITENTIARY GLEN RESERVATION
HOLDEN ARBORETUM
Pierson Creek
Arborhurst Ln
Foxhill Dr
Singlefoot Tr
Deerfield Dr
Wrenwood Dr
Glenstone Dr
Old South Church
EAGLE RD
Eagle Rd
Buckeye Tr
Alpine Dr
Applewood Dr
Partridge Tr
Quail Cir
Valley View
Owl
Ptarmigan Ct
Pheasant Ln
Sperry Rd
CHAPIN FOREST RESERVATION
Farmbrook Ln
Highland Ct
Emerald Glen Dr
Courtney Ln
Hillcrest Rd
Billings Rd
Blair Ln
A
1 Gildersleeve Dr
2 Springer Dr
N Locust Dr
S Locust Dr
Wilbert Dr
Loreto Ridge Dr
Christina Dr
KIRTLAND SOUTH CEM
Farbar Rd
Crary Ln
6
306
CHARDON RD
Ascot Pl
Horse Tr
Gaitside Tr
Walkers Ln
Shetland Ct
Rocking Ln
Lake County Ln
EAST BRANCH CHAGRIN RIVER
B
1 Parkwood Dr
CHILLICOTHE RD
Bridlehurst Tr
Appaloosa Tr
BROWN CEM
LAKE FARM PARK
Heath Rd
C
1 Monterey Dr
Palomino Tr
Prelog Ln
RAND McNALLY
41°37'20"
41°36'54"
41°36'28"
41°36'02"
41°35'36"
41°35'10"
41°34'44"
41°34'18"
81°20'59"
81°20'24"
81°19'50"
81°19'15"
81°18'40"
81°18'05"
A B C D E
1 2 3 4 5 6 7

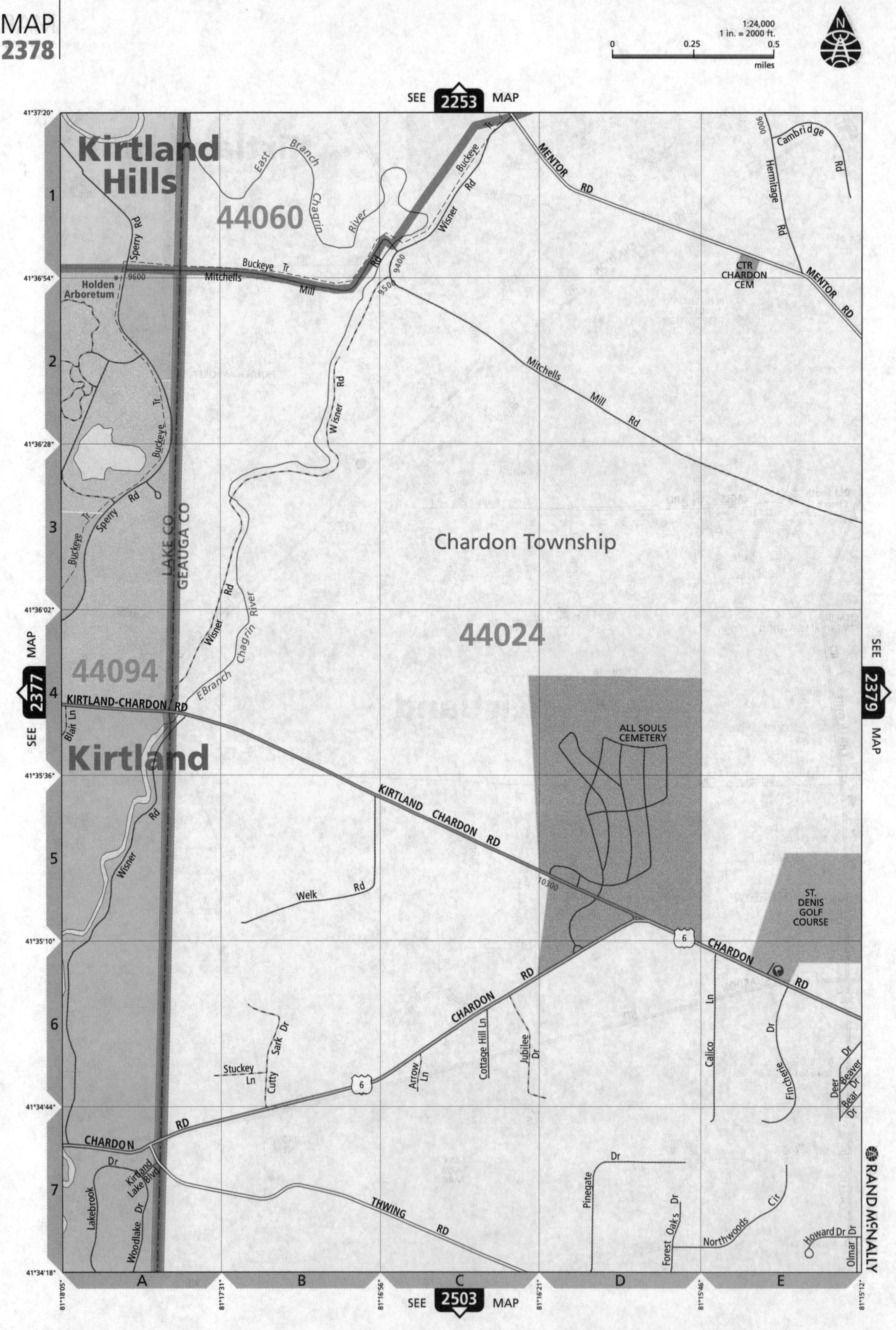
1:24,000
1 in. = 2000 ft.
0 0.25 0.5
miles
SEE 2253 MAP
SEE 2377 MAP
SEE 2379 MAP
SEE 2503 MAP
Kirtland Hills
44060
East Branch Chagrin River
Buckeye Tr
Wisner Rd
MENTOR RD
Cambridge Rd
Hermitage Rd
9000
Sperry Rd
Mitchells Mill Rd
9600
9400
9500
Holden Arboretum
CTR CHARDON CEM
Mitchells Mill Rd
LAKE CO
GEAUGA CO
Chardon Township
44024
44094
KIRTLAND-CHARDON RD
Blair Ln
Kirtland
E Branch Chagrin River
ALL SOULS CEMETERY
KIRTLAND CHARDON RD
10300
Welk Rd
ST. DENIS GOLF COURSE
6
CHARDON RD
Sark Dr
Stuckey Ln
Cutty
Arrow Ln
Cottage Hill Ln
Jubilee Dr
Calico Ln
Finchelie Dr
Deer Dr
Beaver Dr
Bear Dr
CHARDON RD
Lakebrook Dr
Kirtland Lake Blvd
Woodlake Dr
THWING RD
Pinegate Dr
Forest Oaks Dr
Northwoods Cir
Howard Dr
Olmar Dr
A B C D E
1 2 3 4 5 6 7
41°37'20"
41°36'54"
41°36'28"
41°36'02"
41°35'36"
41°35'10"
41°34'44"
41°34'18"
81°18'05"
81°17'31"
81°16'56"
81°16'21"
81°15'46"
81°15'12"
RAND McNALLY

1:24,000
1 in. = 2000 ft.
0 0.25 0.5
miles

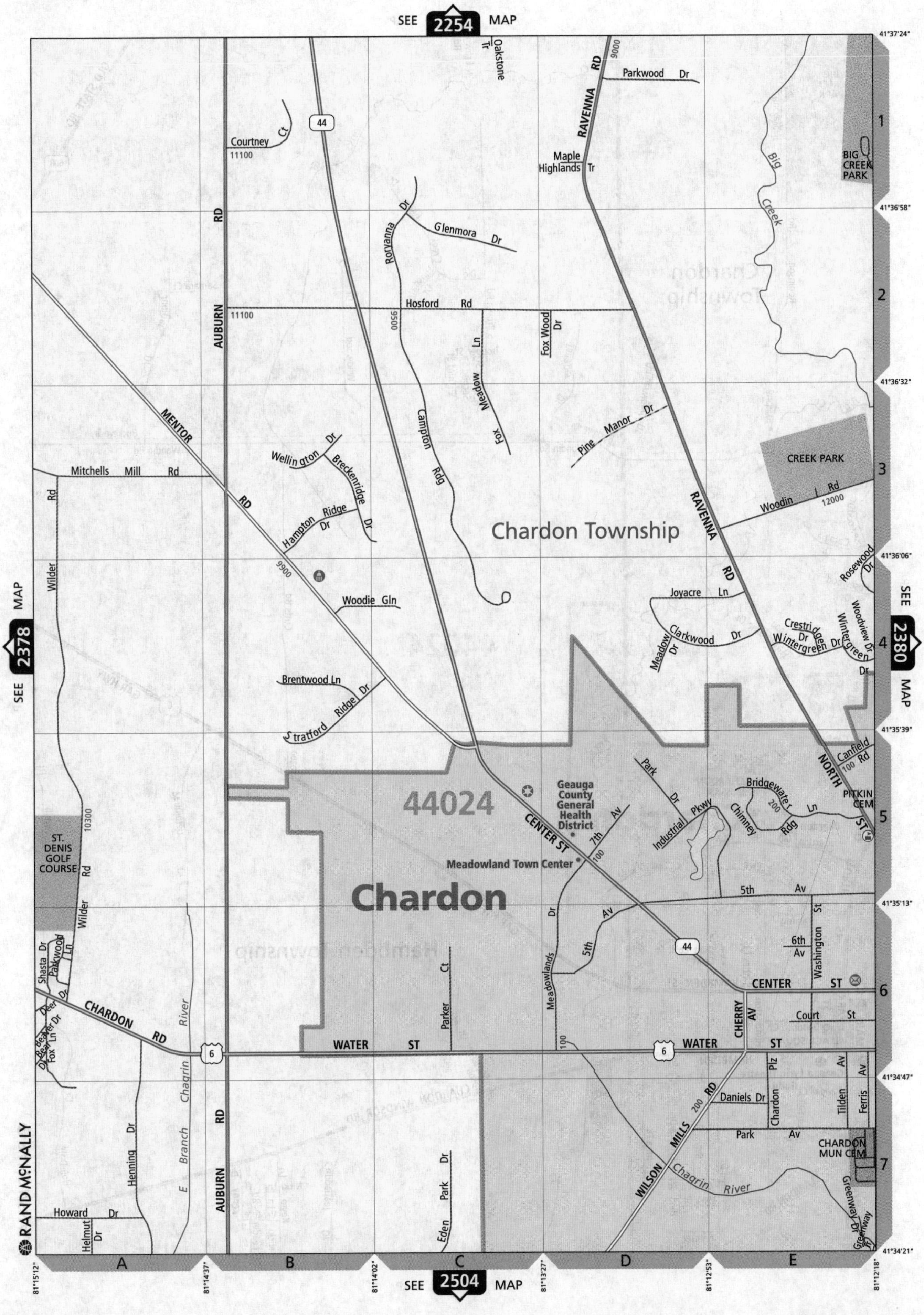
SEE 2254 MAP
SEE 2378 MAP
SEE 2380 MAP
SEE 2504 MAP
Chardon Township
Chardon
44024
Hampden Township
Oakstone Tr
Parkwood Dr
RAVENNA RD
9000
Courtney Ct
11100
44
Maple Highlands Tr
BIG CREEK PARK
Big Creek
AUBURN RD
Rorvanna Dr
Glenmora Dr
Hosford Rd
11100
9500
Fox Wood Dr
Meadow Ln
Fox Meadow
Campton Rdg
Pine Manor Dr
CREEK PARK
MENTOR RD
Mitchells Mill Rd
Wellington Dr
Breckenridge Dr
Hampton Ridge Dr
Woodin Rd
12000
9900
Wilder Rd
Woodie Gln
Rosewood Dr
Joyacre Ln
Clarkwood Dr
Meadow Dr
Crestridge Dr
Wintergreen Dr
Woodview Dr
Brentwood Ln
Stratford Ridge Dr
Canfield Rd
100
NORTH ST
Park Dr
Geauga County General Health District
Bridgewater Ln
200
Chimney Rdg
PITKIN CEM
7th Av
Industrial Pkwy
CENTER ST
100
ST. DENIS GOLF COURSE
10300
Meadowland Town Center
5th Av
Washington St
6th Av
Meadowlands Dr
Shasta Dr
Parkwood Ln
Dr
CHARDON RD
Deer
Beaver Dr
Fox Ln
Bear Dr
Parker Ct
CENTER ST
CHERRY AV
Court St
E Branch Chagrin River
6
WATER ST
100
Daniels Dr
Plz
Av
Av
RD
200
MILLS
WILSON
Chardon
Tilden
Ferris
Park Av
CHARDON MUN CEM
Henning Dr
Eden Park Dr
Chagrin River
Greenway Dr
Greenway Tr
Howard Dr
Helmut Dr
RAND McNALLY
1 2 3 4 5 6 7
A B C D E
41°37'24" 41°36'58" 41°36'32" 41°36'06" 41°35'39" 41°35'13" 41°34'47" 41°34'21"
81°15'12" 81°14'37" 81°14'02" 81°13'27" 81°12'53" 81°12'18"

1:24,000
1 in. = 2000 ft.
0 0.25 0.5
miles

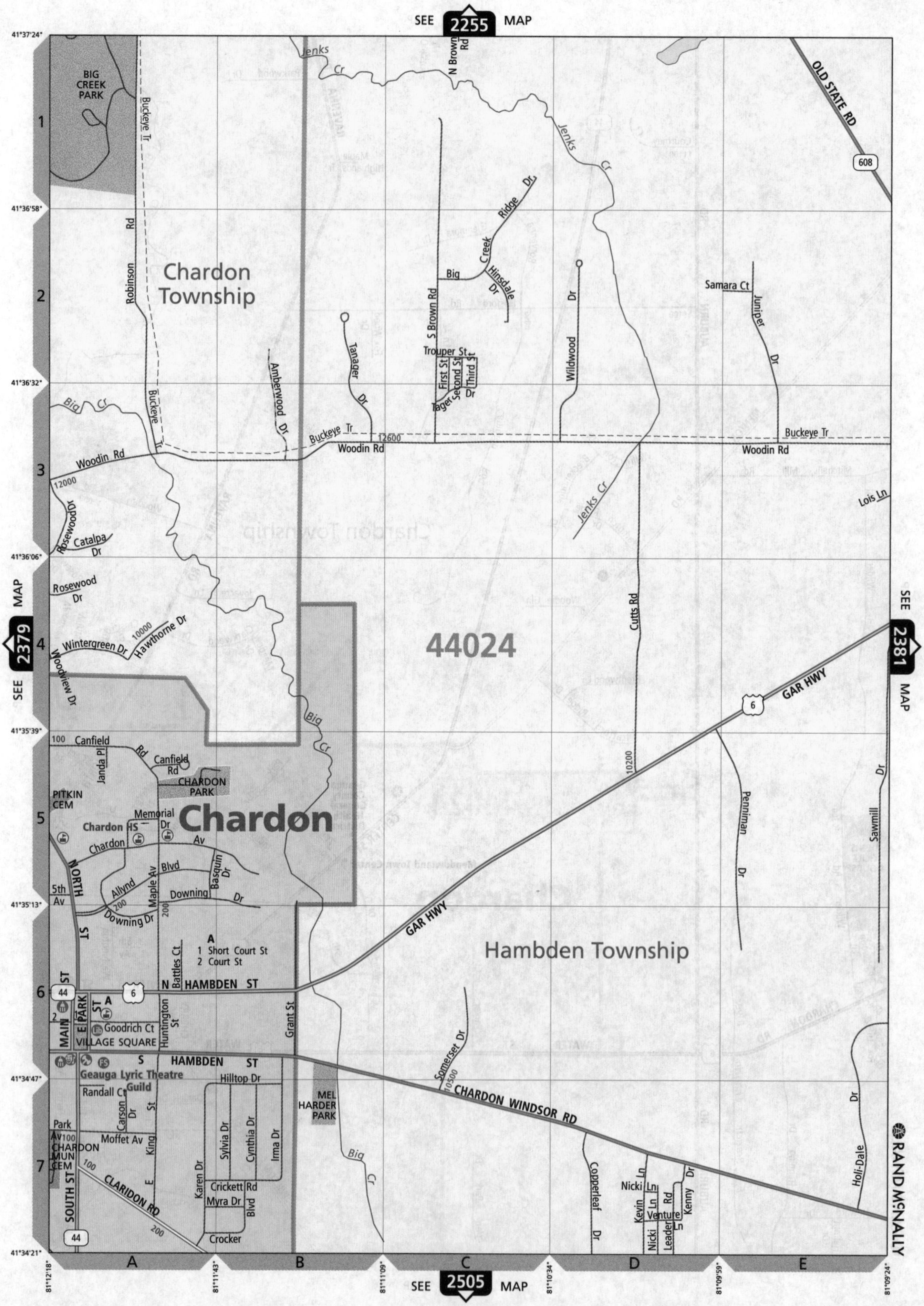
SEE 2255 MAP
SEE 2379 MAP
SEE 2381 MAP
SEE 2505 MAP
BIG CREEK PARK
Chardon Township
Chardon
44024
Hambden Township
Jenks Cr
N Brown Rd
OLD STATE RD
608
Buckeye Tr
Robinson Rd
Big Creek Ridge Dr
Hinsdale Dr
S Brown Rd
Samara Ct
Juniper Dr
Wildwood Dr
Tanager Dr
Amberwood Dr
Trouper St
First St
Second St
Third St
Tager St
Big Cr
Woodin Rd
12600
12000
Lois Ln
Rosewood Dr
Catalpa Dr
Wintergreen Dr
10000
Hawthorne Dr
Woodview Dr
Cutts Rd
GAR HWY
6
10200
Penniman Dr
Sawmill Dr
100 Canfield Rd
Janda Pl
Canfield Rd
CHARDON PARK
PITKIN CEM
Memorial Dr
Chardon HS
Chardon Av
Blvd
Basquin Dr
Allynd
Maple Av
5th Av
200
Downing Dr
NORTH ST
Battles Ct
A
1 Short Court St
2 Court St
N HAMBDEN ST
44
MAIN ST
E PARK ST
Goodrich Ct
VILLAGE SQUARE
Huntington St
Grant St
Somerset Dr
10500
S HAMBDEN ST
Geauga Lyric Theatre Guild
Hilltop Dr
Randall Ct
Carson Dr
King St
Sylvia Dr
Cynthia Dr
Irma Dr
MEL HARDER PARK
CHARDON WINDSOR RD
Park Av
Moffet Av
CHARDON MUN CEM
SOUTH ST
CLARIDON RD
Karen Dr
Crickett Rd
Myra Dr
Blvd
Crocker
Copperleaf Dr
Nicki Ln
Kevin Ln
Venture Rd
Leader Ln
Kenny Dr
Holi-Dale Dr
RAND McNALLY
A
B
C
D
E
1
2
3
4
5
6
7
41°37'24"
41°36'58"
41°36'32"
41°36'06"
41°35'39"
41°35'13"
41°34'47"
41°34'21"
81°12'18"
81°11'43"
81°11'09"
81°10'34"
81°09'59"
81°09'24"

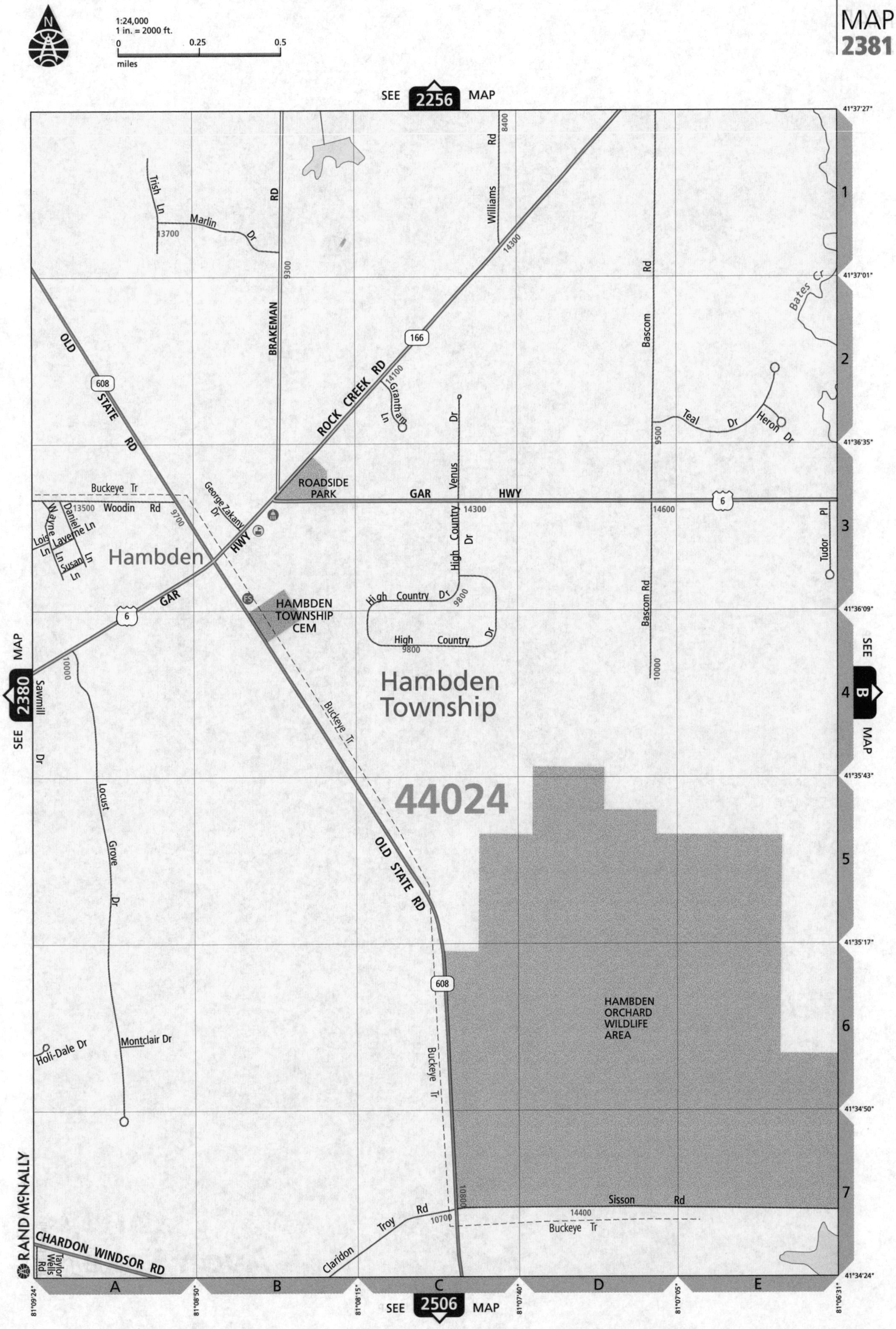
1:24,000
1 in. = 2000 ft.
0
0.25
0.5
miles
SEE 2256 MAP
SEE 2380 MAP
SEE B MAP
SEE 2506 MAP
Hambden
Hambden Township
44024
ROADSIDE PARK
HAMBDEN TOWNSHIP CEM
HAMBDEN ORCHARD WILDLIFE AREA
OLD STATE RD
ROCK CREEK RD
BRAKEMAN RD
GAR HWY
CHARDON WINDSOR RD
Trish Ln
Marlin Dr
Williams Rd
Bascom Rd
Bates Cr
Grantham Ln
Venus Dr
Teal Dr
Heron Dr
Buckeye Tr
Woodin Rd
George Zakany Dr
High Country Dr
Tudor Pl
Daniel Ln
Wayne Ln
Lois Ln
Laverne Ln
Susan Ln
Sawmill Dr
Locust Grove Dr
Montclair Dr
Holi-Dale Dr
Sisson Rd
Claridon Troy Rd
Taylor Wells Rd
608
166
6
RAND McNALLY
A
B
C
D
E
1
2
3
4
5
6
7
41°37'27"
41°37'01"
41°36'35"
41°36'09"
41°35'43"
41°35'17"
41°34'50"
41°34'24"
81°09'24"
81°08'50"
81°08'15"
81°07'40"
81°07'05"
81°06'31"

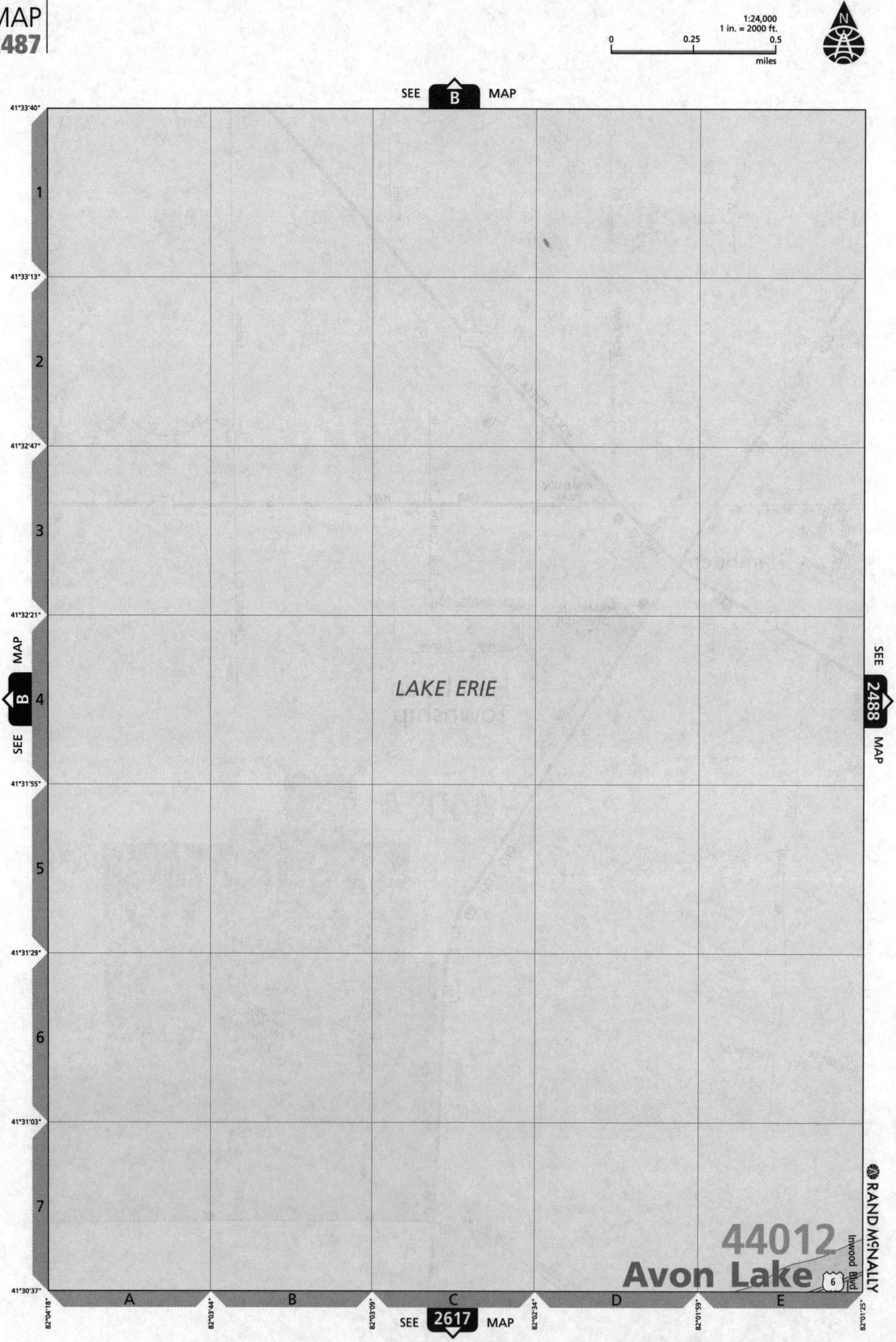
1:24,000
1 in. = 2000 ft.
0
0.25
0.5
miles
N
SEE B MAP
SEE B MAP
SEE 2488 MAP
SEE 2617 MAP
41°33'40"
41°33'13"
41°32'47"
41°32'21"
41°31'55"
41°31'29"
41°31'03"
41°30'37"
82°04'18"
82°03'44"
82°03'09"
82°02'34"
82°01'59"
82°01'25"
1
2
3
4
5
6
7
A
B
C
D
E
LAKE ERIE
44012
Avon Lake
Inwood Blvd
6
RAND McNALLY

1:24,000
1 in. = 2000 ft.
0 0.25 0.5
miles

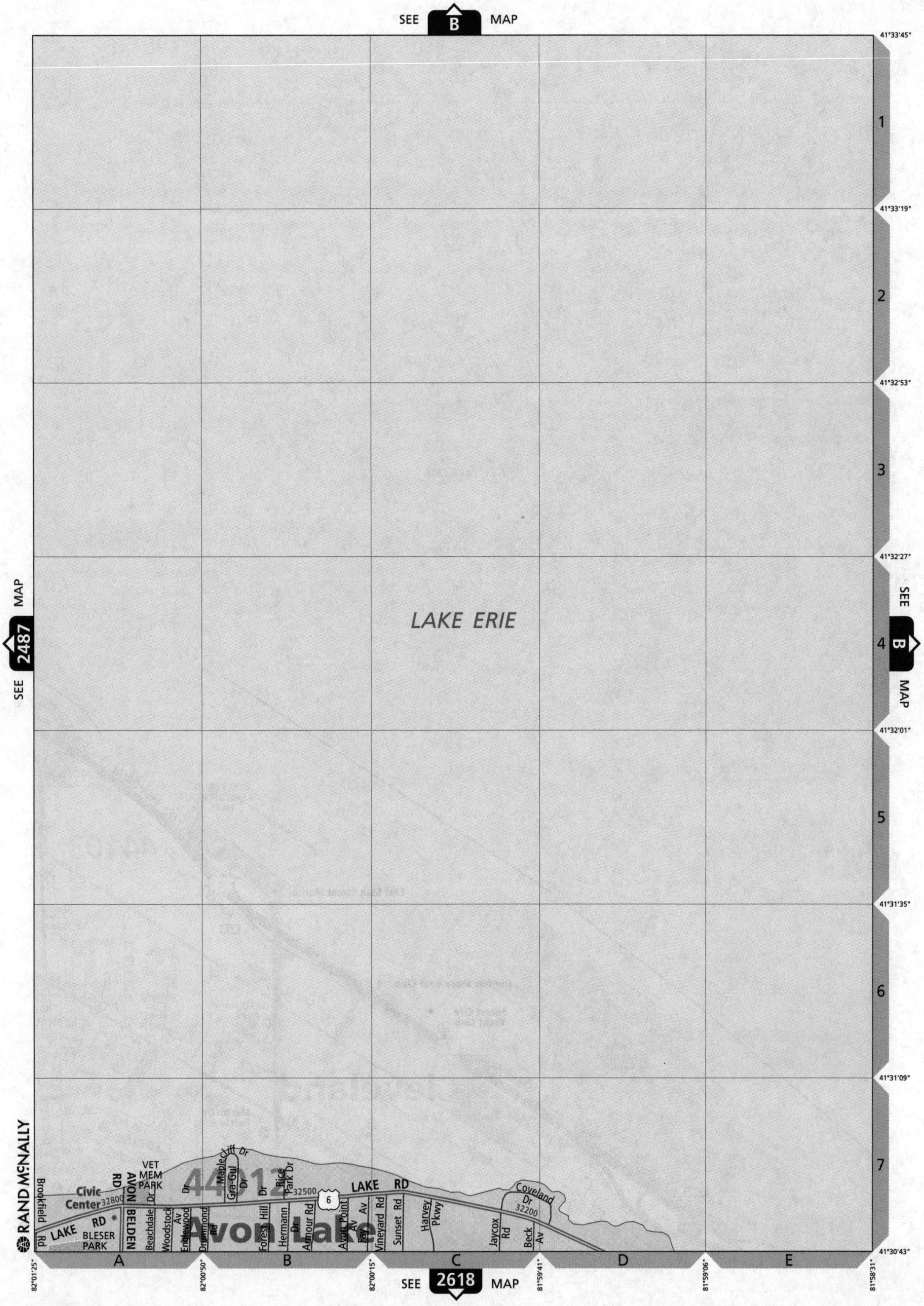
SEE B MAP
SEE 2487 MAP
SEE B MAP
SEE 2618 MAP
LAKE ERIE
1
2
3
4
5
6
7
A
B
C
D
E
41°33'45"
41°33'19"
41°32'53"
41°32'27"
41°32'01"
41°31'35"
41°31'09"
41°30'43"
82°01'25"
82°00'50"
82°00'15"
81°59'41"
81°59'06"
81°58'31"
44012
Avon Lake
LAKE RD
Civic Center
32800
32500
32200
BLESER PARK
VET MEM PARK
AVON BELDEN RD
Brookfield Rd
Beachdale Dr
Woodstock Av
Englewood Dr
Drummond Rd
Maple
Cliff Dr
Gra-Gul Dr
Forest Hill Dr
Hermann Dr
Rice Park Dr
Armour Rd
Avon Point Av
Lear Av
Vineyard Rd
Sunset Rd
6
Harvey Pkwy
Jaycox Rd
Beck Av
Coveland Dr
RAND McNALLY

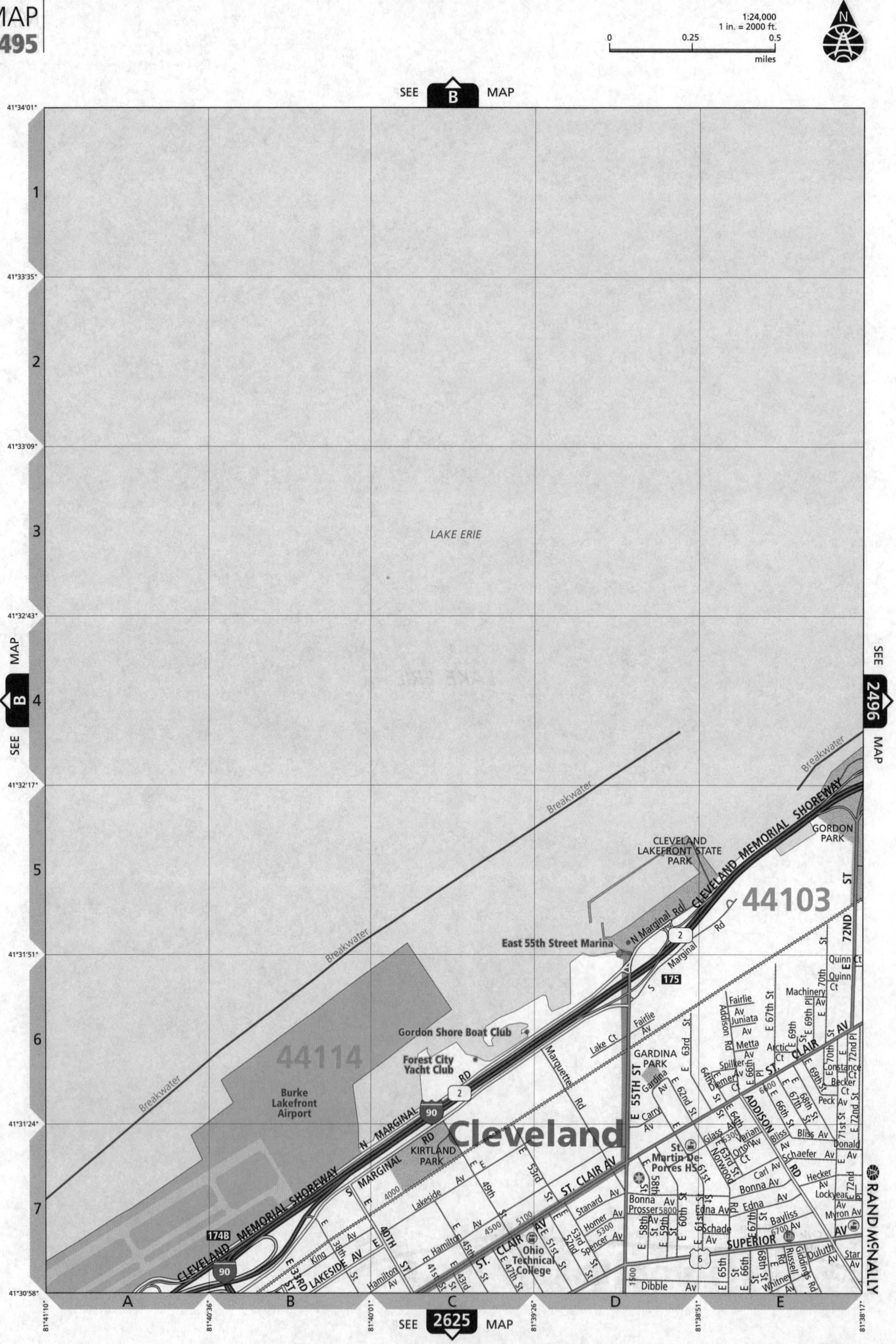
1:24,000
1 in. = 2000 ft.
0
0.25
0.5
miles
SEE B MAP
SEE B MAP
SEE 2496 MAP
SEE 2625 MAP
41°34'01"
41°33'35"
41°33'09"
41°32'43"
41°32'17"
41°31'51"
41°31'24"
41°30'58"
81°41'10"
81°40'36"
81°40'01"
81°39'26"
81°38'51"
81°38'17"
1
2
3
4
5
6
7
A
B
C
D
E
LAKE ERIE
Breakwater
Breakwater
Breakwater
Breakwater
CLEVELAND LAKEFRONT STATE PARK
GORDON PARK
CLEVELAND MEMORIAL SHOREWAY
44103
44114
East 55th Street Marina
N Marginal Rd
S Marginal Rd
Gordon Shore Boat Club
Forest City Yacht Club
Burke Lakefront Airport
N MARGINAL RD
S MARGINAL RD
KIRTLAND PARK
Cleveland
GARDINA PARK
St. Martin De Porres HS
Ohio Technical College
ST. CLAIR AV
SUPERIOR AV
LAKESIDE AV
ADDISON RD
E 55TH ST
E 72ND ST
E 40TH ST
E 33RD ST
Marquette Rd
Lakeside Av
Hamilton Av
King Av
Dibble Av
Fairlie Av
Juniata Av
Metta Av
Lake Ct
Carry Av
Gardina Av
Bonna Av
Prosser Av
Edna Av
Schade Av
Bayliss Av
Bliss Av
Schaefer Av
Hecker Av
Lockyear Av
Myron Av
Carl Av
Glass Av
Orton Av
Varian Ct
Norwood Rd
Spiller Av
Diemer Ct
Addison Rd
Arctic Ct
Machinery Av
Quinn Ct
Constance Ct
Becker Ct
Peck Av
Donald Av
Star Av
Duluth Av
Giddings Rd
Russell Rd
Whitney Av
Stanard Av
Homer Av
Spencer Av
90
90
2
2
6
175
174B
RAND McNALLY

1:24,000
1 in. = 2000 ft.
0 0.25 0.5
miles

SEE B MAP

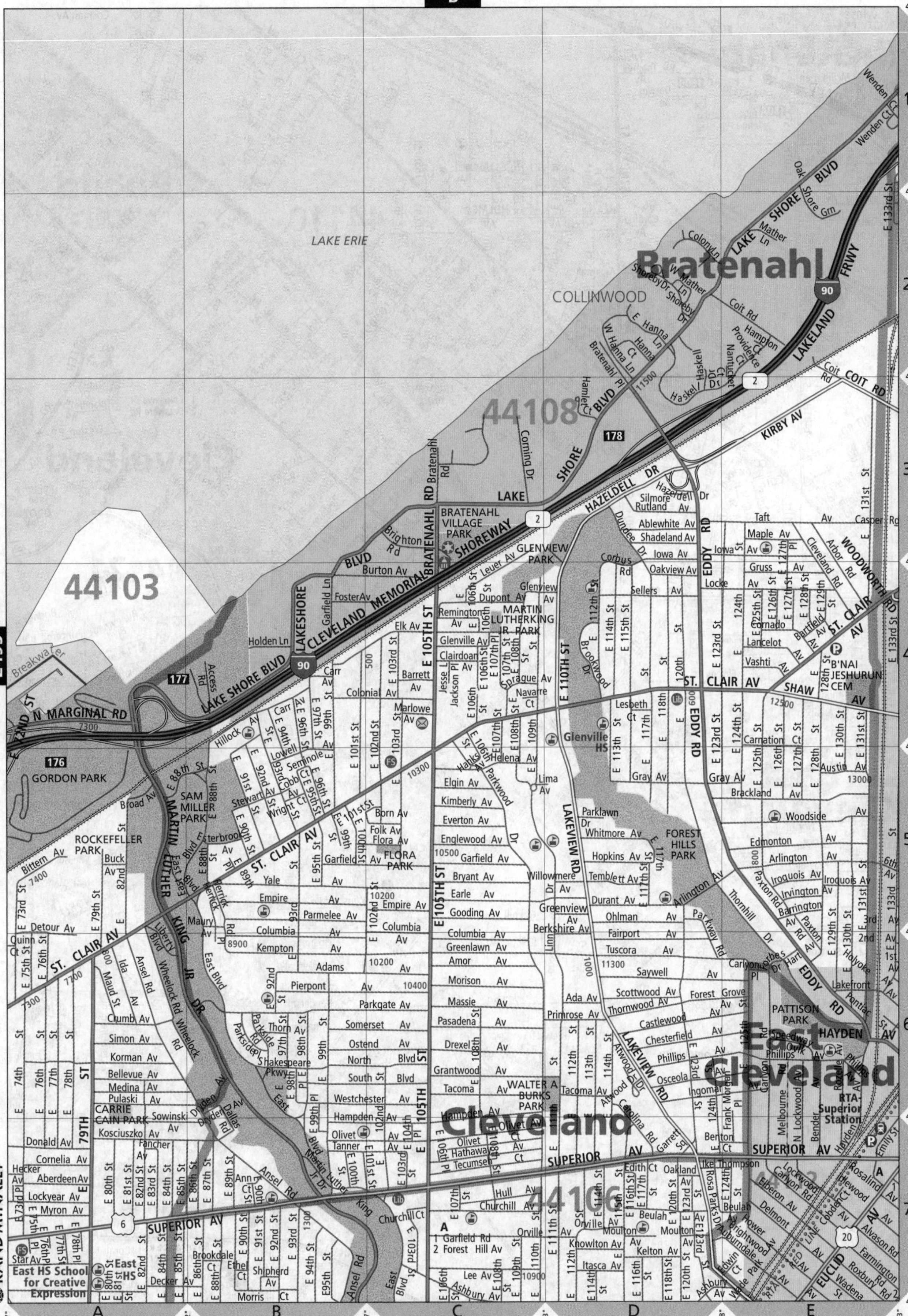

LAKE ERIE
Bratenahl
COLLINWOOD
44108
44103
44106
Cleveland
East Cleveland
LAKE SHORE BLVD
CLEVELAND MEMORIAL SHOREWAY
LAKELAND FRWY
N MARGINAL RD
ST. CLAIR AV
SUPERIOR AV
MARTIN LUTHER KING JR DR
E 105TH ST
E 110TH ST
EDDY RD
LAKEVIEW RD
HAZELDELL DR
KIRBY AV
COIT RD
WOODWORTH RD
SHAW AV
HAYDEN AV
EUCLID AV
GORDON PARK
ROCKEFELLER PARK
SAM MILLER PARK
BRATENAHL VILLAGE PARK
GLENVIEW PARK
MARTIN LUTHER KING JR PARK
FLORA PARK
FOREST HILLS PARK
PATTISON PARK
WALTER A BURKS PARK
CARRIE CAIN PARK
B'NAI JESHURUN CEM
Glenville HS
East HS
East HS School for Creative Expression
RTA-Superior Station
1 Garfield Rd
2 Forest Hill Av
A B C D E
1 2 3 4 5 6 7
41°34'06"
41°33'39"
41°33'13"
41°32'47"
41°32'21"
41°31'55"
41°31'29"
41°31'03"
81°38'17"
81°37'42"
81°37'07"
81°36'33"
81°35'58"
81°35'23"

SEE 2495 MAP

SEE 2497 MAP

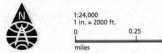

SEE 2626 MAP

1:24,000
1 in. = 2000 ft.
0 0.25 0.5
miles

SEE 2372 MAP

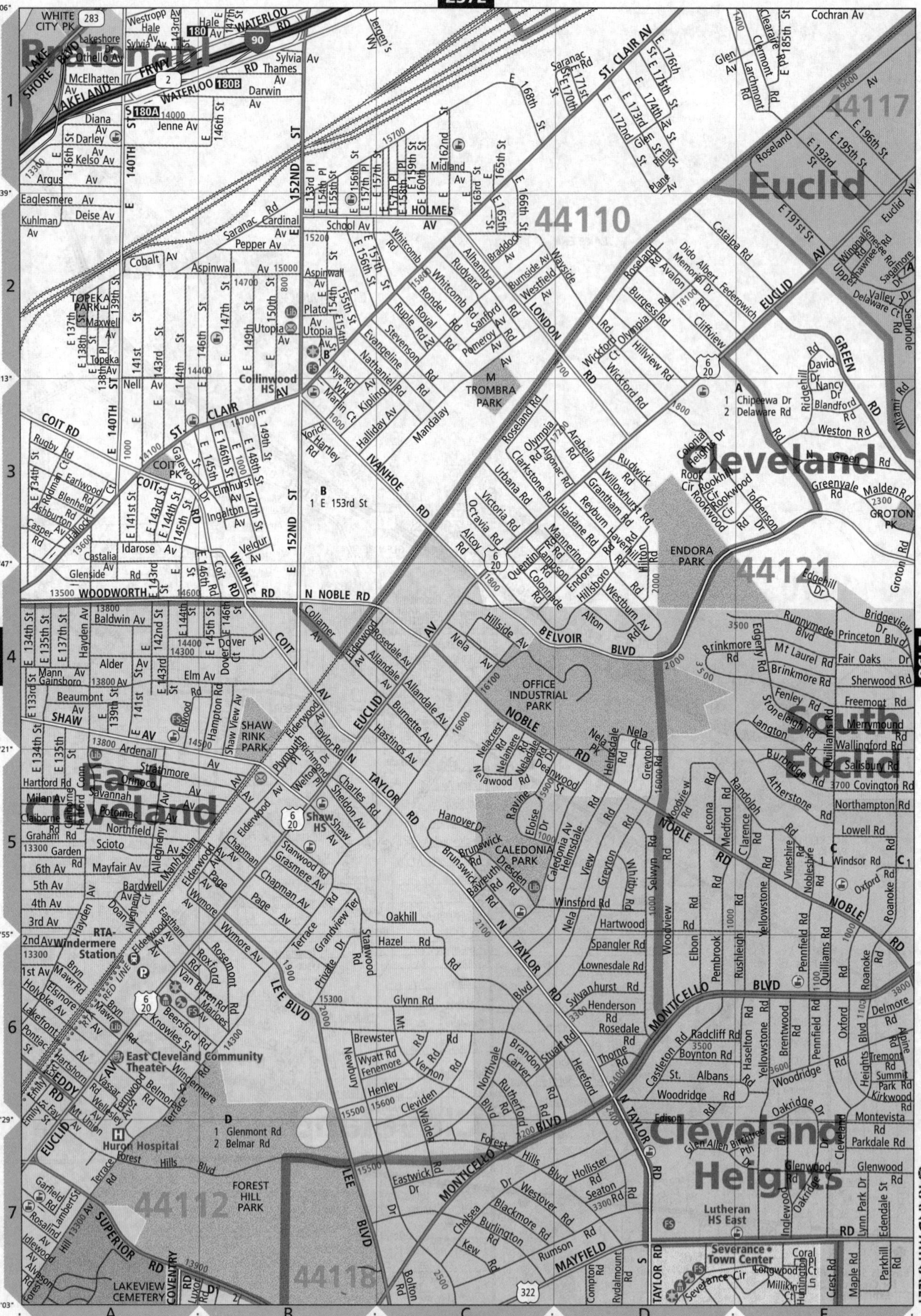
Bratenahl
Euclid
44110
44117
44121
44112
44118
Cleveland
South Euclid
East Cleveland
Cleveland Heights
WHITE CITY PK
TOPEKA PARK
COIT PK
M TROMBRA PARK
ENDORA PARK
GROTON PK
SHAW RINK PARK
OFFICE INDUSTRIAL PARK
CALEDONIA PARK
FOREST HILL PARK
LAKEVIEW CEMETERY
Collinwood HS
Shaw HS
Lutheran HS East
RTA-Windermere Station
East Cleveland Community Theater
Huron Hospital
Severance Town Center
LAKE SHORE BLVD
LAKELAND FRWY
WATERLOO RD
ST. CLAIR AV
EUCLID AV
IVANHOE RD
LONDON RD
WOODWORTH RD
N NOBLE RD
BELVOIR BLVD
NOBLE RD
N TAYLOR RD
TAYLOR RD
MONTICELLO BLVD
LEE BLVD
MAYFIELD RD
SUPERIOR RD
COVENTRY RD
GREEN RD
COIT RD
152ND ST
140TH ST
A
1 Chippewa Dr
2 Delaware Rd
B
1 E 153rd St
C
1 Windsor Rd
D
1 Glenmont Rd
2 Belmar Rd
1
2
3
4
5
6
7
A
B
C
D
E
41°34'06"
41°33'39"
41°33'13"
41°32'47"
41°32'21"
41°31'55"
41°31'29"
41°31'03"
81°35'23"
81°34'48"
81°34'14"
81°33'39"
81°33'04"
81°32'30"

SEE 2496 MAP

SEE 2498 MAP

SEE 2627 MAP

1:24,000
1 in. = 2000 ft.
0 0.25 0.5
miles

SEE 2373 MAP

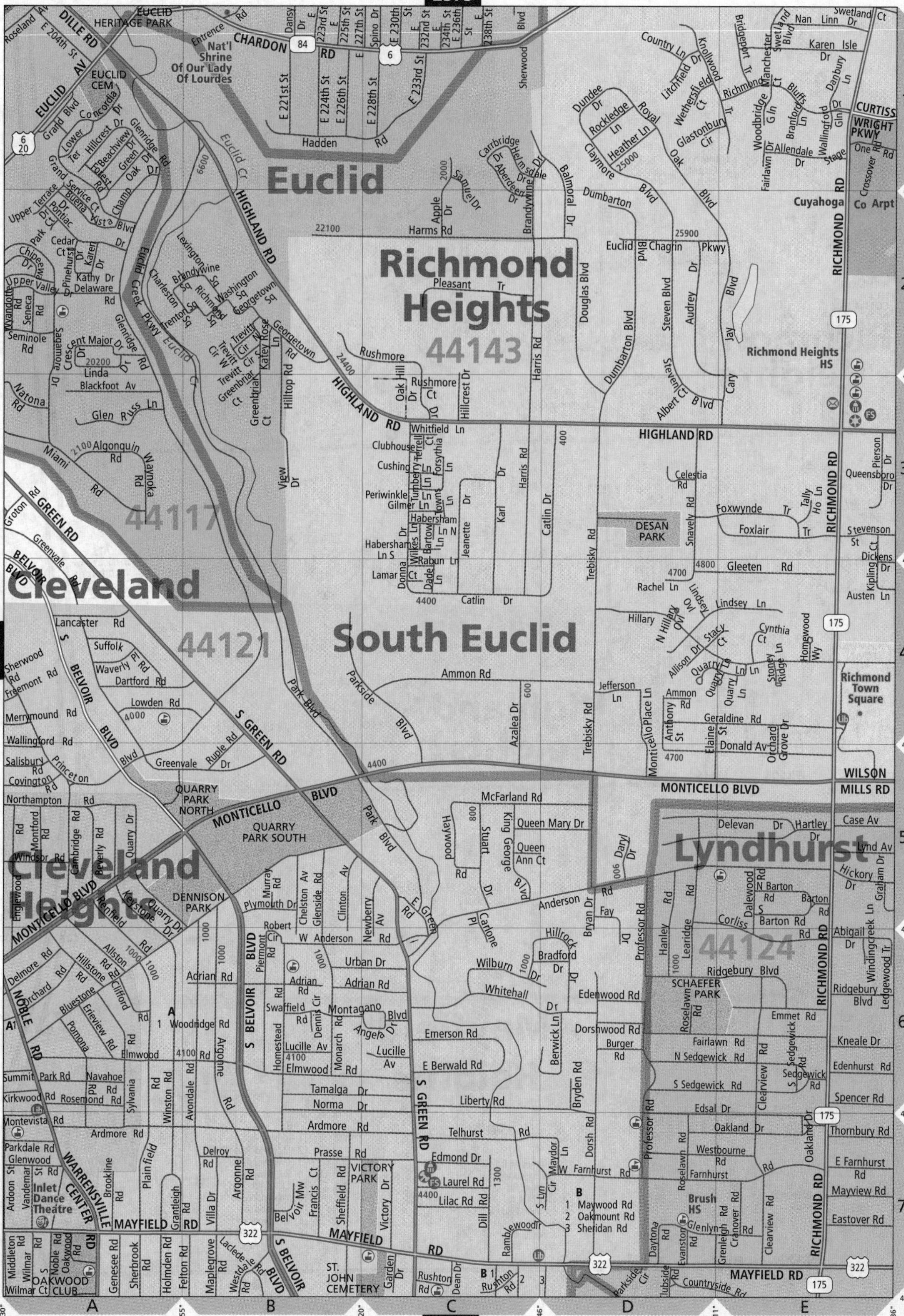
Euclid
Richmond Heights
44143
44117
Cleveland
44121
South Euclid
Cleveland Heights
Lyndhurst
44124
EUCLID HERITAGE PARK
Nat'l Shrine Of Our Lady Of Lourdes
EUCLID CEM
CHARDON RD
HIGHLAND RD
Cuyahoga Co Arpt
Richmond Heights HS
DESAN PARK
Richmond Town Square
QUARRY PARK NORTH
QUARRY PARK SOUTH
DENNISON PARK
MONTICELLO BLVD
WILSON MILLS RD
SCHAEFER PARK
VICTORY PARK
Brush HS
ST. JOHN CEMETERY
OAKWOOD CLUB
Inlet Dance Theatre
MAYFIELD RD
RICHMOND RD
S GREEN RD
S BELVOIR BLVD
WARRENSVILLE CENTER RD
NOBLE RD
A B C D E
1 2 3 4 5 6 7

SEE MAP 2497

SEE 2499 MAP

SEE 2628 MAP

1:24,000
1 in. = 2000 ft.
0 0.25 0.5
miles

SEE 2374 MAP

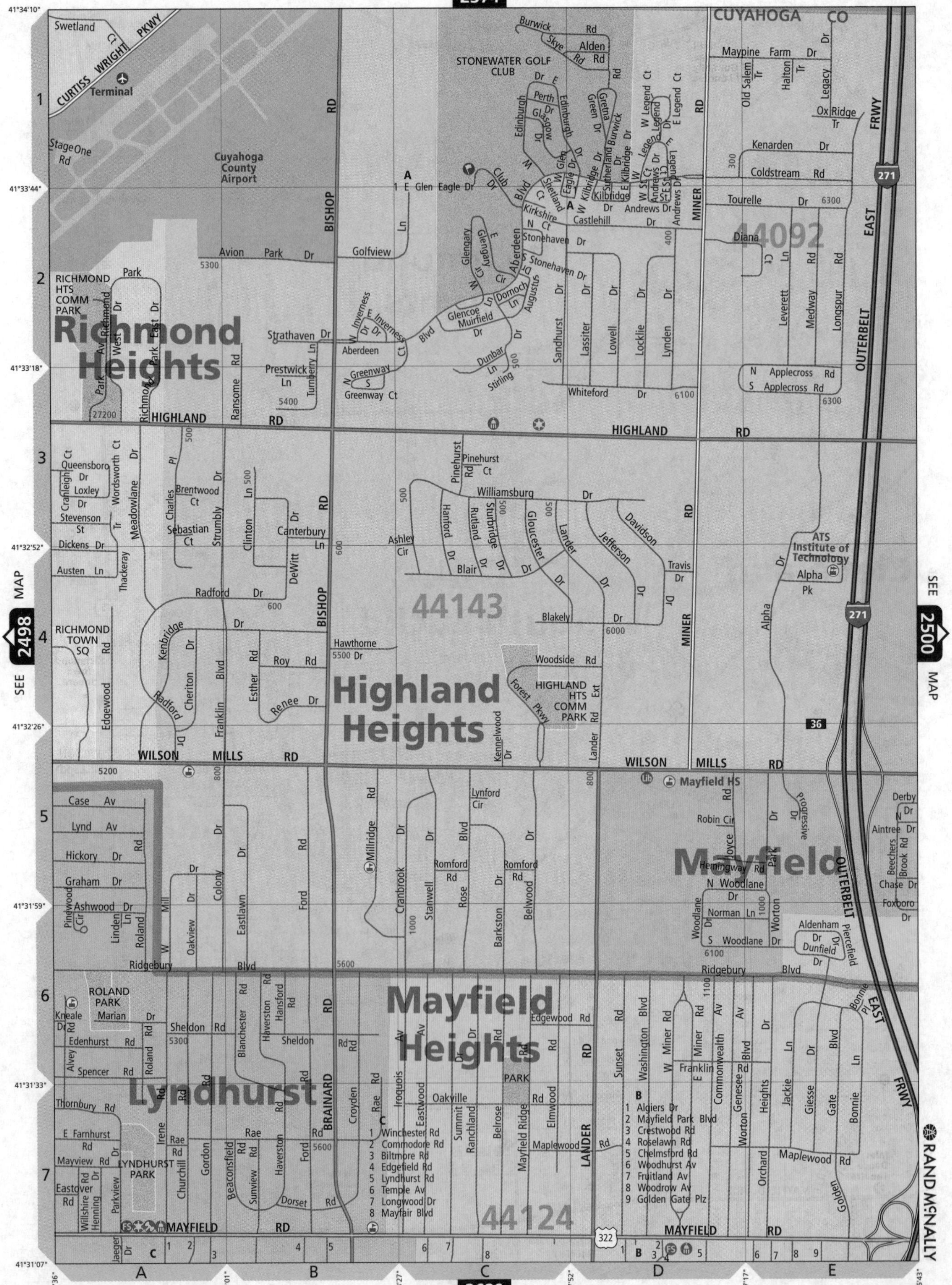
CUYAHOGA CO
Swetland Ct
CURTISS WRIGHT PKWY
Terminal
Stage One Rd
Cuyahoga County Airport
STONEWATER GOLF CLUB
Burwick Rd
Skye Rd
Alden Rd
Maypine Farm Dr
Old Salem Tr
Halton Tr
Legacy Dr
Ox Ridge Tr
Kenarden Dr
Coldstream Rd
Tourelle Dr
Glen Eagle Dr
Club Blvd
Kirkshire Ct
Castlehill Dr
Andrews Dr
Stonehaven Dr
Avion Park Dr
Golfview Ln
RICHMOND HTS COMM PARK
Richmond Heights
Strathaven Dr
Aberdeen
Prestwick Ln
Turnberry Ln
Greenway Ct
Glencoe
Muirfield Dr
Dunbar Ln
Stirling
Sandhurst Dr
Lassiter Dr
Lowell Dr
Locklie Dr
Lynden Dr
Whiteford Dr
44092
Diana Ct
Leverett Rd
Medway Rd
Longspur Rd
N Applecross Rd
S Applecross Rd
EAST OUTERBELT FRWY
271
HIGHLAND RD
Queensboro Dr
Loxley Dr
Stevenson St
Dickens Dr
Austen Ln
Cranleigh Ct
Wordsworth Ct
Meadowlane Dr
Thackeray
Brentwood Ct
Sebastian Ct
Charles Pl
Strumbly Dr
Clinton Ln
Canterbury Ln
DeWitt Dr
Pinehurst Ct
Williamsburg Dr
Ashley Cir
Hanford Dr
Rutland Dr
Sturbridge Dr
Gloucester Dr
Lander Dr
Jefferson Dr
Davidson Dr
Blair Dr
Travis Dr
Blakely Dr
ATS Institute of Technology
Alpha Pk
Alpha Dr
44143
Radford Dr
Kenbridge Dr
Cheriton Dr
RICHMOND TOWN SQ
Edgewood Rd
Franklin Blvd
Esther Rd
Roy Rd
Renee Dr
Hawthorne Dr
Highland Heights
Woodside Rd
HIGHLAND HTS COMM PARK
Forest Pkwy
Kennelwood Dr
BISHOP RD
MINER RD
WILSON MILLS RD
Mayfield HS
36
Case Av
Lynd Av
Hickory Dr
Graham Dr
Ashwood Dr
Pinewood Cir
Linden Ln
Roland Rd
Mill
Oakview Dr
Colony Dr
Eastlawn Dr
Ford Rd
Millridge Rd
Cranbrook Dr
Stanwell Dr
Lynford Cir
Romford Rd
Rose Blvd
Barkston Dr
Belwood Dr
Robin Cir
Joyce
Progressive Dr
Mayfield
Hemingway Rd
N Woodlane Dr
Norman Ln
Woodlane
Worton Dr
S Woodlane Dr
Aldenham Dr
Dunfield Dr
Piercefield
Derby Dr
Aintree Dr
Beechers Brook Rd
Chase Dr
Foxboro Dr
Ridgebury Blvd
ROLAND PARK
Marian Dr
Kneale Dr
Sheldon Rd
Edenhurst Rd
Alvey
Spencer Rd
Blanchester Rd
Haverston Rd
Hansford Rd
Mayfield Heights
Edgewood Rd
Bonnie Pl
Lyndhurst
BRAINARD RD
Croyden
Rae Rd
Iroquois Av
Eastwood Av
Oakville
Summit
Ranchland
Belrose
Mayfield Ridge
Elmwood
PARK
Maplewood Rd
LANDER RD
Sunset
Washington Blvd
W Miner Rd
E Miner Rd
Franklin
Commonwealth Av
Genesee Av
Worton
Heights
Orchard
Jackie Ln
Giesse Dr
Gate Blvd
Bonnie Ln
Golden
Thornbury Rd
E Farnhurst Rd
Mayview Rd
LYNDHURST PARK
Eastover Rd
Wilshire
Henning
Parkview
Irene
Churchill
Gordon
Beaconsfield
Sunview
Dorset Rd
C
1 Winchester Rd
2 Commodore Rd
3 Biltmore Rd
4 Edgefield Rd
5 Lyndhurst Rd
6 Temple Av
7 Longwood Dr
8 Mayfair Blvd
B
1 Algiers Dr
2 Mayfield Park Blvd
3 Crestwood Rd
4 Roselawn Rd
5 Chelmsford Rd
6 Woodhurst Av
7 Fruitland Av
8 Woodrow Av
9 Golden Gate Plz
44124
MAYFIELD RD
322
Jaeger
A B C D E
1 2 3 4 5 6 7
RAND McNALLY

SEE 2498 MAP
SEE 2500 MAP
SEE 2629 MAP

1:24,000
1 in. = 2000 ft.
0 0.25 0.5
miles

SEE 2375 MAP

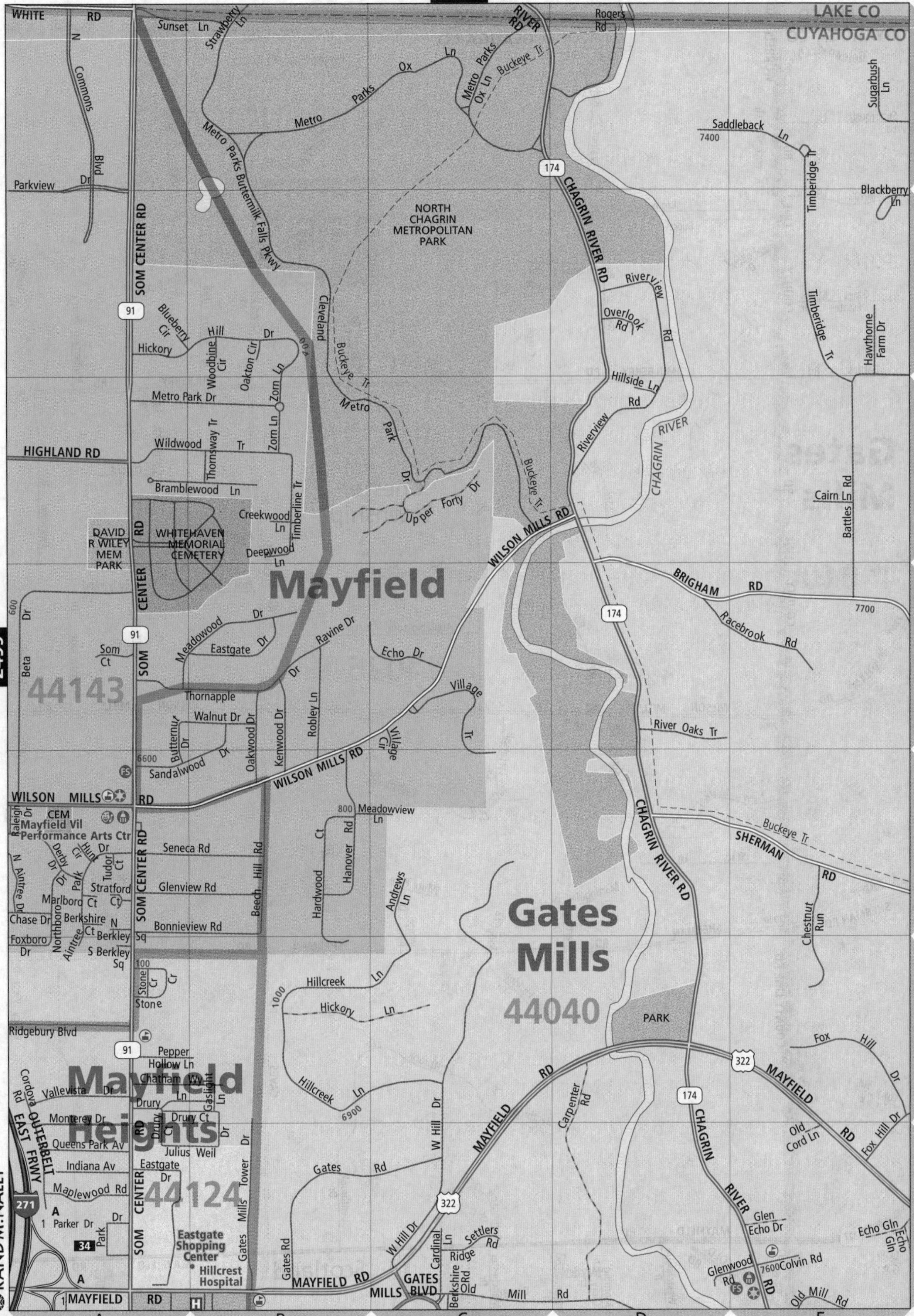
LAKE CO
CUYAHOGA CO
WHITE RD
Sunset Ln
Strawberry Ln
RIVER RD
Rogers Rd
N Commons Blvd
Metro Parks Ox Ln
Buckeye Tr
Metro Parks Ox Ln
Sugarbush Ln
Saddleback Ln
7400
Metro Parks Buttermilk Falls Pkwy
174
CHAGRIN RIVER RD
Timberidge Tr
Blackberry Ln
Parkview Dr
NORTH CHAGRIN METROPOLITAN PARK
SOM CENTER RD
91
Blueberry Cir
Hill Dr
Hickory
Woodbine Cir
Oakton Cir
Zorn Ln
Cleveland
Buckeye Tr
Riverview Rd
Overlook Rd
Hawthorne Farm Dr
Hillside Ln
Metro Park Dr
Riverview Rd
CHAGRIN RIVER
HIGHLAND RD
Wildwood Tr
Thornsway Tr
Zorn Ln
Bramblewood Ln
Buckeye Tr
Upper Forty Dr
Cairn Ln
Battles Rd
Creekwood Ln
Timberline Tr
DAVID R WILEY MEM PARK
WHITEHAVEN MEMORIAL CEMETERY
Deepwood Ln
WILSON MILLS RD
BRIGHAM RD
7700
Mayfield
600
Beta Dr
Som Ct
Meadowood Dr
Eastgate Dr
Ravine Dr
Echo Dr
Racebrook Rd
44143
Thornapple
Village Tr
Walnut Dr
Butternut Dr
Oakwood Dr
Kenwood Dr
Robley Ln
Village Cir
River Oaks Tr
6600
Sandalwood Dr
WILSON MILLS RD
CEM
Mayfield Vil Performance Arts Ctr
Raleigh Dr
800
Meadowview Ln
Buckeye Tr
SHERMAN RD
Seneca Rd
Beech Hill Rd
Hanover Rd
Hunt Dr
Derby Cir
Tudor Ct
N Aintree Dr
Park Dr
Stratford Ct
Glenview Rd
Hardwood Ct
Andrews Ln
Marlboro Ct
Chase Dr
Berkshire Ct
N Berkley Sq
Bonnieview Rd
Foxboro Dr
Northboro Dr
Aintree Dr
S Berkley Sq
Gates Mills
Chestnut Run
100
Stone Cr
Stone Cr
Hillcreek Ln
1000
Hickory Ln
44040
PARK
Ridgebury Blvd
Pepper Hollow Ln
Chatham Wy
Fox Hill Dr
322
MAYFIELD RD
Mayfield Heights
Cordova Rd
Vallevista Dr
Drury Ln
Gaslight Ln
Hillcreek Ln
6900
Carpenter Rd
174
Monterey Dr
Drury Ct
Drury Ct
EAST OUTERBELT FRWY
Queens Park Av
Julius Weil Dr
W Hill Dr
CHAGRIN RIVER RD
Old Cord Ln
Fox Hill Dr
Indiana Av
Eastgate Dr
Tower Dr
Gates Rd
Maplewood Rd
44124
271
A
1 Parker Dr
34
Park Dr
Eastgate Shopping Center
Mills Gates
Gates Rd
W Hill Dr
Cardinal Ln
Settlers Rd
Ridge Rd
Glen Echo Dr
Echo Gln
Hillcrest Hospital
Berkshire Rd
7600 Colvin Rd
Glenwood Rd
MAYFIELD RD
GATES MILLS BLVD
Old Mill Rd
Old Mill Rd
MAYFIELD RD
1 2 3 4 5 6 7
A B C D E
41°34'14"
41°33'48"
41°33'22"
41°32'56"
41°32'30"
41°32'04"
41°31'37"
41°31'11"
81°26'43"
81°26'08"
81°25'33"
81°24'58"
81°24'24"
81°23'49"

SEE 2499 MAP

SEE 2501 MAP

SEE 2630 MAP

1:24,000
1 in. = 2000 ft.
0 0.25 0.5
miles

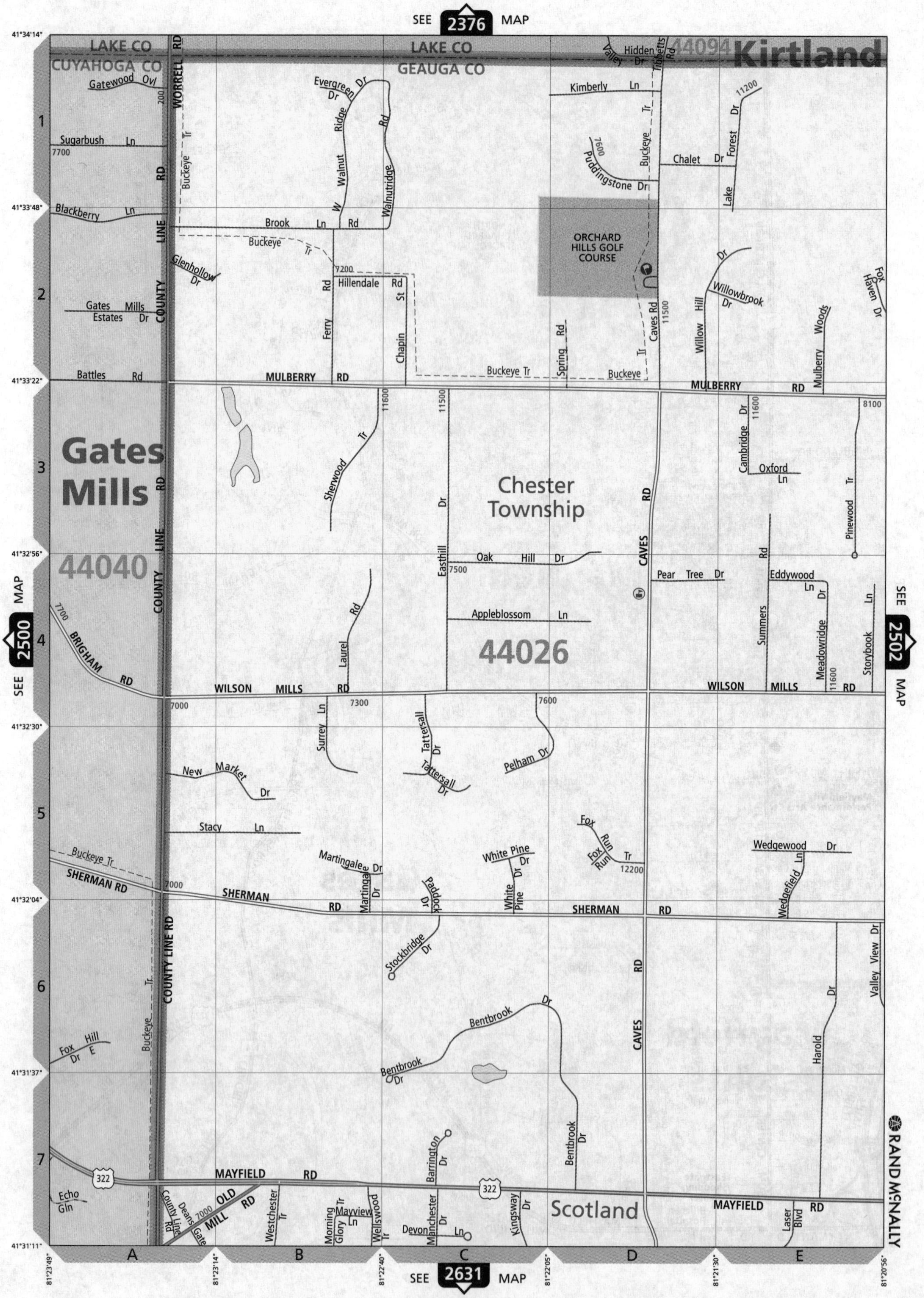
SEE 2376 MAP
SEE 2500 MAP
SEE 2502 MAP
SEE 2631 MAP
LAKE CO
CUYAHOGA CO
GEAUGA CO
Kirtland
44094
Gates Mills
44040
Chester Township
44026
Scotland
ORCHARD HILLS GOLF COURSE
RAND McNALLY
Gatewood Ovl
Sugarbush Ln
Blackberry Ln
Gates Mills Estates Dr
Battles Rd
WORRELL RD
COUNTY LINE RD
Buckeye Tr
Evergreen Dr
Ridge Rd
W Walnut
Walnutridge
Brook Ln Rd
Glenhollow Dr
Hillendale Rd
Ferry Rd
Chapin St
MULBERRY RD
Hidden Valley Dr
Tibbetts Rd
Kimberly Ln
Puddingstone Dr
Chalet Dr
Lake Forest Dr
Caves Rd
Spring Rd
Willowbrook Dr
Willow Hill
Fox Haven Dr
Mulberry Woods
Sherwood Tr
Easthill Dr
Oak Hill Dr
Appleblossom Ln
Laurel Rd
CAVES RD
Pear Tree Dr
Cambridge Dr
Oxford Ln
Summers Rd
Eddywood Ln
Meadowridge Dr
Pinewood Tr
Storybook Ln
BRIGHAM RD
WILSON MILLS RD
Surrey Ln
Tattersall Dr
Pelham Dr
New Market Dr
Stacy Ln
Martingale Dr
Paddock Dr
White Pine Dr
Fox Run Tr
Wedgewood Dr
Wedgefield Ln
SHERMAN RD
Stockbridge Dr
Valley View Dr
Bentbrook Dr
Harold Dr
Fox Hill Dr E
Barrington Dr
MAYFIELD RD
322
Echo Gln
OLD MILL RD
Deans Gate
County Line Rd
Westchester Tr
Morning Glory Tr
Mayview Ln
Wellswood Tr
Devon Ln
Manchester Dr
Kingsway Dr
Laser Blvd
A
B
C
D
E
1
2
3
4
5
6
7
41°34'14"
41°33'48"
41°33'22"
41°32'56"
41°32'30"
41°32'04"
41°31'37"
41°31'11"
81°23'49"
81°23'14"
81°22'40"
81°22'05"
81°21'30"
81°20'56"

SEE 2377 MAP

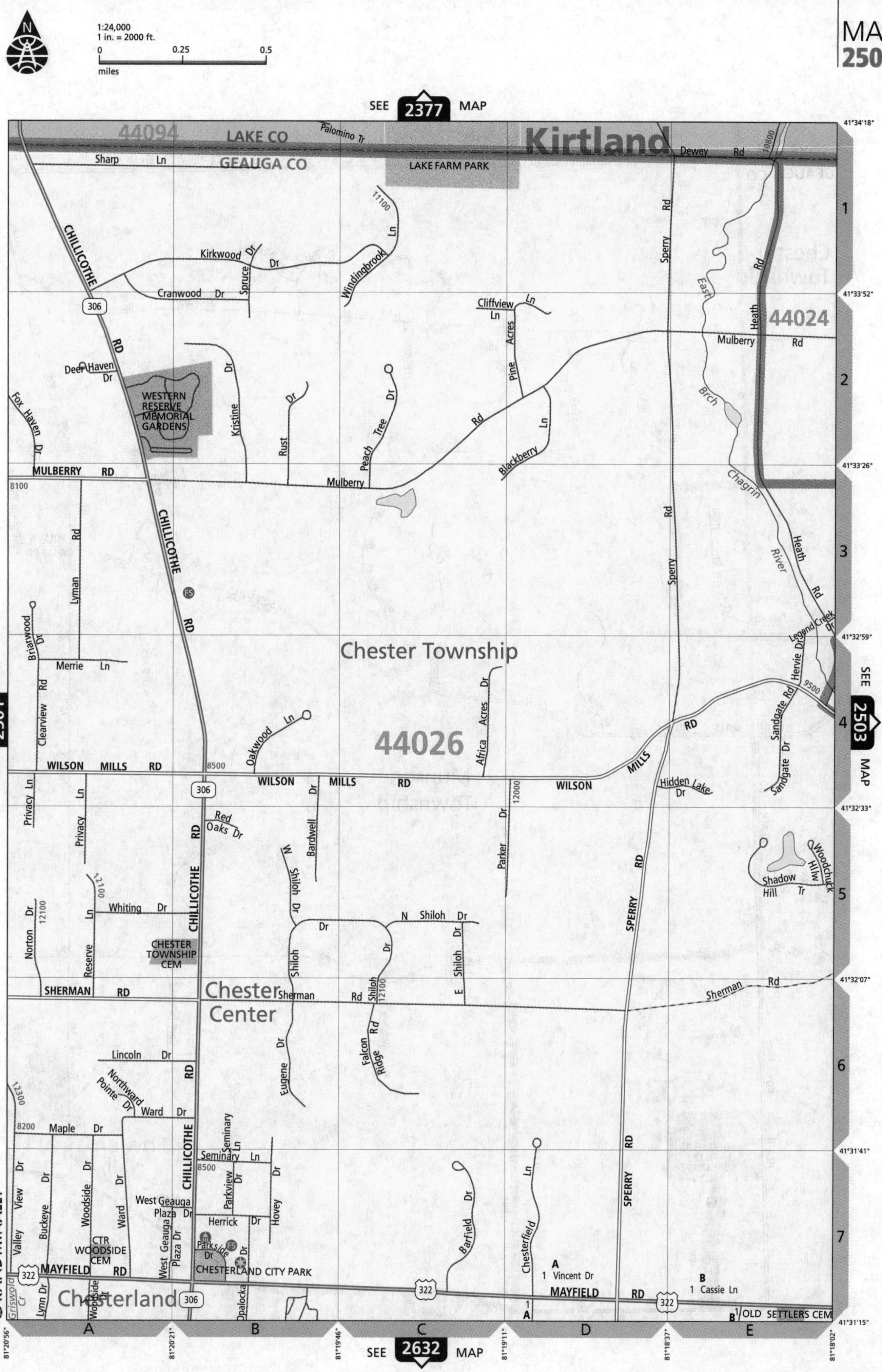
N
1:24,000
1 in. = 2000 ft.
0
0.25
0.5
miles
44094
LAKE CO
Palomino Tr
Kirtland
Dewey Rd
10800
Sharp Ln
GEAUGA CO
LAKE FARM PARK
11100
Windingbrook Ln
Kirkwood Dr
Spruce Dr
CHILLICOTHE RD
306
Cranwood Dr
Cliffview Ln
Pine Acres
44024
Heath Rd
East Brch
Mulberry Rd
Deer Haven Dr
WESTERN RESERVE MEMORIAL GARDENS
Fox Haven Dr
Kristine Dr
Rust Dr
Peach Tree Dr
Blackberry Ln
MULBERRY RD
Mulberry Rd
8100
Chagrin River
Sperry Rd
Lyman Rd
FS
Heath Rd
Legend Creek Dr
Briarwood Dr
Chester Township
Merrie Ln
Clearview Rd
Hervie Dr
9500
Sandgate Rd
Sandgate Dr
Africa Acres Dr
Oakwood Ln
44026
WILSON MILLS RD
8500
WILSON MILLS RD
12000
WILSON MILLS RD
Hidden Lake Dr
Privacy Ln
Privacy Ln
Red Oaks Dr
Bardwell Dr
Parker Dr
W Shiloh Dr
Woodchuck Hllw
Shadow Hill Tr
12100
Whiting Dr
Norton Dr
Reserve Ln
N Shiloh Dr
Shiloh Dr
E Shiloh Dr
CHESTER TOWNSHIP CEM
SHERMAN RD
Chester Center
Sherman Rd
Shiloh Rd
Sherman Rd
SPERRY RD
Falcon Ridge Rd
Eugene Dr
Lincoln Dr
Northward Pointe Dr
12300
Ward Dr
8200
Maple Dr
Seminary Ln
Seminary Ln
8500
Parkview Dr
Hovey Dr
Valley View Dr
Buckeye Dr
Woodside Dr
Ward Dr
West Geauga Plaza Dr
Herrick Dr
Barfield Dr
Chesterfield Ln
CTR WOODSIDE CEM
Parkside Dr
FS
A 1 Vincent Dr
B 1 Cassie Ln
322
MAYFIELD RD
CHESTERLAND CITY PARK
Griswold Cr
Lynn Dr
Woodside Dr
Chesterland
Opalocka Dr
MAYFIELD RD
OLD SETTLERS CEM
41°34'18"
41°33'52"
41°33'26"
41°32'59"
41°32'33"
41°32'07"
41°31'41"
41°31'15"
81°20'56"
81°20'21"
81°19'46"
81°19'11"
81°18'37"
81°18'02"
A B C D E
1 2 3 4 5 6 7
RAND McNALLY

SEE 2501 MAP

SEE 2503 MAP

SEE 2632 MAP

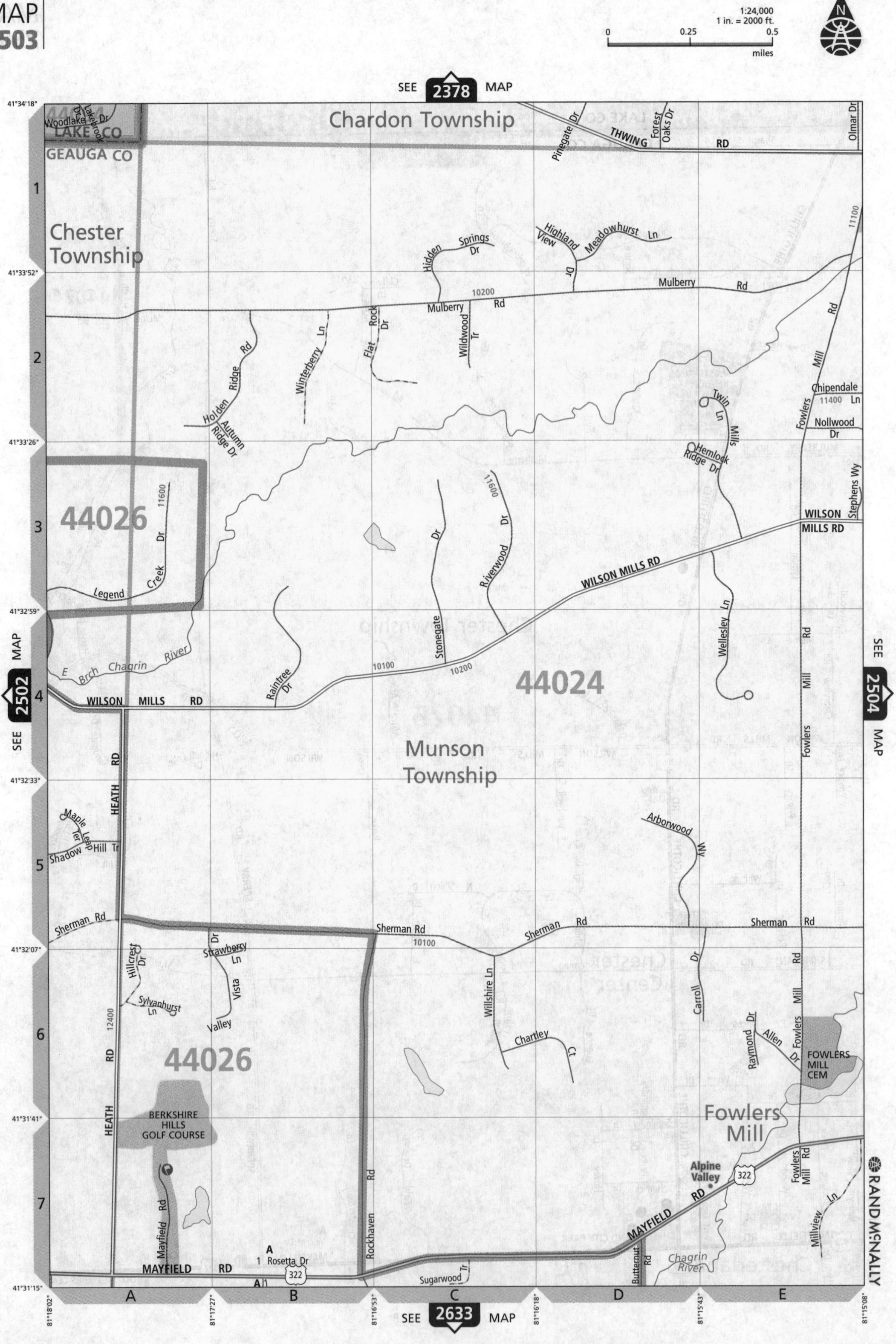
1:24,000
1 in. = 2000 ft.
0
0.25
0.5
miles
N
SEE 2378 MAP
SEE 2633 MAP
SEE 2502 MAP
SEE 2504 MAP
Chardon Township
Chester Township
Munson Township
Fowlers Mill
LAKE CO
GEAUGA CO
44026
44024
44026
Woodlake Dr
Lakebrook Dr
Pinegate Dr
THWING RD
Forest Oaks Dr
Olmar Dr
Hidden Springs Dr
Highland View Dr
Meadowhurst Ln
Mulberry Rd
10200
Holden Ridge Rd
Autumn Ridge Dr
Winterberry Ln
Flat Rock Dr
Wildwood Tr
Fowlers Mill Rd
Chipendale Ln
11400
Nollwood Dr
Twin Mills Ln
Hemlock Ridge Dr
Stephens Wy
WILSON MILLS RD
Legend Creek Dr
11600
Stonegate Dr
Riverwood Dr
E Brch Chagrin River
Raintree Dr
10100
Wellesley Ln
WILSON MILLS RD
HEATH RD
Maple Leaf Ter
Shadow Hill Tr
Arborwood Wy
Sherman Rd
Strawberry Ln
Hillcrest Dr
Vista
Valley
Sylvanhurst Ln
Wilshire Ln
Carroll Dr
Chartley Ct
12400
Raymond Dr
Allen Dr
FOWLERS MILL CEM
BERKSHIRE HILLS GOLF COURSE
Mayfield Rd
Rockhaven Rd
Alpine Valley
322
MAYFIELD RD
Millview Ln
Rosetta Dr
Sugarwood Tr
Butternut Rd
Chagrin River
A
B
C
D
E
1
2
3
4
5
6
7
41°34'18"
41°33'52"
41°33'26"
41°32'59"
41°32'33"
41°32'07"
41°31'41"
41°31'15"
81°18'02"
81°17'27"
81°16'53"
81°16'18"
81°15'43"
81°15'08"
RAND McNALLY

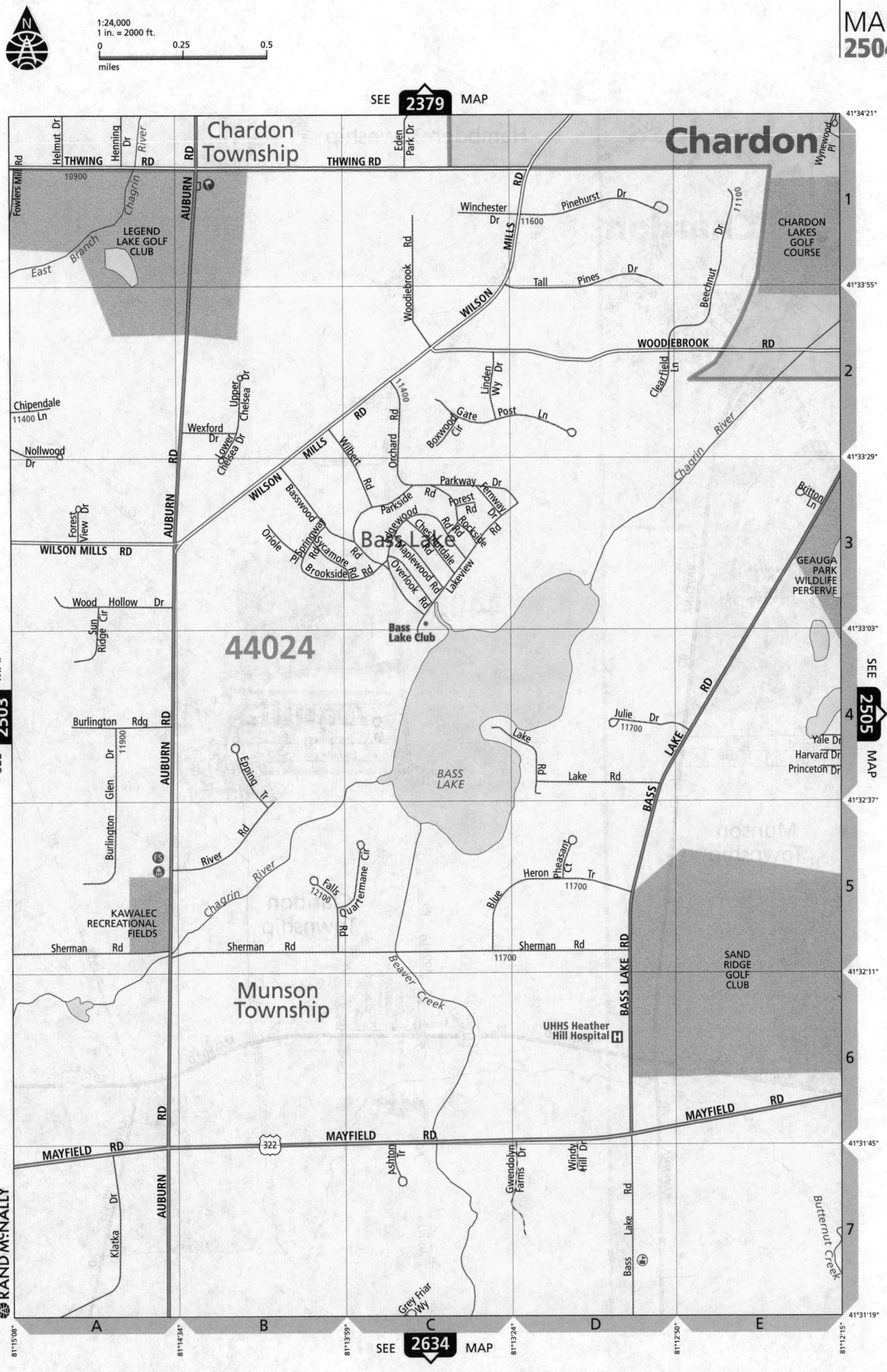
1:24,000
1 in. = 2000 ft.
0 0.25 0.5
miles
SEE 2379 MAP
SEE 2503 MAP
SEE 2505 MAP
SEE 2634 MAP
Chardon Township
Chardon
Munson Township
44024
Bass Lake
BASS LAKE
Bass Lake Club
LEGEND LAKE GOLF CLUB
CHARDON LAKES GOLF COURSE
GEAUGA PARK WILDLIFE PERSERVE
KAWALEC RECREATIONAL FIELDS
SAND RIDGE GOLF CLUB
UHHS Heather Hill Hospital
THWING RD
AUBURN RD
WILSON MILLS RD
WOODIEBROOK RD
BASS LAKE RD
MAYFIELD RD
322
Sherman Rd
River Rd
Lake Rd
Chagrin River
East Branch Chagrin River
Beaver Creek
Butternut Creek
Fowlers Mill Rd
Helmut Dr
Henning Dr
Eden Park Dr
Wynewood Pl
Winchester Dr
Pinehurst Dr
Tall Pines Dr
Beechnut Dr
Clearfield Ln
Woodiebrook Rd
Linden Wy Dr
Post Gate Ln
Boxwood Cir
Chipendale Ln
Nollwood Dr
Wexford Dr
Upper Chelsea Dr
Lower Chelsea Dr
Wilbert Rd
Orchard Rd
Parkway Dr
Fernway Dr
Forest Rd
Parkside Rd
Edgewood Rd
Chesterdale Rd
Rockside Rd
Basswood Rd
Oriole Pl
Springway Rd
Sycamore Rd
Brookside Rd
Maplewood Rd
Overlook Rd
Lakeview
Forest View Dr
Wood Hollow Dr
Sun Ridge Cir
Burlington Rdg
Glen Dr
Burlington
Epping Tr
Britton Ln
Julie Dr
Yale Dr
Harvard Dr
Princeton Dr
Pheasant Ct
Blue Heron Tr
Falls
Quartermane Cir
Ashton Tr
Gwendolyn Farms Dr
Windy Hill Dr
Klatka Dr
Grey Friar Wy
10900
11100
11400
11600
11700
11900
12100
41°34'21"
41°33'55"
41°33'29"
41°33'03"
41°32'37"
41°32'11"
41°31'45"
41°31'19"
81°15'08"
81°14'34"
81°13'59"
81°13'24"
81°12'50"
81°12'15"
A B C D E
1 2 3 4 5 6 7
RAND McNALLY

1:24,000
1 in. = 2000 ft.
0 0.25 0.5
miles

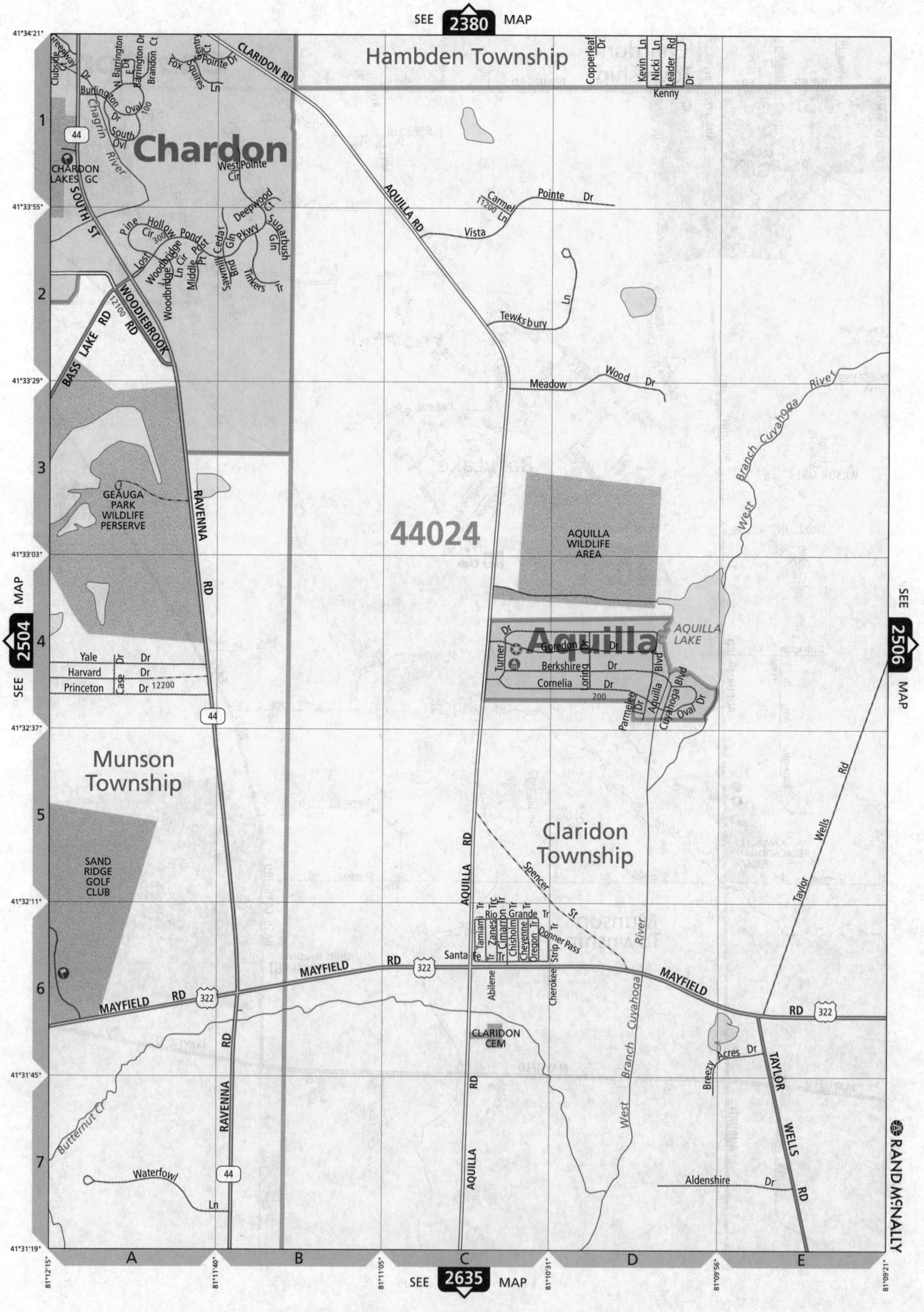
SEE 2380 MAP
SEE 2635 MAP
SEE MAP 2504
SEE MAP 2506
Hambden Township
Chardon
Munson Township
Claridon Township
Aquilla
44024
CHARDON LAKES GC
GEAUGA PARK WILDLIFE PERSERVE
AQUILLA WILDLIFE AREA
AQUILLA LAKE
SAND RIDGE GOLF CLUB
CLARIDON CEM
CLARIDON RD
AQUILLA RD
RAVENNA RD
SOUTH ST
WOODIEBROOK RD
BASS LAKE RD
MAYFIELD RD
TAYLOR WELLS RD
Taylor Wells Rd
Chagrin River
West Branch Cuyahoga River
Butternut Cr
44
322
Clubside
Greenway Ct
Dr
Burlington
N Barrington
Barrington Dr
Brandon Ct
Oval
South Ovl
Fox
Squires
Gentry Ct
Pointe Dr
Ln
West Pointe Cir
Deepwood Ct
Sugarbush Gln
Pine Hollow
Cir
Pond
Lost
Woodbridge
Ln Cir
Middle Pt
Post
Cedar Gln
Pkwy
Sawmill Ln
Bridle
Tinkers Tr
Copperleaf Dr
Kevin Ln
Nicki Ln
Leader Rd
Kenny
Dr
Carmel Ln
11200
Pointe Dr
Vista
Tewksbury Ln
Meadow Wood Dr
Turner Dr
Goredon Dr
Berkshire Dr
Cornelia Dr
Loring
Aquilla Blvd
Cuyahoga Blvd
Oval Dr
Parmelee Dr
200
Yale Dr
Harvard Dr
Princeton Dr
Case Dr
12200
12100
Spencer St
Tamiami Tr
Rio Grande Tr
Zanes Tr
Cimarron Tr
Chisholm Tr
Cheyenne Tr
Oregon Tr
Strip Tr
Donner Pass
Santa Fe Tr
Abilene
Cherokee
Breezy Acres Dr
Aldenshire Dr
Waterfowl Ln
41°34'21"
41°33'55"
41°33'29"
41°33'03"
41°32'37"
41°32'11"
41°31'45"
41°31'19"
81°12'15"
81°11'40"
81°11'05"
81°10'31"
81°09'56"
81°09'21"
A
B
C
D
E
1
2
3
4
5
6
7
RAND McNALLY

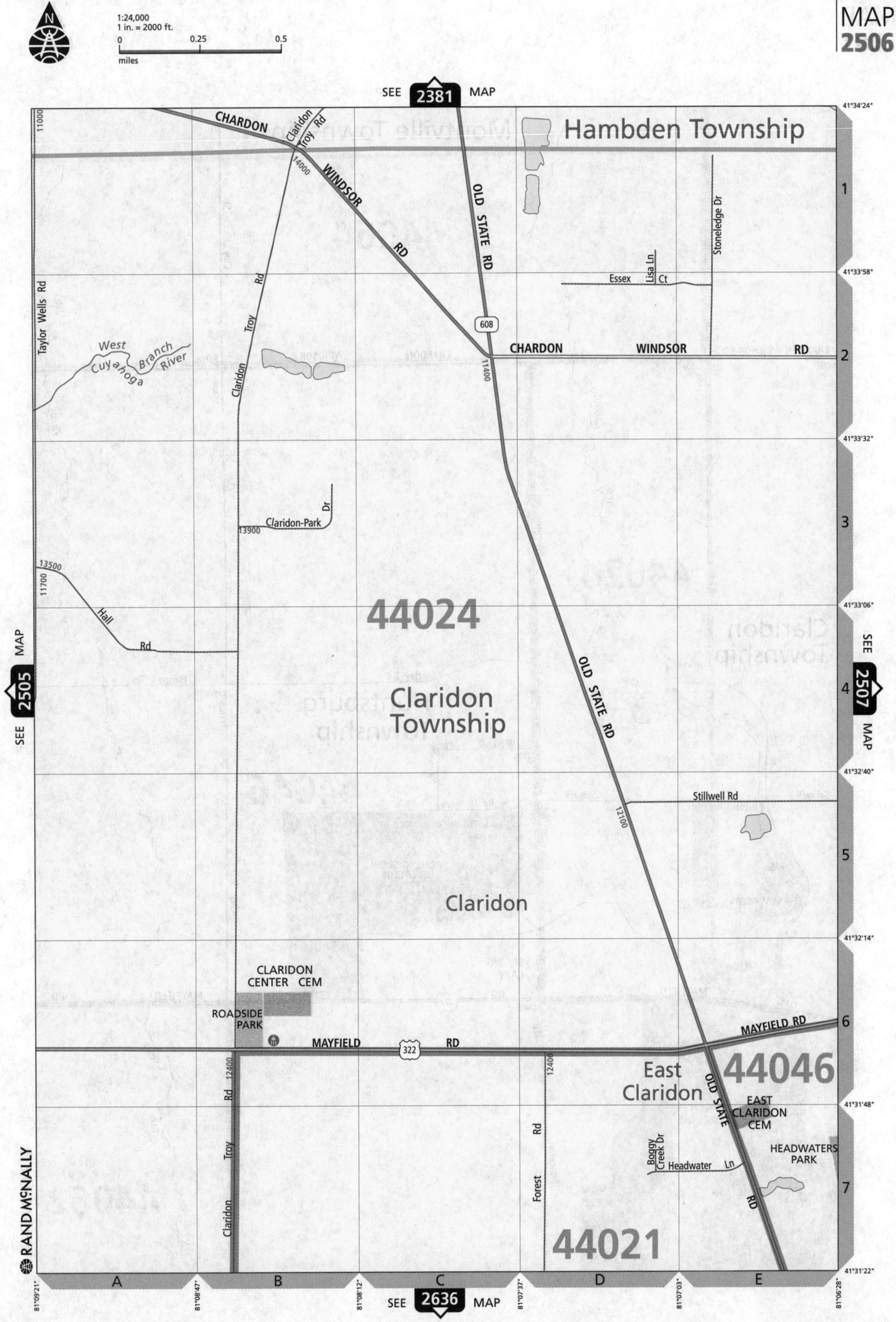
1:24,000
1 in. = 2000 ft.
0 0.25 0.5
miles
SEE 2381 MAP
Hambden Township
CHARDON
Claridon Troy Rd
WINDSOR RD
14000
OLD STATE RD
Stoneledge Dr
Lisa Ln
Essex Ct
608
CHARDON WINDSOR RD
11400
Taylor Wells Rd
West Branch Cuyahoga River
Claridon Troy Rd
Claridon-Park Dr
13900
13500
11700
Hall Rd
44024
Claridon Township
SEE 2505 MAP
SEE 2507 MAP
OLD STATE RD
Stillwell Rd
12100
Claridon
CLARIDON CENTER CEM
ROADSIDE PARK
MAYFIELD 322 RD
MAYFIELD RD
12400
East Claridon
44046
OLD STATE RD
EAST CLARIDON CEM
HEADWATERS PARK
Boggy Creek Dr
Headwater Ln
Claridon Troy Rd
Forest Rd
44021
RAND McNALLY
A B C D E
1 2 3 4 5 6 7
41°34'24"
41°33'58"
41°33'32"
41°33'06"
41°32'40"
41°32'14"
41°31'48"
41°31'22"
81°09'21"
81°08'47"
81°08'12"
81°07'37"
81°07'03"
81°06'28"
SEE 2636 MAP

1:24,000
1 in. = 2000 ft.
0 0.25 0.5
miles

SEE B MAP

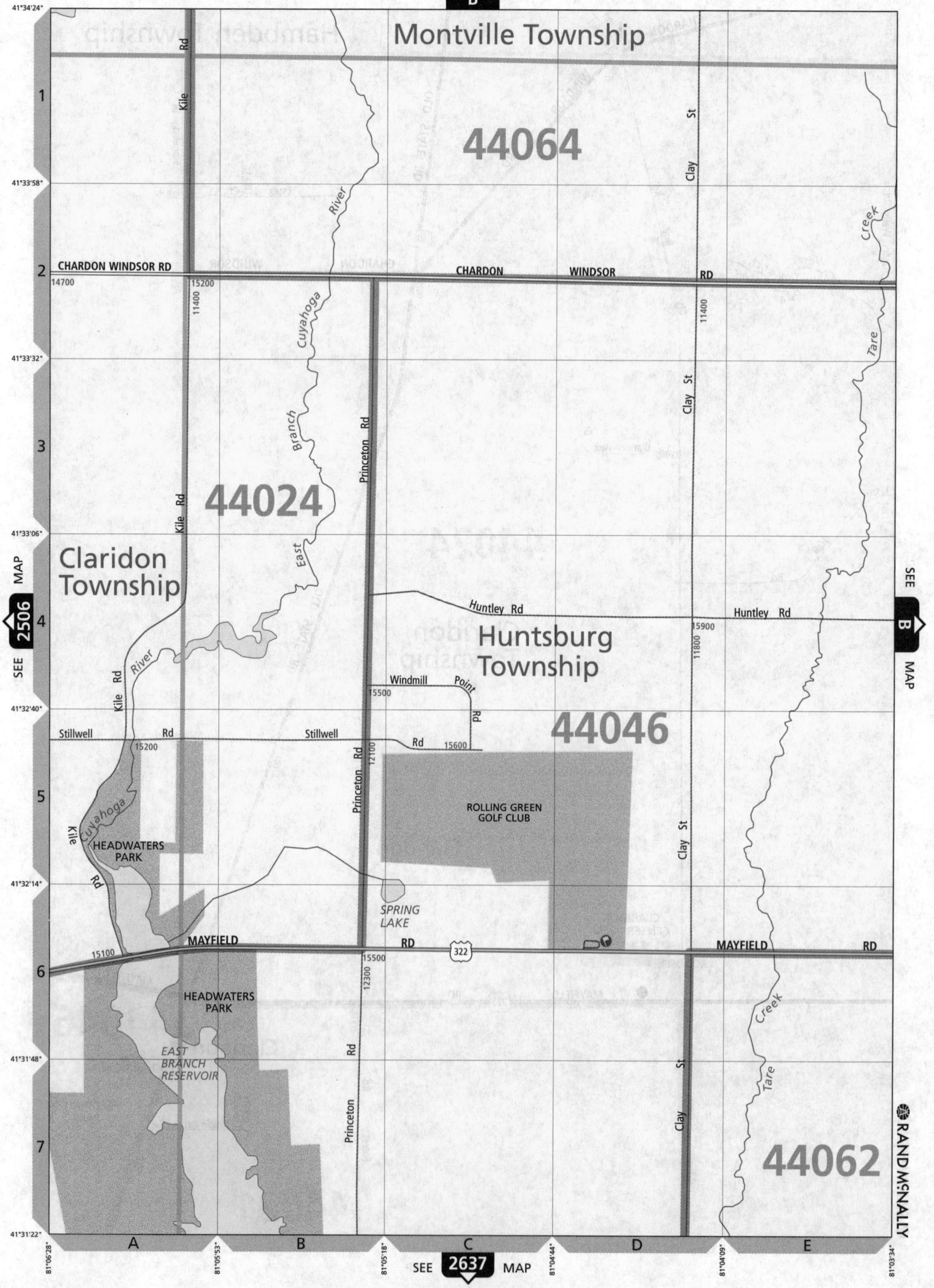
Montville Township
44064
Kile Rd
Clay St
River
Creek
CHARDON WINDSOR RD
14700
15200
11400
Cuyahoga
CHARDON
WINDSOR
RD
Tare
Branch
Princeton Rd
44024
East
Claridon Township
Huntley Rd
15900
11800
Huntsburg Township
Windmill Point Rd
15500
44046
Stillwell Rd
15200
12100
15600
ROLLING GREEN GOLF CLUB
HEADWATERS PARK
SPRING LAKE
MAYFIELD RD
15100
322
12300
EAST BRANCH RESERVOIR
44062
41°34'24"
41°33'58"
41°33'32"
41°33'06"
41°32'40"
41°32'14"
41°31'48"
41°31'22"
81°06'28"
81°05'53"
81°05'18"
81°04'44"
81°04'09"
81°03'34"
1
2
3
4
5
6
7
A
B
C
D
E

SEE 2506 MAP

SEE B MAP

SEE 2637 MAP

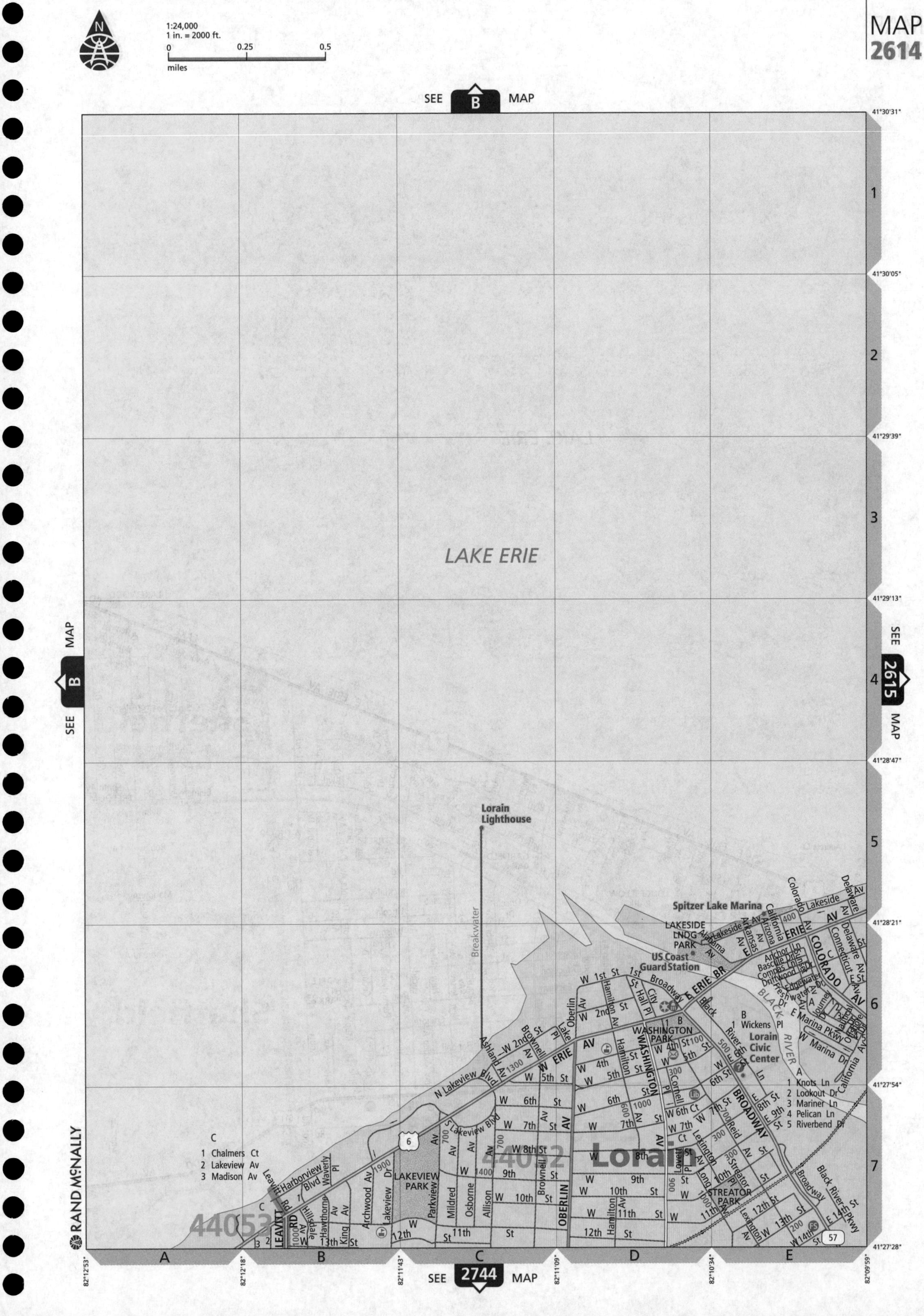
N
1:24,000
1 in. = 2000 ft.
0 0.25 0.5
miles
SEE B MAP
SEE 2615 MAP
SEE 2744 MAP
41°30'31"
41°30'05"
41°29'39"
41°29'13"
41°28'47"
41°28'21"
41°27'54"
41°27'28"
82°12'53"
82°12'18"
82°11'43"
82°11'09"
82°10'34"
82°09'59"
A B C D E
1 2 3 4 5 6 7
LAKE ERIE
Lorain Lighthouse
Breakwater
Spitzer Lake Marina
LAKESIDE LNDG PARK
US Coast Guard Station
WASHINGTON PARK
Lorain Civic Center
LAKEVIEW PARK
STREATOR PARK
BLACK RIVER
44052
44053
Lorain
W ERIE AV
E ERIE AV
COLORADO AV
BROADWAY
OBERLIN AV
WASHINGTON AV
LEAVITT RD
N Lakeview Blvd
1 Knots Ln
2 Lookout Dr
3 Mariner Ln
4 Pelican Ln
5 Riverbend Dr
C
1 Chalmers Ct
2 Lakeview Av
3 Madison Av
1 Wickens Pl
RAND McNALLY

1:24,000
1 in. = 2000 ft.
0 0.25 0.5
miles
SEE B MAP
SEE 2614 MAP
SEE 2616 MAP
SEE 2745 MAP
LAKE ERIE
E ERIE AV
E LAKE RD
LAKEWOOD BCH PARK
Sheffield Lake
Sheffield
44054
Lorain
44052
44052
COLORADO AV
HENDERSON DR
KANSAS AV
LONGFELLOW PARK
GARFIELD PARK
G STREET PARK
HIGHVIEW PARK
MAPLE HTS PARK
FREEDOM PK
BLACK RIVER
Black River
Root Rd
Pin Oak Dr
Industrial
A 1 Andress Ct
RAND McNALLY

1:24,000
1 in. = 2000 ft.
0 0.25 0.5
miles

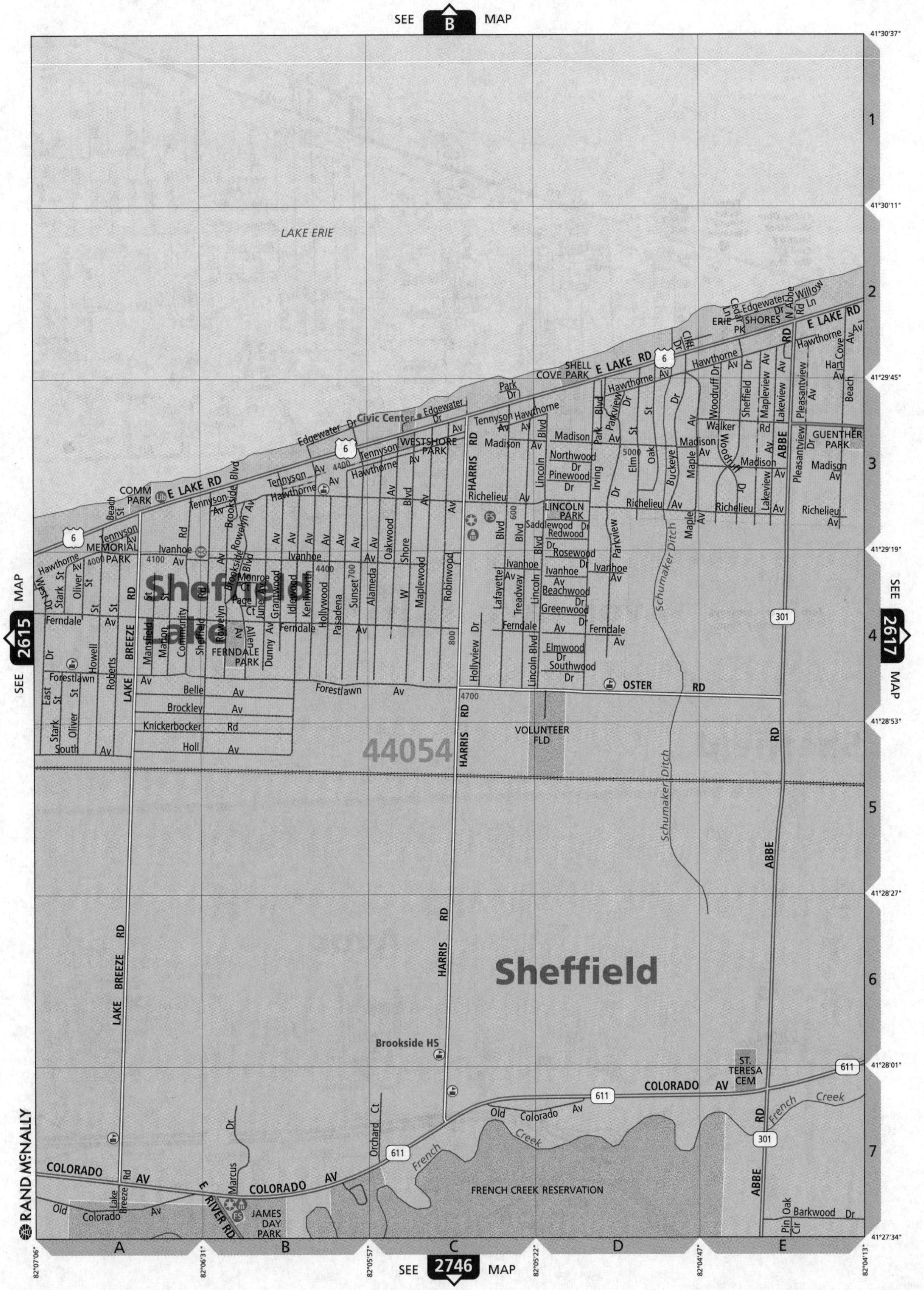
SEE B MAP
SEE 2615 MAP
SEE 2617 MAP
SEE 2746 MAP
LAKE ERIE
Sheffield Lake
Sheffield
44054
E LAKE RD
HARRIS RD
ABBE RD
LAKE BREEZE RD
OSTER RD
COLORADO AV
Old Colorado Av
E RIVER RD
Forestlawn Av
Belle Av
Brockley Av
Knickerbocker Rd
Holl Av
Ferndale Av
Ivanhoe Av
Richelieu Av
Madison Av
Hawthorne Av
Tennyson Av
Edgewater Dr
Civic Center
COMM PARK
MEMORIAL PARK
FERNDALE PARK
WESTSHORE PARK
SHELL COVE PARK
LINCOLN PARK
GUENTHER PARK
ERIE SHORES
VOLUNTEER FLD
Schumaker Ditch
French Creek
Brookside HS
ST. TERESA CEM
FRENCH CREEK RESERVATION
JAMES DAY PARK
Barkwood Dr
Orchard Ct
Marcus Dr
RAND McNALLY
A B C D E
1 2 3 4 5 6 7

1:24,000
1 in. = 2000 ft.
0 0.25 0.5
miles

SEE 2487 MAP

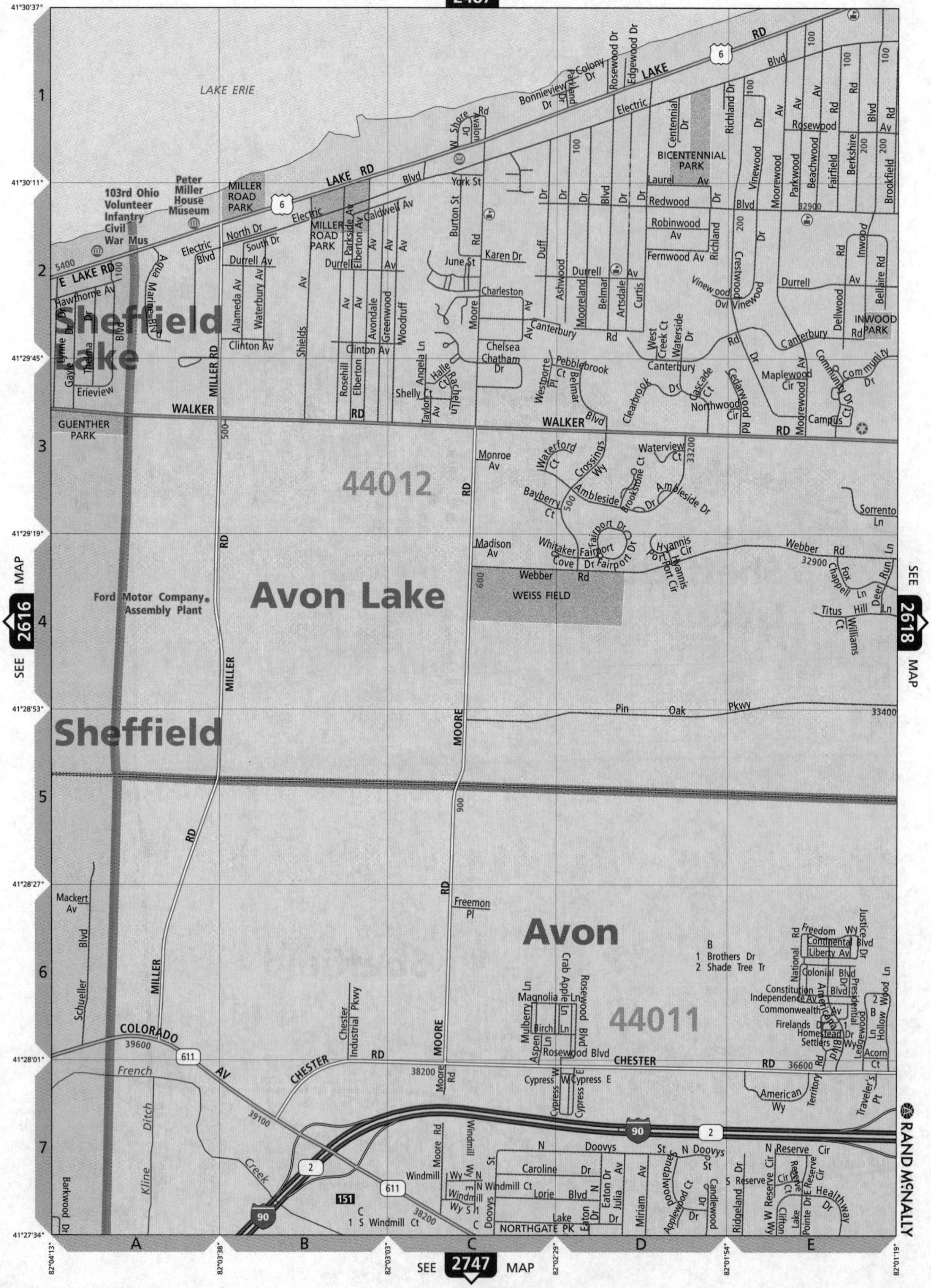
LAKE ERIE
Sheffield Lake
Sheffield
Avon Lake
Avon
44012
44011
103rd Ohio Volunteer Infantry Civil War Mus
Peter Miller House Museum
MILLER ROAD PARK
BICENTENNIAL PARK
INWOOD PARK
GUENTHER PARK
WEISS FIELD
Ford Motor Company Assembly Plant
LAKE RD
E LAKE RD
Electric Blvd
WALKER RD
MILLER RD
MOORE RD
CHESTER RD
COLORADO AV
Pin Oak Pkwy
Webber Rd
Canterbury Rd
Durrell Av
Clinton Av
French Creek
Kline Ditch
Freemon Pl
Chester Industrial Pkwy
Rosewood Blvd
N Doorys St
Northgate PK
Windmill Ct
B
1 Brothers Dr
2 Shade Tree Tr
C
1 S Windmill Ct
1
2
3
4
5
6
7
A
B
C
D
E
41°30'37"
41°30'11"
41°29'45"
41°29'19"
41°28'53"
41°28'27"
41°28'01"
41°27'34"
82°04'13"
82°03'38"
82°03'03"
82°02'29"
82°01'54"
82°01'19"

SEE 2616 MAP
SEE 2618 MAP
SEE 2747 MAP

RAND McNALLY

1:24,000
1 in. = 2000 ft.
0 0.25 0.5
miles

SEE 2488 MAP

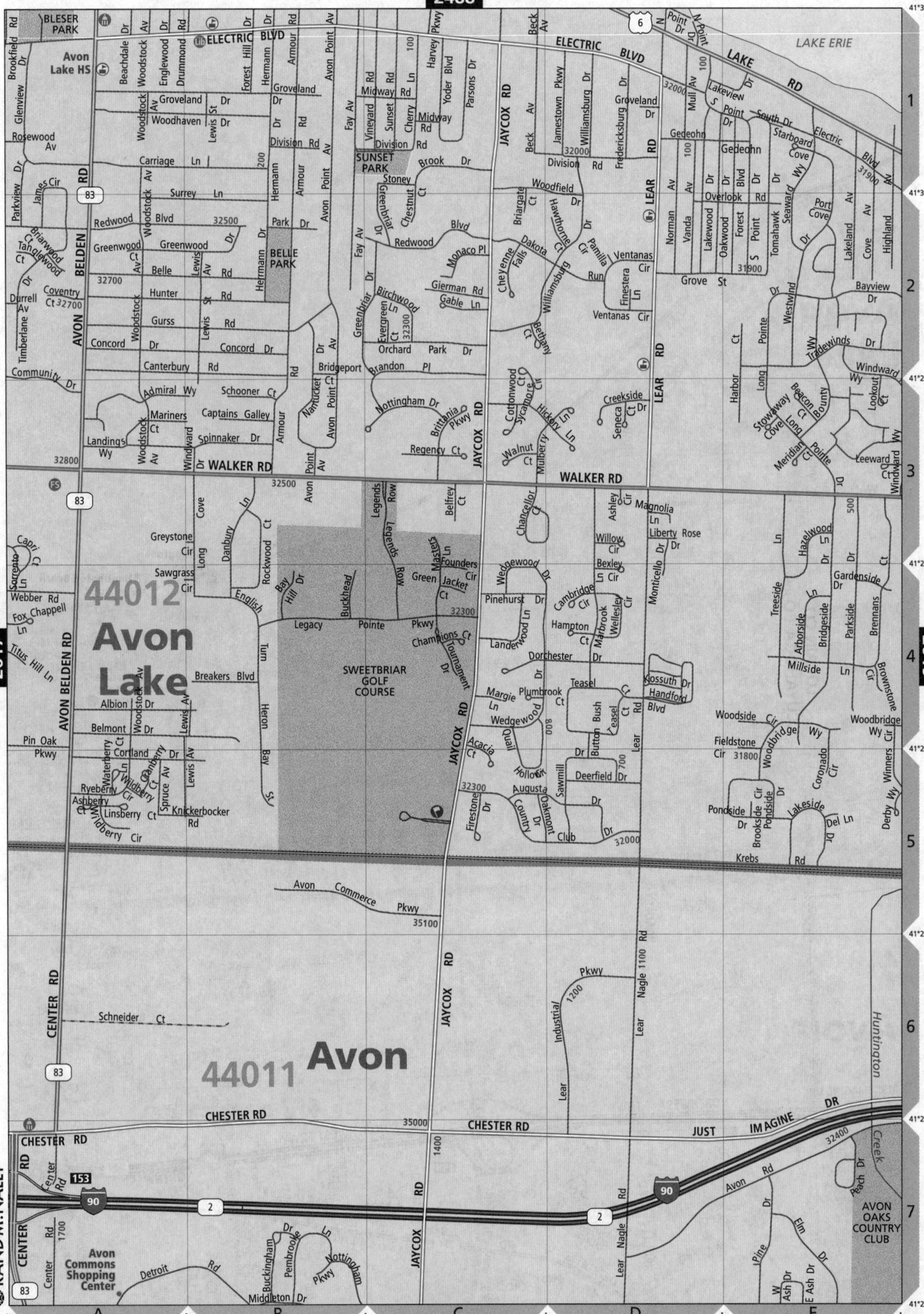
Avon Lake
44012
Avon
44011
LAKE ERIE
BLESER PARK
Avon Lake HS
SUNSET PARK
BELLE PARK
SWEETBRIAR GOLF COURSE
AVON OAKS COUNTRY CLUB
Avon Commons Shopping Center
ELECTRIC BLVD
LAKE RD
WALKER RD
CHESTER RD
JUST IMAGINE DR
AVON BELDEN RD
CENTER RD
JAYCOX RD
LEAR RD
Lear Nagle Rd
Avon Commerce Pkwy
Industrial Pkwy
Schneider Ct
Detroit Rd
Avon Rd
Huntington
Legacy Pointe Pkwy
Groveland Dr
Woodhaven Dr
Carriage Ln
Surrey Ln
Redwood Blvd
Greenwood Dr
Belle Rd
Hunter Rd
Gurss Rd
Concord Dr
Canterbury Rd
Admiral Wy
Schooner Ct
Captains Galley
Mariners Ct
Spinnaker Dr
Landings Wy
Division Rd
Brook Dr
Woodfield Dr
Orchard Park Dr
Brandon Pl
Bridgeport
Nottingham Dr
Regency Ct
Greystone Cir
Sawgrass Cir
Danbury Ln
Rockwood Ct
English
Breakers Blvd
Albion Dr
Belmont Dr
Pin Oak Pkwy
Cortland Dr
Knickerbocker Rd
Wildberry Cir
Pinehurst Dr
Dorchester Dr
Teasel Ct
Deerfield Dr
Augusta Dr
Oakmont Dr
Club Dr
Kossuth Dr
Handford Blvd
Magnolia Ln
Liberty Rose Dr
Monticello Dr
Gedeohn
Overlook Rd
Grove St
Ventanas Cir
Bayview Dr
Tradewinds Dr
Windward
Leeward
Hazelwood Ln
Gardenside Dr
Millside Ln
Woodside Cir
Fieldstone Cir
Woodbridge Wy
Coronado Cir
Pondside Dr
Lakeside Dr
Del Ln
Krebs Rd
Middleton Dr
Nottingham Pkwy
6
83
90
2
153
41°30'43"
41°30'17"
41°29'51"
41°29'25"
41°28'58"
41°28'32"
41°28'06"
41°27'40"
82°01'19"
82°00'45"
82°00'10"
81°59'35"
81°59'01"
81°58'26"
A
B
C
D
E
1
2
3
4
5
6
7
RAND McNALLY

SEE 2617 MAP

SEE 2619 MAP

SEE 2748 MAP

1:24,000
1 in. = 2000 ft.
0 0.25 0.5
miles

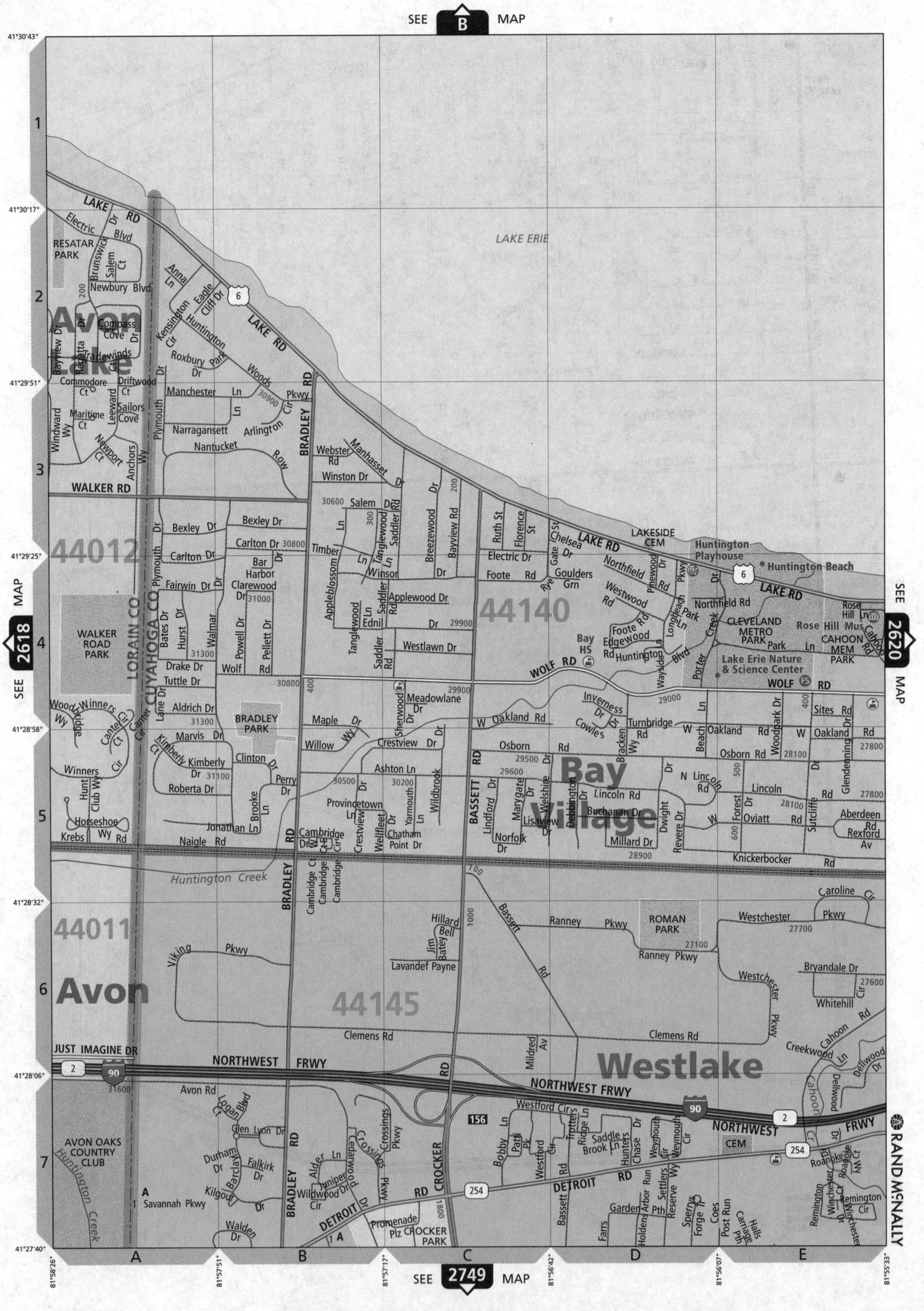
SEE B MAP
SEE 2618 MAP
SEE 2620 MAP
SEE 2749 MAP
41°30'43"
41°30'17"
41°29'51"
41°29'25"
41°28'58"
41°28'32"
41°28'06"
41°27'40"
81°58'26"
81°57'51"
81°57'17"
81°56'42"
81°56'07"
81°55'33"
LAKE ERIE
LAKE RD
Electric Blvd
RESATAR PARK
Brunswick Dr
Salem Ct
Newbury Blvd
Avon Lake
Compass Cove
Bayview Dr
Regatta Dr
Tradewinds Cir
Commodore Ct
Driftwood Ct
Windward Wy
Maritime Ct
Leeward Ct
Sailors Cove
Newport Ct
Anchors Wy
Plymouth Dr
WALKER RD
Anna Ln
Eagle Cliff Dr
Kensington Cir
Huntington Park
Roxbury Dr
Woods
Manchester Ln
30900
Pkwy
Arlington Cir
Narragansett
Nantucket
Row
BRADLEY RD
Webster Rd
Manhasset Dr
Winston Dr
30600
Salem Dr
Saddler Rd
Breezewood Dr
Bayview Rd
200
Ruth St
Florence St
Chelsea Dr
Gate St
LAKESIDE CEM
Huntington Playhouse
Huntington Beach
Electric Dr
Foote Rd
Rye Goulders Grn
Northfield Rd
Pinewood Dr
Pkwy
Westwood Rd
Longbeach Park Ln
Northfield Rd
Porter Creek Dr
CLEVELAND METRO PARK
Rose Hill Ln
Rose Hill Mus
Cahoon Rd
CAHOON MEM PARK
Park Ln
Lake Erie Nature & Science Center
WOLF RD
44012
Bexley Dr
Bexley Dr
Carlton Dr
Carlton Dr
30800
Timber Ln
Tanglewood Ln
Bar Harbor Clarewood Dr
Fairwin Dr
Appleblossom Ln
Winsor Dr
Applewood Dr
Saddler Ln
31000
Tanglewood Ednil
29900
44140
Bay HS
Foote Rd
Edgewood Rd
Huntington
Wayside Blvd
WALKER ROAD PARK
LORAIN CO
CUYAHOGA CO
Bates Dr
Hurst Dr
Walmar Dr
Powell Dr
Pellett Dr
31300
Westlawn Dr
Drake Dr
Wolf Rd
Tuttle Dr
30800
400
Sherwood Dr
Meadowlane Dr
Inverness Dr
29000
Cowles Rd
Turnbridge
Sites Rd
Woodbridge Wy
Winners Cir
Canter Cir
Camer Cir
Lane Dr
Aldrich Dr
31300
BRADLEY PARK
Maple Dr
W Oakland Rd
Bracken Wy Rd
Beach Ln
Oakland Rd
W Oakland Rd
Woodpark Dr
Marvis Dr
Kimberly Ct
Kimberly Dr
Willow Wy
Crestview Dr
Osborn Rd
29500
Osborn Rd
28100
Glendenning Dr
27800
Winners
Hunt Club Wy
31100
Clinton Dr
Perry Dr
Ashton Ln
29600
Bay Village
N Lincoln Rd
500
Lincoln Rd
Lincoln Rd
28100
Roberta Dr
30500
30200
Provincetown Ln
Yarmouth Ln
Wildbrook Ln
BASSETT RD
Lindford Dr
Marygate Dr
Welshire Dr
Debbington Dr
Buchanan Dr
Dwight
Revere Dr
Forest Dr
Oviatt Rd
Sutcliffe Dr
Aberdeen Rd
Rexford Av
Horseshoe Wy
Krebs
Jonathan Ln
Brooke Ln
Naigle Rd
Cambridge Dr
Crestview Ln
Wellfleet Ln
Chatham Point Dr
Norfolk Dr
Lisaview Dr
Millard Dr
28900
600
Knickerbocker Rd
Huntington Creek
700
Cambridge Ct
Cambridge Cir
Cambridge
Caroline Cir
44011
Hillard Bell
1000
Bassett Rd
Ranney Pkwy
ROMAN PARK
27100
Westchester Pkwy
27700
Ranney Pkwy
Viking Pkwy
Jim Batey
Lavandef Payne
Westchester Pkwy
Bryandale Dr
27600
Whitehill Cir
Avon
44145
Cahoon Rd
Clemens Rd
Mildred Av
Clemens Rd
Creekwood Ln
Dellwood Dr
JUST IMAGINE DR
NORTHWEST FRWY
2
90
31600
CROCKER RD
Westlake
NORTHWEST FRWY
Avon Rd
Logan Blvd Ct
Westford Cir
156
90
2
NORTHWEST FRWY
Glen Lyon Dr
Crossings Pkwy
Bobby Ln
Path Dr
Trotters Ridge Ln
Saddle Brook Ln
Hunters Chase Dr
Weymouth Cir
Weymouth Cir
CEM
254
Roanoke Dr
Dellwood Dr
AVON OAKS COUNTRY CLUB
Durham Dr
Barclay
Falkirk Dr
Alder Ln
Cedarwood Dr
Juniper
Westford Cir
Rd
DETROIT RD
Roanoke Wy Ct
Huntington Creek
A
1 Savannah Pkwy
Kilgour Dr
Wildwood Cir
254
Settlers Reserve Wy
Sperry Forge Tr
Coes Post Run
Halls Carriage Pth
Remington Rd
Winchester Ct
Remington Cir
Winchester Dr
Walden Dr
DETROIT RD
1 A
Promenade Plz
CROCKER PARK
1800
Bassett Rd
Farrs
Garden Holdens Arbor Run Pth
A B C D E
1 2 3 4 5 6 7
RAND McNALLY

1:24,000
1 in. = 2000 ft.
0 0.25 0.5
miles

SEE B MAP

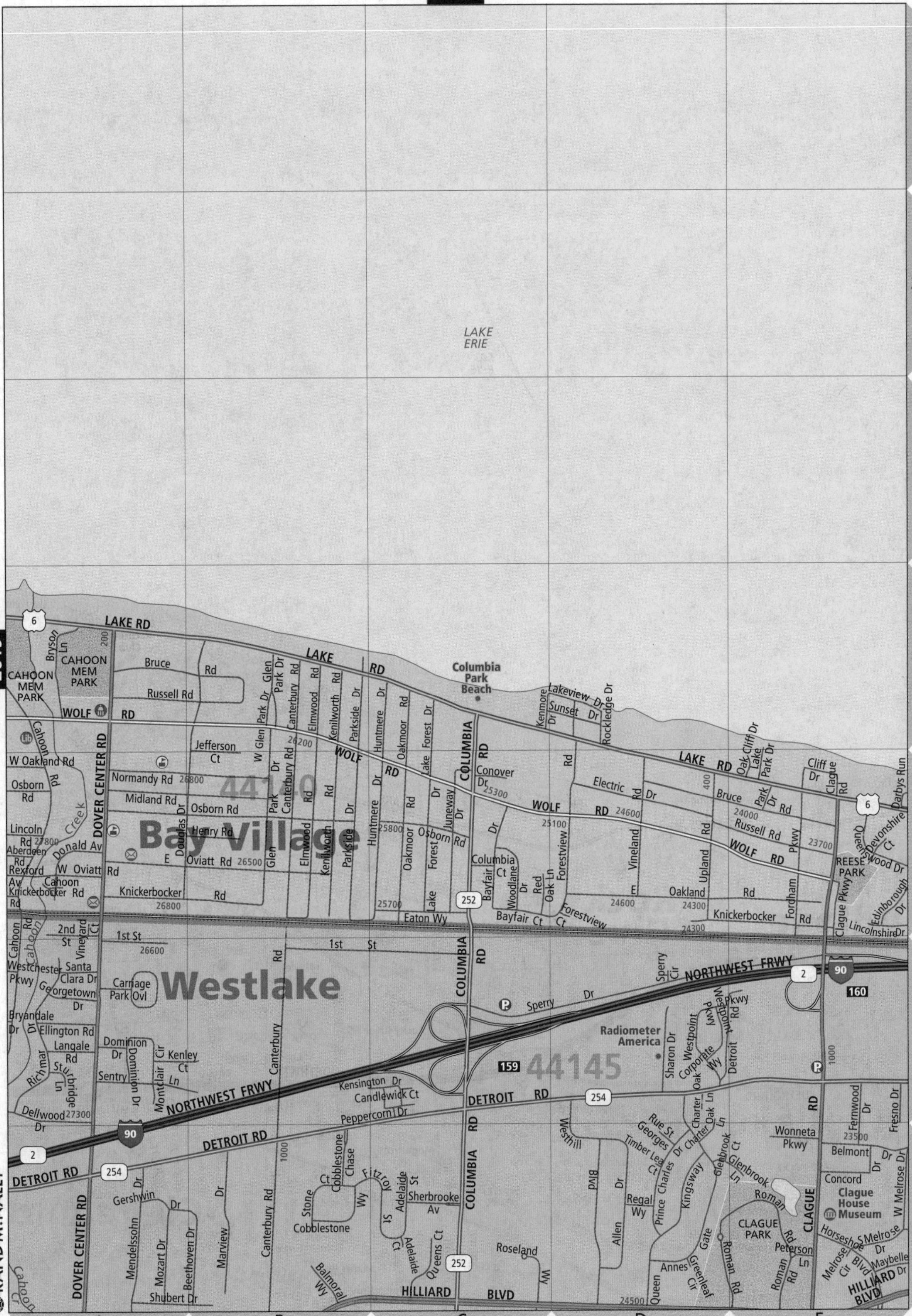

LAKE ERIE
Bay Village
Westlake
44140
44145
Columbia Park Beach
CAHOON MEM PARK
REESE PARK
CLAGUE PARK
Clague House Museum
Radiometer America
LAKE RD
WOLF RD
DOVER CENTER RD
COLUMBIA RD
CLAGUE RD
NORTHWEST FRWY
DETROIT RD
HILLIARD BLVD
Knickerbocker Rd
Oviatt Rd
Osborn Rd
Normandy Rd
Midland Rd
Henry Rd
Russell Rd
Bruce Rd
Jefferson Ct
W Oakland Rd
Oakland Rd
Electric Rd
Lakeview Dr
Sunset Dr
Rockledge Dr
Kenmore Dr
Conover Dr
Bayfair Ct
Forestview Ct
Eaton Wy
1st St
2nd St
Sperry Dr
Kensington Dr
Candlewick Ct
Peppercorn Dr
Gershwin Dr
Mendelssohn Dr
Mozart Dr
Beethoven Dr
Shubert Dr
Marview Dr
Canterbury Rd
Cobblestone Chase
Stone Ct
Fitzroy Wy
Adelaide St
Sherbrooke Av
Queens Ct
Balmoral Wy
Roseland Wy
Westhill Blvd
Allen Dr
Regal Wy
Kingsway
Glenbrook Ln
Roman Rd
Peterson Ln
Wonneta Pkwy
Fernwood Dr
Fresno Dr
Belmont Dr
Concord
Horseshoe Blvd
Melrose Cir
Maybelle Dr
W Melrose Dr
Lincolnshire Dr
Edinborough Dr
Devonshire Ct
Queenswood Dr
Darbys Run
Cliff Dr
6
2
90
252
254
159
160
A
B
C
D
E
1
2
3
4
5
6
7
41°30'48"
41°30'22"
41°29'56"
41°29'30"
41°29'04"
41°28'38"
41°28'12"
41°27'46"
81°55'33"
81°54'58"
81°54'23"
81°53'49"
81°53'14"
81°52'39"

SEE 2619 MAP

SEE 2621 MAP

SEE 2750 MAP

1:24,000
1 in. = 2000 ft.
0 0.25 0.5
miles

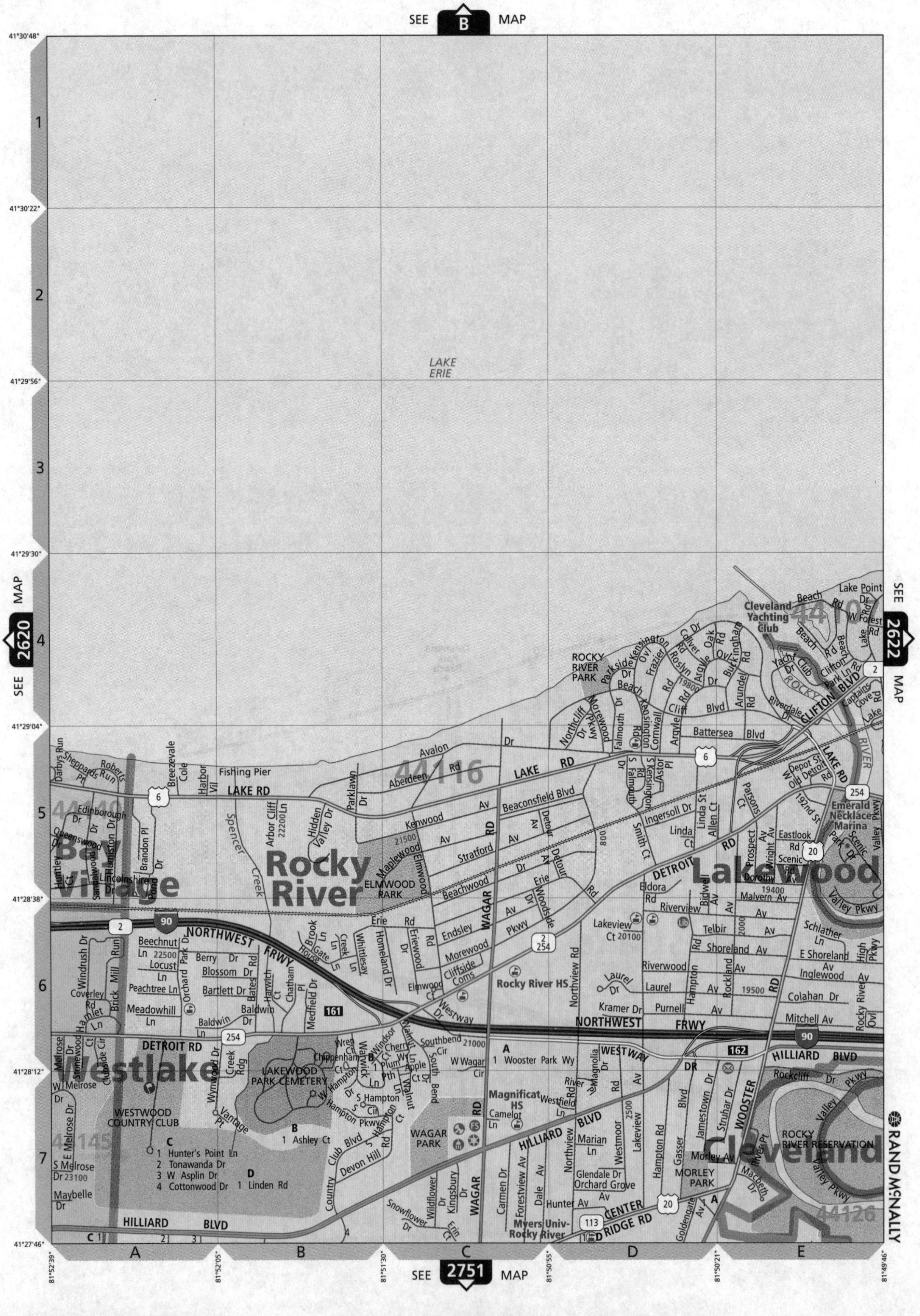
SEE B MAP
SEE 2620 MAP
SEE 2622 MAP
SEE 2751 MAP
41°30'48"
41°30'22"
41°29'56"
41°29'30"
41°29'04"
41°28'38"
41°28'12"
41°27'46"
81°52'39"
81°52'05"
81°51'30"
81°50'55"
81°50'21"
81°49'46"
1
2
3
4
5
6
7
A
B
C
D
E
LAKE ERIE
Rocky River
Bay Village
Westlake
Lakewood
Cleveland
44116
44140
44145
44107
44126
ROCKY RIVER PARK
Cleveland Yachting Club
Fishing Pier
LAKE RD
LAKE RD
DETROIT RD
DETROIT RD
NORTHWEST FRWY
NORTHWEST FRWY
HILLIARD BLVD
HILLIARD BLVD
WAGAR RD
WOOSTER RD
CLIFTON BLVD
CENTER RIDGE RD
WESTWAY DR
ELMWOOD PARK
LAKEWOOD PARK CEMETERY
WESTWOOD COUNTRY CLUB
WAGAR PARK
MORLEY PARK
Rocky River HS
Magnificat HS
Myers Univ-Rocky River
Emerald Necklace Marina
ROCKY RIVER RESERVATION
Spencer Creek
A 1 Wooster Park Wy
B 1 Ashley Ct
C 1 Hunter's Point Ln 2 Tonawanda Dr 3 W Asplin Dr 4 Cottonwood Dr
D 1 Linden Rd
Avalon Dr
Aberdeen Rd
Kenwood Av
Beaconsfield Blvd
Stratford Av
Beachwood Dr
Maplewood
Elmwood
Erie Rd
Endsley Av
Morewood Pkwy
Cliffside Cons
Homeland Dr
Eriewood Dr
Whittlesay
Parklawn Dr
Hidden Valley Dr
Arbor Cliff Ln
Edinborough Dr
Queenswood Dr
Huntley Ct
Sandalwood Dr
Humiston Dr
Brandon Pl
Lincolnshire Dr
Pond Dr
Darbys Run
Sheppards Pt
Roberts Run
Breezevale Cole
Harbor Vil
Beechnut Ln
Locust Ln
Peachtree Ln
Berry Dr
Blossom Dr
Bartlett Dr
Baldwin Dr
Meadowhill Ln
Windrush Dr
Coverley Rd
Brick Mill Run
Orchard Park Dr
Chatham Pl
Medfield Dr
Harwich Ct
Bates
Melrose Dr
W Melrose Dr
E Melrose Dr
S Melrose Dr
Maybelle Dr
Stonewood Ct
Clubside Cir
Wynwood Dr
Creek Rdg
Vantage Pt
Country Club Blvd
Devon Hill
Hampton Rd
S Hampton Cir
W Hampton Dr
Plum Wy
Walnut Ln
Apple Ct
South Bend Dr
Southbend Cir
W Wagar Cir
Chippenham Ct
Windsor Ct
Warwick
Wren Ct
Snowflower Dr
Wildflower Dr
Kingsbury Dr
Erin Ct
Carmen Dr
Forestview Av
Dale Av
Hunter Av
Northview Rd
Magnolia Dr
River Rd
Westfield Ln
Camelot Dr
Marian Ln
Glendale Dr
Orchard Grove Av
Westmoor
Lakeview Av
Hampton Rd
Gasser Blvd
Jamestown Dr
Struhar Dr
Goldengate Av
Northcliff Dr
Morewood Pkwy
Falmouth Dr
S Falmouth Dr
Kensington Rd
S Kensington Rd
Astor Pl
Parkside Dr
Beach Rd
Cornwall
Frazier
Roslyn
Argyle Rd
Oak Ovl
Buckingham Rd
Arundel Rd
Cliff Blvd
Battersea Blvd
Ingersoll Dr
Smith Ct
Linda Ct
Linda St
Allen Ct
Parsons Ct
Prospect Av
Wright Av
Eldora Rd
Riverview Av
Bidwell Av
Telbir Av
Shoreland Av
Riverwood Av
Laurel Av
Laurel Dr
Rockland
Purnell Av
Kramer Dr
Lakeview Ct
Dorothy Av
Malvern Av
Valley Pkwy
Eastlook Rd
Scenic Park Dr
Schlather Ln
E Shoreland Av
Inglewood Av
Colahan Dr
Mitchell Av
Rocky River Ovl
High Pkwy
Rockcliff Dr
Yacht Club Dr
Beach Rd
Lake Point Dr
W Forest Rd
Clifton Park Ln
Riverdale Dr
Captains Cove
Depot St
Old Detroit Rd
192nd St
River Pt
MacBeth Dr
Morley Av
Valley Pkwy
ROCKY RIVER
RAND McNALLY

1:24,000
1 in. = 2000 ft.
0 0.25 0.5
miles

SEE B MAP

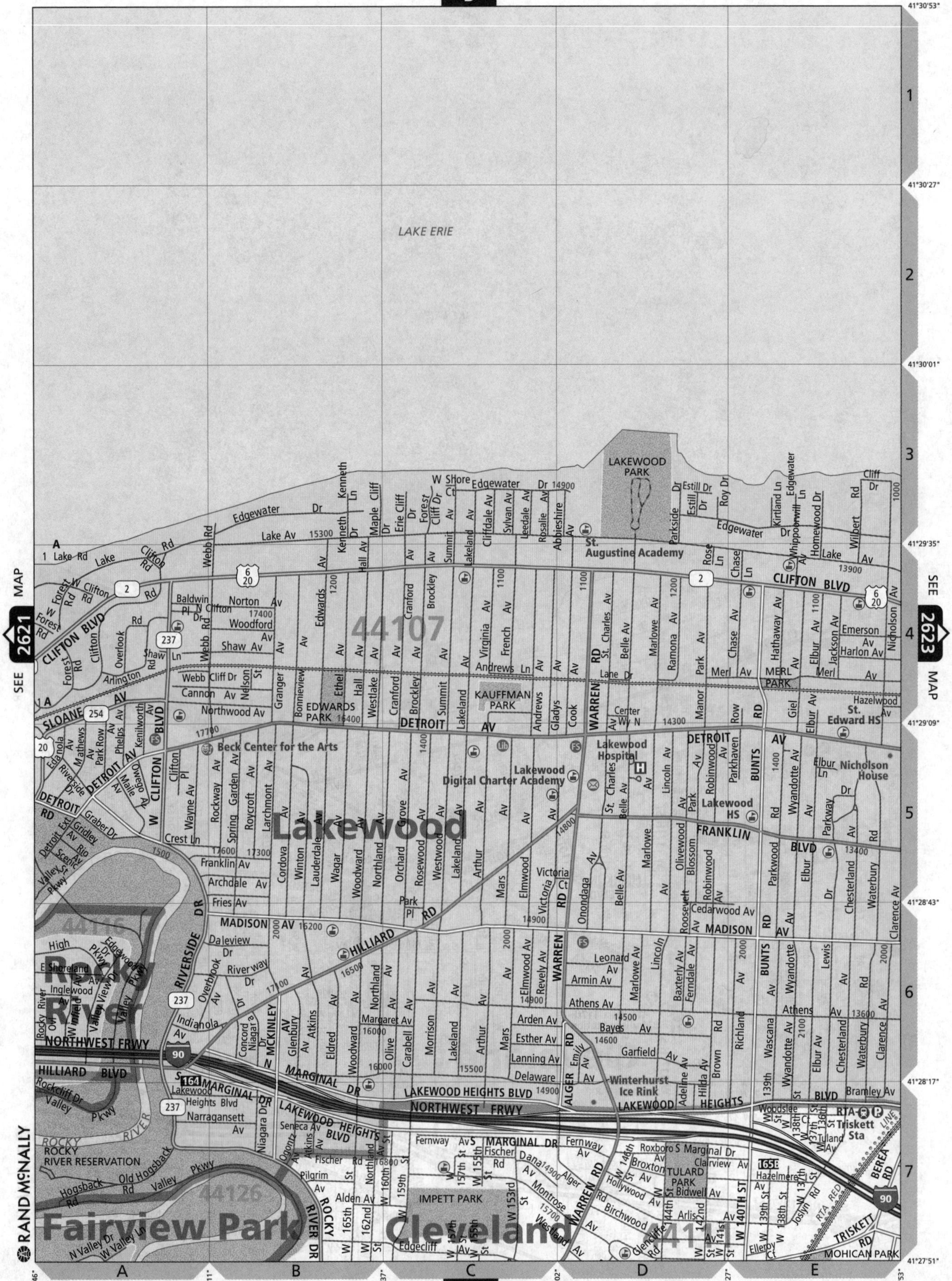
LAKE ERIE
1
2
3
4
5
6
7
A
B
C
D
E
41°30'53"
41°30'27"
41°30'01"
41°29'35"
41°29'09"
41°28'43"
41°28'17"
41°27'51"
81°49'46"
81°49'11"
81°48'37"
81°48'02"
81°47'27"
81°46'53"
Lakewood
44107
LAKEWOOD PARK
St. Augustine Academy
KAUFFMAN PARK
EDWARDS PARK
Beck Center for the Arts
Lakewood Hospital
Lakewood Digital Charter Academy
Lakewood HS
St. Edward HS
Nicholson House
MERL PARK
Winterhurst Ice Rink
TULARD PARK
IMPETT PARK
RTA Triskett Sta
Rocky River
44116
ROCKY RIVER RESERVATION
Fairview Park
44126
Cleveland
4411
CLIFTON BLVD
DETROIT AV
MADISON AV
FRANKLIN BLVD
HILLIARD RD
WARREN RD
BUNTS RD
RIVERSIDE DR
SLOANE AV
NORTHWEST FRWY
LAKEWOOD HEIGHTS BLVD
MARGINAL DR
Edgewater Dr
Lake Av
MOHICAN PARK
TRISKETT RD
BEREA RD

SEE 2621 MAP
SEE 2623 MAP
SEE 2752 MAP

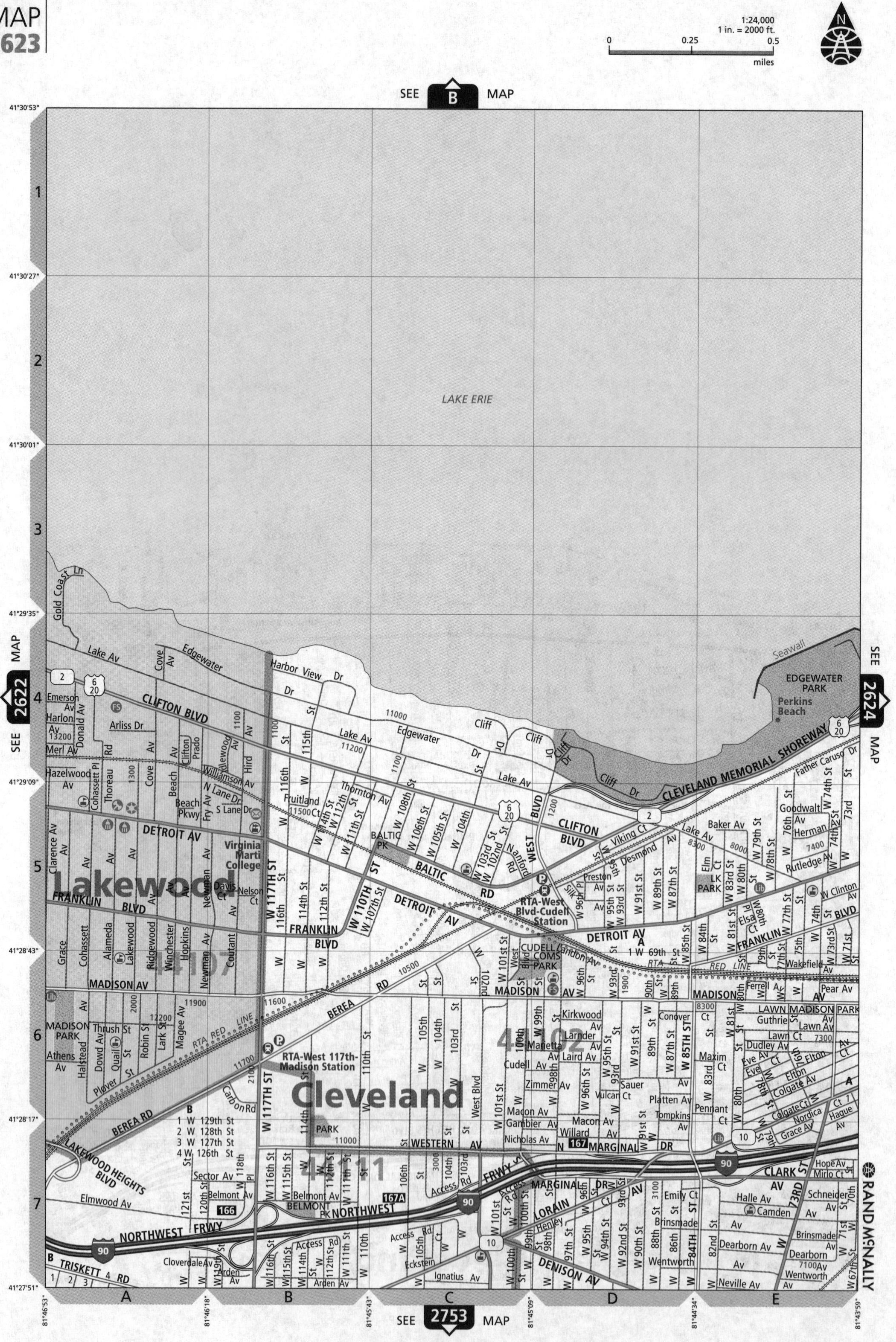
1:24,000
1 in. = 2000 ft.
0
0.25
0.5
miles
SEE B MAP
SEE 2622 MAP
SEE 2624 MAP
SEE 2753 MAP
LAKE ERIE
Lakewood
Cleveland
EDGEWATER PARK
Perkins Beach
Seawall
CLEVELAND MEMORIAL SHOREWAY
CLIFTON BLVD
DETROIT AV
FRANKLIN BLVD
MADISON AV
BEREA RD
LAKEWOOD HEIGHTS BLVD
NORTHWEST FRWY
WESTERN AV
MARGINAL DR
LORAIN AV
DENISON AV
TRISKETT RD
CLARK AV
BALTIC RD
W 117TH ST
W 110TH ST
WEST BLVD
W 85TH ST
84TH ST
73RD ST
Virginia Marti College
RTA-West Blvd-Cudell Station
RTA-West 117th-Madison Station
MADISON PARK
BALTIC PK
CUDELL COMS PARK
LK PARK
BELMONT PK
RTA RED LINE
Lake Av
Edgewater
Harbor View Dr
Gold Coast Ln
Elmwood Av
Ignatius Av
Dearborn Av
Wentworth
Neville Av
RAND McNALLY
A
B
C
D
E
1
2
3
4
5
6
7
41°30'53"
41°30'27"
41°30'01"
41°29'35"
41°29'09"
41°28'43"
41°28'17"
41°27'51"
81°46'53"
81°46'18"
81°45'43"
81°45'09"
81°44'34"
81°43'59"

1:24,000
1 in. = 2000 ft.
0 0.25 0.5
miles

SEE B MAP

41°30'58"
Burke Lakefront Arpt
International Women's Air & Space Museum
Terminal
A
1 Hamilton Av
2 Canfield Ct
Steamship William G Mather Mus
USS Cod WWII Submarine Museum
VOINOVICH PARK
Breakwater
MARGINAL RD
B
1 Frantz Pastorius Blvd
2 W Mall Dr
3 E 3rd St
Rock & Roll Hall of Fame and Mus
Great Lakes Science Ctr
Federal Bur of Investigation
41°30'32"
LAKE ERIE
ERIESIDE AV
44114
Cleveland Browns Stadium
RTA-North Coast Sta
Anthony J Celebrezze Federal Bldg
WILLARD PK
C
1 E 2nd St
2 E 1st St
3 W 6th St
4 W 3rd St
5 W 2nd St
RTA-W 3rd Street Sta
Amtrak-Cleveland Sta
LAKESIDE AV
Cleveland Convention Ctr
Federal Reserve Bank of Cleveland
RTA WATERFRONT LINE
US Coast Guard Station
D
1 W Superior Av
41°30'06"
Cuyahoga Co Jail
PUBLIC SQ
SUPERIOR AV
EUCLID AV
CHESTER AV
Old River Rd
RTA-Flats East Bank Sta
Rockefeller Bldg
Capital Univ-Cleveland
PROSPECT AV
Whiskey Island Marina
Ships Channel
Sherwin-Williams
RTA-Settlers Lndg Sta
Frank J Lausche State Office Bldg
W HURON RD
ONTARIO ST
Quicken Loans Arena
Jacobs Fld
Olde River Yacht Club
HERITAGE PK
E
1 Ontario St
41°29'40"
Seawall
EDGEWATER PARK
Edgewater Marina
Whiskey Island Dr
Channel Park Marina
CUYAHOGA RIVER
CLEVELAND MEMORIAL
SHOREWAY
Division Av
F
1 Henry Speeth Ct
2 Bunnell Ct
Crescent Av
DETROIT W 25TH PARK
Tower City Ampitheater
CARNEGIE AV
COLUMBUS RD
Commodore's Club
HERMAN PARK
Lutheran Hosp
G
1 Harrison St
INNERBELT FRWY
41°29'14"
DETROIT AV
FRANKLIN BLVD
Garrett Morgan School of Science
FAIRVIEW PARK
ABBEY PARK
ABBEY AV
UNIVERSITY RD
Cleveland Public Theatre
W Clinton Av
RANDALL RD
LORAIN AV
FRANK NOVAK PK
RTA-West 25th-Ohio City Sta
St Ignatius HS
Grace Hospital
H
1 Penn Ct
2 Fulton Pl
3 W 43rd Pl
44113
44102
41°28'48"
LINCOLN PARK
MONROE CEM
J
1 W 40th St
GREENWOOD PK
MADISON AV
TRAIN AV
MEDINA FRWY
RTA RED LINE
NORTHWEST FRWY
TREMONT PARK
L
1 W 68th Pl
SCRANTON CEMETERY
ROBERTO CLEMENTE PARK
K
1 Parafine Av
2 Moltke Ct
3 Starkweather Av
4 Branch Av
41°28'22"
ST. MARY'S CEM
CLARK AV
Cleveland
44109
TRENT PARK
M
1 Rhodes Ct
Lincoln-West HS
41°27'56"
A B C D E
1 2 3 4 5 6 7
81°43'59" 81°43'25" 81°42'50" 81°42'15" 81°41'40" 81°41'06"

SEE 2623 MAP

SEE 2625 MAP

SEE 2754 MAP

1:24,000
1 in. = 2000 ft.
0 0.25 0.5
miles

SEE 2495 MAP

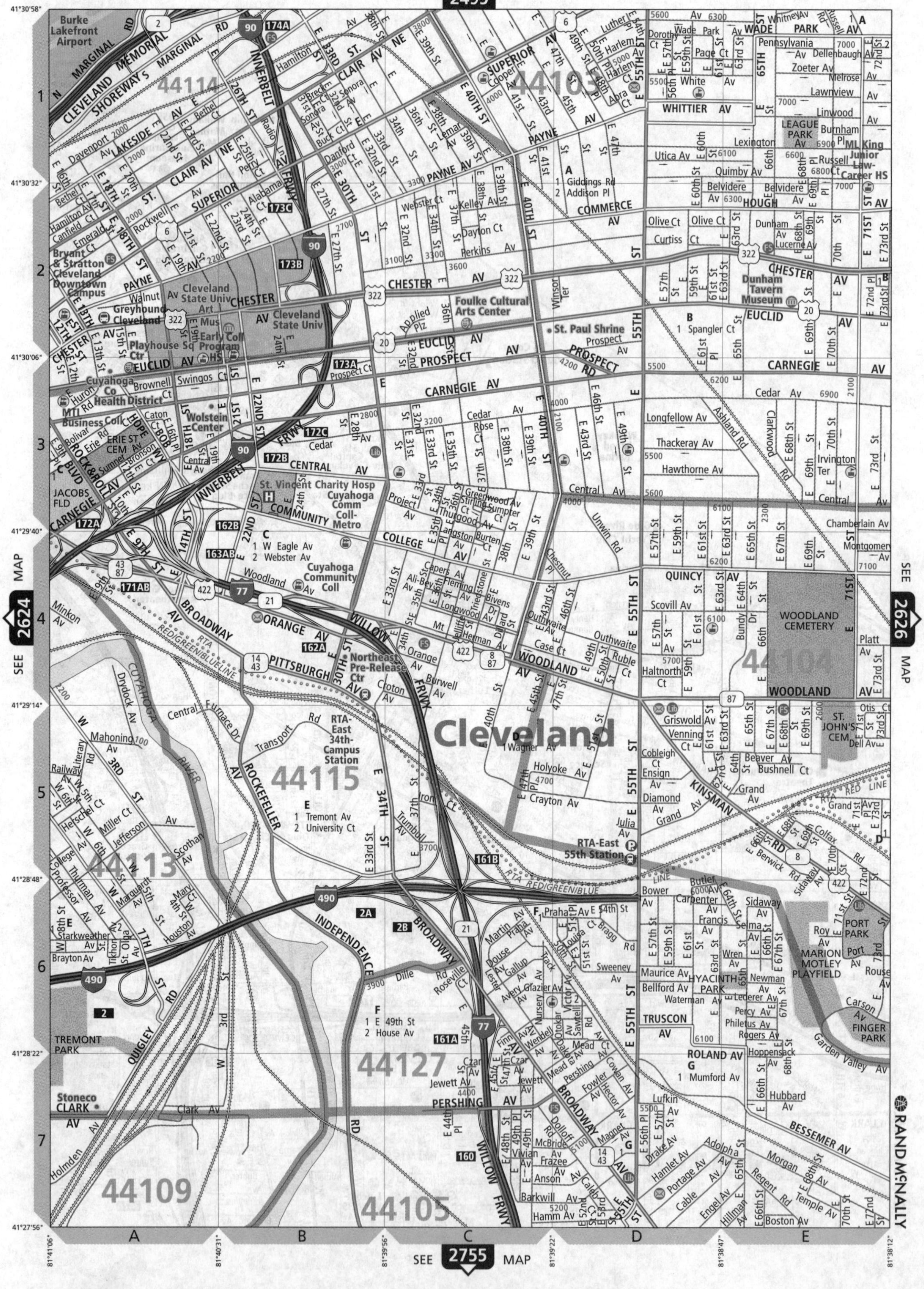
Burke Lakefront Airport
CLEVELAND MEMORIAL SHOREWAY
44114
44103
44104
44115
44113
44127
44109
44105
Cleveland
SUPERIOR AV
CHESTER AV
EUCLID AV
PROSPECT AV
CARNEGIE AV
CENTRAL AV
COMMUNITY COLL
COLLEGE AV
WOODLAND AV
BROADWAY AV
ORANGE AV
PITTSBURGH AV
KINSMAN RD
PERSHING AV
BESSEMER AV
HOUGH AV
WHITTIER AV
COMMERCE AV
QUINCY AV
TRUSCON AV
ROLAND AV
INDEPENDENCE
ROCKEFELLER AV
QUIGLEY RD
WILLOW FRWY
INNERBELT FRWY
E 55TH ST
E 40TH ST
E 30TH ST
E 22ND ST
E 34TH ST
E 9TH ST
CUYAHOGA RIVER
Cleveland State Univ
Cleveland State Univ Art Mus
Bryant & Stratton Cleveland Downtown Campus
Greyhound Cleveland
Playhouse Sq Ctr
Early Coll Program HS
Cuyahoga Co Health District
MTI Business Coll
Wolstein Center
ERIE ST CEM
JACOBS FLD
St. Vincent Charity Hosp
Cuyahoga Comm Coll-Metro
Cuyahoga Community Coll
Foulke Cultural Arts Center
St. Paul Shrine
Northeast Pre-Release Ctr
RTA-East 34th-Campus Station
RTA-East 55th Station
LEAGUE PARK
ML King Junior Law-Career HS
Dunham Tavern Museum
WOODLAND CEMETERY
ST. JOHN'S CEM
PORT PARK
MARION MOTLEY PLAYFIELD
FINGER PARK
TREMONT PARK
Stoneco CLARK
HYACINTH PARK
RTA RED/GREEN/BLUE LINE
A
1 Giddings Rd
2 Addison Pl
B
1 Spangler Ct
C
1 W Eagle Av
2 Webster Av
D
1 Wagner Av
E
1 Tremont Av
2 University Ct
F
1 E 49th St
2 House Av
G
1 Mumford Av
RAND McNALLY

SEE 2624 MAP

SEE 2626 MAP

SEE 2755 MAP

1:24,000
1 in. = 2000 ft.
0 0.25 0.5
miles

SEE 2496 MAP

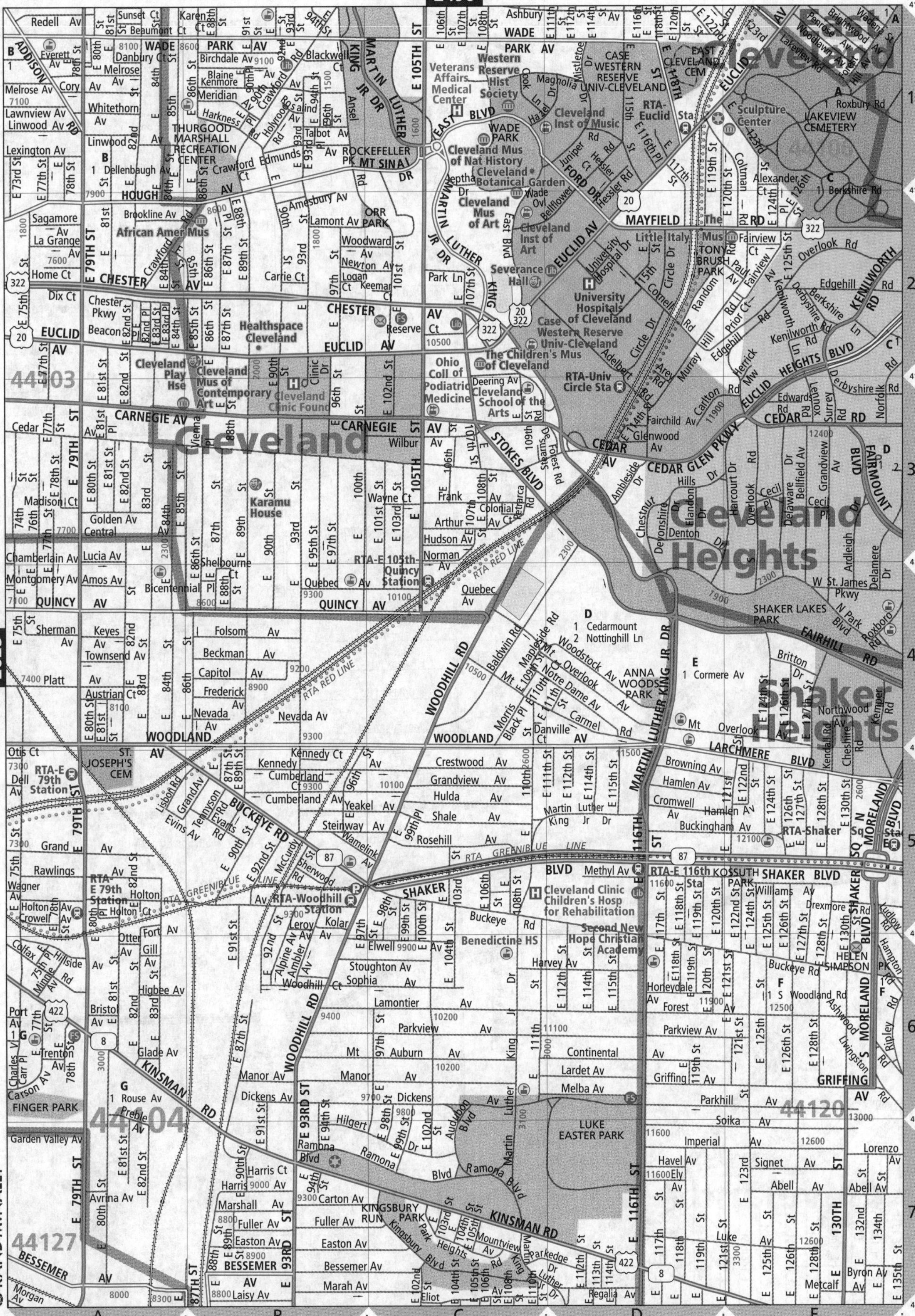
East Cleveland
Cleveland
Cleveland Heights
Shaker Heights
44106
44103
44104
44127
44120
EUCLID AV
CHESTER AV
CARNEGIE AV
QUINCY AV
WOODLAND AV
BUCKEYE RD
KINSMAN RD
SHAKER BLVD
MAYFIELD RD
CEDAR RD
FAIRHILL RD
LARCHMERE BLVD
WOODHILL RD
STOKES BLVD
MARTIN LUTHER KING JR DR
MARTIN LUTHER KING JR BLVD
E 105TH ST
E 116TH ST
E 79TH ST
E 93RD ST
HOUGH AV
WADE PARK AV
LAKEVIEW CEMETERY
WADE PARK
Cleveland Mus of Nat History
Cleveland Botanical Garden
Cleveland Mus of Art
Cleveland Inst of Music
Western Reserve Hist Society
Veterans Affairs Medical Center
CASE WESTERN RESERVE UNIV-CLEVELAND
University Hospitals of Cleveland
Severance Hall
The Children's Mus of Cleveland
Cleveland Clinic Found
Cleveland Play Hse
Cleveland Mus of Contemporary Art
Healthspace Cleveland
Karamu House
African Amer Mus
THURGOOD MARSHALL RECREATION CENTER
ORR PARK
TONY BRUSH PARK
SHAKER LAKES PARK
ANNA WOODS PARK
ST. JOSEPH'S CEM
FINGER PARK
LUKE EASTER PARK
KINGSBURY RUN PARK
HELEN SIMPSON PK
Cleveland Clinic Children's Hosp for Rehabilitation
Benedictine HS
Second New Hope Christian Academy
RTA-Univ Circle Sta
RTA-E 105th-Quincy Station
RTA-E 79th Station
RTA-Woodhill Station
RTA-E 116th St Sta
RTA-Shaker Sq Sta
RTA RED LINE
RTA GREEN/BLUE LINE
Sculpture Center
Little Italy
Ohio Coll of Podiatric Medicine
Cleveland School of the Arts
A
B
C
D
E
1
2
3
4
5
6
7
41°31'03"
41°30'37"
41°30'11"
41°29'45"
41°29'19"
41°28'53"
41°28'26"
41°28'00"
81°38'12"
81°37'38"
81°37'03"
81°36'28"
81°35'54"
81°35'19"
RAND McNALLY

SEE 2625 MAP

SEE 2627 MAP

SEE 2756 MAP

1:24,000
1 in. = 2000 ft.
0 0.25 0.5
miles

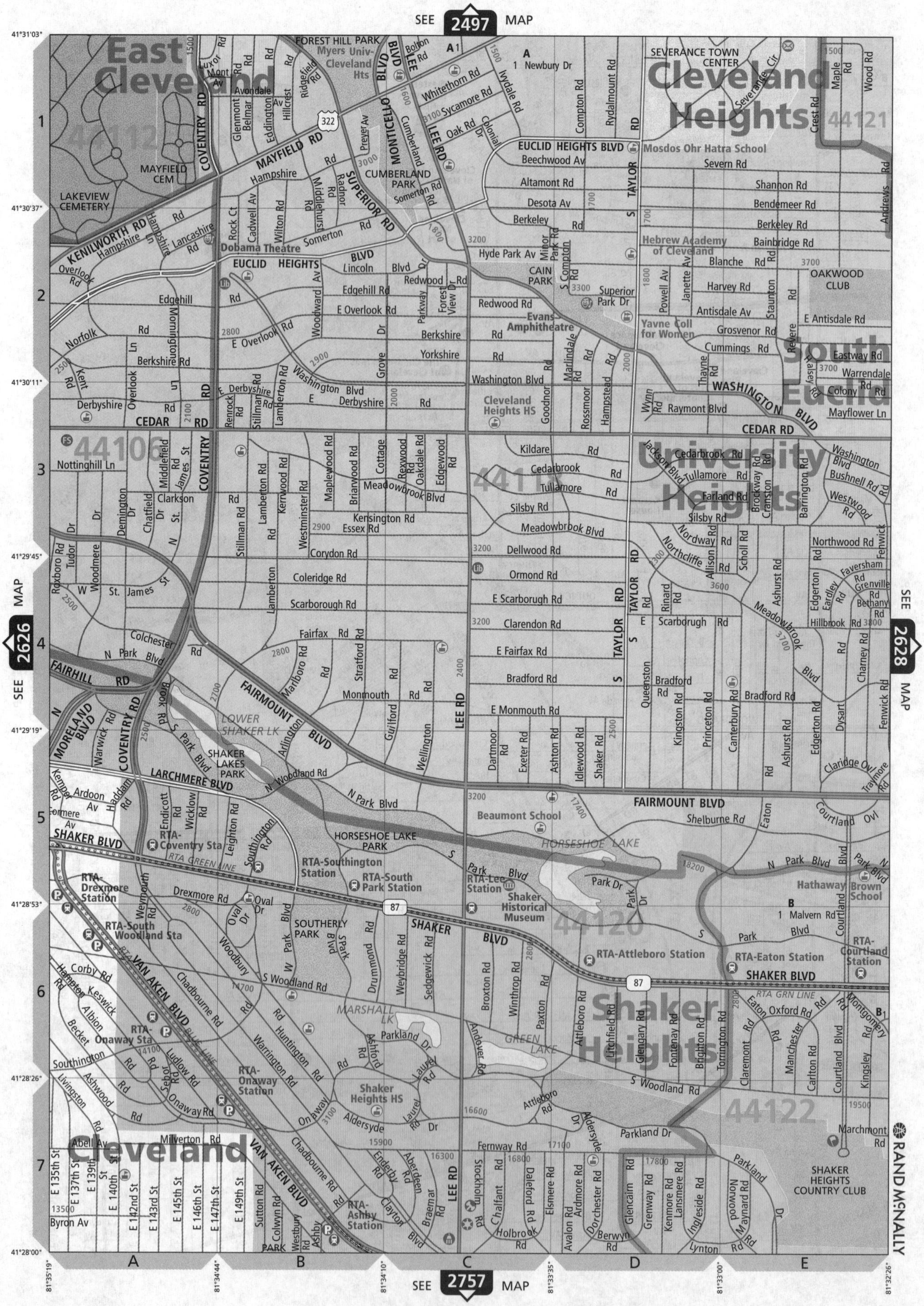
SEE 2497 MAP
SEE 2626 MAP
SEE 2628 MAP
SEE 2757 MAP
East Cleveland
Cleveland Heights
South Euclid
University Heights
Shaker Heights
Cleveland
44112
44121
44106
44118
44120
44122
MAYFIELD CEM
LAKEVIEW CEMETERY
FOREST HILL PARK
Myers Univ-Cleveland Hts
SEVERANCE TOWN CENTER
Mosdos Ohr Hatra School
CUMBERLAND PARK
Dobama Theatre
Hebrew Academy of Cleveland
OAKWOOD CLUB
CAIN PARK
Evans Amphitheatre
Yavne Coll for Women
Cleveland Heights HS
LOWER SHAKER LK
SHAKER LAKES PARK
Beaumont School
HORSESHOE LAKE PARK
HORSESHOE LAKE
RTA-Coventry Sta
RTA-Southington Station
RTA-South Park Station
RTA-Lee Station
Shaker Historical Museum
RTA-Drexmore Station
RTA-South Woodland Sta
SOUTHERLY PARK
RTA-Attleboro Station
RTA-Eaton Station
Hathaway Brown School
RTA-Courtland Station
RTA-Onaway Sta
RTA-Onaway Station
MARSHALL LK
GREEN LAKE
Shaker Heights HS
RTA-Ashby Station
SHAKER HEIGHTS COUNTRY CLUB
MAYFIELD RD
EUCLID HEIGHTS BLVD
COVENTRY RD
CEDAR RD
LEE RD
TAYLOR RD
WASHINGTON BLVD
FAIRMOUNT BLVD
SHAKER BLVD
VAN AKEN BLVD
MORELAND BLVD
FAIRHILL RD
KENILWORTH RD
LARCHMERE BLVD
SUPERIOR RD
MONTICELLO BLVD
Meadowbrook Blvd
S Woodland Rd
Parkland Dr
N Park Blvd
S Park Blvd
322
87
RAND McNALLY

1:24,000
1 in. = 2000 ft.
0 0.25 0.5
miles

SEE 2498 MAP

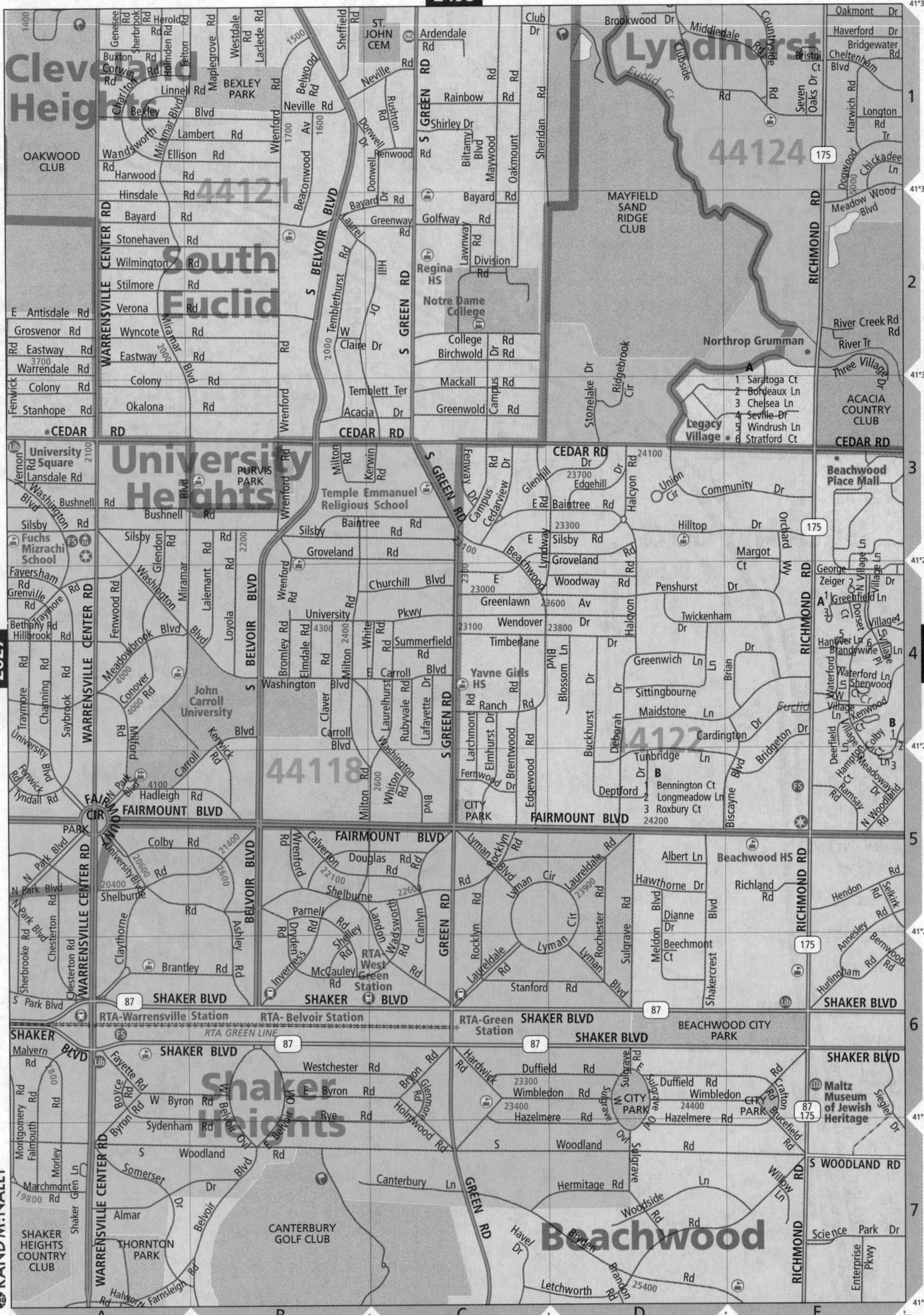
Cleveland Heights
South Euclid
University Heights
Lyndhurst
Shaker Heights
Beachwood
44121
44124
44118
44122
OAKWOOD CLUB
BEXLEY PARK
ST. JOHN CEM
MAYFIELD SAND RIDGE CLUB
Regina HS
Notre Dame College
Northrop Grumman
Legacy Village
A
1 Saratoga Ct
2 Bordeaux Ln
3 Chelsea Ln
4 Seville Dr
5 Windrush Ln
6 Stratford Ct
ACACIA COUNTRY CLUB
Beachwood Place Mall
PURVIS PARK
Temple Emmanuel Religious School
Fuchs Mizrachi School
University Square
John Carroll University
Yavne Girls HS
CITY PARK
B
1 Bennington Ct
2 Longmeadow Ln
3 Roxbury Ct
Beachwood HS
RTA-West Green Station
RTA-Warrensville Station
RTA-Belvoir Station
RTA-Green Station
RTA GREEN LINE
BEACHWOOD CITY PARK
Maltz Museum of Jewish Heritage
CANTERBURY GOLF CLUB
SHAKER HEIGHTS COUNTRY CLUB
THORNTON PARK
WARRENSVILLE CENTER RD
S BELVOIR BLVD
BELVOIR BLVD
S GREEN RD
GREEN RD
RICHMOND RD
CEDAR RD
FAIRMOUNT BLVD
FAIRMOUNT CIR
SHAKER BLVD
S WOODLAND RD
175
87
41°31'07"
41°30'41"
41°30'15"
41°29'49"
41°29'23"
41°28'57"
41°28'31"
41°28'05"
81°32'26"
81°31'51"
81°31'16"
81°30'42"
81°30'07"
81°29'32"
A
B
C
D
E
1
2
3
4
5
6
7
RAND McNALLY

SEE 2627 MAP

SEE 2629 MAP

SEE 2758 MAP

1:24,000
1 in. = 2000 ft.
0 0.25 0.5
miles

SEE 2499 MAP

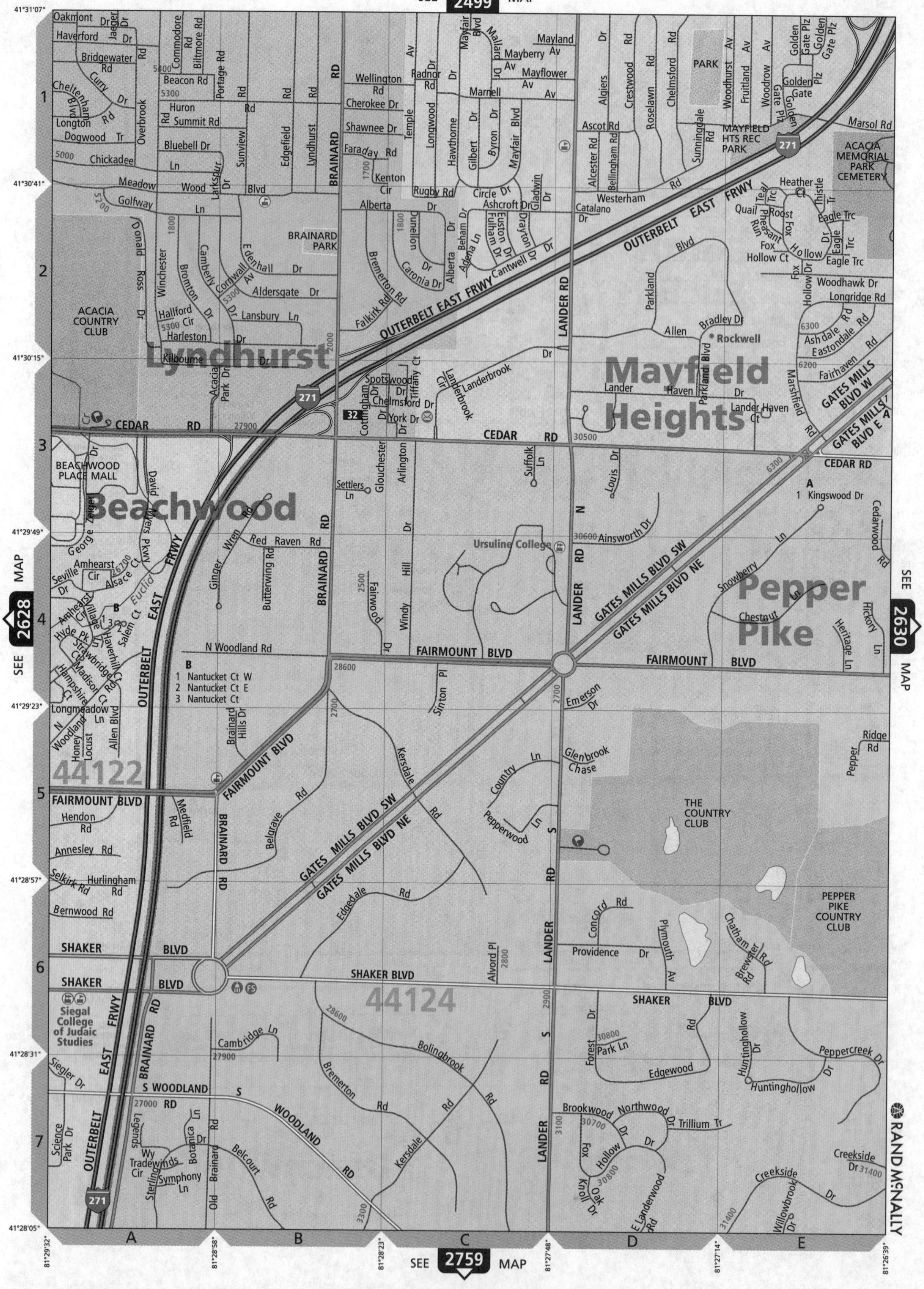
Lyndhurst
Mayfield Heights
Beachwood
Pepper Pike
44122
44124
ACACIA COUNTRY CLUB
BRAINARD PARK
MAYFIELD HTS REC PARK
ACACIA MEMORIAL PARK CEMETERY
PARK
BEACHWOOD PLACE MALL
Ursuline College
THE COUNTRY CLUB
PEPPER PIKE COUNTRY CLUB
Siegal College of Judaic Studies
Rockwell
OUTERBELT EAST FRWY
CEDAR RD
FAIRMOUNT BLVD
SHAKER BLVD
GATES MILLS BLVD SW
GATES MILLS BLVD NE
GATES MILLS BLVD W
GATES MILLS BLVD E
BRAINARD RD
LANDER RD N
LANDER RD S
S WOODLAND RD
N Woodland Rd
Mayfield Rd
Meadow Wood Blvd
Golfway Ln
Chickadee Ln
Bluebell Dr
Huron Rd
Summit Rd
Beacon Rd
Bridgewater Rd
Haverford Dr
Oakmont Dr
Jaeger Rd
Commodore Rd
Biltmore Rd
Portage Rd
Overbrook Rd
Sunview Rd
Edgefield Rd
Lyndhurst Rd
Wellington Rd
Cherokee Dr
Shawnee Dr
Faraday Rd
Kenton Cir
Alberta Dr
Rugby Rd
Marnell Av
Mayfair Blvd
Mayfield Av
Mayberry Av
Mayflower Av
Mallard Dr
Circle Dr
Ashcroft Dr
Algiers Dr
Crestwood Rd
Roselawn Rd
Chelmsford Rd
Sunningdale Rd
Woodhurst Av
Fruitland Av
Woodrow Av
Golden Gate Plz
Marsol Rd
Ascot Rd
Alcester Rd
Bellingham Rd
Westerham Rd
Catalano Dr
Heather Ct
Quail Run
Pleasant Run
Fox Hollow Ct
Fox Hollow Dr
Eagle Trc
Woodhawk Dr
Longridge Rd
Ashdale Rd
Eastondale Rd
Fairhaven Rd
Marshfield Rd
Parkland Blvd
Bradley Dr
Allen Dr
Lander Haven Dr
Lander Haven Ct
Landerbrook Dr
Spotswood Dr
Tiffany Ct
Chelmsford Dr
York Dr
Cottingham Dr
Gloucester Dr
Arlington Dr
Settlers Ln
Suffolk Ln
Louis Dr
Ainsworth Dr
Kingswood Dr
Cedarwood Rd
Snowberry Ln
Chestnut Ln
Hickory Ln
Heritage Ln
Red Raven Rd
Ginger Wren Rd
Butterwing Rd
Fairwood Dr
Windy Hill Dr
Sinton Pl
Emerson Dr
Glenbrook Chase
Country Ln
Pepperwood Ln
Ridge Rd
Pepper Rd
Kersdale Rd
Belgrave Rd
Edgedale Rd
Alvord Pl
Concord Rd
Providence Dr
Plymouth Av
Chatham Rd
Brewster Rd
Medfield Rd
Brainard Hills Dr
Nantucket Ct W
Nantucket Ct E
Nantucket Ct
Hendon Rd
Annesley Rd
Selkirk Rd
Hurlingham Rd
Bernwood Rd
Longmeadow Ln
Honey Locust
Allen Blvd
Woodland
Hampshire Ct
Madison Ct
Strawbridge Ct
Haverhill Ct
Salem Ct
Hyde Pk
Amherst Cir
Seville Dr
Alsace Ct
Euclid
George Zeiger Dr
David Myers Pkwy
Donald Ross Dr
Winchester Rd
Bromton Dr
Camberly Dr
Cornwall Dr
Edenhall Dr
Aldersgate Dr
Lansbury Ln
Hallford Cir
Harleston Dr
Kilbourne Dr
Acacia Park Dr
Falkirk Rd
Bremerton Rd
Caronia Dr
Beham Dr
Adena Ln
Fulham Dr
Euston Dr
Drayton Dr
Cantwell Dr
Gladwin Dr
Dunellon Dr
Cambridge Ln
Bolingbrook Rd
Bremerton Rd
Forest Dr
Park Ln
Edgewood Rd
Huntinghollow Dr
Peppercreek Dr
Brookwood Dr
Northwood Dr
Trillium Tr
Fox Hollow Dr
Oak Knoll Dr
E Landerwood Rd
Creekside Dr
Willowbrook Dr
Siegler Dr
Science Park Dr
Legends Wy
Tradewinds Cir
Botanica Dr
Symphony Ln
Sterling
Old Brainard Rd
Belcourt Rd
271
32

SEE 2628 MAP
SEE 2630 MAP
SEE 2759 MAP

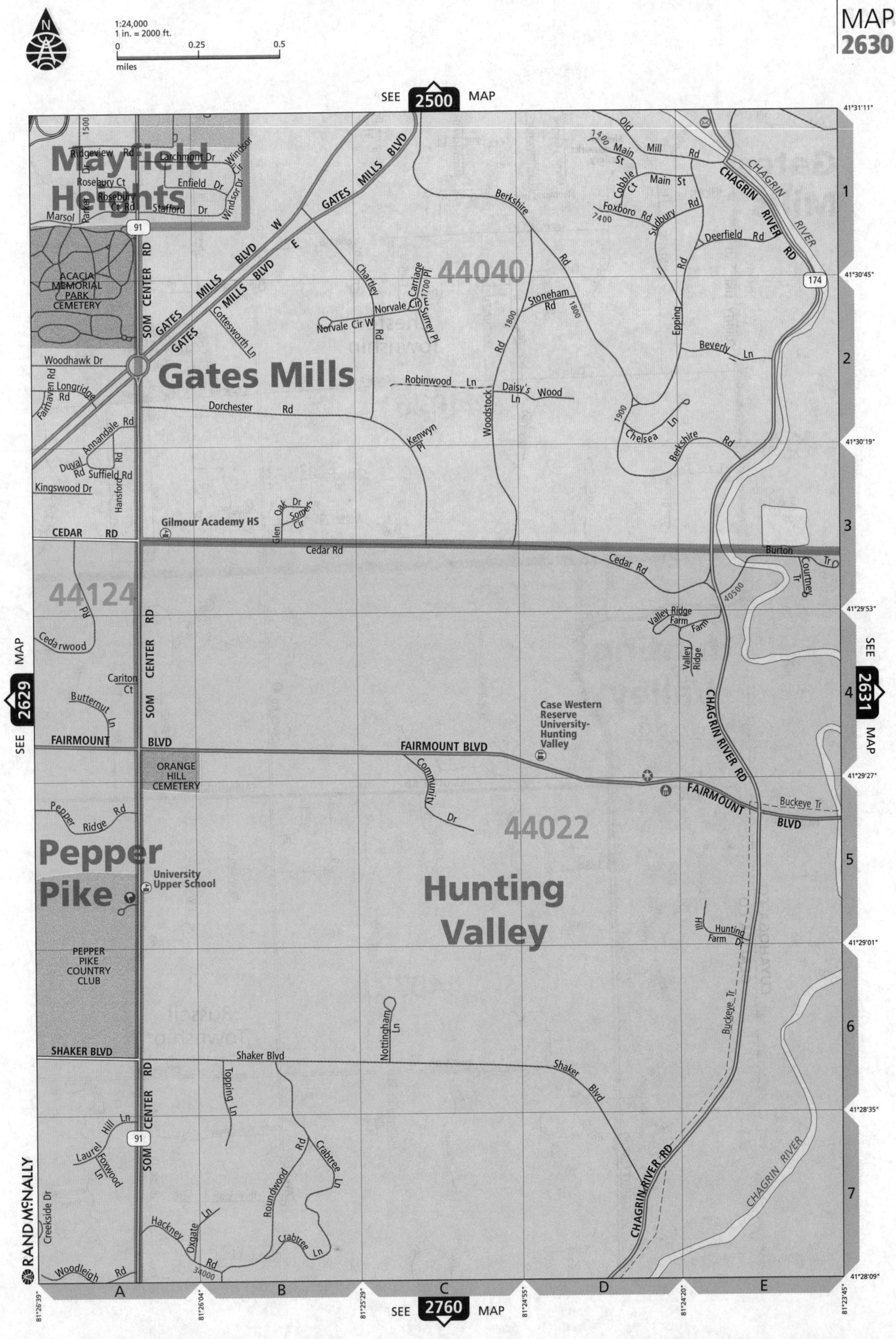
1:24,000
1 in. = 2000 ft.
0 0.25 0.5
miles
SEE 2500 MAP
SEE 2760 MAP
SEE 2629 MAP
SEE 2631 MAP
A B C D E
1 2 3 4 5 6 7
41°31'11"
41°30'45"
41°30'19"
41°29'53"
41°29'27"
41°29'01"
41°28'35"
41°28'09"
81°26'39"
81°26'04"
81°25'29"
81°24'55"
81°24'20"
81°23'45"
Mayfield Heights
Gates Mills
Pepper Pike
Hunting Valley
44040
44124
44022
ACACIA MEMORIAL PARK CEMETERY
ORANGE HILL CEMETERY
PEPPER PIKE COUNTRY CLUB
Gilmour Academy HS
University Upper School
Case Western Reserve University-Hunting Valley
GATES MILLS BLVD W
GATES MILLS BLVD E
SOM CENTER RD
CEDAR RD
Cedar Rd
FAIRMOUNT BLVD
SHAKER BLVD
Shaker Blvd
CHAGRIN RIVER RD
CHAGRIN RIVER
Old Mill Rd
Main St
Cobble Ct
Foxboro Rd
Sudbury Rd
Deerfield Rd
Berkshire Rd
Chartley
Carriage
Norvale Cir
Norvale Cir W
Surrey Pl
Stoneham Rd
Epping Rd
Beverly Ln
Robinwood Ln
Daisy's Wood Ln
Woodstock Rd
Chelsea Ln
Kenwyn Pl
Dorchester Rd
Cottesworth Ln
Ridgeview Rd
Larchmont Dr
Windsor Cir
Windsor Dr
Enfield Dr
Rosebury Ct
Rosebury Ct Rd
Stafford Dr
Parker Dr
Marsol
Woodhawk Dr
Fairhaven Rd
Longridge Rd
Annandale Rd
Duval Rd
Suffield Rd
Hansford Rd
Kingswood Dr
Glen Oak Dr
Somers Cir
Burton Tr
Courtney Tr
Valley Ridge Farm
Valley Ridge
Cedarwood Rd
Carlton Ct
Butternut Ln
Community Dr
Buckeye Tr
Pepper Ridge Rd
Hunting Hill Farm Dr
Nottingham Ln
Topping Ln
Laurel Hill Ln
Foxwood Ln
Roundwood Rd
Crabtree Ln
Hackney Rd
Oxgate Ln
Creekside Dr
Woodleigh Rd
91
174
1400
7400
1700
1800
1900
1500
40500
34000
RAND McNALLY

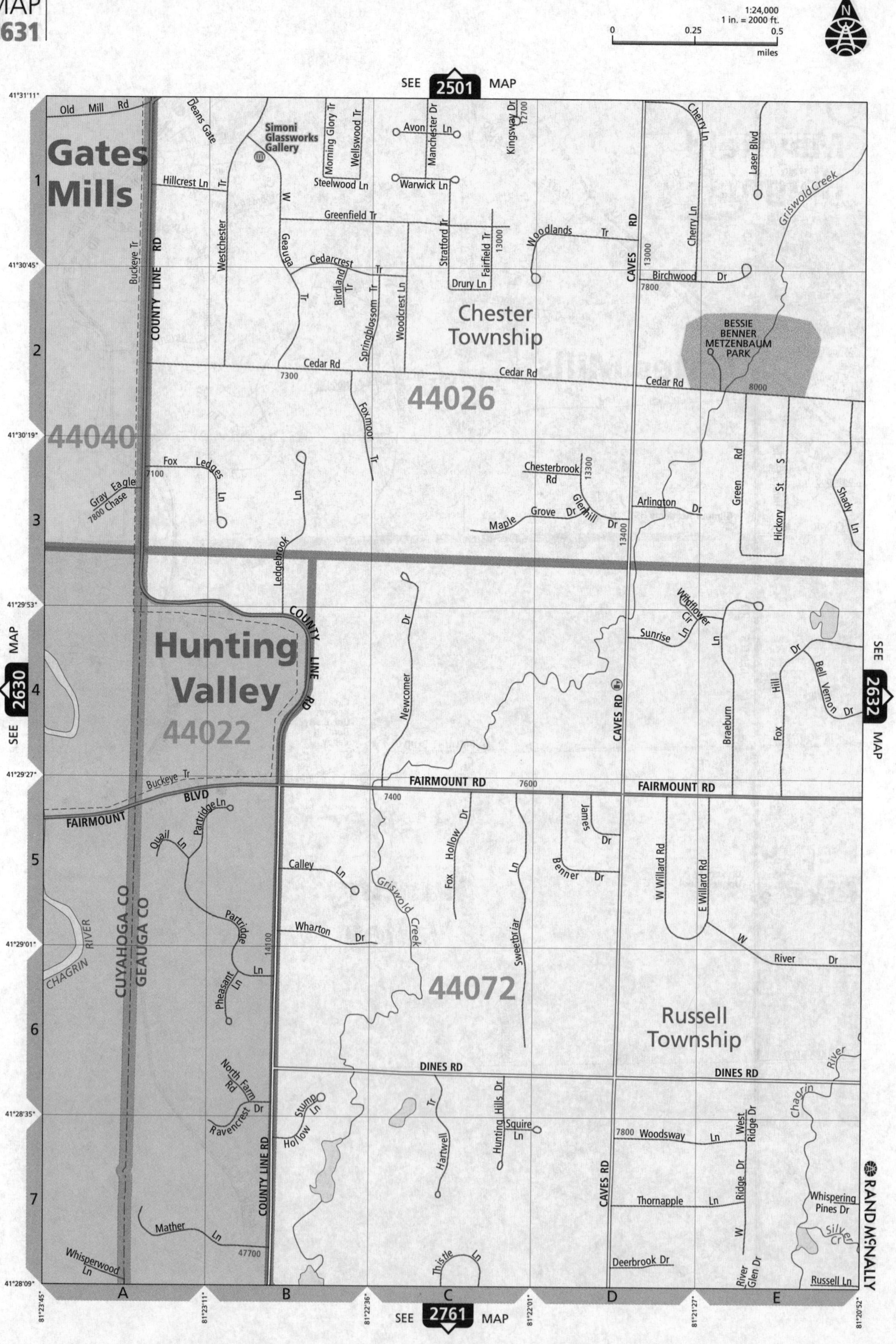
1:24,000
1 in. = 2000 ft.
0
0.25
0.5
miles
N
SEE 2501 MAP
SEE 2761 MAP
SEE 2630 MAP
SEE 2632 MAP
Gates Mills
Hunting Valley
Chester Township
Russell Township
44040
44022
44026
44072
Simoni Glassworks Gallery
BESSIE BENNER METZENBAUM PARK
CUYAHOGA CO
GEAUGA CO
COUNTY LINE RD
CAVES RD
FAIRMOUNT RD
FAIRMOUNT BLVD
DINES RD
Cedar Rd
Old Mill Rd
Deans Gate
Hillcrest Ln
Buckeye Tr
Westchester Tr
W Geauga Tr
Morning Glory Tr
Wellswood Tr
Steelwood Ln
Avon Ln
Manchester Dr
Warwick Ln
Kingsway Dr
Greenfield Tr
Cedarcrest Tr
Birdland Tr
Springblossom Tr
Woodcrest Ln
Stratford Tr
Fairfield Tr
Drury Ln
Woodlands Tr
Cherry Ln
Laser Blvd
Griswold Creek
Birchwood Dr
Foxmoor Tr
Fox Ledges Ln
Gray Eagle Chase
Ledgebrook Ln
Chesterbrook Rd
Maple Grove Dr
Glenhill Dr
Arlington Dr
Green Rd
Hickory St S
Shady Ln
Newcomer Dr
Wildflower Cir
Sunrise Ln
Fox Hill Dr
Bell Vernon Dr
Braeburn Ln
Partridge Ln
Quail Ln
Pheasant Ln
Calley Ln
Wharton Dr
Fox Hollow Dr
Sweetbriar Ln
James Dr
Benner Dr
W Willard Rd
E Willard Rd
W River Dr
CHAGRIN RIVER
North Farm Rd
Ravencrest Dr
Stump Hollow Ln
Hartwell Tr
Hunting Hills Dr
Squire Ln
Woodsway Ln
West Ridge Dr
Thornapple Ln
Deerbrook Dr
River Glen Dr
Chagrin River
Whispering Pines Dr
Silver Cr
Russell Ln
Mather Ln
Whisperwood Ln
Thistle Ln
7100
7300
7400
7600
7800
8000
12700
13000
13300
13400
14100
47700
A
B
C
D
E
1
2
3
4
5
6
7
41°31'11"
41°30'45"
41°30'19"
41°29'53"
41°29'27"
41°29'01"
41°28'35"
41°28'09"
81°23'45"
81°23'11"
81°22'36"
81°22'01"
81°21'27"
81°20'52"
RAND McNALLY

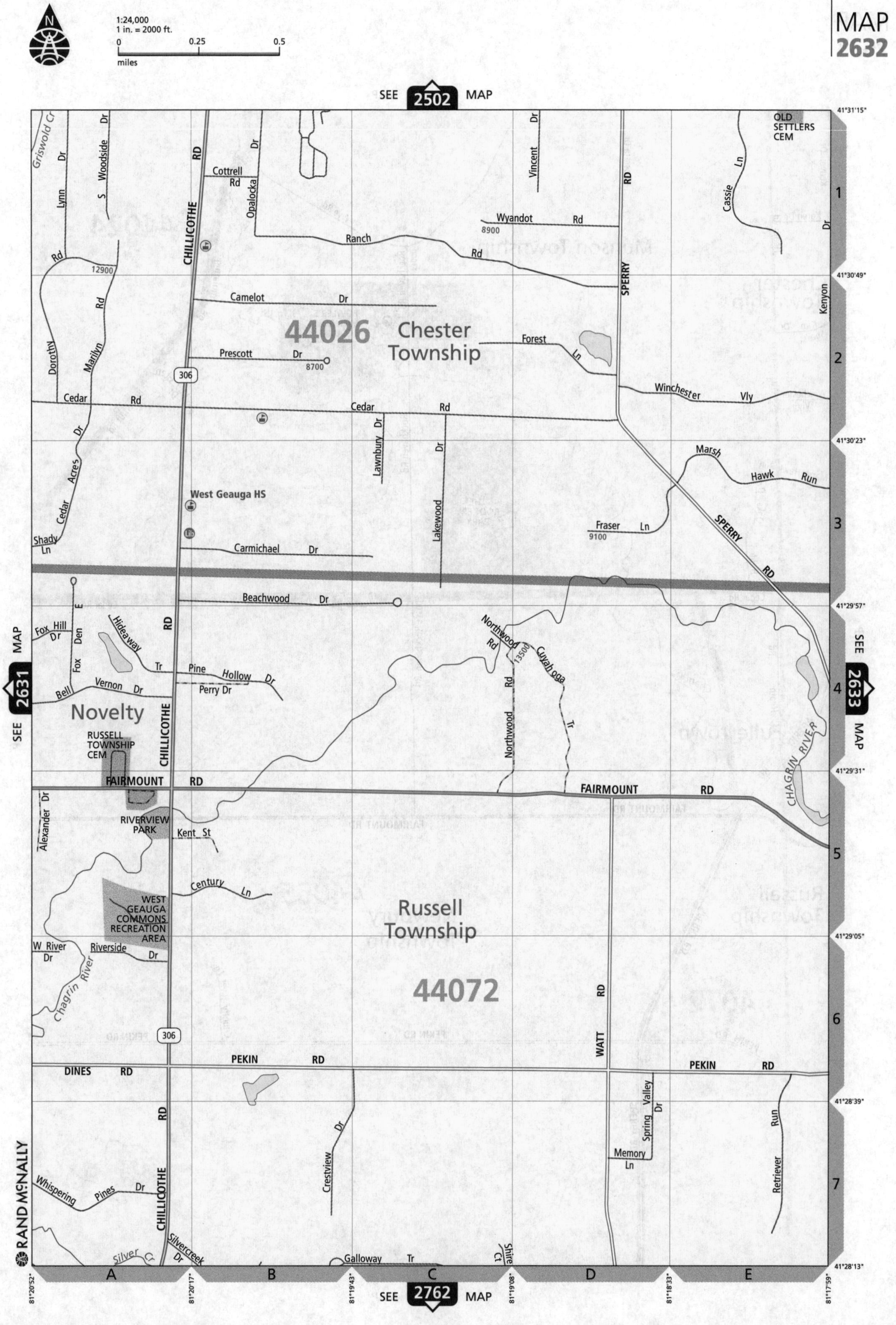
1:24,000
1 in. = 2000 ft.
0
0.25
0.5
miles
SEE 2502 MAP
SEE 2631 MAP
SEE 2633 MAP
SEE 2762 MAP
44026
Chester
Township
44072
Russell
Township
Novelty
Griswold Cr
Woodside Dr
S
Lynn Dr
Rd
12900
CHILLICOTHE RD
Cottrell Rd
Opalocka Dr
Ranch Rd
Wyandot Rd
8900
Vincent Dr
SPERRY RD
OLD SETTLERS CEM
Cassie Ln
Dr
Kenyon
Camelot Dr
Prescott Dr
8700
Forest Ln
Winchester Vly
Dorothy
Marilyn Rd
306
Cedar Rd
Cedar Rd
Lawnbury Dr
Lakewood Dr
Acres Dr
Cedar
Marsh
Hawk Run
West Geauga HS
Fraser Ln
9100
SPERRY RD
Shady Ln
Carmichael Dr
Beachwood Dr
Fox Hill Dr
Fox Den E
Hideaway Tr
Pine Hollow Dr
Perry Dr
Bell
Vernon Dr
Northwood Rd
Northwood Rd
1350
Cuyahoga Tr
CHAGRIN RIVER
RUSSELL TOWNSHIP CEM
FAIRMOUNT RD
FAIRMOUNT RD
Alexander Dr
RIVERVIEW PARK
Kent St
Century Ln
WEST GEAUGA COMMONS RECREATION AREA
W River Dr
Riverside Dr
Chagrin River
WATT RD
306
PEKIN RD
PEKIN RD
DINES RD
Spring Valley Dr
Memory Ln
Crestview Dr
Retriever Run
Whispering Pines Dr
Silver Cr
Silvercreek Dr
Galloway Tr
Shire Ct
A
B
C
D
E
1
2
3
4
5
6
7
41°31'15"
41°30'49"
41°30'23"
41°29'57"
41°29'31"
41°29'05"
41°28'39"
41°28'13"
81°20'52"
81°20'17"
81°19'43"
81°19'08"
81°18'33"
81°17'59"
RAND McNALLY

SEE 2503 MAP

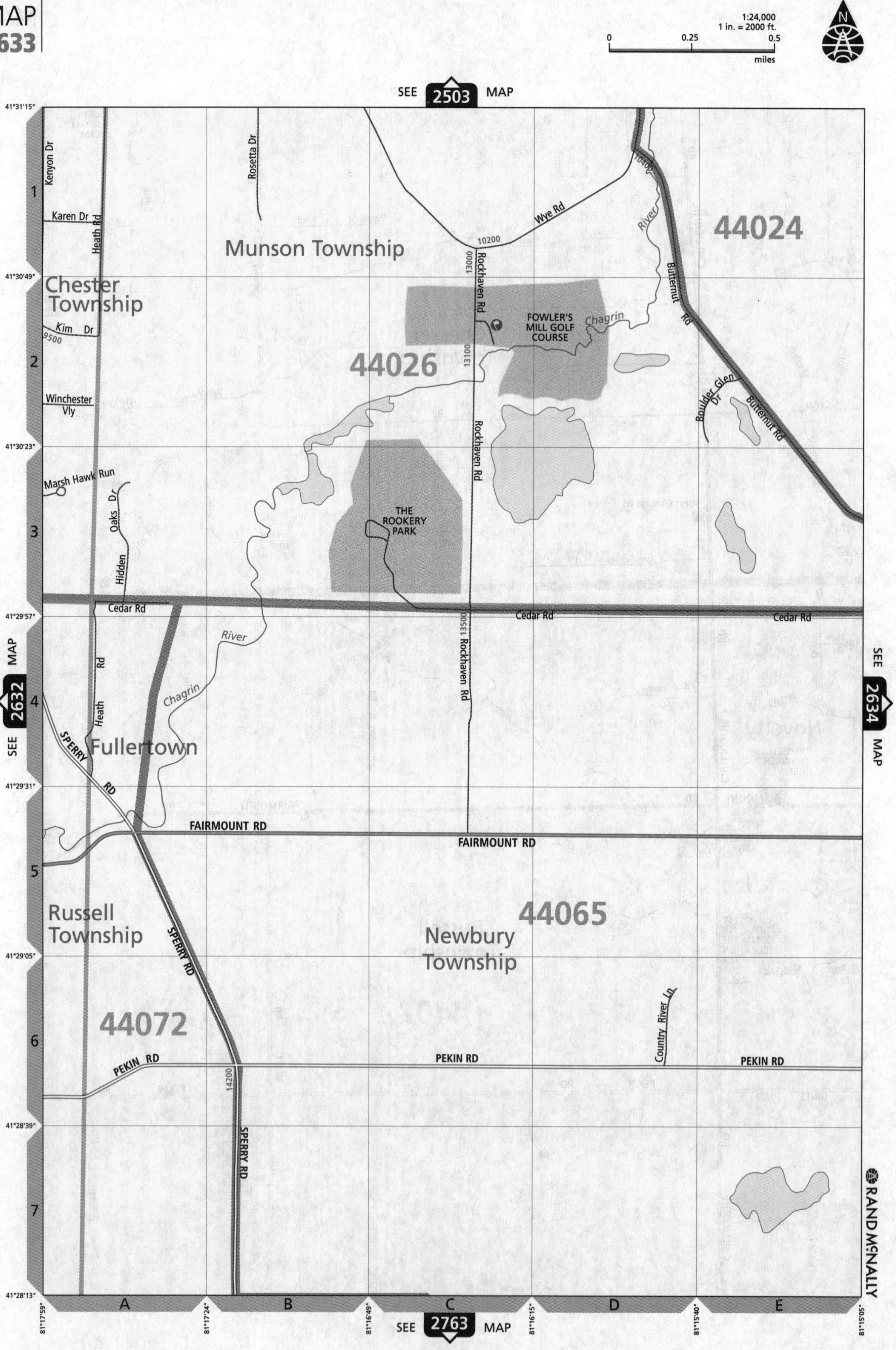
1:24,000
1 in. = 2000 ft.
0
0.25
0.5
miles
N
Munson Township
Chester Township
44024
44026
44065
44072
Fullertown
Russell Township
Newbury Township
Kenyon Dr
Karen Dr
Heath Rd
Rosetta Dr
Wye Rd
10200
10400
13000
13100
13500
14200
9500
Rockhaven Rd
Butternut Rd
Kim Dr
FOWLER'S MILL GOLF COURSE
Chagrin River
Winchester Vly
Boulder Glen Dr
Marsh Hawk Run
Hidden Oaks Dr
THE ROOKERY PARK
Cedar Rd
SPERRY RD
FAIRMOUNT RD
PEKIN RD
Country River Ln
41°31'15"
41°30'49"
41°30'23"
41°29'57"
41°29'31"
41°29'05"
41°28'39"
41°28'13"
81°17'59"
81°17'24"
81°16'49"
81°16'15"
81°15'40"
81°15'05"
A
B
C
D
E
1
2
3
4
5
6
7
RAND McNALLY

SEE 2632 MAP

SEE 2634 MAP

SEE 2763 MAP

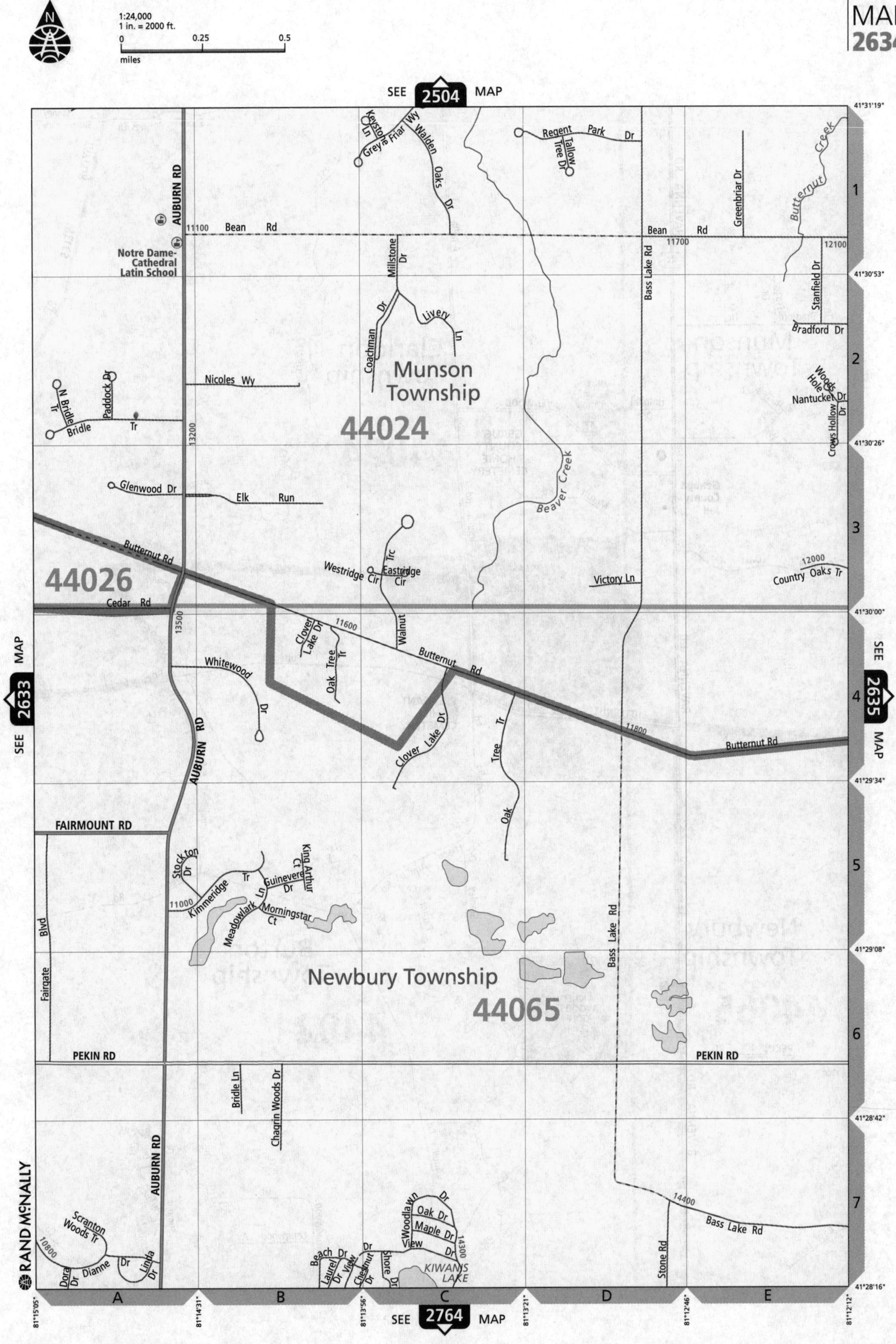
1:24,000
1 in. = 2000 ft.
0
0.25
0.5
miles
SEE 2504 MAP
SEE 2633 MAP
SEE 2635 MAP
SEE 2764 MAP
Munson Township
44024
44026
Newbury Township
44065
Notre Dame-Cathedral Latin School
AUBURN RD
Bean Rd
11100
11700
12100
Bass Lake Rd
Keystone Ln
Greye Friar Wy
Walden Oaks Dr
Regent Park Dr
Tallow Tree Dr
Greenbriar Dr
Butternut Creek
Millstone Dr
Coachman Dr
Livery Ln
Stanfield Dr
Bradford Dr
Woods Hole Dr
Nantucket Dr
Crows Hollow Dr
Nicoles Wy
N Bridle Tr
Paddock Dr
Bridle Tr
13200
Glenwood Dr
Elk Run
Beaver Creek
Butternut Rd
Cedar Rd
Westridge Cir
Eastridge Cir
Trc
Victory Ln
12000
Country Oaks Tr
13500
Clover Lake Dr
11600
Walnut
Oak Tree Tr
Whitewood Dr
Butternut Rd
11800
Clover Lake Dr
Tree Tr
Oak
FAIRMOUNT RD
Stockton Dr
Kimmeridge Tr
11000
Guinevere Dr
King Arthur Ct
Meadowlark Ln
Morningstar Ct
Fairgate Blvd
PEKIN RD
Bridle Ln
Chagrin Woods Dr
14400
Bass Lake Rd
Stone Rd
Scranton Woods Tr
10800
Dora Dr
Dianne Dr
Linda Dr
Woodlawn Dr
Oak Dr
Maple Dr
View Dr
14300
Beach Dr
Laurel Dr
View
Chestnut Dr
Shore Dr
KIWANIS LAKE
1
2
3
4
5
6
7
A
B
C
D
E
41°31'19"
41°30'53"
41°30'26"
41°30'00"
41°29'34"
41°29'08"
41°28'42"
41°28'16"
81°15'05"
81°14'31"
81°13'56"
81°13'21"
81°12'46"
81°12'12"
RAND McNALLY

1:24,000
1 in. = 2000 ft.
0 0.25 0.5
miles

SEE 2505 MAP

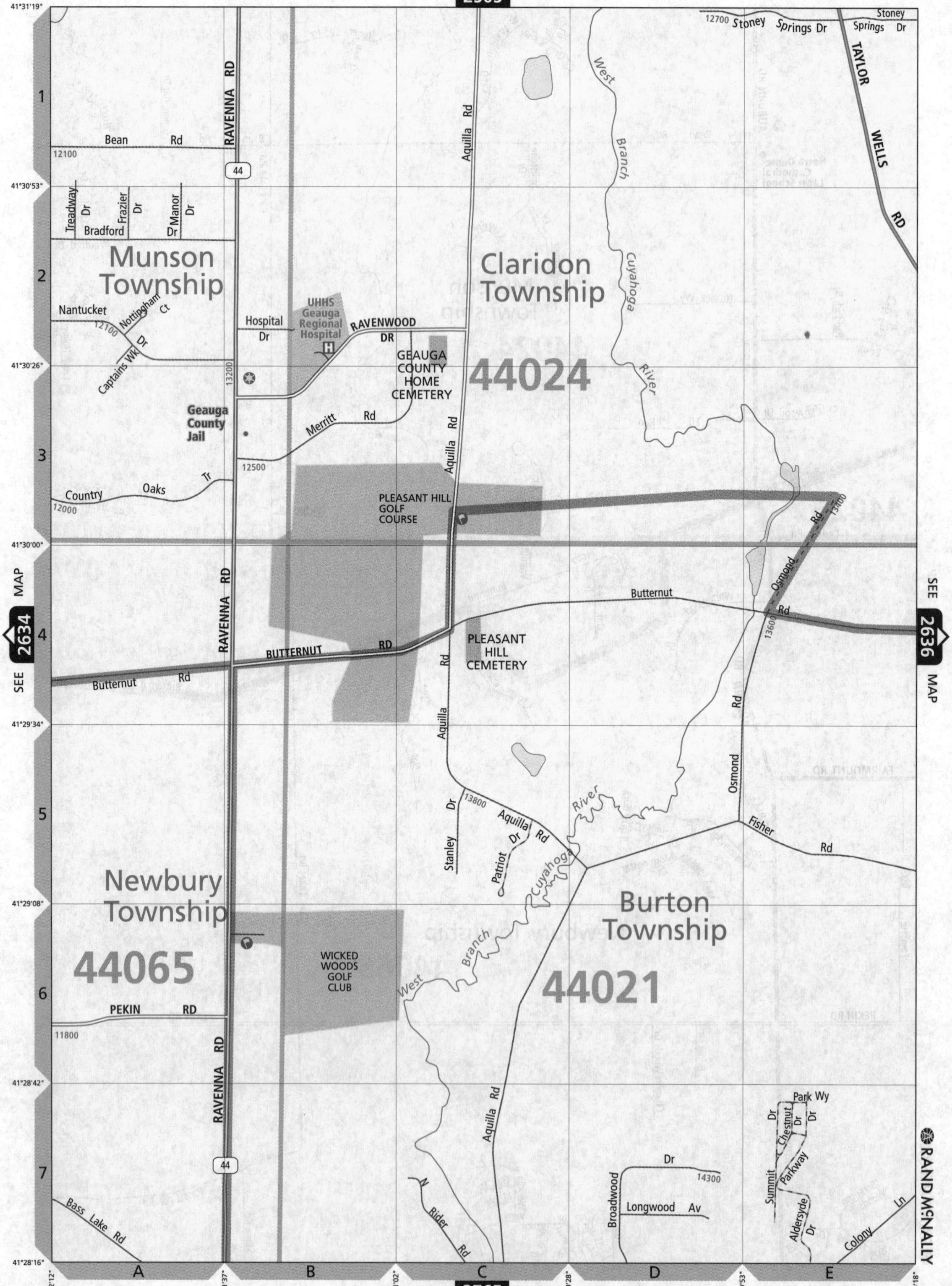
Munson Township
Claridon Township
Newbury Township
Burton Township
44024
44065
44021
RAVENNA RD
44
Bean Rd
12100
Treadway Dr
Frazier Dr
Manor Dr
Bradford Dr
Nantucket
Nottingham Ct
12100 Dr
Captains Wk
Hospital Dr
UHHS Geauga Regional Hospital
RAVENWOOD DR
GEAUGA COUNTY HOME CEMETERY
13200
Geauga County Jail
Merritt Rd
12500
Country Oaks Tr
12000
PLEASANT HILL GOLF COURSE
Aquilla Rd
BUTTERNUT RD
Butternut Rd
Butternut Rd
PLEASANT HILL CEMETERY
12700 Stoney Springs Dr
Stoney Springs Dr
TAYLOR WELLS RD
West Branch Cuyahoga River
Osmond Rd
13400
13600
Fisher Rd
13800
Stanley Dr
Patriot Dr
Aquilla Rd
WICKED WOODS GOLF CLUB
PEKIN RD
11800
Bass Lake Rd
Rider Rd
Broadwood Dr
14300
Longwood Av
Park Wy
Chestnut Dr
Summit Dr
Parkway
Aldersyde Dr
Colony Ln
41°31'19"
41°30'53"
41°30'26"
41°30'00"
41°29'34"
41°29'08"
41°28'42"
41°28'16"
81°12'12"
81°11'37"
81°11'02"
81°10'28"
81°09'53"
81°09'18"
1
2
3
4
5
6
7
A
B
C
D
E

SEE 2634 MAP

SEE 2636 MAP

SEE 2765 MAP

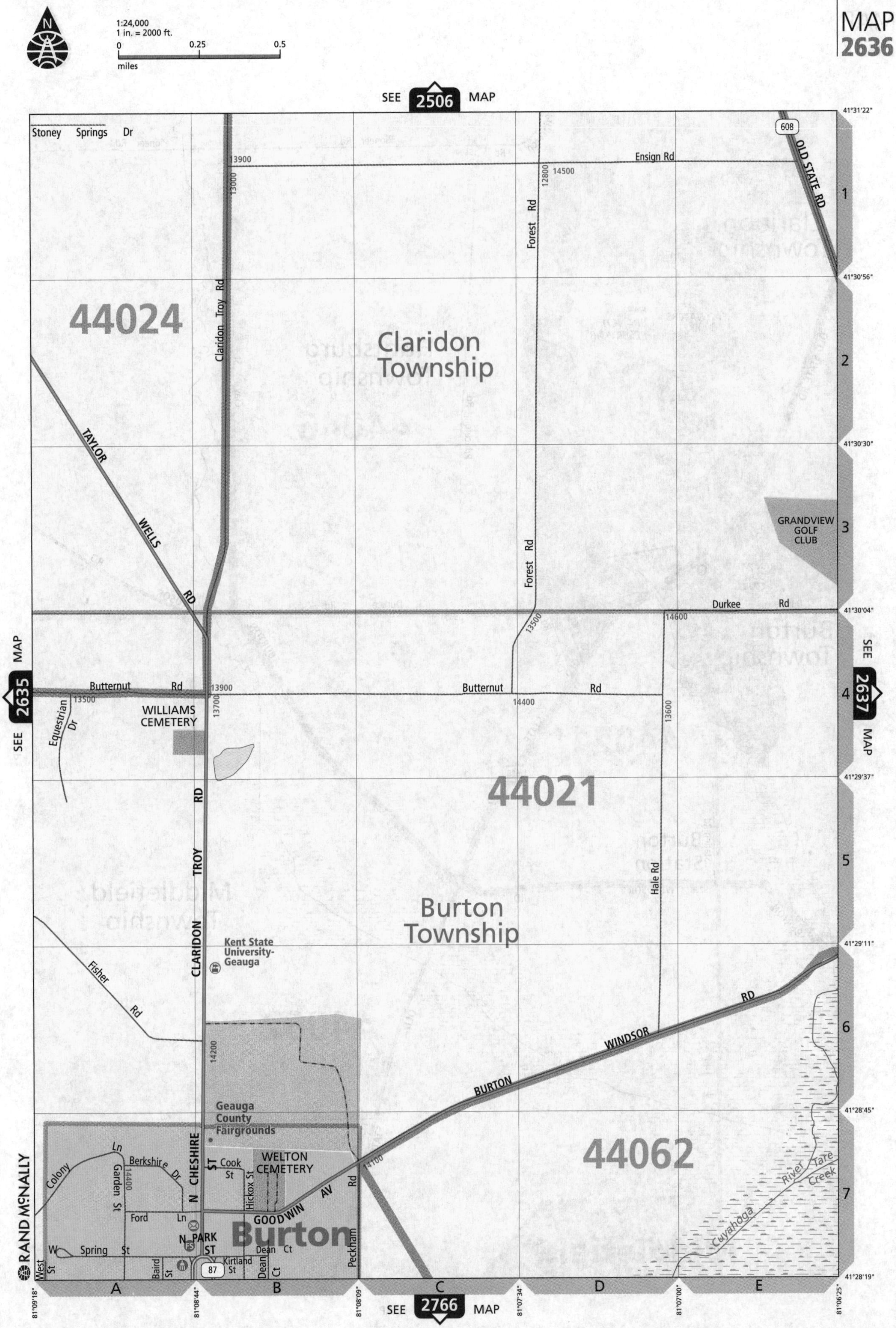
1:24,000
1 in. = 2000 ft.
0
0.25
0.5
miles
Stoney Springs Dr
Ensign Rd
13900
14500
13000
12800
608
OLD STATE RD
Forest Rd
44024
Claridon Troy Rd
Claridon
Township
TAYLOR
WELLS
RD
GRANDVIEW
GOLF
CLUB
Durkee Rd
14600
13500
Butternut Rd
13500
13900
13700
14400
13600
WILLIAMS
CEMETERY
Equestrian Dr
44021
CLARIDON TROY RD
Hale Rd
Burton
Township
Kent State
University-
Geauga
Fisher Rd
BURTON WINDSOR RD
14200
Geauga
County
Fairgrounds
44062
WELTON
CEMETERY
Colony Ln
Berkshire Dr
14400
Garden St
N CHESHIRE ST
Cook St
Hickox St
GOODWIN AV
Rd
14100
Ford Ln
N PARK ST
Burton
Spring St
W
West St
Baird St
87
Kirtland St
Dean Ct
Dean Ct
Peckham
Cuyahoga River
Tare Creek
RAND McNALLY
41°31'22"
41°30'56"
41°30'30"
41°30'04"
41°29'37"
41°29'11"
41°28'45"
41°28'19"
81°09'18"
81°08'44"
81°08'09"
81°07'34"
81°07'00"
81°06'25"
A
B
C
D
E
1
2
3
4
5
6
7

SEE 2506 MAP
SEE 2635 MAP
SEE 2637 MAP
SEE 2766 MAP

1:24,000
1 in. = 2000 ft.
0 0.25 0.5
miles

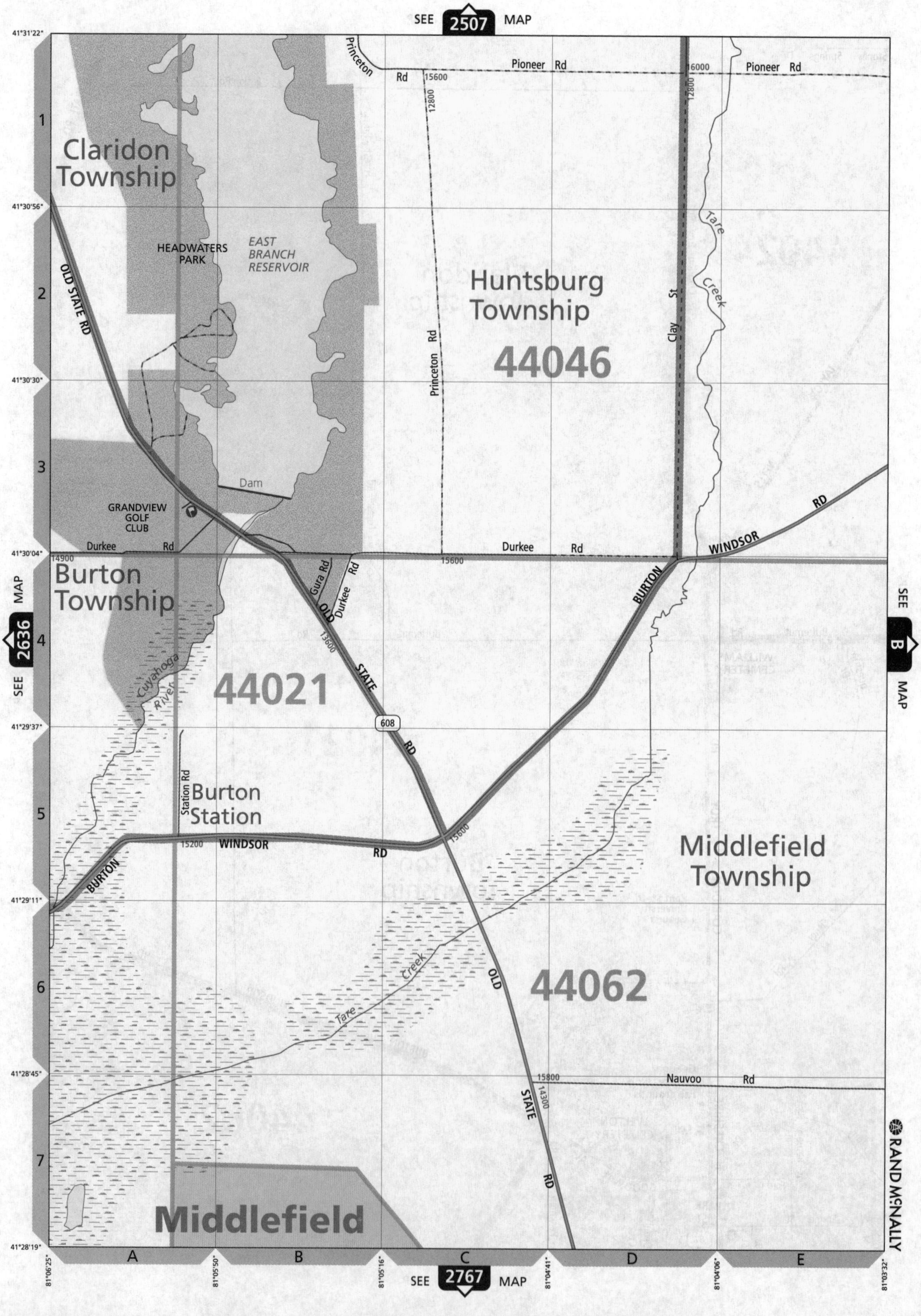
SEE 2507 MAP
SEE 2636 MAP
SEE B MAP
SEE 2767 MAP
41°31'22"
41°30'56"
41°30'30"
41°30'04"
41°29'37"
41°29'11"
41°28'45"
41°28'19"
81°06'25"
81°05'50"
81°05'16"
81°04'41"
81°04'06"
81°03'32"
1
2
3
4
5
6
7
A
B
C
D
E
Claridon Township
HEADWATERS PARK
EAST BRANCH RESERVOIR
Dam
GRANDVIEW GOLF CLUB
Princeton Rd
Pioneer Rd
15600
12800
16000
Huntsburg Township
44046
Clay St
Tare Creek
OLD STATE RD
Durkee Rd
14900
15600
WINDSOR RD
Burton Township
Gura Rd
Durkee Rd
OLD STATE RD
13600
608
BURTON
Cuyahoga River
44021
Station Rd
Burton Station
15200
WINDSOR RD
BURTON
15600
Middlefield Township
44062
15800
Nauvoo Rd
14300
Middlefield

1:24,000
1 in. = 2000 ft.
0 0.25 0.5
miles

SEE B MAP

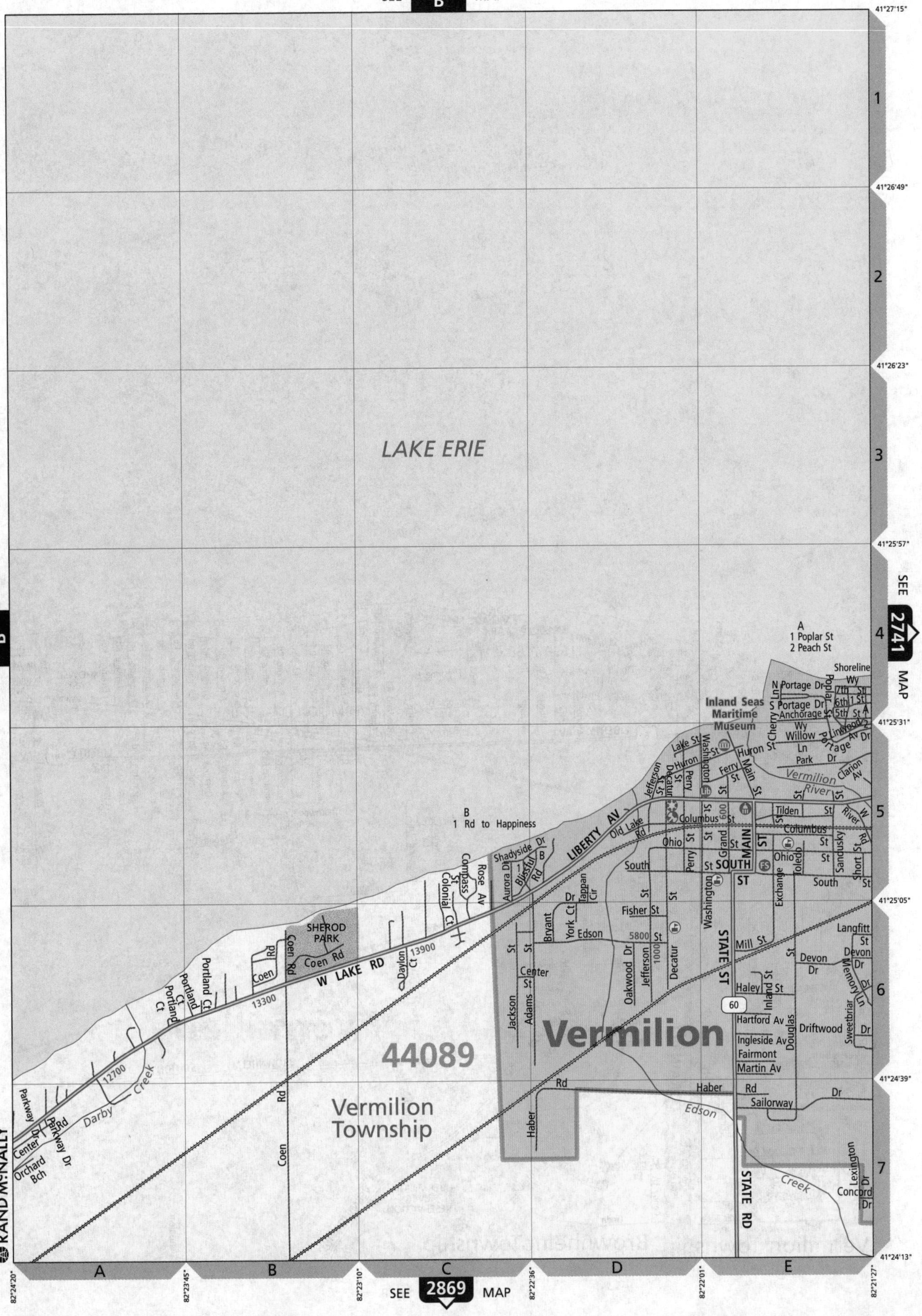
LAKE ERIE
A
1 Poplar St
2 Peach St
B
1 Rd to Happiness
Inland Seas Maritime Museum
Shoreline Wy
N Portage Dr
S Portage Dr
Anchorage Wy
Willow Ln
Park Dr
Linwood
Portage Av
Cherry Ln
Poplar
7th St
6th St
5th St
1 St
Huron St
Vermilion River
Clarion Av
River Rd
Lake St
Huron St
Washington St
Decatur St
Perry St
Jefferson St
Ferry St
Main St
LIBERTY AV
Old Lake Rd
Columbus St
Tilden
Columbus
Ohio St
Grand St
MAIN ST
SOUTH ST
Toledo
Sandusky St
Short St
South
Exchange
Fisher St
Edson
5800
Mill St
Devon Dr
Langfitt St
Memorial Dr
Haley St
Inland St
60
Hartford Av
Ingleside Av
Fairmont
Martin Av
Douglas
Driftwood
Sweetbriar
Vermilion
44089
Vermilion Township
Haber Rd
Sailorway Dr
Edson Creek
STATE ST
STATE RD
Lexington Dr
Concord Dr
Shadyside Dr
Blissful Rd
Aurora Dr
Rose Av
Compass St
Colonial Ct
Tappan Cir
York Ct
Bryant Dr
Center St
Jackson St
Adams St
Oakwood Dr
Jefferson
1000
Decatur
Washington
SHEROD PARK
Coen Rd
Daylon Ct
13900
W LAKE RD
13300
12700
Portland Ct
Darby Creek
Parkway
Center Rd
Parkway Dr
Orchard Bch
Haber
Coen
1
2
3
4
5
6
7
A
B
C
D
E
41°27'15"
41°26'49"
41°26'23"
41°25'57"
41°25'31"
41°25'05"
41°24'39"
41°24'13"
82°24'20"
82°23'45"
82°23'10"
82°22'36"
82°22'01"
82°21'27"

SEE B MAP
SEE 2741 MAP
SEE 2869 MAP

1:24,000
1 in. = 2000 ft.
0 0.25 0.5
miles

SEE B MAP

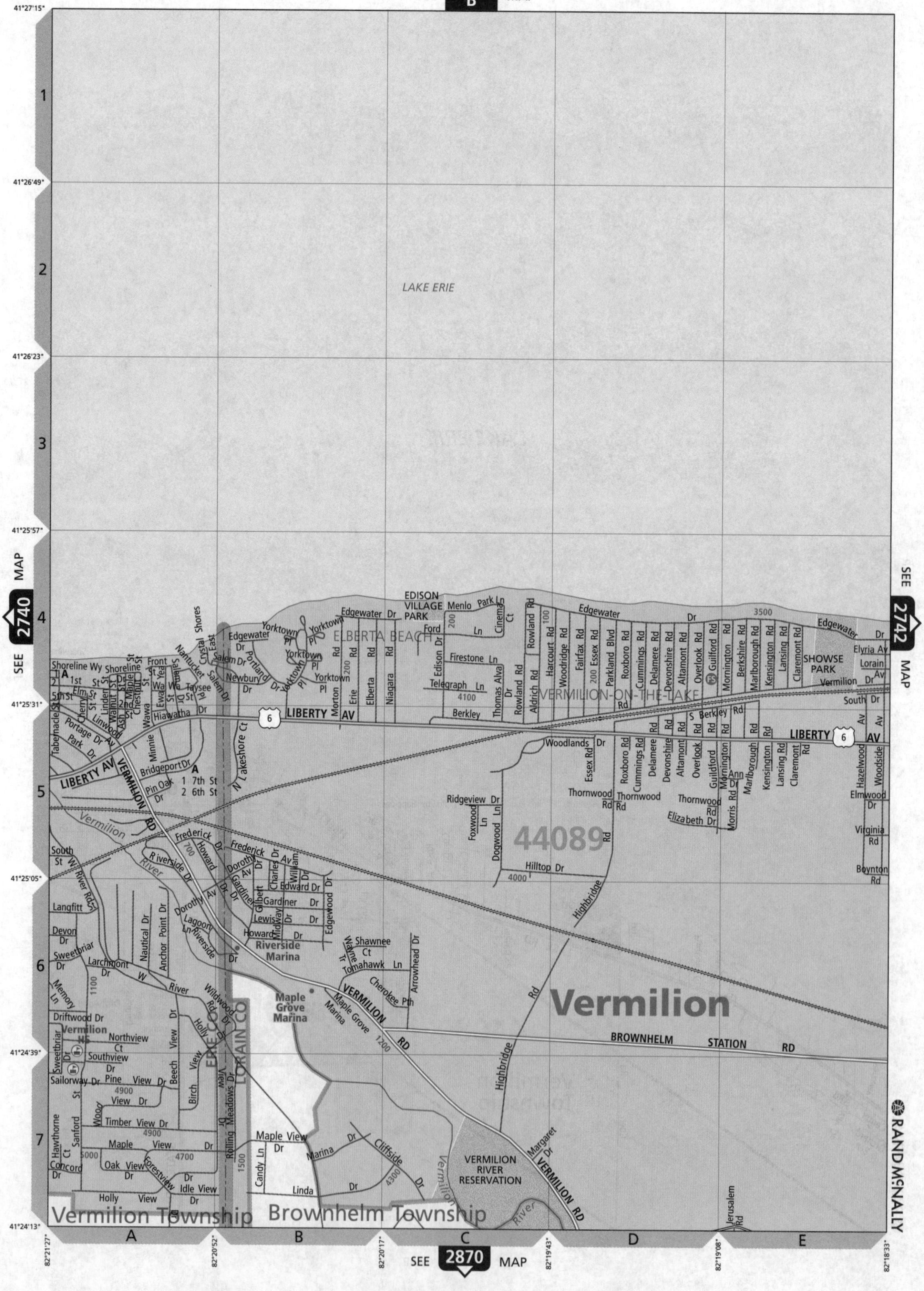
LAKE ERIE
EDISON VILLAGE PARK
ELBERTA BEACH
VERMILION-ON-THE-LAKE
SHOWSE PARK
Edgewater Dr
LIBERTY AV
VERMILION RD
BROWNHELM STATION RD
44089
Vermilion
Riverside Marina
Maple Grove Marina
Vermilion HS
VERMILION RIVER RESERVATION
Vermilion River
ERIE CO
LORAIN CO
Vermilion Township
Brownhelm Township
Highbridge Rd
Thornwood Rd
Woodlands Dr
Ridgeview Dr
Hilltop Dr
Berkley
Telegraph Ln
Firestone Ln
Menlo Park Ln
Jerusalem Rd
Margaret Dr
Cliffside Dr
Marina Dr
Linda
Holly View Dr
Maple View Dr
Oak View Dr
Timber View Dr
Pine View Dr
Sailorway Dr
Rolling Meadows Dr
Riverside Dr
Frederick Av
Dorothy Av
Howard Dr
Lagoon Dr
Larchmont Dr
W River Rd
Nautical Dr
Anchor Point Dr
Sweetbriar Dr
Langfitt
Devon Dr
Memory Ln
Driftwood Dr
Northview Ct
Southview Dr
Shoreline Wy
Hiawatha Dr
Bridgeport Dr
Pin Oak Dr
Portage Dr
Park Dr
Tabernacle St
Nantucket Dr
Crystal Shores
Newbury Dr
Portland Dr
Yorktown Pl
N Lakeshore Ct
Shawnee Ct
Tomahawk Ln
Cherokee Pth
Arrowhead Dr
Foxwood Ln
Dogwood Ln
Elyria Av
Lorain Av
Vermilion Dr
South Dr
Virginia Rd
Boynton Rd
Elmwood Dr
Hazelwood Av
Woodside Av
Elizabeth Dr
Morris Rd

SEE 2740 MAP

SEE 2742 MAP

SEE 2870 MAP

RAND McNALLY

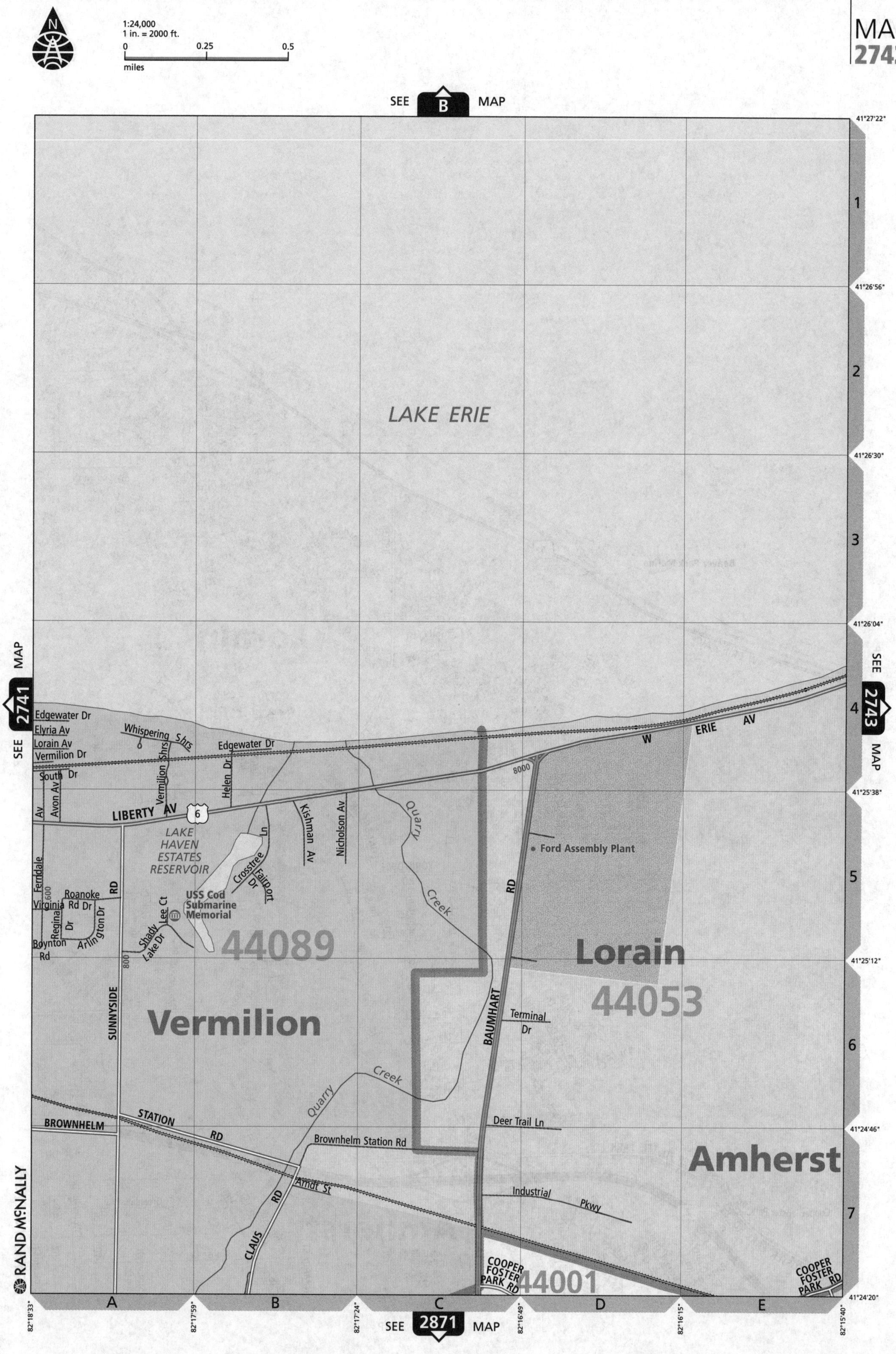
1:24,000
1 in. = 2000 ft.
0
0.25
0.5
miles
SEE B MAP
SEE 2741 MAP
SEE 2743 MAP
SEE 2871 MAP
41°27'22"
41°26'56"
41°26'30"
41°26'04"
41°25'38"
41°25'12"
41°24'46"
41°24'20"
82°18'33"
82°17'59"
82°17'24"
82°16'49"
82°16'15"
82°15'40"
A
B
C
D
E
1
2
3
4
5
6
7
LAKE ERIE
Edgewater Dr
Elyria Av
Lorain Av
Vermilion Dr
South Dr
Whispering Shrs
Vermilion Shrs
Helen Dr
W ERIE AV
8000
LIBERTY AV
6
Avon Av
Av
Kishman Av
Nicholson Av
Quarry Creek
LAKE HAVEN ESTATES RESERVOIR
Crosstree Ln
Dr
Fairport Dr
Ford Assembly Plant
Ferndale
600
Roanoke Rd Dr
Virginia
Regina Dr
Arlington Dr
RD
USS Cod Submarine Memorial
Lee Ct
Shady Lake Dr
Boynton Rd
800
44089
Lorain
44053
BAUMHART RD
SUNNYSIDE
Terminal Dr
Vermilion
Deer Trail Ln
BROWNHELM STATION RD
Brownhelm Station Rd
Amherst
Arndt St
Industrial Pkwy
CLAUS RD
COOPER FOSTER PARK RD
44001
RAND McNALLY

SEE B MAP

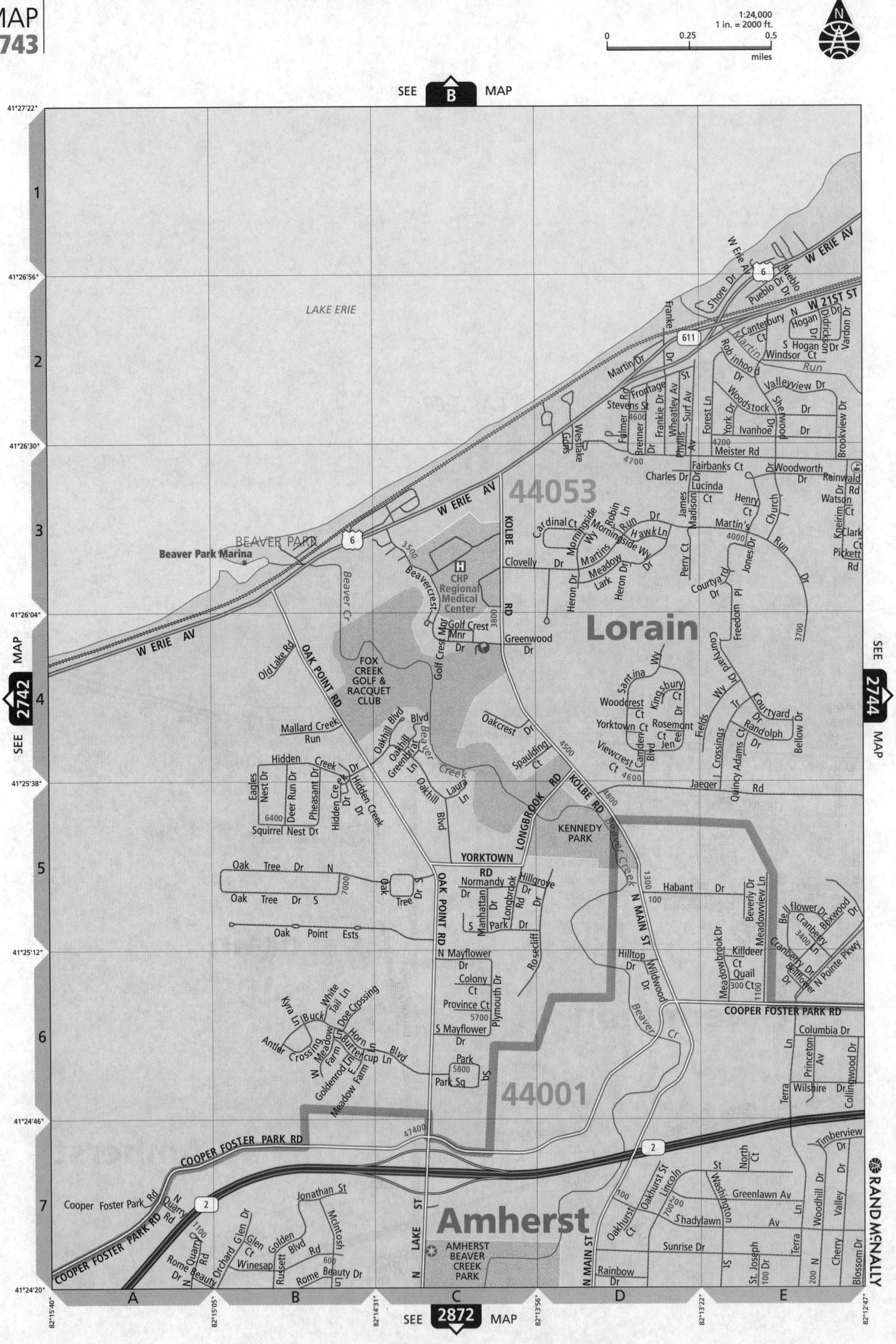
1:24,000
1 in. = 2000 ft.
0 0.25 0.5
miles
N
LAKE ERIE
Lorain
Amherst
44053
44001
W ERIE AV
W 21ST ST
W Erie Av
Shore Dr
Pueblo Dr
Franke Dr
Martin Dr
Martin Run
Canterbury Ct
Hogan Dr
Didrickson Dr
Vardon Dr
S Hogan Ct
Windsor Ct
Robinhood Dr
Valleyview Dr
Frontage Rd
Stevens St
Fulmer Rd
Brenner Dr
Frankie Dr
Wheatley Av
Phyllis St
Surf Av
Forest Ln
Woodstock Dr
York Dr
Ivanhoe Dr
Sherwood Dr
Brookview Dr
Westlake Gdns
Meister Rd
Fairbanks Ct
Charles Dr
Woodworth Dr
Rainwald Dr
Watson Rd
Kneirim Ct
Clark Ct
Pickett Rd
Lucinda Ct
James Madison Dr
Henry Ct
Church Dr
Martin's Run
Jones Dr
Perry Ct
Courtyard Dr
Freedom Pl
KOLBE RD
Cardinal Ct
Morningside Wy
Morningside Dr
Robin Ln
Hawk Ln
Martins Run
Meadow Lark
Heron Dr
Clovelly Dr
BEAVER PARK
Beaver Park Marina
Beaver Cr
Beavercrest
CHP Regional Medical Center
Golf Crest Mnr
Golf Crest Mnr Dr
Greenwood Dr
FOX CREEK GOLF & RACQUET CLUB
Old Lake Rd
OAK POINT RD
Mallard Creek Run
Oakhill Blvd
Greenbriar Ln
Beaver Creek
Oakcrest Dr
Spaulding Ct
LONGBROOK RD
Laura Ln
Santina Wy
Woodcrest Ct
Kingsbury Ct
Yorktown Ct
Rosemont Ct
Camden Blvd
Jen Ct
Viewcrest Ct
Fields Wy
Crossings Tr
Quincy Adams Ct
Randolph Dr
Bellow Dr
Jaeger Rd
Hidden Creek Dr
Eagles Nest Dr
Deer Run Dr
Pheasant Dr
Squirrel Nest Dr
KENNEDY PARK
YORKTOWN RD
Oak Tree Dr N
Oak Tree Dr S
Oak Tree Dr
Oak Point Ests
Normandy Dr
Manhattan Dr
Longbrook Rd
Hillgrove Dr
S Park Dr
Rosecliff
N MAIN ST
Habant Dr
Beverly Dr
Meadowview Ln
Bellflower Dr
Cranberry Ln
Boxwood Dr
N Pointe Pkwy
Hilltop Dr
Wildwood Dr
Meadowbrook Dr
Killdeer Ct
Quail Ct
N Mayflower Dr
Colony Ct
Province Ct
Plymouth Dr
S Mayflower Dr
Kyra Ln
Buck Ln
White Tail Ln
Doe Crossing
Horn Blvd
Antler Crossing
W Meadow Farm
Buttercup Ln
Goldenrod Ln
Meadow Farm
Park Sq
COOPER FOSTER PARK RD
Columbia Dr
Princeton Av
Collingwood Dr
Terra Ln
Wilshire Dr
Timberview Dr
Cooper Foster Park Rd
N Quarry Rd
Rome Beauty Dr
Orchard Glen Dr
Glen Golden Ct
Winesap
Russett Blvd
Jonathan St
McIntosh Ln
Golden Rd
Rome Beauty Dr
N LAKE ST
AMHERST BEAVER CREEK PARK
Oakhurst Ct
Oakhurst St
Lincoln
Washington
North Ct
Greenlawn Av
Shadylawn Av
Woodhill Dr
Valley Dr
Sunrise Dr
St. Joseph
Cherry
Blossom Dr
Rainbow Dr
RAND McNALLY

SEE 2742 MAP

SEE 2744 MAP

SEE 2872 MAP

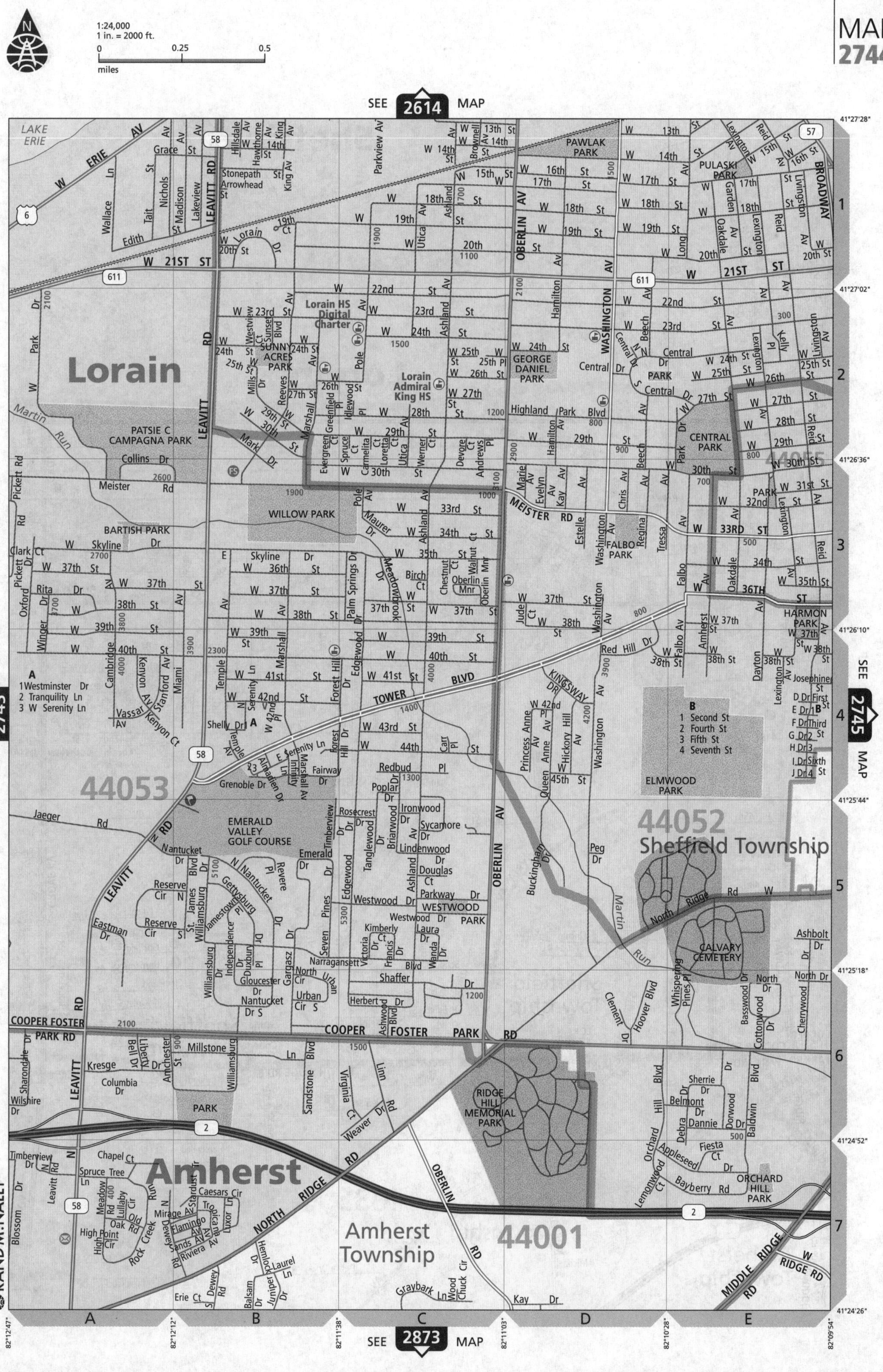
1:24,000
1 in. = 2000 ft.
0
0.25
0.5
miles
SEE 2614 MAP
SEE 2743 MAP
SEE 2745 MAP
SEE 2873 MAP
LAKE ERIE
Lorain
Amherst
Amherst Township
Sheffield Township
44053
44052
44055
44001
PATSIE C CAMPAGNA PARK
WILLOW PARK
BARTISH PARK
SUNNY ACRES PARK
GEORGE DANIEL PARK
CENTRAL PARK
FALBO PARK
PAWLAK PARK
PULASKI PARK
HARMON PARK
ELMWOOD PARK
EMERALD VALLEY GOLF COURSE
WESTWOOD PARK
CALVARY CEMETERY
RIDGE HILL MEMORIAL PARK
ORCHARD HILL PARK
PARK
Lorain HS Digital Charter
Lorain Admiral King HS
W ERIE AV
W 21ST ST
LEAVITT RD
OBERLIN AV
WASHINGTON AV
BROADWAY
MEISTER RD
TOWER BLVD
KINGSWAY DR
W 33RD ST
36TH ST
COOPER FOSTER PARK RD
NORTH RIDGE RD
MIDDLE RIDGE RD
W RIDGE RD
OBERLIN RD
N RIDGE RD
Martin Run
A
1 Westminster Dr
2 Tranquility Ln
3 W Serenity Ln
B
1 Second St
2 Fourth St
3 Fifth St
4 Seventh St
RAND McNALLY
41°27'28"
41°27'02"
41°26'36"
41°26'10"
41°25'44"
41°25'18"
41°24'52"
41°24'26"
82°12'47"
82°12'12"
82°11'38"
82°11'03"
82°10'28"
82°09'54"

1:24,000
1 in. = 2000 ft.
0 0.25 0.5
miles

SEE 2615 MAP

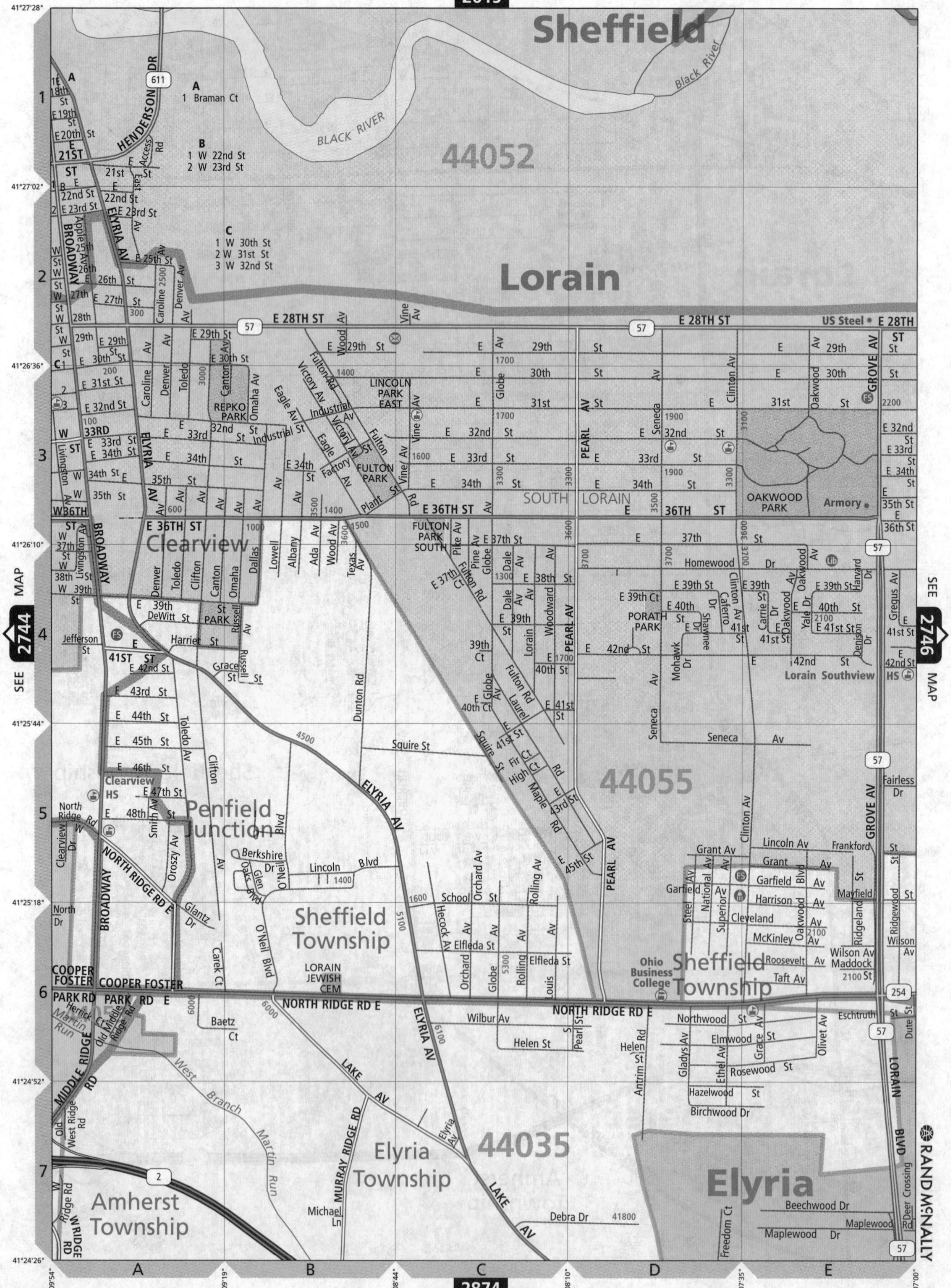
Sheffield
Lorain
Black River
BLACK RIVER
44052
44055
44035
Clearview
Penfield Junction
Sheffield Township
Elyria Township
Amherst Township
Elyria
SOUTH LORAIN
A
1 Braman Ct
B
1 W 22nd St
2 W 23rd St
C
1 W 30th St
2 W 31st St
3 W 32nd St
E 28TH ST
E 36TH ST
HENDERSON DR
BROADWAY
ELYRIA AV
PEARL AV
GROVE AV
LORAIN BLVD
NORTH RIDGE RD E
COOPER FOSTER PARK RD
MIDDLE RIDGE RD
LAKE AV
MURRAY RIDGE RD
W RIDGE RD
REPKO PARK
LINCOLN PARK EAST
FULTON PARK
FULTON PARK SOUTH
PORATH PARK
OAKWOOD PARK
Armory
US Steel
Clearview HS
Lorain Southview HS
Ohio Business College
LORAIN JEWISH CEM
Squire St
Seneca Av
Homewood Dr
Lincoln Av
Grant Av
Garfield Av
Harrison Av
Cleveland Av
McKinley Av
Roosevelt Av
Taft Av
Wilbur Av
Helen St
Northwood St
Elmwood St
Rosewood St
Hazelwood St
Birchwood Dr
Beechwood Dr
Maplewood Dr
Debra Dr
West Branch Martin Run
Martin Run
Baetz Ct
Berkshire Dr
Lincoln Blvd
O'Neill Blvd
School St
Elfleda St
Dunton Rd
Fulton Rd
Clinton Av
Freedom Ct
Deer Crossing Rd
57
611
2
254
A B C D E
1 2 3 4 5 6 7
41°27'28"
41°27'02"
41°26'36"
41°26'10"
41°25'44"
41°25'18"
41°24'52"
41°24'26"
82°09'54"
82°09'19"
82°08'44"
82°08'10"
82°07'35"
82°07'00"

SEE 2744 MAP

SEE 2746 MAP

SEE 2874 MAP

1:24,000
1 in. = 2000 ft.
0 0.25 0.5
miles

SEE 2616 MAP

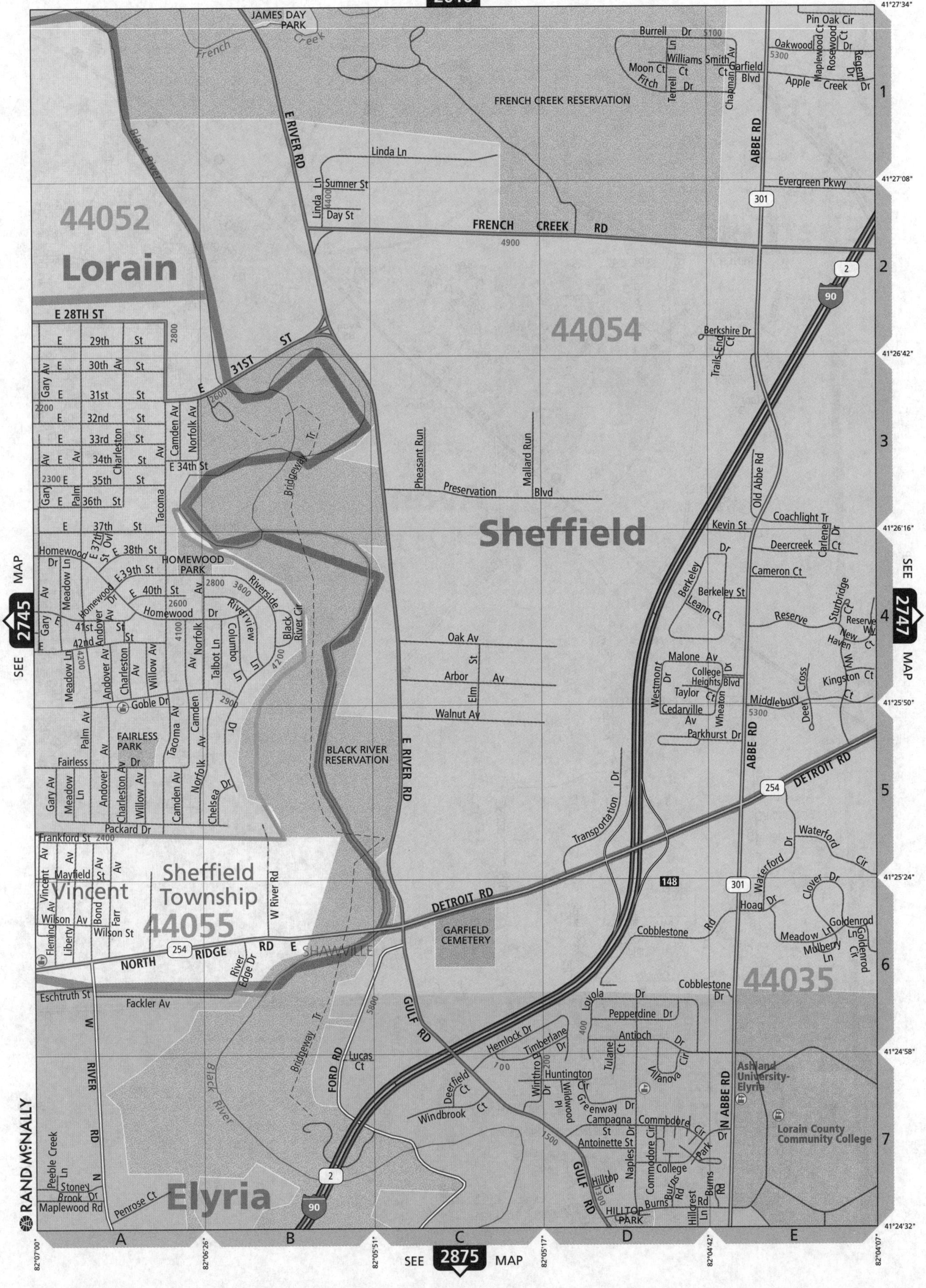
JAMES DAY PARK
French Creek
Burrell Dr 5100
Williams Smith Ct
Moon Ct
Fitch Dr
Terrell Ln
Chapman Av
Garfield Blvd
Pin Oak Cir
Oakwood Ct
Maplewood Ct
Rosewood Ct
Regent Dr
Apple Creek Dr
5300
FRENCH CREEK RESERVATION
E RIVER RD
ABBE RD
Black River
Linda Ln
Sumner St
Day St
4400
Evergreen Pkwy
301
44052
Lorain
FRENCH CREEK RD
4900
2
90
E 28TH ST
E 29th St
E 30th Av St
Gary Av
E 31st St
31ST ST
2800
2600
2200
E 32nd St
E 33rd St
E 34th St
Charleston
Camden Av
Norfolk Av
E 34th St
2300 E 35th St
E 36th St
Palm
Tacoma
E 37th St
E 37th St Ovl
E 38th St
Homewood Dr
HOMEWOOD PARK
E 39th St
E 40th St
Homewood Dr
Riverside
Riverview
Black River Cir
Columbo Ln
Talbot Ln
Meadow Ln
Andover Av
41st St
42nd St
Willow Av
4100
4200
Goble Dr
2900
FAIRLESS PARK
Fairless Dr
Tacoma Av
Camden Av
Norfolk Av
Chelsea Dr
Packard Dr
Frankford St 2400
Bridgeway Tr
44054
Berkshire Dr
Trails End Ct
Pheasant Run
Mallard Run
Preservation Blvd
Old Abbe Rd
Sheffield
Kevin St
Coachlight Tr
Carlene Dr
Deercreek Ct
Cameron Ct
Berkeley Dr
Berkeley St
Leann Ct
Reserve
Sturbridge Ct
Reserve Wy
New Haven Wy
Oak Av
Elm St
Arbor Av
Walnut Av
Malone Av
Westmont Dr
College Heights Blvd
Taylor Ct
Wheaton Dr
Cedarville Av
Parkhurst Dr
Middlebury
5300
Deer Cross Ct
Kingston Ct
BLACK RIVER RESERVATION
DETROIT RD
254
Transportation Dr
Waterford Dr
Waterford Cir
148
301
Clover Dr
Hoag Dr
Goldenrod Ln
Goldenrod Cir
Meadow Ln
Mulberry Ln
Vincent Av
Mayfield St
Bond Av
Farr Av
Sheffield Township
44055
W River Rd
Wilson Av
Wilson St
Fleming Av
Liberty Av
GARFIELD CEMETERY
Cobblestone Rd
Cobblestone Dr
44035
NORTH RIDGE RD E
SHAWVILLE
River Edge Dr
Eschtruth St
Fackler Av
Loyola Dr
Pepperdine Dr
Antioch Dr
Tulane Ct
Villanova Cir
W RIVER RD N
GULF RD
5800
FORD RD
Lucas Ct
Hemlock Dr
Timberlane Dr
Winthrop Dr
Huntington Cir
Wildwood Pl
Greenway Dr
Deerfield Ct
Windbrook Ct
100
200
400
Campagna St
Commodore Cir
Antoinette St
Park Dr
N ABBE RD
Ashland University-Elyria
Lorain County Community College
Peeble Creek Ln
Stoney Brook Dr
Maplewood Rd
Penrose Ct
Elyria
1500
Hilltop Cir
Naples Dr
Commodore Cir
College
Burns Rd
Hillcrest Ln
Burns Rd
HILLTOP PARK
3300
A B C D E
1 2 3 4 5 6 7
41°27'34"
41°27'08"
41°26'42"
41°26'16"
41°25'50"
41°25'24"
41°24'58"
41°24'32"
82°07'00"
82°06'26"
82°05'51"
82°05'17"
82°04'42"
82°04'07"

SEE 2745 MAP

SEE 2747 MAP

SEE 2875 MAP

1:24,000
1 in. = 2000 ft.
0 0.25 0.5
miles

SEE 2617 MAP

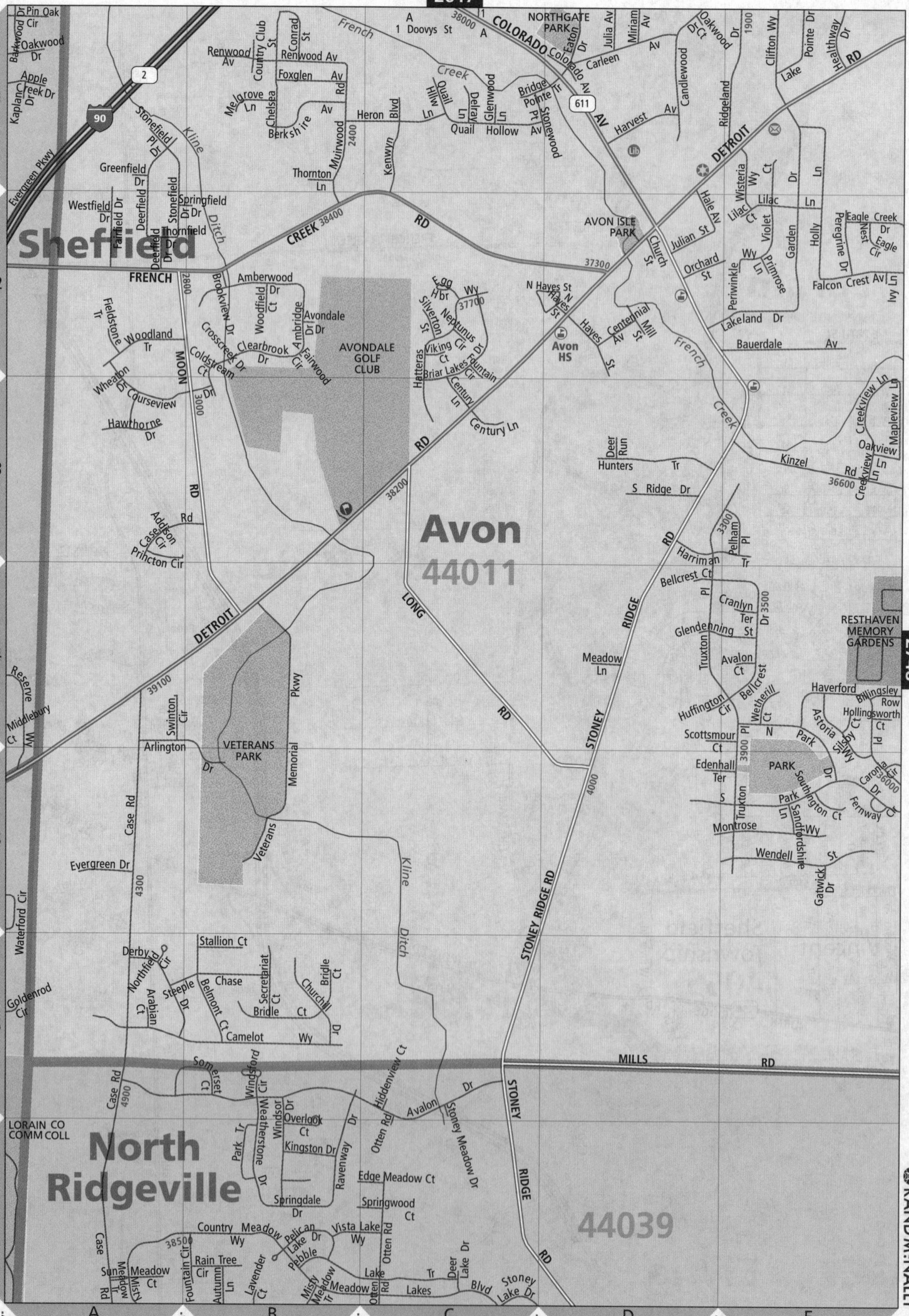
Sheffield
Avon
44011
North Ridgeville
44039
NORTHGATE PARK
AVON ISLE PARK
AVONDALE GOLF CLUB
VETERANS PARK
RESTHAVEN MEMORY GARDENS
PARK
Avon HS
LORAIN CO COMM COLL
COLORADO AV
DETROIT RD
FRENCH CREEK RD
MOON RD
LONG RD
STONEY RIDGE RD
MILLS RD
Case Rd
Evergreen Pkwy
French Creek
Kline Ditch
Pin Oak Cir
Barkwood Dr
Oakwood Dr
Apple Creek Dr
Kaplan Dr
Stonefield Pl
Greenfield Dr
Westfield Dr
Fairfield Dr
Deerfield Dr
Stonefield Dr
Springfield Dr
Thornfield Dr
Renwood Av
Country Club St
Conrad St
Foxglen Av
Melgrove Ln
Chelsea
Berkshire Av
Muirwood
Heron Blvd
Thornton Ln
Kenwyn
Quail Hllw
Delray Ln
Glenwood Ln
Quail Hollow Av
Bridge Pointe Tr
Stonewood
Doovys St
Eaton Dr
Julia Av
Miriam Av
Carleen Av
Harvest Av
Candlewood
Oakwood Dr Ct
Ridgeland Dr
Clifton Wy
Pointe Dr
Lake
Healthway Dr
Hale Av
Wisteria Wy
Lilac Ct
Lilac Ln
Violet
Holly
Garden Dr
Julian St
Orchard St
Periwinkle
Primrose
Church St
Eagle Creek Dr
Peregrine Dr
Eagle Nest Cir
Falcon Crest Av
Ivy Ln
Amberwood Dr
Brookview Dr
Woodfield Ct
Ambridge Dr
Avondale Dr
Crosscreek Dr
Clearbrook Dr
Fairwood Cir
Coldstream Ct
Fieldstone Tr
Woodland Tr
Wheaton Dr
Courseview Dr
Hawthorne Dr
Egg Hbr
Silverton St
Neptunus Cir
Viking Ct
Briar Lakes Dr
Fountain
Hatteras
Century Ln
Century Cir
N Hayes St
Hayes St
Centennial Av
Mill St
Lakeland Dr
Bauerdale Av
Deer Run
Hunters Tr
S Ridge Dr
Kinzel Rd
Creekview Ln
Mapleview Ln
Oakview Ln
Addison Ct
Case Ct
Princton Cir
Harriman Tr
Pelham Pl
Bellcrest Ct
Cranlyn Ter
Glendenning St
Truxton Pl
Avalon Ct
Meadow Ln
Huffington Cir
Bellcrest
Wetherill Ct
Haverford
Billingsley Row
Hollingsworth Ct
Astoria Park
Silsby Wy
Scottsmour Ct
Edenhall Ter
Southington Ct
Caronia Cir
Fernway Ct
Park Ln
Sandfordshire
Montrose Wy
Wendell St
Gatwick Dr
Reserve
Middlebury Wy
Swinton Cir
Arlington Dr
Memorial Pkwy
Veterans
Evergreen Dr
Waterford Cir
Goldenrod Cir
Stallion Ct
Derby Cir
Northfield Ct
Arabian Ct
Steeple Dr
Chase
Belmont Ct
Secretariat Ct
Bridle Ct
Churchill Dr
Camelot Wy
Somerset Ct
Windsford Cir
Weatherstone Dr
Windsor Dr
Overlook Ct
Kingston Dr
Park Tr
Ravenway Dr
Hiddenview Ct
Otten Rd
Avalon Dr
Stoney Meadow Dr
Edge Meadow Ct
Springwood Ct
Springdale Dr
Country Meadow Wy
Pelican Lake Dr
Vista Lake Wy
Pebble
Rain Tree Cir
Fountain Cir
Autumn Ln
Lavender Ct
Sun Meadow Ct
Misty Meadow Tr
Lake Tr
Deer Lake Dr
Lakes Blvd
Stoney Lake Dr
41°27'34"
41°27'08"
41°26'42"
41°26'16"
41°25'50"
41°25'24"
41°24'58"
41°24'32"
82°04'07"
82°03'33"
82°02'58"
82°02'23"
82°01'49"
82°01'14"
RAND McNALLY

SEE 2746 MAP

SEE 2748 MAP

SEE 2876 MAP

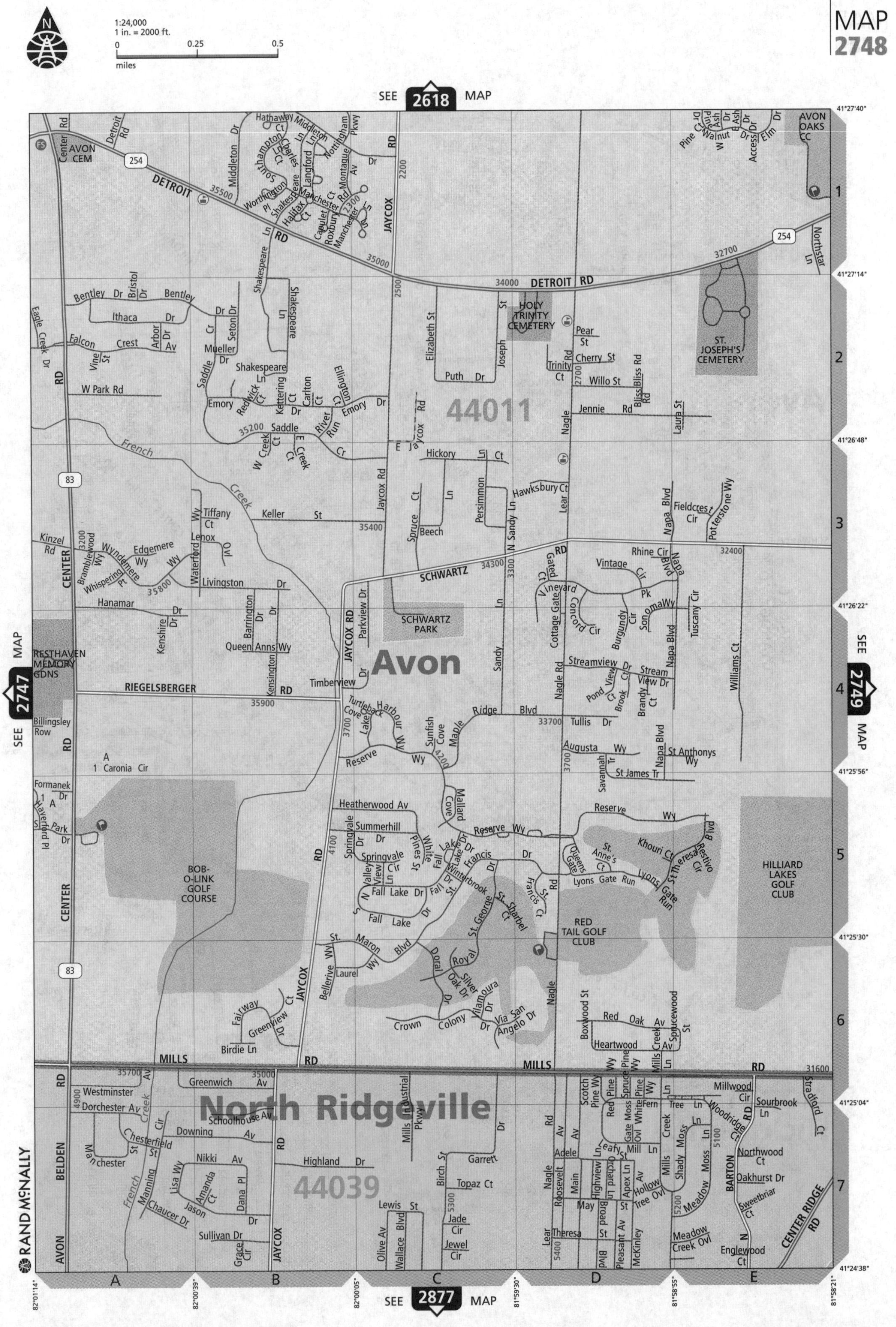
1:24,000
1 in. = 2000 ft.
0 0.25 0.5
miles
SEE 2618 MAP
SEE 2747 MAP
SEE 2749 MAP
SEE 2877 MAP
Avon
North Ridgeville
44011
44039
DETROIT RD
SCHWARTZ RD
RIEGELSBERGER RD
MILLS RD
CENTER RD
JAYCOX RD
NAGLE RD
AVON CEM
HOLY TRINITY CEMETERY
ST. JOSEPH'S CEMETERY
AVON OAKS CC
SCHWARTZ PARK
RESTHAVEN MEMORY GDNS
BOB-O-LINK GOLF COURSE
RED TAIL GOLF CLUB
HILLIARD LAKES GOLF CLUB
French Creek
Keller St
Livingston Dr
Hanamar Dr
Queen Anns Wy
Reserve Wy
Ridge Blvd
Tullis Dr
Streamview Dr
Napa Blvd
Williams Ct
Lyons Gate Run
St. Maron Blvd
Red Oak Av
Heartwood Av
Westminster
Dorchester Av
Chesterfield St
Schoolhouse Av
Downing Av
Highland Dr
Mills Industrial Pkwy
Garrett Dr
Topaz Ct
Lewis St
BARTON RD
CENTER RIDGE RD
BELDEN
AVON
A B C D E
1 2 3 4 5 6 7
RAND McNALLY

1:24,000
1 in. = 2000 ft.
0 0.25 0.5
miles

SEE 2619 MAP

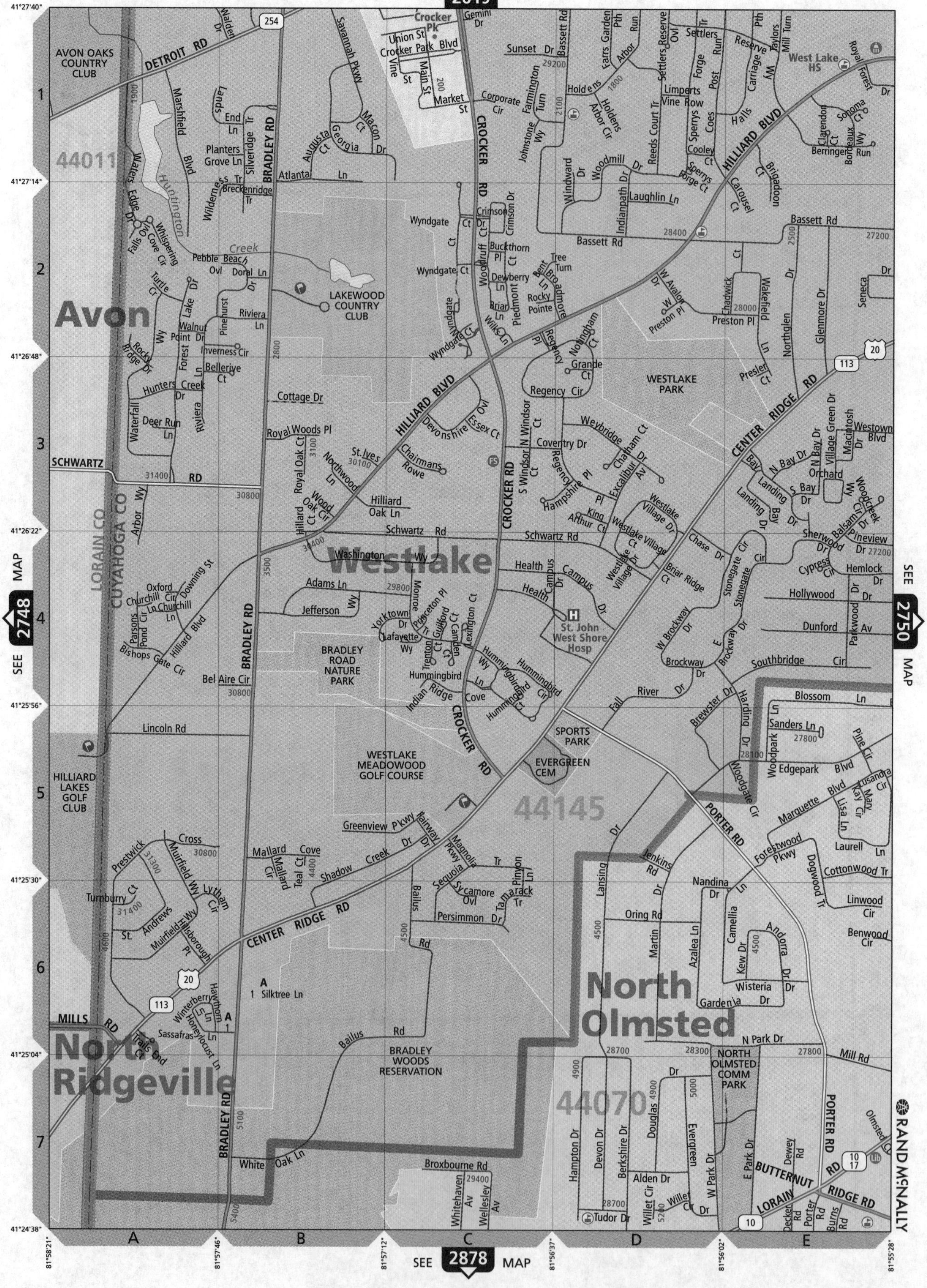
AVON OAKS COUNTRY CLUB
DETROIT RD
254
44011
Avon
LAKEWOOD COUNTRY CLUB
Crocker Pk
Crocker Park Blvd
Union St
Main St
Market St
CROCKER RD
BRADLEY RD
HILLIARD BLVD
Sunset Dr
Bassett Rd
Settlers Reserve
West Lake HS
Westlake
WESTLAKE PARK
SCHWARTZ RD
Schwartz Rd
Washington Wy
Adams Ln
Jefferson Wy
Cottage Dr
Royal Woods Pl
Hilliard Oak Ln
Regency Cir
Coventry Dr
Health Campus Dr
St. John West Shore Hosp
LORAIN CO
CUYAHOGA CO
Hilliard Blvd
Bishops Gate Cir
Bel Aire Cir
BRADLEY ROAD NATURE PARK
Lincoln Rd
HILLIARD LAKES GOLF CLUB
WESTLAKE MEADOWOOD GOLF COURSE
SPORTS PARK
EVERGREEN CEM
44145
CENTER RIDGE RD
20
113
Greenview Pkwy
Mallard Cove
Shadow Creek Dr
Fall River Dr
Brockway Dr
Southbridge Cir
Dunford Av
Hollywood Dr
Hemlock Dr
Westown Blvd
Blossom Ln
Sanders Ln
Edgepark Blvd
Marquette Blvd
PORTER RD
Forestwood Pkwy
Cottonwood Tr
Linwood Cir
Benwood Cir
Laurell Ln
Nandina Dr
Oring Rd
Andorra Dr
Wisteria Dr
Gardenia Dr
North Olmsted
N Park Dr
Mill Rd
NORTH OLMSTED COMM PARK
44070
MILLS RD
North Ridgeville
BRADLEY WOODS RESERVATION
Bailus Rd
White Oak Ln
Broxbourne Rd
Persimmon Dr
Hampton Dr
Devon Dr
Berkshire Dr
Douglas Dr
Evergreen
Alden Dr
Tudor Dr
Willet Cir
BUTTERNUT RIDGE RD
LORAIN RD
10
17
E Park Dr
Dewey Rd
A
1 Silktree Ln
A B C D E
1 2 3 4 5 6 7
RAND McNALLY

SEE 2748 MAP

SEE 2750 MAP

SEE 2878 MAP

1:24,000
1 in. = 2000 ft.
0 0.25 0.5
miles

SEE 2620 MAP

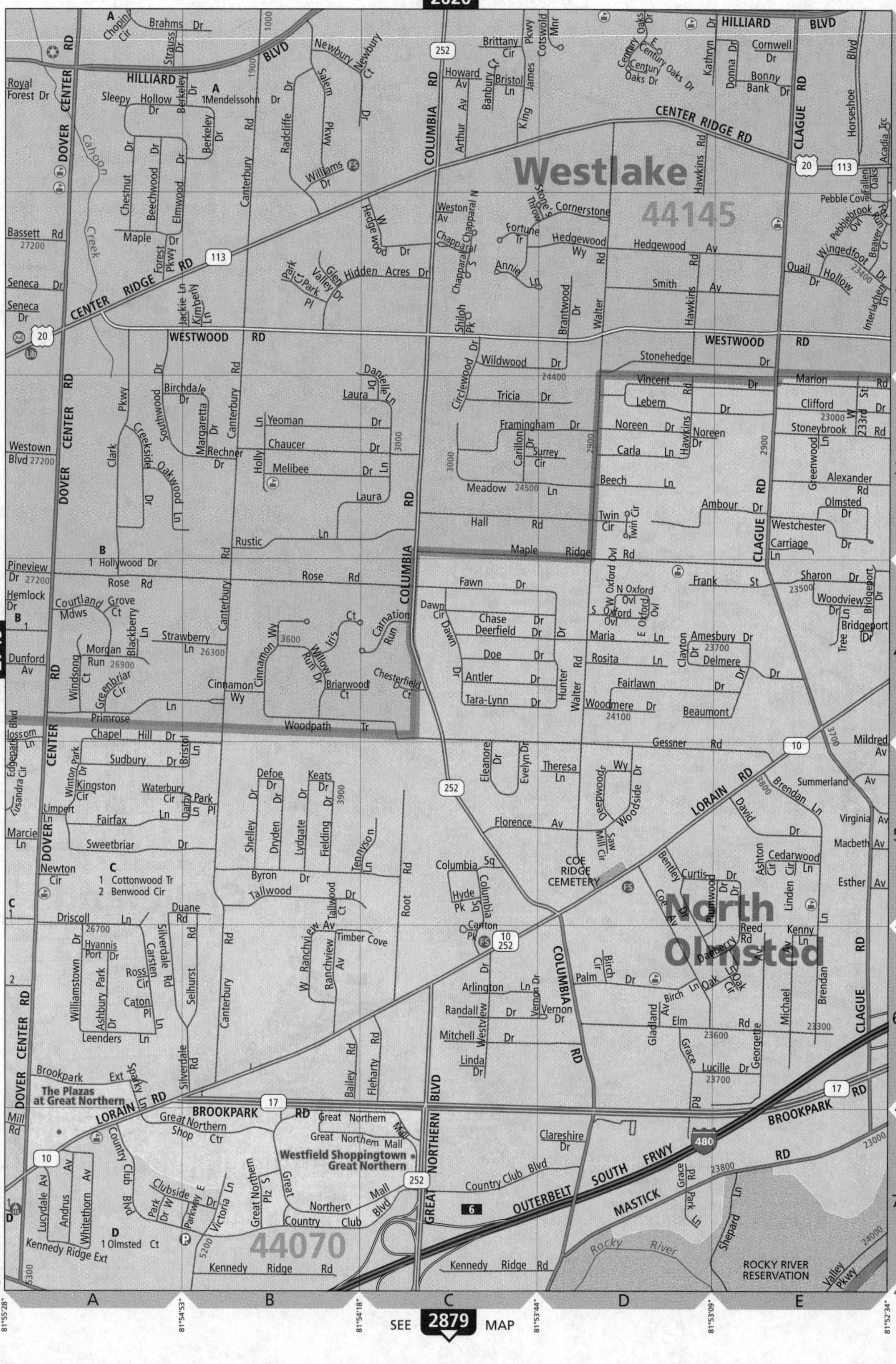
Westlake
44145
North Olmsted
44070
HILLIARD BLVD
CENTER RIDGE RD
WESTWOOD RD
DOVER CENTER RD
COLUMBIA RD
CLAGUE RD
LORAIN RD
BROOKPARK RD
GREAT NORTHERN BLVD
OUTERBELT SOUTH FRWY
MASTICK RD
Canterbury Rd
Rose Rd
Gessner Rd
Maple Ridge Rd
Hall Rd
Stonehedge
Marion Rd
Hedgewood Av
Smith Av
Hawkins Rd
Walter Rd
Columbia Sq
COE RIDGE CEMETERY
The Plazas at Great Northern
Westfield Shoppingtown Great Northern
Great Northern Mall
Country Club Blvd
Kennedy Ridge Rd
Rocky River
ROCKY RIVER RESERVATION
Valley Pkwy
Cahoon Creek
A
B
C
D
E
1
2
3
4
5
6
7
41°27'46"
41°27'20"
41°26'53"
41°26'27"
41°26'01"
41°25'35"
41°25'09"
41°24'43"
81°55'28"
81°54'53"
81°54'18"
81°53'44"
81°53'09"
81°52'34"

SEE 2749 MAP
SEE 2751 MAP
SEE 2879 MAP

1:24,000
1 in. = 2000 ft.
0 0.25 0.5
miles

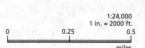

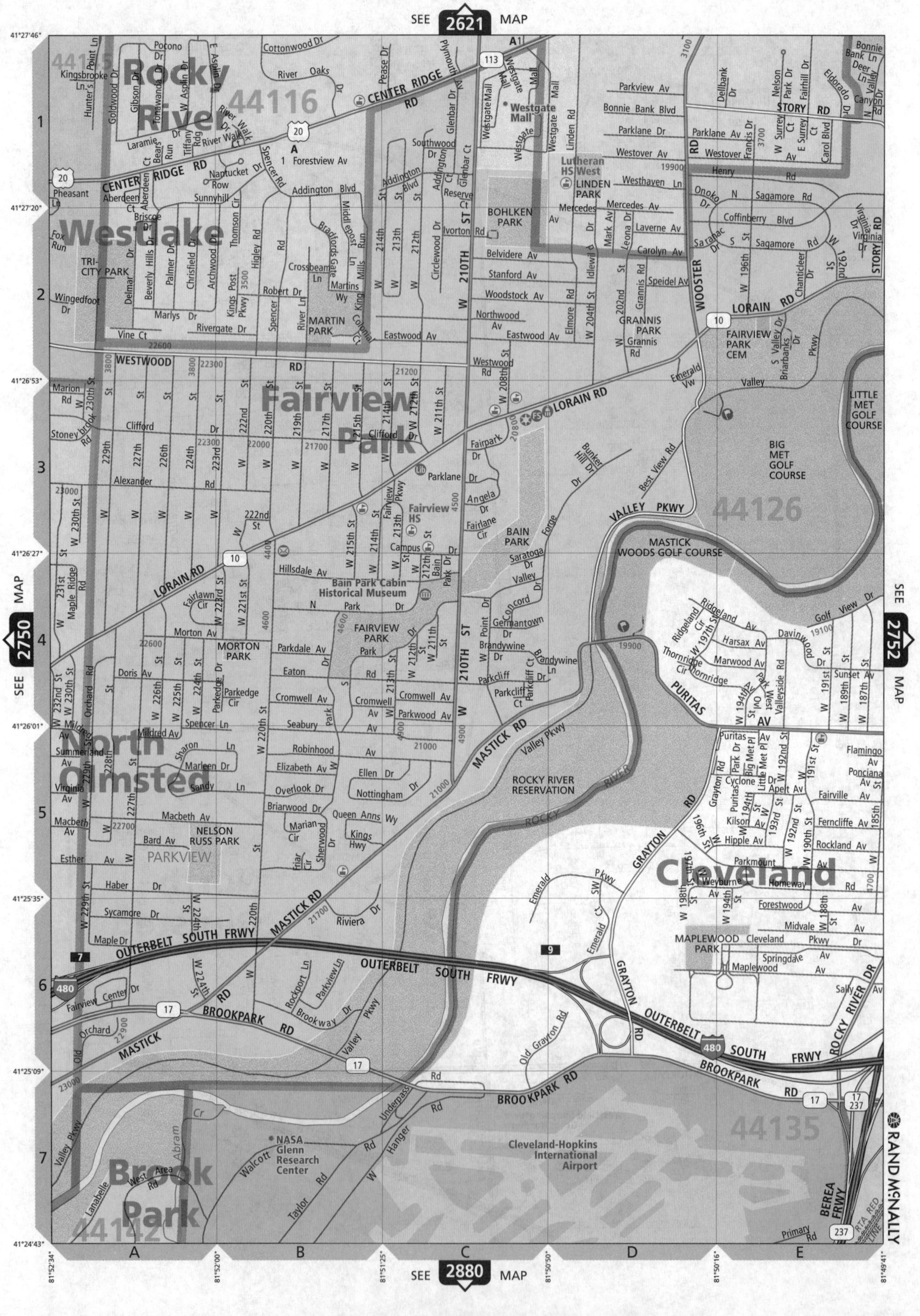
SEE 2621 MAP
SEE 2880 MAP
SEE 2750 MAP
SEE 2752 MAP
Rocky River
44116
Westlake
Fairview Park
North Olmsted
Cleveland
Brook Park
44126
44135
44142
44145
CENTER RIDGE RD
LORAIN RD
WESTWOOD RD
MASTICK RD
W 210TH ST
WOOSTER RD
STORY RD
VALLEY PKWY
PURITAS AV
GRAYTON RD
BROOKPARK RD
OUTERBELT SOUTH FRWY
ROCKY RIVER DR
BEREA FRWY
Westgate Mall
Lutheran HS West
LINDEN PARK
BOHLKEN PARK
TRI-CITY PARK
MARTIN PARK
GRANNIS PARK
FAIRVIEW PARK CEM
LITTLE MET GOLF COURSE
BIG MET GOLF COURSE
MASTICK WOODS GOLF COURSE
Fairview HS
BAIN PARK
Bain Park Cabin Historical Museum
FAIRVIEW PARK
MORTON PARK
NELSON RUSS PARK
PARKVIEW
ROCKY RIVER RESERVATION
MAPLEWOOD PARK
NASA Glenn Research Center
Cleveland-Hopkins International Airport
A B C D E
1 2 3 4 5 6 7
RAND McNALLY

1:24,000
1 in. = 2000 ft.
0 0.25 0.5
miles

SEE 2622 MAP

SEE 2751 MAP

SEE 2753 MAP

Fairview Park
ROCKY RIVER RESERVATION
44126
LORAIN RD
BIG MET GC
LITTLE MET GOLF COURSE
Fairview Hospital
ROCKY RIVER DR
St. Joseph Academy
MUNN PARK
MUNN RD
WARREN RD
TRISKETT RD
LORAIN AV
RAINBOW PARK
RTA-West Park Station
MOHICAN PARK
JEFFERSON PARK
44111
ALGER CEM
DRAKEFIELD PARK
John Marshall HS
Chatfield Av
Clifford Av
MEDINA FRWY
RTA-West 150th-Puritas Station
TERMINAL PARK
W 150TH ST
W 140TH ST
F Carl Shuler School
BELLAIRE RD
EMERY PARK
GUNNING PARK
Campus Hospital of Cleveland
PURITAS AV
GILMORE PARK
RIVERSIDE PARK
Cleveland
Industrial Pkwy
44135
CROSSBURN PARK
BEREA FRWY
OUTERBELT SOUTH FRWY
BROOKPARK RD
RTA-Brookpark Station
Ford Motor Company
FORD MOTOR COMPANY
44142
ENGLE RD
SMITH RD
HOLY CROSS CEMETERY
CAVANAUGH PARK
44130
Parma
Brook Park
W 130TH ST
A
B
C
D
E
1
2
3
4
5
6
7

SEE 2881 MAP

1:24,000
1 in. = 2000 ft.
0 0.25 0.5
miles

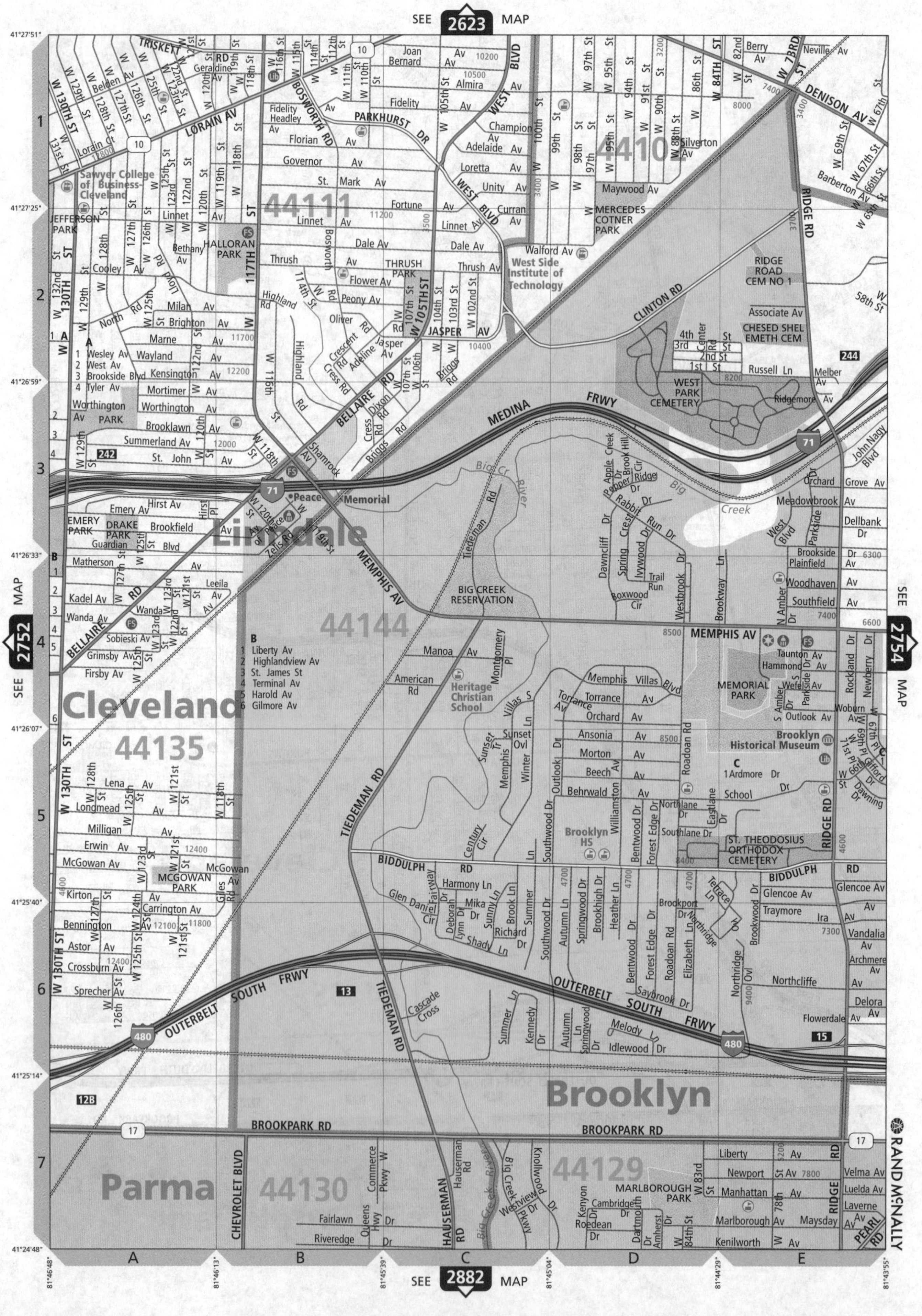
SEE 2623 MAP
SEE 2882 MAP
SEE 2752 MAP
SEE 2754 MAP
Cleveland
44135
Linndale
44111
44144
4410
Brooklyn
Parma
44130
44129
MEDINA FRWY
OUTERBELT SOUTH FRWY
BROOKPARK RD
MEMPHIS AV
BIDDULPH RD
TIEDEMAN RD
RIDGE RD
W 130TH ST
LORAIN AV
BELLAIRE RD
BOSWORTH RD
PARKHURST DR
WEST BLVD
DENISON AV
CLINTON RD
JASPER AV
HAUSERMAN RD
CHEVROLET BLVD
TRISKETT RD
W 117TH ST
W 105TH ST
W 84TH ST
W 73RD ST
BIG CREEK RESERVATION
WEST PARK CEMETERY
RIDGE ROAD CEM NO 1
CHESED SHEL EMETH CEM
MERCEDES COTNER PARK
HALLORAN PARK
THRUSH PARK
JEFFERSON PARK
WORTHINGTON PARK
EMERY PARK
DRAKE PARK
MCGOWAN PARK
MEMORIAL PARK
MARLBOROUGH PARK
ST. THEODOSIUS ORTHODOX CEMETERY
Sawyer College of Business-Cleveland
West Side Institute of Technology
Heritage Christian School
Brooklyn HS
Brooklyn Historical Museum
Peace Memorial
Big Creek
A
1 Wesley Av
2 West Av
3 Brookside Blvd
4 Tyler Av
B
1 Liberty Av
2 Highlandview Av
3 St. James St
4 Terminal Av
5 Harold Av
6 Gilmore Av
C
1 Ardmore Dr
A B C D E
1 2 3 4 5 6 7
41°27'51"
41°27'25"
41°26'59"
41°26'33"
41°26'07"
41°25'40"
41°25'14"
41°24'48"
81°46'48"
81°46'13"
81°45'39"
81°45'04"
81°44'29"
81°43'55"
RAND McNALLY

1:24,000
1 in. = 2000 ft.
0 0.25 0.5
miles

SEE 2624 MAP

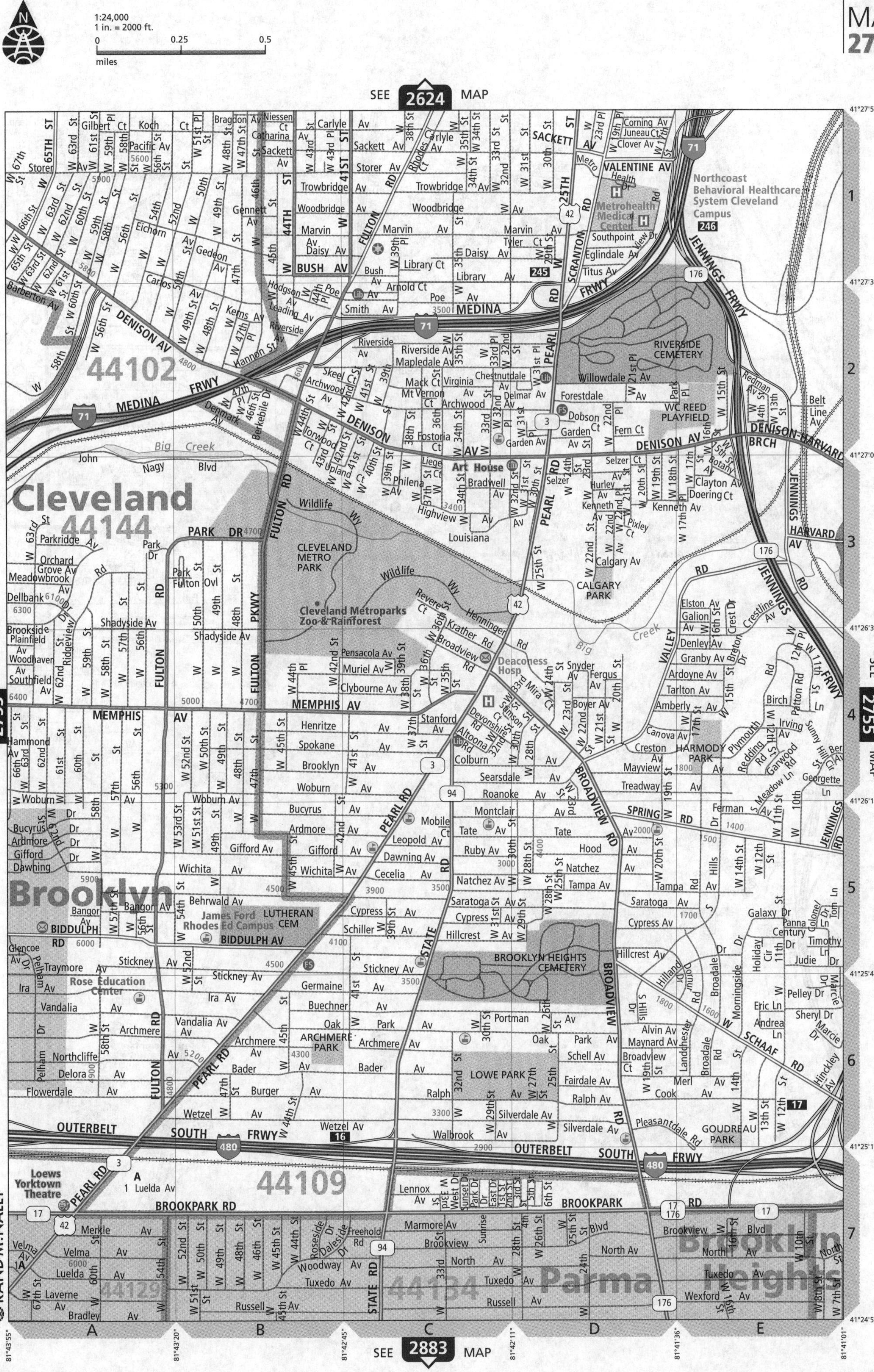
Cleveland
44144
44102
Brooklyn
44109
44129
44134
Parma
Brooklyn Heights
MEDINA FRWY
DENISON AV
FULTON RD
FULTON PKWY
PEARL RD
STATE RD
BROADVIEW RD
JENNINGS FRWY
MEMPHIS AV
BIDDULPH AV
BROOKPARK RD
OUTERBELT SOUTH FRWY
SCRANTON RD
VALENTINE AV
SACKETT AV
DENISON-HARVARD BRCH
SPRING RD
W SCHAAF RD
BUSH AV
PARK DR
Northcoast Behavioral Healthcare System Cleveland Campus
Metrohealth Medical Center
RIVERSIDE CEMETERY
WC REED PLAYFIELD
Art House
CLEVELAND METRO PARK
Cleveland Metroparks Zoo & Rainforest
CALGARY PARK
Deaconess Hosp
HARMODY PARK
James Ford Rhodes Ed Campus
LUTHERAN CEM
Rose Education Center
BROOKLYN HEIGHTS CEMETERY
ARCHMERE PARK
LOWE PARK
GOUDREAU PARK
Loews Yorktown Theatre
Big Creek
John Nagy Blvd
Wildlife Wy
A B C D E
1 2 3 4 5 6 7

SEE 2753 MAP

SEE 2755 MAP

SEE 2883 MAP

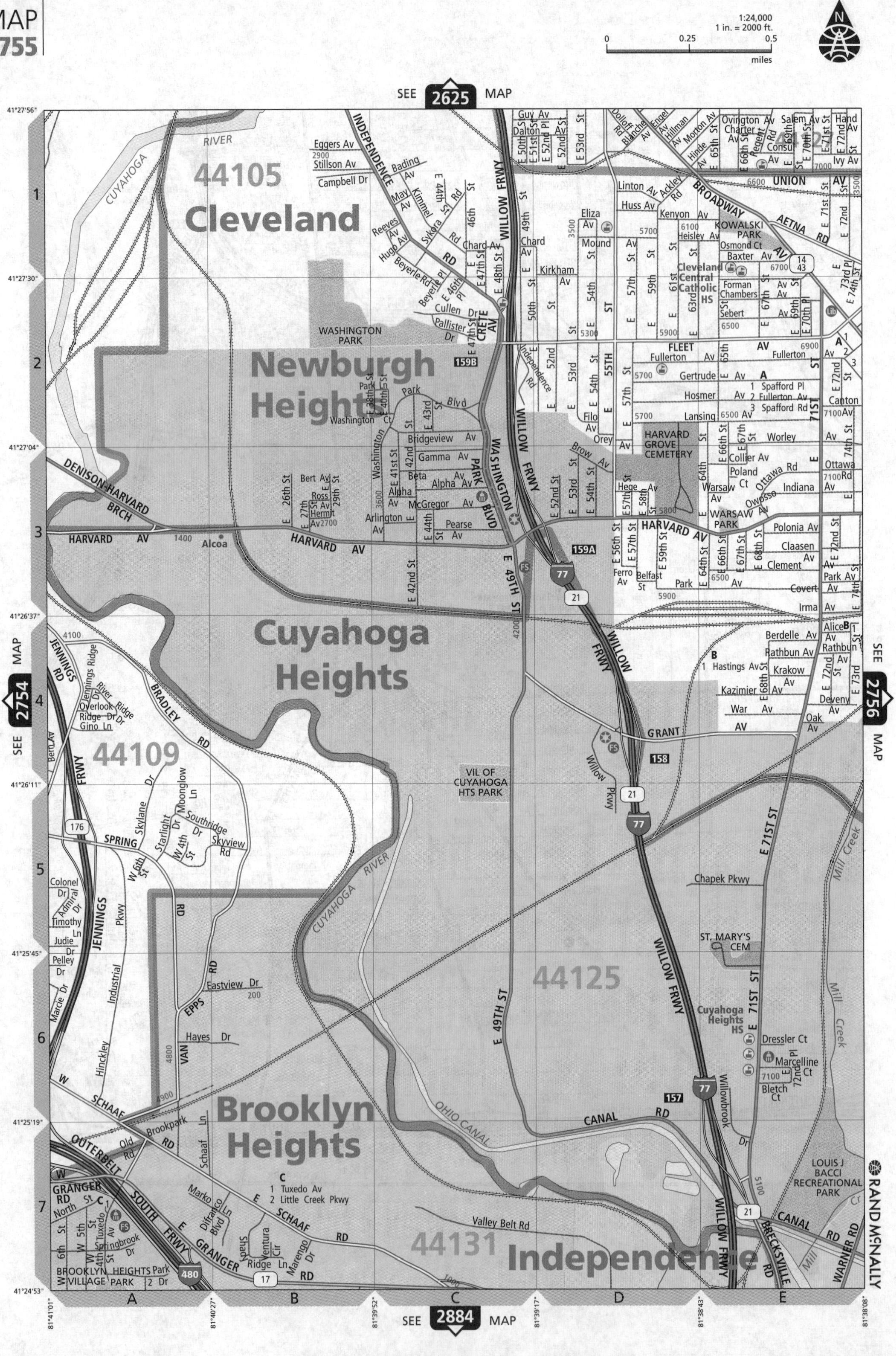
1:24,000
1 in. = 2000 ft.
0 0.25 0.5
miles
SEE 2625 MAP
SEE 2884 MAP
SEE 2754 MAP
SEE 2756 MAP
44105
Cleveland
Newburgh Heights
Cuyahoga Heights
44109
44125
Brooklyn Heights
44131
Independence
CUYAHOGA RIVER
WASHINGTON PARK
HARVARD GROVE CEMETERY
KOWALSKI PARK
Cleveland Central Catholic HS
WARSAW PARK
VIL OF CUYAHOGA HTS PARK
ST. MARY'S CEM
Cuyahoga Heights HS
LOUIS J BACCI RECREATIONAL PARK
BROOKLYN VILLAGE PARK
OHIO CANAL
Mill Creek
Alcoa
WILLOW FRWY
INDEPENDENCE RD
WASHINGTON PARK BLVD
HARVARD AV
DENISON-HARVARD BRCH
BROADWAY AV
UNION AV
AETNA RD
FLEET AV
GRANT AV
E 49TH ST
E 71ST ST
E 55TH ST
BRADLEY RD
JENNINGS RD
JENNINGS FRWY
SPRING RD
VAN EPPS RD
W SCHAAF RD
E SCHAAF RD
CANAL RD
OUTERBELT SOUTH FRWY
GRANGER RD
E GRANGER RD
BRECKSVILLE RD
WARNER RD
Valley Belt Rd
Chapek Pkwy
Willow Pkwy
Willowbrook Dr
Industrial Pkwy
B 1 Hastings Av
C 1 Tuxedo Av 2 Little Creek Pkwy
A 1 Spafford Pl 2 Fullerton Av 3 Spafford Rd
159B
159A
158
157
RAND McNALLY

1:24,000
1 in. = 2000 ft.
0 0.25 0.5
miles

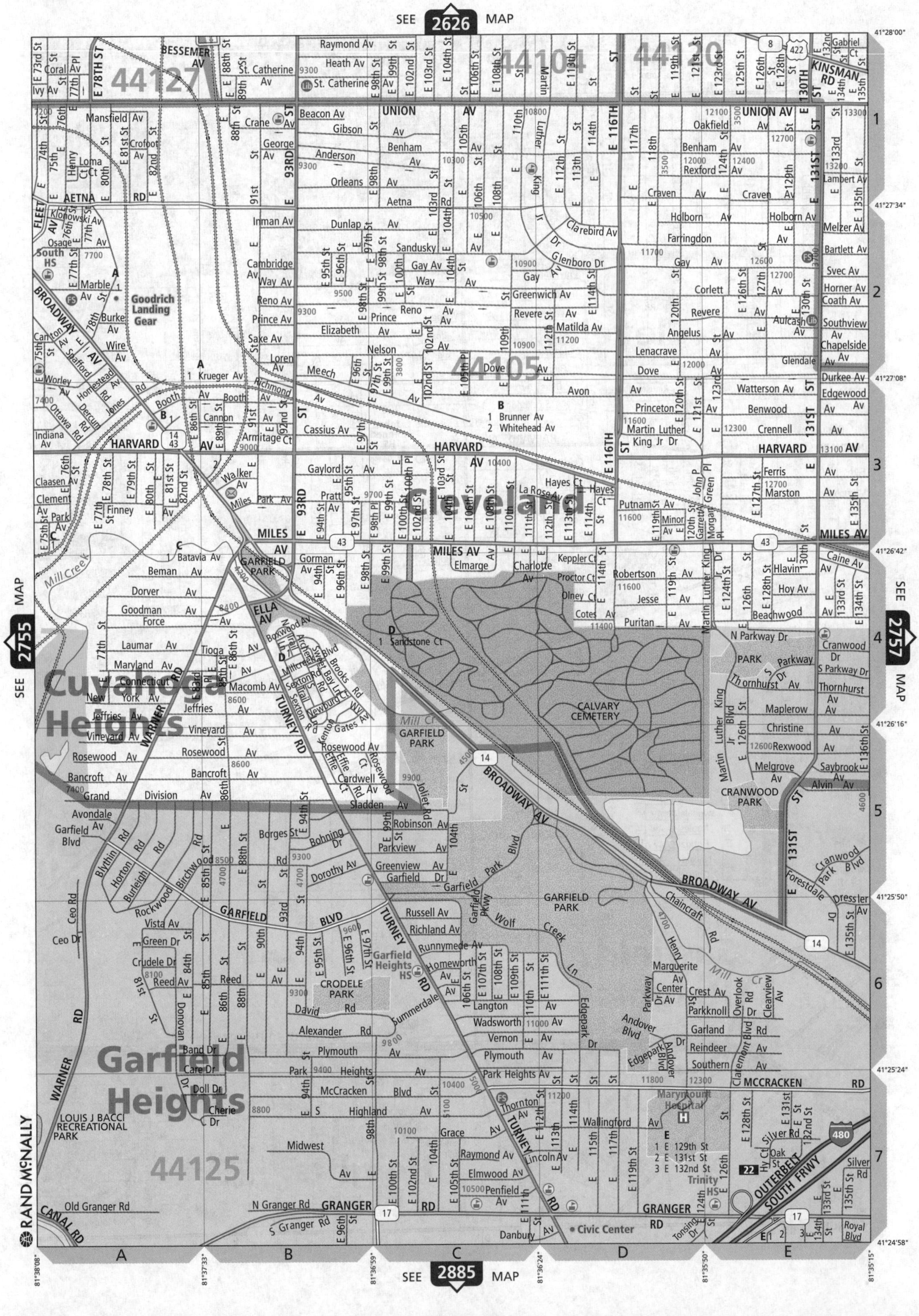
SEE 2626 MAP
SEE 2885 MAP
SEE 2755 MAP
SEE 2757 MAP
44127
44104
44120
44105
44125
Cleveland
Cuyahoga Heights
Garfield Heights
UNION AV
HARVARD AV
MILES AV
BROADWAY AV
TURNEY RD
GARFIELD BLVD
MCCRACKEN RD
GRANGER RD
WARNER RD
KINSMAN RD
E 93RD ST
E 116TH ST
131ST ST
E 78TH ST
ELLA AV
CALVARY CEMETERY
GARFIELD PARK
CRANWOOD PARK
CRODELE PARK
Garfield Heights HS
South HS
Trinity HS
Marymount Hospital
Goodrich Landing Gear
LOUIS J BACCI RECREATIONAL PARK
Civic Center
OUTERBELT SOUTH FRWY
Mill Creek
Wolf Creek
Old Granger Rd
CANAL RD
A 1 Krueger Av
B 1 Brunner Av 2 Whitehead Av
C 1 Batavia Av
D 1 Sandstone Ct
E 1 E 129th St 2 E 131st St 3 E 132nd St
41°28'00"
41°27'34"
41°27'08"
41°26'42"
41°26'16"
41°25'50"
41°25'24"
41°24'58"
81°38'08"
81°37'33"
81°36'59"
81°36'24"
81°35'50"
81°35'15"
RAND McNALLY

1:24,000
1 in. = 2000 ft.
0 0.25 0.5
miles

SEE 2627 MAP

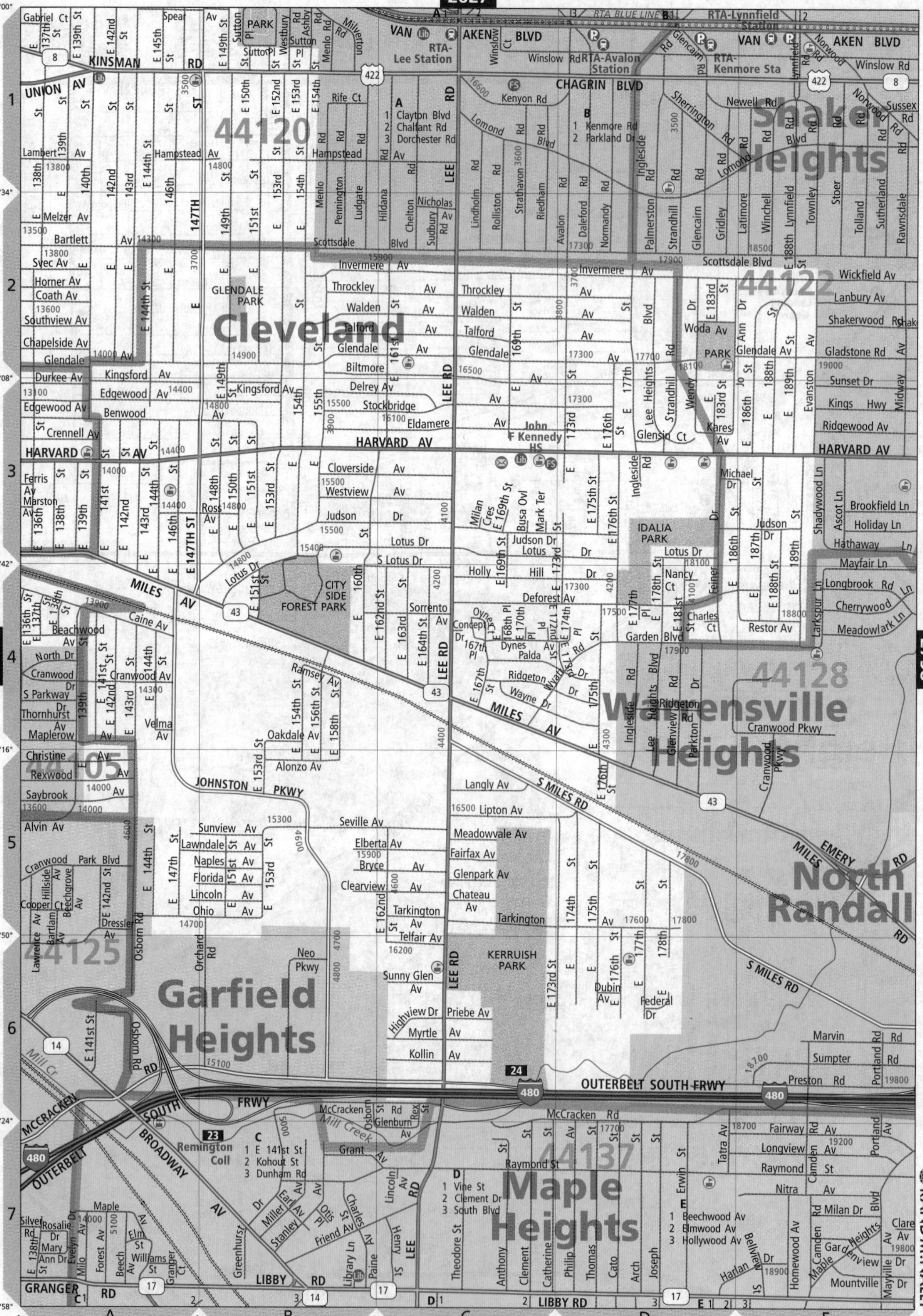
41°28'00"
41°27'34"
41°27'08"
41°26'42"
41°26'16"
41°25'50"
41°25'24"
41°24'58"
44120
44122
44128
44105
44125
44137
Cleveland
Shaker Heights
Warrensville Heights
North Randall
Garfield Heights
Maple Heights
KINSMAN RD
UNION AV
VAN AKEN BLVD
RTA-Lee Station
RTA-Avalon Station
RTA-Kenmore Sta
RTA BLUE LINE
RTA-Lynnfield Station
CHAGRIN BLVD
Scottsdale Blvd
HARVARD AV
MILES AV
S MILES RD
EMERY RD
JOHNSTON PKWY
LEE RD
E 147TH ST
OUTERBELT SOUTH FRWY
McCracken Rd
BROADWAY AV
LIBBY RD
GRANGER RD
GLENDALE PARK
CITY SIDE FOREST PARK
IDALIA PARK
KERRUISH PARK
John F Kennedy HS
Remington Coll
A
1 Clayton Blvd
2 Chalfant Rd
3 Dorchester Rd
B
1 Kenmore Rd
2 Parkland Dr
C
1 E 141st St
2 Kohout St
3 Dunham Rd
D
1 Vine St
2 Clement Dr
3 South Blvd
E
1 Beechwood Av
2 Elmwood Av
3 Hollywood Av
A B C D E
1 2 3 4 5 6 7
81°35'15"
81°34'40"
81°34'06"
81°33'31"
81°32'56"
81°32'22"

SEE 2756 MAP
SEE 2758 MAP
SEE 2886 MAP

RAND McNALLY

1:24,000
1 in. = 2000 ft.
0 0.25 0.5
miles

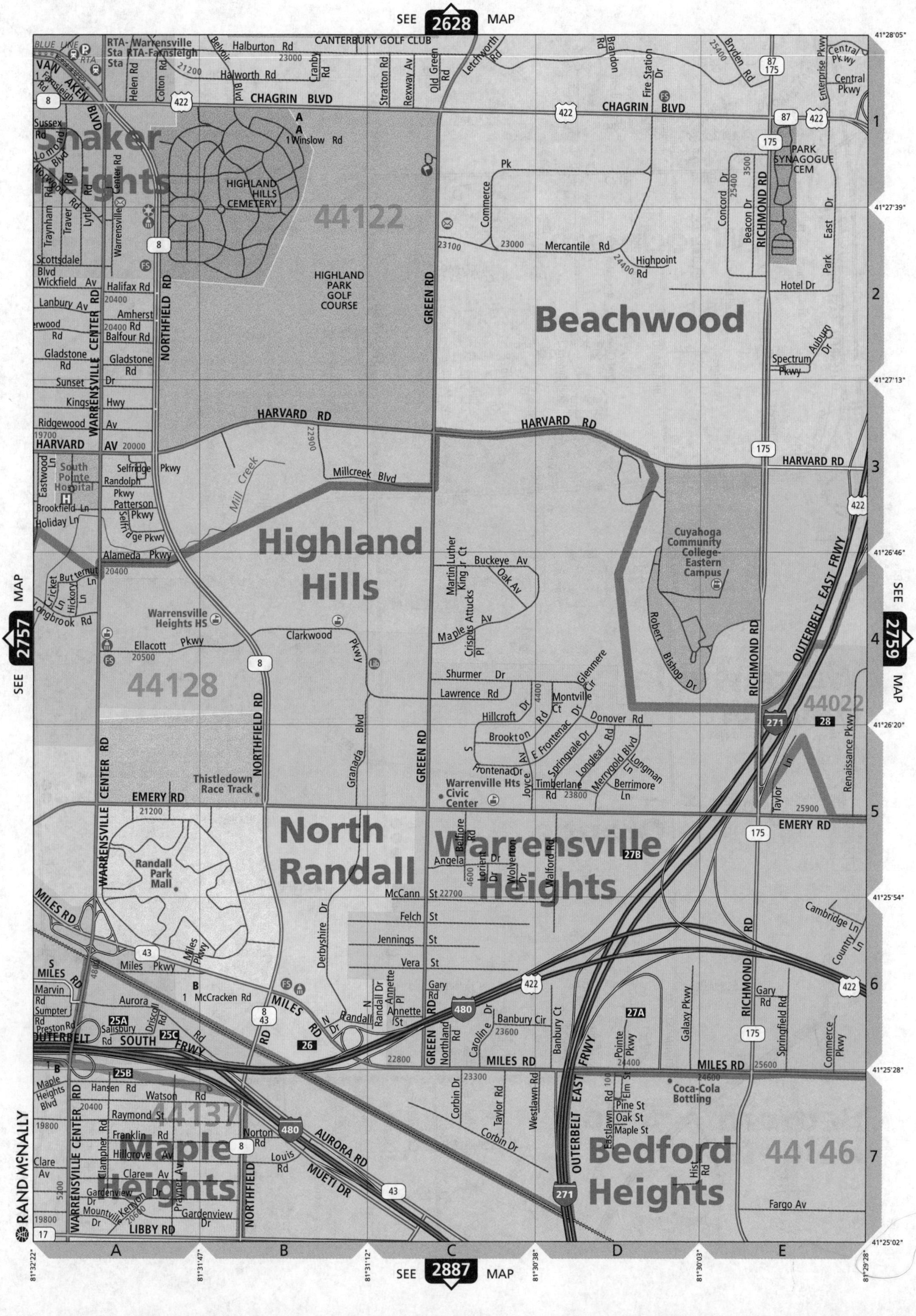
SEE 2628 MAP
SEE 2887 MAP
SEE 2757 MAP
SEE 2759 MAP
Shaker Heights
Beachwood
Highland Hills
North Randall
Warrensville Heights
Maple Heights
Bedford Heights
44122
44128
44022
44137
44146
CANTERBURY GOLF CLUB
HIGHLAND HILLS CEMETERY
HIGHLAND PARK GOLF COURSE
PARK SYNAGOGUE CEM
Cuyahoga Community College-Eastern Campus
Warrensville Heights HS
South Pointe Hospital
Thistledown Race Track
Randall Park Mall
Warrensville Hts Civic Center
Coca-Cola Bottling
RTA-Warrensville Sta
RTA-Farnsleigh Sta
BLUE LINE
VAN AKEN BLVD
CHAGRIN BLVD
Halburton Rd
Halworth Rd
Belvoir Blvd
Cranby Rd
Stratton Rd
Rexway Av
Old Green Rd
Letchworth Rd
Brandon Rd
Fire Station Dr
Bryden Rd
Enterprise Pkwy
Central Pkwy
Winslow Rd
Commerce Pk
Mercantile Rd
Highpoint Rd
Concord Dr
Beacon Dr
RICHMOND RD
Park East Dr
Hotel Dr
Spectrum Pkwy
Auburn Dr
Sussex Rd
Lomond Blvd
Norwood Rd
Traynham Rd
Traver Rd
Lytle Rd
Center Rd
Warrensville Rd
Scottsdale Blvd
Wickfield Av
Halifax Rd
Lanbury Av
Amherst Rd
Balfour Rd
Gladstone Rd
Sunset Dr
Kings Hwy
Ridgewood Av
HARVARD AV
HARVARD RD
NORTHFIELD RD
WARRENSVILLE CENTER RD
GREEN RD
Millcreek Blvd
Mill Creek
Eastwood Ln
Selfridge Pkwy
Randolph Pkwy
Patterson Pkwy
Brookfield Ln
Holiday Ln
Alameda Pkwy
Cricket Ln
Butternut Ln
Hickory Ln
Longbrook Rd
Ellacott Pkwy
Clarkwood Pkwy
Granada Blvd
Martin Luther King Jr Ct
Buckeye Av
Oak Av
Maple Av
Crispus Attucks Pl
Robert Bishop Dr
Shurmer Dr
Lawrence Rd
Glenmere Cir
Montville Ct
Hillcroft Dr
Brookton Rd
E Frontenac Dr
Donover Rd
Springvale Dr
Longleaf Rd
Merrygold Blvd
Longman Ln
Frontenac Dr
Joyce Av
Timberlane Rd
Berrimore Ln
Taylor Ln
Renaissance Pkwy
OUTERBELT EAST FRWY
EMERY RD
Bellflore Rd
Angela
Lorient Dr
Wolverton Dr
Walford Rd
McCann St
Felch St
Jennings St
Vera St
Derbyshire Dr
Cambridge Ln
Country Ln
MILES RD
S MILES RD
Miles Pkwy
Marvin Rd
Sumpter Rd
Preston Rd
Aurora Rd
Salisbury Rd
Driscoll Rd
McCracken Rd
OUTERBELT SOUTH FRWY
Randall Dr
N Randall Dr
Annette Pl
Annette St
Gary Rd
Northland Rd
Caroline Dr
Banbury Cir
Banbury Ct
Pointe Pkwy
Galaxy Pkwy
Springfield Rd
Commerce Pkwy
Maple Heights Blvd
Hansen Rd
Watson Rd
Raymond St
Franklin Rd
Hillgrove Av
Clare Av
Gardenview Dr
Mountville Dr
Kenyon Dr
Clampher Rd
Prayner Av
LIBBY RD
Norton Rd
Louis Rd
AURORA RD
MUETI DR
Corbin Dr
Taylor Rd
Westlawn Rd
Eastlawn Rd
Elm St
Pine St
Oak St
Maple St
Hist Rd
Fargo Av
A B C D E
1 2 3 4 5 6 7
RAND McNALLY

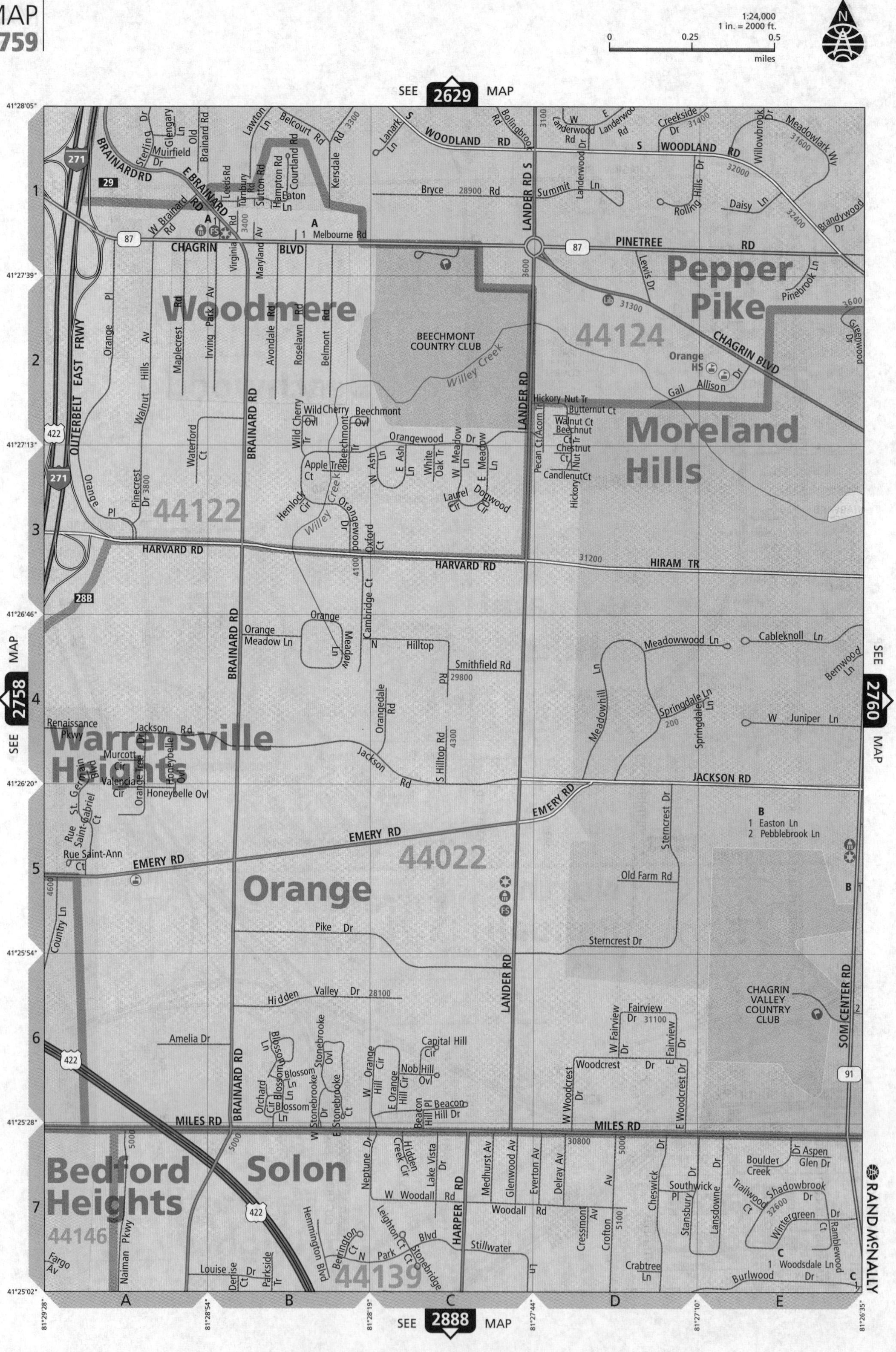
1:24,000
1 in. = 2000 ft.
0 0.25 0.5
miles
SEE 2629 MAP
SEE 2888 MAP
SEE 2758 MAP
SEE 2760 MAP
Woodmere
Pepper Pike
Moreland Hills
Warrensville Heights
Orange
Bedford Heights
Solon
44122
44124
44022
44146
44139
BEECHMONT COUNTRY CLUB
CHAGRIN VALLEY COUNTRY CLUB
Willey Creek
CHAGRIN BLVD
PINETREE RD
WOODLAND RD
HARVARD RD
HIRAM TR
JACKSON RD
EMERY RD
MILES RD
BRAINARD RD
E BRAINARD RD
LANDER RD
LANDER RD S
SOM CENTER RD
HARPER RD
OUTERBELT EAST FRWY
Orange HS
B
1 Easton Ln
2 Pebblebrook Ln
C
1 Woodsdale Ln
A
1 Melbourne Rd
RAND McNALLY

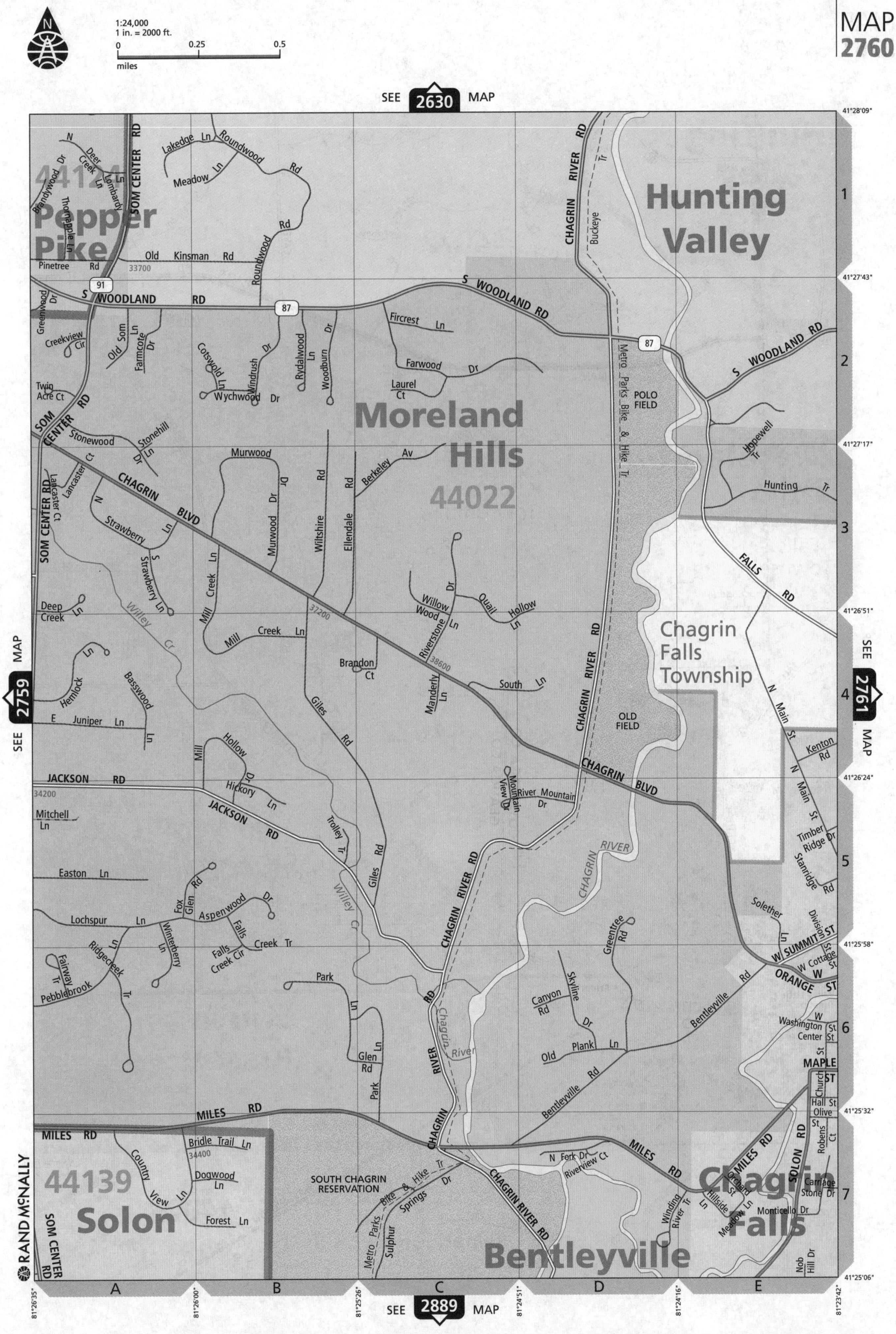
N
1:24,000
1 in. = 2000 ft.
0
0.25
0.5
miles
SEE 2630 MAP
SEE 2759 MAP
SEE 2761 MAP
SEE 2889 MAP
41°28'09"
41°27'43"
41°27'17"
41°26'51"
41°26'24"
41°25'58"
41°25'32"
41°25'06"
81°26'35"
81°26'00"
81°25'26"
81°24'51"
81°24'16"
81°23'42"
A
B
C
D
E
1
2
3
4
5
6
7
44124
Pepper Pike
Hunting Valley
Moreland Hills
44022
Chagrin Falls Township
44139
Solon
Bentleyville
Chagrin Falls
SOM CENTER RD
N Deer Creek Ln
Brandywood Dr
Thornapple Ln
Lombardy Ln
Lakedge Ln
Roundwood Rd
Meadow Ln
Old Kinsman Rd
Pinetree Rd
33700
91
S WOODLAND RD
87
Greenwood Dr
Creekview Cir
Old Som Ln
Farmcote Dr
Cotswold Ln
Windrush Dr
Rydalwood Ln
Woodburn Dr
Fircrest Ln
Farwood Dr
Laurel Ct
Wychwood Dr
Twin Acre Ct
SOM CENTER RD
Stonewood Dr
Stonehill Ln
Lancaster Ct
CHAGRIN BLVD
N Strawberry Ln
S Strawberry Ln
Murwood Dr
Wiltshire Rd
Ellendale Rd
Berkeley Av
CHAGRIN RIVER RD
Buckeye Tr
Metro Parks Bike & Hike Tr
POLO FIELD
Hopewell Tr
Hunting Tr
FALLS RD
Willow Wood Dr
Quail Hollow Ln
Riverstone Ln
Deep Creek Ln
Willey Cr
Mill Creek Ln
37200
Brandon Ct
38600
South Ln
Manderly Ln
OLD FIELD
N Main St
Kenton Rd
Hemlock Ln
Basswood Ln
E Juniper Ln
Giles Rd
Mill Hollow Dr
Hickory Ln
JACKSON RD
34200
Mitchell Ln
Trolley Tr
Mountain View Dr
River Mountain Dr
CHAGRIN BLVD
Timber Ridge Dr
Stanridge Rd
CHAGRIN RIVER
Easton Ln
Fox Glen Rd
Aspenwood Dr
Lochspur Ln
Winterberry Ln
Falls Creek Tr
Falls Creek Cir
Ridgecreek Tr
Fairway Tr
Pebblebrook
Solether
Division St
W SUMMIT ST
W Cottage St
ORANGE ST
Greentree Rd
Skyline Dr
Canyon Rd
Park Ln
Glen Rd
Glen Ln
Chagrin River
Bentleyville Rd
Old Plank Ln
W Washington St
Center St
MAPLE ST
Church St
Hall St
Olive St
MILES RD
Bridle Trail Ln
34400
Country View Ln
Dogwood Ln
Forest Ln
SOUTH CHAGRIN RESERVATION
Sulphur Springs Dr
N Fork Dr
Riverview Ct
Winding River Tr
Hillside Ln
Orchard St
Meadow Ln
Robens Ct
SOLON RD
Carriage Stone Dr
Monticello Dr
Nob Hill Dr
RAND McNALLY

1:24,000
1 in. = 2000 ft.
0 0.25 0.5
miles

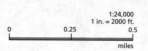

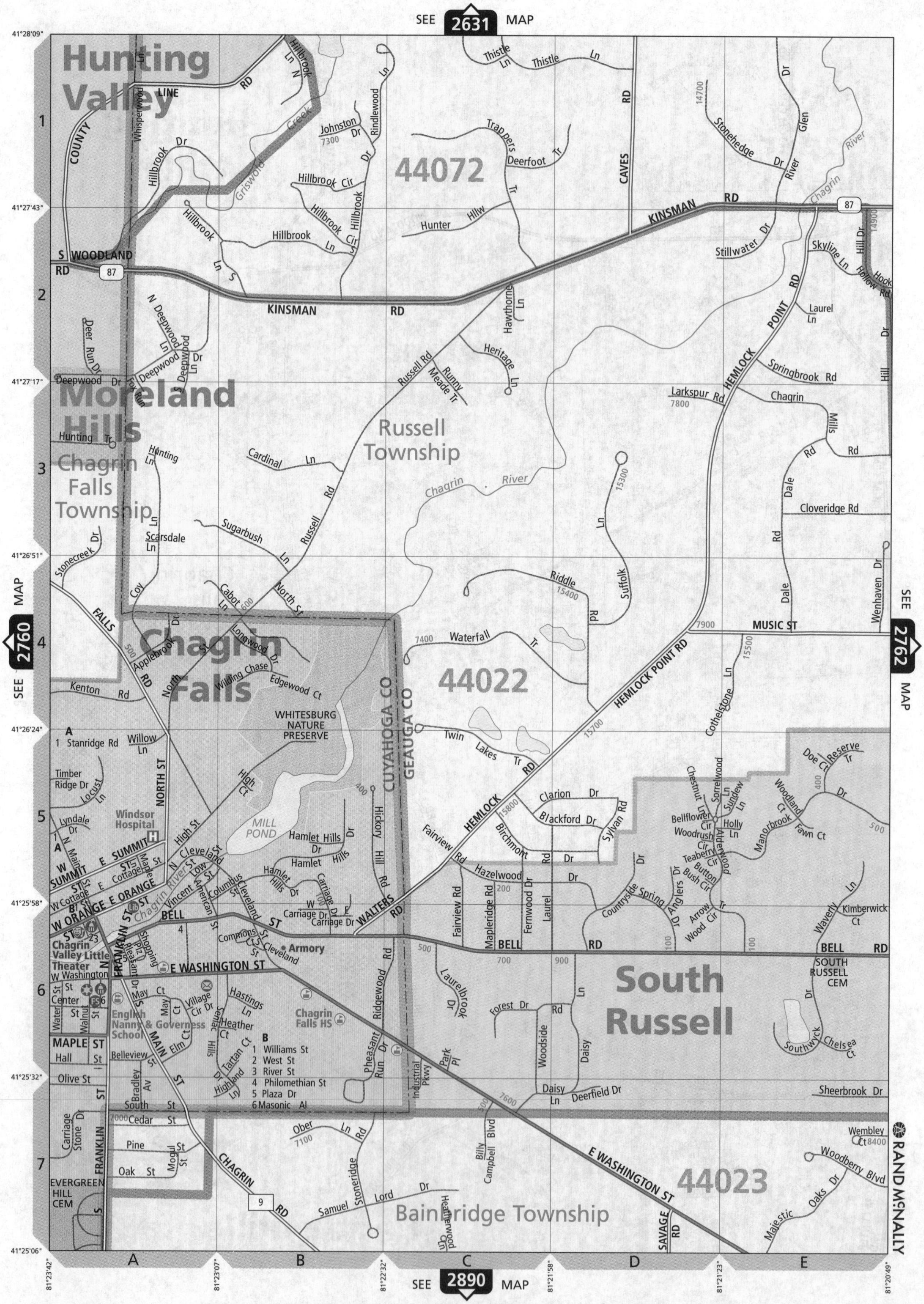
SEE 2631 MAP
SEE 2760 MAP
SEE 2762 MAP
SEE 2890 MAP
Hunting Valley
Moreland Hills
Chagrin Falls Township
Chagrin Falls
Russell Township
South Russell
Bainbridge Township
44072
44022
44023
KINSMAN RD
S WOODLAND RD
87
9
COUNTY LINE RD
CAVES RD
HEMLOCK POINT RD
MUSIC ST
BELL RD
E WASHINGTON ST
CHAGRIN RD
NORTH ST
FALLS RD
FRANKLIN ST
S MAIN ST
W ORANGE
E ORANGE ST
W SUMMIT ST
E SUMMIT ST
MAPLE ST
WALTERS RD
SAVAGE RD
CUYAHOGA CO
GEAUGA CO
Chagrin River
Griswold Creek
Hillbrook Dr
Hillbrook Ln N
Hillbrook Cir
Hillbrook Ln S
Johnston Dr
Rindlewood Dr
Thistle Ln
Trappers Tr
Deerfoot Tr
Hunter Hllw
Stonehedge Dr
River Glen Dr
Stillwater Dr
Skyline Ln
Hollow Rd
Hook Hill Dr
Laurel Ln
Hawthorne Ln
Heritage Ln
Russell Rd
Runny Meade Tr
Springbrook Rd
Larkspur Rd
Chagrin Mills Rd
Dale Rd
Cloveridge Rd
Wenhaven Dr
N Deepwood Ln
S Deepwood Ln
Deepwood Dr
Deer Run Dr
Fox Run
Hunting Tr
Hunting Ln
Cardinal Ln
Sugarbush Ln
Scarsdale Ln
Stonecreek Dr
Coy
Cabot Ln
North St
Riddle Rd
Suffolk Ln
Waterfall Tr
Applebrook Rd
Longwood Dr
Wilding Chase
Edgewood Ct
Kenton Rd
WHITESBURG NATURE PRESERVE
Twin Lakes Tr
Cothelstone Ln
Doe Ct
Reserve Tr
Willow Ln
Stanridge Rd
Timber Ridge Dr
Locust Ln
Lyndale Dr
Windsor Hospital
High St
High Ct
MILL POND
Hamlet Hills Dr
Hickory Hill Rd
Clarion Dr
Blackford Dr
Sylvan Rd
Birchmont Rd
Fairview Rd
Hazelwood Dr
Chestnut Ln
Sorrelwood Ln
Sundew Ln
Woodland Ct
Manorbrook Dr
Fawn Ct
Bellflower Cir
Woodrush Cir
Holly Ln
Alderwood Tr
Teaberry Cir
Burton Bush Cir
Countryside Dr
Spring Dr
Anglers Dr
Arrow Wood Cir
Waverly Ln
Kimberwick Ct
Cleveland St
N Cleveland St
Low St
American St
Columbus St
Vincent St
Commons Ct
Armory
Carriage Dr
W Carriage Dr
Fairview Rd
Mapleridge Rd
Fernwood Dr
Laurel
Laurelbrook Dr
Forest Dr
Woodside Rd
Daisy Ln
Deerfield Dr
SOUTH RUSSELL CEM
Southwyck Dr
Chelsea Ct
Sheerbrook Dr
Wembley Ct
Woodberry Blvd
Oaks Dr
Majestic
Chagrin Valley Little Theater
W Washington St
Center St
Water St
Walnut St
May Ct
Village Cir Dr
Hastings Ln
Chagrin Falls HS
English Nanny & Governess School
Heather Ct
Seneca Hills
Tartan Ct
Highland Dr
Elm Ct
Belleview St
Bradley Av
Ridgewood Rd
Pheasant Run Dr
Industrial Pkwy
Park Pl
Hall St
Olive St
South St
Cedar St
Pine St
Oak St
Mogul St
Carriage Stone Dr
EVERGREEN HILL CEM
Ober Ln
Ober Rd
Stoneridge
Samuel Lord Dr
Heatherwood Ln
Billy Campbell Blvd
A
1 Stanridge Rd
B
1 Williams St
2 West St
3 River St
4 Philomethian St
5 Plaza Dr
6 Masonic Al
RAND McNALLY

SEE 2632 MAP

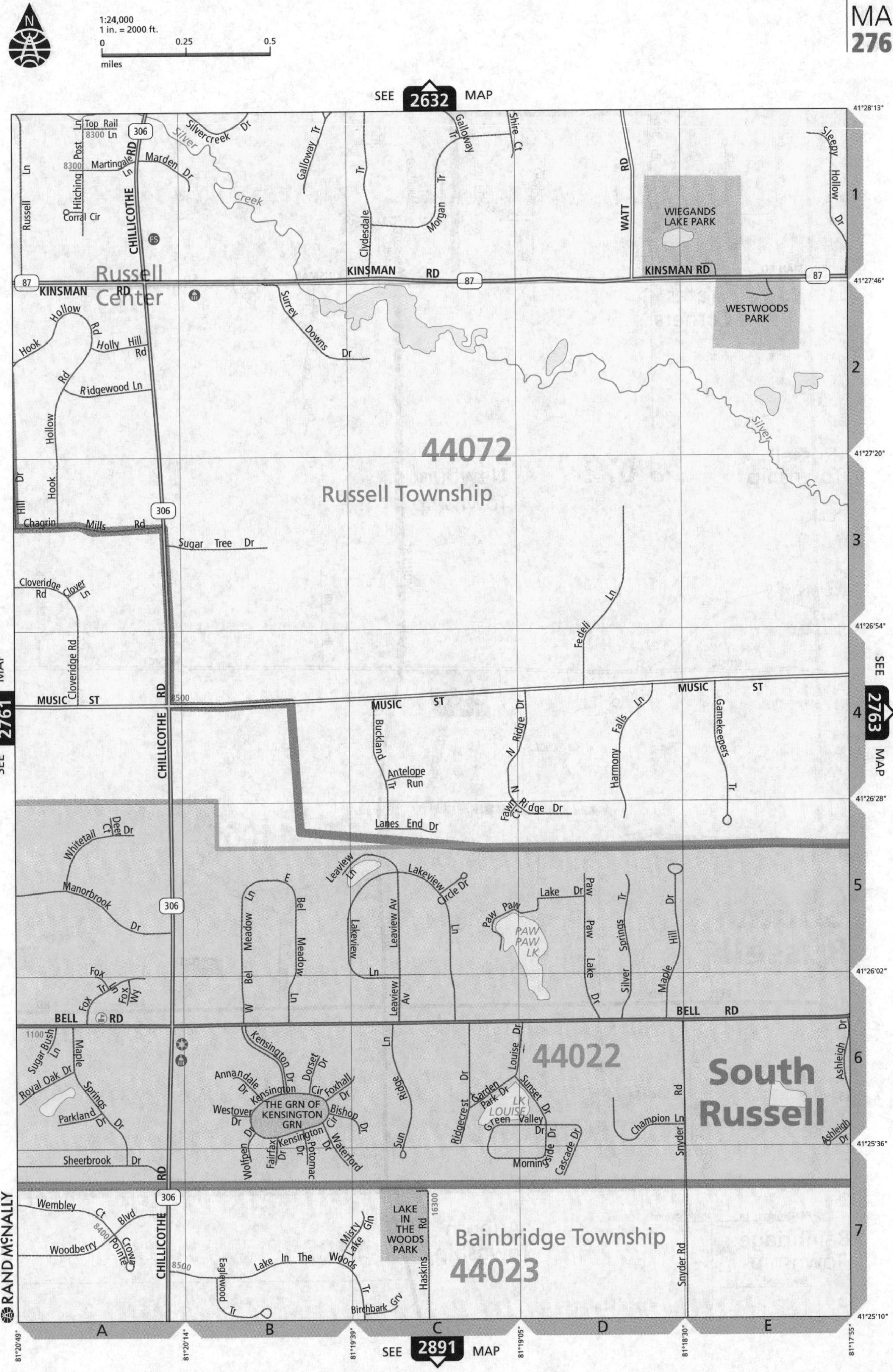
N
1:24,000
1 in. = 2000 ft.
0 0.25 0.5
miles
Russell Center
Russell Township
44072
44022
44023
South Russell
Bainbridge Township
WIEGANDS LAKE PARK
WESTWOODS PARK
LAKE IN THE WOODS PARK
THE GRN OF KENSINGTON GRN
PAW PAW LK
LK LOUISE
KINSMAN RD
KINSMAN RD
CHILLICOTHE RD
WATT RD
MUSIC ST
BELL RD
Chagrin Mills Rd
Silvercreek Dr
Silver Creek
Top Rail Ln
8300
Hitching Post Ln
Martingale Ln
Marden Dr
Russell Ln
Corral Cir
Galloway Tr
Clydesdale Tr
Morgan Tr
Shire Ct
Sleepy Hollow Dr
Surrey Downs Dr
Hook Hollow Rd
Holly Hill Rd
Ridgewood Ln
Hill Dr
Sugar Tree Dr
Cloveridge Rd
Clover Ln
Fedeli Ln
Buckland Tr
Antelope Run
Lanes End Dr
N Ridge Dr
Fawn Ct
Harmony Falls Ln
Gamekeepers Tr
Whitetail Deer Dr
Manorbrook Dr
Leaview Ln
Lakeview Circle Dr
Lakeview Ln
Leaview Av
E Bel Meadow Ln
W Bel Meadow Ln
Paw Paw Lake Dr
Silver Springs Tr
Maple Hill Dr
Fox Tr
Fox Wy
Sugar Bush Ln
Royal Oak Dr
Maple Springs Dr
Parkland Dr
Sheerbrook Dr
Kensington Dr
Annandale Dr
Dorset Dr
Foxhall Dr
Kensington Cir
Bishop Dr
Westover Dr
Wolfpen Dr
Fairfax Dr
Potomac Dr
Waterford Dr
Sun Ridge Ln
Ridgecrest Dr
Garden Park Dr
Louise Dr
Sunset Dr
Green Valley Dr
Morningside Dr
Cascade Dr
Champion Ln
Snyder Rd
Ashleigh Dr
Wembley Ct
Crown Pointe Blvd
Woodberry
8400
Lake In The Woods Tr
Eaglewood Tr
Misty Lake Gln
Birchbark Grv
Haskins Rd
16300
8500
1100
87
306
41°28'13"
41°27'46"
41°27'20"
41°26'54"
41°26'28"
41°26'02"
41°25'36"
41°25'10"
81°20'49"
81°20'14"
81°19'39"
81°19'05"
81°18'30"
81°17'55"
A B C D E
1 2 3 4 5 6 7
RAND McNALLY

SEE 2761 MAP

SEE 2763 MAP

SEE 2891 MAP

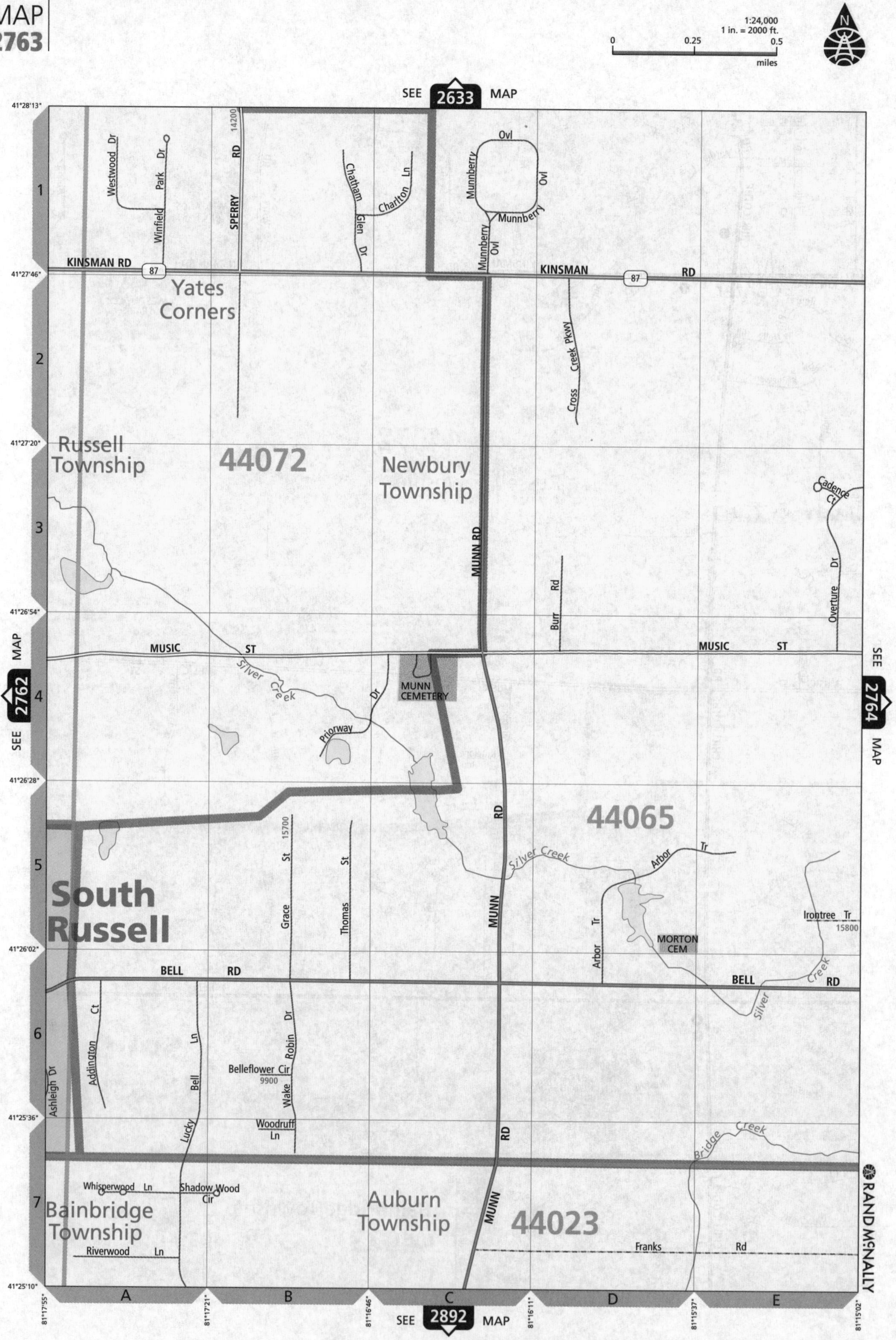
1:24,000
1 in. = 2000 ft.
0
0.25
0.5
miles
SEE 2633 MAP
SEE 2762 MAP
SEE 2764 MAP
SEE 2892 MAP
KINSMAN RD
87
KINSMAN
RD
Yates
Corners
Westwood Dr
Winfield
Park
Dr
SPERRY
RD
14200
Chatham
Glen
Dr
Charlton Ln
Munnberry
Ovl
Munnberry Ovl
Cross Creek Pkwy
Russell
Township
44072
Newbury
Township
MUNN RD
Cadence Ct
Overture Dr
Burr Rd
MUSIC
ST
MUSIC
ST
Silver Creek
MUNN
CEMETERY
Priorway Dr
44065
Silver Creek
Arbor
Tr
Arbor Tr
15700
Grace St
Thomas St
MUNN RD
South
Russell
Irontree Tr
15800
MORTON
CEM
BELL
RD
BELL
RD
Silver Creek
Addington Ct
Ashleigh Dr
Lucky Bell Ln
Robin Dr
Belleflower Cir
9900
Wake
Woodruff Ln
Bridge Creek
Whisperwood Ln
Shadow Wood Cir
Bainbridge
Township
Auburn
Township
MUNN RD
44023
Riverwood Ln
Franks Rd
A
B
C
D
E
1
2
3
4
5
6
7
41°28'13"
41°27'46"
41°27'20"
41°26'54"
41°26'28"
41°26'02"
41°25'36"
41°25'10"
81°17'55"
81°17'21"
81°16'46"
81°16'11"
81°15'37"
81°15'02"
RAND McNALLY

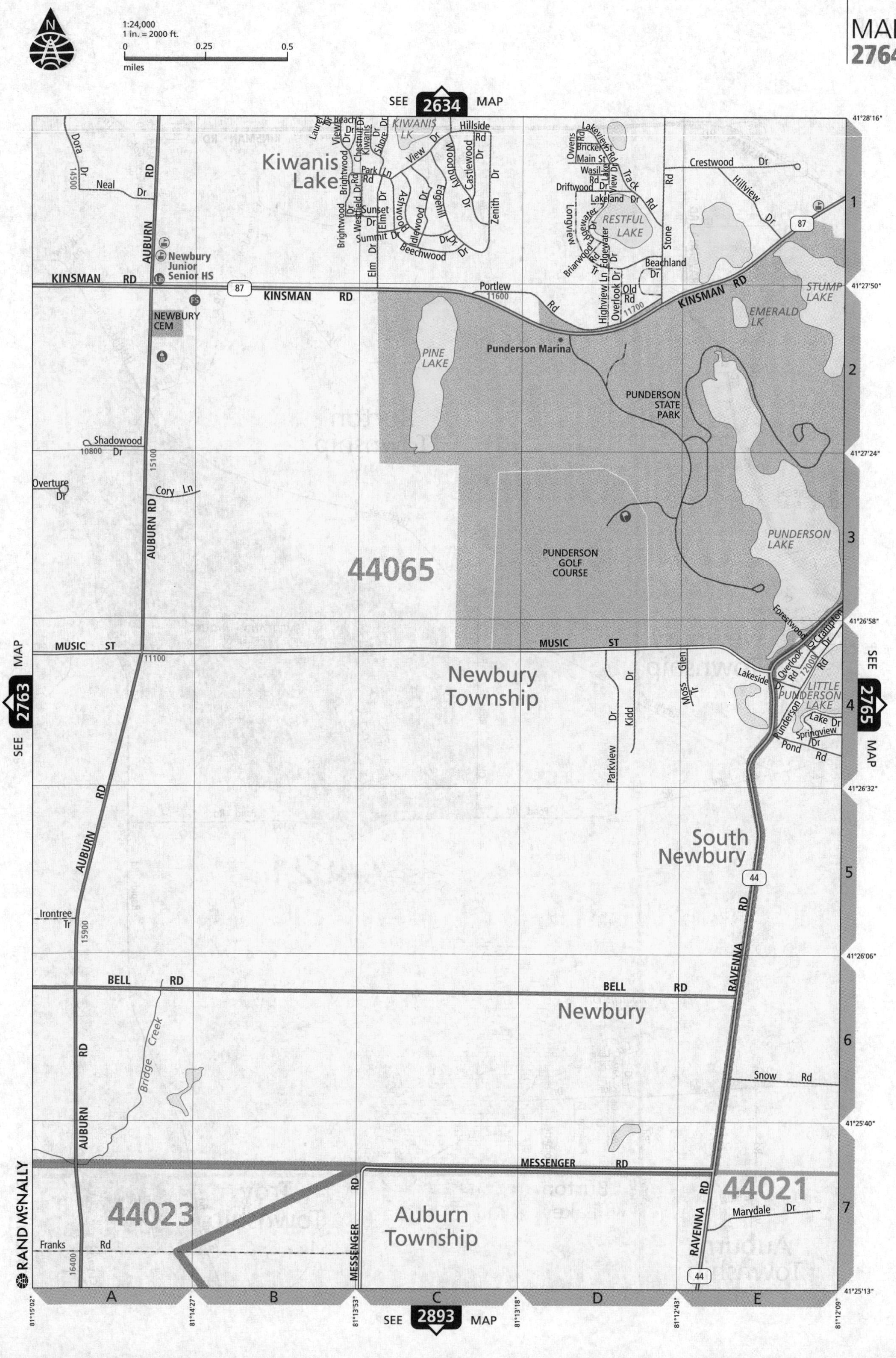
1:24,000
1 in. = 2000 ft.
0
0.25
0.5
miles
SEE 2634 MAP
SEE 2763 MAP
SEE 2765 MAP
SEE 2893 MAP
Kiwanis Lake
KIWANIS LK
Hillside Rd
Castlewood Dr
Woodbury Dr
Zenith Dr
Edgehill Dr
Idlewood Dr
Ashwood Dr
Beechwood Dr
Summit Dr
Sunset Dr
Brightwood Dr
Westfield Dr
Park Ln
Elm Dr
Chestnut Dr
Kiwanis Shore Dr
Laurel Dr
Beach Dr
View Dr
Dora Dr
Neal Dr
14500
AUBURN RD
Newbury Junior Senior HS
KINSMAN RD
87
NEWBURY CEM
Portlew Rd
11600
Lakeview Rd
Owens
Bricker
Main St
Wasil Rd
Driftwood Dr
Lakeland Dr
Longview
Edgewater Dr
Briarwood Tr
Highview Ln
Overlook Dr
Old Rd
11700
Track Rd
RESTFUL LAKE
Stone Rd
Beachland Dr
Crestwood Dr
Hillview Dr
STUMP LAKE
EMERALD LK
Punderson Marina
PINE LAKE
PUNDERSON STATE PARK
PUNDERSON GOLF COURSE
PUNDERSON LAKE
Shadowood Dr
10800
15100
Overture Dr
Cory Ln
44065
MUSIC ST
11100
Newbury Township
Forestwood
Crampton
Overlook Rd
12000
Lakeside
LITTLE PUNDERSON LAKE
Punderson Rd
Lake Dr
Springview Dr
Pond Rd
Parkview Dr
Kidd Dr
Moss Glen Tr
South Newbury
44
RAVENNA RD
Irontree Tr
15900
BELL RD
Newbury
Bridge Creek
Snow Rd
MESSENGER RD
44021
44023
Auburn Township
Marydale Dr
Franks Rd
16400
A
B
C
D
E
1
2
3
4
5
6
7
41°28'16"
41°27'50"
41°27'24"
41°26'58"
41°26'32"
41°26'06"
41°25'40"
41°25'13"
81°15'02"
81°14'27"
81°13'53"
81°13'18"
81°12'43"
81°12'09"
RAND McNALLY

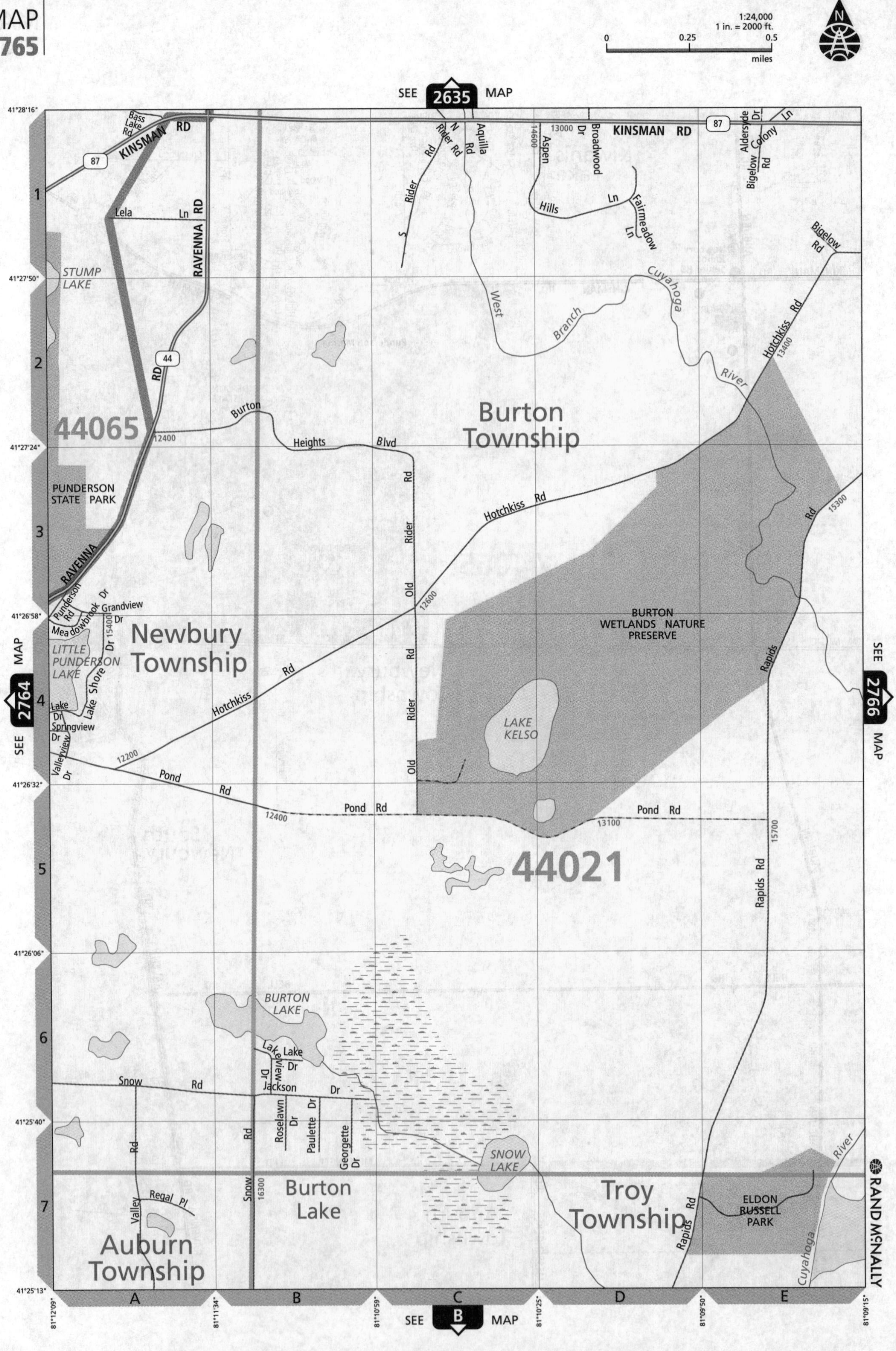
1:24,000
1 in. = 2000 ft.
0 0.25 0.5
miles
N
SEE 2635 MAP
SEE 2764 MAP
SEE 2766 MAP
SEE B MAP
KINSMAN RD
87
Bass Lake Rd
RAVENNA RD
44
Lela Ln
STUMP LAKE
44065
PUNDERSON STATE PARK
Burton Heights Blvd
12400
N Rider Rd
S Rider Rd
Aquilla Rd
Aspen
14600
13000
Broadwood Dr
Hills Ln
Fairmeadow Ln
Aldersyde Dr
Bigelow Colony Rd
Bigelow Rd
Ln
Cuyahoga
West Branch
River
Hotchkiss Rd
13400
Burton Township
Old Rider Rd
12600
15300
BURTON WETLANDS NATURE PRESERVE
Punderson Rd
Meadowbrook Dr
Grandview Dr
15400
LITTLE PUNDERSON LAKE
Lake Shore Dr
Lake Dr
Springview Dr
Valleyview Dr
Newbury Township
Hotchkiss Rd
12200
Pond Rd
12400
13100
LAKE KELSO
Rapids Rd
15700
44021
BURTON LAKE
Lakeview Dr
Lake Dr
Jackson Dr
Snow Rd
Roselawn Dr
Paulette Dr
Georgette Dr
16300
SNOW LAKE
Burton Lake
Valley Rd
Regal Pl
Auburn Township
Troy Township
ELDON RUSSELL PARK
RAND McNALLY
41°28'16"
41°27'50"
41°27'24"
41°26'58"
41°26'32"
41°26'06"
41°25'40"
41°25'13"
81°12'09"
81°11'34"
81°10'59"
81°10'25"
81°09'50"
81°09'15"
1
2
3
4
5
6
7
A
B
C
D
E

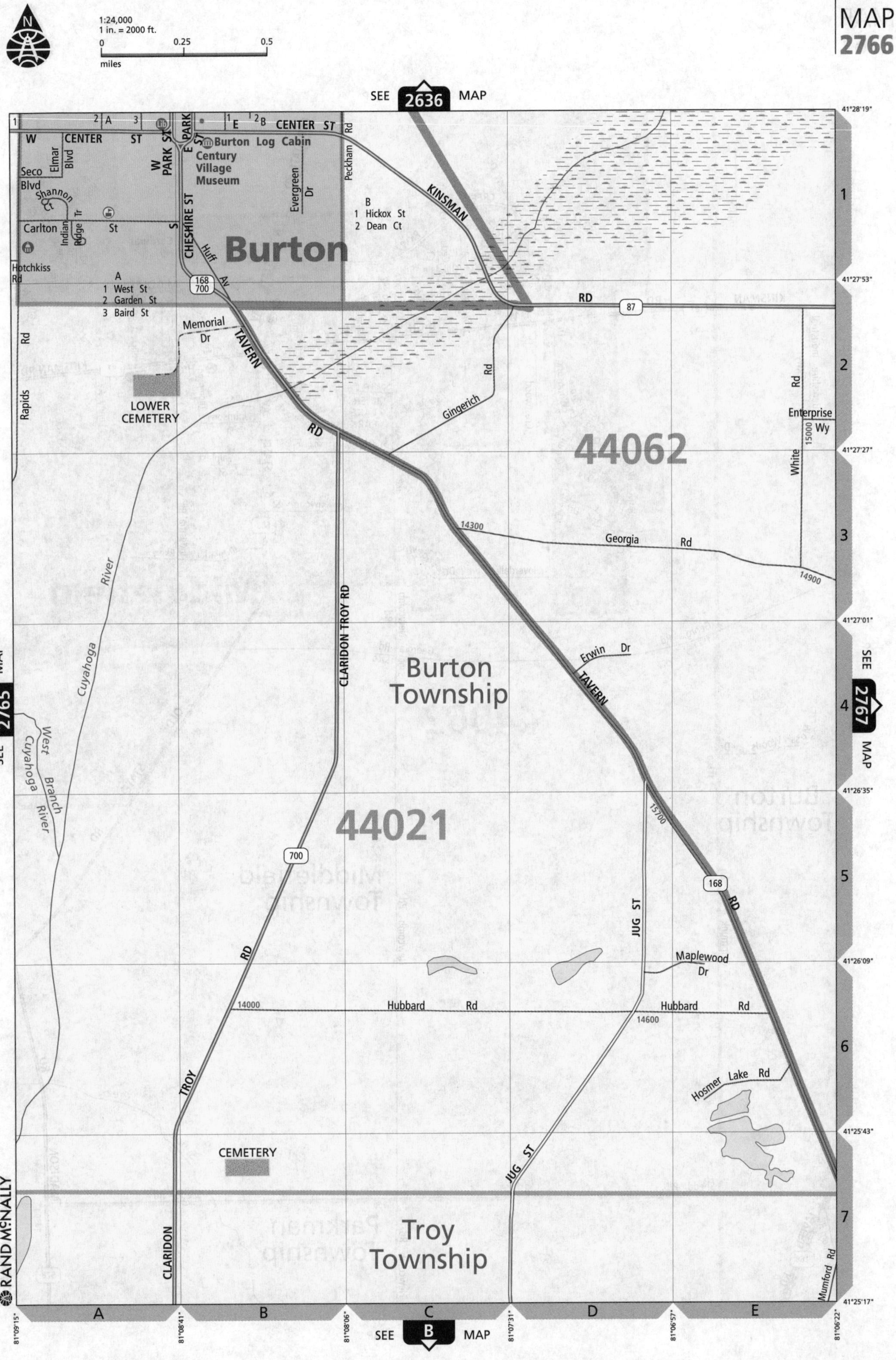
1:24,000
1 in. = 2000 ft.
0
0.25
0.5
miles
SEE 2636 MAP
SEE 2765 MAP
SEE 2767 MAP
SEE B MAP
W CENTER ST
CENTER ST
W PARK ST
E PARK ST
Burton Log Cabin
Century Village Museum
Seco Blvd
Elmar Blvd
Shannon Ct
Indian Ridge Tr
Carlton St
Hotchkiss Rd
CHESHIRE ST
Huff Av
Burton
Evergreen Dr
Peckham Rd
B
1 Hickox St
2 Dean Ct
A
1 West St
2 Garden St
3 Baird St
KINSMAN RD
87
168
700
Memorial Dr
TAVERN RD
Rapids Rd
LOWER CEMETERY
Gingerich Rd
Enterprise Wy
White Rd
15000
44062
14300
Georgia Rd
14900
Cuyahoga River
West Branch Cuyahoga River
CLARIDON TROY RD
Erwin Dr
Burton Township
44021
15700
JUG ST
Maplewood Dr
14000
Hubbard Rd
14600
Hosmer Lake Rd
TROY RD
CEMETERY
CLARIDON
Troy Township
Mumford Rd
RAND McNALLY
41°28'19"
41°27'53"
41°27'27"
41°27'01"
41°26'35"
41°26'09"
41°25'43"
41°25'17"
81°09'15"
81°08'41"
81°08'06"
81°07'31"
81°06'57"
81°06'22"
A
B
C
D
E
1
2
3
4
5
6
7

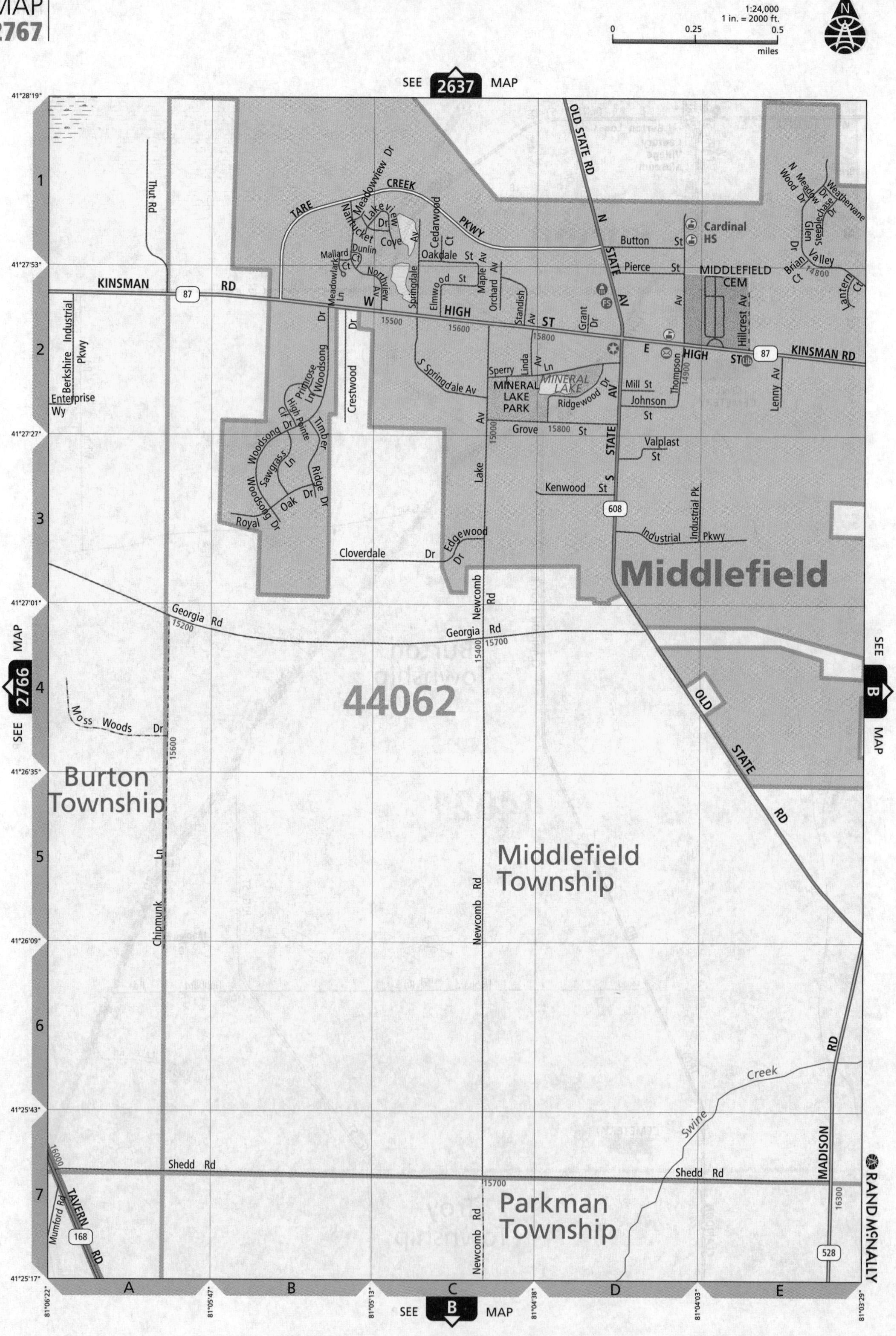
1:24,000
1 in. = 2000 ft.
0
0.25
0.5
miles
N
SEE 2637 MAP
SEE 2766 MAP
SEE B MAP
SEE B MAP
Middlefield
44062
Burton Township
Middlefield Township
Parkman Township
KINSMAN RD
87
W HIGH ST
E HIGH ST
KINSMAN RD
OLD STATE RD
N STATE AV
S STATE AV
608
OLD STATE RD
TARE CREEK PKWY
Meadowview Dr
Lakeview Dr
Nantucket
Cove
Mallard Ct
Dunlin Ct
Northview Av
Meadowlark Ln
Cedarwood Ct
Oakdale St
Elmwood St
Maple Av
Orchard Av
Springdale
Standish Av
Grant Dr
Button St
Pierce St
Cardinal HS
MIDDLEFIELD CEM
Hillcrest Av
Thompson
Lenny Av
N Meadow Wood Dr
Weathervane Dr
Steeplechase Dr
Glen Valley Dr
Brian Ct
Lantern Ct
Thut Rd
Berkshire Industrial Pkwy
Enterprise Wy
Crestwood Dr
Primrose Ln
Woodsong Dr
High Pointe Cir
Timber Ridge Dr
Sawgrass Ln
Oak Dr
Royal Woodsong Dr
S Springdale Av
Sperry
Linda Av
Ln
MINERAL LAKE PARK
MINERAL LAKE
Ridgewood Dr
Mill St
Johnson St
Grove St
Valplast St
Kenwood St
Lake Av
Industrial Pk
Industrial Pkwy
Cloverdale Dr
Edgewood Dr
Newcomb Rd
Georgia Rd
Georgia Rd
Moss Woods Dr
Chipmunk Ln
Shedd Rd
Shedd Rd
Swine Creek
MADISON RD
528
TAVERN RD
Mumford Rd
168
15500
15600
15800
15800
15000
15200
15400
15700
15600
15700
14800
14900
16000
16300
41°28'19"
41°27'53"
41°27'27"
41°27'01"
41°26'35"
41°26'09"
41°25'43"
41°25'17"
81°06'22"
81°05'47"
81°05'13"
81°04'38"
81°04'03"
81°03'29"
A
B
C
D
E
1
2
3
4
5
6
7
RAND McNALLY

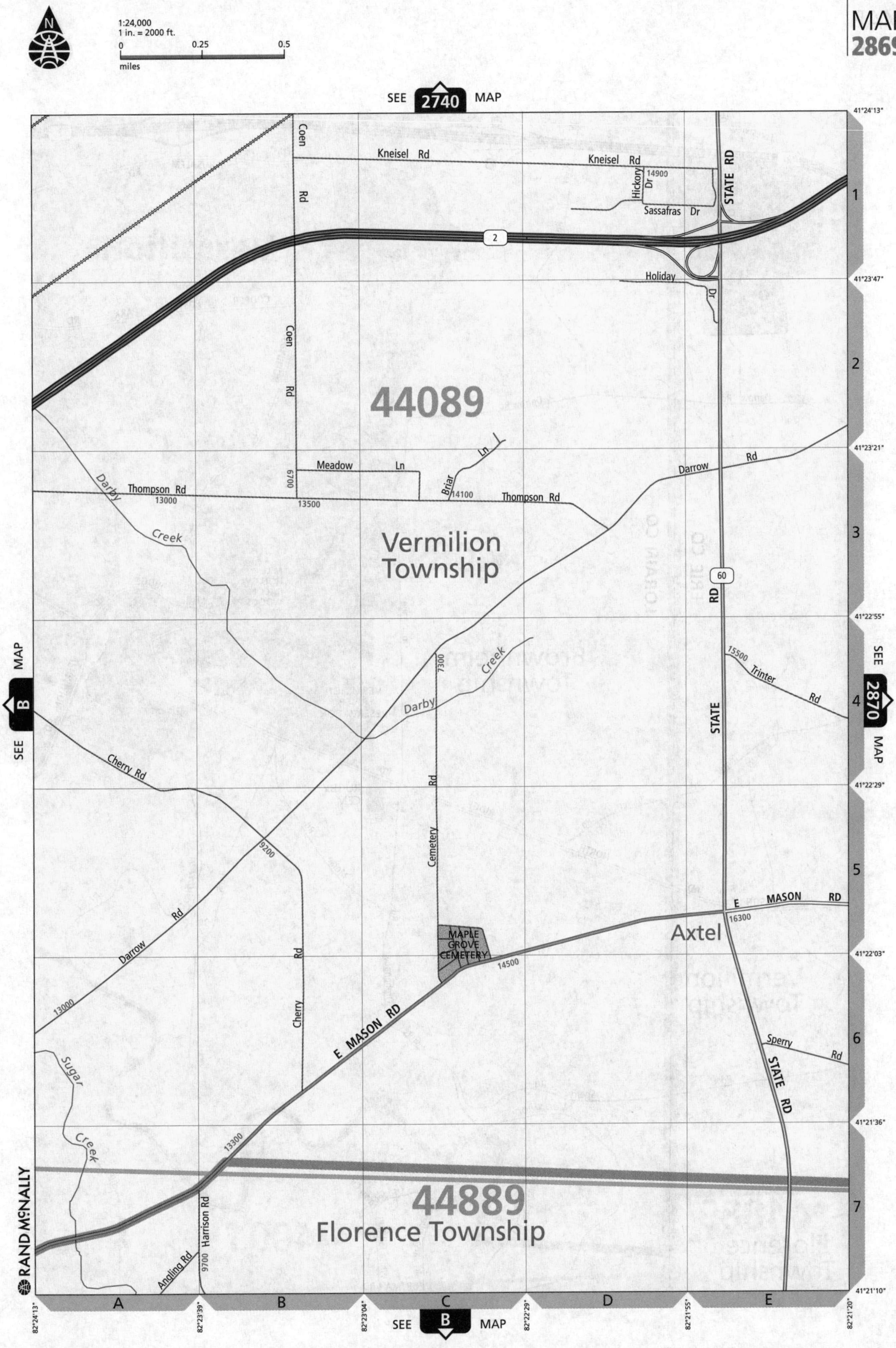
1:24,000
1 in. = 2000 ft.
0 0.25 0.5
miles
SEE 2740 MAP
SEE B MAP
SEE 2870 MAP
SEE B MAP
44089
Vermilion Township
44889
Florence Township
Axtel
Kneisel Rd
Coen Rd
Hickory Dr
14900
Sassafras Dr
STATE RD
2
Holiday Dr
Meadow Ln
Briar Ln
6700
Thompson Rd
13000
13500
14100
Darrow Rd
Darby Creek
60
RD
7300
15500
Trinter Rd
STATE
Cherry Rd
9200
Cemetery Rd
E MASON RD
16300
MAPLE GROVE CEMETERY
14500
Cherry Rd
Darrow Rd
13000
Sperry Rd
STATE RD
Sugar Creek
13300
Harrison Rd
9700
Angling Rd
RAND McNALLY
A
B
C
D
E
1
2
3
4
5
6
7
41°24'13"
41°23'47"
41°23'21"
41°22'55"
41°22'29"
41°22'03"
41°21'36"
41°21'10"
82°24'13"
82°23'39"
82°23'04"
82°22'29"
82°21'55"
82°21'20"

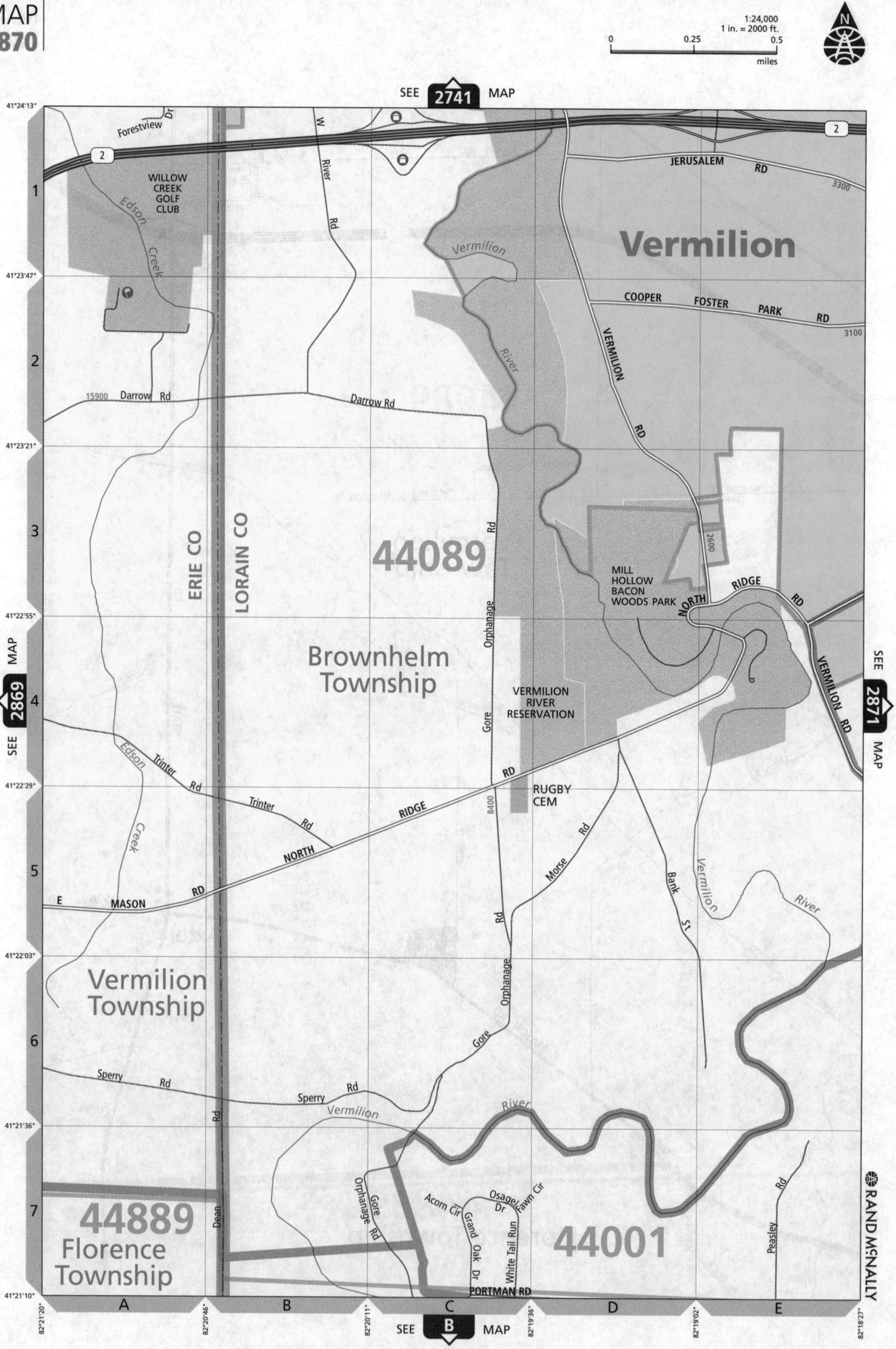
1:24,000
1 in. = 2000 ft.
0 0.25 0.5
miles
SEE 2741 MAP
SEE 2869 MAP
SEE 2871 MAP
SEE B MAP
Forestview Dr
WILLOW CREEK GOLF CLUB
Edson Creek
W River Rd
JERUSALEM RD
3300
Vermilion
COOPER FOSTER PARK RD
3100
VERMILION RD
Vermilion River
15900 Darrow Rd
Darrow Rd
ERIE CO
LORAIN CO
44089
Orphanage Rd
2600
MILL HOLLOW BACON WOODS PARK
NORTH RIDGE RD
Brownhelm Township
VERMILION RIVER RESERVATION
Gore Rd
Trinter Rd
RUGBY CEM
8400
NORTH RIDGE RD
Morse Rd
Bank St
E MASON RD
Vermilion Township
Sperry Rd
Vermilion River
Dean Rd
44889
Florence Township
Gore Orphanage Rd
Acorn Cir
Grand Oak Dr
Osage Dr
Fawn Cir
White Tail Run
44001
PORTMAN RD
Peasley Rd
RAND McNALLY
A B C D E
1 2 3 4 5 6 7
41°24'13"
41°23'47"
41°23'21"
41°22'55"
41°22'29"
41°22'03"
41°21'36"
41°21'10"
82°21'20"
82°20'46"
82°20'11"
82°19'36"
82°19'02"
82°18'27"

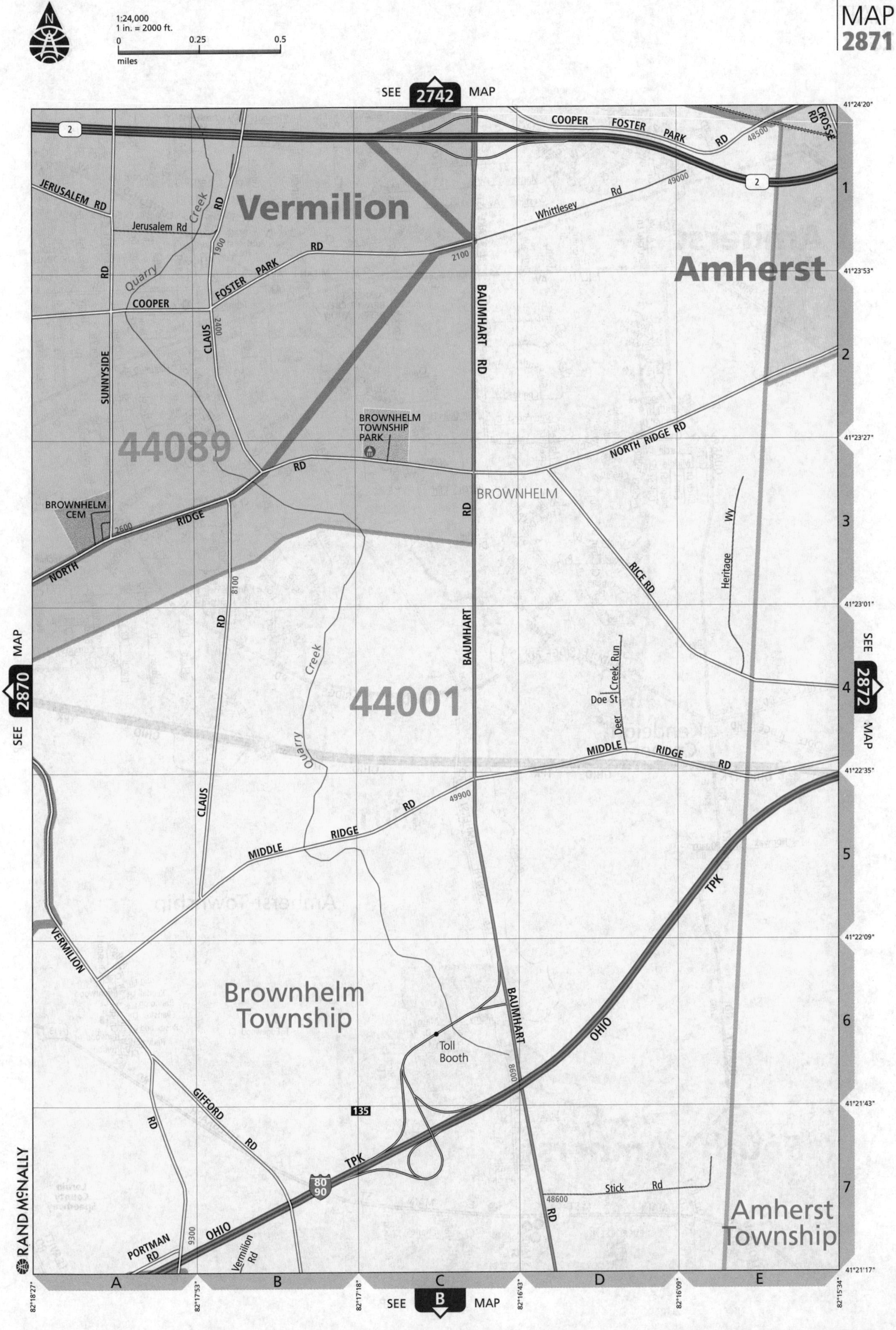
1:24,000
1 in. = 2000 ft.
0 0.25 0.5
miles
SEE 2742 MAP
SEE 2870 MAP
SEE 2872 MAP
SEE B MAP
Vermilion
Amherst
44089
44001
Brownhelm Township
Amherst Township
BROWNHELM
BROWNHELM TOWNSHIP PARK
BROWNHELM CEM
COOPER FOSTER PARK RD
CROSSE RD
JERUSALEM RD
Jerusalem Rd
Whittlesey Rd
Quarry Creek
CLAUS RD
SUNNYSIDE RD
BAUMHART RD
NORTH RIDGE RD
RICE RD
Heritage Wy
Creek Run
Doe St
Deer
MIDDLE RIDGE RD
VERMILION RD
GIFFORD RD
PORTMAN RD
Vermilion Rd
OHIO TPK
Toll Booth
Stick Rd
135
80
90
2
48500
49000
2100
1900
2400
2600
8100
49900
8600
48600
9300
1
2
3
4
5
6
7
A
B
C
D
E
41°24'20"
41°23'53"
41°23'27"
41°23'01"
41°22'35"
41°22'09"
41°21'43"
41°21'17"
82°18'27"
82°17'53"
82°17'18"
82°16'43"
82°16'09"
82°15'34"
RAND McNALLY

1:24,000
1 in. = 2000 ft.
0 0.25 0.5
miles

SEE 2743 MAP

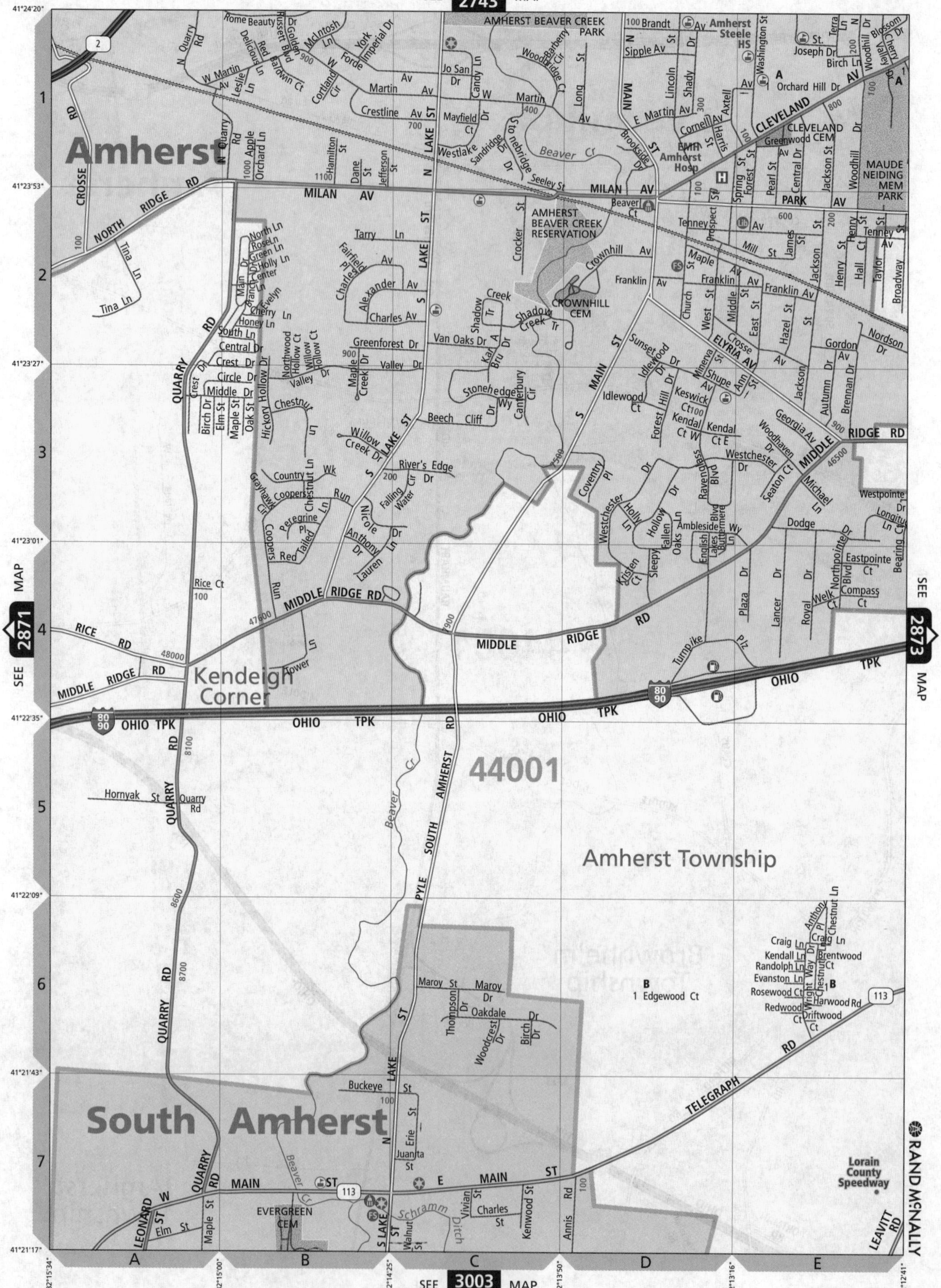
Amherst
South Amherst
Kendeigh Corner
Amherst Township
44001
AMHERST BEAVER CREEK PARK
AMHERST BEAVER CREEK RESERVATION
CROWNHILL CEM
CLEVELAND CEM
MAUDE NEIDING MEM PARK
EVERGREEN CEM
Amherst Steele HS
EMH Amherst Hosp
Lorain County Speedway
MILAN AV
NORTH RIDGE RD
CROSSE RD
QUARRY RD
N LAKE ST
S LAKE ST
S MAIN ST
MAIN ST
CLEVELAND AV
ELYRIA AV
MIDDLE RIDGE RD
RICE RD
OHIO TPK
SOUTH AMHERST RD
PYLE SOUTH AMHERST RD
TELEGRAPH RD
LEAVITT RD
LEONARD ST
W MAIN ST
E MAIN ST
Hornyak St
Quarry Rd
Tina Ln
Rice Ct
Martin Av
W Martin Av
Crestline Av
Tarry Ln
Alexander Av
Charles Av
Greenforest Dr
Van Oaks Dr
Valley Dr
Beech Cliff Dr
River's Edge Dr
Tenney Av
Franklin Av
Crownhill Av
Park Av
Seeley St
Westchester Dr
Dodge
Plaza Dr
Lancer Dr
Royal Dr
Northpointe Dr
Eastpointe Ct
Compass Ct
Westpointe Dr
Turnpike Plz
Maroy St
Maroy Dr
Oakdale Dr
Thompson Dr
Woodcrest Dr
Birch Dr
Buckeye St
Erie St
Juanita St
Charles St
Kenwood St
Vivian St
Walnut St
Annis Rd
Elm St
Maple St
Beaver Cr
Schramm Ditch
Craig Ln
Kendall Ln
Randolph Ln
Evanston Ln
Rosewood Ct
Redwood Ct
Harwood Rd
Driftwood Ct
Brentwood Ct
Chestnut Ln
1 Edgewood Ct
2
80 90
113
A B C D E
1 2 3 4 5 6 7
41°24'20" 41°23'53" 41°23'27" 41°23'01" 41°22'35" 41°22'09" 41°21'43" 41°21'17"
82°15'34" 82°15'00" 82°14'25" 82°13'50" 82°13'16" 82°12'41"

SEE 2871 MAP

SEE 2873 MAP

SEE 3003 MAP

1:24,000
1 in. = 2000 ft.
0 0.25 0.5
miles

SEE 2744 MAP

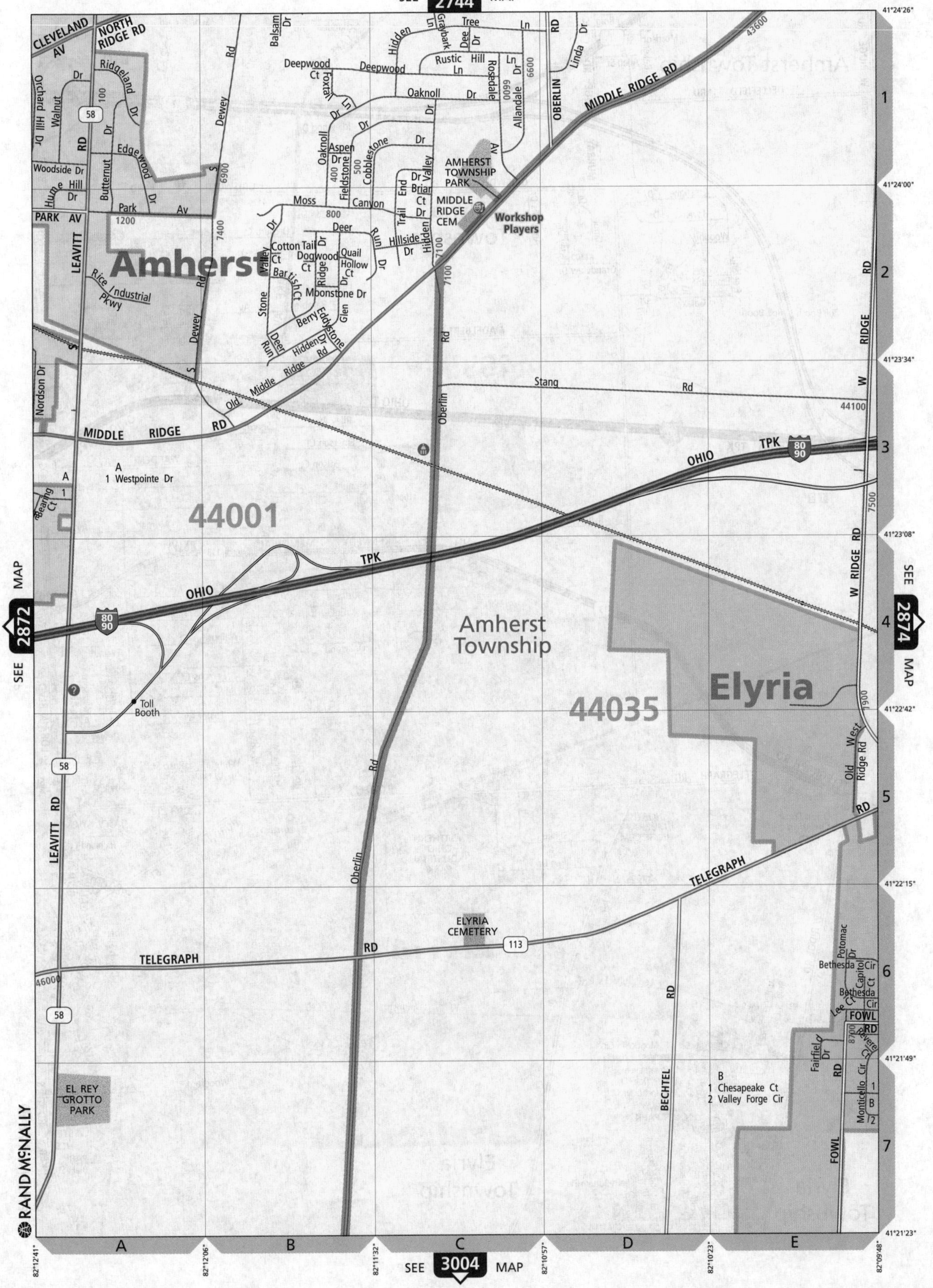

Amherst
Amherst Township
Elyria
44001
44035
CLEVELAND AV
NORTH RIDGE RD
MIDDLE RIDGE RD
Old Middle Ridge Rd
OHIO TPK
80 90
LEAVITT RD
58
Dewey Rd
Oberlin Rd
OBERLIN RD
W RIDGE RD
Old West Ridge Rd
Stang Rd
TELEGRAPH RD
113
BECHTEL RD
FOWL RD
PARK AV
Park Av
Orchard Hill Dr
Walnut Dr
Ridgeland Dr
Butternut Dr
Edgewood Dr
Woodside Dr
Hume Hill Dr
Rice Industrial Pkwy
Nordson Dr
Bearing Ct
Deepwood Ct
Deepwood
Foxtail Ln
Oaknoll Dr
Aspen Dr
Fieldstone
Cobblestone Dr
Moss
Canyon
Deer Run Dr
Valley Dr
Cotton Tail Ct
Dogwood Ct
Bartish Ct
Ridge Dr
Quail Hollow Ct
Moonstone Dr
Stone
Berry
Eddystone Dr
Glen
Deer Run
Hidden Ridge Rd
Hillside Dr
Trail End Ct
Briar Dr
Hidden Valley Dr
Hidden Ln
Graybark Ln
Tree Ln
Dee Dr
Rustic Hill Ln
Rosedale Dr
Allandale Av
Balsam Dr
Linda Dr
AMHERST TOWNSHIP PARK
MIDDLE RIDGE CEM
Workshop Players
ELYRIA CEMETERY
EL REY GROTTO PARK
Toll Booth
A
1 Westpointe Dr
B
1 Chesapeake Ct
2 Valley Forge Cir
Potomac Dr
Bethesda Cir
Capitol Ct
Bethesda Cir
Lee Ct
Revere
Fairfield Dr
Monticello Cir
100
500
400
800
1200
6900
7400
7100
6600
6600
7500
1900
44100
43600
46000
8700
1 2 3 4 5 6 7
A B C D E
41°24'26"
41°24'00"
41°23'34"
41°23'08"
41°22'42"
41°22'15"
41°21'49"
41°21'23"
82°12'41"
82°12'06"
82°11'32"
82°10'57"
82°10'23"
82°09'48"
SEE 2872 MAP
SEE 2874 MAP
RAND McNALLY

SEE 3004 MAP

1:24,000
1 in. = 2000 ft.
0 0.25 0.5
miles

SEE 2745 MAP

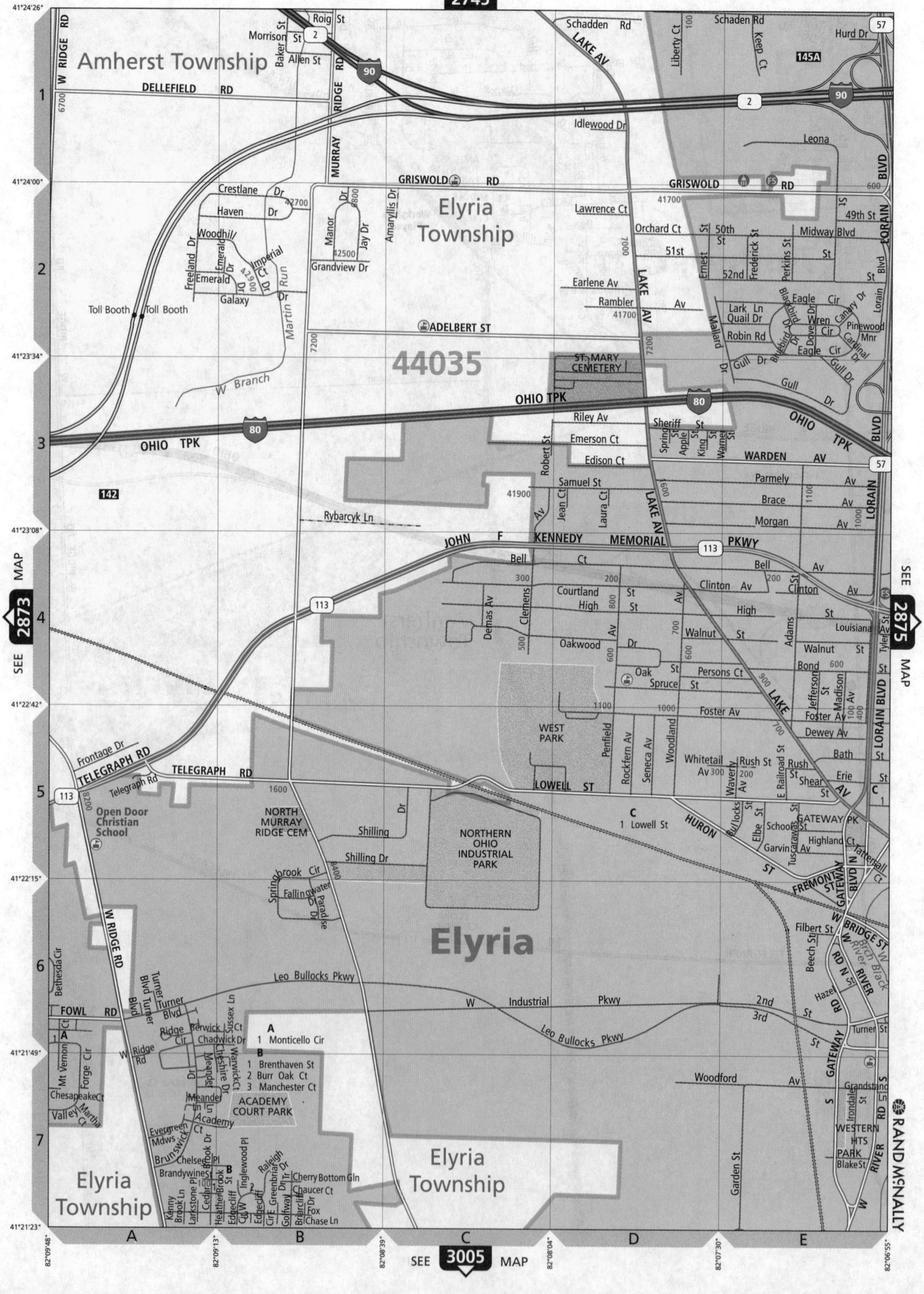
Amherst Township
Elyria Township
44035
Elyria
Elyria Township
Elyria Township
W RIDGE RD
DELLEFIELD RD
Roig St
Morrison St
Baker St
Allen St
MURRAY RIDGE RD
Schadden Rd
Schaden Rd
LAKE AV
Liberty Ct
Keep Ct
Hurd Dr
145A
Idlewood Dr
Leona
GRISWOLD RD
Crestlane Dr
Haven Dr
Woodhill Dr
Freeland Dr
Emerald Dr
Imperial Ct
Galaxy Dr
Manor Dr
Jay Dr
Amaryllis Dr
Grandview Dr
Martin Run
Toll Booth
Toll Booth
ADELBERT ST
W Branch
Lawrence Ct
Orchard Ct
50th St
51st St
52nd St
Ernest St
Frederick St
Perkins St
Midway Blvd
49th St
LORAIN BLVD
Earlene Av
Rambler Av
Lark Ln
Quail Dr
Robin Rd
Mallard Dr
Bluebird Dr
Eagle Cir
Wren Cir
Canary Dr
Pinewood Mnr
Cardinal Dr
Gull Dr
ST. MARY CEMETERY
OHIO TPK
Riley Av
Emerson Ct
Edison Ct
Sheriff St
Spring St
Apple St
King St
Warner St
WARDEN AV
Parmely Av
Brace Av
Morgan Av
Robert St Av
Samuel St
Jean Ct
Laura Ct
142
Rybarcyk Ln
JOHN F KENNEDY MEMORIAL PKWY
Bell Ct
Bell Av
Clinton Av
Courtland St
High St
Demas Av
Clemens Av
Oakwood Dr
Walnut St
Oak St
Spruce St
Persons Ct
Adams St
Louisiana Av
Tyler St
Bond St
Jefferson St
Madison Av
Foster Av
Dewey Av
Bath St
Erie St
WEST PARK
Penfield Av
Rockfern Av
Seneca Av
Woodland Av
Whitetail Av
Rush St
Waverly Av
E Railroad St
Shear St
Frontage Dr
TELEGRAPH RD
Telegraph Rd
LOWELL ST
C
1 Lowell St
HURON ST
Bullocks St
Elbe St
Schools St
Garvin Av
Tuscarawas St
GATEWAY PK
Highland Ct
Tattersall Ct
FREMONT ST
GATEWAY BLVD N
Open Door Christian School
NORTH MURRAY RIDGE CEM
Shilling Dr
Shilling Dr
NORTHERN OHIO INDUSTRIAL PARK
Springbrook Cir
Fallingwater Dr
Paradise Dr
Filbert St
W BRIDGE ST
Beech St
N RIVER RD
Hazel St
Leo Bullocks Pkwy
W Industrial Pkwy
2nd St
3rd St
Turner St
Bethesda Cir
FOWL RD
Turner Blvd
A
1 Monticello Cir
B
1 Brenthaven St
2 Burr Oak Ct
3 Manchester Ct
Berwick Ct
Chadwick Dr
Cheshire Dr
Warwick Ct
Meander Ln
ACADEMY COURT PARK
Academy
Evergreen Mdws
Brunswick
Chelsea Pl
Brandywine St
Mt Vernon Ct
Forge Cir
Chesapeake Ct
Valley
Martha Ct
Kenny Brook Ln
Larkstone Pl
Cedar Brook
Heatherbrook
Edgecliff Cir W
Inglewood Pl
Raleigh Dr
Greenbriar Dr
Golfway Dr
Briarcliff
Cherry Bottom Gln
Chaucer Ct
Fox Chase Ln
Woodford Av
Garden St
Grandstand St
Irondale St
WESTERN HTS PARK
Blake St
S RIVER RD
W RIVER RD
A
B
C
D
E
SEE 2873 MAP
SEE 2875 MAP

SEE 3005 MAP

1:24,000
1 in. = 2000 ft.
0 0.25 0.5
miles

SEE 2746 MAP

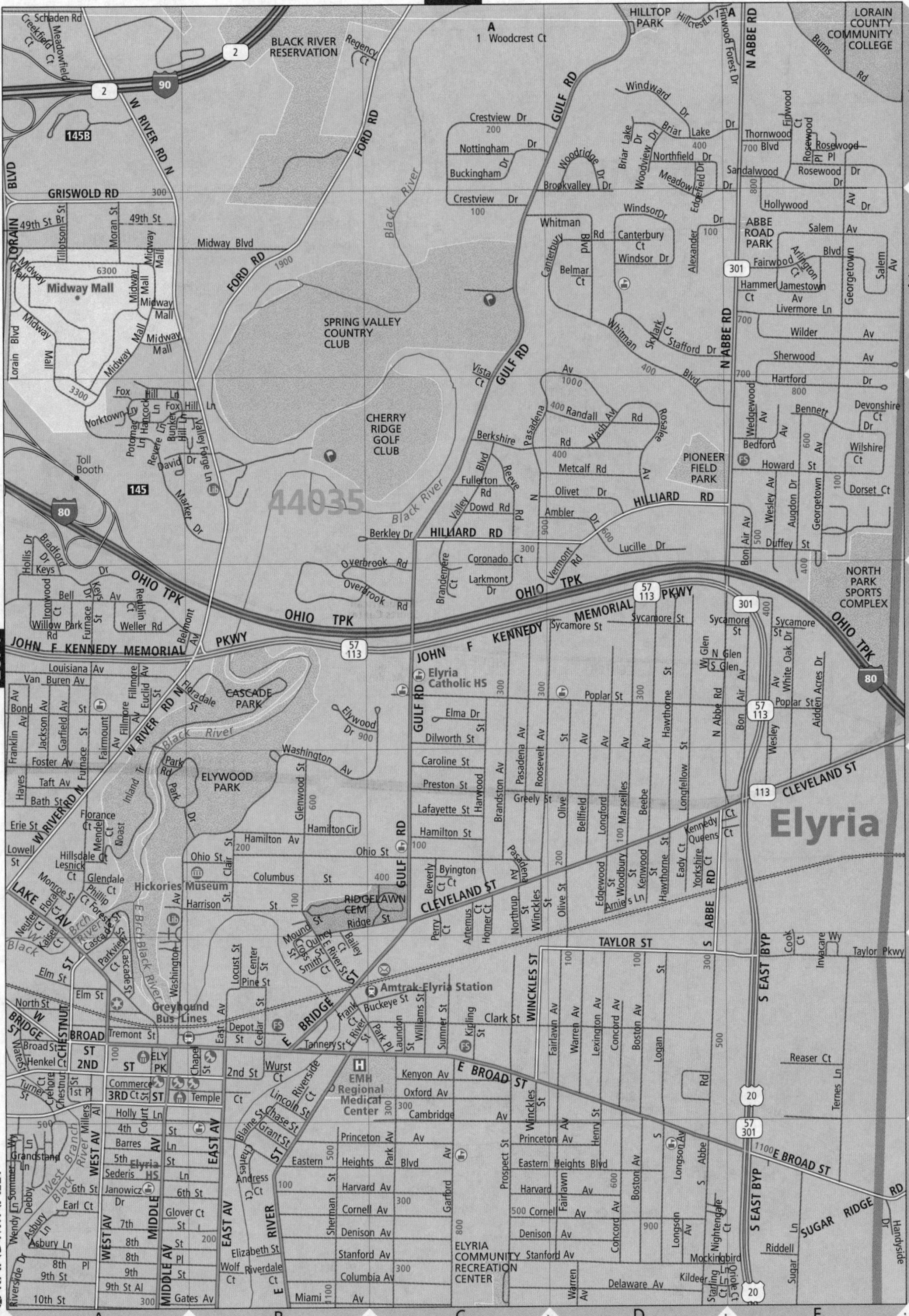
BLACK RIVER RESERVATION
HILLTOP PARK
LORAIN COUNTY COMMUNITY COLLEGE
Midway Mall
SPRING VALLEY COUNTRY CLUB
CHERRY RIDGE GOLF CLUB
44035
ABBE ROAD PARK
PIONEER FIELD PARK
NORTH PARK SPORTS COMPLEX
CASCADE PARK
ELYWOOD PARK
Hickories Museum
RIDGELAWN CEM
Amtrak-Elyria Station
Greyhound Bus Lines
Elyria Catholic HS
EMH Regional Medical Center
Elyria HS
ELYRIA COMMUNITY RECREATION CENTER
Elyria
OHIO TPK
JOHN F KENNEDY MEMORIAL PKWY
GULF RD
FORD RD
W RIVER RD N
N ABBE RD
S EAST BYP
CLEVELAND ST
E BROAD ST
HILLIARD RD
GRISWOLD RD
LORAIN BLVD
SUGAR RIDGE RD
TAYLOR ST
E BRIDGE ST
MIDDLE AV
EAST AV
WEST AV
E RIVER ST
Toll Booth
145B
145
1
2
3
4
5
6
7
A
B
C
D
E

SEE 2874 MAP

SEE 2876 MAP

SEE 3006 MAP

41°24'32" 41°24'06" 41°23'40" 41°23'14" 41°22'48" 41°22'21" 41°21'55" 41°21'29"

82°06'55" 82°06'20" 82°05'46" 82°05'11" 82°04'36" 82°04'02"

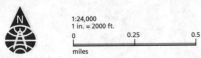

1:24,000
1 in. = 2000 ft.
0 0.25 0.5
miles

SEE 2747 MAP

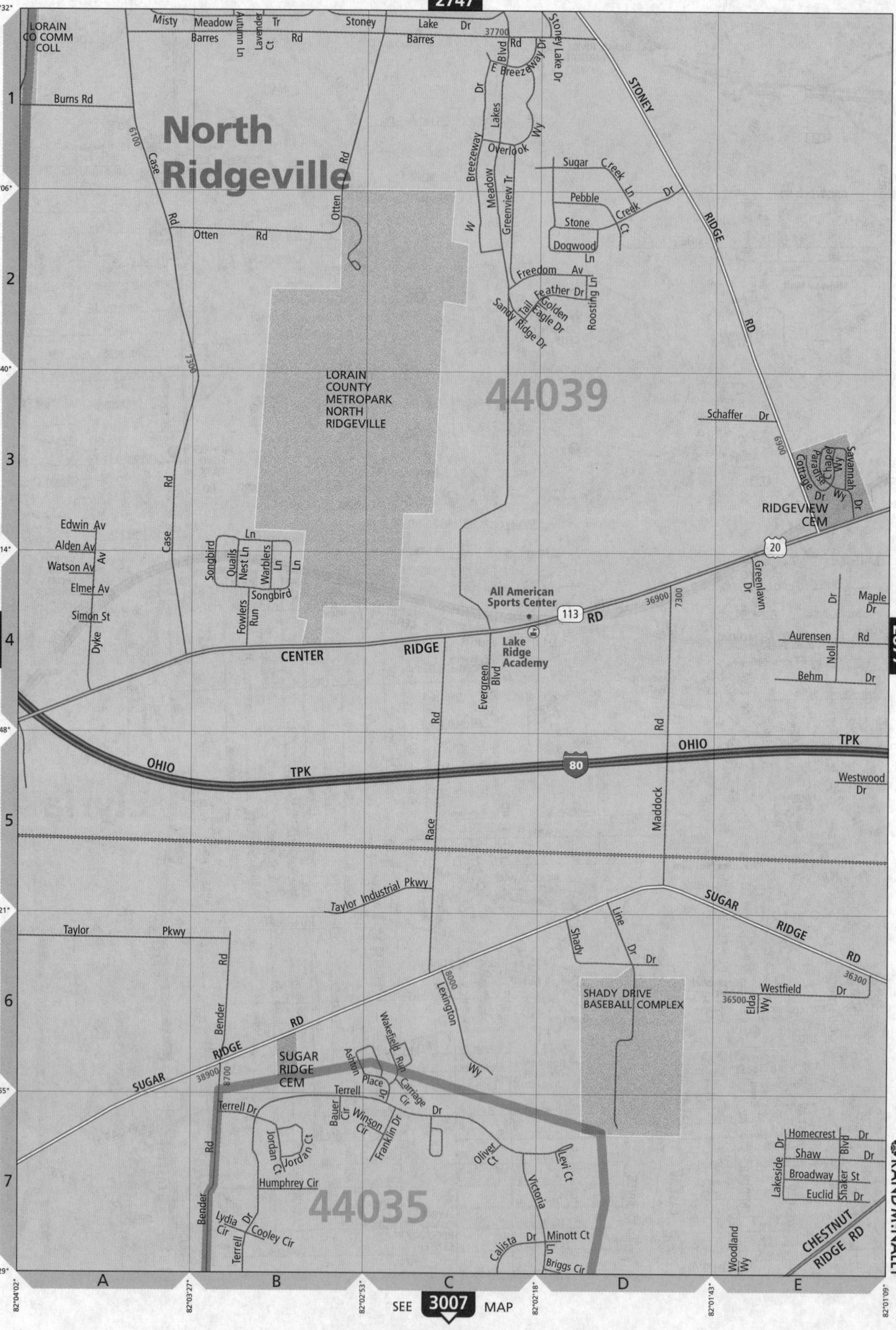
North Ridgeville
LORAIN CO COMM COLL
Misty Meadow Tr
Barres Rd
Autumn Ln
Lavender Ct
Stoney Lake Dr
Barres
37700
Blvd Rd
Stoney Lake Dr
Breezeway Dr
STONEY RIDGE RD
Burns Rd
6100
Case Rd
Otten Rd
Lakes
Overlook Wy
Breezeway Dr
Meadow
W
Greenview Tr
Sugar Creek Ln
Pebble Creek Dr
Stone Ct
Dogwood Ln
Freedom Av
Feather Dr
Golden Eagle Dr
Tail
Sandy Ridge Dr
Roosting Ln
7300
LORAIN COUNTY METROPARK NORTH RIDGEVILLE
44039
Schaffer Dr
6900
Savannah Dr
Chapel Wy
Paradise Wy
Cottage Dr
RIDGEVIEW CEM
Edwin Av
Alden Av
Watson Av
Elmer Av
Simon St
Dyke Av
Songbird Ln
Quails Nest Ln
Warblers Ln
Fowlers Run
20
Greenlawn Dr
All American Sports Center
113
Lake Ridge Academy
36900
7300
Maple Dr
Aurensen Rd
Noll Dr
Behm Dr
CENTER RIDGE RD
Evergreen Blvd
Race Rd
Maddock Rd
OHIO TPK
80
Westwood Dr
Taylor Industrial Pkwy
Taylor Pkwy
SUGAR RIDGE RD
Line Dr
Shady Dr
SHADY DRIVE BASEBALL COMPLEX
36300
Westfield Dr
36500
Elda Wy
Bender Rd
8000
Lexington Wy
38900
8700
SUGAR RIDGE CEM
Ashton Place Dr
Wakefield Run
Carriage Cir
Terrell Dr
Bauer Cir
Winson Cir
Franklin Dr
Jordan Ct
Oliver Ct
Levi Ct
Victoria Ln
Humphrey Cir
44035
Lydia Cir
Cooley Cir
Terrell
Calista Dr
Minott Ct
Briggs Cir
Woodland Wy
Homecrest Dr
Shaw Dr
Broadway St
Euclid Dr
Lakeside Dr
Blvd
Shaker
CHESTNUT RIDGE RD
1
2
3
4
5
6
7
A
B
C
D
E
41°24'32"
41°24'06"
41°23'40"
41°23'14"
41°22'48"
41°22'21"
41°21'55"
41°21'29"
82°04'02"
82°03'27"
82°02'53"
82°02'18"
82°01'43"
82°01'09"

SEE 2875 MAP

SEE 2877 MAP

SEE 3007 MAP

1:24,000
1 in. = 2000 ft.
0 0.25 0.5
miles

SEE 2748 MAP

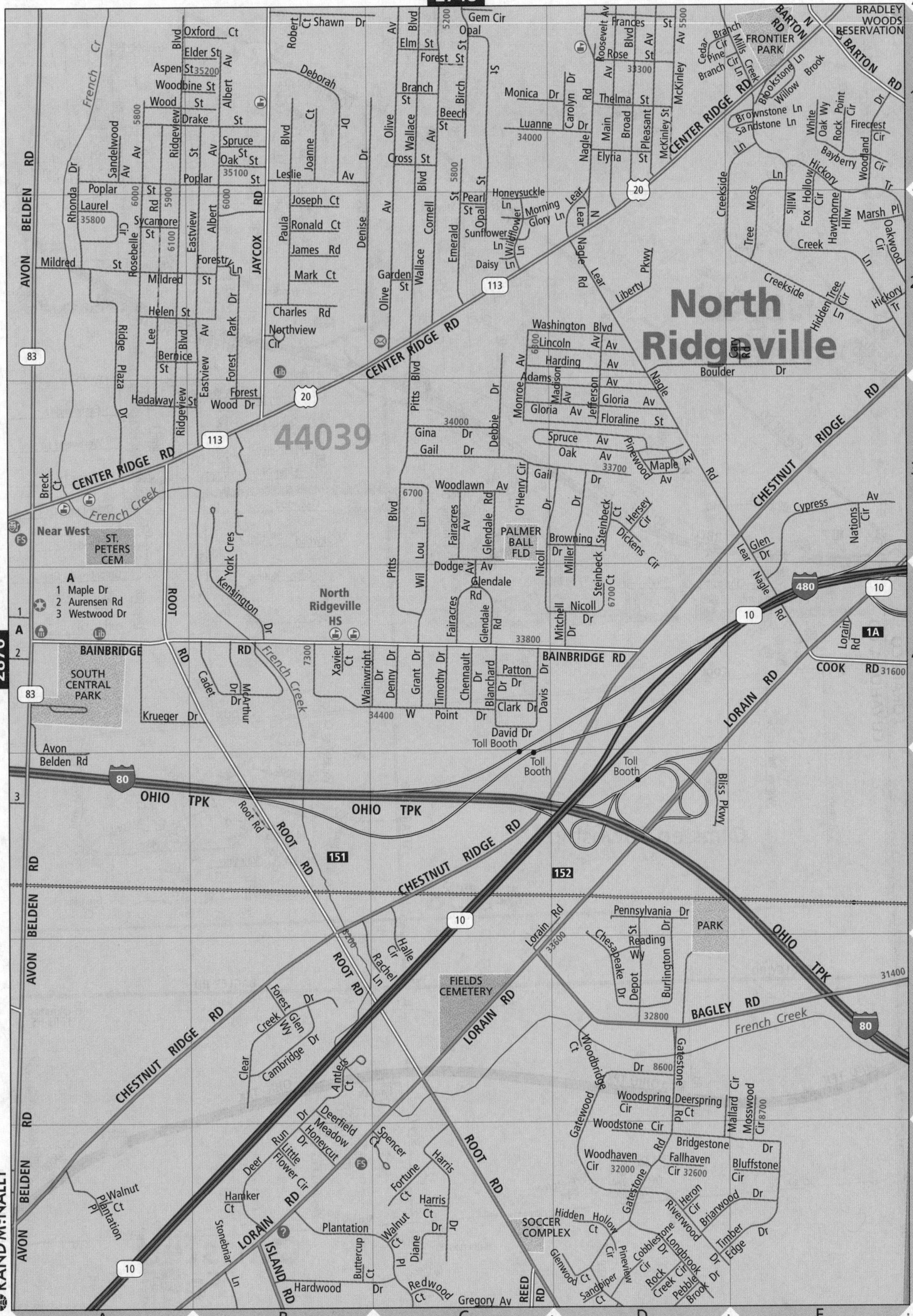
North Ridgeville
44039
CENTER RIDGE RD
AVON BELDEN RD
CHESTNUT RIDGE RD
LORAIN RD
ROOT RD
BAINBRIDGE RD
BAGLEY RD
OHIO TPK
NAGLE RD
JAYCOX RD
BARTON RD
COOK RD
French Creek
French Cr
FRONTIER PARK
BRADLEY WOODS RESERVATION
ST. PETERS CEM
SOUTH CENTRAL PARK
PALMER BALL FLD
North Ridgeville HS
FIELDS CEMETERY
SOCCER COMPLEX
PARK
Near West
Toll Booth
Mildred St
Center Ridge Rd
Washington Blvd
Lincoln Av
Harding Av
Boulder Dr
Woodlawn Av
Krueger Dr
Pennsylvania Dr
Island Rd
Reed Rd
Gregory Av
Hardwood Dr
Plantation Dr
Bliss Pkwy
Liberty Pkwy
A
1 Maple Dr
2 Aurensen Rd
3 Westwood Dr
RAND McNALLY

SEE 2876 MAP

SEE 2878 MAP

SEE 3008 MAP

1:24,000
1 in. = 2000 ft.
0 0.25 0.5
miles

SEE 2749 MAP

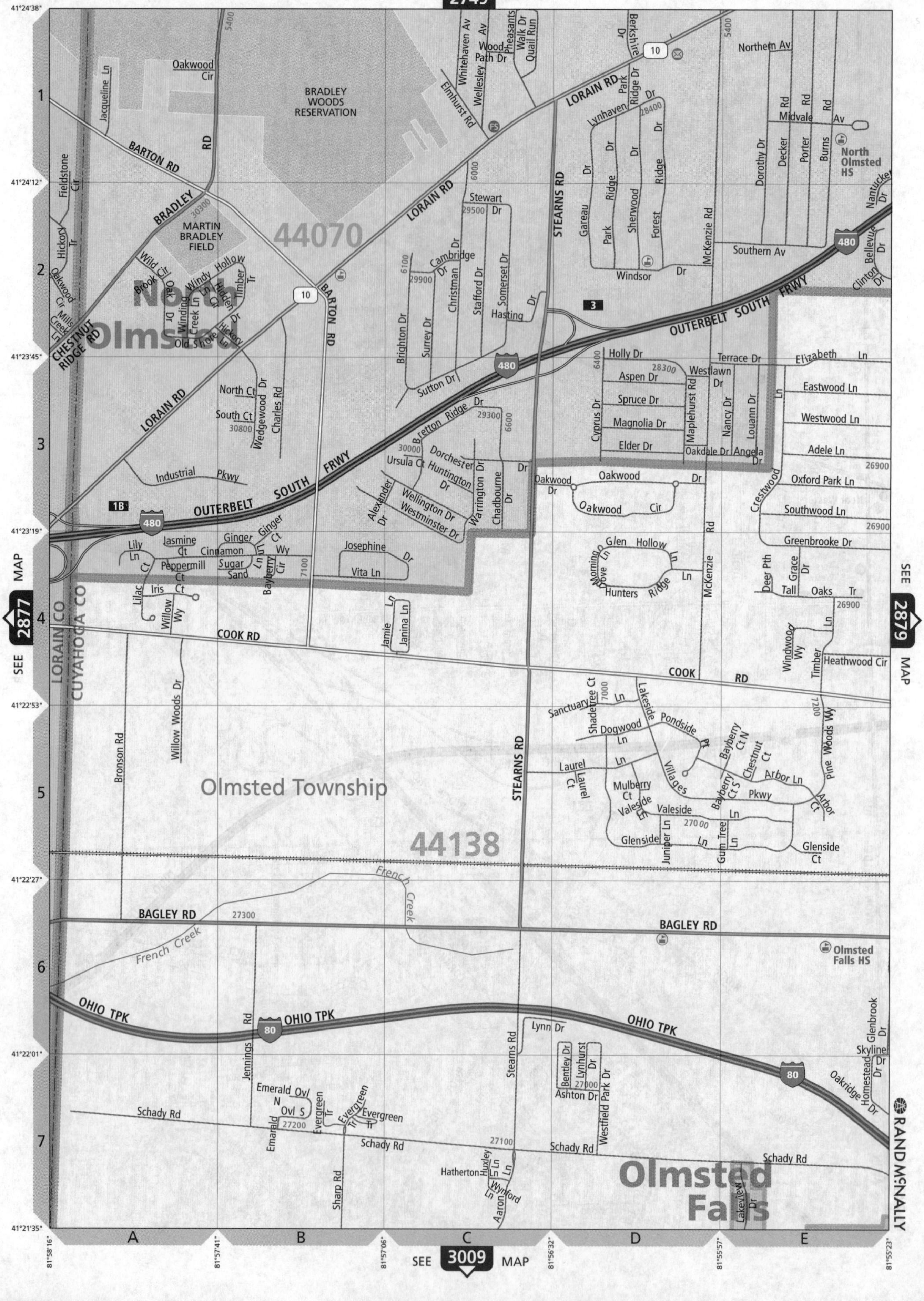
BRADLEY WOODS RESERVATION
MARTIN BRADLEY FIELD
44070
North Olmsted
Olmsted Township
44138
Olmsted Falls
LORAIN CO
CUYAHOGA CO
North Olmsted HS
Olmsted Falls HS
LORAIN RD
BARTON RD
BRADLEY RD
STEARNS RD
COOK RD
BAGLEY RD
OHIO TPK
OUTERBELT SOUTH FRWY
CHESTNUT RIDGE RD
Industrial Pkwy
McKenzie Rd
Bronson Rd
Jennings Rd
Schady Rd
Sharp Rd
Stearns Rd
Willow Woods Dr
Pine Woods Wy
French Creek
Villages Pkwy
Oakwood Cir
Jacqueline Ln
Fieldstone Cir
Hickory Tr
Oakwood Cir
Mills Creek Ln
Wild Cir
Brook Cir
Windy Hollow Ln
Hidden Ct
Timber Tr
Winding Creek Ln
Old Shore Dr
Hickory Ln
North Ct
South Ct
Wedgewood Dr
Charles Rd
Whitehaven Av
Wellesley Av
Wood Path Dr
Pheasants Walk Dr
Quail Run
Elmhurst Rd
Stewart Dr
Cambridge Dr
Christman Dr
Stafford Dr
Somerset Dr
Hasting Dr
Brighton Dr
Surrey Dr
Sutton Dr
Bretton Ridge Dr
Dorchester Dr
Ursula Ct
Huntington Dr
Warrington Dr
Chadbourne Dr
Alexander Dr
Wellington Dr
Westminster Dr
Josephine Dr
Vita Ln
Lily Ln
Jasmine Ct
Ginger Ct
Ginger Wy
Cinnamon Ln
Peppermill Ct
Sugar Ln
Sand
Bayberry Cir
Lilac Ct
Iris Ct
Willow Wy
Jamie Ln
Janina Ln
Berkshire Dr
Park Ridge Dr
Lynhaven Dr
Gareau Dr
Ridge Dr
Sherwood Dr
Forest Ridge Dr
Park
Windsor Dr
Northern Av
Midvale Av
Dorothy Dr
Decker Rd
Porter Rd
Burns Rd
Nantucket Dr
Southern Av
Bellevue Dr
Clinton Dr
Holly Dr
Aspen Dr
Spruce Dr
Magnolia Dr
Elder Dr
Cyprus Dr
Maplehurst Rd
Westlawn Dr
Terrace Dr
Nancy Dr
Louann Dr
Oakdale Dr
Angela Dr
Elizabeth Ln
Eastwood Ln
Westwood Ln
Adele Ln
Oxford Park Ln
Southwood Ln
Crestwood Ln
Greenbrooke Dr
Oakwood Dr
Oakwood Cir
Glen Hollow Ln
Morning Dove Ln
Hunters Ridge Ln
Deer Pth
Grace Dr
Tall Oaks Tr
Windwood Wy
Timber Ln
Heathwood Cir
Sanctuary Ln
Shadetree Ct
Lakeside
Pondside Pt
Dogwood Ln
Bayberry Ct N
Chestnut Ct
Arbor Ln
Arbor Ct
Laurel Ln
Laurel Ct
Mulberry Ct
Valeside Ln
Valeside
Bayberry Ct S
Glenside Ln
Juniper Ln
Gum Tree Ln
Glenside Ct
Lynn Dr
Bentley Dr
Lynhurst Dr
Ashton Dr
Westfield Park Dr
Emerald Ovl N
Emerald Ovl S
Emerald
Evergreen Tr
Evergreen
Hatherton Ln
Huxley Ln
Aaron Ln
Wynford
Lakeview Dr
Glenbrook Dr
Skyline Dr
Homestead Dr
Oakridge Dr
10
480
80
1B
3
5400
30300
6000
29500
6100
29900
6400
28300
28400
6600
29300
30000
30800
7100
26900
7000
7200
27000
27300
27200
27100
A
B
C
D
E
1
2
3
4
5
6
7
41°24'38"
41°24'12"
41°23'45"
41°23'19"
41°22'53"
41°22'27"
41°22'01"
41°21'35"
81°58'16"
81°57'41"
81°57'06"
81°56'32"
81°55'57"
81°55'23"
RAND McNALLY

SEE 2877 MAP
SEE 2879 MAP
SEE 3009 MAP

SEE 2750 MAP

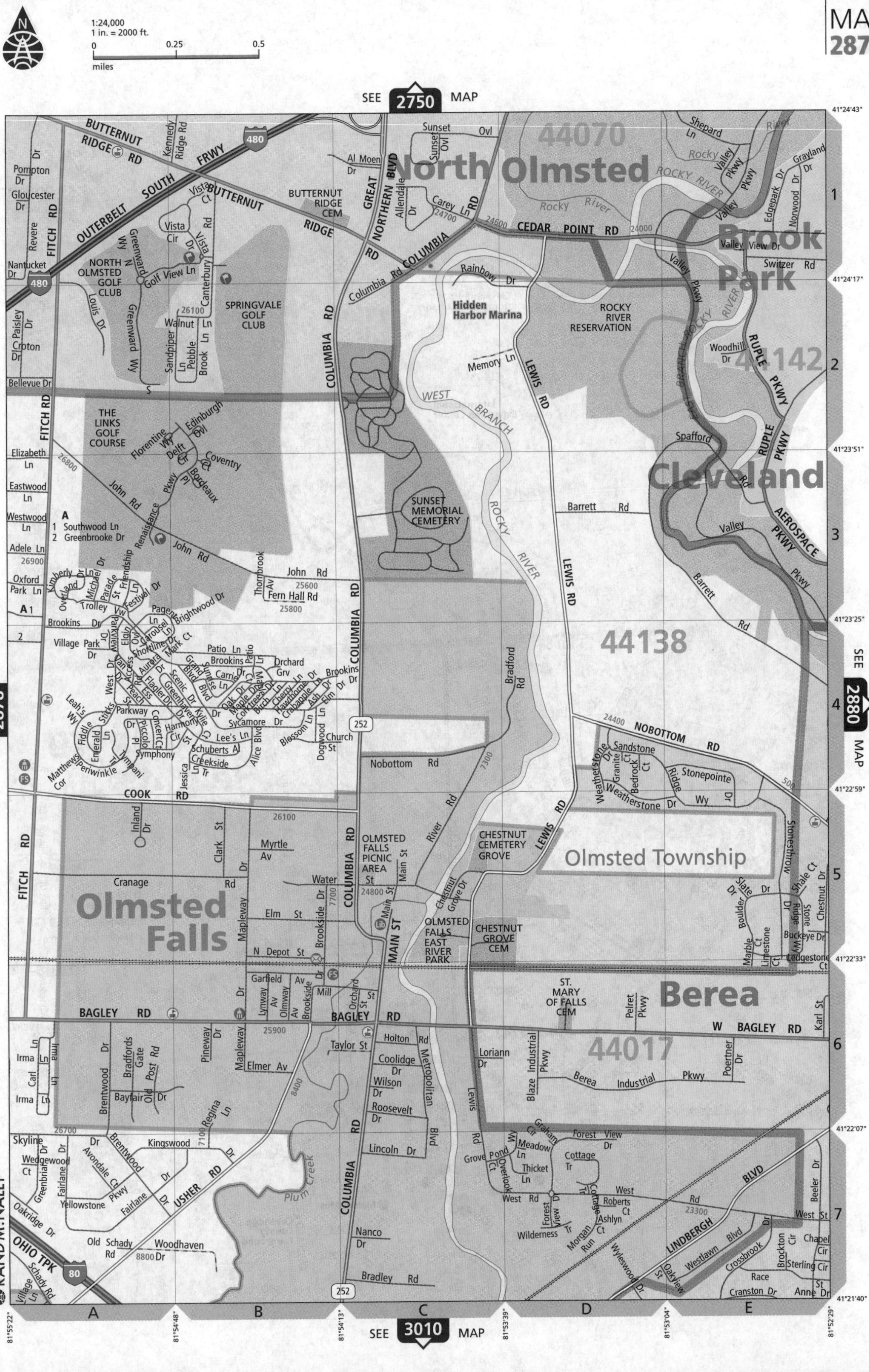
1:24,000
1 in. = 2000 ft.
0 0.25 0.5
miles
North Olmsted
44070
Brook Park
44142
Cleveland
44138
Olmsted Township
Olmsted Falls
Berea
44017
BUTTERNUT RIDGE RD
OUTERBELT SOUTH FRWY
CEDAR POINT RD
COLUMBIA RD
GREAT NORTHERN BLVD
LEWIS RD
NOBOTTOM RD
COOK RD
BAGLEY RD
W BAGLEY RD
USHER RD
LINDBERGH BLVD
RUPLE PKWY
AEROSPACE PKWY
MAIN ST
FITCH RD
OHIO TPK
NORTH OLMSTED GOLF CLUB
SPRINGVALE GOLF CLUB
BUTTERNUT RIDGE CEM
THE LINKS GOLF COURSE
Hidden Harbor Marina
ROCKY RIVER RESERVATION
SUNSET MEMORIAL CEMETERY
CHESTNUT CEMETERY GROVE
OLMSTED FALLS PICNIC AREA
OLMSTED FALLS EAST RIVER PARK
CHESTNUT GROVE CEM
ST. MARY OF FALLS CEM
WEST BRANCH ROCKY RIVER
Plum Creek
A 1 Southwood Ln 2 Greenbrooke Dr
A B C D E
1 2 3 4 5 6 7
41°24'43" 41°24'17" 41°23'51" 41°23'25" 41°22'59" 41°22'33" 41°22'07" 41°21'40"
81°55'22" 81°54'48" 81°54'13" 81°53'39" 81°53'04" 81°52'29"
RAND McNALLY

SEE 2878 MAP

SEE 2880 MAP

SEE 3010 MAP

1:24,000
1 in. = 2000 ft.
0 0.25 0.5
miles

SEE 2751 MAP

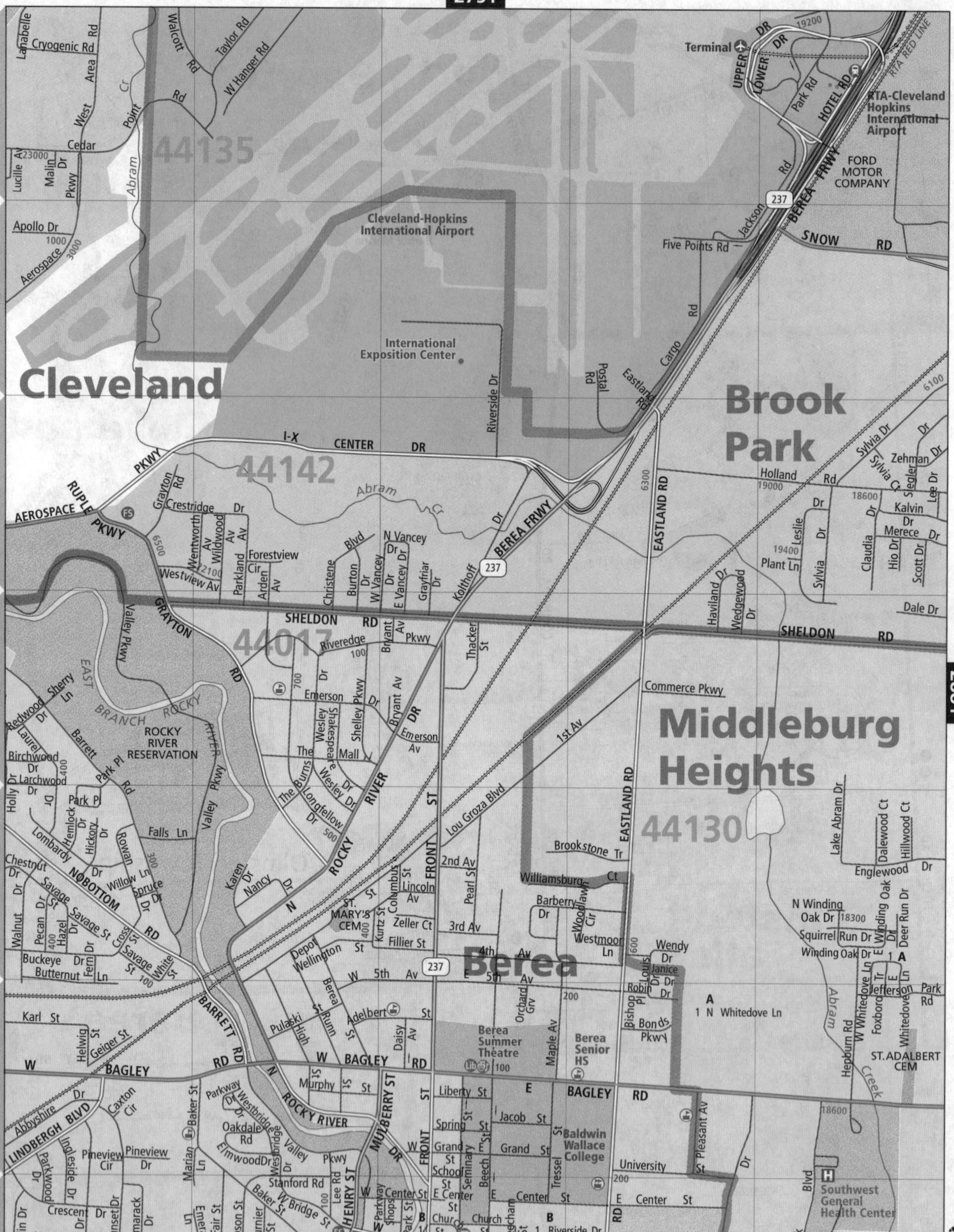
Cleveland
Brook Park
Middleburg Heights
Berea
44135
44142
44017
44130
Cleveland-Hopkins International Airport
RTA-Cleveland Hopkins International Airport
Terminal
FORD MOTOR COMPANY
International Exposition Center
ROCKY RIVER RESERVATION
ST. MARY'S CEM
Berea Summer Theatre
Berea Senior HS
Baldwin Wallace College
Mahler Mus
Cuyahoga County Fairground
Southwest General Health Center
ST. ADALBERT CEM
WALLACE LAKE
BALDWIN LAKE
PARK
I-X CENTER DR
BEREA FRWY
SHELDON RD
EASTLAND RD
SNOW RD
W BAGLEY RD
E BAGLEY RD
N ROCKY RIVER DR
FRONT ST
BARRETT RD
GRAYTON RD
RUPLE PKWY
AEROSPACE PKWY
LINDBERGH BLVD
NOBOTTOM RD
MULBERRY ST
PROSPECT ST
HENRY ST
BRIDGE ST
S ROCKY RIVER DR
Lou Groza Blvd
1st Av
Commerce Pkwy
Holland Rd
Five Points Rd
Cargo Rd
Abram Cr
East Branch Rocky River
237
A B C D E
1 2 3 4 5 6 7

SEE 2879 MAP
SEE 2881 MAP
SEE 3011 MAP

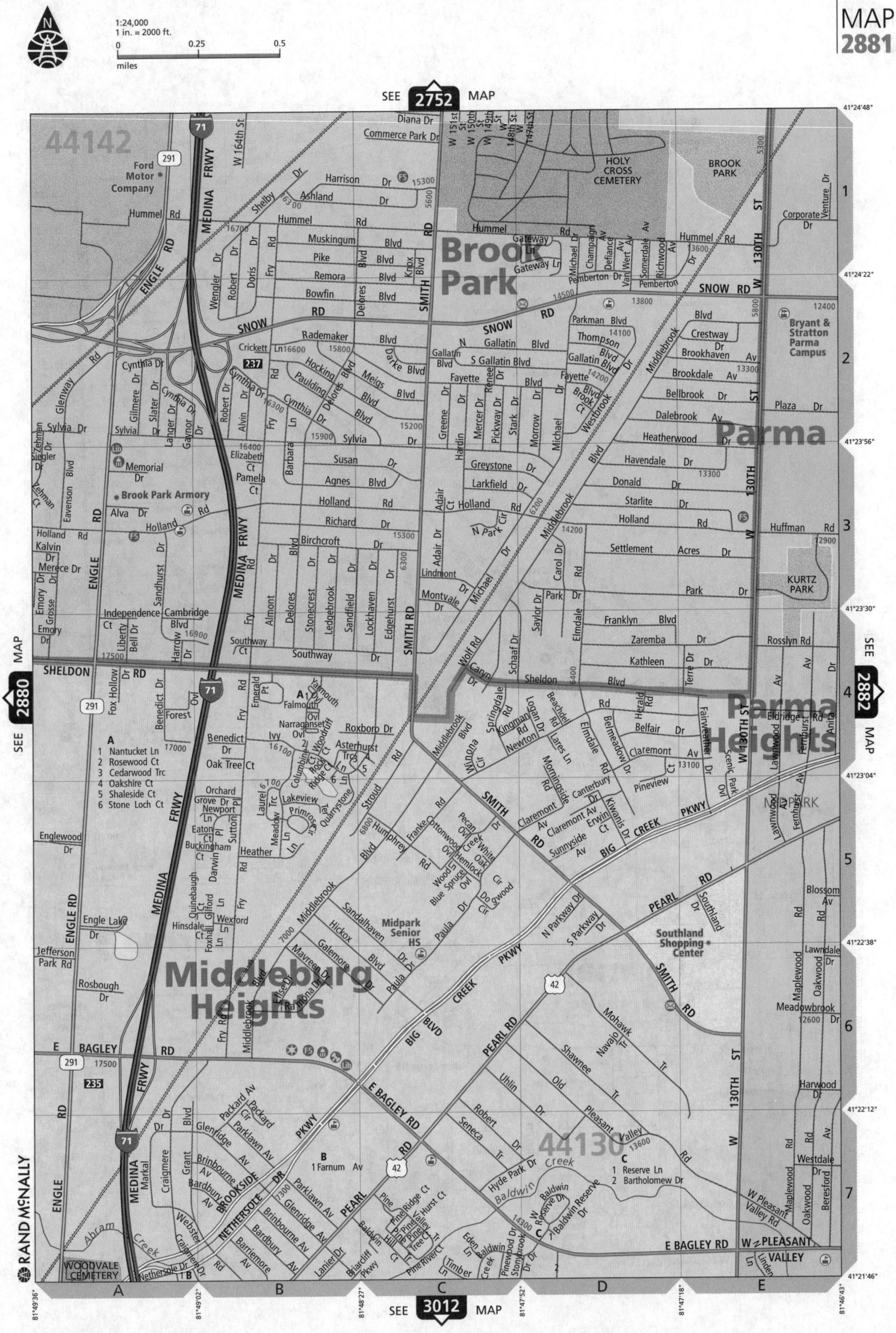
1:24,000
1 in. = 2000 ft.
0
0.25
0.5
miles
SEE 2752 MAP
SEE 2880 MAP
SEE 2882 MAP
SEE 3012 MAP
44142
44130
Brook Park
Parma
Parma Heights
Middleburg Heights
Ford Motor Company
HOLY CROSS CEMETERY
BROOK PARK
Bryant & Stratton Parma Campus
KURTZ PARK
Brook Park Armory
Memorial Dr
Midpark Senior HS
Southland Shopping Center
WOODVALE CEMETERY
MEDINA FRWY
SNOW RD
SMITH RD
W 130TH ST
SHELDON RD
ENGLE RD
E BAGLEY RD
BIG CREEK PKWY
PEARL RD
W PLEASANT VALLEY
Middlebrook Blvd
Hummel Rd
Holland Rd
A
1 Nantucket Ln
2 Rosewood Ct
3 Cedarwood Trc
4 Oakshire Ct
5 Shaleside Ct
6 Stone Loch Ct
B
1 Farnum Av
C
1 Reserve Ln
2 Bartholomew Dr
RAND McNALLY
41°24'48"
41°24'22"
41°23'56"
41°23'30"
41°23'04"
41°22'38"
41°22'12"
41°21'46"
81°49'36"
81°49'02"
81°48'27"
81°47'52"
81°47'18"
81°46'43"

1:24,000
1 in. = 2000 ft.
0 0.25 0.5 miles

SEE 2753 MAP

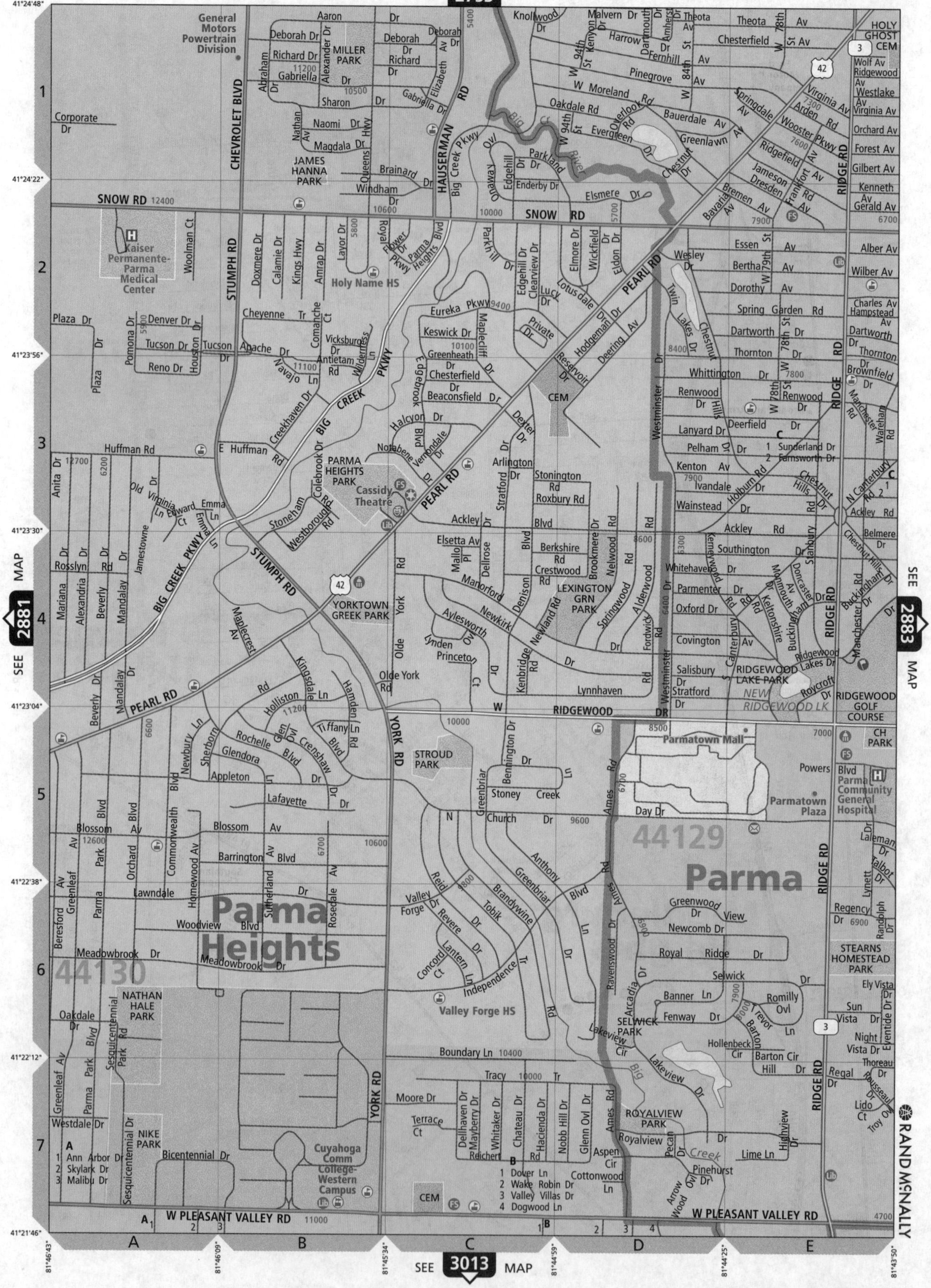
General Motors Powertrain Division
CHEVROLET BLVD
MILLER PARK
JAMES HANNA PARK
HAUSERMAN RD
SNOW RD
Kaiser Permanente-Parma Medical Center
STUMPH RD
Holy Name HS
BIG CREEK PKWY
PEARL RD
PARMA HEIGHTS PARK
Cassidy Theatre
CEM
YORKTOWN GREEK PARK
LEXINGTON GRN PARK
Westminster
RIDGE RD
HOLY GHOST CEM
RIDGEWOOD LAKE PARK
NEW RIDGEWOOD LK
RIDGEWOOD GOLF COURSE
W RIDGEWOOD DR
YORK RD
STROUD PARK
Parmatown Mall
Parmatown Plaza
Parma Community General Hospital
CH PARK
44129
Parma
Parma Heights
44130
NATHAN HALE PARK
Valley Forge HS
SELWICK PARK
STEARNS HOMESTEAD PARK
ROYALVIEW PARK
NIKE PARK
Cuyahoga Comm College-Western Campus
W PLEASANT VALLEY RD
Big Creek
A
1 Ann Arbor Dr
2 Skylark Dr
3 Malibu Dr
B
1 Dover Ln
2 Wake Robin Dr
3 Valley Villas Dr
4 Dogwood Ln
C
1 Sunderland Dr
2 Farnsworth Dr
A B C D E
1 2 3 4 5 6 7

SEE 2881 MAP

SEE 2883 MAP

SEE 3013 MAP

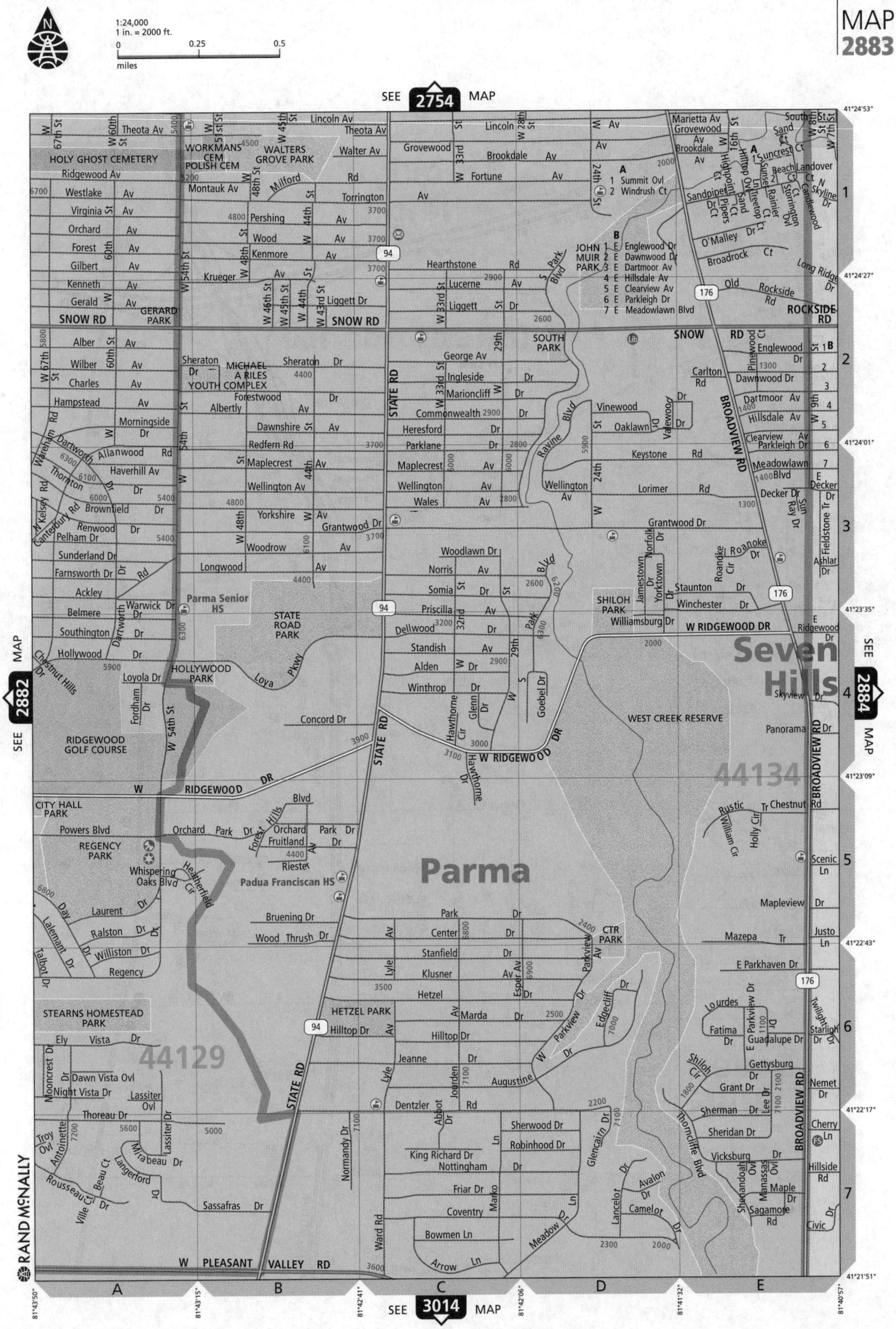
1:24,000
1 in. = 2000 ft.
0
0.25
0.5
miles
SEE 2754 MAP
SEE 3014 MAP
SEE 2882 MAP
SEE 2884 MAP
HOLY GHOST CEMETERY
WORKMANS CEM
POLISH CEM
WALTERS GROVE PARK
GERARD PARK
SNOW RD
MICHAEL A RILES YOUTH COMPLEX
Parma Senior HS
STATE ROAD PARK
HOLLYWOOD PARK
RIDGEWOOD GOLF COURSE
CITY HALL PARK
REGENCY PARK
Padua Franciscan HS
Parma
STEARNS HOMESTEAD PARK
HETZEL PARK
44129
JOHN MUIR PARK
SOUTH PARK
SHILOH PARK
WEST CREEK RESERVE
CTR PARK
Seven Hills
44134
STATE RD
BROADVIEW RD
W RIDGEWOOD DR
W PLEASANT VALLEY RD
ROCKSIDE RD
94
176
A
1 Summit Ovl
2 Windrush Ct
B
1 E Englewood Dr
2 E Dawnwood Dr
3 E Dartmoor Av
4 E Hillsdale Av
5 E Clearview Av
6 E Parkleigh Dr
7 E Meadowlawn Blvd
A
B
C
D
E
1
2
3
4
5
6
7
41°24'53"
41°24'27"
41°24'01"
41°23'35"
41°23'09"
41°22'43"
41°22'17"
41°21'51"
81°43'50"
81°43'15"
81°42'41"
81°42'06"
81°41'32"
81°40'57"
RAND McNALLY

1:24,000
1 in. = 2000 ft.
0 0.25 0.5
miles

SEE 2755 MAP

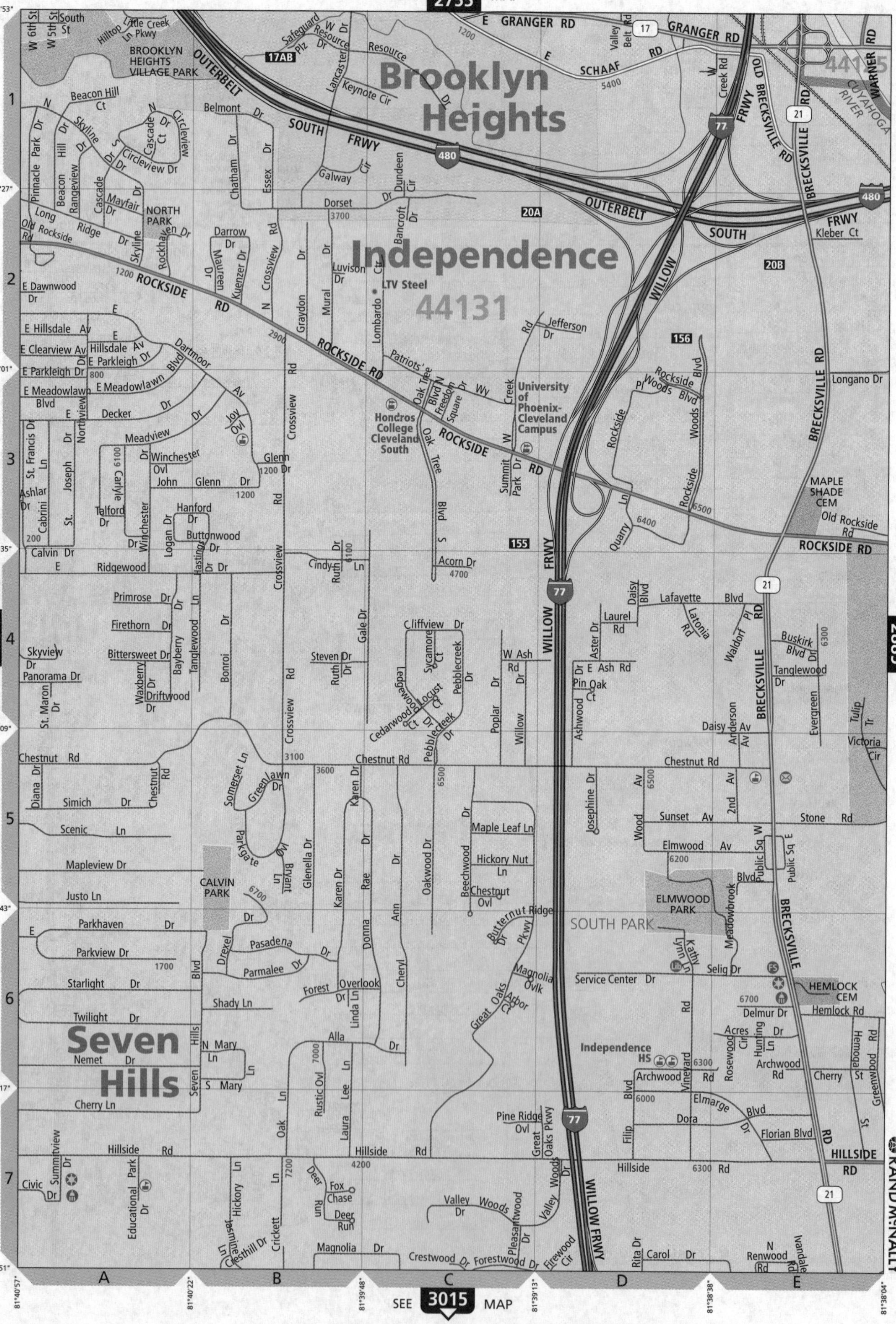
Brooklyn
Heights
Independence
44131
44125
Seven
Hills
SOUTH PARK
BROOKLYN
HEIGHTS
VILLAGE PARK
NORTH
PARK
CALVIN
PARK
ELMWOOD
PARK
MAPLE
SHADE
CEM
HEMLOCK
CEM
LTV Steel
Hondros
College
Cleveland
South
University
of
Phoenix-
Cleveland
Campus
Independence
HS
CUYAHOGA
RIVER
OUTERBELT
SOUTH
FRWY
WILLOW
FRWY
WILLOW FRWY
E GRANGER RD
GRANGER RD
E SCHAAF RD
ROCKSIDE RD
BRECKSVILLE RD
OLD BRECKSVILLE RD
WARNER RD
HILLSIDE RD
Chestnut Rd
Resource Dr
Safeguard Plz
Keynote Cir
Beacon Hill Ct
Belmont Dr
Circleview Dr
Cascade Ct
Skyline Dr
Pinnacle Park Dr
Rangeview Dr
Mayfair Dr
Long Ridge Dr
Old Rockside Rd
Chatham Dr
Essex Dr
Galway Cir
Dundeen Cir
Dorset Dr
Bancroft Dr
Darrow Dr
Maureen Dr
Kuenzer Dr
Crossview Rd
Graydon Dr
Mural Dr
Luvison Dr
Lombardo Ctr
E Dawnwood Dr
E Hillsdale Av
E Clearview Av
E Parkleigh Dr
E Meadowlawn Blvd
Dartmoor Blvd
Decker Dr
Meadview Dr
Joy Ovl
Glenn Dr
John Glenn Dr
Winchester Ovl
St. Francis Dr
Joseph St.
Carlyle Dr
Ashlar Dr
Cabrini Ln
Talford Dr
Hanford Dr
Buttonwood Dr
Logan Dr
Calvin Dr
E Ridgewood Dr
Hastings Dr
Cindy Ln
Ruth Dr
Patriots' Wy
Oak Tree Blvd
Freedom Square Dr
Jefferson Dr
Creek Rd
Summit Park Dr
Acorn Dr
Quarry Ln
Rockside Woods Blvd
Rockside Pl
Longano Dr
Kleber Ct
Primrose Dr
Firethorn Dr
Bittersweet Dr
Bayberry Dr
Tanglewood Ln
Bonroi Dr
Waxberry Dr
Driftwood Dr
Skyview Dr
Panorama Dr
St. Maron Dr
Gale Dr
Steven Dr
Cliffview Dr
Sycamore Ct
Pebblecreek Dr
Locust Ct
Cedarwood Ct
Poplar Dr
W Ash Rd
E Ash Rd
Pin Oak Ct
Ashwood Dr
Aster Dr
Laurel Rd
Daisy Blvd
Lafayette Blvd
Latonia Rd
Waldorf Pl
Buskirk Blvd
Tanglewood Dr
Evergreen Dr
Anderson Av
Daisy Av
Tulip Tr
Victoria Cir
Diana Dr
Simich Dr
Chestnut Rd
Scenic Ln
Mapleview Dr
Justo Ln
Somerset Ln
Greenlawn Dr
Parkgate Ovl
Bryant Ln
Glenella Dr
Karen Dr
Rae Dr
Donna Dr
Ann Dr
Oakwood Dr
Beechwood Dr
Maple Leaf Ln
Hickory Nut Ln
Chestnut Ovl
Butternut Ridge Dr
Josephine Dr
Wood Av
Sunset Av
2nd Av
Elmwood Av
Public Sq W
Public Sq E
Stone Rd
Meadowbrook Blvd
Kathy Lynn Ln
Selig Dr
Service Center Dr
Parkhaven Dr
Parkview Dr
Starlight Dr
Twilight Dr
Drexel Dr
Pasadena Dr
Parmalee Dr
Forest Dr
Overlook Dr
Linda Ln
Cheryl Dr
Shady Ln
Magnolia Ovlk
Great Oaks Pkwy
Arbor Ct
Seven Hills Blvd
N Mary Ln
S Mary Ln
Nemet Dr
Cherry Ln
Alla Dr
Rustic Ovl
Lee Ln
Laura Ln
Oak Ln
Pine Ridge Ovl
Archwood Rd
Vineyard Rd
Filip Blvd
Elmarge Blvd
Dora Dr
Florian Blvd
Delmur Dr
Hemlock Rd
Acres Dr
Rosewood Cir
Hunting Ln
Cherry St
Hemogard Rd
Greenwood Rd
Summitview Dr
Civic Dr
Educational Park Dr
Hickory Ln
Jasmine Ln
Chesthill Dr
Crickett Ln
Deer Run
Fox Chase
Deer Run
Magnolia Dr
Crestwood Dr
Forestwood Dr
Firewood Cir
Pleasantwood Dr
Valley Woods Dr
Rita Dr
Carol Dr
N Renwood Rd
Ivandale Rd
17AB
20A
20B
156
155
17
21
77
480
1 2 3 4 5 6 7
A B C D E
41°24'53"
41°24'27"
41°24'01"
41°23'35"
41°23'09"
41°22'43"
41°22'17"
41°21'51"
81°40'57"
81°40'22"
81°39'48"
81°39'13"
81°38'38"
81°38'04"

SEE 2883 MAP

SEE 2885 MAP

SEE 3015 MAP

1:24,000
1 in. = 2000 ft.
0 0.25 0.5
miles

SEE 2756 MAP

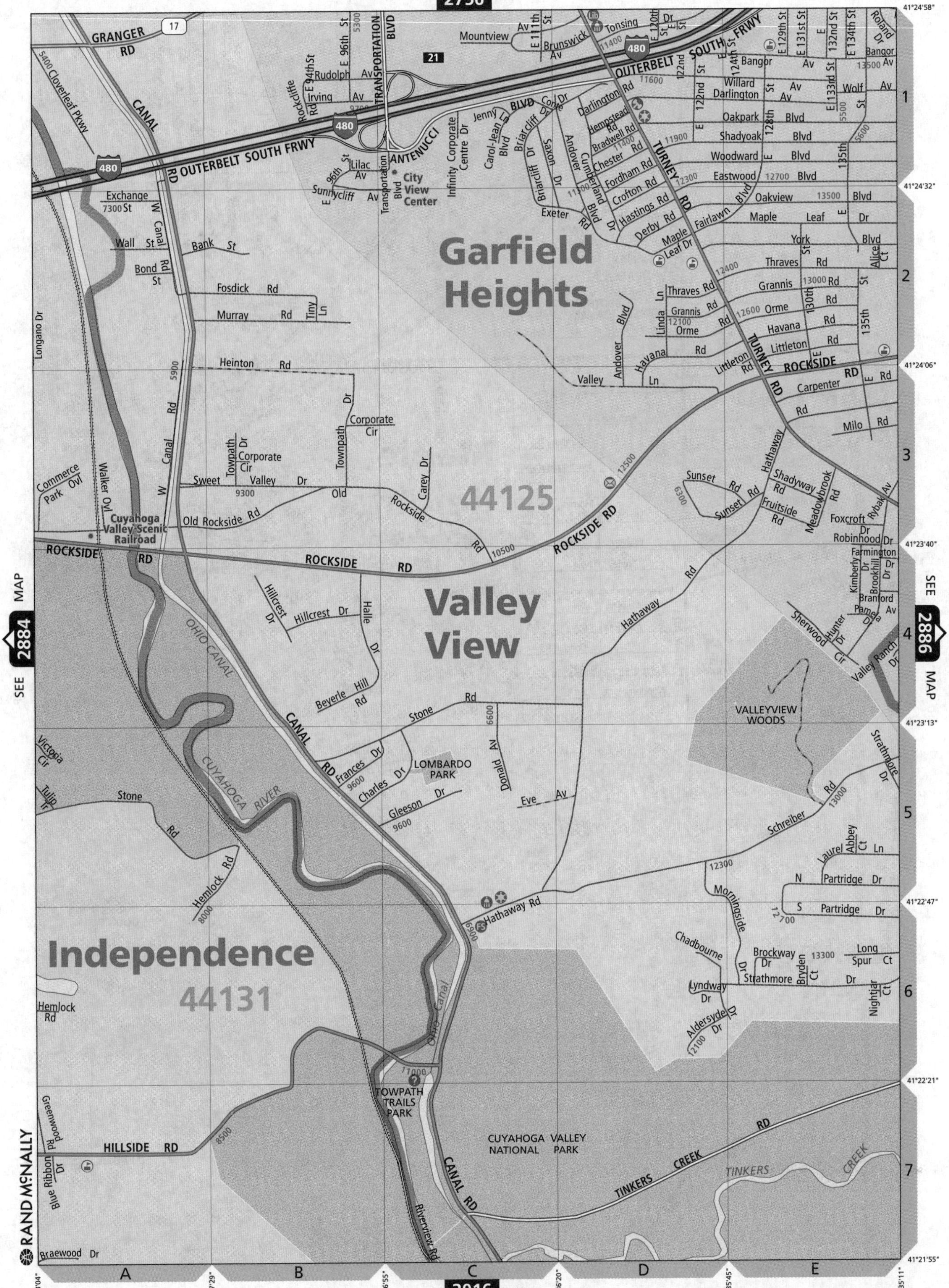

Garfield Heights
Valley View
Independence
44125
44131
GRANGER RD
17
CANAL RD
OUTERBELT SOUTH FRWY
480
21
TRANSPORTATION BLVD
ANTENUCCI BLVD
TURNEY RD
ROCKSIDE RD
Old Rockside Rd
Hathaway Rd
Stone Rd
Schreiber Rd
HILLSIDE RD
TINKERS CREEK RD
TINKERS CREEK
OHIO CANAL
Ohio Canal
CUYAHOGA RIVER
Cuyahoga Valley Scenic Railroad
City View Center
LOMBARDO PARK
VALLEYVIEW WOODS
TOWPATH TRAILS PARK
CUYAHOGA VALLEY NATIONAL PARK
Cloverleaf Pkwy
Exchange St
Wall St
Bond St
Bank St
Fosdick Rd
Murray Rd
Tiny Ln
Heinton Rd
Corporate Cir
Towpath Dr
Sweet Valley Dr
Carey Dr
Commerce Park Ovl
Walker Ovl
W Canal Rd
Longano Dr
Hillcrest Dr
Halle Dr
Beyerle Hill Rd
Frances Dr
Charles Dr
Gleeson Dr
Donald Av
Eve Av
Victoria Cir
Tulip Tr
Hemlock Rd
Greenwood Rd
Blue Ribbon Dr
Braewood Dr
Riverview Rd
Mountview Av
Brunswick Av
Tonsing Dr
Rudolph Av
Irving Av
Rockcliffe Rd
Lilac Av
Sunnycliff Av
Infinity Corporate Centre Dr
Jenny Ln
Carol-Jean Blvd
Briarcliff Dr
Saxon Dr
Andover Blvd
Cumberland Blvd
Exeter Rd
Darlington Rd
Hempstead Rd
Bradwell Rd
Chester Rd
Fordham Rd
Crofton Rd
Hastings Rd
Derby Rd
Maple Leaf Dr
Fairlawn Blvd
Bangor Av
Willard Av
Darlington Av
Wolf Av
Oakpark Blvd
Shadyoak Blvd
Woodward Blvd
Eastwood Blvd
Oakview Blvd
Maple Leaf Dr
York Blvd
Alice Ct
Thraves Rd
Grannis Rd
Orme Rd
Havana Rd
Littleton Rd
Linda Ln
Valley Ln
Carpenter Rd
Milo Rd
Sunset Rd
Shadyway Rd
Fruitside Rd
Meadowbrook Rd
Rybak Av
Foxcroft Dr
Robinhood Dr
Farmington Dr
Kimberly Dr
Brookhill Dr
Branford Av
Pamela Dr
Sherwood Cir
Hunter Dr
Valley Ranch Dr
Strathmore Dr
Laurel Ln
Abbey Ct
N Partridge Dr
S Partridge Dr
Morningside Dr
Chadbourne Dr
Brockway Dr
Bryden Ct
Long Spur Ct
Lyndway Dr
Aldersyde Dr
Nightjar Ct
E 96th St
E 94th St
E 111th St
E 120th St
122nd St
124th St
E 129th St
E 131st St
E 132nd St
E 133rd St
E 134th St
128th St
130th St
135th St
Roland Dr
1
2
3
4
5
6
7
A
B
C
D
E
41°24'58"
41°24'32"
41°24'06"
41°23'40"
41°23'13"
41°22'47"
41°22'21"
41°21'55"
81°38'04"
81°37'29"
81°36'55"
81°36'20"
81°35'45"
81°35'11"
SEE 2884 MAP
SEE 2886 MAP

SEE 3016 MAP

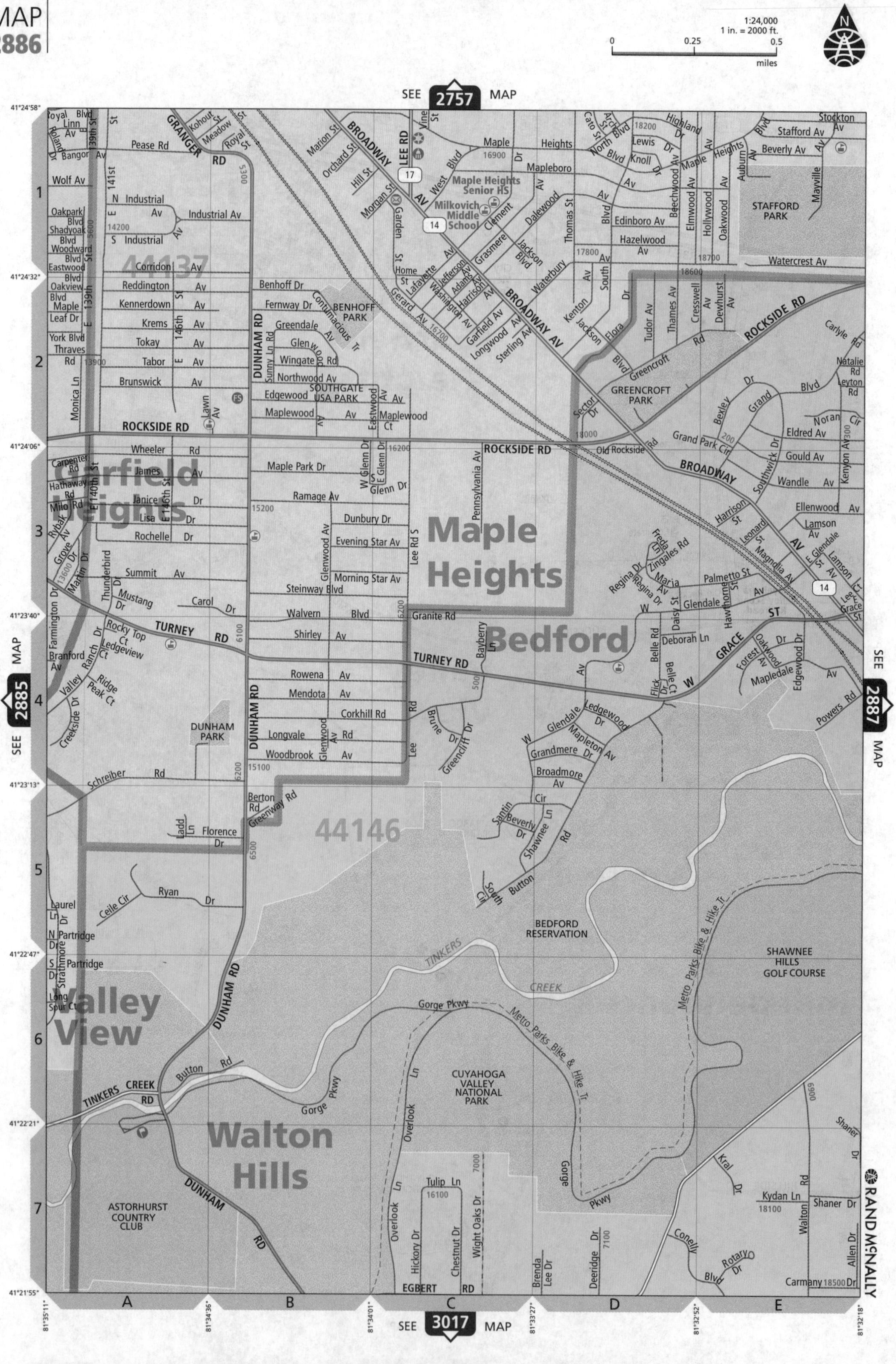
1:24,000
1 in. = 2000 ft.
0
0.25
0.5
miles
N
SEE 2757 MAP
SEE 2885 MAP
SEE 2887 MAP
SEE 3017 MAP
Garfield Heights
Maple Heights
Bedford
Valley View
Walton Hills
44137
44146
BROADWAY AV
GRANGER RD
LEE RD
ROCKSIDE RD
DUNHAM RD
TURNEY RD
W GRACE ST
TINKERS CREEK RD
EGBERT RD
BROADWAY
Maple Heights Senior HS
Milkovich Middle School
BENHOFF PARK
SOUTHGATE USA PARK
GREENCROFT PARK
STAFFORD PARK
DUNHAM PARK
BEDFORD RESERVATION
SHAWNEE HILLS GOLF COURSE
CUYAHOGA VALLEY NATIONAL PARK
ASTORHURST COUNTRY CLUB
TINKERS CREEK
Metro Parks Bike & Hike Tr
Gorge Pkwy
Pease Rd
Industrial Av
Corridon Av
Reddington Av
Kennerdown Av
Krems Av
Tokay Av
Tabor Av
Brunswick Av
Wheeler Rd
James Av
Janice Dr
Lisa Dr
Rochelle Dr
Summit Av
Carol Dr
Schreiber Rd
Florence Dr
Ryan Dr
Benhoff Dr
Fernway Dr
Greendale Av
Wingate Rd
Northwood Av
Edgewood Av
Maplewood Av
Maple Park Dr
Ramage Av
Dunbury Dr
Evening Star Av
Morning Star Av
Steinway Blvd
Walvern Blvd
Shirley Av
Rowena Av
Mendota Av
Corkhill Rd
Longvale Rd
Woodbrook Av
Granite Rd
Pennsylvania Av
Maple Heights Blvd
Mapleboro Av
Edinboro Av
Hazelwood Av
Watercrest Av
Stafford Av
Beverly Av
Carlyle Rd
Grand Blvd
Eldred Av
Gould Av
Wandle Av
Ellenwood Av
Lamson Av
Palmetto St
Glendale Av
Deborah Ln
Mapledale Av
Powers Rd
Broadmore Av
Grandmere Dr
Button Rd
Overlook Ln
Tulip Ln
Hickory Dr
Chestnut Dr
Wight Oaks Dr
Deeridge Dr
Brenda Lee Dr
Kydan Ln
Shaner Dr
Walton Rd
Conelly Blvd
Rotary Dr
Kral Dr
Allen Dr
Carmany Dr
A
B
C
D
E
1
2
3
4
5
6
7
RAND McNALLY

1:24,000
1 in. = 2000 ft.
0 0.25 0.5
miles

SEE 2758 MAP

Maple Heights
44137
Southgate USA
Greyhound-Maple Heights
STAFFORD PARK
Southgate Park Blvd
NORTHFIELD RD
BARTLETT RD
ZION MEMORIAL PARK
EVERGREEN MEMORIAL PARK
ROCKSIDE RD
CANNON RD
AURORA RD
RICHMOND RD
OUTERBELT EAST FRWY
Meadowbrook Market Square
St. Peter Chanel HS
Bedford Senior HS
HILLCREST MEMORIAL PARK CEMETERY
COLUMBUS RD
Bedford Heights
WARRENSVILLE CENTER RD
TAFT PARK
44146
Bedford
UHHS Bedford Medical Ctr
BROADWAY
LINCOLNCOWLES PARK
REED PARK
SOLON RD
BEDFORD CEM
BEDFORD RESERVATION
TINKERS CREEK
UNION ST
BEDFORD CHAGRIN PKWY
Chagrin Pkwy
SHAWNEE HILLS GOLF COURSE
EGBERT RD
INTERSTATE PARK
FORBES RD
Walton Hills
Oakwood
Woodline Rd
Hawthorn Pkwy
Lincolnville Av
OAKLEAF RD
A B C D E
1 2 3 4 5 6 7

SEE 2886 MAP
SEE 2888 MAP
SEE 3018 MAP

1:24,000
1 in. = 2000 ft.
0 0.25 0.5
miles

SEE 2759 MAP
SEE 3019 MAP
SEE MAP 2887
SEE MAP 2889
Bedford Heights
44146
Oakwood
Solon
44139
Glenwillow
RICHMOND RD
CANNON RD
AURORA RD
SOLON RD
HARPER RD
COCHRAN RD
BRAINARD RD
FORBES RD
COLUMBUS RD
Hawthorn Pkwy
Metro Parks Bike & Hike Tr
Wedgewood Dr
Woodsdale Ln
Brighton Park Blvd
SOUTH CHAGRIN RESERVATION
MOUNT OLIVE CEMETERY
HILLCREST MEM PARK CEM
HAWTHORNE VALLEY COUNTRY CLUB
Nestle USA
Nestle's
Cleveland Clinic Solon Family Health Center
Bainbridge Rd
Old South Miles Rd
St. Vincent Solon Medical Campus
ROSELAWN CEM
Patrons of Arts in Vatican Museum
Loreal USA
Carter St
SHADOW LK
TINKERS CREEK
Bruce Industrial Pkwy
Solon Industrial Pkwy
Beaver Meadow Pkwy
Fountain Pkwy
Ambina Dr
Hall St
Tinkers Ct
Pergl Rd
Tinkers Valley Dr
Willow Tree Ln
Arnold Miller Pkwy
Parkland Blvd
Davis Industrial Pkwy
Arthur Rd
Camp Industrial Rd
Enterprise Pkwy
Old Harper Rd
Emerald Ridge Pkwy
Briarwood Ln
Wagon Wheel Dr
Kruse Dr
Orchard Rd
Nimrod St W
Warwickshire Ln
Longview
A
1 Cambridge Dr
2 Morning Glory Ln
B
1 Hawthorn Pkwy
2 Buckthorn Rd
41°25'02"
41°24'36"
41°24'10"
41°23'44"
41°23'18"
41°22'52"
41°22'26"
41°22'00"
81°29'24"
81°28'50"
81°28'15"
81°27'41"
81°27'06"
81°26'31"

RAND McNALLY

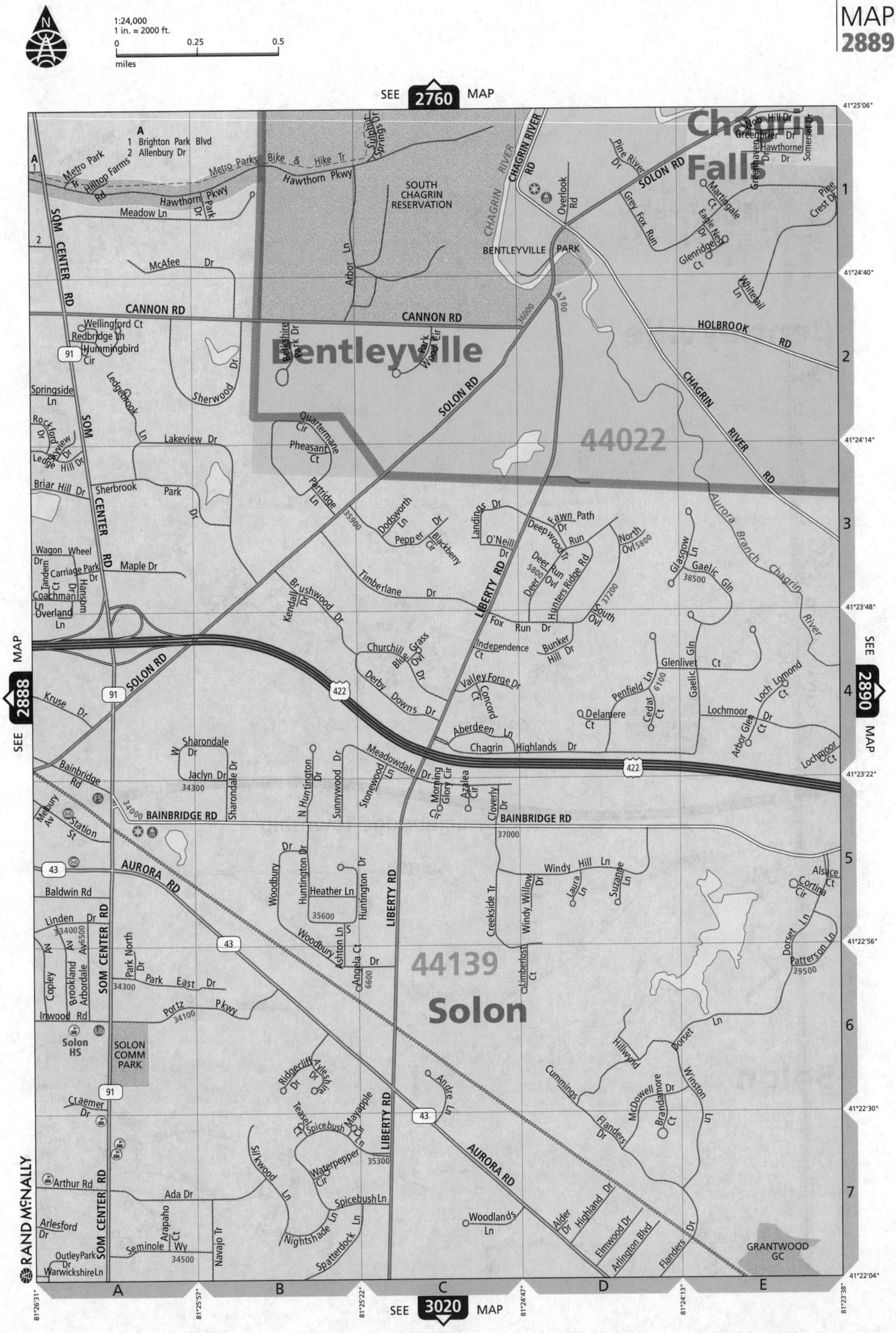
1:24,000
1 in. = 2000 ft.
0
0.25
0.5
miles
SEE 2760 MAP
SEE 3020 MAP
SEE 2888 MAP
SEE 2890 MAP
A
1 Brighton Park Blvd
2 Allenbury Dr
Chagrin Falls
Bentleyville
Solon
44022
44139
SOUTH CHAGRIN RESERVATION
BENTLEYVILLE PARK
SOLON COMM PARK
Solon HS
GRANTWOOD GC
Metro Parks Bike & Hike Tr
Metro Park Tr
Hilltop Farms Rd
Hawthorn Pkwy
Hawthorn Park Dr
Meadow Ln
Sulphur Springs Dr
Arbor Ln
McAfee Dr
CANNON RD
SOM CENTER RD
Wellingford Ct
Redbridge Ln
Hummingbird Cir
Springside Ln
Ledgebrook Ln
Sherwood Dr
Berkshire Park Dr
Park Wood Cir
SOLON RD
CHAGRIN RIVER RD
Chagrin River
Overlook Rd
Pine River Dr
Grey Fox Run
Martingale Ct
Eagle Nest Dr
Glenridge Ct
Whitetail Ln
Nob Hill Dr
Greenbrier Dr
Greenhaven Dr
Hawthorne Dr
Somerset Dr
Pine Crest Dr
HOLBROOK RD
Rockford Dr
Ivyview Dr
Ledge Hill Dr
Briar Hill Dr
Lakeview Dr
Quartermane Cir
Pheasant Ct
Partridge Ln
Sherbrook Park Dr
Dodsworth Ln
Pepper Dr
Blackberry Cir
Landings Dr
O'Neill Dr
Fawn Path Dr
Deepwood Tr
Run
Deer Run
Deer Ovl
Hunters Ridge Rd
North Ovl
South Ovl
Glasgow Ln
Gaelic Gln
Aurora Branch Chagrin River
Wagon Wheel Dr
Carriage Park Dr
Tandem Ct
Hansom Dr
Coachman Ln
Overland Ln
Maple Dr
Brushwood Dr
Kendall Dr
Timberlane Dr
LIBERTY RD
Fox Run Dr
Independence Ct
Bunker Hill Dr
Churchill Dr
Blue Grass Ovl
Derby Downs Dr
Valley Forge Dr
Concord Ct
Penfield Ln
Cedar Ct
Glenlivet Ct
Gaelic Gln
Loch Lomond Ct
Lochmoor Dr
Arbor Glen Ct
Lochmoor Ct
Delamere Ct
Aberdeen Ln
Chagrin Highlands Dr
Kruse Dr
W Sharondale Dr
Jaclyn Dr
Sharondale Dr
Bainbridge Rd
BAINBRIDGE RD
N Huntington Dr
Sunnywood Dr
Stonewood Ln
Meadowdale Dr
Morning Glory Cir
Azalea Cir
Cloverly Dr
Melbury Av
Station St
AURORA RD
Baldwin Rd
Linden Dr
Copley Av
Brookland Av
Arbordale Av
Park North Dr
Park East Dr
Portz Pkwy
Inwood Rd
Woodbury Dr
Huntington Dr
Heather Ln
Ashton Ln
Angela Ct
Windy Hill Ln
Windy Willow Dr
Laura Ln
Suzanne Ln
Creekside Tr
Limberlost Ct
Alsace Ct
Cortina Cir
Dorset Ln
Patterson Ln
Hillwynd
Cummings
Winston Ln
McDowell Dr
Brandamore Ct
Flanders Dr
Ridgecliff Dr
Aylesbire Dr
Teasel Ct
Spicebush Ct
Mayapple Cir
Andre Ln
Craemer Dr
Silkwood Ln
Waterpepper Cir
Spicebush Ln
Nightshade Ln
Spatterdock Ln
Arthur Rd
Ada Dr
Arlesford Dr
Arapaho Ct
Seminole Wy
Navajo Tr
Outley Park Dr
Warwickshire Ln
Woodlands Ln
Alder Dr
Highland Dr
Elmwood Dr
Arlington Blvd
Flanders Dr
91
422
43
RAND McNALLY

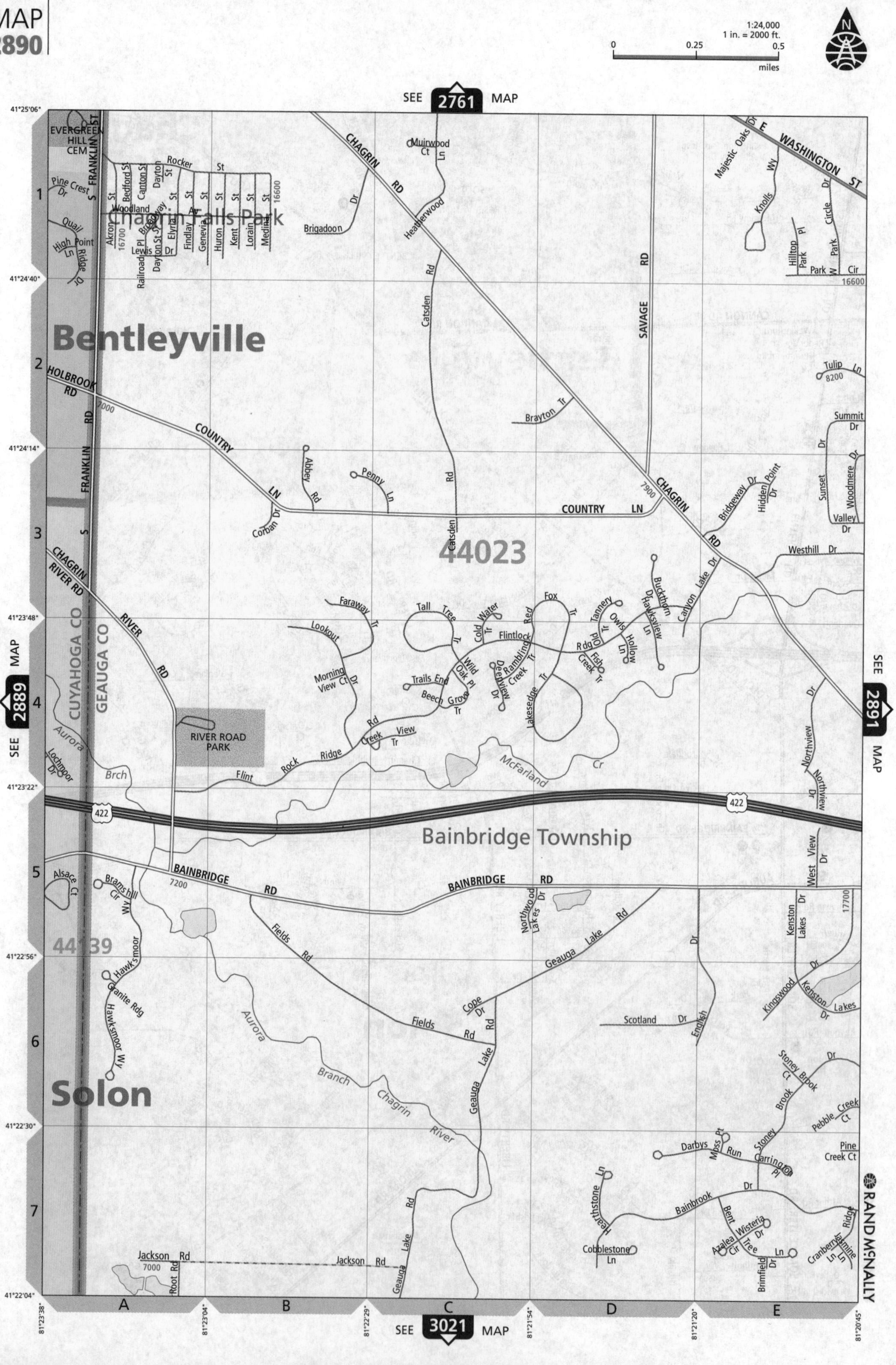
1:24,000
1 in. = 2000 ft.
0
0.25
0.5
miles
N
SEE 2761 MAP
SEE 2889 MAP
SEE 2891 MAP
SEE 3021 MAP
Bentleyville
Chagrin Falls Park
Bainbridge Township
Solon
44023
44139
EVERGREEN HILL CEM
RIVER ROAD PARK
CUYAHOGA CO
GEAUGA CO
S FRANKLIN ST
FRANKLIN RD
HOLBROOK RD
COUNTRY LN
CHAGRIN RD
CHAGRIN RIVER RD
RIVER RD
SAVAGE RD
E WASHINGTON ST
BAINBRIDGE RD
Fields Rd
Geauga Lake Rd
Catsden Rd
Heatherwood
Flint Rock Ridge Rd
Jackson Rd
422
Aurora Branch Chagrin River
McFarland Cr
Brch
Canyon Lake Dr
Scotland Dr
English Dr
Kenston Lakes Dr
Northview Dr
West View Dr
Bainbrook Dr
Stoney Brook Dr
Hawksmoor Wy
Hearthstone Ln
Cobblestone Ln
Muirwood Ct
Brigadoon Dr
Abbey Rd
Penny Ln
Corban Dr
Brayton Tr
Faraway Tr
Lookout
Morning View Ct
Tall Tree Tr
Cold Water Tr
Flintlock
Fox Tr
Tannery
Buckthorn
Hawksview Ln
Owls Hollow Ln
Rdg Pl
Fish Creek Tr
Ramblin Creek Tr
Deerview Dr
Lakesedge Tr
Wild Oak Pl
Trails End
Beech Grove Tr
Creek View Tr
Majestic Oaks Dr
Knolls Wy
Hilltop Pl
Park Pl
Circle Dr
W Park Cir
Tulip Ln
Summit Dr
Woodmere Dr
Sunset Dr
Valley Dr
Hidden Point Dr
Bridgeway Dr
Westhill Dr
Kingswood Dr
Northwood Lakes Dr
Cope Dr
Alsace Ct
Bramshill Cir
Granite Rdg
Lochmoor Dr
Pine Crest Dr
Quail
High Point Ln
Ridge Dr
Rocker St
Woodland Av
Railroad
Lewis
Dayton St
Akron St
Bedford St
Canton St
Broadway
Elyria St
Findlay St
Genevia St
Huron St
Kent St
Lorain St
Medina St
Darbys Run
Moss Pt
Carrington Pl
Pebble Creek Ct
Pine Creek Ct
Bent Tree Ln
Wisteria Dr
Azalea Cir
Brimfield Dr
Cranberry Ln
Jasmine Ln
Root Rd
7000
7200
7900
8200
16600
16700
17700
41°25'06"
41°24'40"
41°24'14"
41°23'48"
41°23'22"
41°22'56"
41°22'30"
41°22'04"
81°23'38"
81°23'04"
81°22'29"
81°21'54"
81°21'20"
81°20'45"
A
B
C
D
E
1
2
3
4
5
6
7
RAND McNALLY

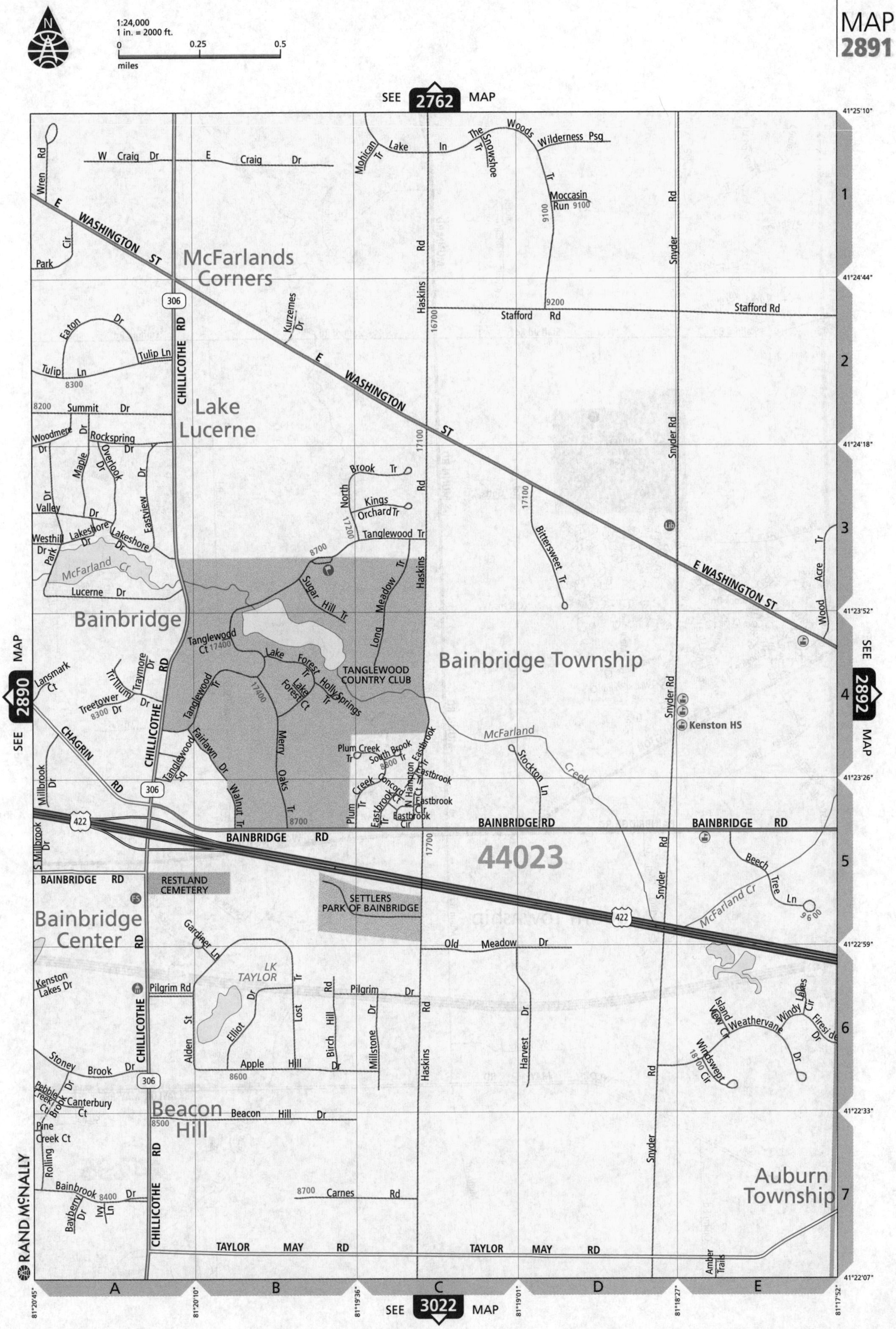
N
1:24,000
1 in. = 2000 ft.
0 0.25 0.5
miles
SEE 2762 MAP
SEE 2890 MAP
SEE 2892 MAP
SEE 3022 MAP
McFarlands Corners
Lake Lucerne
Bainbridge
Bainbridge Township
Bainbridge Center
Beacon Hill
Auburn Township
44023
TANGLEWOOD COUNTRY CLUB
RESTLAND CEMETERY
SETTLERS PARK OF BAINBRIDGE
Kenston HS
LK TAYLOR
E WASHINGTON ST
CHILLICOTHE RD
CHAGRIN RD
BAINBRIDGE RD
TAYLOR MAY RD
Haskins Rd
Snyder Rd
Stafford Rd
W Craig Dr
E Craig Dr
Wren Rd
Park Cir
Mohican Tr
Lake In
The Snowshoe Tr
Woods Tr
Wilderness Psg
Moccasin Run
Kurzemes Dr
Eaton Dr
Tulip Ln
Summit Dr
Woodmere Dr
Rockspring Dr
Maple Dr
Overlook Dr
Eastview Dr
Valley Dr
Westhill Dr
Lakeshore Dr
McFarland Cr
Lucerne Dr
Brook Tr
North Tr
Kings Orchard Tr
Tanglewood Tr
Sugar Hill Tr
Long Meadow Tr
Bittersweet Tr
Wood Acre Tr
Tanglewood Ct
Lake Forest Tr
Lake Forest Ct
Holly Springs Tr
Lansmark Ct
Trillium Dr
Traymore Dr
Treetower Dr
Tanglewood Sq
Fairlawn Dr
Walnut Tr
Merry Oaks Tr
Millbrook Dr
S Millbrook Dr
Plum Creek Tr
South Brook Tr
Eastbrook Tr
Concord Tr
N Hampton Ct
Eastbrook Cir
Stockton Ln
McFarland Creek
Beech Tree Ln
Old Meadow Dr
Gardiner Ln
Lost Tr
Pilgrim Dr
Pilgrim Rd
Kenston Lakes Dr
Alden St
Elliot Dr
Birch Hill Rd
Millstone Dr
Apple Hill Dr
Harvest Dr
Island View Ct
Weathervane Dr
Windy Lakes Cir
Fireside Dr
Windswept Cir
Stoney Brook Dr
Pebble Creek Cir
Brook Ct
Canterbury Ct
Pine Creek Ct
Beacon Hill Dr
Rolling
Bainbrook Dr
Bayberry Dr
Ivy Ln
Carnes Rd
Amber Trails
306
422
8200
8300
8400
8500
8600
8700
8800
9100
9200
9600
16700
17000
17100
17200
17400
17700
18000
41°25'10"
41°24'44"
41°24'18"
41°23'52"
41°23'26"
41°22'59"
41°22'33"
41°22'07"
81°20'45"
81°20'10"
81°19'36"
81°19'01"
81°18'27"
81°17'52"
A B C D E
1 2 3 4 5 6 7
RAND McNALLY

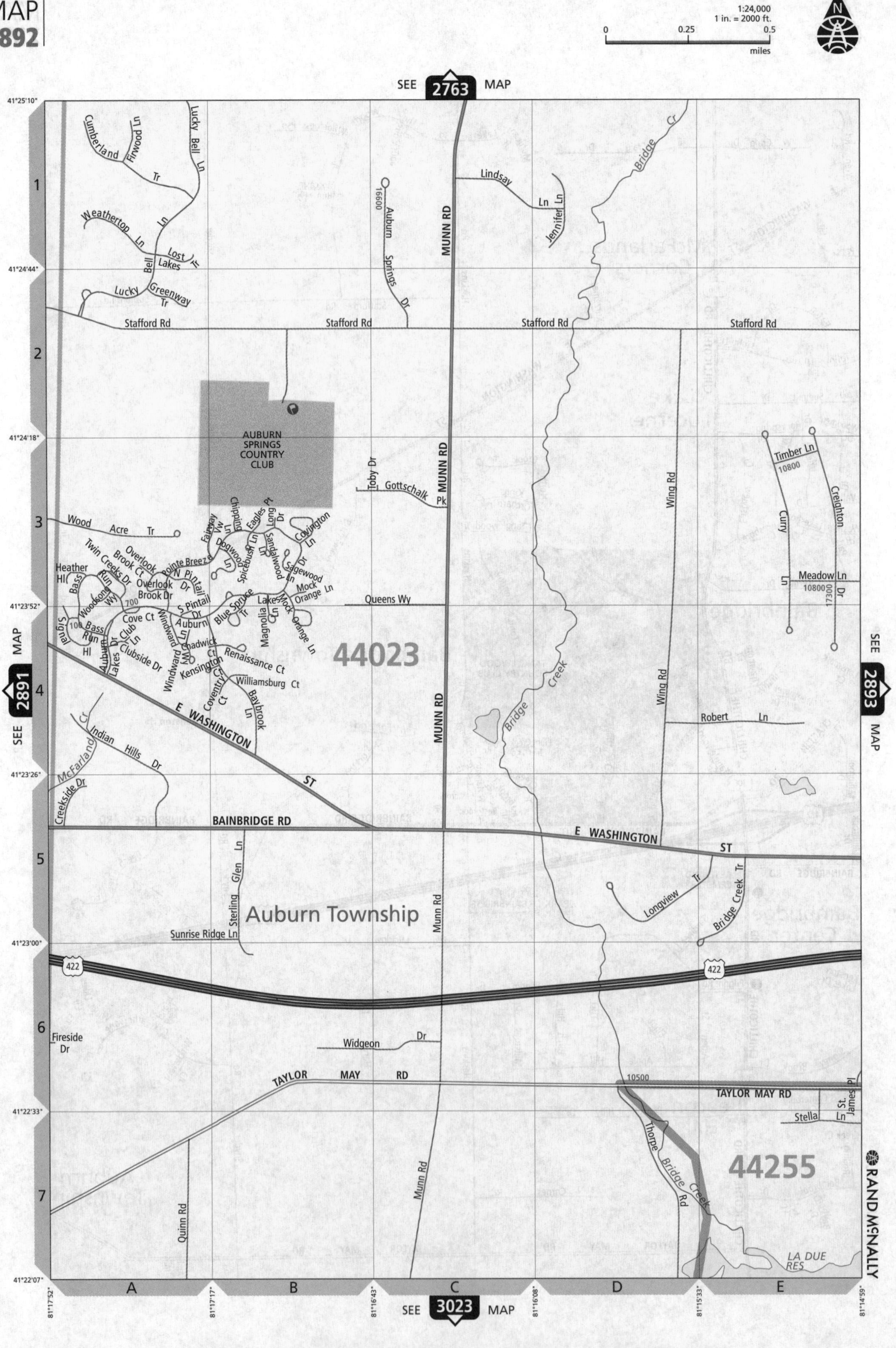
1:24,000
1 in. = 2000 ft.
0
0.25
0.5
miles
N
SEE 2763 MAP
SEE 2891 MAP
SEE 2893 MAP
SEE 3023 MAP
Cumberland
Firwood Ln
Lucky Bell Ln
Tr
Weathertop Ln
Ln
Lost Lakes Tr
Bell
Lucky Greenway Tr
Stafford Rd
Stafford Rd
Stafford Rd
Stafford Rd
Lindsay Ln
Jennifer Ln
Bridge Cr
16600
Auburn Springs Dr
MUNN RD
AUBURN SPRINGS COUNTRY CLUB
Toby Dr
Gottschalk Pk
Wood Acre Tr
Twin Creeks Dr
Heather Hl
Bass Run
Overlook Brook Ct
Overlook Brook Dr
Pointe Breeze Dr
N Pintail Dr
S Pintail Dr
Woodsong Wy
700
100
Bass Run Hl
Signal
Cove Ct
Club Ln
Clubside Dr
Auburn Lakes Dr
Windward Dr
Windward Ln
Auburn Dr
Chadwick Ct
Kensington Ct
Coventry Ct
Renaissance Ct
Williamsburg Ct
Baybrook Ln
Blue Spruce Tr
Magnolia Ln
Lakes
Mock Orange Ln
Fairway Vw
Chipping Ln
Dogwood Ln
Spicebush Ln
Eagles Pt
Long Pt Dr
Sandalwood Ln
Covington Ln
Sagewood Dr
Queens Wy
44023
E WASHINGTON ST
Bridge Creek
Wing Rd
Timber Ln
10800
Creighton Dr
Curry Ln
Meadow Ln
108000
17300
Robert Ln
McFarland Cr
Indian Hills Dr
Creekside Dr
BAINBRIDGE RD
Sterling Glen Ln
Auburn Township
Munn Rd
Sunrise Ridge Ln
Longview Tr
Bridge Creek Tr
422
422
Fireside Dr
Widgeon Dr
TAYLOR MAY RD
10500
TAYLOR MAY RD
Stella Ln
St. James Pl
Thorpe Rd
Bridge Creek
44255
Munn Rd
Quinn Rd
LA DUE RES
A
B
C
D
E
1
2
3
4
5
6
7
41°25'10"
41°24'44"
41°24'18"
41°23'52"
41°23'26"
41°23'00"
41°22'33"
41°22'07"
81°17'52"
81°17'17"
81°16'43"
81°16'08"
81°15'33"
81°14'59"
RAND McNALLY

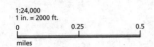

1:24,000
1 in. = 2000 ft.
0 0.25 0.5
miles

SEE 2764 MAP

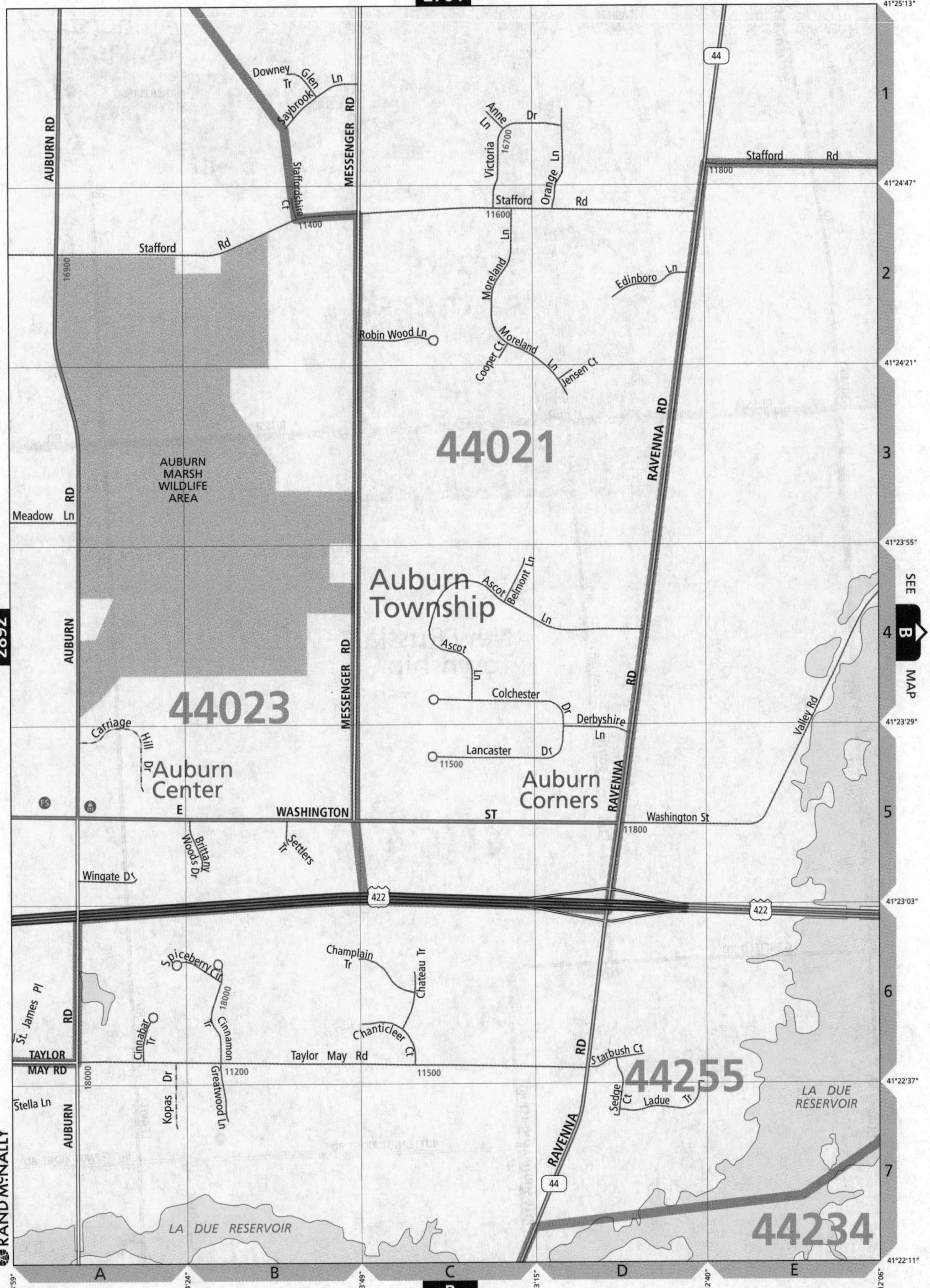

Downey Tr
Glen Ln
Saybrook
Staffordshire Ct
11400
MESSENGER RD
AUBURN RD
Anne Dr
Victoria Ln
16700
Orange Ln
Stafford Rd
11600
11800
44
Stafford Rd
16900
Moreland Ln
Edinboro Ln
Robin Wood Ln
Moreland Ln
Cooper Ct
Jensen Ct
RAVENNA RD
44021
AUBURN MARSH WILDLIFE AREA
Meadow Ln
RD
Auburn Township
Ascot Ln
Belmont Ln
Ascot Ln
Colchester Dr
Derbyshire Ln
Lancaster Dr
11500
Valley Rd
AUBURN
44023
Carriage Hill Dr
Auburn Center
Auburn Corners
RAVENNA RD
E WASHINGTON ST
Washington St
11800
Brittany Woods Dr
Settlers Tr
Wingate Dr
422
422
Champlain Tr
Chateau Tr
Spiceberry Cir
18000
Cinnamon Tr
St. James Pl
RD
Cinnabar Tr
Chanticleer Ct
TAYLOR MAY RD
Taylor May Rd
11200
11500
RD
Starbush Ct
44255
18000
Kopas Dr
Greatwood Ln
Stella Ln
AUBURN
Sedge Ct
Ladue Tr
LA DUE RESERVOIR
RAVENNA
44
LA DUE RESERVOIR
44234
1
2
3
4
5
6
7
A
B
C
D
E
41°25'13"
41°24'47"
41°24'21"
41°23'55"
41°23'29"
41°23'03"
41°22'37"
41°22'11"
81°14'59"
81°14'24"
81°13'49"
81°13'15"
81°12'40"
81°12'06"

SEE 2892 MAP

SEE B MAP

SEE B MAP

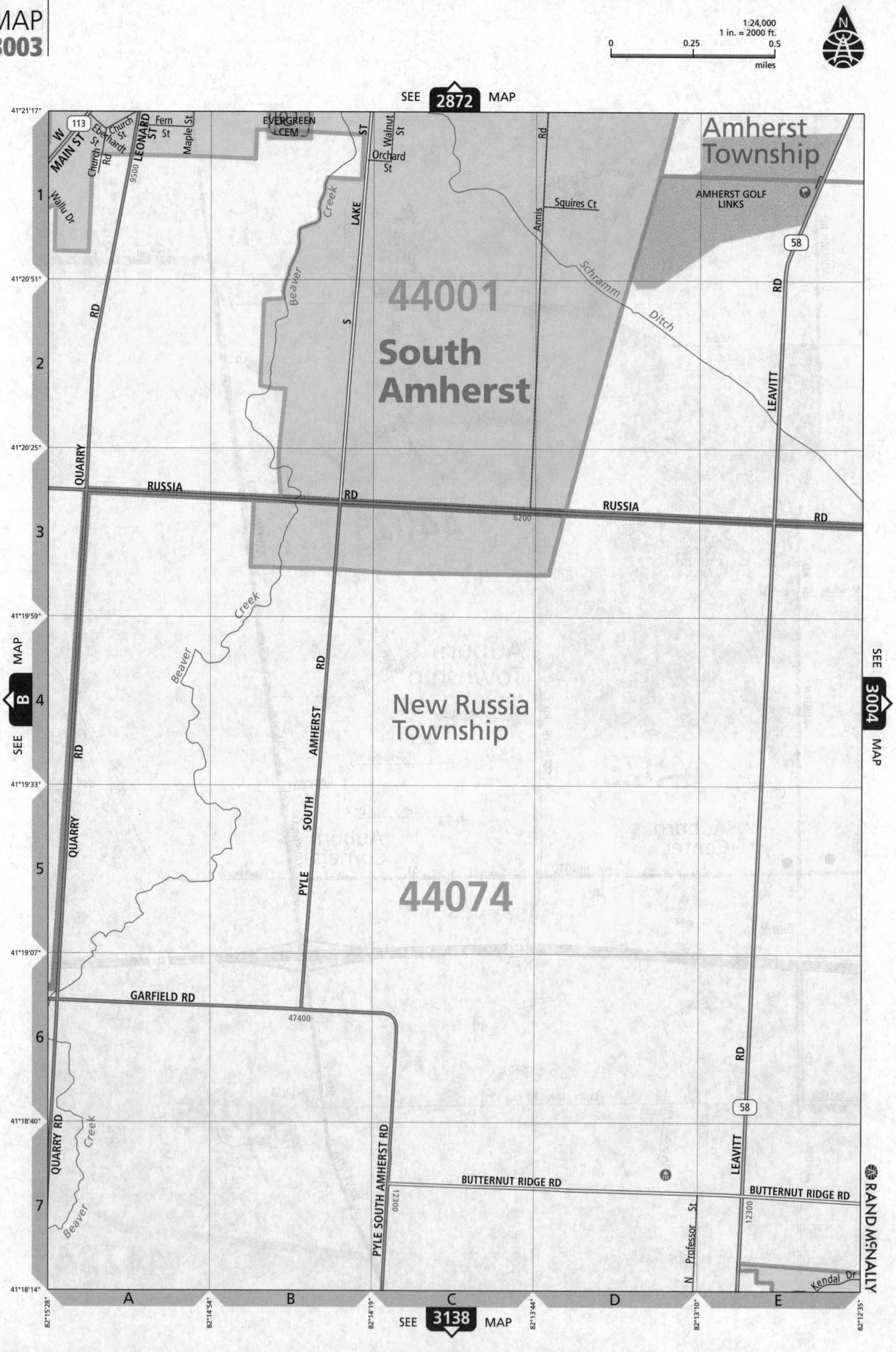
1:24,000
1 in. = 2000 ft.
0
0.25
0.5
miles
N
SEE 2872 MAP
SEE 3138 MAP
SEE B MAP
SEE 3004 MAP
Amherst Township
AMHERST GOLF LINKS
44001
South Amherst
New Russia Township
44074
EVERGREEN CEM
W MAIN ST
113
Church St
Eberhardt St
Church St
Church Rd
LEONARD ST
Fern St
Maple St
Walnut St
Orchard St
Wallu Dr
9500
Squires Ct
Annis Rd
Schramm Ditch
Beaver Creek
LAKE S ST
58
LEAVITT RD
QUARRY RD
RUSSIA RD
6200
SOUTH AMHERST RD
PYLE
GARFIELD RD
47400
PYLE SOUTH AMHERST RD
12300
BUTTERNUT RIDGE RD
N Professor St
Kendal Dr
RAND McNALLY
41°21'17"
41°20'51"
41°20'25"
41°19'59"
41°19'33"
41°19'07"
41°18'40"
41°18'14"
82°15'28"
82°14'54"
82°14'19"
82°13'44"
82°13'10"
82°12'35"
A
B
C
D
E
1
2
3
4
5
6
7

1:24,000
1 in. = 2000 ft.
0 0.25 0.5
miles

SEE 2873 MAP

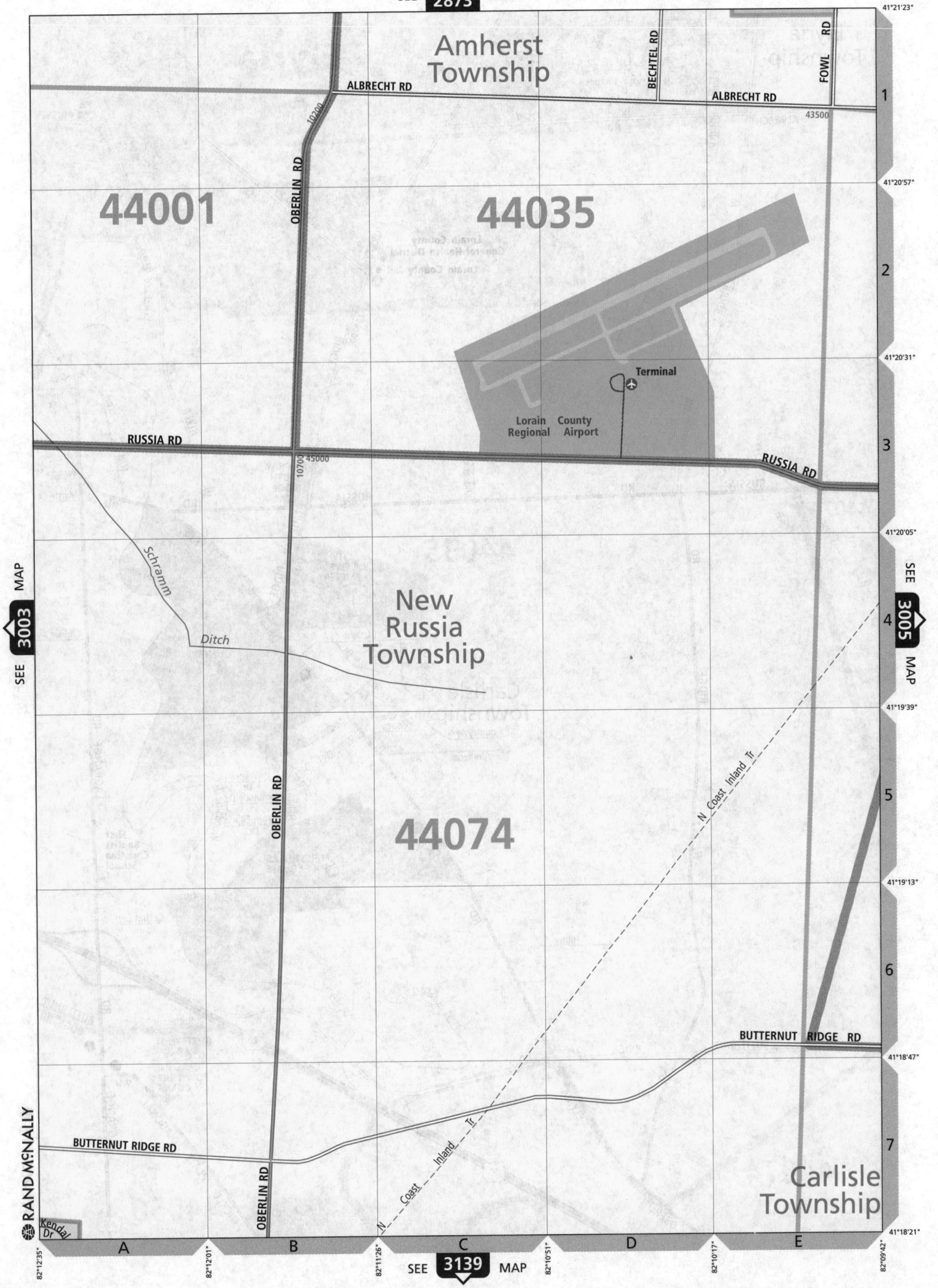
Amherst Township
ALBRECHT RD
BECHTEL RD
FOWL RD
ALBRECHT RD
43500
10200
OBERLIN RD
44001
44035
Terminal
Lorain County Regional Airport
RUSSIA RD
45000
10700
RUSSIA RD
Schramm Ditch
New Russia Township
N Coast Inland Tr
OBERLIN RD
44074
BUTTERNUT RIDGE RD
BUTTERNUT RIDGE RD
OBERLIN RD
Carlisle Township
Kendal Dr
A
B
C
D
E
1
2
3
4
5
6
7
41°21'23"
41°20'57"
41°20'31"
41°20'05"
41°19'39"
41°19'13"
41°18'47"
41°18'21"
82°12'35"
82°12'01"
82°11'26"
82°10'51"
82°10'17"
82°09'42"
RAND McNALLY

SEE 3003 MAP

SEE 3005 MAP

SEE 3139 MAP

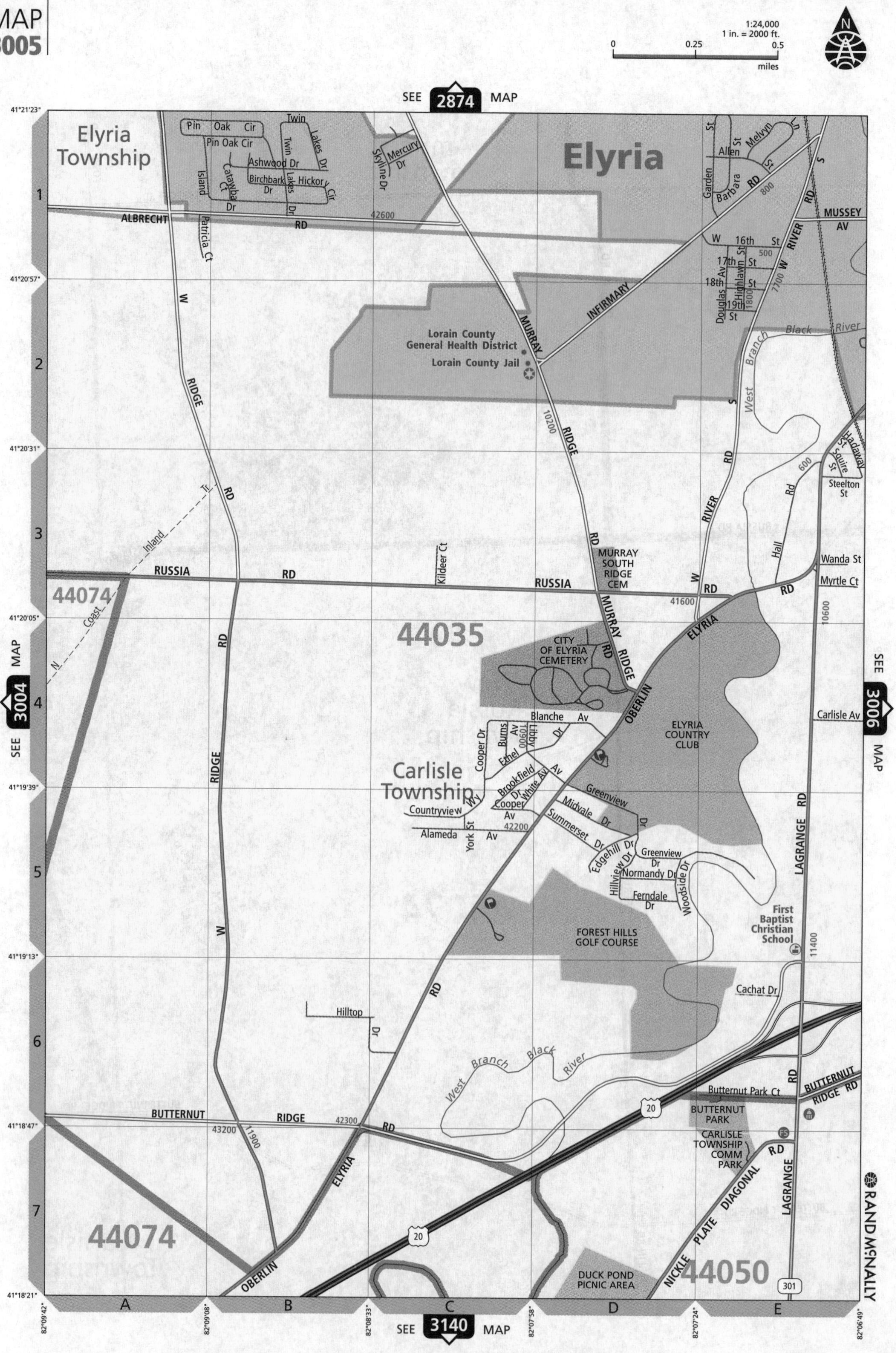
1:24,000
1 in. = 2000 ft.
0
0.25
0.5
miles
N
SEE 2874 MAP
SEE 3004 MAP
SEE 3006 MAP
SEE 3140 MAP
Elyria Township
Elyria
Carlisle Township
44074
44035
44050
Pin Oak Cir
Twin Lakes Dr
Ashwood Dr
Birchbark Dr
Hickory Cir
Catawba Ct
Island Dr
Skyline Dr
Mercury Dr
ALBRECHT RD
Patricia Ct
42600
Garden St
Barbara RD
Allen St
Melvyn Ln
800
MUSSEY AV
W 16th St
17th St
18th St
19th St
Douglas Av
Highlawn St
500
1800
7300
W RIVER RD S
INFIRMARY
MURRAY RIDGE RD
Lorain County General Health District
Lorain County Jail
Black River
West Branch
W RIDGE RD
10200
Hadaway St
Squire St
600
Hall Rd
Steelton St
Inland Tr
N Coast
RUSSIA RD
Kildeer Ct
MURRAY SOUTH RIDGE CEM
41600
Wanda St
Myrtle Ct
ELYRIA RD
10600
CITY OF ELYRIA CEMETERY
OBERLIN
ELYRIA COUNTRY CLUB
Carlisle Av
Blanche Av
Burns Av
Libby Dr
10900
Cooper Dr
Ethel
Brookfield Dr
White Av
Cooper Av
Countryview Wy
Alameda Av
York St
42200
Greenview Dr
Midvale Dr
Summerset Dr
Edgehill Dr
Hillview Dr
Normandy Dr
Ferndale Dr
Woodside Dr
LAGRANGE RD
First Baptist Christian School
11400
FOREST HILLS GOLF COURSE
Cachat Dr
Hilltop Dr
West Branch Black River
Butternut Park Ct
BUTTERNUT RIDGE RD
BUTTERNUT PARK
CARLISLE TOWNSHIP COMM PARK
BUTTERNUT RIDGE
42300
43200
11900
20
NICKLE PLATE DIAGONAL RD
DUCK POND PICNIC AREA
301
A
B
C
D
E
1
2
3
4
5
6
7
41°21'23"
41°20'57"
41°20'31"
41°20'05"
41°19'39"
41°19'13"
41°18'47"
41°18'21"
82°09'42"
82°09'08"
82°08'33"
82°07'58"
82°07'24"
82°06'49"
RAND McNALLY

1:24,000
1 in. = 2000 ft.
0 0.25 0.5
miles

SEE 2875 MAP

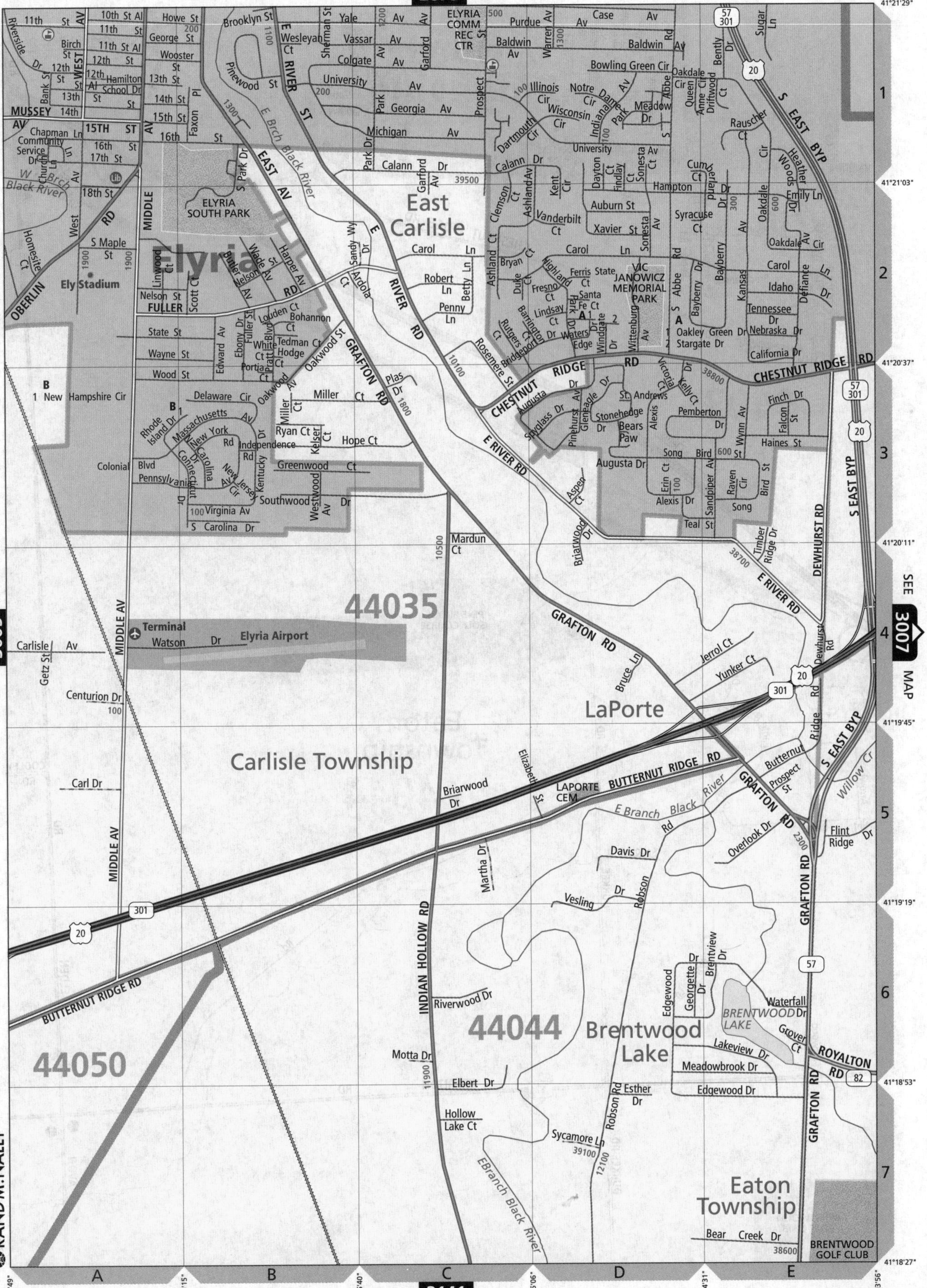
Elyria
East Carlisle
LaPorte
Carlisle Township
Brentwood Lake
Eaton Township
44035
44044
44050
ELYRIA SOUTH PARK
ELYRIA COMM REC CTR
VIC JANOWICZ MEMORIAL PARK
Ely Stadium
Elyria Airport
Terminal
Watson Dr
LAPORTE CEM
BRENTWOOD LAKE
BRENTWOOD GOLF CLUB
E Brch Black River
W Brch Black River
E Branch Black River
Willow Cr
GRAFTON RD
E RIVER RD
EAST AV
MIDDLE AV
WEST AV
OBERLIN RD
CHESTNUT RIDGE RD
BUTTERNUT RIDGE RD
S EAST BYP
INDIAN HOLLOW RD
DEWHURST RD
ROYALTON RD
MUSSEY AV
FULLER RD
15TH ST
Robson Rd
Sycamore Ln
Bear Creek Dr
Brooklyn St
Wesleyan Ct
Pinewood St
Yale Av
Vassar Av
Colgate Av
University Av
Georgia Av
Michigan Av
Calann Dr
Purdue Av
Case Av
Baldwin Av
Bowling Green Cir
Illinois Cir
Wisconsin Cir
Notre Dame Av
Meadow Dr
Hampton Dr
Auburn St
Xavier St
Vanderbilt Ct
Carol Ln
Robert Ln
Penny Ln
Betty Ln
Sandy Wy
Ardola Ct
Louden Ct
Bohannon Ct
Tedman Ct
Hodge Ct
Oakwood St
Miller Ct
Ryan Ct
Hope Ct
Independence Rd
Greenwood Ct
Southwood Dr
Westwood Av
Virginia Av
S Carolina Dr
New Hampshire Cir
Delaware Cir
Massachusetts Av
New York Rd
Colonial Blvd
Pennsylvania Dr
State St
Wayne St
Wood St
Edward Av
Nelson St
Linwood Ct
Scott Ct
S Maple St
Homesite Ct
Chapman Ln
Community Service Dr
Church Ln
Oakley Green Dr
Stargate Dr
Nebraska Dr
California Dr
Tennessee Dr
Idaho Dr
Finch Dr
Haines St
Pemberton Dr
Augusta Dr
Song Bird Ct
Alexis Dr
Teal St
Raven Cir
Timber Ridge Dr
Jerrol Ct
Yunker Ct
Bruce Ln
Mardun Ct
Briarwood Dr
Elizabeth St
Martha Dr
Davis Dr
Vesling Dr
Overlook Dr
Prospect St
Flint Ridge Dr
Riverwood Dr
Motta Dr
Elbert Dr
Hollow Lake Ct
Esther Dr
Edgewood Dr
Meadowbrook Dr
Lakeview Dr
Waterfall Dr
Grover Ct
Georgette Dr
Brentview Dr
Carlisle Av
Getz St
Centurion Dr
Carl Dr
20
57
82
301

SEE 3005 MAP
SEE 3007 MAP
SEE 3141 MAP

1:24,000
1 in. = 2000 ft.
0 0.25 0.5
miles

SEE 2876 MAP

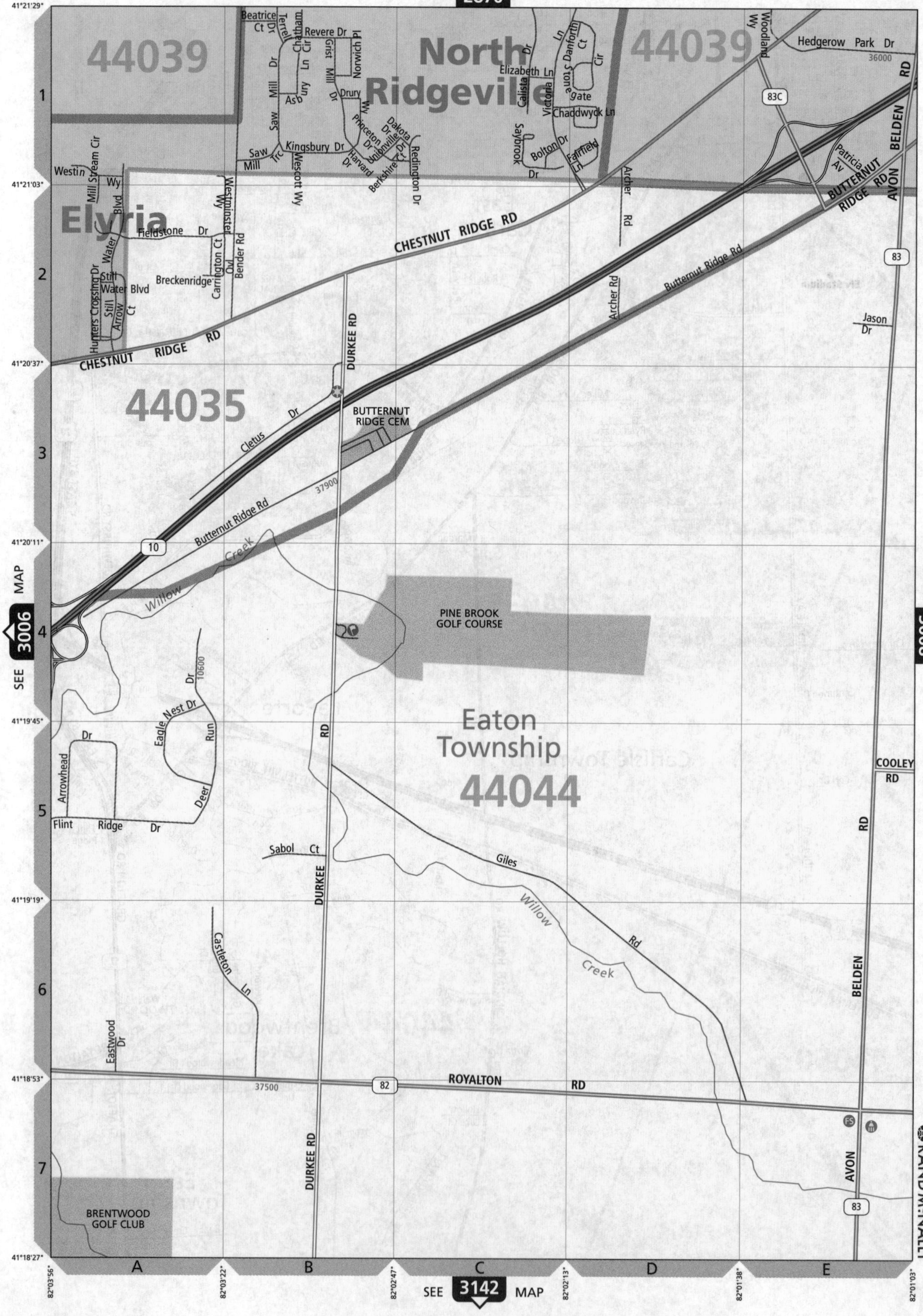
44039
North Ridgeville
44039
Elyria
44035
Eaton Township
44044
CHESTNUT RIDGE RD
BUTTERNUT RIDGE RD
Butternut Ridge Rd
DURKEE RD
AVON BELDEN RD
ROYALTON RD
COOLEY RD
Hedgerow Park Dr
Woodland Wy
Beatrice Ct
Terrel Dr
Revere Dr
Chatham Cir
Grist Mill Dr
Norwich Pl
Asbury Ln
Saw Mill Dr
Drury Ln
Princeton Dr
Dakota Dr
Unionville Dr
Kingsbury Dr
Saw Mill Trc
Wescott Wy
Harvard Dr
Berkshire Ct
Redington Dr
Elizabeth Ln
Calista Dr
Victoria Ln
Danforth Ct
Stonegate Cir
Chaddwyck Ln
Saybrook Dr
Bolton Dr
Fairfield Ln
Archer Rd
Patricia Av
Westin Wy
Mill Stream Cir
Westminster Wy
Blvd
Fieldstone Dr
Bender Rd
Carrington Ct
Owl
Breckenridge
Hunters Crossing Dr
Still Water Blvd
Still Arrow Ct
Water
Jason Dr
Cletus Dr
BUTTERNUT RIDGE CEM
37900
36000
10
83C
83
Willow Creek
PINE BROOK GOLF COURSE
Eagle Nest Dr
10600
Deer Run
Arrowhead Dr
Flint Ridge Dr
Sabol Ct
Giles Rd
Castleton Ln
Eastwood Dr
37500
82
BRENTWOOD GOLF CLUB
A B C D E
1 2 3 4 5 6 7
41°21'29"
41°21'03"
41°20'37"
41°20'11"
41°19'45"
41°19'19"
41°18'53"
41°18'27"
82°03'56"
82°03'22"
82°02'47"
82°02'13"
82°01'38"
82°01'03"

SEE 3006 MAP

SEE 3008 MAP

SEE 3142 MAP

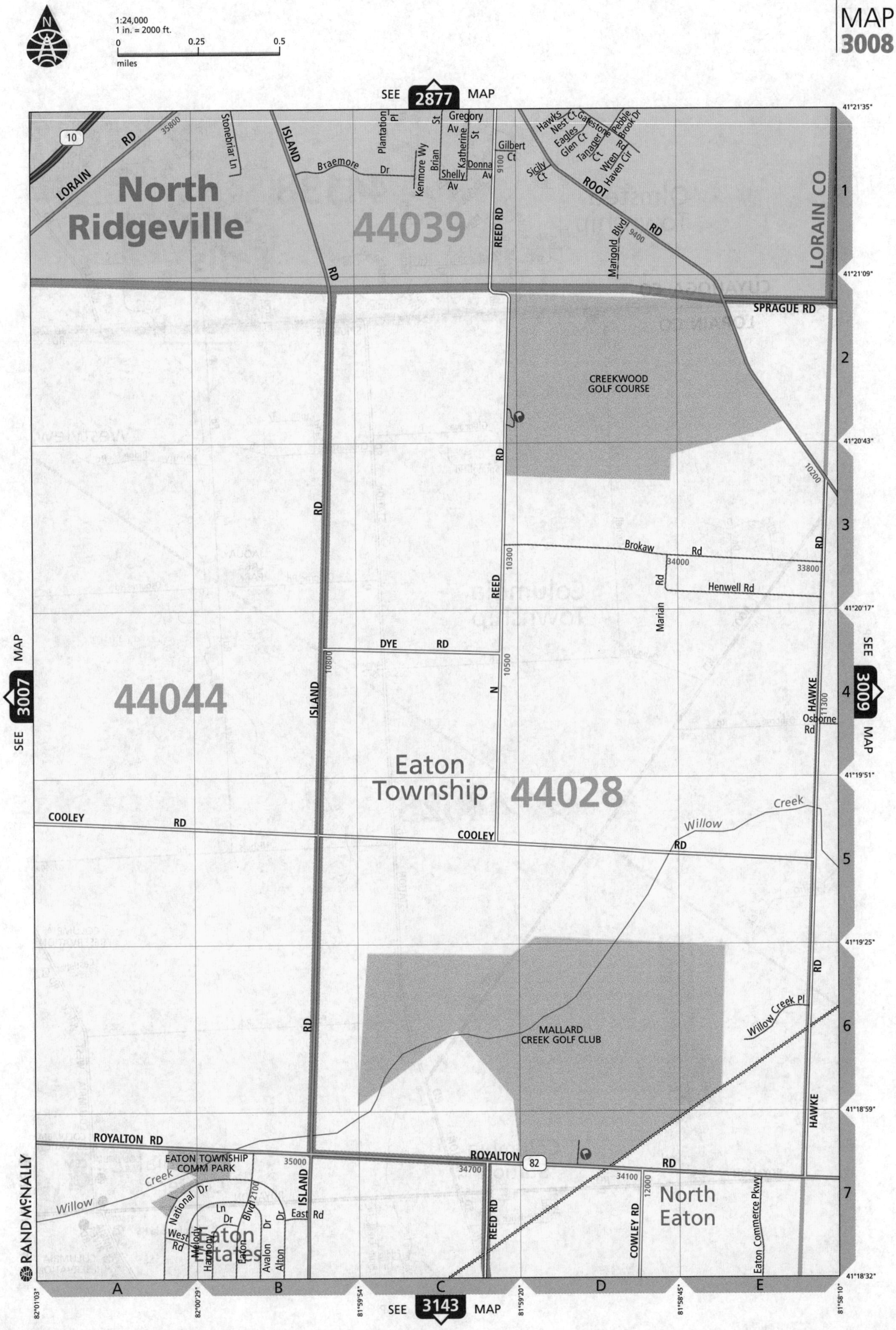
1:24,000
1 in. = 2000 ft.
0 0.25 0.5
miles
SEE 2877 MAP
SEE 3007 MAP
SEE 3009 MAP
SEE 3143 MAP
North Ridgeville
44039
44044
44028
Eaton Township
North Eaton
Eaton Estates
LORAIN RD
10
Stonebriar Ln
ISLAND RD
Braemore Dr
Plantation Pl
Kenmore Wy
Brian St
Gregory Av
Katherine St
Shelly Av
Donna Av
Gilbert Ct
REED RD
Hawks Nest Ct
Eagles Glen Ct
Galestone Ct
Tanager Ct
Pebble Brook Dr
Wren Haven Cir
Sicily Ct
ROOT RD
Marigold Blvd
LORAIN CO
CUYAHOGA CO
SPRAGUE RD
CREEKWOOD GOLF COURSE
Brokaw Rd
Marian Rd
Henwell Rd
HAWKE RD
DYE RD
N REED RD
Osborne Rd
COOLEY RD
Willow Creek
MALLARD CREEK GOLF CLUB
Willow Creek Pl
ROYALTON RD
82
EATON TOWNSHIP COMM PARK
National Dr
West Rd
Melody Ln
Harmony Dr
Eaton Blvd
Avalon Dr
Alton Dr
East Rd
COWLEY RD
Eaton Commerce Pkwy
35800 9100 9400 10200 10300 10500 10800 11300 34000 33800 35000 34700 34100 12000 2100
A B C D E
1 2 3 4 5 6 7
41°21'35" 41°21'09" 41°20'43" 41°20'17" 41°19'51" 41°19'25" 41°18'59" 41°18'32"
82°01'03" 82°00'29" 81°59'54" 81°59'20" 81°58'45" 81°58'10"
RAND McNALLY

1:24,000
1 in. = 2000 ft.
0 0.25 0.5
miles

SEE 2878 MAP

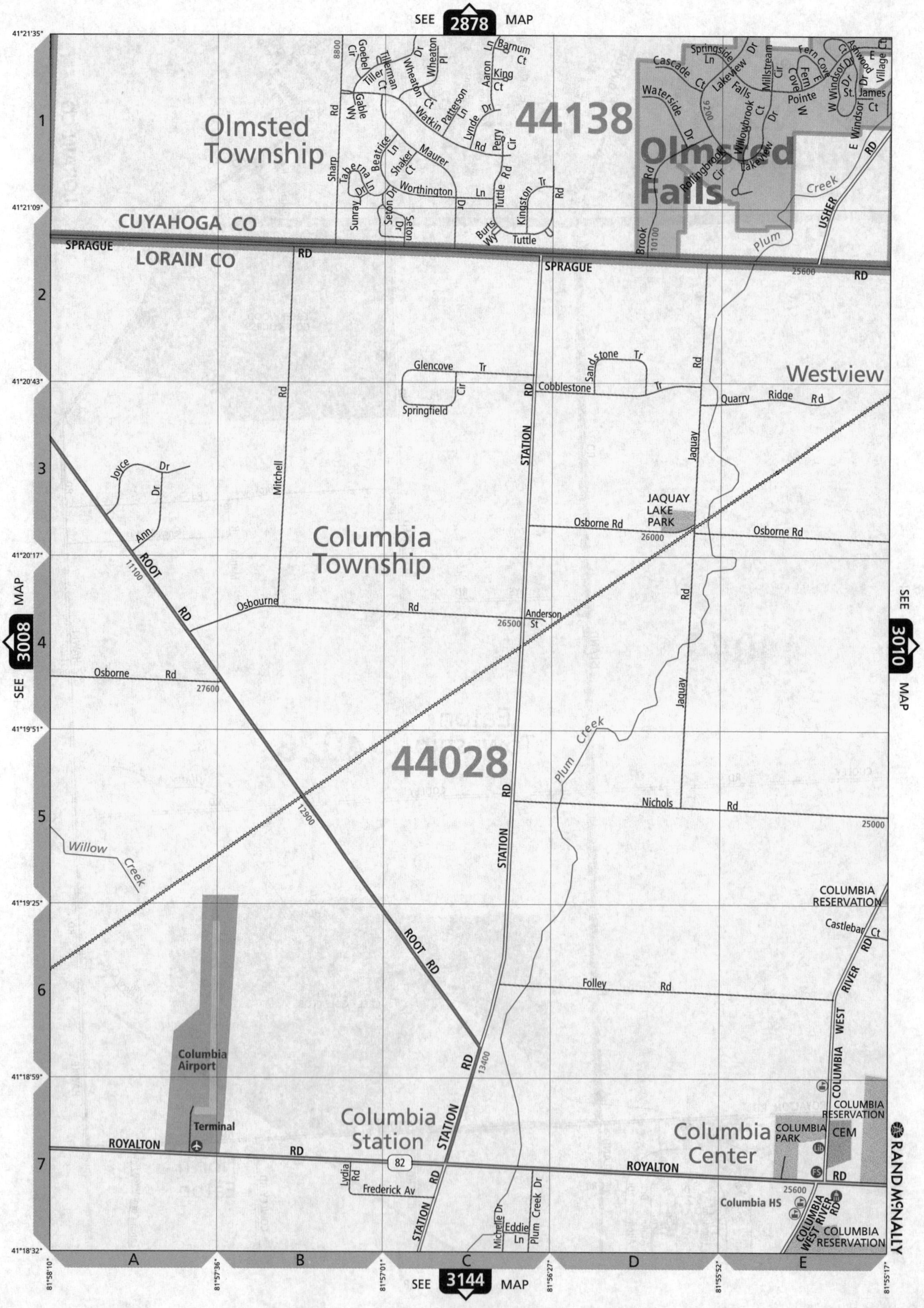
Olmsted Township
44138
Olmsted Falls
CUYAHOGA CO
LORAIN CO
SPRAGUE RD
SPRAGUE
USHER RD
Plum Creek
Westview
Quarry Ridge Rd
Glencove Tr
Springfield Cir
Cobblestone Tr
Sandstone Tr
STATION RD
Jaquay Rd
Mitchell Rd
Joyce Dr
Ann Dr
ROOT RD
JAQUAY LAKE PARK
Osborne Rd
Columbia Township
Osbourne Rd
Anderson St
44028
Nichols Rd
Willow Creek
COLUMBIA RESERVATION
Castlebar Ct
WEST RIVER RD
Folley Rd
COLUMBIA WEST
Columbia Airport
Terminal
ROYALTON RD
82
Columbia Station
Lydia Rd
Frederick Av
Michelle Dr
Eddie Ln
Plum Creek Dr
Columbia Center
COLUMBIA PARK
CEM
Columbia HS
COLUMBIA WEST RIVER RD
RAND McNALLY

SEE 3008 MAP

SEE 3010 MAP

SEE 3144 MAP

1:24,000
1 in. = 2000 ft.
0 0.25 0.5
miles

SEE 2879 MAP

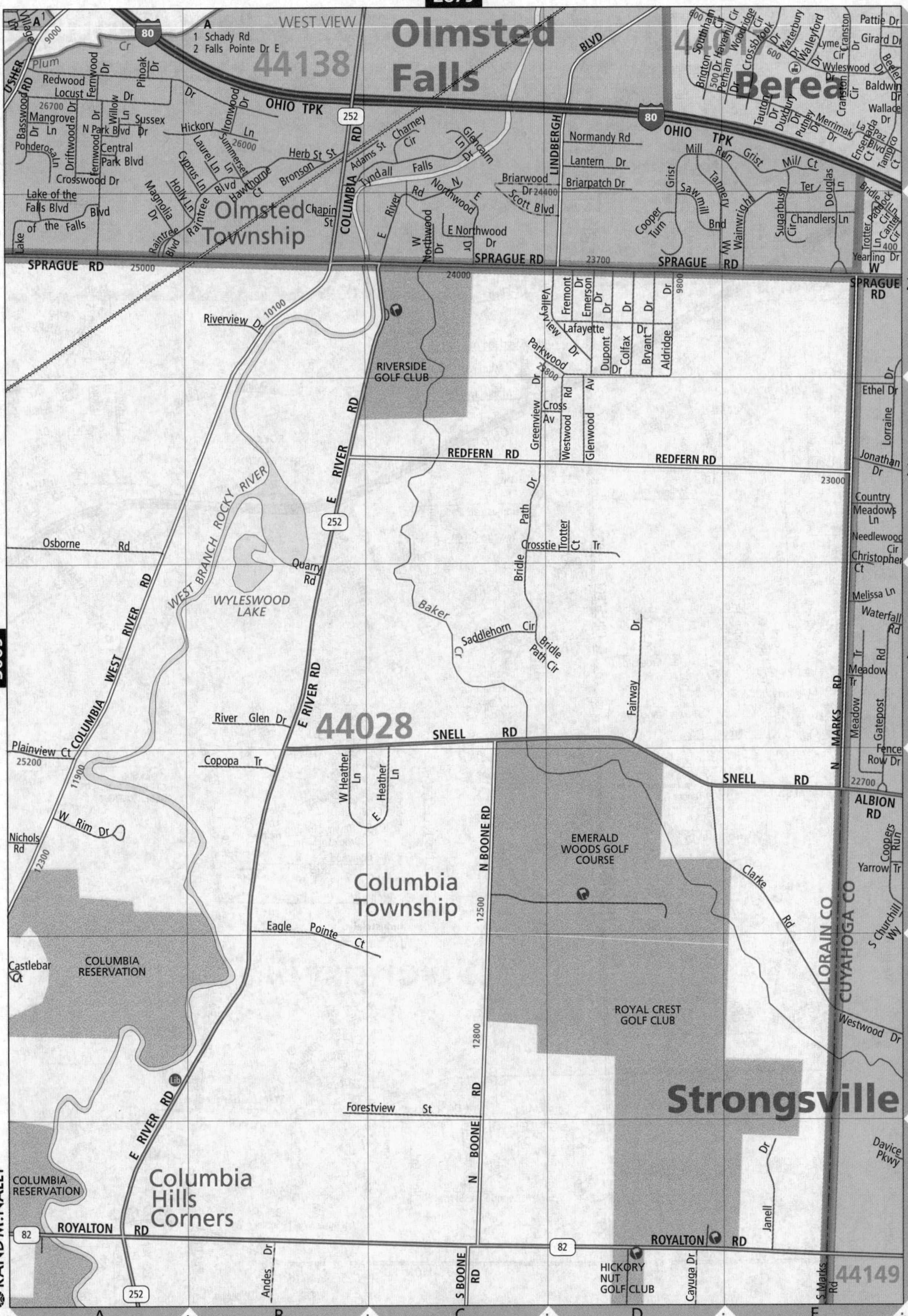

Olmsted Falls
44138
Berea
Olmsted Township
Columbia Township
Columbia Hills Corners
Strongsville
44028
44149
WEST VIEW
A
1 Schady Rd
2 Falls Pointe Dr E
OHIO TPK
SPRAGUE RD
REDFERN RD
SNELL RD
ALBION RD
ROYALTON RD
COLUMBIA RD
E RIVER RD
COLUMBIA WEST RIVER RD
N BOONE RD
S BOONE RD
N MARKS RD
LINDBERGH BLVD
USHER RD
RIVERSIDE GOLF CLUB
EMERALD WOODS GOLF COURSE
ROYAL CREST GOLF CLUB
HICKORY NUT GOLF CLUB
COLUMBIA RESERVATION
WYLESWOOD LAKE
WEST BRANCH ROCKY RIVER
LORAIN CO
CUYAHOGA CO
Osborne Rd
Riverview Dr
Quarry Rd
Plainview Ct
Copopa Tr
River Glen Dr
W Rim Dr
Nichols Rd
Eagle Pointe Ct
Castlebar Ct
Forestview St
Andes Dr
Cayuga Dr
Janell
Clarke Rd
Westwood Dr
Davice Pkwy
Fairway Dr
Saddlehorn Cir
Bridle Path Cir
Bridle Path Dr
Crosstie Ct
Trotter Tr
Baker Cr
Greenview Dr
Westwood Rd
Glenwood Av
Cross Av
Parkwood Dr
Valley View Dr
Fremont Dr
Emerson Dr
Lafayette
Dupont Dr
Colfax Dr
Bryant Dr
Aldridge Dr
W Heather Ln
E Heather Ln
Normandy Rd
Lantern Dr
Briarpatch Dr
Briarwood Dr
Scott Blvd
Mill Run Dr
Grist Mill Ct
Sawmill Bnd
Tannery Wy
Wainwright Dr
Sugarbush Cir
Chandlers Ln
Cooper Turn
Ter
Douglas Ln
E Northwood Dr
Northwood Dr
Lake of the Falls Blvd
Redwood Dr
Locust Dr
Mangrove Dr
Basswood Dr
Ponderosa Ln
Driftwood Dr
Fernwood Dr
N Park Blvd
Central Park Blvd
Crosswood Dr
Sussex Dr
Willow Ln
Pinoak Dr
Hickory Ln
Ironwood Dr
Laurel Ln
Cyprus Ln
Holly Ln
Magnolia Dr
Raintree Blvd
Summerset Ln
Hawthorne Ct
Bronson
Herb St
Adams St
Tyndall Falls
Charney Cir
Glencairn Dr
Chapin St
Plum Cr
Ethel Dr
Lorraine
Jonathan Dr
Country Meadows Ln
Needlewood Cir
Christopher Ct
Melissa Ln
Waterfall Rd
Meadow Tr
Meadowgate Rd
Gatepost
Fence Row Dr
Coopers Run
Yarrow Tr
S Churchill Wy
Yearling Dr
Pattie Dr
Girard Dr
Baldwin Dr
Wallace Dr
Merrimak Dr
Lyme Cir
Wyleswood Dr
Cranston
Walleyford
Waterbury
Woodridge Cir
Crossbrook
Southam Ct
Haverhill Cir
Brigton Dr
Perham Dr
Taunton Dr
Duxbury Dr
Putney Dr
Ensenada
La Paz Blvd
Tampico Ct
Bridle Ct
Trotter Ln
Paddock Cir
Canter Cir
S Marks Rd
BLVD
80
252
82
26700
26000
25000
24400
24000
23800
23700
23000
25200
11900
12300
12500
12800
22700
10100
9000
9800
400
500
600
41°21'40"
41°21'14"
41°20'48"
41°20'22"
41°19'56"
41°19'30"
41°19'04"
41°18'38"
81°55'17"
81°54'43"
81°54'08"
81°53'34"
81°52'59"
81°52'24"
A B C D E
1 2 3 4 5 6 7

SEE 3009 MAP

SEE 3011 MAP

SEE 3145 MAP

1:24,000
1 in. = 2000 ft.
0 0.25 0.5
miles

SEE 2880 MAP

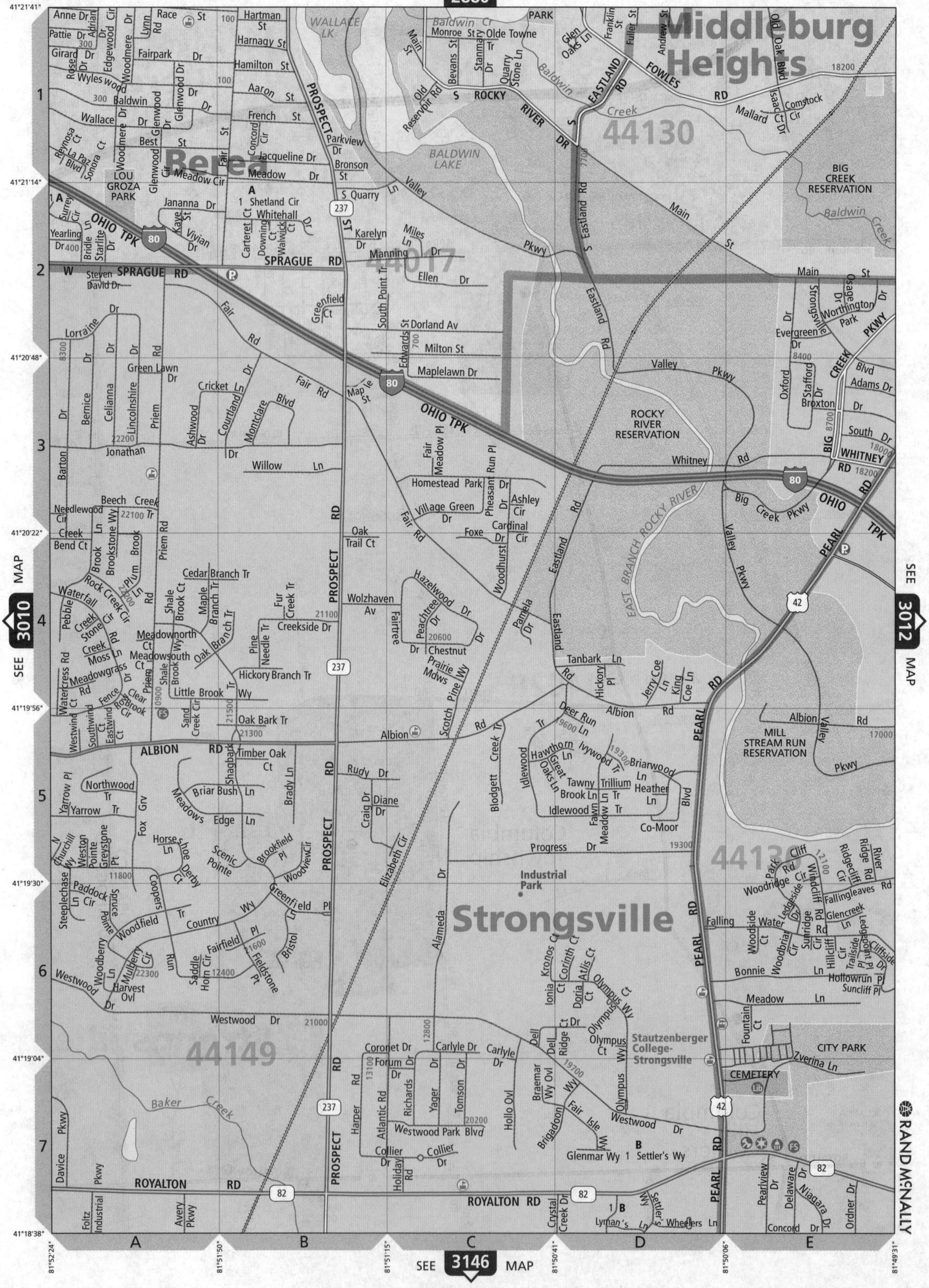
Middleburg Heights
Berea
Strongsville
44130
44017
44149
44136
BIG CREEK RESERVATION
ROCKY RIVER RESERVATION
MILL STREAM RUN RESERVATION
LOU GROZA PARK
CITY PARK
CEMETERY
Industrial Park
Stautzenberger College-Strongsville
BALDWIN LAKE
WALLACE LK
OHIO TPK
PROSPECT RD
PEARL RD
ROYALTON RD
ALBION RD
SPRAGUE RD
W SPRAGUE RD
S ROCKY RIVER DR
EASTLAND RD
FOWLES RD
BIG CREEK PKWY
WHITNEY RD
Valley Pkwy
Big Creek Pkwy
Main St
Fair Rd
Westwood Dr
Progress Dr
Alameda Dr
EAST BRANCH ROCKY RIVER
Baldwin Creek
Baker Creek
80
237
42
82
A
B
C
D
E
1
2
3
4
5
6
7
41°21'41"
41°21'14"
41°20'48"
41°20'22"
41°19'56"
41°19'30"
41°19'04"
41°18'38"
81°52'24"
81°51'50"
81°51'15"
81°50'41"
81°50'06"
81°49'31"

SEE 3010 MAP

SEE 3012 MAP

SEE 3146 MAP

1:24,000
1 in. = 2000 ft.
0 0.25 0.5
miles

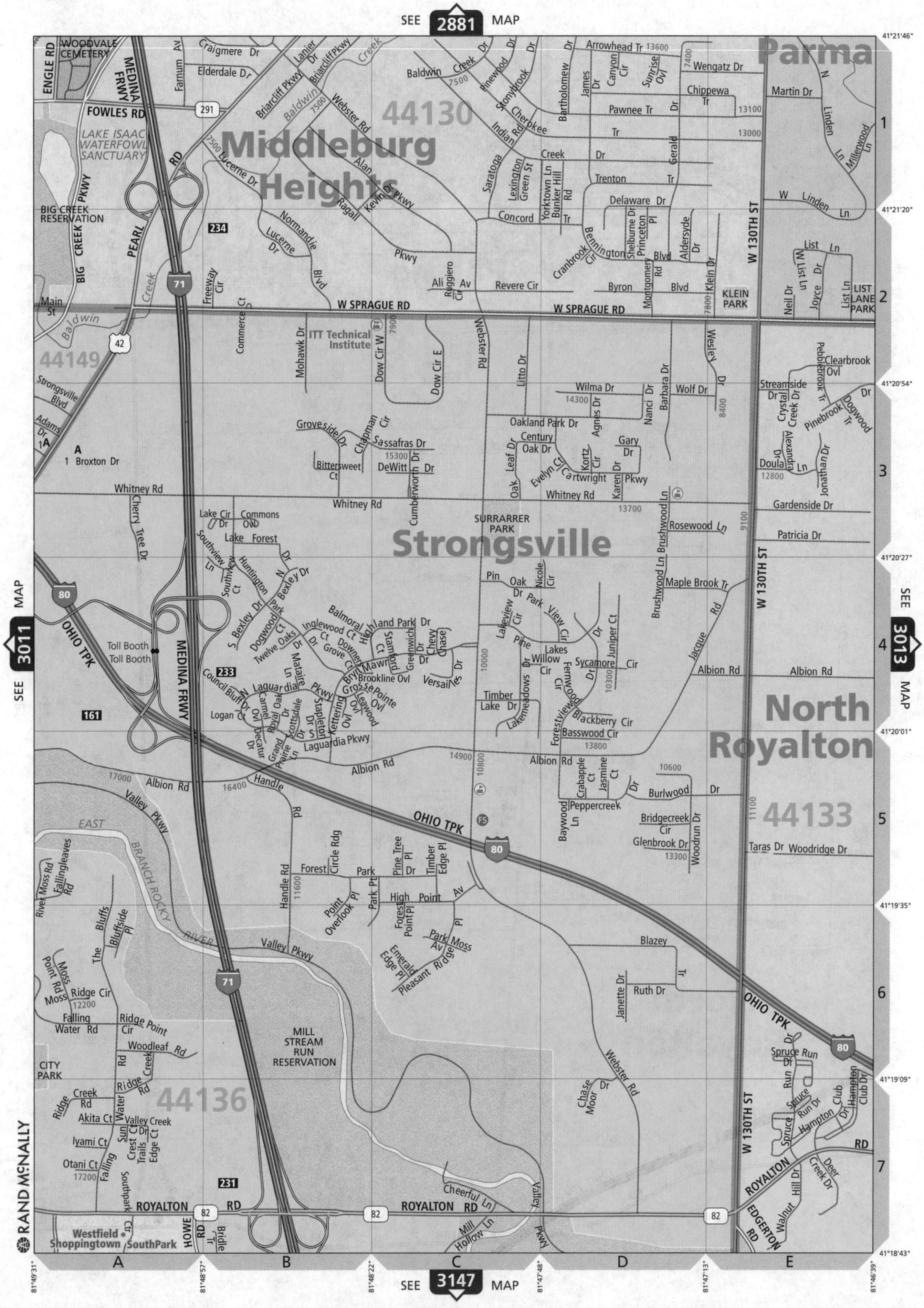
SEE 2881 MAP
SEE 3147 MAP
SEE 3011 MAP
SEE 3013 MAP
Middleburg Heights
Strongsville
Parma
North Royalton
44130
44149
44133
44136
WOODVALE CEMETERY
ENGLE RD
MEDINA FRWY
FOWLES RD
LAKE ISAAC WATERFOWL SANCTUARY
BIG CREEK RESERVATION
BIG CREEK PKWY
PEARL RD
Craigmere Dr
Elderdale Dr
Farnum Av
Lanier Dr
Briarcliff Pkwy
Baldwin Creek
Webster Rd
Lucerne Dr
Normandie Blvd
Alan Dr
Kevin Dr
Ragall Pkwy
Baldwin Creek Dr
Pinewood Dr
Stonybrook Dr
Cherokee Tr
Indian Rd
Bartholomew Dr
James Dr
Canyon Cir
Sunrise Ovl
Arrowhead Tr
Wengatz Dr
Chippewa Tr
Pawnee Tr
Gerald Tr
Creek Dr
Trenton Tr
Saratoga
Lexington Green St
Yorktown Ln
Bunker Hill Tr
Concord
Delaware Dr
Bennington Dr
Shelburne Dr
Princeton Pl
Aldersyde Dr
Cranbrook Cir
Montgomery Rd
Byron Blvd
Klein Dr
KLEIN PARK
Martin Dr
Linden Ln
Millerwood Ln
W Linden Ln
List Ln
W List Ln
Joyce Dr
Neil Dr
LIST LANE PARK
W 130TH ST
Freeway Cir
Ali Av
Ruggiero Cir
Revere Cir
W SPRAGUE RD
Main St
Baldwin Creek
Commerce Ct
Mohawk Dr
ITT Technical Institute
Dow Cir W
Dow Cir E
Litto Dr
Wilma Dr
Nanci Dr
Barbara Dr
Wolf Dr
Wesley Dr
Strongsville Blvd
Adams Dr
Broxton Dr
Groveside Dr
Chapman Cir
Sassafras Dr
Bittersweet Ct
DeWitt Dr
Cumberworth Dr
Oakland Park Dr
Agnes Dr
Century Oak Dr
Leaf Dr
Oak
Evelyn Ct
Kortz Cir
Karen Dr
Cartwright Pkwy
Gary Dr
Whitney Rd
Clearbrook Ovl
Pebblebrook Tr
Streamside Dr
Crystal Creek Dr
Pinebrook Tr
Dogwood Dr
Alexandra Dr
Jonathan Dr
Doula Ln
Gardenside Dr
Patricia Dr
Cherry Tree Dr
Lake Cir Dr
Commons Ovl
Lake Forest Dr
SURRARRER PARK
Rosewood Ln
Brushwood Ln
Southview Ln
Southview Ct
Huntington
Bexley Dr
S. Bexley Dr
Dogwood Park
Balmoral Highland Park Dr
Inglewood Ct
Twelve Oaks
Grove Ct
Downers Ct
Stamford Ct
Greenwich Dr
Chevy Chase
Bryn Mawr
Brookline Ovl
Versailles Dr
Pin Oak Dr
Nicole Cir
Park View Cir
Lakeview Cir
Pine Lakes
Willow Cir
Sycamore Cir
Juniper Ct
Maple Brook Tr
Jacque Rd
Albion Rd
Timber Lake Dr
Lakemeadows Dr
Fernwood Cir
Forestview Dr
Blackberry Cir
Basswood Cir
Toll Booth
Toll Booth
OHIO TPK
MEDINA FRWY
Council Bluff Dr
Laguardia Pkwy
Matairie Ln
Royal Oak Dr
Camel Ovl
Scottsdale Dr
Stapleton Dr
Kettering Ovl
Grosse Pointe
Leawood Ovl
Logan Ct
Decatur Dr
Grand Prairie Ln
Albion Rd
Handle Rd
Valley Pkwy
EAST BRANCH ROCKY RIVER
Crabapple Ct
Jasmine Ct
Burlwood Dr
Baywood Ln
Peppercreek
Bridgecreek Cir
Glenbrook Dr
Woodrun Dr
Taras Dr
Woodridge Dr
River Moss Rd
Fallingleaves Rd
The Bluffs
Bluffside Pl
Forest Circle Rdg
Forest Park
Pine Tree Pl
Timber Edge Pl
High Point Av
Point Overlook Pl
Park Pl
Forest Point Pl
Park Moss Av
Emerald Edge Pl
Pleasant Ridge Pl
Blazey Tr
Janette Dr
Ruth Dr
Moss Point Rd
Moss Ridge Cir
Falling Water Rd
Ridge Point Cir
Woodleaf Rd
CITY PARK
MILL STREAM RUN RESERVATION
Ridge Creek Rd
Ridge Creek
Akita Ct
Water Rd
Valley Creek Dr
Iyami Ct
Sun Crest Ct
Trails Edge Ct
Otani Ct
Falling
Southpark Ct
Spruce Run Dr
Hampton Club Dr
Spruce Run Dr
Chase Moor Dr
Webster Rd
Cheerful Ln
Valley Pkwy
ROYALTON RD
ROYALTON RD
EDGERTON RD
Walnut Hill Dr
Deer Creek Dr
HOWE RD
Bridle Tr
Mill Hollow Ln
Westfield Shoppingtown SouthPark
RAND McNALLY

1:24,000
1 in. = 2000 ft.
0 0.25 0.5 miles

SEE 2882 MAP

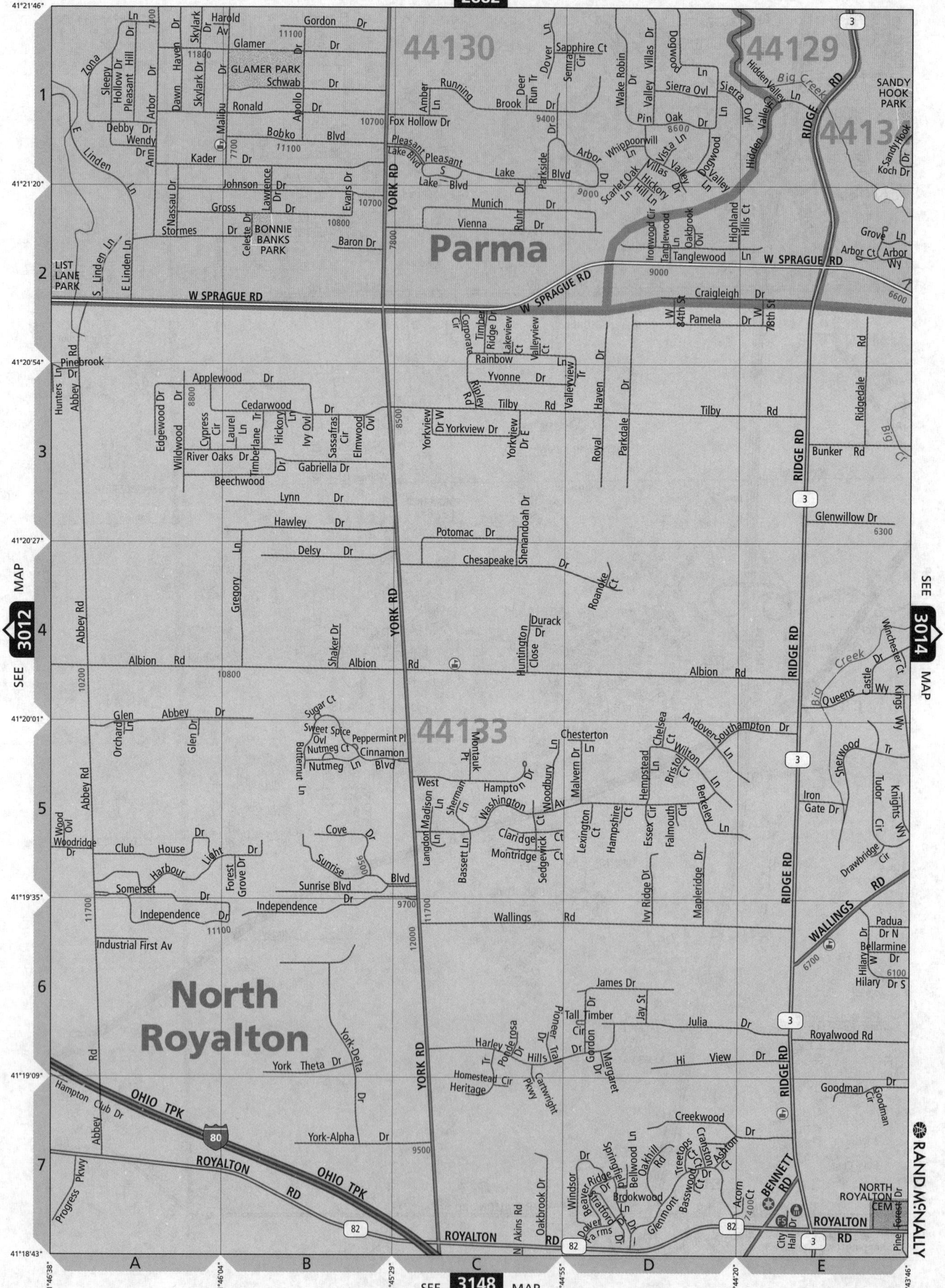
Parma
North Royalton
44130
44129
44134
44133
GLAMER PARK
BONNIE BANKS PARK
LIST LANE PARK
SANDY HOOK PARK
NORTH ROYALTON CEM
City Hall
W SPRAGUE RD
YORK RD
RIDGE RD
ABBEY RD
ALBION RD
WALLINGS RD
ROYALTON RD
BENNETT RD
OHIO TPK
80
82
3
Big Creek
Gordon Dr
Glamer Dr
Schwab Dr
Ronald Dr
Bobko Blvd
Kader Dr
Johnson Dr
Gross Dr
Stormes Dr
Baron Dr
Fox Hollow Dr
Pleasant Lake Blvd
Munich Dr
Vienna Dr
Running Brook Dr
Sapphire Ct
Sierra Ovl
Tanglewood Ln
Craigleigh Dr
Pamela Dr
Applewood Dr
Cedarwood Dr
River Oaks Dr
Gabriella Dr
Beechwood
Lynn Dr
Hawley Dr
Potomac Dr
Delsy Dr
Chesapeake Dr
Rainbow
Yvonne Dr
Tilby Rd
Yorkview Dr
Bunker Rd
Glenwillow Dr
Glen Abbey Dr
Chesterton Ln
Andover
Southampton Dr
Washington Av
Claridge Ct
Montridge Ct
Club House Dr
Harbour Light Dr
Somerset Dr
Independence Dr
Sunrise Blvd
Wallings Rd
Industrial First Av
James Dr
Julia Dr
Royalwood Rd
Hi View Dr
Goodman Dr
Creekwood Dr
York Theta Dr
York-Alpha Dr
York-Delta Dr
Hampton Club Dr
Progress Pkwy
Iron Gate Dr
Hilary Dr S
41°21'46"
41°21'20"
41°20'54"
41°20'27"
41°20'01"
41°19'35"
41°19'09"
41°18'43"
81°46'38"
81°46'04"
81°45'29"
81°44'55"
81°44'20"
81°43'46"
A
B
C
D
E
1
2
3
4
5
6
7

SEE 3012 MAP

SEE 3014 MAP

SEE 3148 MAP

1:24,000
1 in. = 2000 ft.
0 0.25 0.5
miles

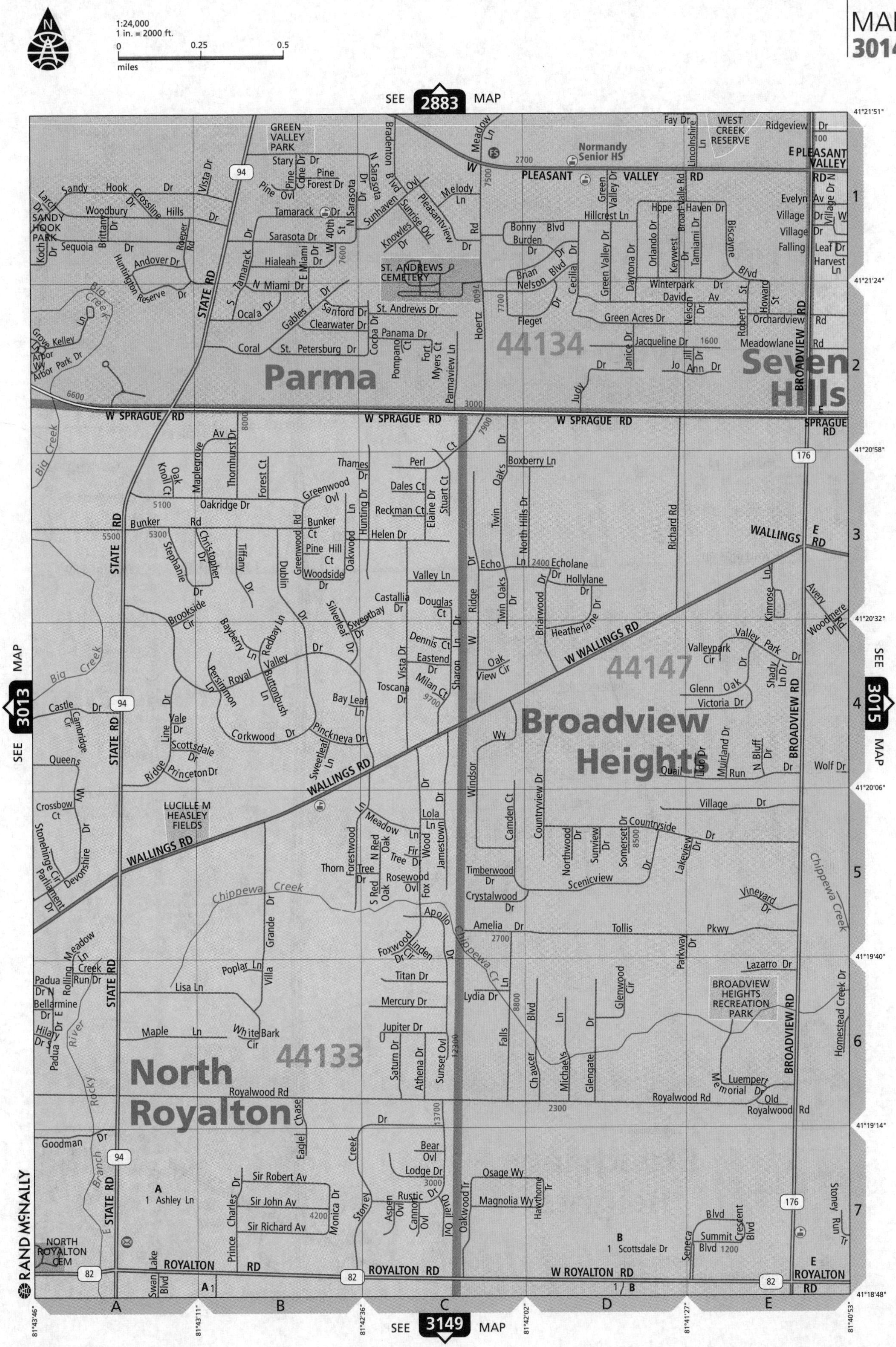
SEE 2883 MAP
SEE 3013 MAP
SEE 3015 MAP
SEE 3149 MAP
Parma
Seven Hills
Broadview Heights
North Royalton
44134
44147
44133
GREEN VALLEY PARK
WEST CREEK RESERVE
Normandy Senior HS
ST. ANDREWS CEMETERY
SANDY HOOK PARK
LUCILLE M HEASLEY FIELDS
BROADVIEW HEIGHTS RECREATION PARK
NORTH ROYALTON CEM
W PLEASANT VALLEY RD
E PLEASANT VALLEY RD
W SPRAGUE RD
E SPRAGUE RD
W WALLINGS RD
WALLINGS RD
E WALLINGS RD
ROYALTON RD
W ROYALTON RD
E ROYALTON RD
STATE RD
BROADVIEW RD
Royalwood Rd
Old Royalwood Rd
Tollis Pkwy
Bunker Rd
Oakridge Dr
Ridge Rd
Big Creek
Chippewa Creek
Rocky River
E Branch
A 1 Ashley Ln
B 1 Scottsdale Dr
A B C D E
1 2 3 4 5 6 7
41°21'51"
41°21'24"
41°20'58"
41°20'32"
41°20'06"
41°19'40"
41°19'14"
41°18'48"
81°43'46"
81°43'11"
81°42'36"
81°42'02"
81°41'27"
81°40'53"
RAND McNALLY

1:24,000
1 in. = 2000 ft.
0 0.25 0.5
miles

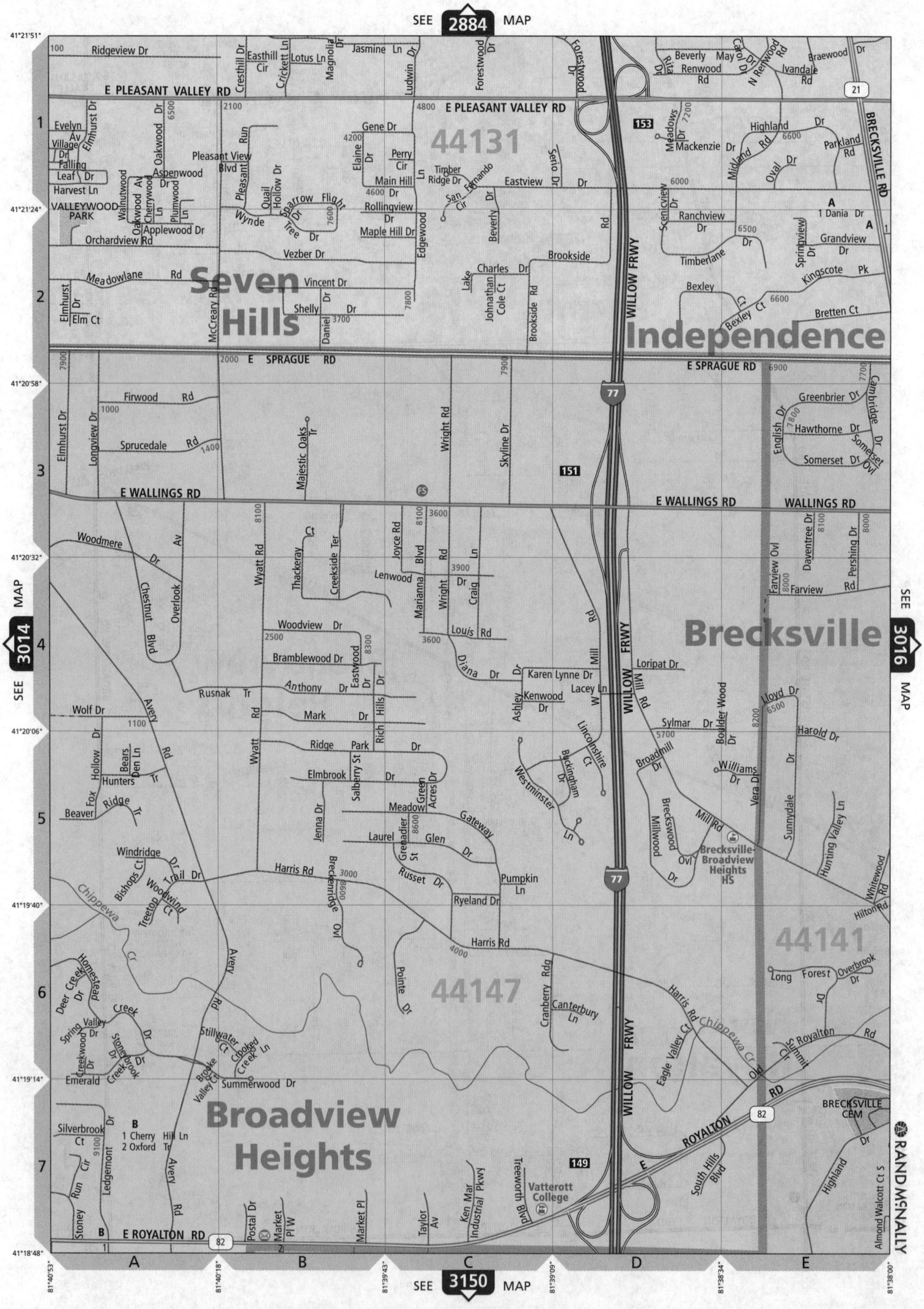
SEE 2884 MAP
SEE 3014 MAP
SEE 3016 MAP
SEE 3150 MAP
Seven Hills
Independence
Brecksville
Broadview Heights
44131
44147
44141
E PLEASANT VALLEY RD
E SPRAGUE RD
E WALLINGS RD
WALLINGS RD
E ROYALTON RD
WILLOW FRWY
BRECKSVILLE RD
Harris Rd
Avery Rd
Wyatt Rd
Wright Rd
Skyline Dr
Mill Rd
Royalton Rd
Ridgeview Dr
Meadowlane Rd
Vezber Dr
Vincent Dr
Eastview Dr
Brookside Rd
Firwood Rd
Sprucedale Rd
Longview Dr
Elmhurst Dr
Majestic Oaks Tr
Woodmere Dr
Chestnut Blvd
Overlook Av
Rusnak Tr
Woodview Dr
Bramblewood Dr
Anthony Dr
Mark Dr
Ridge Park Dr
Elmbrook Dr
Lenwood
Diana Dr
Karen Lynne Dr
Loripat Dr
Sylmar Dr
Broadmill Dr
Westminster
Lincolnshire Ct
Gateway
Pumpkin Ln
Ryeland Dr
Chippewa Cr
Homestead
Deer Creek Dr
Spring Valley Dr
Stillwater Ct
Crooked Creek Ln
Summerwood Dr
Emerald
Silverbrook Ct
Ledgemont Dr
Stoney Run Cir
Cranberry Rdg
Canterbury Ln
Eagle Valley Ct
South Hills Blvd
Vatterott College
Brecksville-Broadview Heights HS
BRECKSVILLE CEM
Farview Ovl
Farview Rd
Greenbrier Dr
Hawthorne Dr
Somerset Dr
Cambridge Dr
Harold Dr
Sunnydale Dr
Hunting Valley Ln
Overbrook Dr
Long Forest
Kingscote Pk
Bretten Ct
Bexley Ct
Grandview Dr
Timberlane Dr
Ranchview Dr
Parkland Rd
Highland Dr
Mackenzie Dr
1 Dania Dr
1 Cherry Hill Ln
2 Oxford Tr
77
82
21
149
151
153
A B C D E
1 2 3 4 5 6 7
RAND McNALLY

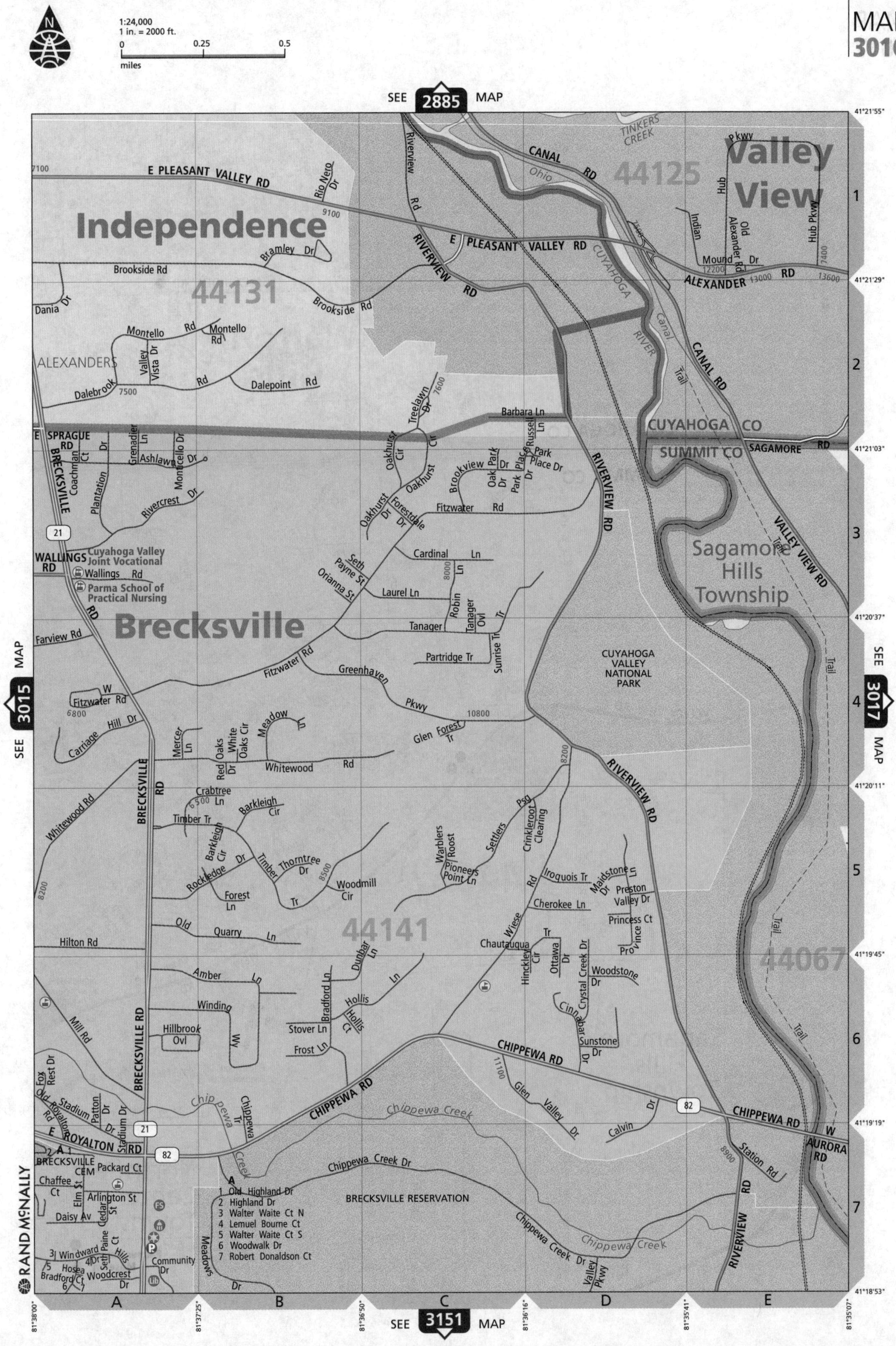
1:24,000
1 in. = 2000 ft.
0
0.25
0.5
miles
SEE 2885 MAP
SEE 3015 MAP
SEE 3017 MAP
SEE 3151 MAP
Independence
Valley View
Brecksville
Sagamore Hills Township
44131
44125
44141
44067
ALEXANDERS
CUYAHOGA CO
SUMMIT CO
CUYAHOGA VALLEY NATIONAL PARK
BRECKSVILLE RESERVATION
TINKERS CREEK
CUYAHOGA RIVER
Ohio Canal
Canal Trail
Chippewa Creek
E PLEASANT VALLEY RD
CANAL RD
ALEXANDER RD
RIVERVIEW RD
BRECKSVILLE RD
CHIPPEWA RD
VALLEY VIEW RD
SAGAMORE RD
E SPRAGUE RD
WALLINGS RD
E ROYALTON RD
AURORA RD
W
Brookside Rd
Bramley Dr
Rio Nero Dr
Dania Dr
Montello Rd
Valley Vista Dr
Dalebrook Rd
Dalepoint Rd
Treelawn Dr
Oakhurst Cir
Oakhurst Dr
Barbara Ln
Russel Ln
Park Place Dr
Oak Park Dr
Brookview Dr
Forestdale Dr
Fitzwater Rd
Coachman Ct
Plantation Dr
Grenadier Ln
Ashlawn Dr
Monticello Dr
Rivercrest Dr
Cuyahoga Valley Joint Vocational
Wallings Rd
Parma School of Practical Nursing
Seth Payne St
Orianna St
Cardinal Ln
Robin Ln
Laurel Ln
Tanager Ovl
Tanager Tr
Sunrise Tr
Partridge Tr
Farview Rd
Greenhaven Pkwy
Glen Forest Tr
W Fitzwater Rd
Carriage Hill Dr
Mercer Ln
Red Oaks Dr
White Oaks Cir
Meadow Ln
Whitewood Rd
Crabtree Ln
Timber Tr
Barkleigh Cir
Rockledge Dr
Forest Ln
Thorntree Dr
Woodmill Cir
Warblers Roost
Pioneers Point Ln
Settlers Psg
Crinkleroot Clearing
Iroquois Tr
Maidstone Dr
Preston Valley Dr
Princess Ct
Province Ct
Cherokee Ln
Wiese Rd
Chautauqua Tr
Hinckley Cir
Ottawa Dr
Crystal Creek Dr
Woodstone Dr
Cinnabar Dr
Sunstone Dr
Old Quarry Ln
Hilton Rd
Amber Ln
Dunbar Ln
Bradford Ln
Hollis Ln
Hollis Ct
Winding Wy
Hillbrook Ovl
Stover Ln
Frost Ln
Mill Rd
Fox Rest Dr
Old Royalton Rd
Stadium Dr
Patton Dr
Chippewa Tr
Glen Valley Dr
Calvin Dr
Station Rd
Chippewa Creek Dr
Valley Pkwy
Meadows Dr
BRECKSVILLE CEM
Packard Ct
Chaffee Ct
Elm St
Arlington St
Daisy Av
Cedar St
Windward Dr
Paine Ct
Hills
Community Dr
Hosea
Bradford Ct
Woodcrest Dr
1 Old Highland Dr
2 Highland Dr
3 Walter Waite Ct N
4 Lemuel Bourne Ct
5 Walter Waite Ct S
6 Woodwalk Dr
7 Robert Donaldson Ct
Pkwy
Hub Pkwy
Indian Mound Dr
Old Alexander Rd
21
82
A
B
C
D
E
1
2
3
4
5
6
7
41°21'55"
41°21'29"
41°21'03"
41°20'37"
41°20'11"
41°19'45"
41°19'19"
41°18'53"
81°38'00"
81°37'25"
81°36'50"
81°36'16"
81°35'41"
81°35'07"
RAND McNALLY

1:24,000
1 in. = 2000 ft.
0 0.25 0.5
miles

SEE 2886 MAP

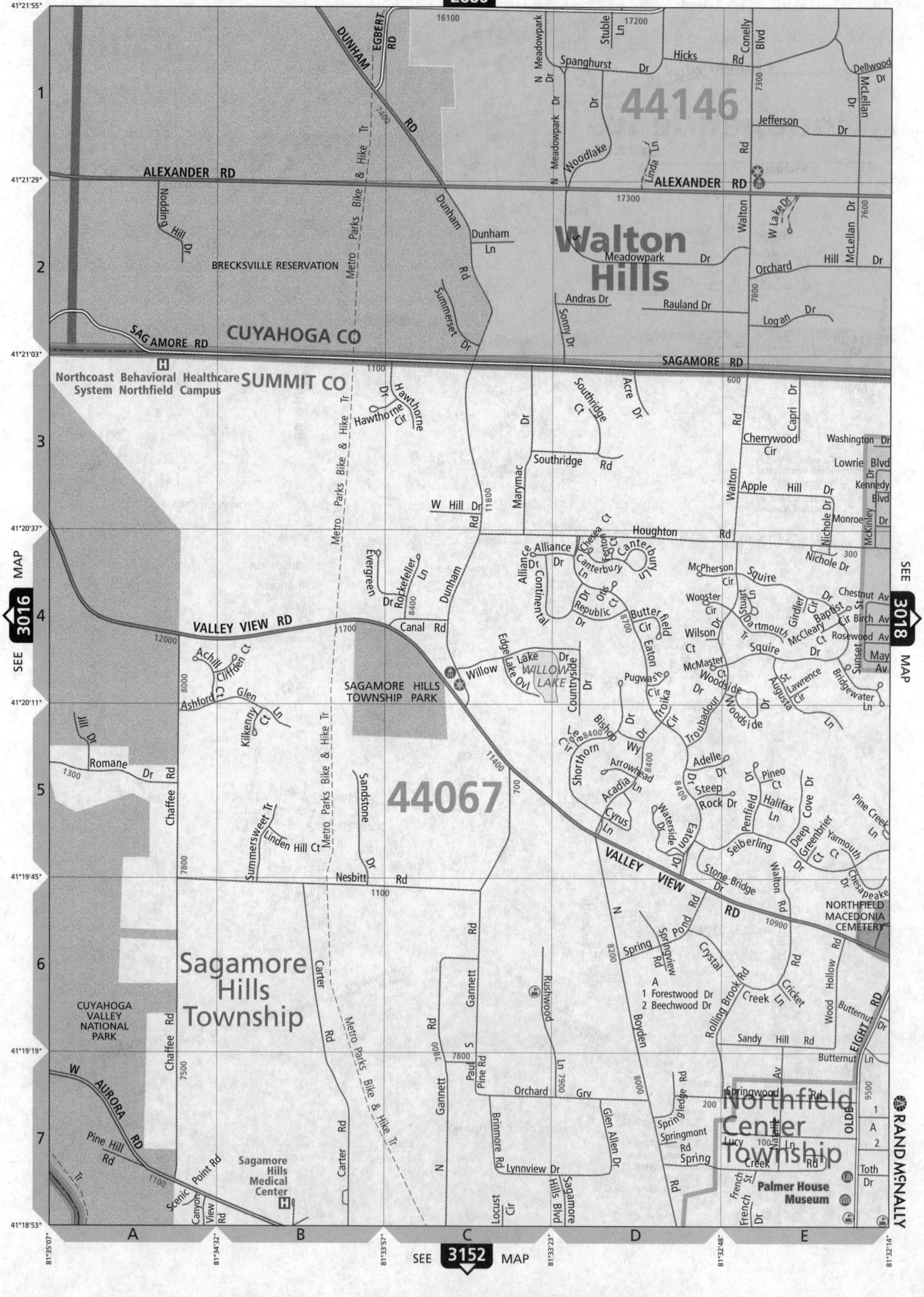
44146
Walton Hills
44067
Sagamore Hills Township
Northfield Center Township
CUYAHOGA CO
SUMMIT CO
BRECKSVILLE RESERVATION
CUYAHOGA VALLEY NATIONAL PARK
SAGAMORE HILLS TOWNSHIP PARK
Northcoast Behavioral Healthcare System Northfield Campus
Sagamore Hills Medical Center
NORTHFIELD MACEDONIA CEMETERY
Palmer House Museum
WILLOW LAKE
ALEXANDER RD
SAGAMORE RD
VALLEY VIEW RD
DUNHAM RD
EGBERT RD
W AURORA RD
EIGHT RD
Metro Parks Bike & Hike Tr
Spanghurst Dr
Hicks Rd
Conelly Blvd
Jefferson Dr
Dellwood Dr
McLellan Dr
Woodlake Dr
Linda Ln
Meadowpark Dr
Orchard Hill Dr
Andras Dr
Rauland Dr
Logan Dr
Sonny Dr
Summerset Dr
Dunham Ln
Nodding Hill Dr
Southridge Ct
Southridge Rd
Acre Dr
Marymac Dr
Cherrywood Cir
Capri Dr
Washington Dr
Lowrie Blvd
Kennedy Blvd
McKinley Dr
Apple Hill Dr
Monroe Dr
Nichole Dr
W Hill Dr
Houghton Rd
Hawthorne Cir
Hawthorne Dr
Evergreen Dr
Rockefeller Ln
Canal Rd
Alliance Dr
Continental Dr
Canterbury Ln
Republic Dr
Butterfield Cir
Eaton Dr
Pugwash Cir
Troika Cir
Troubadour Dr
Woodside Dr
McPherson Cir
Squire Dr
Wooster Cir
Stuart Ln
Dartmouth Ct
McCleary Ct
Girdler Cir
Baptist Cir
Chestnut Av
Birch Av
Rosewood Av
May Av
Sunset St
Wilson Ct
McMaster Ct
Augusta Cir
Lawrence Cir
St. Bridgewater Ln
Willow Dr
Edge Lake Ovl
Lake Dr
Countryside Dr
Achill Ct
Cliffden Ct
Ashford Ct
Glen Ln
Kilkenny Ct
Jill Dr
Romane Dr
Chaffee Rd
Summersweet Tr
Linden Hill Ct
Sandstone Dr
Nesbitt Rd
Bishop Dr
Lee Cir
Shorthorn Wy
Arrowhead Ln
Acadia Ln
Cyrus Ln
Adelle Dr
Steep Rock Dr
Waterside Dr
Pineo Ct
Penfield Dr
Halifax Ln
Cove Dr
Pine Creek Ln
Deep Greenbrier Ct
Yarmouth Ct
Chesapeake Dr
Seiberling Dr
Stone Bridge Dr
Walton Rd
Pond Rd
Spring Rd
Springview Rd
Crystal Dr
Rolling Brook Rd
Creek Ln
Cricket Rd
Hollow Rd
Wood Dr
Butternut Ln
Sandy Hill Rd
A
1 Forestwood Dr
2 Beechwood Dr
Carter Rd
Gannett Rd
Paul S
Pine Rd
Rushwood Ln
Boyden Rd
Orchard Grv
Brinmore Rd
Glen Allen Dr
Lynnview Dr
Locust Cir
Sagamore Hills Blvd
Springledge Rd
Springmont Rd
Springwood Rd
Lucy Ln
Creek Rd
French St
French Dr
Toth Dr
Pine Hill Rd
Scenic Point Rd
Canyon View Rd
OLDE
RAND McNALLY

SEE 3016 MAP

SEE 3018 MAP

SEE 3152 MAP

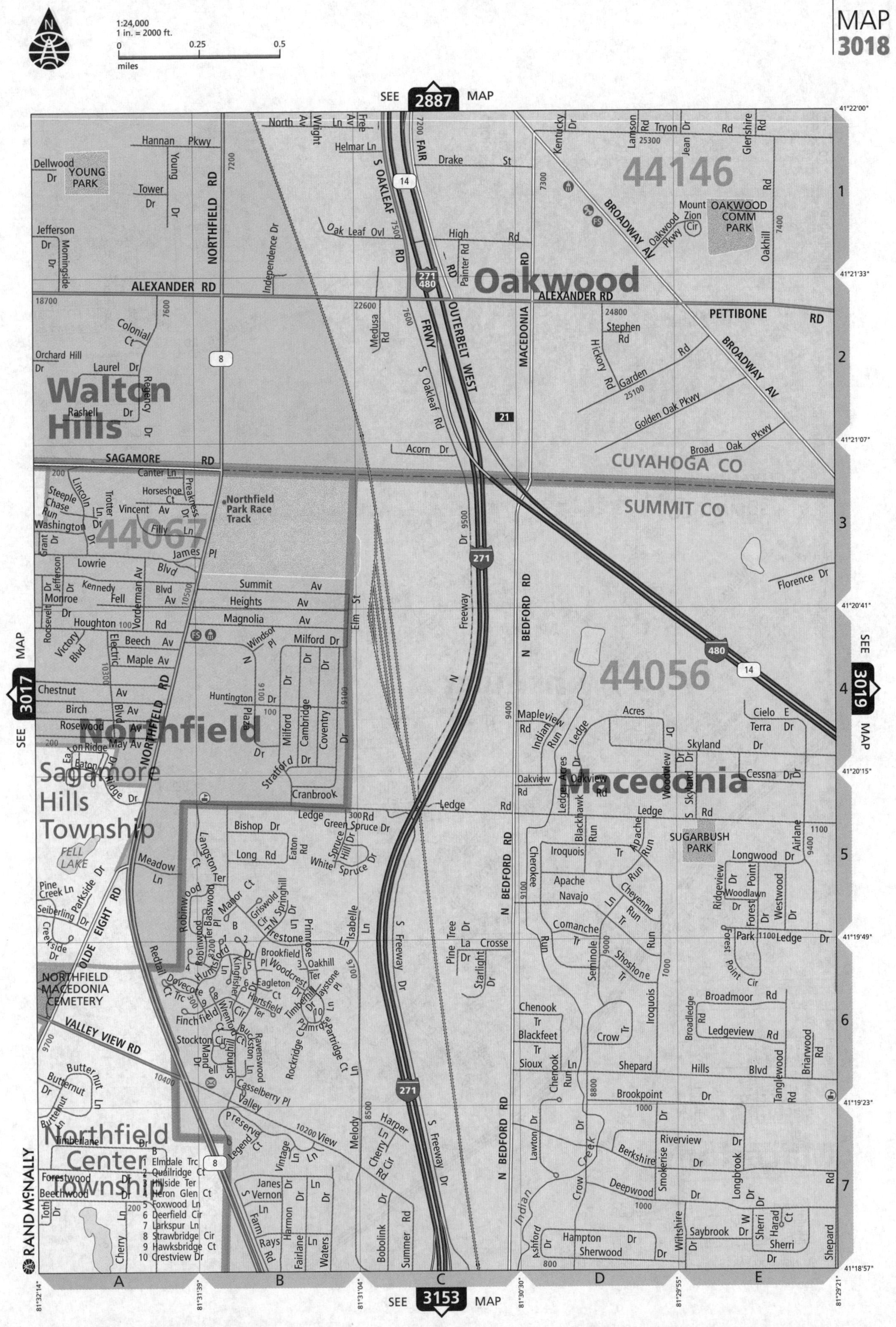
1:24,000
1 in. = 2000 ft.
0
0.25
0.5
miles
N
SEE 2887 MAP
SEE 3153 MAP
SEE 3017 MAP
SEE 3019 MAP
Oakwood
Walton Hills
Northfield
Sagamore Hills Township
Macedonia
Northfield Center Township
44146
44067
44056
CUYAHOGA CO
SUMMIT CO
YOUNG PARK
OAKWOOD COMM PARK
SUGARBUSH PARK
Northfield Park Race Track
FELL LAKE
NORTHFIELD MACEDONIA CEMETERY
ALEXANDER RD
SAGAMORE RD
NORTHFIELD RD
MACEDONIA RD
N BEDFORD RD
BROADWAY AV
PETTIBONE RD
VALLEY VIEW RD
OLDE EIGHT RD
OUTERBELT WEST
FAIR RD
FRWY
S OAKLEAF RD
Ledge Rd
Summit Av
Heights Av
Magnolia Av
Chestnut Av
Birch Av
Rosewood Av
Hannan Pkwy
Drake St
High Rd
Oak Leaf Ovl
Golden Oak Pkwy
Broad Oak Pkwy
Florence Dr
Acres
Skyland Dr
Cessna Dr
Longwood Dr
Broadmoor Rd
Ledgeview Rd
Hills Blvd
Brookpoint Dr
Riverview Dr
Berkshire Dr
Deepwood Dr
Saybrook Dr
Hampton Dr
Sherwood Dr
Shepard Rd
Freeway Dr
S Freeway Dr
Harper Ln
Cherry Rd
Valley View
1 Elmdale Trc
2 Quailridge Ct
3 Hillside Ter
4 Heron Glen Ct
5 Foxwood Ln
6 Deerfield Cir
7 Larkspur Ln
8 Strawbridge Cir
9 Hawksbridge Ct
10 Crestview Dr
14
8
21
271
480
A
B
C
D
E
1
2
3
4
5
6
7
41°22'00"
41°21'33"
41°21'07"
41°20'41"
41°20'15"
41°19'49"
41°19'23"
41°18'57"
81°32'14"
81°31'39"
81°31'04"
81°30'30"
81°29'55"
81°29'21"

1:24,000
1 in. = 2000 ft.
0 0.25 0.5
miles

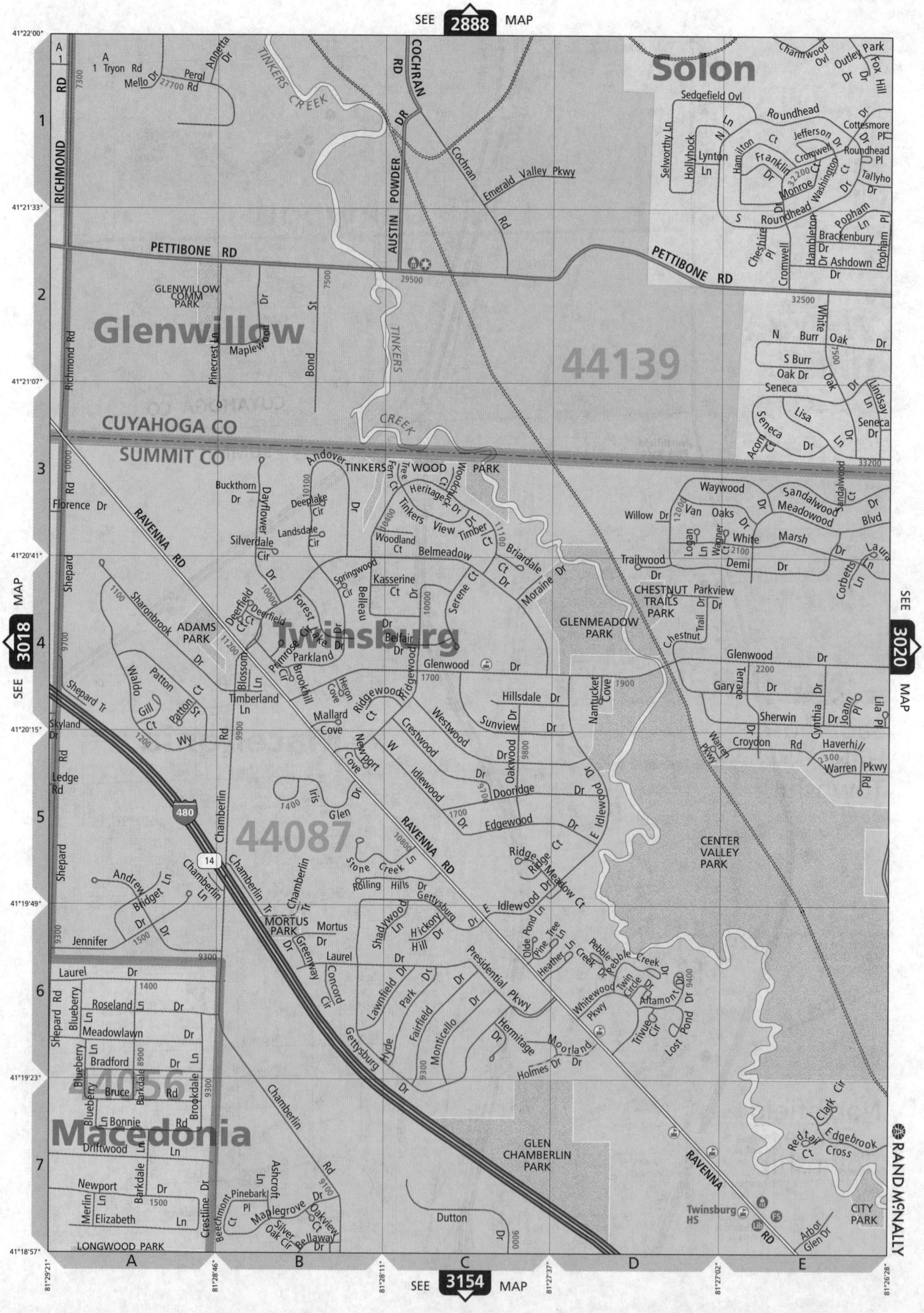
SEE 2888 MAP
SEE 3018 MAP
SEE 3020 MAP
SEE 3154 MAP
41°22'00"
41°21'33"
41°21'07"
41°20'41"
41°20'15"
41°19'49"
41°19'23"
41°18'57"
81°29'21"
81°28'46"
81°28'11"
81°27'37"
81°27'02"
81°26'28"
A
B
C
D
E
1
2
3
4
5
6
7
Solon
Glenwillow
Twinsburg
Macedonia
44139
44087
44056
CUYAHOGA CO
SUMMIT CO
RICHMOND RD
Richmond Rd
PETTIBONE RD
RAVENNA RD
COCHRAN RD
AUSTIN POWDER DR
TINKERS CREEK
Tryon Rd
Mello Dr
Pergl Rd
Annetta Dr
Emerald Valley Pkwy
Cochran Rd
GLENWILLOW COMM PARK
Pinecrest Ln
Maplewood Dr
Bond St
Sedgefield Ovl
Roundhead Dr
Charmwood Ovl
Outley Dr
Park Dr
Fox Hill
Selworthy Ln
Hollyhock Ln
Lynton Ln
Hamilton Ct
Franklin Dr
Jefferson Dr
Cromwell Ct
Monroe Ct
Washington Dr
Cottesmore Pl
Roundhead Pl
Tallyho Dr
Popham Ln
Popham Pl
Brackenbury Dr
Ashdown Dr
Cheshire Pl
Cromwell Dr
Hambleton Dr
N Burr Oak Dr
S Burr Oak Dr
White Oak Dr
Seneca Dr
Lisa Ln
Lindsay Ln
Acorn Ct
TINKERS WOOD PARK
Andover Dr
Buckthorn Dr
Dayflower Dr
Deeplake Cir
Landsdale Cir
Silverdale Cir
Fern Ct
Tree Ct
Woodchuck Ct
Heritage Dr
Tinkers View Dr
Timber Ct
Woodland Ct
Belmeadow Dr
Briardale Ct
Moraine Dr
Waywood Dr
Sandalwood Dr
Meadowood Blvd
Van Oaks Dr
Willow Dr
Logan Ln
Wagner Ct
White Marsh Dr
Trailwood Dr
Demi Dr
Laura Ln
Corbetts Ln
CHESTNUT TRAILS PARK
Parkview Dr
Chestnut Trail Dr
Florence Dr
Shepard Rd
Sharonbrook Dr
ADAMS PARK
Deerfield Ct
Springwood Cir
Kasserine Ct
Belleau Dr
Serene Ct
Forest Lake Dr
Primrose Cir
Parkland Dr
Belfair Dr
Brookhill Dr
Glenwood Dr
GLENMEADOW PARK
Waldo Dr
Patton Ct
Gill Ct
Patton St
Patton Wy
Shepard Tr
Skyland Dr
Blossom Ln
Timberland Ln
Heron Cove
Ridgewood Ct
Ridgewood Dr
Hillsdale Dr
Nantucket Cove
Sunview Dr
Gary Dr
Terrace Dr
Sherwin Dr
Cynthia Dr
Joann Pl
Lila Pl
Warren Pkwy
Croydon Rd
Haverhill Pkwy
Mallard Cove
Newport Cove
Westwood Dr
Crestwood Dr
W Idlewood Dr
Oakwood Dr
Dooridge Dr
E Idlewood Dr
Ledge Rd
Iris Glen Dr
Edgewood Dr
Chamberlin Rd
CENTER VALLEY PARK
Stone Creek Ln
Ridge Meadow Ct
Andrew Dr
Bridget Ln
Chamberlin Ln
Chamberlin Tr
Rolling Hills Dr
Gettysburg Dr
E Idlewood Dr
Jennifer
MORTUS PARK
Mortus Dr
Shadywood Ln
Hickory Hill Dr
Olde Pond Ln
Pine Tree Ln
Heather Ln
Creek Dr
Pebble Creek Dr
Laurel Dr
Greenway Dr
Concord Cir
Lawnfield Dr
Park Dr
Fairfield Dr
Monticello Dr
Presidential Pkwy
Whitewood Pkwy
Twin Circle Dr
Altamont Dr
Trivue Cir
Lost Pond Dr
Hermitage Dr
Moorland Dr
Holmes Dr
Gettysburg Dr
Hyde
Roseland Dr
Meadowlawn Dr
Blueberry Ln
Bradford Dr
Bruce Rd
Barkdale Dr
Brookdale Dr
Bonnie Rd
Driftwood Ln
Newport Dr
Merlin Ln
Elizabeth Ln
Crestline Dr
LONGWOOD PARK
Beechmont Ct
Pinebark Pl
Ashcroft Ln
Maplegrove Dr
Oakview Dr
Silver Oak Cir
Bellaway
GLEN CHAMBERLIN PARK
Dutton Dr
Twinsburg HS
Clark Cir
Edgebrook
Redtail Ct
Cross
Arbor Glen Dr
CITY PARK
RAVENNA RD
480
14
RAND McNALLY

SEE 2889 MAP

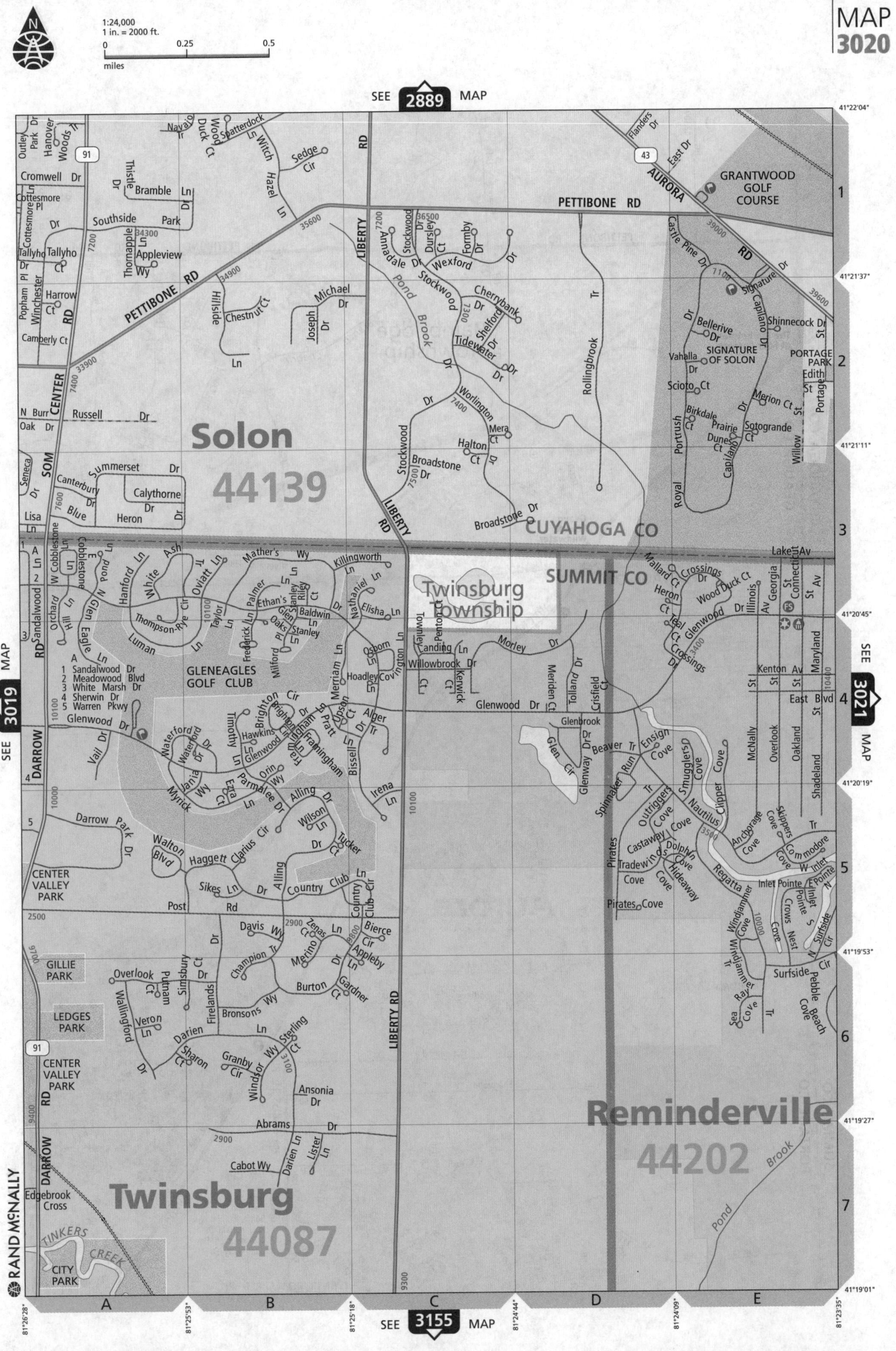
1:24,000
1 in. = 2000 ft.
0
0.25
0.5
miles
N
Solon
44139
Twinsburg Township
Twinsburg
44087
Reminderville
44202
CUYAHOGA CO
SUMMIT CO
GRANTWOOD GOLF COURSE
SIGNATURE OF SOLON
GLENEAGLES GOLF CLUB
PORTAGE PARK
CENTER VALLEY PARK
GILLIE PARK
LEDGES PARK
CITY PARK
TINKERS CREEK
PETTIBONE RD
AURORA RD
LIBERTY RD
SOM CENTER RD
DARROW RD
Glenwood Dr
Post Rd
Abrams Dr
Rollingbrook Tr
Pond Brook
Cromwell Dr
Southside Park
Stockwood Dr
Worlington Dr
Broadstone Dr
Castle Pine Dr
Capilano Dr
Royal Portrush
Mather's Wy
Killingworth Ln
Darrow Park Dr
Walton Blvd
Country Club Ln
Pirates Cove
Regatta
Commodore
Surfside Cir
Kenton Av
East Blvd
McNally
Overlook
Oakland
Shadeland
Maryland
Georgia
Connecticut
Illinois
Lake Av
1 Sandalwood Dr
2 Meadowood Blvd
3 White Marsh Dr
4 Sherwin Dr
5 Warren Pkwy
91
43
A
B
C
D
E
1
2
3
4
5
6
7
41°22'04"
41°21'37"
41°21'11"
41°20'45"
41°20'19"
41°19'53"
41°19'27"
41°19'01"
81°26'28"
81°25'53"
81°25'18"
81°24'44"
81°24'09"
81°23'35"
RAND MCNALLY

SEE 3019 MAP

SEE 3021 MAP

SEE 3155 MAP

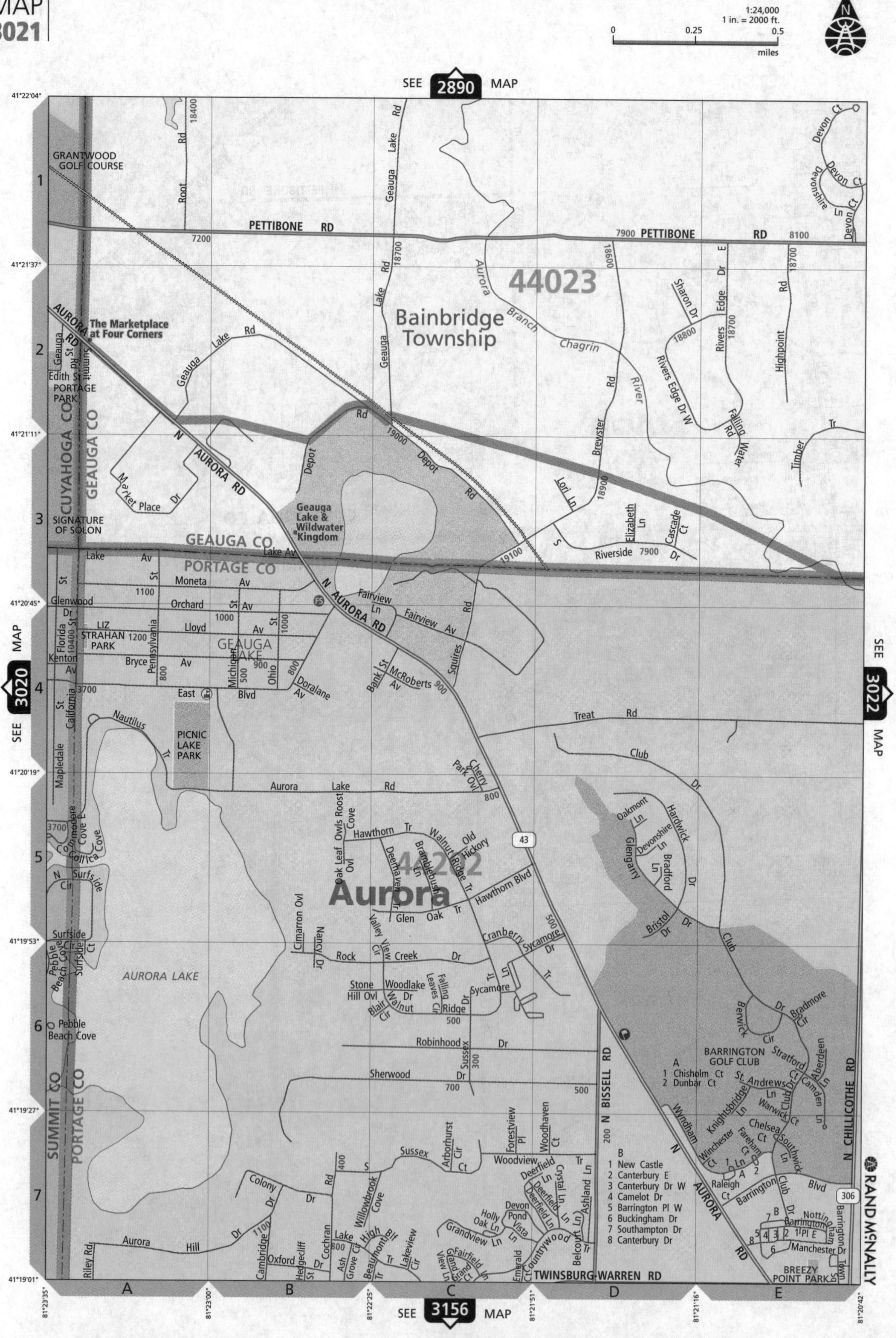
1:24,000
1 in. = 2000 ft.
0
0.25
0.5
miles
SEE 2890 MAP
SEE 3020 MAP
SEE 3022 MAP
SEE 3156 MAP
Bainbridge Township
44023
44202
Aurora
GRANTWOOD GOLF COURSE
The Marketplace at Four Corners
PORTAGE PARK
SIGNATURE OF SOLON
Geauga Lake & Wildwater Kingdom
LIZ STRAHAN PARK
GEAUGA LAKE
PICNIC LAKE PARK
AURORA LAKE
BARRINGTON GOLF CLUB
BREEZY POINT PARK
CUYAHOGA CO
GEAUGA CO
PORTAGE CO
SUMMIT CO
PETTIBONE RD
AURORA RD
N AURORA RD
TWINSBURG-WARREN RD
N BISSELL RD
N CHILLICOTHE RD
Geauga Lake Rd
Depot Rd
Root Rd
Brewster Rd
Aurora Branch Chagrin River
Rivers Edge Dr
Rivers Edge Dr W
Sharon Dr
Highpoint Rd
Falling Water Rd
Timber Tr
Devon Ct
Devonshire Ln
Lori Ln
Elizabeth Ln
Cascade Ct
Riverside Dr
Market Place Dr
Lake Av
Moneta Av
Orchard Av
Lloyd Av
Bryce Av
Glenwood Dr
Kenton Av
Florida St
Pennsylvania Av
Michigan St
Ohio St
East Blvd
Doralane Av
Fairview Ln
Fairview Av
Squires Rd
McRoberts Av
Bank St
Treat Rd
Club Dr
Aurora Lake Rd
Nautilus Tr
Mapledale
California St
Cherry Park Ovl
Hawthorn Tr
Hawthorn Blvd
Owls Roost Cove
Oak Leaf Ovl
Walnut Ridge Tr
Old Hickory
Deerhaven Tr
Bramblebush Ln
Glen Oak Tr
Valley View Cir
Rock Creek Dr
Cimarron Ovl
Nancy Dr
Cranberry
Sycamore Dr
Stone Hill Ovl
Woodlake Dr
Falling Leaves Cir
Blair Cir
Walnut Ridge
Robinhood Dr
Sherwood Dr
Sussex Dr
Sussex S
Arborhurst Cir
Forestview Pl
Woodhaven Ct
Woodview Tr
Deerfield Ln
Crystal Ln
Ashland Ln
Colony Dr
Willowbrook Cove
Aurora Hill Dr
Riley Rd
Cambridge Dr
Oxford St
Hedgecliff Dr
Cochran Rd
Ash Grove Cir
High Blf
Beaumont Tr
Lakeview Cir
Grandview Ln
Holly Oak Ln
Devon Pond Vista
Countrywood Tr
Belcourt Ln
Emerald Ct
Fairfield Ln
Oakmont Ln
Hardwick Dr
Glengarry
Bradford Ln
Bristol Dr
Surfside
Pebble Beach Cove
Commodore Cove E
Collica Cove
Berwick Cir
Bradmore Cir
Stratford
Aberdeen
Camden Ln
St. Andrews Ln
Warwick Ct
Knightsbridge
Chelsea Ct
Southwick Ln
Fareham Ct
Winchester Ct
Wyndham
Raleigh Ct
Barrington Blvd
Nottingham
Manchester Dr
A
1 Chisholm Ct
2 Dunbar Ct
B
1 New Castle
2 Canterbury E
3 Canterbury Dr W
4 Camelot Dr
5 Barrington Pl W
6 Buckingham Dr
7 Southampton Dr
8 Canterbury Dr
43
306
RAND McNALLY
41°22'04"
41°21'37"
41°21'11"
41°20'45"
41°20'19"
41°19'53"
41°19'27"
41°19'01"
81°23'35"
81°23'00"
81°22'25"
81°21'51"
81°21'16"
81°20'42"

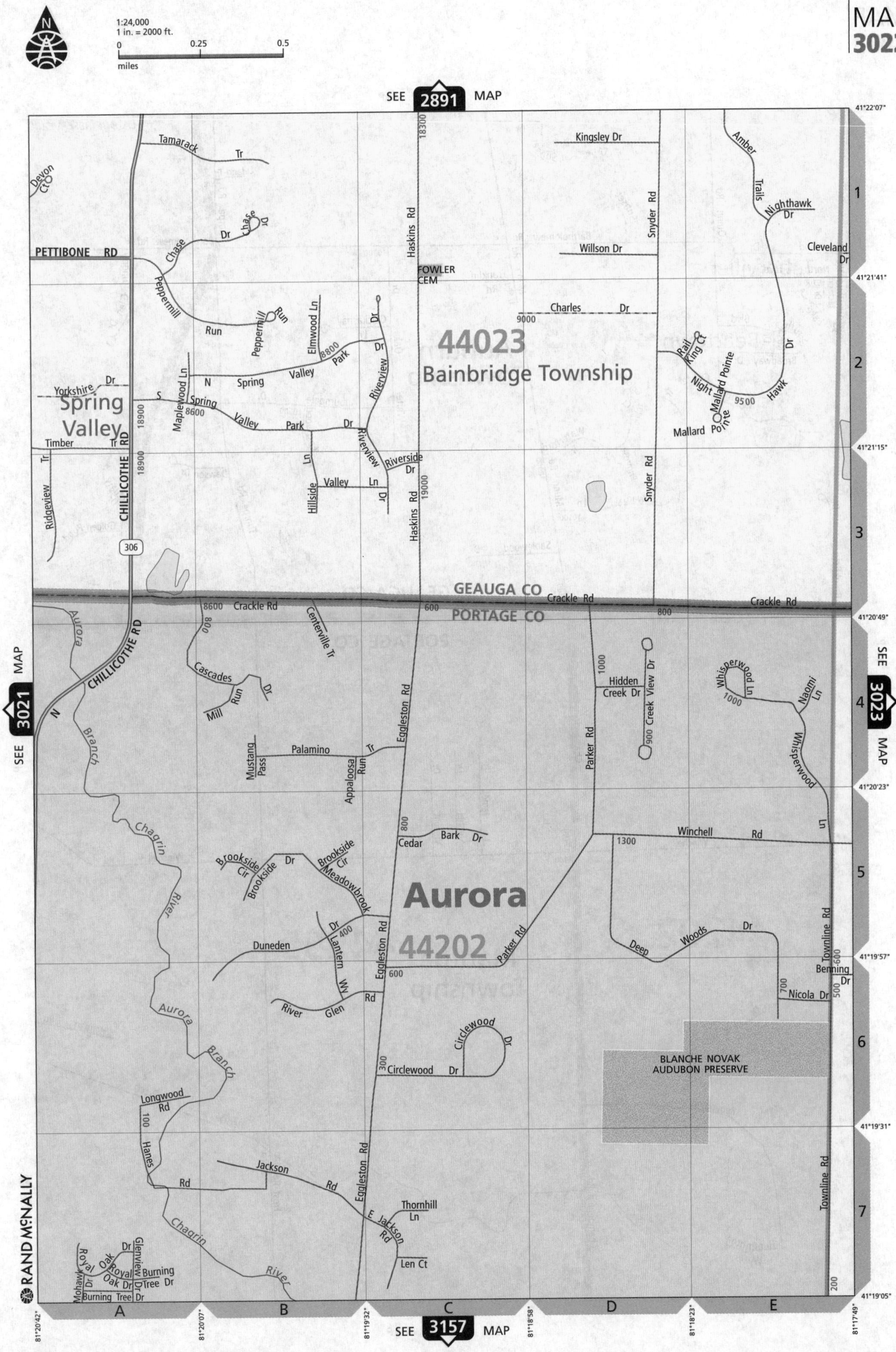
1:24,000
1 in. = 2000 ft.
0
0.25
0.5
miles
SEE 2891 MAP
SEE 3021 MAP
SEE 3023 MAP
SEE 3157 MAP
44023
Bainbridge Township
Spring Valley
Aurora
44202
GEAUGA CO
PORTAGE CO
FOWLER CEM
BLANCHE NOVAK AUDUBON PRESERVE
Tamarack Tr
Devon Ct
Chase Dr
PETTIBONE RD
Peppermill Run
Elmwood Ln
Park Dr
Riverview Dr
Haskins Rd
Kingsley Dr
Willson Dr
Snyder Rd
Charles Dr
Amber Trails Dr
Nighthawk Dr
Cleveland Dr
Rail King Ct
Mallard Pointe
Night Hawk
Yorkshire Dr
N Spring Valley
S Spring Valley Park Dr
Maplewood Ln
Timber Tr
CHILLICOTHE RD
Ridgeview Tr
Hillside Ln
Valley Ln
Riverside Dr
306
Crackle Rd
Centerville Tr
Cascades Dr
Mill Run
Aurora Branch
Chagrin River
Eggleston Rd
Palamino Tr
Mustang Pass
Appaloosa Run
Hidden Creek Dr
Creek View Dr
Parker Rd
Whisperwood Ln
Naomi Ln
Winchell Rd
Cedar Bark Dr
Brookside Cir
Brookside Dr
Meadowbrook
Lantern Wy
Duneden Dr
Deep Woods Dr
Townline Rd
Benning Dr
Nicola Dr
River Glen Rd
Circlewood Dr
Longwood Rd
Hanes Rd
Jackson Rd
E Jackson Rd
Thornhill Ln
Len Ct
Royal Oak Dr
Glenview Dr
Burning Tree Dr
Mohawk Dr
RAND McNALLY
A
B
C
D
E
1
2
3
4
5
6
7
41°22'07"
41°21'41"
41°21'15"
41°20'49"
41°20'23"
41°19'57"
41°19'31"
41°19'05"
81°20'42"
81°20'07"
81°19'32"
81°18'58"
81°18'23"
81°17'49"

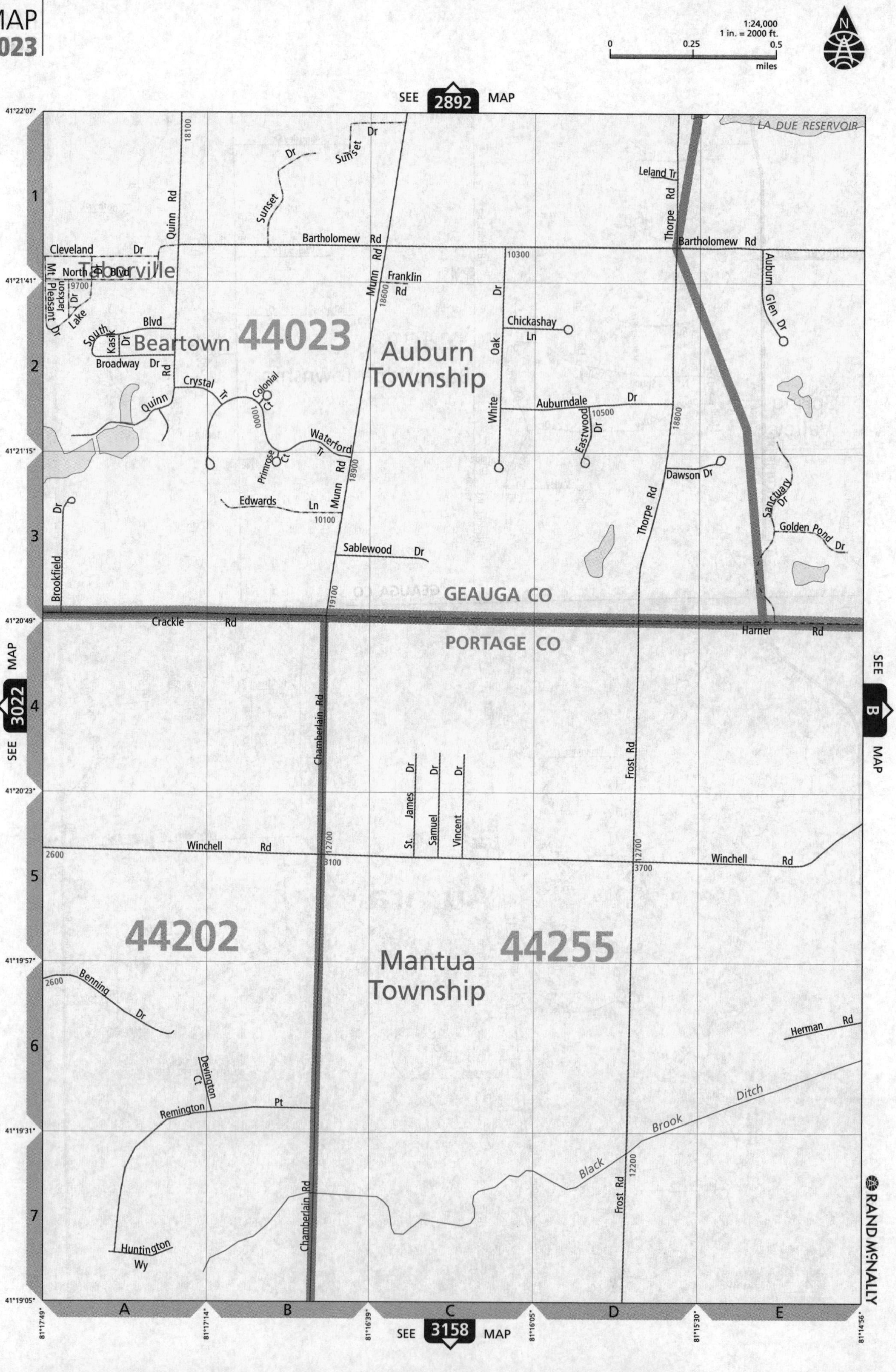
1:24,000
1 in. = 2000 ft.
0
0.25
0.5
miles
N
SEE 2892 MAP
SEE 3022 MAP
SEE B MAP
SEE 3158 MAP
LA DUE RESERVOIR
44023
Auburn Township
Beartown
Tiborville
GEAUGA CO
PORTAGE CO
44202
44255
Mantua Township
Quinn Rd
Sunset Dr
Sunset Dr
Bartholomew Rd
Leland Tr
Thorpe Rd
Cleveland Dr
North Blvd
Mt. Pleasant Dr
Jackson Dr
Lake Dr
South Blvd
Kasik Dr
Broadway Dr
Munn Rd
Franklin Rd
White Oak Dr
Chickashay Ln
Auburn Glen Dr
Crystal Tr
Colonial Ct
Waterford Tr
Primrose Ct
Auburndale Dr
Eastwood Dr
Dawson Dr
Sanctuary Dr
Golden Pond Dr
Edwards Ln
Sablewood Dr
Brookfield Dr
Crackle Rd
Harner Rd
Chamberlain Rd
Frost Rd
St. James Dr
Samuel Dr
Vincent Dr
Winchell Rd
Benning Dr
Devington Ct
Remington Pt
Herman Rd
Black Brook Ditch
Huntington Wy
18100
10300
19700
18600
10000
10500
18800
18900
10100
19100
12700
3100
3700
2600
12200
41°22'07"
41°21'41"
41°21'15"
41°20'49"
41°20'23"
41°19'57"
41°19'31"
41°19'05"
81°17'49"
81°17'14"
81°16'39"
81°16'05"
81°15'30"
81°14'56"
1
2
3
4
5
6
7
A
B
C
D
E
RAND McNALLY

1:24,000
1 in. = 2000 ft.
0 0.25 0.5
miles

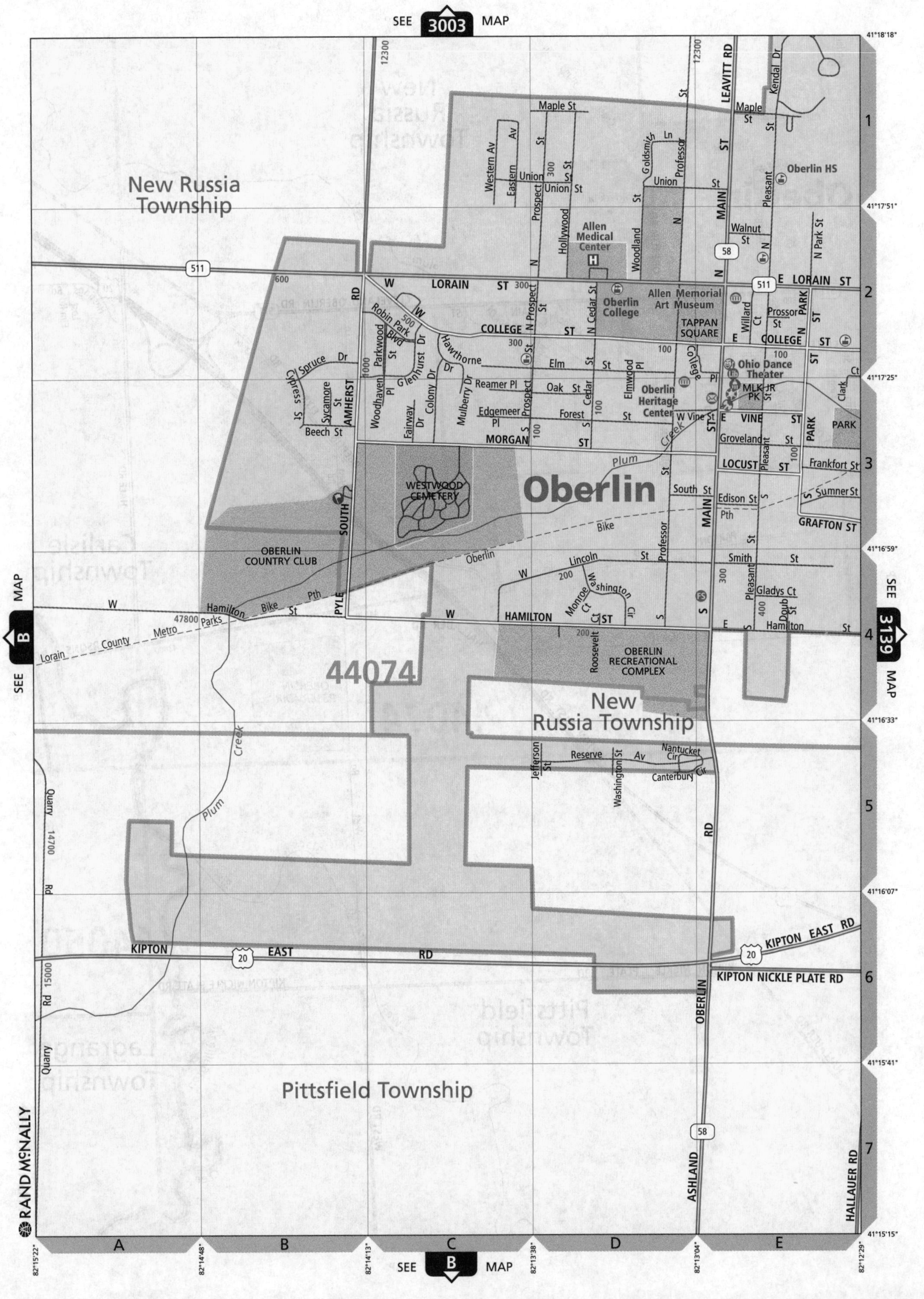
SEE 3003 MAP
SEE B MAP
SEE 3139 MAP
New Russia Township
Oberlin
44074
Pittsfield Township
OBERLIN COUNTRY CLUB
WESTWOOD CEMETERY
OBERLIN RECREATIONAL COMPLEX
Allen Medical Center
Oberlin College
Allen Memorial Art Museum
TAPPAN SQUARE
Oberlin HS
Ohio Dance Theater
MLK JR PK
Oberlin Heritage Center
PARK
W LORAIN ST
E LORAIN ST
COLLEGE ST
MORGAN ST
W HAMILTON ST
E VINE ST
LOCUST ST
GRAFTON ST
S MAIN ST
N MAIN ST
LEAVITT RD
AMHERST
SOUTH
PYLE
KIPTON EAST RD
KIPTON NICKLE PLATE RD
OBERLIN ASHLAND RD
HALLAUER RD
Quarry Rd
Lorain County Metro Parks Bike Pth
Oberlin Bike Pth
Plum Creek
Maple St
Union St
Walnut St
Elm St
Oak St
Forest St
Reamer Pl
Edgemeer Pl
Spruce Dr
Sycamore St
Cypress St
Beech St
Woodhaven Pl
Parkwood St
Glenhurst Dr
Robin Park Blvd
Hawthorne Dr
Fairway Dr
Colony Dr
Mulberry Dr
Western Av
Eastern Av
Prospect St
Hollywood St
Woodland St
Cedar St
Elmwood Pl
Goldsmith Ln
Professor St
Pleasant St
Willard Ct
Prossor St
Park St
Clark
Frankfort St
Sumner St
Edison St
Groveland St
South St
Smith St
Lincoln St
Washington Cir
Monroe Ct
Roosevelt Ct
Gladys Ct
Doub St
Kendal Dr
Reserve Av
Nantucket Cir
Canterbury Cir
Jefferson St
Washington St
KIPTON
511
58
20
A B C D E
1 2 3 4 5 6 7
41°18'18"
41°17'51"
41°17'25"
41°16'59"
41°16'33"
41°16'07"
41°15'41"
41°15'15"
82°15'22"
82°14'48"
82°14'13"
82°13'38"
82°13'04"
82°12'29"
RAND McNALLY

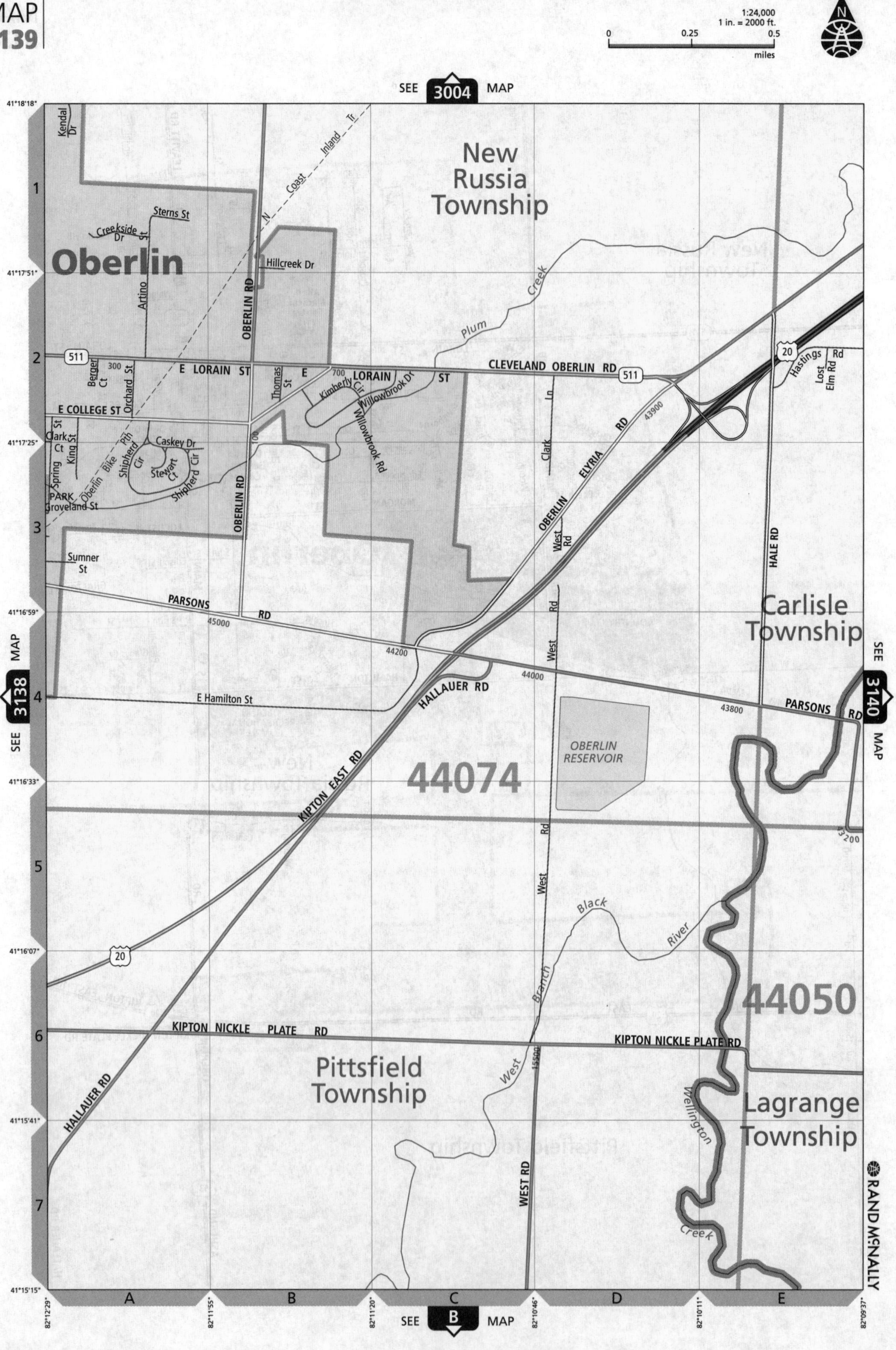
1:24,000
1 in. = 2000 ft.
0
0.25
0.5
miles
N
SEE 3004 MAP
SEE B MAP
SEE 3138 MAP
SEE 3140 MAP
New Russia Township
Oberlin
Carlisle Township
Pittsfield Township
Lagrange Township
44074
44050
OBERLIN RESERVOIR
Kendal Dr
Sterns St
Creekside Dr
Hillcreek Dr
Artino St
OBERLIN RD
N Coast Inland Tr
E LORAIN ST
CLEVELAND OBERLIN RD
511
20
Berger Ct
Orchard St
Thomas St
Kimberly Cir
Willowbrook Dr
Willowbrook Rd
E COLLEGE ST
Clark Ct
King St
Spring St
Caskey Dr
Shipherd Cir
Stewart Ct
Oberlin Bike Pth
PARK
Groveland St
Sumner St
Clark Ln
OBERLIN ELYRIA RD
West Rd
Hastings Rd
Lost Elm Rd
HALE RD
PARSONS RD
E Hamilton St
HALLAUER RD
KIPTON EAST RD
Plum Creek
Black River
West Branch
Wellington Creek
KIPTON NICKLE PLATE RD
WEST RD
A
B
C
D
E
1
2
3
4
5
6
7
RAND McNALLY

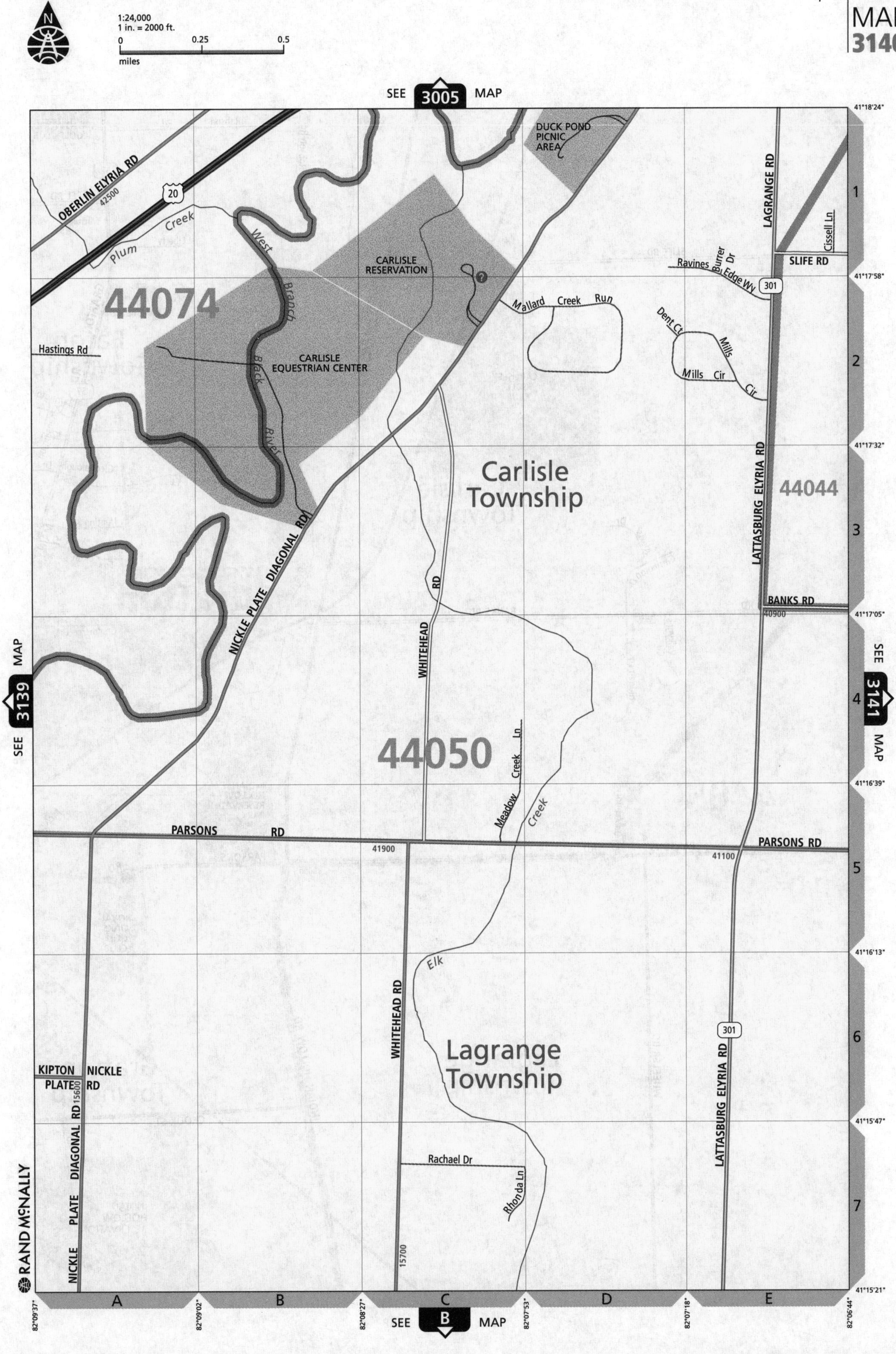
1:24,000
1 in. = 2000 ft.
0
0.25
0.5
miles
SEE 3005 MAP
SEE 3139 MAP
SEE 3141 MAP
SEE B MAP
DUCK POND PICNIC AREA
OBERLIN ELYRIA RD
42500
20
Plum Creek
West Branch Black River
CARLISLE RESERVATION
44074
Hastings Rd
CARLISLE EQUESTRIAN CENTER
Mallard Creek Run
LAGRANGE RD
Cissell Ln
SLIFE RD
Ravines
Burrer Dr
Edge Wy
301
Dent Ct
Mills Cir
Carlisle Township
44044
LATTASBURG ELYRIA RD
NICKLE PLATE DIAGONAL RD
WHITEHEAD RD
BANKS RD
40900
44050
Creek Ln
Meadow
Creek
PARSONS RD
41900
41100
Elk
Lagrange Township
KIPTON NICKLE PLATE RD
15600
Rachael Dr
Rhonda Ln
15700
RAND McNALLY
A
B
C
D
E
1
2
3
4
5
6
7
41°18'24"
41°17'58"
41°17'32"
41°17'05"
41°16'39"
41°16'13"
41°15'47"
41°15'21"
82°09'37"
82°09'02"
82°08'27"
82°07'53"
82°07'18"
82°06'44"

SEE 3006 MAP

1:24,000
1 in. = 2000 ft.
0
0.25
0.5
miles
N
41°18'24"
41°17'58"
41°17'32"
41°17'05"
41°16'39"
41°16'13"
41°15'47"
41°15'21"
82°06'44"
82°06'09"
82°05'35"
82°05'00"
82°04'25"
82°03'51"
1
2
3
4
5
6
7
A
B
C
D
E
Robson Rd
Robson Rd
38600
3100
BRENTWOOD GOLF CLUB
57
CAPEL RD
Midview HS
Liberty Ln
SLIFE RD
INDIAN HOLLOW RD
ST. MARY'S CEMETERY
GRAFTON RD
Eaton Township
River Ridge Ct
57
Barrington Dr
Kensington Dr
CARLISLE GOLF CLUB
Rader Ln
Fox Rd
Oak Rd
Glendalough Dr
Arbor Ct
39000
Carlisle Township
East Branch
Hunting Hllw St
MAIN ST
Alexis Dr
Carrington Dr
Fox Run
Grafton
BANKS RD
BANKS RD
40200
3800
Kelly Dr
Commerce Dr
Valkyries Cir
44044
Black River
Hidden Ln
INDIAN HOLLOW RESERVATION PARK
44050
Gondawood Dr
McAlpin Ct
PARSONS RD
39800
PARSONS RD
39000
ROYAL OAKS GOLF CLUB
WHEELER RD
Lagrange Township
INDIAN HOLLOW RD
Grafton Township
CROOK ST
Yarish Rd
INDIAN HOLLOW RESERVATION
East Branch Black River
RAND McNALLY

SEE 3140 MAP

SEE 3142 MAP

SEE B MAP

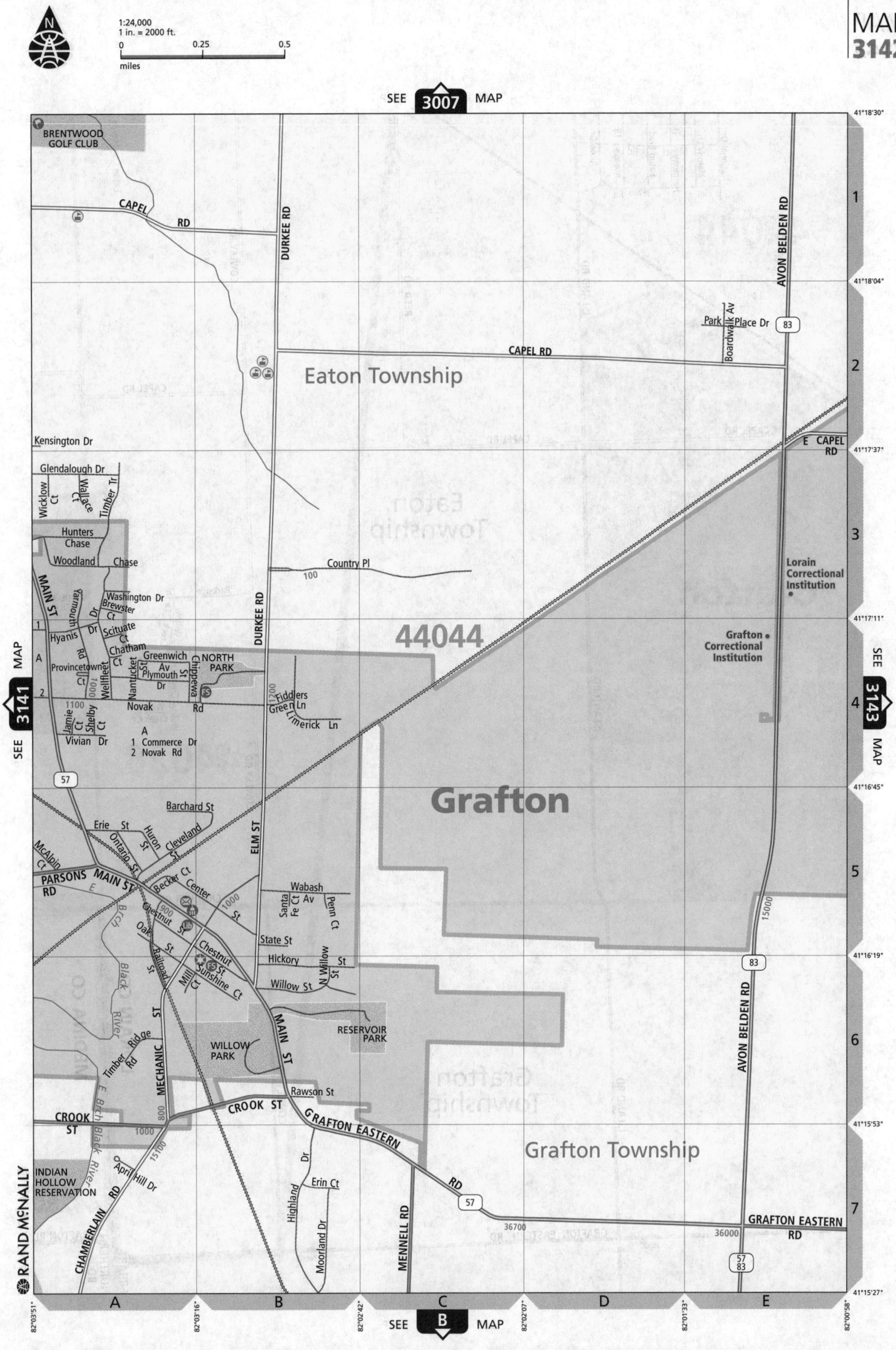
N
1:24,000
1 in. = 2000 ft.
0
0.25
0.5
miles
SEE 3007 MAP
SEE 3141 MAP
SEE 3143 MAP
SEE B MAP
BRENTWOOD GOLF CLUB
CAPEL RD
DURKEE RD
Eaton Township
Park Place Dr
Boardwalk Av
AVON BELDEN RD
83
Kensington Dr
Glendalough Dr
Wicklow Ct
Wallace Ct
Timber Tr
E CAPEL RD
Hunters Chase
Woodland Chase
Country Pl
100
Lorain Correctional Institution
Grafton Correctional Institution
44044
MAIN ST
Yarmouth Dr
Washington Dr
Brewster Ct
Scituate Ct
Hyanis Rd
Chatham Ct
Greenwich Av
Plymouth Dr
NORTH PARK
Chippewa Rd
Provincetown Ct
Wellfleet Ct
Nantucket St
Fiddlers Green Ln
Limerick Ln
1200
1100
Novak Rd
Jamie Ct
Shelby Ct
Vivian Dr
A
1 Commerce Dr
2 Novak Rd
57
Grafton
Barchard St
Erie St
Huron St
Ontario St
Cleveland St
ELM ST
McAlpin Ct
PARSONS RD
MAIN ST
Becker Ct
Center St
1000
Wabash Av
Santa Fe Ct
Penn Ct
Chestnut St
900
Oak St
Railroad St
State St
Hickory
N Willow St
Chestnut St
Sunshine Ct
Mill Ct
Willow St
15000
Black River
MECHANIC ST
Ridge Rd
Timber Rd
RESERVOIR PARK
WILLOW PARK
Rawson St
CROOK ST
800
GRAFTON EASTERN RD
Grafton Township
INDIAN HOLLOW RESERVATION
April Hill Dr
15100
Highland Dr
Erin Ct
Moorland Dr
MENNELL RD
CHAMBERLAIN RD
36700
36000
GRAFTON EASTERN RD
57
83
1
2
3
4
5
6
7
A
B
C
D
E
41°18'30"
41°18'04"
41°17'37"
41°17'11"
41°16'45"
41°16'19"
41°15'53"
41°15'27"
82°03'51"
82°03'16"
82°02'42"
82°02'07"
82°01'33"
82°00'58"
RAND McNALLY

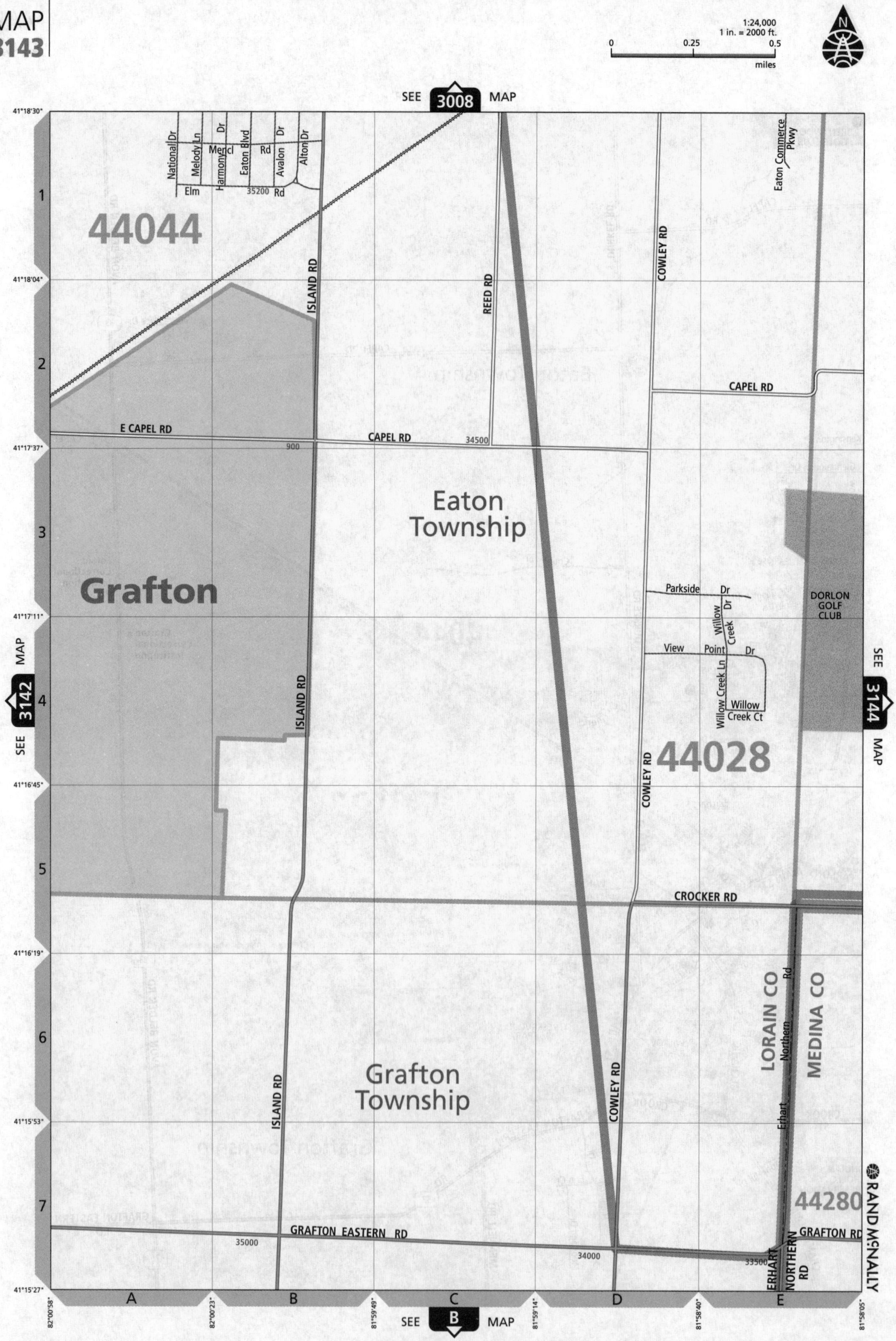
1:24,000
1 in. = 2000 ft.
0 0.25 0.5
miles
N
SEE 3008 MAP
SEE 3142 MAP
SEE 3144 MAP
SEE B MAP
National Dr
Melody Ln
Harmony
Dr
Mercl
Eaton Blvd
Rd
Avalon
Dr
Alton Dr
Elm
35200 Rd
44044
ISLAND RD
REED RD
COWLEY RD
Eaton Commerce Pkwy
CAPEL RD
E CAPEL RD
900
34500
Eaton
Township
Grafton
Parkside
Dr
Willow
Creek
Dr
View
Point
Dr
Willow Creek Ln
Willow
Willow Creek Ct
DORLON
GOLF
CLUB
44028
CROCKER RD
LORAIN CO
MEDINA CO
Northern
Rd
Erhart
Grafton
Township
44280
GRAFTON EASTERN RD
35000
34000
33500
GRAFTON RD
ERHART
NORTHERN
RD
1
2
3
4
5
6
7
A
B
C
D
E
41°18'30"
41°18'04"
41°17'37"
41°17'11"
41°16'45"
41°16'19"
41°15'53"
41°15'27"
82°00'58"
82°00'23"
81°59'49"
81°59'14"
81°58'40"
81°58'05"

1:24,000
1 in. = 2000 ft.
0 0.25 0.5 miles

SEE 3009 MAP

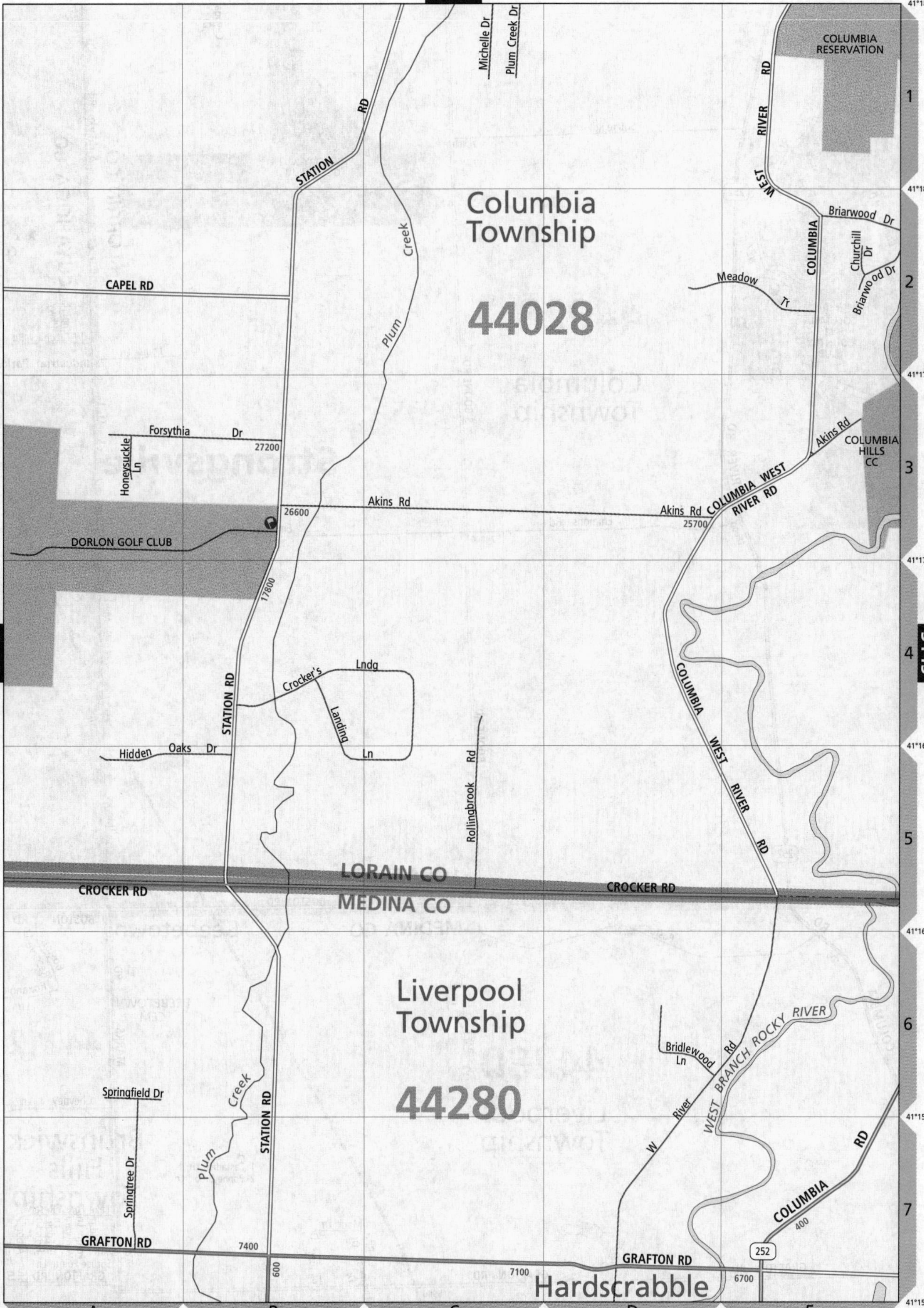

Columbia Township
44028
COLUMBIA RESERVATION
COLUMBIA HILLS CC
STATION RD
CAPEL RD
Plum Creek
Michelle Dr
Plum Creek Dr
WEST RIVER RD
Briarwood Dr
Churchill Dr
Meadow Tr
COLUMBIA
Forsythia Dr
27200
Honeysuckle Ln
Akins Rd
26600
25700
COLUMBIA WEST RIVER RD
DORLON GOLF CLUB
17800
Crocker's Lndg
Landing Ln
Hidden Oaks Dr
Rollingbrook Rd
LORAIN CO
MEDINA CO
CROCKER RD
Liverpool Township
44280
Bridlewood Ln
Rd
WEST BRANCH ROCKY RIVER
W River Rd
Springfield Dr
Springtree Dr
GRAFTON RD
7400
600
7100
6700
252
400
Hardscrabble
1
2
3
4
5
6
7
A
B
C
D
E
41°18'35"
41°18'09"
41°17'43"
41°17'17"
41°16'51"
41°16'25"
41°15'59"
41°15'33"
81°58'05"
81°57'31"
81°56'56"
81°56'21"
81°55'47"
81°55'12"

SEE 3143 MAP

SEE 3145 MAP

SEE B MAP

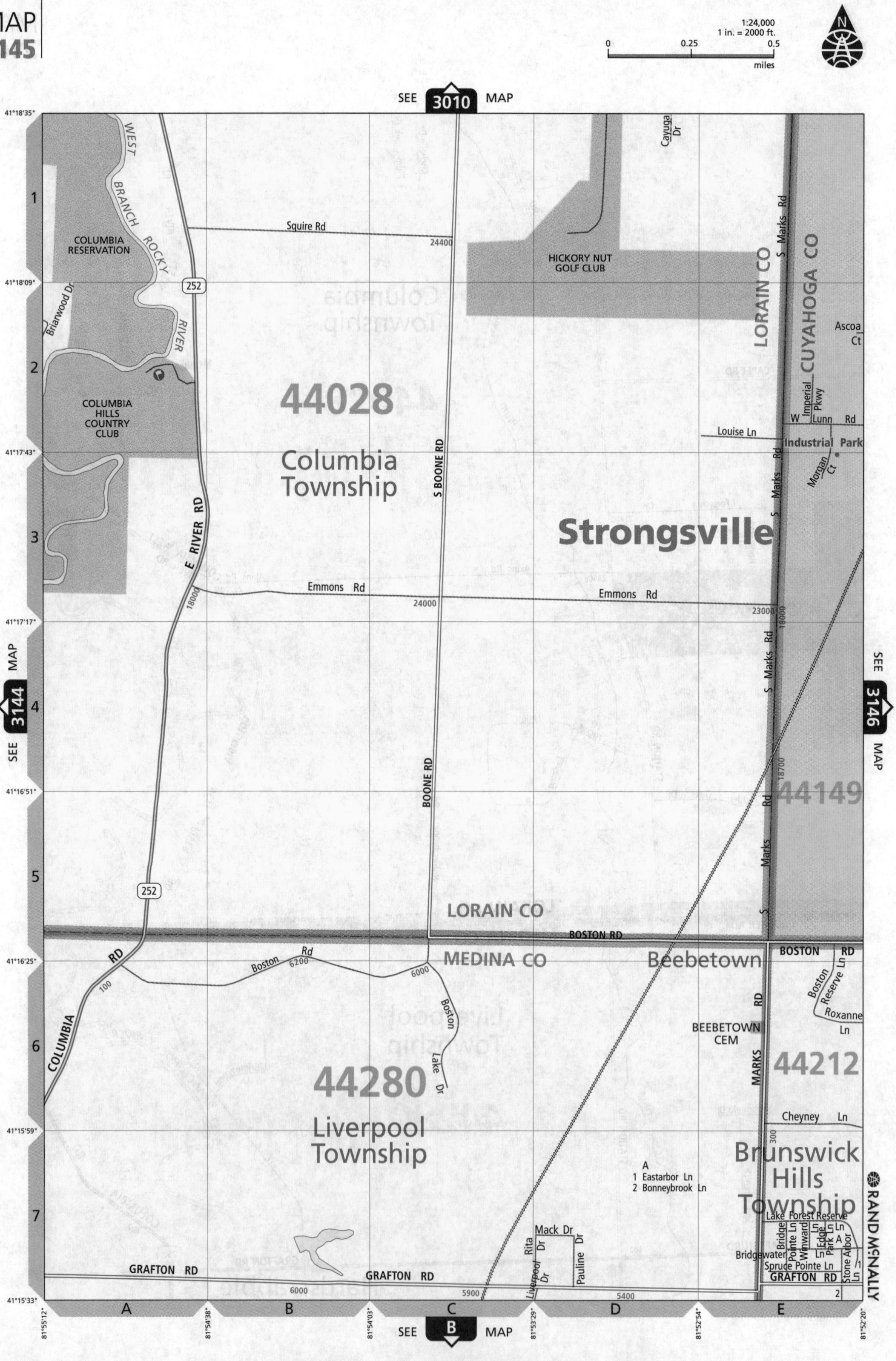
1:24,000
1 in. = 2000 ft.
0
0.25
0.5
miles
N
SEE 3010 MAP
SEE 3144 MAP
SEE 3146 MAP
SEE B MAP
41°18'35"
41°18'09"
41°17'43"
41°17'17"
41°16'51"
41°16'25"
41°15'59"
41°15'33"
81°55'12"
81°54'38"
81°54'03"
81°53'29"
81°52'54"
81°52'20"
A
B
C
D
E
1
2
3
4
5
6
7
WEST BRANCH ROCKY RIVER
COLUMBIA RESERVATION
COLUMBIA HILLS COUNTRY CLUB
Briarwood Dr
252
Squire Rd
24400
HICKORY NUT GOLF CLUB
Cayuga Dr
44028
Columbia Township
S BOONE RD
E RIVER RD
Strongsville
LORAIN CO
CUYAHOGA CO
S Marks Rd
Ascoa Ct
Imperial Pkwy
W Lunn Rd
Louise Ln
Industrial Park
Morgan Ct
Emmons Rd
18000
24000
Emmons Rd
23000
18000
18700
44149
BOONE RD
S Marks Rd
LORAIN CO
BOSTON RD
MEDINA CO
Beebetown
BOSTON RD
COLUMBIA RD
100
Boston Rd
6200
6000
Boston Lake Dr
Boston Reserve Ln
Roxanne Ln
BEEBETOWN CEM
MARKS RD
44212
44280
Liverpool Township
Cheyney Ln
300
Brunswick Hills Township
A
1 Eastarbor Ln
2 Bonneybrook Ln
Lake Forest Reserve
Bridge Pointe Ln
Winward Ln
Edge Park Ln
Ln
A
Bridgewater
Spruce Pointe Ln
Stone Arbor Ln
1
2
Mack Dr
Rita Dr
Pauline Dr
Liverpool Dr
GRAFTON RD
GRAFTON RD
GRAFTON RD
6000
5900
5400
RAND McNALLY

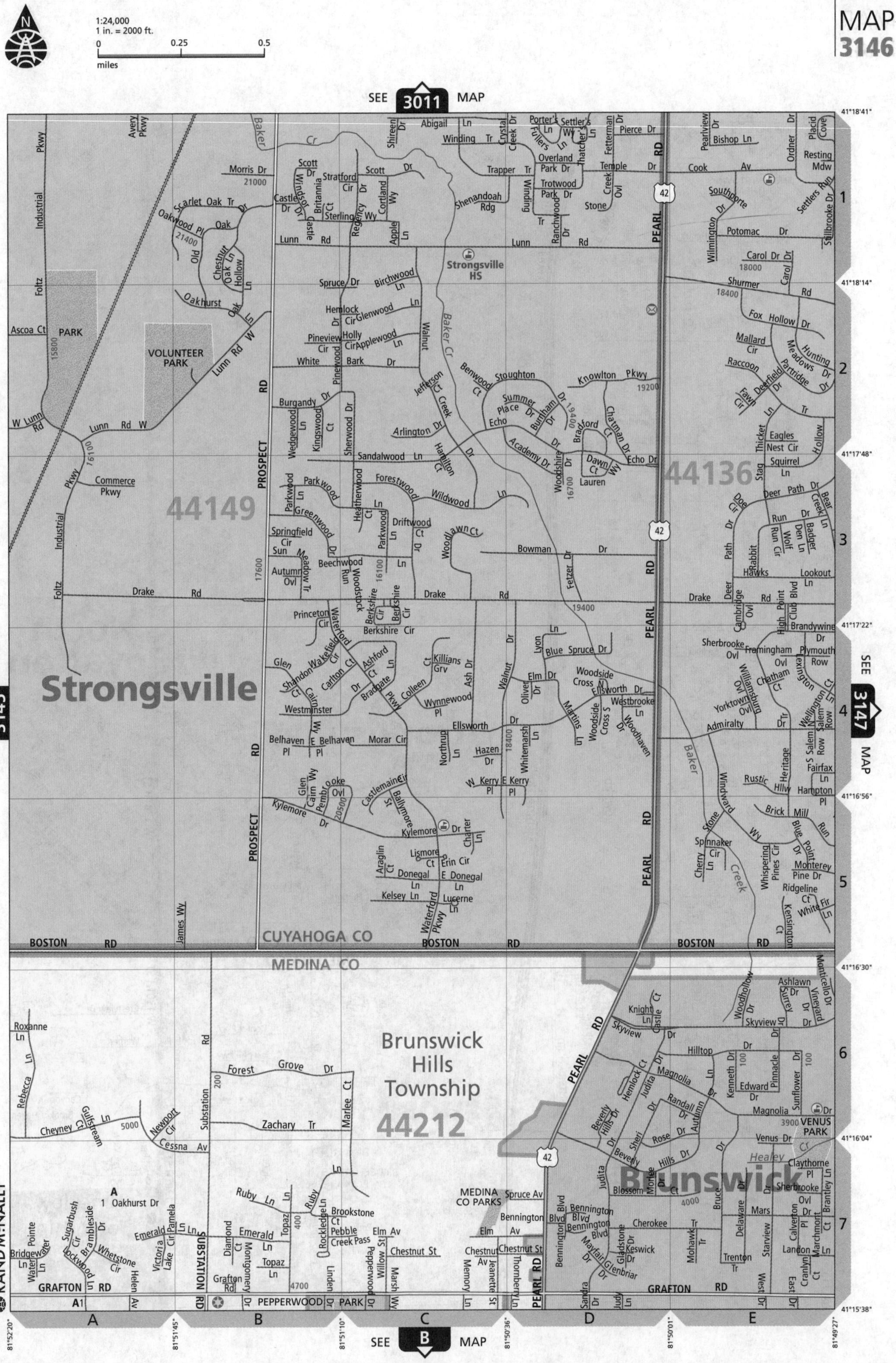
1:24,000
1 in. = 2000 ft.
0
0.25
0.5
miles
SEE 3011 MAP
SEE 3145 MAP
SEE 3147 MAP
SEE B MAP
Strongsville
44149
44136
Brunswick Hills Township
44212
Brunswick
CUYAHOGA CO
MEDINA CO
Strongsville HS
VOLUNTEER PARK
PARK
MEDINA CO PARKS
VENUS PARK
PEPPERWOOD PARK
PEARL RD
PROSPECT RD
BOSTON RD
GRAFTON RD
SUBSTATION RD
Drake Rd
Lunn Rd
Lunn Rd W
W Lunn Rd
Shurmer Rd
Cook Av
Ellsworth Dr
Bowman Dr
Industrial Pkwy
Foltz Pkwy
Commerce Pkwy
Knowlton Pkwy
Waterford Pkwy
Kylemore Dr
Magnolia Dr
Skyview Dr
Forest Grove Dr
Zachary Tr
Cessna Av
Cheyney Ct
Newport Cir
Baker Cr
Healey Cr
Creek
42
1
2
3
4
5
6
7
A
B
C
D
E
A
1 Oakhurst Dr
RAND McNALLY
41°18'41"
41°18'14"
41°17'48"
41°17'22"
41°16'56"
41°16'30"
41°16'04"
41°15'38"
81°52'20"
81°51'45"
81°51'10"
81°50'36"
81°50'01"
81°49'27"

1:24,000
1 in. = 2000 ft.
0 0.25 0.5
miles

SEE 3012 MAP

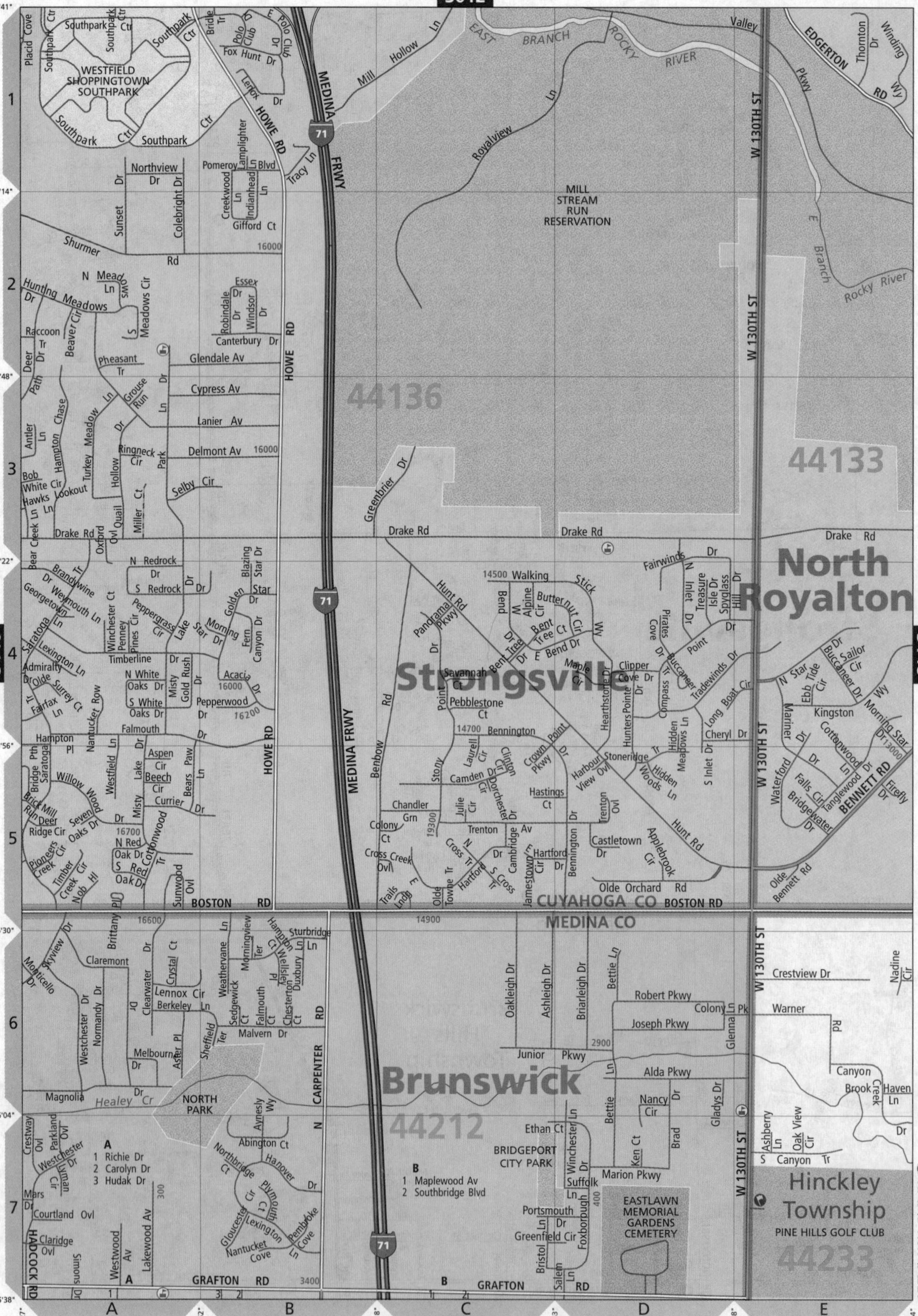

WESTFIELD SHOPPINGTOWN SOUTHPARK
MILL STREAM RUN RESERVATION
EAST BRANCH ROCKY RIVER
MEDINA FRWY
HOWE RD
W 130TH ST
EDGERTON RD
Drake Rd
Shurmer Rd
Hunt Rd
BOSTON RD
CUYAHOGA CO
MEDINA CO
CARPENTER
GRAFTON RD
BENNETT RD
44136
44133
44212
44233
North Royalton
Strongsville
Brunswick
Hinckley Township
PINE HILLS GOLF CLUB
NORTH PARK
BRIDGEPORT CITY PARK
EASTLAWN MEMORIAL GARDENS CEMETERY
Healey Cr
A
1 Richie Dr
2 Carolyn Dr
3 Hudak Dr
B
1 Maplewood Av
2 Southbridge Blvd

SEE 3146 MAP
SEE 3148 MAP

A B C D E

SEE B MAP

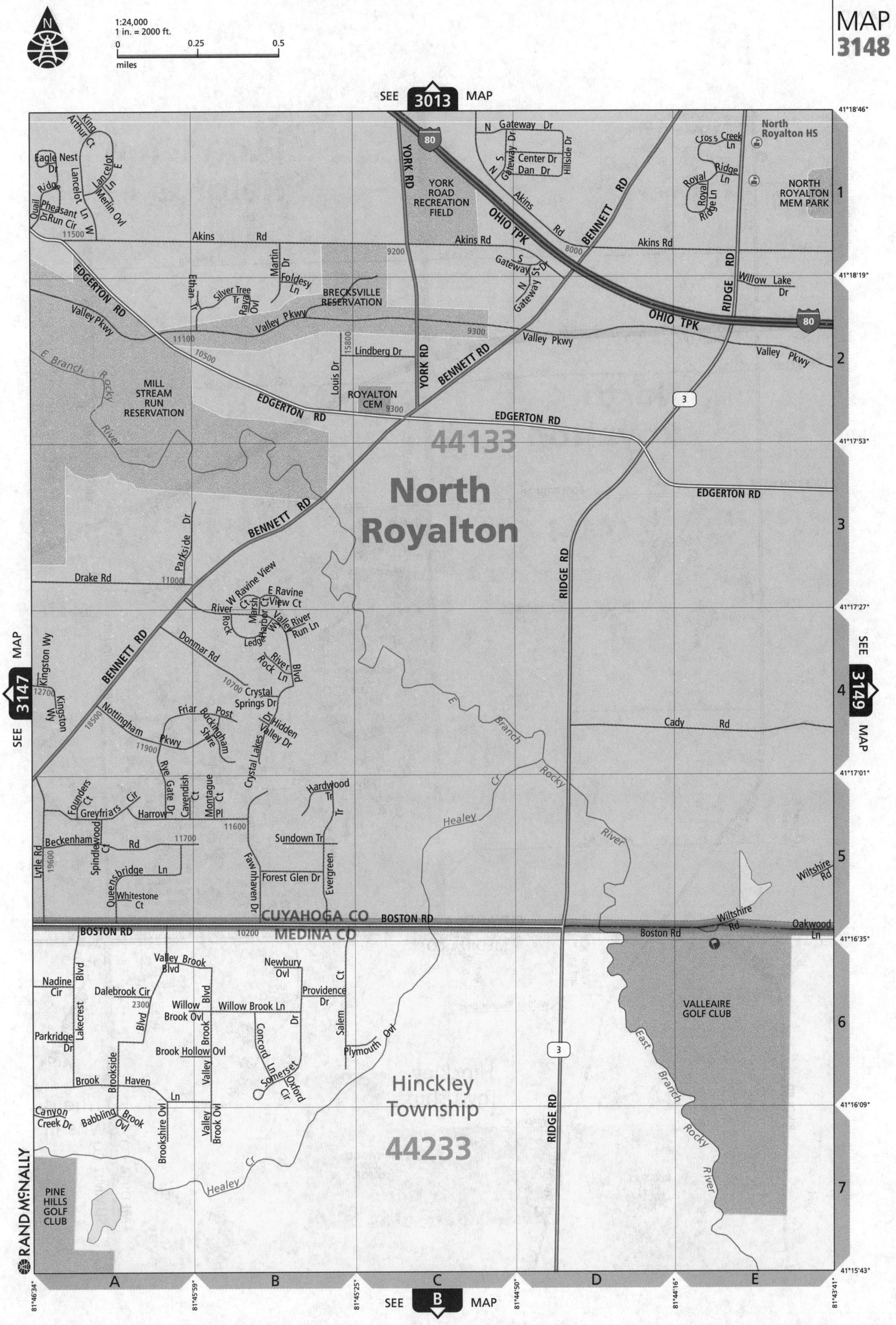
1:24,000
1 in. = 2000 ft.
0 0.25 0.5
miles
SEE 3013 MAP
SEE 3147 MAP
SEE 3149 MAP
SEE B MAP
North Royalton
44133
Hinckley Township
44233
CUYAHOGA CO
MEDINA CO
BOSTON RD
Boston Rd
RIDGE RD
BENNETT RD
YORK RD
EDGERTON RD
OHIO TPK
80
3
Akins Rd
Valley Pkwy
Cady Rd
Drake Rd
Donmar Rd
Nottingham Pkwy
Crystal Springs Dr
Crystal Lakes Dr
Hidden Valley Dr
River Rock Ln
River Run Ln
Valley River Blvd
W Ravine View Ct
E Ravine View Ct
Marsh Ct
Ledge Harbor Ct
Friar Ct
Buckingham Shire
Post
Parkside Dr
Lindberg Dr
Louis Dr
Martin Dr
Foldesy Ln
Silver Tree Tr
Raya Ovl
Ethan Tr
King Arthur Ct
Eagle Nest Dr
Lancelot Ln E
Lancelot Ln W
Merlin Ovl
Quail Ridge Dr
Pheasant Run Cir
N Gateway Dr
S Gateway Dr
Center Dr
Dan Dr
Hillside Dr
Cross Creek Ln
Royal Ridge Ln
Willow Lake Dr
North Royalton HS
NORTH ROYALTON MEM PARK
YORK ROAD RECREATION FIELD
BRECKSVILLE RESERVATION
MILL STREAM RUN RESERVATION
ROYALTON CEM
E Branch Rocky River
Healey Cr
Kingston Wy
Founders Ct
Greyfriars Cir
Harrow
Rye Gate Dr
Cavendish Ct
Montague Ct
Pl
Beckenham Rd
Spindlewood Ct
Queensbridge Ln
Whitestone Ct
Lytle Rd
Hardwood Tr
Sundown Tr
Evergreen Tr
Fawnhaven Dr
Forest Glen Dr
Wiltshire Rd
Oakwood Ln
VALLEAIRE GOLF CLUB
PINE HILLS GOLF CLUB
Nadine Cir
Lakecrest Blvd
Dalebrook Cir
Valley Brook Blvd
Willow Brook Ovl
Willow Brook Ln
Newbury Ovl
Providence Dr
Salem Ct
Concord Ln
Somerset Cir
Oxford Cir
Plymouth Ovl
Brook Hollow Ovl
Parkridge Dr
Brookside
Brook Haven Ln
Canyon Creek Dr
Babbling Brook Ovl
Brookshire Ovl
Valley Brook Ovl
A B C D E
1 2 3 4 5 6 7
41°18'46"
41°18'19"
41°17'53"
41°17'27"
41°17'01"
41°16'35"
41°16'09"
41°15'43"
81°46'34"
81°45'59"
81°45'25"
81°44'50"
81°44'16"
81°43'41"
RAND McNALLY

1:24,000
1 in. = 2000 ft.
0 0.25 0.5
miles

SEE 3014 MAP

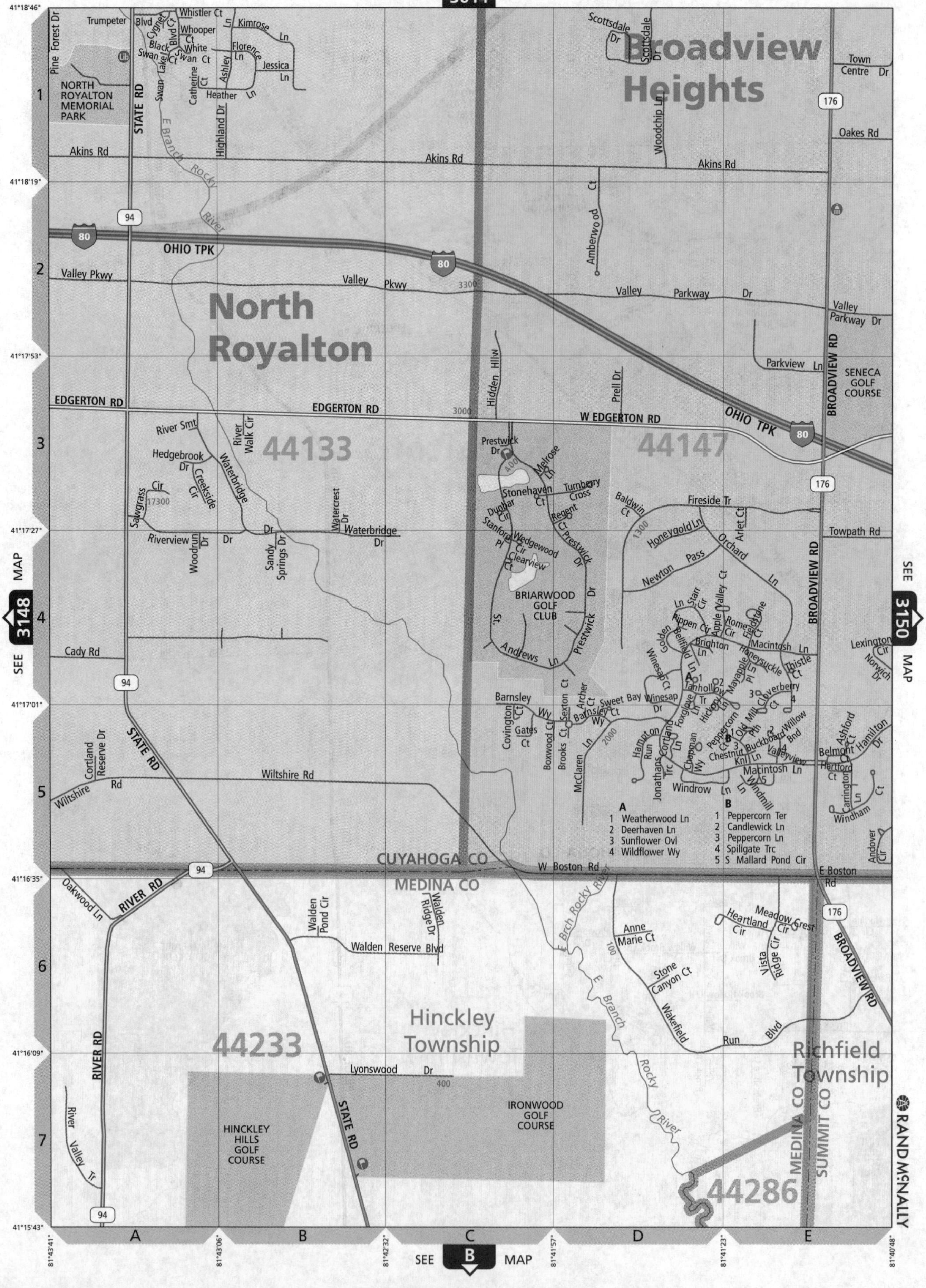

Broadview Heights
North Royalton
Hinckley Township
Richfield Township
44133
44147
44233
44286
NORTH ROYALTON MEMORIAL PARK
BRIARWOOD GOLF CLUB
SENECA GOLF COURSE
HINCKLEY HILLS GOLF COURSE
IRONWOOD GOLF COURSE
CUYAHOGA CO
MEDINA CO
SUMMIT CO
STATE RD
BROADVIEW RD
RIVER RD
OHIO TPK
EDGERTON RD
W EDGERTON RD
Akins Rd
Valley Pkwy
Valley Parkway Dr
Wiltshire Rd
W Boston Rd
E Boston Rd
Cady Rd
Towpath Rd
Oakes Rd
Town Centre Dr
Parkview Ln
Fireside Tr
Walden Reserve Blvd
Lyonswood Dr
Wakefield Run Blvd
E Branch Rocky River
A
1 Weatherwood Ln
2 Deerhaven Ln
3 Sunflower Ovl
4 Wildflower Wy
B
1 Peppercorn Ter
2 Candlewick Ln
3 Peppercorn Ln
4 Spillgate Trc
5 S Mallard Pond Cir
41°18'46"
41°18'19"
41°17'53"
41°17'27"
41°17'01"
41°16'35"
41°16'09"
41°15'43"
81°43'41"
81°43'06"
81°42'32"
81°41'57"
81°41'23"
81°40'48"
1 2 3 4 5 6 7
A B C D E

SEE 3148 MAP

SEE 3150 MAP

SEE B MAP

SEE 3015 MAP

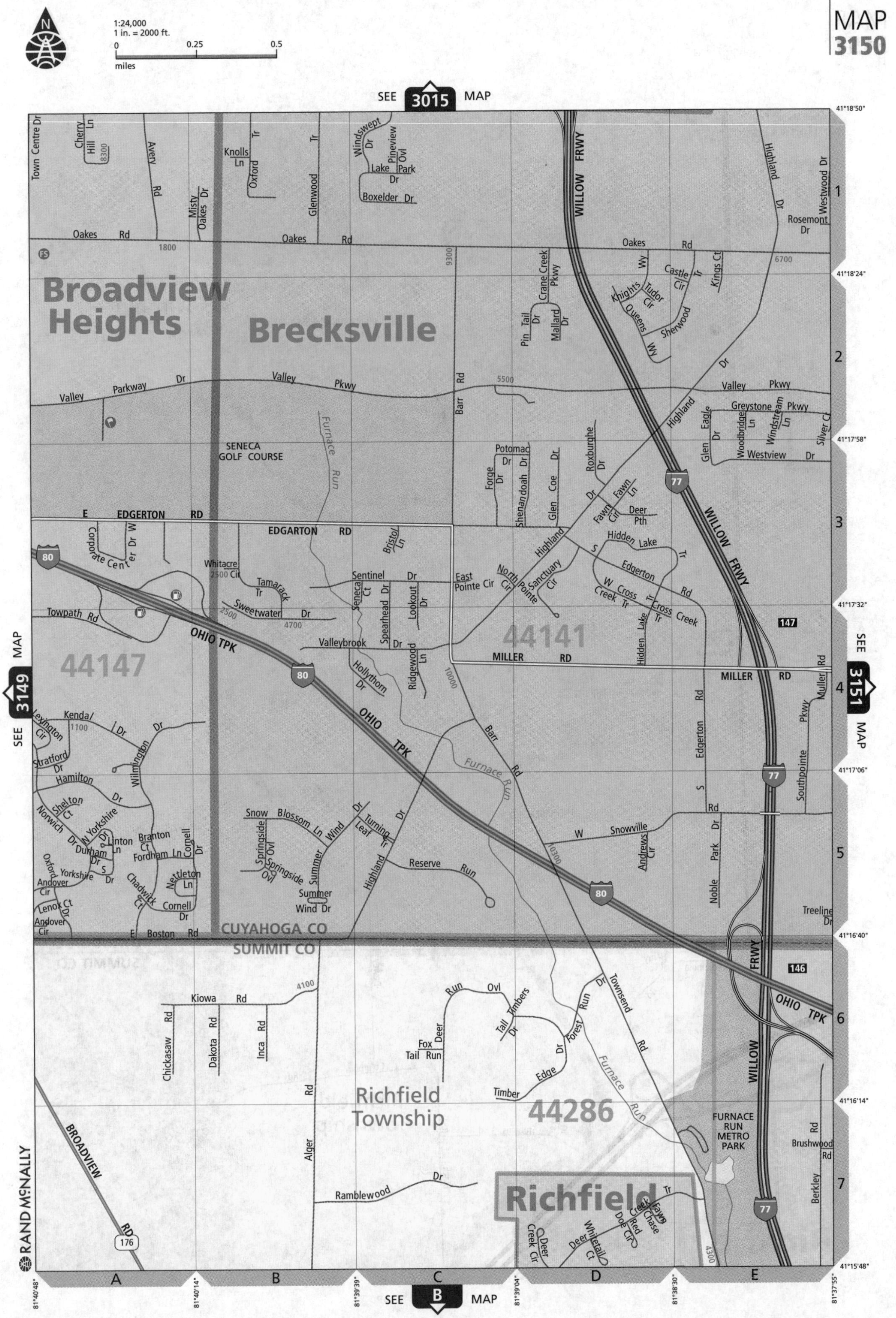
1:24,000
1 in. = 2000 ft.
0 0.25 0.5
miles
Broadview Heights
Brecksville
Richfield Township
Richfield
44147
44141
44286
SENECA GOLF COURSE
FURNACE RUN METRO PARK
CUYAHOGA CO
SUMMIT CO
WILLOW FRWY
OHIO TPK
E EDGERTON RD
EDGARTON RD
MILLER RD
BROADVIEW RD
Oakes Rd
Valley Parkway Dr
Valley Pkwy
Barr Rd
Highland Dr
Townsend Rd
Alger Rd
Kiowa Rd
Ramblewood Dr
Snowville Rd
Furnace Run
RAND McNALLY
A B C D E
1 2 3 4 5 6 7

SEE 3149 MAP

SEE 3151 MAP

SEE B MAP

SEE 3016 MAP

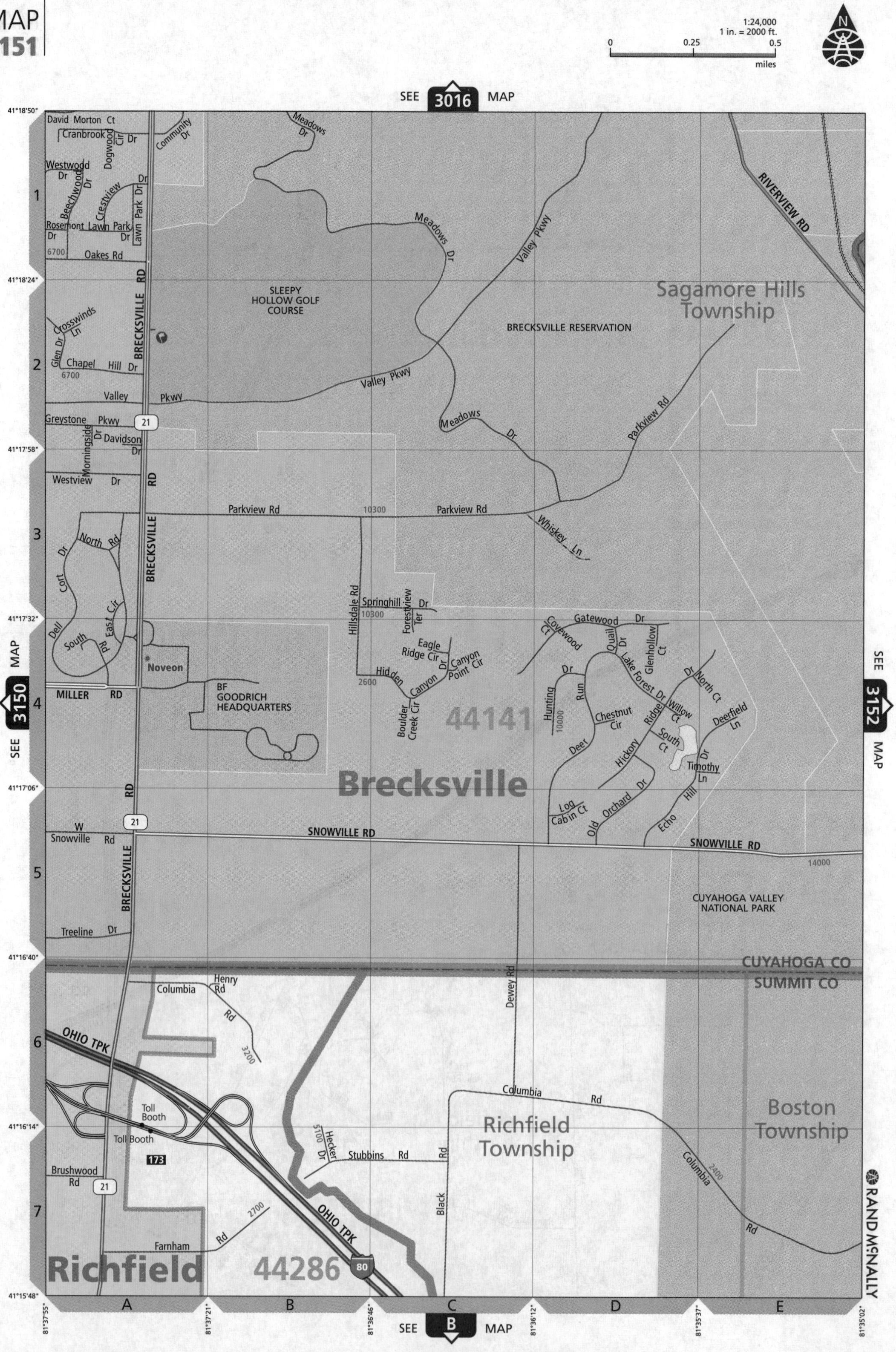
1:24,000
1 in. = 2000 ft.
0
0.25
0.5
miles
N
David Morton Ct
Cranbrook
Dogwood Cir
Dr
Community Dr
Meadows Dr
Westwood Dr
Beechwood Dr
Crestview Dr
Lawn Park Dr
Rosemont Lawn Park Dr
6700
Oakes Rd
RIVERVIEW RD
Meadows Dr
Valley Pkwy
SLEEPY HOLLOW GOLF COURSE
BRECKSVILLE RD
Sagamore Hills Township
BRECKSVILLE RESERVATION
Crosswinds Ln
Glen Dr
Chapel Hill Dr
Valley Pkwy
Greystone Pkwy
21
Morningside Dr
Davidson Dr
Westview Dr
Meadows Dr
Parkview Rd
10300
North Rd
Cort Dr
Whiskey Ln
Hillsdale Rd
Springhill Dr
Forestview Ter
Gatewood Dr
Covewood Ct
Quail Dr
Glenhollow Ct
Dell
South
East Cir
Noveon
Eagle Ridge Cir
Canyon Point Cir
Hidden Canyon Dr
2600
MILLER RD
BF GOODRICH HEADQUARTERS
Boulder Creek Cir
44141
Hunting Run Dr
10000
Chestnut Cir
Lake Forest Dr
North Ct
Willow Ct
Deerfield Ln
Hickory Ridge Dr
South Ct
Deer
Timothy Ln
Breckville
Log Cabin Ct
Old Orchard Dr
Echo Hill Dr
W Snowville Rd
SNOWVILLE RD
14000
CUYAHOGA VALLEY NATIONAL PARK
Treeline Dr
CUYAHOGA CO
SUMMIT CO
Columbia
Henry Rd
Dewey Rd
3200
OHIO TPK
Toll Booth
Toll Booth
173
Columbia Rd
Richfield Township
Boston Township
Hecker Dr
5100
Stubbins Rd
Black Rd
2400
Brushwood Rd
2700
Farnham Rd
Richfield
44286
80
OHIO TPK
A
B
C
D
E
1
2
3
4
5
6
7
41°18'50"
41°18'24"
41°17'58"
41°17'32"
41°17'06"
41°16'40"
41°16'14"
41°15'48"
81°37'55"
81°37'21"
81°36'46"
81°36'12"
81°35'37"
81°35'02"
RAND McNALLY

SEE 3150 MAP
SEE 3152 MAP
SEE B MAP

1:24,000
1 in. = 2000 ft.
0 0.25 0.5
miles

SEE 3017 MAP

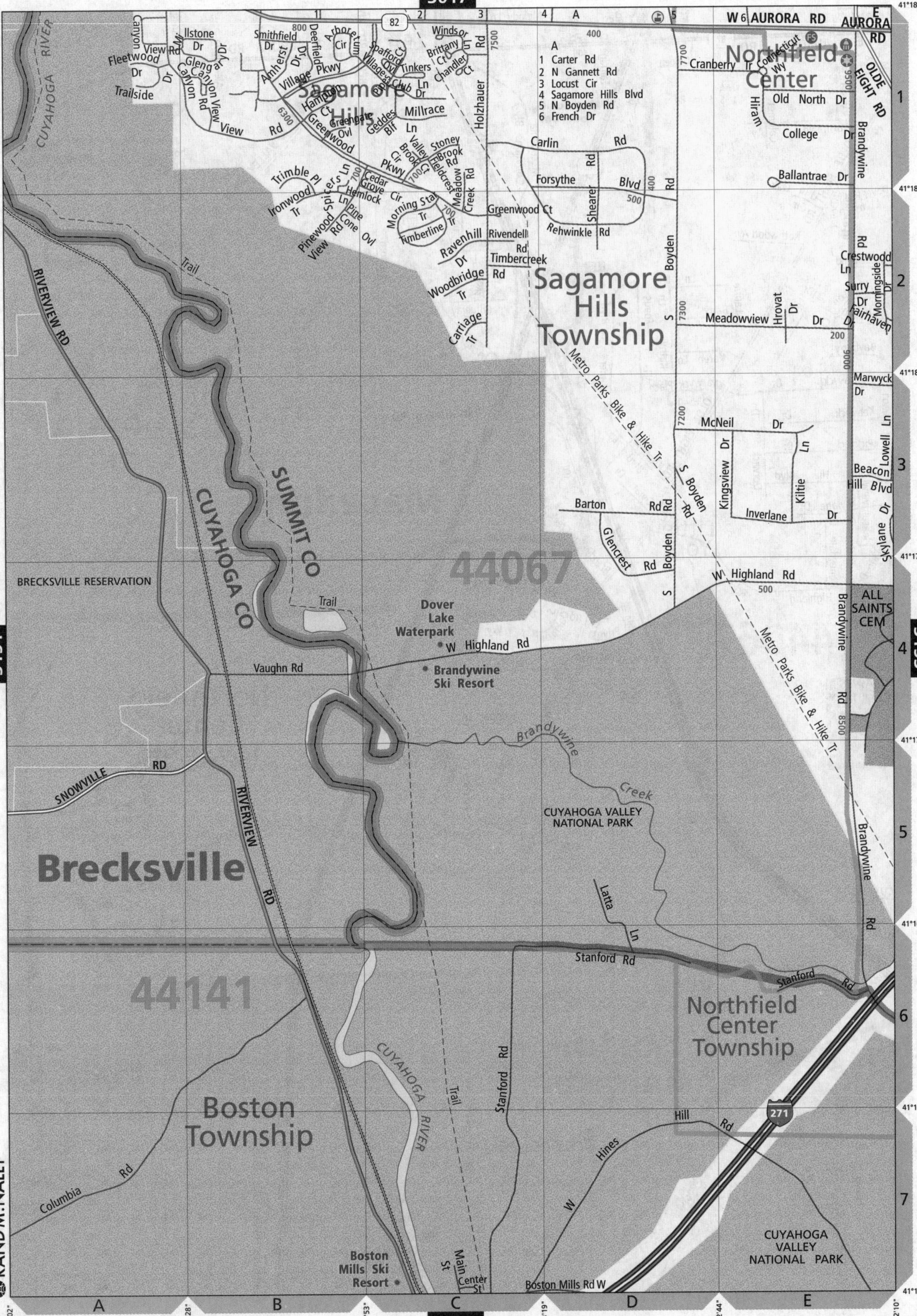
CUYAHOGA RIVER
Canyon View Rd
Millstone Dr
Fleetwood Dr
Glengary Dr
Canyon View Rd
Trailside
View Rd
Smithfield Dr
Deerfield Dr
Arboretum Cir
Amherst Dr
Village Pkwy
Spafford
Windsor
Brittany Ct
Chandler Ct
Tinkers
Club Dr
Sagamore Hills
Hampton Ct
Greengate Ovl
Greenwood
Geddes Blf
Millrace Ln
Holzhauer Rd
1 Carter Rd
2 N Gannett Rd
3 Locust Cir
4 Sagamore Hills Blvd
5 N Boyden Rd
6 French Dr
W AURORA RD
AURORA RD
Cranberry Tr
Connecticut Wy
Northfield Center
OLDE EIGHT RD
Old North Dr
Hiram
College Dr
Brandywine Rd
Carlin Rd
Forsythe Blvd
Shearer Rd
Ballantrae Dr
Stoney Brook Rd
Valley Brook Ct
Meadow Creek Rd
Fieldcrest
Trimble Pl
Ironwood Tr
Spicers Ln
Cedar Grove Cir
Hemlock
Pine Cone Ovl
Pinewood View
Morning Star Tr
Timberline Tr
Greenwood Ct
Rehwinkle Rd
Ravenhill Dr
Rivendell Rd
Timbercreek
Woodbridge Tr
Carriage Tr
Sagamore Hills Township
Boyden Rd
Crestwood Ln
Surry Dr
Morningside Dr
Fairhaven
Meadowview Dr
Hrovat Dr
Metro Parks Bike & Hike Tr
Marwyck Dr
McNeil Dr
Lowell Ln
Beacon Hill Blvd
Kingsview Dr
Kiltie Ln
Inverlane Dr
Skylane Dr
Barton Rd
S Boyden Rd
Glencrest Rd
44067
W Highland Rd
ALL SAINTS CEM
RIVERVIEW RD
CUYAHOGA CO
SUMMIT CO
Trail
BRECKSVILLE RESERVATION
Dover Lake Waterpark
Vaughn Rd
Brandywine Ski Resort
Brandywine Creek
SNOWVILLE RD
CUYAHOGA VALLEY NATIONAL PARK
Breckville
Latta Ln
Stanford Rd
44141
Northfield Center Township
Boston Township
Hill Rd
271
W Hines
Columbia Rd
Boston Mills Ski Resort
Main St
Center St
Boston Mills Rd W
A
B
C
D
E
1
2
3
4
5
6
7

SEE 3151 MAP

SEE 3153 MAP

SEE B MAP

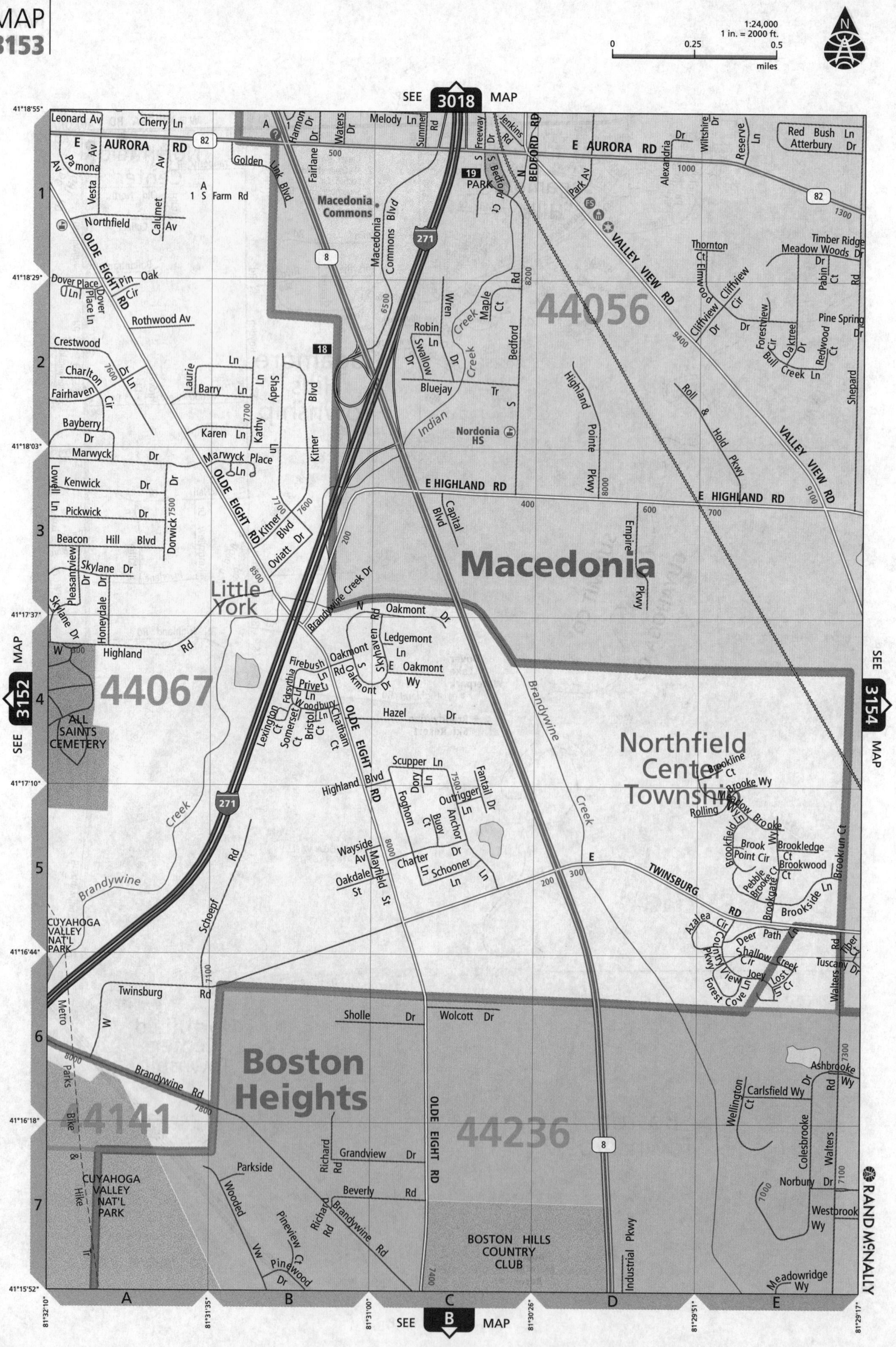
1:24,000
1 in. = 2000 ft.
0 0.25 0.5
miles
SEE 3018 MAP
SEE 3152 MAP
SEE 3154 MAP
SEE B MAP
Macedonia
Northfield Center Township
Boston Heights
Little York
44056
44067
44141
44236
Macedonia Commons
Nordonia HS
ALL SAINTS CEMETERY
CUYAHOGA VALLEY NAT'L PARK
BOSTON HILLS COUNTRY CLUB
E AURORA RD
E HIGHLAND RD
VALLEY VIEW RD
OLDE EIGHT RD
E TWINSBURG RD
N BEDFORD RD
Leonard Av
Cherry Ln
Pamona Av
Vesta Av
Golden Link Blvd
Fairlane Dr
Harmon Dr
Waters Dr
Melody Ln
Summer Rd
Freeway Dr
Jenkins Rd
Alexandria Dr
Wiltshire Dr
Reserve Ln
Red Bush Ln
Atterbury Dr
Farm Rd
Calumet Av
Northfield
Macedonia Commons Blvd
Park Av
Thornton Ct
Timber Ridge Dr
Meadow Woods Dr
Elmwood Ct
Cliffview Cir
Cliffview Dr
Pabin Ct
Forestview Cir
Oaktree Dr
Redwood Ct
Pine Spring Dr
Bull Creek Ln
Shepard Rd
Roll & Hold Pkwy
Dover Place Ln
Pin Oak Cir
Rothwood Av
Crestwood
Charlton Dr
Fairhaven Cir
Bayberry Dr
Marwyck Dr
Lowell Ln
Kenwick Dr
Pickwick Dr
Dorwick Dr
Beacon Hill Blvd
Skylane Dr
Pleasantview Dr
Honeydale Dr
W Highland Rd
Laurie Ln
Barry Ln
Shady Ln
Kathy Ln
Karen Ln
Marwyck Place Ln
Kitner Blvd
Oviatt Dr
Robin Ln
Swallow Dr
Wren Dr
Maple Ct
Bedford Rd
Bluejay Tr
Indian Creek
Highland Pointe Pkwy
Capital Blvd
Empire Pkwy
Brandywine Creek Dr
N Oakmont Dr
Ledgemont Ln
Skyhaven Dr
E Oakmont Wy
Oakmont Rd
S Oakmont Dr
Firebush Ln
Forsythia Ln
Privet Ln
Woodbury Ct
Lexington Ct
Somerset Ct
Bristol Ct
Chatham Ct
Hazel Dr
Scupper Ln
Dory Ln
Fogghorn Ct
Outrigger Ln
Fantail Dr
Buoy Ct
Anchor Dr
Highland Blvd
Wayside Av
Mayfield St
Oakdale St
Charter Ln
Schooner Ln
Brandywine Creek
Brookline Ct
Brooke Wy
Rolling Wy
Meadow Brooke
Brookfield Ln
Brook Point Cir
Brookledge Ct
Brookwood Ct
Pebble Brooke Ct
Brookgate Ct
Brookside Ln
Brookrun Ct
Azalea Cir
Country View Pkwy
Deer Path Ln
Shallow Creek Cir
Joey Ln
Lost Ln
Forest Cove Ln
Tuscany Dr
Tiber Ct
Walters Rd
Schoepf Rd
Twinsburg Rd
Metro Parks Bike & Hike Tr
Brandywine Rd
Sholle Dr
Wolcott Dr
Ashbrooke Wy
Carlsfield Wy
Wellington Ct
Grandview Dr
Richard Rd
Parkside
Wooded Vw
Beverly Rd
Pineview Ct
Pinewood Dr
Colesbrooke Dr
Norbury Dr
Westbrook Wy
Meadowridge Wy
Industrial Pkwy
82
8
271
18
19
PARK
A B C D E
1 2 3 4 5 6 7
41°18'55"
41°18'29"
41°18'03"
41°17'37"
41°17'10"
41°16'44"
41°16'18"
41°15'52"
81°32'10"
81°31'35"
81°31'00"
81°30'26"
81°29'51"
81°29'17"
RAND McNALLY

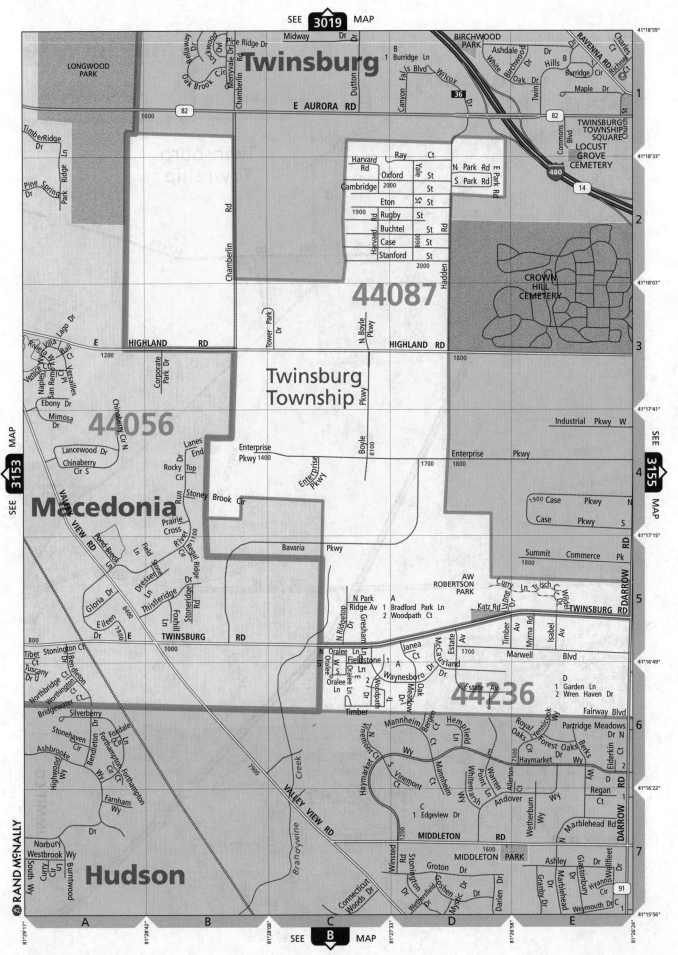

1:24,000
1 in. = 2000 ft.
0 0.25 0.5
miles

SEE 3019 MAP

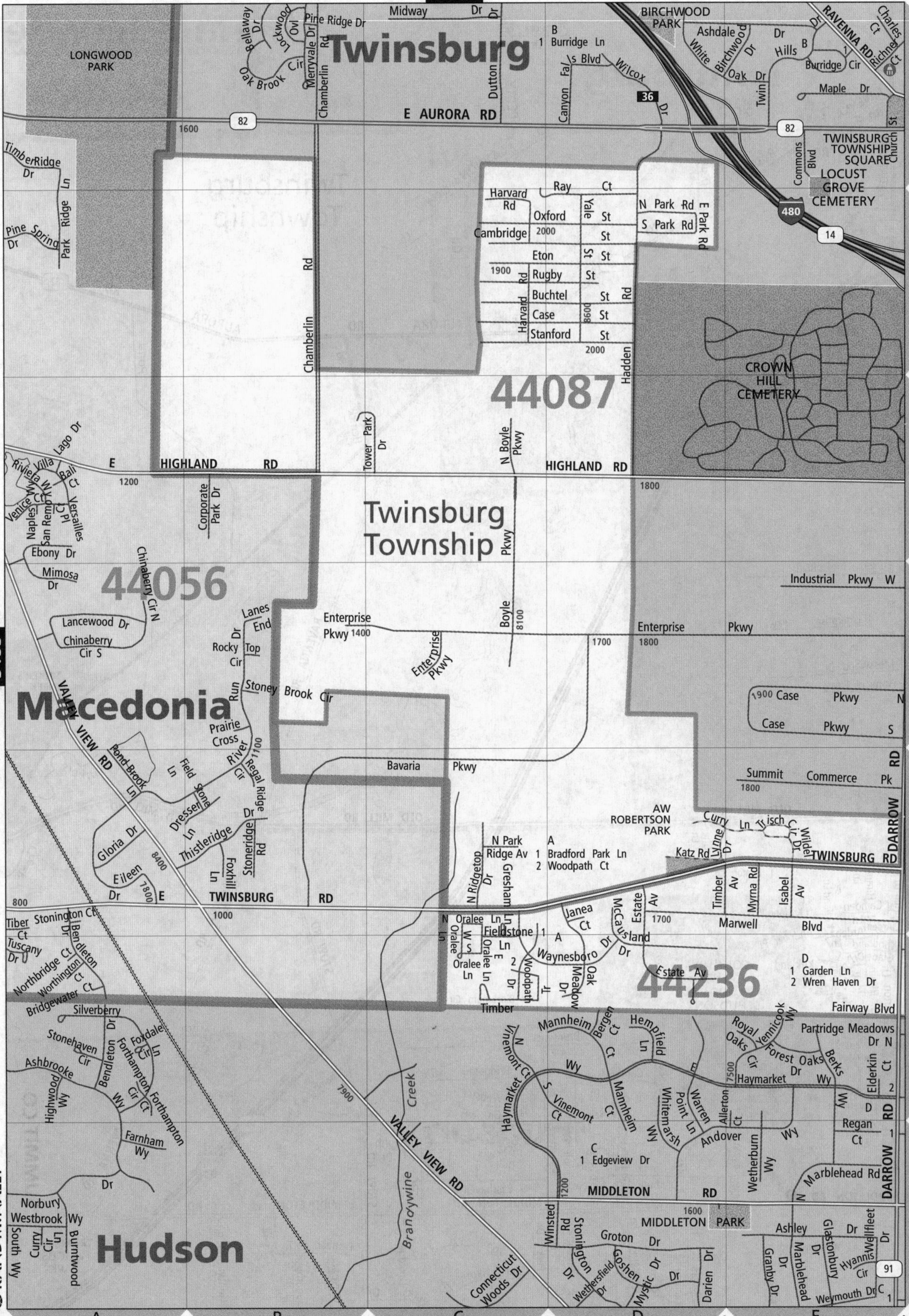
Twinsburg
Twinsburg Township
Macedonia
Hudson
44087
44056
44236
LONGWOOD PARK
BIRCHWOOD PARK
TWINSBURG TOWNSHIP SQUARE
LOCUST GROVE CEMETERY
CROWN HILL CEMETERY
AW ROBERTSON PARK
MIDDLETON PARK
E AURORA RD
E HIGHLAND RD
HIGHLAND RD
TWINSBURG RD
MIDDLETON RD
VALLEY VIEW RD
DARROW RD
RAVENNA RD
Chamberlin Rd
Dutton Rd
Midway Dr
Pine Ridge Dr
Merryvale Dr
Bellaway Dr
Lockwood Ovl
Oak Brook Cir
Canyon Fal
Wilcox Dr
Burridge Ln
Ashdale
White Birchwood
Oak Dr
Twin
Hills
Burridge Cir
Maple Dr
Charles Ct
Richner Ct
Church St
Commons Blvd
Timber Ridge Dr
Pine Spring Dr
Park Ridge Ln
Harvard Rd
Ray Ct
Oxford St
Yale St
Cambridge
Eton St
Rugby St
Buchtel St
Case St
Stanford St
N Park Rd
S Park Rd
E Park Rd
Hadden Rd
Tower Park Dr
N Boyle Pkwy
Boyle Pkwy
Corporate Park Dr
Lago Dr
Riviera Wy
Villa
Bali Ct
Venice Ct
Naples Ct
San Remo Pl
Versailles
Ebony Dr
Mimosa Dr
Chinaberry Cir N
Chinaberry Cir S
Lancewood Dr
Lanes End
Rocky Top Cir
Run Dr
Stoney Brook Cir
Prairie Cross
River Cir
Regal Ridge Dr
Enterprise Pkwy
Industrial Pkwy W
Case Pkwy N
Case Pkwy S
Summit Commerce Pk
Bavaria Pkwy
Pond Brook Ln
Field Stone Ln
Dresser Ln
Thistleridge
Stoneridge Rd
Foxhill Ln
Gloria Dr
Eileen Dr
Curry Ln
Trisch Cir
Wilde Dr
Katz Rd
Lynne Dr
N Park Ridge Av
Bradford Park Ln
Woodpath Ct
N Ridgetop Dr
Gresham Ln
Timber Av
Myrna Rd
Isabel Av
Estate Av
Marwell Blvd
Janea Ct
McCausland Dr
Oralee Ln
Fieldstone Ln
Waynesboro Dr
Oak Meadow Dr
Timber Tr
Garden Ln
Wren Haven Dr
Fairway Blvd
Tiber Ct
Stonington Ct
Tuscany Dr
Bendleton Dr
Worthington Ct
Northbridge Ct
Bridgewater Ct
Silverberry Dr
Stonehaven Cir
Foxdale Ln
Forthampton Cir
Ashbrooke Wy
Highwood Wy
Farnham Wy
Norbury Dr
Westbrook Wy
South Wy
Curry Cir
Buntwood Ln
Mannheim Ct
Bergen Ct
Hempfield Ln
N Vinemont Ct
S Vinemont Ct
Haymarket Dr
Whitemarsh Wy
Point Ln
Warren Ct
Allerton Ct
Andover Wy
Royal Oaks Cir
Fennicook Wy
Forest Oaks Dr
Partridge Meadows Dr N
Berks Wy
Elderkin Ct
Regan Ct
Wetherburn Wy
N Marblehead Rd
Edgeview Dr
Brandywine Creek
Connecticut Woods Dr
Winsted Rd
Stonington Dr
Groton Dr
Wethersfield Dr
Goshen Dr
Mystic Dr
Darien Dr
Ashley Dr
Granby Dr
Marblehead Dr
Glastonbury Dr
Hyannis Cir
Wellfleet Dr
Weymouth Dr
82
480
14
36
91
RAND McNALLY

SEE 3153 MAP

SEE 3155 MAP

SEE B MAP

1:24,000
1 in. = 2000 ft.
0 0.25 0.5
miles

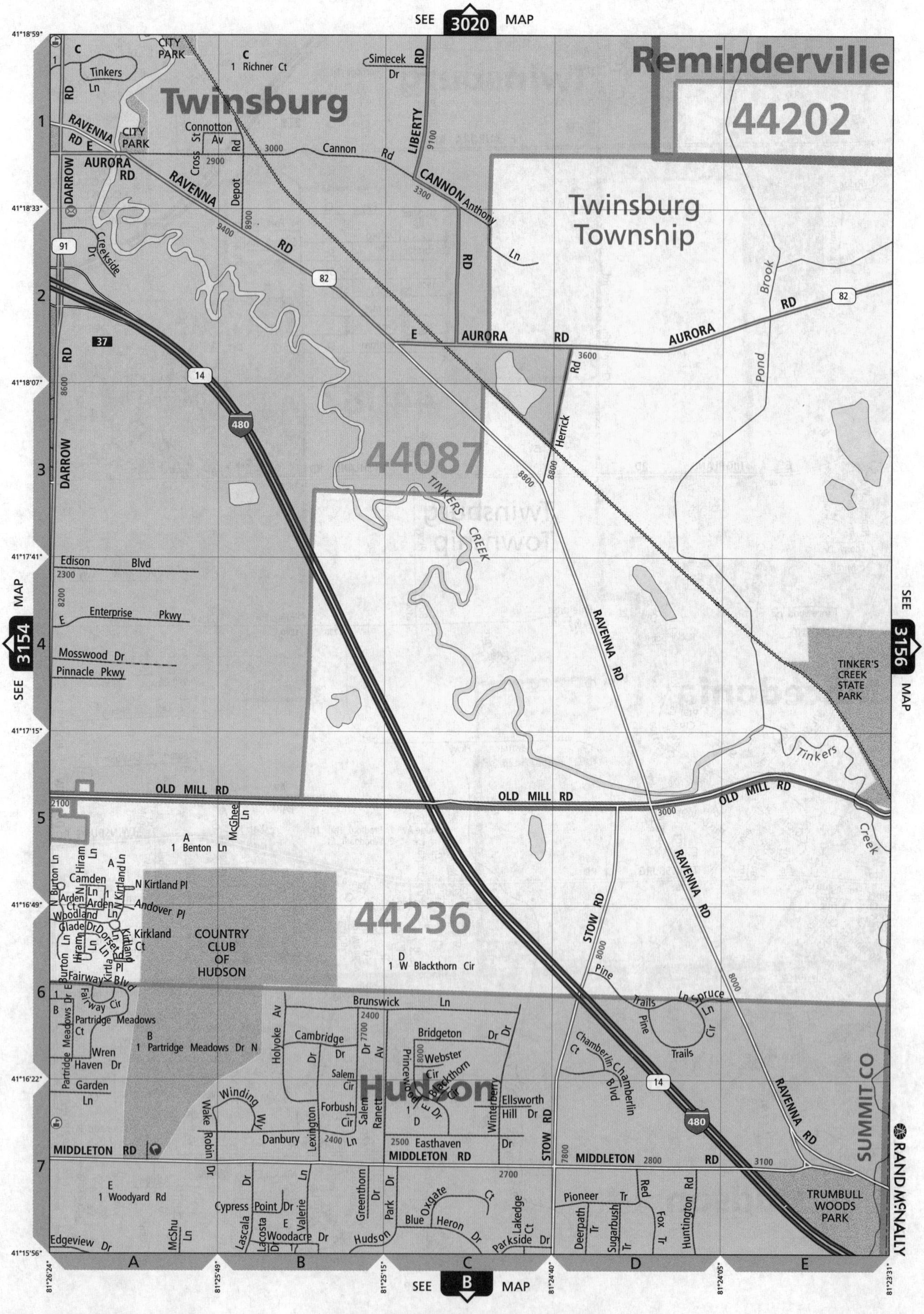
SEE 3020 MAP
SEE 3154 MAP
SEE 3156 MAP
SEE B MAP
Twinsburg
Reminderville
44202
Twinsburg Township
44087
44236
Hudson
CITY PARK
Tinkers Ln
RAVENNA RD E
AURORA RD
DARROW RD
Connotton Av
Cross St
Cannon Rd
1 Richner Ct
Simecek Dr
LIBERTY RD
CANNON Anthony Ln
Depot Rd
Creekside Dr
E AURORA RD
Herrick Rd
TINKERS CREEK
RAVENNA RD
Pond Brook
Edison Blvd
Enterprise Pkwy
Mosswood Dr
Pinnacle Pkwy
TINKER'S CREEK STATE PARK
Tinkers Creek
OLD MILL RD
McGhee Ln
1 Benton Ln
Hiram Ln
N Burton Ln
Camden
Arden Ct
Woodland
Glade Dr
N Kirtland Pl
Andover Pl
Kirkland Ct
Dorset Rd
Fairway Blvd
Fairway Cir
COUNTRY CLUB OF HUDSON
1 W Blackthorn Cir
STOW RD
Pine Ln
Spruce Ln
Trails Cir
Brunswick Ln
Cambridge Dr
Holyoke Av
Salem Cir
Bridgeton Dr
Webster Cir
Blackthorn Ct
Princewood Dr
Chamberlin Ct
Chamberlin Blvd
Partridge Meadows Ct
1 Partridge Meadows Dr N
Wren Haven Dr
Garden Ln
Winding Wy
Wake Robin Dr
Danbury Ln
Lexington
Forbush Cir
Ranett Av
Winterberry
Ellsworth Hill Dr
Easthaven Dr
MIDDLETON RD
1 Woodyard Rd
Cypress Point Dr
Lascala
Lacosta Dr
Valerie Ln
Woodacre Dr
Greenthorn Dr
Hudson Park Dr
Oxgate Ct
Blue Heron Dr
Lakedge Ct
Parkside Dr
Edgeview Dr
McShu Ln
Pioneer Tr
Deerpath Tr
Sugarbush Tr
Red Fox Tr
Huntington Rd
TRUMBULL WOODS PARK
SUMMIT CO
RAND McNALLY

SEE 3021 MAP

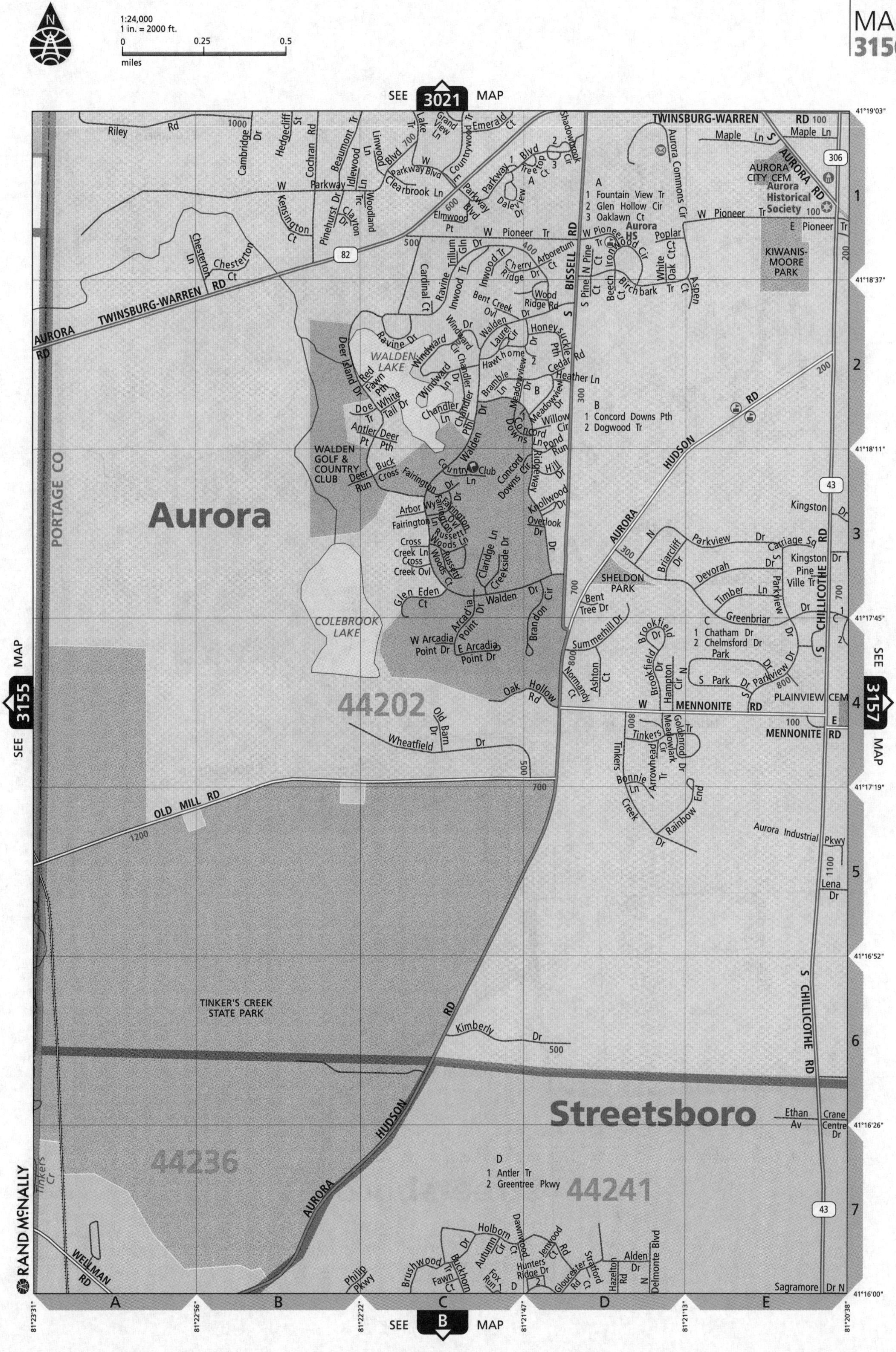
1:24,000
1 in. = 2000 ft.
0
0.25
0.5
miles
Aurora
Streetsboro
44202
44236
44241
PORTAGE CO
TWINSBURG-WARREN RD
AURORA RD
BISSELL RD
OLD MILL RD
AURORA HUDSON RD
S CHILLICOTHE RD
W MENNONITE RD
MENNONITE RD
WELLMAN RD
W Pioneer Tr
E Pioneer Tr
WALDEN LAKE
WALDEN GOLF & COUNTRY CLUB
COLEBROOK LAKE
TINKER'S CREEK STATE PARK
SHELDON PARK
KIWANIS-MOORE PARK
AURORA CITY CEM
Aurora Historical Society
Aurora HS
PLAINVIEW CEM
Tinkers Cr
Aurora Industrial Pkwy
A
1 Fountain View Tr
2 Glen Hollow Cir
3 Oaklawn Ct
B
1 Concord Downs Pth
2 Dogwood Tr
C
1 Chatham Dr
2 Chelmsford Dr
D
1 Antler Tr
2 Greentree Pkwy
82
306
43
41°19'03"
41°18'37"
41°18'11"
41°17'45"
41°17'19"
41°16'52"
41°16'26"
41°16'00"
81°23'31"
81°22'56"
81°22'22"
81°21'47"
81°21'13"
81°20'38"
A
B
C
D
E
1
2
3
4
5
6
7
RAND McNALLY

SEE 3155 MAP

SEE 3157 MAP

SEE B MAP

1:24,000
1 in. = 2000 ft.
0 0.25 0.5
miles

SEE 3022 MAP

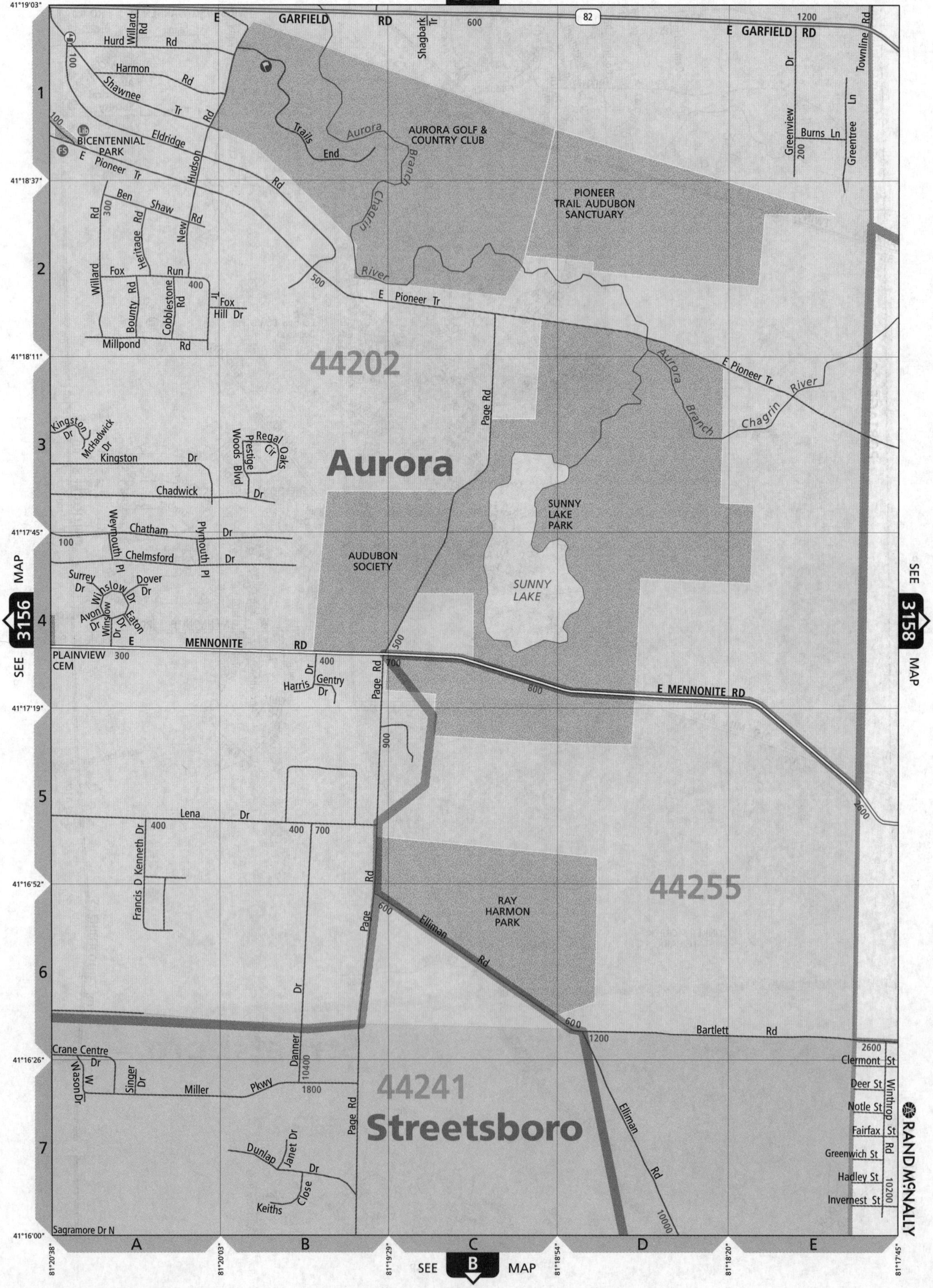
41°19'03"
41°18'37"
41°18'11"
41°17'45"
41°17'19"
41°16'52"
41°16'26"
41°16'00"
1
2
3
4
5
6
7
E GARFIELD RD
82
600
1200
E GARFIELD RD
Hurd Rd
Willard Rd
Harmon Rd
Shawnee Tr
Hudson Rd
Shagbark Tr
Townline Rd
Greenview Dr
Burns Ln
Greentree Ln
200
100
Lib
FS
BICENTENNIAL PARK
Eldridge Rd
E Pioneer Tr
Trails End
Aurora Branch
Chagrin River
AURORA GOLF & COUNTRY CLUB
PIONEER TRAIL AUDUBON SANCTUARY
Ben Shaw Rd
Willard Rd
300
Heritage Rd
New Hudson Rd
Fox Run
400
Bounty Rd
Cobblestone Rd
Fox Hill Dr
Fox Tr
Millpond Rd
500
E Pioneer Tr
44202
Page Rd
Aurora Branch
E Pioneer Tr
Chagrin River
Kingston Dr
McHadwick Dr
Kingston Dr
Regal Cir
Oaks
Prestige
Woods Blvd
Aurora
Chadwick Dr
SUNNY LAKE PARK
Weymouth Pl
Chatham Dr
Plymouth Pl
100
Chelmsford Dr
AUDUBON SOCIETY
SUNNY LAKE
Surrey Dr
Winslow Dr
Dover Dr
Avon Dr
Winslow Dr
Eaton Dr
E MENNONITE RD
500
PLAINVIEW CEM
300
400
Harris Dr
Gentry Dr
Page Rd
700
800
E MENNONITE RD
900
Lena Dr
400
400
700
2600
Kenneth Dr
Francis D
44255
Page Rd
600
Elliman Rd
RAY HARMON PARK
Dr
600
1200
Bartlett Rd
2600
Crane Centre Dr
W Wason Dr
Singer Dr
Miller Pkwy
Danner
10400
1800
44241
Streetsboro
Page Rd
Elliman Rd
Clermont St
Deer St
Notle St
Fairfax St
Greenwich St
Hadley St
Invernest St
Winthrop Rd
10200
Dunlap Janet Dr
Close
Keiths
10000
Sagramore Dr N
A
B
C
D
E
81°20'38"
81°20'03"
81°19'29"
81°18'54"
81°18'20"
81°17'45"

SEE 3156 MAP

SEE 3158 MAP

SEE B MAP

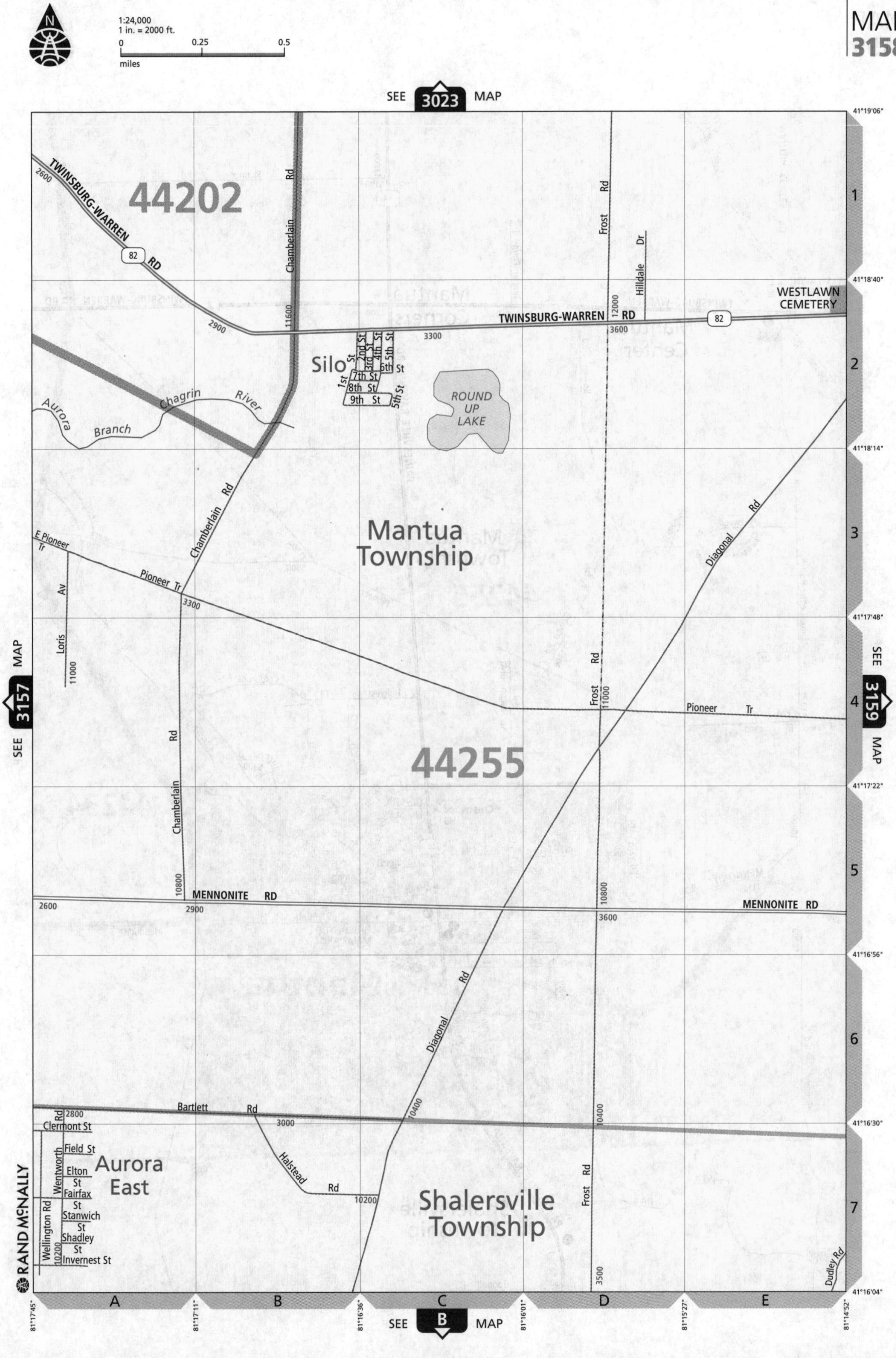
1:24,000
1 in. = 2000 ft.
0
0.25
0.5
miles
SEE 3023 MAP
SEE 3157 MAP
SEE 3159 MAP
SEE B MAP
44202
44255
TWINSBURG-WARREN RD
82
Chamberlain Rd
Frost Rd
Hilldale Dr
WESTLAWN CEMETERY
Silo
1st St
2nd St
3rd St
4th St
5th St
6th St
7th St
8th St
9th St
ROUND UP LAKE
Aurora Branch Chagrin River
Mantua Township
Diagonal Rd
E Pioneer Tr
Pioneer Tr
Loris Av
MENNONITE RD
Bartlett Rd
Halstead Rd
Clermont St
Field St
Elton St
Fairfax St
Stanwich St
Shadley St
Invernest St
Wentworth
Wellington Rd
Aurora East
Shalersville Township
Dudley Rd
2600
2900
11600
3300
12000
3600
11000
10800
3000
10400
10200
3500
2800
A
B
C
D
E
1
2
3
4
5
6
7
41°19'06"
41°18'40"
41°18'14"
41°17'48"
41°17'22"
41°16'56"
41°16'30"
41°16'04"
81°17'45"
81°17'11"
81°16'36"
81°16'01"
81°15'27"
81°14'52"
RAND McNALLY

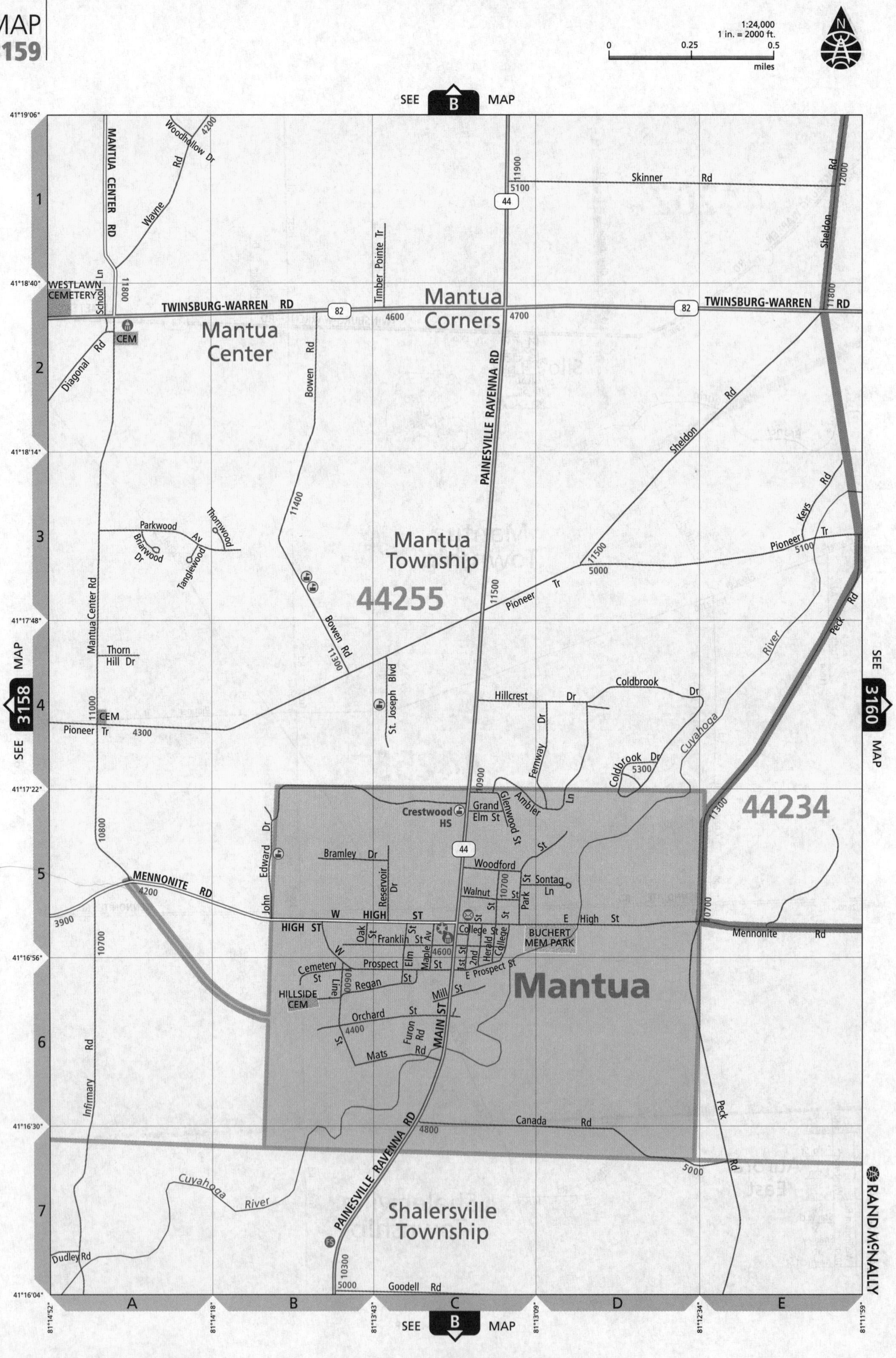
1:24,000
1 in. = 2000 ft.
0
0.25
0.5
miles
N
SEE B MAP
SEE 3158 MAP
SEE 3160 MAP
A
B
C
D
E
1
2
3
4
5
6
7
41°19'06"
41°18'40"
41°18'14"
41°17'48"
41°17'22"
41°16'56"
41°16'30"
41°16'04"
81°14'52"
81°14'18"
81°13'43"
81°13'09"
81°12'34"
81°11'59"
MANTUA CENTER RD
Woodhallow Dr
Rd
Wayne
4200
11900
5100
44
Skinner Rd
Rd
12000
Sheldon
Timber Pointe Tr
WESTLAWN CEMETERY
School Ln
11800
TWINSBURG-WARREN RD
82
4600
Mantua Corners
4700
Mantua Center
CEM
Diagonal Rd
Bowen Rd
PAINESVILLE RAVENNA RD
Sheldon Rd
Keys Rd
Pioneer Tr
5100
Parkwood Av
Briarwood Dr
Thornwood
Tanglewood
11400
Mantua Township
44255
11500
5000
Pioneer Tr
Peck Rd
River
Mantua Center Rd
Thorn Hill Dr
Bowen Rd
11300
St. Joseph Blvd
Coldbrook Dr
Hillcrest Dr
Dr
Fernway
Cuyahoga
Coldbrook Dr
5300
11000
CEM
Pioneer Tr
4300
10900
Ambler Ln
Grand Elm St
Glenwood St
Crestwood HS
44234
11300
John Edward Dr
Bramley Dr
Reservoir Dr
44
Woodford St
Sontag Ln
Walnut
10700
Park
10800
MENNONITE RD
4200
3900
W HIGH ST
HIGH ST
E High St
10700
Mennonite Rd
10700
Oak St
Franklin St
Maple Av
College St
BUCHERT MEM PARK
4600
W
Prospect
Elm
St
1st St
2nd
Herald
College
E Prospect St
Cemetery St
Line
10600
Regan
St
HILLSIDE CEM
Mill St
Mantua
Orchard St
MAIN ST
4400
St
Furon Rd
Mats Rd
Infirmary Rd
Canada Rd
4800
Peck Rd
5000
PAINESVILLE RAVENNA RD
Cuyahoga
River
Shalersville Township
FS
Dudley Rd
10300
5000
Goodell Rd
RAND MCNALLY

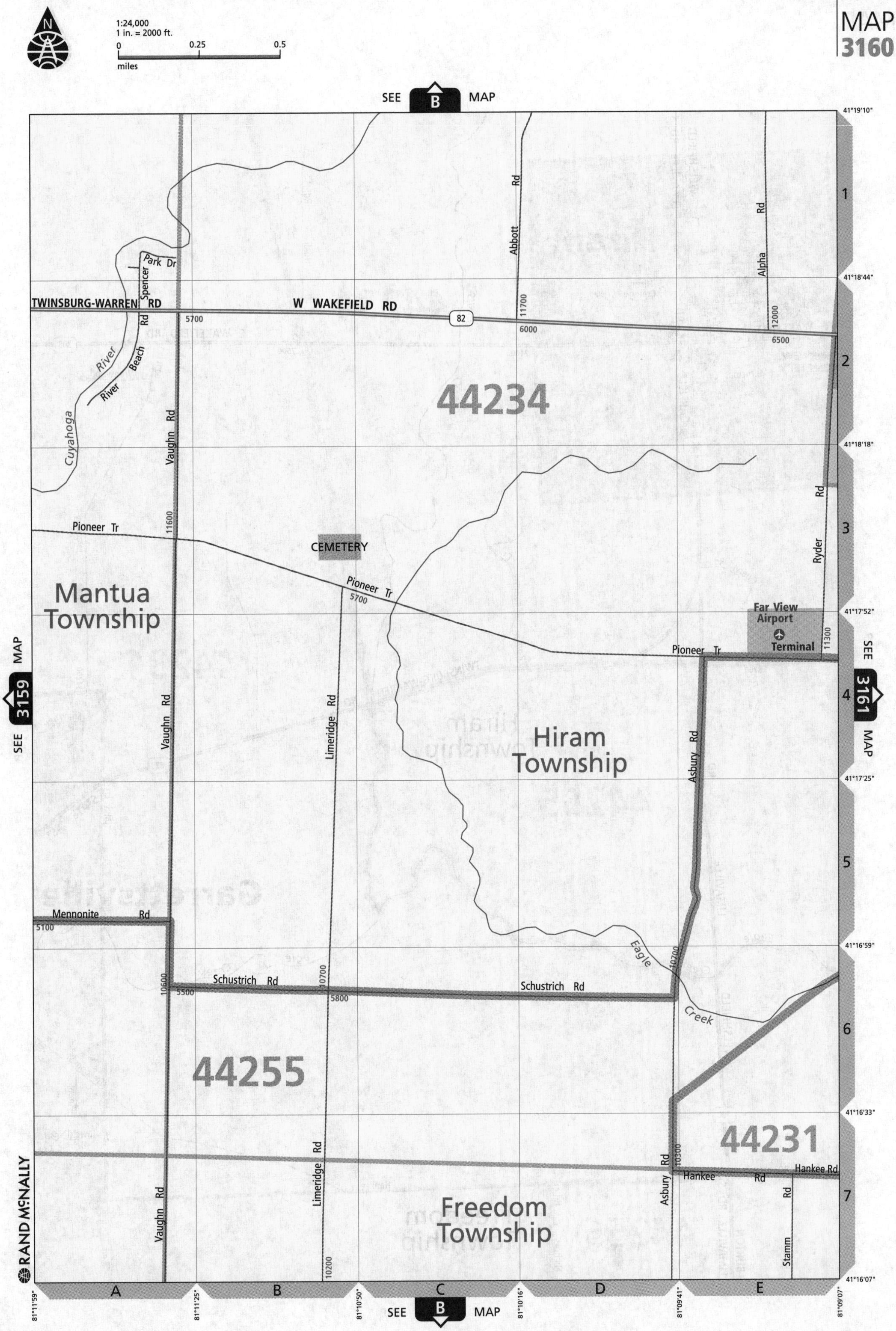
1:24,000
1 in. = 2000 ft.
0 0.25 0.5
miles
SEE B MAP
SEE 3159 MAP
SEE 3161 MAP
TWINSBURG-WARREN RD
W WAKEFIELD RD
82
Park Dr
Spencer Rd
River Beach Rd
Cuyahoga River
Vaughn Rd
Abbott Rd
Alpha Rd
Ryder Rd
5700
6000
6500
11700
12000
11600
44234
Pioneer Tr
CEMETERY
Mantua Township
Far View Airport
Terminal
11300
Limeridge Rd
Hiram Township
Asbury Rd
Mennonite Rd
5100
Schustrich Rd
5500
5800
10600
10700
Eagle Creek
44255
44231
Hankee Rd
10300
Stamm Rd
10200
Freedom Township
A
B
C
D
E
1
2
3
4
5
6
7
41°19'10"
41°18'44"
41°18'18"
41°17'52"
41°17'25"
41°16'59"
41°16'33"
41°16'07"
81°11'59"
81°11'25"
81°10'50"
81°10'16"
81°09'41"
81°09'07"
RAND McNALLY

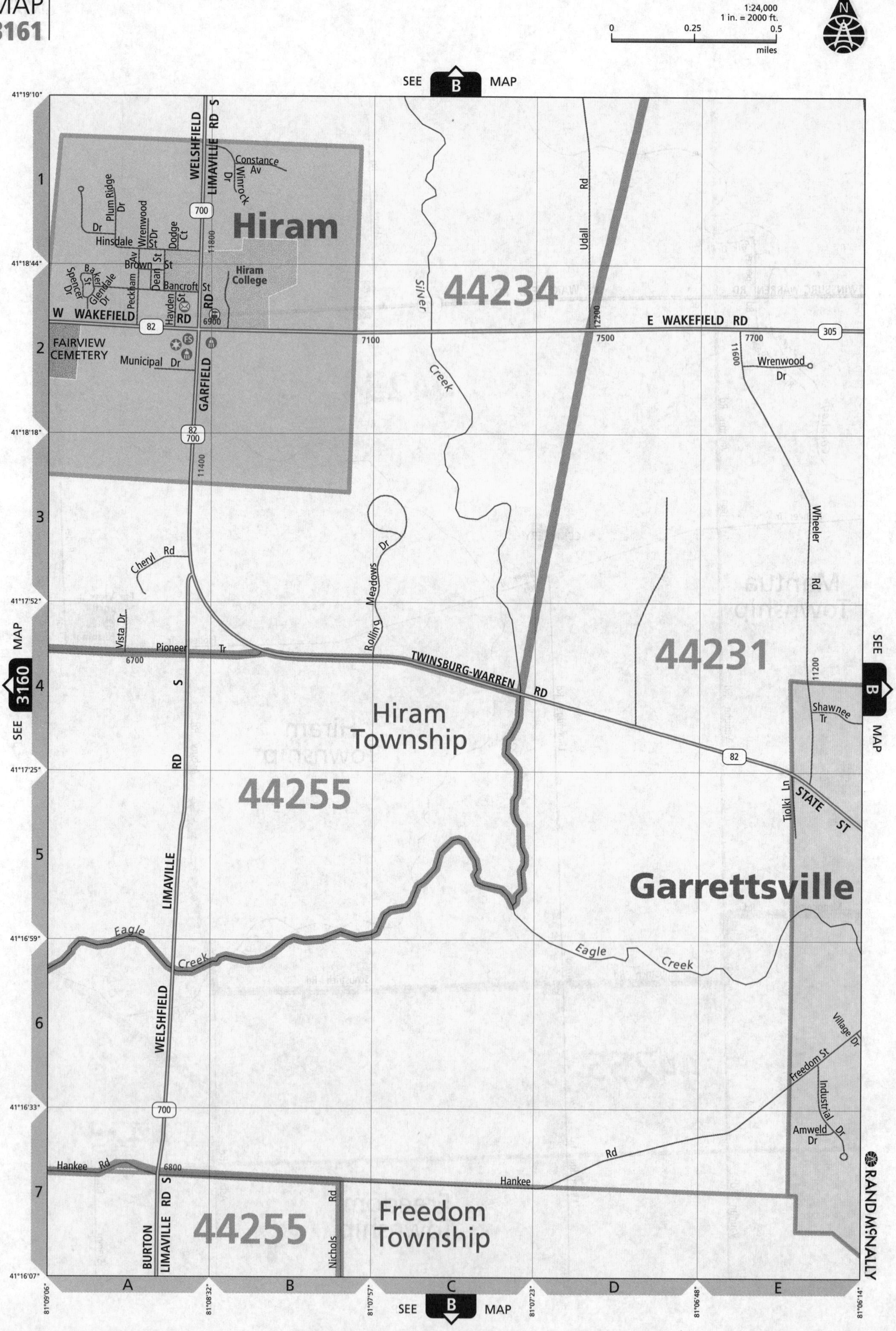
1:24,000
1 in. = 2000 ft.
0
0.25
0.5
miles
SEE B MAP
SEE 3160 MAP
SEE B MAP
SEE B MAP
Hiram
Hiram College
FAIRVIEW CEMETERY
44234
44231
44255
44255
Hiram Township
Freedom Township
Garrettsville
WELSHFIELD LIMAVILLE RD S
Constance Av
Winrock Dr
Plum Ridge Dr
Dr
Hinsdale
Wrenwood St
Dr
Dodge Ct
Brown Av St
Baker St
Spencer Dr
Glendale Dr
Peckham
Dean St
Bancroft St
Hayden St
W WAKEFIELD RD
E WAKEFIELD RD
Municipal Dr
GARFIELD RD
Udall Rd
Silver Creek
Wrenwood Dr
Wheeler Rd
Rolling Meadows Dr
Cheryl Rd
Vista Dr
Pioneer Tr
TWINSBURG-WARREN RD
Shawnee Tr
Tiolki Ln
STATE ST
WELSHFIELD LIMAVILLE RD S
Eagle Creek
Eagle Creek
Village Dr
Freedom St
Industrial Dr
Amweld Dr
Hankee Rd
Hankee Rd
Nichols Rd
BURTON LIMAVILLE RD S
RAND McNALLY
700
82
305
82 700
82
700
11800
6900
7100
12200
7500
7700
11600
11400
6700
11200
6800
1
2
3
4
5
6
7
A
B
C
D
E
41°19'10"
41°18'44"
41°18'18"
41°17'52"
41°17'25"
41°16'59"
41°16'33"
41°16'07"
81°09'06"
81°08'32"
81°07'57"
81°07'23"
81°06'48"
81°06'14"

Cities and Communities

Community Name	Abbr.	County	ZIP Code	Map Page
*Amherst	AMHT	Lorain	44001	2872
Amherst Township	AhtT	Lorain	44001	2873
*Aquilla	AQLA	Geauga	44024	2505
--Ashtabula County	AshC			
Auburn Center		Geauga	44023	2893
Auburn Corners		Geauga	44021	2893
Auburn Township	AbnT	Geauga	44023	2893
*Aurora	AURA	Portage	44202	3156
Aurora East		Portage	44255	3158
*Avon	AVON	Lorain	44011	2618
*Avon Lake	AVLK	Lorain	44012	2618
Axtel		Erie	44089	2869
Bainbridge		Geauga	44023	2891
Bainbridge Center		Geauga	44023	2891
Bainbridge Township	BbgT	Geauga	44023	2891
Bass Lake		Geauga	44024	2504
*Bay Village	BYVL	Cuyahoga	44140	2620
*Beachwood	BHWD	Cuyahoga	44122	2628
Beacon Hill		Geauga	44023	2891
Beartown		Geauga	44023	3023
*Bedford	BDFD	Cuyahoga	44146	2887
*Bedford Heights	BDHT	Cuyahoga	44146	2887
Beebetown		Medina	44280	3145
*Bentleyville	BTVL	Cuyahoga	44022	2889
*Berea	BERA	Cuyahoga	44017	2880
*Boston Heights	BSHT	Summit	44236	3153
Boston Township	BosT	Summit	44141	3152
*Bratenahl	BTNH	Cuyahoga	44108	2496
*Brecksville	BKVL	Cuyahoga	44141	3016
Brentwood Lake		Lorain	44044	3006
*Broadview Heights	BWHT	Cuyahoga	44147	3149
*Brooklyn	BKLN	Cuyahoga	44144	2753
*Brooklyn Heights	BNHT	Cuyahoga	44131	2755
*Brook Park	BKPK	Cuyahoga	44142	2881
Brownhelm Township	BhmT	Lorain	44001	2871
*Brunswick	BNWK	Medina	44212	3147
Brunswick Hills Township	BHIT	Medina	44212	3145
*Burton	BURT	Geauga	44021	2766
Burton Lake		Geauga	44021	2765
Burton Station		Geauga	44021	2637
Burton Township	BtnT	Geauga	44021	2765
Carlisle Township	CrlT	Lorain	44050	3005
*Chagrin Falls	CNFL	Cuyahoga	44022	2761
Chagrin Falls Park		Geauga	44023	2890
Chagrin Falls Township	CFIT	Cuyahoga	44022	2760
*Chardon	CRDN	Geauga	44024	2380
Chardon Township	CdnT	Geauga	44024	2379
Chester Center		Geauga	44026	2502
Chesterland		Geauga	44026	2502
Chester Township	CsTp	Geauga	44026	2502
Claridon		Geauga	44024	2506
Claridon Township	ClrT	Geauga	44024	2506
Clearview		Lorain	44052	2745
*Cleveland	CLEV	Cuyahoga	44114	2624
*Cleveland Heights	CVHT	Cuyahoga	44118	2497
Columbia Center		Lorain	44028	3009
Columbia Hills Corners		Lorain	44028	3010
Columbia Station		Lorain	44028	3009
Columbia Township	ClbT	Lorain	44028	3009
Concord		Lake	44077	2146
Concord Township	CcdT	Lake	44077	2254
--Cuyahoga County	CyhC			
*Cuyahoga Heights	CHHT	Cuyahoga	44125	2755
Driftwood		Ashtabula	44041	1844
East Carlisle		Lorain	44035	3006
East Claridon		Geauga	44024	2506
*East Cleveland	ECLE	Cuyahoga	44112	2497
*Eastlake	ETLK	Lake	44095	2250
Eaton Estates		Lorain	44044	3008
Eaton Township	EatT	Lorain	44044	3007
*Elyria	ELYR	Lorain	44035	2875
Elyria Township	EyrT	Lorain	44035	2874
--Erie County	EreC			
*Euclid	EUCL	Cuyahoga	44123	2373
*Fairport Harbor	FTHR	Lake	44077	2039
*Fairview Park	FWPK	Cuyahoga	44126	2751
Florence Township	FrnT	Erie	44889	2869

Community Name	Abbr.	County	ZIP Code	Map Page
Fowlers Mill		Geauga	44024	2503
Freedom Township	FdmT	Portage	44255	3160
Fullertown		Geauga	44072	2633
*Garfield Heights	GDHT	Cuyahoga	44125	2885
*Garrettsville	GTVL	Portage	44231	3161
*Gates Mills	GSML	Cuyahoga	44040	2500
--Geauga County	GegC			
*Geneva	GNVA	Ashtabula	44041	1944
*Geneva On The Lake	GOTL	Ashtabula	44041	1844
Geneva Township	GnvT	Ashtabula	44041	1943
*Glenwillow	GNWL	Cuyahoga	44139	3019
*Grafton	GFTN	Lorain	44044	3142
Grafton Township	GftT	Lorain	44044	3142
*Grand River	GDRV	Lake	44077	2039
Hambden		Geauga	44024	2381
Hambden Township	HmbT	Geauga	44024	2381
Hardscrabble		Medina	44280	3144
Harpersfield Township	HpfT	Ashtabula	44041	1943
Henrietta Township	HetT	Lorain	44889	2870
*Highland Heights	HDHT	Cuyahoga	44143	2499
*Highland Hills	HIHL	Cuyahoga	44128	2758
Hinckley Township	HkyT	Medina	44233	3148
*Hiram	HRM	Portage	44234	3161
Hiram Township	HrmT	Portage	44234	3160
*Hudson	HDSN	Summit	44236	3154
*Hunting Valley	HGVL	Geauga	44022	2761
*Hunting Valley	HGVL	Cuyahoga	44022	2630
Huntsburg Township	HtbT	Geauga	44046	2507
*Independence	INDE	Cuyahoga	44131	2884
Kendeigh Corner		Lorain	44001	2872
*Kirtland	KTLD	Lake	44094	2376
*Kirtland Hills	KDHL	Lake	44060	2252
Kiwanis Lake		Geauga	44065	2764
Lagrange Township	LrgT	Lorain	44050	3140
--Lake County	LkeC			
*Lakeline	LKLN	Lake	44095	2249
Lake Lucerne		Geauga	44023	2891
*Lakewood	LKWD	Cuyahoga	44107	2623
Lane		Lake	44077	2041
LaPorte		Lorain	44035	3006
Leroy Township	LryT	Lake	44077	2147
*Linndale	LNDL	Cuyahoga	44135	2753
Little Mountain		Geauga	44060	2253
Little York		Summit	44067	3153
Liverpool Township	LvpT	Medina	44280	3144
*Lorain	LORN	Lorain	44052	2614
--Lorain County	LrnC			
*Lyndhurst	LNHT	Cuyahoga	44124	2499
*Macedonia	MCDN	Summit	44056	3153
*Madison	MDSN	Lake	44057	2044
Madison-on-the-Lake		Lake	44057	1843
Madison Township	MadT	Lake	44057	1942
*Mantua	MNTU	Portage	44255	3159
Mantua Center		Portage	44255	3159
Mantua Corners		Portage	44255	3159
Mantua Township	ManT	Portage	44255	3159
*Maple Heights	MPHT	Cuyahoga	44137	2886
*Mayfield	MAYF	Cuyahoga	44143	2500
*Mayfield Heights	MDHT	Cuyahoga	44124	2499
McFarlands Corners		Geauga	44023	2891
--Medina County	MdnC			
*Mentor	MNTR	Lake	44060	2144
*Mentor On The Lake	MONT	Lake	44060	2143
*Middleburg Heights	MDBH	Cuyahoga	44130	2881
*Middlefield	MDFD	Geauga	44062	2767
Middlefield Township	MdfT	Geauga	44062	2637
Montville Township	MtlT	Geauga	44024	2257
*Moreland Hills	MDHL	Cuyahoga	44022	2759
Munson Township	MsnT	Geauga	44024	2504
*Newburgh Heights	NBGH	Cuyahoga	44105	2755
Newbury		Geauga	44065	2764
Newbury Township	NbyT	Geauga	44065	2764
New Russia Township	NRsT	Lorain	44074	3003
North Eaton		Lorain	44028	3008
*Northfield	NHFD	Summit	44067	3018
Northfield Center		Summit	44067	3152
Northfield Center Township	NCtT	Summit	44067	3152

Community Name	Abbr.	County	ZIP Code	Map Page
North Madison		Lake	44057	1843
*North Olmsted	NOSD	Cuyahoga	44070	2750
*North Perry	NPRY	Lake	44081	1940
*North Randall	NRDL	Cuyahoga	44128	2758
*North Ridgeville	NRDV	Lorain	44039	2877
*North Royalton	NRYN	Cuyahoga	44133	3013
Novelty		Geauga	44072	2632
*Oakwood	OKWD	Cuyahoga	44146	3018
*Oberlin	OBLN	Lorain	44074	3138
*Olmsted Falls	ODFL	Cuyahoga	44138	2879
Olmsted Township	OmsT	Cuyahoga	44138	2879
*Orange	ORNG	Cuyahoga	44022	2759
*Painesville	PNVL	Lake	44077	2040
Painesville on the Lake		Lake	44077	2040
Painesville Township	PnvT	Lake	44077	2145
Parkman Township	PkmT	Geauga	44062	2767
*Parma	PRMA	Cuyahoga	44129	2882
*Parma Heights	PMHT	Cuyahoga	44130	2882
Penfield Junction		Lorain	44052	2745
*Pepper Pike	PRPK	Cuyahoga	44124	2629
*Perry	PRRY	Lake	44081	2042
Perry Township	PryT	Lake	44081	2042
Pittsfield Township	PtfT	Lorain	44074	3138
--Portage County	PtgC			
Redbird		Lake	44057	1941
*Reminderville	RMDV	Summit	44202	3020
*Richfield	RHFD	Summit	44286	3151
Richfield Township	RchT	Summit	44286	3150
*Richmond Heights	RDHT	Cuyahoga	44143	2498
*Rocky River	RKRV	Cuyahoga	44116	2621
Russell Center		Geauga	44072	2762
Russell Township	RslT	Geauga	44072	2762
Sagamore Hills		Summit	44067	3152
Sagamore Hills Township	SgHT	Summit	44067	3017
Scotland		Geauga	44026	2501
*Seven Hills	SVHL	Cuyahoga	44131	2884
*Shaker Heights	SRHT	Cuyahoga	44122	2758
Shalersville Township	ShvT	Portage	44255	3158
*Sheffield	SFLD	Lorain	44054	2616
*Sheffield Lake	SDLK	Lorain	44054	2616
Sheffield Township	ShfT	Lorain	44055	2745
Shoreland		Lake	44077	2040
Silo		Portage	44202	3158
*Solon	SLN	Cuyahoga	44139	2889
*South Amherst	SAHT	Lorain	44001	2872
*South Euclid	SELD	Cuyahoga	44121	2498
South Newbury		Geauga	44065	2764
*South Russell	SRSL	Geauga	44022	2762
Spring Valley		Geauga	44023	3022
*Streetsboro	STBR	Portage	44241	3156
*Strongsville	SGVL	Cuyahoga	44136	3011
--Summit County	SmtC			
Sunset Point		Lake	44077	2040
Taborville		Geauga	44023	3023
Thompson Township	TpnT	Geauga	44086	2257
*Timberlake	TMLK	Lake	44095	2249
Troy Township	TroT	Geauga	44021	2766
*Twinsburg	TNBG	Summit	44087	3019
Twinsburg Township	TwbT	Summit	44087	3154
Unionville		Ashtabula	44041	1943
*University Heights	UNHT	Cuyahoga	44118	2628
*Valley View	VLVW	Cuyahoga	44125	2885
*Vermilion	VMLN	Lorain	44001	2871
*Vermilion	VMLN	Erie	44089	2740
Vermilion Township	VmnT	Erie	44089	2869
Vincent		Lorain	44055	2746
*Waite Hill	WTHL	Lake	44094	2376
*Walton Hills	WNHL	Cuyahoga	44146	3017
*Warrensville Heights	WVHT	Cuyahoga	44128	2758
*Westlake	WTLK	Cuyahoga	44145	2749
Westview		Lorain	44028	3009
*Wickliffe	WKLF	Lake	44092	2374
*Willoughby	WLBY	Lake	44094	2250
*Willoughby Hills	WBHL	Lake	44094	2375
*Willowick	WLWK	Lake	44095	2249
*Woodmere	WDMR	Cuyahoga	44122	2759
Yates Corners		Geauga	44072	2763

*Indicates incorporated city

List of Abbreviations

Admin	Administration
Agri	Agricultural
Ag	Agriculture
AFB	Air Force Base
Arpt	Airport
Al	Alley
Amer	American
Anx	Annex
Arc	Arcade
Arch	Archaeological
Aud	Auditorium
Avd	Avenida
Av	Avenue
Bfld	Battlefield
Bch	Beach
Bnd	Bend
Bio	Biological
Blf	Bluff
Blvd	Boulevard
Brch	Branch
Br	Bridge
Brk	Brook
Bldg	Building
Bur	Bureau
Byp	Bypass
Bywy	Byway
Cl	Calle
Cljn	Callejon
Cmto	Caminito
Cm	Camino
Cap	Capitol
Cath	Cathedral
Cswy	Causeway
Cem	Cemetery
Ctr	Center
Ctr	Centre
Cir	Circle
Crlo	Circulo
CH	City Hall
Clf	Cliff
Clfs	Cliffs
Clb	Club
Cltr	Cluster
Col	Coliseum
Coll	College
Com	Common
Coms	Commons
Comm	Community
Co.	Company
Cons	Conservation
Conv & Vis Bur	Convention and Visitors Bureau
Cor	Corner
Cors	Corners
Corp	Corporation
Corr	Corridor
Cte	Corte
CC	Country Club
Co	County
Ct	Court
Ct Hse	Court House
Cts	Courts
Cr	Creek
Cres	Crescent
Cross	Crossing
Curv	Curve
Cto	Cut Off
Dept	Department
Dev	Development
Diag	Diagonal
Div	Division
Dr	Drive
Drwy	Driveway
E	East
El	Elevation
Env	Environmental
Est	Estate
Ests	Estates
Exh	Exhibition
Expm	Experimental
Expo	Exposition
Expwy	Expressway
Ext	Extension
Frgds	Fairgrounds
ft	Feet
Fy	Ferry
Fld	Field
Flds	Fields
Flt	Flat
Flts	Flats
For	Forest
Fk	Fork
Ft	Fort
Found	Foundation
Frwy	Freeway
Gdn	Garden
Gdns	Gardens
Gen Hosp	General Hospital
Gln	Glen
GC	Golf Course
Grn	Green
Grds	Grounds
Grv	Grove
Hbr	Harbor/Harbour
Hvn	Haven
HQs	Headquarters
Ht	Height
Hts	Heights
HS	High School
Hwy	Highway
Hl	Hill
Hls	Hills
Hist	Historical
Hllw	Hollow
Hosp	Hospital
Hse	House
Ind Res	Indian Reservation
Info	Information
Inst	Institute
Int'l	International
I	Island
Is	Islands
Isl	Isle
Jct	Junction
Knl	Knoll
Knls	Knolls
Lk	Lake
Lndg	Landing
Ln	Lane
Lib	Library
Ldg	Lodge
Lp	Loop
Mnr	Manor
Mkt	Market
Mdw	Meadow
Mdws	Meadows
Med	Medical
Mem	Memorial
Metro	Metropolitan
Mw	Mews
Mil	Military
Ml	Mill
Mls	Mills
Mon	Monument
Mtwy	Motorway
Mnd	Mound
Mnds	Mounds
Mt	Mount
Mtn	Mountain
Mtns	Mountains
Mun	Municipal
Mus	Museum
Nat'l	National
Nat'l For	National Forest
Nat'l Hist Pk	National Historic Park
Nat'l Hist Site	National Historic Site
Nat'l Mon	National Monument
Nat'l Park	National Park
Nat'l Rec Area	National Recreation Area
Nat'l Wld Ref	National Wildlife Refuge
Nat	Natural
NAS	Naval Air Station
Nk	Nook
N	North
Orch	Orchard
Ohwy	Outer Highway
Ovl	Oval
Ovlk	Overlook
Ovps	Overpass
Pk	Park
Pkwy	Parkway
Pas	Paseo
Psg	Passage
Pass	Passenger
Pth	Path
Pn	Pine
Pns	Pines
Pl	Place
Pln	Plain
Plns	Plains
Plgnd	Playground
Plz	Plaza
Pt	Point
Pnd	Pond
PO	Post Office
Pres	Preserve
Prov	Provincial
Rwy	Railway
Rec	Recreation
Reg	Regional
Res	Reservoir
Rst	Rest
Rdg	Ridge
Rd	Road
Rds	Roads
St.	Saint
Ste.	Sainte
Sci	Science
Sci	Sciences
Sci	Scientific
Shop Ctr	Shopping Center
Shr	Shore
Shrs	Shores
Skwy	Skyway
S	South
Spr	Spring
Sprs	Springs
Sq	Square
Stad	Stadium
St For	State Forest
St Hist Site	State Historic Site
St Nat Area	State Natural Area
St Pk	State Park
St Rec Area	State Recreation Area
Sta	Station
St	Street
Smt	Summit
Sys	Systems
Tech	Technical
Tech	Technological
Tech	Technology
Ter	Terrace
Terr	Territory
Theol	Theological
Thwy	Throughway
Toll Fy	Toll Ferry
TIC	Tourist Information Center
Trc	Trace
Trfwy	Trafficway
Tr	Trail
Tun	Tunnel
Tpk	Turnpike
Unps	Underpass
Univ	University
Vly	Valley
Vet	Veterans
Vw	View
Vil	Village
Wk	Walk
Wall	Wall
Wy	Way
W	West
WMA	Wildlife Management Area

STREET Block City ZIP Map# Grid

HIGHWAYS

ALT - Alternate Route
BUS - Business Route
CO - County Highway/Road
FM - Farm To Market Road
HIST - Historic Highway
I - Interstate Highway
LP - State Loop
P - Provincial Highway
PK - Park & Recreation Road
RTE - Other Route
SPR - State Spur
SR - State Route/Highway
US - United States Highway

CO-9
7100 BbgT 44022 2761 A7
7100 BbgT 44023 2761 B7
CO-9 Chagrin Rd
7100 BbgT 44022 2761 A7
7100 BbgT 44023 2761 B7
I-71
- BKLN - 2753 E3
- BKPK - 2752 B7
- BKPK - 2881 B2
- BNWK - 3147 B5
- CLEV - 2624 E7
- CLEV - 2752 D4
- CLEV - 2753 E3
- CLEV - 2754 C2
- LNDL - 2753 B3
- MDBH - 2881 A7
- MDBH - 3012 A2
- SGVL - 3012 A2
- SGVL - 3147 C7
I-71 Innerbelt Frwy
- CLEV - 2624 E6
I-71 Medina Frwy
- BKLN - 2753 E3
- BKPK - 2752 B7
- BKPK - 2881 B1
- BNWK - 3147 B5
- CLEV - 2624 E7
- CLEV - 2752 D4
- CLEV - 2753 B3
- CLEV - 2754 A2
- LNDL - 2753 B3
- MDBH - 2881 B4
- MDBH - 3012 A2
- SGVL - 3012 A2
- SGVL - 3147 B4
I-77
- BKVL - 3015 D7
- BKVL - 3150 D1
- BWHT - 3015 D2
- CHHT - 2755 D3
- CLEV - 2625 B4
- CLEV - 2755 D4
- INDE - 2755 E7
- INDE - 2884 D7
- INDE - 3015 D3
- NBGH - 2755 D3
- RHFD - 3150 E5
I-77 Willow Frwy
- BKVL - 3015 D7
- BKVL - 3150 E5
- BWHT - 3015 D2
- CHHT - 2755 D5
- CLEV - 2625 B4
- CLEV - 2755 C1
- INDE - 2755 E7
- INDE - 2884 D2
- INDE - 3015 D1
- NBGH - 2755 C2
- RHFD - 3150 E5
I-80
- AhtT - 2871 E5
- AhtT - 2872 A5
- AhtT - 2873 E3
- AMHT - 2872 E4
- BERA - 3010 D1
- BERA - 3011 E3
- BhmT - 2871 E5
- BKVL - 3150 B4
- BWHT - 3149 C2
- BWHT - 3150 B4
- ELYR - 2874 E3
- ELYR - 2875 E4
- EyrT - 2873 E3
- EyrT - 2874 B3
- NRDV - 2875 E4
- NRDV - 2876 D5
- NRDV - 2877 A5
- NRDV - 2878 B6
- NRYN - 3012 C5
- NRYN - 3013 A7
- NRYN - 3148 E2
- NRYN - 3149 A2
- ODFL - 3010 A1
- OmsT - 2878 B6
- OmsT - 2879 A7
- OmsT - 3010 D1
- RchT - 3150 E6
- RchT - 3151 B7
- RHFD - 3150 E6
- RHFD - 3151 B7
- SGVL - 3011 A2
- SGVL - 3012 C5
I-80 Ohio Tpk
- AhtT - 2871 E5
- AhtT - 2872 A5
- AhtT - 2873 E3
- AMHT - 2872 E4
- BERA - 3010 D1
- BERA - 3011 C3
- BhmT - 2871 C6
- BKVL - 3150 B4
- BWHT - 3149 C2
- BWHT - 3150 A3
- ELYR - 2874 E3
- ELYR - 2875 A3
- EyrT - 2873 E3
- EyrT - 2874 B3
- NRDV - 2875 E4
- NRDV - 2876 D5
- NRDV - 2877 A5
- NRDV - 2878 B6
- NRYN - 3012 C5
- NRYN - 3013 A7
- NRYN - 3148 E2
- NRYN - 3149 A2
- ODFL - 3010 A1
- OmsT - 2878 B6

I-80 Ohio Tpk
- OmsT - 2879 A7
- OmsT - 3010 D1
- RchT - 3150 E6
- RchT - 3151 B7
- RHFD - 3150 E6
- RHFD - 3151 B7
- SGVL - 3011 E3
- SGVL - 3012 C5
I-90
- AhtT - 2871 E5
- AhtT - 2872 A5
- AhtT - 2873 D3
- AMHT - 2872 E4
- AVON - 2617 D7
- AVON - 2618 D7
- AVON - 2619 A7
- AVON - 2747 A1
- BhmT - 2871 C6
- BTNH - 2496 B4
- BTNH - 2497 A1
- CcdT - 2146 C7
- CcdT - 2147 A5
- CcdT - 2253 D2
- CcdT - 2254 B1
- CLEV - 2372 D7
- CLEV - 2373 A6
- CLEV - 2495 B7
- CLEV - 2496 E1
- CLEV - 2497 B1
- CLEV - 2622 B7
- CLEV - 2623 E7
- CLEV - 2624 B6
- CLEV - 2625 B2
- CyhC - 2495 E5
- ELYR - 2746 B7
- ELYR - 2874 E1
- ELYR - 2875 A1
- EUCL - 2373 B5
- EUCL - 2374 A3
- EyrT - 2874 B1
- KDHL - 2252 E4
- KDHL - 2253 B3
- LKWD - 2622 B7
- LryT - 2042 E7
- LryT - 2043 B6
- LryT - 2147 A5
- MadT - 2043 B6
- MadT - 2044 A3
- MDSN - 2043 E4
- MDSN - 2044 A3
- MNTR - 2251 E4
- MNTR - 2252 A4
- MNTR - 2253 B3
- PryT - 2043 B6
- RKRV - 2621 A6
- RKRV - 2622 A6
- SFLD - 2746 E2
- SFLD - 2747 A1
- WBHL - 2250 E7
- WBHL - 2374 D5
- WBHL - 2375 A4
- WKLF - 2374 A3
- WKLF - 2375 A4
- WLBY - 2250 E7
- WLBY - 2251 A6
- WLBY - 2375 C1
- WTHL - 2250 E7
- WTHL - 2251 A6
- WTLK - 2619 A7
- WTLK - 2620 E6
- WTLK - 2621 E6
I-90 Cleveland Mem Shoreway
- BTNH - 2496 E2
- CLEV - 2495 B7
- CLEV - 2496 A4
- CyhC - 2495 E5
I-90 Cleveland Mem Shrwy Frwy
- BTNH - 2496 D3
- CLEV - 2495 C6
- CLEV - 2496 A4
I-90 Innerbelt Frwy
- CLEV - 2624 E4
- CLEV - 2625 B2
I-90 Lakeland Frwy
- BTNH - 2496 E1
- BTNH - 2497 A1
- CLEV - 2372 D7
- CLEV - 2373 A6
- CLEV - 2496 E1
- CLEV - 2497 B1
- EUCL - 2373 D3
I-90 North South Frwy
- CcdT - 2146 C7
- CcdT - 2253 D2
- CcdT - 2254 B1
- KDHL - 2252 E4
- KDHL - 2253 B3
- LryT - 2147 E2
- MadT - 2044 E3
- MDSN - 2044 B3
- MNTR - 2251 E4
- MNTR - 2252 A4
- MNTR - 2253 B3
I-90 Northwest Frwy
- AVON - 2619 A6
- CLEV - 2622 B7
- CLEV - 2623 A7
- CLEV - 2624 B6
- LKWD - 2622 A6
- RKRV - 2621 A6
- RKRV - 2622 E7
- WTLK - 2619 D7
- WTLK - 2620 E6
- WTLK - 2621 E6
I-90 Ohio Tpk
- AhtT - 2871 E5
- AhtT - 2872 A5
- AhtT - 2873 D3
- AMHT - 2872 E4
- BhmT - 2871 A7
I-271
- BDFD - 2887 D3
- BDHT - 2758 D7
- BDHT - 2887 D3
- BHWD - 2629 A7
- BHWD - 2758 E3
- BHWD - 2759 A1
- BosT - 3152 E7
- HDHT - 2499 E1
- LNHT - 2629 B3
- MAYF - 2499 E1
- MCDN - 3018 C6

I-271
- MCDN - 3153 C1
- MDHT - 2499 E6
- MDHT - 2500 A7
- MDHT - 2629 E1
- NCtT - 3152 E7
- NCtT - 3153 B3
- OKWD - 2887 C7
- OKWD - 3018 C3
- ORNG - 2758 E4
- ORNG - 2759 A3
- PRPK - 2629 A7
- PRPK - 2759 A1
- WBHL - 2374 E7
- WBHL - 2375 A4
- WBHL - 2499 E1
- WVHT - 2758 E4
I-271 Outerbelt East Frwy
- BDFD - 2887 D3
- BDHT - 2758 D7
- BDHT - 2887 D3
- BHWD - 2629 E1
- BHWD - 2758 E3
- BHWD - 2759 A1
- HDHT - 2499 E4
- LNHT - 2629 B3
- MCDN - 3018 C6
- MDHT - 2499 E6
- MDHT - 2500 A7
- MDHT - 2629 E1
- OKWD - 2887 C7
- OKWD - 3018 C3
- ORNG - 2758 E3
- ORNG - 2759 A3
- PRPK - 2629 E1
- PRPK - 2759 A1
- WVHT - 2758 E4
I-271 Outerbelt West Frwy
- OKWD - 3018 C1
I-480
- BDFD - 2887 D3
- BDHT - 2758 B7
- BDHT - 2887 C1
- BKLN - 2753 E6
- BNHT - 2755 A7
- BNHT - 2884 E2
- CLEV - 2751 D6
- CLEV - 2752 C7
- CLEV - 2753 E6
- CLEV - 2754 B7
- CLEV - 2755 A7
- CLEV - 2757 C6
- FWPK - 2751 C6
- GDHT - 2756 E7
- GDHT - 2757 A7
- GDHT - 2885 E1
- HDSN - 3155 D7
- INDE - 2884 D1
- INDE - 2885 A1
- MCDN - 3018 E4
- MCDN - 3019 A5
- MPHT - 2757 A7
- MPHT - 2758 B7
- NOSD - 2750 D7
- NOSD - 2751 A6
- NOSD - 2878 E2
- NOSD - 2879 B1
- NRDL - 2758 B7
- NRDV - 2877 E4
- NRDV - 2878 C3
- OKWD - 2887 C7
- OKWD - 3018 E4
- OmsT - 2878 E2
- TNBG - 3019 A5
- TNBG - 3154 E2
- TNBG - 3155 B3
- TwbT - 3155 C5
- VLVW - 2885 B1
- WVHT - 2757 E6
- WVHT - 2758 B7
I-480 Outerbelt East Frwy
- BDFD - 2887 D3
- BDHT - 2887 D3
- OKWD - 2887 C7
- OKWD - 3018 C1
I-480 Outerbelt South Frwy
- BKLN - 2753 B6
- BNHT - 2755 A7
- BNHT - 2884 E2
- CLEV - 2751 C6
- CLEV - 2752 C7
- CLEV - 2753 A6
- CLEV - 2754 B6
- CLEV - 2755 A7
- CLEV - 2757 C6
- FWPK - 2751 A6
- GDHT - 2756 E7
- GDHT - 2757 C6
- GDHT - 2885 D1
- INDE - 2884 D2
- INDE - 2885 A1
- MPHT - 2757 A6
- NOSD - 2750 D7
- NOSD - 2751 A6
- NOSD - 2878 E2
- NOSD - 2879 B1
- NRDV - 2878 A4
- OmsT - 2878 E2
- VLVW - 2885 B1
- WVHT - 2757 E6
- WVHT - 2758 A6
I-480 Outerbelt West Frwy
- OKWD - 3018 C1
I-490
- CLEV - 2624 E6
- CLEV - 2625 C6
SR-2
- AhtT - 2744 E7
- AhtT - 2745 A7
- AMHT - 2743 D7
- AMHT - 2744 B6
- AMHT - 2871 E1
- AMHT - 2872 A1
- AVON - 2617 B7
- AVON - 2618 D7
- AVON - 2619 A6
- AVON - 2747 A1
- BhmT - 2870 D1
- BhmT - 2871 A1
- BTNH - 2496 C3

SR-2
- BTNH - 2497 A1
- CLEV - 2372 C7
- CLEV - 2373 A6
- CLEV - 2495 D5
- CLEV - 2496 E1
- CLEV - 2497 A1
- CLEV - 2624 E1
- CLEV - 2625 A1
- CLEV 44102 2624 A4
- CyhC - 2495 D5
- ELYR - 2746 B7
- ELYR - 2874 E1
- ELYR - 2875 A1
- ETLK - 2249 E7
- ETLK - 2250 B5
- EUCL - 2373 A6
- EUCL - 2374 B2
- EyrT - 2745 A7
- EyrT - 2874 B1
- LKWD 44107 2621 E4
- LORN - 2744 E7
- MNTR - 2143 E6
- MNTR - 2144 A6
- MNTR - 2145 A1
- MNTR - 2251 C1
- PNVL - 2039 E6
- PNVL - 2040 D5
- PNVL - 2145 B1
- PnvT - 2039 E7
- PnvT - 2040 A6
- PnvT - 2041 A3
- PnvT - 2145 B1
- RKRV 44107 2621 E4
- SFLD - 2746 D5
- SFLD - 2747 A1
- VMLN - 2870 E1
- VMLN - 2871 C1
- VmnT - 2869 C1
- VmnT - 2870 A1
- WKLF - 2249 E7
- WKLF - 2374 C1
- WLBY - 2250 E3
- WLBY - 2251 B2
- WLWK - 2249 E7
- WTLK - 2619 A6
- WTLK - 2620 A7
- WTLK - 2621 A6
9200 CLEV 44102 2623 D5
11600 LKWD 44102 2623 B4
11600 LKWD 44107 2623 A4
12900 LKWD 44107 2622 A4
19500 RKRV 44116 2621 C6
SR-2 Cleveland Mem Shoreway
- BTNH - 2496 E3
- CLEV - 2495 C6
- CLEV - 2496 A4
- CLEV - 2624 E1
- CLEV - 2625 A1
- CLEV 44102 2623 E4
- CLEV 44102 2624 A4
- CyhC - 2495 D5
SR-2 Cleveland Mem Shrwy Frwy
- BTNH - 2496 D3
- CLEV - 2495 C6
- CLEV - 2496 B4
SR-2 Clifton Blvd
- LKWD 44107 2621 E4
- RKRV 44107 2621 E4
- RKRV 44116 2621 E4
9200 CLEV 44102 2623 D5
11600 LKWD 44102 2623 B4
11600 LKWD 44107 2623 A4
12900 LKWD 44107 2622 A4
SR-2 Detroit Rd
19500 RKRV 44116 2621 C6
SR-2 Lake Rd
19200 RKRV 44116 2621 E5
SR-2 Lakeland Frwy
- BTNH - 2496 E1
- BTNH - 2497 A1
- CLEV - 2372 C7
- CLEV - 2373 A6
- CLEV - 2496 E1
- CLEV - 2497 B1
- ETLK - 2249 E7
- ETLK - 2250 B5
- EUCL - 2373 C4
- EUCL - 2374 A2
- MNTR - 2143 E6
- MNTR - 2144 A6
- MNTR - 2145 A1
- MNTR - 2251 C1
- PNVL - 2145 B1
- PnvT - 2145 B1
- WKLF - 2249 E7
- WKLF - 2374 B2
- WLBY - 2250 E3
- WLBY - 2251 B2
- WLWK - 2249 E7
SR-2 Northwest Frwy
- AVON - 2619 A6
- RKRV - 2621 A6
- WTLK - 2619 E7
- WTLK - 2620 A7
- WTLK - 2621 A6
SR-3
10 HkyT 44133 3148 D5
10 HkyT 44233 3148 D6
10 NRYN 44133 3148 D5
1400 CLEV 44113 2624 D6
3000 CLEV 44109 2624 D7
3200 CLEV 44109 2754 A7
4500 CLEV 44144 2754 C5
5000 CLEV 44129 2754 A7
5000 PRMA 44109 2754 A7
5000 PRMA 44129 2754 A7
5300 PRMA 44129 2753 E7
5300 PRMA 44129 2882 E1
7300 PRMA 44134 2882 E7
7400 PRMA 44129 3013 E1
7400 PRMA 44134 3013 E1
7800 NRYN 44129 3013 E2
7800 NRYN 44133 3013 E7
7800 NRYN 44134 3013 E2
SR-3 W 25th St
1400 CLEV 44113 2624 D6
3000 CLEV 44109 2624 D7
3200 CLEV 44109 2754 D1
SR-3 Pearl Rd
3600 CLEV 44109 2754 A7
4500 CLEV 44144 2754 C5
5000 CLEV 44129 2754 A7

SR-3 Pearl Rd
5000 PRMA 44109 2754 A7
5000 PRMA 44129 2754 A7
5300 PRMA 44129 2753 E7
5300 PRMA 44129 2882 E1
SR-3 Ridge Rd
10 HkyT 44133 3148 D5
10 HkyT 44233 3148 D6
10 NRYN 44133 3148 D5
5400 PRMA 44129 2882 E6
7300 PRMA 44134 2882 E7
7400 PRMA 44129 3013 E1
7400 PRMA 44134 3013 E1
7800 NRYN 44129 3013 E2
7800 NRYN 44133 3013 E7
7800 NRYN 44134 3013 E2
SR-8
- BSHT 44067 3153 D6
- BSHT 44236 3153 D6
- MCDN 44056 3018 A6
- MCDN 44056 3153 B1
- MCDN 44067 3018 A6
- MPHT 44146 2758 B6
- NCtT 44056 3018 B7
- NCtT 44056 3153 C3
- NCtT 44067 3018 B7
- NCtT 44067 3153 C3
- NCtT 44236 3153 D6
- NHFD 44067 3018 B7
- SgHT 44067 3018 B7
10 BDFD 44146 2887 B4
300 OKWD 44146 2887 B7
400 BDFD 44137 2887 B2
400 BDHT 44146 2887 B2
400 MPHT 44137 2887 B2
400 MPHT 44146 2887 B2
1400 CLEV 44115 2625 C4
1900 CLEV 44114 2624 E4
1900 CLEV 44115 2624 E4
2000 CLEV 44113 2624 E4
3500 HIHL 44122 2758 A2
3500 SRHT 44122 2758 B4
3600 WVHT 44122 2758 A2
3800 CLEV 44104 2625 E5
4100 HIHL 44128 2758 A4
4300 NRDL 44128 2758 B4
4600 WVHT 44128 2758 B5
4900 WVHT 44146 2758 B6
5000 BDHT 44146 2758 B7
5000 MPHT 44137 2758 B7
6900 WNHL 44146 2887 B7
7100 WNHL 44146 3018 B2
7200 CLEV 44104 2626 A6
7600 NHFD 44146 3018 B3
11300 CLEV 44120 2626 D7
12300 CLEV 44120 2756 E1
13700 CLEV 44120 2757 A1
15400 SRHT 44120 2757 B1
17600 SRHT 44122 2757 E1
SR-8 Broadway Av
800 CLEV 44115 2625 A4
SR-8 Chagrin Blvd
15600 CLEV 44120 2757 B1
15600 SRHT 44120 2757 B1
17600 SRHT 44122 2757 E1
19400 SRHT 44122 2758 A1
SR-8 Kinsman Rd
5500 CLEV 44104 2625 E5
7200 CLEV 44104 2626 A6
11300 CLEV 44120 2626 D7
12300 CLEV 44120 2756 E1
13700 CLEV 44120 2757 A1
15400 SRHT 44120 2757 B1
SR-8 Northfield Rd
- MPHT 44146 2758 B6
10 BDFD 44146 2887 B4
300 OKWD 44146 2887 B7
400 BDFD 44137 2887 B2
400 BDHT 44146 2887 B2
400 MPHT 44137 2887 B2
400 MPHT 44146 2887 B2
3500 HIHL 44122 2758 A2
3500 SRHT 44122 2758 B4
3600 WVHT 44122 2758 A2
4100 HIHL 44128 2758 A4
4300 NRDL 44128 2758 B4
4600 WVHT 44128 2758 B5
4900 WVHT 44146 2758 B6
5000 BDHT 44146 2758 B7
5000 MPHT 44137 2758 B7
6900 WNHL 44146 2887 B7
7100 WNHL 44146 3018 B2
7600 NHFD 44067 3018 B3
7600 NHFD 44146 3018 B3
10100 SgHT 44067 3018 A5
SR-8 Ontario St
1900 CLEV 44114 2624 E4
1900 CLEV 44115 2624 E4
2000 CLEV 44113 2624 E4
SR-8 Orange Av
1400 CLEV 44115 2625 A4
SR-8 Woodland Av
2500 CLEV 44115 2625 C4
3800 CLEV 44104 2625 C4
SR-10
- EatT - 3006 E4
- EatT - 3007 A4
- NRDV - 2877 E4
- NRDV - 3007 E1
- NRDV - 3008 A1
10 CLEV 44113 2624 E4
10 CLEV 44115 2624 E4
4400 CLEV 44102 2624 E4
7100 CLEV 44102 2623 E7
9900 CLEV 44111 2623 C7
10600 CLEV 44111 2753 A1
13200 CLEV 44111 2752 C2
18000 FWPK 44111 2752 A2
18000 FWPK 44126 2752 A2
18900 FWPK 44126 2751 E2
22900 NOSD 44070 2751 B4
22900 NOSD 44126 2751 A4
23200 NOSD 44070 2750 A7
27300 NOSD 44070 2749 E7
28200 NOSD 44070 2878 D1
31400 NRDV 44039 2878 B2
31400 NRDV 44070 2878 A3
SR-10 Carnegie Av
10 CLEV 44113 2624 E4
10 CLEV 44115 2624 E4
SR-10 Lorain Av
2000 CLEV 44113 2624 D5
4400 CLEV 44102 2624 E4
7100 CLEV 44102 2623 E7
9900 CLEV 44111 2623 C7

SR-10 Lorain Av
10600 CLEV 44111 2753 A1
13200 CLEV 44111 2752 C2
18000 FWPK 44111 2752 A2
18000 FWPK 44126 2752 A2
SR-10 Lorain Rd
- NRDV 44039 2877 E4
18800 FWPK 44126 2752 A2
18900 FWPK 44126 2751 E2
22900 NOSD 44070 2751 B4
22900 NOSD 44126 2751 A4
23200 NOSD 44070 2750 A7
27300 NOSD 44070 2749 E7
28200 NOSD 44070 2878 D1
31400 NRDV 44039 2878 B2
31400 NRDV 44070 2878 A3
SR-14
- HDSN - 3155 D7
- MCDN - 3018 E4
- MCDN - 3019 A5
- OKWD - 2887 C7
- OKWD - 3018 E4
- TNBG - 3019 A5
- TNBG - 3154 E2
- TNBG - 3155 D7
- TwbT - 3155 B4
10 BDFD 44137 2886 D2
10 BDFD 44146 2886 D2
10 MPHT 44137 2886 C1
10 MPHT 44146 2886 D2
500 BDFD 44146 2887 B5
1900 CLEV 44114 2624 E4
1900 CLEV 44115 2624 E4
1900 CLEV 44115 2625 D7
2000 CLEV 44113 2624 E4
3900 CLEV 44127 2625 C6
5800 CLEV 44127 2755 E1
6200 CLEV 44105 2755 D1
7400 CLEV 44105 2756 A3
9300 CLEV 44125 2756 C5
9300 GDHT 44105 2756 C5
9300 GDHT 44125 2756 C5
13500 GDHT 44125 2757 A6
14100 GDHT 44128 2757 A6
14100 MPHT 44125 2757 A6
14100 MPHT 44128 2757 A6
14100 MPHT 44137 2757 B7
SR-14 E 34th St
2700 CLEV 44115 2625 B5
SR-14 Broadway Av
10 BDFD 44137 2886 D2
10 BDFD 44146 2886 D2
10 MPHT 44137 2886 C1
10 MPHT 44146 2886 D2
500 BDFD 44146 2887 B5
1400 OKWD 44146 2887 C7
3900 CLEV 44115 2625 C6
3900 CLEV 44127 2625 C6
5800 CLEV 44127 2755 E1
6200 CLEV 44105 2755 D1
7400 CLEV 44105 2756 A3
9300 CLEV 44125 2756 C5
9300 GDHT 44105 2756 C5
9300 GDHT 44125 2756 C5
13500 GDHT 44125 2757 A6
14100 GDHT 44128 2757 A6
14100 MPHT 44125 2757 A6
14100 MPHT 44128 2757 A6
14100 MPHT 44137 2757 B7
SR-14 Oakleaf Rd
- OKWD 44146 2887 C7
SR-14 Ontario St
1900 CLEV 44114 2624 E4
1900 CLEV 44115 2624 E4
2000 CLEV 44113 2624 E4
SR-14 Outerbelt East Frwy
- OKWD - 2887 C7
- OKWD - 3018 C1
SR-14 Outerbelt West Frwy
- OKWD - 3018 C1
SR-14 Pittsburgh Av
2200 CLEV 44115 2625 D7
SR-14 Warner Rd
- CLEV 44105 2756 B3
SR-17
- INDE 44125 2884 E1
10 BNHT 44131 2755 B7
700 BNHT 44109 2754 E7
700 BNHT 44131 2754 E7
700 CLEV 44109 2754 D7
700 PRMA 44109 2754 D7
700 PRMA 44131 2754 E7
700 PRMA 44134 2754 D7
900 BNHT 44131 2884 D1
1200 INDE 44131 2884 D1
1500 CLEV 44134 2754 D7
5200 PRMA 44129 2754 A7
5300 MPHT 44137 2886 C1
6000 CLEV 44129 2754 A7
6700 BKLN 44129 2753 E7
6700 BKLN 44144 2753 E7
6700 CLEV 44129 2753 E7
6700 PRMA 44129 2753 E7
6700 PRMA 44144 2753 E7
6900 VLVW 44131 2884 E1
7500 VLVW 44125 2884 E1
7500 VLVW 44125 2885 A1
7700 GDHT 44125 2885 A1
8900 GDHT 44125 2756 C7
10100 PRMA 44130 2753 E7
11700 CLEV 44135 2753 E7
11700 CLEV 44144 2753 E7
11700 PRMA 44135 2753 E7
13000 BKPK 44130 2752 E7
13000 BKPK 44135 2752 C7
13000 BKPK 44142 2752 C7
13000 CLEV 44135 2752 C7
13000 PRMA 44130 2752 E7
13000 PRMA 44135 2752 E7
13600 GDHT 44125 2757 A7
13600 GDHT 44137 2757 A7
13600 MPHT 44137 2757 C7
18200 BKPK 44135 2751 E7
18200 BKPK 44142 2751 E7
18200 CLEV 44135 2751 E7
18200 CLEV 44142 2751 E7
19800 MPHT 44137 2758 C7
21200 BDHT 44146 2758 C7
22400 FWPK 44126 2751 B6
22500 NOSD 44070 2751 B6
22500 NOSD 44126 2751 B6
23000 NOSD 44070 2750 B6
27300 NOSD 44070 2749 E7

SR-17 Brookpark Rd
700 BNHT 44109 2754 E7
700 BNHT 44131 2754 E7
700 CLEV 44109 2754 D7
700 PRMA 44109 2754 D7
700 PRMA 44131 2754 E7
700 PRMA 44134 2754 D7
1500 CLEV 44134 2754 D7
5200 PRMA 44129 2754 A7
6000 CLEV 44129 2754 A7
6700 BKLN 44129 2753 E7
6700 BKLN 44144 2753 E7
6700 CLEV 44129 2753 E7
6700 PRMA 44129 2753 E7
6700 PRMA 44144 2753 E7
10100 PRMA 44130 2753 E7
11700 CLEV 44135 2753 E7
11700 CLEV 44144 2753 E7
11700 PRMA 44135 2753 E7
13000 BKPK 44130 2752 E7
13000 BKPK 44135 2752 C7
13000 BKPK 44142 2752 C7
13000 CLEV 44135 2752 C7
13000 PRMA 44130 2752 E7
13000 PRMA 44135 2752 E7
18200 BKPK 44135 2751 E7
18200 BKPK 44142 2751 E7
18200 CLEV 44135 2751 E7
18200 CLEV 44142 2751 E7
22400 FWPK 44126 2751 B6
22500 NOSD 44070 2751 B6
22500 NOSD 44126 2751 B6
23000 NOSD 44070 2750 B6
SR-17 Granger Rd
- INDE 44125 2884 E1
5500 BNHT 44131 2884 D1
5500 INDE 44131 2884 D1
6900 VLVW 44131 2884 E1
7500 VLVW 44125 2884 E1
7500 VLVW 44125 2885 A1
7700 GDHT 44125 2885 A1
8900 GDHT 44125 2756 C7
13600 GDHT 44125 2757 A7
13600 GDHT 44137 2757 A7
13600 MPHT 44137 2757 A7
SR-17 E Granger Rd
10 BNHT 44131 2755 A7
900 BNHT 44131 2884 D1
1200 INDE 44131 2884 D1
SR-17 W Granger Rd
300 BNHT 44131 2755 B7
SR-17 Lee Rd
5300 MPHT 44137 2886 C1
SR-17 Libby Rd
14400 MPHT 44137 2757 C7
19800 MPHT 44137 2758 C7
21200 BDHT 44146 2758 C7
SR-17 Lorain Rd
- NOSD 44070 2750 A6
27300 NOSD 44070 2749 E7
SR-20
- CrlT - 3006 E4
- EatT - 3006 E4
SR-21
- CHHT - 2755 D3
- CHHT 44125 2755 E7
- CHHT 44131 2755 E7
- CLEV - 2625 C6
- CLEV - 2755 C2
- INDE 44125 2755 E7
- INDE 44131 2755 E7
- NBGH - 2755 D3
- VLVW 44125 2755 E7
- VLVW 44131 2755 E7
4700 RHFD 44286 3151 A7
5200 RHFD 44141 3151 A6
5400 INDE 44125 2884 E1
5400 INDE 44131 2884 E4
5400 VLVW 44125 2884 E1
5400 VLVW 44131 2884 E1
7100 INDE 44131 3015 E1
7600 INDE 44131 3016 A3
7700 BKVL 44131 3016 A2
8600 BKVL 44141 3016 A7
9000 BKVL 44141 3151 A2
SR-21 Brecksville Rd
- CHHT 44125 2755 E7
- CHHT 44131 2755 E7
- INDE 44125 2755 E7
- INDE 44131 2755 E7
- VLVW 44125 2755 E7
- VLVW 44131 2755 E7
4700 RHFD 44286 3151 A7
5200 RHFD 44141 3151 A6
5400 INDE 44125 2884 E1
5400 INDE 44131 2884 E4
5400 VLVW 44125 2884 E1
5400 VLVW 44131 2884 E1
7100 INDE 44131 3015 E1
7600 INDE 44131 3016 A3
7700 BKVL 44131 3016 A2
8600 BKVL 44141 3016 A7
9000 BKVL 44141 3151 A2
SR-21 Willow Frwy
- CHHT - 2755 D5
- CLEV - 2625 B4
- CLEV - 2755 C2
- NBGH - 2755 C2
SR-43
- MPHT 44137 2758 B6
10 AURA 44202 3021 C5
10 AURA 44202 3156 E7
10 BbgT 44023 3021 A2
10 BbgT 44139 3021 A2
10 BbgT 44202 3021 A2
10 SLN 44139 3021 A2
1200 STBR 44202 3156 E6
1900 CLEV 44115 2625 A4
3900 CLEV 44127 2625 C6
4900 NRDL 44128 2758 B6
4900 WVHT 44128 2758 A6
4900 WVHT 44146 2758 B6
5800 CLEV 44127 2755 E1
6200 CLEV 44105 2755 D1
7400 CLEV 44105 2756 A3
10100 STBR 44241 3156 E7
13000 CLEV 44128 2756 E3
13500 CLEV 44105 2757 B4
13500 CLEV 44128 2757 B4
17500 WVHT 44128 2757 D5
19400 NRDL 44128 2757 E5
21700 BDHT 44146 2758 B7
21700 MPHT 44146 2758 B6
23100 BDHT 44146 2887 C1
26700 BDHT 44146 2888 A2

Block	City	ZIP	Map#	Grid
SR-43				
26700	SLN	44139	2888	A2
33200	SLN	44139	2889	C7
37800	SLN	44139	3020	D1
SR-43 E 34th St				
2700	CLEV	44115	2625	B5
SR-43 Aurora Rd				
21700	BDHT	44146	2758	B7
21700	MPHT	44146	2758	B7
23100	BDHT	44146	2887	C1
26700	BDHT	44146	2888	A2
26700	SLN	44139	2888	A2
33200	SLN	44139	2889	C7
37800	SLN	44139	3020	D1
39700	SLN	44139	3021	A2
40000	BbgT	44023	3021	A2
40000	BbgT	44139	3021	A2
40000	BbgT	44202	3021	A2
SR-43 N Aurora Rd				
10	AURA	44202	3021	C5
10	BbgT	44023	3021	A2
10	BbgT	44139	3021	A2
10	BbgT	44202	3021	A2
10	SLN	44139	3021	A2
SR-43 S Aurora Rd				
10	AURA	44202	3156	E1
SR-43 Bartlett Rd				
-	BDHT	44146	2758	C7
SR-43 Broadway Av				
800	CLEV	44115	2625	A4
3900	CLEV	44127	2625	C6
5800	CLEV	44127	2755	E1
6200	CLEV	44105	2755	D1
7400	CLEV	44105	2756	A3
SR-43 S Chillicothe Rd				
100	AURA	44202	3156	E7
1200	STBR	44202	3156	E6
10100	STBR	44241	3156	E7
SR-43 Miles Av				
9100	CLEV	44105	2756	B3
13000	CLEV	44128	2756	E3
13500	CLEV	44105	2757	B4
13500	CLEV	44128	2757	B4
17500	WVHT	44128	2757	D5
SR-43 Miles Rd				
17700	WVHT	44128	2757	D5
19400	NRDL	44128	2757	E5
20000	NRDL	44128	2758	A6
20000	WVHT	44128	2758	A6
SR-43 Mueti Dr				
-	BDHT	44146	2758	B7
-	MPHT	44137	2758	B7
SR-43 Northfield Rd				
-	BDHT	44146	2758	B6
-	MPHT	44137	2758	B6
-	MPHT	44146	2758	B6
4900	NRDL	44128	2758	B6
4900	WVHT	44128	2758	B6
4900	WVHT	44146	2758	B6
SR-43 Pittsburgh Av				
2200	CLEV	44115	2625	D7
SR-44				
-	CcdT	-	2145	E4
-	CcdT	-	2146	A5
-	CcdT	44024	2254	B5
-	CcdT	44077	2254	A1
-	CdnT	44024	2254	B5
-	CdnT	44024	2379	B1
-	GDRV	44077	2039	B4
-	MNTR	-	2145	B1
-	MNTR	44060	2039	B4
-	PNVL	-	2145	D3
-	PnvT	-	2145	B1
-	PnvT	44060	2039	B6
-	PnvT	44077	2039	B6
100	CRDN	44024	2379	E6
100	CRDN	44024	2380	A6
300	CRDN	44024	2505	A1
600	MsnT	44024	2505	B7
10300	MNTU	44255	3159	C7
10300	ShvT	44255	3159	B7
10900	ManT	44255	3159	C5
12600	MsnT	44024	2635	B1
13400	NbyT	44021	2635	B4
13400	NbyT	44024	2635	B4
13400	NbyT	44065	2635	B4
14200	NbyT	44021	2765	A2
14200	NbyT	44065	2765	A2
15400	NbyT	44021	2764	E7
15400	NbyT	44065	2764	E7
16200	AbnT	44021	2764	E7
16400	AbnT	44021	2893	E1
16400	AbnT	44255	2893	E1
18200	AbnT	44234	2893	C7
SR-44 Center St				
100	CRDN	44024	2379	E6
100	CRDN	44024	2380	A6
SR-44 N Hambden St				
100	CRDN	44024	2380	A6
SR-44 S Hambden St				
100	CRDN	44024	2380	A6
SR-44 Heisley Rd				
-	GDRV	44077	2039	B4
-	MNTR	44060	2039	B4
-	MNTR	44060	2145	A1
-	PnvT	44060	2039	B6
-	PnvT	44077	2039	B6
SR-44 Lakeland Frwy				
-	MNTR	-	2145	B1
-	PNVL	-	2145	B1
-	PnvT	-	2145	B1
SR-44 Main St				
100	CRDN	44024	2380	A6
10400	MNTU	44255	3159	C7
10400	ShvT	44255	3159	C7
SR-44 Painesville Ravenna Rd				
10300	MNTU	44255	3159	C7
10300	ShvT	44255	3159	B7
10900	ManT	44255	3159	C5
SR-44 E Park St				
100	CRDN	44024	2380	A6
SR-44 Ravenna Rd				
11600	CRDN	44024	2505	A3
11600	MsnT	44024	2505	B7
12600	MsnT	44024	2635	B1
13400	NbyT	44021	2635	B4
13400	NbyT	44024	2635	B4
13400	NbyT	44065	2635	B4
14200	NbyT	44021	2765	A2
14200	NbyT	44065	2765	A2
15400	NbyT	44021	2764	E7
15400	NbyT	44065	2764	E7
16200	AbnT	44021	2764	E7
16400	AbnT	44021	2893	E1
16400	AbnT	44255	2893	E1
18200	AbnT	44234	2893	C7
SR-44 South St				
100	CRDN	44024	2380	A7
300	CRDN	44024	2505	A1
600	MsnT	44024	2505	A2
SR-44 Water St				
100	CRDN	44024	2380	A6
SR-57				
-	EatT	44035	3006	E3
-	EatT	44044	3007	A4
-	ELYR	44035	2875	E4
-	ELYR	44035	3006	E1
100	LORN	44055	2745	E5
300	EatT	44044	3141	E2
300	GFTN	44044	3141	E3
300	GFTN	44044	3142	C7
300	LORN	44052	2614	E7
1100	GftT	44044	3142	C7
1500	LORN	44052	2744	E1
2000	LORN	44052	2745	A1
2400	CrlT	44044	3006	E6
2400	EatT	44044	3006	E6
3000	CrlT	44044	3141	E1
4800	ShfT	44055	2745	E5
6000	EyrT	44035	2745	E7
6000	ShfT	44035	2745	E6
6200	ELYR	44035	2745	E7
6500	ELYR	44035	2874	E1
SR-57 E 28th St				
100	LORN	44055	2745	A2
SR-57 Avon Belden Rd				
15500	GftT	44044	3142	E7
SR-57 Broadway				
300	LORN	44052	2614	E7
1500	LORN	44052	2744	E1
2000	LORN	44052	2745	A1
2600	LORN	44055	2745	A2
SR-57 S East Byp				
-	CrlT	44044	3006	E5
-	EatT	44035	3006	E3
-	EatT	44044	3006	E4
-	EatT	44044	3007	A4
-	ELYR	44035	2875	E7
-	ELYR	44035	3006	E1
SR-57 Grafton Rd				
2400	CrlT	44044	3006	E6
2400	EatT	44044	3006	E6
3000	CrlT	44044	3141	E1
3000	EatT	44044	3141	E2
13300	GFTN	44044	3141	E3
SR-57 Grafton Eastern Rd				
36000	GftT	44044	3142	C7
36700	GFTN	44044	3142	C7
SR-57 Grove Av				
-	ShfT	44035	2745	E6
2700	LORN	44055	2745	E5
4800	ShfT	44055	2745	E5
SR-57 John F Kennedy Mem Pkwy				
-	ELYR	44035	2874	E4
-	ELYR	44035	2875	E4
SR-57 Lorain Blvd				
6000	EyrT	44035	2745	E7
6000	ShfT	44035	2745	E6
6000	ShfT	44055	2745	E6
6200	ELYR	44035	2745	E7
6500	ELYR	44035	2874	E1
SR-57 Main St				
300	EatT	44044	3141	E3
300	GFTN	44044	3141	E3
300	GFTN	44044	3142	A4
1100	GftT	44044	3142	B6
SR-58				
-	PtfT	44074	3138	E5
10	OBLN	44074	3138	E7
100	AhtT	44001	2873	A6
100	AMHT	44001	2744	B4
100	AMHT	44001	2873	A1
200	NRsT	44074	3138	E1
800	AMHT	44053	2744	A6
800	LORN	44001	2744	A6
800	LORN	44053	2744	B1
1000	LORN	44052	2614	B7
1000	LORN	44053	2614	B7
1300	LORN	44052	2744	B1
9200	AhtT	44001	2872	E7
9200	AhtT	44001	3003	E1
9500	NRsT	44001	3003	E1
9800	NRsT	44074	3003	E6
12300	OBLN	44074	3003	E7
SR-58 Ashland Oberlin Rd				
-	NRsT	44074	3138	E5
-	OBLN	44074	3138	E5
-	PtfT	44074	3138	E5
SR-58 Leavitt Rd				
1000	LORN	44052	2614	B7
1000	LORN	44053	2614	B7
1300	LORN	44052	2744	B1
1300	LORN	44053	2744	B1
5300	AMHT	44001	2744	A6
5300	AMHT	44053	2744	A6
5300	LORN	44001	2744	A6
7400	AhtT	44001	2873	A6
7400	AMHT	44001	2873	A3
9200	AhtT	44001	2872	E7
9200	AhtT	44001	3003	E1
9500	NRsT	44001	3003	E1
9800	NRsT	44074	3003	E6
12300	OBLN	44074	3003	E7
12400	NRsT	44074	3138	E1
12400	OBLN	44074	3138	E1
SR-58 N Leavitt Rd				
100	AMHT	44001	2744	B4
800	AMHT	44053	2744	A6
800	LORN	44001	2744	A6
800	LORN	44053	2744	A6
SR-58 S Leavitt Rd				
100	AhtT	44001	2873	A1
100	AMHT	44001	2873	A1
SR-58 N Main St				
10	OBLN	44074	3138	E2
200	NRsT	44074	3138	E1
SR-58 S Main St				
10	OBLN	44074	3138	E7
300	NRsT	44074	3138	E4
SR-60				
600	VMLN	44089	2740	E6
1200	VmnT	44089	2740	E7
1400	VmnT	44089	2869	E3
4700	FrnT	44889	2869	E7
4700	VmnT	44889	2869	E7
SR-60 Main St				
600	VMLN	44089	2740	E5
SR-60 South St				
5500	VMLN	44089	2740	E5
SR-60 State Rd				
1400	VmnT	44089	2740	E7
1400	VmnT	44089	2869	E3
4700	FrnT	44889	2869	E7
4700	VmnT	44889	2869	E7
SR-60 State St				
800	VMLN	44089	2740	E6
1200	VmnT	44089	2740	E7
SR-82				
-	BKVL	44141	3015	E7
-	CrlT	44044	3006	E6
10	AURA	44202	3157	D1
10	NCtT	44067	3152	E1
10	NCtT	44067	3153	A1
100	BWHT	44147	3014	E7
100	SgHT	44067	3152	C1
300	MCDN	44056	3153	B1
500	AURA	44202	3021	D7
500	AURA	44202	3156	B1
900	SgHT	44067	3017	B7
1100	AURA	44087	3156	A2
1100	TwbT	44087	3156	A2
1200	ManT	44202	3157	E1
1300	BKVL	44141	3016	A7
1300	SgHT	44067	3016	E7
1300	SgHT	44141	3016	E7
1400	MCDN	44056	3154	B1
1500	TNBG	44087	3154	B1
2400	BKVL	44147	3015	B7
2400	BWHT	44141	3015	B7
2600	ManT	44202	3158	A1
2800	TNBG	44087	3155	B2
2900	NRYN	44133	3014	A7
2900	NRYN	44147	3014	C7
3000	ManT	44255	3158	B2
3400	TwbT	44087	3155	C2
3700	ManT	44255	3159	B2
4700	ManT	44234	3159	B2
4800	BWHT	44147	3015	E7
5300	ManT	44234	3160	C2
5500	HrmT	44234	3160	A2
6200	NRYN	44133	3013	D7
6500	HRM	44234	3160	E2
6600	HRM	44234	3161	A2
7100	GTVL	44231	3161	E5
7100	HrmT	44231	3161	D4
7100	HrmT	44234	3161	E4
7100	HrmT	44255	3161	E4
11700	NRYN	44133	3012	E7
12700	SGVL	44133	3012	E7
12700	SGVL	44136	3012	C7
17800	SGVL	44136	3011	E7
18600	SGVL	44149	3011	D7
22300	ClbT	44028	3010	D7
22300	ClbT	44149	3010	E7
22300	SGVL	44149	3010	E7
25100	ClbT	44028	3009	C7
27400	ClbT	44028	3008	E7
27400	EatT	44028	3008	D7
34500	EatT	44044	3008	C7
35700	EatT	44044	3007	B7
38100	EatT	44044	3006	E6
SR-82 Aurora Rd				
3600	TNBG	44087	3155	D2
3600	TwbT	44087	3155	E2
SR-82 E Aurora Rd				
10	NCtT	44067	3152	E1
10	NCtT	44067	3153	A1
300	MCDN	44056	3153	B1
1400	MCDN	44056	3154	B1
1500	TNBG	44087	3154	B1
2800	TNBG	44087	3155	B2
3400	TwbT	44087	3155	C2
SR-82 W Aurora Rd				
10	NCtT	44067	3152	E1
100	SgHT	44067	3152	C1
900	SgHT	44067	3017	B7
1300	BKVL	44141	3016	E7
1300	SgHT	44067	3016	E7
1300	SgHT	44141	3016	E7
SR-82 Chippewa Rd				
7300	BKVL	44141	3016	E6
13000	SgHT	44067	3016	E7
13000	SgHT	44141	3016	E7
SR-82 Garfield Rd				
11400	HRM	44234	3161	A2
SR-82 E Garfield Rd				
10	AURA	44202	3157	D1
1200	ManT	44202	3157	E1
SR-82 Ravenna Rd				
9100	TNBG	44087	3155	C2
SR-82 Royalton Rd				
-	CrlT	44044	3006	E6
3000	BWHT	44147	3014	C7
3000	NRYN	44133	3014	A7
3000	NRYN	44147	3014	C7
6200	NRYN	44133	3013	D7
11700	NRYN	44133	3012	E7
12700	SGVL	44133	3012	E7
12700	SGVL	44136	3012	B7
17800	SGVL	44136	3011	E7
18600	SGVL	44149	3011	D7
22300	ClbT	44028	3010	D7
22300	ClbT	44149	3010	E7
22300	SGVL	44149	3010	E7
25100	ClbT	44028	3009	C7
27400	ClbT	44028	3008	E7
27400	EatT	44028	3008	D7
34500	EatT	44044	3008	C7
35700	EatT	44044	3007	B7
38100	EatT	44044	3006	E6
SR-82 E Royalton Rd				
-	BKVL	44141	3015	E7
100	BWHT	44147	3014	E7
2400	BKVL	44147	3015	B7
2400	BWHT	44141	3015	B7
4800	BWHT	44147	3015	E7
6900	BKVL	44141	3016	A7
SR-82 W Royalton Rd				
1000	BWHT	44147	3014	E7
2900	NRYN	44133	3014	C7
2900	NRYN	44147	3014	C7
SR-82 State St				
7800	GTVL	44231	3161	E5
7800	HrmT	44231	3161	E5
SR-82 Twinsburg-Warren Rd				
500	AURA	44202	3021	D7
500	AURA	44202	3156	B1
1100	AURA	44087	3156	A2
1100	TwbT	44087	3156	A2
2600	AURA	44202	3157	E1
2600	ManT	44202	3157	E1
2600	ManT	44202	3158	A1
3000	ManT	44255	3158	B2
3700	ManT	44255	3159	B2
4700	ManT	44234	3159	B2
5300	ManT	44234	3160	C2
5500	HrmT	44234	3160	A2
7100	GTVL	44231	3161	E5
7100	HrmT	44231	3161	D4
7100	HrmT	44234	3161	B4
7100	HrmT	44255	3161	B4
SR-82 W Wakefield Rd				
5700	HrmT	44234	3160	B2
5700	ManT	44234	3160	A2
6500	HRM	44234	3160	E2
6600	HRM	44234	3161	A2
SR-82 Welshfield Limavle Rd S				
11300	HRM	44234	3161	A3
11300	HrmT	44234	3161	A3
SR-83				
-	AVON	44011	2618	A7
100	AVLK	44012	2488	A7
100	AVLK	44012	2618	A6
700	AVON	44012	2618	A5
1600	EatT	44044	3142	E2
1600	GFTN	44044	3142	E6
2000	AVON	44011	2748	A6
4200	NRDV	44011	2748	A6
4200	NRDV	44039	2748	A6
5000	NRDV	44039	2877	A2
9000	NRDV	44039	3007	E7
9000	NRDV	44039	3008	A1
9400	EatT	44039	3007	E7
9400	EatT	44044	3007	E7
14700	GftT	44044	3142	E6
SR-83 Avon Belden Rd				
100	AVLK	44012	2488	A7
100	AVLK	44012	2618	A6
700	AVON	44011	2618	A5
700	AVON	44012	2618	A5
1600	EatT	44044	3142	E2
1600	GFTN	44044	3142	E6
4900	AVON	44011	2748	A6
4900	NRDV	44011	2748	A6
4900	NRDV	44039	2748	A6
5000	NRDV	44039	2877	A2
9000	NRDV	44039	3007	E7
9000	NRDV	44039	3008	A1
9400	EatT	44039	3007	E7
9400	EatT	44044	3007	E7
14700	GftT	44044	3142	E6
SR-83 Center Rd				
-	AVON	44011	2618	A7
800	AVLK	44012	2618	A5
800	AVON	44012	2618	A5
2000	AVON	44011	2748	A6
4200	NRDV	44011	2748	A6
4200	NRDV	44039	2748	A6
SR-83 Chester Rd				
36000	AVON	44011	2618	A7
SR-83C				
10800	EatT	44035	3007	E2
10800	EatT	44039	3007	E2
10800	EatT	44044	3007	E2
10800	NRDV	44039	3007	E1
SR-83C Butternut Ridge Rd				
10800	EatT	44035	3007	E2
10800	EatT	44039	3007	E2
10800	EatT	44044	3007	E2
10800	NRDV	44039	3007	E2
SR-84				
10	GNVA	44041	1944	B6
10	MDSN	44057	2044	B1
10	PnvT	44077	2146	E2
200	HpfT	44041	1944	B6
200	PNVL	44077	2146	C2
400	MadT	44057	2044	D1
500	GnvT	44041	1944	B6
700	MadT	44057	2043	E2
700	MDSN	44057	2043	E2
800	PnvT	44077	2147	A1
1400	PryT	44077	2147	B1
2400	WKLF	44092	2374	B4
2500	PryT	44077	2041	C7
2500	PryT	44081	2041	C7
2800	PryT	44081	2042	B5
4400	PRRY	44081	2042	D4
4500	PryT	44057	2042	D4
5000	MadT	44081	2043	A3
5000	PryT	44057	2043	A3
5000	PryT	44081	2043	A3
5800	HpfT	44041	1943	C7
6800	HpfT	44057	1943	B7
6800	MadT	44057	1943	B7
7300	MadT	44057	1942	E7
7300	MNTR	44060	2251	B5
8000	MNTR	44060	2252	B2
8400	KDHL	44060	2252	B2
9300	MNTR	44060	2253	A2
9600	CcdT	44060	2253	A1
9800	CcdT	44060	2145	C6
9800	CcdT	44077	2145	C6
9800	CcdT	44077	2253	C1
10600	CcdT	44077	2146	C2
21000	EUCL	44117	2498	B1
23500	EUCL	44143	2498	C1
23800	RDHT	44143	2498	C1
24400	RDHT	44143	2373	D7
26500	RDHT	44143	2374	B6
27200	WBHL	44092	2374	B6
30600	WKLF	44092	2375	A3
30600	WLBY	44094	2375	A3
36800	WLBY	44094	2250	E7
38500	WLBY	44094	2251	C4
38900	MNTR	44094	2251	B5
SR-84 Bank St				
800	PNVL	44077	2146	C2
800	PnvT	44077	2146	C2
SR-84 Bishop Rd				
2400	WKLF	44092	2374	B4
2700	WBHL	44092	2374	B5
SR-84 Chardon Rd				
21000	EUCL	44117	2498	B1
23500	EUCL	44143	2498	C1
23800	RDHT	44143	2498	C1
24400	RDHT	44143	2373	D7
26500	RDHT	44143	2374	B6
27200	WBHL	44092	2374	B6
SR-84 Johnnycake Ridge Rd				
10	PnvT	44077	2146	B3
7300	MNTR	44060	2251	B5
8000	MNTR	44060	2252	B2
8400	KDHL	44060	2252	B2
9300	MNTR	44060	2253	A2
9600	CcdT	44060	2253	A1
9800	CcdT	44060	2145	C6
9800	CcdT	44077	2145	C6
9800	CcdT	44077	2253	C1
10600	CcdT	44077	2146	C2
38200	WLBY	44094	2250	E7
38500	WLBY	44094	2251	C4
38900	MNTR	44094	2251	B5
SR-84 E Main St				
10	MDSN	44057	2044	D1
400	MadT	44057	2044	D1
SR-84 W Main St				
10	MDSN	44057	2044	B1
700	MadT	44057	2043	E2
700	MDSN	44057	2043	E2
SR-84 Ridge Rd				
28700	WKLF	44092	2374	B4
30600	WKLF	44092	2375	A3
30600	WLBY	44094	2375	A3
36800	WLBY	44094	2250	C7
SR-84 S Ridge Rd				
2600	PryT	44077	2041	C7
2600	PryT	44081	2041	C7
2800	PryT	44081	2042	B5
4400	PRRY	44081	2042	D4
4500	PryT	44057	2042	D4
5000	MadT	44057	2043	A3
5000	MadT	44081	2043	A3
5000	PryT	44057	2043	A3
5000	PryT	44081	2043	A3
5900	MDSN	44057	2043	E2
7100	MadT	44057	2044	D1
7100	MDSN	44057	2044	D1
7300	MadT	44057	1942	E7
7400	MadT	44057	1943	A7
7800	HpfT	44041	1943	B7
7800	HpfT	44057	1943	B7
SR-84 S Ridge Rd E				
10	GNVA	44041	1944	B6
500	GnvT	44041	1944	B6
SR-84 S Ridge Rd W				
10	GNVA	44041	1944	B6
200	HpfT	44041	1944	B6
5800	HpfT	44041	1943	C7
6800	HpfT	44057	1943	B7
6800	MadT	44057	1943	B7
SR-84 Riverside Dr				
400	PnvT	44077	2146	E2
800	PnvT	44077	2147	A1
1400	PryT	44077	2147	B1
2500	PryT	44077	2041	C7
2500	PryT	44081	2041	C7
SR-84 S State St				
400	PNVL	44077	2146	C2
700	PnvT	44077	2146	C2
SR-84 E Walnut Av				
200	PNVL	44077	2146	C1
400	PnvT	44077	2146	D2
SR-86				
10	PNVL	44077	2040	B6
10	PNVL	44077	2146	C2
700	PnvT	44077	2146	C3
6100	CcdT	44077	2146	C3
7800	LryT	44086	2257	B4
7800	TpnT	44024	2257	B4
7800	TpnT	44086	2257	B4
8200	TpnT	44064	2257	E6
8300	MtlT	44064	2257	E6
12000	CcdT	44077	2147	A5
12400	LryT	44077	2147	B5
13000	LryT	44077	2255	E1
13000	LryT	44077	2256	A1
14000	LryT	44086	2256	C3
SR-86 Painesville Warren Rd				
6100	CcdT	44077	2146	C3
6100	PnvT	44077	2146	C3
12000	CcdT	44077	2147	A5
12400	LryT	44077	2147	B5
13000	LryT	44077	2255	E1
13000	LryT	44077	2256	A1
14000	LryT	44086	2256	C3
14700	LryT	44086	2257	A3
14800	TpnT	44024	2257	A3
14800	TpnT	44086	2257	A3
SR-86 Plank Rd				
7800	LryT	44086	2257	B4
7800	TpnT	44024	2257	B4
7800	TpnT	44086	2257	B4
8200	TpnT	44064	2257	E6
8300	MtlT	44064	2257	E6
SR-86 N State St				
10	PNVL	44077	2040	B6
SR-86 S State St				
10	PNVL	44077	2040	B7
10	PNVL	44077	2146	C2
700	PnvT	44077	2146	C2
SR-87				
1400	CLEV	44115	2625	A4
1900	CLEV	44114	2624	E3
1900	CLEV	44115	2624	E3
2000	CLEV	44113	2624	E3
2900	BHWD	44122	2628	E7
3000	BHWD	44122	2758	E1
3800	CLEV	44104	2625	E4
7000	HGVL	44022	2761	A2
7000	HGVL	44072	2761	A2
7000	RslT	44022	2761	A2
7000	RslT	44072	2761	A2
7500	CLEV	44104	2626	D5
8200	RslT	44072	2762	A1
9600	NbyT	44072	2763	A1
9600	RslT	44072	2763	A1
10100	NbyT	44065	2763	C1
10400	NbyT	44065	2764	B2
11000	CLEV	44120	2626	D5
12000	NbyT	44065	2765	A1
12100	NbyT	44021	2765	A1
12400	BtnT	44021	2765	E1
13300	CLEV	44120	2627	C6
13400	SRHT	44120	2627	A5
13800	BURT	44021	2636	B7
13800	BURT	44021	2766	D2
14000	BtnT	44021	2766	C1
14300	BtnT	44062	2766	D2
15000	BtnT	44062	2767	A2
15100	MDFD	44062	2767	B2
15100	MdfT	44062	2767	B2
18400	SRHT	44122	2627	E6
19500	SRHT	44122	2628	A6
26900	BHWD	44122	2759	A1
26900	ORNG	44122	2759	A1
26900	WDMR	44122	2759	A1
28900	ORNG	44124	2759	B1
29800	PRPK	44122	2759	C1
30400	PRPK	44124	2759	D1
32900	PRPK	44124	2760	B2
33200	PRPK	44022	2760	B2
33700	HGVL	44022	2760	A2
33700	MDHL	44022	2760	A2
SR-87 Broadway Av				
800	CLEV	44115	2625	A4
SR-87 Buckeye Rd				
8400	CLEV	44104	2626	A5
SR-87 E Center St				
13800	BURT	44021	2766	D2
14000	BtnT	44021	2766	B1
SR-87 W Center St				
13500	BtnT	44021	2766	A1
13500	BURT	44021	2766	A1
SR-87 Chagrin Blvd				
25600	BHWD	44122	2758	E1
26900	BHWD	44122	2759	A1
26900	ORNG	44122	2759	A1
26900	WDMR	44122	2759	A1
28900	ORNG	44124	2759	B1
28900	PRPK	44124	2759	B1
29800	PRPK	44122	2759	C1
SR-87 E High St				
15900	MDFD	44062	2767	D2
SR-87 W High St				
15300	MDFD	44062	2767	B2
15400	MdfT	44062	2767	B2
SR-87 Kinsman Rd				
7000	HGVL	44022	2761	A2
7000	HGVL	44072	2761	A2
7000	RslT	44022	2761	A2
7000	RslT	44072	2761	A2
8200	RslT	44072	2762	A1
9600	NbyT	44072	2763	A1
9600	RslT	44072	2763	A1
10100	NbyT	44065	2763	C1
10400	NbyT	44065	2764	B2
12000	NbyT	44065	2765	A1
12100	NbyT	44021	2765	A1
12400	BtnT	44021	2765	E1
14000	BtnT	44021	2766	C1
14000	BURT	44021	2766	C1
14300	BtnT	44062	2766	D2
15000	BtnT	44062	2767	A2
15100	MDFD	44062	2767	B2
15100	MdfT	44062	2767	B2
SR-87 Ontario St				
1900	CLEV	44114	2624	E3
1900	CLEV	44115	2624	E3
2000	CLEV	44113	2624	E3
SR-87 Orange Av				
1400	CLEV	44115	2625	A4
SR-87 E Park St				
14500	BURT	44021	2766	B1
SR-87 N Park St				
13800	BURT	44021	2636	B7
SR-87 W Park St				
-	BURT	44021	2766	A1
SR-87 Pinetree Rd				
30400	PRPK	44124	2759	D1
SR-87 Richmond Rd				
2900	BHWD	44122	2628	E7
3000	BHWD	44122	2758	E1
SR-87 Shaker Blvd				
10000	CLEV	44104	2626	D5
11000	CLEV	44120	2626	D5
13300	CLEV	44120	2627	C6
13400	SRHT	44120	2627	A5
18400	SRHT	44122	2627	E6
19500	SRHT	44122	2628	C6
23100	BHWD	44122	2628	D6
SR-87 Woodland Av				
2500	CLEV	44115	2625	C4
3800	CLEV	44104	2625	E4
7500	CLEV	44104	2626	B5
SR-87 S Woodland Rd				
32900	PRPK	44124	2759	E1
32900	PRPK	44124	2760	B2
33200	PRPK	44022	2760	B2
33700	HGVL	44022	2760	A2
33700	MDHL	44022	2760	A2
45800	HGVL	44022	2761	A2
45800	HGVL	44072	2761	A2
SR-91				
-	WLBY	44094	2250	B5
-	WLBY	44095	2250	B5
200	MAYF	44040	2500	A1
200	MAYF	44092	2500	A1
200	MAYF	44094	2500	A1
200	MAYF	44143	2500	A2
200	WBHL	44092	2500	A1
200	WBHL	44094	2500	A1
400	ETLK	44095	2250	B5
400	TMLK	44095	2250	A2
900	MDHT	44124	2500	A6
900	MDHT	44143	2500	A6
1600	GSML	44040	2630	A1
1600	GSML	44124	2630	A1
1900	MDHT	44124	2630	A7
2000	HGVL	44022	2630	A3
2000	HGVL	44040	2630	A3
2000	PRPK	44124	2630	A3
2300	PRPK	44022	2630	A4
2500	WBHL	44094	2375	A6
2600	HGVL	44124	2630	A4
2900	WBHL	44092	2375	A7
3300	HGVL	44022	2760	A1
3300	PRPK	44124	2760	A2
3400	PRPK	44022	2760	A2
3600	MDHL	44022	2760	A2
3600	MDHL	44124	2760	A2
4200	MDHL	44022	2759	E6
4900	SLN	44022	2759	E7
4900	SLN	44139	2759	E7
5100	SLN	44139	2760	A7
5200	SLN	44139	2889	A6
5200	WLBY	44094	2375	A1
7000	SLN	44139	3020	A1
7300	HDSN	44236	3154	E7
7600	TNBG	44139	3020	A3
7700	TwbT	44236	3154	E6
7900	TNBG	44087	3154	E7
7900	TNBG	44236	3154	E5
7900	TwbT	44087	3154	E5
8700	TNBG	44087	3155	A2
9200	TNBG	44087	3020	A6
9700	TNBG	44087	3019	E5
SR-91 Darrow Rd				
7300	HDSN	44236	3154	E7
7700	TwbT	44236	3154	E6
7900	TNBG	44087	3154	E7
7900	TNBG	44236	3154	E5
7900	TwbT	44087	3154	E5
8700	TNBG	44087	3155	A2
9200	TNBG	44087	3020	A6
9700	TNBG	44087	3019	E5
10300	SLN	44139	3020	A3
10300	TNBG	44139	3020	A3
SR-91 Som Center Rd				
-	WLBY	44094	2250	B5
-	WLBY	44095	2250	B5
200	MAYF	44092	2500	A1
200	MAYF	44094	2500	A1
200	MAYF	44143	2500	A2
200	WBHL	44092	2500	A1
200	WBHL	44094	2500	A1
400	ETLK	44095	2250	B5
400	TMLK	44095	2250	A2
700	MAYF	44040	2500	A4
900	MDHT	44124	2500	A6
900	MDHT	44143	2500	A6
1500	MDHT	44124	2630	A1
1600	GSML	44124	2630	A1
1900	GSML	44040	2630	A7
2000	HGVL	44022	2630	A3
2000	HGVL	44040	2630	A3
2000	PRPK	44124	2630	A3
2300	PRPK	44022	2630	A4
2500	WBHL	44094	2375	A6
2600	HGVL	44124	2630	A4
2900	WBHL	44092	2375	A7
3300	HGVL	44022	2760	A1
3300	PRPK	44124	2760	A2
3400	PRPK	44022	2760	A2
3600	MDHL	44022	2760	A2
3600	MDHL	44124	2760	A2
4200	MDHL	44022	2759	E6
4900	SLN	44022	2759	E7
4900	SLN	44139	2759	E7
5100	SLN	44139	2760	A7
5200	SLN	44139	2889	A6
5200	WLBY	44094	2375	A1
7000	SLN	44139	3020	A1
7600	TNBG	44087	3020	A3
7600	TNBG	44139	3020	A3
SR-94				
10	HkyT	44133	3149	A5
10	HkyT	44233	3149	A5
4200	CLEV	44109	2754	C4
4900	CLEV	44134	2754	C7
4900	PRMA	44109	2754	C7
4900	PRMA	44134	2754	C7
5400	PRMA	44134	2883	C3
7000	PRMA	44129	2883	B6
7400	PRMA	44134	3014	B1
7800	NRYN	44133	3014	A4
7800	NRYN	44134	3014	A2
14200	NRYN	44133	3149	A2
SR-94 River Rd				
10	HkyT	44133	3149	A5
10	HkyT	44233	3149	A5
10	NRYN	44133	3149	A5
SR-94 State Rd				
4200	CLEV	44109	2754	C4
4900	CLEV	44134	2754	C7
4900	PRMA	44109	2754	C7
4900	PRMA	44134	2754	C7
5400	PRMA	44134	2883	C3
7000	PRMA	44129	2883	B6
7400	PRMA	44134	3014	B1
7800	NRYN	44133	3014	A4
7800	NRYN	44134	3014	A2
14200	NRYN	44133	3149	A2
20000	HkyT	44133	3149	B5
20000	HkyT	44233	3149	B5
SR-113				
100	SAHT	44001	2872	B7
300	AhtT	44001	2872	D7
400	SAHT	44001	3003	A1
500	NRsT	44001	3003	A1
700	ELYR	44035	2875	E4
900	ELYR	44039	2875	E5
900	NRDV	44039	2875	E5
1500	RKRV	44116	2621	D7
2500	LKWD	44126	2621	E7
2500	RKRV	44126	2621	E7
20600	FWPK	44116	2751	C1
20600	FWPK	44126	2751	C1
20600	RKRV	44116	2751	C1
22800	WTLK	44116	2751	A1
22800	WTLK	44145	2751	A1
23100	WTLK	44145	2750	B2
27200	WTLK	44145	2749	A6
31400	NRDV	44039	2749	A7
31400	NRDV	44145	2749	A7
31600	NRDV	44039	2748	E7
31600	NRDV	44039	2877	B3
36100	NRDV	44039	2876	D4
43100	EyrT	44035	2874	B4
43300	ELYR	44035	2873	E5
43300	ELYR	44035	2874	A5
43300	EyrT	44035	2873	E5
43400	AhtT	44035	2873	C6
44000	AhtT	44001	2873	C6
SR-113 Center Ridge Rd				
19400	RKRV	44116	2621	D7
20600	FWPK	44116	2751	C1
20600	FWPK	44126	2751	C1
20600	RKRV	44116	2751	C1
22800	WTLK	44116	2751	A1
22800	WTLK	44145	2751	A1
23100	WTLK	44145	2750	B2
27200	WTLK	44145	2749	A6
31400	NRDV	44039	2749	A7
31400	NRDV	44145	2749	A7
31600	NRDV	44039	2748	E7
31600	NRDV	44039	2877	B3
36100	NRDV	44039	2876	D4
SR-113 Cleveland St				
700	ELYR	44035	2875	E5
900	ELYR	44039	2875	E5
900	NRDV	44039	2875	E5
SR-113 John F Kennedy Mem Pkwy				
-	ELYR	44035	2874	C4
-	ELYR	44035	2875	E4
-	EyrT	44035	2874	C4
SR-113 E Main St				
100	SAHT	44001	2872	C7
300	AhtT	44001	2872	D7
SR-113 W Main St				
100	SAHT	44001	2872	B7

Cleveland Street Index

Block	City	ZIP	Map#	Grid
SR-113 W Main St				
400	SAHT	44001	3003	A1
500	NRsT	44001	3003	A1
SR-113 Telegraph Rd				
43100	ELYR	44035	2874	B4
43300	ELYR	44035	2873	E5
43300	EyrT	44035	2873	E5
43300	EyrT	44035	2874	A5
43400	AhtT	44035	2873	C6
44000	AhtT	44001	2873	C6
46100	AhtT	44001	2872	E6
SR-113 Wooster Rd				
1500	RKRV	44116	2621	E5
2500	LKWD	44126	2621	E7
2500	RKRV	44126	2621	E7
SR-166				
13900	HmbT	44024	2381	C2
14300	HmbT	44024	2256	E7
14800	HmbT	44024	2257	A6
14800	MtlT	44024	2257	B5
14800	TpnT	44024	2257	B5
15500	TpnT	44086	2257	D3
SR-166 Rock Creek Rd				
13900	HmbT	44024	2381	C2
14300	HmbT	44024	2256	E7
14800	HmbT	44024	2257	A6
14800	MtlT	44024	2257	B5
14800	TpnT	44024	2257	B5
15500	TpnT	44086	2257	D3
SR-168				
-	BURT	44021	2766	B1
14700	BtnT	44021	2766	E5
14700	BtnT	44062	2766	E5
16300	BtnT	44021	2767	A7
16300	BtnT	44062	2767	A7
16300	TroT	44021	2767	A7
16300	TroT	44062	2767	A7
SR-168 S Cheshire Rd				
-	BtnT	44021	2766	B2
-	BtnT	44062	2766	B2
-	BURT	44021	2766	B2
SR-168 S Cheshire St				
-	BURT	44021	2766	B1
14700	BtnT	44021	2766	B2
14700	BtnT	44062	2766	B2
SR-168 Tavern Rd				
14800	BtnT	44021	2766	E5
14800	BtnT	44062	2766	E5
14800	BURT	44021	2766	B2
16300	BtnT	44021	2767	A7
16300	BtnT	44062	2767	A7
16300	TroT	44021	2767	A7
16300	TroT	44062	2767	A7
SR-174				
-	WBHL	44094	2250	D7
400	GSML	44040	2500	D6
1400	GSML	44040	2630	E2
2000	HGVL	44022	2630	E3
2000	HGVL	44040	2630	E3
2100	WBHL	44094	2375	D6
2900	GSML	44094	2500	C1
2900	WBHL	44094	2500	C1
4100	WLBY	44094	2250	D7
SR-174 Chagrin River Rd				
-	GSML	44094	2500	C1
-	WBHL	44094	2500	C1
400	GSML	44040	2500	D6
1500	GSML	44040	2630	E2
2000	HGVL	44022	2630	E3
2000	HGVL	44040	2630	E3
SR-174 Old Mill Rd				
-	GSML	44040	2630	E1
SR-174 Ridge Rd				
37700	WLBY	44094	2250	E7
SR-174 River Rd				
-	WBHL	44094	2250	D7
-	WLBY	44094	2250	D7
2100	WBHL	44094	2375	D6
2900	GSML	44040	2500	C1
2900	GSML	44094	2500	C1
2900	WBHL	44094	2500	C1
SR-174 River St				
4100	WLBY	44094	2250	E5
SR-175				
100	EUCL	44117	2373	E7
100	EUCL	44143	2373	E7
100	RDHT	44117	2373	E6
100	RDHT	44143	2373	E6
200	EUCL	44132	2373	E7
300	RDHT	44143	2498	E1
700	LNHT	44124	2498	E7
700	LNHT	44143	2498	E5
1500	LNHT	44124	2628	E1
2000	BHWD	44122	2628	E7
2000	BHWD	44124	2628	E3
3000	BHWD	44122	2758	E3
3700	HIHL	44122	2758	E1
3700	WVHT	44122	2758	E1
4300	WVHT	44122	2758	E5
4400	WVHT	44128	2758	E5
4800	BDHT	44128	2758	E7
4800	BDHT	44146	2758	E7
5500	BDHT	44146	2888	A1
5500	SLN	44139	2888	A1
25700	BDHT	44146	2887	E1
26000	SLN	44146	2888	A1
SR-175 E 260th St				
200	EUCL	44132	2373	E4
1500	EUCL	44117	2373	E5
1500	EUCL	44143	2373	E5
SR-175 Cannon Rd				
27200	BDHT	44146	2888	A2
27200	SLN	44139	2888	A2
27300	SLN	44146	2888	A2
SR-175 Richmond Rd				
-	EUCL	44132	2373	E7
100	EUCL	44117	2373	E7
100	EUCL	44143	2373	E7
100	RDHT	44117	2373	E6
100	RDHT	44143	2373	E6
300	RDHT	44143	2498	E1
700	LNHT	44124	2498	E7
700	LNHT	44143	2498	E5
1500	LNHT	44124	2628	E1
2000	BHWD	44122	2628	E7
2000	BHWD	44124	2628	E3
3000	BHWD	44122	2758	E3
3700	HIHL	44122	2758	E1
3700	WVHT	44122	2758	E1
4300	WVHT	44122	2758	E5
4400	WVHT	44128	2758	E5
4800	BDHT	44128	2758	E7
4800	BDHT	44146	2758	E7
5500	BDHT	44146	2888	A1
5500	SLN	44139	2888	A1

Block	City	ZIP	Map#	Grid
SR-175 Richmond Rd				
25700	BDHT	44146	2887	E1
26000	SLN	44146	2888	A1
SR-176				
-	CLEV	-	2754	E3
-	CLEV	-	2755	A5
1500	PRMA	44109	2754	D7
1500	PRMA	44134	2754	D7
4800	RchT	44286	3149	E6
4800	RchT	44286	3150	A7
4900	CLEV	44134	2754	D7
5300	BWHT	44147	3149	E6
5300	PRMA	44134	2883	E6
5300	RchT	44147	3149	E6
5300	RchT	44233	3149	E6
6300	PRMA	44131	2883	E4
6300	SVHL	44131	2883	E4
7400	PRMA	44131	3014	E3
7400	PRMA	44134	3014	E3
7400	SVHL	44131	3014	E3
7800	BWHT	44131	3014	E3
7800	BWHT	44134	3014	E3
7800	BWHT	44147	3014	E7
SR-176 Broadview Rd				
4800	RchT	44286	3149	E6
4800	RchT	44286	3150	A7
4900	CLEV	44109	2754	D7
4900	CLEV	44134	2754	D7
5000	PRMA	44134	2754	D7
5300	BWHT	44147	3149	E6
5300	PRMA	44134	2883	E6
5300	RchT	44147	3149	E5
5300	RchT	44233	3149	E6
6300	PRMA	44131	2883	E4
6300	SVHL	44131	2883	E4
7400	PRMA	44131	3014	E3
7400	PRMA	44134	3014	E3
7400	SVHL	44131	3014	E3
7800	BWHT	44131	3014	E3
7800	BWHT	44134	3014	E3
7800	BWHT	44147	3014	E7
SR-176 Brookpark Rd				
1500	CLEV	44109	2754	D7
1500	CLEV	44134	2754	D7
1500	PRMA	44109	2754	D7
1500	PRMA	44134	2754	D7
SR-176 Jennings Frwy				
-	CLEV	-	2754	E3
-	CLEV	-	2755	A5
SR-237				
-	BKPK	-	2751	E7
-	BKPK	-	2880	E1
-	CLEV	-	2880	E1
-	CLEV	44142	2880	D3
10	BERA	44017	2880	C5
200	BERA	44017	3011	B7
700	SGVL	44017	3011	B2
700	SGVL	44149	3011	B2
800	BERA	44142	2880	C4
800	BKPK	44142	2880	E1
1100	LKWD	44107	2622	A6
2300	CLEV	44107	2622	A7
3100	CLEV	44111	2622	B7
3100	LKWD	44111	2622	B7
3200	CLEV	44111	2752	B1
3900	CLEV	44135	2752	A5
4800	CLEV	44135	2751	E7
4900	BKPK	44135	2751	E7
4900	CLEV	44142	2751	E7
18200	BKPK	44135	2752	A7
18200	BKPK	44142	2752	A7
SR-237 W Bagley Rd				
10	BERA	44017	2880	C6
SR-237 Berea Frwy				
-	BKPK	-	2751	E7
-	BKPK	-	2880	E1
-	CLEV	-	2880	E1
-	CLEV	44142	2880	D3
SR-237 Brookpark Rd				
18200	BKPK	44135	2751	E7
18200	BKPK	44135	2752	A7
18200	BKPK	44142	2751	E7
18200	BKPK	44142	2752	A7
18200	CLEV	44135	2751	E7
18200	CLEV	44135	2752	A7
18200	CLEV	44142	2751	E7
SR-237 W Clifton Blvd				
1100	LKWD	44107	2622	A4
SR-237 Front St				
200	BERA	44017	2880	C6
SR-237 Henry St				
10	BERA	44017	2880	B7
SR-237 Kolthoff Dr				
6500	BERA	44017	2880	C4
6500	BERA	44142	2880	C4
6500	BKPK	44142	2880	C4
SR-237 Mulberry St				
200	BERA	44017	2880	C6
SR-237 Prospect Rd				
8500	BERA	44017	3011	B2
8500	SGVL	44017	3011	B2
8500	SGVL	44149	3011	B3
SR-237 Prospect St				
10	BERA	44017	2880	C5
200	BERA	44017	3011	B7
700	SGVL	44017	3011	B2
700	SGVL	44149	3011	B2
SR-237 Riverside Dr				
1500	LKWD	44107	2622	A6
2300	CLEV	44107	2622	A7
17100	CLEV	44111	2622	B7
17100	LKWD	44111	2622	B7
SR-237 Rocky River Dr				
3100	CLEV	44107	2622	B7
3100	CLEV	44111	2622	B7
3100	LKWD	44107	2622	B7
3100	LKWD	44111	2622	B7
3200	CLEV	44111	2752	B1
3900	CLEV	44135	2752	A5
4800	CLEV	44135	2751	E6
4900	BKPK	44135	2751	E7
4900	BKPK	44142	2751	E7
4900	CLEV	44142	2751	E7
SR-237 N Rocky River Dr				
800	BERA	44017	2880	C3
800	BERA	44142	2880	C4
800	BKPK	44142	2880	C4
SR-252				
10	ClbT	44028	3145	A5
10	LvpT	44028	3145	A5
10	LvpT	44280	3144	E7
10	LvpT	44280	3145	A5
300	BYVL	44140	2620	C5
600	WTLK	44140	2620	C5
600	WTLK	44145	2620	C7

Block	City	ZIP	Map#	Grid
SR-252				
1700	WTLK	44145	2750	D6
3200	NOSD	44070	2750	C7
3200	NOSD	44145	2750	C3
3200	WTLK	44070	2750	D6
5200	NOSD	44070	2879	C1
6200	OmsT	44070	2879	C2
6200	OmsT	44138	2879	C2
6600	ODFL	44138	2879	C7
9000	ODFL	44138	3010	B3
9700	ClbT	44028	3010	B3
9800	ClbT	44138	3010	B3
SR-252 Columbia Rd				
10	ClbT	44028	3145	A5
10	LvpT	44028	3145	A5
10	LvpT	44280	3144	E7
10	LvpT	44280	3145	A5
300	BYVL	44140	2620	C5
600	WTLK	44140	2620	C5
600	WTLK	44145	2620	C7
1700	WTLK	44145	2750	D6
3200	NOSD	44070	2750	D6
3200	NOSD	44145	2750	C3
3200	WTLK	44070	2750	D6
5900	NOSD	44070	2879	C2
6200	OmsT	44070	2879	C2
6200	OmsT	44138	2879	C2
8000	ODFL	44138	2879	B7
9000	ODFL	44138	3010	B1
9700	ClbT	44028	3010	B2
9700	ClbT	44138	3010	B2
SR-252 Great Northern Blvd				
4500	NOSD	44070	2750	C7
5200	NOSD	44070	2879	C1
SR-252 Lorain Rd				
24600	NOSD	44070	2750	C6
SR-252 Main St				
7900	ODFL	44138	2879	C5
SR-252 E River Rd				
9800	ClbT	44028	3010	A7
9800	ClbT	44138	3010	C2
9800	ODFL	44138	3010	C2
14000	ClbT	44028	3145	A5
17700	LvpT	44028	3145	A5
17700	LvpT	44280	3145	A5
SR-252 Sprague Rd				
24400	ClbT	44028	3010	B3
24400	ClbT	44138	3010	B3
24400	ODFL	44138	3010	B3
SR-254				
-	LKWD	44107	2621	E5
-	RKRV	44107	2621	E5
1300	LKWD	44107	2622	A4
2200	ShfT	44035	2746	E6
2200	ShfT	44055	2745	E6
2300	ShfT	44055	2746	A6
3200	SFLD	44035	2746	E5
3200	SFLD	44054	2746	E5
3200	ShfT	44035	2746	C6
3200	ShfT	44054	2746	C6
5400	AVON	44011	2747	A5
5400	SFLD	44011	2747	A5
5400	SFLD	44035	2747	A5
5400	SFLD	44054	2747	A5
19000	RKRV	44116	2621	C6
22800	WTLK	44116	2621	A6
22800	WTLK	44145	2621	B6
23300	WTLK	44145	2620	A7
27300	WTLK	44145	2619	C7
30400	WTLK	44145	2749	B1
31400	AVON	44145	2749	A1
32000	AVON	44011	2749	B1
32200	AVON	44011	2748	E1
SR-254 Detroit Rd				
-	LKWD	44107	2621	E5
-	RKRV	44107	2621	E5
4700	SFLD	44035	2746	E5
4700	SFLD	44054	2746	E5
5400	AVON	44011	2747	A5
5400	SFLD	44011	2747	A5
5400	SFLD	44035	2747	A5
5400	SFLD	44054	2747	A5
19000	RKRV	44116	2621	C6
22800	WTLK	44116	2621	A6
22800	WTLK	44145	2621	B6
23300	WTLK	44145	2620	A7
27300	WTLK	44145	2619	C7
30400	WTLK	44145	2749	B1
31400	AVON	44145	2749	A1
32000	AVON	44011	2749	B1
32200	AVON	44011	2748	E1
SR-254 North Ridge Rd E				
2200	ShfT	44035	2745	E6
2200	ShfT	44055	2745	E6
2300	ShfT	44055	2746	A6
3200	SFLD	44035	2746	C6
3200	SFLD	44054	2746	C6
3200	ShfT	44035	2746	C6
3200	ShfT	44054	2746	C6
SR-254 Sloane Av				
1300	LKWD	44107	2622	A4
SR-283				
-	PNVL	44077	2039	E7
10	PnvT	44077	2040	A7
100	GDRV	44077	2039	C6
300	PnvT	44077	2039	C6
600	MNTR	44060	2039	C6
600	PnvT	44060	2039	B7
5500	MONT	44060	2143	E1
6100	MNTR	44060	2143	E3
8000	MNTR	44060	2144	A1
8000	MONT	44060	2144	E1
9100	MNTR	44060	2038	E7
13600	BTNH	44108	2497	A1
13600	BTNH	44110	2497	A1
13700	BTNH	44108	2372	A7
13700	BTNH	44110	2372	A7
13700	CLEV	44110	2372	A7
16900	CLEV	44119	2372	D6
18400	EUCL	44119	2372	E4
19500	EUCL	44119	2373	A3
19900	EUCL	44123	2373	C1
24800	EUCL	44132	2373	D1
25700	EUCL	44132	2248	E7
27200	EUCL	44132	2249	A7
28100	WLWK	44095	2249	C5
33000	ETLK	44095	2249	D3
33500	LKLN	44095	2249	D3
34400	TMLK	44095	2249	E2
34700	ETLK	44095	2250	C1
34700	TMLK	44095	2250	A2
35900	ETLK	44095	2142	C7
37700	WLBY	44094	2142	E5
37700	WLBY	44095	2142	E5

Block	City	ZIP	Map#	Grid
SR-283				
38400	WLBY	44094	2143	E1
38800	MNTR	44094	2143	B4
SR-283 Andrews Rd				
5500	MONT	44060	2143	E1
6100	MNTR	44060	2143	E3
SR-283 Lake Shore Blvd				
500	PnvT	44077	2039	C6
600	MNTR	44060	2039	C6
600	PnvT	44060	2039	B7
7000	MNTR	44060	2143	B4
7700	MONT	44060	2143	E1
8000	MNTR	44060	2144	A1
8000	MONT	44060	2144	E1
9100	MNTR	44060	2038	E7
13600	BTNH	44108	2497	A1
13600	BTNH	44110	2497	A1
13700	BTNH	44108	2372	A7
13700	BTNH	44110	2372	A7
13700	CLEV	44110	2372	A7
16900	CLEV	44119	2372	D6
18400	EUCL	44119	2372	E4
19500	EUCL	44119	2373	A3
19900	EUCL	44123	2373	C1
24800	EUCL	44132	2373	D1
25700	EUCL	44132	2248	E7
27200	EUCL	44132	2249	A7
28100	WLWK	44095	2249	C5
33000	ETLK	44095	2249	D3
33500	LKLN	44095	2249	D3
34400	TMLK	44095	2249	E2
34700	ETLK	44095	2250	C1
34700	TMLK	44095	2250	A2
35900	ETLK	44095	2142	C7
37700	WLBY	44094	2142	E5
37700	WLBY	44095	2142	E5
38400	WLBY	44094	2143	E1
38800	MNTR	44094	2143	B4
SR-283 Richmond Rd				
800	PNVL	44077	2039	E7
800	PnvT	44077	2039	E7
1000	GDRV	44077	2039	D6
SR-283 Richmond St				
-	PNVL	44077	2039	E7
10	PnvT	44077	2040	A7
600	PnvT	44077	2039	E7
SR-283 River St				
600	GDRV	44077	2039	C6
700	PnvT	44077	2039	C6
SR-283 Singer Av				
100	GDRV	44077	2039	C6
300	PnvT	44077	2039	C6
SR-291				
5000	BKPK	44135	2752	A7
5000	BKPK	44142	2752	A7
5000	BKPK	44142	2881	A1
5000	CLEV	44135	2752	A7
6400	MDBH	44130	2881	A6
6400	MDBH	44142	2881	A4
7500	MDBH	44130	3012	B1
SR-291 Engle Rd				
5000	BKPK	44135	2752	A7
5000	BKPK	44142	2752	A7
5000	BKPK	44142	2881	A1
5000	CLEV	44135	2752	A7
6400	MDBH	44130	2881	A6
6400	MDBH	44142	2881	A4
7500	MDBH	44130	3012	A1
SR-291 Fowles Rd				
16600	MDBH	44130	3012	A1
SR-301				
-	CrlT	-	3006	E4
-	CrlT	44044	3140	E3
-	CrlT	44050	3140	E6
-	EatT	44035	3006	E3
-	EatT	44044	3006	E4
-	ELYR	44035	3006	E1
-	LrgT	44050	3140	E5
100	SDLK	44054	2616	E2
400	ELYR	44035	2875	E7
500	SFLD	44054	2616	E7
800	ELYR	44035	2746	E6
1200	SFLD	44035	2746	E6
2300	SFLD	44054	2746	E2
11900	CrlT	44035	3005	E7
11900	CrlT	44050	3005	E6
SR-301 Abbe Rd				
100	SDLK	44054	2616	E2
500	SFLD	44054	2616	E7
2300	SFLD	44035	2746	E2
4400	SFLD	44035	2745	E5
SR-301 N Abbe Rd				
400	ELYR	44035	2875	E2
800	ELYR	44035	2746	E6
1200	SFLD	44035	2746	E6
5000	SFLD	44054	2746	E5
SR-301 S East Byp				
-	EatT	44035	3006	E3
-	EatT	44044	3006	E4
-	ELYR	44035	2875	E7
-	ELYR	44035	3006	E1
SR-301 John F Kennedy Mem Pkwy				
-	ELYR	44035	2875	E4
SR-301 Lagrange Rd				
-	CrlT	44050	3140	E6
11900	CrlT	44035	3005	E7
11900	CrlT	44050	3005	E6
SR-301 Lattasburg Elyria Rd				
-	CrlT	44044	3140	E3
-	CrlT	44050	3140	E1
-	LrgT	44050	3140	E5
SR-305				
6900	HRM	44234	3161	B2
6900	HrmT	44234	3161	B2
7100	HrmT	44231	3161	E2
SR-305 E Wakefield Rd				
6900	HRM	44234	3161	B2
6900	HrmT	44234	3161	B2
7100	HrmT	44231	3161	E2
SR-306				
-	WLBY	44060	2251	D7
-	WLBY	44094	2251	D7
10	AURA	44202	3021	E7
10	AURA	44202	3156	E1
500	AURA	44202	3022	A5
1000	AURA	44023	3022	A3
1000	BbgT	44023	3022	A3
5000	SRSL	44022	2762	A5
5200	BbgT	44022	2762	A7
5200	BbgT	44023	2762	A7
6200	MNTR	44060	2143	C7
7300	MNTR	44060	2251	C1
8800	KTLD	44094	2251	D6

Block	City	ZIP	Map#	Grid
SR-306				
9100	KTLD	44094	2376	E2
9700	KTLD	44094	2377	A7
11000	CsTp	44026	2502	B7
11000	CsTp	44094	2502	A2
11000	KTLD	44094	2502	A2
12700	CsTp	44026	2632	B1
13400	CsTp	44072	2632	A3
13400	RslT	44072	2632	A6
14600	RslT	44072	2762	A7
15000	RslT	44022	2762	A3
16400	BbgT	44023	2891	A6
SR-306 Broadmoor Rd				
-	WLBY	44060	2251	D7
-	WLBY	44094	2251	D7
8000	MNTR	44060	2251	D7
SR-306 Chillicothe Rd				
5000	SRSL	44022	2762	A5
5200	BbgT	44022	2762	A7
5200	BbgT	44023	2762	A7
8800	KTLD	44094	2251	D6
9100	KTLD	44094	2376	E2
9700	KTLD	44094	2377	A7
11000	CsTp	44026	2502	B7
11000	CsTp	44094	2502	A2
11000	KTLD	44094	2502	A2
12700	CsTp	44026	2632	B1
13400	CsTp	44072	2632	A3
13400	RslT	44072	2632	A6
14600	RslT	44072	2762	A7
15000	RslT	44022	2762	A3
16400	BbgT	44023	2891	A6
18400	BbgT	44023	3022	A3
18900	AURA	44023	3022	A3
18900	AURA	44202	3022	A3
SR-306 N Chillicothe Rd				
10	AURA	44202	3021	E7
10	AURA	44202	3156	E1
500	AURA	44202	3022	A5
1000	AURA	44023	3022	A3
1000	BbgT	44023	3022	A3
SR-306 S Chillicothe Rd				
10	AURA	44202	3156	E1
SR-306 Reynolds Rd				
6200	MNTR	44060	2143	C7
7300	MNTR	44060	2251	C1
SR-307				
6700	MadT	44057	2044	E3
6700	MDSN	44057	2044	E3
SR-307 Warner Rd				
6700	MadT	44057	2044	E3
6700	MDSN	44057	2044	E3
SR-511				
10	OBLN	44074	3138	E2
200	OBLN	44074	3139	A2
300	NRsT	44074	3138	A2
600	NRsT	44074	3139	D2
SR-511 Cleveland Oberlin Rd				
-	OBLN	44074	3139	C2
43700	NRsT	44074	3139	D2
SR-511 E Lorain St				
10	OBLN	44074	3138	E2
200	OBLN	44074	3139	A2
600	NRsT	44074	3139	B2
SR-511 W Lorain St				
10	OBLN	44074	3138	E2
300	NRsT	44074	3138	C2
SR-528				
10	MDSN	44057	2044	B1
200	MDSN	44057	1942	B7
800	MadT	44057	1942	B7
4300	MadT	44057	2044	B1
15900	MdfT	44062	2767	E7
15900	PkmT	44062	2767	E7
SR-528 Chardon-Madison Rd				
4300	MadT	44057	2044	B1
4300	MDSN	44057	2044	B3
SR-528 Hubbard Rd				
2700	MadT	44057	1942	B7
2700	MDSN	44057	1942	B7
SR-528 N Lake St				
10	MDSN	44057	2044	B1
200	MDSN	44057	1942	B7
800	MadT	44057	1942	B6
SR-528 Madison Rd				
15900	MdfT	44062	2767	E7
15900	PkmT	44062	2767	E7
SR-528 W Main St				
10	MDSN	44057	2044	B1
SR-528 River St				
10	MDSN	44057	2044	B1
SR-534				
10	GNVA	44041	1944	B4
500	GnvT	44041	1944	C2
2200	HpfT	44041	1944	C7
SR-534 N Broadway				
10	GNVA	44041	1944	C4
500	GnvT	44041	1944	C2
SR-534 S Broadway				
10	GNVA	44041	1944	B4
SR-534 N Broadway St				
700	GNVA	44041	1944	C2
700	GnvT	44041	1944	C2
SR-534 S Broadway St				
1200	GNVA	44041	1944	C6
SR-535				
10	PnvT	44077	2040	B3
500	FTHR	44077	2039	D5
600	PNVL	44077	2039	E7
600	PnvT	44077	2039	E7
SR-535 East St				
600	FTHR	44077	2039	D5
SR-535 Fairport Nursery Rd				
10	PnvT	44077	2040	B3
500	FTHR	44077	2039	D4
500	PnvT	44077	2039	E3
SR-535 Richmond St				
600	PNVL	44077	2039	E7
600	PnvT	44077	2039	E7
900	FTHR	44077	2039	D6
SR-608				
8400	CcdT	44024	2255	C5
8400	HmbT	44024	2255	D6
8400	HmbT	44077	2255	C5
8800	HmbT	44024	2380	E1
8800	HmbT	44024	2381	C6
10900	ClrT	44024	2506	C2
10900	HmbT	44024	2506	C2
11500	CcdT	44077	2146	D7
11500	CcdT	44077	2254	E1
11900	CcdT	44077	2255	B4
12100	ClrT	44021	2506	E6

Block	City	ZIP	Map#	Grid
SR-608				
12100	ClrT	44046	2506	E6
12600	ClrT	44021	2636	E1
12600	ClrT	44046	2636	E1
12800	ClrT	44021	2637	A2
12800	ClrT	44046	2637	A2
13400	HtbT	44021	2637	A3
13400	HtbT	44046	2637	A3
13500	MdfT	44021	2637	C5
13500	MdfT	44046	2637	B5
13600	MdfT	44062	2637	B5
14300	MdfT	44062	2767	D1
14700	MDFD	44062	2767	D3
SR-608 Concord-Hambden Rd				
11500	CcdT	44077	2146	D7
11500	CcdT	44077	2254	E1
11900	CcdT	44077	2255	B4
12700	CcdT	44024	2255	C5
12700	HmbT	44024	2255	C5
12700	HmbT	44077	2255	C5
SR-608 Old State Rd				
8400	CcdT	44024	2255	C5
8400	CcdT	44077	2255	C5
8400	HmbT	44024	2255	D6
8400	HmbT	44077	2255	C5
8800	HmbT	44024	2380	E1
8800	HmbT	44024	2381	C6
10900	ClrT	44024	2506	C2
10900	HmbT	44024	2506	C2
12100	ClrT	44021	2506	E6
12100	ClrT	44046	2506	E6
12600	ClrT	44021	2636	E1
12600	ClrT	44046	2636	E1
12800	ClrT	44021	2637	A2
12800	ClrT	44046	2637	A2
13400	HtbT	44021	2637	A3
13400	HtbT	44046	2637	A3
13500	MdfT	44021	2637	B5
13500	MdfT	44046	2637	B5
13600	MdfT	44062	2637	B5
14300	MdfT	44062	2767	D1
15000	MDFD	44062	2767	D4
SR-608 N State Av				
14700	MDFD	44062	2767	D1
14700	MdfT	44062	2767	D1
SR-608 S State Av				
14900	MDFD	44062	2767	D3
15300	MdfT	44062	2767	D4
SR-611				
-	LORN	44053	2743	D2
-	LORN	44054	2615	D7
100	LORN	44052	2744	D1
100	LORN	44052	2745	A1
1400	LORN	44052	2615	D7
2300	LORN	44053	2744	A1
3500	SFLD	44054	2615	E7
3900	SFLD	44054	2616	C7
5300	AVON	44011	2617	C7
5300	SFLD	44011	2617	B7
5300	SFLD	44054	2617	B7
37000	AVON	44011	2747	D1
SR-611 E 21st St				
100	LORN	44052	2745	A1
SR-611 W 21st St				
100	LORN	44052	2744	D1
2300	LORN	44053	2744	A1
3300	LORN	44053	2743	E2
SR-611 Colorado Av				
-	LORN	44054	2615	D7
1400	LORN	44052	2615	D7
3500	SFLD	44054	2615	E7
3900	SFLD	44054	2616	C7
5300	AVON	44011	2617	B7
5300	SFLD	44011	2617	B7
5300	SFLD	44054	2617	B7
37000	AVON	44011	2747	D1
SR-611 Henderson Dr				
1700	LORN	44052	2615	B7
2000	LORN	44052	2745	A1
SR-615				
-	KDHL	44060	2251	E6
-	KDHL	44094	2251	E6
-	KTLD	44060	2251	E6
6300	MNTR	44060	2144	B7
7300	MNTR	44060	2252	B1
7700	MNTR	44060	2143	E3
7700	MONT	44060	2143	E3
8200	KDHL	44060	2252	A5
8400	KDHL	44094	2252	A5
8400	KTLD	44060	2252	A5
8400	KTLD	44094	2252	A5
8800	KTLD	44094	2251	E6
SR-615 Center St				
6300	MNTR	44060	2144	B7
7300	MNTR	44060	2252	B1
8200	KDHL	44060	2252	B4
SR-615 Chillicothe Rd				
-	KDHL	44060	2251	E6
-	KDHL	44094	2251	E6
-	KTLD	44060	2251	E6
8400	KDHL	44060	2252	A5
8400	KDHL	44094	2252	A5
8400	KTLD	44060	2252	A5
8400	KTLD	44094	2252	A5
8800	KTLD	44094	2251	E6
SR-615 Munson Rd				
7700	MNTR	44060	2143	E3
7700	MONT	44060	2143	E3
8000	MNTR	44060	2144	A3
SR-633				
200	EUCL	44132	2249	A7
400	EUCL	44132	2374	B2
400	WKLF	44092	2374	B2
SR-633 Lloyd Rd				
200	EUCL	44132	2249	A7
400	EUCL	44132	2374	B2
400	WKLF	44092	2374	B2
SR-640				
31000	WLWK	44095	2249	E5
32500	ETLK	44095	2249	E4
33700	ETLK	44095	2250	A5
36300	ETLK	44094	2250	B5
36300	WLBY	44094	2250	B5
SR-640 Vine St				
31000	WLWK	44095	2249	E5
32500	ETLK	44095	2249	E4
33700	ETLK	44095	2250	A5
36300	ETLK	44094	2250	B5
36300	WLBY	44094	2250	B5
SR-700				
-	BURT	44021	2766	B1
10000	FdmT	44255	3161	A7
10000	HrmT	44231	3161	A7
10000	HrmT	44255	3161	A7

Block	City	ZIP	Map#	Grid
SR-700				
10800	HrmT	44234	3161	A7
11300	HRM	44234	3161	A3
14400	BtnT	44021	2766	B5
14400	BtnT	44062	2766	B2
16000	TroT	44021	2766	A7
SR-700 Burton Limaville Rd S				
10000	FdmT	44255	3161	A7
10000	HrmT	44231	3161	A7
10000	HrmT	44255	3161	A7
SR-700 S Cheshire Rd				
-	BtnT	44021	2766	B2
-	BtnT	44062	2766	B2
-	BURT	44021	2766	B2
SR-700 S Cheshire St				
-	BURT	44021	2766	B1
14700	BtnT	44021	2766	B2
14700	BtnT	44062	2766	B2
SR-700 Claridon Troy Rd				
14400	BtnT	44021	2766	B5
14400	BtnT	44062	2766	B2
16000	TroT	44021	2766	A7
SR-700 Garfield Rd				
11400	HRM	44234	3161	A2
11900	HrmT	44234	3161	A1
SR-700 Tavern Rd				
14800	BtnT	44021	2766	B2
14800	BtnT	44062	2766	B2
14800	BURT	44021	2766	B2
SR-700 Welshfield Limavle Rd S				
10400	FdmT	44255	3161	A7
10400	HrmT	44231	3161	A6
10400	HrmT	44255	3161	A7
11300	HRM	44234	3161	A3
11900	HrmT	44234	3161	A1
US-6				
-	CLEV	44102	2624	A4
-	LKWD	44107	2621	E4
-	RKRV	44107	2621	E4
10	CLEV	44114	2624	E2
100	CLEV	44113	2624	C4
100	CLEV	44115	2624	E3
100	CRDN	44024	2380	A6
100	LORN	44052	2614	C7
200	CRDN	44024	2379	E6
400	HmbT	44024	2380	E4
600	CdnT	44024	2379	B6
800	LORN	44052	2615	A5
1200	CLEV	44114	2625	D1
1600	LORN	44053	2742	C4
1600	VMLN	44053	2742	C4
1600	VMLN	44089	2742	B5
2300	LORN	44052	2614	B7
2700	LORN	44053	2744	A1
3100	LORN	44053	2743	B3
3500	LORN	44054	2615	D4
3500	SDLK	44054	2615	C4
3800	CLEV	44103	2625	C1
3800	SDLK	44054	2616	A3
4500	VMLN	44089	2741	B5
5100	CLEV	44103	2495	E7
5100	VMLN	44089	2740	E5
5400	SDLK	44054	2617	A2
5500	AVLK	44012	2617	B2
5500	SDLK	44012	2617	A2
7000	KTLD	44094	2376	B6
7000	WBHL	44094	2376	A5
7100	CLEV	44103	2496	A7
8200	KTLD	44094	2377	A6
8300	CLEV	44106	2496	A7
8300	CLEV	44108	2496	A7
9200	CLEV	44102	2623	C5
9600	CdnT	44024	2378	A7
9600	CdnT	44094	2378	A7
9600	KTLD	44094	2378	B6
11600	LKWD	44102	2623	B4
11600	LKWD	44107	2623	B4
12400	CLEV	44112	2496	E7
12400	ECLE	44112	2496	E7
12500	VmnT	44089	2740	A7
12900	LKWD	44107	2622	E4
13500	ECLE	44112	2497	C4
13500	HmbT	44024	2381	A4
16300	CLEV	44112	2497	C4
18000	CLEV	44121	2497	D2
18400	CLEV	44117	2497	E2
18400	EUCL	44117	2497	E2
19200	RKRV	44116	2621	E5
19600	EUCL	44117	2498	A1
20400	EUCL	44143	2498	A1
22800	BYVL	44116	2621	A5
22800	BYVL	44140	2621	D5
23400	BYVL	44140	2620	A4
23800	RDHT	44143	2498	C1
24400	RDHT	44143	2373	D7
26500	RDHT	44143	2374	A6
27200	WBHL	44092	2374	D6
27500	BYVL	44140	2619	E4
29300	WBHL	44094	2374	D6
31400	AVLK	44012	2619	B2
31400	AVLK	44140	2619	A2
31700	AVLK	44012	2618	D1
31900	WBHL	44094	2375	A5
32000	AVLK	44012	2488	B7
32800	AVLK	44012	2487	E7
US-6 W 25th St				
-	CLEV	44113	2624	C4
US-6 Buckley Blvd				
-	CLEV	44113	2624	C4
US-6 Center St				
100	CRDN	44024	2380	A6
US-6 Chardon Rd				
7000	KTLD	44094	2376	B6
7000	WBHL	44094	2376	A5
8200	KTLD	44094	2377	A6
9600	CdnT	44024	2378	A7
9600	CdnT	44094	2378	A7
9600	KTLD	44094	2378	B6
10800	CdnT	44024	2379	B6
11100	CRDN	44024	2379	B6
21000	EUCL	44117	2498	C1
23500	EUCL	44143	2498	C1
23800	RDHT	44143	2498	C1
24400	RDHT	44143	2373	D7
26500	RDHT	44143	2374	A6
27200	WBHL	44092	2374	D6
29300	WBHL	44094	2374	D6
31900	WBHL	44094	2375	A5
US-6 Cleveland Mem Shoreway				
-	CLEV	44102	2623	E4
-	CLEV	44102	2624	A4
-	CLEV	44113	2624	C4

STREET Block	City	ZIP	Map#	Grid
US-6 Clifton Blvd				
-	LKWD	44107	2621	E4
-	RKRV	44107	2621	E4
-	RKRV	44116	2621	E4
9200	CLEV	44102	2623	C5
11600	LKWD	44102	2623	B4
11600	LKWD	44107	2623	B4
12900	LKWD	44107	2622	E4
US-6 Detroit Av				
2400	CLEV	44113	2624	C4
US-6 E Erie Av				
100	LORN	44052	2614	E6
800	LORN	44052	2615	A5
3500	LORN	44054	2615	D4
3500	SDLK	44054	2615	D4
US-6 W Erie Av				
100	LORN	44052	2614	C7
2300	LORN	44053	2614	B7
2700	LORN	44053	2744	A1
3100	LORN	44053	2743	B3
6100	LORN	44053	2742	E4
8000	VMLN	44053	2742	C4
8000	VMLN	44089	2742	C4
US-6 E Erie Br				
-	LORN	44052	2614	D6
US-6 Euclid Av				
13500	ECLE	44112	2497	C4
16300	CLEV	44112	2497	C4
18000	CLEV	44121	2497	D2
18400	CLEV	44117	2497	E2
18400	EUCL	44117	2497	E2
19600	EUCL	44117	2498	A1
20400	EUCL	44143	2498	A1
US-6 Gar Hwy				
12500	CRDN	44024	2380	B6
US-6 GAR Hwy				
12700	HmbT	44024	2380	E4
13500	HmbT	44024	2381	A4
US-6 N Hambden St				
100	CRDN	44024	2380	A6
400	HmbT	44024	2380	B6
US-6 S Hambden St				
100	CRDN	44024	2380	A6
US-6 Lake Rd				
19200	RKRV	44116	2621	E5
22800	BYVL	44116	2621	A5
22800	BYVL	44140	2621	D5
23400	BYVL	44140	2620	A4
27500	BYVL	44140	2619	E4
31400	AVLK	44012	2619	B2
31400	AVLK	44140	2619	A2
31700	AVLK	44012	2618	D1
32000	AVLK	44012	2488	B7
32800	AVLK	44012	2487	E7
32900	AVLK	44012	2617	B2
33700	SDLK	44012	2617	A2
33700	SDLK	44054	2617	A2
US-6 E Lake Rd				
-	LORN	44052	2615	D4
-	LORN	44054	2615	D4
3500	SDLK	44054	2615	C4
3800	SDLK	44054	2616	A3
5400	SDLK	44054	2617	A2
5500	AVLK	44012	2617	A2
5500	SDLK	44012	2617	A2
US-6 W Lake Rd				
12500	VmnT	44089	2740	A7
14200	VMLN	44089	2740	C6
US-6 Liberty Av				
1600	LORN	44053	2742	C4
1600	VMLN	44053	2742	C4
1600	VMLN	44089	2742	A5
4500	VMLN	44089	2741	B5
5100	VMLN	44089	2740	E5
US-6 Main St				
100	CRDN	44024	2380	A6
US-6 E Park St				
100	CRDN	44024	2380	A6
US-6 Superior Av				
-	CLEV	44113	2624	D3
4000	CLEV	44103	2625	C1
4000	CLEV	44114	2625	C1
5100	CLEV	44103	2495	D7
7100	CLEV	44103	2496	A7
8300	CLEV	44106	2496	A7
8300	CLEV	44108	2496	A7
12400	CLEV	44112	2496	E7
12400	ECLE	44112	2496	E7
US-6 Superior Av E				
10	CLEV	44114	2624	E2
1200	CLEV	44114	2625	D1
3800	CLEV	44103	2625	C1
US-6 W Superior Av				
100	CLEV	44113	2624	E3
100	CLEV	44114	2624	E3
100	CLEV	44115	2624	E3
US-6 Water St				
100	CRDN	44024	2380	A6
200	CRDN	44024	2379	E6
600	CdnT	44024	2379	C6
US-20				
-	CLEV	44102	2624	A4
-	CrlT	-	3005	C7
-	CrlT	-	3006	E4
-	CrlT	-	3139	E2
-	CrlT	-	3140	A1
-	EatT	-	3006	E4
-	ELYR	44035	2875	E7
-	ELYR	44035	3006	E1
-	LKWD	44107	2621	E5
-	NRsT	44074	3139	A6
-	OBLN	44074	3138	B6
-	PtfT	44074	3138	B6
-	PtfT	44074	3139	A6
-	RKRV	44107	2621	E5
10	CLEV	44114	2624	E3
10	CLEV	44115	2624	E3
10	GNVA	44041	1944	E3
10	PNVL	44077	2040	E4
10	PNVL	44077	2146	A1
200	CLEV	44113	2624	C4
400	PnvT	44077	2040	C6
500	PNVL	44077	2145	E2
900	CLEV	44114	2625	E2
900	ELYR	44039	2875	E4
900	GnvT	44041	1944	D3
900	NRDV	44039	2875	E4
1100	LKWD	44107	2622	A5
1100	PnvT	44077	2145	D3
1200	CLEV	44115	2625	A3
1500	RKRV	44116	2621	D7
1700	PnvT	44077	2041	C2
2100	MNTR	44060	2145	D3
2100	PnvT	44060	2145	B6
2400	PryT	44077	2041	B3
US-20				
2400	PryT	44081	2041	B3
2500	LKWD	44126	2621	E7
2500	RKRV	44126	2621	E7
3400	PryT	44081	1940	A7
3600	CLEV	44103	2625	C2
3700	NPRY	44081	1940	E6
4000	WLBY	44094	2250	A7
4700	MadT	44057	1941	C5
4700	MadT	44081	1941	C5
4700	NPRY	44081	1941	C5
4700	PryT	44081	1941	C5
5900	GnvT	44041	1943	B4
6200	MadT	44057	1942	B4
6700	GnvT	44057	1943	B4
7000	MNTR	44060	2251	C3
7000	MNTR	44094	2251	B4
7000	WLBY	44060	2251	B4
7000	WLBY	44094	2251	B4
7300	CLEV	44103	2626	A2
7500	MadT	44057	1943	A5
8000	MNTR	44060	2252	A1
8400	CLEV	44106	2626	C2
8700	MNTR	44060	2144	D7
9200	CLEV	44102	2623	C5
11600	LKWD	44102	2623	B4
11600	LKWD	44107	2623	B4
12200	ECLE	44106	2626	E1
12400	ECLE	44112	2626	E1
12500	ECLE	44112	2496	E7
13500	ECLE	44112	2497	C4
16300	CLEV	44112	2497	C4
18000	CLEV	44121	2497	D2
18400	CLEV	44117	2497	E2
18400	EUCL	44117	2497	E2
19600	EUCL	44117	2498	A1
20400	EUCL	44143	2498	A1
20600	FWPK	44116	2751	C1
20600	FWPK	44126	2751	C1
20600	RKRV	44116	2751	B1
20700	EUCL	44117	2373	B7
22800	WTLK	44116	2751	A1
22800	WTLK	44145	2751	A1
23100	WTLK	44145	2750	A2
25400	EUCL	44132	2373	E4
26000	EUCL	44143	2373	E4
27000	EUCL	44132	2374	D1
27200	WTLK	44145	2749	A6
28300	WKLF	44092	2374	A4
30300	WLWK	44092	2374	D1
30500	WKLF	44092	2249	E7
30500	WLWK	44092	2249	E7
30700	WKLF	44094	2249	E7
30700	WLBY	44094	2249	E7
31400	NRDV	44039	2749	A7
31400	NRDV	44145	2749	A7
31600	NRDV	44039	2748	E7
31600	NRDV	44039	2877	B3
36100	NRDV	44039	2876	E3
US-20 W 25th St				
-	CLEV	44113	2624	C4
US-20 Buckley Blvd				
-	CLEV	44113	2624	C4
US-20 Casement Av				
400	PnvT	44077	2040	C6
US-20 Center Ridge Rd				
19400	RKRV	44116	2621	D7
20600	FWPK	44116	2751	C1
20600	FWPK	44126	2751	C1
20600	RKRV	44116	2751	B1
22800	WTLK	44116	2751	A1
22800	WTLK	44145	2751	A1
23100	WTLK	44145	2750	A2
27200	WTLK	44145	2749	A6
31400	NRDV	44039	2749	A7
31400	NRDV	44145	2749	A7
31600	NRDV	44039	2748	E7
31600	NRDV	44039	2877	B3
36100	NRDV	44039	2876	E3
US-20 Cleveland St				
700	ELYR	44035	2875	E5
900	ELYR	44039	2875	E4
900	NRDV	44039	2875	E4
US-20 Cleveland Mem Shoreway				
-	CLEV	44102	2623	E4
-	CLEV	44102	2624	A4
-	CLEV	44113	2624	C4
US-20 Clifton Blvd				
9200	CLEV	44102	2623	C5
11600	LKWD	44102	2623	B4
11600	LKWD	44107	2623	B4
12900	LKWD	44107	2622	E4
US-20 W Clifton Blvd				
1100	LKWD	44107	2622	A4
US-20 Detroit Av				
2400	CLEV	44113	2624	C4
US-20 Detroit Rd				
-	LKWD	44107	2621	E5
-	RKRV	44107	2621	E5
-	RKRV	44116	2621	E5
US-20 S East Byp				
-	EatT	44035	3006	E3
-	EatT	44044	3006	E4
-	ELYR	44035	2875	E7
-	ELYR	44035	3006	E1
US-20 Erie St				
4000	WLBY	44094	2250	E5
US-20 E Erie St				
10	PNVL	44077	2040	E4
800	PnvT	44077	2040	C6
US-20 W Erie St				
10	PNVL	44077	2146	A1
US-20 Euclid Av				
100	CLEV	44114	2624	E3
100	CLEV	44115	2624	E3
900	CLEV	44114	2625	E2
1200	CLEV	44115	2625	A3
3600	CLEV	44103	2625	C2
7300	CLEV	44103	2626	A2
8400	CLEV	44106	2626	C2
12200	ECLE	44106	2626	E1
12400	ECLE	44112	2626	E1
12500	ECLE	44112	2496	E7
13500	ECLE	44112	2497	C4
16300	CLEV	44112	2497	C4
18000	CLEV	44121	2497	D2
18400	CLEV	44117	2497	E2
18400	EUCL	44117	2497	E2
19600	EUCL	44117	2498	A1
20400	EUCL	44143	2498	A1
20700	EUCL	44117	2373	B7
25400	EUCL	44132	2373	E4
26000	EUCL	44143	2373	E4
27000	EUCL	44132	2374	D1
US-20 Euclid Av				
28300	WKLF	44092	2374	A4
30300	WLWK	44092	2374	D1
30500	WKLF	44092	2249	E7
30500	WLWK	44092	2249	E7
30700	WKLF	44094	2249	E7
30700	WLBY	44094	2249	E7
34000	WLBY	44094	2250	A7
US-20 Kipton East Rd				
-	NRsT	44074	3139	A6
-	OBLN	44074	3138	B6
-	PtfT	44074	3138	B6
-	PtfT	44074	3139	A6
US-20 E Main St				
10	GNVA	44041	1944	C4
900	GnvT	44041	1944	D3
US-20 W Main St				
10	GNVA	44041	1944	E3
1000	GnvT	44041	1944	A4
US-20 Mentor Av				
100	PNVL	44077	2146	A1
500	PNVL	44077	2145	E2
1100	PnvT	44077	2145	D3
2100	MNTR	44060	2145	D3
2100	PnvT	44060	2145	B6
7000	MNTR	44060	2251	C3
7000	MNTR	44094	2251	B4
7000	WLBY	44060	2251	B4
7000	WLBY	44094	2251	B4
8000	MNTR	44060	2252	A1
8700	MNTR	44060	2144	D7
38100	WLBY	44094	2250	E5
US-20 Public Sq				
10	CLEV	44113	2624	E3
10	CLEV	44114	2624	E3
10	CLEV	44115	2624	E3
US-20 N Ridge Rd				
1200	PnvT	44077	2040	D5
1700	PnvT	44077	2041	C2
2400	PryT	44077	2041	B3
2400	PryT	44081	2041	B3
3400	PryT	44081	1940	A7
3700	NPRY	44081	1940	E6
4700	MadT	44057	1941	C5
4700	MadT	44081	1941	C5
4700	NPRY	44081	1941	C5
4700	PryT	44081	1941	C5
6200	MadT	44057	1942	B4
7500	GnvT	44041	1943	B4
7500	GnvT	44057	1943	B4
7500	MadT	44057	1943	A5
US-20 N Ridge Rd E				
4500	GnvT	44041	1944	E3
US-20 N Ridge Rd W				
5900	GnvT	44041	1943	B4
6700	GnvT	44057	1943	B4
US-20 River St				
4100	WLBY	44094	2250	E5
US-20 Sloane Av				
1300	LKWD	44107	2622	A5
US-20 Superior Av				
-	CLEV	44113	2624	D3
US-20 Superior Av E				
10	CLEV	44114	2624	E3
US-20 W Superior Av				
100	CLEV	44113	2624	E3
100	CLEV	44114	2624	E3
100	CLEV	44115	2624	E3
US-20 Wooster Rd				
1500	RKRV	44116	2621	E5
2500	LKWD	44126	2621	E7
2500	RKRV	44126	2621	E7
US-42				
10	BHIT	44212	3146	D7
10	BNWK	44136	3146	D5
10	BNWK	44149	3146	D5
10	BNWK	44212	3146	D7
10	SGVL	44136	3146	D5
10	SGVL	44149	3146	D5
1400	CLEV	44113	2624	D7
3000	CLEV	44109	2624	D7
3200	CLEV	44109	2754	A7
4500	CLEV	44144	2754	C5
5000	CLEV	44129	2754	A7
5000	PRMA	44109	2754	A7
5000	PRMA	44129	2754	A7
5300	PRMA	44129	2753	E7
5300	PRMA	44129	2882	E1
5700	PRMA	44130	2882	D2
5800	PMHT	44129	2882	D2
5800	PMHT	44130	2882	B4
6600	MDBH	44130	2881	D6
6600	PMHT	44130	2881	E5
7400	MDBH	44130	3012	B1
7700	SGVL	44130	3012	A2
7700	SGVL	44136	3012	A2
7700	SGVL	44149	3012	A2
9100	SGVL	44136	3011	D7
9100	SGVL	44149	3011	D7
US-42 W 25th St				
1400	CLEV	44113	2624	D7
3000	CLEV	44109	2624	D7
3200	CLEV	44109	2754	D1
US-42 Pearl Rd				
10	BHIT	44212	3146	D7
10	BNWK	44136	3146	D5
10	BNWK	44149	3146	D5
10	BNWK	44212	3146	D7
10	SGVL	44136	3146	D5
10	SGVL	44149	3146	D5
3600	CLEV	44109	2754	A7
4500	CLEV	44144	2754	C5
5000	CLEV	44129	2754	A7
5000	PRMA	44109	2754	A7
5000	PRMA	44129	2754	A7
5300	PRMA	44129	2753	E7
5300	PRMA	44129	2882	E1
5700	PRMA	44130	2882	D2
5800	PMHT	44129	2882	D2
5800	PMHT	44130	2882	B4
6600	MDBH	44130	2881	D6
6600	PMHT	44130	2881	E5
7400	MDBH	44130	3012	B1
7700	SGVL	44130	3012	A2
7700	SGVL	44136	3012	A2
7700	SGVL	44149	3012	A2
9100	SGVL	44136	3011	D7
9100	SGVL	44149	3011	D7
US-322				
10	CLEV	44114	2624	E2
100	CLEV	44113	2624	E3
100	CLEV	44115	2624	E3
2200	CLEV	44114	2625	C2
2500	CLEV	44106	2626	C2
2500	CVHT	44106	2626	E2
US-322				
2500	CVHT	44106	2627	B1
2500	CVHT	44112	2627	B1
2700	CVHT	44118	2627	A1
3200	CVHT	44118	2497	C7
3400	CVHT	44121	2497	D7
3600	CLEV	44103	2625	C2
3800	CVHT	44121	2498	B7
3900	SELD	44121	2498	D7
4600	LNHT	44121	2498	D7
4600	LNHT	44124	2498	E7
4700	SELD	44124	2498	D7
5000	LNHT	44124	2499	D7
5600	MDHT	44124	2499	B7
6800	GSML	44040	2500	E6
6800	MDHT	44124	2500	B7
7000	GSML	44040	2501	A7
7300	CLEV	44103	2626	A2
7300	CsTp	44026	2501	C7
8100	CsTp	44026	2502	C7
9400	CsTp	44026	2503	B7
9500	MsnT	44026	2503	A7
9900	MsnT	44024	2503	B7
10800	MsnT	44024	2504	B7
12100	MsnT	44024	2505	A6
12400	ClrT	44024	2505	C6
13400	ClrT	44024	2506	C6
13800	ClrT	44021	2506	C6
14400	ClrT	44046	2506	E6
14900	ClrT	44024	2507	A6
14900	ClrT	44046	2507	A6
15100	HtbT	44024	2507	C6
15100	HtbT	44046	2507	C6
15800	HtbT	44062	2507	D6
US-322 E 13th St				
1700	CLEV	44114	2625	A2
US-322 Chester Av				
2200	CLEV	44114	2625	C2
3600	CLEV	44103	2625	C2
7300	CLEV	44103	2626	A2
8400	CLEV	44106	2626	A2
US-322 Detroit Av				
2400	CLEV	44113	2624	C4
US-322 Euclid Av				
10900	CLEV	44106	2626	C2
US-322 Mayfield Rd				
2500	CLEV	44106	2626	E2
2500	CVHT	44106	2626	E2
2500	CVHT	44106	2627	B1
2500	CVHT	44112	2627	B1
2700	CVHT	44118	2627	A1
3200	CVHT	44118	2497	C7
3400	CVHT	44121	2497	D7
3800	CVHT	44121	2498	B7
3900	SELD	44121	2498	D7
4600	LNHT	44121	2498	D7
4600	LNHT	44124	2498	E7
4700	SELD	44124	2498	D7
5000	LNHT	44124	2499	D7
5600	MDHT	44124	2499	B7
6800	GSML	44040	2500	E6
6800	MDHT	44124	2500	B7
7000	GSML	44040	2501	A7
7300	CsTp	44026	2501	C7
8100	CsTp	44026	2502	C7
9400	CsTp	44026	2503	B7
9500	MsnT	44026	2503	A7
9900	MsnT	44024	2503	B7
10800	MsnT	44024	2504	B7
12100	MsnT	44024	2505	A6
12400	ClrT	44024	2505	C6
13400	ClrT	44024	2506	C6
13800	ClrT	44021	2506	C6
14400	ClrT	44046	2506	E6
14900	ClrT	44024	2507	A6
14900	ClrT	44046	2507	A6
15100	HtbT	44024	2507	C6
15100	HtbT	44046	2507	C6
15800	HtbT	44062	2507	D6
US-322 Superior Av				
-	CLEV	44113	2624	D3
US-322 Superior Av E				
10	CLEV	44114	2624	E2
1200	CLEV	44114	2625	A2
US-322 W Superior Av				
100	CLEV	44113	2624	E3
100	CLEV	44114	2624	E3
100	CLEV	44115	2624	E3
US-422				
-	AbnT	-	2892	A6
-	AbnT	-	2893	E6
-	BbgT	-	2890	E5
-	BbgT	-	2891	D5
-	BbgT	-	2892	A6
-	BDHT	-	2758	B7
-	MPHT	-	2758	A6
-	NRDL	-	2758	B6
-	ORNG	-	2758	E4
-	ORNG	-	2759	A2
-	SLN	-	2759	A7
-	SLN	-	2888	B1
-	SLN	-	2889	B4
-	SLN	-	2890	A5
-	WVHT	-	2758	E4
-	WVHT	-	2759	A6
1400	CLEV	44115	2625	A4
1900	CLEV	44114	2624	E3
1900	CLEV	44115	2624	E3
2000	CLEV	44113	2624	E3
3800	CLEV	44104	2625	E6
7200	CLEV	44104	2626	D7
11300	CLEV	44120	2626	D7
12300	CLEV	44120	2756	E1
13700	CLEV	44120	2757	A1
15400	SRHT	44120	2757	B1
17600	SRHT	44122	2757	E1
19400	SRHT	44122	2758	D1
20800	BHWD	44122	2758	E1
20800	HIHL	44122	2758	A1
26900	BHWD	44122	2759	A1
US-422 Broadway Av				
800	CLEV	44115	2625	A4
US-422 Chagrin Blvd				
15600	CLEV	44120	2757	B1
15600	SRHT	44120	2757	B1
17600	SRHT	44122	2757	E1
19400	SRHT	44122	2758	D1
20800	BHWD	44122	2758	E1
20800	HIHL	44122	2758	A1
26900	BHWD	44122	2759	A1
US-422 Kinsman Rd				
5500	CLEV	44104	2625	E6
7200	CLEV	44104	2626	D7
11300	CLEV	44120	2626	D7
12300	CLEV	44120	2756	E1
US-422 Kinsman Rd				
13700	CLEV	44120	2757	A1
15400	SRHT	44120	2757	B1
US-422 Ontario St				
1900	CLEV	44114	2624	E3
1900	CLEV	44115	2624	E3
2000	CLEV	44113	2624	E3
US-422 Orange Av				
1400	CLEV	44115	2625	A4
US-422 Outerbelt East Frwy				
-	BHWD	-	2758	E3
-	BHWD	-	2759	A2
-	ORNG	-	2758	E4
-	ORNG	-	2759	A2
-	WVHT	-	2758	E5
US-422 Woodland Av				
2500	CLEV	44115	2625	C4
3800	CLEV	44104	2625	C4
A				
Aaron Av				
26000	EUCL	44132	2373	E3
Aaron Dr				
10400	PRMA	44130	2882	B1
Aaron Ln				
-	OmsT	44138	2878	C7
9000	OmsT	44138	3009	C1
Aaron St				
10	BERA	44017	3011	B1
Abbe Rd				
100	SDLK	44054	2616	E2
500	SFLD	44054	2616	E3
2300	SFLD	44054	2746	E1
4400	SFLD	44035	2746	E5
Abbe Rd SR-301				
100	SDLK	44054	2616	E2
500	SFLD	44054	2616	E3
2300	SFLD	44054	2746	E5
4400	SFLD	44035	2746	E5
N Abbe Rd				
-	SDLK	44054	2616	E2
200	ELYR	44035	2875	D4
800	ELYR	44035	2746	E7
1200	SFLD	44035	2746	E7
5000	SFLD	44054	2746	E5
N Abbe Rd SR-301				
400	ELYR	44035	2875	E2
800	ELYR	44035	2746	E7
1200	SFLD	44035	2746	E7
5000	SFLD	44054	2746	E5
S Abbe Rd				
100	ELYR	44035	2875	D5
1200	ELYR	44035	3006	D1
Abbey Av				
1100	CLEV	44113	2624	D5
Abbey Ct				
6600	VLVW	44125	2885	E5
Abbey Dr				
900	MadT	44057	2043	E2
900	MDSN	44057	2043	E2
Abbey Rd				
4200	LryT	44057	2042	E7
7900	NRYN	44130	3013	A2
7900	NRYN	44133	3013	A7
7900	PRMA	44130	3013	A2
17100	BbgT	44023	2890	B3
Abbeyshire Wy				
9600	CcdT	44060	2145	A6
9600	MNTR	44060	2145	B7
Abbieshire Av				
1000	LKWD	44107	2622	D4
Abbot Dr				
7100	PRMA	44134	2883	C7
Abbotsford Dr				
100	SDLK	44054	2615	D4
Abbott Rd				
11700	HrmT	44234	3160	D1
Abbott's Mill Dr				
3400	WLBY	44094	2250	D3
Abby Av				
18600	CLEV	44119	2372	E5
18600	EUCL	44119	2372	E5
Abby Ct				
7300	MNTR	44060	2251	C1
Abbyshire Dr				
400	BERA	44017	2880	A6
Abell Av				
12300	CLEV	44120	2626	E7
13400	CLEV	44120	2627	A7
Abels Av				
300	PnvT	44077	2039	C6
Aberdeen Av				
7400	CLEV	44103	2496	A7
Aberdeen Blvd				
-	HDHT	44143	2499	B2
Aberdeen Ct				
10	RKRV	44116	2751	A1
Aberdeen Dr				
2100	EUCL	44143	2498	C1
2100	RDHT	44143	2498	C1
Aberdeen Ln				
200	AURA	44202	3021	E6
36400	SLN	44139	2889	C4
Aberdeen Rd				
1700	MadT	44057	1941	D1
3200	SRHT	44120	2627	C7
21000	RKRV	44116	2621	C5
27800	BYVL	44140	2619	E5
27800	BYVL	44140	2620	A5
Abiding Wy				
5600	MadT	44057	1941	C3
Abigail Dr				
5100	LNHT	44124	2498	E6
Abigail Ln				
19900	SGVL	44149	3146	C1
Abilene Tr				
100	ClrT	44024	2505	C6
Abington Ct				
3400	BNWK	44212	3147	B7
Ablewhite Av				
11400	CLEV	44108	2496	D3
Abra Ct				
4800	CLEV	44103	2625	D1
Abraham Dr				
5400	PRMA	44130	2882	B1
Abrams Dr				
2900	TNBG	44087	3020	B7
Acacia Av				
7500	MNTR	44060	2252	B1
Acacia Ct				
32200	AVLK	44012	2618	C4
Acacia Dr				
400	WLWK	44095	2249	B7
Acacia Dr				
4300	SELD	44121	2628	B3
16000	SGVL	44136	3147	B4
Acacia Park Dr				
2100	BHWD	44122	2629	A3
2100	BHWD	44124	2629	A3
2100	LNHT	44124	2629	A3
Academy Ct				
100	ELYR	44035	2874	A7
900	PNVL	44077	2145	E3
Academy Dr				
16100	SGVL	44149	3146	D2
Acadia Dr				
8300	SgHT	44067	3017	D5
Acadia Trc				
2000	WTLK	44145	2750	E1
Access Dr				
-	AVON	44011	2748	E1
Access Rd				
-	CLEV	44102	2623	C7
-	CLEV	44111	2623	C7
-	OmsT	44138	2879	A4
500	CLEV	44108	2496	B4
2000	LORN	44052	2745	A1
Acheivement Av				
-	PRRY	44081	2042	B1
-	PryT	44081	2042	B1
Achievement Av				
-	PRRY	44081	2042	B1
-	PryT	44081	2042	B1
Achill Ct				
7900	SgHT	44067	3017	A4
Achilles Dr				
11700	CcdT	44077	2254	D4
Ackley Blvd				
8500	PMHT	44129	2882	C3
8500	PMHT	44130	2882	C3
8500	PRMA	44129	2882	C3
Ackley Rd				
5400	PRMA	44129	2883	A3
5400	PRMA	44134	2883	A3
5900	CLEV	44105	2755	D1
5900	CLEV	44127	2755	D1
6600	PRMA	44129	2882	E3
Acorn Cir				
52300	BhmT	44001	2870	C7
Acorn Ct				
7400	NRYN	44133	3013	E7
7500	SLN	44139	3019	E3
36100	AVON	44011	2617	E6
Acorn Dr				
10	OKWD	44146	3018	C3
4700	INDE	44131	2884	C4
Acorn Tr				
3700	ORNG	44022	2759	D2
3700	ORNG	44124	2759	D2
3700	PRPK	44124	2759	D2
Acre Dr				
8900	SgHT	44067	3017	D3
8900	SgHT	44146	3017	D3
8900	WNHL	44146	3017	D3
Acres Dr				
6300	INDE	44131	2884	E6
Ada Av				
3500	LORN	44055	2745	B4
3500	ShfT	44055	2745	B4
11100	CLEV	44108	2496	D6
Ada Dr				
34000	SLN	44139	2889	A7
Adair Ct				
6200	BKPK	44142	2881	C3
Adair Dr				
6200	BKPK	44142	2881	C3
Adams Av				
5600	MPHT	44137	2886	C2
9200	CLEV	44108	2496	B6
33600	NRDV	44039	2877	C3
Adams Ct				
7500	MNTR	44060	2143	D6
Adams Dr				
17900	SGVL	44136	3012	A3
17900	SGVL	44149	3011	E3
17900	SGVL	44149	3012	A3
Adams Ln				
29800	WTLK	44145	2749	B4
Adams St				
10	BERA	44017	2880	C7
300	ELYR	44035	2874	E4
600	BDFD	44146	2887	A4
900	VMLN	44089	2740	D6
2100	LORN	44052	2615	B6
25300	ODFL	44138	3010	B1
Addington Blvd				
21000	FWPK	44126	2751	C1
21800	RKRV	44116	2751	B1
Addington Ct				
-	NbyT	44065	2763	A6
3700	FWPK	44126	2751	C1
Addison Cir				
-	AVON	44011	2747	A3
Addison Pl				
7200	CLEV	44103	2625	D2
Addison Rd				
800	CLEV	44103	2495	E6
1400	CLEV	44103	2626	A1
Adelaide Av				
10	PnvT	44077	2039	D7
10100	CLEV	44102	2753	C1
10100	CLEV	44111	2753	C1
Adelaide Ct				
1300	WTLK	44145	2620	C7
Adelaide St				
1300	WTLK	44145	2620	C7
Adelbert Rd				
2000	CLEV	44106	2626	D2
Adelbert St				
10	BERA	44017	2880	B6
41700	ELYR	44035	2874	C2
41700	EyrT	44035	2874	C2
Adele Ln				
26900	OmsT	44138	2878	E3
26900	OmsT	44138	2879	A3
Adele St				
-	NRDV	44039	2748	D7
Adeline Av				
2200	CLEV	44107	2622	D7
2200	CLEV	44111	2622	D7
2200	LKWD	44107	2622	D7
Adeline Rd				
10700	CLEV	44111	2753	B2
Adelle Dr				
400	SgHT	44067	3017	D5
Adena Ln				
1900	MDHT	44124	2629	C2
Adkins Rd				
7000	MNTR	44060	2251	A1
7000	MNTR	44094	2251	B1
7000	WLBY	44094	2251	B1
Admiral Dr				
10	ETLK	44095	2142	B7
100	ETLK	44095	2250	B1
4500	CLEV	44109	2755	A5
Admiral Wy				
32600	AVLK	44012	2618	A3
Admiralty Dr				
17500	SGVL	44136	3146	E4
17500	SGVL	44136	3147	A4
18500	SGVL	44149	3146	D4
Adolpha Av				
5700	CLEV	44127	2625	D7
Adrian Av				
14200	CLEV	44111	2752	D1
Adrian Dr				
300	BERA	44017	2880	A7
400	BERA	44017	3011	A1
Adrian Rd				
4100	SELD	44121	2498	B6
Aerospace Pkwy				
2000	BKPK	44142	2880	A2
5000	BKPK	44142	2879	E3
5000	CLEV	44142	2880	A3
Aetna Rd				
7000	CLEV	44105	2755	E1
7400	CLEV	44105	2756	A1
Africa Acres Dr				
11800	CsTp	44026	2502	C4
Agard Ct				
9000	MNTR	44060	2144	D7
Agnes Blvd				
15400	BKPK	44142	2881	B3
Agnes Ct				
1700	CLEV	44113	2624	D7
Agnes Dr				
8500	SGVL	44136	3012	D3
Aidden Acres Dr				
300	ELYR	44035	2875	E4
Aileen Dr				
7900	MNTR	44060	2252	D3
Aimee Ln				
4200	WLBY	44094	2251	B5
Ainsworth Dr				
30600	PRPK	44124	2629	D4
N Aintree Dr				
800	MAYF	44143	2500	A5
6400	MAYF	44143	2499	E5
Aintree Park Dr				
800	MAYF	44143	2500	A6
Airlane Dr				
9300	MCDN	44056	3018	E5
Airport Pkwy				
38100	WLBY	44094	2142	E7
Akins Rd				
-	ClbT	44028	3144	E3
1200	BWHT	44147	3149	C1
2200	NRYN	44133	3149	A1
2200	NRYN	44147	3149	C1
5900	NRYN	44133	3148	D1
N Akins Rd				
8000	NRYN	44133	3148	D1
8300	NRYN	44133	3013	C7
Akita Ct				
17200	SGVL	44136	3012	A7
Akron St				
16600	BbgT	44023	2890	A1
Alabama Av				
100	LORN	44052	2614	D6
Alabama Ct				
-	CLEV	44114	2625	B2
Alameda Av				
-	AVLK	44012	2617	B2
-	CrlT	44035	3005	C5
500	SDLK	44054	2616	C4
1400	LKWD	44107	2623	A6
Alameda Dr				
11200	SGVL	44149	3011	C6
Alameda Pkwy				
20400	HIHL	44122	2758	A4
20400	HIHL	44128	2758	A4
20400	WVHT	44122	2758	A4
Alan Dr				
2400	WBHL	44092	2374	D4
Alan Pkwy				
7500	MDBH	44130	3012	B1
Albany Av				
3400	LORN	44055	2745	B4
3400	ShfT	44055	2745	B3
Alber Av				
5400	PRMA	44129	2883	A2
5400	PRMA	44134	2883	A2
6700	PRMA	44129	2882	E2
Albers Av				
16800	CLEV	44111	2752	B2
Albert Av				
5800	NRDV	44039	2877	B2
Albert Ct				
400	RDHT	44143	2498	D3
Albert Ln				
24400	BHWD	44122	2628	D5
Alberta Dr				
5600	LNHT	44124	2629	C2
Albertly Av				
3700	PRMA	44134	2883	B2
4800	PRMA	44129	2883	A2
Alberton Rd				
24900	EUCL	44123	2373	D3
24900	EUCL	44132	2373	D3
Albion Dr				
-	AVLK	44012	2618	A4
Albion Rd				
3000	CLEV	44120	2627	A6
3000	SRHT	44120	2627	A6
7100	NRYN	44133	3013	A4
11800	NRYN	44133	3012	E4
11800	SGVL	44133	3012	E4
11800	SGVL	44136	3012	E4
17000	SGVL	44136	3011	E5
19000	SGVL	44149	3011	D4
22700	ClbT	44028	3010	E5
22700	ClbT	44149	3010	E5
22700	SGVL	44149	3010	E5
Albrecht Rd				
42100	ELYR	44035	3005	A1
42100	EyrT	44035	3005	A1
43000	AhtT	44035	3004	E1
43000	CrlT	44035	3004	E1
43000	CrlT	44035	3005	A1
43000	EyrT	44035	3004	E1
43000	NRsT	44035	3004	E1
44000	AhtT	44001	3004	B1

STREET Block City ZIP Map# Grid

Albrecht Rd
44000 NRsT 44001 3004 B1
Albrus Av
14400 CLEV 44111 2752 D3
14400 CLEV 44135 2752 D3
Alcester Rd
1700 MDHT 44124 2629 D1
Alcina Av
- ETLK 44095 2250 A3
Alcott Pl
100 PNVL 44077 2146 B2
Alcoy Rd
1700 CLEV 44112 2497 C3
1800 ECLE 44112 2497 C4
Alda Pkwy
2700 BNWK 44212 3147 D6
2700 BNWK 44233 3147 E6
2700 HkyT 44233 3147 E6
Alden Av
15900 CLEV 44111 2622 B7
38900 NRDV 44039 2876 A3
Alden Dr
900 STBR 44241 3156 D7
2900 PRMA 44134 2883 C4
10600 MsnT 44024 2503 E6
28400 NOSD 44070 2749 D7
Alden Rd
- HDHT 44143 2499 D1
Alden St
17900 BbgT 44023 2891 A6
Aldene Av
15000 CLEV 44135 2752 C4
Aldenham Dr
6200 MDHT 44143 2499 E6
Aldenshire Dr
13100 ClrT 44024 2505 D7
Alder Av
13800 ECLE 44112 2497 A4
Alder Ct
9600 CcdT 44060 2253 A4
9600 MNTR 44060 2253 A4
Alder Dr
- SLN 44139 2889 D7
Alder Ln
1500 WTLK 44145 2619 B7
Aldersgate Dr
1800 LNHT 44124 2629 B2
Aldersyde Dr
7600 MDBH 44130 3012 D2
12100 VLVW 44125 2885 D6
14400 BtnT 44021 2635 E7
14400 BtnT 44021 2765 E1
15500 SRHT 44120 2627 B7
Alderwood Rd
6200 PMHT 44130 2882 D4
Alderwood Tr
100 SRSL 44022 2761 D5
Aldrich Dr
31300 BYVL 44140 2619 A4
Aldrich Rd
100 VMLN 44089 2741 C5
Aldridge Dr
9800 ClbT 44028 3010 D2
9800 ClbT 44138 3010 D2
9800 ODFL 44138 3010 D2
Aletha Av
500 GNVA 44041 1944 B5
Alexander Av
100 AMHT 44001 2872 B2
300 LORN 44052 2615 B5
Alexander Ct
12200 CLEV 44106 2626 E1
Alexander Dr
100 ELYR 44035 2875 D2
5400 PRMA 44130 2882 B1
7100 NOSD 44070 2878 B3
13900 RslT 44072 2632 A5
Alexander Rd
7000 CcdT 44077 2146 E7
7000 CcdT 44077 2254 D1
9300 GDHT 44125 2756 B6
12000 VLVW 44125 3016 E2
13600 VLVW 44125 3017 A1
13600 WNHL 44146 3017 A1
18700 WNHL 44146 3018 A2
21400 OKWD 44146 3018 D2
22000 FWPK 44126 2751 A3
22900 NOSD 44070 2751 A3
22900 NOSD 44126 2751 A3
23100 NOSD 44070 2750 E3
Alexandra Dr
8500 NRYN 44133 3012 E3
Alexandria Dr
6200 PMHT 44130 2882 A4
6200 PRMA 44130 2882 A3
8600 MCDN 44056 3153 D1
Alexco Rd
4100 CLEV 44135 2752 E3
Alexis Dr
- CrlT 44044 3141 B3
100 ELYR 44035 3006 D3
Alfred Dr
5200 MNTR 44060 2038 E7
Alfred Lerner Wy
100 CLEV 44114 2624 D2
Alger Rd
- CLEV 44107 2622 D7
2100 LKWD 44107 2622 D7
4700 RchT 44286 3150 B7
5300 BKVL 44141 3150 B7
5300 RchT 44141 3150 B7
14400 CLEV 44111 2622 D7
Alger Tr
10100 TNBG 44087 3020 C4
Algiers Dr
1500 MDHT 44124 2499 D7
1500 MDHT 44124 2629 D1
Algonac Rd
1700 CLEV 44112 2497 C3
Algonquin Rd
2100 EUCL 44117 2498 A3
Alhambra Rd
700 CLEV 44110 2497 C2
Ali Av
- MDBH 44130 3012 C2
Ali-Bey Av
3500 CLEV 44115 2625 C4
Alice Av
7100 CLEV 44105 2755 E4
Alice Blvd
10 OmsT 44138 2879 B4
Alice Ct
- GDHT 44125 2885 E2
Alla Dr
3100 SVHL 44131 2884 B6

Allandale Av
1700 ECLE 44112 2497 B4
Allandale Dr
6500 AhtT 44001 2873 C1
Allanwood Rd
5400 PRMA 44129 2883 A3
5400 PRMA 44134 2883 A3
Allegheny Av
1400 ECLE 44112 2497 A5
Allegheny Cir
1600 ECLE 44112 2497 A5
Allegheny Rd
7500 CcdT 44060 2253 B2
Allen Av
- SDLK 44054 2616 B4
10 PnvT 44077 2039 D6
Allen Blvd
2300 BHWD 44122 2629 A5
Allen Ct
1200 RKRV 44116 2621 D5
Allen Dr
1400 WTLK 44145 2620 D7
7100 WNHL 44146 2886 E7
10600 MsnT 44024 2503 E6
Allen St
- EyrT 44035 2874 B1
800 ELYR 44035 3005 E1
Allen Bradley Dr
10 MDHT 44124 2629 D2
Allenbury Dr
32500 SLN 44139 2888 E1
33100 SLN 44139 2889 A1
Allendale Dr
4800 RDHT 44143 2498 E1
5600 NOSD 44070 2879 C1
7100 MNTR 44060 2251 B1
Allen Troy Ct
8700 MNTR 44060 2252 C1
Allerton Ct
7500 HDSN 44236 3154 E6
Alliance Dr
400 SgHT 44067 3017 C4
Allien Av
17800 CLEV 44111 2752 A2
Alling Dr
2800 TNBG 44087 3020 B5
Allison Av
600 LORN 44052 2614 C7
13600 CLEV 44111 2752 E1
Allison Dr
600 RDHT 44143 2498 D4
Allison Rd
2200 UNHT 44118 2627 D4
Allman Ct
1600 CLEV 44113 2624 E6
Allston Rd
1000 CVHT 44121 2498 A6
Allynd Blvd
10 CRDN 44024 2380 A5
Almadien Dr
4300 LORN 44053 2744 B4
Almar Dr
20400 BHWD 44122 2628 A7
20400 SRHT 44122 2628 A7
Almira Av
8000 CLEV 44102 2753 E1
9900 CLEV 44111 2753 C1
Al Moen Dr
25300 NOSD 44070 2879 C1
Almond Walcott Ct S
6700 BKVL 44141 3015 E7
Almont Dr
6300 BKPK 44142 2881 B4
Alonzo Av
15300 CLEV 44128 2757 B5
Alpha Av
4200 NBGH 44105 2755 C3
Alpha Dr
600 HDHT 44143 2499 E4
600 MAYF 44143 2499 E5
Alpha Pk
10 HDHT 44143 2499 E4
Alpha Rd
11600 HrmT 44234 3160 E1
Alpine Av
2800 CLEV 44104 2626 B6
Alpine Cir
17900 SGVL 44136 3147 C4
Alpine Dr
8200 KTLD 44094 2377 A3
W Alpine Dr
8200 KTLD 44094 2377 A3
Alpine Rd
1100 CVHT 44121 2497 E6
Alsace Ct
- SLN 44139 2889 E5
26700 BHWD 44122 2629 A4
39700 SLN 44139 2890 A5
Altamont Dr
9400 TNBG 44087 3019 D6
Altamont Rd
200 VMLN 44089 2741 D4
3200 CVHT 44118 2627 C1
Althea Dr
6100 CcdT 44077 2145 E4
6100 CcdT 44077 2146 A3
Althen Av
2100 CLEV 44109 2624 D7
Alton Dr
12100 EatT 44044 3008 B7
12200 EatT 44044 3143 B1
Alton Rd
2000 CLEV 44112 2497 D4
2000 ECLE 44112 2497 D4
28900 WKLF 44092 2374 B3
Altoona Rd
3100 CLEV 44109 2754 C4
Alva Dr
- BKPK 44142 2881 A3
Alva St
32800 ETLK 44095 2249 E6
32800 WLWK 44095 2249 E6
Alvason Rd
1800 ECLE 44112 2496 E7
1800 ECLE 44112 2497 A7
Alvey Rd
1100 LNHT 44124 2499 A6
Alvin Av
1700 CLEV 44109 2754 D6
13100 GDHT 44105 2756 E5
13100 GDHT 44125 2756 E5
13600 GDHT 44105 2757 A5
13600 GDHT 44125 2757 A5
Alvin Dr
6000 BKPK 44142 2881 B2

Alvord Pl
2800 PRPK 44124 2629 C6
Alyssa Ct
10500 CcdT 44077 2253 E1
Amanda Ct
5200 NRDV 44039 2748 B7
Amanda Pl
7300 CcdT 44077 2253 C1
Amaryllis Dr
6900 EyrT 44035 2874 C2
Amber Ct
5700 WLBY 44094 2375 A2
Amber Dr
17000 CLEV 44111 2752 B1
N Amber Dr
4100 BKLN 44144 2753 E4
S Amber Dr
4300 BKLN 44144 2753 E4
Amber Ln
7300 BKVL 44141 3016 B6
7500 PRMA 44130 3013 C1
Amberly Av
1500 CLEV 44109 2754 D4
Amber Trails
- BbgT 44023 2891 E7
- BbgT 44023 3022 E1
Amberwood Ct
9500 BWHT 44147 3149 D2
Amber Wood Dr
9200 KTLD 44094 2377 B1
Amberwood Dr
12400 CdnT 44024 2380 B2
38700 AVON 44011 2747 B2
Amberwood Ln
1400 PnvT 44077 2041 A7
Ambina Dr
28600 SLN 44139 2888 B7
Ambler Av
2700 CLEV 44104 2626 B6
Ambler Dr
400 ELYR 44035 2875 D3
Ambler Ln
10800 ManT 44255 3159 C5
10800 MNTU 44255 3159 C5
Ambleside Dr
2100 CLEV 44104 2626 D3
2100 CLEV 44106 2626 D3
2100 CVHT 44106 2626 D3
9000 MNTR 44060 2252 D1
33100 AVLK 44012 2617 D3
Ambleside Wy
100 AMHT 44001 2872 D3
Ambour Dr
23700 NOSD 44070 2750 D3
Ambridge Dr
- AVON 44011 2747 B2
Ambrose Dr
6300 MNTR 44060 2143 B4
Amchester St
900 AMHT 44001 2744 A6
900 AMHT 44053 2744 A6
900 LORN 44053 2744 A6
Amelia Av
4100 WLBY 44094 2251 B5
Amelia Dr
- ORNG 44022 2759 A6
2500 BWHT 44147 3014 C5
American Rd
10 BKLN 44144 2753 C4
American St
10 CNFL 44022 2761 A5
American Wy
- AVON 44011 2617 E7
Americana Blvd
300 AVON 44011 2617 E6
American Legion Pkwy
10 BERA 44017 2880 C7
Amerwood Ct
1500 PnvT 44077 2041 A7
Ames Rd
6600 PMHT 44129 2882 D5
6600 PMHT 44130 2882 D5
6600 PRMA 44129 2882 D6
7200 PRMA 44130 2882 D7
Amesbury Av
9200 CLEV 44106 2626 B2
Amesbury Dr
- MNTR 44060 2252 A2
23700 NOSD 44070 2750 D4
Amhearst Cir
26400 BHWD 44122 2629 A4
Amherst Av
3000 LORN 44052 2744 E4
3000 LORN 44055 2744 E3
Amherst Dr
5200 PRMA 44129 2753 D7
5300 PRMA 44129 2882 D1
6800 SgHT 44067 3152 B1
Amherst Rd
20400 HIHL 44122 2758 A2
20400 WVHT 44122 2758 A2
Amity Dr
7000 MadT 44057 1843 D6
Ammon Rd
- RDHT 44143 2498 D4
4300 SELD 44143 2498 C4
Amor Av
10500 CLEV 44108 2496 C6
Amos Av
7900 CLEV 44104 2626 A4
Amrap Dr
5800 PMHT 44130 2882 B2
5800 PRMA 44130 2882 B2
Amsterdam Rd
1200 CLEV 44110 2372 B6
Amweld Dr
1500 GTVL 44231 3161 E7
Amy Av
100 MDSN 44057 2043 E2
Amy Ct
34800 ETLK 44095 2250 A3
Anaconda Av
5500 MNTR 44060 2144 A1
Anchor Ct
7500 MNTR 44060 2143 D4
Anchor Curv
- PNVL 44077 2040 A5
Anchor Dr
200 SDLK 44054 2615 D4
Anchor Ln
- LORN 44052 2614 E6
7300 NCtT 44067 3153 C5
Anchorage Wy
5300 VMLN 44089 2740 E4

Anchorage Cove
10100 RMDV 44202 3020 E5
Anchor Point Dr
- VMLN 44089 2741 A6
Anchors Wy
400 AVLK 44012 2619 A3
Anderson Av
6500 INDE 44131 2884 E5
9300 CLEV 44105 2756 B1
Anderson Rd
4400 SELD 44121 2498 D5
4600 SELD 44143 2498 C5
4700 LNHT 44124 2498 D5
4700 SELD 44124 2498 D5
28900 WKLF 44092 2374 B3
W Anderson Rd
4200 SELD 44121 2498 B6
Anderson St
26400 ClbT 44028 3009 C4
Andes Dr
14000 ClbT 44028 3010 B7
Andorra Dr
4500 NOSD 44070 2749 E6
Andover Av
4100 LORN 44055 2746 A4
Andover Blvd
5000 GDHT 44125 2756 D6
5400 GDHT 44125 2885 D1
Andover Cir
- WBHL 44092 2374 A6
500 BWHT 44147 3149 E5
500 BWHT 44147 3150 A5
Andover Dr
5100 PRMA 44134 3014 A1
7000 MNTR 44060 2143 B7
7000 WLBY 44094 2143 B7
10000 TNBG 44087 3019 B3
Andover Ln
7500 NRYN 44133 3013 D5
Andover Pl
2100 TwbT 44236 3155 A6
Andover Rd
- SRHT 44120 2627 C6
Andover Wy
7400 HDSN 44236 3154 D7
Andras Dr
17000 WNHL 44146 3017 D2
Andre Ln
6600 SLN 44139 2889 C6
Andrea Dr
7400 CcdT 44060 2253 B2
Andrea Ln
4700 CLEV 44109 2754 E6
Andress Ct
10 LORN 44052 2615 A5
100 ELYR 44035 2875 B7
Andrew Dr
9300 TNBG 44087 3019 A5
Andrew St
10 BERA 44017 2880 D7
10 BERA 44017 3011 D1
10 MDBH 44017 3011 D1
10 MDBH 44130 3011 D1
Andrews Av
1100 LKWD 44107 2622 C5
Andrews Cir
10 BKVL 44141 3150 D5
Andrews Ln
800 GSML 44040 2500 C5
15300 LKWD 44107 2622 C4
Andrews Pl
2900 LORN 44052 2744 C3
38800 WLBY 44094 2251 A5
Andrews Rd
1700 CVHT 44118 2627 E2
1700 CVHT 44121 2627 E2
1700 SELD 44118 2627 E2
1700 SELD 44121 2627 E2
5500 MONT 44060 2143 E3
6100 MNTR 44060 2143 E3
Andrews Rd SR-283
5500 MONT 44060 2143 E3
6100 MNTR 44060 2143 E3
Andrus Av
5000 NOSD 44070 2750 A7
Angela Cir
10 PnvT 44077 2145 E3
Angela Ct
6600 SLN 44139 2889 C6
Angela Dr
4300 SELD 44121 2498 B6
4400 FWPK 44126 2751 C3
10700 KTLD 44094 2376 E7
23000 WVHT 44128 2758 C5
27900 NOSD 44070 2878 E3
Angela Ln
300 AVLK 44012 2617 C3
7600 MadT 44057 1844 A5
Angelina Cir
9200 MNTR 44060 2144 E1
Angelus Av
11600 CLEV 44105 2756 D2
12700 CLEV 44120 2756 E2
Anglers Dr
100 SRSL 44022 2761 D6
Angling Rd
9200 FrnT 44889 2869 A7
Anita Dr
6200 PMHT 44130 2881 E4
6200 PMHT 44130 2882 A3
6200 PRMA 44130 2882 A3
Ann Ct
8900 CLEV 44108 2496 B7
Ann Dr
3500 VMLN 44089 2741 E5
27600 ClbT 44028 3009 A3
Ann St
- AMHT 44001 2872 E3
Anna Ct
5600 MONT 44060 2143 D2
Anna Dr
10500 KTLD 44094 2376 B6
Anna Ln
31500 BYVL 44140 2619 A2
Annadale Dr
7200 SLN 44139 3020 C1
Annandale Dr
10 SRSL 44022 2762 B6
Annandale Rd
6500 GSML 44040 2630 A3
6500 MDHT 44124 2630 A3
Ann Arbor Dr
7400 PRMA 44130 2882 A7
7400 PRMA 44130 3013 A1

Anne Dr
300 BERA 44017 2879 E7
300 BERA 44017 3010 E1
300 BERA 44017 3011 A1
Anne Ln
16600 AbnT 44021 2893 C1
Anne Marie Ct
200 HkyT 44233 3149 D6
Annesley Rd
25700 BHWD 44122 2628 E6
26200 BHWD 44122 2629 A5
Annetta Dr
27800 GNWL 44139 3019 A1
Annette Pl
4800 WVHT 44128 2758 C6
Annette St
22900 WVHT 44128 2758 C6
Annie Ln
24400 WTLK 44145 2750 C2
Annis Rd
100 AhtT 44001 2872 D7
100 SAHT 44001 2872 D7
100 SAHT 44001 3003 D1
300 SAHT 44074 3003 C3
Ansel Rd
10 GNVA 44041 1944 D4
800 CLEV 44103 2496 A6
1000 CLEV 44108 2496 B7
1200 CLEV 44106 2496 B7
1300 CLEV 44106 2626 B1
Anson Av
4900 CLEV 44127 2625 C7
Ansonia Av
1400 MadT 44057 1843 C7
8500 BKLN 44144 2753 D5
Ansonia Dr
3000 TNBG 44087 3020 B6
Antelope Run
8800 RslT 44072 2762 C4
Antenucci Blvd
- GDHT 44125 2885 C1
Anthony Ct
7100 MadT 44057 1843 D6
Anthony Dr
400 AMHT 44001 2872 B3
3300 BWHT 44147 3015 B4
Anthony Ln
3300 TNBG 44087 3155 C1
3300 TwbT 44087 3155 C1
6700 PMHT 44130 2882 C5
Anthony Pl
- AhtT 44001 2872 E6
Anthony St
600 RDHT 44143 2498 D4
5000 MPHT 44137 2757 C7
Antietam Rd
10700 PMHT 44130 2882 B3
Antioch Dr
100 ELYR 44035 2746 D6
Antioch Rd
2300 NPRY 44081 1940 E4
2300 PryT 44081 1940 E4
Antisdale Av
3400 CVHT 44118 2627 D2
E Antisdale Rd
3700 CVHT 44118 2627 E2
3700 SELD 44118 2627 E2
3700 SELD 44118 2628 A2
3800 SELD 44121 2628 A2
Antler Dr
24600 NOSD 44070 2750 C4
Antler Ln
16900 SGVL 44136 3146 E3
16900 SGVL 44136 3147 A3
Antler Pt
463-00 AURA 44202 3156 B2
Antler Tr
- STBR 44241 3156 C7
Antler Crossing
- LORN 44053 2743 B6
Antlers Ct
8400 NRDV 44039 2877 B6
Antoinette Dr
6300 MNTR 44060 2143 B4
7000 PRMA 44129 2883 A7
Antoinette St
100 ELYR 44035 2746 D7
Antrim Rd
6000 EyrT 44035 2745 D7
6000 EyrT 44055 2745 D7
6000 LORN 44055 2745 D7
6100 ELYR 44035 2745 D7
Apache Dr
- PRMA 44130 2882 B2
11100 PMHT 44130 2882 B2
Apache Run
9300 MCDN 44056 3018 D5
Apache Tr
10 MadT 44057 2043 A5
10 PryT 44057 2043 A5
Apelt Av
19100 CLEV 44135 2751 E5
Apex Ln
- NRDV 44039 2748 D7
Apollo Dr
500 ETLK 44095 2249 E2
600 ETLK 44095 2250 A2
1000 BKPK 44142 2880 A2
3100 NRYN 44133 3014 C5
7500 PRMA 44130 3013 B1
Apollo Pkwy
- WLBY 44094 2251 A4
38000 WLBY 44094 2250 E4
Appaloosa Run
800 AURA 44202 3022 B5
Appaloosa Tr
10 MadT 44057 2043 E2
10 MDSN 44057 2043 E2
8400 KTLD 44094 2377 B7
Apple Av
2300 LORN 44052 2745 A2
2300 LORN 44055 2745 A2
4200 CLEV 44113 2624 B6
Apple Ct
21600 RKRV 44116 2621 C6
Apple Dr
2000 EUCL 44143 2498 C2
2100 RDHT 44143 2498 C2
Apple Ln
15000 SGVL 44149 3146 C1
Apple St
10 ELYR 44035 2874 D3
10 EyrT 44035 2874 D3
Appleblossom Ln
300 BYVL 44140 2619 B4

Appleblossom Ln
7500 CsTp 44026 2501 C4
Applebrook Cir
19500 SGVL 44136 3147 D5
Applebrook Dr
200 CNFL 44022 2761 A4
200 RslT 44022 2761 A4
Appleby Ln
3000 TNBG 44087 3020 C5
Apple Creek Dr
4000 BKLN 44144 2753 D3
5300 SFLD 44054 2746 E1
5300 SFLD 44054 2747 A1
N Applecross Rd
400 HDHT 44143 2499 E2
S Applecross Rd
500 HDHT 44143 2499 E3
Applegate Rd
20600 MPHT 44137 2887 A1
20700 BDHT 44146 2887 B1
Apple Hill Dr
200 SgHT 44067 3017 E3
8500 BbgT 44023 2891 B6
Apple Orchard Ln
1000 AMHT 44001 2872 B1
Appleseed Dr
500 LORN 44053 2744 D7
Appleton Ct
6900 MNTR 44060 2143 E6
Appleton Dr
10600 PMHT 44130 2882 A5
Apple Tree Ct
10 ORNG 44122 2759 B3
Appletree Ct
400 PnvT 44077 2146 E2
Appletree Dr
300 PnvT 44077 2146 E1
Apple Valley Ct
1300 BWHT 44147 3149 D4
Appleview Wy
34300 SLN 44139 3020 A1
Applewood Ct
1900 AVON 44011 2617 D7
Applewood Ct E
8700 MNTR 44060 2144 C4
Applewood Ct W
8600 MNTR 44060 2144 C3
Applewood Dr
600 SVHL 44131 3015 A2
9500 NRYN 44133 3013 A3
9800 KTLD 44094 2377 A3
30000 BYVL 44140 2619 C4
Applewood Ln
20200 SGVL 44149 3146 C2
Applied Plz
10 CLEV 44114 2625 C2
10 CLEV 44115 2625 C2
April Hill Dr
10 GftT 44044 3142 A7
Aqua Marine Blvd
- AVLK 44012 2617 A2
Aquarius Pkwy
38100 WLBY 44094 2142 E6
Aquilla Blvd
- AQLA 44024 2505 D4
- ClrT 44024 2505 D4
Aquilla Rd
11100 ClrT 44024 2505 C5
11100 CRDN 44024 2505 B1
11800 AQLA 44024 2505 C4
12400 ClrT 44024 2635 C1
13400 BtnT 44021 2635 C5
13400 BtnT 44024 2635 C5
13400 ClrT 44021 2635 C3
14000 BtnT 44021 2765 C1
Arabella Rd
1600 CLEV 44112 2497 D3
Arabian Ct
4700 AVON 44011 2747 A6
Araglin Ct
19300 SGVL 44149 3146 C5
Arapaho Ct
6900 SLN 44139 2889 A7
Arbor Av
- SFLD 44054 2746 C4
20100 EUCL 44119 2373 A4
20100 EUCL 44123 2373 A4
Arbor Ct
5300 INDE 44131 2884 C6
6700 PRMA 44134 3013 E2
7300 OmsT 44138 2878 E5
38200 CrlT 44044 3141 D3
38200 EatT 44044 3141 D3
Arbor Dr
- AVON 44011 2748 A2
7700 PRMA 44130 3013 D1
Arbor Ln
- BTVL 44022 2889 B2
1900 PnvT 44077 2041 A5
26900 OmsT 44138 2878 E5
Arbor Rd
300 CLEV 44108 2496 E3
Arbor St
1500 WKLF 44092 2374 D1
1500 WLWK 44092 2374 D1
2100 MadT 44057 1942 C2
Arbor Tr
15800 NbyT 44065 2763 D6
Arbor Wy
600 AURA 44202 3156 C3
3300 WTLK 44145 2749 A4
6600 PRMA 44134 3014 A2
7800 PRMA 44134 3013 E2
Arbor Cliff Ln
22200 RKRV 44116 2621 B5
Arbordale Av
6500 SLN 44139 2889 A6
Arbordale Ln
10 PnvT 44077 2145 B5
Arboretum Cir
700 SgHT 44067 3152 B1
Arboretum Ct
300 AURA 44202 3156 D1
Arbor Glen Ct
6100 SLN 44139 2889 E4
Arbor Glen Dr
2600 TNBG 44087 3019 E7
11700 CdnT 44024 2254 D6
Arbor Glenn Pl
7300 CcdT 44060 2253 C1
Arborhurst Cir
200 AURA 44202 3021 C7
Arborhurst Ln
8700 KTLD 44094 2377 C2

Arbor Park Dr
7800 PRMA 44134 3013 E2
7800 PRMA 44134 3014 A2
Arborside Ln
500 AVLK 44012 2618 E4
Arborvine Ln
300 MDSN 44057 1942 B7
Arborwood Wy
- MsnT 44024 2503 D5
Arbutus Rd
24800 OKWD 44146 2887 D7
Arcade Av
15600 CLEV 44110 2372 C7
Arcadia Dr
7000 PRMA 44129 2882 D6
Arcadia Point Dr
700 AURA 44202 3156 C4
E Arcadia Point Dr
500 AURA 44202 3156 C4
W Arcadia Point Dr
600 AURA 44202 3156 C4
Arch St
5000 MPHT 44137 2757 D7
5300 MPHT 44137 2886 D1
Archdale Av
17300 LKWD 44107 2622 B5
Archer Ct
2600 BWHT 44147 3149 D5
Archer Rd
600 BDFD 44146 2887 C3
4300 CLEV 44105 2756 B4
9500 EatT 44035 3007 D1
9500 EatT 44039 3007 D1
9500 NRDV 44039 3007 D1
9700 EatT 44044 3007 D2
Archmere Av
4300 CLEV 44109 2754 A6
4500 CLEV 44144 2754 B6
5800 BKLN 44144 2754 A6
6200 BKLN 44144 2753 E6
Archwood Av
- CLEV 44102 2754 B2
- CLEV 44109 2754 B2
900 LORN 44052 2614 B7
Archwood Dr
3300 RKRV 44116 2751 A2
Archwood Rd
6900 INDE 44131 2884 E6
Arcola Rd
2800 MadT 44057 1942 E5
Arctic Ct
6700 CLEV 44103 2495 E6
Arden Av
800 BERA 44017 2880 B4
800 BERA 44142 2880 B4
800 BKPK 44142 2880 B4
800 PnvT 44077 2040 C2
11700 CLEV 44111 2623 B7
14900 LKWD 44107 2622 C6
Arden Ct
2000 TwbT 44236 3155 A5
Arden Dr
8900 MNTR 44060 2144 D3
N Arden Dr
5900 MNTR 44060 2144 D3
Arden Ln
2000 TwbT 44236 3155 A6
Arden Rd
7400 PRMA 44129 2882 E1
Ardenall Av
13800 ECLE 44112 2497 A5
Ardendale Rd
4400 SELD 44121 2628 C1
Ardleigh Dr
- CVHT 44106 2626 E4
Ardmore Av
100 PNVL 44077 2146 A2
3900 CLEV 44109 2754 B5
4200 CLEV 44144 2754 B5
Ardmore Dr
5800 BKLN 44144 2754 A5
5800 CLEV 44144 2754 A5
Ardmore Rd
3200 SRHT 44120 2627 D7
3900 CVHT 44121 2498 A7
4000 SELD 44121 2498 B7
Ardola Ct
10 CrlT 44035 3006 B2
Ardoon Av
13400 CLEV 44120 2627 A5
Ardoon St
1200 CVHT 44121 2498 A7
Ardoye Av
800 PnvT 44077 2040 D2
Ardoyne Av
1400 CLEV 44109 2754 D4
Ardwell Dr
20000 EUCL 44123 2373 A3
Arey Rd
2100 CLEV 44106 2626 D2
Argee Dr
7200 MNTR 44060 2144 B7
Argonne Dr
500 PNVL 44077 2040 A5
Argonne Rd
900 CVHT 44121 2498 B5
900 SELD 44121 2498 B7
Argus Av
13300 CLEV 44110 2497 A1
Argyle Dr
- EUCL 44117 2373 D7
- EUCL 44143 2373 D7
- RDHT 44117 2373 D7
- RDHT 44143 2373 D7
1200 MadT 44057 1843 D6
Argyle Ovl
19400 RKRV 44116 2621 D4
Argyle Rd
200 RKRV 44116 2621 D5
Arizona Av
10 LORN 44052 2614 E5
Arkansas Av
10 LORN 44052 2614 E5
5600 CLEV 44102 2624 A7
Arlesford Dr
32300 SLN 44139 2888 E7
33200 SLN 44139 2889 A7
Arlet Ct
1200 BWHT 44147 3149 E4
Arline Av
700 ETLK 44095 2250 B2
Arlington Av
100 PnvT 44077 2146 D1
3800 NBGH 44105 2755 B3
12000 CLEV 44108 2496 D5

STREET Block City ZIP Map# Grid

Arlington Blvd
6900 SLN 44139 2889 D7
Arlington Cir
10 WKLF 44092 2374 C3
28400 WLWK 44095 2249 A7
30900 BYVL 44140 2619 B3
Arlington Ct
800 ELYR 44035 2875 E2
Arlington Dr
- AVON 44011 2747 A4
600 VMLN 44089 2742 A5
2300 LNHT 44124 2629 C3
2300 PRPK 44124 2629 C3
7800 CsTp 44026 2631 D3
9600 PMHT 44130 2882 C3
20100 SGVL 44149 3146 C2
37200 WLBY 44094 2250 D7
Arlington Ln
24600 NOSD 44070 2750 C6
Arlington Rd
1200 LKWD 44107 2622 A4
2400 CVHT 44118 2627 B5
Arlington St
6900 BKVL 44141 3016 A7
Arlis Av
13800 CLEV 44111 2622 D7
Arliss Dr
12500 LKWD 44107 2623 A4
Armadale Av
29200 WKLF 44092 2374 C4
Armi Cir
400 PnvT 44077 2147 A2
Armin Av
14600 LKWD 44107 2622 D6
Armitage Av
10 PnvT 44077 2040 D2
Armitage Ct
9200 CLEV 44105 2756 B3
Armour Rd
100 AVLK 44012 2488 B7
100 AVLK 44012 2618 B1
Arms Av
- EUCL 44117 2373 B4
22200 EUCL 44119 2373 B4
22200 EUCL 44123 2373 B4
Arndt St
2100 LORN 44089 2742 B7
2100 VMLN 44089 2742 B7
Arnie's Ln
- ELYR 44035 2875 D5
Arnold Ct
3800 CLEV 44109 2754 C2
Arnold Dr
30200 WLWK 44095 2249 C6
Arnold Miller Pkwy
6000 SLN 44139 2888 D6
Arrow Ct
100 EatT 44035 3007 A2
100 ELYR 44035 3007 A2
Arrow Ln
2800 PRMA 44134 2883 C7
10600 CdnT 44024 2378 C6
Arrowhead Av
18500 CLEV 44119 2372 E5
19300 CLEV 44119 2373 A5
19700 EUCL 44119 2373 A5
Arrowhead Dr
1000 VMLN 44089 2741 C6
11100 EatT 44044 3007 A5
Arrowhead Ln
500 SgHT 44067 3017 D5
Arrowhead St
2300 LORN 44052 2744 B1
2300 LORN 44053 2744 B1
Arrowhead Tr
900 AURA 44202 3156 D4
13500 MDBH 44130 3012 D1
Arrowood Ct
8800 MNTR 44060 2144 C3
Arrowood Dr
8700 MNTR 44060 2144 C3
Arrow Wood Cir
100 SRSL 44022 2761 D6
Arrow Wood Ovl
7300 PRMA 44129 2882 D7
Artemus Ct
10 ELYR 44035 2875 C6
Arthur Av
1300 LKWD 44107 2622 C5
1900 WTLK 44145 2750 C1
2200 CLEV 44107 2622 C6
2200 CLEV 44111 2622 C6
10500 CLEV 44106 2626 C3
29400 WKLF 44092 2249 B7
Arthur Ct
1200 MadT 44057 1843 D6
Arthur Rd
31200 SLN 44139 2888 E7
32800 SLN 44139 2889 A7
Arthur St
37300 WLBY 44094 2250 D7
Artino St
100 OBLN 44074 3139 A2
Artmar Dr
6000 CcdT 44077 2145 E4
Artsdale Dr
- AVLK 44012 2617 D2
Arundel Rd
200 RKRV 44116 2621 E4
Asbury Ln
- ELYR 44035 2875 A7
- NRDV 44035 3007 B1
Asbury Rd
9800 FdmT 44231 3160 D7
9800 FdmT 44255 3160 D7
9800 HrmT 44231 3160 D7
9800 HrmT 44255 3160 E5
10300 HrmT 44234 3160 E4
Ascoa Ct
22300 SGVL 44149 3145 E2
22300 SGVL 44149 3146 A2
Ascot Ln
4000 WVHT 44122 2757 E3
4100 WVHT 44128 2757 E3
11500 AbnT 44021 2893 C4
11700 AbnT 44255 2893 C4
Ascot Pl
8700 KTLD 44094 2377 C6
Ascot Rd
6000 MDHT 44124 2629 D1
Ash Av
- EUCL 44132 2374 A2
Ash Dr
10 OmsT 44138 2879 B4
17600 SGVL 44149 3146 C4

STREET Block City ZIP Map# Grid

E Ash Dr
1600 AVON 44011 2618 E7
1600 AVON 44011 2748 E1
W Ash Dr
1600 AVON 44011 2618 E7
1600 AVON 44011 2748 E1
E Ash Ln
3900 ORNG 44122 2759 C3
W Ash Ln
3900 ORNG 44122 2759 C3
Ash Rd
2500 WLBY 44094 2250 E1
E Ash Rd
5600 INDE 44131 2884 D4
W Ash Rd
4900 INDE 44131 2884 C4
Ash St
400 VMLN 44089 2741 A5
Ashberry Ct
600 AVLK 44012 2618 A5
Ashberry Ln
300 HkyT 44233 3147 E7
Ashbolt Dr
- LORN 44053 2744 E5
Ashbrooke Wy
600 BSHT 44236 3153 E6
600 HDSN 44236 3153 E6
700 HDSN 44236 3154 A6
Ashburton Av
13400 CLEV 44110 2497 A3
Ashbury Av
10200 CLEV 44106 2496 C7
10800 CLEV 44106 2626 C1
12300 CLEV 44112 2496 E7
Ashbury Park Dr
4400 NOSD 44070 2750 A6
Ashby Rd
3300 SRHT 44120 2627 B7
3400 CLEV 44120 2757 B1
3400 SRHT 44120 2757 B1
Ashcroft Dr
5800 MDHT 44124 2629 C2
Ashcroft Ln
9100 TNBG 44087 3019 B7
Ashdale Dr
2300 TNBG 44087 3154 D1
Ashdale Rd
6300 MDHT 44124 2629 E2
Ashdown Dr
32500 SLN 44139 3019 E2
Ashford Ct
300 BWHT 44147 3149 E5
20400 SGVL 44149 3146 C4
Ashford Dr
8500 MCDN 44056 3018 D7
Ashford Rd
3000 SRHT 44120 2627 B6
Ashford St
8200 CcdT 44077 2254 E5
Ashford Glen Ln
1300 SgHT 44067 3017 A5
Ash Grove Cir
200 AURA 44202 3021 B7
Ashland Av
100 ELYR 44035 3006 D2
100 LORN 44052 2614 C6
1300 LORN 44052 2744 C1
3000 LORN 44053 2744 C3
Ashland Ct
400 ELYR 44035 3006 C2
Ashland Dr
15300 BKPK 44142 2881 B1
Ashland Ln
10 AURA 44202 3021 D7
Ashland Rd
2100 CLEV 44103 2625 D3
2200 CLEV 44104 2625 D3
Ashland Oberlin Rd
- NRsT 44074 3138 E5
- OBLN 44074 3138 D7
- PtfT 44074 3138 D7
Ashland Oberlin Rd SR-58
- NRsT 44074 3138 E5
- OBLN 44074 3138 D7
- PtfT 44074 3138 D7
Ashlar Dr
100 SVHL 44131 2883 E3
100 SVHL 44131 2884 A3
Ashlawn Dr
3800 BNWK 44212 3146 E6
7000 BKVL 44141 3016 A3
Ashleigh Dr
10 BNWK 44136 3147 C6
10 BNWK 44212 3147 C6
10 SGVL 44136 3147 C6
100 SRSL 44022 2762 E6
100 SRSL 44022 2763 A6
Ashley Cir
500 AVLK 44012 2618 D3
5600 HDHT 44143 2499 B4
20200 SGVL 44149 3011 C3
Ashley Ct
10 RKRV 44116 2621 B7
Ashley Dr
1700 HDSN 44236 3154 E7
8400 BWHT 44147 3015 C4
Ashley Ln
9800 CcdT 44060 2253 B1
14000 NRYN 44133 3014 A7
14000 NRYN 44133 3149 B1
Ashley Rd
2600 SRHT 44122 2628 B5
Ashlyn Ct
8800 ODFL 44138 2879 D7
Ashton Cir
4100 NOSD 44070 2750 E5
Ashton Ct
800 AURA 44202 3156 D4
7500 NRYN 44133 3013 D7
8400 MNTR 44060 2251 C5
Ashton Dr
26900 OmsT 44138 2878 D7
Ashton Ln
6500 SLN 44139 2889 B6
30000 BYVL 44140 2619 B5
Ashton Rd
2500 CVHT 44118 2627 D5
Ashton Tr
12500 MsnT 44024 2504 C7
Ashton Place Dr
- NRDV 44035 2876 B6
- NRDV 44039 2876 C6
Ashurst Rd
2200 UNHT 44118 2627 E4
2500 SRHT 44118 2627 E5

STREET Block City ZIP Map# Grid

Ashview Dr
900 MadT 44057 1844 A5
Ashview Dr Ext
- MadT 44057 1844 A5
Ashwood Blvd
5900 AMHT 44001 2744 C6
5900 AMHT 44053 2744 C6
5900 LORN 44053 2744 C6
Ashwood Ct
8900 ODFL 44138 3009 E1
Ashwood Dr
- NbyT 44065 2764 C1
100 AVLK 44012 2617 D2
100 ELYR 44035 3005 B1
5100 LNHT 44124 2499 A6
6400 INDE 44131 2884 D5
8600 SGVL 44149 3011 A3
29200 WKLF 44092 2374 C4
Ashwood Ln
- MNTR 44060 2144 E7
Ashwood Rd
3000 CLEV 44120 2626 E6
3100 CLEV 44120 2627 A7
3100 SRHT 44120 2627 A7
Ashwood Tr
9800 CcdT 44060 2253 B3
Aspen Cir
8800 PRMA 44129 2882 D7
8800 PRMA 44130 2882 D7
16600 SGVL 44136 3147 A5
Aspen Ct
- CLEV 44102 2624 A6
300 AURA 44202 3156 E2
9900 CcdT 44060 2253 B2
10200 CrlT 44035 3006 D3
Aspen Dr
10 AhtT 44001 2873 B1
28300 NOSD 44070 2878 D3
Aspen Ln
1400 AVON 44011 2617 C6
Aspen Ovl
13900 NRYN 44133 3014 C7
Aspen St
35200 NRDV 44039 2877 A1
Aspen Glen Dr
32700 SLN 44139 2759 E7
Aspen Hills Ln
14600 BtnT 44021 2765 D1
Aspenwood Ct
8800 MNTR 44060 2144 D3
Aspenwood Dr
100 MDHL 44022 2760 B5
600 SVHL 44131 3015 A1
Aspenwood Ln
34800 WLBY 44094 2375 A1
Asper St
100 PNVL 44077 2040 A7
Aspinwall Av
13500 CLEV 44110 2497 A2
E Asplin Dr
2600 RKRV 44116 2751 A1
W Asplin Dr
- RKRV 44116 2621 A7
2600 RKRV 44116 2751 A1
Associate Av
7300 BKLN 44144 2753 E2
7300 CLEV 44144 2753 E2
Aster Dr
5900 INDE 44131 2884 D4
7600 MNTR 44060 2143 D5
Aster Pl
100 BNWK 44212 3147 A6
Asterhurst Trc
6700 MDBH 44130 2881 B4
Astor Av
12400 CLEV 44135 2753 A6
13000 CLEV 44135 2752 E6
Astor Pl
10 RKRV 44116 2621 D5
Astoria Wy
3900 AVON 44011 2747 E4
Athena Dr
12300 NRYN 44133 3014 C6
Athens Av
10 PnvT 44077 2041 B5
13000 LKWD 44107 2623 A6
13300 LKWD 44107 2622 E6
Atherstone Rd
3500 CVHT 44121 2497 E5
Atkins Av
2000 LKWD 44107 2622 B6
2300 CLEV 44107 2622 B7
2300 CLEV 44111 2622 B7
Atlanta Ln
30500 WTLK 44145 2749 B1
Atlantic Rd
12800 SGVL 44149 3011 B7
Atlas Dr
300 LORN 44052 2615 C5
Atlis Ct
12200 SGVL 44149 3011 D6
Atterbury Dr
1100 MCDN 44056 3153 E1
Attica Rd
3500 CLEV 44111 2752 D1
Attleboro Rd
2700 SRHT 44120 2627 D6
Atwater Dr
1100 MadT 44057 1843 E6
Atwood Dr
1100 CLEV 44108 2496 D6
Atwood Pl
5800 WLBY 44094 2375 A2
Auburn Av
1000 CLEV 44113 2624 E6
5300 MPHT 44137 2886 E1
Auburn Dr
2000 BHWD 44122 2758 E2
Auburn Rd
- CcdT 44077 2146 B5
7200 CcdT 44077 2254 B1
8200 CcdT 44024 2254 B5
8200 CdnT 44024 2254 B7
9000 CdnT 44024 2379 B7
9800 CRDN 44024 2379 B7
10700 CdnT 44024 2504 B1
10700 MsnT 44024 2504 A4
12500 MsnT 44024 2634 A7
13300 MsnT 44026 2634 A7
13300 MsnT 44065 2634 A7
13400 NbyT 44026 2634 A3
13400 NbyT 44065 2634 A3
14600 NbyT 44065 2764 A1
16000 AbnT 44023 2764 A7
16000 NbyT 44023 2764 A7

STREET Block City ZIP Map# Grid

Auburn Rd
16400 AbnT 44023 2893 A7
17800 AbnT 44255 2893 A6
Auburn Rdg
6900 CcdT 44077 2146 A7
Auburn St
400 ELYR 44035 3006 D2
400 PNVL 44077 2040 A7
Auburndale Av
1600 CLEV 44112 2496 D7
1600 ECLE 44112 2496 E7
12300 CLEV 44106 2496 D7
Auburndale Dr
10400 AbnT 44023 3023 D2
Auburn Glen Dr
18600 AbnT 44255 3023 E1
Auburn Lakes Dr
10 AbnT 44023 2892 A4
Auburn Springs Dr
16600 AbnT 44023 2892 C1
Audrey Dr
300 RDHT 44143 2498 D2
800 ETLK 44095 2250 B3
Audubon Blvd
3000 CLEV 44104 2626 C7
Augdon Dr
400 ELYR 44035 2875 E3
Augusta Av
200 LORN 44052 2615 A6
Augusta Ct
2100 WTLK 44145 2749 B1
Augusta Dr
100 CrlT 44035 3006 D3
100 ELYR 44035 3006 C3
32100 AVLK 44012 2618 C5
Augusta Ln
7900 CcdT 44077 2253 E3
8000 SgHT 44067 3017 E4
Augusta Wy
33200 AVON 44011 2748 D4
Augustine Dr
2200 PRMA 44134 2883 C6
Augustus Dr
400 HDHT 44143 2499 C2
Aulcash Av
- CLEV 44105 2756 E2
- CLEV 44120 2756 E2
Aurensen Rd
36000 NRDV 44039 2876 E4
36000 NRDV 44039 2877 A4
Aurora Dr
10 OmsT 44138 2879 A4
700 VMLN 44089 2740 C5
Aurora Rd
3600 AURA 44087 3156 A2
3600 AURA 44202 3156 A2
3600 TNBG 44087 3155 D2
3600 TwbT 44087 3155 E2
3600 TwbT 44087 3156 A2
20600 WVHT 44128 2758 A6
20600 WVHT 44146 2758 A6
21700 BDHT 44146 2758 B7
21700 MPHT 44146 2758 B7
23100 BDHT 44146 2887 D1
26700 BDHT 44146 2888 A2
26700 SLN 44139 2888 E5
33200 SLN 44139 2889 C7
37800 SLN 44139 3020 D1
39700 SLN 44139 3021 A2
40000 BbgT 44023 3021 A2
40000 BbgT 44139 3021 A2
40000 BbgT 44202 3021 A2
Aurora Rd SR-43
21700 BDHT 44146 2758 B7
21700 MPHT 44146 2758 B7
23100 BDHT 44146 2887 E2
26700 BDHT 44146 2888 A2
26700 SLN 44139 2888 E5
33200 SLN 44139 2889 C7
37800 SLN 44139 3020 D1
39700 SLN 44139 3021 A2
40000 BbgT 44023 3021 A2
40000 BbgT 44139 3021 A2
40000 BbgT 44202 3021 A2
Aurora Rd SR-82
3600 AURA 44087 3156 A2
3600 AURA 44202 3156 A2
3600 TNBG 44087 3155 D2
3600 TwbT 44087 3155 E2
3600 TwbT 44087 3156 A2
E Aurora Rd
10 NCtT 44067 3152 E1
10 NCtT 44067 3153 D1
300 MCDN 44056 3153 B1
1400 MCDN 44056 3154 C1
1500 TNBG 44087 3154 C1
3400 TNBG 44087 3155 C2
3400 TwbT 44087 3155 C2
E Aurora Rd SR-82
10 NCtT 44067 3152 E1
10 NCtT 44067 3153 D1
300 MCDN 44056 3153 B1
1400 MCDN 44056 3154 C1
1500 TNBG 44087 3154 C1
3400 TNBG 44087 3155 C2
3400 TwbT 44087 3155 C2
N Aurora Rd
10 AURA 44202 3021 E7
10 BbgT 44023 3021 A3
10 BbgT 44139 3021 A2
10 BbgT 44202 3021 A3
10 SLN 44139 3021 A2
N Aurora Rd SR-43
10 AURA 44202 3021 D7
10 BbgT 44023 3021 A3
10 BbgT 44139 3021 A2
10 BbgT 44202 3021 A3
10 SLN 44139 3021 A2
S Aurora Rd
10 AURA 44202 3156 E1
S Aurora Rd SR-43
10 AURA 44202 3156 E1
W Aurora Rd
10 NCtT 44067 3152 E1
100 SgHT 44067 3152 E1
900 SgHT 44067 3017 B7
1100 SgHT 44067 3016 E7
1300 BKVL 44141 3016 E7
1300 SgHT 44141 3016 E7
W Aurora Rd SR-82
10 NCtT 44067 3152 E1
100 SgHT 44067 3152 E1
900 SgHT 44067 3017 B7
1100 SgHT 44067 3016 E7
1300 BKVL 44141 3016 E7

STREET Block City ZIP Map# Grid

W Aurora Rd SR-82
1300 SgHT 44141 3016 E7
Aurora Commons Cir
- AURA 44202 3156 D1
Aurora Hill Dr
900 AURA 44202 3021 A7
Aurora Hudson Rd
200 AURA 44202 3156 B7
1400 STBR 44236 3156 C6
1400 STBR 44241 3156 C6
Aurora Industrial Pkwy
10 AURA 44202 3156 E5
Aurora Lake Rd
600 AURA 44202 3021 B5
Austen Ln
5100 RDHT 44143 2498 E4
5100 RDHT 44143 2499 A4
Austin Av
12800 CLEV 44108 2496 E5
Austin Rd
100 GNVA 44041 1944 D3
100 GnvT 44041 1944 D3
Austin St
200 BERA 44017 2880 D7
400 BERA 44130 2880 D7
400 MDBH 44130 2880 D7
Austin Point Dr
7000 CcdT 44077 2146 C7
Austin Powder Dr
7200 GNWL 44139 3019 C2
Austrian Ct
7900 CLEV 44104 2626 A4
Autumn Cir
10200 STBR 44241 3156 C7
Autumn Dr
600 AMHT 44001 2872 E3
8000 LryT 44024 2256 C4
Autumn Ln
100 BNWK 44212 3146 E6
4700 BKLN 44144 2753 D6
5400 NRDV 44039 2747 B7
5400 NRDV 44039 2876 B1
Autumn Ovl
20600 SGVL 44149 3146 B3
Autumn Ridge Dr
- MsnT 44024 2503 B2
6300 MadT 44057 1942 A4
Avalon Ct
36700 AVON 44011 2747 E4
Avalon Dr
- RKRV 44116 2621 C5
10 AVLK 44012 2617 C1
10 BDFD 44146 2887 A3
1300 MadT 44057 1843 C6
2000 PRMA 44134 2883 D7
12100 EatT 44044 3008 B7
12100 EatT 44044 3143 B1
37700 NRDV 44039 2747 C6
W Avalon Dr
2600 WTLK 44145 2749 D2
Avalon Rd
- CLEV 44120 2757 D2
- CLEV 44128 2757 D2
1600 CLEV 44112 2497 D2
1700 CLEV 44121 2497 E2
3100 SRHT 44120 2627 D7
3400 SRHT 44120 2757 D2
Avenue Sq
2500 PryT 44077 2041 B7
Avenue of Peace
- LNDL 44111 2753 B3
11900 LNDL 44135 2753 B3
Avery Av
4600 CLEV 44127 2625 C6
Avery Pkwy
- SGVL 44149 3011 A7
- SGVL 44149 3146 A1
Avery Rd
8100 BWHT 44147 3014 E3
8200 BWHT 44147 3015 B6
9200 BWHT 44147 3150 A1
Avery St
300 BDFD 44146 2887 B4
Avery Ter
200 PNVL 44077 2040 B7
Avion Park Dr
5300 HDHT 44143 2499 B2
Avon Av
300 VMLN 44089 2742 A5
10200 CLEV 44105 2756 D3
Avon Dr
- AURA 44202 3157 A4
7300 MNTR 44060 2251 C1
Avon Ln
7400 CsTp 44026 2631 C1
Avon Rd
31200 AVON 44011 2619 A7
31200 AVON 44145 2619 A7
31200 WTLK 44145 2619 A7
31500 AVON 44011 2618 E7
Avon Belden Rd
- LmC 44012 2488 A7
100 AVLK 44012 2488 A7
100 AVLK 44012 2618 A4
700 AVON 44011 2618 A5
700 AVON 44012 2618 A5
1600 EatT 44044 3142 E6
1600 GFTN 44044 3142 E3
4900 AVON 44011 2748 A7
4900 NRDV 44011 2748 A7
4900 NRDV 44039 2748 A7
5000 NRDV 44039 2877 A5
9000 NRDV 44039 3007 E2
9000 NRDV 44039 3008 A1
9400 EatT 44039 3007 E2
9400 EatT 44044 3007 E7
14700 GftT 44044 3142 E6
Avon Belden Rd SR-57
15500 GftT 44044 3142 E7
Avon Belden Rd SR-83
100 AVLK 44012 2488 A7
100 AVLK 44012 2618 A4
700 AVON 44011 2618 A5
700 AVON 44012 2618 A5
1600 EatT 44044 3142 E6
1600 GFTN 44044 3142 E3
4900 AVON 44011 2748 A7
4900 NRDV 44011 2748 A7
4900 NRDV 44039 2748 A7
5000 NRDV 44039 2877 A7
9000 NRDV 44039 3007 E2
9000 NRDV 44039 3008 A1
9400 EatT 44039 3007 E2
9400 EatT 44044 3007 E7
14700 GftT 44044 3142 E6

STREET Block City ZIP Map# Grid

Avon Commerce Pkwy
35100 AVON 44011 2618 B5
Avondale Av
100 AVLK 44012 2617 B2
2700 CVHT 44112 2627 A1
2700 CVHT 44118 2627 B1
7600 GDHT 44125 2756 A5
Avondale Ct
8500 OmsT 44138 2879 A7
Avondale Dr
- AVON 44011 2747 B2
Avondale Rd
- WLBY 44094 2250 C6
1000 CVHT 44121 2498 B5
1000 SELD 44121 2498 B7
3600 WDMR 44122 2759 B2
Avon Point Av
100 AVLK 44012 2488 B7
100 AVLK 44012 2618 B1
Avrina Av
7900 CLEV 44104 2626 A7
7900 CLEV 44127 2626 A7
Axtell Av
10 PNVL 44077 2040 A7
100 AMHT 44001 2872 D1
Ayleshire Dr
6600 SLN 44139 2889 B6
Aylesworth Dr
6300 PMHT 44130 2882 C4
Aynesly Wy
200 BNWK 44212 3147 B7
Azalea Cir
500 NCtT 44067 3153 D5
6200 SLN 44139 2889 C5
8000 BbgT 44023 2890 E7
Azalea Dr
600 SELD 44143 2498 C4
Azalea Ln
10 MNTR 44060 2144 E7
4400 NOSD 44070 2749 D6
Azalea Ridge Dr
- PryT 44081 1940 E6

B

Babbitt Rd
200 EUCL 44123 2373 C2
900 EUCL 44117 2373 D4
900 EUCL 44132 2373 D4
Babbling Brook Ovl
200 HkyT 44233 3148 A7
Bacon Rd
400 PnvT 44077 2041 A2
Bader Av
3200 CLEV 44109 2754 B6
4600 CLEV 44144 2754 B6
Badger Den Ln
16700 SGVL 44136 3146 E3
Bading Av
3400 CLEV 44105 2755 C1
Baetz Ct
6000 EyrT 44035 2745 A6
6000 EyrT 44055 2745 A6
6000 ShfT 44055 2745 A6
Bagley Dr
- BERA 44017 2880 D7
- BERA 44130 2880 D7
- MDBH 44017 2880 D7
- MDBH 44130 2880 D7
Bagley Rd
24600 BERA 44017 2879 C6
24600 ODFL 44017 2879 C6
24600 ODFL 44138 2879 C6
26700 OmsT 44138 2879 A6
26900 OmsT 44138 2878 A6
27300 NRDV 44039 2878 A6
27300 NRDV 44138 2878 A6
31400 NRDV 44039 2877 D6
E Bagley Rd
10 BERA 44017 2880 D6
12800 PRMA 44130 2881 E7
12900 MDBH 44130 2881 C6
17800 MDBH 44130 2880 E6
18800 BERA 44130 2880 D6
19300 MDBH 44017 2880 D6
W Bagley Rd
10 BERA 44017 2880 A6
500 BERA 44017 2879 E6
1300 ODFL 44017 2879 C6
1300 ODFL 44138 2879 C6
W Bagley Rd SR-237
10 BERA 44017 2880 C6
Bailey Av
3500 CLEV 44113 2624 C6
4400 CLEV 44102 2624 B6
Bailey Ct
- CLEV 44113 2624 C6
100 ELYR 44035 2875 B6
Bailey Dr
1200 WKLF 44092 2374 C1
Bailey Rd
4600 NOSD 44070 2750 B6
4800 MadT 44057 2044 B5
Bailus Rd
- NOSD 44070 2749 B7
- NOSD 44145 2749 B7
4400 WTLK 44145 2749 C6
Bainbridge Rd
3400 CVHT 44118 2627 E2
3700 SELD 44118 2627 E2
7100 BbgT 44023 2890 A5
7100 BbgT 44139 2890 A5
7100 SLN 44139 2890 A5
8500 BbgT 44023 2891 E5
9500 AbnT 44023 2892 B5
9500 BbgT 44023 2892 B5
29800 SLN 44139 2888 D3
32700 SLN 44139 2889 C5
33300 NRDV 44039 2877 A4
Bainbrook Dr
7800 BbgT 44023 2890 D7
8300 BbgT 44023 2891 A7
Bain Farm Ct
11100 CcdT 44077 2146 B4
Bain Park Dr
4500 FWPK 44126 2751 C4
Baintree Rd
4300 UNHT 44118 2628 B3
4300 UNHT 44121 2628 C3
E Baintree Rd
23200 BHWD 44122 2628 D3
Baird St
14500 BURT 44021 2636 A7
14500 BURT 44021 2766 A2

STREET Block City ZIP Map# Grid

Baker Av
8000 CLEV 44102 2623 E5
8600 MNTR 44060 2144 B7
Baker Rd
4900 LryT 44057 2042 E7
Baker St
- EyrT 44035 2874 B1
10 BERA 44017 2880 B6
6600 HRM 44234 3161 A2
Balboa Ct
900 PnvT 44077 2146 D2
Baldwin Av
500 ELYR 44035 3006 C1
13800 ECLE 44112 2497 A4
Baldwin Blvd
6000 LORN 44053 2744 E6
Baldwin Ct
10 AMHT 44001 2872 B1
1300 BWHT 44147 3149 D3
15300 MDBH 44130 2881 B7
Baldwin Dr
- RKRV 44116 2621 B6
100 BERA 44017 3011 A1
300 BERA 44017 3010 E1
Baldwin Ln
10 RKRV 44116 2621 A6
11200 TNBG 44087 3020 B3
Baldwin Pl
17800 LKWD 44107 2622 A4
Baldwin Rd
2300 CLEV 44104 2626 C4
4300 PryT 44081 2042 D4
4500 PryT 44057 2042 D5
8300 KDHL 44060 2252 B5
9300 KDHL 44060 2253 A6
32700 SLN 44139 2888 E5
33300 SLN 44139 2889 A5
Baldwin Creek Dr
7300 MDBH 44130 2881 C7
7400 MDBH 44130 3012 C1
Baldwin Reserve Dr
7200 MDBH 44130 2881 D7
W Baldwin Reserve Dr
7200 MDBH 44130 2881 D7
Balfour Rd
20400 HIHL 44122 2758 A2
20400 WVHT 44122 2758 A2
Bali Ct
1000 MCDN 44056 3154 A3
Ball Av
20100 EUCL 44119 2373 A4
20100 EUCL 44123 2373 A4
Ballantrae Dr
100 NCtT 44067 3152 E1
100 SgHT 44067 3152 E1
Ballymore St
18800 SGVL 44149 3146 C4
Balmoral Ct
15600 SGVL 44136 3012 B4
Balmoral Dr
300 EUCL 44143 2498 D1
300 RDHT 44143 2498 D1
Balmoral Wy
1500 WTLK 44145 2620 B7
Balsam Dr
3200 WTLK 44145 2749 E4
6300 AhtT 44001 2744 B7
6300 AhtT 44001 2873 B1
6600 BDHT 44146 2887 E6
7200 OKWD 44146 2887 E7
Baltic Rd
9500 CLEV 44102 2623 C5
Banbury Cir
23600 WVHT 44128 2758 C6
Banbury Ct
1800 WTLK 44145 2750 C1
4800 WVHT 44128 2758 D6
4900 BDHT 44128 2758 D6
Banbury Dr
5400 SLN 44139 2888 E2
Banbury Ovl
5600 MadT 44057 1941 C3
Bancroft Av
7400 GDHT 44105 2756 A5
8000 CLEV 44105 2756 A5
Bancroft Dr
5700 BNHT 44131 2884 C2
5700 INDE 44131 2884 C2
Bancroft St
6700 HRM 44234 3161 A2
Band Dr
8300 GDHT 44125 2756 A6
Bangor Av
5400 CLEV 44144 2754 A5
5800 BKLN 44144 2754 A5
12100 GDHT 44125 2885 E1
13500 GDHT 44125 2886 A1
13900 GDHT 44137 2886 A1
13900 MPHT 44137 2886 A1
Bank Rd
7300 MadT 44057 1843 E5
Bank St
600 PnvT 44077 2146 C1
800 AURA 44202 3021 C4
800 PNVL 44077 2146 C3
1200 ELYR 44035 3006 A1
8200 BhmT 44089 2870 D5
9000 VLVW 44125 2885 A2
Bank St SR-84
800 PNVL 44077 2146 C3
800 PnvT 44077 2146 C3
Banks Rd
39600 CrlT 44044 3141 C3
40100 CrlT 44050 3141 C3
40600 CrlT 44044 3140 E3
40600 CrlT 44050 3140 E3
Banks Landing Dr
- PNVL 44077 2146 C1
Banner Ln
6900 PRMA 44129 2882 D6
Bannerstone Dr
10 PnvT 44077 2041 A7
Baptist Cir
200 SgHT 44067 3017 E4
Bar Hbr
37600 WLBY 44094 2250 D3
Barbara Av
15600 CLEV 44135 2752 C4
Barbara Dr
7900 MDBH 44130 3012 D2
7900 SGVL 44130 3012 D2
7900 SGVL 44136 3012 D3
8400 MNTR 44060 2144 B2
Barbara Ln
- INDE 44131 3016 C2

STREET Block City ZIP Map# Grid

Barbara Ln
- INDE 44141 3016 C2
6000 BKPK 44142 2881 B3
Barbara St
1000 ELYR 44035 3005 E1
32800 ETLK 44095 2249 E5
32800 WLWK 44095 2249 E5
Barber Av
1700 CLEV 44113 2624 C6
37000 WLBY 44094 2250 D6
Barber Ct
2600 CLEV 44113 2624 D6
Barberry Cir
900 AMHT 44001 2872 C1
Barberry Dr
10 BERA 44017 2880 C5
100 BERA 44130 2880 D5
100 MDBH 44130 2880 D5
Barberry Hill Dr
8000 MNTR 44060 2251 E1
8000 MNTR 44060 2252 A1
Barberton Av
6100 CLEV 44102 2754 A2
6300 CLEV 44102 2753 E1
Barchard St
700 GFTN 44044 3142 A5
Barchester Dr
10000 CcdT 44077 2145 C7
10100 CcdT 44077 2253 D1
Barclay Blvd
1400 WTLK 44145 2619 B7
Barclay St
10 GDRV 44077 2039 C6
Bard Av
22400 FWPK 44126 2751 A5
Bardbury Av
16600 MDBH 44130 2881 A7
Bardwell Av
14000 ECLE 44112 2497 A5
Bardwell Dr
12000 CsTp 44026 2502 B5
Barfield Dr
12500 CsTp 44026 2502 C7
Bar Harbor Dr
300 BYVL 44140 2619 B4
Bar Harbour Ln
7500 MNTR 44060 2251 B2
Barjode Rd
30000 WLWK 44095 2249 C7
Barkdale Ln
8900 MCDN 44056 3019 A7
Barkleigh Cir
6500 BKVL 44141 3016 B5
Barkston Dr
800 HDHT 44143 2499 C6
900 MDHT 44124 2499 C6
900 MDHT 44143 2499 C6
Barkwill Av
4800 CLEV 44127 2625 C7
Barkwood Ct
5800 MNTR 44060 2144 C3
Barkwood Dr
2500 SFLD 44054 2747 A1
5300 SFLD 44054 2616 E7
5300 SFLD 44054 2617 A7
Barley Dr
10 PnvT 44077 2040 E7
10 PnvT 44077 2146 E1
Barnaby Ln
7700 MNTR 44060 2143 D6
Barnes Av
100 PNVL 44077 2040 A7
Barnes Ct
37900 WLBY 44094 2250 D6
Barnsley Wy
2300 BWHT 44147 3149 D5
Barnum Ct
9100 OmsT 44138 3009 C1
Barnum Rd
1900 HpfT 44041 1944 E5
2300 GnvT 44041 1944 E5
Baron Dr
10700 PRMA 44130 3013 B2
Barr Rd
9300 BKVL 44141 3150 C4
10300 RchT 44141 3150 D6
10300 RchT 44286 3150 D6
Barres Ln
200 ELYR 44035 2875 A7
Barres Rd
37500 NRDV 44039 2876 B1
Barrett Av
10300 CLEV 44108 2496 C4
Barrett Rd
10 BERA 44017 2880 B6
600 BERA 44017 2879 E4
600 OmsT 44017 2879 E4
600 OmsT 44138 2879 E3
Barriemore Av
16200 MDBH 44130 2881 B7
Barrington Av
12600 CLEV 44108 2496 E5
Barrington Blvd
10 AURA 44202 3021 E7
10600 PMHT 44130 2882 B5
Barrington Ct
100 ELYR 44035 3006 C2
Barrington Dr
- EatT 44044 3141 E2
3300 AVON 44011 2748 B4
12600 CsTp 44026 2501 C7
E Barrington Dr
400 CRDN 44024 2505 A1
W Barrington Dr
300 CRDN 44024 2505 A1
Barrington Pl E
10 AURA 44202 3021 E7
Barrington Pl W
200 AURA 44202 3021 D7
Barrington Rd
2100 UNHT 44118 2627 E3
Barrington Rdg
200 PnvT 44077 2145 C5
Barrington Town Sq
10 AURA 44202 3021 E7
Barristers Ct
- KTLD 44094 2376 E2
Barry Ct
6100 MNTR 44060 2144 A3
Barry Ln
10 NCtT 44067 3153 A2
Bartfield Av
12700 CLEV 44108 2496 E4
Bartholomew Dr
7300 MDBH 44130 2881 D7

Bartholomew Dr
7300 MDBH 44130 3012 D1
Bartholomew Rd
9900 AbnT 44023 3023 B1
10300 AbnT 44255 3023 B1
Bartish Ct
600 AhtT 44001 2873 B2
Bartlam Av
4700 GDHT 44125 2757 A6
Bartlett Av
13100 CLEV 44105 2756 E2
13100 CLEV 44120 2756 E2
13100 CLEV 44120 2757 A2
14300 CLEV 44128 2757 A2
15400 SRHT 44120 2757 A2
Bartlett Dr
22200 RKRV 44116 2621 A6
Bartlett Rd
- BDHT 44146 2758 C7
500 AURA 44241 3157 D6
500 AURA 44255 3157 D6
500 STBR 44241 3157 D6
500 STBR 44255 3157 D6
700 ManT 44255 3157 E6
700 ShvT 44255 3157 E6
2700 ManT 44255 3158 A6
2700 ShvT 44255 3158 A6
5200 BDHT 44146 2887 C2
5500 BDFD 44146 2887 C2
Bartlett Rd SR-43
- BDHT 44146 2758 C7
Bartley Ln
8400 MNTR 44060 2144 B3
Barton Cir
7200 PRMA 44129 2882 E6
Barton Dr
7000 MNTR 44060 2144 D7
8300 SGVL 44149 3011 A3
Barton Rd
- LNHT 44124 2498 E5
700 SgHT 44067 3152 D3
5300 NOSD 44070 2878 B2
5300 NRDV 44039 2877 E1
5300 NRDV 44039 2878 A1
5300 NRDV 44070 2878 A1
7100 OmsT 44070 2878 B2
7100 OmsT 44138 2878 B2
N Barton Rd
4800 AVON 44011 2748 E6
4800 NRDV 44011 2748 E6
4800 NRDV 44039 2748 E6
5000 LNHT 44124 2498 E5
5200 NRDV 44039 2877 E1
S Barton Rd
5000 LNHT 44124 2498 E5
Barton Hill Dr
7200 PRMA 44129 2882 E6
Bartow Ln
500 RDHT 44143 2498 C3
Bartter Av
14500 CLEV 44111 2752 D2
Bartwood Dr
2500 PnvT 44077 2041 B5
2500 PryT 44077 2041 B5
Barwick Ct
800 PnvT 44077 2040 E2
Bascom Rd
9000 HmbT 44024 2256 D7
9000 HmbT 44024 2381 D4
Bascule Dr
- LORN 44052 2614 E6
Base Dr
10 PnvT 44077 2041 A4
Basquin Dr
200 CRDN 44024 2380 B5
Bass Run
10 AbnT 44023 2892 A4
Bassett Ln
9300 NRYN 44133 3013 C5
Bassett Rd
200 BYVL 44140 2619 C5
500 BYVL 44140 2619 C6
500 WTLK 44140 2619 C6
1600 WTLK 44145 2749 D2
27200 WTLK 44145 2750 A2
Bass Lake Rd
11400 CRDN 44024 2505 A3
11400 MsnT 44024 2504 D7
11400 MsnT 44024 2505 A3
12500 MsnT 44024 2634 D2
13500 NbyT 44024 2634 D4
13500 NbyT 44065 2634 D4
14400 NbyT 44021 2765 A1
14400 NbyT 44065 2635 A7
14400 NbyT 44065 2765 A1
Basswood Cir
13800 SGVL 44136 3012 D5
Basswood Ct
7500 NRYN 44133 3013 D7
Basswood Dr
5700 LORN 44053 2744 E6
6500 BDHT 44146 2887 D6
9200 ODFL 44138 3010 A1
Basswood Ln
10 MDHL 44022 2760 A4
7500 MNTR 44060 2251 D4
Basswood Pl
8700 MCDN 44056 3018 B5
Basswood Rd
11500 MsnT 44024 2504 B3
Batavia Av
7500 CLEV 44105 2756 A4
Bates Dr
300 BYVL 44140 2619 A4
Bates Ln
2600 WBHL 44094 2375 B4
Bates Rd
200 MadT 44057 2044 D2
200 MDSN 44057 2044 D2
700 RKRV 44116 2621 B6
3100 MadT 44057 1942 D7
3100 MDSN 44057 1942 D7
Bath St
100 ELYR 44035 2875 A5
200 ELYR 44035 2874 E5
Bathgate Dr
1600 MadT 44057 1842 E7
1600 MadT 44057 1941 E1
Battersea Blvd
19200 RKRV 44116 2621 D5
Battles Ct
10 CRDN 44024 2380 A6
Battles Rd
400 GSML 44040 2500 E3
7700 CsTp 44026 2501 A2

Battles Rd
7700 CsTp 44040 2501 A2
7700 GSML 44040 2501 A2
Bauer Cir
8800 NRDV 44035 2876 B7
Bauer Ln
7200 MNTR 44060 2143 C4
Bauerdale Av
8100 PRMA 44129 2882 D1
36600 AVON 44011 2747 E2
Baumhart Rd
1100 LORN 44053 2742 C6
1100 LORN 44089 2742 C7
1400 BhmT 44001 2742 C7
1400 BhmT 44053 2742 C7
1400 BhmT 44089 2742 C7
1400 VMLN 44001 2742 C7
1400 VMLN 44089 2742 C7
1700 BhmT 44001 2871 C6
1700 VMLN 44001 2871 C6
1700 VMLN 44089 2871 C1
Bavaria Av
5700 PRMA 44129 2882 D2
Bavaria Pkwy
7800 MCDN 44087 3154 C5
7800 TwbT 44087 3154 C5
8000 MCDN 44056 3154 C5
Baxter Av
6500 CLEV 44105 2755 E1
Baxterly Av
2000 LKWD 44107 2622 D6
Bay Ct
5600 WLBY 44094 2375 A2
N Bay Dr
2000 WLBY 44094 2143 A7
2100 WLBY 44094 2251 A1
2800 WTLK 44145 2749 E3
S Bay Dr
2900 WTLK 44145 2749 E3
Bayard Rd
- SELD 44121 2628 C2
4000 CVHT 44121 2628 A2
4000 SELD 44118 2628 A2
Bayberry Cir
5600 NRDV 44039 2877 E1
7100 NOSD 44070 2878 B4
Bayberry Ct
33300 AVLK 44012 2617 C3
Bayberry Ct E
400 PnvT 44077 2146 E2
Bayberry Ct N
7200 OmsT 44138 2878 E5
Bayberry Ct S
7300 OmsT 44138 2878 D5
Bayberry Ct W
1000 PnvT 44077 2146 E2
Bayberry Dr
10 NCtT 44067 3153 A2
200 ELYR 44035 3006 D2
6300 SVHL 44131 2884 A4
18200 BbgT 44023 2891 A7
Bayberry Ln
100 BDFD 44146 2886 C4
9600 NRYN 44133 3014 B4
Bayberry Rd
500 LORN 44053 2744 E7
Baybrook Ln
- AbnT 44023 2892 B4
S Bay Cove
500 PnvT 44077 2145 B6
Bayes Av
14200 LKWD 44107 2622 D6
Bayfair Ct
24900 BYVL 44140 2620 C5
Bayfair Dr
500 BYVL 44140 2620 C5
26400 ODFL 44138 2879 A6
Bay Hill Dr
- AVLK 44012 2618 B4
Bay Landing Dr
3000 WTLK 44145 2749 E3
Bay Leaf Ln
6000 NRYN 44133 3014 B4
Bayliss Av
6700 CLEV 44103 2495 E7
Bay Meadow St
2300 MadT 44057 1941 D3
Bay Point Cove
7100 MNTR 44060 2251 B1
Bayreuth Rd
1600 CVHT 44112 2497 C5
1600 ECLE 44112 2497 C5
Bayridge Blvd
300 WLWK 44095 2249 D5
900 WLWK 44092 2249 E7
Bay Ridge Ct
7500 MNTR 44060 2143 D4
Bayshore Dr
100 ETLK 44095 2142 C7
Bayside Dr
6500 MadT 44057 1942 B1
Baythorne Dr
- MNTR 44060 2252 A3
Bayview Dr
200 AVLK 44012 2619 A2
31700 AVLK 44012 2618 E2
36900 ETLK 44095 2142 D6
Bayview Rd
200 BYVL 44140 2619 C3
Baywood Ln
- SGVL 44136 3012 D5
Beach Av
1200 LKWD 44107 2623 A5
Beach Ct
5500 PRMA 44134 2883 E1
Beach Dr
- NbyT 44065 2634 B7
- NbyT 44065 2764 B1
6700 MadT 44057 1843 B6
Beach Ln
400 BYVL 44140 2619 D5
Beach Pkwy
1300 LKWD 44107 2623 A5
Beach Rd
- CyhC 44107 2621 E4
800 LKWD 44107 2621 E4
Beach St
- SDLK 44054 2616 A3
10 GNVA 44041 1944 C4
Beach Cliff Blvd
19200 RKRV 44116 2621 D4
Beachdale Dr
10 AVLK 44012 2488 A7
100 AVLK 44012 2618 A1

Beachdell Rd
6400 MDBH 44130 2881 D4
Beachland Dr
11800 NbyT 44065 2764 D1
24300 EUCL 44123 2373 D1
Beachpark Dr
33800 ETLK 44095 2249 E2
33800 LKLN 44095 2249 E2
33900 ETLK 44095 2250 A2
Beachview Dr
20000 EUCL 44117 2498 A1
S Beachview Dr
38300 WLBY 44094 2142 E5
38300 WLBY 44094 2143 A5
Beachview Rd
1000 WLBY 44094 2142 E4
N Beachview Rd
38300 WLBY 44094 2142 E4
38400 WLBY 44094 2143 A4
S Beachview Rd
1100 WLBY 44094 2142 E5
Beachwood Av
- CLEV 44105 2757 A4
100 AVLK 44012 2617 E1
12300 CLEV 44105 2756 E4
13300 CLEV 44105 2757 A4
Beachwood Blvd
2300 BHWD 44122 2628 C3
23000 UNHT 44118 2628 C3
23000 UNHT 44121 2628 C3
Beachwood Dr
4800 SDLK 44054 2616 D4
8500 RslT 44072 2632 B3
20500 RKRV 44116 2621 C6
Beacon Av
9300 CLEV 44105 2756 B1
Beacon Ct
300 AVLK 44012 2618 E3
Beacon Dr
- PNVL 44077 2040 A5
3500 BHWD 44122 2758 E2
6800 MNTR 44060 2143 E6
34000 WLBY 44094 2375 A2
Beacon Pl
8100 CLEV 44103 2626 A2
Beacon Rd
5300 LNHT 44124 2629 A1
Beacon Hill Blvd
10 NCtT 44067 3153 A3
200 NCtT 44067 3152 E3
200 SgHT 44067 3152 E3
Beacon Hill Ct
5400 SVHL 44131 2884 A1
Beacon Hill Dr
600 ORNG 44022 2759 C6
5500 SVHL 44131 2884 A2
8500 BbgT 44023 2891 B7
Beacon Hill Pl
- ORNG 44022 2759 C7
- SLN 44022 2759 C7
- SLN 44139 2759 C7
Beaconsfield Blvd
20500 RKRV 44116 2621 C5
Beaconsfield Dr
9900 PMHT 44130 2882 C3
Beaconsfield Rd
1300 LNHT 44124 2499 B7
Beaconwood Av
1600 SELD 44121 2628 B2
Beall Dr
- PnvT 44077 2146 B3
10 PNVL 44077 2146 B2
Bean Rd
11100 MsnT 44024 2634 D1
12100 MsnT 44024 2635 A1
Bear Dr
500 CdnT 44024 2378 E6
500 CdnT 44024 2379 A6
Bear Ovl
3000 NRYN 44133 3014 C7
Bear Creek Dr
5800 BDHT 44146 2887 C3
38500 CrlT 44044 3006 E7
38500 EatT 44044 3006 E7
Bear Creek Ln
16900 SGVL 44136 3146 E3
16900 SGVL 44136 3147 A4
Bearing Ct
- AMHT 44001 2872 E4
- AMHT 44001 2873 A3
Bears Run
10 RKRV 44116 2751 A1
Bears Den Ln
8500 BWHT 44147 3015 A5
Bears Paw
100 ELYR 44035 3006 D3
Bears Paw Ln
18800 SGVL 44136 3147 A5
Beatrice Ct
- NRDV 44035 3007 B1
- NRDV 44039 3007 B1
Beatrice Ln
9500 OmsT 44138 3009 B1
Beau Ct
7200 PRMA 44129 2883 A7
Beaumont Av
13400 ECLE 44112 2497 A4
Beaumont Ct
8000 CLEV 44103 2626 A1
Beaumont Dr
- MNTR 44060 2252 A3
3400 NOSD 44070 2750 D4
Beaumont Tr
100 AURA 44202 3021 C7
100 AURA 44202 3156 B1
Beaver Av
6200 CLEV 44104 2625 E5
Beaver Cir
16900 SGVL 44136 3147 A2
Beaver Cr
2300 WTLK 44145 2750 E2
Beaver Ct
100 AMHT 44001 2872 D2
Beaver Dr
400 CdnT 44024 2378 E6
400 CdnT 44024 2379 A6
Beaver Tr
10200 RMDV 44087 3020 D4
10200 RMDV 44202 3020 D4
Beaver Creek Dr
7600 MNTR 44060 2253 A2
Beavercrest Dr
3500 LORN 44053 2743 C3
Beaver Meadow Pkwy
29600 GNWL 44139 2888 C7

Beaver Meadow Pkwy
29600 SLN 44139 2888 C7
Beaver Ridge Dr
8000 NRYN 44133 3013 D7
Beaver Ridge Tr
500 BWHT 44147 3015 A5
Bechtel Rd
8400 AhtT 44035 2873 D7
8400 AhtT 44035 3004 D1
8400 NRsT 44035 3004 D1
Beck Av
100 AVLK 44012 2488 C7
100 AVLK 44012 2618 C1
Beckenham Rd
11700 NRYN 44133 3148 A5
Becker Av
5200 MNTR 44060 2038 C7
5400 MNTR 44060 2144 C1
Becker Ct
900 ETLK 44095 2250 C3
900 GFTN 44044 3142 A5
7000 CLEV 44103 2495 E6
Becket Rd
2900 CLEV 44120 2627 A6
3100 SRHT 44120 2627 A6
Beckford Av
22200 EUCL 44119 2373 B5
22200 EUCL 44123 2373 B4
Beckman Av
8600 CLEV 44104 2626 B4
Becky Av
10 CcdT 44077 2146 B4
Bedford Av
700 ELYR 44035 2875 E3
S Bedford Ct
8400 MCDN 44056 3153 C1
N Bedford Rd
8500 MCDN 44056 3018 C5
8500 MCDN 44056 3153 C1
9400 MCDN 44146 3018 D3
9400 OKWD 44146 3018 D3
S Bedford Rd
7900 MCDN 44056 3153 C2
Bedford St
5300 BDHT 44146 2887 D1
16600 BbgT 44023 2890 A1
Bedford Chagrin Pkwy
- BDFD 44146 2887 B5
- BDHT 44146 2887 D5
Bedford Glen Rd
10 BDFD 44146 2887 B4
Bedford Glens Pk
- BDFD 44146 2887 A5
Bedrock Ct
- BERA 44138 2879 D4
Beebe Av
100 ELYR 44035 2875 D5
Beech Av
10 NHFD 44067 3018 A4
800 PnvT 44077 2040 C2
2000 LORN 44052 2744 D2
5100 MPHT 44137 2757 A7
8500 BKLN 44144 2753 D5
14000 CLEV 44111 2752 D2
Beech Cir
16600 SGVL 44136 3147 A5
Beech Ct
200 AURA 44202 3156 D2
Beech Dr
500 EUCL 44132 2374 A1
5600 MONT 44060 2143 D1
Beech Ln
3200 AVON 44011 2748 C3
24100 NOSD 44070 2750 D3
24100 WTLK 44070 2750 D3
24100 WTLK 44145 2750 D3
Beech St
- NRDV 44039 2877 C1
- WLBY 44094 2142 E5
10 BERA 44017 2880 C7
300 ELYR 44035 2874 E6
500 OBLN 44074 3138 B3
Beech Cliff Dr
10 AMHT 44001 2872 C3
Beech Creek Tr
22100 SGVL 44149 3011 A3
Beechersbrook Dr
2300 MadT 44057 1941 C3
Beechers Brook Rd
800 MAYF 44143 2499 E5
Beechfront Dr
- PnvT 44077 2040 D2
Beechgrove Av
4600 GDHT 44125 2757 A5
Beech Grove Tr
17400 BbgT 44023 2890 C4
Beech Hill Rd
800 MAYF 44040 2500 B5
800 MAYF 44143 2500 B5
Beech Hills Dr
36700 WBHL 44094 2375 D4
Beechmont Ct
9100 TNBG 44087 3019 B7
24500 BHWD 44122 2628 D6
Beechmont Ovl
3800 ORNG 44122 2759 B2
Beechmont Tr
3800 ORNG 44122 2759 B3
Beechnut Ct
3800 ORNG 44022 2759 D2
Beechnut Dr
11100 MsnT 44024 2504 E2
Beechnut Ln
22500 RKRV 44116 2621 A6
Beech Tree Ln
9400 BbgT 44023 2891 E5
Beech View Dr
1100 VMLN 44089 2741 A7
Beechwood Av
3200 CVHT 44118 2627 C1
5300 MPHT 44137 2757 D7
5300 MPHT 44137 2886 D1
Beechwood Dr
10 NCtT 44067 3017 D6
10 NCtT 44067 3018 A7
300 NCtT 44067 3153 A1
300 WLWK 44095 2249 B7
2200 WTLK 44145 2750 A2
6500 INDE 44131 2884 C5
7200 MNTR 44060 2144 D7
7200 MNTR 44060 2252 D1
8000 KTLD 44094 2376 E7
9200 BKVL 44141 3151 A1
9600 NRYN 44133 3013 A3
14600 NbyT 44065 2764 C1

Beechwood Dr
29200 WKLF 44092 2374 C4
41100 ELYR 44035 2745 E7
Beechwood Ln
400 PNVL 44077 2145 B3
20200 SGVL 44149 3146 C3
Beeler Dr
100 BERA 44017 2879 E7
400 BERA 44017 3010 E1
Beersford Rd
1800 ECLE 44112 2497 A6
Beery Dr
100 WLWK 44092 2249 D7
100 WLWK 44095 2249 D7
Beethoven Dr
1300 WTLK 44145 2620 B7
Beham Dr
1800 MDHT 44124 2629 C2
Behm Dr
36100 NRDV 44039 2876 E4
Behrwald Av
3500 CLEV 44109 2754 C5
3900 CLEV 44144 2754 B5
8600 BKLN 44144 2753 D5
Beidler Rd
4400 ETLK 44095 2250 B6
4400 WLBY 44094 2250 B6
4400 WLBY 44095 2250 B6
Bel Aire Cir
30800 WTLK 44145 2749 A4
Belcourt Ln
100 AURA 44202 3021 D7
Belcourt Rd
27700 PRPK 44124 2629 B7
28300 PRPK 44124 2759 B1
Belden Av
12000 CLEV 44111 2753 A1
13000 CLEV 44111 2752 E1
Belfair Dr
1600 TNBG 44087 3019 C4
13300 MDBH 44130 2881 D4
Belfast St
5700 CLEV 44105 2755 D3
Belfiore Rd
4600 WVHT 44128 2758 C5
Belfrey Ct
500 AVLK 44012 2618 C3
Belglo Ln
- MNTR 44060 2251 E4
Belgrave Rd
2700 PRPK 44124 2629 B5
Belhaven Pl
20800 SGVL 44149 3146 B4
E Belhaven Pl
20700 SGVL 44149 3146 B4
Bell Av
100 ELYR 44035 2874 E4
500 ELYR 44035 2875 A4
Bell Ct
1000 ELYR 44035 2874 C4
1100 EyrT 44035 2874 C4
Bell Rd
400 CNFL 44022 2761 C6
400 SRSL 44022 2761 E6
1100 SRSL 44022 2762 A6
1600 NbyT 44022 2763 A6
1600 NbyT 44065 2763 A6
1600 SRSL 44022 2763 A6
10400 NbyT 44065 2764 D6
10900 NbyT 44021 2764 E6
38400 WLBY 44094 2250 E2
38400 WLBY 44094 2251 A2
Bell St
10 CNFL 44022 2761 A6
400 SRSL 44022 2761 A6
Bella Dr
18800 CLEV 44119 2372 E6
Bellaire Dr
10 PnvT 44077 2146 D2
Bellaire Rd
200 AVLK 44012 2617 E2
10600 CLEV 44111 2753 B3
11000 LNDL 44111 2753 B3
11500 LNDL 44135 2753 B3
11800 CLEV 44135 2753 A4
13000 CLEV 44135 2752 E4
Bellarmine Dr
6100 NRYN 44133 3013 E6
6100 NRYN 44133 3014 A6
Bellaston Rd
- EUCL 44117 2373 D7
- EUCL 44143 2373 D7
- RDHT 44117 2373 D7
100 RDHT 44143 2373 D7
Bellaway Dr
1600 TNBG 44087 3019 B7
1600 TNBG 44087 3154 B1
Bellbrook Dr
13300 BKPK 44130 2881 D2
13300 BKPK 44142 2881 D2
13300 PRMA 44130 2881 D2
Bellcrest Ct
36700 AVON 44011 2747 D4
Bellcrest Dr
3500 AVON 44011 2747 E4
Belle Av
1100 LKWD 44107 2622 D4
4100 SDLK 44054 2616 A4
4200 SFLD 44054 2616 B4
Belle Ct
600 BDFD 44146 2886 D4
Belle Rd
400 BDFD 44146 2886 D4
32500 AVLK 44012 2618 A2
Belleair Av
1300 MadT 44057 1843 B6
Belleau Dr
10200 TNBG 44087 3019 B4
Belleflower Cir
9900 NbyT 44065 2763 B6
Belle Meadow Rd
4600 MNTR 44060 2038 E6
Bellerive Ct
30900 WTLK 44145 2749 A3
Bellerive Dr
7300 SLN 44139 3020 E2
Bellerive Wy
4500 AVON 44011 2748 B6
Belleshire Av
13500 CLEV 44135 2752 E4
Belleview St
10 CNFL 44022 2761 A6
Bellevue Av
800 PnvT 44077 2040 D2
7900 CLEV 44103 2496 A6

Bellevue Dr
800 WLBY 44094 2143 A4
6000 NOSD 44070 2878 E2
27000 NOSD 44070 2879 A2
Bellfield Av
100 ELYR 44035 2875 D5
2100 CVHT 44106 2626 E3
Bellfield Ln
1500 BWHT 44147 3149 D4
Bellflower Cir
100 SRSL 44022 2761 D5
Bellflower Ct
6800 MNTR 44060 2143 B6
Bellflower Dr
3400 LORN 44053 2743 E5
Bellflower Rd
7100 MNTR 44060 2143 C6
8000 MNTR 44060 2144 A5
11000 CLEV 44106 2626 D2
Bellford Av
5500 CLEV 44127 2625 D6
Bellingham Rd
1700 MDHT 44124 2629 D1
Bellmore St
- PnvT 44077 2040 D7
Bellow Dr
- LORN 44053 2743 E4
Bell Vernon Dr
8100 RslT 44072 2631 E4
8100 RslT 44072 2632 A4
Bellview St
1300 WKLF 44092 2374 C2
5200 MPHT 44137 2757 E7
Bellwood Ln
7900 NRYN 44133 3013 D7
Belmar Blvd
100 AVLK 44012 2617 D2
Belmar Ct
1000 ELYR 44035 2875 D2
Belmar Rd
1500 CVHT 44118 2627 B1
1500 ECLE 44112 2497 B7
1500 ECLE 44118 2497 B7
1500 ECLE 44118 2627 B1
Belmeadow Dr
6400 MDBH 44130 2881 D4
9900 TNBG 44087 3019 C3
E Bel Meadow Ln
10 SRSL 44022 2762 B5
W Bel Meadow Ln
10 SRSL 44022 2762 B6
Belmere Av
- SFLD 44054 2615 E5
Belmere Dr
5400 PRMA 44129 2883 A4
5400 PRMA 44134 2883 A4
6600 PRMA 44129 2882 E4
Belmere Rd
- SDLK 44054 2615 E5
- SFLD 44054 2615 E5
Belmont Av
100 ELYR 44035 2875 B4
11000 CLEV 44111 2623 B7
Belmont Ct
100 BWHT 44147 3149 E5
4500 AVON 44011 2747 B6
Belmont Dr
400 PNVL 44077 2146 A2
600 LORN 44053 2744 E6
600 PNVL 44077 2145 E2
2200 BNHT 44131 2884 B1
2200 SVHL 44131 2884 B1
23200 WTLK 44145 2620 E7
32500 AVLK 44012 2618 A4
Belmont Ln
17300 AbnT 44021 2893 C4
Belmont Rd
3600 WDMR 44122 2759 B2
Belmore Rd
1800 ECLE 44112 2497 A6
Belrose Rd
1100 HDHT 44143 2499 C6
1100 MDHT 44124 2499 C7
1100 MDHT 44143 2499 C6
Belt Line Av
1000 CLEV 44109 2754 E2
Belvedere Dr
7300 MNTR 44060 2253 A2
Belvidere Av
6000 CLEV 44103 2625 D2
20500 FWPK 44126 2751 C2
Belvoir Blvd
1800 CLEV 44112 2497 C4
1800 ECLE 44112 2497 C4
1900 CVHT 44112 2497 D4
1900 CVHT 44121 2497 D4
1900 ECLE 44121 2497 D4
2000 CLEV 44121 2497 C4
2400 CLEV 44121 2498 A4
2400 SELD 44121 2498 A3
2600 SRHT 44118 2628 B5
2600 SRHT 44122 2628 B5
3100 BHWD 44122 2628 B7
3300 BHWD 44122 2758 B1
3400 HIHL 44122 2758 B1
S Belvoir Blvd
100 CLEV 44121 2498 A4
100 SELD 44121 2498 A4
600 CVHT 44121 2498 A5
1400 SELD 44121 2628 B2
2100 UNHT 44118 2628 B4
2100 UNHT 44121 2628 B2
2500 SRHT 44118 2628 B5
Belvoir Ct
6500 CcdT 44077 2145 D5
Belvoir Mw
1300 SELD 44121 2498 B7
E Belvoir Ovl
2900 SRHT 44122 2628 B7
W Belvoir Ovl
2900 SRHT 44122 2628 B6
Belwood Dr
800 HDHT 44143 2499 C6
900 MDHT 44124 2499 C6
900 MDHT 44143 2499 C6
Belwood Rd
1600 SELD 44121 2628 B1
Beman Av
7800 CLEV 44105 2756 A4
Benbow Rd
18000 SGVL 44136 3147 C5
19700 BNWK 44136 3147 C5
19700 BNWK 44212 3147 C5
E Bend Dr
13900 SGVL 44136 3147 C4

Cleveland Street Index

STREET
Block City ZIP Map# Grid

W Bend Dr
4200 WLBY 44094 2251 B5
18000 SGVL 44136 3147 C4
Bendemeer Rd
3400 CVHT 44118 2627 E1
3700 CVHT 44121 2627 E1
Bender Av
1100 ECLE 44112 2496 E7
Bender Rd
- EatT 44035 3007 B2
8700 NRDV 44035 2876 B7
8700 NRDV 44039 2876 B7
8800 NRDV 44035 3007 B2
8800 NRDV 44039 3007 B1
Bendleton Dr
- MCDN 44056 3154 A5
- MCDN 44236 3154 A6
7500 HDSN 44236 3154 A6
Benedict Dr
6600 BKPK 44142 2881 A4
6600 MDBH 44130 2881 A4
6600 MDBH 44142 2881 A4
Benham Av
9300 CLEV 44105 2756 D1
12900 CLEV 44120 2756 E1
Benhoff Dr
15300 MPHT 44137 2886 B2
Ben Hur Av
3900 WLBY 44094 2250 C4
Benjamin Rd
1700 MadT 44057 1842 D7
1700 MadT 44057 1941 D1
Benner Dr
13800 RsIT 44072 2631 D5
Bennett Ct
100 GNVA 44041 1944 B4
Bennett Dr
800 ELYR 44035 2875 E3
Bennett Rd
- SGVL 44133 3147 E5
- SGVL 44136 3147 E5
1200 MadT 44057 1843 D6
1500 MadT 44057 1942 D1
13600 NRYN 44133 3013 E7
14200 NRYN 44133 3148 C2
19000 NRYN 44133 3147 E5
Benning Dr
2600 AURA 44202 3022 E6
2600 ManT 44202 3022 E6
2600 ManT 44202 3023 A6
Bennington Av
12000 CLEV 44135 2753 A6
13000 CLEV 44135 2752 E6
Bennington Blvd
4200 BNWK 44212 3146 D7
4300 BHIT 44212 3146 C7
13300 MDBH 44130 3012 D2
Bennington Ct
10 BHWD 44122 2628 D5
Bennington Dr
6500 PMHT 44130 2882 C5
14200 SGVL 44136 3147 D5
19600 BNWK 44136 3147 D5
19600 BNWK 44212 3147 D5
Bennington Hamlet Cir
- EUCL 44123 2373 C3
Ben Shaw Rd
100 AURA 44202 3157 A2
Bentbrook Dr
12400 CsTp 44026 2501 D7
Bent Creek Ovl
400 AURA 44202 3156 C2
Bentley Dr
4100 NOSD 44070 2750 D5
8500 OmsT 44138 2878 D7
35900 AVON 44011 2748 A2
Bentley Pl
7000 CcdT 44077 2145 D7
Bentleyville Rd
200 CNFL 44022 2760 E6
200 MDHL 44022 2760 D7
300 BTVL 44022 2760 D7
Bently Dr
100 ELYR 44035 3006 E1
Benton Av
25300 EUCL 44132 2373 E3
Benton Ct
12400 CLEV 44108 2496 D7
12400 CLEV 44112 2496 E7
12400 ECLE 44112 2496 E7
Benton Ln
7700 TwbT 44236 3155 A5
Bent Tree Ct
14100 SGVL 44136 3147 C4
Bent Tree Dr
300 AURA 44202 3156 D3
14300 SGVL 44136 3147 C4
Bent Tree Ln
18200 BbgT 44023 2890 E7
Bent Tree Turn
29100 WTLK 44145 2749 C2
Bentwood Dr
4500 BKLN 44144 2753 D5
Benwood Av
12300 CLEV 44105 2756 E3
13600 CLEV 44105 2757 A3
13600 CLEV 44128 2757 A3
Benwood Cir
27200 NOSD 44070 2749 E6
27200 NOSD 44070 2750 A5
Benwood Ct
19800 SGVL 44149 3146 C2
Berdelle Av
6800 CLEV 44105 2755 E4
Berea Coms
10 BERA 44017 2880 C7
Berea Frwy
- BKPK - 2751 E7
- BKPK - 2880 E2
- CLEV - 2751 E7
- CLEV - 2752 A6
- CLEV - 2880 E2
- CLEV 44142 2880 E2
Berea Frwy SR-237
- BKPK - 2751 E7
- BKPK - 2880 E2
- CLEV - 2880 E2
- CLEV 44142 2880 E2
Berea Rd
3000 CLEV 44111 2623 A7
3100 CLEV 44111 2622 E7
3200 CLEV 44111 2752 E1
10200 CLEV 44102 2623 B6
11500 LKWD 44102 2623 B6
11500 LKWD 44107 2623 B6
Berea Rd
11700 CLEV 44107 2623 A7
Berea St
200 BERA 44017 2880 B5
Berea Industrial Pkwy
700 BERA 44017 2879 D6
Beres Dr
6200 CcdT 44077 2146 A4
Beresford Av
6600 PMHT 44130 2882 A6
7000 PRMA 44130 2882 A6
7100 PRMA 44130 2881 E7
Bergen Ct
7600 HDSN 44236 3154 D6
7600 TwbT 44236 3154 D6
Berger Ct
10 OBLN 44074 3139 A2
Berkebile Dr
4500 CLEV 44102 2754 B2
4500 CLEV 44109 2754 B2
Berkeley Av
37900 MDHL 44022 2760 C3
Berkeley Dr
1900 WTLK 44145 2750 B1
4000 SFLD 44054 2746 D4
Berkeley Ln
3500 BNWK 44212 3147 A6
7400 NRYN 44133 3013 D5
Berkeley Rd
3200 CVHT 44118 2627 C2
3700 CVHT 44121 2627 E2
3700 SELD 44118 2627 E2
3700 SELD 44121 2627 E2
Berkeley St
- SFLD 44054 2746 D4
Berkley Dr
100 ELYR 44035 2875 C3
Berkley Rd
3400 VMLN 44089 2741 C5
4600 RHFD 44286 3150 E7
S Berkley Rd
- VMLN 44089 2741 D5
N Berkley Sq
6600 MAYF 44143 2500 A6
S Berkley Sq
6600 MAYF 44143 2500 A6
Berks Wy
7400 HDSN 44236 3154 E6
Berkshire Av
11100 CLEV 44108 2496 C6
38400 AVON 44011 2747 B1
Berkshire Cir
- SGVL 44149 3146 C3
Berkshire Ct
- MAYF 44143 2500 A5
- NRDV 44035 3007 B2
Berkshire Dr
100 AQLA 44024 2505 C4
100 BDFD 44146 2887 A3
400 ShfT 44055 2745 B5
800 MCDN 44056 3018 D7
4900 NOSD 44070 2749 D7
5200 SFLD 44054 2746 E2
5300 NOSD 44070 2878 D1
6500 MNTR 44060 2144 A5
13700 BURT 44021 2636 A7
Berkshire Ln
2400 CVHT 44106 2626 E2
Berkshire Rd
100 AVLK 44012 2617 E1
100 ELYR 44035 2875 C3
100 VMLN 44089 2741 E4
1500 GSML 44040 2500 C7
1500 GSML 44040 2630 C1
2500 CVHT 44106 2626 E2
2500 CVHT 44106 2627 A2
2700 CVHT 44118 2627 A2
9100 PMHT 44130 2882 C4
Berkshire Hills Dr
7000 KTLD 44094 2376 B5
7000 WBHL 44094 2376 A5
Berkshire Industrial Pkwy
14900 BtnT 44062 2767 A2
Berkshire Park Dr
10 BTVL 44022 2889 B2
Bern Av
900 CLEV 44109 2754 E4
900 CLEV 44109 2755 A4
Bernard Av
10200 CLEV 44111 2753 C1
Bernard Dr
8700 MNTR 44060 2252 C2
Bernice Dr
8300 SGVL 44149 3011 A3
Bernice St
- NRDV 44039 2877 A2
Bernwood Ct
9100 MNTR 44060 2252 E3
Bernwood Ln
10 MDHL 44022 2759 E4
Bernwood Rd
26300 BHWD 44122 2628 E6
26300 BHWD 44122 2629 A6
Berrimore Ln
24400 WVHT 44128 2758 D5
Berringer Run
27700 WTLK 44145 2749 E1
Berrington Ct
5100 SLN 44139 2759 B7
Berry Av
7300 CLEV 44102 2753 E1
Berry Dr
22200 RKRV 44116 2621 A6
Berry Ridge Dr
400 AhtT 44001 2873 B2
Bert Av
2800 NBGH 44105 2755 B3
Bertha Av
7400 PRMA 44129 2882 E2
Bertha Ct
900 ETLK 44095 2250 B3
Berton Rd
- MPHT 44137 2886 B5
E Berwald Rd
4400 SELD 44121 2498 C6
Berwick Cir
400 AURA 44202 3021 E6
Berwick Ct
100 ELYR 44035 2874 A6
Berwick Ln
1100 SELD 44121 2498 D6
Berwick Rd
6200 MadT 44057 1842 E7
6200 MadT 44057 1843 A7
Berwick Rd
6600 CLEV 44104 2625 E5
Berwyn Av
14000 CLEV 44111 2752 D2
Berwyn Dr
500 BbgT 44022 2761 C7
10 BDFD 44146 2887 B3
Berwyn Rd
17400 SRHT 44120 2627 D7
17400 SRHT 44122 2627 D7
Bessemer Av
- CLEV 44104 2756 A1
- CLEV 44127 2756 A1
6500 CLEV 44127 2625 E7
6700 CLEV 44127 2626 A7
9300 CLEV 44104 2626 B7
Best St
10 BDFD 44146 2887 B6
100 BERA 44017 3011 A1
Best View Rd
- FWPK 44126 2751 D3
Beta Av
4100 NBGH 44105 2755 C3
Beta Dr
600 MAYF 44143 2500 A4
Bethany Av
12200 CLEV 44111 2753 A2
Bethany Ct
300 AVLK 44012 2618 C2
37300 WLBY 44094 2250 D3
Bethany Rd
3800 UNHT 44118 2627 E4
3800 UNHT 44118 2628 A4
Bethel Ct
- CLEV 44114 2624 E2
- CLEV 44114 2625 A1
Bethesda Cir
100 ELYR 44035 2873 E6
100 ELYR 44035 2874 A6
Bettie Ln
10 BNWK 44212 3147 D7
Betty Ln
9800 CrlT 44035 3006 C2
Beulah Av
11500 CLEV 44106 2496 D7
12400 CLEV 44112 2496 D7
12400 ECLE 44112 2496 D7
Bevans St
200 BERA 44017 3011 C1
Beverly Av
19100 MPHT 44137 2886 E1
Beverly Ct
100 ELYR 44035 2875 C5
900 ETLK 44095 2250 B3
Beverly Dr
10 BDFD 44146 2886 C5
1200 AMHT 44001 2743 E5
6200 PMHT 44130 2882 A4
6200 PRMA 44130 2882 A3
7500 INDE 44131 3015 C2
Beverly Ln
7500 GSML 44040 2630 E2
Beverly Rd
10 BSHT 44236 3153 B7
300 CVHT 44121 2498 A5
Beverly Hills Dr
1600 EUCL 44117 2373 D6
1900 RDHT 44117 2373 D7
1900 RDHT 44143 2373 D7
3200 RKRV 44116 2751 A2
4200 BNWK 44212 3146 D6
Beverly May Dr
6600 INDE 44131 3015 D1
Bexley Blvd
4000 CVHT 44121 2628 A1
4000 SELD 44121 2628 A1
Bexley Cir
32000 AVLK 44012 2618 D4
Bexley Ct
6600 INDE 44131 3015 D2
Bexley Dr
100 BDFD 44146 2886 E2
30800 BYVL 44140 2619 B3
N Bexley Dr
9500 SGVL 44136 3012 B4
S Bexley Dr
9800 SGVL 44136 3012 B4
Beyerle Pl
4000 CLEV 44105 2755 C2
Beyerle Rd
3400 CLEV 44105 2755 C1
Beyerle Hill Rd
6400 VLVW 44125 2885 B4
Bicentennial Dr
- PRMA 44130 2882 A7
Bicentennial Pl
8600 CLEV 44106 2626 A4
Biddulph Av
3500 CLEV 44109 2754 C5
4500 CLEV 44109 2754 B5
5800 BKLN 44144 2754 A5
Biddulph Rd
6000 BKLN 44144 2754 A5
6000 CLEV 44144 2754 A5
6500 BKLN 44144 2753 E5
Bidwell Av
1500 RKRV 44116 2621 D6
14000 CLEV 44111 2622 D7
Bierce Cir
3000 TNBG 44087 3020 C5
Big Creek Ct
11300 CcdT 44077 2146 C4
Big Creek Pkwy
5200 BKLN 44144 2753 C7
5200 PRMA 44129 2753 C7
5200 PRMA 44144 2753 C7
5400 PRMA 44129 2882 C2
5400 PRMA 44130 2882 C3
5600 PMHT 44130 2882 B3
6500 PMHT 44130 2881 D5
6600 MDBH 44130 2881 C6
7500 MDBH 44130 3012 A2
7800 SGVL 44130 3012 A2
7800 SGVL 44149 3012 A2
8300 SGVL 44149 3011 E3
Big Creek Ridge Dr
- HmbT 44024 2380 C2
Bigelow Rd
14700 BtnT 44021 2765 E1
Big Met Pl
4500 CLEV 44135 2751 E5
Big Rock Dr
10 PnvT 44077 2041 A7
Billings Rd
8200 KTLD 44094 2377 A5
Billingsley Row
36000 AVON 44011 2747 E4
36000 AVON 44011 2748 A4
Billy Campbell Blvd
500 BbgT 44022 2761 C7
500 BbgT 44023 2761 C7
500 SRSL 44022 2761 C7
Biltamy Blvd
1700 SELD 44121 2628 C1
Biltmore Av
15500 CLEV 44128 2757 B2
Biltmore Pl
36400 WLBY 44094 2250 C6
Biltmore Rd
1400 LNHT 44124 2499 B7
1400 LNHT 44124 2629 A1
7500 MNTR 44060 2252 C2
Birch Av
10 NHFD 44067 3018 A4
100 NHFD 44067 3017 E4
500 EUCL 44132 2374 A2
Birch Cir
4300 NOSD 44070 2750 D6
31200 SLN 44139 2888 D1
Birch Ct
1400 LORN 44053 2744 C3
Birch Dr
- AhtT 44001 2872 A3
- SAHT 44001 2872 C6
100 PnvT 44077 2041 B4
Birch Ln
10 OmsT 44138 2879 B4
800 AMHT 44001 2872 E1
1000 CLEV 44109 2754 E4
5800 MONT 44060 2143 E2
23900 NOSD 44070 2750 D6
37800 AVON 44011 2617 C6
Birch St
- ELYR 44035 3006 A1
5100 NRDV 44039 2748 C7
5400 NRDV 44039 2877 C1
Birchbark Dr
100 ELYR 44035 3005 B1
Birchbark Grv
8800 BbgT 44023 2762 C7
Birchbark Tr
200 AURA 44202 3156 D2
Birchcroft Dr
15200 BKPK 44142 2881 B3
Birchdale Av
8600 CLEV 44106 2626 B1
Birchdale Dr
26400 WTLK 44145 2750 A3
Birch Hill Rd
17900 BbgT 44023 2891 B6
Birchmont Dr
7600 RsIT 44022 2761 C5
Birchtree Pth
3500 CVHT 44121 2497 E7
Birch View Dr
1200 VMLN 44089 2741 A7
Birchwold Rd
4400 SELD 44121 2628 C2
Birchwood Av
14200 CLEV 44111 2622 D7
Birchwood Dr
400 BERA 44017 2880 A4
600 WLBY 44094 2143 A4
5600 MNTR 44060 2143 E2
7800 CsTp 44026 2631 D2
8900 TNBG 44087 3154 E1
41500 EyrT 44035 2745 D7
Birchwood Ln
300 PNVL 44077 2145 B3
20200 SGVL 44149 3146 C2
32300 AVLK 44012 2618 C2
Birchwood Rd
4600 GDHT 44125 2756 A5
Birdie Ln
1500 PnvT 44077 2040 E4
5600 MNTR 44060 2144 D2
35100 AVON 44011 2748 B6
Birdland Tr
13100 CsTp 44026 2631 B2
Birkdale Ct
7400 SLN 44139 3020 E2
Birmingham Av
10800 CcdT 44077 2146 B7
Biscayne Blvd
2500 BHWD 44122 2628 E5
7500 PRMA 44134 3014 E1
Bishop Ct
7500 MNTR 44060 2252 B2
Bishop Dr
10 SRSL 44022 2762 B6
200 MCDN 44056 3018 B5
Bishop Ln
18200 SGVL 44136 3146 E1
Bishop Pl
500 BERA 44017 2880 D6
Bishop Rd
200 HDHT 44092 2374 B7
200 HDHT 44143 2374 B7
400 HDHT 44143 2499 B4
200 WBHL 44092 2374 B7
1000 WBHL 44092 2374 B5
Bishop Rd SR-84
2400 WKLF 44092 2374 B5
2700 WBHL 44092 2374 B5
Bishop Wy
300 SgHT 44067 3017 D5
Bishop Park Dr
27000 WBHL 44092 2374 B5
Bishops Ct
8100 BWHT 44147 3015 A5
Bishops Gate Cir
31200 WTLK 44145 2749 A4
Bissell Dr
10000 TNBG 44087 3020 C4
N Bissell Rd
10 AURA 44202 3021 D6
S Bissell Rd
10 AURA 44202 3156 D2
Bittern Av
7400 CLEV 44103 2496 A5
Bittersweet Ct
15600 SGVL 44136 3012 B3
Bittersweet Dr
800 SVHL 44131 2884 A4
Bittersweet Tr
17100 BbgT 44023 2891 D3
Bivens Dr
3800 CLEV 44115 2625 C4
Black Rd
4900 RchT 44141 3151 C7
Blackberry Cir
13700 SGVL 44136 3012 D4
36600 SLN 44139 2889 C3
Blackberry Ln
3500 WTLK 44145 2750 A4
7700 CsTp 44026 2501 A2
7700 CsTp 44040 2501 A2
7700 GSML 44040 2500 E2
7700 GSML 44040 2501 A2
11400 CsTp 44026 2502 C3
Blackbird Dr
200 ELYR 44035 2874 E2
Blackbrook Rd
10 PnvT 44077 2039 C7
10 PnvT 44077 2145 B1
600 MNTR 44060 2145 B1
600 PnvT 44060 2145 B1
9600 MNTR 44060 2039 A7
Blackburn Rd
23000 OKWD 44146 2887 C7
Blackfeet Tr
800 MCDN 44056 3018 D6
Blackfoot Av
20200 EUCL 44117 2498 A3
Blackford Dr
7600 RsIT 44022 2761 C5
Blackhawk Run
9100 MCDN 44056 3018 D5
Blackmore Rd
1300 CVHT 44118 2497 C7
3300 PryT 44081 2041 D1
Black River Cir
4100 LORN 44055 2746 B4
Black River Ln
1300 LORN 44052 2614 D6
Black River Pkwy
- LORN 44052 2614 E7
Blackstone Av
23100 EUCL 44123 2373 C3
Blackstone Ct
- CLEV 44113 2624 D3
Black Swan Ct
5300 NRYN 44133 3149 A1
E Blackthorn Cir
2600 HDSN 44236 3155 C7
W Blackthorn Cir
2500 HDSN 44236 3155 C6
Blackwell Ct
9500 CLEV 44106 2626 B1
Blaine Av
10 BDFD 44146 2887 A3
600 CLEV 44106 2626 B1
Blaine St
100 ELYR 44035 2875 B7
400 GNVA 44041 1944 C4
Blair Cir
300 AURA 44202 3021 C6
Blair Dr
5600 HDHT 44143 2499 C4
Blair Ln
10100 KTLD 44094 2377 E5
10100 KTLD 44094 2378 A4
Blair Pl
500 PNVL 44077 2040 C6
Blair Rd
5100 PryT 44057 2042 B7
5100 PryT 44081 2042 B6
5200 LryT 44057 2042 C7
5200 LryT 44077 2042 C7
5200 PryT 44077 2042 C7
Blake St
100 ELYR 44035 2874 E7
Blakely Dr
5800 HDHT 44143 2499 C4
Blanch Av
35400 ETLK 44095 2250 B4
Blanchard Dr
7300 NRDV 44039 2877 C4
Blanche Av
5200 CLEV 44127 2755 D1
41600 CrlT 44035 3005 D4
Blanche Rd
3300 CVHT 44118 2627 D2
3700 SELD 44118 2627 D2
Blanchester Rd
1000 HDHT 44143 2499 B6
1000 LNHT 44124 2499 B6
1000 LNHT 44143 2499 B6
Blandford Rd
18000 CLEV 44121 2497 E3
Blase Av
13500 CLEV 44111 2752 E1
Blase Nemeth Rd
1500 PnvT 44077 2040 E4
1700 PnvT 44077 2041 A3
Blatt Ct
2500 CLEV 44109 2624 D7
Blaze Industrial Pkwy
10 BERA 44017 2879 D6
Blazey Tr
12100 SGVL 44136 3012 D6
13100 NRYN 44133 3012 D6
13100 SGVL 44133 3012 D6
Blazing Star Dr
17700 SGVL 44136 3147 B4
Blenheim Rd
13400 CLEV 44110 2497 A3
Bletch Ct
7100 CHHT 44125 2755 E6
Blish Av
10 PnvT 44077 2145 B4
Bliss Av
6600 CLEV 44103 2495 E7
Bliss Ln
- EUCL 44123 2373 B2
Bliss Ovl
500 MDSN 44057 2044 A3
Bliss Pkwy
- NRDV 44039 2877 D5
Bliss Rd
- AVON 44011 2748 D2
Blissfield Dr
300 WLWK 44095 2249 B7
Blissful Rd
700 VMLN 44089 2740 C5
Blodgett Creek Tr
5600 SGVL 44149 3011 C5
Blossom Av
10600 PMHT 44130 2881 A2
12600 PMHT 44130 2881 E5
Blossom Ct
4000 BNWK 44212 3146 D7
Blossom Dr
200 AMHT 44001 2743 E7
200 AMHT 44001 2744 A7
Blossom Dr
200 AMHT 44001 2872 E1
600 LORN 44052 2615 D5
8600 MNTR 44060 2252 C1
22200 RKRV 44116 2621 A6
Blossom Ln
- SLN 44022 2759 B7
- SLN 44139 2759 B7
10 OmsT 44138 2879 B4
200 ORNG 44022 2759 B6
2400 BHWD 44122 2628 D4
9900 TNBG 44087 3019 B4
27200 NOSD 44070 2750 A4
27300 NOSD 44070 2749 E4
Blossom Park Av
1400 LKWD 44107 2622 D5
Blue Bell Ct
9400 MNTR 44060 2145 A6
Bluebell Dr
5300 LNHT 44124 2629 A1
Blueberry Cir
400 MAYF 44143 2500 A2
Blueberry Hl
10700 KTLD 44094 2376 D6
Blueberry Ln
9300 MCDN 44056 3019 A6
Bluebird Dr
100 ELYR 44035 2874 E3
Blue Grass Ovl
36300 SLN 44139 2889 C4
Blue Heron Dr
2600 HDSN 44236 3155 C7
33700 SLN 44139 3020 A3
Blue Heron Tr
11600 MsnT 44024 2504 C5
Blue Heron Wy
- MNTR 44060 2144 C1
Bluejay Ln
8900 MNTR 44060 2144 D2
Bluejay Tr
400 MCDN 44056 3153 C2
Blue Point Dr
19100 SGVL 44136 3146 E5
Blue Pond Tr
28400 SLN 44139 2888 B2
Blue Ribbon Dr
7100 INDE 44131 2885 A7
Blue Ridge Dr
7400 CcdT 44060 2253 B1
Blue Spruce Dr
18900 SGVL 44149 3146 D4
Blue Spruce Ovl
6800 MDBH 44130 2881 C5
Blue Spruce St
2900 PryT 44081 2041 D3
Blue Spruce Tr
600 AbnT 44023 2892 B4
Bluestone Ln
3000 BDFD 44146 2887 C2
3000 BDHT 44146 2887 C2
Bluestone Rd
3900 CVHT 44121 2498 A6
4000 SELD 44121 2498 A6
N Bluff Dr
8400 BWHT 44147 3014 E4
Bluff St
8900 KTLD 44094 2251 D7
Bluffside Pl
12200 SGVL 44136 3012 A6
Bluffstone Cir
32400 NRDV 44039 2877 E7
Blythin Rd
4600 CLEV 44105 2756 A5
4600 GDHT 44105 2756 A5
4600 GDHT 44125 2756 A5
Boardwalk Av
- EatT 44044 3142 E2
Bobby Ln
1300 WTLK 44145 2619 C7
Bob Hope Wy
2000 CLEV 44114 2625 A3
2000 CLEV 44115 2625 A3
Bobko Blvd
10700 PRMA 44130 3013 B1
Bobolink Dr
8300 MCDN 44056 3018 C7
Bob White Cir
16900 SGVL 44136 3147 A3
Boggy Creek Dr
12600 ClrT 44021 2506 D7
Bogie Ln
1500 PnvT 44077 2040 E4
Bohannon Ct
100 ELYR 44035 3006 B2
Bohning Dr
9300 GDHT 44125 2756 B5
Bolingbrook Rd
28500 PRPK 44124 2629 C6
29800 PRPK 44124 2759 C1
Bolivar Rd
700 CLEV 44115 2624 E3
700 CLEV 44115 2625 A3
Bolton Dr
37100 NRDV 44035 3007 C1
Bolton Rd
2500 CVHT 44118 2497 C7
2500 CVHT 44118 2627 C1
Bon Air Av
100 ELYR 44035 2875 E3
Bond Av
4900 ShfT 44055 2746 A6
Bond St
- VLVW 44125 2885 A2
100 ELYR 44035 2875 A4
500 ELYR 44035 2874 E4
7500 GNWL 44139 3019 B2
Bonds Pkwy
200 BERA 44017 2880 D6
Bonna Av
5600 CLEV 44103 2495 D7
Bonneybrook Ln
500 BHIT 44212 3145 D7
Bonnie Ct
30500 WKLF 44092 2374 E1
Bonnie Ln
200 AURA 44202 3156 D4
1100 MDHT 44124 2499 E7
18000 SGVL 44136 3011 E6
18000 SGVL 44149 3011 E6
Bonnie Pl
1100 MDHT 44124 2499 E6
Bonnie Rd
1400 MCDN 44056 3019 A7
Bonnie Bank Blvd
19900 RKRV 44116 2751 D1
Bonnie Bank Ln
18900 FWPK 44126 2751 E1
Bonnieview Av
1200 LKWD 44107 2622 B4
Bonnieview Dr
30100 WKLF 44092 2374 D3
33200 AVLK 44012 2617 C1
Bonnieview Rd
6600 MAYF 44040 2500 A5
6600 MAYF 44143 2500 A5
Bonniewood Dr
200 CLEV 44110 2372 B7
Bonny Blvd
2400 PRMA 44134 3014 C1
Bonny Bank Dr
23800 WTLK 44145 2750 E1
Bonroi Dr
6300 SVHL 44131 2884 B4
Booker Av
24500 OKWD 44146 2887 D7
Boone Rd
17900 ClbT 44028 3145 C5
17900 ClbT 44280 3145 C5
17900 LvpT 44280 3145 C5
N Boone Rd
11800 ClbT 44028 3010 C7
S Boone Rd
14000 ClbT 44028 3010 C7
14000 ClbT 44028 3145 C3
Booth Av
8100 CLEV 44105 2756 A3
Booth Rd
8700 KDHL 44060 2252 D7
9100 KDHL 44060 2377 D1
9100 KTLD 44060 2377 D1
9100 KTLD 44094 2377 C2
Bordeaux Ln
10 BHWD 44122 2628 E3
Bordeaux Pl
10 OmsT 44138 2879 B3
Bordeaux Wy
1800 WTLK 44145 2749 E1
Borges St
9200 GDHT 44125 2756 B5
Born Av
10100 CLEV 44108 2496 C5
Bosley Cove
6600 MNTR 44060 2145 A5
Boston Av
100 ELYR 44035 2875 D6
6600 CLEV 44127 2625 E7
Boston Rd
1300 HkyT 44133 3148 A5
1300 HkyT 44233 3148 A5
1300 NRYN 44133 3148 A5
2500 BNWK 44133 3147 E5
2500 BNWK 44136 3147 D5
2500 BNWK 44212 3147 D5
2500 BNWK 44233 3147 E5
2500 HkyT 44133 3147 E5
2500 HkyT 44233 3147 E5
2500 NRYN 44133 3147 E5
2500 SGVL 44133 3147 E5
2500 SGVL 44136 3147 D5
3700 BHIT 44136 3146 E5
3700 BNWK 44212 3146 E5
3700 SGVL 44136 3146 E5
3900 BNWK 44136 3146 D5
3900 BNWK 44149 3146 D5
3900 SGVL 44149 3146 E5
3900 SGVL 44212 3146 E5
4100 BHIT 44149 3146 E5
4800 BHIT 44212 3146 E5
4900 BHIT 44149 3145 D5
4900 BHIT 44212 3145 D5
4900 SGVL 44149 3145 D5
5200 ClbT 44028 3145 D5
5200 ClbT 44149 3145 D5
5200 LvpT 44028 3145 D5
5200 LvpT 44149 3145 D5
5200 LvpT 44212 3145 D5
5200 LvpT 44280 3145 D5
5400 ClbT 44280 3145 D5
E Boston Rd
100 BWHT 44147 3149 E5
100 BWHT 44147 3150 A5
100 RchT 44147 3149 E5
100 RchT 44233 3149 E5
100 RchT 44286 3149 E5
100 RchT 44286 3150 A5
1600 BKVL 44141 3150 A5
1600 BWHT 44141 3150 B5
1600 RchT 44141 3150 A5
W Boston Rd
10 BWHT 44147 3149 D5
10 HkyT 44147 3149 C5
10 HkyT 44233 3149 C5
10 RchT 44147 3149 C5
10 RchT 44233 3149 C5
10 RchT 44286 3149 C5
Boston Lake Dr
- LvpT 44280 3145 C6
Boston Mills Rd W
1400 BosT 44141 3152 C7
Boston Reserve Ln
10 BHIT 44149 3145 E6
10 BHIT 44212 3145 E6
10 SGVL 44149 3145 E6
Bosworth Rd
3300 CLEV 44111 2753 B1
Botanica Ln
- PRPK 44124 2629 A7
Botany Av
1400 CLEV 44109 2754 E3
Boulder Dr
- BERA 44138 2879 E5
32700 NRDV 44039 2877 D2
Boulder Creek Cir
5200 BKVL 44141 3151 C4
Boulder Creek Dr
5000 MDHL 44022 2759 E7
5000 SLN 44022 2759 E7
5000 SLN 44139 2759 E7
Boulder Glen Dr
13100 MsnT 44024 2633 E2
13100 MsnT 44026 2633 E2
Boulder Ridge Pl
10 PnvT 44077 2041 A7
10 PnvT 44077 2147 A1
Boulder Wood Dr
7200 BWHT 44147 3015 E5
Boundary Ln
9100 PRMA 44130 2882 C6
Bounty Rd
400 AURA 44202 3157 A2

STREET Block	City	ZIP	Map#	Grid
Bounty Wy				
300	AVLK	44012	2618	E3
Bowdoin Dr				
1200	PnvT	44077	2147	A1
Bowen Rd				
11100	ManT	44255	3159	B4
Bower Av				
5400	CLEV	44127	2625	D6
Bowfin Blvd				
15300	BKPK	44142	2881	B2
Bowhall Rd				
400	PnvT	44077	2040	E5
600	PnvT	44077	2041	A5
Bowling Green Cir				
600	ELYR	44035	3006	D1
Bowling Green Rd				
20600	MPHT	44137	2887	A1
Bowman Dr				
19100	SGVL	44136	3146	D3
19100	SGVL	44149	3146	D3
Bowmen Ln				
2700	PRMA	44134	2883	C7
Boxberry Ln				
2400	BWHT	44147	3014	C3
Boxelder Dr				
3500	BKVL	44141	3150	C1
Boxwood Av				
-	CLEV	44105	2756	B4
Boxwood Cir				
8900	BKLN	44144	2753	D4
11400	MsnT	44024	2504	C2
Boxwood Ct				
-	BWHT	44147	3149	C5
Boxwood Dr				
5500	LORN	44053	2743	E5
Boxwood St				
4800	AVON	44011	2748	D6
Boxwood Tr				
1900	PnvT	44077	2145	B5
Boyce Rd				
2900	SRHT	44122	2628	A6
Boyd Ct				
35600	WLBY	44094	2375	B2
N Boyden Rd				
7800	NCtT	44067	3152	D1
7800	SgHT	44067	3017	D6
7800	SgHT	44067	3152	D1
S Boyden Rd				
7100	SgHT	44067	3152	D3
7700	NCtT	44067	3152	D2
Boyer Av				
2100	CLEV	44109	2754	D4
Boyer Ln				
9000	KDHL	44060	2252	E4
Boyle Pkwy				
8100	TwbT	44087	3154	C4
N Boyle Pkwy				
8400	TwbT	44087	3154	C3
Boynton Rd				
3200	VMLN	44089	2741	E5
3200	VMLN	44089	2742	A5
3400	CVHT	44121	2497	D6
Brace Av				
100	ELYR	44035	2874	E3
Bracken Wy				
400	BYVL	44140	2619	D5
Brackenbury Dr				
32700	SLN	44139	3019	E2
Brackland Av				
12300	CLEV	44108	2496	E5
Brad Dr				
200	BNWK	44212	3147	D7
Braddock Av				
16400	CLEV	44110	2497	C2
Bradenton Blvd				
7400	PRMA	44134	3014	C1
Bradford Av				
1600	CLEV	44113	2624	D5
Bradford Ct				
19200	SGVL	44149	3146	D2
Bradford Dr				
900	ELYR	44035	2875	A3
1400	MCDN	44056	3019	A6
4600	SELD	44121	2498	D6
12000	MsnT	44024	2634	E2
12100	MsnT	44024	2635	A2
Bradford Ln				
400	AURA	44202	3021	D5
8600	BKVL	44141	3016	B6
Bradford Rd				
3200	CVHT	44118	2627	C4
3600	UNHT	44118	2627	E4
7100	ODFL	44138	2879	D4
7100	OmsT	44138	2879	D4
Bradford Park Ln				
7700	TwbT	44236	3154	D5
Bradfords Gate				
3300	RKRV	44116	2751	B2
8200	ODFL	44138	2879	A6
Bradgate Av				
16300	CLEV	44111	2752	A3
17200	CLEV	44135	2752	A3
Bradgate Ln				
20000	SGVL	44149	3146	C4
Bradley Av				
100	BbgT	44022	2761	A7
100	CNFL	44022	2761	A7
100	CyhC	44022	2761	A7
5400	PRMA	44129	2754	A7
5400	PRMA	44129	2883	A1
5400	PRMA	44134	2883	A1
6700	PRMA	44129	2753	E7
Bradley Ct				
10800	CcdT	44077	2146	A4
Bradley Rd				
-	BYVL	44140	2619	B3
-	ODFL	44138	2879	C7
600	WTLK	44140	2619	B6
600	WTLK	44145	2619	B7
1900	WTLK	44145	2749	B4
4100	CLEV	44109	2755	A4
5200	NOSD	44070	2749	B4
5200	NOSD	44145	2749	B4
5400	NOSD	44070	2878	A2
30900	NRDV	44039	2878	A2
30900	NRDV	44070	2878	A2
Bradmore Cir				
400	AURA	44202	3021	E6
Bradwell Av				
2900	CLEV	44109	2754	C3
Bradwell Rd				
11400	GDHT	44125	2885	D1
Brady Ln				
11100	SGVL	44149	3011	B5
Braeburn Ln				
13500	RslT	44072	2631	E4
Braeburn Park Dr				
1700	EUCL	44117	2373	D7
Braemar Rd				
3200	SRHT	44120	2627	C7
Braemar Wy Ovl				
19700	SGVL	44149	3011	C7
Braemore Dr				
-	NRDV	44039	3008	B1
Braewood Dr				
7200	INDE	44131	2885	A7
7200	INDE	44131	3015	E1
Bragdon Av				
4600	CLEV	44102	2754	B1
4600	CLEV	44109	2754	B1
Bragg Rd				
5300	CLEV	44127	2625	D6
Brahms Dr				
26600	WTLK	44145	2750	A1
Brainard Av				
1600	CLEV	44109	2624	D7
Brainard Ct				
7500	MNTR	44060	2143	D6
Brainard Dr				
10400	PRMA	44130	2882	B1
Brainard Rd				
-	PRPK	44124	2759	A1
800	HDHT	44143	2499	B5
1000	LNHT	44124	2499	B7
1000	LNHT	44143	2499	B6
1400	LNHT	44124	2629	B1
2700	PRPK	44124	2629	B5
3600	ORNG	44122	2759	B4
3600	WDMR	44122	2759	B4
3800	ORNG	44022	2759	B3
4800	SLN	44022	2759	B7
4800	SLN	44139	2759	B7
5200	SLN	44139	2888	A1
E Brainard Rd				
3400	PRPK	44122	2759	B1
3400	PRPK	44124	2759	B1
3400	WDMR	44122	2759	A1
3400	WDMR	44124	2759	B1
W Brainard Rd				
3400	ORNG	44122	2759	A1
3400	PRPK	44124	2759	A1
3400	WDMR	44122	2759	A1
3400	WDMR	44124	2759	A1
Brainard Hills Dr				
2700	PRPK	44124	2629	B5
Braintree Ln				
10	CcdT	44060	2145	C6
Brakeman Rd				
7500	HmbT	44024	2256	B4
7500	HmbT	44077	2256	B4
7500	LryT	44077	2256	B4
8400	LryT	44024	2256	B5
8900	HmbT	44024	2381	B2
Braman Ct				
-	LORN	44052	2745	A1
Bramble Ct				
5500	WLBY	44094	2375	A1
Bramble Ln				
404-00	AURA	44202	3156	C2
34200	SLN	44139	3020	A1
Bramblebush Ln				
-	AURA	44202	3021	C5
Brambleside Dr				
400	BHIT	44212	3146	A7
Brambleside Ln				
6100	MNTR	44060	2143	C3
Bramblewood Dr				
2500	BWHT	44147	3015	B4
Bramblewood Ln				
6600	MAYF	44143	2500	A3
Bramblewood Pl				
6100	MNTR	44060	2143	D3
Bramblewood Wy				
3200	AVON	44011	2748	A3
Bramley Av				
-	LKWD	44107	2622	E7
Bramley Dr				
4400	MNTU	44255	3159	B5
8700	INDE	44131	3016	B1
Bramshill Cir				
7000	BbgT	44023	2890	A5
Branch Av				
10	PnvT	44077	2040	C7
1600	CLEV	44113	2624	E7
Branch Dr				
-	AhtT	44001	2872	B2
Branch St				
-	NRDV	44039	2877	C1
Brandamore Ct				
6600	SLN	44139	2889	D7
Brandemere Ct				
100	ELYR	44035	2875	C4
Brandon Cir				
800	AURA	44202	3156	D4
Brandon Ct				
10	MDHL	44022	2760	B4
500	CRDN	44024	2505	A1
Brandon Pl				
10	RKRV	44116	2621	A5
32200	AVLK	44012	2618	C2
Brandon Rd				
1000	CVHT	44112	2497	C6
1100	CVHT	44118	2497	D7
3300	BHWD	44122	2628	D7
3300	BHWD	44122	2758	D1
Brandston Av				
100	ELYR	44035	2875	C5
Brandt Av				
100	AMHT	44001	2872	D1
Brandy Ct				
-	AVON	44011	2748	D4
Brandywine Dr				
2000	EUCL	44143	2498	C2
2000	RDHT	44143	2498	C2
7000	CcdT	44060	2145	A7
7000	MNTR	44060	2145	A7
17400	SGVL	44136	3146	E4
17400	SGVL	44136	3147	A4
20700	FWPK	44126	2751	C4
Brandywine Ln				
-	BHWD	44122	2628	E4
20700	FWPK	44126	2751	C4
Brandywine Rd				
2700	PMHT	44130	2882	C6
7300	BSHT	44236	3153	C7
7500	NCtT	44067	3153	B7
7500	NCtT	44141	3153	B7
8000	NCtT	44067	3152	E5
8000	NCtT	44141	3152	E6
Brandywine Rd				
8200	SgHT	44067	3152	E5
Brandywine Sq				
10	EUCL	44143	2498	A2
Brandywine St				
100	ELYR	44035	2874	A7
Brandywine Creek Dr				
7600	MCDN	44056	3153	B4
7600	NCtT	44056	3153	B4
7600	NCtT	44067	3153	B4
Brandywood Dr				
10	PRPK	44124	2759	E1
10	PRPK	44124	2760	A1
Branford Av				
13600	GDHT	44125	2885	E4
13600	GDHT	44125	2886	A4
Branford Ln				
300	RDHT	44143	2498	E1
Brantley Ln				
300	BNWK	44212	3146	E7
Brantley Rd				
20600	SRHT	44122	2628	A6
Branton Ct				
1700	BWHT	44147	3150	A5
Brantwood Dr				
2400	WTLK	44145	2750	D2
Bratenahl Pl				
10	BTNH	44108	2496	D2
Bratenahl Rd				
100	BTNH	44108	2496	C4
Brayes Manor Dr				
9500	MNTR	44060	2253	A3
Brayton Av				
700	CLEV	44113	2624	E6
700	CLEV	44113	2625	A6
Brayton Tr				
7700	BbgT	44023	2890	C2
Brazil Rd				
17600	CLEV	44119	2372	D5
Breakers Blvd				
-	AVLK	44012	2618	B4
Breakwater Av				
5900	CLEV	44102	2624	A4
Breck Ct				
3200	CLEV	44114	2625	B1
6800	NRDV	44039	2877	A3
Breckenridge Dr				
9700	CdnT	44024	2379	B3
25500	EUCL	44117	2373	D6
Breckenridge Ovl				
-	EatT	44035	3007	A2
8600	BWHT	44147	3015	B5
Breckenridge Tr				
30800	WTLK	44145	2749	B2
Brecksville Rd				
-	CHHT	44125	2755	E7
-	CHHT	44131	2755	E7
-	INDE	44125	2755	E7
-	INDE	44131	2755	E7
-	VLVW	44125	2755	E7
-	VLVW	44131	2755	E7
4700	RHFD	44286	3151	A5
5200	RHFD	44141	3151	A6
5400	INDE	44125	2884	E1
5400	VLVW	44125	2884	E3
5400	VLVW	44131	2884	E3
6600	INDE	44131	2884	E5
7300	INDE	44131	3015	E1
7600	INDE	44131	3016	A2
7700	BKVL	44131	3016	A2
7700	BKVL	44141	3016	A3
9000	BKVL	44141	3151	A3
Brecksville Rd SR-21				
-	CHHT	44125	2755	E7
-	CHHT	44131	2755	E7
-	INDE	44125	2755	E7
-	INDE	44131	2755	E7
-	VLVW	44125	2755	E7
-	VLVW	44131	2755	E7
4700	RHFD	44286	3151	A5
5200	RHFD	44141	3151	A6
5400	INDE	44125	2884	E1
5400	VLVW	44125	2884	E3
5400	VLVW	44131	2884	E3
6400	INDE	44131	2884	E4
7300	INDE	44131	3015	E1
7600	INDE	44131	3016	A2
7700	BKVL	44131	3016	A2
7700	BKVL	44141	3016	A2
9000	BKVL	44141	3151	A3
Breckswood Ovl				
5500	BWHT	44147	3015	D5
Breezevale Cole				
22600	RKRV	44116	2621	A5
E Breezeway Dr				
5600	NRDV	44039	2876	C1
W Breezeway Dr				
5600	NRDV	44039	2876	C1
Breezewood Dr				
200	BYVL	44140	2619	C4
6500	CcdT	44077	2146	E6
6500	CcdT	44077	2147	A5
Breezy Acres Dr				
12100	ClrT	44024	2505	D7
Bremen Av				
7900	PRMA	44129	2882	D2
Bremerton Rd				
1800	LNHT	44124	2629	B2
3000	PRPK	44124	2629	B7
Brenda Lee Dr				
7000	WNHL	44146	2886	D7
Brendan Ln				
3800	NOSD	44070	2750	E6
Brenel Dr				
7300	CcdT	44060	2253	C1
7300	CcdT	44077	2253	C1
Brennan Dr				
600	AMHT	44001	2872	E3
Brennans Ct				
500	AVLK	44012	2618	E4
Brenner Dr				
2800	LORN	44053	2743	D3
Brenthaven St				
100	ELYR	44035	2874	B7
Brentview Dr				
100	CrlT	44044	3006	E6
Brentwood Cir				
-	AhtT	44001	2872	E6
3300	HDHT	44143	2499	A3
Brentwood Dr				
200	PNVL	44077	2145	E3
8200	ODFL	44138	2879	A6
8400	OmsT	44138	2879	A7
Brentwood Ln				
11100	CdnT	44024	2379	B4
Brentwood Rd				
1100	CVHT	44121	2497	E6
2400	BHWD	44122	2628	C5
2600	SRHT	44122	2628	C5
7800	MNTR	44060	2251	D3
Breton Dr				
4100	CLEV	44109	2754	E4
Brett Dr				
30100	WBHL	44092	2374	D5
Bretten Ct				
-	INDE	44131	3016	A2
6400	INDE	44131	3015	E2
Bretton Ct				
5500	WLBY	44094	2375	A1
Bretton Ridge Dr				
6600	NOSD	44070	2878	C3
Brevier Av				
-	CLEV	44113	2624	D5
Brewer Ct				
6300	MNTR	44060	2144	A4
Brewster Ct				
1000	GFTN	44044	3142	A3
Brewster Dr				
4000	WTLK	44145	2749	D5
N Brewster Pl				
7100	CcdT	44077	2146	B7
S Brewster Pl				
7200	CcdT	44077	2146	B7
Brewster Rd				
2800	PRPK	44124	2629	E6
15300	ECLE	44112	2497	B6
16200	CVHT	44112	2497	B6
18600	BbgT	44023	3021	D3
18600	BbgT	44202	3021	D3
19100	AURA	44202	3021	C3
Brian Av				
17800	CLEV	44119	2372	D6
Brian Ct				
-	PNVL	44077	2146	B1
16000	MDFD	44062	2767	E2
Brian Dr				
2300	BHWD	44122	2628	E4
2400	PRMA	44134	3014	C1
10200	CcdT	44077	2145	D6
Brian St				
9000	NRDV	44039	3008	C1
Briar Ct				
10	AhtT	44001	2873	C2
30400	WKLF	44092	2374	E2
Briar Ln				
500	BDFD	44146	2887	B3
6800	VmnT	44089	2869	C3
11100	NRYN	44133	3147	E5
29300	WTLK	44145	2749	C2
Briar Rd				
4700	CLEV	44135	2752	D6
Briarbanks Dr				
4400	FWPK	44126	2751	E2
Briar Bush Ln				
21300	SGVL	44149	3011	A5
Briarcliff Ct				
7100	MNTR	44060	2145	A7
Briarcliff Dr				
100	ELYR	44035	2874	B7
600	AURA	44202	3156	D3
5500	GDHT	44125	2885	C1
Briarcliff Pkwy				
7400	MDBH	44130	2881	B7
7400	MDBH	44130	3012	B1
Briardale Av				
23100	EUCL	44123	2373	C3
25100	EUCL	44132	2373	D2
Briardale Ct				
1100	TNBG	44087	3019	C3
Briardale Ln				
5800	SLN	44139	2888	E3
Briargate Ct				
200	AVLK	44012	2618	C2
Briar Hill Dr				
5800	SLN	44139	2888	E3
5800	SLN	44139	2889	A3
7300	KTLD	44094	2376	B5
Briar Hill Rd				
100	PnvT	44077	2147	A2
Briar Lake Dr				
100	ELYR	44035	2875	D1
Briar Lakes Dr				
37800	AVON	44011	2747	C2
Briarleigh Dr				
10	BNWK	44136	3147	D6
10	BNWK	44212	3147	D6
10	SGVL	44136	3147	D6
Briarpatch Dr				
24000	ODFL	44138	3010	D1
Briar Ridge Ct				
3400	WTLK	44145	2749	D4
Briarwood Ct				
25700	WTLK	44145	2750	B4
32700	AVLK	44012	2618	A2
Briarwood Dr				
4100	ManT	44255	3159	A3
4500	LORN	44053	2744	C5
7300	MNTR	44060	2252	E1
8100	BWHT	44147	3014	D4
10500	CrlT	44035	3006	D3
11700	CsTp	44026	2502	A4
21700	FWPK	44126	2751	B5
24400	ODFL	44138	3010	C1
25200	ClbT	44028	3144	E2
25200	ClbT	44028	3145	A2
32400	NRDV	44039	2877	D7
Briarwood Ln				
5800	SLN	44139	2888	D3
19200	SGVL	44149	3011	D5
Briarwood Rd				
2100	CVHT	44118	2627	B3
9100	MCDN	44056	3018	E6
14700	NbyT	44065	2764	D1
Briarwyck Woods Av				
11700	CcdT	44077	2254	E5
Brichford Rd				
7900	MNTR	44060	2251	E3
Bricker Ct				
8500	MNTR	44060	2144	B3
Bricker St				
-	NbyT	44065	2764	D1
Brick Mill Run				
600	RKRV	44116	2621	A6
600	WTLK	44116	2621	A6
600	WTLK	44145	2621	A6
17600	SGVL	44136	3146	E5
17600	SGVL	44136	3147	A5
Bridge Av				
2300	CLEV	44113	2624	D5
4400	CLEV	44102	2624	A5
Bridge Ct				
4500	CLEV	44102	2624	B5
4500	CLEV	44113	2624	B5
Bridge Dr				
1000	LORN	44052	2615	A7
Bridge Pth				
18900	SGVL	44136	3147	A5
E Bridge St				
10	BERA	44017	2880	C7
100	ELYR	44035	2875	B6
W Bridge St				
10	BERA	44017	2880	B7
10	ELYR	44035	2875	A6
200	ELYR	44035	2874	E6
Bridgecreek Cir				
13300	SGVL	44136	3012	D5
Bridge Creek Tr				
17800	AbnT	44023	2892	E5
Bridge Pointe Ln				
-	BHIT	44212	3145	E7
Bridge Pointe Tr				
37500	AVON	44011	2747	C1
Bridgeport Ct				
32400	AVLK	44012	2618	B2
Bridgeport Dr				
100	CrlT	44035	3006	D3
100	ELYR	44035	3006	C2
3200	NOSD	44070	2750	E4
4600	VMLN	44089	2741	A5
Bridgeport Ln				
8400	MNTR	44060	2144	B5
Bridgeport Tr				
300	RDHT	44143	2498	E1
Bridgeside Dr				
200	AVLK	44012	2618	E4
Bridgestone Dr				
32400	NRDV	44039	2877	D7
Bridget Ln				
1200	TNBG	44087	3019	A6
Bridgeton Dr				
2500	HDSN	44236	3155	C6
25000	BHWD	44122	2628	E5
Bridgeview Av				
3900	NBGH	44105	2755	C2
Bridgeview Dr				
3700	CLEV	44121	2497	E4
3700	SELD	44121	2497	E4
Bridgewater Ct				
700	MCDN	44056	3154	A6
Bridgewater Dr				
4500	PryT	44081	2042	C5
11100	NRYN	44133	3147	E5
Bridgewater Ln				
-	BHIT	44212	3145	E7
-	BHIT	44212	3146	A7
100	CRDN	44024	2379	E5
100	SgHT	44067	3017	E4
Bridgewater Rd				
5100	LNHT	44124	2628	E1
5100	LNHT	44124	2629	A1
Bridgeway Dr				
17100	BbgT	44023	2890	E3
Bridle Ct				
8300	MNTR	44060	2251	D5
38700	AVON	44011	2747	B6
Bridle Ln				
-	NbyT	44065	2634	B6
400	BERA	44017	3010	E1
400	BERA	44017	3011	A2
700	SGVL	44017	3011	A2
Bridle Pth				
1500	PnvT	44077	2041	B7
1600	PryT	44077	2041	B7
Bridle Tr				
10800	MsnT	44024	2634	A2
14100	SGVL	44136	3012	B7
14100	SGVL	44136	3147	B1
N Bridle Tr				
13100	MsnT	44024	2634	A2
Bridlehurst Tr				
8200	KTLD	44094	2377	A7
Bridle Path Cir				
11000	ClbT	44028	3010	C4
Bridle Path Dr				
10600	ClbT	44028	3010	C4
Bridle Path Tr				
30300	WKLF	44092	2374	E3
Bridle Trail Ln				
34400	SLN	44139	2760	A7
Bridlewood Dr				
6900	CcdT	44077	2146	E7
7200	CcdT	44077	2254	E1
Bridlewood Ln				
6700	LvpT	44280	3144	D6
N Brier Patch Ln				
400	MDSN	44057	1942	B7
S Brier Patch Ln				
400	MDSN	44057	1942	B7
Brigadoon Ct				
2200	WTLK	44145	2749	E1
Brigadoon Dr				
16600	BbgT	44023	2890	B1
Brigadoon Wy				
13600	SGVL	44149	3011	C7
Briggs Cir				
37000	NRDV	44035	2876	D7
Briggs Rd				
10200	CLEV	44111	2753	C2
Brigham Rd				
7200	GSML	44040	2500	D4
7700	CsTp	44026	2501	A4
7700	GSML	44040	2501	A4
Brighton Av				
11700	CLEV	44111	2753	A2
Brighton Cir				
10100	TNBG	44087	3020	B4
Brighton Dr				
6100	NOSD	44070	2878	C3
Brighton Ln				
1500	BWHT	44147	3149	D4
Brighton Pl				
2200	MadT	44057	1942	C3
Brighton Pth				
38200	WLBY	44094	2250	E2
Brighton Rd				
2800	SRHT	44120	2627	D6
4400	MNTR	44060	2039	A4
10300	BTNH	44108	2496	C3
Brighton Park Blvd				
32300	SLN	44139	2888	E1
32500	SLN	44139	2889	A1
Brightwood Av				
1800	CVHT	44112	2626	E1
1800	ECLE	44112	2496	E7
1800	ECLE	44112	2626	E1
Brightwood Dr				
-	NbyT	44065	2764	B1
10	OmsT	44138	2879	B4
7000	CcdT	44060	2145	C7
7000	CcdT	44077	2145	C7
Brightwood Rd				
14600	NbyT	44065	2764	B1
Brigton Dr				
500	BERA	44017	3010	D1
Brimfield Dr				
-	BbgT	44023	2890	E7
9400	MNTR	44060	2145	A7
Brinbourne Av				
16500	MDBH	44130	2881	B7
Bringman Ct				
9200	MNTR	44060	2252	E3
Brinkmore Rd				
3500	CVHT	44121	2497	D4
3600	SELD	44121	2497	E4
Brinmore Rd				
7500	SgHT	44067	3017	C7
Brinsmade Av				
7300	CLEV	44102	2623	D7
Briscoe Dr				
22600	RKRV	44116	2751	A2
Bristlewood Dr				
7000	CcdT	44077	2146	C6
Bristol Av				
10	PnvT	44077	2041	B6
2500	PryT	44077	2041	B6
7900	CLEV	44104	2626	A6
Bristol Ct				
5000	LNHT	44124	2628	E1
7200	NCtT	44067	3153	B4
11100	NRYN	44133	3013	D5
Bristol Dr				
500	AURA	44202	3021	D5
2400	AVON	44011	2748	A2
Bristol Ln				
400	BNWK	44212	3147	C7
3800	NOSD	44070	2750	B5
7500	BKVL	44141	3150	C3
12200	SGVL	44149	3011	B6
25000	WTLK	44145	2750	C1
Bristol Rd				
10	CLEV	44110	2372	C6
Britannia Ct				
14800	SGVL	44149	3146	B1
Brittania Pkwy				
300	AVLK	44012	2618	C3
Brittany Cir				
25300	WTLK	44145	2750	C1
Brittany Ct				
600	SgHT	44067	3152	C1
9800	CcdT	44060	2145	B7
Brittany Dr				
7600	PRMA	44134	3014	A1
Brittany Pl				
16900	BNWK	44136	3147	A6
16900	BNWK	44212	3147	A6
16900	SGVL	44136	3147	A6
Brittany Woods Dr				
17700	AbnT	44023	2893	B5
Brittney Ct				
800	WLWK	44092	2249	D7
800	WLWK	44095	2249	D7
Britton Dr				
300	GNVA	44041	1944	A5
12400	CLEV	44120	2626	E4
12500	SRHT	44120	2626	E4
Britton Ln				
-	MsnT	44024	2504	E3
Broad Av				
-	CLEV	44103	2496	A5
-	CLEV	44108	2496	A5
Broad Blvd				
5200	NRDV	44039	2748	D7
5400	NRDV	44039	2877	D1
Broad St				
10	ELYR	44035	2875	A6
E Broad St				
10	ELYR	44035	2875	E7
1200	ELYR	44039	2875	E7
1200	NRDV	44039	2875	E7
Broadale Rd				
4200	CLEV	44109	2754	E6
Broadledge Rd				
9000	MCDN	44056	3018	E6
Broadmill Dr				
5500	BWHT	44147	3015	D5
Broadmoor Cir				
7400	MNTR	44060	2251	C3
Broadmoor Rd				
-	WLBY	44060	2251	C3
-	WLBY	44094	2251	C3
1000	MCDN	44056	3018	E6
8000	MNTR	44060	2251	C3
Broadmoor Rd SR-306				
-	WLBY	44060	2251	C3
-	WLBY	44094	2251	C3
8000	MNTR	44060	2251	C3
Broadmore Av				
10	BDFD	44146	2886	D4
Broadmore Ln				
2600	WTLK	44145	2749	C2
Broad Oak Pkwy				
-	OKWD	44146	3018	E3
Broadrock Ct				
1000	PRMA	44134	2883	E1
Broadstone Dr				
36700	SLN	44139	3020	C3
Broad-Valle Rd				
7500	PRMA	44134	3014	E1
Broadview Ct				
1900	CLEV	44109	2754	D6
Broadview Rd				
2000	CLEV	44109	2754	D4
4800	RchT	44286	3149	E6
4800	RchT	44286	3150	A7
4900	CLEV	44134	2754	D7
5000	PRMA	44134	2754	D5
5300	BWHT	44147	3149	E6
5300	RchT	44147	3149	E5
5300	RchT	44233	3149	E6
5400	PRMA	44134	2883	E5
6300	PRMA	44131	2883	E5
6300	SVHL	44131	2883	E5
7300	PRMA	44131	3014	E2
7300	PRMA	44134	3014	E2
7300	SVHL	44131	3014	E2
7800	BWHT	44131	3014	E2
7800	BWHT	44134	3014	E2
7800	BWHT	44147	3014	E6
Broadview Rd SR-176				
4800	RchT	44286	3150	A7
Broadview Rd SR-176				
4900	CLEV	44109	2754	D6
4900	CLEV	44134	2754	D7
5000	PRMA	44134	2754	D5
5300	BWHT	44147	3149	E6
5300	RchT	44147	3149	E5
5300	RchT	44233	3149	E6
5300	RchT	44286	3149	E6
5400	PRMA	44134	2883	E5
6300	PRMA	44131	2883	E5
6300	SVHL	44131	2883	E5
7300	PRMA	44131	3014	E2
7300	PRMA	44134	3014	E2
7300	SVHL	44131	3014	E2
7800	BWHT	44131	3014	E2
7800	BWHT	44134	3014	E2
7800	BWHT	44147	3014	E4
Broadway				
100	LORN	44052	2614	E7
1400	LORN	44052	2744	E1
2000	LORN	44052	2745	A2
2600	LORN	44055	2745	A2
3600	ShfT	44052	2745	A6
3600	ShfT	44055	2745	A4
4900	LORN	44053	2745	A6
4900	ShfT	44053	2745	A6
Broadway SR-57				
300	LORN	44052	2614	E7
1400	LORN	44052	2744	E1
2000	LORN	44052	2745	A2
2600	LORN	44055	2745	A2
N Broadway				
10	GNVA	44041	1944	C3
500	GnvT	44041	1944	C3
N Broadway SR-534				
10	GNVA	44041	1944	C3
500	GnvT	44041	1944	C3
S Broadway				
10	GNVA	44041	1944	B5
S Broadway SR-534				
10	GNVA	44041	1944	B5
Broadway Av				
-	GNWL	44139	3019	A3
-	MCDN	44056	3019	A3
-	MCDN	44146	3019	A3
-	Okwd	44146	3019	A3
-	TNBG	44056	3019	A3
-	TNBG	44087	3019	A3
-	TNBG	44139	3019	A3
10	BDFD	44137	2886	D2
10	BDFD	44146	2886	D3
10	MPHT	44137	2886	B1
10	MPHT	44146	2886	D2
500	BDFD	44146	2887	B5
1400	OKWD	44146	2887	C7
1900	CLEV	44115	2625	A4
3900	CLEV	44127	2625	D7
5800	CLEV	44127	2755	D1
6200	CLEV	44105	2755	D1
7300	CLEV	44105	2756	D5
9300	CLEV	44125	2756	C4
9300	GDHT	44105	2756	C4
9300	GDHT	44125	2756	C4
13600	GDHT	44125	2757	A6
14100	GDHT	44128	2757	A6
14100	MPHT	44125	2757	A6
14100	MPHT	44128	2757	A6
14100	MPHT	44137	2757	A7
23900	OKWD	44146	3018	E2
Broadway Av SR-8				
800	CLEV	44115	2625	A4
Broadway Av SR-14				
10	BDFD	44137	2886	D2
10	BDFD	44146	2886	D3
10	MPHT	44137	2886	B1
10	MPHT	44146	2886	D2
500	BDFD	44146	2887	B5
1400	OKWD	44146	2887	C7
1900	CLEV	44115	2625	A4
3900	CLEV	44127	2625	D7
5800	CLEV	44127	2755	D1
6200	CLEV	44105	2755	D1
7300	CLEV	44105	2756	D5
9300	CLEV	44125	2756	C4
9300	GDHT	44105	2756	C4
9300	GDHT	44125	2756	C4
13600	GDHT	44125	2757	A6
14100	GDHT	44128	2757	A6
14100	MPHT	44125	2757	A6
14100	MPHT	44128	2757	A6
14100	MPHT	44137	2757	A7
Broadway Av SR-43				
1900	CLEV	44115	2625	A4
3900	CLEV	44127	2625	D7
5800	CLEV	44127	2755	D1
6200	CLEV	44105	2755	D1
7300	CLEV	44105	2756	A2
Broadway Av SR-87				
800	CLEV	44115	2625	A4
Broadway Av US-422				
800	CLEV	44115	2625	A4
Broadway Dr				
9700	AbnT	44023	3023	A2
Broadway St				
100	AhtT	44001	2872	E2
100	AMHT	44001	2872	E2
16700	BbgT	44023	2890	A1
36000	NRDV	44039	2876	E7
N Broadway St				
700	GNVA	44041	1944	C2
700	GnvT	44041	1944	C1
N Broadway St SR-534				
700	GNVA	44041	1944	C2
700	GnvT	44041	1944	C1
S Broadway St				
1200	GNVA	44041	1944	C6
S Broadway St SR-534				
1200	GNVA	44041	1944	C6
Broadwood Dr				
14300	BtnT	44021	2635	D7
14500	BtnT	44021	2765	D1
Brock Ct				
-	EUCL	44123	2373	B2
Brockley Av				
1100	LKWD	44107	2622	C4
4100	SDLK	44054	2616	A4
4200	SFLD	44054	2616	B4
Brockton Cir				
300	BERA	44017	2879	E7
Brockway Dr				
12600	VLVW	44125	2885	E6
28500	WTLK	44145	2749	D4
E Brockway Dr				
28500	WTLK	44145	2749	D4

Cleveland Street Index

STREET
Block City ZIP Map# Grid

W Brockway Dr
29000 WTLK 44145 2749 D4
Brockway Rd
2100 UNHT 44118 2627 E3
Brokaw Rd
33500 ClbT 44028 3008 D3
33500 EatT 44028 3008 D3
Bromley Rd
2300 UNHT 44118 2628 B4
Bromton Dr
1800 LNHT 44124 2629 A2
Bronson Ct
- CLEV 44115 2625 A3
Bronson Rd
7400 OmsT 44138 2878 A5
Bronson St
10 BERA 44017 3011 B1
25500 ODFL 44138 3010 B1
Bronsons Wy
2600 TNBG 44087 3020 B6
Brook Cir
6000 NOSD 44070 2878 A2
Brook Ct
3400 AVON 44011 2748 D4
6000 BKPK 44142 2881 D2
Brook Dr
400 ETLK 44095 2250 D1
Brook Ln
1000 RKRV 44116 2621 B6
4700 BKLN 44144 2753 C6
Brook Rd
- CVHT 44118 2627 A4
- SRHT 44118 2627 A4
- SRHT 44120 2627 A4
9300 ODFL 44138 3009 D2
9400 ClbT 44028 3009 D2
9400 ClbT 44138 3009 D2
Brookdale Av
1600 PRMA 44134 2883 C1
13300 BKPK 44130 2881 D2
13300 BKPK 44142 2881 D2
13300 PRMA 44130 2881 D2
Brookdale Ct
- CLEV 44106 2496 B7
Brookdale Dr
400 ETLK 44095 2142 D7
Brookdale Ln
9200 MCDN 44056 3019 A7
25600 EUCL 44117 2373 D6
Brookdale Rd
1900 EUCL 44117 2373 E7
1900 RDHT 44117 2373 E7
1900 RDHT 44143 2373 E7
Brooke Ln
500 BYVL 44140 2619 B5
Brooke Lyn Wy
11700 CcdT 44077 2254 D2
Brooke Valley Ct
1400 BWHT 44147 3015 A6
Brookfield Av
11700 CLEV 44135 2753 A3
11700 LNDL 44135 2753 A3
Brookfield Dr
700 AURA 44202 3156 D4
10000 CcdT 44060 2253 C1
10000 CcdT 44077 2253 C1
11000 CrlT 44035 3005 C5
19000 AbnT 44023 3023 A3
19000 ManT 44023 3023 A3
19000 ManT 44202 3023 A3
Brookfield Ln
7400 NCtT 44067 3153 E5
19300 WVHT 44122 2757 E3
19300 WVHT 44122 2758 A3
Brookfield Pl
200 MCDN 44056 3018 B6
21400 SGVL 44149 3011 B5
Brookfield Rd
100 AVLK 44012 2488 A7
100 AVLK 44012 2617 E2
100 AVLK 44012 2618 A1
Brookgate Wy
7500 NCtT 44067 3153 E5
Brookhaven Av
13300 BKPK 44130 2881 E2
13300 BKPK 44142 2881 E2
13300 PRMA 44130 2881 E2
Brookhaven Dr
6700 MNTR 44060 2144 A6
Brook Haven Ln
2200 HkyT 44233 3148 A6
2400 HkyT 44233 3147 E6
Brookhigh Dr
4700 BKLN 44144 2753 D6
Brook Hill Cir
4000 BKLN 44144 2753 D3
Brookhill Cir
9900 TNBG 44087 3019 B4
Brookhill Dr
6300 GDHT 44125 2885 E4
Brook Hollow Ovl
2200 HkyT 44233 3148 A6
Brookins Dr
10 OmsT 44138 2879 A4
Brookland Av
6500 SLN 44139 2889 A6
Brooklawn Av
11800 CLEV 44111 2753 A3
Brookledge Ct
600 NCtT 44067 3153 E5
Brookline Av
8200 CLEV 44103 2626 A2
8200 CLEV 44106 2626 A2
Brookline Ct
500 NCtT 44067 3153 E4
Brookline Ovl
9600 SGVL 44136 3012 B4
Brookline Pl
1100 WLBY 44094 2142 E5
Brookline Rd
1300 CVHT 44121 2498 A7
1300 SELD 44121 2498 A7
Brook Ln Rd
7000 CsTp 44026 2501 B2
7000 CsTp 44040 2501 A2
7000 GSML 44040 2501 A2
Brooklyn Av
3600 CLEV 44109 2754 B4
4500 CLEV 44144 2754 B4
Brooklyn St
100 ELYR 44035 3006 B1
Brookmere Dr
6200 PMHT 44130 2882 D4
Brookpark Ext
26600 NOSD 44070 2750 A6
Brookpark Rd
700 BNHT 44109 2754 E7
700 BNHT 44131 2754 E7
700 CLEV 44109 2754 E7
700 PRMA 44109 2754 E7
700 PRMA 44131 2754 E7
700 PRMA 44134 2754 D7
1500 CLEV 44134 2754 D7
5200 PRMA 44129 2754 A7
6000 CLEV 44129 2754 A7
6700 BKLN 44129 2753 E7
6700 BKLN 44144 2753 B7
6700 CLEV 44129 2753 E7
6700 PRMA 44129 2753 E7
6700 PRMA 44144 2753 B7
10100 PRMA 44130 2753 B7
11700 CLEV 44135 2753 B7
11700 CLEV 44144 2753 B7
11700 PRMA 44135 2753 B7
12800 CLEV 44135 2752 B7
12800 PRMA 44130 2752 B7
12800 PRMA 44135 2752 B7
13000 BKPK 44130 2752 D7
13000 BKPK 44135 2752 D7
13000 BKPK 44142 2752 D7
18200 BKPK 44135 2751 E7
18200 BKPK 44142 2751 E7
18200 CLEV 44135 2751 D6
18200 CLEV 44142 2751 E7
22400 FWPK 44126 2751 A6
22500 NOSD 44070 2751 A6
22500 NOSD 44126 2751 A6
23000 NOSD 44070 2750 E7
Brookpark Rd SR-17
700 BNHT 44109 2754 E7
700 BNHT 44131 2754 E7
700 CLEV 44109 2754 E7
700 PRMA 44109 2754 E7
700 PRMA 44131 2754 E7
700 PRMA 44134 2754 D7
1500 CLEV 44134 2754 D7
5200 PRMA 44129 2754 A7
6000 CLEV 44129 2754 A7
6700 BKLN 44129 2753 E7
6700 BKLN 44144 2753 B7
6700 CLEV 44129 2753 E7
6700 PRMA 44129 2753 E7
6700 PRMA 44144 2753 B7
10100 PRMA 44130 2753 B7
11700 CLEV 44135 2753 B7
11700 CLEV 44144 2753 B7
11700 PRMA 44135 2753 B7
12800 CLEV 44135 2752 B7
12800 PRMA 44130 2752 B7
12800 PRMA 44135 2752 B7
13000 BKPK 44130 2752 D7
13000 BKPK 44135 2752 D7
13000 BKPK 44142 2752 D7
18200 BKPK 44135 2751 E7
18200 BKPK 44142 2751 E7
18200 CLEV 44135 2751 D6
18200 CLEV 44142 2751 E7
22400 FWPK 44126 2751 A6
22500 NOSD 44070 2751 A6
22500 NOSD 44126 2751 A6
23000 NOSD 44070 2750 E7
Brookpark Rd SR-176
1500 CLEV 44109 2754 E7
1500 CLEV 44134 2754 D7
1500 PRMA 44109 2754 E7
1500 PRMA 44134 2754 E7
Brookpark Rd SR-237
18200 BKPK 44135 2751 E7
18200 BKPK 44135 2752 A7
18200 BKPK 44142 2751 E7
18200 BKPK 44142 2752 A7
18200 CLEV 44135 2751 E7
18200 CLEV 44135 2752 A7
18200 CLEV 44142 2751 E7
Brook Point Cir
500 NCtT 44067 3153 E5
Brookpoint Dr
900 MCDN 44056 3018 D6
Brookport Dr
8400 BKLN 44144 2753 D6
Brookridge Ln
- CcdT 44077 2253 C1
Brookrun Ct
7600 NCtT 44067 3153 E5
Brooks Blvd
6100 MNTR 44060 2143 D4
Brooks Ct
2800 BWHT 44147 3149 D5
Brooks Dr
- WLBY 44094 2142 E5
N Brooks Dr
- WLBY 44094 2142 E5
Brooks Rd
4300 CLEV 44105 2756 B4
Brooksdale Rd
4600 MNTR 44060 2038 D6
Brookshire Ovl
200 HkyT 44233 3148 A7
Brookside Blvd
10 HkyT 44133 3148 A5
10 HkyT 44233 3148 A6
10 NRYN 44133 3148 A5
600 SDLK 44054 2616 B3
3800 CLEV 44111 2752 E3
3800 CLEV 44111 2753 A2
3900 CLEV 44135 2752 E3
Brookside Cir
300 AURA 44202 3022 B5
700 AVLK 44012 2618 E5
8900 MNTR 44060 2144 D7
10000 NRYN 44133 3014 A3
Brookside Dr
- AURA 44202 3022 B5
100 AMHT 44001 2872 D1
5800 CLEV 44144 2754 A4
6300 BKLN 44144 2753 E3
6300 CLEV 44144 2753 E3
7700 ODFL 44138 2879 B5
Brookside Ln
400 NCtT 44067 3153 E5
700 MCDN 44056 3153 E5
Brookside Pkwy
7300 MDBH 44130 2881 B7
Brookside Rd
5000 BWHT 44131 3015 C2
5000 BWHT 44147 3015 C2
5000 INDE 44131 3015 D2
7200 INDE 44131 3016 A1
11200 MsnT 44024 2504 B3
Brookstone Blvd
- PNVL 44077 2145 B2
Brookstone Ct
500 AVLK 44012 2617 D3
4600 BHIT 44212 3146 B7
Brookstone Ln
10 WLBY 44094 2375 B2
32700 NRDV 44039 2877 E1
Brookstone Tr
20300 MDBH 44130 2880 C5
Brookstone Wy
9500 SGVL 44149 3011 A4
Brookton Rd
4400 WVHT 44128 2758 C5
Brookvalley Dr
100 ELYR 44035 2875 D1
Brookview Blvd
1000 PRMA 44134 2754 D7
Brookview Dr
2600 AVON 44011 2747 B2
2800 LORN 44053 2743 E3
10900 BKVL 44141 3016 C3
Brookway Dr
21600 FWPK 44126 2751 B6
Brookway Ln
4100 BKLN 44144 2753 E4
Brookwood Ct
600 NCtT 44067 3153 E5
Brookwood Dr
- CLEV 44108 2496 D4
4600 BKLN 44144 2753 E6
4700 LNHT 44124 2628 D1
30400 PRPK 44124 2629 D7
Brookwood Ln
7900 NRYN 44133 3013 D7
Brothers Dr
1400 AVON 44011 2617 D6
Brow Av
5200 NBGH 44105 2755 D3
5400 CLEV 44105 2755 D3
Brown Av
37800 WLBY 44094 2250 D6
Brown Ln
10 BDFD 44146 2887 A4
Brown Rd
2000 LKWD 44107 2622 D6
2200 CLEV 44107 2622 D7
2200 CLEV 44111 2622 D7
N Brown Rd
8700 HmbT 44024 2255 C7
8700 HmbT 44024 2380 C1
S Brown Rd
9200 HmbT 44024 2380 C2
Brown St
10 CLEV 44110 2372 B6
6700 HRM 44234 3161 A2
Brownell Av
100 LORN 44052 2614 C7
1100 LORN 44052 2744 C1
Brownell Ct
1200 CLEV 44115 2625 A3
Brownell Dr
7000 MNTR 44060 2251 B1
Brownfield Dr
5400 PRMA 44129 2883 A3
5400 PRMA 44134 2883 A3
6500 PRMA 44129 2882 E3
Brownhelm Station Rd
- LORN 44053 2742 B7
- VMLN 44053 2742 B7
1600 LORN 44089 2742 B7
3000 VMLN 44089 2741 D6
3000 VMLN 44089 2742 A7
Browning Av
- CLEV 44104 2626 D5
11700 CLEV 44120 2626 D5
Browning Ct
- CcdT 44077 2253 B4
8200 CcdT 44060 2253 B5
Browning Dr
33500 NRDV 44039 2877 D3
Brownstone Cir
600 AVLK 44012 2618 E4
Brownstone Ct
6100 MNTR 44060 2144 D3
Brownstone Ln
32800 NRDV 44039 2877 E1
Broxbourne Rd
29400 NOSD 44070 2749 C7
Broxton Av
14400 CLEV 44111 2622 D7
Broxton Dr
18000 SGVL 44136 3012 A3
18000 SGVL 44149 3011 E3
18000 SGVL 44149 3012 A3
Broxton Rd
2800 SRHT 44120 2627 C6
Bruce Av
21500 EUCL 44123 2373 B3
Bruce Dr
200 BNWK 44212 3146 E7
29500 WLWK 44095 2249 B6
Bruce Ln
- WLWK 44095 2249 B6
100 CrlT 44035 3006 D4
Bruce Rd
1400 MCDN 44056 3019 A7
26500 BYVL 44140 2620 A4
Brucefield Rd
25200 BHWD 44122 2628 E6
Bruce Industrial Pkwy
30100 SLN 44139 2888 C6
Bruening Dr
4300 PRMA 44134 2883 B5
Brune Dr
10 BDFD 44146 2886 C4
Brunner Av
8100 CLEV 44105 2756 C3
Brunswick Av
10800 GDHT 44125 2885 C1
14100 MPHT 44137 2886 A2
Brunswick Dr
100 AVLK 44012 2619 A2
100 ELYR 44035 2874 A7
100 EyrT 44035 2874 A7
Brunswick Ln
2300 HDSN 44236 3155 B6
Brunswick Rd
2000 CVHT 44112 2497 C5
2000 ECLE 44112 2497 C5
Brush Av
26000 EUCL 44132 2373 E5
26400 EUCL 44132 2374 A4
Brush Rd
- EUCL 44117 2373 E5
100 EUCL 44143 2373 E5
100 RDHT 44143 2373 E5
Brushview Dr
1800 RDHT 44143 2374 A6
Brushwood Dr
10000 STBR 44241 3156 C7
35600 SLN 44139 2889 B3
Brushwood Ln
9400 SGVL 44136 3012 D4
Brushwood Rd
3200 RHFD 44286 3151 A7
4800 RHFD 44286 3150 E7
Brussels Rd
- CLEV 44110 2372 B6
Bryan Ct
100 ELYR 44035 3006 C2
Bryan Dr
900 SELD 44121 2498 D6
900 SELD 44143 2498 D5
Bryandale Dr
27600 WTLK 44145 2619 E6
27600 WTLK 44145 2620 A6
Bryant Av
800 BERA 44017 2880 C4
800 BERA 44142 2880 C4
800 BKPK 44142 2880 C4
10500 CLEV 44108 2496 C5
Bryant Dr
800 VMLN 44089 2740 D6
9800 ClbT 44028 3010 D2
9800 ClbT 44138 3010 D2
9800 ODFL 44138 3010 D2
Bryant Ln
6700 SVHL 44131 2884 B5
Bryce Av
900 AURA 44202 3021 A4
1200 RMDV 44202 3021 A4
15900 CLEV 44128 2757 B5
Bryce Rd
28900 PRPK 44124 2759 C1
Bryden Ct
6800 VLVW 44125 2885 E6
Bryden Rd
- SELD 44121 2498 D6
23200 BHWD 44122 2628 D7
23200 SRHT 44122 2628 D7
25400 BHWD 44122 2758 E1
Bryn Mawr Av
600 WKLF 44092 2249 A7
600 WKLF 44092 2374 A1
Bryn Mawr Dr
10 PnvT 44077 2146 D3
10600 SGVL 44136 3012 B4
Bryn Mawr Rd
1600 ECLE 44112 2497 A6
Bryon Rd
22600 SRHT 44122 2628 C6
Brysdale Av
17600 CLEV 44135 2752 A6
Bryson Dr
6100 MNTR 44060 2143 E3
Bryson Ln
300 BYVL 44140 2620 A4
Buccaneer Dr
18200 NRYN 44133 3147 E4
Buccaneer Tr
18600 SGVL 44136 3147 D4
Buchanan Ct
7100 MNTR 44060 2143 D7
Buchanan Dr
28900 BYVL 44140 2619 D5
Buchtel St
1800 TwbT 44087 3154 C2
2000 TNBG 44087 3154 D2
Buck Av
7900 CLEV 44103 2496 A5
Buck Cross
482-00 AURA 44202 3156 C3
Buck Ct
- CLEV 44114 2625 B1
Buckboard Ln
1300 BWHT 44147 3149 E5
5900 SLN 44139 2888 E3
5900 SLN 44139 2889 A3
8100 CcdT 44060 2253 B4
Buckeye Av
- HIHL 44128 2758 C4
4100 WLBY 44094 2250 D5
Buckeye Ct
2500 CLEV 44109 2624 D7
Buckeye Dr
200 BERA 44017 2880 A5
200 SDLK 44054 2616 D3
300 BERA 44017 2879 E5
12500 CsTp 44026 2502 A7
Buckeye Ln
5800 MONT 44060 2143 E2
Buckeye Rd
10 PnvT 44077 2145 D4
8400 CLEV 44104 2626 B5
11500 CLEV 44120 2626 E6
Buckeye Rd SR-87
8400 CLEV 44104 2626 B5
Buckeye St
100 ELYR 44035 2875 C6
100 SAHT 44001 2872 B7
Buckhead
500 AVLK 44012 2618 B4
Buckhill Ct
9700 CcdT 44060 2253 B3
Buck Horn Blvd
- LORN 44053 2743 B6
Buckhorn Tr
- STBR 44241 3156 C7
Buckhurst Dr
2400 BHWD 44122 2628 D5
Buckhurst Pl
7000 CcdT 44060 2145 B7
Buckingham Av
- CLEV 44120 2626 D5
Buckingham Ct
16800 MDBH 44130 2881 A5
Buckingham Dr
- AVON 44011 2618 B7
100 ELYR 44035 2875 C1
200 AURA 44202 3021 D7
200 GNVA 44041 1944 A5
4700 BWHT 44147 3015 D5
4700 LORN 44052 2744 D5
4700 LORN 44053 2744 D5
6300 PRMA 44129 2882 E4
Buckingham Pl
- CcdT 44077 2253 E4
Buckingham Rd
10 RKRV 44116 2621 E4
Buckingham Shire
19400 NRYN 44133 3148 B4
Buckland Tr
15500 RslT 44072 2762 C4
Buckley Av
- CLEV 44113 2624 B6
Buckley Blvd
- CLEV 44113 2624 C4
Buckley Blvd US-6
- CLEV 44113 2624 C4
Buckley Blvd US-20
- CLEV 44113 2624 C4
Buckner Dr
200 EUCL 44123 2373 C2
Buckston Ct
8500 MCDN 44056 3018 B6
Buckthorn Dr
- TNBG 44087 3019 B3
7800 MNTR 44060 2253 A3
17200 BbgT 44023 2890 D3
Buckthorn Pl
29300 WTLK 44145 2749 C2
Buckthorn Rd
24900 BDHT 44146 2887 E7
26000 OKWD 44146 2887 E6
26300 GNWL 44139 2888 A6
26300 GNWL 44146 2888 A6
26300 Okwd 44146 2888 A6
Bucyrus Av
3800 CLEV 44109 2754 B5
4200 CLEV 44144 2754 B5
Bucyrus Dr
5800 BKLN 44144 2754 A5
5800 CLEV 44144 2754 A5
Buechner Av
3600 CLEV 44109 2754 B6
Buena Vista Dr
1700 EUCL 44117 2498 A2
2100 WKLF 44092 2374 C3
9300 MNTR 44060 2252 E1
Buffalo Ct
18000 CLEV 44119 2372 D7
Bugby Dr
6300 MadT 44057 1942 A3
Buhrer Av
1000 CLEV 44109 2624 E7
Bull Creek Ln
1000 MCDN 44056 3153 E2
Bullocks St
100 ELYR 44035 2874 E5
Bunbury Ln
6900 CcdT 44077 2146 C6
Bundy Dr
2500 CLEV 44104 2625 E4
Bunker Ct
4000 NRYN 44133 3014 B3
Bunker Ln
2400 WLBY 44094 2251 A1
Bunker Rd
300 WLWK 44095 2249 C6
4500 NRYN 44133 3014 A3
5500 NRYN 44133 3013 E3
Bunker Cove
7100 MNTR 44060 2251 B2
Bunker Hill Dr
20400 FWPK 44126 2751 D3
37300 SLN 44139 2889 D4
Bunker Hill Ln
10 ELYR 44035 2875 A3
Bunker Hill Rd
7500 MDBH 44130 3012 D2
Bunnell Ct
2900 CLEV 44113 2624 B4
Bunts Rd
1200 LKWD 44107 2622 D7
2100 CLEV 44107 2622 E7
2100 CLEV 44111 2622 E7
Buoy Ct
7400 NCtT 44067 3153 C5
Burbank Ct
16000 CLEV 44110 2372 C7
Burbridge Rd
3600 CVHT 44121 2497 E5
3600 SELD 44121 2497 E5
Burden Dr
2600 PRMA 44134 3014 C1
Burgandy Dr
20700 SGVL 44149 3146 B2
Burger Av
3500 CLEV 44109 2754 B6
4700 CLEV 44144 2754 B6
Burger Dr
10 EUCL 44123 2373 C1
Burger Rd
4700 LNHT 44124 2498 D6
4700 SELD 44121 2498 D6
Burgess Rd
1600 CLEV 44112 2497 D2
Burgundy Cir
3300 AVON 44011 2748 D4
Burke Av
7800 CLEV 44105 2756 A2
Burleigh Rd
4600 CLEV 44105 2756 A5
4600 GDHT 44105 2756 A5
4600 GDHT 44125 2756 A5
Burlington Dr
- NRDV 44039 2877 D6
Burlington Rd
1200 CVHT 44118 2497 C7
Burlington Rdg
10900 MsnT 44024 2504 A4
Burlington Glen Dr
11900 MsnT 44024 2504 A5
Burlington Oval Dr
10 CRDN 44024 2505 A1
Burlwood Dr
- NRYN 44133 3012 E5
- SGVL 44133 3012 E5
13300 SGVL 44136 3012 D5
31700 SLN 44139 2759 E7
31700 SLN 44139 2888 D1
Burnette Av
1800 ECLE 44112 2497 C4
Burnham Dr
16200 SGVL 44149 3146 D2
Burnham Pl
7000 CLEV 44103 2625 E1
Burning Tree Dr
- AURA 44202 3022 A7
Burns Av
10900 CrlT 44035 3005 C4
Burns Ln
10 AURA 44202 3157 E1
Burns Rd
100 ELYR 44035 2746 D7
200 ELYR 44035 2875 E1
400 ELYR 44035 2876 A1
400 ELYR 44039 2876 A1
400 NRDV 44039 2876 A1
2600 MadT 44057 1941 E5
2600 MDSN 44057 1941 E5
5300 NOSD 44070 2749 E7
5300 NOSD 44070 2878 E1
Burnside Av
16500 CLEV 44110 2497 C2
Burntwood Ln
7300 HDSN 44236 3154 A7
Burr Rd
- NbyT 44065 2763 D4
Burr St
500 GNVA 44041 1944 C4
Burrard Ct
- WLBY 44094 2142 E5
Burrard Ln
- WLBY 44094 2142 E5
Burrell Dr
5000 SFLD 44054 2746 D1
Burrer Dr
- CrlT 44050 3140 E1
Burridge Av
7000 MNTR 44060 2144 C7
7200 MNTR 44060 2252 C1
Burridge Cir
2500 TNBG 44087 3154 E1
Burridge Ln
9000 TNBG 44087 3154 D1
Burr Oak Ct
100 ELYR 44035 2874 B7
N Burr Oak Dr
32200 SLN 44139 3019 E2
32800 SLN 44139 3020 A2
S Burr Oak Dr
32200 SLN 44139 3019 E2
Burrows Rd
15800 MtlT 44064 2257 D5
15800 TpnT 44064 2257 D5
15800 TpnT 44086 2257 D5
Burrows St
100 GNVA 44041 1944 B4
Burten Ct
3700 CLEV 44115 2625 C4
Burton Av
9900 BTNH 44108 2496 C4
Burton Ct
4000 CLEV 44113 2624 C6
Burton Dr
6500 BERA 44017 2880 B3
6500 BERA 44142 2880 B4
6500 BKPK 44142 2880 B4
9700 TNBG 44087 3020 B6
Burton Ln
7900 TwbT 44236 3155 A6
N Burton Ln
7700 TwbT 44236 3155 A5
Burton St
10 PNVL 44077 2040 A7
100 AVLK 44012 2617 C2
200 FTHR 44077 2039 C5
Burton Tr
40500 HGVL 44022 2630 E3
Burton Heights Blvd
12400 BtnT 44021 2765 B2
12400 NbyT 44021 2765 B2
12400 NbyT 44065 2765 B2
Burton Limaville Rd S
10000 FdmT 44255 3161 A7
10000 HrmT 44231 3161 A7
10000 HrmT 44255 3161 A7
Burton Limaville Rd S SR-700
10000 FdmT 44255 3161 A7
10000 HrmT 44231 3161 A7
10000 HrmT 44255 3161 A7
Burton Windsor Rd
14100 BtnT 44021 2636 C6
14100 BtnT 44062 2636 C6
14100 BURT 44021 2636 C7
14700 BtnT 44021 2637 A5
14700 BtnT 44062 2637 A5
15100 MdfT 44021 2637 A5
15100 MdfT 44062 2637 A5
15200 MdfT 44046 2637 C5
15500 HtbT 44046 2637 D4
15500 HtbT 44062 2637 D4
Burts Wy
9700 OmsT 44138 3009 C2
Burwell Av
3500 CLEV 44115 2625 C4
Burwick Rd
300 HDHT 44143 2499 C1
Busa Ovl
4100 CLEV 44128 2757 C3
Bush Av
3900 CLEV 44109 2754 B1
4500 CLEV 44102 2754 B1
Bushnell Ct
6600 CLEV 44104 2625 E5
8400 MNTR 44060 2144 B3
Bushnell Rd
3700 UNHT 44118 2627 E3
3800 UNHT 44118 2628 A3
4000 UNHT 44121 2628 A3
Buskirk Blvd
7100 INDE 44131 2884 E4
Butler Av
- ELYR 44035 3006 B2
6000 CLEV 44127 2625 D6
Butler Hill Dr
- CcdT 44077 2253 D3
Buttercup Ct
- NRDV 44039 2877 B7
Buttercup Ln
- LORN 44053 2743 B6
Butterfield Cir
300 SgHT 44067 3017 D4
Butterfly Ln
7900 CcdT 44077 2254 C3
Buttermere Ln
300 AMHT 44001 2872 D4
Buttermilk Falls Pkwy
- WBHL 44094 2375 B6
Butternut Cir
18200 SGVL 44136 3147 C4
Butternut Ct
3700 MDHL 44022 2759 D2
3700 ORNG 44022 2759 D2
Butternut Dr
10 NCtT 44067 3017 E6
10 NCtT 44067 3018 A6
100 AhtT 44001 2873 A2
100 AMHT 44001 2873 A2
700 MAYF 44040 2500 A5
Butternut Ln
10 NCtT 44067 3017 E7
10 NCtT 44067 3018 A6
10 SgHT 44067 3017 E7
200 BERA 44017 2880 A5
2500 PRPK 44124 2630 A4
7100 MNTR 44060 2143 B5
11100 NRYN 44133 3013 B5
20000 WVHT 44128 2758 A4
20100 HIHL 44122 2758 A4
20100 HIHL 44128 2758 A4
20100 WVHT 44122 2758 A4
Butternut Rd
10300 MsnT 44024 2503 D7
10300 MsnT 44024 2633 D1
10300 MsnT 44026 2503 D7
10300 MsnT 44026 2633 D1
10600 MsnT 44024 2634 A3
10600 MsnT 44026 2634 A3
11000 MsnT 44065 2634 A3
11100 NbyT 44024 2634 E4
11100 NbyT 44065 2634 B3
11800 NbyT 44021 2635 A4
11800 NbyT 44024 2635 A4
11800 NbyT 44065 2635 A4
12400 BtnT 44021 2635 B4
12400 BtnT 44024 2635 B4
13200 BtnT 44021 2636 C4
13200 BtnT 44024 2636 C4
Butternut Park Ct
40900 CrlT 44035 3005 E6
40900 CrlT 44050 3005 E6
Butternut Ridge Dr
4900 INDE 44131 2884 C6
Butternut Ridge Rd
7200 CrlT 44044 3006 E5
10800 EatT 44035 3007 E2
10800 EatT 44039 3007 E2
10800 EatT 44044 3006 E5
10800 EatT 44044 3007 E2
10800 NRDV 44039 3007 E2
25100 NOSD 44070 2879 A1
25100 NOSD 44138 2879 C1
27100 NOSD 44070 2750 A7
27200 NOSD 44070 2749 E7
38700 CrlT 44035 3006 A6
40200 CrlT 44050 3006 A6
40500 CrlT 44050 3005 E6
41100 CrlT 44035 3005 A6
41100 CrlT 44074 3005 A6
42700 CrlT 44035 3004 E6
42700 CrlT 44074 3004 E6
42700 NRsT 44074 3004 A7
45000 NRsT 44074 3003 E7
Butternut Ridge Rd SR-83C
10800 EatT 44035 3007 E2
10800 EatT 44039 3007 E2
10800 EatT 44044 3007 E2
10800 NRDV 44039 3007 E2
Butterwing Rd
2500 PRPK 44124 2629 B4
Button Av
200 PNVL 44077 2039 D7
300 PnvT 44077 2039 D7
Button Rd
500 BDFD 44146 2886 C5
7200 CcdT 44060 2253 C1
7200 CcdT 44077 2253 C1
14500 WNHL 44146 2886 A6
Button St
15900 MDFD 44062 2767 D1
Button Bush
600 AVLK 44012 2618 D5
Button Bush Cir
100 SRSL 44022 2761 D5
Buttonbush Ln
5000 NRYN 44133 3014 B4
Buttonwood Dr
1600 SVHL 44131 2884 A3
Buxton Cir
1600 PnvT 44077 2040 E2
Buxton Rd
4000 CVHT 44121 2628 A1
4000 SELD 44121 2628 A1
Byington Ct
100 ELYR 44035 2875 C5
Byron Av
13200 CLEV 44120 2626 E7
13500 CLEV 44120 2627 A7
Byron Blvd
13300 MDBH 44130 3012 D2
Byron Dr
1600 MDHT 44124 2629 C1
25500 NOSD 44070 2750 B5
Byron Rd
6800 MadT 44057 1942 C2
20400 SRHT 44122 2628 A7
E Byron Rd
21800 SRHT 44122 2628 B6
W Byron Rd
20800 SRHT 44122 2628 A6

C

C St
500 LORN 44052 2614 E6
700 LORN 44052 2615 A6
Cabin Dr
2600 WKLF 44092 2374 B4
Cable Av
5800 CLEV 44127 2625 D7
Cableknoll Ln
10 MDHL 44022 2759 E4
Cabot Ct
6000 MNTR 44060 2144 B3
Cabot Ln
7100 CNFL 44022 2761 B4
7100 RslT 44022 2761 B4
Cabot Wy
3000 TNBG 44087 3020 B7
Cabrini Ln
6000 SVHL 44131 2884 A3
Cabriolet Av
9000 CcdT 44060 2253 B4
Cachat Dr
41100 CrlT 44035 3005 E6
Caddie Ln
11100 CcdT 44077 2254 B1

Cleveland Street Index

STREET Block	City	ZIP	Map#	Grid
Caddy Ln				
1500	PnvT	44077	2040	E4
Cadence Ct				
10800	NbyT	44065	2763	E3
Cadet Dr				
10	NRDV	44039	2877	B4
Cadle Av				
7200	MNTR	44060	2252	A1
Cadwell Av				
1700	CVHT	44118	2627	B2
Cady Rd				
5600	NRYN	44133	3148	D4
5600	NRYN	44133	3149	A4
Caesars Cir				
10	AMHT	44001	2744	B7
Caferro Dr				
3900	LORN	44055	2745	D4
Cahoon Rd				
300	BYVL	44140	2619	E4
400	BYVL	44140	2620	A4
600	WTLK	44140	2620	A4
600	WTLK	44145	2620	A4
900	WTLK	44145	2619	E6
Caine Av				
13100	CLEV	44105	2756	E4
13300	CLEV	44105	2757	A4
13900	CLEV	44128	2757	A4
Cairn Ln				
7500	GSML	44040	2500	E3
Calamie Dr				
5800	PMHT	44130	2882	B2
5800	PRMA	44130	2882	B2
Calann Dr				
600	ELYR	44035	3006	C1
39500	CrlT	44035	3006	C1
Calcutta Av				
15400	CLEV	44110	2372	B7
Caldwell Av				
-	AVLK	44012	2617	B2
14500	CLEV	44111	2752	D1
Caleb Ct				
5400	CLEV	44127	2625	D7
Caledonia Av				
800	CVHT	44112	2497	D5
800	ECLE	44112	2497	C5
Calgary Av				
2200	CLEV	44109	2754	D3
Cali Ct				
11600	CcdT	44077	2254	D1
Cali Dr				
11700	CcdT	44077	2254	D1
Calico Ln				
10500	CdnT	44024	2378	E6
California Av				
10	LORN	44052	2614	E5
California Dr				
100	ELYR	44035	3006	E2
California St				
800	AURA	44202	3021	A4
900	RMDV	44202	3021	A4
1200	AURA	44139	3021	A3
1200	BbgT	44139	3021	A3
1200	BbgT	44202	3021	A3
1200	RMDV	44139	3021	A3
1200	SLN	44139	3021	A3
Calista Dr				
9000	NRDV	44035	2876	C7
9000	NRDV	44035	3007	C1
Call Rd				
3200	NPRY	44081	1940	D7
3200	PryT	44081	1940	D7
3500	PRRY	44081	2042	D2
3500	PryT	44081	2042	D2
Callendar Blvd				
800	PnvT	44077	2039	C7
800	PnvT	44077	2145	C1
Calley Ln				
7300	HGVL	44022	2631	B5
7300	RslT	44022	2631	B5
7300	RslT	44072	2631	B5
Callow Rd				
6900	LryT	44077	2147	D7
7400	HmbT	44024	2255	D2
7400	LryT	44024	2255	D3
7400	LryT	44077	2255	D3
Calumet Av				
-	NCtT	44067	3153	A1
Calverton Pl				
400	BNWK	44212	3146	E7
Calverton Rd				
21900	SRHT	44118	2628	B5
21900	SRHT	44122	2628	B5
Calvin Dr				
200	SVHL	44131	2884	A4
12100	BKVL	44141	3016	D7
Calythorne Dr				
34200	SLN	44139	3020	A3
Camberly Ct				
33800	SLN	44139	3020	A2
Camberly Dr				
1800	LNHT	44124	2629	A2
Cambrian Wy				
2200	MadT	44057	1941	D3
Cambridge Av				
200	ELYR	44035	2875	C6
3500	LORN	44053	2744	A4
9100	CLEV	44105	2756	B2
Cambridge Blvd				
16900	BKPK	44142	2881	A4
Cambridge Cir				
-	WBHL	44092	2374	A6
10500	NRYN	44133	3014	A4
30600	BYVL	44140	2619	B5
32100	AVLK	44012	2618	D4
Cambridge Ct				
4100	ORNG	44022	2759	B4
4100	ORNG	44122	2759	B4
Cambridge Ct E				
30600	BYVL	44140	2619	B5
Cambridge Ct W				
30600	BYVL	44140	2619	B6
Cambridge Dr				
100	AURA	44202	3156	B1
200	AURA	44202	3021	B7
2300	HDSN	44236	3155	B6
7700	BKVL	44131	3015	E2
7700	BKVL	44141	3015	E2
7700	INDE	44131	3015	E2
8500	PRMA	44129	2753	D7
8900	NHFD	44067	3018	B4
11600	CsTp	44026	2501	E3
19400	SGVL	44136	3147	C5
25400	BDHT	44146	2887	D4
25700	OKWD	44146	2887	E4
26200	Okwd	44146	2888	A4
Cambridge Dr				
26200	SLN	44139	2888	A4
29800	NOSD	44070	2878	C2
30600	BYVL	44140	2619	B5
34800	NRDV	44039	2877	B6
Cambridge Ln				
400	WLBY	44094	2250	A7
26000	WVHT	44128	2758	E6
27900	PRPK	44124	2629	B6
Cambridge Ovl				
17700	SGVL	44136	3146	E4
Cambridge Rd				
-	SELD	44121	2498	A5
800	CVHT	44121	2498	A5
9100	CdnT	44024	2378	E1
Cambridge St				
1900	TwbT	44087	3154	C2
2000	TNBG	44087	3154	C2
Cambridge Park Dr				
6100	MNTR	44060	2144	A4
Camden Av				
3100	LORN	44055	2746	A3
6800	CLEV	44102	2623	E7
6800	CLEV	44102	2624	A7
Camden Blvd				
4600	LORN	44053	2743	D4
Camden Ct				
3700	WTLK	44145	2749	C4
8400	BWHT	44147	3014	C5
Camden Dr				
14400	SGVL	44136	3147	C5
Camden Ln				
-	AURA	44202	3021	E6
2000	TwbT	44236	3155	A5
Camden Rd				
4900	WVHT	44128	2757	E6
5000	MPHT	44128	2757	E6
5000	MPHT	44137	2757	E7
Camellia Ln				
4400	NOSD	44070	2749	E6
Camelot Ct				
2800	WBHL	44092	2374	C6
6700	MNTR	44060	2143	E5
Camelot Dr				
100	AURA	44202	3021	D7
100	OBLN	44074	3138	D5
2000	PRMA	44134	2883	D7
6800	MNTR	44060	2143	E6
8400	CsTp	44026	2632	B2
Camelot Ln				
2000	RKRV	44116	2621	C7
Camelot Wy				
38600	AVON	44011	2747	B6
Cameron Av				
27000	EUCL	44132	2373	E1
27000	EUCL	44132	2374	A1
Cameron Ct				
5300	SFLD	44054	2746	E4
Camino Dr				
700	ETLK	44095	2250	B2
Campagna St				
100	ELYR	44035	2746	D7
Campbell Dr				
-	CLEV	44105	2755	B1
6100	MadT	44057	1941	E1
Campbell Rd				
4900	WLBY	44094	2249	E7
4900	WLBY	44094	2250	A7
5900	MONT	44060	2143	C3
6000	MNTR	44060	2143	C3
Campers Dr				
100	ETLK	44095	2249	E2
100	LKLN	44095	2249	E2
Camp Industrial Rd				
6200	SLN	44139	2888	D5
Campton Ct				
5400	BDHT	44146	2887	C1
Campton Rdg				
9500	CdnT	44024	2379	C3
Campus Ct				
10	AVLK	44012	2617	E3
300	ETLK	44095	2142	C7
Campus Dr				
1900	SELD	44121	2628	C3
2100	BHWD	44121	2628	C3
2100	BHWD	44122	2628	C3
21000	FWPK	44126	2751	C3
N Campus Dr				
-	KTLD	44094	2376	D1
S Campus Dr				
-	KTLD	44094	2376	E1
Campus Rd				
2100	BHWD	44121	2628	C3
2100	BHWD	44122	2628	C3
2100	SELD	44121	2628	C3
2100	UNHT	44118	2628	C3
2100	UNHT	44121	2628	C3
Canada Rd				
4600	MNTU	44255	3159	C6
4600	ShvT	44255	3159	C6
5000	ManT	44255	3159	E7
Canal Rd				
600	CLEV	44113	2624	E4
900	SgHT	44067	3017	C4
5100	CHHT	44125	2755	E7
5100	GDHT	44125	2755	E7
5100	GDHT	44125	2756	A7
5100	VLVW	44125	2755	E7
5100	VLVW	44125	2756	A7
5200	GDHT	44125	2885	A1
5200	VLVW	44125	2885	B4
7300	VLVW	44125	3016	D1
7600	SgHT	44067	3016	E2
7600	SgHT	44125	3016	E2
W Canal Rd				
5600	VLVW	44125	2885	A2
Canary Dr				
200	ELYR	44035	2874	E2
Canary Ln				
-	MNTR	44060	2144	D2
Candlenut Ct				
3900	MDHL	44022	2759	D3
3900	ORNG	44022	2759	D3
Candlestick Ln				
10000	CcdT	44077	2145	C7
Candlewick Ct				
25700	WTLK	44145	2620	B6
Candlewick Ln				
1200	BWHT	44147	3149	E5
Candlewood Ct				
5500	PRMA	44134	2883	E1
6300	MNTR	44060	2144	C4
Candlewood Dr				
1900	AVON	44011	2617	D7
1900	AVON	44011	2747	D1
Candy Ln				
300	AMHT	44001	2872	C1
6700	BhmT	44089	2741	B7
Canfield Ct				
1300	CLEV	44114	2625	A2
Canfield Dr				
200	PNVL	44077	2040	A7
Canfield Rd				
100	CRDN	44024	2379	E5
100	CRDN	44024	2380	A5
Cannon Av				
8600	CLEV	44105	2756	B3
17400	LKWD	44107	2622	A4
Cannon Ovl				
13900	NRYN	44133	3014	C7
Cannon Rd				
2800	TNBG	44087	3155	B1
23000	BDHT	44146	2887	C2
26800	BDHT	44146	2888	A2
26800	SLN	44139	2888	C2
27300	SLN	44146	2888	A2
33000	SLN	44139	2889	A2
34900	BTVL	44022	2889	B2
34900	BTVL	44139	2889	B2
Cannon Rd SR-175				
27200	BDHT	44146	2888	A2
27200	SLN	44139	2888	A2
27300	SLN	44146	2888	A2
Cannon Ridge Dr				
7700	MNTR	44060	2253	A2
Canova Av				
1700	CLEV	44109	2754	D4
Canter Cir				
-	AVLK	44012	2619	A4
700	BERA	44017	3010	E2
Canter Ct				
-	AVLK	44012	2619	A5
-	GnvT	44041	1944	C1
Canter Ln				
10	NHFD	44067	3018	A3
Canterbury E				
200	AURA	44202	3021	D7
Canterbury Cir				
10	AMHT	44001	2872	C3
10	OBLN	44074	3138	D5
10	PtfT	44074	3138	D5
Canterbury Ct				
300	ELYR	44035	2875	D2
2900	WBHL	44092	2374	C7
4000	LORN	44053	2743	E2
8300	BbgT	44023	2891	A6
Canterbury Dr				
-	MDBH	44130	2881	D5
300	AURA	44202	3021	D7
6700	MadT	44057	1942	B2
16100	SGVL	44136	3147	B2
33700	SLN	44139	3020	A3
Canterbury Dr W				
100	AURA	44202	3021	D7
Canterbury Ln				
400	SgHT	44067	3017	D4
4700	BWHT	44147	3015	D6
5500	HDHT	44143	2499	B3
9200	MNTR	44060	2252	E1
9300	MNTR	44060	2253	B1
22300	SRHT	44122	2628	C7
Canterbury Rd				
-	AVLK	44012	2618	A2
100	ELYR	44035	2875	D2
200	BYVL	44140	2620	B5
600	WTLK	44140	2620	B6
600	WTLK	44145	2620	B7
1000	WTLK	44145	2750	B4
2200	UNHT	44118	2627	E3
2400	CVHT	44118	2627	E5
3800	NOSD	44070	2750	B4
3800	NOSD	44145	2750	B4
5600	NOSD	44070	2879	B2
17800	CLEV	44119	2372	D4
18000	EUCL	44119	2372	E4
32900	AVLK	44012	2617	D3
N Canterbury Rd				
6100	PRMA	44129	2882	E3
6100	PRMA	44129	2883	A3
S Canterbury Rd				
6400	PRMA	44129	2882	E4
Canterwood Tr				
7500	CcdT	44060	2253	C2
Canton Av				
2900	LORN	44055	2745	B3
7100	CLEV	44105	2755	E2
7500	CLEV	44105	2756	A2
Canton St				
16600	BbgT	44023	2890	A1
Cantor Av				
-	CLEV	44102	2624	B7
Cantwell Dr				
5800	MDHT	44124	2629	C2
Canyon Cir				
7400	MDBH	44130	3012	D1
Canyon Ct				
5400	WLBY	44094	2375	A1
Canyon Rd				
100	MDHL	44022	2760	D6
18800	FWPK	44126	2751	E1
18800	FWPK	44126	2752	A1
S Canyon Tr				
2600	HkyT	44233	3147	E7
2700	BNWK	44212	3147	E7
2700	BNWK	44233	3147	E7
Canyon Creek Dr				
2400	HkyT	44233	3147	E6
2400	HkyT	44233	3148	A7
Canyon Falls Blvd				
8900	TNBG	44087	3154	D1
Canyon Lake Dr				
8000	BbgT	44023	2890	D3
Canyon Point Cir				
7200	BKVL	44141	3151	C4
Canyon Ridge Dr				
5400	PryT	44077	2147	B1
Canyon View Dr				
5600	PryT	44077	2147	B2
Canyon View Rd				
-	SgHT	44067	3017	A7
1200	SgHT	44067	3152	B1
Cape St				
-	PNVL	44077	2039	E5
-	PNVL	44077	2040	A5
Capel Rd				
27000	ClbT	44028	3143	E2
27000	ClbT	44028	3144	A2
27000	EatT	44028	3143	E2
34000	EatT	44044	3143	B2
34500	GFTN	44044	3143	B2
Capel Rd				
37500	CrlT	44044	3141	E1
37500	EatT	44044	3141	E1
37500	EatT	44044	3142	A1
E Capel Rd				
900	EatT	44044	3142	E2
900	GFTN	44044	3142	E2
900	GFTN	44044	3143	A2
Capers Av				
3500	CLEV	44115	2625	C4
Capilano Dr				
7100	SLN	44139	3020	E3
Capital Blvd				
7700	MCDN	44056	3153	C3
Capital Pkwy				
10900	CcdT	44077	2254	A3
Capital Hill Cir				
200	ORNG	44022	2759	C6
Capitol Av				
8600	CLEV	44104	2626	B4
Capitol Ct				
100	ELYR	44035	2873	E6
Capri Ct				
500	AVLK	44012	2618	A3
Capri Dr				
10	SgHT	44067	3017	E3
10	SgHT	44146	3017	E3
10	WNHL	44146	3017	E3
Captain's Ct				
7500	MNTR	44060	2143	D3
Captains Wk				
13200	MsnT	44024	2635	A3
Captains Cove				
17800	LKWD	44107	2621	E4
Captains Galley				
32500	AVLK	44012	2618	B3
Capulet Ct				
2400	AVON	44011	2748	B1
Carabell Av				
2000	LKWD	44107	2622	C6
2200	CLEV	44107	2622	C6
2200	CLEV	44111	2622	C6
Carbon Rd				
2100	CLEV	44111	2623	B6
2100	LKWD	44107	2623	B6
Cardinal Av				
14900	CLEV	44110	2497	B2
Cardinal Cir				
20100	SGVL	44149	3011	C3
Cardinal Ct				
-	LORN	44053	2743	D3
300	AURA	44202	3156	C1
600	ETLK	44095	2250	D1
Cardinal Dr				
-	KDHL	44060	2252	C7
100	ELYR	44035	2874	E2
5500	MNTR	44060	2144	E1
8400	KTLD	44094	2252	B7
8500	KTLD	44060	2252	C7
Cardinal Ln				
1400	GSML	44040	2500	C7
7100	RslT	44022	2761	B3
10600	BKVL	44141	3016	C3
Cardington Dr				
25000	BHWD	44122	2628	D4
Cardwell Av				
9400	CLEV	44105	2756	B5
9400	CLEV	44125	2756	B5
9400	GDHT	44125	2756	C5
Care Dr				
8300	GDHT	44125	2756	A6
Carek Ct				
5300	EyrT	44035	2745	A6
5300	EyrT	44055	2745	A6
5300	ShfT	44055	2745	A6
Carey Dr				
6000	VLVW	44125	2885	C3
Carey Ln				
24700	NOSD	44070	2879	C1
24700	NOSD	44138	2879	C1
Cargo Rd				
5800	CLEV	44135	2880	D2
6100	BKPK	44142	2880	D2
Carillon Dr				
2900	WTLK	44145	2750	C3
Cariton Ct				
2500	HGVL	44022	2630	A4
2500	PRPK	44022	2630	A4
2500	PRPK	44124	2630	A4
Carl Av				
6200	CLEV	44103	2495	E7
Carl Ct				
4200	WLBY	44094	2251	B5
Carl Dr				
40500	CrlT	44035	3006	A5
Carl Ln				
-	ODFL	44138	2879	A6
10	OmsT	44138	2879	A6
Carla Ln				
24000	NOSD	44070	2750	D3
24000	WTLK	44070	2750	D3
24000	WTLK	44145	2750	D3
Carleen Av				
37100	AVON	44011	2747	D1
Carlene Dr				
5300	SFLD	44054	2746	E4
Carlenroy Dr				
10	ETLK	44095	2142	B6
Carlin Rd				
400	SgHT	44067	3152	C1
Carlisle Av				
40500	CrlT	44035	3006	A4
40700	CrlT	44035	3005	E4
Carlone Pl				
900	SELD	44121	2498	C5
Carlos Av				
4600	CLEV	44102	2754	A1
Carlsfield Wy				
400	BSHT	44236	3153	E6
Carlton Ct				
-	AVON	44011	2748	B2
8600	MNTR	44060	2144	C7
20500	SGVL	44149	3146	B4
Carlton Dr				
300	ETLK	44095	2250	B2
5500	BDHT	44146	2887	C2
30800	BYVL	44140	2619	B3
Carlton Pk				
25100	NOSD	44070	2750	C6
Carlton Rd				
1600	PRMA	44134	2883	E2
2800	SRHT	44122	2627	E7
11800	CLEV	44106	2626	E2
11800	CVHT	44106	2626	D3
Carlton St				
13500	BtnT	44021	2766	A1
13500	BURT	44021	2766	A1
Carlyle Av				
3700	CLEV	44109	2754	B1
Carlyle Dr				
900	SVHL	44131	2884	A3
20200	SGVL	44149	3011	C6
Carlyle Rd				
10	BDFD	44146	2886	E2
10	BDFD	44146	2887	A2
Carlyon Pl				
1000	CLEV	44108	2496	E6
1000	CLEV	44112	2496	E6
1000	ECLE	44108	2496	E6
1000	ECLE	44112	2496	E6
Carlyon Rd				
1000	CLEV	44108	2496	E6
1000	CLEV	44112	2496	E6
1000	ECLE	44108	2496	E6
1000	ECLE	44112	2496	E6
Carmany Dr				
18500	WNHL	44146	2886	E7
18700	WNHL	44146	2887	A7
Carmel Ln				
11200	ClrT	44024	2505	C1
Carmel Ovl				
10600	SGVL	44136	3012	B4
Carmelita Ct				
2900	LORN	44052	2744	C3
Carmen Dr				
2600	RKRV	44116	2621	C7
Carmen Pl				
7200	MNTR	44060	2144	E7
7200	MNTR	44060	2252	E1
Carmichael Dr				
8500	CsTp	44026	2632	B3
Carmody Dr				
100	PNVL	44077	2040	A7
100	PNVL	44077	2146	C1
Carnation Ct				
12400	CLEV	44108	2496	E4
Carnation Run				
25600	NOSD	44070	2750	C4
25600	WTLK	44070	2750	C4
25600	WTLK	44145	2750	C4
Carnegie Av				
10	CLEV	44113	2624	E4
10	CLEV	44115	2624	E4
500	CLEV	44115	2625	A3
3600	CLEV	44103	2625	E3
7100	CLEV	44103	2626	A3
8100	CLEV	44106	2626	B3
Carnegie Av SR-10				
10	CLEV	44113	2624	E4
10	CLEV	44115	2624	E4
Carnegie St				
6300	MNTR	44060	2145	A4
Carnes Rd				
8700	BbgT	44023	2891	B7
Carol Av				
21000	EUCL	44119	2373	B4
Carol Blvd				
3700	RKRV	44116	2751	E1
Carol Dr				
6100	BKPK	44142	2881	D3
6600	INDE	44131	2884	D7
6600	INDE	44131	3015	E1
14900	MPHT	44137	2886	A3
15200	SGVL	44136	3146	E1
Carol Ln				
100	ELYR	44035	3006	E2
39500	CrlT	44035	3006	C2
Carole Dr				
7300	MNTR	44060	2252	A1
N Carolina Dr				
200	ELYR	44035	3006	B3
S Carolina Dr				
100	ELYR	44035	3006	B3
Carolina Rd				
11400	CLEV	44106	2496	D7
11400	CLEV	44108	2496	D6
Caroline Av				
2300	LORN	44052	2745	A3
2300	LORN	44055	2745	A2
Caroline Cir				
27600	WTLK	44145	2619	E5
Caroline Dr				
4900	BDHT	44128	2758	C6
4900	WVHT	44128	2758	C6
37500	AVON	44011	2617	C7
Caroline St				
1100	ELYR	44035	2875	C5
Carol-Jean Blvd				
5500	GDHT	44125	2885	C1
Carolyn Av				
19900	FWPK	44116	2751	D2
19900	FWPK	44126	2751	D2
19900	RKRV	44116	2751	D2
19900	RKRV	44126	2751	D2
Carolyn Dr				
500	BNWK	44212	3147	A7
5600	NRDV	44039	2877	D1
6100	MNTR	44060	2143	E4
6100	MONT	44060	2143	E4
Caronia Cir				
36000	AVON	44011	2747	E5
36000	AVON	44011	2748	A4
Caronia Dr				
1800	LNHT	44124	2629	C2
Carousel Ct				
2300	WTLK	44145	2749	E2
Carousel Ln				
10	OmsT	44138	2879	A4
Carpenter Av				
6100	CLEV	44127	2625	D6
Carpenter Dr				
8300	MNTR	44060	2144	A7
Carpenter Rd				
1200	GSML	44040	2500	D7
12800	GDHT	44125	2885	E3
13500	GDHT	44125	2886	A3
13500	GDHT	44137	2886	A3
13500	MPHT	44137	2886	A3
N Carpenter Rd				
10	BNWK	44136	3147	B6
10	BNWK	44212	3147	B6
10	SGVL	44136	3147	B6
Carr Av				
9100	CLEV	44108	2496	B4
9700	BTNH	44108	2496	B4
Carr Pl				
1700	LORN	44053	2744	C4
Carrbridge Dr				
23700	EUCL	44143	2498	C1
Carriage Cir				
-	NRDV	44035	2876	C6
7900	MNTR	44060	2143	E6
Carriage Dr				
10	CNFL	44022	2761	B5
E Carriage Dr				
10	CNFL	44022	2761	B6
W Carriage Dr				
10	CNFL	44022	2761	B6
Carriage Ln				
23400	NOSD	44070	2750	E3
32500	AVLK	44012	2618	A1
36400	WLBY	44094	2375	C1
Carriage Pl				
1700	GSML	44040	2630	C2
Carriage Sq				
10	AURA	44202	3156	E3
Carriage Tr				
700	SgHT	44067	3152	C2
Carriage Hill Dr				
6800	BKVL	44141	3016	A4
11000	AbnT	44023	2893	A5
Carriage Hills Dr				
8000	CcdT	44060	2253	C4
8000	CcdT	44077	2253	C4
Carriage Park Dr				
33600	SLN	44139	2889	A3
Carriage Park Ovl				
700	WTLK	44145	2620	A6
Carriage Stone Dr				
10	BbgT	44022	2761	A7
10	CNFL	44022	2760	E7
10	CNFL	44022	2761	A7
10	CyhC	44022	2761	A7
Carrie Ct				
9000	CLEV	44106	2626	B2
Carrie Dr				
3900	LORN	44055	2745	E4
Carrie Ln				
10	OmsT	44138	2879	B4
Carrington Av				
11800	CLEV	44135	2753	A6
13000	CLEV	44135	2752	E6
Carrington Ct				
-	EatT	44035	3007	A2
600	WLWK	44095	2249	B6
Carrington Dr				
-	CrlT	44044	3141	B3
7400	CcdT	44060	2253	A1
7400	MNTR	44060	2253	A1
Carrington Ln				
400	BWHT	44147	3149	E5
Carrington Pl				
8100	BbgT	44023	2890	E7
Carrmunn Av				
3400	CLEV	44111	2752	C1
Carroll Av				
10	PNVL	44077	2146	A2
2500	CLEV	44113	2624	C5
Carroll Blvd				
4200	UNHT	44118	2628	B4
E Carroll Blvd				
14300	UNHT	44118	2628	C4
14400	BHWD	44122	2628	C4
Carroll Dr				
12200	MsnT	44024	2503	E6
Carry Av				
5500	CLEV	44103	2495	D6
5500	CLEV	44114	2495	D6
Carrydale Av				
14000	CLEV	44111	2752	D2
Carson Av				
300	GDRV	44077	2039	C6
400	PnvT	44077	2039	C6
6900	CLEV	44104	2625	E6
6900	CLEV	44127	2625	E6
7300	CLEV	44104	2626	A6
Carson Dr				
100	CRDN	44024	2380	A7
Carsten Ln				
4400	NOSD	44070	2750	A6
Carter Blvd				
6300	MNTR	44060	2143	C5
Carter Rd				
1800	CLEV	44113	2624	D4
7500	SgHT	44067	3017	B7
7500	SgHT	44067	3152	D1
12100	CcdT	44077	2147	B4
12100	LryT	44077	2147	B4
Carter St				
30000	SLN	44139	2888	C6
Carteret Ct				
700	BERA	44017	3011	B2
Carton Av				
9300	CLEV	44104	2626	B7
Cartwright Pkwy				
12800	NRYN	44133	3013	C6
13600	SGVL	44136	3012	D3
Carver Rd				
1000	CVHT	44112	2497	C6
1100	CVHT	44118	2497	C7
Cary Rd				
6300	NRDV	44039	2877	E2
Cary Jay Blvd				
300	RDHT	44143	2498	E3
Caryl Dr				
1200	BDFD	44146	2887	C6
Caryn Dr				
14700	BKPK	44130	2881	C4
14700	BKPK	44142	2881	C4
14700	MDBH	44130	2881	C4
Casa Bella Dr				
4200	PryT	44081	1940	C7
Cascade Cross				
-	BKLN	44144	2753	C6
Cascade Ct				
300	AVLK	44012	2617	D3
5400	WLBY	44094	2375	A1
5600	SVHL	44131	2884	A1
19100	BbgT	44202	3021	D3
27000	ODFL	44138	3009	D1
Cascade Dr				
10	SRSL	44022	2762	D7
5500	SVHL	44131	2884	A2
Cascade Rd				
6500	CcdT	44077	2147	B7
6500	CcdT	44077	2255	C1
Cascade St				
100	ELYR	44035	2875	A6
Cascades Dr				
800	AURA	44023	3022	B4
800	AURA	44202	3022	A4
800	BbgT	44023	3022	A4
Case Av				
500	ELYR	44035	3006	D1
Case Av				
5000	LNHT	44124	2498	E5
5000	LNHT	44124	2499	A5
7300	MNTR	44060	2252	A1
Case Ct				
4000	CLEV	44104	2625	C4
4000	CLEV	44115	2625	C4
Case Dr				
-	MsnT	44024	2505	A4
Case Pkwy N				
1900	TNBG	44087	3154	E4
Case Pkwy S				
1900	TNBG	44087	3154	E4
Case Rd				
-	AVON	44011	2747	A3
4800	NRDV	44011	2747	A6
4800	NRDV	44039	2747	A7
5500	NRDV	44039	2876	A1
Case St				
1800	TNBG	44087	3154	C2
1800	TwbT	44087	3154	C2
Casement Av				
10	PNVL	44077	2040	C6
100	PnvT	44077	2040	C7
Casement Av US-20				
400	PnvT	44077	2040	C6
Caskey Dr				
400	OBLN	44074	3139	A3
Casper Rd				
13300	CLEV	44110	2496	E3
13300	CLEV	44110	2497	A3
Cass Av				
5500	CLEV	44102	2624	A4
Casselberry Pl				
300	MCDN	44056	3018	B6
Cassie Ln				
12700	CsTp	44026	2502	E7
12700	CsTp	44026	2632	E1
Cassius Av				
9300	CLEV	44105	2756	B3
Castalia Av				
13800	CLEV	44110	2497	A3
Castallia Dr				
-	NRYN	44133	3014	C3
Castaway Cove				
-	RMDV	44202	3020	D5
Castle Av				
1100	CLEV	44113	2624	E7
Castle Cir				
6400	BKVL	44141	3150	D2
Castle Ct				
10	BNWK	44212	3146	D6
Castle Dr				
6100	NRYN	44133	3013	E4
6100	NRYN	44133	3014	A4
20900	SGVL	44149	3146	B1
Castlebar Ct				
25000	ClbT	44028	3010	A6
25100	ClbT	44028	3009	E6
Castlehill Dr				
5900	HDHT	44143	2499	D2
Castlemaine Cir				
20300	SGVL	44149	3146	C5
Castleman Ct				
1100	PnvT	44077	2146	E2
Castle Pine Dr				
7200	SLN	44139	3020	D1
Castle Pines Cir				
10600	CcdT	44077	2253	E3
Castleton Ln				
11700	EatT	44044	3007	A6
Castleton Rd				
1000	CVHT	44121	2497	D6
Castletown Dr				
19400	SGVL	44136	3147	D5
Castlewood Av				
11500	CLEV	44108	2496	D6
12300	CLEV	44112	2496	D6
12300	ECLE	44112	2496	D6
Castlewood Ct				
4000	PRRY	44081	2042	B1
Castlewood Dr				
14600	NbyT	44065	2764	C1
Caswell Ct				
1400	EUCL	44132	2373	D5
Catalano Dr				
6000	MDHT	44124	2629	D2
Catalpa Cir				
9400	MNTR	44060	2253	A3
Catalpa Dr				
12100	CdnT	44024	2380	A3
Catalpa Rd				
1600	CLEV	44112	2497	D2
1600	CLEV	44121	2497	D2
Catawba Ct				
100	ELYR	44035	3005	B1
Catawba St				
29500	WKLF	44092	2374	C2
Catharina Av				
4400	CLEV	44102	2754	B1
4400	CLEV	44109	2754	B1
Catherine Ct				
14100	NRYN	44133	3149	A1
Catherine St				
5000	MPHT	44137	2757	C7
Catlin Dr				
400	RDHT	44143	2498	D3
Cato St				
5000	MPHT	44137	2757	D7
5300	MPHT	44137	2886	D1
Caton Ct				
1300	CLEV	44115	2625	A3
Caton Pl				
26600	NOSD	44070	2750	A6
Catsden Rd				
16800	BbgT	44023	2890	C2
Cat Tail Ct				
-	MNTR	44060	2144	C1
Cavendish Ct				
19400	NRYN	44133	3148	A5
Caves Rd				
11100	CsTp	44026	2501	D2
11100	CsTp	44026	2501	D1
11100	KTLD	44094	2501	D1
12700	CsTp	44026	2631	D4
13400	CsTp	44072	2631	D3
13400	RslT	44072	2631	D7
14600	RslT	44072	2761	D1
14700	RslT	44022	2761	D2
Caxton Cir				
300	BERA	44017	2880	A6
Cayuga Ct				
14000	CLEV	44111	2752	D1
Cayuga Dr				
14000	ClbT	44028	3010	D7

Cleveland Street Index

STREET
Block City ZIP Map# Grid

Cayuga Dr
14000 ClbT 44028 3145 D1
Cecelia Av
3500 CLEV 44109 2754 C5
Cecelia Ct
34200 ETLK 44095 2250 A4
Cecil Pl
- CVHT 44106 2626 E3
Cecilia Dr
7500 PRMA 44134 3014 D2
Cedar Av
2200 CLEV 44115 2625 B3
3900 CLEV 44103 2625 C3
7400 CLEV 44103 2626 A3
10900 CLEV 44106 2626 D3
Cedar Ct
1700 EUCL 44117 2498 A2
6100 SLN 44139 2889 D4
Cedar Dr
1200 LORN 44052 2615 D6
Cedar Gln
100 CRDN 44024 2505 B2
Cedar Ln
- SDLK 44054 2616 E2
Cedar Rd
438-1 AURA 44202 3156 D2
7000 CsTp 44026 2631 B2
7000 GSML 44040 2631 A2
8100 CsTp 44026 2632 C2
9700 MsnT 44026 2633 A3
9700 MsnT 44072 2633 A3
9700 NbyT 44026 2633 A3
10100 NbyT 44026 2633 E4
10100 NbyT 44065 2633 E4
10300 MsnT 44026 2634 A3
10300 MsnT 44065 2634 A3
10300 NbyT 44026 2634 A3
10300 NbyT 44065 2634 A3
12300 CLEV 44106 2626 E3
12300 CVHT 44106 2626 E3
12500 CVHT 44106 2627 A3
12700 CVHT 44118 2627 A3
13400 UNHT 44118 2627 E3
13700 SELD 44118 2627 E3
13800 SELD 44118 2628 A3
13800 SELD 44121 2628 A3
13800 UNHT 44118 2628 A3
13800 UNHT 44121 2628 A3
14400 BHWD 44121 2628 C3
14400 BHWD 44122 2628 C3
23300 LNHT 44122 2628 D3
23300 SELD 44122 2628 C3
24100 BHWD 44124 2628 D3
24100 LNHT 44124 2628 D3
26600 BHWD 44122 2629 A3
26600 BHWD 44124 2629 A3
26600 LNHT 44124 2629 A3
27900 PRPK 44122 2629 B3
27900 PRPK 44124 2629 E3
29000 MDHT 44124 2629 E3
32400 MDHT 44124 2630 A3
32400 PRPK 44124 2630 A3
33300 GSML 44040 2630 A3
33300 HGVL 44022 2630 D3
33300 HGVL 44040 2630 A3
Cedar St
10 ELYR 44035 2875 B6
10 GNVA 44041 1944 C3
7000 BbgT 44022 2761 A7
7000 CNFL 44022 2761 A7
8900 BKVL 44141 3016 A7
N Cedar St
10 OBLN 44074 3138 D2
100 GNVA 44041 1944 C3
S Cedar St
10 GNVA 44041 1944 C4
10 OBLN 44074 3138 D3
Cedar Acres Dr
13200 CsTp 44026 2632 A3
Cedar Bark Dr
600 AURA 44202 3022 C5
Cedar Branch Cir
33000 NRDV 44039 2877 D1
Cedar Branch Tr
21500 SGVL 44149 3011 A4
Cedar Brook Dr
100 ELYR 44035 2874 A7
Cedarbrook Dr
300 PNVL 44077 2146 A3
600 PNVL 44077 2145 E3
Cedarbrook Rd
3200 CVHT 44118 2627 C3
3300 UNHT 44118 2627 C3
Cedar Creek Ct
1300 PnvT 44077 2041 A7
Cedarcrest Tr
7200 CsTp 44026 2631 B1
Cedar Glen Dr
10 PnvT 44077 2041 A7
Cedar Glen Pkwy
11300 CLEV 44106 2626 D3
11300 CVHT 44106 2626 D3
Cedar Grove Cir
800 SgHT 44067 3152 C1
Cedarhurst Dr
1800 WKLF 44092 2374 E2
Cedarmount
2400 CVHT 44106 2626 D4
Cedar Point Rd
- BKPK 44135 2880 A1
- CLEV 44135 2880 A1
- CLEV 44142 2880 A1
- NOSD 44142 2879 D1
22500 BKPK 44142 2880 A1
23000 BKPK 44142 2879 D1
24000 NOSD 44070 2879 D1
24000 NOSD 44138 2879 D1
Cedarview Dr
2100 BHWD 44121 2628 C3
2100 BHWD 44122 2628 C3
2100 SELD 44121 2628 C3
Cedarville Av
5200 SFLD 44054 2746 D5
Cedarwood Av
14100 LKWD 44107 2622 D6
Cedarwood Ct
4100 INDE 44131 2884 C5
14700 MDFD 44062 2767 C1
Cedarwood Dr
1300 WTLK 44145 2619 B7
9500 NRYN 44133 3013 B3
Cedarwood Ln
23400 NOSD 44070 2750 E5
Cedarwood Rd
400 AVLK 44012 2617 E3

Cedarwood Rd
2400 MDHT 44124 2630 A4
2400 PRPK 44124 2629 E3
2400 PRPK 44124 2630 A4
5900 MONT 44060 2143 B3
6000 MNTR 44060 2143 B3
S Cedarwood Rd
6300 MNTR 44060 2143 B4
Cedarwood Trc
- MDBH 44130 2881 A4
Ceile Cir
14000 WNHL 44146 2886 A5
Celeste Dr
- PRMA 44130 3013 B2
Celestia Rd
400 RDHT 44143 2498 D3
Celianna Dr
8200 SGVL 44149 3011 A3
Celizic Ln
- LryT 44077 2147 D6
Cemetery Rd
7300 VmnT 44089 2869 C5
Cemetery St
- MNTU 44255 3159 B6
Centennial Av
37200 AVON 44011 2747 D2
Centennial Dr
- AVLK 44012 2617 D1
Centennial St
100 GNVA 44041 1944 D4
600 GnvT 44041 1944 D5
Center Av
12000 GDHT 44125 2756 D6
Center Ct
10 CLEV 44115 2624 E3
Center Dr
2400 PRMA 44134 2883 C5
8600 NRYN 44133 3148 D1
Center Ln
- AhtT 44001 2872 B2
Center Rd
- BKLN 44144 2753 D2
- CLEV 44144 2753 D2
- VmnT 44089 2740 A7
800 AVLK 44012 2618 A5
800 AVON 44011 2618 A7
800 AVON 44012 2618 A5
900 ETLK 44095 2250 B3
900 PnvT 44077 2041 B3
2000 AVON 44011 2748 A5
3100 NPRY 44081 1940 B5
3100 PryT 44081 1940 B5
3500 PryT 44081 2042 B2
3600 PRRY 44081 2042 B1
4200 NRDV 44011 2748 A5
4200 NRDV 44039 2748 A5
Center Rd SR-83
800 AVLK 44012 2618 A5
800 AVON 44011 2618 A6
800 AVON 44012 2618 A5
2000 AVON 44011 2748 A5
4200 NRDV 44011 2748 A5
4200 NRDV 44039 2748 A5
Center St
- ELYR 44035 2875 B6
10 CLEV 44110 2372 C6
10 CNFL 44022 2760 E6
10 CNFL 44022 2761 A6
100 PnvT 44077 2041 B4
100 CRDN 44024 2379 C5
100 CRDN 44024 2380 A6
900 GFTN 44044 3142 A5
1000 CLEV 44113 2624 D4
1000 VMLN 44089 2740 C6
4200 WLBY 44094 2250 E6
5800 BosT 44141 3152 C7
5900 MNTR 44060 2144 A3
7200 MNTR 44060 2252 A5
8200 KDHL 44060 2252 B4
Center St SR-44
100 CRDN 44024 2379 C5
100 CRDN 44024 2380 A6
Center St SR-615
6300 MNTR 44060 2144 B6
7200 MNTR 44060 2252 A5
8200 KDHL 44060 2252 B4
Center St US-6
100 CRDN 44024 2380 A6
E Center St
- BERA 44017 2880 C7
- BERA 44130 2880 D7
- MDBH 44130 2880 D7
13800 BURT 44021 2766 B1
14000 BtnT 44021 2766 B1
E Center St SR-87
13800 BURT 44021 2766 B1
14000 BtnT 44021 2766 B1
W Center St
10 BERA 44017 2880 C7
13500 BtnT 44021 2766 A1
13500 BURT 44021 2766 A1
W Center St SR-87
13500 BtnT 44021 2766 A1
13500 BURT 44021 2766 A1
Center Wy N
14600 LKWD 44107 2622 D4
Center Ridge Rd
19400 RKRV 44116 2621 D7
20600 FWPK 44116 2751 A1
20600 FWPK 44126 2751 A1
20600 RKRV 44116 2751 A1
22800 WTLK 44116 2751 A1
22800 WTLK 44145 2751 A1
23200 WTLK 44145 2750 A2
27200 WTLK 44145 2749 B6
31400 NRDV 44039 2749 A7
31400 NRDV 44145 2749 A7
31600 NRDV 44039 2748 E7
31600 NRDV 44039 2877 A3
36100 NRDV 44039 2876 B4
Center Ridge Rd SR-113
19400 RKRV 44116 2621 D7
20600 FWPK 44116 2751 A1
20600 FWPK 44126 2751 A1
20600 RKRV 44116 2751 A1
22800 WTLK 44116 2751 A1
22800 WTLK 44145 2751 A1
23200 WTLK 44145 2750 A2
27200 WTLK 44145 2749 B6
31400 NRDV 44039 2749 A7
31400 NRDV 44145 2749 A7
31600 NRDV 44039 2748 E7
31600 NRDV 44039 2877 A3
36100 NRDV 44039 2876 B4

Center Ridge Rd US-20
19400 RKRV 44116 2621 D7
20600 FWPK 44116 2751 A1
20600 FWPK 44126 2751 A1
20600 RKRV 44116 2751 A1
22800 WTLK 44116 2751 A1
22800 WTLK 44145 2751 A1
23200 WTLK 44145 2750 A2
27200 WTLK 44145 2749 B6
31400 NRDV 44039 2749 A7
31400 NRDV 44145 2749 A7
31600 NRDV 44039 2748 E7
31600 NRDV 44039 2877 A3
36100 NRDV 44039 2876 B4
Centerville Tr
700 AURA 44023 3022 B3
700 AURA 44202 3022 B3
700 BbgT 44023 3022 B3
Central Av
1800 CLEV 44115 2625 A3
3900 CLEV 44103 2625 E3
3900 CLEV 44104 2625 E3
7400 CLEV 44103 2626 A3
7400 CLEV 44104 2626 A3
8300 CLEV 44106 2626 A3
Central Dr
- AhtT 44001 2872 B2
100 AMHT 44001 2872 E1
900 LORN 44052 2744 D2
N Central Dr
800 LORN 44052 2744 D2
S Central Dr
800 LORN 44052 2744 D2
Central Pkwy
25900 BHWD 44122 2758 E1
Central Furnace Dr
2000 CLEV 44115 2625 A5
Central Park Blvd
9400 ODFL 44138 3010 A1
Central Via
300 CLEV 44113 2624 E4
300 CLEV 44115 2624 E4
Centurion Dr
100 CrlT 44035 3006 A4
Century Cir
4600 BKLN 44144 2753 C5
Century Dr
1100 CLEV 44109 2754 E5
Century Ln
2900 AVON 44011 2747 C3
6800 RslT 44072 2632 B5
Century Oak Dr
14400 SGVL 44136 3012 C3
Century Oaks Dr
1700 WTLK 44145 2750 D1
E Century Oaks Dr
1700 WTLK 44145 2750 D1
Centuryway Rd
20600 MPHT 44137 2887 A1
Ceo Dr
- GDHT 44125 2756 A6
Ceo Rd
4700 GDHT 44125 2756 A6
Cesko Av
3500 CLEV 44109 2624 C7
Cessna Av
4900 BHIT 44212 3146 A7
Cessna Dr
900 MCDN 44056 3018 E5
Chablis Ct
6800 MNTR 44060 2143 E6
Chadbourne Dr
6600 NOSD 44070 2878 C3
6800 VLVW 44125 2885 D6
Chadbourne Rd
2700 CLEV 44120 2627 A5
2800 SRHT 44120 2627 B7
Chaddwyck Ln
37000 NRDV 44035 3007 C1
Chadwick Ct
- BWHT 44147 3150 A5
100 AbnT 44023 2892 A4
2600 WTLK 44145 2749 E2
Chadwick Dr
- AURA 44202 3156 E3
- AURA 44202 3157 A3
100 ELYR 44035 2874 A6
Chadwick Rd
5100 LryT 44057 2042 E7
Chaffee Ct
6500 BKVL 44141 3016 A7
Chaffee Rd
7400 SgHT 44067 3017 A5
Chagrin Blvd
- PRPK 44124 2759 E2
200 CNFL 44022 2760 E6
200 MDHL 44022 2760 D4
300 CFIT 44022 2760 E5
15600 CLEV 44120 2757 B1
15600 SRHT 44120 2757 B1
17600 SRHT 44122 2757 D1
19400 SRHT 44122 2758 B1
20800 BHWD 44122 2758 D1
20800 HIHL 44122 2758 A1
26900 BHWD 44122 2759 A1
26900 ORNG 44122 2759 A1
26900 WDMR 44122 2759 A1
28900 ORNG 44124 2759 B1
28900 PRPK 44124 2759 B1
29800 PRPK 44122 2759 C1
33000 MDHL 44022 2759 E2
Chagrin Blvd SR-8
15600 CLEV 44120 2757 B1
15600 SRHT 44120 2757 B1
17600 SRHT 44122 2757 C1
19400 SRHT 44122 2758 B1
Chagrin Blvd SR-87
25600 BHWD 44122 2758 D1
26900 BHWD 44122 2759 A1
26900 ORNG 44122 2759 A1
26900 WDMR 44122 2759 A1
28900 ORNG 44124 2759 B1
28900 PRPK 44124 2759 B1
29800 PRPK 44122 2759 C1
Chagrin Blvd US-422
15600 CLEV 44120 2757 B1
15600 SRHT 44120 2757 B1
17600 SRHT 44122 2757 C1
19400 SRHT 44122 2758 B1
20800 BHWD 44122 2758 D1
20800 HIHL 44122 2758 A1
26900 BHWD 44122 2759 A1
Chagrin Dr
2500 WBHL 44094 2375 E3
2500 WTHL 44094 2375 E3
5500 MONT 44060 2143 D2

Chagrin Dr
35800 ETLK 44095 2250 C1
Chagrin Rd
7100 BbgT 44022 2761 B7
7100 BbgT 44023 2761 B7
7100 CNFL 44022 2761 B7
7100 CyhC 44022 2761 B7
7300 BbgT 44023 2890 B1
8200 BbgT 44023 2891 A4
Chagrin Rd CO-9
7100 BbgT 44022 2761 A7
7100 BbgT 44023 2761 B7
Chagrin Highlands Dr
6000 SLN 44139 2889 C4
Chagrin Mills Ct
38600 WLBY 44094 2251 A1
Chagrin Mills Rd
8000 RslT 44022 2761 E3
8200 RslT 44022 2762 A3
8200 RslT 44072 2762 A3
Chagrin River Rd
- GSML 44094 2500 C1
- WBHL 44094 2500 C1
400 GSML 44040 2500 D1
1400 GSML 44040 2630 E1
2000 HGVL 44022 2630 E4
2000 HGVL 44040 2630 E3
3100 HGVL 44022 2760 D1
3400 MDHL 44022 2760 C5
4500 BTVL 44022 2760 C7
6100 BTVL 44022 2889 D1
6600 BbgT 44023 2890 A3
6600 BbgT 44139 2890 A3
6600 BTVL 44139 2889 E2
6600 SLN 44139 2889 E2
6600 SLN 44139 2890 A3
Chagrin River Rd SR-174
- GSML 44094 2500 C1
- WBHL 44094 2500 C1
400 GSML 44040 2500 D1
1400 GSML 44040 2630 E1
2000 HGVL 44022 2630 E4
2000 HGVL 44040 2630 E3
Chagrin Woods Dr
14200 NbyT 44065 2634 B7
Chaincraft Rd
4600 GDHT 44125 2756 D6
Chairmans Ct
6900 CcdT 44060 2145 B7
Chairmans Rowe
29800 WTLK 44145 2749 C3
Chalet Dr
7800 CsTp 44026 2501 D1
Chalfant Rd
3200 SRHT 44120 2627 C7
3300 SRHT 44120 2757 C1
Chalmers Ct
100 LORN 44052 2614 A7
Chamberlain Av
7100 CLEV 44104 2625 E3
7100 CLEV 44104 2626 A3
Chamberlain Rd
800 GFTN 44044 3142 A7
800 GftT 44044 3142 A7
10800 ManT 44255 3158 A5
11200 ManT 44202 3158 A5
11600 ManT 44202 3023 B7
11600 ManT 44255 3023 B7
12700 AbnT 44023 3023 B7
12700 AbnT 44202 3023 B7
12700 AbnT 44255 3023 B7
Chamberlin Blvd
2800 HDSN 44236 3155 D6
Chamberlin Ct
7900 HDSN 44236 3155 D6
Chamberlin Ln
1300 TNBG 44087 3019 A5
Chamberlin Rd
1300 MCDN 44056 3154 B3
1300 TwbT 44087 3154 B3
8400 TNBG 44087 3154 B2
9000 TNBG 44087 3019 B7
9400 MCDN 44056 3019 B6
9500 MCDN 44087 3019 B6
Chamberlin Tr
9600 TNBG 44087 3019 B5
Chambers Av
6900 CLEV 44105 2755 E2
Chambers Ct
6500 MNTR 44060 2144 B5
Champ Dr
19900 EUCL 44117 2498 A2
Champaign Av
5700 BKPK 44142 2881 D1
Champaign Dr
7700 MNTR 44060 2143 D6
Champion Av
10100 CLEV 44102 2753 C1
10100 CLEV 44111 2753 C1
Champion Ln
100 SRSL 44022 2762 D6
Champion Tr
2200 TNBG 44087 3020 B6
Champions Ct
300 AVLK 44012 2618 C4
Champlain Tr
11400 AbnT 44255 2893 B6
Chancellor Ct
500 AVLK 44012 2618 C3
Chandler Ct
7500 SgHT 44067 3152 C1
Chandler Dr
409-00 AURA 44202 3156 C2
Chandler Grn
14900 SGVL 44136 3147 C5
Chandler Ln
805-00 AURA 44202 3156 C2
Chandler Pth
455-00 AURA 44202 3156 C2
Chandlers Ln
23000 ODFL 44138 3010 E2
Channing Ln
7200 CcdT 44060 2145 B7
Channing Rd
2300 UNHT 44118 2628 A4
Chanticleer Ct
18000 AbnT 44255 2893 B6
Chanticleer Dr
4200 FWPK 44126 2751 E2
Chapek Pkwy
6600 CHHT 44125 2755 D5
Chapel Cir
300 BERA 44017 2879 E7
300 BERA 44017 2880 A7

Chapel Ct
1200 AMHT 44001 2744 A7
Chapel Ln
10 PnvT 44077 2041 A4
Chapel Rd
5400 MadT 44057 1941 E2
6200 MadT 44057 1942 D2
Chapel St
100 ELYR 44035 2875 B6
Chapel Wy
6800 NRDV 44039 2876 E3
Chapel Hill Dr
6700 BKVL 44141 3151 A2
26300 NOSD 44070 2750 A4
Chapel Rd Ext
5200 MadT 44057 1941 B2
Chapelside Av
13100 CLEV 44105 2756 E2
13100 CLEV 44120 2756 E2
13100 CLEV 44120 2757 A2
Chapelway Dr
7800 MNTR 44060 2252 D3
Chapin St
11400 CsTp 44026 2501 C2
25500 ODFL 44138 3010 B2
Chapin Falls Ln
7600 KTLD 44094 2376 C5
Chapman Av
1400 MadT 44057 1843 C7
1700 ECLE 44112 2497 B5
5100 SFLD 44054 2746 E1
Chapman Cir
8700 SGVL 44136 3012 B3
Chapman Ln
400 ELYR 44035 3006 A1
Chapman Wy
1500 BWHT 44147 3149 D5
Chapparal
24500 WTLK 44145 2750 C2
Chapparal N
2300 WTLK 44145 2750 C2
Chapparal S
2300 WTLK 44145 2750 C2
Character Cir
- PRRY 44081 2042 B1
- PryT 44081 2042 B1
Chard Av
- CLEV 44105 2755 C1
Chardon Av
100 CRDN 44024 2380 A5
Chardon Plz
10 CRDN 44024 2379 E7
Chardon Rd
- CLEV 44117 2372 E6
- CLEV 44117 2373 A7
- CLEV 44119 2372 E6
1200 EUCL 44117 2373 A7
7000 KTLD 44094 2376 D6
7000 WBHL 44094 2376 A5
8200 KTLD 44094 2377 A6
9400 KTLD 44094 2378 E6
9600 CdnT 44024 2378 E7
9600 CdnT 44094 2378 A7
10700 CdnT 44024 2379 A6
11100 CRDN 44024 2379 B6
21000 EUCL 44117 2498 B1
23500 EUCL 44143 2498 C1
23800 RDHT 44143 2498 C1
24400 RDHT 44143 2373 E7
26000 RDHT 44143 2374 A6
27200 WBHL 44092 2374 C6
29300 WBHL 44094 2374 D6
33700 WBHL 44094 2375 D5
Chardon Rd SR-84
21000 EUCL 44117 2498 B1
23500 EUCL 44143 2498 C1
23800 RDHT 44143 2498 C1
24400 RDHT 44143 2373 E7
26000 RDHT 44143 2374 A6
27200 WBHL 44092 2374 A6
Chardon Rd US-6
7000 KTLD 44094 2376 D6
7000 WBHL 44094 2376 A5
8200 KTLD 44094 2377 A6
9400 KTLD 44094 2378 E6
9600 CdnT 44024 2378 E7
9600 CdnT 44094 2378 A7
10700 CdnT 44024 2379 A6
11100 CRDN 44024 2379 B6
21000 EUCL 44117 2498 B1
23500 EUCL 44143 2498 C1
23800 RDHT 44143 2498 C1
24400 RDHT 44143 2373 E7
26000 RDHT 44143 2374 A6
27200 WBHL 44092 2374 C6
29300 WBHL 44094 2374 D6
33700 WBHL 44094 2375 D5
Chardon St
400 PNVL 44077 2040 A7
Chardon-Madison Rd
4300 MadT 44057 2044 B7
4300 MDSN 44057 2044 B4
Chardon-Madison Rd SR-528
4300 MadT 44057 2044 B7
4300 MDSN 44057 2044 B4
Chardonview Dr
25800 RDHT 44143 2373 E7
26200 RDHT 44143 2374 A6
Chardon Windsor Rd
12400 CRDN 44024 2380 B6
12400 HmbT 44024 2380 C7
13400 HmbT 44024 2381 A7
13500 ClrT 44024 2506 B1
13500 HmbT 44024 2506 B1
14700 ClrT 44024 2507 A2
14700 HtbT 44024 2507 A2
14700 HtbT 44064 2507 C2
15500 HtbT 44046 2507 C2
Chardonwood Dr
8000 KDHL 44060 2252 C4
N Chariot St
8000 CcdT 44060 2253 B4
S Chariot St
8100 CcdT 44060 2253 B4
Charlane Ct
5100 MadT 44057 1941 A2
5100 MadT 44081 1941 A2
5100 NPRY 44081 1941 A2
Charles Av
100 AMHT 44001 2872 B2
5400 PRMA 44129 2883 A2
5400 PRMA 44134 2883 A2
6700 PRMA 44129 2882 E2

Charles Ct
100 ELYR 44035 2875 B7
2100 AVON 44011 2748 B1
9000 TNBG 44087 3154 E1
18200 CLEV 44122 2757 D4
Charles Dr
- VMLN 44089 2741 B6
4400 LORN 44053 2743 D3
9000 BbgT 44023 3022 D2
9700 VLVW 44125 2885 B5
Charles Pl
500 HDHT 44143 2499 A3
Charles Rd
1800 ECLE 44112 2497 B5
4700 NRDV 44039 2877 B2
6400 NOSD 44070 2878 B3
Charles St
10 BDFD 44146 2887 B6
10 GDRV 44077 2039 C5
200 SAHT 44001 2872 C7
700 WLWK 44095 2249 E6
5100 MPHT 44137 2757 B7
Charlesderry Rd
8000 KTLD 44094 2376 E1
Charleston Av
2800 LORN 44055 2746 A3
33300 AVLK 44012 2617 C2
Charleston Sq
10 EUCL 44143 2498 A2
Charles V Carr Pl
3000 CLEV 44104 2626 A6
Charlotte Av
11000 CLEV 44105 2756 C4
Charlotte St
10 PNVL 44077 2146 B2
Charlton Cir
7500 NCtT 44067 3153 A2
Charlton Ln
10100 NbyT 44072 2763 C1
Charlton Rd
4000 SELD 44121 2628 A1
Charmar Dr
- MNTR 44060 2144 C2
Charmwood Ovl
32700 SLN 44139 3019 E1
32800 SLN 44139 2888 E7
Charney Cir
9500 ODFL 44138 3010 C1
Charney Rd
2300 UNHT 44118 2627 E4
Charter Av
6600 CLEV 44127 2755 E1
Charter Dr
10 NCtT 44067 3153 C5
Charter Ln
19100 SGVL 44149 3146 C5
Charter Oak Ln
1100 WTLK 44145 2620 D7
Chartley Ct
10300 MsnT 44024 2503 C6
Chartley Rd
1700 GSML 44040 2630 C1
Chase Av
1200 LKWD 44107 2622 E4
Chase Dr
6200 MNTR 44060 2143 D4
6400 MAYF 44143 2499 E5
6400 MAYF 44143 2500 A5
8600 BbgT 44023 3022 B1
24700 NOSD 44070 2750 C4
28400 WTLK 44145 2749 D4
Chase Ln
10 LKWD 44107 2622 E4
Chase St
100 ELYR 44035 2875 B6
Chase Moor Dr
12900 SGVL 44136 3012 D7
Chateau Av
16500 CLEV 44128 2757 C5
Chateau Dr
7200 PRMA 44130 2882 C7
Chateau Tr
17900 AbnT 44255 2893 C6
Chatfield Av
15000 CLEV 44111 2752 B3
17500 CLEV 44135 2752 A3
Chatfield Dr
10 PNVL 44077 2145 E2
2100 CVHT 44106 2627 A3
Chatham Av
2500 CLEV 44113 2624 C5
Chatham Cir
- NRDV 44035 3007 B1
Chatham Ct
1000 GFTN 44044 3142 A4
3000 WTLK 44145 2749 D3
7200 NCtT 44067 3153 B4
17900 SGVL 44136 3146 E4
Chatham Dr
10 AURA 44202 3156 E4
10 AURA 44202 3157 A3
10 PnvT 44077 2145 B5
5500 BNHT 44131 2884 B2
5500 SVHL 44131 2884 B2
33300 AVLK 44012 2617 C3
Chatham Pl
900 RKRV 44116 2621 B6
Chatham Rd
2800 PRPK 44124 2629 E6
Chatham Wy
100 MDHT 44124 2500 A6
Chatham Glen Dr
14600 NbyT 44072 2763 B1
Chatham Point Dr
30200 BYVL 44140 2619 C5
Chatman Dr
16100 SGVL 44149 3146 D2
Chatworth Dr
25100 EUCL 44117 2373 D6
25500 RDHT 44117 2373 D6
25500 RDHT 44143 2373 D6
Chaucer Blvd
8700 BWHT 44147 3014 D6
Chaucer Ct
100 ELYR 44035 2874 B7
Chaucer Dr
25500 WTLK 44145 2750 B3
35200 NRDV 44039 2748 A7
Chaucer Wy
2200 MadT 44057 1942 B3
Chaumont Rd
- WLWK 44095 2249 C5
Chautauqua Tr
11400 BKVL 44141 3016 C5

Checquers Ct
9800 CcdT 44060 2253 B4
Cheerful Ln
11600 SGVL 44136 3012 C7
Chelford Rd
1900 EUCL 44117 2373 D7
1900 RDHT 44117 2373 D7
1900 RDHT 44143 2373 D7
Chelmsford Dr
10 AURA 44202 3156 E4
10 AURA 44202 3157 A4
5600 LNHT 44124 2629 B3
Chelmsford Rd
1500 MDHT 44124 2499 D7
1500 MDHT 44124 2629 D1
Chelsea Av
33300 AVLK 44012 2617 C2
Chelsea Ct
10 SRSL 44022 2761 E6
200 AURA 44202 3021 E7
11000 NRYN 44133 3013 D5
Chelsea Dr
200 WLBY 44094 2250 A7
200 WLBY 44094 2375 A1
3000 CVHT 44118 2497 C7
4700 LORN 44055 2746 B5
29500 BYVL 44140 2619 D3
Chelsea Ln
10 BHWD 44122 2628 E2
7400 GSML 44040 2630 D2
Chelsea St
- AVON 44011 2747 B1
Chelsee Pl
100 ELYR 44035 2874 A7
Chelston Av
900 SELD 44121 2498 B5
Cheltenham Blvd
5000 LNHT 44124 2628 E1
5100 LNHT 44124 2629 A1
Cheltenham Dr
38200 WLBY 44094 2250 E2
Chelton Rd
3500 SRHT 44120 2757 C2
Chennault Dr
7300 NRDV 44039 2877 C4
Chenook Run
8800 MCDN 44056 3018 D6
Chenook Tr
700 MCDN 44056 3018 D6
Cherie Dr
8400 GDHT 44125 2756 B7
Cheriton Dr
700 HDHT 44143 2499 A4
Cherokee Av
- EUCL 44119 2373 A5
18500 CLEV 44119 2372 E5
19300 CLEV 44119 2373 A5
Cherokee Dr
5600 LNHT 44124 2629 B1
5600 MDHT 44124 2629 B1
Cherokee Ln
11500 BKVL 44141 3016 D5
Cherokee Pth
1200 VMLN 44089 2741 B6
Cherokee Run
8900 MCDN 44056 3018 D5
Cherokee Tr
500 WLBY 44094 2143 B4
4000 BNWK 44212 3146 D7
13000 MDBH 44130 3012 C1
13000 PRMA 44130 3012 E1
Cherokee Strip Tr
10 ClrT 44024 2505 D6
Cherry Av
100 CRDN 44024 2379 E6
Cherry Cir
8500 MCDN 44056 3018 C7
Cherry Ln
- AhtT 44001 2872 B2
- AMHT 44001 2872 B2
- VMLN 44089 2740 E5
10 OmsT 44138 2879 B4
100 AVLK 44012 2618 C1
100 PRMA 44131 2883 E7
100 PRMA 44134 2883 E7
100 SVHL 44131 2883 E7
100 SVHL 44131 2884 A7
8000 NCtT 44067 3018 A7
8000 NCtT 44067 3153 A1
12800 CsTp 44026 2631 D1
Cherry Rd
8500 VmnT 44089 2869 A4
Cherry St
- VMLN 44089 2741 A5
7200 INDE 44131 2884 E6
8000 MONT 44060 2143 E1
8000 MONT 44060 2144 B1
33300 AVON 44011 2748 D2
Cherry Wy
21400 RKRV 44116 2621 C6
Cherrybank Dr
37000 SLN 44139 3020 C2
Cherry Blossom Dr
6800 MNTR 44060 2143 C6
Cherry Bottom Gln
100 ELYR 44035 2874 B7
Cherry Hill Dr
10200 CcdT 44077 2145 D5
Cherry Hill Ln
1200 BWHT 44147 3150 A1
8300 BWHT 44147 3015 A7
Cherry Hollow Dr
11400 CdnT 44024 2254 C6
Cherry Park Ovl
600 AURA 44202 3021 C4
Cherry Ridge Dr
300 AURA 44202 3156 C1
Cherrystone Dr
9200 MNTR 44060 2144 E7
9200 MNTR 44060 2252 E1
Cherry Stone Ln
19000 SGVL 44136 3146 E5
Cherry Tree Dr
9200 SGVL 44136 3012 A3
Cherry Tree Ln
10 PnvT 44077 2146 B3
Cherry Valley Dr
100 AMHT 44001 2743 E7
100 AMHT 44001 2872 E1
Cherrywood Cir
- MNTR 44060 2145 A7
10 GNVA 44041 1944 C7
10 HpfT 44041 1944 C7
400 SgHT 44067 3017 E3

STREET
Block City ZIP Map# Grid

Cherrywood Dr
5600 LORN 44053 2744 E6
Cherry Wood Ln
- PNVL 44077 2145 C3
Cherrywood Ln
300 PNVL 44077 2145 C3
7600 SVHL 44131 3015 A2
19100 WVHT 44128 2757 E4
Cheryl Dr
6100 CcdT 44077 2146 B4
13100 NRYN 44133 3147 D4
13100 SGVL 44133 3147 D4
13100 SGVL 44136 3147 D4
Cheryl Rd
6700 HrmT 44234 3161 A3
Cheryl Ann Dr
6500 INDE 44131 2884 C5
6700 SVHL 44131 2884 C6
Chesapeake Ct
10 ELYR 44035 2873 E7
10 ELYR 44035 2874 A7
Chesapeake Dr
- NRDV 44039 2877 D6
8400 SgHT 44067 3017 E5
9300 NRYN 44133 3013 C4
Chesapeake Pl
100 PnvT 44077 2145 B5
Chesapeake Cove
300 PnvT 44077 2145 B6
Chesea Ct
8700 SgHT 44067 3017 D4
Cheshire Ct
7700 MNTR 44060 2253 A2
Cheshire Dr
100 ELYR 44035 2874 A6
Cheshire Pl
7300 SLN 44139 3019 E2
Cheshire Rd
2500 CLEV 44120 2626 E5
2500 SRHT 44120 2626 E5
S Cheshire Rd
- BtnT 44021 2766 B2
- BtnT 44062 2766 B2
- BURT 44021 2766 B2
S Cheshire Rd SR-168
- BtnT 44021 2766 B2
- BtnT 44062 2766 B2
- BURT 44021 2766 B2
S Cheshire Rd SR-700
- BtnT 44021 2766 B2
- BtnT 44062 2766 B2
- BURT 44021 2766 B2
N Cheshire St
14300 BtnT 44021 2636 B7
14300 BURT 44021 2636 B7
S Cheshire St
14600 BURT 44021 2766 B1
14700 BtnT 44021 2766 B2
14700 BtnT 44062 2766 B2
S Cheshire St SR-168
14600 BURT 44021 2766 B1
14700 BtnT 44021 2766 B2
14700 BtnT 44062 2766 B2
S Cheshire St SR-700
14600 BURT 44021 2766 B1
14700 BtnT 44021 2766 B2
14700 BtnT 44062 2766 B2
Chester Av
900 CLEV 44114 2624 E3
2200 CLEV 44114 2625 C2
3600 CLEV 44103 2625 E2
7300 CLEV 44103 2626 A2
9300 CLEV 44106 2626 B2
Chester Av US-322
2200 CLEV 44114 2625 C2
3600 CLEV 44103 2625 E2
7300 CLEV 44103 2626 A2
9300 CLEV 44106 2626 B2
Chester Pkwy
8100 CLEV 44103 2626 A2
Chester Rd
11300 GDHT 44125 2885 D1
33600 AVON 44011 2618 A7
36100 AVON 44011 2617 B7
Chester Rd SR-83
36000 AVON 44011 2618 A7
Chester St
10 PNVL 44077 2039 E7
10 PNVL 44077 2040 A6
Chesterbrook Rd
7600 CsTp 44026 2631 C3
Chesterfield Av
7500 PRMA 44129 2882 D1
11500 CLEV 44108 2496 D6
12300 CLEV 44112 2496 E6
12300 ECLE 44112 2496 E6
Chesterfield Ct
25600 NOSD 44070 2750 C4
25600 WTLK 44070 2750 C4
25600 WTLK 44145 2750 C4
Chesterfield Dr
10000 PMHT 44130 2882 C3
Chesterfield Ln
12500 CsTp 44026 2502 D7
Chesterfield St
35400 NRDV 44039 2748 A7
Chester Industrial Pkwy
1200 AVON 44011 2617 B6
Chesterland Av
1400 LKWD 44107 2622 E6
2100 CLEV 44107 2622 E7
2100 CLEV 44111 2622 E7
Chesterton Ct
- AURA 44202 3156 B1
100 BNWK 44212 3147 B6
Chesterton Ln
- AURA 44202 3156 A1
8100 NRYN 44133 3013 D5
Chesterton Rd
- SRHT 44122 2628 A6
2600 SRHT 44118 2628 A5
Chestnut Av
- BHIT 44212 3146 C7
10 NHFD 44067 3018 A4
100 NHFD 44067 3017 E4
Chestnut Blvd
8100 BWHT 44147 3015 A4
Chestnut Cir
12200 BKVL 44141 3151 D4
Chestnut Ct
200 AVLK 44012 2618 C2
3500 LORN 44053 2744 C3
3800 ORNG 44022 2759 D3
7200 OmsT 44138 2878 E5
35100 SLN 44139 3020 B2

Chestnut Dr
- BtnT 44021 2635 E7
300 BERA 44017 2879 E5
400 BERA 44017 2880 A5
2000 WTLK 44145 2750 A2
5700 PRMA 44129 2882 D1
7000 WNHL 44146 2886 C7
14500 NbyT 44065 2634 B7
14500 NbyT 44065 2764 C1
20600 SGVL 44149 3011 C4
Chestnut Knl
1300 BWHT 44147 3149 D5
Chestnut Ln
- AhtT 44001 2872 E6
- WBHL 44092 2374 A6
100 RDHT 44143 2374 A6
100 SRSL 44022 2761 D5
800 AMHT 44001 2872 B3
31800 PRPK 44124 2629 E4
Chestnut Ovl
4700 INDE 44131 2884 C5
Chestnut Pl
- CLEV 44104 2625 C4
- CLEV 44115 2625 C4
Chestnut Rd
10 PRMA 44131 2883 E5
10 PRMA 44134 2883 E5
10 SVHL 44131 2883 E5
600 WLBY 44094 2143 A4
1400 SVHL 44131 2884 B5
4000 INDE 44131 2884 B5
Chestnut Run
900 GSML 44040 2500 E6
Chestnut St
10 ELYR 44035 2875 A6
10 GNVA 44041 1944 B5
10 PNVL 44077 2145 E2
300 CcdT 44077 2145 E3
300 FTHR 44077 2039 D3
400 VMLN 44089 2741 A5
600 HpfT 44041 1944 B6
900 GFTN 44044 3142 B5
1200 WLBY 44094 2142 E5
4300 BHIT 44212 3146 C7
4300 BNWK 44212 3146 C7
5400 MONT 44060 2143 E1
N Chestnut Commons Dr
7300 MNTR 44060 2143 C4
S Chestnut Commons Dr
7300 MNTR 44060 2143 C4
Chestnutdale Av
3100 CLEV 44109 2754 C2
Chestnutdale Rd
11600 MsnT 44024 2504 C3
Chestnut Grove Dr
7700 ODFL 44138 2879 C5
Chestnut Hill Dr
5000 WLBY 44094 2250 B7
5000 WLBY 44094 2375 B1
Chestnut Hills Dr
1800 CVHT 44106 2626 D3
2200 CLEV 44106 2626 D3
2200 CVHT 44104 2626 D4
5800 PRMA 44129 2882 D2
6300 PRMA 44129 2883 A4
Chestnut Oak Ln
15200 SGVL 44149 3146 B1
Chestnut Ridge Rd
31500 NOSD 44070 2878 A3
31500 NRDV 44039 2878 A3
31500 NRDV 44070 2878 A3
31700 NRDV 44039 2877 A6
36000 NRDV 44039 2876 E7
36000 NRDV 44039 3007 C2
36800 EatT 44035 3007 A3
36800 EatT 44039 3007 D1
36800 NRDV 44035 3007 D1
37800 ELYR 44035 3007 A3
38200 EatT 44035 3006 E3
38200 ELYR 44035 3006 E3
39200 CrlT 44035 3006 C3
Chestnut Trail Dr
1600 TNBG 44087 3019 D4
Cheswick Dr
5000 ORNG 44022 2759 D7
5000 SLN 44022 2759 D7
5000 SLN 44139 2759 D7
5200 SLN 44139 2888 D1
Cheswick Pl
31400 SLN 44139 2888 D1
Chevrolet Blvd
5000 BKLN 44144 2753 B7
5000 PRMA 44130 2753 B7
5000 PRMA 44130 2882 B1
5000 PRMA 44144 2753 B7
5500 PMHT 44130 2882 B2
Chevy Chase
9900 SGVL 44136 3012 C4
Cheyenne Run
9100 MCDN 44056 3018 D5
Cheyenne Tr
10 ClrT 44024 2505 C6
10000 PMHT 44130 2882 B2
Cheyenne Falls
300 AVLK 44012 2618 C2
Cheyney Ln
5000 BHIT 44212 3146 A6
5100 BHIT 44212 3145 E6
5100 LvpT 44212 3145 E6
5100 LvpT 44280 3145 E6
Chicago St
500 PNVL 44077 2145 D1
500 PnvT 44077 2145 D1
Chickadee Ln
5000 LNHT 44124 2628 E1
5000 LNHT 44124 2629 A1
Chickasaw Av
18500 CLEV 44119 2372 E5
19300 CLEV 44119 2373 A5
Chickasaw Rd
5200 RchT 44286 3150 A6
Chickashay Ln
10400 AbnT 44023 3023 C2
Chillicothe Rd
- KDHL 44060 2251 E6
- KDHL 44094 2251 E6
- KTLD 44060 2251 E6
5000 SRSL 44022 2762 A7
5200 BbgT 44022 2762 A7
5200 BbgT 44023 2762 A7
7000 MNTR 44060 2145 A7
7100 MNTR 44060 2253 A1
7200 MNTR 44060 2252 D3
7500 KDHL 44060 2252 A6
8400 KDHL 44094 2252 A6

Chillicothe Rd
8400 KTLD 44060 2252 A6
8400 KTLD 44094 2252 A6
8800 KTLD 44094 2251 D7
9100 KTLD 44094 2376 E2
9500 KTLD 44094 2377 A4
11000 CsTp 44026 2502 B7
11000 CsTp 44094 2502 A1
11000 KTLD 44094 2502 A1
12700 CsTp 44026 2632 B1
13400 CsTp 44072 2632 A3
13400 RslT 44072 2632 A7
14600 RslT 44072 2762 A4
15000 RslT 44022 2762 A4
16400 BbgT 44023 2891 A2
18400 BbgT 44023 3022 A3
18900 AURA 44023 3022 A3
18900 AURA 44202 3022 A3
Chillicothe Rd SR-306
5000 SRSL 44022 2762 A7
5200 BbgT 44022 2762 A7
5200 BbgT 44023 2762 A7
8800 KTLD 44094 2251 D7
9100 KTLD 44094 2376 E2
9500 KTLD 44094 2377 A4
11000 CsTp 44026 2502 B7
11000 CsTp 44094 2502 A1
11000 KTLD 44094 2502 A1
12700 CsTp 44026 2632 B1
13400 CsTp 44072 2632 A3
13400 RslT 44072 2632 A7
14600 RslT 44072 2762 A4
15000 RslT 44022 2762 A4
16400 BbgT 44023 2891 A2
18400 BbgT 44023 3022 A3
18900 AURA 44023 3022 A3
18900 AURA 44202 3022 A3
Chillicothe Rd SR-615
- KDHL 44060 2251 E6
- KDHL 44094 2251 E6
- KTLD 44060 2251 E6
8400 KDHL 44060 2252 A6
8400 KDHL 44094 2252 A6
8400 KTLD 44060 2252 A6
8400 KTLD 44094 2252 A6
8800 KTLD 44094 2251 E6
N Chillicothe Rd
10 AURA 44202 3021 E7
500 AURA 44202 3022 A4
1000 AURA 44023 3022 A4
1000 BbgT 44023 3022 A4
N Chillicothe Rd SR-306
10 AURA 44202 3021 E7
500 AURA 44202 3022 A4
1000 AURA 44023 3022 A4
1000 BbgT 44023 3022 A4
S Chillicothe Rd
10 AURA 44202 3156 E4
1200 STBR 44202 3156 E6
10100 STBR 44241 3156 E7
S Chillicothe Rd SR-43
100 AURA 44202 3156 E4
1200 STBR 44202 3156 E6
10100 STBR 44241 3156 E7
S Chillicothe Rd SR-306
10 AURA 44202 3156 E1
Chimney Rdg
100 CRDN 44024 2379 E5
Chimney Ridge Dr
2000 MadT 44057 1942 A2
Chimney Ridge Tr
38300 WBHL 44094 2376 A6
Chinaberry Cir N
8700 MCDN 44056 3154 A3
Chinaberry Cir S
900 MCDN 44056 3154 A4
Chinkapin Ct
6700 OKWD 44146 2887 E6
Chipeewa Dr
19600 EUCL 44117 2497 E3
19600 EUCL 44117 2498 A2
Chipendale Ln
11400 MsnT 44024 2503 E2
11400 MsnT 44024 2504 A2
Chipmunk Ln
15400 BtnT 44062 2767 A5
15400 MdfT 44062 2767 A6
Chipmunk Ridge Dr
10000 CcdT 44077 2253 C1
Chippenham Ct
10 RKRV 44116 2621 B6
Chippewa Rd
7300 BKVL 44141 3016 C6
13000 SgHT 44067 3016 E6
13000 SgHT 44141 3016 E6
Chippewa Rd SR-82
7300 BKVL 44141 3016 C6
13000 SgHT 44067 3016 E6
13000 SgHT 44141 3016 E6
Chippewa St
1000 GFTN 44044 3142 A4
Chippewa Tr
- BKVL 44141 3016 B6
7400 MDBH 44130 3012 D1
Chippewa Creek Dr
- BKVL 44141 3016 C7
Chipping Ln
400 AbnT 44023 2892 B3
Chisholm Ct
100 AURA 44202 3021 D6
Chisholm Tr
10 ClrT 44024 2505 C6
Chopin Cir
27000 WTLK 44145 2750 A1
Chris Av
3000 LORN 44052 2744 D3
Chrisfield Dr
3300 RKRV 44116 2751 A2
Christene Blvd
6400 BERA 44017 2880 B4
6400 BERA 44142 2880 B4
6400 BKPK 44142 2880 B4
Christian Av
11700 CcdT 44077 2254 E1
Christina Ct
1000 GDRV 44077 2039 C6
1000 PnvT 44077 2039 C6
Christina Dr
10200 KTLD 44094 2377 C5
Christina Wy Ct
3400 PryT 44081 1940 C7
Christine Av
12600 GDHT 44105 2756 E5
13100 GDHT 44105 2757 A5
13900 CLEV 44105 2757 A5

Christine Av
14000 CLEV 44128 2757 A5
21800 EUCL 44119 2373 B5
21800 EUCL 44123 2373 B5
Christine Ct
100 ETLK 44095 2142 D5
Christine Dr
2800 WBHL 44092 2374 C5
Christman Dr
6000 NOSD 44070 2878 C2
Christopher Ct
5900 MNTR 44060 2144 C3
22400 ClbT 44028 3010 E3
22400 ClbT 44149 3010 E3
22400 SGVL 44149 3010 E3
Christopher Dr
8600 NRYN 44133 3014 B3
Church Av
2500 CLEV 44113 2624 C4
Church Dr
3300 LORN 44053 2743 E3
N Church Dr
9000 PMHT 44129 2882 D5
9000 PMHT 44130 2882 C5
9000 PRMA 44129 2882 D5
9000 PRMA 44130 2882 D5
Church Ln
10 ELYR 44035 3006 A1
Church Rd
- NRsT 44001 3003 A1
- SAHT 44001 3003 A1
Church St
10 BERA 44017 2880 C7
10 CNFL 44022 2760 E6
10 OmsT 44138 2879 B4
100 AMHT 44001 2872 D2
400 SAHT 44001 3003 A1
2500 AVON 44011 2747 D2
3800 WLBY 44094 2250 D4
9000 TNBG 44087 3154 E1
Churchill Av
10500 CLEV 44106 2496 C7
Churchill Blvd
4200 BHWD 44122 2628 C4
4200 UNHT 44118 2628 C4
4200 UNHT 44122 2628 C4
Churchill Ct
10200 CLEV 44106 2496 C7
Churchill Dr
4500 AVON 44011 2747 B6
15900 ClbT 44028 3144 E2
35900 SLN 44139 2889 C4
Churchill Ln
- WTLK 44145 2749 A4
N Churchill Pl
7100 CcdT 44077 2146 A7
S Churchill Pl
7200 CcdT 44077 2146 B7
Churchill Rd
1000 HDHT 44143 2499 A6
1000 LNHT 44124 2499 A7
1000 LNHT 44143 2499 A6
Churchill Sq
7300 MNTR 44060 2143 C6
N Churchill Wy
11800 SGVL 44149 3011 A5
S Churchill Wy
12500 SGVL 44149 3010 E6
12500 SGVL 44149 3011 A5
Cielo E Terra Dr
900 MCDN 44056 3018 E4
Cimarron Ovl
800 AURA 44202 3021 B6
Cimarron Tr
10 ClrT 44024 2505 C6
Cindy Ln
3500 SVHL 44131 2884 B4
Cinema Ct
100 VMLN 44089 2741 C4
Cinnabar Dr
8900 BKVL 44141 3016 D6
Cinnabar Tr
18000 AbnT 44255 2893 A6
Cinnamon Blvd
11100 NRYN 44133 3013 B5
Cinnamon Tr
17900 AbnT 44255 2893 B6
Cinnamon Wy
3600 WTLK 44145 2750 B4
30000 NOSD 44070 2878 A4
Circle Ct
2800 CLEV 44113 2624 C5
Circle Dr
- AhtT 44001 2872 A3
10 SRSL 44022 2762 C5
2000 CLEV 44106 2626 D2
2500 PryT 44077 2041 B7
5800 MDHT 44124 2629 C2
6700 MadT 44057 1843 B6
Circle Rdg
11500 SGVL 44136 3012 B5
N Circleview Dr
1100 SVHL 44131 2884 A1
S Circleview Dr
1100 SVHL 44131 2884 A1
Circlewood Dr
500 AURA 44202 3022 C6
2600 WTLK 44145 2750 C3
3800 FWPK 44126 2751 C2
Cissell Ln
12600 CrlT 44044 3140 E1
City Hall Dr
13900 NRYN 44133 3013 E7
City Hall Pl
100 LORN 44052 2614 D6
Civic Dr
- PRMA 44131 2883 E7
- PRMA 44134 2883 E7
- SVHL 44131 2883 E7
- SVHL 44131 2884 A7
Civic Center Blvd
8400 MNTR 44060 2144 B4
CJ Ct
9200 MNTR 44060 2144 E7
Claasen Av
6700 CLEV 44105 2755 E3
7400 CLEV 44105 2756 A3
Clague Pkwy
500 BYVL 44140 2620 E5
Clague Rd
300 BYVL 44140 2620 E5
500 WTLK 44140 2620 E6
500 WTLK 44145 2620 E7
1500 WTLK 44145 2750 E6
2700 NOSD 44070 2750 E3

Clague Rd
2700 NOSD 44145 2750 E3
2700 WTLK 44070 2750 E3
Claiborne Rd
13300 ECLE 44112 2497 A5
Claiborne Hartford Conn
- ECLE 44112 2497 A5
Clairdoan Av
10500 CLEV 44108 2496 C4
Claire Av
16200 CLEV 44111 2752 B1
W Claire Dr
4300 SELD 44121 2628 B2
Clairidge Dr
5500 WLBY 44094 2375 B2
Clairmont Dr
10 PnvT 44077 2145 C4
Clairview Av
14000 CLEV 44111 2622 D7
Clampher Rd
- MPHT 44146 2758 A7
4900 MPHT 44137 2758 A7
Clare Av
19700 MPHT 44137 2757 E7
19700 MPHT 44137 2758 A7
21200 BDHT 44146 2758 B7
Clarebird Av
11200 CLEV 44105 2756 D2
Claremont Av
13100 MDBH 44130 2881 D4
Claremont Blvd
4700 GDHT 44125 2756 E7
Claremont Dr
10 BNWK 44212 3147 A6
Claremont Rd
100 VMLN 44089 2741 E4
2800 SRHT 44122 2627 E5
Clarence Av
1300 LKWD 44107 2623 A5
2000 LKWD 44107 2622 E6
Clarence Rd
800 CVHT 44121 2497 E5
Clarendon Ct
1900 WTLK 44145 2749 E1
Clarendon Dr
5400 SLN 44139 2888 E2
Clarendon Rd
3200 CVHT 44118 2627 C4
Clareshire Dr
24400 NOSD 44070 2750 D7
Clarewood Dr
30900 BYVL 44140 2619 B4
Claridge Ct
8100 NRYN 44133 3013 C5
Claridge Ln
670-00 AURA 44202 3156 C3
Claridge Ovl
3700 BNWK 44212 3147 A7
3700 SRHT 44118 2627 E5
3700 UNHT 44118 2627 E5
Claridon Rd
100 CRDN 44024 2380 A7
300 ClrT 44024 2505 B1
300 CRDN 44024 2505 B1
Claridon-Park Dr
13900 ClrT 44024 2506 B3
Claridon Troy Rd
10700 ClrT 44024 2506 B2
10700 HmbT 44024 2381 B7
10700 HmbT 44024 2506 B2
12300 ClrT 44021 2506 B7
12400 ClrT 44021 2636 B2
12400 ClrT 44024 2636 B2
13000 BtnT 44021 2636 B6
13000 BtnT 44024 2636 B6
14200 BURT 44021 2636 B7
14400 BtnT 44021 2766 A7
14400 BtnT 44062 2766 B2
16000 TroT 44021 2766 A7
Claridon Troy Rd SR-700
14400 BtnT 44021 2766 A7
14400 BtnT 44062 2766 B2
16000 TroT 44021 2766 A7
Clarion Av
- VMLN 44089 2740 E5
Clarion Dr
7600 RslT 44022 2761 C5
35800 ETLK 44095 2250 C1
Clarius Cir
9800 TNBG 44087 3020 B5
Clark Av
300 CLEV 44109 2625 A7
900 CLEV 44109 2624 E7
900 CLEV 44113 2624 E7
900 CLEV 44113 2625 A7
4000 WLBY 44094 2250 E5
4400 CLEV 44102 2624 C7
6800 CLEV 44102 2623 E7
Clark Cir
9000 TNBG 44087 3019 E7
Clark Ct
10 OBLN 44074 3138 E3
10 OBLN 44074 3139 A2
3500 LORN 44053 2743 E3
3500 LORN 44053 2744 A3
37900 WLBY 44094 2250 D5
Clark Dr
28700 WKLF 44092 2374 B4
33800 NRDV 44039 2877 C4
Clark Ln
13000 NRsT 44074 3139 D3
Clark Pkwy
2700 WTLK 44145 2750 A3
Clark Rd
3400 PryT 44081 1940 A6
3800 NPRY 44081 1940 B6
10600 CdnT 44024 2253 E7
10600 CdnT 44060 2253 E7
10700 CdnT 44024 2254 B7
12000 CcdT 44024 2255 A6
12000 CcdT 44077 2255 A6
12000 CdnT 44024 2255 A6
Clark St
100 BERA 44017 2880 C7
100 ELYR 44035 2875 C6
7500 ODFL 44138 2879 B5
7500 OmsT 44138 2879 B5
Clarke Rd
10000 ClbT 44028 3010 E5
10900 ClbT 44149 3010 E6
10900 SGVL 44149 3010 E6
Clarkson Rd
2600 CVHT 44106 2627 A3
2700 CVHT 44118 2627 A3

Clarkstone Rd
1700 CLEV 44112 2497 C3
Clarkwood Dr
11700 CdnT 44024 2379 D4
Clarkwood Pkwy
4300 HIHL 44128 2758 B4
4300 WVHT 44128 2758 B4
Clarkwood Rd
- CLEV 44104 2625 E3
2100 CLEV 44103 2625 E3
Clarmont Rd
30600 WLWK 44095 2249 C5
Claudia Dr
6300 BKPK 44142 2880 E3
Claus Rd
1200 LORN 44089 2742 B7
1200 VMLN 44089 2742 B7
7800 BhmT 44001 2871 B5
7800 VMLN 44001 2871 B5
7800 VMLN 44089 2871 B5
Claver Rd
2400 UNHT 44118 2628 B4
Clay St
- MdfT 44046 2637 D4
- MdfT 44062 2637 D4
4400 HpfT 44041 1944 E7
4700 GNVA 44041 1944 E7
6700 TpnT 44086 2257 D7
8000 TpnT 44024 2257 D7
8000 TpnT 44064 2257 D7
8400 MtlT 44024 2257 D7
8400 MtlT 44064 2257 D7
10900 HtbT 44064 2507 D3
10900 HtbT 44062 2507 D1
11200 HtbT 44046 2507 D3
11800 HtbT 44062 2507 D7
12400 HtbT 44046 2637 D2
12400 HtbT 44062 2637 D2
Claymoor Av
6800 MadT 44057 1843 C6
Claymore Blvd
300 RDHT 44143 2498 D1
Claythorne Pl
3800 BNWK 44212 3146 E7
Claythorne Rd
2600 SRHT 44122 2628 A6
21400 SRHT 44118 2628 B5
Clayton Av
1600 CLEV 44109 2754 E3
29200 WKLF 44092 2374 B2
Clayton Blvd
3300 SRHT 44120 2627 B7
3300 SRHT 44120 2757 C1
Clayton Dr
700 AURA 44202 3156 B1
3400 NOSD 44070 2750 D4
Clearair Dr
6200 MNTR 44060 2143 C4
Clearaire Rd
1200 CLEV 44110 2372 E7
1200 CLEV 44110 2497 E1
Clear Brook Cir
10800 SGVL 44149 3011 A4
Clearbrook Dr
- AVON 44011 2747 B2
300 AVLK 44012 2617 D3
Clearbrook Ln
10 AURA 44202 3156 C1
Clearbrook Ovl
12600 NRYN 44133 3012 E2
Clear Creek Dr
34700 NRDV 44039 2877 B6
Clearfield Ln
11300 MsnT 44024 2504 D2
Clearlake Dr
10500 CcdT 44077 2145 E5
Clearmont Dr
7200 MNTR 44060 2143 C4
Clearview Av
900 PRMA 44131 2883 E2
900 PRMA 44134 2883 E2
900 SVHL 44131 2883 E2
4900 GDHT 44125 2756 E6
15900 CLEV 44128 2757 B5
E Clearview Av
10 PRMA 44131 2883 D2
10 PRMA 44134 2883 D2
10 SVHL 44131 2883 D2
10 SVHL 44131 2884 A2
Clearview Ct
300 BWHT 44147 3149 C4
Clearview Dr
400 EUCL 44123 2373 B3
4900 LORN 44053 2745 A5
4900 ShfT 44052 2745 A5
4900 ShfT 44053 2745 A5
5800 PMHT 44130 2882 C2
5800 PRMA 44130 2882 C2
Clearview Rd
1000 LNHT 44124 2498 E7
11800 CsTp 44026 2502 A4
Clearwater Dr
10 BNWK 44136 3147 A5
10 BNWK 44212 3147 A6
10 SGVL 44136 3147 A5
3700 PRMA 44134 3014 B2
Clearwater Ln
2500 PryT 44077 2041 B7
Clearway Dr
36900 ETLK 44095 2142 D7
Clemens Av
500 ELYR 44035 2874 C4
900 EyrT 44035 2874 C4
Clemens Rd
27900 WTLK 44145 2619 D6
Clement Av
6500 CLEV 44105 2755 E3
7400 CLEV 44105 2756 A3
Clement Dr
5300 MPHT 44137 2757 C7
5300 MPHT 44137 2886 C1
5800 LORN 44053 2744 D6
Clement St
5000 MPHT 44137 2757 C7
Cleminshaw Rd
14400 CLEV 44135 2752 D3
Clemson Ct
100 ELYR 44035 3006 C2
Clermont Rd
- EUCL 44117 2497 E1
1400 CLEV 44110 2497 E1
Clermont St
2600 ShvT 44255 3157 E7
2600 ShvT 44255 3158 A7
2600 STBR 44255 3157 E7

Cletus Dr
37900 EatT 44035 3007 B3
Cleveland Av
- LORN 44055 2745 D6
100 AMHT 44001 2872 E1
1000 AhtT 44001 2873 A1
1000 AMHT 44001 2873 A1
1200 MadT 44057 1843 D6
2000 ShfT 44055 2745 D6
Cleveland Blvd
1700 LORN 44052 2615 B5
Cleveland Dr
9600 AbnT 44023 3022 E1
9700 AbnT 44023 3023 A1
Cleveland Rd
300 CLEV 44108 2496 E3
Cleveland St
10 CNFL 44022 2761 B5
100 ELYR 44035 2875 C5
900 ELYR 44039 2875 E4
900 NRDV 44039 2875 E4
1000 GFTN 44044 3142 A5
Cleveland St SR-113
700 ELYR 44035 2875 E5
900 ELYR 44039 2875 E4
900 NRDV 44039 2875 E4
Cleveland St US-20
700 ELYR 44035 2875 E5
900 ELYR 44039 2875 E4
900 NRDV 44039 2875 E4
N Cleveland St
200 CNFL 44022 2761 A5
S Cleveland St
10 CNFL 44022 2761 B6
Cleveland Heights Blvd
1100 CVHT 44121 2497 E7
1300 CVHT 44118 2497 E7
Cleveland Memorial Shoreway
- BTNH - 2496 B4
- CLEV - 2495 A7
- CLEV - 2496 A4
- CLEV - 2624 D2
- CLEV - 2625 A1
- CLEV 44102 2623 D5
- CLEV 44102 2624 A4
- CyhC - 2495 E5
Cleveland Mem Shoreway I-90
- BTNH - 2496 B4
- CLEV - 2495 D5
- CLEV - 2496 A4
- CyhC - 2495 D5
Cleveland Mem Shoreway SR-2
- BTNH - 2496 B4
- CLEV - 2495 D5
- CLEV - 2496 A4
- CLEV - 2624 E1
- CLEV - 2625 A1
- CLEV 44102 2623 D5
- CLEV 44102 2624 A4
- CyhC - 2495 D5
Cleveland Mem Shoreway US-6
- CLEV 44102 2623 D5
- CLEV 44102 2624 A4
- CLEV 44113 2624 C4
Cleveland Mem Shoreway US-20
- CLEV 44102 2623 D5
- CLEV 44102 2624 A4
- CLEV 44113 2624 C4
Cleveland Mem Shoreway Frwy
- BTNH - 2496 D3
- CLEV - 2495 C6
- CLEV - 2496 A4
Cleveland Mem Shrwy Frwy I-90
- BTNH - 2496 D3
- CLEV - 2495 E5
- CLEV - 2496 B4
Cleveland Mem Shrwy Frwy SR-2
- BTNH - 2496 D3
- CLEV - 2495 E5
- CLEV - 2496 A4
Cleveland Metro Park Dr
- GSML 44040 2500 B2
- MAYF 44040 2500 C3
Cleveland Oberlin Rd
- OBLN 44074 3139 C2
43700 NRsT 44074 3139 C2
Cleveland Oberlin Rd SR-511
- OBLN 44074 3139 C2
43700 NRsT 44074 3139 C2
Cleveland Pkwy Dr
18300 CLEV 44135 2751 E6
Cleveland Pkwy Dr SW
17900 CLEV 44135 2752 A6
Cleviden Rd
15600 ECLE 44112 2497 C6
16100 CVHT 44112 2497 C6
Cliff Cir
18800 FWPK 44126 2752 A1
Cliff Ct
5600 WLBY 44094 2375 A2
Cliff Dr
- CyhC 44102 2623 D4
5000 SDLK 44054 2616 D2
10000 CLEV 44102 2623 C4
13400 LKWD 44107 2622 E3
23700 BYVL 44140 2620 E5
Cliffdale Av
1000 LKWD 44107 2622 C3
Cliffden Ct
1200 SgHT 44067 3017 B4
Clifford Av
13200 CLEV 44135 2752 E3
13500 CLEV 44111 2752 E3
Clifford Dr
21500 FWPK 44126 2751 A3
22800 NOSD 44070 2751 A3
22800 NOSD 44126 2751 A3
23000 NOSD 44070 2750 E3
Clifford Rd
1100 CVHT 44121 2498 A6
1100 SELD 44121 2498 A6
Cliffside Coms
100 RKRV 44116 2621 C6
Cliffside Dr
6600 VMLN 44089 2741 B7
6700 BhmT 44089 2741 C7

Cleveland Street Index

STREET
Block City ZIP Map# Grid

Cliffside Dr
17800 SGVL 44136 3011 E6
Cliffview Cir
8400 MCDN 44056 3153 E2
Cliffview Dr
1000 ETLK 44095 2250 B4
4100 INDE 44131 2884 C4
8400 MCDN 44056 3153 D2
Cliffview Ln
8900 CsTp 44026 2502 C2
Cliffview Rd
1600 CLEV 44112 2497 D2
1700 CLEV 44121 2497 D2
Cliffwood Ct E
8700 MNTR 44060 2144 C4
Cliffwood Ct W
8600 MNTR 44060 2144 C4
Clifton Av
- SDLK 44054 2615 E4
2900 LORN 44055 2745 A5
3600 ShfT 44055 2745 A4
Clifton Blvd
- RKRV 44107 2621 E4
- RKRV 44116 2621 E4
9200 CLEV 44102 2623 D5
11600 LKWD 44102 2623 B4
11600 LKWD 44107 2623 A4
13400 LKWD 44107 2622 E4
18000 LKWD 44107 2621 E4
Clifton Blvd SR-2
- RKRV 44107 2621 E4
- RKRV 44116 2621 E4
9200 CLEV 44102 2623 D5
11600 LKWD 44102 2623 B4
11600 LKWD 44107 2623 A4
13400 LKWD 44107 2622 E4
18000 LKWD 44107 2621 E5
Clifton Blvd US-6
- RKRV 44107 2621 E4
- RKRV 44116 2621 E4
9200 CLEV 44102 2623 D5
11600 LKWD 44102 2623 B4
11600 LKWD 44107 2623 A4
13400 LKWD 44107 2622 E4
18000 LKWD 44107 2621 E5
Clifton Blvd US-20
9200 CLEV 44102 2623 D5
11600 LKWD 44102 2623 B4
11600 LKWD 44107 2623 A4
13400 LKWD 44107 2622 E4
W Clifton Blvd
1100 LKWD 44107 2622 A5
W Clifton Blvd SR-237
1100 LKWD 44107 2622 A5
W Clifton Blvd US-20
1100 LKWD 44107 2622 A5
Clifton Ct
8100 MNTR 44060 2144 A4
N Clifton Dr
17800 LKWD 44107 2622 B4
Clifton Pl
1400 LKWD 44107 2622 A5
Clifton Rd
18000 LKWD 44107 2622 A4
W Clifton Rd
18100 LKWD 44107 2622 A4
Clifton Wy
2100 AVON 44011 2617 E7
2100 AVON 44011 2747 E1
Clifton Park Ln
17800 LKWD 44107 2621 E4
Clifton Prado
1200 LKWD 44107 2623 A4
Clinic Dr
- CLEV 44106 2626 B3
Clinton Av
- AVLK 44012 2617 B2
200 ELYR 44035 2874 E4
900 SELD 44121 2498 B5
2800 CLEV 44113 2624 B5
2800 LORN 44055 2745 D2
3800 CLEV 44102 2624 B5
4200 ShfT 44055 2745 E5
5500 EyrT 44035 2745 E6
5500 ShfT 44035 2745 E6
W Clinton Av
5800 CLEV 44102 2624 A5
6500 CLEV 44102 2623 E5
Clinton Cir
19000 SGVL 44136 3147 C5
Clinton Dr
27300 NOSD 44070 2878 E2
30800 BYVL 44140 2619 B5
Clinton Ln
500 HDHT 44143 2499 B4
Clinton Rd
7300 BKLN 44144 2753 D2
7300 CLEV 44144 2753 E2
8700 CLEV 44102 2753 C2
Clipper Cove
- SDLK 44054 2615 D4
1500 PnvT 44077 2040 E2
10100 RMDV 44202 3020 E5
Clipper Cove Dr
13500 SGVL 44136 3147 D4
Clocktower Dr
- KTLD 44094 2251 E5
- MNTR 44060 2251 E5
- MNTR 44094 2251 E5
N Clocktower Dr
- KTLD 44094 2251 D5
- MNTR 44094 2251 D5
S Clocktower Dr
- KTLD 44094 2251 D5
Clopton Ct
9300 MNTR 44060 2145 A1
Cloud Av
4100 CLEV 44113 2624 B7
Clovelly Dr
5200 LORN 44053 2743 C3
Clover Av
1700 CLEV 44109 2754 D1
7400 MNTR 44060 2251 C2
Clover Cir
5600 WLBY 44094 2375 A1
Clover Dr
5200 SFLD 44035 2746 E6
Clover Ln
8300 RslT 44022 2762 A3
Cloverberry Ct
1200 BWHT 44147 3149 E4
Cloverdale Av
11900 CLEV 44111 2623 A7
Cloverdale Dr
15400 MDFD 44062 2767 B3
Cloverdale Dr
15400 MdfT 44062 2767 B3
Cloveridge Rd
8000 RslT 44022 2761 E3
8000 RslT 44022 2762 A4
Clover Lake Dr
- NbyT 44065 2634 C4
13500 NbyT 44024 2634 B4
Cloverleaf Pkwy
5400 VLVW 44125 2885 A1
Cloverleigh Dr
1000 MadT 44057 1843 E6
Cloverly Dr
6200 SLN 44139 2889 C5
Cloverside Av
15500 CLEV 44128 2757 B3
Club Ct
6000 MNTR 44060 2144 D3
30400 WKLF 44092 2374 E2
Club Dr
- SELD 44121 2628 C1
10 HDHT 44143 2499 C1
200 AURA 44202 3021 E5
Club Ln
10 AbnT 44023 2892 A4
Clubhouse
400 RDHT 44143 2498 C3
Club House Dr
11600 NRYN 44133 3013 A5
Clubside Cir
1000 WTLK 44145 2621 A7
Clubside Ct
100 CRDN 44024 2505 A1
Clubside Dr
10 AbnT 44023 2892 A4
25300 NOSD 44070 2750 A7
Clubside Rd
1500 LNHT 44124 2498 D7
1500 LNHT 44124 2628 D1
Clybourne Av
3800 CLEV 44109 2754 C4
Clyde Rd
1700 MadT 44057 1941 D1
Clydesdale Tr
14600 RslT 44072 2762 C1
CO-9 Chagrin Rd
7100 BbgT 44022 2761 A7
7100 BbgT 44023 2761 B7
Coachlight Tr
5300 SFLD 44054 2746 E3
Coachman Ct
7700 BKVL 44131 3016 A3
7700 BKVL 44141 3016 A3
7700 INDE 44131 3016 A3
Coachman Dr
13000 MsnT 44024 2634 C2
Coachman Ln
33000 SLN 44139 2889 A3
Coast Guard Rd
10 PnvT 44077 2039 B3
Coath Av
13100 CLEV 44105 2756 E2
13100 CLEV 44120 2756 E2
13100 CLEV 44120 2757 A2
Cobalt Av
13900 CLEV 44110 2497 A2
Cobb Ct
- CLEV 44108 2496 B5
Cobble Ct
- GSML 44040 2630 D1
Cobblestone Cir
- PNVL 44077 2145 B2
33000 NRDV 44039 2877 D7
Cobblestone Dr
- ELYR 44035 2746 D6
- SFLD 44035 2746 D6
600 AhtT 44001 2873 C1
Cobblestone Ln
7000 CcdT 44060 2145 C5
7900 BbgT 44023 2890 D7
E Cobblestone Ln
10400 TNBG 44087 3020 A3
W Cobblestone Ln
10300 TNBG 44087 3020 A3
Cobblestone Rd
400 AURA 44202 3157 A2
5200 SFLD 44035 2746 D6
Cobblestone Tr
26000 ClbT 44028 3009 C3
Cobblestone Wy
1300 WTLK 44145 2620 B7
Cobblestone Chase
1200 WTLK 44145 2620 B7
Cobden Ct
- ECLE 44112 2496 E7
Cobleigh Ct
5500 CLEV 44104 2625 D5
Cochran Av
18500 CLEV 44110 2372 E7
18500 CLEV 44110 2497 E1
Cochran Rd
10 AURA 44202 3156 B1
200 AURA 44202 3021 B7
6000 SLN 44139 2888 C4
6900 GNWL 44139 2888 C7
7000 GNWL 44139 3019 C1
Cockle Cove
- PnvT 44077 2145 B5
Cocoa Dr
7700 PRMA 44134 3014 C2
Code Av
37000 WLBY 44094 2250 C4
Coe Av
4100 NOSD 44070 2750 D5
14400 CLEV 44135 2752 C5
Coe St
100 BERA 44017 2880 C7
Coen Rd
4700 VmnT 44089 2740 B6
5700 VmnT 44089 2869 B2
Coes Post Run
1700 WTLK 44145 2619 D7
1700 WTLK 44145 2749 D1
Coffinberry Blvd
18900 FWPK 44126 2751 E2
19800 RKRV 44116 2751 D2
19800 RKRV 44126 2751 D2
Cohassett Av
1300 LKWD 44107 2623 A6
Cohassett Pl
1300 LKWD 44107 2623 A5
Coit Av
1200 CLEV 44110 2497 B4
1200 ECLE 44110 2497 B4
1200 ECLE 44112 2497 B4
Coit Rd
- CLEV 44110 2496 E3
12100 BTNH 44108 2496 E3
12600 CLEV 44108 2496 E3
13300 CLEV 44110 2497 A3
14700 ECLE 44110 2497 B4
14700 ECLE 44112 2497 B3
Colahan Dr
18900 RKRV 44116 2621 E6
Colbourne Rd
23400 EUCL 44123 2373 C3
Colburn Av
2300 CLEV 44109 2754 C4
Colburn Rd
11100 CcdT 44024 2254 D5
11100 CcdT 44077 2254 D5
11100 CdnT 44024 2254 D5
Colby Ct
10 BHWD 44122 2628 E5
Colby Rd
20700 SRHT 44122 2628 A5
Colchester Dr
11500 AbnT 44021 2893 C4
Colchester Rd
- CVHT 44106 2627 A4
2600 CVHT 44118 2627 A4
Coldbrook Dr
4800 ManT 44255 3159 D4
5200 MNTU 44255 3159 D5
Coldstream Ct
- AVON 44011 2747 B2
Coldstream Rd
6100 HDHT 44143 2499 E1
Cold Water Tr
17300 BbgT 44023 2890 C4
Cole Dr
7300 MNTR 44060 2143 C4
Cole Plz
400 WLWK 44095 2249 C6
Colebright Dr
15100 SGVL 44136 3147 A2
Colebrook Dr
6200 PMHT 44130 2882 B3
Coleridge Rd
2700 CVHT 44106 2627 A4
2700 CVHT 44118 2627 B4
6200 CcdT 44077 2145 E4
6200 PnvT 44077 2145 D4
Colesbrooke Dr
- HDSN 44236 3153 E6
7000 BSHT 44236 3153 E7
Colfax Dr
9800 ClbT 44028 3010 D2
9800 ClbT 44138 3010 D2
9800 ODFL 44138 3010 D2
Colfax Rd
6800 CLEV 44104 2625 E5
7500 CLEV 44104 2626 A6
Colgate Av
200 ELYR 44035 3006 B1
6500 CLEV 44102 2624 A6
7000 CLEV 44102 2623 E6
Colgate Ct
6500 CLEV 44102 2624 A6
7000 CLEV 44102 2623 E6
Collamer Av
1600 ECLE 44110 2497 B4
1600 ECLE 44112 2497 B4
Colleen Ct
19900 SGVL 44149 3146 C4
Colleen Dr
6100 CcdT 44077 2146 B4
College Av
700 CLEV 44113 2625 A5
800 CLEV 44113 2624 E5
College Ct
- PNVL 44077 2146 B1
- WLBY 44094 2142 E4
- WLBY 44094 2143 A5
College Pl
10 OBLN 44074 3138 D2
College Rd
4400 SELD 44121 2628 C2
College St
- MNTU 44255 3159 C5
E College St
10 OBLN 44074 3138 E2
100 OBLN 44074 3139 A2
600 NRsT 44074 3139 B2
W College St
10 OBLN 44074 3138 C2
500 NRsT 44074 3138 C2
College Heights Blvd
5200 SFLD 44054 2746 D4
College Park Dr
1100 ELYR 44035 2746 D7
10000 CcdT 44060 2253 C3
10000 CcdT 44077 2253 C3
Colletta Ln
3400 CLEV 44111 2752 B1
Collica Cove
800 AURA 44202 3021 A5
800 RMDV 44202 3021 A5
Collier Av
6400 CLEV 44105 2755 E3
Collier Dr
20200 SGVL 44149 3011 B7
Collingwood Dr
900 AMHT 44001 2743 E6
Collins Dr
2600 LORN 44053 2744 A3
Collins Rd
5900 MNTR 44060 2144 A3
Collver Rd
10 RKRV 44116 2621 D4
Colonel Dr
600 CLEV 44109 2754 E5
600 CLEV 44109 2755 A5
Colonial Av
9900 CLEV 44108 2496 B4
Colonial Blvd
100 ELYR 44035 3006 A3
2900 AVON 44011 2617 E6
5700 WLBY 44094 2375 A2
Colonial Ct
800 VmnT 44089 2740 C5
3900 RKRV 44116 2751 B2
10800 CLEV 44106 2626 C3
18800 AbnT 44023 3023 B2
19500 WNHL 44146 3018 A2
Colonial Dr
- PNVL 44077 2146 A3
- PnvT 44077 2146 B3
1600 CVHT 44118 2627 C1
6800 MNTR 44060 2143 E6
Colonial St
10 CLEV 44110 2372 C5
Colonial Heights Dr
17700 CLEV 44112 2497 D3
Colonnade Dr
6600 MadT 44057 1942 B4
Colonnade Rd
1800 CLEV 44112 2497 C4
Colony Ct
400 GNVA 44041 1944 A5
500 WLBY 44094 2250 A7
500 WLBY 44094 2375 A1
5800 LORN 44053 2743 C6
9400 MNTR 44060 2253 A2
15000 SGVL 44136 3147 B5
Colony Dr
10 OBLN 44074 3138 C3
800 AURA 44202 3021 B7
800 HDHT 44143 2499 A5
900 LNHT 44124 2499 A6
900 LNHT 44143 2499 A6
33200 AVLK 44012 2617 D1
Colony Ln
10 BTNH 44108 2496 D2
13400 BtnT 44021 2635 E7
13400 BtnT 44021 2765 E1
13600 BtnT 44021 2636 A7
13600 BURT 44021 2636 A7
Colony Pk
100 BNWK 44212 3147 D6
100 BNWK 44233 3147 D6
100 HkyT 44233 3147 D6
Colony Rd
3700 SELD 44118 2627 E3
3700 SELD 44118 2628 A3
4000 SELD 44121 2628 A3
Colorado Av
- LORN 44054 2615 D7
100 LORN 44052 2614 E6
400 LORN 44052 2615 B6
3500 SFLD 44054 2615 E7
3900 SFLD 44054 2616 B7
5300 AVON 44011 2617 A6
5300 SFLD 44011 2617 A6
5300 SFLD 44054 2617 A6
37000 AVON 44011 2747 C1
Colorado Av SR-611
- LORN 44054 2615 D7
1400 LORN 44052 2615 B6
3500 SFLD 44054 2615 E7
3900 SFLD 44054 2616 B7
5300 AVON 44011 2617 A6
5300 SFLD 44011 2617 A6
5300 SFLD 44054 2617 A6
37000 AVON 44011 2747 C1
Colt Dr
7200 MNTR 44060 2253 A1
Coltman Rd
1800 CLEV 44106 2626 E1
Colton Rd
3400 SRHT 44122 2758 A1
Columbia Av
100 ELYR 44035 2875 B7
10200 CLEV 44108 2496 C5
Columbia Ct
900 CcdT 44077 2145 E3
900 PNVL 44077 2145 E3
25400 BYVL 44140 2620 C5
Columbia Dr
800 AMHT 44001 2743 E6
1000 AMHT 44001 2744 A6
5500 BDHT 44146 2887 C2
Columbia Rd
10 ClbT 44028 3145 A6
10 LvpT 44028 3145 A6
10 LvpT 44280 3144 E7
10 LvpT 44280 3145 A6
300 BYVL 44140 2620 C5
600 WTLK 44140 2620 C5
600 WTLK 44145 2620 C7
1500 BosT 44141 3152 A7
1700 WTLK 44145 2750 C4
1900 BosT 44141 3151 E7
1900 RchT 44141 3151 D7
3200 NOSD 44070 2750 D6
3200 NOSD 44145 2750 C3
3200 RchT 44286 3151 A6
3200 RHFD 44286 3151 A6
3200 WTLK 44070 2750 C3
5300 NOSD 44070 2879 C2
5400 NOSD 44138 2879 C1
5800 OmsT 44138 2879 C2
6200 OmsT 44070 2879 C4
8000 ODFL 44138 2879 C7
9000 ODFL 44138 3010 B2
9700 ClbT 44028 3010 B2
9700 ClbT 44138 3010 B2
Columbia Rd SR-252
10 ClbT 44028 3145 A6
10 LvpT 44028 3145 A6
10 LvpT 44280 3144 E7
10 LvpT 44280 3145 A6
300 BYVL 44140 2620 C5
600 WTLK 44140 2620 C5
600 WTLK 44145 2620 C7
1700 WTLK 44145 2750 C4
3200 NOSD 44070 2750 C3
3200 NOSD 44145 2750 C3
3200 WTLK 44070 2750 C3
5900 NOSD 44070 2879 C3
6200 OmsT 44070 2879 C4
6200 OmsT 44138 2879 C4
8000 ODFL 44138 2879 C7
9000 ODFL 44138 3010 B2
9700 ClbT 44028 3010 B2
9700 ClbT 44138 3010 B2
Columbia Sq
4100 NOSD 44070 2750 C5
Columbia West River Rd
9800 ClbT 44028 3010 A4
9800 ClbT 44138 3010 B2
9800 ODFL 44138 3010 B2
12300 ClbT 44028 3009 E7
14200 ClbT 44028 3144 D4
17500 ClbT 44280 3144 E5
17500 LvpT 44280 3144 E5
Columbine Av
15000 CLEV 44111 2752 C1
Columbine Ct
6700 MDBH 44130 2881 B5
Columbo Ln
4100 LORN 44055 2746 B4
Columbus Rd
600 BDFD 44146 2887 E3
600 BDHT 44146 2887 E3
Columbus Rd
1600 CLEV 44113 2624 D4
25700 OKWD 44146 2887 E3
26300 BDHT 44146 2888 A3
26300 Okwd 44146 2888 A3
26300 SLN 44139 2888 A3
Columbus St
- VMLN 44089 2740 D5
10 BDFD 44146 2887 B3
10 BERA 44017 2880 C5
100 CNFL 44022 2761 A5
100 ELYR 44035 2875 B5
500 BDHT 44146 2887 C3
Colvin Rd
7600 GSML 44040 2500 E7
Colwyn Rd
3300 SRHT 44120 2627 B7
Comanche Ct
6000 PMHT 44130 2882 B2
Comanche Tr
700 MCDN 44056 3018 D5
7000 MNTR 44060 2143 A5
7000 MNTR 44094 2143 A5
7000 WLBY 44094 2143 A5
Comet Ct
8200 MNTR 44060 2144 A3
Commerce Av
4000 CLEV 44103 2625 D2
4000 CLEV 44114 2625 C2
Commerce Cir
6000 WLBY 44094 2375 A3
Commerce Ct
300 ELYR 44035 2875 A6
16500 MDBH 44130 3012 B2
16500 SGVL 44130 3012 B2
16500 SGVL 44136 3012 B2
Commerce Dr
900 GFTN 44044 3141 E4
900 GFTN 44044 3142 A4
7100 MNTR 44060 2251 B3
Commerce Pk
- BHWD 44122 2758 C2
23100 HIHL 44122 2758 C2
Commerce Pkwy
4800 BDHT 44128 2758 E6
4800 BDHT 44146 2758 E6
4800 WVHT 44128 2758 E6
19600 MDBH 44130 2880 D4
21800 SGVL 44149 3146 A3
Commerce Pkwy W
5200 BKLN 44144 2753 B7
5200 PRMA 44130 2753 B7
5200 PRMA 44144 2753 B7
Commerce Pl
100 GNVA 44041 1944 C5
Commerce Park Dr
15400 BKPK 44142 2881 C1
Commerce Park Ovl
7600 INDE 44131 2885 A3
Commercial Rd
2600 CLEV 44113 2624 E4
Commodore Cir
200 ELYR 44035 2746 D7
Commodore Ct
31700 AVLK 44012 2619 A3
Commodore Rd
1500 LNHT 44124 2499 B7
1500 LNHT 44124 2629 A1
Commodore Cove
1500 PnvT 44077 2040 E1
Commodore Cove E
3800 RMDV 44202 3021 A5
Commodore Cove W
3700 RMDV 44202 3020 E5
Commons Blvd
8800 TNBG 44087 3154 E1
N Commons Blvd
200 MAYF 44092 2500 A1
200 MAYF 44143 2500 A1
200 WBHL 44092 2500 A1
Commons Ct
10 CNFL 44022 2761 B6
Commons Ovl
16200 SGVL 44136 3012 B3
Commonwealth Av
700 AVON 44011 2617 E6
1100 MAYF 44143 2499 D6
1100 MAYF 44124 2499 D7
1100 MDHT 44143 2499 D6
Commonwealth Blvd
6600 PMHT 44130 2882 A5
Commonwealth Dr
2700 PRMA 44134 2883 C2
Community Dr
- HGVL 44022 2630 C4
10 AVLK 44012 2617 E2
10 AVLK 44012 2618 A2
10 BKVL 44141 3016 A7
10 BKVL 44141 3151 A1
5100 WLBY 44094 2250 B7
5100 WLBY 44094 2375 B1
24000 BHWD 44122 2628 D3
24000 BHWD 44124 2628 D3
24000 LNHT 44122 2628 D3
24000 LNHT 44124 2628 D3
Community Ln
10 ELYR 44035 3006 A1
Community Rd
700 SDLK 44054 2616 A4
Community College Av
2200 CLEV 44115 2625 B3
3900 CLEV 44104 2625 C4
Communitiy Ln
300 PNVL 44077 2145 D1
Co-Moor Blvd
11200 SGVL 44149 3011 D5
Compas Ln
- LORN 44052 2614 E6
Compass Ct
- AMHT 44001 2872 E4
Compass St
4600 VmnT 44089 2740 C5
Compass Cove
31600 AVLK 44012 2619 A2
Compass Point Dr
13000 NRYN 44133 3147 E4
13000 SGVL 44133 3147 E4
13000 SGVL 44136 3147 D4
Compton Rd
1400 CVHT 44118 2497 D7
1400 CVHT 44118 2627 D1
S Compton Rd
1800 CVHT 44118 2627 D2
Compton St
2100 MadT 44057 1942 B2
Comstock Cir
18600 MDBH 44130 3011 E1
Comstock Rd
5400 BDHT 44146 2887 C1
Concept Dr
16600 CLEV 44128 2757 C4
Concert Ct
10 OmsT 44138 2879 A4
Concord Av
200 ELYR 44035 2875 D6
Concord Cir
500 BERA 44017 3011 B1
3300 AVON 44011 2748 D3
9400 TNBG 44087 3019 B6
Concord Ct
6100 SLN 44139 2889 C4
8700 BbgT 44023 2891 C5
10000 PMHT 44130 2882 C6
Concord Dr
- AVLK 44012 2618 B2
- PRMA 44134 2883 B4
300 LORN 44052 2615 D4
1100 WTLK 44145 2620 E7
2000 LKWD 44107 2622 B6
3500 BHWD 44122 2758 E2
4500 FWPK 44126 2751 C4
5100 VMLN 44089 2740 E7
5100 VMLN 44089 2741 A7
5100 VmnT 44089 2740 E7
8100 MNTR 44060 2144 A3
18300 SGVL 44136 3011 E7
18300 SGVL 44136 3146 E1
Concord Ln
100 HkyT 44233 3148 B6
Concord Rd
2800 PRPK 44124 2629 D6
Concord St
- WKLF 44092 2374 C2
Concord Tr
14100 MDBH 44130 3012 C2
Concord Downs Cir
480-00 AURA 44202 3156 C3
Concord Downs Ln
483-00 AURA 44202 3156 C2
Concord Downs Pth
485-00 AURA 44202 3156 D2
Concord-Hambden Rd
11000 CcdT 44077 2254 B1
11200 CcdT 44077 2146 C7
12300 CcdT 44077 2255 B3
12700 CcdT 44024 2255 C5
12700 HmbT 44024 2255 C5
12700 HmbT 44077 2255 C5
Concord-Hambden Rd SR-608
11500 CcdT 44077 2146 D7
11500 CcdT 44077 2254 E1
12300 CcdT 44077 2255 B2
12700 CcdT 44024 2255 C5
12700 HmbT 44024 2255 C5
12700 HmbT 44077 2255 C5
Concordia Dr
20000 EUCL 44117 2498 A1
Concord Point Ct
9900 CcdT 44060 2253 C1
9900 CcdT 44077 2253 C1
Condon Ct
300 PNVL 44077 2040 B7
Conelly Blvd
7100 WNHL 44146 2886 D7
7100 WNHL 44146 3017 E1
Conestoga Tr
8000 CcdT 44060 2253 C3
Congress Dr
- PnvT 44077 2146 B3
Conley Rd
6100 CcdT 44077 2146 E4
6100 CcdT 44077 2147 A4
8900 KTLD 44094 2251 D7
Connecticut Av
200 LORN 44052 2614 E6
7600 CLEV 44105 2756 A4
Connecticut Dr
200 ELYR 44035 3006 B3
Connecticut St
10500 RMDV 44039 3020 E3
10500 RMDV 44202 3020 E3
10500 SLN 44139 3020 E3
Connecticut Wy
200 SgHT 44067 3152 E1
Connecticut Colony Cir
6600 MNTR 44060 2144 D5
Connecticut Woods Dr
1200 HDSN 44236 3154 C7
Connie Ct
300 ETLK 44095 2142 D7
Connie Dr
7000 MNTR 44060 2143 B7
7200 MNTR 44060 2251 B1
Connor Dr
900 ETLK 44095 2250 B3
Connotton Av
2900 TNBG 44087 3155 A1
Conover Ct
8100 MNTR 44060 2144 A4
8300 CLEV 44102 2623 D6
Conover Dr
25300 BYVL 44140 2620 C5
Conover Rd
4000 UNHT 44118 2628 A4
Conrad St
- AVON 44011 2747 B1
Constance Av
- HRM 44234 3161 B1
Constance Ct
7100 CLEV 44103 2495 E6
Constantine Ct
7000 MNTR 44060 2143 B7
Constitution Blvd
1200 AVON 44011 2617 E6
Consul Av
6600 CLEV 44127 2755 E1
Conte Dr
5400 GDHT 44125 2885 C1
Continental Av
11100 CLEV 44104 2626 D6
11100 CLEV 44120 2626 D6
Continental Blvd
4100 AVON 44011 2617 E6
Continental Dr
400 SgHT 44067 3017 C4
Contumacious Tr
- MPHT 44137 2886 B2
Cook Av
1100 LKWD 44107 2622 D4
Cook Av
1200 CLEV 44109 2754 D6
18000 SGVL 44136 3146 E1
18500 SGVL 44149 3146 D1
Cook Ct
100 ELYR 44035 2875 E6
Cook Ln
- CLEV 44106 2626 C1
Cook Rd
25500 ODFL 44138 2879 A5
25500 OmsT 44138 2879 A5
26900 OmsT 44138 2878 B4
27300 NRDV 44039 2878 A4
27300 NRDV 44138 2878 A4
31600 NRDV 44039 2877 E4
Cook St
13800 BURT 44021 2636 B7
Cooley Av
11700 CLEV 44111 2753 A2
13200 CLEV 44111 2752 E2
Cooley Cir
- NRDV 44035 2876 B7
Cooley Ct
28100 WTLK 44145 2749 D1
Cooley Rd
33500 ClbT 44028 3008 E5
33500 EatT 44028 3008 C5
35000 EatT 44044 3007 E5
35000 EatT 44044 3008 C5
Coolidge Ct
7600 MNTR 44060 2143 D6
Coolidge Dr
- ODFL 44138 2879 C6
27500 EUCL 44132 2374 A4
Cooper Av
4000 CLEV 44103 2625 C1
41800 CrlT 44035 3005 C5
Cooper Ct
- AbnT 44021 2893 C3
13600 GDHT 44125 2757 A5
Cooper Dr
10900 CrlT 44035 3005 C4
Cooper Ln
8400 MNTR 44060 2144 B3
Cooper Foster Park Rd
100 LORN 44052 2745 A6
100 LORN 44053 2744 A6
100 LORN 44053 2745 A6
100 ShfT 44052 2745 A6
100 ShfT 44053 2745 A6
500 AMHT 44053 2743 E6
500 LORN 44001 2743 E6
500 LORN 44001 2744 A6
500 LORN 44053 2743 E6
800 AhtT 44001 2744 B6
800 AhtT 44053 2744 B6
1100 AMHT 44001 2744 A6
1100 AMHT 44053 2744 A6
1600 VMLN 44001 2871 C1
1600 VMLN 44089 2871 A2
3000 VMLN 44089 2870 D2
48200 AMHT 44001 2742 E7
48200 AMHT 44001 2743 A7
48200 AMHT 44053 2742 E7
48400 AMHT 44001 2871 D1
48400 AMHT 44053 2871 D1
48400 LORN 44001 2871 D1
48400 LORN 44053 2871 D1
48500 BhmT 44001 2742 C7
48500 BhmT 44001 2871 D1
48500 BhmT 44053 2871 E1
48500 BhmT 44089 2742 C7
48500 VMLN 44089 2742 C7
48500 VMLN 44089 2742 C7
Cooper Foster Park Rd E
100 LORN 44052 2745 A6
100 LORN 44053 2745 A6
100 ShfT 44052 2745 A6
100 ShfT 44053 2745 A6
200 EyrT 44035 2745 A6
200 EyrT 44052 2745 A6
200 EyrT 44053 2745 A6
Cooper Foster Park Rd W
- BhmT 44001 2742 C7
- BhmT 44089 2742 C7
- VMLN 44001 2742 C7
- VMLN 44089 2742 C7
Coopers Run
1000 AMHT 44001 2872 B3
11500 SGVL 44149 3010 E5
11600 SGVL 44149 3011 A5
Cooper Turn
23800 ODFL 44138 3010 D2
Cope Dr
7600 BbgT 44023 2890 C6
Copley Av
6500 SLN 44139 2889 A6
Copopa Tr
24800 ClbT 44028 3010 B5
Copperfield Ct
200 PnvT 44077 2040 E6
Copperleaf Dr
- PnvT 44077 2040 E2
- PnvT 44077 2041 A2
10800 HmbT 44024 2380 D7
10800 HmbT 44024 2505 D1
Coral Av
- CLEV 44127 2756 A1
Coral Pl
- CVHT 44118 2497 E7
Coralberry Ln
700 MDSN 44057 1942 B7
Coral Gables Dr
3800 PRMA 44134 3014 B2
Corban Dr
17200 BbgT 44023 2890 B3
Corbetts Ln
10200 TNBG 44087 3019 E4
Corbin Dr
5000 BDHT 44128 2758 C7
5000 WVHT 44128 2758 C7
Corbus Rd
11200 CLEV 44108 2496 D3
Corby Rd
13500 CLEV 44120 2627 A6
Cordova Av
1400 LKWD 44107 2622 B5
Cordova Rd
1100 MDHT 44124 2500 A6
Corduroy Rd
4600 MNTR 44060 2038 E6
Corinth Ct
12200 SGVL 44149 3011 D6
Corkhill Rd
500 BDFD 44146 2886 B4

Cleveland Street Index

STREET
Block City ZIP Map# Grid

Corkhill Rd
600 MPHT 44137 2886 C4
Corktree Dr
10 OmsT 44138 2879 B4
Corkwood Dr
4900 NRYN 44133 3014 B4
Corlett Av
11400 CLEV 44105 2756 D2
13000 CLEV 44120 2756 E2
Corliss Rd
4800 LNHT 44124 2498 E5
Cormere Av
13300 CLEV 44120 2626 D4
13300 CLEV 44120 2627 A5
Cornado Av
12500 CLEV 44108 2496 E4
Cornelia Av
7400 CLEV 44103 2496 A7
Cornelia Dr
10 AQLA 44024 2505 C4
10 ClrT 44024 2505 C4
Cornell Av
200 AMHT 44001 2872 D1
500 ELYR 44035 2875 C7
5200 NRDV 44039 2748 C7
5200 NRDV 44039 2877 C2
Cornell Ct
900 PNVL 44077 2145 E3
Cornell Dr
400 BWHT 44147 3150 A5
Cornell Ln
7000 MNTR 44060 2251 B2
Cornell Pl
600 LORN 44052 2614 D6
Cornell Rd
2000 CLEV 44106 2626 D2
Cornerstone
2400 WTLK 44145 2750 D2
Cornflower Ln
700 MDSN 44057 1942 B7
Corning Av
1700 CLEV 44109 2754 D1
Corning Dr
200 BTNH 44108 2496 C3
Cornwall Av
5300 LNHT 44124 2629 B2
Cornwall Ct
8500 MNTR 44060 2144 B2
Cornwall Rd
200 RKRV 44116 2621 D5
18000 CLEV 44119 2372 E4
18000 EUCL 44119 2372 E4
Cornwell Dr
23700 WTLK 44145 2750 E1
Coronada Dr
\- MONT 44060 2037 E7
\- MONT 44060 2143 E1
5300 MONT 44060 2038 A7
5400 MNTR 44060 2144 A1
5400 MONT 44060 2144 A1
Coronado Cir
600 AVLK 44012 2618 E5
Coronado Ct
100 ELYR 44035 2875 C3
Coronet Dr
20700 SGVL 44149 3011 B6
Corporate Blvd
7300 MNTR 44060 2143 D7
7300 MNTR 44060 2251 D1
Corporate Cir
800 WTLK 44145 2749 C1
8000 NRYN 44130 3013 C2
8000 NRYN 44133 3013 C2
8000 PRMA 44130 3013 C2
9600 VLVW 44125 2885 B3
Corporate Dr
12600 PRMA 44130 2881 E1
12600 PRMA 44130 2882 A1
12900 BKPK 44130 2881 E1
12900 BKPK 44142 2881 E1
Corporate Wy
800 WTLK 44145 2620 D6
Corporate Center Dr W
10 BWHT 44147 3150 A3
Corporate Park Dr
8200 MCDN 44056 3154 B3
8200 TwbT 44087 3154 B3
Corral Cir
8300 RslT 44072 2762 A1
Corridon Av
14100 MPHT 44137 2886 A1
Corsica Av
15600 CLEV 44110 2372 C6
Cortina Cir
39300 SLN 44139 2889 E5
Cortland Cir
10 AMHT 44001 2872 B1
10 GNVA 44041 1944 C7
Cortland Dr
\- AVLK 44012 2618 A5
Cortland Ln
1700 BWHT 44147 3149 D5
Cortland Wy
14700 SGVL 44149 3146 C1
Cortland Reserve Dr
5300 NRYN 44133 3149 A5
Corwin Dr
10 PNVL 44077 2145 D3
Corwin Rd
4000 CVHT 44121 2628 A1
4000 SELD 44121 2628 A1
Cory Av
5000 NPRY 44081 1941 A4
7900 CLEV 44103 2626 A1
Cory Ln
11000 NbyT 44065 2764 A3
Corydon Ct
\- WLBY 44094 2251 A5
Corydon Rd
2700 CVHT 44106 2627 A3
2700 CVHT 44118 2627 B3
Cotes Av
11300 CLEV 44105 2756 D4
Cothelstone Ln
15500 RslT 44022 2761 D4
Cotswold Ln
10 MDHL 44022 2760 B2
Cotswold Mnr
\- WTLK 44145 2620 D7
\- WTLK 44145 2750 C1
Cottage Ct
10 PnvT 44077 2040 C2
Cottage Dr
6800 NRDV 44039 2876 E3
30500 WTLK 44145 2749 B3
E Cottage St
10 CNFL 44022 2761 A5
W Cottage St
10 CNFL 44022 2760 E6
10 CNFL 44022 2761 A6
Cottage Tr
23600 ODFL 44138 2879 D7
Cottage Gate
\- AVON 44011 2748 D4
Cottage Grove Dr
1900 CVHT 44118 2627 B3
Cottage Hill Ln
\- CdnT 44024 2378 C6
Cottesmore Ln
7100 SLN 44139 3020 A1
Cottesmore Pl
33200 SLN 44139 3019 E1
33200 SLN 44139 3020 A1
Cottesworth Ln
1800 GSML 44040 2630 B2
Cottingham Dr
2100 LNHT 44124 2629 B3
Cotton Tail Ct
200 AhtT 44001 2873 B2
Cottontail Ct
\- PnvT 44077 2041 C7
Cottonwood Ct
300 AVLK 44012 2618 C3
800 ETLK 44095 2250 B3
9900 CcdT 44060 2253 B3
Cottonwood Dr
5700 LORN 44053 2744 E6
21600 RKRV 44116 2621 A7
21600 RKRV 44116 2751 B1
Cottonwood Ln
8800 PRMA 44129 2882 D7
8800 PRMA 44130 2882 D7
12700 NRYN 44133 3147 E4
Cottonwood Ovl
15500 MDBH 44130 2881 C5
Cottonwood Tr
19500 SGVL 44136 3147 A5
19700 BNWK 44136 3147 A5
19700 BNWK 44212 3147 A5
27200 NOSD 44070 2749 E5
27200 NOSD 44070 2750 A5
Cottrell Rd
8500 CsTp 44026 2632 B1
Coudry St
9000 KTLD 44094 2251 D7
Coulby Ct
28800 WKLF 44092 2374 B4
Coulter Av
22300 EUCL 44117 2373 B7
Council Bluff Dr
10100 SGVL 44136 3012 B4
Country Ct
7800 MNTR 44060 2252 E3
Country Ln
10 PnvT 44077 2040 D7
10 PnvT 44077 2146 D1
10 PRPK 44124 2629 C5
300 RDHT 44143 2498 D1
4600 WVHT 44022 2759 A5
4600 WVHT 44128 2758 E6
4600 WVHT 44128 2759 A5
7000 BbgT 44022 2890 A2
7000 BbgT 44023 2890 D3
7000 BTVL 44022 2890 A2
Country Pl
\- EatT 44044 3142 B3
Country Wk
400 AMHT 44001 2872 B3
Country Wy
21600 SGVL 44149 3011 A6
Country Club
\- AVON 44011 2747 B1
Country Club Blvd
2600 RKRV 44116 2621 B7
24400 NOSD 44070 2750 A7
Country Club Cir
\- TNBG 44087 3020 C5
Country Club Dr
2000 WKLF 44092 2374 E3
32000 AVLK 44012 2618 C5
Country Club Ln
500 AURA 44202 3156 C3
2900 TNBG 44087 3020 B5
Country Meadow Wy
38300 NRDV 44039 2747 B7
Country Meadows Ln
22200 ClbT 44028 3010 E3
22200 ClbT 44149 3010 E3
22200 SGVL 44149 3010 E3
Country Oaks Tr
12000 MsnT 44024 2634 E3
12000 MsnT 44024 2635 A3
Country River Ln
14000 NbyT 44065 2633 D6
Country Scene Ln
9600 CcdT 44060 2145 B7
9800 CcdT 44077 2145 C7
Countryside Dr
10 BWHT 44147 3014 D5
10 SRSL 44022 2761 D6
8500 SgHT 44067 3017 D5
Countryside Rd
4800 LNHT 44124 2498 D7
4800 LNHT 44124 2628 E1
Countryview Dr
8400 BWHT 44147 3014 D5
Country View Ln
33700 MDHL 44022 2760 A7
33700 SLN 44022 2760 A7
33700 SLN 44139 2760 A7
Country View Pkwy
\- NCtT 44067 3153 E5
Countryview Wy
11000 CrlT 44035 3005 C5
Countrywood Tr
\- AURA 44202 3021 C7
500 AURA 44202 3156 C1
County Line Rd
200 CsTp 44026 2501 A7
200 CsTp 44040 2501 A1
200 GSML 44040 2501 A7
800 GnvT 44041 1844 B7
800 GnvT 44057 1844 B7
800 MadT 44057 1844 B7
1200 GnvT 44041 1943 B7
1200 GnvT 44057 1943 B7
1200 MadT 44057 1943 B4
1400 CsTp 44026 2631 B4
1400 GSML 44040 2631 B4
1900 HGVL 44040 2631 A3
1900 RslT 44026 2631 A3
2900 HpfT 44041 1943 B6
2900 HpfT 44057 1943 B6
11100 CsTp 44094 2501 A1
11100 GSML 44094 2501 A1
11100 KTLD 44094 2501 A1
11100 WBHL 44094 2501 A1
13400 HGVL 44022 2631 B7
13400 RslT 44022 2631 B7
13500 HGVL 44072 2631 B4
13500 RslT 44072 2631 B7
14500 HGVL 44022 2761 A1
14500 RslT 44022 2761 A1
14500 RslT 44072 2761 A1
14900 HGVL 44072 2761 A2
Courseview Dr
\- AVON 44011 2747 A3
Court St
100 CRDN 44024 2379 E6
100 CRDN 44024 2380 A6
100 ELYR 44035 2875 A7
Courtland Av
13400 CLEV 44111 2752 E3
14300 CLEV 44135 2752 D3
Courtland Blvd
100 ETLK 44095 2142 D5
2600 SRHT 44118 2627 E6
2600 SRHT 44122 2627 E7
Courtland Ct
5400 CLEV 44102 2624 A5
Courtland Dr
8600 SGVL 44149 3011 B3
38400 WLBY 44094 2251 A1
Courtland Mdws
26900 WTLK 44145 2750 A4
Courtland Ovl
2600 SRHT 44118 2627 E5
3700 BNWK 44212 3147 A7
Courtland Rd
3400 PRPK 44122 2759 B1
Courtland St
10 ELYR 44035 2874 D4
200 FTHR 44077 2039 C4
200 PNVL 44077 2040 A7
Courtney Ct
11100 CdnT 44024 2379 B1
Courtney Ln
\- KTLD 44094 2377 B4
Courtney Tr
2500 HGVL 44022 2630 E3
Courtyard Dr
\- LORN 44053 2743 D3
6600 MadT 44057 1942 B2
Coutant Av
1400 LKWD 44107 2623 B6
Cove Av
100 AVLK 44012 2618 E2
1000 LKWD 44107 2623 A4
Cove Ct
10 AbnT 44023 2892 A4
800 ETLK 44095 2250 C3
Cove Dr
9500 NRYN 44133 3013 B5
Cove Beach Av
\- SFLD 44054 2616 E2
200 SDLK 44054 2616 E2
Coveland Dr
10 AVLK 44012 2488 C7
10 LrnC 44012 2488 C7
Coventry Ct
10 OmsT 44138 2879 B3
100 AbnT 44023 2892 B4
32700 AVLK 44012 2618 A2
Coventry Dr
10 PnvT 44077 2145 D4
2000 PRMA 44134 2883 C7
9000 NHFD 44067 3018 B4
29300 WTLK 44145 2749 C3
Coventry Ln
300 WLBY 44094 2250 A7
Coventry Pl
600 AMHT 44001 2872 D3
Coventry Rd
\- SRHT 44106 2627 A4
\- SRHT 44118 2627 A4
1500 CVHT 44112 2627 A1
1500 CVHT 44118 2627 A3
1500 ECLE 44112 2497 A7
1500 ECLE 44112 2627 A1
1500 ECLE 44118 2497 A7
1500 ECLE 44118 2627 A1
1600 CVHT 44106 2627 A3
2500 SRHT 44120 2627 A5
Coverley Rd
800 WTLK 44145 2621 A6
Covert Av
7100 CLEV 44105 2755 E3
Covewood Ct
9900 BKVL 44141 3151 D4
Covington Av
8100 PRMA 44129 2882 D4
Covington Ct
\- BWHT 44147 3149 C5
\- CcdT 44077 2254 B2
Covington Ln
\- AbnT 44023 2892 B3
10300 TNBG 44087 3020 C4
Covington Rd
3700 CVHT 44121 2497 E5
3700 SELD 44121 2497 E5
3800 SELD 44121 2498 A5
Cowan Av
5100 CLEV 44127 2625 D7
Cowles Av
10 BDFD 44146 2887 A4
Cowles Dr
29100 BYVL 44140 2619 D4
Cowley Rd
12000 EatT 44028 3008 D7
12000 EatT 44028 3143 D5
13600 GftT 44028 3143 D6
14500 GftT 44044 3143 D6
Cox Dr
500 GNVA 44041 1944 B6
Coy Ln
500 CNFL 44022 2761 A4
500 RslT 44022 2761 A4
Crabapple Ct
10900 SGVL 44136 3012 D5
Crab Apple Ln
1400 AVON 44011 2617 D6
Crabapple Ln
10 OmsT 44138 2879 B4
Crabtree Ln
3100 HGVL 44022 2630 B7
6400 BKVL 44141 3016 B5
31400 SLN 44139 2759 D7
Crackle Rd
200 AURA 44202 3022 D3
200 BbgT 44023 3022 D3
500 AURA 44023 3022 D3
800 AbnT 44023 3022 E3
800 AbnT 44023 3023 A4
800 ManT 44023 3022 E3
800 ManT 44023 3023 A4
800 ManT 44202 3022 E3
800 ManT 44202 3023 A4
900 AbnT 44202 3023 B3
900 AbnT 44255 3023 B3
900 ManT 44255 3023 B3
Craemer Dr
\- SLN 44139 2889 A6
Crafton Rd
3000 BHWD 44122 2628 E6
Craig Dr
11300 SGVL 44149 3011 B5
E Craig Dr
8500 BbgT 44023 2891 B1
W Craig Dr
8300 BbgT 44023 2891 A1
Craig Ln
\- AhtT 44001 2872 E6
8100 BWHT 44147 3015 C4
Craigleigh Dr
7500 PRMA 44129 3013 D2
7500 PRMA 44134 3013 E2
Craigmere Dr
7200 MDBH 44130 2881 A7
16200 MDBH 44130 3012 A1
Crampton Dr
12000 NbyT 44021 2764 E4
Cranage Rd
26100 ODFL 44138 2879 A5
26100 OmsT 44138 2879 A5
Cranberry Ct
700 AVLK 44012 2618 A5
Cranberry Dr
\- LORN 44053 2743 E5
Cranberry Ln
3400 LORN 44053 2743 E5
7700 MNTR 44060 2143 D6
Cranberry Rdg
8700 BWHT 44147 3015 C6
Cranberry Tr
\- AURA 44202 3021 C5
100 SgHT 44067 3152 D1
Cranberry Ridge Ln
18200 BbgT 44023 2890 E7
Cranbrook Cir
7700 MDBH 44130 3012 D2
Cranbrook Dr
800 HDHT 44143 2499 C6
1000 MDHT 44124 2499 C6
1000 MDHT 44143 2499 C6
6800 BKVL 44141 3151 A1
8900 NHFD 44067 3018 B5
Cranby Rd
3400 BHWD 44122 2758 B1
Crane Av
8800 CLEV 44105 2756 B1
Crane Centre Dr
2500 STBR 44241 3156 E6
2500 STBR 44241 3157 A6
Crane Creek Pkwy
2500 BKVL 44141 3150 D2
Craneing Rd
1300 WKLF 44092 2374 A3
Cranfield Rd
22900 BDHT 44146 2887 C1
Cranford Av
1100 LKWD 44107 2622 C4
Cranleigh Ct
400 RDHT 44143 2499 A3
Cranlyn Ct
400 BNWK 44212 3146 E7
Cranlyn Rd
2600 BHWD 44122 2628 C6
2600 SRHT 44118 2628 C6
2600 SRHT 44122 2628 C6
Cranlyn Ter
36700 AVON 44011 2747 E4
Cranover Rd
1300 LNHT 44124 2498 E7
Cranston Cir
500 BERA 44017 3010 E1
Cranston Ct
7500 NRYN 44133 3013 D7
Cranston Dr
300 BERA 44017 2879 E7
300 BERA 44017 3010 E1
Cranston Rd
2100 UNHT 44118 2627 E3
Cranwood Av
14000 CLEV 44128 2757 A4
14000 GDHT 44105 2757 A4
14000 GDHT 44128 2757 A4
Cranwood Dr
8300 CsTp 44026 2502 A2
13100 GDHT 44105 2756 E4
13100 GDHT 44105 2757 A4
Cranwood Pkwy
4300 WVHT 44128 2757 E4
Cranwood Park Blvd
13100 GDHT 44125 2756 E5
13100 GDHT 44125 2757 A5
14100 GDHT 44128 2757 A5
Crary Ln
10400 KTLD 44094 2377 C6
Craven Av
11600 CLEV 44105 2756 D1
Crawford Ct
700 CLEV 44113 2624 E5
8900 CLEV 44106 2626 B1
Crawford Rd
1400 CLEV 44106 2626 B1
1700 CLEV 44103 2626 A2
Crayton Av
4500 CLEV 44104 2625 C5
4500 CLEV 44115 2625 C5
Creawood Dr
7900 CcdT 44077 2254 A3
Creawood Forest
\- KTLD 44094 2376 D3
9400 WTHL 44094 2376 D2
E Creek Ct
3200 AVON 44011 2748 B3
W Creek Ct
3200 AVON 44011 2748 B3
N Creek Dr
100 PnvT 44077 2041 A3
Creek Ln
1000 RKRV 44116 2621 B6
W Creek Rd
5000 INDE 44131 2884 C3
Creek Rdg
\- RKRV 44116 2621 B6
Creek Bend Ct
22400 SGVL 44149 3011 A4
Creekfield Ct
100 ELYR 44035 2875 A1
Creekhaven Dr
6100 PMHT 44130 2882 B3
Creek Moss Ln
10700 SGVL 44149 3011 A4
Creek Run Dr
5500 NRYN 44133 3014 A6
Creekside Cir
17200 NRYN 44133 3149 A3
Creekside Dr
10 GDHT 44137 2886 A4
300 AVLK 44012 2618 D3
300 OBLN 44074 3139 A1
681-00 AURA 44202 3156 C3
2600 TNBG 44087 3155 A2
2900 WTLK 44145 2750 A3
6700 MadT 44057 1942 B2
8500 SgHT 44067 3018 A5
17600 AbnT 44023 2892 A5
21100 SGVL 44149 3011 B4
31400 PRPK 44124 2629 E7
31400 PRPK 44124 2630 A7
31400 PRPK 44124 2759 D1
Creekside Ln
5600 NRDV 44039 2877 E2
Creekside Ter
8100 BWHT 44147 3015 B4
Creekside Tr
10 OmsT 44138 2879 B4
6300 SLN 44139 2889 C5
Creek Stone Cir
10700 SGVL 44149 3011 A4
Creekview Cir
10 MDHL 44022 2760 A2
Creek View Dr
900 AURA 44202 3022 D4
Creekview Dr
600 ETLK 44095 2250 D1
1000 CLEV 44119 2372 D6
4000 MDSN 44057 1941 E6
Creekview Ln
2700 AVON 44011 2747 E3
Creek View Tr
\- BbgT 44023 2890 C4
Creekwood Dr
7300 NRYN 44133 3013 D7
8900 BWHT 44147 3015 A6
9000 MNTR 44060 2252 D1
Creekwood Ln
1100 WTLK 44145 2619 E6
6800 MAYF 44143 2500 B3
15600 SGVL 44136 3147 B2
Crehore Ct
10 ELYR 44035 2875 A6
Crehore St
1400 LORN 44052 2615 B6
Creighton Dr
17000 AbnT 44023 2892 E3
Crennell Av
12300 CLEV 44105 2756 E3
13100 CLEV 44105 2757 A3
13600 CLEV 44128 2757 A3
Crenshaw Dr
6600 PMHT 44130 2882 B5
Crescent Av
4500 CLEV 44102 2624 B4
4500 CLEV 44113 2624 B4
Crescent Blvd
9100 BWHT 44147 3014 E7
Crescent Dr
300 BERA 44017 2880 A7
500 WLWK 44095 2249 D6
1100 PNVL 44077 2145 D3
2100 EUCL 44117 2498 A2
Crescent Rd
11000 CLEV 44111 2753 B2
Cress Rd
3700 CLEV 44111 2753 B2
Cressmont Av
5000 SLN 44139 2759 D7
Cresswell Av
10 BDFD 44137 2886 D2
10 BDFD 44146 2886 D2
10 MPHT 44137 2886 D2
Crest Av
12300 GDHT 44125 2756 D6
Crest Dr
\- AhtT 44001 2872 A3
4000 CLEV 44109 2754 E4
Crest Ln
17700 LKWD 44107 2622 A5
Crest Rd
1400 CVHT 44118 2497 E7
1400 CVHT 44118 2627 E1
1400 CVHT 44121 2497 E7
1400 CVHT 44121 2627 E1
Cresthaven Dr
28300 WLWK 44095 2249 B6
Cresthill Dr
7800 SVHL 44131 2884 B7
7800 SVHL 44131 3015 B1
Crestland Rd
17400 CLEV 44119 2372 D4
Crestlane Dr
42700 EyrT 44035 2874 B2
Crestline Av
700 AMHT 44001 2872 B1
1300 CLEV 44109 2754 E4
Crestline Dr
9100 MCDN 44056 3019 A7
Creston Av
1700 CLEV 44109 2754 D4
Crestridge Dr
10000 CdnT 44024 2379 E4
21800 BKPK 44142 2880 A3
Crestview Dr
100 ELYR 44035 2875 C1
2500 BNWK 44212 3147 E6
2500 BNWK 44233 3147 E6
2500 HkyT 44233 3147 E6
6900 BKVL 44141 3151 A1
8700 MCDN 44056 3018 A7
14300 RslT 44072 2632 B7
30100 BYVL 44140 2619 B5
Crestway Dr
13300 BKPK 44142 2881 E2
Crestway Ovl
200 BNWK 44212 3147 A7
Crestwood Av
4800 WLBY 44094 2250 E7
10300 CLEV 44104 2626 C5
Crestwood Dr
10 PnvT 44077 2041 B5
100 AVLK 44012 2617 E2
2500 PryT 44077 2041 B5
4600 INDE 44131 2884 C7
4600 INDE 44131 3015 C1
9700 TNBG 44087 3019 C4
10700 KTLD 44094 2376 E7
11800 NbyT 44065 2764 E1
14900 MDFD 44062 2767 B2
14900 MdfT 44062 2767 B2
Crestwood Ln
6500 OmsT 44138 2878 E3
7500 NCtT 44067 3153 A2
7600 NCtT 44067 3152 E2
Crestwood Rd
1500 MDHT 44124 2629 D1
9100 PMHT 44130 2882 C4
Crete Av
3700 CLEV 44105 2755 C2
3700 NBGH 44105 2755 C2
Cricket Ln
2800 WBHL 44092 2374 C6
4200 WVHT 44128 2758 A4
8200 SgHT 44067 3017 E6
21900 SGVL 44149 3011 A3
Crickett Ln
7200 SVHL 44131 2884 B7
7400 SVHL 44131 3015 B1
16600 BKPK 44142 2881 B2
Crickett Rd
400 CRDN 44024 2380 A7
Crile Rd
7600 CcdT 44077 2254 B3
Crimson Ct
7600 MNTR 44060 2252 E2
Crimson Dr
2400 WTLK 44145 2749 C2
Crinkleroot Clearing
8300 BKVL 44141 3016 D5
Crisfield Ct
\- RMDV 44087 3020 D4
Crispus Attucks Pl
\- HIHL 44128 2758 C4
Crocker Blvd
400 CRDN 44024 2380 A7
Crocker Rd
600 WTLK 44145 2619 C7
2000 WTLK 44145 2749 C5
6700 ClbT 44028 3144 E5
6700 ClbT 44280 3144 D5
6700 LvpT 44280 3144 D5
7500 ClbT 44028 3143 D5
7500 ClbT 44280 3143 D5
7500 EatT 44028 3143 D5
7500 GftT 44028 3143 D5
7500 LvpT 44028 3143 D5
7500 LvpT 44280 3143 D5
Crocker St
10 BERA 44017 2880 B7
200 AMHT 44001 2872 C2
Crocker Park Blvd
100 WTLK 44145 2749 B1
Crocker's Lndg
26000 ClbT 44028 3144 B4
Crofoot Av
8100 CLEV 44105 2756 A1
Crofton Av
5000 ORNG 44022 2759 D7
5000 SLN 44022 2759 D7
5000 SLN 44139 2759 D7
5100 SLN 44139 2888 D1
Crofton Rd
11600 GDHT 44125 2885 D2
Cromwell Av
100 WLBY 44094 2250 A7
11600 CLEV 44120 2626 D5
21300 FWPK 44126 2751 B4
Cromwell Dr
100 GNVA 44041 1944 A5
2800 LORN 44052 2615 C7
7300 SLN 44139 3019 E2
33100 SLN 44139 3020 A1
Crook St
1000 GFTN 44044 3142 A6
37400 GftT 44044 3142 B6
38000 GftT 44044 3141 D7
38200 LrgT 44044 3141 E6
38600 LrgT 44050 3141 D6
Crooked Creek Ln
8900 BWHT 44147 3015 B6
Crooked Stick Dr
\- CcdT 44077 2253 E4
Crosby St
10 BERA 44017 2880 B7
Cross Av
\- ClbT 44028 3010 D3
Cross St
\- BDFD 44146 2887 A6
\- ELYR 44035 2875 B6
\- NRDV 44039 2877 C1
200 BERA 44017 2880 A5
7400 MNTR 44060 2252 D1
9000 TNBG 44087 3155 A1
N Cross Tr
19500 SGVL 44136 3147 C5
S Cross Tr
19700 SGVL 44136 3147 C5
Crossbeam Ln
21800 RKRV 44116 2751 B2
Crossbow Ct
6600 NRYN 44133 3014 A5
Crossbrook Av
38300 WLBY 44094 2142 E5
38400 WLBY 44094 2143 A5
Crossbrook Dr
300 BERA 44017 2879 E7
300 BERA 44017 3010 E1
300 BERA 44138 2879 E7
300 ODFL 44138 2879 E7
Crossburn Av
12400 CLEV 44135 2753 A6
13000 CLEV 44135 2752 E6
Cross Creek Dr
\- WLBY 44094 2142 E5
7000 CcdT 44060 2145 B7
Crosscreek Dr
\- AVON 44011 2747 B2
E Cross Creek Dr
\- WLBY 44094 2142 E5
Cross Creek Ln
600 AURA 44202 3156 C3
14500 NRYN 44133 3148 E1
Cross Creek Ovl
600 AURA 44202 3156 C3
19500 SGVL 44136 3147 B5
Cross Creek Pkwy
14800 NbyT 44065 2763 D2
Cross Creek Tr
6500 BKVL 44141 3150 D4
W Cross Creek Tr
7000 BKVL 44141 3150 D3
Crosse Av
400 AMHT 44001 2872 D2
Crosse Rd
100 AMHT 44001 2872 A2
6700 AMHT 44001 2742 E7
6700 AMHT 44001 2871 E1
6700 AMHT 44053 2742 E7
Crossfield Av
7300 MNTR 44060 2251 C4
Crossings Dr
10500 RMDV 44202 3020 E3
Crossings Pkwy
1300 WTLK 44145 2619 B7
Crossings Tr
4500 LORN 44053 2743 E4
Crossings Wy
500 AVLK 44012 2617 D3
Crossline Dr
7600 PRMA 44134 3014 A1
Crossover Rd
\- RDHT 44143 2498 E2
Crossroads Dr
\- CcdT 44077 2255 A4
Crosstie Tr
25000 ClbT 44028 3010 C3
Crosstree Ln
\- VMLN 44089 2742 B5
Crossview Rd
5900 SVHL 44131 2884 B5
N Crossview Rd
5700 BNHT 44131 2884 B2
5700 SVHL 44131 2884 B2
Crosswinds Ln
7300 BKVL 44141 3151 A2
Crosswood Dr
26600 ODFL 44138 3010 A1
Croton Av
3400 CLEV 44115 2625 B4
Croton Dr
6100 NOSD 44070 2879 A2
Crow Dr
8500 MCDN 44056 3018 D7
8500 MCDN 44056 3153 D1
Crow Tr
900 MCDN 44056 3018 D6
Crowell Av
7500 CLEV 44104 2626 A5
N Crowell Av
10 GNVA 44041 1944 D3
S Crowell Av
10 GNVA 44041 1944 D3
Crown Av
1400 CLEV 44113 2624 E5
Crown Ct
5600 WLBY 44094 2375 A2
7400 MNTR 44060 2251 C1
Crown Colony Dr
33700 AVON 44011 2748 C6
Crownhill Av
100 AMHT 44001 2872 D2
Crown Point Dr
10 GNVA 44041 1944 C7
Crown Point Pkwy
14100 SGVL 44136 3147 C5
Crown Pointe
16400 BbgT 44023 2762 A7
Crows Hollow Dr
13000 MsnT 44024 2634 E3
Crows Nest Cove
9900 RMDV 44202 3020 E5
Croyden Av
\- CLEV 44110 2372 C5
\- CLEV 44119 2372 C5
Croyden Rd
10 CLEV 44110 2372 C5
1000 HDHT 44143 2499 B7
1000 LNHT 44124 2499 B7
1000 LNHT 44143 2499 B7
Croydon Rd
2200 TNBG 44087 3019 E5
Crudele Dr
8100 GDHT 44125 2756 A6
Crumb Av
7900 CLEV 44103 2496 A6
Cryogenic Rd
\- BKPK 44142 2880 A1
Crystal Av
20100 EUCL 44119 2373 A3
20100 EUCL 44123 2373 A3
Crystal Ct
10 BNWK 44212 3147 A6
Crystal Ln
10 AURA 44202 3021 D7
Crystal Tr
9900 AbnT 44023 3023 A2
Crystal Creek Dr
6900 BKVL 44141 3016 D6
8100 NRYN 44133 3012 E3
14000 SGVL 44149 3011 D7
14000 SGVL 44149 3146 C1
Crystal Creek Rd
8100 SgHT 44067 3017 D6
Crystal Lakes Dr
18200 NRYN 44133 3148 B5
Crystal Shores East
\- VMLN 44089 2741 A4
Crystal Springs Dr
10200 NRYN 44133 3148 B4
Crystalwood Dr
2500 BWHT 44147 3014 C5
Cudell Av
9800 CLEV 44102 2623 C6
Cullen Dr
3800 CLEV 44105 2755 C2
Culver Blvd
7000 MNTR 44060 2143 B7
7000 MNTR 44094 2143 B7
7000 WLBY 44094 2143 B7
Cumberland Av
10 CLEV 44110 2372 C5
8900 CLEV 44104 2626 B5

STREET
Block City ZIP Map# Grid

Cumberland Ct
100 ELYR 44035 3006 D1
6100 MNTR 44060 2144 A3
9400 CLEV 44104 2626 B5
Cumberland Dr
5500 GDHT 44125 2885 D1
6200 MNTR 44060 2144 A4
Cumberland Rd
1600 CVHT 44118 2627 C1
Cumberland Tr
9700 AbnT 44023 2892 A1
Cumberworth Dr
- SGVL 44136 3012 C3
Cumings Blvd
1300 MadT 44057 1843 C6
Cumings Rd
100 PNVL 44077 2146 C2
200 PnvT 44077 2146 C2
Cummings
- SLN 44139 2889 D6
Cummings Av
10 GNVA 44041 1944 C4
Cummings Rd
200 VMLN 44089 2741 D4
3400 CVHT 44118 2627 D2
Cunningham Rd
7500 GnvT 44041 1943 A1
7500 GnvT 44057 1943 A1
7500 MadT 44057 1942 E1
7500 MadT 44057 1943 A1
Curberry Dr
7700 MNTR 44060 2253 A2
Curran Av
10100 CLEV 44102 2753 C2
10100 CLEV 44111 2753 C2
Currier Dr
16300 SGVL 44136 3147 A5
Curry Cir
7200 HDSN 44236 3154 A7
Curry Dr
1500 LNHT 44124 2629 A1
Curry Ln
1700 TwbT 44087 3154 D5
17000 AbnT 44023 2892 E3
Curtis Blvd
32900 ETLK 44095 2249 E6
32900 WLWK 44095 2249 E6
33600 ETLK 44095 2250 A6
Curtis Dr
100 AVLK 44012 2617 D2
23700 NOSD 44070 2750 D5
Curtiss Ct
5900 CLEV 44103 2625 D2
6400 MNTR 44060 2144 A4
Curtiss Wright Pkwy
26000 RDHT 44143 2498 E1
26000 RDHT 44143 2499 A1
26300 HDHT 44143 2499 A1
26500 HDHT 44092 2374 A7
26500 HDHT 44143 2374 A7
26500 WBHL 44092 2374 A7
Cushing Ln
4400 RDHT 44143 2498 C3
Cutts Rd
9700 HmbT 44024 2380 D4
Cutty Sark Dr
9800 CdnT 44024 2378 B6
Cuyahoga Blvd
- AQLA 44024 2505 D4
- ClrT 44024 2505 D5
Cuyahoga Tr
13500 RslT 44072 2632 D4
Cyclone Dr
19300 CLEV 44135 2751 E5
Cygnet Ct
14000 NRYN 44133 3149 A1
Cynthia Ct
500 RDHT 44143 2498 E4
Cynthia Dr
- BKPK 44142 2881 A2
300 CRDN 44024 2380 B7
9900 TNBG 44087 3019 E5
Cypress E
1600 AVON 44011 2617 D7
Cypress W
- AVON 44011 2617 C7
Cypress Av
- NRDV 44039 2877 E3
3500 CLEV 44109 2754 C5
3900 CLEV 44144 2754 C5
16000 SGVL 44136 3147 A3
Cypress Blvd
10 MadT 44057 1941 B6
Cypress Cir
3400 WTLK 44145 2749 E4
8900 NRYN 44133 3013 A3
9800 CcdT 44060 2253 B3
Cypress St
10 OBLN 44074 3138 B2
Cypress Point Dr
2300 HDSN 44236 3155 B7
Cyprus Dr
6400 NOSD 44070 2878 D3
6700 OmsT 44070 2878 D3
6700 OmsT 44138 2878 D3
Cyprus Ln
9500 ODFL 44138 3010 A1
Cyrano Ct
4100 CLEV 44113 2624 B5
Cyril Av
4100 CLEV 44109 2624 B7
Cyrus Ln
8100 SgHT 44067 3017 D5
Czar Av
4600 CLEV 44127 2625 C7

D

D Dr
- LORN 44052 2744 E4
D St
1400 LORN 44052 2615 A5
Dade Ln
500 RDHT 44143 2498 C4
Dahlia Dr
7300 MONT 44060 2143 C3
Daisy Av
200 BERA 44017 2880 C6
2500 CLEV 44109 2754 C1
6600 INDE 44131 2884 D4
6800 BKVL 44141 3016 A7
Daisy Blvd
6000 INDE 44131 2884 D4
Daisy Ct
9500 MNTR 44060 2145 A5
Daisy Ln
10 BbgT 44022 2761 C7
10 BbgT 44023 2761 C7
10 PRPK 44124 2759 E1
10 SRSL 44022 2761 C7
5700 WLBY 44094 2375 A2
33900 NRDV 44039 2877 C2
Daisy St
400 BDFD 44146 2886 D4
Daisy Hill Ct
- CcdT 44077 2253 D4
Daisy's Wood Ln
7300 GSML 44040 2630 C2
Dakota Av
600 LORN 44052 2615 D5
4800 CLEV 44127 2625 D6
Dakota Dr
- NRDV 44035 3007 B1
Dakota Rd
5200 RchT 44286 3150 B6
Dakota Run
32100 AVLK 44012 2618 C2
Dale Av
2400 RKRV 44116 2621 C7
3700 LORN 44055 2745 C4
10200 CLEV 44102 2753 B2
10200 CLEV 44111 2753 B2
Dale Dr
- BKPK 44142 2880 E4
- BKPK 44142 2881 A4
Dale Rd
15200 RslT 44022 2761 E3
Dalebrook Av
13300 BKPK 44130 2881 D2
13300 BKPK 44142 2881 D2
13300 PRMA 44130 2881 D2
Dalebrook Cir
2300 HkyT 44233 3148 A6
Dalebrook Rd
7400 INDE 44131 3016 A2
Daleford Dr
7700 MNTR 44060 2143 D6
Daleford Rd
3200 SRHT 44120 2627 C7
3400 SRHT 44120 2757 D2
Dalepark Dr
100 BDFD 44146 2887 A5
Dalepoint Rd
8100 INDE 44131 3016 B2
Dales Ct
3200 NRYN 44133 3014 C3
Daleside Dr
5200 CLEV 44109 2754 B7
5200 PRMA 44109 2754 B7
5200 PRMA 44134 2754 B7
Daleview Dr
- AURA 44202 3156 C1
17300 LKWD 44107 2622 B6
Dalewood Av
5400 MPHT 44137 2886 C1
Dalewood Ct
- MDBH 44130 2880 E5
Dalewood Rd
900 LNHT 44124 2498 E5
Dallas Av
3200 LORN 44055 2745 B4
3400 ShfT 44055 2745 B3
Dallas Dr
8200 MNTR 44060 2144 A4
Dallas Rd
1100 CLEV 44108 2496 B6
Dalton Av
4900 CLEV 44127 2755 C1
Dalton Ct
8100 MNTR 44060 2144 A4
Dalton Dr
1100 PnvT 44077 2040 E6
1100 PnvT 44077 2041 A6
Dalwood Dr
300 CLEV 44110 2372 A7
Damon Av
15600 CLEV 44110 2372 C6
Dan Dr
8500 NRYN 44133 3148 D1
Dana Av
14900 CLEV 44111 2622 C7
Dana Pl
5200 NRDV 44039 2748 B7
Danberry Dr
4100 NOSD 44070 2750 D6
Danbury Av
11100 GDHT 44125 2756 C7
Danbury Ct
- CLEV 44103 2626 A1
8100 MNTR 44060 2144 A4
Danbury Dr
8000 MNTR 44060 2144 A4
Danbury Ln
300 RDHT 44143 2498 E1
500 AVLK 44012 2618 B3
2200 HDSN 44236 3155 B7
Dane St
100 AMHT 44001 2872 B1
Danford Ct
3000 CLEV 44114 2625 B1
Danforth Ct
- NRDV 44035 3007 D1
Dania Dr
7200 INDE 44131 3015 E2
7200 INDE 44131 3016 A2
Daniel Av
15300 CLEV 44110 2372 B7
Daniel Dr
7800 BWHT 44131 3015 B2
7800 BWHT 44147 3015 B2
7800 SVHL 44131 3015 B2
31400 WLWK 44095 2249 D6
Daniel Ln
10 HmbT 44024 2381 A3
Danielle Dr
2700 WTLK 44145 2750 C2
Daniels Dr
10 CRDN 44024 2379 E7
Danley Sq S
- LORN 44052 2615 A6
N Danley Sq
1300 LORN 44052 2615 A6
Danner Dr
500 AURA 44202 3157 B7
900 STBR 44202 3157 B6
900 STBR 44241 3157 B6
Dannie Dr
500 LORN 44053 2744 E6
Dansy Dr
1800 EUCL 44117 2373 B7
Dansy Dr
1800 EUCL 44117 2498 B1
Danvers Dr
10100 CcdT 44077 2145 D6
Danville Ct
11000 CLEV 44104 2626 C4
Darby Ct
10 CcdT 44060 2145 C5
Darby Ln
3900 NOSD 44070 2750 B5
Darbys Run
300 BYVL 44140 2620 E5
300 BYVL 44140 2621 A5
7900 BbgT 44023 2890 D7
Darien Dr
7200 HDSN 44236 3154 D7
Darien Ln
2900 TNBG 44087 3020 B7
Darke Blvd
15200 BKPK 44142 2881 C2
Darlene Cir
6100 CcdT 44077 2146 B4
Darley Av
13300 CLEV 44110 2497 A1
Darlington Av
11700 GDHT 44125 2885 D1
Darlington Dr
500 BDFD 44146 2887 B3
Darlington Rd
11400 GDHT 44125 2885 D1
Darrow Dr
5700 SVHL 44131 2884 B2
Darrow Rd
7300 HDSN 44236 3154 E7
7700 TwbT 44236 3154 E6
7900 TNBG 44087 3154 E7
7900 TNBG 44236 3154 E5
7900 TwbT 44087 3154 E5
8700 TNBG 44087 3155 A1
9700 TNBG 44087 3019 E5
9800 TNBG 44087 3020 A4
10300 SLN 44139 3020 A4
10300 TNBG 44139 3020 A4
13000 VmnT 44089 2869 A6
15400 VmnT 44089 2870 A2
52100 BhmT 44089 2870 A2
Darrow Rd SR-91
7300 HDSN 44236 3154 E7
7700 TwbT 44236 3154 E6
7900 TNBG 44087 3154 E7
7900 TNBG 44236 3154 E5
7900 TwbT 44087 3154 E5
8700 TNBG 44087 3155 A1
9700 TNBG 44087 3019 E5
9800 TNBG 44087 3020 A4
10300 SLN 44139 3020 A4
10300 TNBG 44139 3020 A4
Darrow Park Dr
9900 TNBG 44087 3020 A5
Dartford Rd
4000 SELD 44121 2498 A4
Dartmoor Av
900 PRMA 44131 2883 E2
900 PRMA 44134 2883 E2
900 SVHL 44131 2883 E2
E Dartmoor Av
10 PRMA 44131 2883 D1
10 PRMA 44134 2883 D1
10 SVHL 44131 2883 D1
10 SVHL 44131 2884 A2
Dartmoor Rd
2500 CVHT 44118 2627 C5
7900 MNTR 44060 2251 C4
Dartmouth Av
16500 CLEV 44111 2752 B2
Dartmouth Cir
100 ELYR 44035 3006 C1
Dartmouth Dr
1000 PnvT 44077 2146 E1
1100 PnvT 44077 2147 A1
5300 PRMA 44129 2753 D7
5300 PRMA 44129 2882 D1
Dartmouth Tr
300 SgHT 44067 3017 E4
Dartworth Dr
5800 PRMA 44129 2883 A4
7400 PRMA 44129 2882 E2
Darwin Av
14100 CLEV 44110 2497 B1
Darwin Pl
16600 MDBH 44130 2881 B5
Daryl Dr
900 SELD 44121 2498 D5
900 SELD 44143 2498 D5
Dave Dr
6600 MadT 44057 1843 B7
Davenport Av
1400 CLEV 44114 2625 A1
Daventree Dr
8100 BKVL 44141 3015 E4
Davice Pkwy
12800 SGVL 44149 3010 E7
12800 SGVL 44149 3011 A7
David Av
1400 PRMA 44134 3014 D2
David Dr
100 ELYR 44035 2875 A3
10200 CcdT 44077 2145 D6
18000 CLEV 44121 2497 E2
23400 NOSD 44070 2750 E5
23800 BDHT 44146 2887 C1
33800 NRDV 44039 2877 C4
David Rd
9300 GDHT 44125 2756 B6
David Morton Ct
6800 BKVL 44141 3151 A1
David Myers Pkwy
10 BHWD 44122 2629 A3
10 BHWD 44124 2629 A3
10 LNHT 44124 2629 A3
Davids Wy
4100 PRRY 44081 2042 B2
Davidson Dr
600 HDHT 44143 2499 D3
9600 BKVL 44141 3151 A2
Davie Ct
900 MDSN 44057 2043 E2
Davinwood Dr
19100 CLEV 44135 2751 E4
Davis Ct
11800 LKWD 44107 2623 B5
Davis Dr
5500 MONT 44060 2143 D2
7300 NRDV 44039 2877 C4
39000 CrlT 44044 3006 D5
Davis Rd
3000 PryT 44057 2042 E3
3000 PryT 44081 2042 E3
4500 PRRY 44081 2042 D1
Davis Wy
9100 TNBG 44087 3020 B5
Davis Industrial Pkwy
6100 SLN 44139 2888 E5
Davista Av
1300 MadT 44057 1843 C7
Dawn Cir
3400 NOSD 44070 2750 C4
Dawn Ct
7300 CcdT 44060 2253 C1
19200 SGVL 44149 3146 D3
Dawn Dr
500 MDSN 44057 2044 A2
700 MDSN 44057 2043 E2
3400 NOSD 44070 2750 C4
22700 EUCL 44117 2373 C7
Dawncliff Dr
4100 BKLN 44144 2753 D4
Dawn Haven Dr
7400 PRMA 44130 3013 A1
Dawning Av
3500 CLEV 44109 2754 C5
Dawning Dr
5800 BKLN 44144 2754 A5
5800 CLEV 44144 2754 A5
6300 BKLN 44144 2753 E5
Dawnshire Av
3700 PRMA 44134 2883 B2
Dawn Vista Ovl
5800 PRMA 44129 2883 A6
Dawnwood Ct
10100 STBR 44241 3156 C7
Dawnwood Dr
900 PRMA 44131 2883 E2
900 PRMA 44134 2883 E2
900 SVHL 44131 2883 E2
E Dawnwood Dr
10 PRMA 44131 2883 D1
10 PRMA 44134 2883 D1
10 SVHL 44131 2883 D1
10 SVHL 44131 2884 A2
Dawson Blvd
6100 MNTR 44060 2143 D4
Dawson Ct
10 BDFD 44146 2887 A4
Dawson Dr
10600 AbnT 44023 3023 D3
Day Dr
200 LORN 44052 2615 D5
6800 PRMA 44129 2882 D5
6800 PRMA 44129 2883 A5
8700 PMHT 44129 2882 D5
8700 PMHT 44130 2882 D5
8700 PRMA 44130 2882 D5
Day St
4500 SFLD 44054 2746 B2
Dayflower Dr
10000 TNBG 44087 3019 B3
Daylon Ct
4800 VmnT 44089 2740 C6
Dayton Av
3000 LORN 44055 2744 E4
3400 LORN 44052 2744 E3
Dayton Ct
- CLEV 44114 2625 C2
100 ELYR 44035 3006 D1
S Dayton Ext
4600 MadT 44057 2043 D5
Dayton Rd
10 MadT 44057 1941 E7
10 MadT 44057 2043 E1
10 MDSN 44057 1941 E7
10 MDSN 44057 2043 E1
Dayton St
16600 BbgT 44023 2890 A1
Daytona Dr
7500 PRMA 44134 3014 D2
Daytona Rd
1400 LNHT 44124 2498 D7
Dean Ct
14500 BURT 44021 2636 B7
14500 BURT 44021 2766 C1
Dean Dr
1400 SELD 44121 2498 C7
Dean Rd
8700 BhmT 44089 2870 B7
8700 BhmT 44889 2870 B7
8700 FrnT 44889 2870 B7
8700 HetT 44889 2870 B7
8700 VmnT 44089 2870 B7
8700 VmnT 44889 2870 B7
Dean St
11700 HRM 44234 3161 A2
Deanna Ct
24400 EUCL 44123 2373 D3
Deans Gate
- CsTp 44026 2501 A7
- CsTp 44026 2631 A1
Deanwood St
2000 ECLE 44112 2497 C5
Dearborn Av
7300 CLEV 44102 2623 E7
Deb Ann Ct
11900 CcdT 44077 2254 E2
Debbie Dr
6400 NRDV 44039 2877 C3
Debbie Pl
2700 MadT 44057 1941 B4
Debbington Dr
500 BYVL 44140 2619 D5
Debby Dr
12100 PRMA 44130 3013 A1
Debby Ln
- ELYR 44035 2875 A7
Debonair Dr
7500 MNTR 44060 2251 B2
7500 MNTR 44094 2251 B1
7500 WLBY 44094 2251 B1
Deborah Ct
7900 MNTR 44060 2252 D3
Deborah Dr
- PRMA 44130 2882 C1
800 WLWK 44095 2249 D6
2400 BHWD 44122 2628 D4
2700 SRHT 44122 2628 D5
4700 NRDV 44039 2877 B1
Deborah Ln
200 BDFD 44146 2886 D4
Deborah Lynn Dr
4700 BKLN 44144 2753 C6
Debra Dr
6100 LORN 44053 2744 E6
41800 EyrT 44035 2745 C7
Decatur Dr
10400 SGVL 44136 3012 B5
Decatur St
600 VMLN 44089 2740 D6
Decker Av
8200 CLEV 44103 2496 A7
8400 CLEV 44106 2496 A7
Decker Dr
900 PRMA 44131 2883 E3
900 PRMA 44134 2883 E3
900 SVHL 44131 2883 E3
E Decker Dr
10 PRMA 44131 2883 E3
10 PRMA 44134 2883 E3
10 SVHL 44131 2883 E3
200 SVHL 44131 2884 A3
Decker Rd
5300 NOSD 44070 2749 E7
5300 NOSD 44070 2878 E1
Dee Dr
6500 AhtT 44001 2873 C1
Deep Cove Dr
8500 SgHT 44067 3017 E5
Deep Creek Ln
10 MDHL 44022 2760 A3
Deeplake Cir
1500 TNBG 44087 3019 B3
Deepview Dr
17400 BbgT 44023 2890 C4
Deepwood Blvd
7900 MNTR 44060 2251 D4
Deepwood Ct
100 CRDN 44024 2505 B2
300 AhtT 44001 2873 B1
Deepwood Dr
900 MCDN 44056 3018 D7
6000 MDHL 44022 2761 A3
6000 RslT 44022 2761 A3
7100 RslT 44072 2761 A2
Deepwood Ln
200 AhtT 44001 2873 B1
6800 MAYF 44143 2500 B3
N Deepwood Ln
15000 RslT 44022 2761 A2
S Deepwood Ln
15100 RslT 44022 2761 A2
Deepwood Tr
5800 SLN 44139 2889 D3
Deep Woods Dr
400 AURA 44202 3022 D5
Deepwoods Wy
3900 NOSD 44070 2750 D5
Deer Cross
5300 SFLD 44054 2746 E5
Deer Ct
400 SRSL 44022 2762 A5
6600 BDHT 44146 2887 E6
Deer Dr
200 CdnT 44024 2378 E6
200 CdnT 44024 2379 A6
Deer Hllw
9400 MNTR 44060 2039 A7
Deer Ln
18900 FWPK 44126 2751 E1
Deer Pth
462-00 AURA 44202 3156 C2
6900 OmsT 44138 2878 E4
7500 BKVL 44141 3150 D3
Deer Rdg
5100 MNTR 44060 2039 A7
Deer Run
- AVON 44011 2747 D3
500 AhtT 44001 2873 B2
501-00 AURA 44202 3156 B3
2600 WBHL 44094 2375 B4
4000 SVHL 44131 2884 B7
10000 BKVL 44141 3151 D4
37000 SLN 44139 2889 D3
Deer St
2600 ShvT 44255 3157 E7
2600 STBR 44255 3157 E7
Deerborn Av
5500 MNTR 44060 2144 A1
Deerbrook Dr
7800 RslT 44072 2631 D7
Deer Creek Cir
4600 RHFD 44286 3150 D7
Deercreek Ct
5300 SFLD 44054 2746 E4
Deer Creek Dr
8600 BWHT 44147 3015 A6
12400 NRYN 44133 3012 E7
Deercreek Dr
5600 WLBY 44094 2375 B2
N Deer Creek Ln
33200 PRPK 44124 2760 A1
33600 HGVL 44022 2760 A1
Deer Creek Run
- BhmT 44001 2871 D4
Deer Creek Tr
3200 RchT 44286 3150 E7
3200 RHFD 44286 3150 D7
Deer Crossing
- ELYR 44035 2745 E7
Deerfield Cir
8600 MCDN 44056 3018 A7
Deerfield Ct
100 ELYR 44035 2746 C7
10000 TNBG 44087 3019 B4
Deerfield Dr
10 MDSN 44057 1942 B6
10 PnvT 44077 2040 E7
10 PnvT 44077 2146 E1
10 SRSL 44022 2761 D7
2400 AVON 44011 2747 A2
6500 SgHT 44067 3152 B1
7500 PRMA 44129 2882 E3
9700 KTLD 44094 2377 C3
16900 SGVL 44136 3146 E2
24500 NOSD 44070 2750 C4
32000 AVLK 44012 2618 D5
Deerfield Ln
10 AURA 44202 3021 D7
10 BHWD 44122 2628 E5
10000 BKVL 44141 3151 E4
Deerfield Rd
7600 GSML 44040 2630 E1
Deerfield Meadow Ct
8600 NRDV 44039 2877 B6
Deerfoot Tr
7600 RslT 44072 2761 C1
Deer Haven Dr
6400 CcdT 44077 2146 A5
8300 CsTp 44026 2502 A2
Deerhaven Ln
1900 BWHT 44147 3149 D5
Deerhaven Tr
- AURA 44202 3021 C5
Deeridge Dr
7100 WNHL 44146 2886 D7
Deering Av
5800 PMHT 44130 2882 D3
10700 CLEV 44106 2626 C3
Deer Island Dr
400-00 AURA 44202 3156 B2
Deer Lake Dr
5400 NRDV 44039 2747 C7
Deermont Av
1300 MadT 44057 1843 C7
Deer Path Dr
16900 SGVL 44136 3146 E3
16900 SGVL 44136 3147 A2
Deer Path Ln
500 NCtT 44067 3153 E5
Deerpath Tr
7500 HDSN 44236 3155 D7
Deer Ridge Cir
17400 SGVL 44136 3147 A5
Deer Run Dr
- MDBH 44130 2880 E5
800 AhtT 44001 2873 B2
4800 LORN 44053 2743 B5
6000 HGVL 44022 2761 A2
6000 MDHL 44022 2761 A2
10600 EatT 44044 3007 A5
34400 NRDV 44039 2877 B7
Deer Run Ln
500 AVLK 44012 2617 E4
19600 SGVL 44149 3011 D5
31500 WTLK 44145 2749 A3
Deer Run Ovl
3700 RchT 44286 3150 C6
5800 SLN 44139 2889 D3
Deer Run Tr
7500 PRMA 44130 3013 C1
12000 CcdT 44077 2254 E4
Deerspring Ct
32600 NRDV 44039 2877 D6
Deer Trail Ln
7400 LORN 44053 2742 C6
Deer Wood Ct
9300 MNTR 44060 2039 A7
Deerwood Ct
- PNVL 44077 2145 C2
Defiance Av
100 ELYR 44035 3006 E2
5700 BKPK 44142 2881 D1
Defoe Dr
26000 NOSD 44070 2750 B5
Deforest Av
16500 CLEV 44128 2757 C4
17800 CLEV 44122 2757 D4
De Forest Rd
- CLEV 44106 2626 C3
Deise Av
13600 CLEV 44110 2497 A2
Del Ln
31800 AVLK 44012 2618 E5
Delamere Ct
37500 SLN 44139 2889 D4
Delamere Dr
2200 CVHT 44106 2626 E4
Delamere Rd
200 VMLN 44089 2741 D4
Delavan Av
17700 CLEV 44119 2372 D6
Delaware Av
100 LORN 44052 2614 E5
300 LORN 44052 2615 A6
500 ELYR 44035 2875 D7
14200 LKWD 44107 2622 C6
Delaware Cir
100 ELYR 44035 3006 B3
Delaware Ct
19400 EUCL 44117 2497 E2
Delaware Dr
300 BNWK 44212 3146 E7
2100 CVHT 44106 2626 E3
7600 MDBH 44130 3012 D1
13800 SGVL 44136 3011 E7
Delaware Rd
19500 EUCL 44117 2497 E3
19500 EUCL 44117 2498 A2
Delaware St
2400 WKLF 44092 2374 D4
Delevan Dr
4800 LNHT 44124 2498 E5
Delft Cir
10 OmsT 44138 2879 B3
Dell Av
7100 CLEV 44104 2625 E5
7300 CLEV 44104 2626 A5
Dell Dr
19600 SGVL 44149 3011 C6
Dellbank Dr
3400 RKRV 44116 2751 E1
6000 CLEV 44144 2754 A3
6300 BKLN 44144 2753 E3
6300 CLEV 44144 2753 E3
Dell Cort Dr
10 BKVL 44141 3151 A4
Dellefield Rd
42600 AhtT 44035 2874 A1
42600 EyrT 44035 2874 A1
Dellenbaugh Av
7100 CLEV 44103 2625 E1
7100 CLEV 44103 2626 A1
Dellhaven Av
6400 MNTR 44060 2145 A5
Dellhaven Dr
7200 PRMA 44130 2882 C7
Dell Ridge Ct
12800 SGVL 44149 3011 C6
Dellrose Dr
6200 PMHT 44130 2882 C4
Dellwood Dr
1100 WTLK 44145 2619 E7
2600 PRMA 44134 2883 C4
18500 WNHL 44146 3017 E1
18500 WNHL 44146 3018 A1
27300 WTLK 44145 2620 A6
Dellwood Rd
200 AVLK 44012 2617 E2
3200 CVHT 44118 2627 C3
Delmar Av
2600 CLEV 44109 2754 C2
Delmar Dr
3300 RKRV 44116 2751 A2
Delmere Dr
23500 NOSD 44070 2750 D4
Delmont Av
1600 CLEV 44106 2496 E7
1600 CLEV 44112 2496 E7
1600 ECLE 44112 2496 E7
16000 SGVL 44136 3147 A3
N Delmonte Blvd
10000 STBR 44241 3156 D7
Delmore Rd
3700 CVHT 44121 2497 E6
3700 CVHT 44121 2498 A6
Delmur Dr
6700 INDE 44131 2884 E6
Delora Av
5300 CLEV 44109 2754 B6
5300 CLEV 44144 2754 B6
5700 BKLN 44144 2754 A6
6200 BKLN 44144 2753 E6
Delores Blvd
5700 BKPK 44142 2881 B2
Delray Av
5000 ORNG 44022 2759 D7
5000 SLN 44022 2759 D7
5000 SLN 44139 2759 D7
Delray Ln
2300 AVON 44011 2747 C1
Delrey Av
15500 CLEV 44128 2757 B3
Delroy Rd
4100 SELD 44121 2498 B7
Delsy Dr
9900 NRYN 44133 3013 B4
Delta Cir
5600 WLBY 44094 2375 A2
Demas Av
700 ELYR 44035 2874 C4
Demi Dr
2000 TNBG 44087 3019 E4
Demington Dr
2100 CVHT 44106 2627 A3
Demshar Dr
7300 MNTR 44060 2253 A1
Denise Ct
5200 SLN 44139 2759 B7
5200 SLN 44139 2888 B1
Denise Dr
5800 NRDV 44039 2877 B2
Denison Av
500 ELYR 44035 2875 C7
1300 CLEV 44109 2754 D2
4400 CLEV 44102 2754 A2
6600 CLEV 44102 2753 E1
6900 BKLN 44102 2753 E1
6900 BKLN 44144 2753 E1
9200 CLEV 44102 2623 D7
9900 CLEV 44111 2623 C7
Denison Blvd
6000 PMHT 44130 2882 C4
Denison Dr
4100 LORN 44055 2745 E4
Denison-Harvard Brch
- CHHT 44125 2755 A3
800 CHHT 44105 2755 A3
800 CHHT 44109 2755 A3
800 CLEV 44109 2754 E2
800 CLEV 44109 2755 A3
Denley Av
1400 CLEV 44109 2754 E4
Denmark Av
4600 CLEV 44102 2754 B2
Dennis Cir
1100 SELD 44121 2498 B6
Dennis Ct
10 GnvT 44041 1944 C2
9400 NRYN 44133 3014 C4
Dennis Dr
1500 WKLF 44092 2374 E1
Dennison Ct
8400 MNTR 44060 2144 B3
Dennisport Dr
26200 OKWD 44146 2887 E7
Denny Dr
7300 NRDV 44039 2877 C4
Densmore Rd
31600 WLWK 44095 2249 E5
Dent Ct
41300 CrlT 44050 3140 D2
Denton Dr
2000 CVHT 44106 2626 D3
Dentzler Rd
2200 PRMA 44134 2883 C6
3900 PRMA 44129 2883 B6
Denver Av
2500 LORN 44055 2745 A3
3600 ShfT 44055 2745 A4
Denver Dr
11900 PRMA 44130 2882 A2
Depot Rd
8900 TNBG 44087 3155 B1
19000 BbgT 44023 3021 B3
19000 BbgT 44202 3021 B3
Depot St
- NRDV 44039 2877 D6
10 BERA 44017 2880 B5
10 GNVA 44041 1944 B4
200 ELYR 44035 2875 B6
1300 RKRV 44116 2621 E5
4100 PRRY 44081 2042 C3
37800 WLBY 44094 2250 E4
N Depot St
25700 ODFL 44138 2879 B5
Deptford Dr
2500 BHWD 44122 2628 D5
Derby Ct
12000 SGVL 44149 3011 A5
Derby Dr
700 PNVL 44077 2040 A6
4500 AVON 44011 2747 A6
6400 MAYF 44143 2499 E5
6400 MAYF 44143 2500 A5
Derby Rd
11700 GDHT 44125 2885 D2
Derby Run
300 WBHL 44092 2374 B5
Derby Wy
700 AVLK 44012 2618 E5
700 AVLK 44012 2619 A5
Derby Downs Dr
36000 SLN 44139 2889 C4
Derbyshire Dr
4600 NRDL 44128 2758 B6
4600 WVHT 44128 2758 B6

Cleveland Street Index

STREET Block City ZIP Map# Grid

Derbyshire Ln
11700 AbnT 44021 2893 D4
11700 AbnT 44255 2893 D4
Derbyshire Rd
2400 CVHT 44106 2626 E2
2500 CVHT 44106 2627 A3
2700 CVHT 44118 2627 A3
E Derbyshire Rd
2800 CVHT 44106 2627 A3
2800 CVHT 44118 2627 B3
Dercum Rd
7600 CLEV 44105 2756 A3
Derubertis Dr
1500 MadT 44057 1942 A4
Desmond Av
8700 CLEV 44102 2623 D5
Desota Av
3200 CVHT 44118 2627 C1
Detour Av
700 RKRV 44116 2621 C5
7300 CLEV 44103 2496 A5
Detroit Av
2400 CLEV 44113 2624 C4
4300 CLEV 44102 2624 B5
7000 CLEV 44102 2623 C5
11600 LKWD 44102 2623 B5
11600 LKWD 44107 2623 A5
13300 LKWD 44107 2622 A5
Detroit Av US-6
2400 CLEV 44113 2624 C4
Detroit Av US-20
2400 CLEV 44113 2624 C4
Detroit Av US-322
2400 CLEV 44113 2624 C4
Detroit Ext
18600 LKWD 44107 2622 A5
Detroit Rd
- LKWD 44107 2621 E5
- RKRV 44107 2621 E5
4700 SFLD 44035 2746 C6
4700 SFLD 44054 2746 C6
5400 AVON 44011 2747 B4
5400 SFLD 44011 2747 A5
5400 SFLD 44035 2747 A5
5400 SFLD 44054 2747 A5
18600 LKWD 44107 2622 A5
19000 RKRV 44116 2621 D5
22800 WTLK 44116 2621 A6
22800 WTLK 44145 2621 A6
24100 WTLK 44145 2620 E6
27300 WTLK 44145 2619 B7
30400 WTLK 44145 2749 B1
31400 AVON 44145 2749 A1
32000 AVON 44011 2749 A1
35800 AVON 44011 2618 A7
35800 AVON 44011 2748 A1
Detroit Rd SR-2
19500 RKRV 44116 2621 E5
Detroit Rd SR-254
- LKWD 44107 2621 E5
- RKRV 44107 2621 E5
4700 SFLD 44035 2746 C6
4700 SFLD 44054 2746 C6
5400 AVON 44011 2747 B4
5400 SFLD 44011 2747 A5
5400 SFLD 44035 2747 A5
5400 SFLD 44054 2747 A5
19000 RKRV 44116 2621 D5
22800 WTLK 44116 2621 A6
22800 WTLK 44145 2621 A6
23300 WTLK 44145 2620 A7
27300 WTLK 44145 2619 B7
30400 WTLK 44145 2749 B1
31400 AVON 44145 2749 A1
32000 AVON 44011 2749 A1
32200 AVON 44011 2748 A1
Detroit Rd US-20
- LKWD 44107 2621 E5
- RKRV 44107 2621 E5
- RKRV 44116 2621 E5
Deveny Av
7100 CLEV 44105 2755 E4
Devington Ct
12100 ManT 44202 3023 A6
Devoe Av
23700 EUCL 44123 2373 D2
24900 EUCL 44132 2373 D2
Devon Ct
- BbgT 44023 3021 E1
- BbgT 44023 3022 A1
Devon Dr
4900 NOSD 44070 2749 D7
5100 VMLN 44089 2740 E6
5100 VMLN 44089 2741 A6
Devon Ln
7400 CsTp 44026 2501 C7
Devon Rd
17500 CLEV 44119 2372 D5
Devon St
6200 MadT 44057 1843 A7
Devon Hill Rd
2600 RKRV 44116 2621 B7
Devon Pond
200 AURA 44202 3021 C7
Devonshire Av
600 SDLK 44054 2615 E5
Devonshire Ct
100 ELYR 44035 2875 E3
400 BYVL 44140 2620 E5
6500 MNTR 44060 2144 A5
Devonshire Dr
- CVHT 44106 2626 D3
- SDLK 44054 2615 E5
6500 NRYN 44133 3014 A5
Devonshire Ln
- BbgT 44023 3021 E1
400 AURA 44202 3021 D5
Devonshire Ovl
29500 WTLK 44145 2749 C3
Devonshire Rd
200 VMLN 44089 2741 D4
3000 CLEV 44109 2754 C4
Devorah Dr
10 AURA 44202 3156 E3
Devore Ct
2900 LORN 44052 2744 C3
Dewberry Ln
29300 WTLK 44145 2749 C2
Dewey Av
500 ELYR 44035 2874 E5
Dewey Dr
35400 ETLK 44095 2142 B7
Dewey Rd
5100 NOSD 44070 2749 E7
5300 BKVL 44141 3151 C6

Dewey Rd
5300 RchT 44141 3151 C6
6700 TpnT 44086 2257 E5
7800 MtlT 44064 2257 E5
7800 TpnT 44064 2257 E5
9200 CsTp 44024 2502 E1
9200 CsTp 44026 2502 E1
9200 CsTp 44094 2502 E1
9200 KTLD 44094 2502 E1
N Dewey Rd
6000 AMHT 44001 2744 A7
6200 AhtT 44001 2744 B7
S Dewey Rd
6200 AhtT 44001 2744 B7
6200 AMHT 44001 2744 B7
6300 AhtT 44001 2873 A2
6300 AMHT 44001 2873 A2
Dewhurst Av
10 BDFD 44137 2886 E2
10 BDFD 44146 2886 E2
10 MPHT 44137 2886 E2
Dewhurst Rd
10100 EatT 44035 3006 E4
10100 ELYR 44035 3006 E4
10200 CrlT 44035 3006 E4
DeWitt Dr
500 HDHT 44143 2499 B4
15000 SGVL 44136 3012 C3
DeWitt St
500 LORN 44055 2745 A4
500 ShfT 44052 2745 A4
500 ShfT 44055 2745 A4
Dexter Rd
6100 PMHT 44130 2882 C3
Dexter Pl
1500 CLEV 44113 2624 C4
Diagonal Rd
10000 ShvT 44255 3158 C6
10300 ManT 44255 3158 E3
11100 ManT 44255 3159 A2
Diamond Av
5500 CLEV 44104 2625 D5
Diamond Ct
400 BHIT 44212 3146 B7
Diamond Centre Dr
- PNVL 44060 2145 A2
- PNVL 44077 2145 A2
9500 MNTR 44060 2145 A2
Diana Av
13600 CLEV 44110 2497 A1
Diana Ct
300 HDHT 44143 2499 D2
Diana Dr
- BKPK 44142 2752 C7
- BKPK 44142 2881 C1
3800 BWHT 44147 3015 C4
6600 SVHL 44131 2884 A5
Diane Ct
30800 WBHL 44092 2374 D4
Diane Dr
4000 FWPK 44126 2752 A1
8800 NRDV 44039 2877 C7
20600 SGVL 44149 3011 B5
Dianne Dr
10800 NbyT 44065 2634 A7
24500 BHWD 44122 2628 D5
Dibble Av
5500 CLEV 44103 2495 D7
Dickens Av
8900 CLEV 44104 2626 B6
11100 CLEV 44120 2626 D6
Dickens Cir
33400 NRDV 44039 2877 D3
Dickens Dr
5100 RDHT 44143 2498 E3
5100 RDHT 44143 2499 A4
Dickerson Rd
500 WLWK 44095 2249 D5
Dido Albert Federowich Mem Dr
1700 CLEV 44112 2497 D2
1700 CLEV 44121 2497 D2
Didrickson Dr
2300 LORN 44053 2743 E2
Diemer Ct
6200 CLEV 44103 2495 E6
Difranco Blvd
- BNHT 44131 2755 A7
Dill Rd
1200 SELD 44121 2498 C7
Dillard St
2500 CLEV 44115 2625 C4
Dille Rd
1400 CLEV 44110 2373 A7
1400 EUCL 44110 2373 A7
1400 EUCL 44117 2373 A7
1400 EUCL 44117 2498 A1
1500 EUCL 44143 2498 A1
3900 CLEV 44115 2625 C6
3900 CLEV 44127 2625 C6
Dillewood Av
- SFLD 44054 2615 E5
700 SDLK 44054 2615 E5
Dillewood Rd
1000 CLEV 44119 2372 D6
Dilworth St
100 ELYR 44035 2875 C4
Dines Rd
7300 HGVL 44022 2631 B6
7300 RslT 44022 2631 B6
7300 RslT 44072 2631 C6
7800 RslT 44072 2632 A6
Discovery Ln
7500 CcdT 44077 2253 E2
7500 CcdT 44077 2254 A2
Division Av
2500 CLEV 44113 2624 C4
3200 CLEV 44102 2624 B4
Division Dr
1100 MadT 44057 1843 E6
7700 MNTR 44060 2251 D1
Division Rd
- AVLK 44012 2618 C1
4500 SELD 44121 2628 C2
Division St
100 CNFL 44022 2760 E3
7200 BDFD 44146 2887 B7
7200 OKWD 44146 2887 B7
Divot Dr
300 WLWK 44095 2249 C6
Dix Ct
7600 CLEV 44103 2626 A2
Dixon Rd
10800 CLEV 44111 2753 B3
34900 WBHL 44094 2375 A6

Doan Av
1500 ECLE 44112 2497 A5
N Doan Av
10 PnvT 44077 2145 B4
S Doan Av
10 PnvT 44077 2145 C5
Dobson Ct
2400 CLEV 44109 2754 D2
Dock Rd
800 LkeC 44057 1844 A4
800 MadT 44057 1844 A5
1200 MadT 44057 1843 E7
1200 MadT 44057 1942 E1
1900 MadT 44057 1943 A2
Dodd Rd
2400 WBHL 44094 2375 E3
2400 WBHL 44094 2376 A4
Dodd's Lndg
38400 WBHL 44094 2376 A4
Dodd's Hill Rd
38100 WBHL 44094 2375 E4
38100 WBHL 44094 2376 A4
Dodge Av
33900 NRDV 44039 2877 C4
Dodge Ct
- HRM 44234 3161 A1
Dodge Dr
800 AMHT 44001 2872 E3
Dodsworth Ln
9800 SLN 44139 2889 C3
Doe Cir
16600 SGVL 44136 3146 E3
Doe Ct
200 SRSL 44022 2761 E5
Doe Dr
24700 NOSD 44070 2750 C4
Doe St
- BhmT 44001 2871 D4
Doe Tr
443-00 AURA 44202 3156 C2
Doe Crossing
- LORN 44053 2743 B6
Doering Ct
1700 CLEV 44109 2754 E3
Dogwood Cir
4000 ORNG 44122 2759 C3
6800 MDBH 44130 2881 C5
9100 BKVL 44141 3151 A1
Dogwood Ct
300 AhtT 44001 2873 B2
9800 SGVL 44136 3012 B4
Dogwood Ln
10 OmsT 44138 2879 B4
500 AbnT 44023 2892 B3
500 VMLN 44089 2741 C5
6200 NRDV 44039 2876 D2
7000 MNTR 44060 2144 D7
7400 PRMA 44129 2882 C7
7400 PRMA 44130 2882 C7
7400 PRMA 44130 3013 D1
27000 OmsT 44138 2878 D5
34500 SLN 44139 2760 B7
Dogwood Tr
124-00 AURA 44202 3156 D2
4200 NOSD 44070 2749 E5
5000 LNHT 44124 2628 E1
5100 LNHT 44124 2629 A1
12600 NRYN 44133 3012 E3
Doll Dr
8300 GDHT 44125 2756 A7
Dollar Ct
3200 CLEV 44113 2624 C5
Dolloff Rd
4900 CLEV 44127 2625 D7
5400 CLEV 44127 2755 D1
Dolores Dr
38100 ETLK 44095 2250 E1
38200 WLBY 44094 2250 E1
38200 WLBY 44095 2250 E1
Dolphin Rd
5600 MONT 44060 2143 E1
Dolphin Cove
3500 RMDV 44202 3020 D5
Dominion Dr
900 WTLK 44145 2620 A6
Donald Av
1200 LKWD 44107 2623 A4
4700 RDHT 44143 2498 E5
6600 VLVW 44125 2885 C5
7100 CLEV 44103 2495 E7
7200 CLEV 44103 2496 A7
27200 BYVL 44140 2620 A5
Donald Dr
8200 MNTR 44060 2144 A4
13300 BKPK 44130 2881 D3
13300 BKPK 44142 2881 D3
13300 PRMA 44130 2881 D3
Donald Ross Dr
- LNHT 44124 2629 A2
- WBHL 44094 2375 B4
Doncaster Av
6300 PRMA 44129 2882 E4
Doncaster Ct
10 CcdT 44060 2145 B7
Donegal Ln
20300 SGVL 44149 3146 C5
E Donegal Ln
20200 SGVL 44149 3146 C5
Donelly Ct
16000 CLEV 44135 2752 B5
Donmar Rd
10700 NRYN 44133 3148 A4
Donna Av
33900 NRDV 44039 3008 C1
Donna Dr
1700 WTLK 44145 2750 E1
4400 RDHT 44143 2498 C4
Donna Rae Dr
6500 SVHL 44131 2884 C6
Donner Pass
- ClrT 44024 2505 C6
Donnybrook Rd
20500 MPHT 44137 2887 A1
20600 BDHT 44146 2887 A1
20600 MPHT 44146 2887 A1
Donovan Dr
4800 GDHT 44125 2756 A6
Donover Rd
24200 WVHT 44128 2758 D4
Donwell Dr
1600 SELD 44121 2628 B1
Dooridge Dr
1700 TNBG 44087 3019 C5
Doovys St
1800 AVON 44011 2617 C7

Doovys St
1800 AVON 44011 2747 C1
N Doovys St
36800 AVON 44011 2617 D7
Dora Blvd
6000 INDE 44131 2884 D7
Dora Dr
14500 NbyT 44065 2634 A7
14500 NbyT 44065 2764 A1
Doral Dr
4400 AVON 44011 2748 C6
8800 MNTR 44060 2144 C3
Doral Ln
30800 WTLK 44145 2749 B2
Doralane Av
600 AURA 44202 3021 B4
Dorchester Av
- SDLK 44054 2615 E5
35400 NRDV 44039 2748 A7
Dorchester Cir
19100 SGVL 44136 3147 C5
Dorchester Dr
1200 MadT 44057 1843 C6
17000 CLEV 44119 2372 D5
29100 NOSD 44070 2878 C3
29100 NOSD 44138 2878 C3
29100 OmsT 44070 2878 C3
29100 OmsT 44138 2878 C3
32000 AVLK 44012 2618 C4
Dorchester Ln
10 CcdT 44060 2145 C6
Dorchester Rd
10 PnvT 44077 2041 B6
100 PryT 44077 2041 B6
3200 SRHT 44120 2627 D7
3300 SRHT 44120 2757 C1
33900 GSML 44040 2630 B2
33900 MDHT 44124 2630 A2
36200 HGVL 44022 2630 C3
36200 HGVL 44040 2630 C3
Doria Ct
12500 SGVL 44149 3011 D6
Doris Av
22300 FWPK 44126 2751 A4
Doris Cir
700 PNVL 44077 2040 A5
Doris Dr
5700 BKPK 44142 2881 B2
Doris Rd
3400 CLEV 44111 2752 B1
Dorland Av
10 BERA 44017 3011 C2
Dormae Ct
10600 CcdT 44077 2146 A4
Dornback Pkwy
33200 ETLK 44095 2249 E7
Dornoch Ln
- HDHT 44143 2499 C2
Dornur Dr
4600 CLEV 44109 2754 E5
Dorodo Ct
1300 LORN 44052 2615 B6
Dorothea Dr
1100 PnvT 44077 2040 E6
1200 PnvT 44077 2041 A6
Dorothy Av
4600 VMLN 44089 2741 A6
7300 PRMA 44129 2882 E2
9400 GDHT 44125 2756 B5
19100 RKRV 44116 2621 E5
Dorothy Ct
5500 CLEV 44103 2625 D1
Dorothy Dr
5400 NOSD 44070 2878 E1
30000 WKLF 44092 2374 D2
Dorothy Rd
12900 CsTp 44026 2632 A2
Dorrwood Dr
5700 MNTR 44060 2144 C2
Dorset Ct
10 BHWD 44122 2628 E4
100 ELYR 44035 2875 E3
Dorset Dr
100 SRSL 44022 2762 B6
2400 SVHL 44131 2884 B2
2900 BNHT 44131 2884 B2
Dorset Ln
2100 TwbT 44236 3155 A6
6400 SLN 44139 2889 E6
Dorset Rd
5500 LNHT 44124 2499 B7
Dorsh Rd
1000 SELD 44121 2498 D7
1300 LNHT 44121 2498 D7
1300 LNHT 44124 2498 D7
Dorshwood Rd
4700 LNHT 44124 2498 D6
4700 SELD 44121 2498 D6
Dorver Av
7700 CLEV 44105 2756 A4
Dorwick Dr
7300 NCtT 44067 3153 A3
Dorwood Dr
6000 LORN 44053 2744 E6
Dory Ln
7400 NCtT 44067 3153 C5
Doty Rd
7100 MadT 44057 2044 D6
Doub St
- NRsT 44074 3138 E4
- OBLN 44074 3138 E4
Douglas Av
1600 ELYR 44035 3005 E2
Douglas Blvd
300 RDHT 44143 2498 D2
Douglas Ct
1300 LORN 44053 2744 C5
9100 NRYN 44133 3014 C3
Douglas Dr
200 BYVL 44140 2620 A5
4900 NOSD 44070 2749 D7
5900 MadT 44057 1941 E1
31400 WLWK 44095 2249 D6
Douglas Ln
9700 ClbT 44028 3010 E2
9700 ClbT 44138 3010 E2
9700 ODFL 44138 3010 E2
Douglas Rd
1500 WKLF 44092 2249 E7
1500 WKLF 44092 2374 E1
1500 WKLF 44094 2249 E7
1500 WLBY 44094 2249 E7
22000 SRHT 44122 2628 B5
Douglas St
800 VMLN 44089 2740 E6

Doula Ln
12700 NRYN 44133 3012 E3
12800 SGVL 44133 3012 E3
12800 SGVL 44136 3012 E3
Douse Av
4400 CLEV 44127 2625 C6
Dove Av
10200 CLEV 44105 2756 D2
Dove Dr
100 ELYR 44035 2874 E2
Dove Ln
- MNTR 44060 2144 D2
Dovecote Trc
200 MCDN 44056 3018 A6
Dovegate Dr
- MNTR 44060 2252 A3
Dover Av
14300 ECLE 44112 2497 B4
Dover Ct
1200 ECLE 44112 2497 B4
Dover Dr
- AURA 44202 3157 A4
Dover Ln
7300 PRMA 44130 2882 C7
7300 PRMA 44130 3013 C1
Dover Center Rd
200 BYVL 44140 2620 A4
600 WTLK 44140 2620 A5
600 WTLK 44145 2620 A5
1400 WTLK 44145 2750 A1
3700 NOSD 44070 2750 A3
3700 NOSD 44145 2750 A4
Dover Farms Dr
4700 NRYN 44133 3013 D7
Dover Place Ln
10 NCtT 44067 3153 A2
Dow Cir E
7900 MDBH 44130 3012 C3
7900 SGVL 44130 3012 C3
7900 SGVL 44136 3012 C3
Dow Cir W
7900 MDBH 44130 3012 C2
7900 SGVL 44130 3012 C2
7900 SGVL 44136 3012 C2
Dowd Av
2000 LKWD 44107 2623 A6
Dowd Rd
200 ELYR 44035 2875 C3
Downers Grove Ct
9400 SGVL 44136 3012 B4
Downey Glen Tr
16600 AbnT 44021 2893 B1
Downing Av
35100 NRDV 44039 2748 A7
Downing Ct
700 BERA 44017 3011 B2
Downing Dr
300 CRDN 44024 2380 A5
N Downing Pl
7100 CcdT 44077 2146 A7
S Downing Pl
7200 CcdT 44077 2146 A7
Downing St
- WTLK 44145 2749 A4
Doxmere Dr
5800 PMHT 44130 2882 B2
5800 PRMA 44130 2882 B2
Drake Av
5500 CLEV 44127 2625 D7
Drake Dr
33300 BYVL 44140 2619 A4
Drake Rd
11000 NRYN 44133 3147 E3
11000 NRYN 44133 3148 A3
11000 SGVL 44133 3147 E3
11000 SGVL 44136 3147 C3
17500 SGVL 44136 3146 E3
18400 SGVL 44149 3146 D3
Drake St
22600 OKWD 44146 3018 C1
30800 NRDV 44039 2877 B1
Drakefield Av
2500 CLEV 44111 2752 C3
24700 EUCL 44123 2373 D2
24700 EUCL 44132 2373 D2
25000 EUCL 44132 2374 A2
Drawbridge Cir
6600 NRYN 44133 3013 E5
Drayton Dr
23000 MDHT 44124 2629 C2
Dreamhaven Dr
- MadT 44057 1941 B2
Drenik Dr
1600 WKLF 44092 2374 E2
Dresden Av
7400 PRMA 44129 2882 E1
Dresden Rd
800 CVHT 44112 2497 C5
800 ECLE 44112 2497 C5
Dresser Ln
1000 MCDN 44056 3154 A5
Dressler Av
13400 GDHT 44125 2756 E6
13400 GDHT 44125 2757 A5
14200 GDHT 44128 2757 A5
Dressler Ct
7100 CHHT 44125 2755 E6
Drexel Av
10500 CLEV 44108 2496 C6
Drexel Dr
6700 SVHL 44131 2884 B6
Drexmore Rd
12800 CLEV 44120 2626 E5
13400 CLEV 44120 2627 A5
13900 SRHT 44120 2627 A5
Driftwood Ct
- AhtT 44001 2872 E6
100 ELYR 44035 3006 E1
20100 SGVL 44149 3146 C3
31700 AVLK 44012 2619 A2
Driftwood Dr
300 LORN 44052 2614 E6
1100 SVHL 44131 2884 A4
5000 VMLN 44089 2740 E6
5000 VMLN 44089 2741 A6
7700 MONT 44060 2143 E2
9200 ODFL 44138 3010 A1
11700 NbyT 44065 2764 D1
Driftwood Ln
1300 MCDN 44056 3019 A7
1500 TNBG 44056 3019 A7
1500 TNBG 44087 3019 A7
Driscoll Ln
26700 NOSD 44070 2750 A5

Driscoll Rd
4900 WVHT 44146 2758 A6
Drummond Rd
100 AVLK 44012 2488 B7
100 AVLK 44012 2618 B1
2800 SRHT 44120 2627 B6
Drury Ct
1200 MDHT 44124 2500 A7
Drury Ln
- WTHL 44094 2375 E1
10 MDHT 44124 2500 A6
7500 CsTp 44026 2631 C2
38200 WLBY 44094 2250 E1
Drury Wy
- NRDV 44035 3007 B1
Dryden Av
- CLEV 44103 2496 B6
- CLEV 44108 2496 B6
Dryden Dr
3900 NOSD 44070 2750 B5
Dryden Rd
2700 SRHT 44122 2628 B5
Drydock Av
2100 CLEV 44113 2625 A4
D Termination Av
- GNVA 44041 1944 A4
Duane Rd
26200 NOSD 44070 2750 A5
Dubay Ct
600 PNVL 44077 2146 B2
Dubin Av
17500 CLEV 44128 2757 D6
Dublin Dr
4700 NRYN 44133 3014 B3
Dublin Ln
9500 MNTR 44060 2145 A6
Duckworth Ln
7700 MNTR 44060 2143 D5
Dudley Av
7300 CLEV 44102 2623 E6
Dudley Rd
3600 ShvT 44255 3158 E7
3600 ShvT 44255 3159 A7
Duff Dr
100 AVLK 44012 2617 C2
Duffey St
600 ELYR 44035 2875 E3
Duffield Rd
23300 SRHT 44122 2628 C6
24400 BHWD 44122 2628 D6
Duffton Ln
1600 PnvT 44077 2040 E2
1700 PnvT 44077 2041 A2
Dugan Farms
3800 PRRY 44081 2042 B2
Dugans Lndg
3900 PRRY 44081 2042 B2
Duke Av
5000 CLEV 44102 2624 B6
Duke Ct
100 ELYR 44035 3006 C2
7400 MNTR 44060 2251 C1
Duluth Av
7100 CLEV 44103 2495 E7
Dumbarton Blvd
300 RDHT 44143 2498 D2
Dunbar Cir
300 BWHT 44147 3149 C3
Dunbar Ct
10 PnvT 44077 2146 D1
100 AURA 44202 3021 D6
Dunbar Dr
6100 MNTR 44060 2143 E4
Dunbar Ln
400 HDHT 44143 2499 C3
8600 BKVL 44141 3016 B6
Dunbar Rd
1600 MadT 44057 1842 E7
1700 MadT 44057 1941 E1
Dunbury Dr
15600 MPHT 44137 2886 B3
Dundee Dr
300 CLEV 44108 2496 D3
24700 RDHT 44143 2498 D1
Dundee St
6000 MadT 44057 1941 E1
Dundeen Cir
5600 BNHT 44131 2884 C1
Duneden Av
6500 SLN 44139 2888 E6
Duneden Dr
300 AURA 44202 3022 B5
Dunedin Av
1300 MadT 44057 1843 C6
Dunellon Dr
1800 LNHT 44124 2629 C2
Dunfield Dr
6200 MDHT 44143 2499 E6
Dunford Av
27200 WTLK 44145 2749 E4
27200 WTLK 44145 2750 A4
Dunham Av
6600 CLEV 44103 2625 E2
Dunham Ln
16400 WNHL 44146 3017 C2
Dunham Rd
- MPHT 44137 2757 B7
5300 MPHT 44137 2886 A7
6300 WNHL 44137 2886 B5
6300 WNHL 44146 2886 B5
6900 CyhC 44146 2886 A6
7200 WNHL 44146 3017 C4
11500 SghT 44067 3017 C4
11800 SghT 44146 3017 C4
Dunlap Av
9300 CLEV 44105 2756 B2
Dunlap Dr
1600 STBR 44241 3157 B7
Dunlin Ct
14800 MFDD 44062 2767 B1
Dunny Av
600 SDLK 44054 2616 B4
Dunton Rd
3200 LORN 44055 2745 B4
3200 ShfT 44055 2745 B4
Dupont Av
10500 CLEV 44108 2496 C4
Dupont Dr
9800 ClbT 44028 3010 D2
9800 ClbT 44138 3010 D2
9800 ODFL 44138 3010 D2
Durack Dr
9100 NRYN 44133 3013 C4
Durant Av
11300 CLEV 44108 2496 D5

Durham Ct
6500 MNTR 44060 2143 E5
Durham Dr
- WTLK 44145 2619 A7
1200 BWHT 44147 3150 A5
Durkee Av
13100 CLEV 44105 2756 E3
13100 CLEV 44105 2757 A3
13600 CLEV 44128 2757 A3
Durkee Rd
- HtbT 44021 2637 A3
9700 EatT 44035 3007 B2
10300 EatT 44044 3007 B7
12000 EatT 44044 3142 B1
13500 GFTN 44044 3142 B4
14600 BtnT 44021 2636 E3
14600 ClrT 44021 2636 E3
14900 BtnT 44021 2637 A3
14900 ClrT 44021 2637 A3
15400 HtbT 44046 2637 B4
15400 MdfT 44021 2637 B4
15400 MdfT 44046 2637 B4
15700 HtbT 44062 2637 D4
Durrell Av
- AVLK 44012 2618 A2
32800 AVLK 44012 2617 E2
Dursley Ct
7200 SLN 44139 3020 C1
Dusty Ln
8700 CdnT 44024 2254 A7
Dute St
6000 ELYR 44035 2745 E6
6000 ShfT 44035 2745 E6
6000 ShfT 44055 2745 E6
Dutton Dr
8900 TNBG 44087 3154 C1
9000 TNBG 44087 3019 C7
Duval Rd
6400 MDHT 44124 2630 A3
Duxbury Ct
7200 OKWD 44146 2887 E7
Duxbury Dr
600 BERA 44017 3010 E1
Duxbury Ln
10 BNWK 44212 3147 B6
Duxbury Pl
5500 LORN 44053 2744 B6
Dwayne Ct
9900 CcdT 44060 2253 C1
Dwight Dr
500 BYVL 44140 2619 D5
Dye Rd
34400 EatT 44028 3008 C4
34400 EatT 44044 3008 C4
Dyke Av
7100 NRDV 44039 2876 A4
Dynes Av
16700 CLEV 44128 2757 C4
Dysart Rd
2300 UNHT 44118 2627 E4

E

E Dr
- LORN 44052 2744 E4
E St
300 LORN 44052 2615 A6
500 LORN 44052 2614 E6
Eady Ct
100 ELYR 44035 2875 D5
Eagle Av
3100 LORN 44055 2745 B3
W Eagle Av
100 CLEV 44113 2624 E4
100 CLEV 44115 2624 E3
300 CLEV 44115 2625 B4
Eagle Cir
100 ELYR 44035 2874 E2
Eagle Rd
- WTHL 44094 2375 E3
7700 KTLD 44094 2376 D3
7700 WTHL 44094 2376 D3
8200 KTLD 44094 2377 A3
36600 WBHL 44094 2375 D3
Eagle St
- WLWK 44095 2249 C5
10 MDSN 44057 2044 B1
100 FTHR 44077 2039 D4
N Eagle St
10 GNVA 44041 1944 B3
S Eagle St
10 GNVA 44041 1944 B4
W Eagle St
100 PNVL 44077 2145 E1
Eagle Trc
400 MDHT 44124 2629 E2
Eaglebrook Ct
- LryT 44077 2256 A3
Eagle Chase
13000 NRYN 44133 3014 B7
Eagle Cliff Dr
10 BYVL 44140 2619 A2
Eagle Creek Dr
2200 AVON 44011 2747 E2
2200 AVON 44011 2748 A2
Eagle Mills Rd
6700 WBHL 44094 2375 E3
6700 WTHL 44094 2375 E3
6800 WTHL 44094 2376 A3
7600 KTLD 44094 2376 C3
Eagle Nest Cir
2200 AVON 44011 2747 E2
Eagle Nest Dr
10 BTVL 44022 2889 E1
12200 NRYN 44133 3148 A1
37500 EatT 44044 3007 A5
Eagle Nest Ln
8700 KTLD 44094 2252 C7
38300 WBHL 44094 2376 A4
Eagle Point Dr
- MadT 44057 1942 A4
Eagle Pointe Ct
- ClbT 44028 3010 B5
Eagle Ridge Cir
9200 BKVL 44141 3151 C4
Eagle Ridge Dr
8200 CcdT 44077 2253 D5
Eagles Pt
400 AbnT 44023 2892 B3
Eagles Glen Ct
33100 NRDV 44039 3008 D1
Eaglesmere Av
13300 CLEV 44110 2497 A2
Eagles Nest Cir
17000 SGVL 44136 3146 E2

STREET
Block City ZIP Map# Grid

Eagles Nest Dr
4700 LORN 44053 2743 B5
Eagles Nest Rd
6100 MNTR 44060 2144 C3
Eagleton Ct
200 MCDN 44056 3018 B6
Eagle Valley Ct
10 BWHT 44147 3015 D7
Eaglewood Dr
700 WLBY 44094 2143 A4
Eaglewood Tr
8500 BbgT 44023 2762 B7
Eardley Rd
2300 UNHT 44118 2627 E4
Earl Av
6500 MadT 44057 1843 B7
15600 MPHT 44137 2757 B7
Earl Ct
400 ELYR 44035 2875 A7
Earle Av
10500 CLEV 44108 2496 C5
Earlene Av
41700 EyrT 44035 2874 D2
Earlwood Rd
13400 CLEV 44110 2497 A3
East Av
10 ELYR 44035 2875 B7
1100 ELYR 44035 3006 B1
1300 CrlT 44035 3006 B1
2100 LORN 44052 2745 A1
2300 LORN 44055 2745 A2
8500 MNTR 44060 2144 C6
East Blvd
- CLEV 44103 2496 A5
- CLEV 44108 2496 A5
10 RMDV 44202 3020 E4
700 AURA 44202 3021 A4
1200 CLEV 44106 2496 C7
1200 RMDV 44202 3021 A4
10600 CLEV 44106 2626 C1
S East Byp
- CrlT 44035 3006 E5
- EatT 44035 3006 E1
- EatT 44044 3006 E3
- EatT 44044 3007 A4
- ELYR 44035 2875 E6
- ELYR 44035 3006 E1
S East Byp SR-57
- CrlT 44044 3006 E5
- EatT 44035 3006 E1
- EatT 44044 3006 E3
- EatT 44044 3007 A4
- ELYR 44035 2875 E6
- ELYR 44035 3006 E1
S East Byp SR-301
- EatT 44035 3006 E1
- EatT 44044 3006 E4
- ELYR 44035 2875 E6
- ELYR 44035 3006 E1
S East Byp US-20
- EatT 44035 3006 E1
- EatT 44044 3006 E4
- ELYR 44035 2875 E6
- ELYR 44035 3006 E1
East Cir
10 BKVL 44141 3151 A4
East Ct
300 PNVL 44077 2145 E3
21100 OKWD 44146 2887 B7
East Dr
10 CLEV 44134 2754 C7
500 BNWK 44212 3146 E7
700 SDLK 44054 2616 A4
6700 SLN 44139 3020 E1
East Rd
35000 EatT 44044 3008 B7
East St
100 FTHR 44077 2039 D4
400 AMHT 44001 2872 E2
East St SR-535
600 FTHR 44077 2039 D5
Eastarbor Ln
- BHIT 44212 3145 D7
Eastbrook Cir
- BbgT 44023 2891 C5
Eastbrook Dr
100 EUCL 44132 2249 A6
Eastbrook Tr
17600 BbgT 44023 2891 C5
Eastend Dr
9500 NRYN 44133 3014 C4
Eastern Av
100 OBLN 44074 3138 C1
Eastern Heights Blvd
500 ELYR 44035 2875 C7
Eastgate Dr
6600 MDHT 44124 2500 A7
6700 MAYF 44143 2500 B4
Eastham Av
1700 ECLE 44112 2497 A5
Easthaven Dr
2500 HDSN 44236 3155 C7
Easthill Cir
2600 SVHL 44131 3015 B1
Easthill Dr
11500 CsTp 44026 2501 C4
Easthill Wy
11900 CcdT 44077 2254 E2
Eastlake Dr
900 ETLK 44095 2250 B4
Eastland Rd
- CLEV 44135 2880 D2
- CLEV 44142 2880 D2
10 BERA 44017 2880 D7
500 BERA 44130 2880 D5
500 MDBH 44130 2880 D5
6200 BKPK 44142 2880 D5
6300 BERA 44142 2880 D5
6300 MDBH 44142 2880 D5
8200 MDBH 44017 3011 D2
8200 MDBH 44130 3011 D2
8200 SGVL 44017 3011 D2
8200 SGVL 44130 3011 D2
8200 SGVL 44149 3011 D2
S Eastland Rd
7600 BERA 44017 3011 D1
7600 BERA 44130 3011 D1
7600 MDBH 44017 3011 D2
7600 MDBH 44130 3011 D2
Eastlane Dr
4500 BKLN 44144 2753 D5
Eastlawn Dr
800 HDHT 44143 2499 B6
800 LNHT 44124 2499 B6
800 LNHT 44143 2499 B6

STREET
Block City ZIP Map# Grid

Eastlawn Dr
33800 ETLK 44095 2250 A4
Eastlawn Rd
100 BDHT 44128 2758 D7
100 BDHT 44146 2758 D7
100 WVHT 44128 2758 D7
Eastlawn St
300 GNVA 44041 1944 C3
1900 LORN 44052 2615 B6
Eastlook Rd
19100 RKRV 44116 2621 E5
Eastman Dr
5400 LORN 44053 2744 A5
Eastmoor Rd
8200 MNTR 44060 2251 C4
Easton Av
1400 MadT 44057 1843 B7
8800 CLEV 44104 2626 B7
Easton Ln
10 MDHL 44022 2759 E5
10 MDHL 44022 2760 A5
Eastondale Rd
6200 MDHT 44124 2629 E2
Eastover Rd
5000 LNHT 44124 2498 E7
5000 LNHT 44124 2499 A7
East Pointe Cir
9800 BKVL 44141 3150 C3
Eastpointe Ct
- AMHT 44001 2872 E4
Eastridge Cir
11400 MsnT 44024 2634 C3
Eastview Av
- NRDV 44039 2877 B3
Eastview Dr
- BbgT 44023 2891 A3
200 BNHT 44131 2755 A6
4400 INDE 44131 3015 C1
Eastview St
5700 NRDV 44039 2877 B2
Eastway Dr
8000 MNTR 44060 2143 E4
8000 MNTR 44060 2144 A4
Eastway Rd
3700 SELD 44118 2627 E2
3700 SELD 44118 2628 A2
4000 SELD 44121 2628 A2
Eastwick Dr
3000 CVHT 44118 2497 C7
Eastwind Ct
11000 SGVL 44149 3011 A5
Eastwood Av
1100 HDHT 44143 2499 C7
1100 MDHT 44124 2499 C7
1100 MDHT 44143 2499 C7
5600 MPHT 44137 2886 C2
20400 FWPK 44126 2751 C2
Eastwood Blvd
12300 GDHT 44125 2885 D1
13500 GDHT 44125 2886 A1
Eastwood Dr
700 PNVL 44077 2146 C2
8300 BWHT 44147 3015 B4
11800 EatT 44044 3007 A6
18800 AbnT 44023 3023 D2
Eastwood Ln
4000 WVHT 44122 2758 A3
4100 WVHT 44122 2757 E4
4100 WVHT 44128 2757 E4
4100 WVHT 44128 2758 A3
26900 OmsT 44138 2878 E3
26900 OmsT 44138 2879 A3
Eastwood St
10 GNVA 44041 1944 C4
Easy St
25100 BDHT 44146 2887 D3
Eaton Blvd
12000 EatT 44044 3008 B7
12200 EatT 44044 3143 B1
Eaton Cir
5400 MNTR 44060 2145 A1
Eaton Ct
6000 BDHT 44146 2887 D4
16700 MDBH 44130 2881 B5
Eaton Dr
- AURA 44202 3157 A4
2100 AVON 44011 2617 D7
2100 AVON 44011 2747 D1
8300 BbgT 44023 2891 A2
8400 SgHT 44067 3017 D5
N Eaton Dr
1800 AVON 44011 2617 D7
Eaton Ln
- PRPK 44122 2759 B1
- PRPK 44124 2759 B1
- WDMR 44122 2759 B1
- WDMR 44124 2759 B1
Eaton Rd
2400 UNHT 44118 2627 E4
2500 SRHT 44118 2627 E5
2600 SRHT 44120 2627 D6
2800 SRHT 44122 2627 E6
8800 MCDN 44056 3018 B5
20800 FWPK 44126 2751 B4
Eaton Wy
25500 BYVL 44140 2620 C5
Eaton Commerce Pkwy
12100 EatT 44028 3008 E7
12100 EatT 44028 3143 E1
Eaton Ridge Dr
100 SgHT 44067 3018 A4
Eavenson Blvd
6100 BKPK 44142 2881 A3
Ebb Tide Cir
13100 NRYN 44133 3147 E4
Eberhardt St
100 SAHT 44001 3003 A1
Ebony Dr
- ELYR 44035 3006 B2
- MCDN 44056 3154 A3
Echo Dr
- SGVL 44136 3146 D3
600 MAYF 44040 2500 C4
8800 MNTR 44060 2144 C6
19100 SGVL 44149 3146 D3
E Echo Dr
8800 MNTR 44060 2144 D6
Echo Gln
- GSML 44040 2501 A7
1200 GSML 44040 2500 E7
Echo Ln
2400 BWHT 44147 3014 C3
Echo Hill Dr
10000 BKVL 44141 3151 D5

STREET
Block City ZIP Map# Grid

Echolane Dr
2400 BWHT 44147 3014 D3
Eckstein Ct
10400 CLEV 44111 2623 C7
Edanola Av
1200 LKWD 44107 2622 A5
Eddie Ln
- ClbT 44028 3009 C7
Eddie Rd
10 MadT 44057 1844 A6
Eddington Rd
1500 CVHT 44118 2627 B1
1500 ECLE 44112 2627 B1
1500 ECLE 44118 2627 B1
Eddy Rd
100 BTNH 44108 2496 D3
300 CLEV 44108 2496 D4
1000 ECLE 44108 2496 E6
1300 ECLE 44112 2496 E6
1600 ECLE 44112 2497 A6
28700 WBHL 44092 2374 E5
29000 WBHL 44094 2374 E5
30800 WBHL 44094 2375 A5
Eddystone Dr
1100 AhtT 44001 2873 B2
Eddywood Ln
8000 CsTp 44026 2501 E4
Eden Ln
14700 MDBH 44130 2881 C7
Edendale St
1300 CVHT 44121 2497 E7
Edenhall Dr
1700 LNHT 44124 2629 B2
Edenhall Ter
36400 AVON 44011 2747 D5
Edenhurst Rd
5000 LNHT 44124 2498 E6
5000 LNHT 44124 2499 A6
Eden Park Dr
- CdnT 44024 2379 C7
- CdnT 44024 2504 C1
- MsnT 44024 2504 C1
Edenwood Rd
4700 LNHT 44124 2498 D6
4700 SELD 44121 2498 D6
Edgarton Rd
2400 BKVL 44141 3150 B3
2400 BWHT 44141 3150 B3
2400 BWHT 44147 3150 B3
Edgebrook Blvd
5900 PMHT 44130 2882 C3
Edgebrook Cross
2500 TNBG 44087 3019 E7
2600 TNBG 44087 3020 A7
Edgebrook Ct
7800 LryT 44077 2256 A3
Edgecliff Av
15200 CLEV 44111 2622 C7
15200 CLEV 44111 2752 C1
Edgecliff Cir E
100 ELYR 44035 2874 B7
Edgecliff Cir W
100 ELYR 44035 2874 B7
Edgecliff Dr
1100 BDFD 44146 2887 B5
6900 PRMA 44134 2883 D6
19500 EUCL 44119 2372 E3
19900 EUCL 44119 2373 A3
22500 EUCL 44123 2373 B1
25500 EUCL 44132 2373 E1
27100 EUCL 44132 2248 E7
27200 EUCL 44132 2249 A7
Edgecliff Ter
- CLEV 44111 2752 C1
Edgedale Rd
28400 PRPK 44124 2629 B6
Edgefield Dr
100 ELYR 44035 2875 D2
Edgefield Rd
1400 LNHT 44124 2499 B7
1400 LNHT 44124 2629 B1
Edgehill Dr
- SELD 44121 2497 E4
10 PnvT 44077 2146 D3
3700 CLEV 44121 2497 E4
5600 PRMA 44130 2882 C2
5800 PMHT 44130 2882 C2
14600 NbyT 44065 2764 C1
23800 BHWD 44122 2628 D3
41500 CrlT 44035 3005 D5
Edgehill Rd
2200 CLEV 44106 2626 D2
2300 CVHT 44106 2626 E2
2500 CVHT 44106 2627 A2
2900 CVHT 44118 2627 B2
8700 MNTR 44060 2252 C1
Edgehurst Dr
- MDBH 44130 2881 C4
- MDBH 44142 2881 C4
6300 BKPK 44142 2881 C4
Edge Lake Ovl
8400 SgHT 44067 3017 C4
Edge Meadow Ct
38000 NRDV 44039 2747 C7
Edgemeer Pl
300 OBLN 44074 3138 C3
Edgemere Wy
35800 AVON 44011 2748 A3
Edgemont Rd
25000 RDHT 44143 2373 D7
Edgemoor Av
6500 SLN 44139 2888 E6
Edgepark Blvd
3800 NOSD 44070 2750 A5
27300 NOSD 44070 2749 E5
28000 WTLK 44070 2749 E5
28000 WTLK 44145 2749 E5
28200 NOSD 44145 2749 D5
Edgepark Dr
4700 GDHT 44125 2756 D6
5700 BKPK 44142 2879 E1
Edge Park Ln
- BHIT 44212 3145 E7
Edgerly Rd
600 CVHT 44121 2497 E4
Edgerton Rd
2100 UNHT 44118 2627 E4
2500 SRHT 44118 2627 E5
3000 BWHT 44147 3149 C3
3000 NRYN 44133 3149 A3
3000 NRYN 44147 3149 C3
5800 NRYN 44133 3148 C2
11900 NRYN 44133 3147 E1
12200 NRYN 44133 3012 E7
12200 SGVL 44133 3012 E7

STREET
Block City ZIP Map# Grid

Edgerton Rd
12200 SGVL 44136 3012 E7
18300 CLEV 44119 2372 D6
E Edgerton Rd
900 BWHT 44147 3149 E3
900 BWHT 44147 3150 A3
2000 BKVL 44141 3150 B3
2000 BWHT 44141 3150 B3
S Edgerton Rd
6900 BKVL 44141 3150 D3
W Edgerton Rd
1000 BWHT 44147 3149 D3
2800 NRYN 44133 3149 C3
2800 NRYN 44147 3149 C3
Edgeview Dr
2000 HDSN 44236 3154 D7
2000 HDSN 44236 3155 A7
Edgewater Dr
- LORN 44052 2614 E6
3100 VMLN 44089 2741 E4
3100 VMLN 44089 2742 A4
5100 SDLK 44054 2616 E2
9900 CLEV 44102 2623 C4
11500 LKWD 44102 2623 B4
11500 LKWD 44107 2623 A4
14700 NbyT 44065 2764 D1
14900 LKWD 44107 2622 C3
Edgewater Ln
1000 LKWD 44107 2622 E3
Edgewood Av
1000 MadT 44057 1844 A5
13100 CLEV 44105 2756 E3
13100 CLEV 44105 2757 A3
14000 CLEV 44128 2757 A3
15300 MPHT 44137 2886 B2
Edgewood Cir
400 BERA 44017 2880 A7
400 BERA 44017 3011 A1
Edgewood Ct
- AhtT 44001 2872 D6
10 CNFL 44022 2761 B4
Edgewood Dr
- VMLN 44089 2741 B6
10 AVLK 44012 2617 D1
10 BDFD 44146 2886 E4
10 BERA 44017 2880 A7
10 CrlT 44044 3006 D6
10 EatT 44044 3006 E7
100 AhtT 44001 2873 A2
100 AMHT 44001 2873 A1
1800 TNBG 44087 3019 C5
3500 LORN 44053 2744 C4
8800 NRYN 44133 3013 A3
15600 MDFD 44062 2767 C3
15600 MdfT 44062 2767 C3
18300 RKRV 44116 2622 A6
28900 WLWK 44095 2249 B7
Edgewood Ln
5800 WLBY 44094 2375 A2
7500 SVHL 44131 3015 C2
Edgewood Rd
600 RDHT 44143 2499 A4
2100 CVHT 44118 2627 C3
2500 BHWD 44122 2628 C5
2500 SRHT 44122 2628 C5
2900 PRPK 44124 2629 D7
5900 MDHT 44124 2499 C6
8000 MNTR 44060 2143 E5
8000 MNTR 44060 2144 A5
11500 MsnT 44024 2504 C3
28900 BYVL 44140 2619 D4
Edgewood St
100 ELYR 44035 2875 D5
Edinboro Av
17800 MPHT 44137 2886 D1
Edinboro Ln
- AbnT 44021 2893 D2
- AbnT 44255 2893 D2
Edinboro Pl
6700 CcdT 44077 2146 C6
Edinborough Dr
400 BYVL 44140 2621 A5
500 BYVL 44140 2620 E5
E Edinburgh Dr
200 HDHT 44143 2499 C1
W Edinburgh Dr
200 HDHT 44143 2499 C1
Edinburgh Ovl
- OmsT 44138 2879 B2
Edison Blvd
2300 TNBG 44087 3155 A4
Edison Ct
41700 ELYR 44035 2874 D3
41700 EyrT 44035 2874 D3
Edison Dr
10 ETLK 44095 2250 B1
100 VMLN 44089 2741 C4
Edison Rd
3400 CVHT 44118 2497 D7
3400 CVHT 44121 2497 D7
Edison St
10 OBLN 44074 3138 E3
Edith Ct
11500 CLEV 44106 2496 D7
Edith St
2400 LORN 44052 2744 B1
2400 LORN 44053 2744 A1
39600 SLN 44139 3020 E2
39900 SLN 44139 3021 A2
Edmond Dr
4400 SELD 44121 2498 C7
Edmonton Av
12300 CLEV 44108 2496 E5
Edmund Cir
9300 MNTR 44060 2039 A7
Edmunds Av
9000 CLEV 44106 2626 B1
Edna Av
6500 CLEV 44103 2495 E7
Ednil Dr
29900 BYVL 44140 2619 B4
Edolyn Av
15300 CLEV 44111 2752 C2
Edsal Dr
4700 LNHT 44124 2498 D6
4700 SELD 44121 2498 D7
Edson St
5800 VMLN 44089 2740 D6
8600 MNTR 44060 2038 C7
Educational Park Dr
10 SVHL 44131 2884 A7
Edward Av
100 ELYR 44035 3006 B3
32800 ETLK 44095 2249 E5

STREET
Block City ZIP Map# Grid

Edward Ct
6300 PMHT 44130 2882 A3
Edward Dr
- VMLN 44089 2741 B6
3900 BNWK 44212 3146 E6
Edward St
6500 MNTR 44060 2144 A5
Edwards Av
1100 LKWD 44107 2622 B4
Edwards Ln
9900 AbnT 44023 3023 B3
Edwards Rd
2300 CVHT 44106 2626 E3
Edwards St
10 MDSN 44057 1942 B7
10 MDSN 44057 2044 B1
700 BERA 44017 3011 C3
Edward Walsh Dr
38600 WLBY 44094 2251 A1
Edwin Av
38800 NRDV 44039 2876 A3
Edwin Ct
12300 CLEV 44106 2496 E7
12300 CLEV 44112 2496 E7
Effie Ct
- CLEV 44105 2756 B5
Effie Rd
- GDHT 44125 2756 B5
4500 CLEV 44105 2756 B5
4600 GDHT 44105 2756 B5
Effingham Blvd
23400 EUCL 44117 2373 C7
24400 RDHT 44117 2373 D7
24400 RDHT 44143 2373 D7
Egbert Rd
10 BDFD 44146 2887 A6
15500 WNHL 44146 3017 B1
17400 WNHL 44146 2886 D7
17600 CyhC 44146 2886 D7
18300 CyhC 44146 2887 A6
18300 WNHL 44146 2887 A6
Egg Hbr
37900 AVON 44011 2747 C2
Eggers Av
2900 CLEV 44105 2755 B1
Eggleston Rd
900 AURA 44023 3022 C6
900 AURA 44202 3022 C6
900 BbgT 44023 3022 C6
Eglindale Av
1800 CLEV 44109 2754 D1
Eichorn Av
4500 CLEV 44102 2754 A1
4500 CLEV 44109 2754 B1
Eileen Dr
700 MCDN 44056 3154 A5
Eisenhower Dr
7600 KTLD 44094 2251 D7
Elaine Dr
7500 SVHL 44131 3015 B1
8100 NRYN 44133 3014 C3
Elaine St
- RDHT 44143 2498 D5
Elandon Dr
2100 CVHT 44106 2626 D3
Elbe St
100 ELYR 44035 2874 E5
Elberon Av
1600 CLEV 44106 2496 E7
1600 CLEV 44112 2496 E7
1600 ECLE 44112 2496 E7
Elbert Dr
100 CrlT 44044 3006 C7
Elberta Av
15900 CLEV 44128 2757 B5
Elberta Rd
10 PNVL 44077 2145 D2
10 PnvT 44077 2145 D2
200 VMLN 44089 2741 B4
4400 PryT 44081 2042 D4
Elberton Av
- AVLK 44012 2617 B2
Elbon Rd
800 CVHT 44121 2497 D6
Elbur Av
1100 LKWD 44107 2622 E4
2100 CLEV 44107 2622 E7
2100 CLEV 44111 2622 E7
Elbur Ln
13500 LKWD 44107 2622 E5
Elda Wy
- NRDV 44039 2876 E6
Eldamere Av
15500 CLEV 44128 2757 C3
Elder Dr
28300 NOSD 44070 2878 D3
Elder St
35200 NRDV 44039 2877 B1
Elderdale Dr
16400 MDBH 44130 3012 A1
Elderkin Ct
7500 HDSN 44236 3154 E6
Elderwood Av
14600 ECLE 44112 2497 A5
Eldo St
4700 WLBY 44094 2250 D7
Eldon Ct
8200 MNTR 44060 2144 A5
Eldon Dr
1600 WKLF 44092 2374 E2
5700 PMHT 44130 2882 D2
5700 PRMA 44130 2882 D2
Eldora Rd
19800 RKRV 44116 2621 D5
Eldorado Dr
3500 RKRV 44116 2751 E1
Eldred Av
10 BDFD 44146 2886 E2
10 BDFD 44146 2887 A2
2100 LKWD 44107 2622 B6
Eldridge Blvd
6100 BDHT 44146 2887 D4
Eldridge Rd
10 AURA 44202 3157 A1
12500 MDBH 44130 2881 E4
12500 PMHT 44130 2881 E4
Eleanor Ct
7900 MNTR 44060 2251 E4
Eleanore Dr
3800 NOSD 44070 2750 C5
15600 CLEV 44135 2752 C4
Electric Blvd
10200 NHFD 44067 3018 A4
31600 AVLK 44012 2619 A2
32000 AVLK 44012 2618 D1

STREET
Block City ZIP Map# Grid

Electric Blvd
32900 AVLK 44012 2617 D1
Electric Dr
24300 BYVL 44140 2620 D5
29600 BYVL 44140 2619 C4
Elevator Av
10 PNVL 44077 2146 B2
Elfleda St
1600 ShfT 44055 2745 C6
Elgin Av
10500 CLEV 44108 2496 C5
Elgin Ovl
10 OmsT 44138 2879 A4
Elgin Rd
29900 WKLF 44092 2249 C7
Elinore Av
26100 EUCL 44132 2373 E2
26900 EUCL 44132 2374 A2
Eliot Av
10200 CLEV 44104 2626 C7
Elise Dr
7000 MDBH 44130 2881 B6
Elisha Ln
3100 TNBG 44087 3020 C3
Eliza Av
5300 CLEV 44105 2755 D1
Elizabeth Av
5400 PRMA 44130 2882 C1
9300 CLEV 44105 2756 B2
21700 FWPK 44126 2751 B5
Elizabeth Blvd
- PNVL 44077 2145 C3
- PnvT 44077 2145 C3
Elizabeth Cir
11500 SGVL 44149 3011 C6
Elizabeth Ct
6100 BKPK 44142 2881 B3
7000 MNTR 44060 2251 B1
Elizabeth Dr
10 GNVA 44041 1944 C6
3200 PryT 44081 1940 D6
3500 VMLN 44089 2741 D5
Elizabeth Ln
1300 MCDN 44056 3019 A7
4700 BKLN 44144 2753 D6
19000 BbgT 44202 3021 D3
26900 NOSD 44070 2878 E3
26900 NOSD 44138 2878 E3
26900 OmsT 44138 2878 E3
26900 OmsT 44138 2879 A3
37100 NRDV 44035 3007 C1
Elizabeth St
- CrlT 44035 3006 C5
- CrlT 44044 3006 C5
100 ELYR 44035 2875 B7
2500 AVON 44011 2748 C2
Elk Av
9900 CLEV 44108 2496 C4
Elk Run
11200 MsnT 44024 2634 B3
Ella Av
8300 CLEV 44105 2756 B4
Ellacott Pkwy
20500 HIHL 44128 2758 A4
20500 WVHT 44128 2758 A4
Ellen Av
5800 CLEV 44102 2624 A5
Ellen Dr
10 BERA 44017 3011 C2
21200 FWPK 44126 2751 B5
Ellendale Rd
3800 MDHT 44022 2760 B3
Ellenwood Av
10 BDFD 44146 2886 E3
10 BDFD 44146 2887 A3
Elleroy Ct
13900 CLEV 44111 2622 E7
Ellie Pl
7600 MNTR 44060 2253 A2
Elliman Rd
600 AURA 44202 3157 C6
600 AURA 44241 3157 C6
600 AURA 44255 3157 C6
600 STBR 44255 3157 C6
10000 STBR 44241 3157 D7
Ellington Ct
2700 AVON 44011 2748 B2
Ellington Pl
7600 MNTR 44060 2251 B2
Ellington Rd
27200 WTLK 44145 2620 A6
Elliot Dr
17900 BbgT 44023 2891 B6
Ellison Rd
4000 SELD 44121 2628 A1
Ellison Creek Dr
10700 CcdT 44077 2146 A5
Ellsworth Av
25000 EUCL 44123 2373 D1
25000 EUCL 44132 2373 D1
Ellsworth Dr
19300 SGVL 44136 3146 D4
19300 SGVL 44149 3146 C4
Ellsworth Hill Dr
2600 HDSN 44236 3155 C7
Ellwood Av
13500 CLEV 44135 2752 E4
Elm Av
- EUCL 44132 2374 A2
- WKLF 44092 2374 A2
1000 MadT 44057 1844 A5
4300 BHIT 44212 3146 C7
4300 BNWK 44212 3146 D7
13800 ECLE 44112 2497 A4
14700 BKPK 44142 2752 C7
Elm Ct
10 CNFL 44022 2761 A6
300 SVHL 44131 3015 A2
1300 CLEV 44102 2623 E5
Elm Dr
10 OmsT 44138 2879 B4
1600 AVON 44011 2618 E7
1600 AVON 44011 2748 E1
14600 NbyT 44065 2764 C1
19400 SGVL 44149 3146 D4
Elm Rd
23300 NOSD 44070 2750 D6
35000 EatT 44044 3143 A1
Elm St
- AhtT 44001 2872 B3
- NRDV 44039 2877 C1
- SDLK 44054 2616 D3
- SFLD 44054 2616 D3
- SFLD 44054 2746 C4
10 BDFD 44146 2887 A3

STREET
Block City ZIP Map# Grid

Elm St
10 GNVA 44041 1944 B3
100 OBLN 44074 3138 D2
100 SAHT 44001 2872 A7
200 BDHT 44146 2758 D7
400 ELYR 44035 2875 A6
400 PNVL 44077 2040 A5
900 PNVL 44077 2039 E5
1000 GFTN 44044 3142 B5
2000 CLEV 44113 2624 C3
5000 VMLN 44089 2741 A4
8900 BKVL 44141 3016 A7
8900 KTLD 44094 2251 D7
8900 MNTR 44060 2252 D1
8900 WTHL 44094 2251 D7
10400 MCDN 44056 3018 C4
10400 NHFD 44056 3018 C4
10400 NHFD 44067 3018 C4
10600 MNTU 44255 3159 C6
14400 MPHT 44137 2757 A7
25500 ODFL 44138 2879 B5
37800 WLBY 44094 2250 D4
Elma Dr
100 ELYR 44035 2875 C4
Elmar Blvd
14600 BURT 44021 2766 A1
Elmarge Av
10400 CLEV 44105 2756 C4
Elmarge Dr
6000 INDE 44131 2884 D7
Elmbrook Dr
3300 BWHT 44147 3015 B5
Elmdale Rd
2400 UNHT 44118 2628 B4
6100 BKPK 44142 2881 D4
6400 MDBH 44130 2881 D4
6400 MDBH 44142 2881 D4
Elmdale Trc
8700 MCDN 44056 3018 A7
Elmer Av
- NRDV 44039 2876 A4
25800 ODFL 44138 2879 B6
Elm Hill Dr
5500 SLN 44139 2888 D3
Elmhurst Av
14500 CLEV 44110 2497 B3
Elmhurst Dr
2500 BHWD 44122 2628 C5
2600 SRHT 44122 2628 C5
7900 BWHT 44131 3015 A3
7900 BWHT 44147 3015 A3
7900 SVHL 44131 3015 A3
Elmhurst Rd
5700 NOSD 44070 2878 C1
Elmore Dr
5800 PMHT 44130 2882 D2
5800 PRMA 44130 2882 D2
Elmore Rd
3900 FWPK 44116 2751 D2
3900 FWPK 44126 2751 D2
3900 RKRV 44116 2751 D2
Elmwood Av
800 WKLF 44092 2374 B1
1400 LKWD 44107 2622 C5
5300 MPHT 44137 2757 D7
5300 MPHT 44137 2886 D1
6000 INDE 44131 2884 D5
10600 GDHT 44125 2756 C7
11800 CLEV 44111 2623 A7
N Elmwood Av
600 WKLF 44092 2249 A7
600 WKLF 44092 2374 B1
Elmwood Ct
1300 RKRV 44116 2621 C6
Elmwood Dr
200 BERA 44017 2880 B6
800 MCDN 44056 3153 D1
900 WLBY 44094 2142 E4
2100 WTLK 44145 2750 A2
3200 VMLN 44089 2741 E5
4800 SDLK 44054 2616 D4
6800 SLN 44139 2889 D7
8100 KTLD 44094 2376 E6
23800 EUCL 44123 2373 C1
Elmwood Ln
18700 BbgT 44023 3022 B2
Elmwood Ovl
8900 NRYN 44133 3013 B3
Elmwood Pl
10 OBLN 44074 3138 D3
Elmwood Pt
- AURA 44202 3156 C1
Elmwood Rd
200 RKRV 44116 2621 C5
300 BYVL 44140 2620 B5
1100 HDHT 44143 2499 C6
1100 MDHT 44124 2499 C7
1100 MDHT 44143 2499 C6
3900 CVHT 44121 2498 A6
4000 SELD 44121 2498 B6
6400 MNTR 44060 2143 E5
Elmwood St
15500 MDFD 44062 2767 C2
41300 EyrT 44035 2745 D6
Eloise Dr
800 CVHT 44112 2497 C5
800 ECLE 44112 2497 C5
Elsa Ct
8000 CLEV 44102 2623 E5
Elsetta Av
10000 PMHT 44130 2882 C4
14000 CLEV 44135 2752 D3
Elsienna Av
16200 CLEV 44135 2752 B4
Elsinore Av
16000 ECLE 44112 2497 A6
Elsmere Dr
8800 PRMA 44130 2882 D2
24300 EUCL 44117 2373 D6
Elsmere Rd
3200 SRHT 44120 2627 D7
Elston Av
1600 CLEV 44109 2754 E3
Elton Av
6900 CLEV 44102 2623 E6
Elton Ct
6800 CLEV 44102 2623 E6
6800 CLEV 44102 2624 A6
Elton St
2700 ShvT 44255 3158 A7
Elwell Av
9600 CLEV 44104 2626 C6
Elwood Rd
1300 ECLE 44112 2497 A4

STREET
Block City ZIP Map# Grid

Ely Av
11600 CLEV 44104 2626 D7
11600 CLEV 44120 2626 D7
Elyria Av
- LORN 44052 2744 E1
100 AMHT 44001 2872 D2
1700 LORN 44052 2745 A2
2300 LORN 44055 2745 A3
3100 VMLN 44089 2741 E4
3100 VMLN 44089 2742 A4
3600 ShfT 44055 2745 C6
3900 ShfT 44052 2745 A4
5300 EyrT 44035 2745 C7
5300 EyrT 44055 2745 C6
Elyria St
16600 BbgT 44023 2890 A1
33200 NRDV 44039 2877 D1
Ely Vista Dr
5400 PRMA 44129 2883 A6
6500 PRMA 44129 2882 E6
Elywood Dr
900 ELYR 44035 2875 B4
Emarald Ovl S
8600 OmsT 44138 2878 B7
Emerald Ct
500 AURA 44202 3021 C7
500 AURA 44202 3156 C1
1400 CLEV 44114 2625 A2
5600 MNTR 44060 2145 A2
Emerald Ct SW
4800 CLEV 44135 2751 D6
Emerald Dr
1700 LORN 44053 2744 B5
42900 EyrT 44035 2874 B2
Emerald Ln
10 OmsT 44138 2879 A4
100 BERA 44017 2880 B7
4700 BHIT 44212 3146 B7
Emerald Ovl N
8500 OmsT 44138 2878 B7
Emerald Pkwy
20400 CLEV 44135 2751 C6
Emerald Pt
- BKPK 44142 2881 B4
- MDBH 44142 2881 B4
16100 MDBH 44130 2881 B4
Emerald St
5800 NRDV 44039 2877 C2
Emerald Vw
- FWPK 44126 2751 D3
Emerald Creek Dr
1200 BWHT 44147 3015 A6
Emerald Edge Pl
11600 SGVL 44136 3012 C6
Emerald Glen Dr
- KTLD 44094 2377 A4
Emerald Lakes Blvd
2800 WBHL 44092 2374 B6
Emerald Ridge Pkwy
- SLN 44139 2888 B2
Emerald Valley Pkwy
30300 GNWL 44139 3019 C1
Emerson Av
10 BERA 44017 2880 C4
12900 LKWD 44107 2622 E4
12900 LKWD 44107 2623 A4
Emerson Ct
41700 ELYR 44035 2874 D3
41700 EyrT 44035 2874 D3
Emerson Dr
10 BERA 44017 2880 B4
2700 PRPK 44124 2629 D4
9800 ClbT 44028 3010 D2
9800 ClbT 44138 3010 D2
9800 ODFL 44138 3010 D2
Emerson Rd
4400 SELD 44121 2498 C6
4800 MadT 44057 2044 D7
Emery Av
11900 CLEV 44135 2753 A3
13500 CLEV 44135 2752 E3
Emery Cir
6100 MNTR 44060 2143 E3
6100 MONT 44060 2143 E3
Emery Rd
19500 NRDL 44128 2757 E5
19500 WVHT 44128 2757 E5
20100 NRDL 44128 2758 E5
21200 WVHT 44128 2758 E5
25900 WVHT 44022 2758 E5
26700 WVHT 44022 2759 B5
26700 WVHT 44128 2759 A5
26900 ORNG 44022 2759 C5
30600 MDHL 44022 2759 D5
Emily Av
2200 LKWD 44107 2622 D6
Emily Ct
8200 CLEV 44102 2623 D7
Emily Ext
13700 ECLE 44112 2497 A6
Emily Ln
100 ELYR 44035 3006 E2
Emily St
13300 ECLE 44112 2496 E7
13300 ECLE 44112 2497 A7
30900 WKLF 44092 2374 E1
Emma Ln
12100 PMHT 44130 2882 A3
Emmet Rd
4900 LNHT 44124 2498 E6
Emmons Rd
23000 ClbT 44028 3145 B3
23000 ClbT 44149 3145 B3
23000 SGVL 44149 3145 B3
Emory Dr
6400 BKPK 44142 2881 A3
35400 AVON 44011 2748 B2
Empire Av
8800 CLEV 44108 2496 B5
Empire Pkwy
7800 MCDN 44056 3153 D3
Empire Rd
1500 WKLF 44092 2374 E2
1500 WLWK 44092 2374 E2
Emsley Ct
38100 WLBY 44094 2250 E1
Enderby Dr
9500 PRMA 44130 2882 C2
Enderby Rd
3200 SRHT 44120 2627 B7
Endicott Rd
2600 SRHT 44120 2627 A5
Endora Rd
16500 CLEV 44112 2497 D4
16500 ECLE 44112 2497 D4

Endsley Av
20800 RKRV 44116 2621 C6
Enfield Dr
6700 MDHT 44124 2630 A1
7000 MNTR 44060 2251 B1
Engel Av
5900 CLEV 44127 2625 E7
5900 CLEV 44127 2755 D1
Engle Rd
5000 BKPK 44135 2752 A7
5000 BKPK 44142 2752 A7
5000 BKPK 44142 2881 A2
5000 CLEV 44135 2752 A7
6400 MDBH 44130 2881 A7
6400 MDBH 44142 2881 A3
7400 MDBH 44130 3012 A1
Engle Rd SR-291
5000 BKPK 44135 2752 A7
5000 BKPK 44142 2752 A7
5000 BKPK 44142 2881 A2
5000 CLEV 44135 2752 A7
6400 MDBH 44130 2881 A7
6400 MDBH 44142 2881 A3
7400 MDBH 44130 3012 A1
Engle Lake Dr
17500 MDBH 44130 2881 A5
Englewood Av
10500 CLEV 44108 2496 C5
Englewood Ct
32600 NRDV 44039 2748 E7
Englewood Dr
100 AVLK 44012 2488 A7
100 AVLK 44012 2618 A1
900 PRMA 44131 2883 E2
900 PRMA 44134 2883 E2
900 SVHL 44131 2883 E2
17700 MDBH 44130 2881 A5
17800 MDBH 44130 2880 E5
E Englewood Dr
10 PRMA 44131 2883 D1
10 PRMA 44134 2883 D1
10 SVHL 44131 2883 D1
10 SVHL 44131 2884 A2
Englewood Rd
800 CVHT 44121 2498 A5
English Dr
7800 BKVL 44141 3015 E3
17800 BbgT 44023 2890 E6
English Lakes Blvd
200 AMHT 44001 2872 D4
English Turn
- AVLK 44012 2618 B4
Enid Rd
29900 WKLF 44092 2249 C7
Ennis Av
10 BDFD 44146 2887 A3
Ensenada Ct
600 BERA 44017 3010 E1
Ensign Av
5500 CLEV 44104 2625 D5
Ensign Rd
13900 ClrT 44021 2636 D1
13900 ClrT 44024 2636 B1
14500 ClrT 44046 2636 D1
Ensign Cove
3400 RMDV 44202 3020 D4
Enterprise Av
13000 CLEV 44135 2752 E6
Enterprise Dr
7800 MNTR 44060 2251 B2
Enterprise Pkwy
1400 TwbT 44087 3154 D4
1700 TNBG 44087 3154 D4
3200 BHWD 44122 2628 E7
3200 BHWD 44122 2758 E1
6000 SLN 44139 2888 C4
E Enterprise Pkwy
2100 TNBG 44087 3155 A4
Enterprise Wy
14900 BtnT 44062 2766 E2
14900 BtnT 44062 2767 A2
Entrence Rd
- EUCL 44117 2373 B7
- EUCL 44117 2498 B1
Epping Rd
1600 GSML 44040 2630 E2
Epping Tr
12000 MsnT 44024 2504 B4
Equestrian Ct
8000 CcdT 44060 2253 B4
Equestrian Dr
13600 BtnT 44021 2636 A4
13600 BtnT 44024 2636 A4
Erhart Northern Rd
- ClbT 44028 3143 E5
- ClbT 44280 3143 E5
- LvpT 44028 3143 E7
600 GftT 44028 3143 E7
600 GftT 44044 3143 E7
600 LvpT 44044 3143 E7
600 LvpT 44280 3143 E7
Eric Dr
7200 MNTR 44060 2143 C3
Eric Ln
1100 CLEV 44109 2754 E6
Erich Dr
2800 WBHL 44092 2374 D7
Ericson Ln
5500 WLBY 44094 2375 B1
Ericston Ct
600 PNVL 44077 2040 A5
Erie Av
6700 MadT 44057 1843 B6
E Erie Av
100 LORN 44052 2614 E6
800 LORN 44052 2615 D4
3500 LORN 44054 2615 D4
3500 SDLK 44054 2615 D4
E Erie Av US-6
100 LORN 44052 2614 E6
800 LORN 44052 2615 D4
3500 LORN 44054 2615 D4
3500 SDLK 44054 2615 D4
W Erie Av
100 LORN 44052 2614 D6
2300 LORN 44053 2614 B7
2700 LORN 44053 2744 A1
3100 LORN 44053 2743 E1
6100 LORN 44053 2742 E4
8000 VMLN 44053 2742 C4
8000 VMLN 44089 2742 C4
W Erie Av US-6
100 LORN 44052 2614 C6
2300 LORN 44053 2614 B7
2700 LORN 44053 2744 A1

W Erie Av US-6
3100 LORN 44053 2743 A4
6100 LORN 44053 2742 E4
8000 VMLN 44053 2742 C4
8000 VMLN 44089 2742 C4
E Erie Br
- LORN 44052 2614 D6
E Erie Br US-6
- LORN 44052 2614 D6
Erie Ct
100 AhtT 44001 2744 B7
1000 CLEV 44115 2625 A3
Erie Dr
7000 MNTR 44060 2251 B1
Erie Rd
10 ETLK 44095 2142 A7
10 ETLK 44095 2250 C3
200 VMLN 44089 2741 B4
900 ETLK 44094 2250 C3
900 WLBY 44094 2250 D3
1000 WLBY 44095 2250 C3
21400 RKRV 44116 2621 B6
Erie St
10 GNVA 44041 1944 C4
100 ELYR 44035 2875 A5
100 SAHT 44001 2872 C7
200 ELYR 44035 2874 E5
600 GFTN 44044 3142 A5
3700 WLBY 44094 2250 E4
5300 BDHT 44146 2887 D1
Erie St US-20
4000 WLBY 44094 2250 E5
E Erie St
10 PNVL 44077 2040 B7
800 PnvT 44077 2040 C6
E Erie St US-20
10 PNVL 44077 2040 B7
800 PnvT 44077 2040 C6
W Erie St
10 PNVL 44077 2146 A1
W Erie St US-20
10 PNVL 44077 2146 A1
Erie Cliff Dr
1000 LKWD 44107 2622 C3
Erieside Av
300 CLEV 44114 2624 D2
Erie St Ext
900 PnvT 44077 2040 C6
Erieview Blvd
100 SDLK 44054 2617 A3
Erieview Dr
100 ETLK 44095 2142 C6
1200 MadT 44057 1843 E6
Erieview Rd
1100 CVHT 44121 2498 A6
Eriewood Dr
1100 RKRV 44116 2621 C6
Erin Av
2600 CLEV 44113 2624 C7
Erin Cir
19100 SGVL 44149 3146 C5
Erin Ct
- GftT 44044 3142 B7
10 RKRV 44116 2621 C7
100 ELYR 44035 3006 D3
Ernadale Av
16200 CLEV 44111 2752 B2
Ernest Av
16500 CLEV 44111 2752 B2
Ernest St
- ELYR 44035 2874 D2
Erwin Av
11700 BKLN 44144 2753 B5
11700 CLEV 44135 2753 A5
11700 CLEV 44144 2753 B5
Erwin Ct
13900 MDBH 44130 2881 D5
Erwin Dr
14500 BtnT 44021 2766 D4
14500 BtnT 44062 2766 D4
Erwin St
5000 MPHT 44137 2757 D7
Eschtruth St
2200 ELYR 44035 2745 E6
2200 EyrT 44035 2745 E6
2200 ShfT 44035 2745 E6
2300 ELYR 44035 2746 A6
2300 ShfT 44035 2746 A6
2300 ShfT 44055 2746 A6
Esma Ln
8400 MNTR 44060 2144 B3
Esmeralda Av
14400 CLEV 44110 2372 A7
Esper Av
6800 PRMA 44134 2883 D6
Essen Av
7400 PRMA 44129 2882 E2
Essex Cir
11200 NRYN 44133 3013 D5
Essex Ct
14400 ClrT 44024 2506 D2
29700 WTLK 44145 2749 C3
Essex Dr
5500 BNHT 44131 2884 B1
5500 SVHL 44131 2884 B2
7300 MNTR 44060 2251 C1
16100 SGVL 44136 3147 B2
Essex Rd
200 VMLN 44089 2741 D4
2900 CVHT 44118 2627 B3
Estate Av
7500 TwbT 44236 3154 D6
7700 TwbT 44087 3154 D5
Estates Ct
28600 SLN 44139 2888 B1
Estelle Av
3000 LORN 44052 2744 D3
Esterbrook Av
8800 CLEV 44108 2496 B5
Esther Av
14900 LKWD 44107 2622 C6
22700 FWPK 44126 2751 A5
22900 NOSD 44070 2750 E5
22900 NOSD 44070 2751 A5
22900 NOSD 44126 2751 A5
Esther Dr
38900 CrlT 44044 3006 D7
Esther Rd
700 HDHT 44143 2499 B4
Esther St
8400 MNTR 44060 2252 B2
Estill Dr
1000 LKWD 44107 2622 D3
Ethan Av
1200 STBR 44241 3156 E6

Ethan Ct
3000 BNWK 44212 3147 C7
Ethan Tr
15400 NRYN 44133 3148 A2
Ethan's Dr
2500 TNBG 44087 3020 B3
Ethel Av
1100 LKWD 44107 2622 B4
6000 EyrT 44035 2745 D6
6000 ShfT 44035 2745 D6
6000 ShfT 44055 2745 D6
Ethel Ct
8900 CLEV 44106 2496 B7
Ethel Dr
22200 ClbT 44028 3010 E3
22200 ClbT 44149 3010 E3
22200 SGVL 44149 3010 E3
41700 CrlT 44035 3005 C4
Eton St
1900 TwbT 44087 3154 C2
2000 TNBG 44087 3154 C2
Euclid Av
100 CLEV 44114 2624 E3
100 CLEV 44115 2624 E3
200 LORN 44052 2615 C7
900 CLEV 44114 2625 A3
1200 CLEV 44115 2625 A3
3600 CLEV 44103 2625 E2
7300 CLEV 44103 2626 B2
8400 CLEV 44106 2626 E1
12200 ECLE 44106 2626 E1
12400 ECLE 44112 2626 E1
12600 ECLE 44112 2496 E7
13500 ECLE 44112 2497 B4
16300 CLEV 44112 2497 E2
18000 CLEV 44121 2497 D2
18400 CLEV 44117 2497 E2
19400 EUCL 44117 2497 E2
19600 EUCL 44117 2498 A1
20400 EUCL 44143 2498 A1
20700 EUCL 44117 2373 C7
25400 EUCL 44132 2373 D5
26000 EUCL 44143 2373 E5
27000 EUCL 44132 2374 A4
28600 WKLF 44092 2374 B3
30300 WLWK 44092 2374 D1
30500 WKLF 44092 2249 E7
30500 WLWK 44092 2249 E7
30700 WKLF 44094 2249 E7
30700 WLBY 44094 2249 E7
34000 WLBY 44094 2250 C6
Euclid Av US-6
13500 ECLE 44112 2497 B4
16300 CLEV 44112 2497 E2
18000 CLEV 44121 2497 D2
18400 CLEV 44117 2497 E2
18400 EUCL 44117 2497 E2
19600 EUCL 44117 2498 A1
20400 EUCL 44143 2498 A1
Euclid Av US-20
100 CLEV 44114 2624 E3
100 CLEV 44115 2624 E3
900 CLEV 44114 2625 A3
1200 CLEV 44115 2625 A3
3600 CLEV 44103 2625 E2
7300 CLEV 44103 2626 B2
8400 CLEV 44106 2626 E1
12200 ECLE 44106 2626 E1
12400 ECLE 44112 2626 E1
12600 ECLE 44112 2496 E7
13500 ECLE 44112 2497 B4
16300 CLEV 44112 2497 E2
18000 CLEV 44121 2497 D2
18400 CLEV 44117 2497 E2
18400 EUCL 44117 2497 E2
19600 EUCL 44117 2498 A1
20400 EUCL 44143 2498 A1
20700 EUCL 44117 2373 C7
25400 EUCL 44132 2373 D5
26000 EUCL 44143 2373 E5
27000 EUCL 44132 2374 A4
28300 WKLF 44092 2374 B3
30300 WLWK 44092 2374 D1
30500 WKLF 44092 2249 E7
30500 WLWK 44092 2249 E7
30700 WKLF 44094 2249 E7
30700 WLBY 44094 2249 E7
34000 WLBY 44094 2250 C6
Euclid Av US-322
10900 CLEV 44106 2626 D2
Euclid Dr
36000 NRDV 44039 2876 E7
Euclid St
100 ELYR 44035 2875 A4
Euclid Beach Blvd
16000 CLEV 44110 2372 C6
Euclid Chagrin Pkwy
25800 RDHT 44143 2498 D2
Euclid Creek Pkwy
6600 EUCL 44117 2498 B4
6600 EUCL 44143 2498 A2
6600 SELD 44117 2498 B4
6600 SELD 44121 2498 B4
Euclid Heights Blvd
2300 CLEV 44106 2626 E3
2300 CVHT 44106 2626 E3
2500 CVHT 44106 2627 A2
2700 CVHT 44118 2627 B2
Euclid Square Mall
- EUCL 44117 2373 D4
10 EUCL 44132 2373 D4
Euclid Vets Dr
1300 EUCL 44132 2373 E4
Eugene Dr
- CsTp 44026 2502 B6
Eureka Pkwy
9400 PMHT 44130 2882 C2
Euston Dr
1800 MDHT 44124 2629 C2
Evangeline Rd
800 CLEV 44110 2497 B2
Evans Dr
7700 PRMA 44130 3013 B2
Evanston Av
3800 CLEV 44122 2757 E3
3800 WVHT 44122 2757 E3
Evanston Ln
- AhtT 44001 2872 E6
Evanston Rd
1400 LNHT 44124 2498 D7
Evarts Rd
8800 CLEV 44104 2626 B5
Eve Av
6700 VLVW 44125 2885 C5
7600 CLEV 44102 2623 E6

Eve Ct
- CLEV 44102 2623 E6
Evelyn
- AhtT 44001 2872 B2
- AMHT 44001 2872 B2
Evelyn Av
100 PRMA 44131 3014 E1
100 PRMA 44134 3014 E1
100 SVHL 44131 3014 E1
100 SVHL 44131 3015 A1
3000 LORN 44052 2744 D3
Evelyn Ct
14000 SGVL 44136 3012 C3
Evelyn Dr
3800 NOSD 44070 2750 C5
5200 GDHT 44125 2757 A7
Evening Star Av
15700 MPHT 44137 2886 B3
Eventide Dr
6900 PRMA 44129 2882 E6
Everett Av
10 PnvT 44077 2145 B4
7500 CLEV 44103 2626 A1
Everett Rd
100 PnvT 44077 2145 B5
Everett St
100 GDRV 44077 2039 B6
400 PnvT 44077 2039 B6
Evergreen Blvd
7300 NRDV 44039 2876 C4
Evergreen Ct
300 AVLK 44012 2618 C2
2900 LORN 44052 2744 B3
Evergreen Dr
5000 NOSD 44070 2749 D7
6300 INDE 44131 2884 E4
7200 CsTp 44026 2501 B1
8200 PRMA 44129 2882 D1
8400 SgHT 44067 3017 B4
8700 MNTR 44060 2252 D1
14600 BURT 44021 2766 B1
18500 SGVL 44149 3011 E2
28300 WBHL 44092 2374 B6
39300 AVON 44011 2747 A5
Evergreen Mdws
8900 ELYR 44035 2874 A7
8900 EyrT 44035 2874 A7
Evergreen Pkwy
5300 SFLD 44054 2746 E2
Evergreen Pl
10 CLEV 44110 2372 B6
Evergreen Rd
2000 NPRY 44081 1941 A3
Evergreen Tr
- OmsT 44138 2878 B7
20800 NRYN 44133 3148 B5
20900 HkyT 44133 3148 B5
20900 HkyT 44233 3148 B5
Everton Av
5000 ORNG 44022 2759 D7
5000 SLN 44022 2759 D7
5000 SLN 44139 2759 D7
10500 CLEV 44108 2496 C5
Everwood Wy
- MadT 44057 1941 B3
Evins Av
8600 CLEV 44104 2626 A5
Ewa Yea St
400 VMLN 44089 2741 A4
Excalibur Av
3000 WTLK 44145 2749 D3
Excalibur Dr
7100 CcdT 44077 2146 A7
Exchange St
700 VMLN 44089 2740 E6
7300 VLVW 44125 2885 A2
Executive Ct
9600 CcdT 44060 2145 B6
Exeter Rd
2500 CVHT 44118 2627 C5
11100 GDHT 44125 2885 C2
Exmoor Dr
11000 CcdT 44077 2146 C6
Ezmor Ln
500 WKLF 44092 2249 A7
Ezra Ct
10000 TNBG 44087 3020 B4

F

F Dr
- LORN 44052 2744 E4
F St
600 LORN 44052 2615 A6
Fackler Av
2400 ELYR 44035 2746 A6
2400 ShfT 44035 2746 A6
Factory St
1200 LORN 44055 2745 B3
Fair Rd
8000 SGVL 44149 3011 B3
Fair St
100 BERA 44017 2880 B7
400 BERA 44017 3011 B1
Fairacres Av
6800 NRDV 44039 2877 C3
Fairbanks Ct
4200 LORN 44053 2743 D3
Fairchild Av
11400 CLEV 44106 2626 D3
11400 CVHT 44106 2626 D3
Fairdale Av
2100 CLEV 44109 2754 D6
Fairdale Rd
10 PnvT 44077 2145 D4
Fairfax Av
16500 CLEV 44128 2757 C5
Fairfax Dr
10 SRSL 44022 2762 B7
6400 MNTR 44060 2144 A5
Fairfax Ln
17400 SGVL 44136 3146 E4
17400 SGVL 44136 3147 A4
26400 NOSD 44070 2750 A5
Fairfax Rd
200 VMLN 44089 2741 D4
2700 CVHT 44118 2627 B4
E Fairfax Rd
3200 CVHT 44118 2627 C4
Fairfax St
2600 ShvT 44255 3157 E7
2600 ShvT 44255 3158 A7
2600 STBR 44255 3157 E7
Fairfield Av
1000 CLEV 44113 2624 E5

Fairfield Dr
- AVON 44011 2747 A2
- ELYR 44035 2873 E7
9300 TNBG 44087 3019 C6
Fairfield Ln
600 AURA 44202 3021 C7
37000 NRDV 44035 3007 D1
Fairfield Ovl
5200 SLN 44139 2888 D1
Fairfield Pl
400 AMHT 44001 2872 B2
21600 SGVL 44149 3011 A6
Fairfield Rd
10 PnvT 44077 2145 C5
100 AVLK 44012 2617 E2
200 CcdT 44077 2145 C6
Fairfield Tr
12900 CsTp 44026 2631 C2
Fairgate Blvd
13800 NbyT 44065 2634 A6
Fairgrounds Rd
10 PnvT 44077 2145 D4
200 CcdT 44077 2145 D5
Fairhaven Ct
7700 MNTR 44060 2252 D2
Fairhaven Dr
10 NCtT 44067 3153 A2
100 NCtT 44067 3152 E2
Fairhaven Rd
6200 MDHT 44124 2629 E3
6200 MDHT 44124 2630 A2
Fairhill Dr
3200 RKRV 44116 2751 E1
Fairhill Rd
- CVHT 44106 2627 A4
- CVHT 44118 2627 A4
- SRHT 44106 2627 A4
- SRHT 44118 2627 A4
11600 CLEV 44120 2626 E4
12300 CLEV 44106 2626 E4
12300 CVHT 44106 2626 E4
12300 SRHT 44120 2626 E4
13700 SRHT 44120 2627 A4
Fairidge Rd
7700 KTLD 44094 2251 D7
Fairington Dr
666-00 AURA 44202 3156 C3
Fairington Ln
662-00 AURA 44202 3156 C3
Fairington Ovl
613-00 AURA 44202 3156 C3
Fair Isle Wy
19500 SGVL 44149 3011 D7
Fairlane Cir
20900 FWPK 44126 2751 C3
Fairlane Dr
8200 MCDN 44056 3018 B7
8200 MCDN 44056 3153 B1
8500 OmsT 44138 2879 A7
Fairlawn Av
100 ELYR 44035 2875 D6
400 PNVL 44077 2039 E7
7700 MNTR 44060 2252 E2
14300 CLEV 44111 2752 D2
Fairlawn Blvd
12400 GDHT 44125 2885 D2
Fairlawn Cir
22300 FWPK 44126 2751 A4
Fairlawn Dr
300 RDHT 44143 2498 E1
3600 NOSD 44070 2750 D4
10400 PRMA 44130 2753 B7
17500 BbgT 44023 2891 B4
22700 EUCL 44117 2373 C7
Fairlawn Rd
4700 LNHT 44124 2498 D6
4700 SELD 44121 2498 D6
Fairless Dr
2200 LORN 44055 2745 E5
2200 LORN 44055 2746 A5
Fairlie Av
- CLEV 44103 2495 D6
- CLEV 44114 2495 D6
Fairmeadow Ln
14700 BtnT 44021 2765 D1
Fair Meadow Pl
9100 SGVL 44149 3011 C3
Fairmont
- VMLN 44089 2740 E6
Fairmount Av
500 ELYR 44035 2875 A5
Fairmount Blvd
2400 CVHT 44106 2626 E3
2600 CVHT 44106 2627 A3
2700 CVHT 44118 2627 D5
18700 SRHT 44118 2627 E5
20600 SRHT 44118 2628 B5
20600 SRHT 44122 2628 A5
22800 BHWD 44122 2628 C5
26000 BHWD 44122 2629 A5
26700 PRPK 44124 2629 C4
32900 PRPK 44124 2630 A4
33600 HGVL 44022 2630 E5
33600 HGVL 44124 2630 A4
33600 PRPK 44022 2630 A4
39000 HGVL 44022 2631 A5
47000 RslT 44022 2631 A5
47000 RslT 44072 2631 A5
Fairmount Cir
- SRHT 44118 2628 A5
- UNHT 44118 2628 A5
Fairmount Rd
7300 HGVL 44022 2631 B5
7300 RslT 44022 2631 B5
7300 RslT 44072 2631 D5
8200 RslT 44072 2632 D5
9300 NbyT 44065 2633 A5
9300 NbyT 44072 2633 A5
9300 RslT 44072 2633 A5
10200 NbyT 44065 2634 A5
Fair Oaks Dr
3700 CVHT 44121 2497 E4
3700 SELD 44121 2497 E4
Fair Oaks Rd
7000 BDFD 44146 2887 C7
7000 OKWD 44146 2887 C7
7200 OKWD 44146 3018 C1
Fairpark Dr
100 BERA 44017 3011 A1
20800 FWPK 44126 2751 C3
Fairport Av
11300 CLEV 44108 2496 D6
Fairport Dr
- VMLN 44089 2742 B5
33100 AVLK 44012 2617 D4

Fairport Nursery Rd
10 PnvT 44077 2040 A3
500 FTHR 44077 2039 D4
500 PnvT 44077 2039 E3
Fairport Nursery Rd SR-535
10 PnvT 44077 2040 A3
500 FTHR 44077 2039 D4
500 PnvT 44077 2039 E3
Fairtree Dr
9800 SGVL 44149 3011 C4
Fairtree Rd
5200 BDHT 44146 2887 B1
Fairview Av
600 AURA 44202 3021 C4
2000 CLEV 44106 2626 E2
2000 CVHT 44106 2626 E2
7500 MNTR 44060 2252 A2
Fairview Ct
12200 CLEV 44106 2626 E2
Fairview Dr
7600 KTLD 44094 2251 D7
31100 ORNG 44022 2759 D6
E Fairview Dr
4800 ORNG 44022 2759 D6
W Fairview Dr
4800 ORNG 44022 2759 D6
Fairview Ln
1000 AURA 44202 3021 B3
Fairview Pkwy
4400 FWPK 44126 2751 C3
Fairview Rd
100 GNVA 44041 1944 B6
2800 WBHL 44092 2374 C5
31100 RslT 44022 2761 C5
31100 SRSL 44022 2761 C5
Fairview Center Dr
- FWPK 44126 2751 A6
Fairville Av
17400 CLEV 44135 2752 A5
18200 CLEV 44135 2751 E5
Fairway Av
18700 MPHT 44137 2757 E7
Fairway Blvd
500 WKLF 44092 2249 B7
500 WKLF 44095 2249 B7
1900 HDSN 44236 3154 E6
1900 HDSN 44236 3155 A6
1900 TwbT 44236 3154 E6
1900 TwbT 44236 3155 A6
29800 WLWK 44095 2249 C6
Fairway Cir
2000 HDSN 44236 3155 A6
2000 TwbT 44236 3155 A6
Fairway Dr
10 OBLN 44074 3138 C3
1700 LORN 44053 2744 B4
1900 WKLF 44092 2374 E2
4300 CLEV 44135 2752 A4
4400 WTLK 44145 2749 C5
4700 AVON 44011 2748 B6
4700 BKLN 44144 2753 C5
11000 ClbT 44028 3010 D4
Fairway Tr
10 MDHL 44022 2760 A6
Fairway Vw
400 AbnT 44023 2892 B3
Fairweather Dr
6400 BKPK 44142 2881 E4
6400 MDBH 44130 2881 E4
6400 MDBH 44142 2881 E4
Fairwin Dr
31200 BYVL 44140 2619 A4
Fairwinds Dr
13100 SGVL 44136 3147 D4
Fairwood Blvd
700 ELYR 44035 2875 E2
Fairwood Cir
- AVON 44011 2747 B2
300 BERA 44017 2880 A7
Fairwood Dr
2500 PRPK 44124 2629 B4
13500 CLEV 44111 2752 E2
Falbo Av
3000 LORN 44052 2744 E4
Falcon St
100 ELYR 44035 3006 E3
Falcon Crest Av
35900 AVON 44011 2748 A2
36100 AVON 44011 2747 E2
Falcon Ridge Rd
- CsTp 44026 2502 C6
Falkirk Dr
- WTLK 44145 2619 B7
Falkirk Rd
1600 MadT 44057 1843 A7
1600 MadT 44057 1942 A1
5600 LNHT 44124 2629 B2
Fall St
1600 CLEV 44113 2624 D4
Fallen Oaks
2200 WTLK 44145 2750 E1
Fallen Oaks Ln
10 AMHT 44001 2872 D3
Fallhaven Cir
32600 NRDV 44039 2877 D7
Falling Leaf Dr
100 SVHL 44131 3014 E1
100 SVHL 44131 3015 A1
Falling Leaves Cir
400 AURA 44202 3021 C6
Fallingleaves Rd
17600 SGVL 44136 3012 A5
17800 SGVL 44136 3011 E6
Falling Rock Ln
1200 PnvT 44077 2147 A1
Falling Water Cir
300 AMHT 44001 2872 B3
Fallingwater Dr
- ELYR 44035 2874 B6
Falling Water Rd
12800 SGVL 44136 3012 A6
17700 SGVL 44136 3011 D6
18800 SGVL 44149 3011 D6
18900 BbgT 44023 3021 E2
Fall Lake Dr
4200 AVON 44011 2748 C5
N Fall Lake Dr
33700 AVON 44011 2748 C5
S Fall Lake Dr
4200 AVON 44011 2748 C5
Fall River Dr
28700 WTLK 44145 2749 D5
Falls Cir
15000 NRYN 44133 3147 E5

STREET
Block City ZIP Map# Grid

Falls Ln
- BERA 44017 2880 A5
8700 BWHT 44147 3014 C6
Falls Ovl
2100 WTLK 44145 2749 A2
Falls Rd
200 CNFL 44022 2761 A4
500 CFIT 44022 2761 A4
600 CFIT 44022 2760 E4
3800 HGVL 44022 2760 E3
3800 MDHL 44022 2760 E3
12100 MsnT 44024 2504 B5
Falls Creek Cir
10 MDHL 44022 2760 B6
Falls Creek Tr
10 MDHL 44022 2760 B5
Falls Pointe Dr E
- ODFL 44138 3010 B1
26900 ODFL 44138 3009 E1
Falmouth Cir
11200 NRYN 44133 3013 D5
Falmouth Ct
100 BNWK 44212 3147 B6
Falmouth Dr
200 RKRV 44116 2621 D5
16000 SGVL 44136 3147 A4
S Falmouth Dr
500 RKRV 44116 2621 D5
Falmouth Ovl
15800 MDBH 44130 2881 B4
Falmouth Rd
2800 SRHT 44122 2628 A7
Fancher Av
8200 CLEV 44103 2496 A7
Fanta Ct
4800 CLEV 44102 2624 B7
Fantail Dr
7300 NCtT 44067 3153 C4
Fanwood Ct
1000 PnvT 44077 2146 E1
Fanwood Dr
300 PnvT 44077 2146 E1
Faraday Rd
5600 LNHT 44124 2629 B1
Faraway Tr
7400 BbgT 44023 2890 B3
Farbar Rd
8700 KTLD 44094 2377 C6
Fareham Ct
100 AURA 44202 3021 E7
Fargo Av
25900 BDHT 44146 2758 E7
25900 BDHT 44146 2759 A7
Far Hills Dr
7200 CcdT 44077 2254 D1
Farland Rd
3500 CVHT 44118 2627 D3
3500 UNHT 44118 2627 D3
Farley Dr
4500 MNTR 44060 2038 E5
Farm Dr
31500 SLN 44139 2888 D3
S Farm Rd
8100 MCDN 44056 3018 B7
8100 MCDN 44056 3153 B1
Farmbrook Ln
8200 KTLD 44094 2377 A4
Farmcote Dr
10 HGVL 44022 2760 A2
10 MDHL 44022 2760 A2
Farmingdale Ln
6700 MNTR 44060 2143 B5
Farmington Ct
9800 CcdT 44060 2145 B7
Farmington Dr
6400 GDHT 44125 2885 E4
6400 GDHT 44125 2886 A4
Farmington Rd
1800 ECLE 44112 2496 E7
1800 ECLE 44112 2497 A7
Farmington Turn
1900 WTLK 44145 2749 C1
Farnham Dr
7000 MNTR 44060 2143 B7
Farnham Rd
2700 RchT 44286 3151 A7
2700 RHFD 44286 3151 A7
Farnham Wy
800 HDSN 44236 3154 A7
Farnhurst Rd
4700 LNHT 44124 2498 D7
4700 SELD 44121 2498 D7
4700 SELD 44124 2498 D7
E Farnhurst Rd
5000 LNHT 44124 2498 E7
5000 LNHT 44124 2499 A7
W Farnhurst Rd
4600 SELD 44121 2498 D7
4700 LNHT 44124 2498 D7
4700 SELD 44124 2498 D7
Farnsleigh Rd
3400 SRHT 44122 2758 A1
20100 SRHT 44122 2628 A7
20700 BHWD 44122 2628 A7
Farnsworth Dr
5700 PRMA 44129 2883 A3
6600 PRMA 44129 2882 E3
Farnum Av
7400 MDBH 44130 2881 A7
7400 MDBH 44130 3012 A1
Farr Av
4900 ShfT 44055 2746 A6
Farragut Dr
35000 ETLK 44095 2142 B7
Farringdon Av
11600 CLEV 44105 2756 D2
12900 CLEV 44120 2756 E2
24700 EUCL 44123 2373 D2
24700 EUCL 44132 2373 D2
26800 EUCL 44132 2374 A2
Farrs Garden Pth
1700 WTLK 44145 2619 D7
1700 WTLK 44145 2749 D1
Farview Ovl
8000 BKVL 44141 3015 E4
Farview Rd
6300 BKVL 44141 3015 E4
6300 BWHT 44141 3015 E4
6300 BWHT 44147 3015 E4
6800 BKVL 44141 3016 A4
Farwood Dr
- HGVL 44022 2760 C2
10 MDHL 44022 2760 C2
Father Caruso Dr
- CLEV 44102 2623 E4

Father Caruso Dr
- CLEV 44102 2624 A4
Fatima Dr
1400 PRMA 44134 2883 E6
Faversham Rd
3800 UNHT 44118 2627 E4
3800 UNHT 44118 2628 A4
Fawn Cir
- BhmT 44001 2870 C7
5800 BKVL 44141 3150 D3
18100 SGVL 44136 3146 E2
Fawn Ct
500 SRSL 44022 2761 E5
700 STBR 44241 3156 C7
9000 RslT 44072 2762 C5
9700 CcdT 44060 2253 B3
Fawn Dr
24600 NOSD 44070 2750 C4
25300 WTLK 44070 2750 C4
25300 WTLK 44145 2750 C4
Fawn Ln
5800 BKVL 44141 3150 D3
Fawn Chase
2400 RHFD 44286 3150 D7
Fawnhaven Dr
20800 NRYN 44133 3148 B5
20900 HkyT 44133 3148 B5
20900 HkyT 44233 3148 B5
Fawn Hill Pl
36100 WLBY 44094 2375 B2
Fawn Meadow Ln
10800 SGVL 44149 3011 D5
Fawn Path Dr
37400 SLN 44139 2889 D3
Faxon Pl
1400 ELYR 44035 3006 B1
Fay Av
100 AVLK 44012 2488 B7
100 AVLK 44012 2618 B1
Fay Dr
1800 PRMA 44134 3014 D1
4700 SELD 44121 2498 D5
Fay Rd
6300 CcdT 44077 2146 C6
Fay St
1700 ECLE 44112 2497 A6
Faye Ln
7300 MNTR 44060 2143 C5
Fayette Blvd
14400 BKPK 44142 2881 C2
Fayette Rd
20600 SRHT 44122 2628 A6
Fedeli Ln
- RslT 44072 2762 D4
Federal Dr
17700 CLEV 44128 2757 D6
Feiner Dr
4000 CLEV 44122 2757 D4
4000 CLEV 44128 2757 D4
4200 WVHT 44122 2757 D4
4200 WVHT 44128 2757 D4
Felch St
22400 NRDL 44128 2758 C6
22400 WVHT 44128 2758 C6
Fell Av
10 NHFD 44067 3018 A3
Felton Rd
1400 SELD 44121 2498 B7
1400 SELD 44121 2628 B1
Fence Row Dr
10800 SGVL 44149 3010 E5
10800 SGVL 44149 3011 A4
Fenemore Rd
15600 ECLE 44112 2497 B6
Fenlake Rd
5400 BDHT 44146 2887 C1
Fenley Rd
3500 CVHT 44121 2497 E4
3600 SELD 44121 2497 E4
Fenton Ct
8700 SgHT 44067 3017 D4
Fenway Dr
2100 BHWD 44121 2628 C3
2100 BHWD 44122 2628 C3
2100 SELD 44121 2628 C3
2100 UNHT 44121 2628 C3
7900 PRMA 44129 2882 D6
Fenwick Av
4200 CLEV 44113 2624 B6
4800 CLEV 44102 2624 B6
Fenwick Dr
28900 WKLF 44092 2374 C4
Fenwick Rd
1900 SELD 44118 2628 A2
2100 SELD 44118 2627 E3
2100 UNHT 44118 2627 E4
2500 UNHT 44118 2628 A5
Fenwood Ct
5700 MONT 44060 2143 E2
Fenwood Rd
2300 UNHT 44118 2628 A4
Fergus Av
2000 CLEV 44109 2754 D4
Ferman Av
1100 CLEV 44109 2754 E5
Fern Ct
2000 CLEV 44109 2754 D2
Fern Dr
10 PNVL 44077 2145 D3
300 BERA 44017 2880 A5
7300 MONT 44060 2143 D2
30000 WLWK 44095 2249 C6
Fern St
300 SAHT 44001 3003 A1
Fern Canyon Dr
18000 SGVL 44136 3147 B4
Ferncliffe Av
18200 CLEV 44135 2751 E5
18200 CLEV 44135 2752 A5
Fern Cove E
9000 ODFL 44138 3009 E1
Fern Cove W
9000 ODFL 44138 3009 E1
Ferndale Av
300 VMLN 44089 2742 A5
2000 LKWD 44107 2622 D6
3700 SDLK 44054 2615 E4
3800 SDLK 44054 2616 A4
16500 CLEV 44111 2752 B2
Ferndale Dr
- CrlT 44035 3005 D5
Fern Hall Rd
25800 OmsT 44138 2879 B3
Fernhill Av
7700 PRMA 44129 2882 D1

Fernhurst Av
6300 PMHT 44130 2881 E5
Fernshaw Av
17100 CLEV 44111 2752 A3
Fern Tree Ln
33000 NRDV 44039 2748 D7
Fernway Av
15300 CLEV 44111 2622 C7
Fernway Cir
36200 AVON 44011 2747 E5
Fernway Ct
- CcdT 44077 2255 A4
Fernway Dr
- MsnT 44024 2504 C3
10800 ManT 44255 3159 D4
10800 MNTU 44255 3159 C4
15300 MPHT 44137 2886 B2
Fernway Rd
15600 SRHT 44120 2627 C7
17600 SRHT 44122 2627 C7
Fernwood Av
300 AVLK 44012 2617 D2
13700 ECLE 44112 2497 A6
Fernwood Cir
14100 SGVL 44136 3012 D4
Fernwood Dr
10 SRSL 44022 2761 C6
100 RslT 44022 2761 C6
1000 WTLK 44145 2620 E7
9200 ODFL 44138 3010 A1
9500 ClbT 44028 3010 A2
9500 ClbT 44138 3010 A2
23100 BHWD 44122 2628 C5
23100 UNHT 44118 2628 C5
Ferrell Av
7900 CLEV 44102 2623 E6
Ferris Av
100 CRDN 44024 2379 E7
12300 CLEV 44105 2756 E3
13100 CLEV 44105 2757 A3
Ferris State Ct
100 ELYR 44035 3006 D2
Ferro Av
5600 CLEV 44105 2755 D3
Ferry Rd
11400 CsTp 44026 2501 B2
Ferry St
5500 VMLN 44089 2740 E5
Festival Dr
10 OmsT 44138 2879 A3
Fetterman Dr
14200 SGVL 44149 3146 D1
Fetzer Dr
17300 SGVL 44149 3146 D3
Fiddlers Wy
100 PnvT 44077 2145 B1
Fiddlers Green Ln
- GFTN 44044 3142 B4
Fiddle Sticks
10 OmsT 44138 2879 A4
Fidelity Av
10100 CLEV 44102 2753 C1
11400 CLEV 44111 2753 B1
Field Av
4800 CLEV 44102 2624 B7
Field St
2700 ShfT 44255 3158 A7
Fieldcrest Cir
- AVON 44011 2748 E3
Fieldcrest Ct
700 SgHT 44067 3152 C1
Fielding Dr
3900 NOSD 44070 2750 B5
Fields Rd
7300 BbgT 44023 2890 B5
Fields Wy
4500 LORN 44053 2743 E4
Fieldstone Cir
5800 NRDV 44039 2878 A2
31800 AVLK 44012 2618 D4
Fieldstone Ct
1300 BWHT 44147 3149 E4
7900 CcdT 44060 2253 C3
Fieldstone Dr
100 EatT 44035 3007 A2
100 ELYR 44035 3007 A2
500 AhtT 44001 2873 B2
Field Stone Ln
7900 MCDN 44056 3154 A5
Fieldstone Ln
1400 TwbT 44236 3154 C6
Fieldstone Pt
12300 SGVL 44149 3011 B6
Fieldstone Tr
- AVON 44011 2747 A2
6000 SVHL 44131 2883 E3
Fiesta Ct
6300 LORN 44053 2744 E7
Fifth St
- LORN 44052 2744 E4
- ShfT 44052 2744 E4
Figgie Dr
4600 WLBY 44094 2251 B6
Figgie Rd
300 PNVL 44077 2039 E7
Filbert St
100 ELYR 44035 2874 E6
Filip Blvd
6900 INDE 44131 2884 D7
Fillier St
10 BERA 44017 2880 C5
Fillmore Av
500 ELYR 44035 2875 A4
1500 LORN 44052 2615 B6
Fillmore Cir
1200 LORN 44052 2615 B6
Fillmore Ct
7100 MNTR 44060 2143 D7
Filly Ln
10 NHFD 44067 3018 A3
Filo Av
5300 CLEV 44105 2755 D2
Finch Dr
100 ELYR 44035 3006 E3
Fincherie Dr
10500 CdnT 44024 2378 E6
Finchfield Cir
200 MCDN 44056 3018 A6
Findlay Ct
100 ELYR 44035 3006 D2
Findlay St
16600 BbgT 44023 2890 A1
Findley Dr
8200 MNTR 44060 2144 A4

Finestera Ln
- AVLK 44012 2618 D2
Finn Av
4800 CLEV 44127 2625 C6
Finney Av
7600 CLEV 44105 2756 A3
Finwood Ct
700 ELYR 44035 2875 E1
Finwood Forest Dr
- ELYR 44035 2875 D1
Fir Av
5800 CLEV 44102 2624 A6
Fir Ct
1700 LORN 44055 2745 C5
Fircrest Ln
10 MDHL 44022 2760 C2
Firebush Ln
10 NCtT 44067 3153 B4
Firecrest Cir
5600 NRDV 44039 2877 E1
Firefly Dr
11900 NRYN 44133 3147 E5
Firelands Dr
600 AVON 44011 2617 E6
9600 TNBG 44087 3020 B6
Fireside Ct
6800 MNTR 44060 2143 B6
Fireside Dr
- AbnT 44023 2891 E6
- AbnT 44023 2892 A6
- BbgT 44023 2891 E6
Fireside Tr
1000 BWHT 44147 3149 D3
Fire Station Dr
- BHWD 44122 2758 D1
Firestone Dr
700 AVLK 44012 2618 C5
Firestone Ln
4100 VMLN 44089 2741 C4
9700 MCDN 44056 3018 B5
10000 MCDN 44067 3018 B5
10000 NHFD 44067 3018 B5
Firethorn Dr
800 SVHL 44131 2884 A4
Firewood Cir
7300 INDE 44131 2884 D7
7300 INDE 44131 3015 D1
Firsby Av
12500 CLEV 44135 2753 A4
First St
- HmbT 44024 2380 C3
- LORN 44052 2744 E4
Fir Tree Dr
3100 NRYN 44133 3014 C5
Firwood Ln
- AbnT 44023 2892 A1
Firwood Rd
1000 BWHT 44147 3015 A3
6000 MNTR 44060 2143 B3
6000 MONT 44060 2143 B3
19000 CLEV 44110 2372 E7
Fischer Rd
16500 CLEV 44107 2622 B7
16500 CLEV 44111 2622 B7
16500 LKWD 44107 2622 B7
16800 LKWD 44111 2622 B7
Fish Creek Tr
17300 BbgT 44023 2890 D4
Fisher Rd
13400 BtnT 44021 2635 E5
13400 BtnT 44021 2636 A6
24800 EUCL 44117 2373 B6
Fisher St
5700 VMLN 44089 2740 D6
Fishermans Tr
1800 MadT 44057 1941 D1
Fitch Dr
5000 SFLD 44054 2746 D1
Fitch Rd
5400 NOSD 44070 2879 A1
6200 OmsT 44070 2879 A2
6200 OmsT 44138 2879 A1
Fitzroy St
1300 WTLK 44145 2620 B7
Fitzwater Rd
7000 BKVL 44141 3016 C3
W Fitzwater Rd
6800 BKVL 44141 3016 A4
Five Points Rd
- BKPK 44135 2880 E2
- BKPK 44142 2880 E2
19400 CLEV 44135 2880 D2
Flagler Dr
10 OmsT 44138 2879 A4
Flamingo Av
10 AMHT 44001 2744 B7
18000 CLEV 44135 2752 A5
18300 CLEV 44135 2751 E5
Flanders Dr
- SLN 44139 3020 D1
37700 SLN 44139 2889 D6
Flat Rock Dr
10400 MsnT 44024 2503 C2
Fleet Av
- NBGH 44105 2755 C2
4900 CLEV 44105 2755 D2
7300 CLEV 44105 2756 A2
Fleetwood Dr
1000 SgHT 44067 3152 A1
Fleger Dr
2600 PRMA 44134 3014 C2
Fleharty Rd
4600 NOSD 44070 2750 C6
Fleming Av
3700 CLEV 44115 2625 C4
4900 ShfT 44055 2746 A6
Flick Dr
400 BDFD 44146 2886 D4
Flintlock Rdg
7800 BbgT 44023 2890 C4
Flint Ridge Dr
- CrlT 44044 3006 E5
37500 EatT 44044 3007 A5
38400 EatT 44044 3006 E5
Flint Rock Ridge Rd
- BbgT 44023 2890 B4
Flora Av
10000 CLEV 44108 2496 C5
Flora Dr
10 BDFD 44137 2886 D2
10 BDFD 44146 2886 D2
10 MPHT 44137 2886 D2
10 MPHT 44146 2886 D2
Floradale St
100 ELYR 44035 2875 A4

Floral Ct
100 ELYR 44035 2875 A5
Floraline St
33600 NRDV 44039 2877 D3
Florance Ct
100 ELYR 44035 2875 A5
Florence Av
10 PnvT 44077 2039 D7
24500 NOSD 44070 2750 C5
Florence Dr
900 MCDN 44056 3018 E3
900 MCDN 44056 3019 A3
900 TNBG 44056 3019 A3
900 TNBG 44087 3019 A3
14900 MPHT 44137 2886 A5
14900 WNHL 44146 2886 B5
38400 WLBY 44094 2376 A6
Florence Ln
14000 NRYN 44133 3149 B1
Florence Rd
9100 KTLD 44094 2251 E7
9100 KTLD 44094 2376 E1
Florence St
300 BYVL 44140 2619 C3
Florence Wy Ct
3400 PryT 44081 1940 D7
Florentine Wy
10 OmsT 44138 2879 A3
Florian Av
10600 CLEV 44111 2753 B1
Florian Blvd
- INDE 44131 2884 E7
Florida Av
200 LORN 44052 2615 A6
14800 CLEV 44128 2757 A5
Florida St
4100 PryT 44081 2041 D4
10400 RMDV 44202 3021 A4
10500 RMDV 44139 3021 A4
10500 SLN 44139 3021 A4
Flower Av
10700 CLEV 44111 2753 B2
Flower Dr
5800 PMHT 44130 2882 C2
5800 PRMA 44130 2882 B2
Flowerdale Av
5400 CLEV 44109 2754 A6
5400 CLEV 44144 2754 A6
5700 BKLN 44144 2753 E6
5700 CLEV 44144 2753 E6
Fobes St
500 PNVL 44077 2040 C6
Foghorn Ln
7300 NCtT 44067 3153 C5
Foldesy Ln
- NRYN 44133 3148 B2
Folk Av
10000 CLEV 44108 2496 C5
Folkstone Dr
10900 CcdT 44077 2146 A6
Follett Ct
- CLEV 44113 2624 D5
Folley Rd
25600 ClbT 44028 3009 D6
Folsom Av
8600 CLEV 44104 2626 B4
Foltz Industrial Pkwy
14000 SGVL 44149 3011 A7
14000 SGVL 44149 3146 A2
Fontenay Rd
2800 SRHT 44120 2627 D6
Foote Rd
29600 BYVL 44140 2619 C4
Foothill Blvd
3600 WLBY 44094 2250 D4
Foothill Rd
8700 MNTR 44060 2252 C1
Foraker Ct
8400 MNTR 44060 2144 B3
Forbes Ct
6500 MNTR 44060 2144 B5
Forbes Dr
- CLEV 44108 2496 E6
- ECLE 44108 2496 E6
- ECLE 44112 2496 E6
Forbes Rd
10 BDFD 44146 2887 B7
10 OKWD 44146 2887 D7
24000 BDHT 44146 2887 D7
26400 GNWL 44139 2888 A7
26400 Okwd 44146 2888 A7
Forbush Cir
7600 HDSN 44236 3155 B7
Force Av
7700 CLEV 44105 2756 A4
Ford Dr
1900 CLEV 44106 2626 D1
Ford Ln
4000 VMLN 44089 2741 C4
13700 BURT 44021 2636 A7
Ford Rd
800 HDHT 44143 2499 B6
800 LNHT 44124 2499 B7
800 LNHT 44143 2499 B6
1100 ELYR 44035 2746 B7
1200 ELYR 44035 2875 B2
5300 SFLD 44035 2746 C6
7300 MNTR 44060 2143 C4
Forde Av
700 AMHT 44001 2872 B1
Fordham Dr
6300 PRMA 44129 2883 A4
Fordham Ln
2000 BWHT 44147 3150 A5
Fordham Pkwy
300 BYVL 44140 2620 E5
600 WTLK 44140 2620 E5
Fordham Rd
11500 GDHT 44125 2885 D1
Fordwick Rd
6400 PMHT 44130 2882 D4
Forest Av
- MadT 44057 1843 C6
5100 MPHT 44137 2757 A7
5400 PRMA 44129 2883 A1
5400 PRMA 44134 2883 A1
6700 PRMA 44129 2882 E1
11000 CLEV 44104 2626 C6
11500 CLEV 44120 2626 D6
Forest Blvd
100 AVLK 44012 2618 E2
Forest Ct
8000 NRYN 44133 3014 B3
Forest Dr
10 BDFD 44146 2886 E4

Forest Dr
10 ETLK 44095 2142 C7
10 PNVL 44077 2145 E2
10 SRSL 44022 2761 C6
500 BYVL 44140 2619 E5
2900 PRPK 44124 2629 D7
5600 WLBY 44094 2375 A2
S Forest Dr
11300 CcdT 44077 2254 C2
Forest Ln
2600 LORN 44053 2743 E2
2800 WBHL 44094 2375 B6
5500 BKVL 44141 3016 B5
8100 MNTR 44060 2251 D4
8900 CsTp 44026 2632 D2
34000 SLN 44139 2760 B7
Forest Ovl
16800 MDBH 44130 2881 A4
Forest Pkwy
- HDHT 44143 2499 C4
2400 WTLK 44145 2750 A2
Forest Rd
1100 LKWD 44107 2622 A4
1700 EUCL 44117 2498 A1
4600 MNTR 44060 2038 D6
7500 MadT 44057 1844 A5
11500 MsnT 44024 2504 C3
12400 ClrT 44021 2506 D7
12400 ClrT 44021 2636 D3
12400 ClrT 44024 2506 D7
13500 BtnT 44021 2636 C4
28300 EUCL 44095 2249 A7
28300 EUCL 44132 2249 A7
28300 WLWK 44095 2249 A7
W Forest Rd
1000 LKWD 44107 2621 E4
1000 LKWD 44107 2622 A4
Forest St
- GNVA 44041 1944 C4
10 ELYR 44035 2875 A5
100 AMHT 44001 2872 E2
100 OBLN 44074 3138 D3
34300 NRDV 44039 2877 C1
N Forest St
10 GNVA 44041 1944 C4
S Forest St
10 GNVA 44041 1944 C4
Forestbrook Ln
- PNVL 44077 2145 B2
Forest Cliff Dr
1000 LKWD 44107 2622 C3
Forest Cove Ln
7200 NCtT 44067 3153 E6
Forestdale Av
1800 CLEV 44109 2754 D2
Forestdale Dr
4800 GDHT 44125 2756 E5
7800 BKVL 44141 3016 C3
8000 KTLD 44094 2251 E7
8000 KTLD 44094 2252 A7
13100 GDHT 44105 2756 E5
Forest Edge Dr
4500 BKLN 44144 2753 D5
8800 KTLD 44094 2377 C1
Forest Glen Av
6500 SLN 44139 2888 E6
Forest Glen Dr
10000 NRYN 44133 3148 B5
Forest Glen Rd
2300 MadT 44057 1941 B3
Forest Glen Wy
8200 NRDV 44039 2877 B6
Forest Grove Av
12300 CLEV 44108 2496 D6
12300 CLEV 44112 2496 D6
12300 ECLE 44112 2496 D6
Forest Grove Dr
- NRYN 44133 3013 B5
4600 BHIT 44212 3146 B6
Forestgrove Rd
28900 WLWK 44095 2249 C7
30200 WLWK 44092 2249 D7
Forest Hill Av
12500 CLEV 44106 2626 E1
12500 CLEV 44112 2626 E1
12600 CVHT 44112 2626 E1
12600 ECLE 44112 2626 E1
12900 ECLE 44112 2496 C7
12900 ECLE 44112 2497 A7
Forest Hill Dr
100 AMHT 44001 2872 D3
100 AVLK 44012 2488 B7
100 AVLK 44012 2618 B1
4000 LORN 44053 2744 B4
Forest Hills Blvd
1200 CVHT 44112 2497 C7
1200 CVHT 44118 2497 C7
1800 ECLE 44112 2497 C7
1800 ECLE 44118 2497 B7
4200 PRMA 44134 2883 B5
Forest Lake Dr
2700 WTLK 44145 2749 A3
9900 TNBG 44087 3019 B4
Forestlawn Av
- SFLD 44054 2616 B4
3700 SDLK 44054 2615 E4
3900 SDLK 44054 2616 A4
Forest Oaks Dr
1700 HDSN 44236 3154 E6
10800 CdnT 44024 2378 D7
10900 CdnT 44024 2503 D1
10900 MsnT 44024 2503 D1
Forest Overlook Dr
3200 SVHL 44131 2884 B6
Forest Park Dr
6100 NRDV 44039 2877 B2
15200 SGVL 44136 3012 B5
Forest Point Cir
9200 MCDN 44056 3018 E5
Forest Point Dr
9200 MCDN 44056 3018 E5
Forest Point Pl
11600 SGVL 44136 3012 C6
Forest Ridge Dr
5600 NOSD 44070 2878 D2
Forest Run Dr
3600 RchT 44286 3150 D6
Forestry Ln
- NRDV 44039 2877 B2
Forest Valley Ln
7000 CcdT 44077 2255 A3
Forestview Av
- EUCL 44092 2374 A1
- WKLF 44092 2374 A1
2600 FWPK 44116 2751 B1

Forestview Av
2600 FWPK 44126 2751 B1
2600 RKRV 44116 2621 C7
2600 RKRV 44116 2751 B1
8400 MNTR 44060 2252 B2
25500 EUCL 44132 2373 E1
27000 EUCL 44132 2374 A1
Forestview Cir
8300 MCDN 44056 3153 E2
21600 BKPK 44142 2880 B3
Forestview Ct
24900 BYVL 44140 2620 D5
Forest View Dr
1800 CVHT 44118 2627 C2
8400 ODFL 44138 2879 D7
11500 MsnT 44024 2504 A3
Forestview Dr
1400 VMLN 44089 2741 A7
1500 VmnT 44089 2741 A7
1500 VmnT 44089 2870 A1
9700 SGVL 44136 3012 D5
Forestview Pl
100 AURA 44202 3021 C7
Forestview Rd
300 BYVL 44140 2620 D5
Forestview St
24000 ClbT 44028 3010 B6
Forestview Ter
9900 BKVL 44141 3151 C4
Forestwood Av
18400 CLEV 44135 2751 E6
18400 CLEV 44135 2752 B6
Forest Wood Dr
35100 NRDV 44039 2877 B3
Forestwood Dr
10 NCtT 44067 3017 D6
10 NCtT 44067 3018 A7
3700 PRMA 44134 2883 B2
4900 PRMA 44129 2883 A2
7200 INDE 44131 2884 C7
7200 INDE 44131 3015 C1
12000 NbyT 44021 2764 E3
12000 NbyT 44065 2764 E4
15000 SGVL 44149 3146 C3
Forestwood Ln
10100 NRYN 44133 3014 B5
Forestwood Pkwy
27800 NOSD 44070 2749 E5
Forge Dr
9600 BKVL 44141 3150 C3
N Fork Dr
10 BTVL 44022 2760 D7
10 MDHL 44022 2760 D7
Forman Av
6500 CLEV 44105 2755 E2
Formanek Dr
36000 AVON 44011 2748 A5
Formby Dr
7200 SLN 44139 3020 C1
Forsythe Blvd
400 SgHT 44067 3152 D1
Forsythe Ln
9200 MNTR 44060 2144 E7
9200 MNTR 44060 2145 A6
Forsythia Dr
27100 ClbT 44028 3144 A3
Forsythia Ln
400 RDHT 44143 2498 C3
7300 NCtT 44067 3153 B4
Fort Av
8200 CLEV 44104 2626 A6
Forthampton Cir
7500 HDSN 44236 3154 A6
Forthampton Ct
7400 HDSN 44236 3154 A6
Fort Myers Ct
7700 PRMA 44134 3014 C2
Fortuna Dr
5600 MNTR 44060 2144 E2
Fortune Av
2400 PRMA 44134 2883 C1
10400 CLEV 44111 2753 C2
Fortune Ct
34300 NRDV 44039 2877 C7
Fortune Tr
24500 WTLK 44145 2750 C2
Forum Dr
20600 SGVL 44149 3011 B7
Fosdick Rd
8300 VLVW 44125 2885 B2
Foster Av
100 ELYR 44035 2875 A5
500 ELYR 44035 2874 D5
9900 BTNH 44108 2496 B4
Fostoria Ct
- CLEV 44109 2754 C2
Founders Cir
300 AVLK 44012 2618 C4
Founders Ct
19400 NRYN 44133 3148 A5
Fountain Av
300 PNVL 44077 2145 E1
Fountain Cir
2900 AVON 44011 2747 C2
5400 NRDV 44039 2747 B7
Fountain Ct
12800 SGVL 44136 3011 E6
Fountain Pkwy
28600 SLN 44139 2888 B7
Fountain View Tr
- AURA 44202 3156 D1
Fournier St
100 BERA 44017 2880 B7
Fourth St
- LORN 44052 2744 E4
Fowl Rd
1900 ELYR 44035 2873 E6
1900 ELYR 44035 2874 A6
9000 EyrT 44035 2873 E7
9300 AhtT 44035 3004 E1
9300 CrlT 44035 3004 E1
9300 ELYR 44035 3004 E1
9300 EyrT 44035 3004 E1
9300 NRsT 44035 3004 E1
Fowler Av
5000 CLEV 44127 2625 D7
Fowler Dr
2700 WBHL 44094 2375 A6
Fowlers Run
7300 NRDV 44039 2876 B4
Fowlers Mill Rd
11100 CdnT 44024 2504 A1
11100 MsnT 44024 2503 E4
11100 MsnT 44024 2504 A1

Cleveland Street Index

STREET Block	City	ZIP	Map#	Grid
Fowles Rd				
200	BERA	44017	3011	D1
300	BERA	44130	3011	D1
300	MDBH	44130	3011	D1
16600	MDBH	44130	3012	A1
Fowles Rd SR-291				
16600	MDBH	44130	3012	A1
Fox Av				
22600	EUCL	44123	2373	B3
Fox Grv				
11200	SGVL	44149	3011	A5
Fox Ln				
10	CdnT	44024	2379	A6
200	SRSL	44022	2762	A5
Fox Rd				
-	CrlT	44044	3141	D3
Fox Run				
-	CsTp	44026	2501	D5
-	EatT	44044	3141	E3
-	GFTN	44044	3141	E3
-	STBR	44241	3156	C7
2300	WTLK	44145	2750	E2
2300	WTLK	44145	2751	A2
15200	RslT	44022	2761	A3
Fox Tr				
100	SRSL	44022	2762	A6
Fox Wy				
300	SRSL	44022	2762	A6
Foxboro Dr				
6400	MAYF	44143	2499	E6
6400	MAYF	44143	2500	A6
Foxboro Rd				
7400	GSML	44040	2630	D1
Foxboro St				
28800	WLWK	44095	2249	B6
Foxboro Tr				
6900	MDBH	44130	2880	E6
Foxborough Dr				
300	BNWK	44212	3147	D7
Fox Chappell Ln				
32700	AVLK	44012	2618	A4
32800	AVLK	44012	2617	E4
Fox Chase				
4000	SVHL	44131	2884	B7
Fox Chase Ln				
100	ELYR	44035	2874	B7
Foxcroft Dr				
13500	GDHT	44125	2885	E3
Foxcroft Pl				
7000	CcdT	44077	2145	C7
Foxdale Cir				
7500	HDSN	44236	3154	A6
Fox Den E				
13500	RslT	44072	2632	A4
Fox Den Ln				
1300	WLBY	44094	2143	A5
Foxe Dr				
20200	SGVL	44149	3011	C4
Foxfire Dr				
1100	PnvT	44077	2040	E7
1200	PnvT	44077	2041	A6
Foxglen Av				
38400	AVON	44011	2747	B1
Fox Glen Rd				
10	MDHL	44022	2760	A5
Foxglove Ln				
2000	BWHT	44147	3149	D5
Foxhall Dr				
10	SRSL	44022	2762	B6
Foxhall Ln				
-	MDBH	44130	2881	B6
Fox Haven Dr				
11400	CsTp	44026	2501	E2
11400	CsTp	44026	2502	A2
Fox Hill Dr				
400	AURA	44202	3157	B2
1000	GSML	44040	2500	E7
6900	SLN	44139	2888	E7
7000	SLN	44139	3019	E1
13500	RslT	44072	2631	E4
13500	RslT	44072	2632	A4
Foxhill Dr				
8800	KTLD	44094	2377	C3
Fox Hill Dr E				
7800	GSML	44040	2501	A6
Fox Hill Ln				
100	ELYR	44035	2875	A3
Foxhill Ln				
7800	MCDN	44056	3154	B5
Fox Hill Tr				
9600	CcdT	44060	2253	B3
Fox Hollow Cir				
5700	NRDV	44039	2877	E2
Fox Hollow Ct				
100	MDHT	44124	2629	E2
Fox Hollow Dr				
-	BKPK	44142	2881	A4
-	MDBH	44130	2881	A4
-	MDBH	44142	2881	A4
100	MDHT	44124	2629	E2
3100	PRPK	44124	2629	D7
8400	BWHT	44147	3015	A5
10000	PRMA	44130	3013	B1
13800	RslT	44072	2631	C5
17800	SGVL	44136	3146	E2
Fox Hollow Ln				
8700	KDHL	44060	2252	B6
Fox Hunt Dr				
16000	SGVL	44136	3147	B1
Foxlair Tr				
4800	RDHT	44143	2498	E3
Fox Ledges Ln				
7100	CsTp	44026	2631	A3
7100	GSML	44040	2631	A3
Fox Meadow Ln				
9500	CdnT	44024	2379	C3
Fox Mill Rd				
7200	MNTR	44060	2144	D7
7200	MNTR	44060	2252	D1
Foxmoor Tr				
13200	CsTp	44026	2631	B2
Fox Pointe Dr				
100	CRDN	44024	2505	A1
Fox Rest Dr				
8600	BKVL	44141	3016	A6
Fox Run Dr				
1300	WLBY	44094	2143	A5
37000	SLN	44139	2889	C4
Fox Run Tr				
100	AURA	44202	3157	A2
12200	CsTp	44026	2501	D5
Foxtail Ln				
6500	AhtT	44001	2873	B1
Fox Tail Run				
3900	RchT	44286	3150	C6
Foxwood Ct				
6200	MNTR	44060	2144	D4
Fox Wood Dr				
9500	CdnT	44024	2379	D2
10000	NRYN	44133	3014	C5
Foxwood Dr				
3200	NRYN	44133	3014	C5
Foxwood Ln				
10	PRPK	44124	2630	A7
600	VMLN	44089	2741	C5
8600	MCDN	44056	3018	A7
Foxwood Tr				
9800	KTLD	44094	2376	D3
Foxwynde Tr				
4800	RDHT	44143	2498	E3
Fracci Ct				
7000	MNTR	44060	2144	B6
Framingham Dr				
24500	NOSD	44070	2750	C3
24500	WTLK	44070	2750	C3
24500	WTLK	44145	2750	C3
Framingham Ln				
2900	TNBG	44087	3020	B4
Framingham Ovl				
17800	SGVL	44136	3146	E4
Frances Dr				
1900	WKLF	44092	2374	E2
9600	VLVW	44125	2885	B5
Frances St				
34400	NRDV	44039	2877	D1
Francis Av				
5500	CLEV	44127	2625	D6
Francis Ct				
1300	SELD	44121	2498	B7
Francis Dr				
3700	RKRV	44116	2751	E1
3800	FWPK	44116	2751	E1
3800	FWPK	44126	2751	E1
5400	LORN	44053	2744	C5
Francis St				
5500	MNTR	44060	2144	C1
Francis D Kenneth Dr				
10	AURA	44202	3157	A6
Frank Av				
10500	CLEV	44106	2626	C3
Frank Ct				
10	ELYR	44035	2875	B6
Frank Dr				
30000	WKLF	44092	2374	D2
Frank St				
23700	NOSD	44070	2750	D4
Franke Dr				
2000	LORN	44053	2743	D2
Franke Rd				
6700	MDBH	44130	2881	C5
Frankford St				
-	LORN	44055	2745	E5
-	ShfT	44055	2745	E5
2300	ShfT	44055	2746	A5
Frankfort Av				
200	CLEV	44113	2624	D3
5600	PRMA	44129	2882	E2
Frankfort St				
-	OBLN	44074	3138	E3
Frankie Dr				
-	LORN	44053	2743	D2
Franklin Av				
10	BDFD	44146	2887	A4
100	AMHT	44001	2872	D2
100	ELYR	44035	2875	A5
2000	CLEV	44113	2624	D4
17300	LKWD	44107	2622	A5
29600	WKLF	44092	2249	B7
Franklin Blvd				
600	HDHT	44143	2499	A5
2500	CLEV	44113	2624	C5
4500	CLEV	44102	2624	A5
7100	CLEV	44102	2623	E5
11600	LKWD	44102	2623	B5
11600	LKWD	44107	2623	B5
13300	LKWD	44107	2622	E5
Franklin Dr				
-	NRDV	44035	2876	C7
100	BERA	44017	2880	A7
32200	SLN	44139	3019	E1
Franklin Rd				
6100	MDHT	44124	2499	D6
10200	AbnT	44023	3023	C1
20500	MPHT	44137	2758	A7
21200	BDHT	44146	2758	B7
S Franklin Rd				
1100	BbgT	44022	2890	A3
1100	BbgT	44023	2890	A3
1100	BbgT	44139	2890	A3
1100	BTVL	44022	2890	A3
1100	SLN	44022	2890	A3
1100	SLN	44139	2890	A3
16600	CNFL	44022	2890	A3
Franklin St				
100	BERA	44017	2880	D7
100	BERA	44017	3011	D1
500	PNVL	44077	2146	B2
4400	MNTU	44255	3159	C5
N Franklin St				
10	CNFL	44022	2761	A6
S Franklin St				
10	CNFL	44022	2761	A7
100	BbgT	44022	2761	A7
100	CyhC	44022	2761	A7
16400	BbgT	44023	2761	A7
16500	BbgT	44022	2890	A1
16500	BbgT	44023	2890	A1
16500	CNFL	44022	2890	A1
16500	CyhC	44023	2761	A7
Franklin Park St				
-	BDFD	44146	2887	B4
Franklyn Blvd				
5000	WLBY	44094	2250	A7
5100	WLBY	44094	2375	A1
6300	BKPK	44142	2881	D4
Frank Morgan Pl				
-	CLEV	44108	2496	E7
Franks Rd				
10400	AbnT	44023	2763	D7
10400	AbnT	44023	2764	A7
11000	AbnT	44021	2764	A7
Frantz Pastorius Blvd				
-	CLEV	44114	2624	C1
Fraser Ln				
9100	CsTp	44026	2632	D3
Frazee Av				
4900	CLEV	44127	2625	C7
Frazier Dr				
13000	MsnT	44024	2635	A2
19200	RKRV	44116	2621	D4
Freas Av				
3800	CLEV	44113	2624	C6
Freda Ln				
300	BDFD	44146	2886	D3
Frederick Av				
-	VMLN	44089	2741	B5
8600	CLEV	44104	2626	B4
26700	ClbT	44028	3009	B7
Frederick Dr				
4600	VMLN	44089	2741	A5
5600	MNTR	44060	2144	B2
Frederick Ln				
11200	TNBG	44087	3020	B4
Frederick St				
-	ELYR	44035	2874	E2
10	PNVL	44077	2146	B2
Fredericksburg Dr				
100	AVLK	44012	2618	D1
Fredle Dr				
7500	CcdT	44077	2254	B2
Free Av				
7200	BDFD	44146	2887	C7
7200	OKWD	44146	2887	C7
7200	OKWD	44146	3018	C1
Freed Ct				
35900	ETLK	44095	2250	B3
Freed Dr				
35400	ETLK	44095	2250	B3
Freedom Av				
-	NRDV	44039	2876	C2
Freedom Ct				
10	ELYR	44035	2745	D7
Freedom Pl				
-	LORN	44053	2743	E4
Freedom Rd				
100	PNVL	44077	2145	C1
100	PnvT	44077	2145	C1
Freedom St				
10400	GTVL	44231	3161	E6
10400	HrmT	44231	3161	E6
Freedom Wy				
4500	AVON	44011	2617	E6
Freedom Square Dr				
5700	INDE	44131	2884	C3
Freehold Rd				
3700	PRMA	44134	2754	C7
Freeland Dr				
6900	EyrT	44035	2874	A2
Freeman Av				
1900	CLEV	44113	2624	D5
Freemon Pl				
-	AVON	44011	2617	C6
Freemont Rd				
3700	CVHT	44121	2497	E4
3700	SELD	44121	2497	E4
3700	SELD	44121	2498	A4
Freeport Ln				
9400	MNTR	44060	2145	A5
Freeway Cir				
7800	MDBH	44130	3012	B2
7800	SGVL	44130	3012	B2
7800	SGVL	44136	3012	B2
N Freeway Dr				
8500	MCDN	44056	3018	C4
9500	MCDN	44146	3018	C3
9500	OKWD	44146	3018	C3
S Freeway Dr				
8500	MCDN	44056	3018	C7
8800	MCDN	44056	3153	C1
Fremont Av				
800	PnvT	44077	2040	D2
Fremont Dr				
9800	ClbT	44028	3010	D2
9800	ClbT	44138	3010	D2
9800	ODFL	44138	3010	D2
Fremont St				
100	ELYR	44035	2874	E6
French Av				
1100	LKWD	44107	2622	C4
French Blvd				
5600	MNTR	44060	2144	C1
French Dr				
7800	NCtT	44067	3017	E7
7800	NCtT	44067	3152	D1
French St				
-	NCtT	44067	3017	E7
10	BERA	44017	3011	B1
1000	CLEV	44113	2624	D4
French Creek Rd				
4500	SFLD	44054	2746	C2
5300	AVON	44011	2747	A2
5300	SFLD	44011	2747	A2
5300	SFLD	44054	2747	A2
Freshwater Dr				
-	LORN	44052	2614	E6
Fresno Ct				
100	ELYR	44035	3006	D2
Fresno Dr				
1000	WTLK	44145	2620	E7
Friar Cir				
5400	FWPK	44126	2751	B5
Friar Dr				
2400	PRMA	44134	2883	C7
Friar Post				
11700	NRYN	44133	3148	A4
Frick Ct				
15500	CLEV	44111	2752	C1
Friend Av				
15200	MPHT	44137	2757	B7
Friendship Ln				
10	OmsT	44138	2879	A3
Fries Av				
17300	LKWD	44107	2622	B6
Front Av				
900	CLEV	44113	2624	C3
Front St				
10	BERA	44017	2880	C6
4800	VMLN	44089	2741	A4
Front St SR-237				
200	BERA	44017	2880	C5
Frontage Dr				
-	EyrT	44035	2874	A5
Frontage St				
4400	LORN	44053	2743	D2
E Frontenac Dr				
4400	WVHT	44128	2758	D5
S Frontenac Dr				
4500	WVHT	44128	2758	C5
Frontier Av				
5800	CLEV	44102	2624	A7
Frontier Dr				
7800	MNTR	44060	2253	A3
Frost Ln				
8800	BKVL	44141	3016	B6
Frost Rd				
3400	ShvT	44255	3158	D7
11000	ManT	44255	3158	D1
11400	ManT	44255	3023	D4
12700	AbnT	44023	3023	D4
12700	AbnT	44255	3023	D4
Fruit Av				
900	CLEV	44113	2624	E6
Fruitland Av				
10	PnvT	44077	2041	A5
1500	MDHT	44124	2499	D7
1500	MDHT	44124	2629	E1
Fruitland Ct				
11500	CLEV	44102	2623	B5
Fruitland Dr				
4000	PRMA	44134	2883	B5
Fruitside Rd				
12800	GDHT	44125	2885	E3
Fry Av				
1200	LKWD	44107	2623	B5
Fry Rd				
5700	BKPK	44142	2881	B1
6500	MDBH	44130	2881	B6
6500	MDBH	44142	2881	B4
Fulham Dr				
1800	MDHT	44124	2629	C2
Fuller Av				
9300	CLEV	44104	2626	B7
20100	EUCL	44119	2373	A3
21500	EUCL	44123	2373	B3
28900	EUCL	44132	2374	A1
28900	WKLF	44092	2374	A1
Fuller Rd				
100	CrlT	44035	3006	C2
200	ELYR	44035	3006	A2
Fuller St				
10	BERA	44017	2880	D7
10	BERA	44017	3011	D1
10	MDBH	44017	3011	D1
10	MDBH	44130	3011	D1
300	ELYR	44035	3006	B2
Fullers Ln				
14300	SGVL	44149	3146	D1
Fullerton Av				
5700	CLEV	44105	2755	E2
Fullerton Rd				
200	ELYR	44035	2875	C3
Fullerwood Dr				
27000	EUCL	44132	2373	E1
27100	EUCL	44132	2374	A1
27200	EUCL	44132	2249	A7
Fulmer Rd				
2800	LORN	44053	2743	D2
Fulton Ct				
3800	CLEV	44113	2624	B5
Fulton Pkwy				
4000	CLEV	44109	2754	B4
4000	CLEV	44144	2754	B4
Fulton Pl				
1900	CLEV	44113	2624	B5
Fulton Rd				
1600	CLEV	44113	2624	C5
2800	LORN	44055	2745	B3
3000	CLEV	44109	2624	C7
3200	CLEV	44109	2754	C1
3700	CLEV	44102	2754	B2
4000	CLEV	44144	2754	A4
Fur Creek Tr				
-	SGVL	44149	3011	B4
Furnace St				
100	ELYR	44035	2875	A5
G				
G Dr				
-	LORN	44052	2744	E4
G St				
1800	LORN	44052	2615	D5
Gable Ln				
32200	AVLK	44012	2618	C2
Gable Wy				
27300	OmsT	44138	3009	B1
Gabriel Ct				
6800	MNTR	44060	2144	E6
13200	CLEV	44120	2756	E1
13500	CLEV	44120	2757	A1
Gabriella Dr				
9900	NRYN	44133	3013	B3
10500	PRMA	44130	2882	B1
Gabriels Lndg				
7200	CcdT	44077	2146	C7
Gaelic Gln				
6000	SLN	44139	2889	E3
Gail Dr				
33700	NRDV	44039	2877	C3
Gail Allison Dr				
-	MDHL	44022	2759	D2
-	MDHT	44124	2759	D2
-	PRPK	44124	2759	D2
Gailway Dr				
6100	OKWD	44146	2887	E4
Gainsboro Av				
13300	ECLE	44112	2497	A4
Gaitside Tr				
-	KTLD	44094	2377	C6
N Galahad Pl				
7100	CcdT	44077	2146	A7
S Galahad Pl				
7200	CcdT	44077	2146	A6
Galalina Blvd				
35600	ETLK	44095	2142	B7
Galaxie Dr				
5900	MNTR	44060	2144	A3
Galaxy Dr				
1100	CLEV	44109	2754	E5
42700	EyrT	44035	2874	B2
Galaxy Pkwy				
4800	BDHT	44128	2758	D6
4800	BDHT	44146	2758	D6
4800	WVHT	44128	2758	D6
Gale Dr				
6200	INDE	44131	2884	C4
6200	SVHL	44131	2884	C4
Gale Rd				
2900	WLBY	44094	2250	E2
Galemore Dr				
15300	MDBH	44130	2881	B6
Galewood Dr				
1000	CLEV	44110	2497	A3
Galion Av				
1600	CLEV	44109	2754	E3
Gallant Wy				
7300	CcdT	44077	2254	C1
Gallatin Blvd				
15000	BKPK	44142	2881	C2
N Gallatin Blvd				
14400	BKPK	44142	2881	C2
S Gallatin Blvd				
14400	BKPK	44142	2881	C2
Gallowae Ct				
7800	MNTR	44060	2143	E5
Galloway Tr				
8700	RslT	44072	2632	B7
8800	RslT	44072	2762	C1
Gallup Av				
4600	CLEV	44127	2625	C6
Galway Cir				
3600	BNHT	44131	2884	B1
Gambier Av				
9800	CLEV	44102	2623	C7
Gamekeeper Ct				
9700	CcdT	44060	2145	B7
Gamekeepers Tr				
15500	RslT	44072	2762	E4
Gamma Av				
4300	NBGH	44105	2755	C3
N Gannett Rd				
7500	SgHT	44067	3017	C7
7500	SgHT	44067	3152	D1
S Gannett Rd				
7800	SgHT	44067	3017	C6
Gar Hwy				
12500	CRDN	44024	2380	B6
GAR Hwy				
12700	HmbT	44024	2380	E4
13500	HmbT	44024	2381	C3
Gar Hwy US-6				
12500	CRDN	44024	2380	B6
GAR Hwy US-6				
12700	HmbT	44024	2380	E4
13500	HmbT	44024	2381	C3
Garden Av				
1700	LORN	44052	2744	E1
2600	CLEV	44109	2754	C2
Garden Blvd				
17500	CLEV	44128	2757	D4
17500	WVHT	44128	2757	D4
17900	CLEV	44122	2757	D4
17900	CLEV	44128	2757	D4
17900	WVHT	44122	2757	D4
Garden Ct				
10	PnvT	44077	2040	D1
Garden Dr				
1400	SELD	44121	2498	C7
1900	WKLF	44092	2374	E3
2200	AVON	44011	2747	E2
24300	EUCL	44123	2373	C4
Garden Ln				
2000	HDSN	44236	3154	E6
2000	HDSN	44236	3155	A7
8700	MNTR	44060	2038	D6
Garden Rd				
900	WLBY	44094	2143	A5
13300	ECLE	44112	2497	A5
24500	OKWD	44146	3018	D2
Garden St				
-	NRDV	44039	2877	C2
100	BDFD	44146	2887	A3
500	ELYR	44035	2874	E7
1000	ELYR	44035	3005	E1
5500	MPHT	44137	2886	C1
14400	BURT	44021	2636	A7
14400	BURT	44021	2766	A2
Gardenia Dr				
27800	NOSD	44070	2749	D6
Garden Park Dr				
10	SRSL	44022	2762	C6
Gardenside Dr				
9800	WTHL	44094	2376	B3
12600	NRYN	44133	3012	E3
12600	SGVL	44133	3012	E3
12600	SGVL	44136	3012	E3
31700	AVLK	44012	2618	E4
38800	WLBY	44094	2251	A5
Garden Valley Av				
6900	CLEV	44104	2625	E6
6900	CLEV	44104	2626	A7
6900	CLEV	44127	2625	E6
6900	CLEV	44127	2626	A7
Gardenview Dr				
19300	MPHT	44137	2757	E7
19800	MPHT	44137	2758	A7
21200	BDHT	44146	2758	B7
Gardina Av				
6100	CLEV	44103	2495	D6
Gardiner Dr				
-	VMLN	44089	2741	B6
Gardiner Ln				
17800	BbgT	44023	2891	A5
Gardner Ct				
2400	TNBG	44087	3020	B6
Gareau Dr				
5700	NOSD	44070	2878	D2
Garfield Av				
-	LORN	44055	2745	D5
500	ELYR	44035	2875	A4
2000	ShfT	44055	2745	D5
5600	MPHT	44137	2886	C2
10500	CLEV	44108	2496	C5
14200	LKWD	44107	2622	D6
25700	ODFL	44138	2879	B6
Garfield Blvd				
1500	LORN	44052	2615	B6
5200	SFLD	44054	2746	E1
7500	GDHT	44125	2756	B6
Garfield Dr				
10	PnvT	44077	2145	B4
9800	GDHT	44125	2756	C5
Garfield Ln				
10	BTNH	44108	2496	B4
Garfield Pkwy				
-	GDHT	44125	2756	C6
Garfield Rd				
1800	ECLE	44112	2496	C7
1800	ECLE	44112	2497	A7
7600	MNTR	44060	2251	E2
7800	KDHL	44060	2251	E6
7800	KDHL	44094	2251	E6
7800	KTLD	44060	2251	E6
7800	KTLD	44094	2251	E6
8300	MNTR	44094	2251	E5
11400	HRM	44234	3161	A2
11900	HrmT	44234	3161	A2
47000	NRsT	44074	3003	A6
Garfield Rd SR-82				
11400	HRM	44234	3161	A2
Garfield Rd SR-700				
11400	HRM	44234	3161	A2
11900	HrmT	44234	3161	A2
E Garfield Rd				
10	AURA	44202	3157	B1
1200	ManT	44202	3157	E1
E Garfield Rd SR-82				
10	AURA	44202	3157	B1
1200	ManT	44202	3157	E1
Garfield St				
300	GNVA	44041	1944	C4
Garfield Park Blvd				
-	GDHT	44125	2756	C5
Garford Av				
-	CrlT	44035	3006	C2
100	ELYR	44035	2875	C7
1200	ELYR	44035	3006	C1
Gargasz Dr				
5100	LORN	44053	2744	B6
5900	AMHT	44001	2744	B6
5900	AMHT	44053	2744	B6
Garland Rd				
12300	GDHT	44125	2756	D6
Garrett Dr				
4900	AVON	44011	2748	C7
4900	NRDV	44011	2748	C7
4900	NRDV	44039	2748	C7
Garrett Sq				
-	CLEV	44106	2496	D7
-	CLEV	44108	2496	D7
Garrett A Morgan Pl				
4100	CLEV	44105	2756	E3
Garretts Cove Dr				
36500	ETLK	44095	2250	C3
Garvin Av				
100	ELYR	44035	2874	E5
Garwood Dr				
1100	PnvT	44077	2146	E1
1200	PnvT	44077	2147	A1
Garwood Rd				
4300	CLEV	44109	2754	E4
Gary Av				
2800	LORN	44055	2746	A3
5400	BDHT	44146	2887	D1
26800	EUCL	44132	2373	E2
26800	EUCL	44132	2374	A2
Gary Ct				
1000	WKLF	44092	2374	B1
Gary Dr				
2000	TNBG	44087	3019	D4
13300	SGVL	44136	3012	D3
Gary Rd				
-	WVHT	44128	2758	C6
Gaslight Ln				
100	MDHT	44124	2500	B6
Gasser Blvd				
2400	RKRV	44116	2621	D7
Gated Ct				
3300	AVON	44011	2748	D3
Gate House Ln				
21700	RKRV	44116	2621	B6
Gate Moss Ovl				
4900	NRDV	44039	2748	D7
Gate Post Ln				
11400	MsnT	44024	2504	C2
Gatepost Rd				
10700	SGVL	44149	3010	E4
Gates Av				
200	ELYR	44035	2875	A7
9700	CLEV	44105	2756	B5
Gates Ct				
-	BWHT	44147	3149	C5
Gates Rd				
6900	GSML	44040	2500	B7
Gates Mills Blvd				
-	GSML	44040	2500	C7
6900	GSML	44040	2630	B1
Gates Mills Blvd E				
-	PRPK	44124	2629	E3
6300	MDHT	44124	2629	E3
6400	MDHT	44124	2630	A2
6600	GSML	44040	2630	A2
Gates Mills Blvd NE				
30600	PRPK	44124	2629	D4
32400	MDHT	44124	2629	D4
Gates Mills Blvd SW				
-	MDHT	44124	2629	D4
6300	PRPK	44124	2629	D4
Gates Mills Blvd W				
-	PRPK	44124	2629	E3
6400	MDHT	44124	2629	E3
6400	MDHT	44124	2630	A2
6600	GSML	44040	2630	A2
Gates Mills Estates Dr				
7700	CsTp	44026	2501	A2
7700	CsTp	44040	2501	A2
7700	GSML	44040	2501	A2
Gates Mills Tower Dr				
-	GSML	44040	2500	B7
-	MDHT	44040	2500	B7
6800	MDHT	44124	2500	B7
Gatestone Rd				
8500	NRDV	44039	2877	D7
8800	NRDV	44039	3008	D1
Gateway				
10	CLEV	44119	2373	A5
10	EUCL	44119	2373	A5
Gateway Blvd N				
100	ELYR	44035	2874	E6
N Gateway Dr				
8600	NRYN	44133	3148	C1
S Gateway Dr				
14200	NRYN	44133	3148	C1
Gateway Ln				
5700	BKPK	44142	2881	D1
S Gateway Rd				
6100	ELYR	44035	2874	E7
N Gateway St				
-	NRYN	44133	3148	D2
Gatewood Dr				
6100	MNTR	44060	2144	C4
8600	NRDV	44039	2877	D7
9900	BKVL	44141	3151	D4
Gatewood Ovl				
7800	CsTp	44026	2501	A1
7800	CsTp	44040	2501	A1
7800	GSML	44040	2501	A1
Gatsby Ln				
2900	WBHL	44092	2374	D7
Gatwick Dr				
-	AVON	44011	2747	E5
Gay Av				
11600	CLEV	44105	2756	D2
12900	CLEV	44120	2756	E2
Gay St				
23100	EUCL	44123	2373	C2
Gayle Dr				
200	SDLK	44054	2617	A3
Gaylord Av				
9300	CLEV	44105	2756	B3
Gaynor Dr				
6000	BKPK	44142	2881	A2
Geauga St				
7300	SLN	44139	3021	A2
W Geauga Tr				
12800	CsTp	44026	2631	B1
Geauga Lake Rd				
-	BbgT	44202	3021	A2
17700	BbgT	44023	2890	C7
18400	BbgT	44023	3021	C2
Gebhart Pl				
30100	WLWK	44095	2249	D6
Geddes Blf				
700	SgHT	44067	3152	C1
Gedeohn				
31900	AVLK	44012	2618	E1
Gedeon Av				
4700	CLEV	44102	2754	B1
Gehring St				
2000	CLEV	44113	2624	D5
Geiger St				
400	BERA	44017	2880	A6
Gem Cir				
34100	NRDV	44039	2877	C1
Gemini Ct				
5600	SLN	44139	2888	D2
Gemini Dr				
-	WTLK	44145	2749	C1
Gene Dr				
4200	SVHL	44131	3015	B1
Genesee Av				
1100	MAYF	44143	2499	D6
1100	MDHT	44124	2499	D7
1100	MDHT	44143	2499	D6
Genesee Rd				
1400	SELD	44121	2498	A7
1400	SELD	44121	2628	A1
18900	EUCL	44117	2497	E2
Genevia St				
16600	BbgT	44023	2890	A1
Gennett Av				
-	CLEV	44102	2754	B1
-	CLEV	44109	2754	B1
Gentry Cir				
7600	CcdT	44077	2254	C2
Gentry Ct				
100	CRDN	44024	2505	A1
Gentry Dr				
300	AURA	44202	3157	B4
Genung St				
3100	MadT	44057	1942	B6
3100	MDSN	44057	1942	B6
George Av				
2500	PRMA	44134	2883	C2
9100	CLEV	44105	2756	B1
George St				
200	ELYR	44035	3006	A1
Georgeanne Ct				
5100	MNTR	44060	2039	A7
Georgetown Av				
500	ELYR	44035	2875	E3
Georgetown Dr				
6700	MNTR	44060	2143	D6
27200	WTLK	44145	2620	A6
Georgetown Ln				
16400	SGVL	44136	3147	A4
Georgetown Rd				
24300	EUCL	44143	2498	B2
24300	RDHT	44143	2498	B2
Georgetown Sq				
10	EUCL	44143	2498	B2
Georgette Av				
4300	NOSD	44070	2750	E6
Georgette Dr				
100	CrlT	44044	3006	D6
16200	BtnT	44021	2765	B7
Georgette Ln				
900	CLEV	44109	2754	E4
George Zakany Dr				
-	HmbT	44024	2381	B3
George Zeiger Dr				
-	BHWD	44124	2629	A3
-	LNHT	44124	2629	A3
26000	BHWD	44122	2628	E4
26400	BHWD	44122	2629	A4
Georgia Av				
100	LORN	44052	2615	A5
200	ELYR	44035	3006	C1
800	AMHT	44001	2872	E3
Georgia Dr				
2000	WTLK	44145	2749	B1
Georgia Rd				
14300	BtnT	44021	2766	D3
14300	BtnT	44062	2766	D3
14900	BtnT	44062	2767	C4
14900	MdfT	44062	2767	C4
Georgia St				
10500	RMDV	44139	3020	E3
10500	RMDV	44202	3020	E3
10500	SLN	44139	3020	E3
Georgie Ct				
8700	MNTR	44060	2144	C7
Gerald Av				
5400	PRMA	44129	2883	A2
5400	PRMA	44134	2883	A2
6700	PRMA	44129	2882	E2
Gerald Dr				
7400	MDBH	44130	3012	D1
Geraldine Av				
11700	CLEV	44111	2753	A1
Geraldine Rd				
4700	RDHT	44143	2498	D4
Gerard Av				
16700	MPHT	44137	2886	C2
Germaine Av				
3500	CLEV	44109	2754	B6
4500	CLEV	44144	2754	B6
Germantown Dr				
20700	FWPK	44126	2751	C4
Gershwin Dr				
26600	WTLK	44145	2620	A7
Gertrude Av				
5700	CLEV	44105	2755	D2
Gessner Rd				
23600	NOSD	44070	2750	D5
25300	NOSD	44145	2750	D5
25300	WTLK	44070	2750	D5
25300	WTLK	44145	2750	D5
Gettysburg Dr				
1000	PRMA	44131	2883	E6
1000	PRMA	44134	2883	E6
1000	SVHL	44131	2883	E6
1700	LORN	44053	2744	B5

Cleveland Street Index

STREET Block	City	ZIP	Map#	Grid
Gettysburg Dr				
8600	TNBG	44087	3019	B6
Getz St				
10800	CrlT	44035	3006	A4
Gibson Av				
9300	CLEV	44105	2756	B1
Gibson Dr				
2600	RKRV	44116	2751	A1
Gibson St				
100	BERA	44017	2880	B7
Giddings Rd				
1300	CLEV	44103	2495	E7
1300	CLEV	44103	2625	D2
Giel Av				
1200	LKWD	44107	2622	E4
Gierman Rd				
-	AVLK	44012	2618	C2
Giesse Dr				
-	MDHT	44143	2499	E7
1000	MDHT	44124	2499	E7
Gifford Av				
4000	CLEV	44109	2754	B5
4200	CLEV	44144	2754	B5
Gifford Ct				
15600	SGVL	44136	3147	B2
Gifford Dr				
5800	BKLN	44144	2754	A5
5800	CLEV	44144	2754	A5
6300	BKLN	44144	2753	E5
Gifford Rd				
8800	BhmT	44001	2871	A6
Gilbert Av				
5400	PRMA	44129	2883	A1
5400	PRMA	44134	2883	A1
6700	PRMA	44129	2882	E1
Gilbert Ct				
5800	CLEV	44102	2754	A1
33800	NRDV	44039	3008	C1
Gilbert Dr				
-	BDFD	44146	2887	B5
-	VMLN	44089	2741	B6
10	ETLK	44095	2250	C1
1600	MDHT	44124	2629	C1
Gilchrist Dr				
27700	EUCL	44132	2249	A6
28200	WLWK	44095	2249	A6
Gildersleeve Cir				
7800	KTLD	44094	2376	D5
Gildersleeve Dr				
-	KTLD	44094	2377	A5
7700	KTLD	44094	2376	E5
Giles Rd				
4000	MDHL	44022	2760	B4
4600	CLEV	44135	2753	B5
36300	EatT	44044	3007	C5
Gilford Ln				
-	MDBH	44130	2881	B5
Gill Av				
8200	CLEV	44104	2626	A6
Gill Ct				
1200	TNBG	44087	3019	A4
Gillett St				
10	PNVL	44077	2146	A2
Gilmer Ln				
4400	RDHT	44143	2498	C3
Gilmere Dr				
6000	BKPK	44142	2881	A2
Gilmore Av				
13000	CLEV	44135	2752	E4
13000	CLEV	44135	2753	B4
25500	EUCL	44132	2373	D1
Gina Dr				
34000	NRDV	44039	2877	C3
Ginger Ct				
30000	NOSD	44070	2878	B4
Ginger Ln				
30100	NOSD	44070	2878	B4
Gingerich Rd				
15000	BtnT	44021	2766	C2
15000	BtnT	44062	2766	C2
Ginger Wren Rd				
2400	PRPK	44124	2629	A4
Gino Ln				
700	CLEV	44109	2755	A4
Girard Dr				
300	BERA	44017	3010	E1
300	BERA	44017	3011	A1
Girdled Rd				
10500	CcdT	44024	2253	E5
10500	CcdT	44060	2253	E5
10500	CcdT	44077	2253	E5
10500	CdnT	44024	2253	E5
10500	CdnT	44060	2253	E5
10600	CcdT	44077	2254	A5
12000	CcdT	44077	2255	B2
12800	LryT	44077	2255	D1
13200	LryT	44077	2256	A1
Girdler Cir				
200	SgHT	44067	3017	E4
Giuliano Dr				
-	KTLD	44094	2376	B6
Givens Ct				
3000	PryT	44081	2041	D3
Glade Av				
8200	CLEV	44104	2626	A6
Gladland Av				
4500	NOSD	44070	2750	D6
Gladstone Dr				
-	BNWK	44212	3146	D7
Gladstone Rd				
19000	CLEV	44122	2757	E2
19000	WVHT	44122	2757	E2
19700	WVHT	44122	2758	A2
20400	HIHL	44122	2758	A2
Gladwin Dr				
1700	MDHT	44124	2629	C2
Gladys Av				
-	EyrT	44055	2745	D6
-	ShfT	44055	2745	D6
1100	LKWD	44107	2622	C5
6100	EyrT	44035	2745	D6
Gladys Ct				
10	OBLN	44074	3138	E4
Gladys Dr				
200	BNWK	44212	3147	D7
Glamer Dr				
10700	PRMA	44130	3013	B1
Glantz Dr				
700	ShfT	44052	2745	A6
700	ShfT	44055	2745	A6
Glasgow Dr				
300	HDHT	44143	2499	C1
Glasgow Ln				
5800	SLN	44139	2889	E3
Glasgow St				
6000	MadT	44057	1941	E1
Glass Av				
6000	CLEV	44103	2495	E7
Glastonbury Cir				
4700	RDHT	44143	2498	D1
Glastonbury Dr				
7200	HDSN	44236	3154	E7
Glazier Av				
5000	CLEV	44127	2625	C6
Gleeson Dr				
9600	VLVW	44125	2885	C5
Gleeten Rd				
4800	RDHT	44143	2498	E4
N Glen				
100	ELYR	44035	2875	E4
S Glen				
100	ELYR	44035	2875	D4
W Glen				
300	ELYR	44035	2875	D4
Glen Av				
18300	CLEV	44110	2497	D1
Glen Cir				
10300	RMDV	44087	3020	D4
Glen Ct				
1200	AMHT	44001	2743	B7
7700	MONT	44060	2143	D1
Glen Dr				
9500	BKVL	44141	3151	A2
10500	NRYN	44133	3013	A5
32700	NRDV	44039	2877	E3
33800	ETLK	44095	2250	A3
33900	ETLK	44095	2249	E3
Glen Ovl				
1800	RDHT	44143	2373	E7
6900	CcdT	44077	2145	C7
11200	PMHT	44130	2882	B5
Glen Rd				
10	MDHL	44022	2760	C6
Glen Abbey Dr				
10600	NRYN	44133	3013	A4
Glenallen Av				
6300	SLN	44139	2888	E6
Glen Allen Dr				
3400	CVHT	44121	2497	D7
7700	SgHT	44067	3017	D7
Glen Arbor Ct				
7900	MNTR	44060	2252	D3
Glen Arden Dr				
32200	WLWK	44095	2249	D4
Glenbar Ct				
3700	FWPK	44126	2751	C1
Glenbar Dr				
3200	FWPK	44116	2751	C1
3200	FWPK	44126	2751	C1
3200	RKRV	44116	2751	C1
Glenboro Dr				
11100	CLEV	44105	2756	D2
Glenbriar Dr				
-	BNWK	44212	3146	D7
Glenbrook Blvd				
23500	EUCL	44117	2373	D7
Glenbrook Ct				
1300	WTLK	44145	2620	D7
Glenbrook Dr				
3200	RMDV	44087	3020	D4
8400	OmsT	44138	2878	E6
8400	OmsT	44138	2879	A6
13300	SGVL	44136	3012	D5
Glenbrook Ln				
1300	WTLK	44145	2620	E7
Glenbrook Rd				
4300	WLBY	44094	2250	C6
Glenbrook Chase				
-	PRPK	44124	2629	D5
Glenburn Av				
16000	MPHT	44128	2757	C7
Glenbury Av				
2100	LKWD	44107	2622	B6
Glenbury Ln				
2600	WLBY	44094	2250	E1
Glencairn Ct				
6800	MNTR	44060	2143	D6
Glencairn Dr				
7100	PRMA	44134	2883	D7
Glencairn Ln				
9500	ODFL	44138	3010	C1
Glencairn Rd				
3200	SRHT	44120	2627	D7
3200	SRHT	44122	2627	D7
3300	SRHT	44120	2757	D1
3400	SRHT	44122	2757	D2
Glen Cairn Wy				
18000	SGVL	44149	3146	B4
Glencliffe Rd				
14400	CLEV	44111	2622	D7
14400	CLEV	44111	2752	D1
Glencoe Av				
6200	BKLN	44144	2753	E5
6200	BKLN	44144	2754	A5
15300	CLEV	44110	2372	B6
Glen Coe Dr				
6500	BKVL	44141	3150	D3
Glencoe Ln				
400	HDHT	44143	2499	C2
Glencove Tr				
-	ClbT	44028	3009	C2
Glencreek Ln				
18200	SGVL	44136	3011	E6
Glencrest Rd				
800	SgHT	44067	3152	D3
Glendale Av				
13100	CLEV	44105	2756	E2
13100	CLEV	44105	2757	A2
13100	CLEV	44120	2756	E2
13100	CLEV	44120	2757	A2
14000	CLEV	44128	2757	C2
16000	SGVL	44136	3147	A2
18400	CLEV	44122	2757	E2
18900	WVHT	44122	2757	E2
W Glendale Av				
10	BDFD	44146	2886	D3
Glendale Ct				
100	ELYR	44035	2875	A5
Glendale Dr				
1100	HRM	44234	3161	A2
20200	RKRV	44116	2621	D7
Glendale Rd				
6800	NRDV	44039	2877	C3
E Glendale St				
10	BDFD	44146	2886	E3
Glendalough Dr				
1000	EatT	44044	3141	E3
1000	EatT	44044	3142	A3
Glen Daniel Cir				
10400	BKLN	44144	2753	C5
Glendenning Dr				
400	BYVL	44140	2619	E5
Glendenning St				
36700	AVON	44011	2747	D4
Glendon Rd				
2200	UNHT	44118	2628	A4
Glendora Ln				
10400	PMHT	44130	2882	B5
Glen Eagle Dr				
4500	BKVL	44141	3150	E3
Gleneagle Dr				
100	ELYR	44035	3006	D3
E Glen Eagle Dr				
300	HDHT	44143	2499	C2
W Glen Eagle Dr				
300	HDHT	44143	2499	C1
Glen Eagle Ln				
10000	TNBG	44087	3020	A3
Glen Eagles Ct				
11200	CcdT	44077	2146	B6
Glen Echo Dr				
7600	GSML	44040	2500	E7
Glen Eden Ct				
600	AURA	44202	3156	C3
Glenella Dr				
6600	SVHL	44131	2884	B5
Glenfield Rd				
18500	CLEV	44119	2372	E6
Glenforest Rd				
24200	EUCL	44123	2373	D3
Glen Forest Tr				
10600	BKVL	44141	3016	C4
Glengarry Dr				
200	AURA	44202	3021	D5
E Glengary Cir				
300	HDHT	44143	2499	C2
W Glengary Cir				
300	HDHT	44143	2499	C2
Glengary Dr				
7200	SgHT	44067	3152	B1
Glengary Ln				
-	PRPK	44124	2759	A1
Glengary Rd				
2800	SRHT	44120	2627	D6
Glengate Dr				
7700	BWHT	44147	3014	D6
Glengate Rd				
2300	WBHL	44094	2375	D2
Glenhill Dr				
13300	CsTp	44026	2631	D3
23700	BHWD	44122	2628	C3
23700	LNHT	44122	2628	C3
Glen Hollow Cir				
-	AURA	44202	3156	D1
Glenhollow Ct				
10000	BKVL	44141	3151	D4
Glenhollow Dr				
11400	CsTp	44026	2501	A2
11400	CsTp	44040	2501	A2
11400	GSML	44040	2501	A2
Glen Hollow Ln				
28700	OmsT	44138	2878	D4
Glenhurst Dr				
10	OBLN	44074	3138	C3
Glenhurst Rd				
600	WLWK	44095	2249	D6
Glen Kyle Ln				
34900	WBHL	44094	2375	A4
Glenlivet Ct				
38600	SLN	44139	2889	D4
Glen Lodge Rd				
4700	MNTR	44060	2038	D6
Glenlyn Rd				
4800	LNHT	44124	2498	D7
Glen Lyon Dr				
-	WTLK	44145	2619	B7
Glenmar Wy				
19500	SGVL	44149	3011	D7
Glenmere Cir				
4300	WVHT	44128	2758	D4
Glenmont Dr				
7400	NRYN	44133	3013	D7
Glenmont Rd				
1500	CVHT	44118	2627	B1
1500	ECLE	44112	2497	B7
1500	ECLE	44118	2497	B7
1500	ECLE	44118	2627	B1
Glenmora Dr				
11300	CdnT	44024	2379	C2
Glenmore Dr				
2500	WTLK	44145	2749	E2
Glenmore Rd				
2800	SRHT	44122	2628	C6
Glenn Av				
38200	WLBY	44094	2250	E5
Glenn Dr				
1200	SVHL	44131	2884	B3
6400	PRMA	44134	2883	C4
E Glenn Dr				
5800	MPHT	44137	2886	C3
S Glenn Dr				
16100	MPHT	44137	2886	C3
W Glenn Dr				
5800	MPHT	44137	2886	B3
Glenna Ln				
100	BNWK	44212	3147	E6
Glenn Oak Dr				
8200	BWHT	44147	3014	E4
Glenn Ovl Dr				
7200	PRMA	44130	2882	D7
Glen Oak Dr				
-	GSML	44040	2630	B3
-	HGVL	44022	2630	B3
-	HGVL	44040	2630	B3
Glen Oak Tr				
-	AURA	44202	3021	C5
Glen Oaks				
11200	TNBG	44087	3020	B3
Glen Oaks Blvd				
600	ShfT	44055	2745	B5
Glen Oaks Ln				
10	BERA	44017	3011	D1
Glenpark Av				
16500	CLEV	44128	2757	C5
Glen Park Dr				
200	BYVL	44140	2620	B4
W Glen Park Dr				
300	BYVL	44140	2620	B4
Glenpark Rd				
8000	KTLD	44094	2376	E2
Glenridge Av				
15600	MDBH	44130	2881	B7
Glenridge Ct				
10	BTVL	44022	2889	E1
Glenridge Rd				
1700	EUCL	44117	2498	A1
2200	SELD	44117	2498	B4
2200	SELD	44121	2498	B4
Glen Russ Ln				
20200	EUCL	44117	2498	A3
Glenshire Av				
17400	CLEV	44135	2752	A5
Glenshire Rd				
7200	BDHT	44146	2887	E7
7200	OKWD	44146	2887	E7
7200	OKWD	44146	3018	E1
Glenside Ct				
26900	OmsT	44138	2878	E5
Glenside Ln				
7300	OmsT	44138	2878	D5
Glenside Rd				
900	SELD	44121	2498	B5
13400	CLEV	44110	2497	A4
Glensin Ct				
-	CLEV	44128	2757	D3
Glenstone Dr				
9600	KTLD	44094	2377	B3
Glen Valley Dr				
2300	WTLK	44145	2750	B2
11100	BKVL	44141	3016	C6
14700	MDFD	44062	2767	E1
Glenview Av				
1500	MadT	44057	1843	A7
10800	CLEV	44108	2496	C4
Glenview Dr				
10	AURA	44202	3022	A7
100	AVLK	44012	2618	A1
Glenview Rd				
4300	CLEV	44122	2757	D4
4300	CLEV	44128	2757	D5
4300	WVHT	44122	2757	D5
4300	WVHT	44128	2757	D5
6600	MAYF	44040	2500	A5
6600	MAYF	44143	2500	A5
Glenville Av				
10500	CLEV	44108	2496	C4
Glenway Dr				
10200	RMDV	44087	3020	D5
Glenway Rd				
5900	BKPK	44142	2881	A2
Glenwillow Dr				
6300	NRYN	44133	3013	E3
Glenwood Av				
-	ClbT	44028	3010	D3
4600	WLBY	44094	2250	D6
5000	ORNG	44022	2759	C7
5000	SLN	44022	2759	C7
5000	SLN	44139	2759	C7
11400	CLEV	44106	2626	D3
11400	CVHT	44106	2626	D3
15300	MPHT	44137	2886	B2
Glenwood Cir				
600	BERA	44017	3011	A2
7700	BWHT	44147	3014	D6
Glenwood Ct				
33000	NRDV	44039	2877	D7
Glenwood Dr				
400	PNVL	44077	2146	A3
500	BERA	44017	3011	A1
1600	TNBG	44087	3019	C4
2500	TNBG	44087	3020	A4
3200	RMDV	44087	3020	D4
3200	RMDV	44202	3020	E4
3700	AURA	44202	3021	A4
3700	RMDV	44202	3021	A4
6100	MNTR	44060	2144	A3
10800	MsnT	44024	2634	A3
Glenwood Ln				
2300	AVON	44011	2747	C1
20200	SGVL	44149	3146	C2
Glenwood Rd				
3600	CVHT	44121	2497	E7
3700	CVHT	44121	2498	A7
7500	GSML	44040	2500	D7
Glenwood St				
100	ELYR	44035	2875	B5
4600	MNTU	44255	3159	C5
Glenwood Tr				
9100	BKVL	44141	3150	B1
Globe Av				
2800	LORN	44055	2745	C4
5200	ShfT	44055	2745	C6
5300	EyrT	44035	2745	C6
5300	EyrT	44055	2745	C6
Gloria Av				
33700	NRDV	44039	2877	C3
Gloria Dr				
800	MCDN	44056	3154	A5
Gloucester Cir				
400	BNWK	44212	3147	B7
Gloucester Dr				
500	HDHT	44143	2499	C3
1800	LORN	44053	2744	B6
27100	NOSD	44070	2879	A1
Gloucester Rd				
10000	STBR	44241	3156	D7
Glouchester Dr				
2100	LNHT	44124	2629	B3
Glover Ct				
10	ELYR	44035	2875	A7
Glynn Rd				
15300	ECLE	44112	2497	C6
15700	CVHT	44112	2497	C6
Goble Dr				
2400	LORN	44055	2746	A5
Goebel Cir				
9100	OmsT	44138	3009	B1
Goebel Dr				
6300	PRMA	44134	2883	D4
Gold Coast Ln				
-	LKWD	44107	2623	A4
Golden Av				
7900	CLEV	44103	2626	A3
Golden Ln				
1400	BWHT	44147	3149	D4
Golden Eagle Dr				
-	NRDV	44039	2876	D2
Goldengate Av				
3100	RKRV	44116	2621	D7
3100	RKRV	44116	2751	D1
Golden Gate Blvd				
1100	MDHT	44124	2499	E7
Golden Gate Plz				
1500	MDHT	44124	2499	D7
1500	MDHT	44124	2629	E1
Golden Link Blvd				
8100	MCDN	44056	3153	B1
8100	NCtT	44067	3153	B1
Golden Oak Pkwy				
300	OKWD	44146	3018	D2
Golden Pond Dr				
-	AbnT	44255	3023	E3
Goldenrod Cir				
5300	SFLD	44035	2746	E6
5300	SFLD	44035	2747	A6
Goldenrod Dr				
200	AURA	44202	3156	D4
7300	MONT	44060	2143	C3
Goldenrod Ln				
-	LORN	44053	2743	B6
5300	SFLD	44035	2746	E6
Goldenrod Rd				
7400	MONT	44060	2143	D3
Golden Russett Blvd				
300	AMHT	44001	2872	B1
400	AMHT	44001	2743	B7
Golden Star Dr				
17100	SGVL	44136	3147	B4
Gold Finch Ct				
9000	MNTR	44060	2144	D1
Gold Rush Dr				
-	WLBY	44094	2250	E2
-	WLBY	44094	2251	A2
17100	SGVL	44136	3147	A4
Goldsmith Ln				
-	OBLN	44074	3138	D1
Goldwood Dr				
2600	RKRV	44116	2751	A1
Golf Dr				
10	PnvT	44077	2146	D3
Golf Crest Mnr				
-	LORN	44053	2743	C4
Golf View Dr				
18400	CLEV	44135	2752	A4
18500	CLEV	44135	2751	E4
Golf View Ln				
10	NOSD	44070	2879	A1
Golfview Ln				
-	HDHT	44143	2499	B2
Golfway Dr				
300	PnvT	44077	2040	E4
Golfway Ln				
5200	LNHT	44124	2629	A2
Golfway Rd				
4400	SELD	44121	2628	C2
Golfway Tr				
100	ELYR	44035	2874	B7
Goller Av				
20100	EUCL	44119	2373	A5
Gondawood Dr				
49500	CrlT	44044	3141	B5
49500	CrlT	44050	3141	B5
49500	LrgT	44044	3141	B5
49500	LrgT	44050	3141	B5
Goodell Ct				
9300	MNTR	44060	2252	E3
Goodell Rd				
4400	ShvT	44255	3159	C7
Gooding Av				
10500	CLEV	44108	2496	C5
Goodman Av				
7700	CLEV	44105	2756	A4
Goodman Cir				
5700	NRYN	44133	3013	E7
Goodman Dr				
5500	NRYN	44133	3013	E7
5500	NRYN	44133	3014	A7
Goodnor Rd				
1900	CVHT	44118	2627	C3
Goodrich Ct				
100	CRDN	44024	2380	A6
Goodwalt Av				
7400	CLEV	44102	2623	E5
Goodwin Av				
-	BtnT	44021	2636	B7
-	BtnT	44062	2636	B7
13800	BURT	44021	2636	B7
Gordon Av				
400	AMHT	44001	2872	E2
Gordon Dr				
10700	PRMA	44130	3013	B1
12600	NRYN	44133	3013	D6
Gordon Rd				
1000	HDHT	44143	2499	A7
1000	LNHT	44124	2499	A7
1000	LNHT	44143	2499	A7
Goredon Dr				
10	AQLA	44024	2505	C4
10	ClrT	44024	2505	C4
Gore Orphanage Rd				
-	BhmT	44889	2870	C7
-	HetT	44889	2870	C7
7400	BhmT	44089	2870	C4
52200	BhmT	44001	2870	C7
Gorge Pkwy				
-	BDFD	44146	2887	A5
-	CyhC	44146	2886	B6
-	CyhC	44146	2887	A5
-	WNHL	44146	2886	B6
-	WNHL	44146	2887	A5
Gorman Av				
9300	CLEV	44105	2756	B4
Goshen Dr				
1500	HDSN	44236	3154	D7
Gosling Wy				
8300	MNTR	44060	2144	B2
Gottschalk Pk				
-	AbnT	44023	2892	C3
Gould Av				
10	BDFD	44146	2886	E3
10	BDFD	44146	2887	A3
Gould Ct				
-	CLEV	44113	2624	D5
Goulders Grn				
29300	BYVL	44140	2619	D4
Governor Av				
10500	CLEV	44111	2753	B1
Governors Pl				
6100	MNTR	44060	2144	B3
Graber Dr				
1400	LKWD	44107	2622	A5
Grace Av				
1400	LKWD	44107	2623	A6
6000	EyrT	44035	2745	E6
6000	ShfT	44035	2745	E6
6000	ShfT	44055	2745	E6
7300	CLEV	44102	2623	E7
9000	GDHT	44125	2756	C7
Grace Cir				
5400	NRDV	44039	2748	B7
Grace Ct				
8700	MNTR	44060	2038	C7
Grace Dr				
5400	MNTR	44060	2038	D7
5400	MNTR	44060	2144	D1
6900	OmsT	44138	2878	E4
Grace Rd				
4600	NOSD	44070	2750	D6
Grace St				
900	ShfT	44055	2745	A4
2500	LORN	44052	2744	B1
2500	LORN	44053	2744	A1
15700	NbyT	44065	2763	B5
E Grace St				
10	BDFD	44146	2886	E3
10	BDFD	44146	2887	A3
W Grace St				
10	BDFD	44146	2886	E4
Grafton Rd				
1500	CrlT	44035	3006	B2
2000	CrlT	44044	3006	E6
2400	EatT	44044	3006	E7
2700	BNWK	44212	3147	A7
2700	BNWK	44233	3147	E7
2700	HkyT	44233	3147	E7
3000	CrlT	44044	3141	E2
3000	EatT	44044	3141	E2
3800	BNWK	44212	3146	D7
4800	BHIT	44212	3146	B7
5000	BHIT	44212	3145	E7
5300	LvpT	44212	3145	A7
5300	LvpT	44280	3145	A7
6000	LvpT	44280	3144	D7
7400	LvpT	44280	3143	E7
7800	GftT	44028	3143	E7
7800	GftT	44044	3143	E7
7800	LvpT	44028	3143	E7
7800	LvpT	44044	3143	E7
13300	GFTN	44044	3141	E3
Grafton Rd SR-57				
2300	CrlT	44044	3006	E6
2400	EatT	44044	3006	E7
3000	CrlT	44044	3141	E2
3000	EatT	44044	3141	E2
13300	GFTN	44044	3141	E3
Grafton St				
100	NRsT	44074	3139	A3
100	OBLN	44074	3138	E3
100	OBLN	44074	3139	A3
Grafton Eastern Rd				
33500	GftT	44028	3143	B7
33500	GftT	44044	3143	B7
33500	LvpT	44028	3143	B7
33500	LvpT	44044	3143	B7
33500	LvpT	44280	3143	B7
35000	GftT	44044	3142	B6
36700	GFTN	44044	3142	C7
Grafton Eastern Rd SR-57				
36000	GftT	44044	3142	B6
36700	GFTN	44044	3142	C7
Gra-Gul Dr				
10	AVLK	44012	2488	B7
Graham Cir				
8600	ODFL	44138	2879	D6
Graham Dr				
5100	LNHT	44124	2498	E5
5100	LNHT	44124	2499	A5
Graham Rd				
13300	ECLE	44112	2497	A5
Gramatan Av				
14000	CLEV	44111	2752	D1
Granada Blvd				
4400	NRDL	44128	2758	B5
4400	WVHT	44128	2758	B5
Granada Dr				
5400	MONT	44060	2144	A1
Granby Av				
1400	CLEV	44109	2754	E4
Granby Cir				
2900	TNBG	44087	3020	B6
Granby Dr				
7200	HDSN	44236	3154	E7
Grand Av				
1000	MadT	44057	1843	E6
2600	CLEV	44104	2626	A5
6200	CLEV	44104	2625	E5
Grand Blvd				
10	BDFD	44146	2886	E2
10	OmsT	44138	2879	B4
300	BDFD	44146	2887	A2
20000	EUCL	44117	2498	A1
29100	EUCL	44092	2374	A1
29100	EUCL	44132	2374	A1
29100	WKLF	44092	2374	A1
29600	WKLF	44092	2249	B7
29800	WKLF	44095	2249	B7
29800	WLWK	44095	2249	B7
Grand Ct				
600	AURA	44202	3021	C7
600	AURA	44202	3156	C1
Grand Pl				
5500	WLBY	44094	2375	A2
Grand St				
500	VMLN	44089	2740	E5
E Grand St				
10	BERA	44017	2880	C6
W Grand St				
10	BERA	44017	2880	C6
Grand Division Av				
7400	CLEV	44105	2756	A5
7400	GDHT	44105	2756	A5
7400	GDHT	44125	2756	A5
Grande Ct				
29200	WTLK	44145	2749	D3
Grand Elm St				
4700	MNTU	44255	3159	C5
Grand Harbor Dr				
10	GDRV	44077	2039	D6
Grand Haven Ct				
200	PnvT	44077	2039	C7
Grand Key Dr				
10	GDRV	44077	2039	C6
Grandmere Dr				
10	BDFD	44146	2886	D4
Grand Oak Dr				
9300	BhmT	44001	2870	C7
9300	HetT	44001	2870	C7
9300	HetT	44889	2870	C7
Grand Park Cir				
200	BDFD	44146	2886	D2
Grand Prairie Ln				
10600	SGVL	44136	3012	B5
Grandridge Pt				
6100	CcdT	44077	2146	C4
Grand River Av				
100	PNVL	44077	2146	C1
Grandstand Ln				
-	ELYR	44035	2874	E7
-	ELYR	44035	2875	A7
Grandview Av				
2100	CVHT	44106	2626	E3
10300	CLEV	44104	2626	C5
Grandview Dr				
10	BSHT	44236	3153	B7
6700	INDE	44131	3015	E2
10400	KTLD	44094	2376	B5
12200	NbyT	44021	2765	A3
42500	EyrT	44035	2874	B2
Grand View Ln				
600	AURA	44202	3021	C7
600	AURA	44202	3156	C1
Grandview Ln				
-	AURA	44202	3021	C7
Grandview Ter				
14900	ECLE	44112	2497	B6
Granger Av				
100	PnvT	44077	2039	C7
1200	LKWD	44107	2622	B4
Granger Ct				
5200	MPHT	44137	2757	A7
Granger Rd				
-	INDE	44125	2884	E1
5500	BNHT	44131	2884	D1
5500	INDE	44131	2884	D1
6900	VLVW	44131	2884	E1
7500	VLVW	44125	2884	D1
7500	VLVW	44125	2885	A1
7700	GDHT	44125	2885	A1
8900	GDHT	44125	2756	B7
13600	GDHT	44125	2757	A7
13600	GDHT	44137	2757	A7
13600	MPHT	44137	2757	A7
14500	MPHT	44137	2886	A1
Granger Rd SR-17				
-	INDE	44125	2884	E1
5500	BNHT	44131	2884	D1
5500	INDE	44131	2884	D1
6900	VLVW	44131	2884	E1
7500	VLVW	44125	2884	D1
7500	VLVW	44125	2885	A1
7700	GDHT	44125	2885	A1
8900	GDHT	44125	2756	B7
13600	GDHT	44125	2757	A7
13600	GDHT	44137	2757	A7
13600	MPHT	44137	2757	A7
E Granger Rd				
10	BNHT	44131	2755	A7
1200	BNHT	44131	2884	C1
1200	INDE	44131	2884	D1
E Granger Rd SR-17				
10	BNHT	44131	2755	A7
1200	BNHT	44131	2884	C1
1200	INDE	44131	2884	D1
N Granger Rd				
9000	GDHT	44125	2756	B7
S Granger Rd				
9200	GDHT	44125	2756	B7
W Granger Rd				
300	BNHT	44131	2755	A7
W Granger Rd SR-17				
300	BNHT	44131	2755	A7
Granite Ct				
-	BERA	44138	2879	D4
Granite Dr				
-	WLBY	44094	2143	A5
Granite Rd				
16600	BDFD	44137	2886	C4
16600	BDFD	44146	2886	C4
16600	MPHT	44137	2886	C4
Granite Rdg				
-	BbgT	44023	2890	A6
Grannis Rd				
4200	FWPK	44116	2751	D2
4200	FWPK	44126	2751	D2
4200	RKRV	44116	2751	D2
12400	GDHT	44125	2885	E2
Grant Av				
2000	LORN	44055	2745	E5
2000	ShfT	44055	2745	E5
4900	CHHT	44125	2755	D4
5700	CHHT	44105	2755	D4
5700	CLEV	44105	2755	D4
15800	MPHT	44137	2757	B7
Grant Blvd				
7200	MDBH	44130	2881	A7
Grant Dr				
1200	PRMA	44134	2883	E6
7300	NRDV	44039	2877	C4
9200	NHFD	44067	3018	A3
14800	MDFD	44062	2767	D2
Grant Rd				
30400	WKLF	44092	2374	E1
Grant St				
10	PNVL	44077	2145	E2
100	CRDN	44024	2380	B6
100	ELYR	44035	2875	B7
100	GNVA	44041	1944	C4
100	HmbT	44024	2380	B6
2800	LORN	44052	2615	D5
7100	MNTR	44060	2143	C7
Grantham Ln				
9500	HmbT	44024	2381	C2
Grantham Rd				
1800	CLEV	44112	2497	D3
Grantleigh Rd				
1300	SELD	44121	2498	A7
Granton Av				
3400	CLEV	44111	2752	C1
Grantwood Av				
500	SDLK	44054	2616	B4
10500	CLEV	44108	2496	C6
Grantwood Dr				
1400	PRMA	44134	2883	B3
4800	PRMA	44129	2883	A3
Grape Arbor Dr				
6400	MadT	44057	1942	B3
Grapeland Av				
14500	CLEV	44111	2752	C1
Grasmere Av				
1800	ECLE	44112	2497	B5
5400	MPHT	44137	2886	C1
Gray Av				
11300	CLEV	44108	2496	D5
Gray Rd				
6300	CcdT	44077	2146	D4
Graybark Ln				
100	AhtT	44001	2744	C7
100	AhtT	44001	2873	C1

STREET
Block City ZIP Map# Grid

Graydon Dr
5700 BNHT 44131 2884 B2
5700 SVHL 44131 2884 B2
Gray Eagle Chase
7800 CsTp 44026 2631 A3
7800 GSML 44040 2631 A3
Grayfriar Dr
6400 BERA 44017 2880 C4
6400 BERA 44142 2880 C4
6400 BKPK 44142 2880 C4
Grayhawk Cir
600 AMHT 44001 2872 B3
Grayland Dr
5600 BKPK 44142 2879 E1
Graylock Dr
2600 KTLD 44094 2376 A5
2600 WBHL 44094 2376 A5
Graystone Ln
9400 MNTR 44060 2145 A5
Grayton Rd
500 BERA 44017 2880 A4
800 BERA 44142 2880 A4
800 BKPK 44142 2880 A3
4400 CLEV 44135 2751 D5
Grayview Ct
11500 CcdT 44077 2146 D4
Great Northern Blvd
4500 NOSD 44070 2750 C7
5200 NOSD 44070 2879 C1
Great Northern Blvd SR-252
4500 NOSD 44070 2750 C7
5200 NOSD 44070 2879 C1
Great Northern Plz S
5000 NOSD 44070 2750 B7
Great Northern Mall
100 NOSD 44070 2750 B7
Great Northern Shop Ctr
5000 NOSD 44070 2750 A7
Great Oaks Ln
20000 SGVL 44149 3011 C5
Great Oaks Pkwy
4800 INDE 44131 2884 C6
Greatwood Ln
18100 AbnT 44255 2893 B6
Greely St
- ELYR 44035 2875 C5
Green Cir
5700 WLBY 44094 2375 A1
Green Ct
300 PNVL 44077 2145 E2
Green Dr
8100 GDHT 44125 2756 A6
29200 WLWK 44095 2249 B6
37100 ETLK 44095 2142 E6
Green Ln
- AhtT 44001 2872 B2
- AMHT 44001 2872 B2
Green Rd
- MadT 44057 1842 D7
1700 MadT 44057 1941 D3
1800 CLEV 44112 2497 E2
1800 CLEV 44121 2497 E2
2100 CLEV 44121 2498 A3
2100 SELD 44121 2498 A4
2600 BHWD 44122 2628 C7
2600 SRHT 44118 2628 C6
2600 SRHT 44122 2628 C7
3200 BHWD 44122 2758 C1
3400 HIHL 44122 2758 C1
3700 HIHL 44128 2758 C2
4300 WVHT 44128 2758 C6
4900 BDHT 44128 2758 C6
13200 CsTp 44026 2631 E3
E Green Rd
800 SELD 44121 2498 C5
N Green Rd
1900 CLEV 44112 2497 E3
1900 CLEV 44121 2497 E3
S Green Rd
100 CLEV 44121 2498 A4
100 SELD 44121 2498 B4
1500 SELD 44121 2628 C3
2100 UNHT 44118 2628 C3
2100 UNHT 44121 2628 C3
2200 BHWD 44122 2628 C3
2200 UNHT 44122 2628 C4
2600 SRHT 44118 2628 C5
2600 SRHT 44122 2628 C5
Green St
3800 PRRY 44081 2042 C2
Green Acres Dr
1400 PRMA 44134 3014 D2
8500 BWHT 44147 3015 C5
Greenbriar Cir
3700 WTLK 44145 2750 A4
Greenbriar Ct
100 EUCL 44143 2498 B3
Greenbriar Dr
10 AURA 44202 3156 E4
100 ELYR 44035 2874 B7
200 AVLK 44012 2618 C1
6600 PMHT 44130 2882 C5
8500 OmsT 44138 2879 A7
12700 MsnT 44024 2634 E1
Greenbriar Ln
- MadT 44057 1941 B3
- MadT 44081 1941 A3
- NPRY 44081 1941 A3
4700 LORN 44053 2743 C4
Greenbrier Ct
8500 SgHT 44067 3017 E5
Greenbrier Dr
100 CNFL 44022 2889 E1
6600 BKVL 44141 3015 E3
17000 SGVL 44136 3147 B3
Greenbrook Dr
2600 MadT 44057 1942 A4
Greenbrooke Dr
26900 OmsT 44138 2878 E4
26900 OmsT 44138 2879 A3
Greencliff Dr
10 BDFD 44146 2886 C4
Greencroft Rd
10 BDFD 44146 2886 D2
Greendale Av
15300 MPHT 44137 2886 B2
Greene Dr
6000 BKPK 44142 2881 C2
Greenfield Cir
3000 BNWK 44212 3147 C7
Greenfield Ct
10 BERA 44017 3011 B2
Greenfield Dr
- AVON 44011 2747 A1
300 PnvT 44077 2041 A6
Greenfield Ln
- BHWD 44122 2628 E4
1400 PNVL 44077 2145 C3
Greenfield Pl
2700 LORN 44052 2744 B2
21100 SGVL 44149 3011 B6
Greenfield Tr
7200 CsTp 44026 2631 B1
Greenforest Dr
700 AMHT 44001 2872 B2
Greengate Ovl
800 SgHT 44067 3152 B1
Greenhaven Dr
10 OmsT 44138 2879 A4
400 CNFL 44022 2889 E1
Greenhaven Pkwy
9500 BKVL 44141 3016 B4
Greenheath Dr
10000 PMHT 44130 2882 C3
Greenhill Rd
15100 CLEV 44111 2752 C3
15300 CLEV 44135 2752 C3
Greenhurst Dr
5000 MPHT 44137 2757 B7
Greening Av
4500 PryT 44057 2042 D4
4500 PryT 44081 2042 D4
Green Jacket Ct
300 AVLK 44012 2618 C4
Greenlawn Av
200 AMHT 44001 2743 E7
8200 PRMA 44129 2882 D1
10500 CLEV 44108 2496 C6
23000 BHWD 44122 2628 C4
23000 UNHT 44118 2628 C4
23000 UNHT 44122 2628 C4
Green Lawn Dr
22100 SGVL 44149 3011 A3
Greenlawn Dr
- NRDV 44039 2876 E4
2500 SVHL 44131 2884 B5
Greenleaf Av
6600 PMHT 44130 2882 A7
7000 PRMA 44130 2882 A7
Greenleaf Cir
1500 WTLK 44145 2620 D7
Green Oak Av
5500 MNTR 44060 2144 A1
Green Oak Dr
19900 EUCL 44117 2498 A1
Green Ridge Av
6700 SLN 44139 2888 E7
Green Ridge Ct
7900 MNTR 44060 2251 E3
Green Ridge Dr
2100 WKLF 44092 2374 C3
6200 BDHT 44146 2887 E4
Greenridge Dr
10 GNVA 44041 1944 C7
Greenside Dr
500 PnvT 44077 2040 E3
Green Spruce Dr
300 MCDN 44056 3018 B5
Greenthorn Dr
7500 HDSN 44236 3155 B7
Greentree Ln
10 AURA 44202 3157 E1
Greentree Pkwy
- STBR 44241 3156 C7
Greentree Rd
10 MDHL 44022 2760 D6
Greenvale Dr
100 SELD 44121 2498 A5
Greenvale Rd
2300 CLEV 44112 2497 E3
2300 CLEV 44121 2497 E3
2400 CLEV 44121 2498 A3
2400 SELD 44121 2498 A3
Green Valley Dr
- PRMA 44134 3014 D1
10 SRSL 44022 2762 C6
Greenvalley Dr
7100 MNTR 44060 2145 A7
Greenview Av
9800 GDHT 44125 2756 C5
11100 CLEV 44108 2496 D5
Greenview Ct
4600 AVON 44011 2748 B6
Greenview Dr
10 AURA 44202 3157 E1
200 CrlT 44035 3005 D5
10000 ClbT 44028 3010 C3
Greenview Pkwy
29900 WTLK 44145 2749 B5
Greenview Tr
- NRDV 44039 2876 C2
Greenward Wy N
10 NOSD 44070 2879 A1
Greenward Wy S
100 NOSD 44070 2879 A2
N Greenway Ct
5500 HDHT 44143 2499 B3
S Greenway Ct
5600 HDHT 44143 2499 B3
Greenway Dr
100 CRDN 44024 2505 A1
100 ELYR 44035 2746 D7
300 CRDN 44024 2379 E7
9500 TNBG 44087 3019 B6
Greenway Rd
- MPHT 44137 2886 B5
- WNHL 44137 2886 B5
- WNHL 44146 2886 B5
4300 SELD 44121 2628 C2
15400 CLEV 44111 2752 C1
Greenway Tr
300 CRDN 44024 2379 E7
9700 AbnT 44023 2892 A2
Greenwich Av
1000 GFTN 44044 3142 A4
10900 CLEV 44105 2756 C2
35100 AVON 44011 2748 A6
35100 NRDV 44011 2748 A6
35100 NRDV 44039 2748 A6
Greenwich Ct
1500 PnvT 44077 2041 B6
Greenwich Dr
9800 SGVL 44136 3012 C4
Greenwich Ln
24400 BHWD 44122 2628 D4
Greenwich St
2600 ShvT 44255 3157 E7
2600 STBR 44255 3157 E7
Greenwold Rd
4400 SELD 44121 2628 C3
4500 SELD 44122 2628 C3
Greenwood Av
- AMHT 44001 2872 E1
- AVLK 44012 2617 C2
- CLEV 44115 2625 C3
17000 CLEV 44111 2752 B1
Greenwood Ct
300 ELYR 44035 3006 B3
600 SgHT 44067 3152 C2
32700 AVLK 44012 2618 A2
Greenwood Dr
- LORN 44053 2743 C4
3600 MDHL 44022 2759 E2
3600 MDHL 44124 2759 E2
3600 PRPK 44124 2759 E2
3600 PRPK 44124 2760 A2
4800 SDLK 44054 2616 D4
7100 MNTR 44060 2143 B3
16900 SGVL 44149 3146 B3
32500 AVLK 44012 2618 A2
Greenwood Ln
23400 NOSD 44070 2750 E3
Greenwood Ovl
4000 NRYN 44133 3014 B3
Greenwood Pkwy
800 SgHT 44067 3152 B1
Greenwood Rd
6900 INDE 44131 2884 E7
6900 INDE 44131 2885 A7
8500 NRYN 44133 3014 B3
23600 EUCL 44117 2373 C7
Greenwood View Dr
7900 PRMA 44129 2882 D6
Gregory Av
33900 NRDV 44039 2877 C7
Gregory Ct
9000 MNTR 44060 2144 D6
Gregory Ln
10800 NRYN 44133 3013 B4
Gregus Av
3800 LORN 44055 2745 E4
Grenadier Ln
7700 BKVL 44131 3016 A3
7700 BKVL 44141 3016 A3
7700 INDE 44131 3016 A3
Grenadier St
8600 BWHT 44147 3015 C5
Grenleigh Rd
1400 LNHT 44124 2498 E7
Grenney Ln
100 PNVL 44077 2146 C3
Grenoble Dr
2100 LORN 44053 2744 B4
Grenville Rd
3800 UNHT 44118 2627 E4
3800 UNHT 44118 2628 A4
Grenway Dr
8400 MNTR 44060 2252 B2
Grenway Rd
3200 SRHT 44120 2627 D7
3200 SRHT 44122 2627 D7
Gresham Ln
7700 TwbT 44236 3154 C5
Gretna Green Dr
300 HDHT 44143 2499 D1
Grey Fox Run
10 BTVL 44022 2889 D1
Grey Friar Wy
11300 MsnT 44024 2634 C1
11400 MsnT 44024 2504 C7
Greyfriars Cir
11800 NRYN 44133 3148 A5
Greystone Cir
- AVLK 44012 2618 A3
Greystone Dr
14500 BKPK 44142 2881 C3
Greystone Pkwy
9400 BKVL 44141 3150 E2
9400 BKVL 44141 3151 A2
Greystone Pt
11700 SGVL 44149 3011 A5
Greyton Rd
800 CVHT 44112 2497 D5
800 ECLE 44112 2497 D5
Gridley Av
1400 LKWD 44107 2622 A5
Gridley Rd
3500 SRHT 44122 2757 D2
Griffing Av
11600 CLEV 44104 2626 D6
11600 CLEV 44120 2626 D6
Grimes Rd
- BDHT 44146 2887 B1
Grimsby Av
12300 CLEV 44135 2753 A4
Grist Mill Ct
23100 ODFL 44138 3010 E1
Grist Mill Dr
- NRDV 44035 3007 B1
Gristmill Dr
10 PNVL 44077 2040 C7
10 PNVL 44077 2146 C1
Grist Mill Run
9500 ODFL 44138 3010 D1
Griswold Av
5700 CLEV 44104 2625 D5
Griswold Cir
8900 MCDN 44056 3018 B5
Griswold Rd
300 ELYR 44035 2875 A2
600 ELYR 44035 2874 D2
800 EyrT 44035 2874 C1
6800 MadT 44057 2044 C6
10100 CdnT 44024 2253 C7
10100 CdnT 44060 2253 C7
Gross Dr
10800 PRMA 44130 3013 A2
Grosse Dr
6300 BKPK 44142 2881 A4
6500 MDBH 44130 2881 A4
6500 MDBH 44142 2881 A4
Grosse Pointe Ovl
15500 SGVL 44136 3012 B4
Grosvenor Rd
3500 CVHT 44118 2627 D2
3700 SELD 44118 2627 D2
3700 SELD 44118 2628 A2
3800 SELD 44121 2628 A2
Groton Dr
1400 HDSN 44236 3154 D7
Groton Rd
18100 CLEV 44121 2497 E4
18100 CLEV 44121 2498 A3
Grouse Run
16600 SGVL 44136 3147 A3
Grouse Ridge Dr
8500 CdnT 44024 2254 E5
Grove Av
- ShfT 44035 2745 E6
10 PnvT 44077 2040 E7
1500 MadT 44057 1843 A7
2700 LORN 44055 2745 E3
4100 WLBY 44094 2250 D6
4800 ShfT 44055 2745 E5
5500 MNTR 44060 2144 A1
7200 OKWD 44146 2887 D7
Grove Av SR-57
- ShfT 44035 2745 E6
2700 LORN 44055 2745 E3
4800 ShfT 44055 2745 E5
Grove Ct
1900 CLEV 44113 2624 D4
27000 WTLK 44145 2750 A4
Grove Dr
13600 GDHT 44125 2886 A3
13800 GDHT 44137 2886 A3
13800 MPHT 44137 2886 A3
Grove Ln
6500 PRMA 44134 3013 E2
6500 PRMA 44134 3014 A2
Grove St
15700 MDFD 44062 2767 C2
31900 AVLK 44012 2618 D2
38500 WLBY 44094 2143 A4
Groveland Av
17900 CLEV 44111 2752 A2
Groveland Dr
32500 AVLK 44012 2618 B1
Groveland Rd
4200 UNHT 44118 2628 B3
4300 BHWD 44122 2628 C3
E Groveland Rd
23000 BHWD 44122 2628 D4
23000 UNHT 44118 2628 C4
23000 UNHT 44122 2628 C4
Groveland St
10 OBLN 44074 3138 E3
100 OBLN 44074 3139 A3
Groveland Club Dr
300 CLEV 44110 2372 B7
Grove Pond Wy
24400 ODFL 44138 2879 C7
Grover Ct
10 CrlT 44044 3006 E6
10 EatT 44044 3006 E6
Grover Rd
35100 ETLK 44095 2250 B2
Groveside Dr
8300 SGVL 44136 3012 B3
Grovewood Av
1600 PRMA 44134 2883 E1
15200 CLEV 44110 2372 D7
17000 CLEV 44119 2372 D7
35300 ETLK 44095 2250 B3
Grovewood Dr
5600 MNTR 44060 2144 A2
7900 MONT 44060 2143 E2
8000 MNTR 44060 2143 E1
Gruss Av
12400 CLEV 44108 2496 E4
Guadalupe Dr
1000 PRMA 44131 2883 E6
1000 PRMA 44134 2883 E6
1000 SVHL 44131 2883 E6
Guardian Blvd
11600 CLEV 44135 2753 A3
11600 LNDL 44135 2753 A3
Guilbert Rd
33500 ETLK 44095 2249 E3
Guildford Rd
500 VMLN 44089 2741 D5
Guilford Ct
3600 WTLK 44145 2749 C4
Guilford Rd
200 VMLN 44089 2741 D4
2400 CVHT 44118 2627 C5
Guinevere Dr
11200 NbyT 44065 2634 B5
Gulf Rd
100 ELYR 44035 2875 C4
1200 ELYR 44035 2746 D7
1800 SFLD 44035 2746 C6
5300 SFLD 44054 2746 C6
Gulfstream Ct
200 BHIT 44212 3146 A6
Gull Dr
200 ELYR 44035 2874 E2
Gulls Cove
200 PnvT 44077 2145 B6
Gullybrook Ln
- WBHL 44094 2375 B2
10 WLBY 44094 2375 B3
Gum Tree Ln
- OmsT 44138 2878 E5
Gura Rd
13500 HtbT 44046 2637 B4
13500 MdfT 44021 2637 B4
13500 MdfT 44046 2637 B4
Gurss Rd
32400 AVLK 44012 2618 A2
Guthrie Av
6500 CLEV 44102 2623 E6
6500 CLEV 44102 2624 A6
Guy Av
4900 CLEV 44127 2755 C1
Gwendolyn Farms Dr
12500 MsnT 44024 2504 C7

H

H Dr
- LORN 44052 2744 E4
H St
900 LORN 44052 2615 A7
Habant Dr
100 AMHT 44001 2743 D5
Haber Dr
22000 FWPK 44126 2751 A5
Haber Rd
5600 VMLN 44089 2740 E7
5600 VmnT 44089 2740 D7
Habersham Ln N
4400 RDHT 44143 2498 C3
Habersham Ln S
4400 RDHT 44143 2498 C3
Hacienda Dr
7200 PRMA 44130 2882 C7
Hackberry Dr
7900 MNTR 44060 2253 A3
Hackney Ct
8000 MNTR 44060 2143 E6
8000 MNTR 44060 2144 A6
Hackney Rd
33900 HGVL 44022 2630 A7
33900 PRPK 44022 2630 A7
33900 PRPK 44124 2630 A7
Hadaway St
100 CrlT 44035 3005 E2
35300 NRDV 44039 2877 A3
Hadcock Rd
500 BNWK 44212 3147 A7
Haddam Dr
300 LORN 44052 2615 D5
Haddam Rd
2600 CLEV 44120 2627 A5
2600 SRHT 44120 2627 A5
Hadden Rd
2000 EUCL 44117 2498 B1
8400 TNBG 44087 3154 D3
8400 TwbT 44087 3154 D3
Hadleigh Rd
- SRHT 44122 2628 B5
4100 SRHT 44118 2628 A5
4100 UNHT 44118 2628 A5
Hadley Rd
31800 WLWK 44095 2249 E5
Hadley St
2600 ShvT 44255 3157 E7
2600 STBR 44255 3157 E7
Hafely Dr
300 LORN 44052 2615 B5
Haggett Dr
2700 TNBG 44087 3020 B5
Hague Av
6700 CLEV 44102 2623 E6
6700 CLEV 44102 2624 A6
Haines Rd
1800 MadT 44057 1941 C1
Haines St
100 ELYR 44035 3006 E3
300 EatT 44035 3006 E3
Halburton Rd
20800 BHWD 44122 2758 B1
20800 SRHT 44122 2758 B1
Halcyon Dr
10000 PMHT 44130 2882 C3
Halcyon Rd
2100 BHWD 44122 2628 D3
2100 LNHT 44122 2628 D3
Haldane Rd
1800 CLEV 44112 2497 D3
Hale Av
2500 AVON 44011 2747 D2
14000 BTNH 44110 2497 A1
14400 CLEV 44110 2497 B1
Hale Rd
10 PnvT 44077 2041 A4
2500 PryT 44077 2041 B4
2600 PryT 44081 2041 C4
13000 CrlT 44074 3139 E3
13000 NRsT 44074 3139 E3
13300 BtnT 44021 2636 D5
13300 ClrT 44021 2636 D4
13600 BtnT 44062 2636 D5
Haley St
5400 VMLN 44089 2740 E6
Halifax Ct
2400 AVON 44011 2748 B1
Halifax Ln
300 SgHT 44067 3017 E5
Halifax Rd
20400 HIHL 44122 2758 A2
20400 WVHT 44122 2758 A2
Halifax St
29900 WKLF 44092 2249 C7
Hall Av
1100 LKWD 44107 2622 B4
6500 MadT 44057 1843 B7
Hall Ct
300 AMHT 44001 2872 E2
1400 EUCL 44117 2373 D5
1400 EUCL 44132 2373 D5
Hall Rd
500 CrlT 44035 3005 E3
13500 ClrT 44024 2506 A4
24500 NOSD 44070 2750 C3
24500 WTLK 44070 2750 C3
24500 WTLK 44145 2750 C3
Hall St
10 CNFL 44022 2760 E6
10 CNFL 44022 2761 A6
29100 SLN 44139 2888 B6
Hallauer Rd
14500 NRsT 44074 3139 B5
14500 PtfT 44074 3139 C4
15000 PtfT 44074 3138 E7
Halle Av
7400 CLEV 44102 2623 E7
Halle Cir
8200 NRDV 44039 2877 C6
Halle Ct
- AVLK 44012 2617 C3
Halle Dr
200 EUCL 44132 2373 D1
6000 VLVW 44125 2885 B4
34000 WLBY 44094 2375 A2
Halle Farm Dr
- WLBY 44094 2375 A3
Hallford Cir
5300 LNHT 44124 2629 A2
Halliday Av
15600 CLEV 44110 2497 B3
Hallnorth Dr
8400 MNTR 44060 2252 B2
Hallock Ct
900 CLEV 44110 2497 A3
Halls Carriage Pth
1700 WTLK 44145 2619 E7
1700 WTLK 44145 2749 E1
Halsey Dr
35000 ETLK 44095 2142 A7
Halsey Rd
2000 CVHT 44118 2627 E2
2000 SELD 44118 2627 E2
Halstead Av
2000 LKWD 44107 2623 A6
Halstead Rd
10200 ManT 44255 3158 B7
10200 ShvT 44255 3158 B7
Haltnorth Ct
5500 CLEV 44104 2625 D4
Halton Ct
36800 SLN 44139 3020 C2
Halton Tr
- HDHT 44143 2499 E1
Halworth Rd
20600 SRHT 44122 2628 A7
20600 SRHT 44122 2758 B1
20900 BHWD 44122 2758 A1
Hamann Pkwy
4200 WLBY 44094 2250 C6
N Hambden St
100 CRDN 44024 2380 A6
400 HmbT 44024 2380 B6
N Hambden St SR-44
100 CRDN 44024 2380 A6
N Hambden St US-6
100 CRDN 44024 2380 A6
400 HmbT 44024 2380 B6
S Hambden St
100 CRDN 44024 2380 A6
400 HmbT 44024 2380 A6
S Hambden St SR-44
100 CRDN 44024 2380 A6
S Hambden St US-6
100 CRDN 44024 2380 A6
Hambleton Dr
7300 SLN 44139 3019 E2
Hamden Rd
6400 PMHT 44130 2882 B4
Hamden St
2100 MadT 44057 1942 C2
Hamilton Av
- CLEV 44103 2495 C7
100 LORN 44052 2614 D6
200 ELYR 44035 2875 B5
1200 CLEV 44114 2624 E2
1400 LORN 44052 2744 D2
2600 CLEV 44114 2625 B1
4000 CLEV 44114 2495 C7
Hamilton Cir
300 ELYR 44035 2875 B5
Hamilton Ct
16700 SGVL 44149 3146 C2
32000 SLN 44139 3019 E1
Hamilton Dr
300 BWHT 44147 3149 E5
300 BWHT 44147 3150 A5
9300 MNTR 44060 2144 E5
9300 MNTR 44060 2145 A4
Hamilton St
10 BERA 44017 3011 B1
100 AMHT 44001 2872 B1
100 ELYR 44035 2875 C5
E Hamilton St
10 NRsT 44074 3138 E4
10 OBLN 44074 3138 E4
100 NRsT 44074 3139 A4
100 OBLN 44074 3139 A4
W Hamilton St
100 NRsT 44074 3138 B4
100 OBLN 44074 3138 C4
Hamilton School Dr
- ELYR 44035 3006 A1
Hamker Ct
8900 NRDV 44039 2877 B7
Hamlen Av
- CLEV 44104 2626 D5
11600 CLEV 44120 2626 D5
Hamlet Av
5600 CLEV 44127 2625 D7
Hamlet Ct
100 BTNH 44108 2496 D3
Hamlet Ln
800 WTLK 44145 2621 A6
Hamlet Hills Dr
200 CNFL 44022 2761 B5
Hamm Av
4900 CLEV 44127 2625 C7
Hammer Ct
700 ELYR 44035 2875 E2
Hammond Av
6600 BKLN 44144 2753 E4
6600 CLEV 44144 2753 E4
6600 CLEV 44144 2754 A4
Hampden Av
9900 CLEV 44108 2496 B7
Hampshire Ct
10 BHWD 44122 2629 A4
11200 NRYN 44133 3013 D5
Hampshire Ln
1700 CVHT 44106 2627 A2
1700 CVHT 44112 2627 A2
Hampshire Pl
27200 WTLK 44145 2749 C3
Hampshire Rd
2500 CVHT 44106 2627 A2
2700 CVHT 44118 2627 A2
Hampshire Cove
100 PnvT 44077 2145 B6
Hampstead Av
5400 PRMA 44129 2883 A2
5400 PRMA 44134 2883 A2
6700 PRMA 44129 2882 E2
14900 CLEV 44120 2757 B1
15400 SRHT 44120 2757 B1
Hampstead Rd
2000 CVHT 44118 2627 D3
Hampton Cir
700-00 AURA 44202 3156 D4
S Hampton Cir
10 RKRV 44116 2621 B7
Hampton Ct
10 BHWD 44122 2628 E5
10 BNWK 44212 3147 B5
100 BTNH 44108 2496 E2
900 SgHT 44067 3152 B1
1500 PnvT 44077 2041 B5
5400 WLBY 44094 2375 A1
32100 AVLK 44012 2618 D4
N Hampton Ct
17600 BbgT 44023 2891 C5
S Hampton Ct
10 RKRV 44116 2621 B7
10100 CcdT 44060 2253 C3
Hampton Dr
400 ELYR 44035 3006 D2
800 MCDN 44056 3018 D7
4900 NOSD 44070 2749 D7
W Hampton Dr
1400 RKRV 44116 2621 B7
S Hampton Pkwy
10 RKRV 44116 2621 B7
Hampton Pl
17400 SGVL 44136 3146 E4
17400 SGVL 44136 3147 A4
Hampton Rd
1300 ECLE 44112 2497 B4
1500 RKRV 44116 2621 D6
2800 CLEV 44120 2626 E6
2900 CLEV 44120 2627 A6
3500 PRPK 44122 2759 B1
3500 WDMR 44122 2759 B1
Hampton Run
1800 BWHT 44147 3149 D5
Hampton Bay Ln
11200 CcdT 44077 2146 B7
Hampton Chase
16400 SGVL 44136 3147 A3
Hampton Club Dr
12700 NRYN 44133 3013 A7
12800 NRYN 44133 3012 E7
Hampton Ridge Dr
11200 CdnT 44024 2379 B3
Hanamar Dr
35900 AVON 44011 2748 A3
Hancock Av
2900 CLEV 44113 2624 C6
Hancock Ln
10 ELYR 44035 2875 A3
Hancock St
1800 LORN 44052 2615 B6
Hand Av
7100 CLEV 44127 2755 E1
Handford Blvd
32000 AVLK 44012 2618 D4
Handle Rd
11100 SGVL 44136 3012 B5
Handyside Dr
9000 NRDV 44039 2875 E7
Hanes Rd
100 AURA 44202 3022 A7
Hanford Dr
500 HDHT 44143 2499 C3
1600 SVHL 44131 2884 A3
Hanford Ln
10300 TNBG 44087 3020 A3
W Hanger Rd
5200 CLEV 44135 2751 C7
5200 CLEV 44135 2880 B1
Hankee Rd
6400 FdmT 44231 3160 E7
6400 FdmT 44255 3160 E7
6400 HrmT 44231 3160 E7
6400 HrmT 44255 3160 E7
6500 FdmT 44231 3161 A7
6500 FdmT 44255 3161 C7
6500 HrmT 44231 3161 C7
6500 HrmT 44255 3161 A7
7100 GTVL 44231 3161 C7
Hanks Av
10500 CLEV 44108 2496 C5
Hanley Rd
900 LNHT 44124 2498 D6
Hanna Ct
10 BTNH 44108 2496 D2
E Hanna Ln
10 BTNH 44108 2496 D2
W Hanna Ln
10 BTNH 44108 2496 D2
Hanna Rd
2500 WBHL 44094 2375 B3
Hannan Pkwy
20200 WNHL 44146 3018 A1
Hannon St
- CLEV 44102 2754 B2
- CLEV 44109 2754 B2
Hanover Dr
1900 CVHT 44112 2497 C5
1900 ECLE 44112 2497 C5
3400 BNWK 44212 3147 B7
Hanover Ln
10 BHWD 44122 2628 E4
Hanover Rd
700 MAYF 44040 2500 B5
Hanover Woods Tr
33300 SLN 44139 3020 A1
Hansen Rd
20500 MPHT 44137 2758 A7
20700 MPHT 44146 2758 A7
Hansford Rd
1000 HDHT 44143 2499 B6
1000 LNHT 44124 2499 B6
1000 LNHT 44143 2499 B6
2000 MDHT 44124 2630 A3
Hansom Dr
5900 SLN 44139 2889 A3
Hansom Pl
7900 CcdT 44060 2253 B4
Harad Ct
8800 MCDN 44056 3018 E7
Harbor Ct
- AVLK 44012 2618 E3
Harbor Dr
- MNTR 44060 2038 B7
8200 MNTR 44060 2144 A1
Harbor Vil
- RKRV 44116 2621 A5
Harbor Creek Dr
100 MONT 44060 2144 A1
Harbor Ridge Ln
200 FTHR 44077 2039 D5
Harborside Lndg
6600 MNTR 44060 2145 A5
Harborview Blvd
2100 LORN 44052 2614 B7
2200 LORN 44053 2614 B7
Harbor View Dr
11200 CLEV 44102 2623 B4
Harbour Light Dr
11400 NRYN 44133 3013 A5
Harbour View Ovl
14000 SGVL 44136 3147 D5
Harcourt Dr
2100 CLEV 44106 2626 E3
2100 CVHT 44106 2626 E3
Harcourt Rd
100 VMLN 44089 2741 D4
Hardin Dr
6000 BKPK 44142 2881 C3
Harding Av
33800 NRDV 44039 2877 D2
Harding Dr
1500 WKLF 44092 2249 E7
1500 WKLF 44092 2374 E1
1500 WLWK 44092 2249 E7
4000 WTLK 44145 2749 E4
Harding St
7400 MNTR 44060 2143 C7
Hardwick Dr
500 AURA 44202 3021 D5

STREET
Block City ZIP Map# Grid

Hardwick Rd
23100 SRHT 44122 2628 C6
Hardwood Ct
800 MAYF 44040 2500 B5
Hardwood Dr
- NRDV 44039 2877 B7
Hardwood Tr
10000 NRYN 44133 3148 B5
Hardy Rd
600 PnvT 44077 2040 C3
Harkness Rd
8600 CLEV 44106 2626 B1
Harlan Dr
18600 MPHT 44137 2757 D7
Harland Av
17300 CLEV 44119 2372 D5
Harlem Av
4900 CLEV 44103 2625 D1
Harlem Ct
4900 CLEV 44103 2625 D1
Harleston Dr
5300 LNHT 44124 2629 A2
Harley Av
14500 CLEV 44111 2752 D1
Harley Ln
5500 MNTR 44060 2144 C1
Harley Hills Dr
7400 NRYN 44133 3013 C6
Harlon Av
12900 LKWD 44107 2622 E4
12900 LKWD 44107 2623 A4
Harlow Dr
37200 WLBY 44094 2250 D7
Harlowe St
- EUCL 44117 2373 C7
- RDHT 44117 2373 C7
- RDHT 44143 2373 C7
Harmon Av
10 PNVL 44077 2145 D2
Harmon Dr
8200 MCDN 44056 3018 B7
8200 MCDN 44056 3153 B1
Harmon Rd
10 AURA 44202 3157 A1
Harmondale Dr
38800 WLBY 44094 2251 B5
Harmony Cir
10 OmsT 44138 2679 A4
Harmony Dr
12200 EatT 44044 3008 B7
12300 EatT 44044 3143 B1
Harmony Ln
5000 WLBY 44094 2250 B7
5000 WLBY 44094 2375 B1
10200 BKLN 44144 2753 C5
Harmony Falls Ln
15500 RslT 44072 2762 D4
Harms Rd
22100 EUCL 44143 2498 B2
22100 RDHT 44143 2498 C2
Harnagy St
10 BERA 44017 3011 B1
Harner Rd
3700 AbnT 44023 3023 E4
3700 AbnT 44255 3023 E4
3700 ManT 44255 3023 E4
Harnessfield Ln
- CcdT 44077 2254 C2
Harold Av
11600 PRMA 44130 3013 A1
13000 CLEV 44135 2752 E4
13000 CLEV 44135 2753 B4
Harold Dr
6600 BKVL 44141 3015 E5
12300 CsTp 44026 2501 E6
Harold St
- WKLF 44092 2375 A2
- WLBY 44094 2375 A2
Harper Av
- ELYR 44035 3006 B2
Harper Dr
6800 CcdT 44077 2145 E6
Harper Ln
600 MCDN 44056 3018 C7
Harper Rd
5000 ORNG 44022 2759 C7
5000 SLN 44022 2759 C7
5000 SLN 44139 2759 C7
5100 SLN 44139 2888 C3
13100 SGVL 44149 3011 B7
Harper St
4000 PRRY 44081 2042 C3
Harriet St
600 LORN 44055 2745 A4
600 ShfT 44052 2745 A4
600 ShfT 44055 2745 A4
Harriman St
10 BDFD 44146 2887 A4
Harriman Tr
36800 AVON 44011 2747 D3
Harris Av
8800 CLEV 44104 2626 B7
Harris Ct
8700 NRDV 44039 2877 C7
9000 CLEV 44104 2626 B7
Harris Dr
300 AURA 44202 3157 B4
8600 NRDV 44039 2877 C7
Harris Rd
300 BWHT 44147 3015 D6
300 ECLE 44143 2498 C3
300 RDHT 44143 2498 D3
300 SDLK 44054 2616 C3
800 SFLD 44054 2616 C4
Harris St
100 AMHT 44001 2872 D1
Harrison Av
2000 ShfT 44055 2745 E5
5600 MPHT 44137 2886 C2
Harrison Dr
15300 BKPK 44142 2881 B1
Harrison Rd
9000 FrnT 44089 2869 A7
9000 FrnT 44889 2869 B7
30800 WKLF 44092 2374 E1
30800 WKLF 44092 2375 A1
30800 WLBY 44094 2375 A1
Harrison St
10 BDFD 44146 2886 E3
100 ELYR 44035 2875 B5
600 CLEV 44113 2624 E4
5900 MNTR 44060 2144 A3
30000 WKLF 44095 2249 C6
Harrow Ct
6200 BDHT 44146 2887 D4

Harrow Ct
33700 SLN 44139 3020 A2
Harrow Dr
6500 BKPK 44142 2881 A4
6500 MDBH 44130 2881 A4
6500 MDBH 44142 2881 A4
8600 PRMA 44129 2882 D1
Harrow Pl
11600 NRYN 44133 3148 A5
Harsax Av
19400 CLEV 44135 2751 E4
Hart Av
- CLEV 44108 2496 E6
- SDLK 44054 2616 E2
Hart Rd
7900 KDHL 44060 2252 D5
7900 MNTR 44060 2252 D4
Hart St
7100 MNTR 44060 2144 B7
7200 MNTR 44060 2252 B1
Hartford Av
5400 VMLN 44089 2740 E6
Hartford Ct
100 BWHT 44147 3149 E5
Hartford Dr
300 ETLK 44095 2250 C1
500 ELYR 44035 2875 E3
E Hartford Dr
14400 SGVL 44136 3147 C5
Hartford Rd
13300 ECLE 44112 2497 A5
Hartland Dr
24000 EUCL 44123 2373 D3
Hartley Dr
4800 LNHT 44124 2498 E5
Hartley Rd
1000 CLEV 44110 2497 B3
Hartman St
10 BERA 44017 3011 B1
Hartsfield Ter
200 MCDN 44056 3018 B6
Hartshire Dr
5600 WLBY 44094 2375 B2
Hartshorn Dr
10 PNVL 44077 2145 E2
Hartshorn Rd
1700 ECLE 44112 2497 A6
Hartwell Tr
14300 RslT 44072 2631 C7
Hartwood Rd
3300 CVHT 44112 2497 D5
3400 CVHT 44121 2497 D5
Harvard Av
500 CHHT 44105 2754 E3
500 CHHT 44125 2754 E3
500 CLEV 44105 2754 E3
500 CLEV 44109 2754 E3
500 CLEV 44125 2754 E3
500 ELYR 44035 2875 C7
600 CHHT 44105 2755 A3
600 CHHT 44125 2755 A3
1600 NBGH 44105 2755 B3
5400 CLEV 44105 2755 D3
11600 CLEV 44105 2756 E3
13100 CLEV 44105 2757 A3
13900 CLEV 44128 2757 B3
18200 CLEV 44122 2757 D3
18900 WVHT 44122 2757 E3
19800 WVHT 44122 2758 A3
20000 HIHL 44122 2758 A3
Harvard Dr
- MsnT 44024 2504 E4
- NRDV 44035 3007 B1
3700 WLBY 44094 2250 C4
3800 LORN 44055 2745 A6
12200 MsnT 44024 2505 A4
Harvard Rd
- ORNG 44122 2758 E3
8400 TwbT 44087 3154 C2
20800 HIHL 44122 2758 C3
20800 WVHT 44122 2758 E3
22500 BHWD 44122 2758 E3
22500 HIHL 44128 2758 C3
26800 ORNG 44022 2759 C3
26800 ORNG 44122 2759 C3
30500 MDHL 44022 2759 D3
Harvest Av
37100 AVON 44011 2747 D1
Harvest Dr
17900 BbgT 44023 2891 D6
Harvest Ln
200 SVHL 44131 3014 E1
200 SVHL 44131 3015 A1
Harvest Ovl
22200 SGVL 44149 3011 A6
Harvest Home Dr
8500 MNTR 44060 2144 B2
Harvey Av
11000 CLEV 44104 2626 C6
11500 CLEV 44120 2626 D6
Harvey Pkwy
100 AVLK 44012 2488 C7
100 AVLK 44012 2618 C1
Harvey Rd
3500 CVHT 44118 2627 D2
Harwich Ct
1000 RKRV 44116 2621 B6
Harwich Rd
1600 LNHT 44124 2628 E1
Harwood Dr
- PMHT 44130 2881 E6
- PRMA 44130 2881 E6
Harwood Ln
8200 CcdT 44077 2253 C4
Harwood Rd
- AhtT 44001 2872 E6
4000 CVHT 44121 2628 A1
4000 SELD 44121 2628 A1
Harwood St
10 ELYR 44035 2875 C5
Haselton Rd
1100 CVHT 44121 2497 E6
Haskell Dr
10 BTNH 44108 2496 D2
Haskins Rd
16300 BbgT 44023 2762 C7
16400 BbgT 44023 2891 C6
18300 BbgT 44023 3022 C1
19000 AURA 44023 3022 C3
19000 AURA 44202 3022 C3
Hasting Dr
6200 NOSD 44070 2878 C2
Hastings Av
1800 ECLE 44112 2497 C4
7300 CLEV 44105 2755 E4

Hastings Ct
14100 SGVL 44136 3147 C5
Hastings Dr
6200 SVHL 44131 2884 B4
Hastings Ln
10 CNFL 44022 2761 B6
Hastings Rd
11600 GDHT 44125 2885 D2
42900 CrlT 44074 3139 E2
42900 CrlT 44074 3140 A2
42900 NRsT 44074 3139 E2
Hastings St
37900 WLBY 44094 2250 E7
Hathaway Av
1200 LKWD 44107 2622 E4
10500 CLEV 44108 2496 C7
Hathaway Ct
2100 AVON 44011 2748 B1
Hathaway Dr
9400 MNTR 44060 2039 A7
Hathaway Ln
19000 WVHT 44122 2757 E3
19000 WVHT 44128 2757 E3
Hathaway Rd
6100 GDHT 44125 2885 E3
6200 VLVW 44125 2885 D4
13500 GDHT 44125 2886 A3
13500 GDHT 44137 2886 A3
13500 MPHT 44137 2886 A3
Hatherton Ln
27200 OmsT 44138 2878 C7
Hatteras Wy
3000 AVON 44011 2747 C3
Hauserman Rd
5200 BKLN 44144 2753 C7
5200 PRMA 44130 2753 C7
5200 PRMA 44144 2753 C7
5400 PRMA 44130 2882 C2
5700 PMHT 44130 2882 C2
Havana Rd
12700 GDHT 44125 2885 E2
Havel Av
11600 CLEV 44104 2626 D7
11600 CLEV 44120 2626 D7
Havel Dr
3200 BHWD 44122 2628 C7
Haven Ct
5400 WLBY 44094 2375 A1
Haven Dr
42700 EyrT 44035 2874 B2
Havendale Dr
5900 BKPK 44142 2881 D3
Havenhurst Ct
6700 MNTR 44060 2144 A6
Haverford Blvd
7100 MNTR 44060 2143 B7
7100 MNTR 44060 2251 B1
Haverford Dr
5000 LNHT 44124 2628 E1
5000 LNHT 44124 2629 A1
Haverford Pl
3900 AVON 44011 2747 E4
36000 AVON 44011 2748 A5
Haverhill Av
5400 PRMA 44129 2883 A3
5400 PRMA 44134 2883 A3
Haverhill Cir
400 BERA 44017 3010 D1
Haverhill Ct
10 BHWD 44122 2629 A4
Haverhill Dr
31900 SLN 44139 2888 E3
Haverhill Rd
1900 CLEV 44112 2497 D3
2300 TNBG 44087 3019 E5
Haverston Rd
1000 HDHT 44143 2499 B6
1000 LNHT 44124 2499 B7
1000 LNHT 44143 2499 B6
Haviland Dr
6400 BKPK 44142 2880 D4
6400 MDBH 44130 2880 D4
6400 MDBH 44142 2880 D4
Hawaiian Dr
10 MadT 44057 1941 B6
Hawk Av
7300 MNTR 44060 2143 C6
Hawk Ln
- LORN 44053 2743 D3
Hawke Rd
10000 ClbT 44028 3008 E7
10000 EatT 44028 3008 E7
Hawkins Dr
400 PNVL 44077 2146 A3
Hawkins Ln
2800 TNBG 44087 3020 B4
Hawkins Rd
- NOSD 44145 2750 D3
2000 WTLK 44145 2750 D1
2900 NOSD 44070 2750 D3
Hawk Ridge Dr
200 PnvT 44077 2040 E6
200 PnvT 44077 2041 A6
Hawksbridge Ct
8500 MCDN 44056 3018 A7
Hawksbury Ct
33600 AVON 44011 2748 D3
Hawks Lookout Ln
17000 SGVL 44136 3146 E3
17000 SGVL 44136 3147 A3
Hawksmoor Wy
17800 BbgT 44023 2890 A6
Hawks Nest Ct
33100 NRDV 44039 2877 D7
33100 NRDV 44039 3008 D1
Hawksview Ln
17300 BbgT 44023 2890 D3
Hawley Dr
9800 NRYN 44133 3013 B3
Hawthorn Blvd
- AURA 44202 3021 C5
Hawthorn Ln
4800 WTLK 44145 2749 A6
19900 SGVL 44149 3011 C5
Hawthorn Pkwy
- BDHT 44146 2887 E6
- BTVL 44022 2889 B1
- GNWL 44139 2888 A6
- OKWD 44146 2887 E6
- Okwd 44146 2888 A6
- SLN 44139 2888 B2
- SLN 44139 2889 B1
Hawthorn Tr
- AURA 44202 3021 B5

Hawthorne Av
1000 LORN 44052 2614 B7
1300 LORN 44052 2744 B1
3800 SDLK 44054 2615 E4
5200 SDLK 44054 2616 E2
5200 SDLK 44054 2617 A2
5500 CLEV 44103 2625 D3
Hawthorne Cir
1000 SgHT 44067 3017 B3
6400 PRMA 44134 2883 C4
Hawthorne Ct
1400 VMLN 44089 2741 A7
26100 ODFL 44138 3010 B2
32200 AVLK 44012 2618 D2
Hawthorne Dr
- AVON 44011 2747 A3
10 OBLN 44074 3138 C2
10 OmsT 44138 2879 B4
10 PnvT 44077 2145 D3
100 CNFL 44022 2889 E1
125-00 AURA 44202 3156 C2
1500 MDHT 44124 2629 C1
1700 LNHT 44124 2629 C1
5500 HDHT 44143 2499 B4
6500 PRMA 44134 2883 C4
6600 BKVL 44141 3015 A3
7100 MNTR 44060 2143 B7
9000 CdnT 44024 2380 A4
11900 SgHT 44067 3017 C3
11900 SgHT 44146 3017 C3
11900 WNHL 44146 3017 C3
24300 EUCL 44117 2373 D6
24400 BHWD 44122 2628 D5
24400 SRHT 44122 2628 D5
Hawthorne Hllw
5800 NRDV 44039 2877 E2
Hawthorne Ln
15000 RslT 44022 2761 C2
15000 RslT 44072 2761 C2
Hawthorne St
10 ELYR 44035 2875 D5
400 BDFD 44146 2886 E4
Hawthorne Tr
3500 BWHT 44147 3014 D7
Hawthorne Farm Dr
400 GSML 44040 2500 E2
Hayden Av
- ECLE 44108 2496 E7
1100 CLEV 44110 2497 A3
1200 ECLE 44110 2497 A3
1200 ECLE 44112 2497 A4
1900 ECLE 44112 2496 E7
Hayden St
11600 HRM 44234 3161 A2
Hayer Dr
100 PNVL 44077 2145 E1
Hayes Av
100 ELYR 44035 2875 A5
800 WLBY 44094 2143 A4
Hayes Blvd
7000 MNTR 44060 2143 C7
7300 MNTR 44060 2251 C1
Hayes Ct
- CLEV 44105 2756 D3
Hayes Dr
100 BNHT 44131 2755 A6
2800 WBHL 44094 2375 D6
Hayes St
10 PNVL 44077 2145 E1
10 PNVL 44077 2146 A2
2900 AVON 44011 2747 D2
N Hayes St
2800 AVON 44011 2747 C2
Haymarket Wy
1200 HDSN 44236 3154 C7
E Haymarket Wy
1500 HDSN 44236 3154 C7
Haywood Av
6400 MadT 44057 1843 B7
Haywood Rd
800 SELD 44121 2498 C5
Hazel Av
1400 MadT 44057 1843 B7
28700 WKLF 44092 2374 B3
Hazel Dr
10 NCtT 44067 3153 C4
400 BERA 44017 2880 A5
1500 CLEV 44106 2626 C1
11400 CcdT 44077 2146 C4
Hazel Rd
15600 ECLE 44112 2497 C6
Hazel St
100 ELYR 44035 2874 E6
500 AMHT 44001 2872 E2
Hazeldell Dr
11800 CLEV 44108 2496 D3
Hazelmere Av
13700 CLEV 44111 2622 E7
Hazelmere Rd
23300 SRHT 44122 2628 C7
24300 BHWD 44122 2628 D7
Hazelton Rd
9900 STBR 44241 3156 D7
Hazelwood Av
300 VMLN 44089 2741 E5
13000 LKWD 44107 2623 A4
13300 LKWD 44107 2622 E4
17800 MPHT 44137 2886 D1
Hazelwood Cir
10 GNVA 44041 1944 C7
Hazelwood Dr
- RslT 44022 2761 C5
100 SRSL 44022 2761 C5
9600 SGVL 44149 3011 C4
Hazelwood Ln
31800 AVLK 44012 2618 E3
Hazelwood St
41500 EyrT 44035 2745 D7
Hazen Dr
19800 SGVL 44149 3146 C4
Headlands Rd
9200 MNTR 44060 2038 E4
9300 MNTR 44060 2039 A4
9600 PnvT 44060 2039 B4
9600 PnvT 44077 2039 A4
Headley Av
11300 CLEV 44111 2753 B1
Headwater Ln
14600 ClrT 44021 2506 D7
14600 ClrT 44046 2506 E7
Health Campus Dr
29200 WTLK 44145 2749 C4
Healthway Dr
1900 AVON 44011 2617 E7
1900 AVON 44011 2747 E1

Hearn Dr
1100 MadT 44057 1843 D6
Hearthstone Dr
18400 SGVL 44136 3147 D4
Hearthstone Ln
18200 BbgT 44023 2890 D7
Hearthstone Rd
2600 PRMA 44134 2883 C1
Heartland Cir
10 HkyT 44233 3149 E6
Heartwood Av
32700 AVON 44011 2748 D6
Heath Av
9300 CLEV 44104 2756 B1
Heath Rd
10800 CsTp 44094 2502 E1
10800 KTLD 44094 2377 E7
10800 KTLD 44094 2502 E1
11700 CsTp 44024 2502 E2
11700 CsTp 44026 2502 E2
11900 CsTp 44024 2503 A5
11900 CsTp 44026 2503 A7
11900 MsnT 44026 2503 A5
12100 MsnT 44026 2503 A7
12700 CsTp 44026 2633 A1
13500 MsnT 44026 2633 A4
13500 MsnT 44072 2633 A4
13500 NbyT 44072 2633 A4
13500 RslT 44072 2633 A4
Heather Ct
10 CNFL 44022 2761 B6
200 MDHT 44124 2629 E1
Heather Hl
200 AbnT 44023 2892 A3
Heather Ln
100 ETLK 44095 2142 C7
420-00 AURA 44202 3156 D2
500 BDFD 44146 2887 B2
2200 TNBG 44087 3019 C6
4600 NRYN 44133 3149 A1
4700 BKLN 44144 2753 D6
16200 MDBH 44130 2881 B5
19200 SGVL 44149 3011 D5
25000 RDHT 44143 2498 D1
35600 SLN 44139 2889 B5
E Heather Ln
13000 ClbT 44028 3010 C5
W Heather Ln
14000 ClbT 44028 3010 B5
Heather Rd
1600 MadT 44057 1842 E7
1700 MadT 44057 1941 E1
Heather Brook St
100 ELYR 44035 2874 B7
Heatherfield Cir
5200 PRMA 44129 2883 A5
Heathergreen Ct
5500 WLBY 44094 2375 A1
Heather Hill Dr
5400 MNTR 44060 2144 E1
Heatherlane Dr
2000 BWHT 44147 3014 D4
Heatherstone Dr
1000 PnvT 44077 2146 E2
1100 PnvT 44077 2147 A2
Heatherwood Av
34300 AVON 44011 2748 B5
Heatherwood Ct
15000 SGVL 44149 3146 C3
Heatherwood Dr
13300 BKPK 44130 2881 D2
13300 BKPK 44142 2881 D2
13300 PRMA 44130 2881 D2
Heatherwood Ln
16500 BbgT 44023 2761 C7
16500 BbgT 44023 2890 C1
Heather Woods Dr
500 ELYR 44035 3006 E1
Heathwood Cir
26900 OmsT 44138 2878 E4
Heckathorne Dr
10 PnvT 44077 2041 A5
Hecker Av
6900 CLEV 44103 2495 E7
7100 CLEV 44103 2496 A7
Hecker Dr
5100 RchT 44141 3151 B7
Hecock Av
5000 ShfT 44055 2745 C6
5300 EyrT 44035 2745 C6
5300 EyrT 44055 2745 C6
Hector Av
5100 CLEV 44127 2625 D7
Hedgebrook Dr
5400 NRYN 44133 3149 A3
Hedgecliff St
100 AURA 44202 3021 B7
100 AURA 44202 3156 B1
Hedgeline Dr
6600 BDHT 44146 2887 E7
Hedgerow Park Dr
36000 NRDV 44039 3007 E1
Hedgewood Av
23700 WTLK 44145 2750 D2
W Hedgewood Dr
2300 WTLK 44145 2750 C2
Hedgewood Wy
24400 WTLK 44145 2750 D2
Hege Av
5600 CLEV 44105 2755 D3
5600 NBGH 44105 2755 D3
Heidi Ct
7400 CcdT 44060 2253 C2
Heights Av
10 MCDN 44056 3018 B3
10 NHFD 44056 3018 B3
10 NHFD 44067 3018 B3
Heinton Rd
5600 VLVW 44125 2885 B2
Heisley Av
6100 CLEV 44105 2755 D1
Heisley Rd
- GDRV 44077 2039 B4
- MNTR 44060 2039 A7
- PnvT 44060 2039 B7
- PnvT 44077 2039 A7
5600 MNTR 44060 2145 A1
5800 MNTR 44060 2144 E3
Heisley Rd SR-44
- GDRV 44077 2039 B4
- MNTR 44060 2039 A7
- MNTR 44060 2145 A1
- PnvT 44060 2039 A7
- PnvT 44077 2039 A7

E Heisley Rd
5200 MNTR 44060 2039 B7
5400 MNTR 44060 2145 A1
W Heisley Rd
5300 MNTR 44060 2039 A7
5300 MNTR 44060 2145 A1
Heisley Park Ln
400 PNVL 44077 2145 C3
Helen Av
500 BHIT 44212 3146 A7
25600 EUCL 44132 2373 D2
Helen Dr
300 VMLN 44089 2742 B5
3100 NRYN 44133 3014 C3
Helen Rd
3400 SRHT 44122 2758 A1
Helen St
- NRDV 44039 2877 A2
41800 EyrT 44035 2745 C6
Helena Av
10500 CLEV 44108 2496 C5
Helene Dr
- PnvT 44077 2040 E7
- PnvT 44077 2146 E1
Helmar Ln
- OKWD 44146 3018 B1
Helmsdale Dr
2000 EUCL 44143 2498 C1
2000 RDHT 44143 2498 C1
Helmsdale Rd
800 CVHT 44112 2497 D5
16100 ECLE 44112 2497 D5
Helmut Dr
10900 CdnT 44024 2379 A7
10900 CdnT 44024 2504 A1
10900 MsnT 44024 2504 A1
Helper Dr
500 BDFD 44146 2887 B3
Helwig Dr
10 GNVA 44041 1944 D7
Helwig St
400 BERA 44017 2880 A6
Hemingway Ln
8200 CcdT 44060 2253 B4
Hemingway Rd
6100 MAYF 44143 2499 D5
Hemlock Av
1200 CLEV 44113 2624 C3
Hemlock Cir
4000 ORNG 44122 2759 B3
20500 SGVL 44149 3146 B2
Hemlock Ct
100 PnvT 44077 2040 E7
100 PnvT 44077 2041 A6
200 BNWK 44212 3146 D6
Hemlock Dr
100 ELYR 44035 2746 C6
300 BERA 44017 2880 A5
500 EUCL 44132 2374 A2
2300 NPRY 44081 1940 D3
2800 WBHL 44094 2375 E7
6200 AhtT 44001 2744 B7
6200 AMHT 44001 2744 B7
27300 WTLK 44145 2749 E4
27300 WTLK 44145 2750 A4
Hemlock Ln
10 MDHL 44022 2760 A4
800 SgHT 44067 3152 B2
15200 MDBH 44130 2881 C5
Hemlock Rd
500 CNFL 44022 2761 C5
500 RslT 44022 2761 C5
500 SRSL 44022 2761 C5
7200 INDE 44131 2884 E6
8000 INDE 44131 2885 A5
Hemlock Point Rd
15000 RslT 44022 2761 D4
15000 RslT 44072 2761 E1
Hemlock Ridge Dr
8400 KTLD 44094 2252 B7
8400 KTLD 44094 2377 B1
10500 MsnT 44024 2503 E3
Hemmington Blvd
5100 SLN 44139 2759 B7
Hemoga St
6900 INDE 44131 2884 E6
Hempfield Ln
7500 HDSN 44236 3154 D6
Hempstead Ln
11100 NRYN 44133 3013 D5
Hempstead Rd
11400 GDHT 44125 2885 D1
Henderson Dr
1700 LORN 44052 2615 A7
2000 LORN 44052 2745 A1
Henderson Dr SR-611
1700 LORN 44052 2615 A7
2000 LORN 44052 2745 A1
Henderson Rd
3300 CVHT 44112 2497 D6
Hendon Rd
25700 BHWD 44122 2628 E5
26200 BHWD 44122 2629 A5
Hendricks Rd
8300 MNTR 44060 2144 B3
Henkel Ct
10 ELYR 44035 2875 A6
Henley Ct
- CLEV 44102 2623 D7
Henley Rd
15500 ECLE 44112 2497 B6
Henning Dr
1300 LNHT 44124 2499 A7
10700 CdnT 44024 2379 A7
10900 CdnT 44024 2504 A1
10900 MsnT 44024 2504 A1
Henninger Rd
3400 CLEV 44109 2754 C3
Henritze Av
3500 CLEV 44109 2754 B4
4500 CLEV 44144 2754 B4
Henry Ct
3600 CLEV 44105 2756 A1
4000 LORN 44053 2743 E3
Henry Rd
3200 RchT 44286 3151 B6
19100 FWPK 44126 2751 D1
19600 RKRV 44116 2751 D1
19600 RKRV 44126 2751 D1
26500 BYVL 44140 2620 B5
Henry St
10 BDFD 44146 2887 A4
10 BERA 44017 2880 B7
100 GDRV 44077 2039 C5
200 AMHT 44001 2872 E2

Henry St
300 ELYR 44035 2875 D7
400 PNVL 44077 2040 B6
4700 GDHT 44125 2756 D6
5000 MPHT 44137 2757 C7
Henry St SR-237
10 BERA 44017 2880 B7
Henry Speeth Ct
3000 CLEV 44113 2624 B4
Henwell Rd
33500 ClbT 44028 3008 E3
33500 EatT 44028 3008 E3
Hepburn Rd
6900 MDBH 44130 2880 E6
Herald Rd
- BKPK 44142 2881 D4
- MDBH 44130 2881 D3
- MDBH 44142 2881 D4
Herald St
10600 MNTU 44255 3159 C5
Herb St
25600 ODFL 44138 3010 B1
Herbert Dr
1400 LORN 44053 2744 C6
Hereford Rd
1000 CVHT 44112 2497 C6
1000 CVHT 44118 2497 D6
Heresford Dr
2700 PRMA 44134 2883 C2
Heritage
- EUCL 44117 2373 C6
Heritage Av
5700 MadT 44057 1941 C2
Heritage Ct
- WLBY 44094 2251 A1
Heritage Dr
11000 TNBG 44087 3019 C3
Heritage Ln
2600 PRPK 44124 2629 E4
15000 RslT 44022 2761 C2
Heritage Rd
300 AURA 44202 3157 A2
Heritage Tr
12700 NRYN 44133 3013 C7
17800 SGVL 44136 3146 E4
Heritage Wy
7500 BhmT 44001 2871 E3
Herman Av
6500 CLEV 44102 2624 A5
7300 CLEV 44102 2623 E5
Herman Rd
3800 ManT 44255 3023 E6
Hermann Dr
100 AVLK 44012 2488 B7
100 AVLK 44012 2618 B1
Hermit Av
2700 NBGH 44105 2755 B3
Hermitage Dr
2000 TNBG 44087 3019 C6
Hermitage Rd
7100 CcdT 44077 2145 E7
7200 CcdT 44077 2253 E1
8300 CcdT 44024 2253 E5
8300 CcdT 44060 2253 E5
8300 CdnT 44024 2253 E5
8300 CdnT 44060 2253 E5
9000 CdnT 44024 2378 E1
23600 BHWD 44122 2628 D7
23600 SRHT 44122 2628 D7
Herold Rd
4000 CVHT 44121 2628 A1
4000 SELD 44121 2628 A1
Heron Cir
32600 NRDV 44039 2877 D7
Heron Ct
3300 RMDV 44202 3020 D3
Heron Dr
- HmbT 44024 2381 E2
- LORN 44053 2743 D3
Heron Ln
37900 AVON 44011 2747 B1
Heron Bay St
- AVLK 44012 2618 B4
Heron Cove
1900 TNBG 44087 3019 B4
Heron Glen Ct
1900 MCDN 44056 3018 A7
Herrick Ct
- LORN 44053 2745 A6
Herrick Dr
8500 CsTp 44026 2502 B7
Herrick Mw
10 CLEV 44106 2626 E2
10 CVHT 44106 2626 E3
Herrick Pl
800 CLEV 44108 2496 B5
Herrick Rd
10 TwbT 44087 3155 D3
800 CLEV 44108 2496 B5
8800 TNBG 44087 3155 D3
Herrmann Dr
- AVLK 44012 2618 B2
Herschel Ct
500 CLEV 44113 2625 A5
Hersey Cir
6500 NRDV 44039 2877 D3
Hervie Dr
11700 CsTp 44026 2502 E4
Hessler Ct
1900 CLEV 44106 2626 D1
Hessler Rd
11200 CLEV 44106 2626 D2
Hetzel Dr
2400 PRMA 44134 2883 C6
Hialeah Dr
3900 PRMA 44134 3014 B1
Hiawatha Blvd
10 ETLK 44095 2142 B7
Hiawatha Dr
4800 VMLN 44089 2741 A5
Hickory Cir
100 ELYR 44035 3005 B1
Hickory Ct
27300 EUCL 44132 2374 A2
33900 AVON 44011 2748 C3
Hickory Dr
200 BERA 44017 2880 A5
2000 VmnT 44089 2869 D1
5000 LNHT 44124 2498 E5
5100 LNHT 44124 2499 A5
7000 WNHL 44146 2886 C7
Hickory Ln
100 MDHL 44022 2760 B5
200 PNVL 44077 2146 A2
1800 BWHT 44147 3149 D5

STREET Block City ZIP Map# Grid

Hickory Ln
2500 PRPK 44124 2629 E4
4200 WVHT 44128 2758 A4
5200 WLBY 44094 2374 E1
6200 NOSD 44070 2878 B2
6800 GSML 44040 2500 B6
7200 SVHL 44131 2884 B7
8900 NRYN 44133 3013 B3
26000 ODFL 44138 3010 B1
32100 AVLK 44012 2618 C3
Hickory Pl
10500 SGVL 44149 3011 D4
Hickory Rd
7500 OKWD 44146 3018 D2
Hickory St
1100 GFTN 44044 3142 B6
1100 GftT 44044 3142 B6
5500 MONT 44060 2143 E1
Hickory St S
8000 CsTp 44026 2631 E3
Hickory Tr
5600 NRDV 44039 2877 E1
6000 NRDV 44039 2878 A2
Hickory Branch Tr
21300 SGVL 44149 3011 B4
Hickory Hill Av
4200 LORN 44052 2744 D4
Hickory Hill Ct
10500 KTLD 44094 2376 B6
Hickory Hill Dr
400 MAYF 44143 2500 A2
9500 TNBG 44087 3019 C6
Hickory Hill Ln
7800 PRMA 44130 3013 D1
Hickory Hill Rd
10 PnvT 44077 2147 B2
200 CNFL 44022 2761 B5
Hickory Hollow Dr
10 AMHT 44001 2872 B3
8600 CdnT 44024 2254 D6
Hickory Nut Ln
4800 INDE 44131 2884 C5
Hickory Nut Tr
- ORNG 44122 2759 C2
- ORNG 44124 2759 D2
- PRPK 44122 2759 C2
- PRPK 44124 2759 D2
3700 ORNG 44022 2759 D3
Hickory Ridge Dr
10000 BKVL 44141 3151 D4
Hickox Blvd
15200 MDBH 44130 2881 B5
Hickox St
14400 BURT 44021 2636 B7
14500 BURT 44021 2766 C1
Hicks Rd
17500 WNHL 44146 3017 D1
Hidden Cir
30800 NOSD 44070 2878 A2
Hidden Hllw
9800 BWHT 44147 3149 C3
Hidden Ln
13900 CrlT 44044 3141 B4
Hidden Acres Dr
25500 WTLK 44145 2750 B2
Hidden Canyon Dr
2500 BKVL 44141 3151 C4
Hidden Creek Cir
5000 ORNG 44022 2759 C7
5000 SLN 44022 2759 C7
5000 SLN 44139 2759 C7
Hidden Creek Dr
900 AURA 44202 3022 D4
6200 LORN 44053 2743 B4
Hidden Glen Dr
7100 AhtT 44001 2873 B2
Hidden Glenn Dr
9000 MNTR 44060 2252 D3
Hidden Harbor Dr
500 FTHR 44077 2039 D6
Hidden Hollow Ct
33000 NRDV 44039 2877 D7
Hidden Hollow Dr
7700 MNTR 44060 2252 E3
Hidden Lake Dr
9300 CsTp 44026 2502 D4
Hidden Lake Tr
6400 BKVL 44141 3150 D4
Hidden Meadows Ln
18800 SGVL 44136 3147 D4
Hidden Oaks Dr
- ClbT 44028 3144 A5
13100 MsnT 44026 2633 A3
13100 MsnT 44072 2633 A3
13100 NbyT 44072 2633 A3
Hidden Point Dr
17100 BbgT 44023 2890 E3
Hidden Springs Dr
11200 MsnT 44024 2503 C1
Hidden Tree Cir
32600 NRDV 44039 2877 E2
Hidden Tree Ln
100 AhtT 44001 2873 C1
Hidden Valley Cir
7600 PRMA 44129 3013 E1
7600 PRMA 44130 3013 E1
Hidden Valley Ct
9200 MNTR 44060 2252 E3
Hidden Valley Dr
10 RKRV 44116 2621 B5
6600 AhtT 44001 2873 C2
7600 KTLD 44094 2376 C7
7600 KTLD 44094 2501 D1
10200 NRYN 44133 3148 B4
28100 ORNG 44022 2759 B6
Hidden Valley Ln
7500 PRMA 44129 3013 E1
7500 PRMA 44130 3013 E1
7500 PRMA 44134 3013 E1
Hiddenview Ct
- NRDV 44039 2747 C6
Hidden Woods Ln
19200 SGVL 44136 3147 D5
Hideaway Tr
- RslT 44072 2632 A4
Hideaway Cove
- PnvT 44077 2040 E2
10000 RMDV 44202 3020 D5
Higbee Av
8200 CLEV 44104 2626 A6
High Blf
300 AURA 44202 3021 B7
High Ct
10 CNFL 44022 2761 B5
1700 LORN 44055 2745 C5

High Pkwy
18400 RKRV 44116 2621 E6
18400 RKRV 44116 2622 A6
High Rd
22000 OKWD 44146 3018 C1
High St
10 CLEV 44113 2624 E3
10 CLEV 44115 2624 E3
100 CNFL 44022 2761 A5
100 ELYR 44035 2874 D4
200 BERA 44017 2880 B6
200 FTHR 44077 2039 D5
600 BDFD 44146 2887 B4
4400 MNTU 44255 3159 B5
E High St
10 PNVL 44077 2146 B1
4600 MNTU 44255 3159 D5
4900 ManT 44234 3159 D5
4900 ManT 44255 3159 D5
15900 MDFD 44062 2767 D2
E High St SR-87
15900 MDFD 44062 2767 D2
W High St
10 PNVL 44077 2146 B1
4400 MNTU 44255 3159 B5
15300 MDFD 44062 2767 C2
15400 MdfT 44062 2767 B2
W High St SR-87
15300 MDFD 44062 2767 C2
15400 MdfT 44062 2767 B2
High Bluff Ct
7200 CcdT 44077 2253 E1
Highbridge Ct
9400 MNTR 44060 2145 A7
Highbridge Rd
500 VMLN 44089 2741 D6
High Country Dr
9700 HmbT 44024 2381 C3
Highgate Ct
9800 CcdT 44060 2145 B7
Highgate Bluff Ln
- WLBY 44094 2250 E4
Highland Av
10 AVLK 44012 2618 E2
S Highland Av
8800 GDHT 44125 2756 B7
Highland Blvd
- NCtT 44067 3153 B5
Highland Ct
100 ELYR 44035 2874 E5
8500 KTLD 44094 2377 B4
9000 MNTR 44060 2252 D1
Highland Dr
- GftT 44044 3142 B7
4600 WLBY 44094 2250 D6
6500 INDE 44131 3015 E1
6800 SLN 44139 2889 D7
8900 BKVL 44141 3015 E7
9000 BKVL 44141 3016 A7
9000 BKVL 44141 3150 E1
10300 RchT 44141 3150 B5
10300 RchT 44286 3150 B5
14900 NRYN 44133 3149 B1
18200 MPHT 44137 2886 D1
34600 NRDV 44039 2748 B7
35800 ETLK 44095 2250 C2
Highland Ln
10 CNFL 44022 2761 A7
Highland Rd
- EUCL 44117 2498 A1
- EUCL 44143 2498 A1
1300 MCDN 44056 3154 B3
1300 TwbT 44087 3154 D3
1700 TNBG 44087 3154 D3
3600 CLEV 44111 2753 B2
3700 LNDL 44111 2753 B2
5300 HDHT 44143 2499 D3
5300 RDHT 44143 2499 A3
6300 MAYF 44143 2499 E3
6400 MAYF 44143 2500 A3
24400 RDHT 44143 2498 D3
E Highland Rd
10 MCDN 44056 3153 C3
10 MCDN 44067 3153 B3
10 NCtT 44067 3153 B3
1000 MCDN 44056 3154 A3
1200 TwbT 44087 3154 A3
W Highland Rd
10 NCtT 44067 3153 A4
400 NCtT 44067 3152 E4
400 SgHT 44067 3152 C4
1100 BKVL 44141 3152 C4
Highland Hills Ct
7900 PRMA 44129 3013 D2
Highland Park Blvd
800 LORN 44052 2744 D2
Highland Park Dr
100 ELYR 44035 3006 D2
500 CrlT 44035 3006 D2
15200 SGVL 44136 3012 B4
Highland Pointe Pkwy
8000 MCDN 44056 3153 D2
Highlandview Av
- CLEV 44135 2752 D4
13000 CLEV 44135 2753 B4
Highland View Dr
6900 CcdT 44077 2145 D6
11200 MsnT 44024 2503 D1
Highlawn St
1600 ELYR 44035 3005 E2
High Meadow Rd
400 AMHT 44001 2744 A7
High Point Av
15200 SGVL 44136 3012 C5
High Point Cir
1200 AMHT 44001 2744 A7
Highpoint Ct
5500 PRMA 44134 2883 E1
High Point Dr
5500 SLN 44139 2888 E2
High Point Ln
10 BTVL 44022 2890 A1
10 WLBY 44094 2375 A2
Highpoint Rd
18700 BbgT 44023 3021 E2
24400 BHWD 44122 2758 D2
High Point Club Blvd
17800 SGVL 44136 3146 E4
High Pointe Cir
15100 MDFD 44062 2767 B2
High Tech Av
10 PNVL 44077 2146 C2
High Tee St
300 WLWK 44095 2249 C6

Highview Av
3300 CLEV 44109 2754 C3
Highview Dr
6900 SLN 44139 2888 D7
7200 PRMA 44129 2882 E7
16200 CLEV 44128 2757 C6
Highview Ln
- NRDV 44039 2748 D7
14700 NbyT 44065 2764 D2
Highwood Wy
7400 HDSN 44236 3154 A6
Higley Rd
3200 RKRV 44116 2751 B2
4000 FWPK 44116 2751 B2
4000 FWPK 44126 2751 B2
Hikers Tr
- CdnT 44024 2254 B7
Hilary Dr S
6100 NRYN 44133 3013 E6
6100 NRYN 44133 3014 A6
Hilary Dr W
11900 NRYN 44133 3013 E6
Hilda Av
2200 CLEV 44107 2622 D7
2200 CLEV 44111 2622 D7
2200 LKWD 44107 2622 D7
Hildana Rd
3500 SRHT 44120 2757 C2
Hilgert Dr
9400 CLEV 44104 2626 B7
Hill Dr
415-00 AURA 44202 3156 D3
14900 RslT 44022 2761 E2
14900 RslT 44072 2761 E2
15000 RslT 44022 2762 A3
15000 RslT 44072 2762 A3
W Hill Dr
700 GSML 44040 2500 C7
900 SgHT 44067 3017 C3
Hill Pl
- WLBY 44094 2251 A1
Hill St
5400 MPHT 44137 2886 B1
Hilland Dr
4500 CLEV 44109 2754 D6
Hillandale Dr
1600 EUCL 44092 2374 A4
1600 EUCL 44132 2374 A4
1600 WKLF 44092 2374 A4
Hillard Ct
30400 WTLK 44145 2749 B3
Hillard Bell
- WTLK 44145 2619 C6
Hillary Ln
4700 RDHT 44143 2498 D4
4700 SELD 44143 2498 D4
N Hillary Ovl
4800 RDHT 44143 2498 D4
Hillbrook Cir
14000 RslT 44072 2761 B2
Hillbrook Dr
14700 RslT 44072 2761 B2
14800 HGVL 44022 2761 A1
14800 HGVL 44072 2761 A1
14800 RslT 44022 2761 A1
Hillbrook Ln N
14600 HGVL 44022 2761 B1
14600 RslT 44022 2761 B1
Hillbrook Ln S
7100 RslT 44022 2761 B2
7200 RslT 44072 2761 A2
Hillbrook Ovl
7500 BKVL 44141 3016 A6
Hillbrook Rd
3700 UNHT 44118 2627 E4
3800 UNHT 44118 2628 A4
Hillcliff Cir
12300 SGVL 44136 3011 E6
Hillcreek Dr
- NRsT 44074 3139 B1
- OBLN 44074 3139 B1
Hillcreek Ln
900 GSML 44040 2500 B6
Hillcrest Av
2900 CLEV 44109 2754 C5
5500 MNTR 44060 2144 B1
14700 MDFD 44062 2767 E2
Hillcrest Dr
400 RDHT 44143 2498 C3
4700 ManT 44255 3159 C4
6000 VLVW 44125 2885 B4
12300 CsTp 44026 2503 A6
12300 MsnT 44026 2503 A6
19900 EUCL 44117 2498 A1
36000 ETLK 44095 2142 C7
Hillcrest Ln
100 ELYR 44035 2746 D7
100 ELYR 44035 2875 D1
2100 PRMA 44134 3014 D1
7000 CsTp 44026 2631 A1
7000 GSML 44040 2631 A1
Hillcrest Rd
1500 CVHT 44118 2627 B1
1500 ECLE 44112 2627 B1
1500 ECLE 44118 2627 B1
10000 KTLD 44094 2377 B4
Hillcroft Dr
4400 WVHT 44128 2758 C4
Hilldale Dr
11600 ManT 44255 3158 D2
Hillendale Rd
7200 CsTp 44026 2501 B2
Hiller Av
18000 CLEV 44119 2372 D5
Hillgrove Av
17800 CLEV 44119 2372 D5
20500 MPHT 44137 2758 A7
21200 BDHT 44146 2758 B7
Hillgrove Dr
5200 LORN 44053 2743 C5
Hilliard Blvd
- LKWD 44107 2622 A6
- RKRV 44107 2622 A6
18500 RKRV 44116 2621 E6
18500 RKRV 44116 2622 A6
22800 WTLK 44116 2621 A7
22800 WTLK 44145 2621 A7
23000 WTLK 44145 2620 E7
23200 WTLK 44145 2750 E1
27300 WTLK 44145 2749 E4
31200 AVON 44011 2749 A4
31200 AVON 44145 2749 A4
Hilliard Rd
100 ELYR 44035 2875 D3
14800 LKWD 44107 2622 B6

Hilliard Oak Ln
29600 WTLK 44145 2749 B3
Hillman Av
6000 CLEV 44127 2625 E7
6000 CLEV 44127 2755 D1
Hillock Av
9100 CLEV 44108 2496 B4
Hillrock Dr
1000 SELD 44121 2498 D6
S Hills Dr
4200 CLEV 44109 2754 E5
Hillsboro Av
- CcdT 44077 2146 A7
Hillsboro Rd
1700 CLEV 44112 2497 D4
1700 ECLE 44112 2497 D4
Hillsborough Pt
4800 WTLK 44145 2749 A6
Hillsdale Av
900 PRMA 44131 2883 E2
900 PRMA 44134 2883 E2
900 SVHL 44131 2883 E2
1000 LORN 44052 2614 B7
1300 LORN 44052 2744 B1
21200 FWPK 44126 2751 B4
E Hillsdale Av
10 PRMA 44131 2883 D2
10 PRMA 44134 2883 D2
10 SVHL 44131 2883 D2
10 SVHL 44131 2884 A2
Hillsdale Ct
100 ELYR 44035 2875 A5
Hillsdale Dr
1800 TNBG 44087 3019 C4
Hillsdale Rd
9800 BKVL 44141 3151 B4
Hillside Av
1800 ECLE 44112 2497 C4
2800 CLEV 44104 2626 A6
4600 GDHT 44125 2757 A5
Hillside Cir
10 GNVA 44041 1944 C6
Hillside Dr
10 ETLK 44095 2142 B7
10 PNVL 44077 2040 B7
900 AhtT 44001 2873 C2
14200 NRYN 44133 3148 D1
Hillside Ln
200 CNFL 44022 2760 E7
400 GSML 44040 2500 D3
7200 SLN 44139 3020 B2
18900 BbgT 44023 3022 B3
Hillside Rd
- VLVW 44131 2885 C6
10 PRMA 44131 2883 E7
10 PRMA 44134 2883 E7
10 SVHL 44131 2883 E7
10 SVHL 44131 2884 A7
4200 INDE 44131 2884 A7
7500 INDE 44131 2885 A7
11000 VLVW 44125 2885 C6
11400 NbyT 44065 2764 C1
Hillside Ter
300 MCDN 44056 3018 A7
Hillsover Dr
10300 KTLD 44094 2376 A5
Hillstone Rd
1000 CVHT 44121 2498 A6
Hilltop Cir
100 ELYR 44035 2746 D7
Hilltop Dr
- CrlT 44035 3005 B6
100 AMHT 44001 2743 D6
100 CRDN 44024 2380 B7
3500 PRMA 44134 2883 B6
3900 BNWK 44212 3146 E6
3900 VMLN 44089 2741 C5
8400 MNTR 44060 2144 C2
24200 BHWD 44122 2628 D3
Hilltop Ln
5100 BNHT 44131 2884 A1
Hilltop Ovl
5500 PRMA 44134 2883 E1
Hilltop Rd
2200 EUCL 44143 2498 B3
2200 RDHT 44143 2498 B3
N Hilltop Rd
4200 ORNG 44022 2759 C4
S Hilltop Rd
4300 ORNG 44022 2759 C4
Hilltop Farms Rd
- SLN 44139 2889 A1
Hilltop Park Pl
16600 BbgT 44023 2890 E1
Hillview Dr
- CrlT 44035 3005 D5
11900 NbyT 44065 2764 E1
Hillview Rd
1600 CLEV 44112 2497 D2
Hillward St
3500 WLBY 44094 2250 D4
Hillwood Ct
- MDBH 44130 2880 E5
Hillwynd
- SLN 44139 2889 D6
Hilo Farm Dr
9100 KDHL 44060 2252 E5
Hilton Rd
1900 CLEV 44112 2497 D4
6800 BKVL 44141 3015 E6
6800 BKVL 44141 3016 A5
Hinckley Av
4300 CLEV 44109 2754 E6
Hinckley Cir
8500 BKVL 44141 3016 D6
Hinckley Industrial Pkwy
4500 CLEV 44109 2755 A6
Hinde Av
6200 CLEV 44127 2755 D1
Hine Av
700 PNVL 44077 2039 E6
900 PNVL 44077 2040 A5
W Hines Hill Rd
600 BosT 44141 3152 D7
1100 NCtT 44141 3152 D7
Hinsdale Ct
- MDBH 44130 2881 A5
Hinsdale Dr
- HmbT 44024 2380 C2
Hinsdale Rd
4000 CVHT 44121 2628 A2
4000 SELD 44121 2628 A2
Hinsdale St
6700 HRM 44234 3161 A1

Hio Dr
6400 BKPK 44142 2880 E3
Hipple Av
19200 CLEV 44135 2751 E5
Hiram Ln
2100 TwbT 44236 3155 A6
N Hiram Ln
7700 TwbT 44236 3155 A5
Hiram Tr
31200 MDHL 44022 2759 D3
31200 ORNG 44022 2759 D3
Hiram College Dr
10 NCtT 44067 3152 E1
10 SgHT 44067 3152 E1
Hird Av
1100 LKWD 44107 2623 B4
Hirst Av
11900 CLEV 44135 2753 A3
Hirst Pl
- CLEV 44135 2753 A3
Hist Rd
5000 BDHT 44146 2758 E7
Hitching Post Ln
14400 RslT 44072 2762 A1
Hi View Dr
7200 NRYN 44133 3013 D6
Hlavin Av
12800 CLEV 44105 2756 E4
Hoadley Ln
2900 TNBG 44087 3020 C4
Hoag Dr
5300 SFLD 44054 2746 E6
Hobart Rd
9300 WTHL 44094 2376 B3
9800 KTLD 44094 2376 C5
Hobbie Dr
35400 ETLK 44095 2250 B3
Hobbit Ct
10800 CcdT 44077 2146 A6
Hobby Horse Ln
7500 CcdT 44060 2253 C2
Hocking Blvd
15200 BKPK 44142 2881 B2
Hodge Ct
100 ELYR 44035 3006 B2
Hodgeman Dr
5800 PMHT 44129 2882 D2
5800 PMHT 44130 2882 D2
5800 PRMA 44129 2882 D2
Hodgson Av
4200 CLEV 44109 2754 B2
Hodgson Rd
7000 MNTR 44060 2143 A7
7000 MNTR 44094 2143 A7
7000 WLBY 44094 2143 A7
Hoertz Rd
7500 PRMA 44134 3014 C2
7700 BWHT 44134 3014 C2
7700 BWHT 44147 3014 C2
N Hogan Dr
3700 LORN 44053 2743 E2
S Hogan Dr
3700 LORN 44053 2743 E2
Hogsback Rd
- CLEV 44107 2622 A7
- CLEV 44126 2622 A7
Holborn Av
12700 CLEV 44105 2756 E2
12900 CLEV 44120 2756 E2
Holborn Rd
700 STBR 44241 3156 C7
Holbrook Rd
16700 SRHT 44120 2627 C7
35100 BbgT 44022 2890 A2
35100 BbgT 44023 2890 A2
35100 BTVL 44022 2889 E2
35100 BTVL 44022 2890 A2
Holburn Rd
6000 PRMA 44129 2882 E3
Holden Ct
- KDHL 44060 2253 A4
200 GNVA 44041 1944 B4
Holden Ln
9300 BTNH 44108 2496 B4
Holden Rdg
- CcdT 44060 2253 A4
Holden Ridge Rd
- MsnT 44024 2503 B2
Holdens Arbor Cir
1900 WTLK 44145 2749 D1
Holdens Arbor Run
1600 WTLK 44145 2619 D7
1700 WTLK 44145 2749 D1
Holi-Dale Dr
10600 HmbT 44024 2380 E7
10600 HmbT 44024 2381 A6
Holiday Cir
4500 CLEV 44109 2754 E5
Holiday Dr
15000 VmnT 44089 2869 D1
Holiday Ln
19300 WVHT 44122 2757 E3
19300 WVHT 44122 2758 A3
Holiday Rd
13900 SGVL 44149 3011 C7
Holiday Hills Ct
6300 BDHT 44146 2887 E5
Holl Av
4100 SDLK 44054 2616 A5
4200 SFLD 44054 2616 B5
Holland Rd
13300 BKPK 44130 2881 E3
13300 BKPK 44142 2881 A3
13300 PMHT 44130 2881 E3
13300 PRMA 44130 2881 E3
18200 BKPK 44142 2880 E3
Holland St
- GDRV 44077 2039 C5
Hollenbeck Cir
7900 PRMA 44129 2882 D6
Hollingsworth Ct
36000 AVON 44011 2747 E4
Hollis Ct
8600 BKVL 44141 3016 B6
Hollis Dr
900 ELYR 44035 2875 A4
Hollis Ln
8600 BKVL 44141 3016 B6
Hollister Rd
3300 CVHT 44118 2497 D7
3400 CVHT 44121 2497 D7
Holliston Ln
10700 PMHT 44130 2882 B5
Hollo Ovl
13000 SGVL 44149 3011 C7

Hollow Lake Ct
22000 CrlT 44044 3006 C7
Hollowrun Pl
17800 SGVL 44136 3011 E6
Hollow Tree Ovl
33000 NRDV 44039 2748 D7
Hollow Wood Ln
1400 AVON 44011 2617 E6
Holly Cir
1200 PRMA 44134 2883 E5
20500 SGVL 44149 3146 C2
Holly Dr
300 BERA 44017 2879 E5
300 BERA 44017 2880 A5
7500 MONT 44060 2143 D2
28300 NOSD 44070 2878 D2
Holly Ln
- AhtT 44001 2872 B2
- AMHT 44001 2872 B2
100 SRSL 44022 2761 E5
200 ELYR 44035 2875 A6
2200 AVON 44011 2747 E2
2900 WTLK 44145 2750 B3
8800 ODFL 44138 3010 A1
Holly Rd
5300 BDHT 44146 2887 B1
Hollycroft Ln
7400 MNTR 44060 2251 E2
7400 MNTR 44060 2252 A1
Holly Hill Dr
16500 CLEV 44128 2757 C4
Holly Hill Ln
5300 SLN 44139 2888 C1
Holly Hill Rd
8300 RslT 44072 2762 A2
Hollyhock Ln
7100 SLN 44139 3019 D1
Hollylane Dr
2100 BWHT 44147 3014 D3
Holly Oak Ln
800 AURA 44202 3021 C7
Holly Park Dr
7200 CcdT 44060 2253 B1
Holly Springs Tr
8700 BbgT 44023 2891 B4
Hollythorn Dr
5500 BKVL 44141 3150 C4
Holly View Dr
1100 VMLN 44089 2741 A7
Hollyview Dr
700 SDLK 44054 2616 C4
700 SFLD 44054 2616 C4
Hollywood Av
600 SDLK 44054 2616 B4
5300 MPHT 44137 2757 D7
5300 MPHT 44137 2886 E1
14400 CLEV 44111 2622 D7
Hollywood Dr
800 ELYR 44035 2875 E2
5400 PRMA 44129 2883 A4
5400 PRMA 44134 2883 A4
6600 PRMA 44129 2882 E4
27200 WTLK 44145 2749 E4
27200 WTLK 44145 2750 A4
Hollywood St
100 OBLN 44074 3138 D2
Holmden Av
1000 CLEV 44109 2624 E7
1000 CLEV 44109 2625 A7
1000 CLEV 44113 2625 A7
Holmden Ct
1000 CLEV 44109 2624 D7
Holmden Rd
1400 SELD 44121 2498 A7
1400 SELD 44121 2628 A1
Holmes Av
15200 CLEV 44110 2497 C2
Holmes Dr
2000 TNBG 44087 3019 C6
N Holmes Pl
7100 CcdT 44077 2146 A7
S Holmes Pl
7200 CcdT 44077 2146 A6
Holmwood Rd
22600 SRHT 44122 2628 C6
Holton Av
7900 CLEV 44104 2626 A5
Holton Ct
7900 CLEV 44104 2626 A5
Holton Rd
25300 ODFL 44138 2879 C6
Holyoke Av
1500 ECLE 44112 2496 E6
1500 ECLE 44112 2497 A6
4700 CLEV 44104 2625 C5
7600 HDSN 44236 3155 B6
Holyrood Rd
1600 CLEV 44106 2626 B1
Holzhauer Rd
7100 SgHT 44067 3152 C1
Home Ct
7600 CLEV 44103 2626 A2
Home St
16300 MPHT 44137 2886 C1
Homecrest Dr
- NRDV 44039 2876 E7
Homeland Dr
1000 RKRV 44116 2621 B6
Homer Av
5300 CLEV 44103 2495 D7
Homer Ct
100 ELYR 44035 2875 C6
Homesite Ct
100 ELYR 44035 3006 A2
Homestead Av
7800 CLEV 44105 2756 A3
Homestead Cir
7600 NRYN 44133 3013 C7
Homestead Dr
500 AVON 44011 2617 E6
8500 OmsT 44138 2878 E7
Homestead Rd
1000 SELD 44121 2498 B6
5700 MadT 44057 1941 D1
Homestead Creek Dr
1200 BWHT 44147 3014 E6
1200 BWHT 44147 3015 A6
Homestead Park Dr
20100 SGVL 44149 3011 C3
Homeway Rd
18300 CLEV 44135 2751 E5
18300 CLEV 44135 2752 A5
Homewood Av
5100 MPHT 44137 2757 E7
6700 PMHT 44130 2882 A6

Homewood Dr
800 PNVL 44077 2146 C2
1000 LKWD 44107 2622 E4
1800 LORN 44055 2745 D4
2200 LORN 44055 2746 A4
4600 MNTR 44060 2038 E5
28900 WKLF 44092 2374 A2
Homewood Wy
10 RDHT 44143 2498 E4
Homeworth Av
500 PNVL 44077 2040 A6
10300 GDHT 44125 2756 C6
Honey Ln
- AhtT 44001 2872 B2
- AMHT 44001 2872 B2
Honeybelle Ovl
100 ORNG 44022 2759 A5
Honey Crisp Ct
- WLBY 44094 2251 A2
Honeycut Dr
8700 NRDV 44039 2877 B7
Honeydale Av
11600 CLEV 44104 2626 D6
11600 CLEV 44120 2626 D6
Honeydale Dr
7200 NCtT 44067 3153 A4
Honeygold Ln
1400 BWHT 44147 3149 D4
Honey Locust
- BHWD 44122 2629 A5
Honey Locust Ct
100 PnvT 44077 2041 B7
Honeylocust Ln
4800 WTLK 44145 2749 A6
Honeysuckle Ln
10200 BWHT 44147 3149 E4
17300 ClbT 44028 3144 A3
33800 NRDV 44039 2877 C2
Honeysuckle Pth
390-00 AURA 44202 3156 D2
Hood Av
2000 CLEV 44109 2754 D5
Hook Hollow Rd
14800 RslT 44022 2761 E2
14800 RslT 44072 2761 E2
14800 RslT 44072 2762 A3
15000 RslT 44022 2762 A3
Hoose Rd
9400 KDHL 44060 2252 E4
9400 KDHL 44060 2253 B2
9400 MNTR 44060 2252 E4
9400 MNTR 44060 2253 B2
10200 CcdT 44060 2253 D1
10200 CcdT 44077 2253 D1
Hoover Av
700 CLEV 44119 2372 D5
Hoover Blvd
5700 LORN 44053 2744 D6
Hoover Ct
7700 MNTR 44060 2143 D6
Hoover Dr
7000 MNTR 44060 2143 D7
Hope Av
6700 CLEV 44102 2623 E7
6700 CLEV 44102 2624 A7
Hope Ct
100 CrlT 44035 3006 B3
40000 ELYR 44035 3006 B3
Hope Haven Dr
1600 PRMA 44134 3014 D1
Hopewell Tr
10 MDHL 44022 2760 E3
Hopkins Av
1400 LKWD 44107 2623 A6
11200 CLEV 44108 2496 D5
Hopkins Rd
6500 MNTR 44060 2144 C5
7200 MNTR 44060 2252 D2
Hoppensack Av
6500 CLEV 44127 2625 E7
Horace Ct
3300 CLEV 44113 2624 C6
Horizon Dr
4900 RDHT 44143 2373 E7
Horizons Dr
12800 LryT 44077 2147 D7
Horner Av
13100 CLEV 44105 2756 E2
13100 CLEV 44120 2756 E2
13100 CLEV 44120 2757 A2
Hornyak St
10 AhtT 44001 2872 A5
Horseshoe Blvd
- WTLK 44145 2750 E1
23200 WTLK 44145 2620 E7
Horseshoe Ct
10 NHFD 44067 3018 A3
Horseshoe Ln
22100 SGVL 44149 3011 A5
Horseshoe Wy
700 AVLK 44012 2619 A5
Horton Rd
4600 CLEV 44105 2756 A5
4600 GDHT 44105 2756 A5
4600 GDHT 44125 2756 A5
Hosea Bradford Ct
6900 BKVL 44141 3016 A7
Hosford Rd
11100 CdnT 44024 2379 C2
Hosmer Av
5700 CLEV 44105 2755 D2
Hosmer Lake Rd
- BtnT 44021 2766 E6
- BtnT 44062 2766 E6
Hospital Dr
12400 ClrT 44024 2635 B2
12400 MsnT 44024 2635 B2
Hotchkiss Rd
12200 NbyT 44021 2765 B4
12600 BrtT 44021 2765 C3
13500 BrtT 44021 2766 A1
13500 BURT 44021 2766 A1
Hotel Dr
- BHWD 44122 2758 E2
Hotel Rd
- BKPK 44135 2880 E1
- CLEV 44135 2880 E1
- CLEV 44142 2880 E1
Hough Av
5500 CLEV 44103 2625 E2
7300 CLEV 44103 2626 A2
8200 CLEV 44106 2626 A2
Houghton Ct
10 FTHR 44077 2039 D3

Cleveland Street Index

STREET Block | City | ZIP | Map# | Grid

Houghton Rd
10 NHFD 44067 3018 A4
300 NHFD 44067 3017 E4
300 SgHT 44067 3017 D4
House Av
5000 CLEV 44127 2625 B6
House Ct
200 FTHR 44077 2039 D3
Houston Av
300 CLEV 44113 2625 A6
Houston Dr
5900 PRMA 44130 2882 A3
Hovey Dr
12500 CsTp 44026 2502 B7
Howard Av
1400 CLEV 44113 2624 E6
25300 WTLK 44145 2750 C1
Howard Dr
700 VMLN 44089 2741 A5
10700 CdnT 44024 2378 E7
10800 CdnT 44024 2379 A7
Howard St
700 ELYR 44035 2875 E3
7600 PRMA 44134 3014 E2
Howe Rd
14000 SGVL 44136 3012 A7
14400 SGVL 44136 3147 B1
18800 BNWK 44136 3147 B5
18800 BNWK 44212 3147 B5
Howe St
200 ELYR 44035 3006 A1
Howell Dr
8000 MNTR 44060 2143 E4
Howell St
600 SDLK 44054 2616 A4
Howells Ct
500 ETLK 44094 2142 E7
500 ETLK 44095 2142 E7
Hower Av
1400 CLEV 44112 2496 E7
1400 ECLE 44112 2496 E7
Howlett Av
4100 CLEV 44113 2624 B7
Hoy Av
12800 CLEV 44105 2756 E4
Hoyt Ct
8500 MNTR 44060 2252 B1
Hoyt St
400 PNVL 44077 2146 B1
Hrovat Dr
- SgHT 44067 3152 E2
Hub Pkwy
7400 VLVW 44125 3016 E1
Hubbard Av
6500 CLEV 44127 2625 E7
Hubbard Rd
1300 MadT 44057 1843 B7
1600 MadT 44057 1942 B3
2700 MDSN 44057 1942 B5
14000 BtnT 44021 2766 C6
14600 BtnT 44062 2766 D6
Hubbard Rd SR-528
2700 MadT 44057 1942 B5
2700 MDSN 44057 1942 B5
Huckleberry Dr
26700 RDHT 44143 2374 A5
Hudak Dr
500 BNWK 44212 3147 A7
Hudson Av
6400 MNTR 44060 2145 A5
10500 CLEV 44106 2626 C3
Hudson Blvd
- SLN 44139 2888 E6
Hudson Park Dr
7500 HDSN 44236 3155 B7
Huff Av
14800 BtnT 44021 2766 B2
14800 BtnT 44062 2766 B2
14800 BURT 44021 2766 B1
Huffington Cir
3600 AVON 44011 2747 D4
Huffman Rd
11700 PMHT 44130 2882 A3
11700 PRMA 44130 2882 A3
12900 BKPK 44130 2881 E3
12900 BKPK 44142 2881 E3
12900 PMHT 44130 2881 E3
12900 PRMA 44130 2881 E3
E Huffman Rd
11300 PMHT 44130 2882 B3
11300 PRMA 44130 2882 A3
Hughes St
4200 WLBY 44094 2250 D5
Hugo Av
3400 CLEV 44105 2755 C1
Hulda Av
9900 CLEV 44104 2626 C5
Hulett Av
1200 ETLK 44095 2250 A4
Hull Av
10700 CLEV 44106 2496 C7
Hulls Cove
7100 MNTR 44060 2251 B2
Hume Hill Dr
10 AMHT 44001 2873 A2
Humiston Dr
400 BYVL 44140 2621 A5
Hummel Rd
13300 BKPK 44130 2881 E1
13300 BKPK 44142 2881 E1
13300 PRMA 44130 2881 E1
Hummingbird Cir
5500 SLN 44139 2889 A2
29400 WTLK 44145 2749 C4
Hummingbird Ct
- WTLK 44145 2749 C5
Hummingbird Ln
- WTLK 44145 2749 C4
Hummingbird Wy
29400 WTLK 44145 2749 C4
Humphrey Cir
- NRDV 44035 2876 B7
Humphrey Ct
16700 CLEV 44110 2372 C6
Humphrey Rd
15100 MDBH 44130 2881 C5
Humphrey Hill Dr
7900 CcdT 44077 2253 C4
Hunt Cir
6500 MAYF 44143 2500 A5
Hunt Rd
17600 SGVL 44136 3147 D5
19600 NRYN 44133 3147 E5
19600 SGVL 44133 3147 E5
Hunt Club Dr
- CcdT 44077 2254 B2
Hunt Club Wy
700 AVLK 44012 2619 A5
Hunter Av
- RKRV 44116 2621 D7
Hunter Dr
3300 NOSD 44070 2750 D4
6400 GDHT 44125 2885 E4
Hunter Hllw
7400 RslT 44072 2761 C2
Hunter Rd
- AVLK 44012 2618 A2
Hunters Ln
12500 NRYN 44133 3013 A3
Hunters Tr
900 BWHT 44147 3015 A5
7200 CcdT 44077 2146 C7
7200 CcdT 44077 2254 C1
37100 AVON 44011 2747 D3
Hunters Chase
1000 GFTN 44044 3142 A3
Hunters Chase Dr
1400 WTLK 44145 2619 D7
Hunters Creek Dr
31500 WTLK 44145 2749 A3
Hunters Crossing Dr
- ELYR 44035 3007 A2
Hunter's Point Ln
1700 WTLK 44145 2621 A7
1700 WTLK 44145 2751 A1
Hunters Pointe Dr
18500 SGVL 44136 3147 D4
Hunters Ridge Dr
- STBR 44241 3156 C7
Hunters Ridge Ln
28700 OmsT 44138 2878 D4
Hunters Ridge Rd
37400 SLN 44139 2889 D4
Hunters Woods Ln
2900 WBHL 44094 2375 D7
Hunting Dr
8200 NRYN 44133 3014 C3
10000 BKVL 44141 3151 D4
Hunting Hllw
- EatT 44044 3141 E3
- GFTN 44044 3141 E3
Hunting Ln
6800 INDE 44131 2884 E6
7000 RslT 44022 2761 A3
Hunting Tr
10 MDHL 44022 2760 E3
10 MDHL 44022 2761 A3
Hunting Hill Farm Dr
38200 HGVL 44022 2630 E5
Hunting Hills Dr
8500 KDHL 44060 2251 E6
8500 KDHL 44060 2252 A6
8500 KTLD 44060 2251 E6
8500 KTLD 44094 2252 A6
14300 RslT 44072 2631 C7
Huntinghollow Dr
10 PRPK 44124 2629 E7
Hunting Lake Dr
7200 CcdT 44077 2254 C1
Hunting Meadows Dr
16900 SGVL 44136 3147 A2
17000 SGVL 44136 3146 E2
Huntington Blvd
28000 BYVL 44140 2619 D4
Huntington Cir
100 ELYR 44035 2746 D7
Huntington Dr
100 NHFD 44067 3018 B4
300 MCDN 44056 3018 B4
300 NHFD 44056 3018 B4
6300 SLN 44139 2889 B5
29500 NOSD 44070 2878 C3
N Huntington Dr
6200 SLN 44139 2889 B5
S Huntington Dr
35600 SLN 44139 2889 C5
Huntington Ln
1500 CVHT 44118 2497 E7
Huntington Rd
10 PnvT 44077 2040 C5
2800 SRHT 44120 2627 B6
7500 HDSN 44236 3155 D7
Huntington St
100 CRDN 44024 2380 A6
Huntington Wy
- ManT 44202 3023 A7
Huntington Beach Dr
- FTHR 44077 2039 C3
Huntington Close
10900 NRYN 44133 3013 C4
Huntington Park Dr
9200 SGVL 44136 3012 B4
Huntington Reserve Dr
5000 PRMA 44134 3014 A1
Huntington Woods Dr
100 MDSN 44057 2044 C2
Huntington Woods Pkwy
10 BYVL 44140 2619 A2
Hunting Valley Ln
4500 BKVL 44141 3015 E5
Huntley Ct
500 BYVL 44140 2621 A5
Huntley Rd
15300 HtbT 44024 2507 B4
15300 HtbT 44046 2507 C4
Huntmere Av
15200 CLEV 44110 2372 B7
Huntmere Dr
300 BYVL 44140 2620 C5
Huntoon Rd
12000 CcdT 44077 2146 E6
12000 CcdT 44077 2147 A6
12200 LryT 44077 2147 C6
Huntsford Dr
200 MCDN 44056 3018 B6
Hurd Dr
- ELYR 44035 2874 E1
Hurd Rd
10 AURA 44202 3157 A1
Hurley Av
2100 CLEV 44109 2754 D3
Hurlingham Rd
25700 BHWD 44122 2628 E6
26100 BHWD 44122 2629 A6
Huron Av
6700 MadT 44057 1843 B7
Huron Rd
5300 LNHT 44124 2629 A1
E Huron Rd
100 CLEV 44113 2624 E3
100 CLEV 44115 2624 E3
900 CLEV 44115 2625 A3
1200 CLEV 44114 2625 A3
W Huron Rd
- CLEV 44115 2624 E3
100 CLEV 44113 2624 E3
Huron St
100 ELYR 44035 2874 D5
700 GFTN 44044 3142 A5
5500 VMLN 44089 2740 E5
16600 BbgT 44023 2890 B1
Hurricane Dr
38100 WLBY 44094 2250 E2
Hurst Dr
10 PnvT 44077 2145 C3
300 BYVL 44140 2619 A4
Huss Av
5600 CLEV 44105 2755 D1
Huxley Ln
9000 OmsT 44138 2878 C7
Hy Ct
5200 GDHT 44125 2756 E7
Hyacinth Ln
- PNVL 44077 2145 B3
Hyanis Dr
1000 GFTN 44044 3142 A4
Hyannis Cir
1900 HDSN 44236 3154 E7
Hyannis Dr
7200 OKWD 44146 2887 E7
Hyannis Port Cir
- AVLK 44012 2617 D4
Hyannis Port Dr
26700 NOSD 44070 2750 A6
Hyde Av
3500 CLEV 44109 2624 B7
4400 CLEV 44102 2624 B7
Hyde Pk
10 BHWD 44122 2629 A4
4300 NOSD 44070 2750 C5
Hyde St
6000 MNTR 44060 2143 E3
Hyde Park Av
3200 CVHT 44118 2627 C2
Hyde Park Dr
7200 MDBH 44130 2881 C7
9300 TNBG 44087 3019 C6
Hyder Dr
10 MDSN 44057 2044 C2
100 MadT 44057 2044 C2

I

I Dr
- LORN 44052 2744 E4
I-71
- BKPK - 2881 B2
- BNWK - 3147 B6
- CLEV - 2624 E7
- MDBH - 2881 A7
- MDBH - 3012 A1
- SGVL - 3012 A2
- SGVL - 3147 C7
I-71 Innerbelt Frwy
- CLEV - 2624 E6
I-71 Medina Frwy
- BKLN - 2753 E3
- BKPK - 2752 B7
- BKPK - 2881 B1
- BNWK - 3147 B5
- CLEV - 2624 E7
- CLEV - 2752 D4
- CLEV - 2753 A4
- CLEV - 2754 B2
- LNDL - 2753 B3
- MDBH - 2881 B4
- MDBH - 3012 A2
- SGVL - 3012 A2
- SGVL - 3147 B4
I-77
- BKVL - 3150 D1
- BWHT - 3015 D2
- CHHT - 2755 D3
- CLEV - 2625 C6
- INDE - 2884 D7
- INDE - 3015 D3
- NBGH - 2755 D3
I-77 Willow Frwy
- BKVL - 3015 D7
- BKVL - 3150 E5
- BWHT - 3015 D2
- CHHT - 2755 D5
- CLEV - 2625 C7
- CLEV - 2755 C1
- INDE - 2755 E7
- INDE - 2884 D2
- INDE - 3015 D1
- NBGH - 2755 C2
- RHFD - 3150 E5
I-80 Ohio Tpk
- AhtT - 2871 E5
- AhtT - 2872 A5
- AhtT - 2873 C4
- AMHT - 2872 E4
- BERA - 3010 D1
- BERA - 3011 C3
- BhmT - 2871 C6
- BKVL - 3150 B4
- BWHT - 3149 C2
- BWHT - 3150 B4
- ELYR - 2874 E3
- ELYR - 2875 E4
- EyrT - 2873 E3
- EyrT - 2874 B3
- NRDV - 2875 E4
- NRDV - 2876 D5
- NRDV - 2877 A5
- NRDV - 2878 E7
- NRYN - 3012 C5
- NRYN - 3013 A7
- NRYN - 3148 E2
- NRYN - 3149 C2
- ODFL - 3010 E1
- OmsT - 2878 B6
- OmsT - 2879 A7
- OmsT - 3010 D1
- RchT - 3150 E6
- RchT - 3151 B7
- RHFD - 3150 E6
- RHFD - 3151 B7
- SGVL - 3011 E3
- SGVL - 3012 C5
I-90
- AVON - 2617 D7
- AVON - 2618 D7
- AVON - 2619 A7
- AVON - 2747 A1
- CLEV - 2372 E6
- CLEV - 2373 A6
- CLEV - 2495 B7
- CLEV - 2497 B1
- CLEV - 2623 E7
- CLEV - 2624 E4
- CLEV - 2625 A3
- ELYR - 2746 B7
- ELYR - 2874 E1
- ELYR - 2875 A1
- EUCL - 2373 B5
- EUCL - 2374 A3
- EyrT - 2874 B1
- SFLD - 2746 E2
- SFLD - 2747 A1
- WBHL - 2250 E7
- WBHL - 2374 D5
- WBHL - 2375 A4
- WKLF - 2374 A3
- WKLF - 2375 A4
- WLBY - 2250 E7
- WLBY - 2251 A6
- WLBY - 2375 C1
- WTHL - 2250 E7
- WTHL - 2251 A6
- WTLK - 2619 A7
I-90 Cleveland Mem Shoreway
- BTNH - 2496 E2
- CLEV - 2495 E5
- CLEV - 2496 A4
- CyhC - 2495 E5
I-90 Cleveland Mem Shrwy Frwy
- BTNH - 2496 D3
- CLEV - 2495 C6
- CLEV - 2496 A4
I-90 Innerbelt Frwy
- CLEV - 2624 E4
- CLEV - 2625 B2
I-90 Lakeland Frwy
- BTNH - 2496 E1
- BTNH - 2497 A1
- CLEV - 2372 D7
- CLEV - 2373 A6
- CLEV - 2496 E1
- CLEV - 2497 B1
- EUCL - 2373 B5
I-90 North South Frwy
- CcdT - 2146 C7
- CcdT - 2253 D2
- CcdT - 2254 B1
- KDHL - 2252 E4
- KDHL - 2253 B3
- LryT - 2147 E2
- MadT - 2044 E3
- MDSN - 2044 B3
- MNTR - 2251 E4
- MNTR - 2252 A4
- MNTR - 2253 B3
I-90 Northwest Frwy
- AVON - 2619 A6
- CLEV - 2622 B7
- CLEV - 2623 C7
- CLEV - 2624 B6
- LKWD - 2622 A6
- RKRV - 2621 A6
- RKRV - 2622 A6
- WTLK - 2619 D7
- WTLK - 2620 E6
- WTLK - 2621 E6
I-90 Ohio Tpk
- AhtT - 2871 E5
- AhtT - 2872 A5
- AhtT - 2873 D3
- AMHT - 2872 E4
- BhmT - 2871 A7
I-271
- BDHT - 2887 D2
- BHWD - 2629 A5
- BHWD - 2759 A2
- BosT - 3152 E7
- HDHT - 2499 E1
- MAYF - 2499 E1
- MCDN - 3018 C3
- MCDN - 3153 C1
- MDHT - 2499 E6
- NCtT - 3152 E7
- NCtT - 3153 B3
- OKWD - 3018 C3
- ORNG - 2758 E4
- ORNG - 2759 A2
- PRPK - 2629 A7
- WBHL - 2374 E4
- WBHL - 2375 A4
- WBHL - 2499 E1
- WVHT - 2758 E5
I-271 Outerbelt East Frwy
- BDFD - 2887 D3
- BDHT - 2758 D7
- BDHT - 2887 D3
- BHWD - 2629 E1
- BHWD - 2758 E3
- BHWD - 2759 A1
- HDHT - 2499 E4
- LNHT - 2629 B3
- MCDN - 3018 C6
- MDHT - 2499 E6
- MDHT - 2500 A7
- MDHT - 2629 E1
- OKWD - 2887 C7
- OKWD - 3018 C3
- ORNG - 2758 E3
- ORNG - 2759 A3
- PRPK - 2629 E1
- PRPK - 2759 A1
- WVHT - 2758 E5
I-271 Outerbelt West Frwy
- OKWD - 3018 C1
I-480
- BDHT - 2758 B7
- BDHT - 2887 C1
- BKLN - 2753 E6
- BNHT - 2755 A7
- CLEV - 2751 D6
- CLEV - 2754 B7
- CLEV - 2755 A7
- HDSN - 3155 D7
- MCDN - 3018 E4
- MCDN - 3019 A5
- MPHT - 2758 B7
- NOSD - 2878 A3
- NRDL - 2758 C6
- NRDV - 2877 E4
- NRDV - 2878 C3
- OKWD - 3018 E4
- TNBG - 3019 A5
- TNBG - 3154 E2
- TNBG - 3155 B3
- TwbT - 3155 C5
- WVHT - 2757 E6
- WVHT - 2758 C6
I-480 Outerbelt East Frwy
- BDFD - 2887 D3
- BDHT - 2887 D3
- OKWD - 2887 C7
- OKWD - 3018 C1
I-480 Outerbelt South Frwy
- BKLN - 2753 B6
- BNHT - 2755 A7
- BNHT - 2884 E2
- CLEV - 2751 C6
- CLEV - 2752 C7
- CLEV - 2753 B6
- CLEV - 2754 A6
- CLEV - 2755 A7
- CLEV - 2757 C6
- FWPK - 2751 C6
- GDHT - 2756 E7
- GDHT - 2757 C6
- GDHT - 2885 D1
- INDE - 2884 D2
- INDE - 2885 A1
- MPHT - 2757 A6
- NOSD - 2750 D7
- NOSD - 2751 A6
- NOSD - 2878 E2
- NOSD - 2879 B1
- NRDV - 2878 A4
- OmsT - 2878 E2
- VLVW - 2885 B1
- WVHT - 2757 E6
- WVHT - 2758 A6
I-480 Outerbelt West Frwy
- OKWD - 3018 C1
I-490
- CLEV - 2624 E6
- CLEV - 2625 B6
Ida Av
800 CLEV 44103 2496 A6
Idaho Av
100 LORN 44052 2615 A5
Idaho Dr
100 ELYR 44035 3006 E2
Idarose Av
13800 CLEV 44110 2497 A3
Idlehurst Dr
1700 EUCL 44117 2373 D6
1900 RDHT 44117 2373 D7
1900 RDHT 44143 2373 D7
Idle View Dr
4600 VMLN 44089 2741 A7
Idlewild Dr
3800 RKRV 44116 2751 D2
3900 FWPK 44116 2751 D2
3900 FWPK 44126 2751 D2
Idlewood Av
500 SDLK 44054 2616 B4
800 SFLD 44054 2616 B4
1200 LKWD 44107 2623 B4
1800 ECLE 44112 2496 E7
1800 ECLE 44112 2497 A7
Idlewood Ct
100 AMHT 44001 2872 D3
Idlewood Dr
100 AMHT 44001 2872 D3
9000 MNTR 44060 2252 D1
9400 BKLN 44144 2753 D6
14600 NbyT 44065 2764 C1
41800 EyrT 44035 2874 D1
E Idlewood Dr
9600 TNBG 44087 3019 D5
W Idlewood Dr
1600 TNBG 44087 3019 C5
Idlewood Ln
100 AURA 44202 3156 B1
Idlewood Pl
2700 LORN 44052 2744 C2
Idlewood Rd
2500 CVHT 44118 2627 D5
Idlewood Tr
- SGVL 44136 3011 D5
19100 SGVL 44149 3011 C5
Ignatius Av
10200 CLEV 44111 2623 C7
Ike Thompson
12300 CLEV 44106 2496 D7
Illinois Av
200 LORN 44052 2615 A5
10500 RMDV 44202 3020 E3
Illinois Cir
100 ELYR 44035 3006 D1
Ilsley Sq
10200 CcdT 44060 2253 D1
Imperial Av
11600 CLEV 44104 2626 D7
11600 CLEV 44120 2626 D7
Imperial Ct
7000 EyrT 44035 2874 B2
Imperial Pkwy
- SGVL 44149 3145 E2
Inca Rd
5200 RchT 44286 3150 B6
Independence Av
800 AVON 44011 2617 E6
Independence Blvd
9200 PMHT 44129 2882 D5
9200 PMHT 44130 2882 C6
9200 PRMA 44129 2882 D5
Independence Ct
17300 BKPK 44142 2881 A4
36800 SLN 44139 2889 C4
Independence Dr
5500 LORN 44053 2744 B6
7500 WNHL 44146 3018 B2
7900 MNTR 44060 2143 E6
8000 MNTR 44060 2144 A6
9700 NRYN 44133 3013 B6
Independence Rd
100 ELYR 44035 3006 B3
2900 CLEV 44115 2625 B6
2900 CLEV 44127 2625 B6
3100 CLEV 44105 2625 B6
3800 CLEV 44105 2755 C2
Independence St
400 FTHR 44077 2039 D4
Indian Run
9300 MCDN 44056 3018 D4
Indiana Av
100 ELYR 44035 3006 D1
200 LORN 44052 2615 A5
6500 MDHT 44124 2500 A7
6800 CLEV 44105 2755 E3
7400 CLEV 44105 2756 A3
Indiana St
3600 PryT 44081 2041 E1
Indian Creek Dr
13300 MDBH 44130 3012 C1
Indianhead Ln
15600 SGVL 44136 3147 B2
Indian Hills Dr
17400 AbnT 44023 2892 A4
Indian Hollow Rd
10400 CrlT 44035 3006 C3
10800 CrlT 44044 3006 C6
12000 CrlT 44044 3141 C2
13800 LrgT 44044 3141 D5
13800 LrgT 44050 3141 D5
Indian Mound Dr
7400 VLVW 44125 3016 E1
Indianola Av
10 PnvT 44077 2040 C2
17600 LKWD 44107 2622 A6
Indianola Dr
6500 MadT 44057 1843 A7
Indianpath Dr
2200 WTLK 44145 2749 D2
Indian Point Rd
6100 LryT 44077 2147 E5
Indian Pointe Dr
1300 WLBY 44094 2142 E5
1300 WLBY 44094 2143 A5
Indian Ridge Tr
14700 BURT 44021 2766 A1
Indian Ridge Cove
29500 WTLK 44145 2749 C5
Indigo Tr
- MNTR 44060 2144 C1
Industrial Av
1200 LORN 44055 2745 B3
14700 MPHT 44137 2886 A1
N Industrial Av
14100 MPHT 44137 2886 A1
S Industrial Av
14200 MPHT 44137 2886 A1
Industrial Dr
10200 GTVL 44231 3161 E6
Industrial Ln
16000 CLEV 44135 2752 B6
Industrial Pk
- MDFD 44062 2767 D3
Industrial Pkwy
100 CNFL 44022 2761 C7
100 CRDN 44024 2379 D5
100 SRSL 44022 2761 C7
4400 CLEV 44135 2752 B6
6700 BSHT 44236 3153 D7
6700 NOSD 44070 2878 A3
7300 LORN 44053 2742 C5
7300 LORN 44089 2742 C7
16000 MDFD 44062 2767 D3
Industrial Pkwy W
- TNBG 44087 3154 E4
N Industrial Pkwy
37400 WLBY 44094 2250 D5
W Industrial Pkwy
- ELYR 44035 2874 C6
- EyrT 44035 2874 C6
Industrial St
100 LORN 44055 2745 B3
Industrial First Av
10700 NRYN 44133 3013 A6
Industrial Park Blvd
7100 MNTR 44060 2251 B3
Industry Dr
10 BDFD 44146 2887 A6
10 WNHL 44146 2887 A6
Infinity Ln
4300 LORN 44053 2744 B4
Infinity Corporate Centre Dr
10 GDHT 44125 2885 C2
Infirmary Rd
900 CrlT 44035 3005 D1
1900 ELYR 44035 3005 D2
10100 ShvT 44255 3159 A6
10200 ManT 44255 3159 A6
Ingalton Av
14500 CLEV 44110 2497 B3
Ingersoll Dr
19800 RKRV 44116 2621 D5
Ingleside Av
5400 VMLN 44089 2740 E6
Ingleside Dr
100 BERA 44017 2880 A6
2400 PRMA 44134 2883 C2
Ingleside Rd
3200 SRHT 44120 2627 D7
3200 SRHT 44122 2627 D7
3300 SRHT 44120 2757 D1
3300 SRHT 44122 2757 D1
4000 CLEV 44128 2757 D3
4300 WVHT 44128 2757 D4
17600 CLEV 44119 2372 D4
Inglewood Av
18600 RKRV 44116 2621 E6
18600 RKRV 44116 2622 A6
Inglewood Ct
15800 SGVL 44136 3012 B4
Inglewood Dr
1200 CVHT 44121 2497 E7
1200 CVHT 44118 2497 E7
Inglewood Pl
100 ELYR 44035 2874 B7
Ingomar Av
11900 CLEV 44108 2496 D6
12400 CLEV 44112 2496 D6
12400 ECLE 44112 2496 D6
Inland Dr
7500 ODFL 44138 2879 A5
7500 OmsT 44138 2879 A5
Inland St
1000 VMLN 44089 2740 E6
Inland Shores Dr
6200 MNTR 44060 2143 D4
N Inlet Dr
17600 SGVL 44136 3147 D4
S Inlet Dr
18700 SGVL 44136 3147 D5
Inlet Pointe E
10100 RMDV 44202 3020 E5
Inlet Pointe N
10100 RMDV 44202 3020 E5
Inlet Pointe S
10100 RMDV 44202 3020 E5
Inman Av
9100 CLEV 44105 2756 B2
Innerbelt Frwy
- CLEV - 2624 E5
- CLEV - 2625 A4
Innerbelt Frwy I-71
- CLEV - 2624 E6
Innerbelt Frwy I-90
- CLEV - 2624 E5
- CLEV - 2625 A4
Inner Cir Ct
28700 SLN 44139 2888 B1
Interlachen Ln
2400 WTLK 44145 2750 E2
E Interstate St
10 BDFD 44146 2887 B6
W Interstate St
10 BDFD 44146 2887 A6
Invacare Wy
10 ELYR 44035 2875 E6
Inverlane Dr
500 NCtT 44067 3152 E3
500 SgHT 44067 3152 E3
Invermere Av
15400 CLEV 44128 2757 B2
17900 CLEV 44122 2757 D2
18800 WVHT 44122 2757 E2
Inverness Cir
30800 WTLK 44145 2749 A2
Inverness Ct
9800 CcdT 44060 2145 B7
Inverness Dr
6100 MadT 44057 1941 E1
29100 BYVL 44140 2619 D4
E Inverness Dr
300 HDHT 44143 2499 B2
W Inverness Dr
300 HDHT 44143 2499 B2
Inverness Rd
2600 SRHT 44122 2628 B6
Inverness St
2600 ShvT 44255 3157 E7
2600 STBR 44255 3157 E7
2700 ShvT 44255 3158 A7
Inwood Blvd
100 AVLK 44012 2487 E7
100 AVLK 44012 2617 E2
Inwood Rd
32800 SLN 44139 2888 E6
33600 SLN 44139 2889 A6
Inwood Tr
300 AURA 44202 3156 C2
Ionia Ct
12500 SGVL 44149 3011 C6
Iowa Av
200 LORN 44052 2615 A5
12200 CLEV 44108 2496 D3
Iowa Ct
4300 PryT 44081 2041 D3
Ira Av
4600 CLEV 44109 2754 B6
4600 CLEV 44144 2754 B6
5800 BKLN 44144 2754 A6
6200 BKLN 44144 2753 E6
Irena Ln
3000 TNBG 44087 3020 C5
Irene Rd
1000 HDHT 44143 2499 A6
1000 LNHT 44124 2499 A7
1000 LNHT 44143 2499 A6
Iris Ct
25800 WTLK 44145 2750 B4
30600 OmsT 44138 2878 A4
Iris Ln
33900 ETLK 44095 2250 A3
34300 ETLK 44095 2249 E3
Iris Glen Dr
1500 TNBG 44087 3019 B5
Irma Av
7100 CLEV 44105 2755 E3
Irma Dr
200 CRDN 44024 2380 B7
Irma Ln
100 OmsT 44138 2879 A6
Iron Ct
3800 CLEV 44115 2625 C5
3800 CLEV 44127 2625 C5
Irondale St
100 ELYR 44035 2874 E7
Iron Gate Dr
6800 NRYN 44133 3013 E5
Irontree Tr
15800 NbyT 44065 2763 E5
15800 NbyT 44065 2764 A5
Ironwood Av
18700 CLEV 44110 2372 E7
Ironwood Cir
100 AURA 44202 3156 D1
7900 PRMA 44129 3013 D2
Ironwood Ct
500 ELYR 44035 2875 A4
Ironwood Dr
1400 LORN 44053 2744 C5
9200 ODFL 44138 3010 B1
Ironwood Tr
900 SgHT 44067 3152 B2
Iroquois Av
10 PnvT 44077 2040 C2
1100 HDHT 44143 2499 C7
1100 MDHT 44124 2499 C7
1100 MDHT 44143 2499 C7
1200 LNHT 44124 2499 C7
12800 CLEV 44108 2496 E5
Iroquois Run
800 MCDN 44056 3018 D6
Iroquois Tr
400 MNTR 44060 2143 B4
400 MNTR 44094 2143 B4
400 MONT 44060 2143 B4
400 MONT 44094 2143 B4
400 WLBY 44094 2143 B4
600 MCDN 44056 3018 D5
11500 BKVL 44141 3016 D5

STREET Block City ZIP Map# Grid

Irving Av
- GDHT 44125 2885 B1
1000 CLEV 44109 2754 E4
Irving Park Av
3600 WDMR 44122 2759 B2
Irving Park Blvd
300 SDLK 44054 2616 D3
800 SFLD 44054 2616 D4
Irvington Av
12600 CLEV 44108 2496 E5
Irvington Ter
7000 CLEV 44103 2625 E3
Isaac Dr
7600 MDBH 44130 3011 E1
Isabel Av
7700 TwbT 44087 3154 E5
7700 TwbT 44236 3154 E5
Isabelle Ln
8800 MCDN 44056 3018 B5
Island Dr
100 ELYR 44035 3005 A1
E Island Dr
100 ETLK 44095 2142 C7
W Island Dr
35400 ETLK 44095 2142 B7
35400 ETLK 44095 2250 B1
Island Rd
9000 EatT 44039 3008 B1
9000 EatT 44044 3008 B1
9000 NRDV 44039 2877 B7
9000 NRDV 44039 3008 B1
9500 EatT 44028 3008 B3
12100 EatT 44044 3143 B7
12500 GFTN 44044 3143 B2
13400 GftT 44044 3143 B6
Island View Cir
18000 BbgT 44023 2891 E6
Istra Ln
2800 WBHL 44092 2374 D6
Itasca Av
11200 CLEV 44106 2496 D7
Ithaca Ct
5400 CLEV 44102 2624 A6
Ithaca Dr
2500 AVON 44011 2748 A2
Ivan Av
21500 EUCL 44119 2373 B4
22300 EUCL 44123 2373 B4
23200 EUCL 44117 2373 B4
Ivan Ct
9300 MNTR 44060 2145 A1
Ivana Ct
6500 MNTR 44060 2143 E5
Ivandale Dr
7500 PRMA 44129 2882 D3
Ivandale Rd
6700 INDE 44131 3015 E1
6900 INDE 44131 2884 E7
Ivanhoe Av
4000 SDLK 44054 2616 A4
Ivanhoe Dr
3700 LORN 44053 2743 E2
Ivanhoe Rd
100 BDFD 44146 2887 A4
900 CLEV 44110 2497 B3
1000 CLEV 44112 2497 C3
1000 ECLE 44112 2497 C3
Ivorton Rd
- FWPK 44126 2751 C2
Ivy Av
7000 CLEV 44127 2755 E1
7200 CLEV 44127 2756 A1
Ivy Ct
5500 WLBY 44094 2375 A1
7000 MNTR 44060 2143 B3
Ivy Dr
5500 MONT 44060 2143 D1
Ivy Ln
- AVON 44011 2747 E2
200 CcdT 44077 2145 E3
200 PNVL 44077 2145 E3
6600 BKPK 44142 2881 C4
6600 MDBH 44130 2881 B4
6600 MDBH 44142 2881 C4
18300 BbgT 44023 2891 A7
Ivy Ovl
8900 NRYN 44133 3013 B3
Ivydale Rd
1500 CVHT 44118 2627 C1
Ivy Ridge Dr
11700 NRYN 44133 3013 D6
Ivywood Dr
4100 BKLN 44144 2753 D4
Ivywood Tr
19300 SGVL 44149 3011 D5
I-X Center Dr
- BKPK 44142 2880 B3
Iyami Ct
17200 SGVL 44136 3012 A7

J

J Dr
- LORN 44052 2744 E4
Jackie Ct
9100 MNTR 44060 2144 D6
Jackie Ln
1100 MDHT 44124 2499 E7
2500 WTLK 44145 2750 B2
Jackrabbit Tr
- PnvT 44077 2041 B7
- PryT 44077 2041 B7
Jackson Av
200 ELYR 44035 2875 A4
1200 LKWD 44107 2622 E4
30000 WKLF 44092 2374 D4
30100 WBHL 44092 2374 D4
Jackson Blvd
10 BDFD 44137 2886 D2
10 BDFD 44146 2886 D2
2100 UNHT 44118 2627 D3
16700 MPHT 44137 2886 C1
Jackson Dr
12400 BtnT 44021 2765 B6
12400 NbyT 44021 2765 B6
18600 AbnT 44023 3023 A2
Jackson Rd
100 AURA 44202 3022 B7
100 ORNG 44022 2759 A4
7000 BbgT 44023 2890 B7
19300 CLEV 44135 2880 D2
30400 MDHL 44022 2759 E4
34200 MDHL 44022 2760 B5
E Jackson Rd
500 AURA 44202 3022 C7

Jackson St
100 AMHT 44001 2872 E1
900 VMLN 44089 2740 C6
2100 LORN 44052 2615 B6
7000 MNTR 44060 2144 C7
7200 MNTR 44060 2252 B1
9300 MNTR 44060 2145 A5
9500 PnvT 44060 2145 A5
9500 PnvT 44077 2145 A5
E Jackson St
10 PNVL 44077 2040 B7
W Jackson St
10 PNVL 44077 2040 A7
10 PNVL 44077 2146 A1
200 PNVL 44077 2145 B4
1300 PnvT 44077 2145 B4
1900 MNTR 44060 2145 B4
1900 PnvT 44060 2145 B4
Jaclyn Dr
34300 SLN 44139 2889 A4
Jacob St
100 BERA 44017 2880 C6
Jacque Rd
13000 NRYN 44133 3012 D4
13000 SGVL 44133 3012 D4
13000 SGVL 44136 3012 D4
Jacqueline Dr
10 BERA 44017 3011 B1
1600 PRMA 44134 3014 D2
Jacqueline Ln
5400 NOSD 44070 2878 A1
Jade Cir
34100 NRDV 44039 2748 C7
Jaeger Dr
1400 LNHT 44124 2499 A7
1400 LNHT 44124 2629 A1
Jaeger Rd
2800 LORN 44053 2743 D5
2800 LORN 44053 2744 A5
Jakse Dr
1200 ETLK 44095 2249 E4
James Av
14000 GDHT 44125 2886 A3
14000 GDHT 44137 2886 A3
14000 MPHT 44137 2886 A3
James Cir
200 AVLK 44012 2618 A2
James Dr
7300 NRYN 44133 3013 D6
7400 MDBH 44130 3012 D1
13800 RslT 44072 2631 D5
James Pl
10 NHFD 44067 3018 A3
James Rd
4700 NRDV 44039 2877 B2
James St
300 AMHT 44001 2872 E2
31600 WLWK 44095 2249 E6
31700 ETLK 44095 2249 E6
James Wy
19600 BHIT 44149 3146 B5
19600 BHIT 44212 3146 B5
19600 SGVL 44149 3146 B5
James Madison Dr
- LORN 44053 2743 D3
Jameson Rd
7400 PRMA 44129 2882 E1
Jamestown Av
800 ELYR 44035 2875 E2
Jamestown Cir
19600 SGVL 44136 3147 C5
Jamestown Dr
2400 RKRV 44116 2621 D7
6100 PRMA 44134 2883 D3
9900 NRYN 44133 3014 C5
Jamestown Pkwy
100 AVLK 44012 2618 D1
Jamestown Pl
5200 LORN 44053 2744 B5
Jamestowne Dr
6200 PMHT 44130 2882 A4
6200 PRMA 44130 2882 A3
Jamesway Ct
8700 MNTR 44060 2144 C4
Jamie Ct
1000 GFTN 44044 3142 A4
Jamie Dr
11600 CcdT 44077 2254 D2
Jamie Ln
10 OmsT 44138 2878 C4
Jananna Dr
100 BERA 44017 3011 A2
Janda Pl
- CRDN 44024 2380 A5
Jane Dr
5900 MNTR 44060 2144 D3
Janea Ct
1500 TwbT 44236 3154 D5
Janell Dr
13500 ClbT 44028 3010 E7
Janes Ln
300 MCDN 44056 3018 B7
Janet Blvd
5500 SLN 44139 2888 D2
Janet Dr
10200 STBR 44241 3157 B7
Janette Av
1700 CVHT 44118 2627 D2
Janette Dr
12200 SGVL 44136 3012 D6
Jania Wy
9900 TNBG 44087 3020 B4
Janice Dr
- PRMA 44134 3014 D2
300 BERA 44017 2880 D5
300 BERA 44130 2880 D5
300 MDBH 44130 2880 D5
14000 GDHT 44125 2886 A3
14000 GDHT 44137 2886 A3
14000 MPHT 44137 2886 A3
Janina Ln
100 OmsT 44138 2878 C4
Janowicz Dr
300 ELYR 44035 2875 A7
Japan Ct
2000 CLEV 44113 2624 C5
Jaquay Rd
9800 ClbT 44028 3009 D4
9800 ClbT 44138 3009 D2
Jasani Ct
7300 MNTR 44060 2251 C1
Jasmine Ct
10900 SGVL 44136 3012 D5
30500 NOSD 44070 2878 A4

Jasmine Ln
300 MDSN 44057 1942 A7
2900 SVHL 44131 2884 B7
2900 SVHL 44131 3015 B1
18300 BbgT 44023 2890 E7
Jason Av
11700 CcdT 44077 2254 D1
Jason Dr
35000 NRDV 44039 2748 A7
36000 EatT 44044 3007 E2
Jasper Av
10100 CLEV 44111 2753 C2
Jay Av
2500 CLEV 44113 2624 C5
Jay Dr
6900 EyrT 44035 2874 B2
Jay St
12400 NRYN 44133 3013 D6
Jaycox Rd
100 AVLK 44012 2488 C7
100 AVLK 44012 2618 C6
900 AVON 44011 2618 C7
900 AVON 44012 2618 C5
4900 AVON 44011 2748 B7
4900 NRDV 44011 2748 B7
4900 NRDV 44039 2748 B7
5400 NRDV 44039 2877 B2
E Jaycox Rd
2700 AVON 44011 2748 C3
Jaystone Pl
600 MCDN 44056 3018 B6
Jean Av
14400 CLEV 44110 2372 A7
Jean Ct
100 ELYR 44035 2874 D3
Jean Dr
- OKWD 44146 2887 E7
- OKWD 44146 3018 E1
800 ETLK 44095 2250 B3
Jeanette Dr
400 RDHT 44143 2498 C3
Jeanette St
400 BHIT 44212 3146 C7
Jeanne Dr
2800 PRMA 44134 2883 C6
Jefferson Av
100 CLEV 44113 2625 A5
800 CLEV 44113 2624 E6
5600 MPHT 44137 2886 C2
6300 NRDV 44039 2877 D3
N Jefferson Blvd
2200 LORN 44052 2615 C5
S Jefferson Blvd
2200 LORN 44052 2615 C5
Jefferson Ct
20100 SGVL 44149 3146 C2
26600 BYVL 44140 2620 B4
Jefferson Dr
500 HDHT 44143 2499 D3
6000 INDE 44131 2884 D2
9000 NHFD 44067 3018 A3
18000 WNHL 44146 3017 E1
18500 WNHL 44146 3018 A1
32400 SLN 44139 3019 E1
E Jefferson Dr
7000 MNTR 44060 2143 D7
W Jefferson Dr
7000 MNTR 44060 2143 D7
Jefferson Ln
600 SELD 44143 2498 D4
Jefferson St
- OBLN 44074 3138 D5
- PtfT 44074 3138 D5
10 PNVL 44077 2146 A1
100 AMHT 44001 2872 B1
100 LORN 44052 2745 A4
100 ShfT 44052 2745 A4
200 PNVL 44077 2040 A7
400 ELYR 44035 2874 E4
600 BDFD 44146 2887 A4
600 VMLN 44089 2740 D5
Jefferson Wy
30000 WTLK 44145 2749 B4
Jefferson Park Rd
17800 MDBH 44130 2880 E6
17800 MDBH 44130 2881 A6
Jeffries Av
7500 GDHT 44105 2756 A4
8200 CLEV 44105 2756 A4
Jelliffe St
2500 CLEV 44115 2625 C4
Jenee Dr
4100 LORN 44053 2743 D4
Jenkins Rd
8500 MCDN 44056 3153 C1
28600 NOSD 44070 2749 D5
28600 NOSD 44145 2749 D5
28600 WTLK 44070 2749 D5
28600 WTLK 44145 2749 D5
Jenna Dr
8600 BWHT 44147 3015 B5
Jenne Av
14000 CLEV 44110 2497 A1
Jennie Ln
35800 WBHL 44094 2375 C2
Jennie Rd
33400 AVON 44011 2748 D2
Jennifer Ct
11700 CcdT 44077 2254 D1
Jennifer Dr
1400 MCDN 44056 3019 A6
1400 MCDN 44087 3019 A6
1400 TNBG 44087 3019 A6
Jennifer Ln
16600 AbnT 44023 2892 D1
Jennings Dr
7500 LryT 44077 2256 A3
Jennings Frwy
- CLEV - 2754 E1
- CLEV - 2755 A5
Jennings Frwy SR-176
- CLEV - 2754 E1
- CLEV - 2755 A5
Jennings Rd
3200 CLEV 44109 2754 E3
4000 CLEV 44109 2755 A4
8200 OmsT 44138 2878 B7
Jennings St
22400 NRDL 44128 2758 B6
22400 WNHL 44128 2758 C6
Jennings Ridge Dr
4200 CLEV 44109 2755 A4
Jennison St
33900 ETLK 44095 2250 A4

Jenny Ln
10800 GDHT 44125 2885 C1
Jens Wy
3300 PryT 44081 1940 D7
Jensen Ct
- AbnT 44021 2893 D3
Jenther Dr
7500 MNTR 44060 2251 C1
Jenwood Ct
10100 STBR 44241 3156 D7
Jeptha Dr
- CLEV 44106 2626 C1
Jeremy Av
7300 MNTR 44060 2143 C5
Jergen's Wy
15700 CLEV 44110 2497 B1
Jerrol Ct
100 CrlT 44035 3006 E4
Jerry Coe Ln
10300 SGVL 44149 3011 D4
Jerusalem Rd
- VMLN 44089 2741 E7
3000 VMLN 44089 2870 D1
3000 VMLN 44089 2871 A1
Jesse Av
11600 CLEV 44105 2756 D4
Jesse L Jackson Pl
500 CLEV 44108 2496 C4
Jessica Ln
10 OmsT 44138 2879 B4
4500 NRYN 44133 3149 B1
Jessica Cove
2300 WLBY 44094 2251 A1
N Jester Pl
7100 CcdT 44077 2146 A7
S Jester Pl
7200 CcdT 44077 2146 A6
Jet Center Dr
38300 WLBY 44094 2143 A6
Jewel Cir
34100 NRDV 44039 2748 C7
Jewett Av
4600 CLEV 44127 2625 C7
Jill Dr
7700 PRMA 44134 3014 E2
7900 SgHT 44067 3017 A5
Jim Batey
- WTLK 44145 2619 C6
Joan Av
10200 CLEV 44111 2753 C1
Jo Ann Dr
1600 PRMA 44134 3014 D2
3700 CLEV 44122 2757 E3
Joann Dr
7600 CcdT 44077 2254 E2
Joann Pl
9900 TNBG 44087 3019 E4
Joanne Ct
5600 NRDV 44039 2877 B1
Jodi Dr
12900 LryT 44077 2147 D7
Jody Lynn Dr
4700 MNTR 44060 2038 D6
Joey Ln
- NCtT 44067 3153 E6
- NCtT 44236 3153 E6
John Av
3800 CLEV 44113 2624 B5
4400 CLEV 44102 2624 B5
John Ct
3800 CLEV 44113 2624 B5
John Rd
25600 ODFL 44138 2879 C3
25600 OmsT 44138 2879 B3
John St
10 BDFD 44146 2887 B6
Johnathan Cole Ct
- INDE 44131 3015 C2
John Bailey Dr
- PnvT 44077 2040 C2
John Edward Dr
10700 ManT 44255 3159 B5
10700 MNTU 44255 3159 B5
John F Kennedy Memorial Pkwy
- ELYR 44035 2874 C4
- ELYR 44035 2875 C4
- EyrT 44035 2874 C4
John F Kennedy Mem Pkwy SR-57
- ELYR 44035 2874 E4
- ELYR 44035 2875 C4
John F Kennedy Mem Pkwy SR-113
- ELYR 44035 2874 C4
- ELYR 44035 2875 C4
- EyrT 44035 2874 C4
John F Kennedy Mem Pkwy SR-301
- ELYR 44035 2875 C4
John Glenn Dr
900 SVHL 44131 2884 A3
John Nagy Blvd
3900 BKLN 44144 2753 E3
3900 CLEV 44109 2754 A3
3900 CLEV 44144 2753 E3
3900 CLEV 44144 2754 A3
Johnnycake Ridge Rd
10 PnvT 44077 2146 B3
7300 MNTR 44060 2251 B5
8000 MNTR 44060 2252 B2
8400 KDHL 44060 2252 B2
9300 MNTR 44060 2253 A2
9600 CcdT 44060 2253 A2
9800 CcdT 44060 2145 C7
9800 CcdT 44077 2253 C1
10600 CcdT 44077 2145 C7
10600 CcdT 44077 2146 A4
38200 WLBY 44094 2250 E7
38500 WLBY 44094 2251 B5
38900 MNTR 44094 2251 B5
Johnnycake Ridge Rd SR-84
10 PnvT 44077 2146 B3
7300 MNTR 44060 2251 B5
8000 MNTR 44060 2252 B2
8400 KDHL 44060 2252 B2
9300 MNTR 44060 2253 A2
9600 CcdT 44060 2253 A2
9800 CcdT 44060 2145 C7
9800 CcdT 44077 2253 C1
10600 CcdT 44077 2145 C7
10600 CcdT 44077 2146 A4
38200 WLBY 44094 2250 E7
38500 WLBY 44094 2251 B5

Johnnycake Ridge Rd SR-84
38900 MNTR 44094 2251 B5
John P Green Pl
4000 CLEV 44105 2756 D3
Johnson Av
600 BDFD 44146 2887 B3
Johnson Ct
600 CLEV 44113 2624 D3
Johnson Dr
10700 PRMA 44130 3013 B2
28700 WKLF 44092 2374 B4
Johnson St
15900 MDFD 44062 2767 D2
Johnston Dr
7300 RslT 44072 2761 B1
Johnston Pkwy
4400 CLEV 44128 2757 B5
4600 GDHT 44128 2757 A5
Johnstone Wy
2100 WTLK 44145 2749 C1
Joliet Rd
4500 GDHT 44105 2756 C5
4500 GDHT 44125 2756 C5
Jonathan Cir
10 GNVA 44041 1944 C6
Jonathan Dr
3200 CLEV 44111 2622 D7
3200 CLEV 44111 2752 D1
8500 NRYN 44133 3012 E3
20900 SGVL 44149 3011 A3
22300 ClbT 44028 3010 E3
22300 ClbT 44149 3010 E3
22300 SGVL 44149 3010 E3
Jonathan Ln
31000 BYVL 44140 2619 A5
Jonathan St
800 AMHT 44001 2743 B7
Jonathans Trc
1700 BWHT 44147 3149 D5
Jones Dr
3300 LORN 44053 2743 E3
Jones Rd
7600 CLEV 44105 2756 A3
Jonquil Ln
500 MDSN 44057 1942 A7
Jordan Ct
- NRDV 44035 2876 B7
Jordan Dr
9100 MNTR 44060 2038 E5
9200 MNTR 44060 2039 A4
37400 WLBY 44094 2250 D6
Jo San Dr
600 AMHT 44001 2872 C1
Joseph Ct
4700 NRDV 44039 2877 B2
34200 ETLK 44095 2250 A4
Joseph Dr
7300 SLN 44139 3020 B2
Joseph Ln
2700 MadT 44057 1941 A4
2700 MadT 44081 1941 A4
2700 NPRY 44081 1941 A5
Joseph Pkwy
2800 BNWK 44212 3147 D6
Joseph St
2500 AVON 44011 2748 C2
5000 MPHT 44137 2757 D7
7600 KTLD 44094 2251 D7
7600 WTHL 44094 2251 D7
Josephine Dr
6500 INDE 44131 2884 D5
7000 NOSD 44070 2878 B4
Josephine St
3900 LORN 44052 2744 E4
Joseph Lloyd Pkwy
1700 WLBY 44094 2142 E7
Joslyn Rd
3000 CLEV 44107 2622 E7
3000 CLEV 44111 2622 E7
3000 LKWD 44107 2622 E7
Joughin Al
200 PNVL 44077 2040 C7
Joughin St
600 FTHR 44077 2039 D4
600 PnvT 44077 2039 D4
Jourden Av
6800 PRMA 44134 2883 C6
Journey Dr
- LORN 44052 2614 E6
Jovanna Ct
9300 MNTR 44060 2144 E1
Joy Ct
3000 CLEV 44113 2624 D6
Joy Ovl
900 SVHL 44131 2884 B3
Joyacre Ln
11700 CdnT 44024 2379 D4
Joyce Av
4500 WVHT 44128 2758 C5
Joyce Dr
7800 NRYN 44130 3012 E2
7800 NRYN 44133 3012 E2
7800 PRMA 44130 3012 E2
27600 ClbT 44028 3009 A3
Joyce Rd
800 HDHT 44143 2499 D5
800 MAYF 44143 2499 D5
8100 BWHT 44147 3015 C3
Juanita St
100 SAHT 44001 2872 C7
Jubilee Dr
10200 CdnT 44024 2378 C6
Jude Ct
3700 LORN 44052 2744 D3
Judie Dr
600 CLEV 44109 2754 E5
600 CLEV 44109 2755 A5
Judita Dr
100 BNWK 44212 3146 D6
Judson Dr
14700 CLEV 44128 2757 B3
18300 CLEV 44122 2757 E3
Judy Ct
15500 CLEV 44111 2752 C3
Judy Dr
2000 PRMA 44134 3014 D2
7700 BWHT 44134 3014 D2
7700 BWHT 44147 3014 D2
Judy Ln
500 BNWK 44212 3146 D7
Jug St
14400 BtnT 44021 2766 D7
14400 BtnT 44062 2766 D7
16000 TroT 44021 2766 C7

Julia Av
1800 AVON 44011 2617 D7
2000 AVON 44011 2747 D1
5400 CLEV 44104 2625 D5
Julia Dr
7200 NRYN 44133 3013 D6
Julia St
10 GDRV 44077 2039 C6
Julian Ct
7400 MNTR 44060 2253 A1
Julian St
36900 AVON 44011 2747 D2
Julie Cir
19200 SGVL 44136 3147 C5
Julie Dr
11700 MsnT 44024 2504 D4
Julius Weil Dr
1200 MDHT 44124 2500 A7
Jumpers Crossing Ln
7400 CcdT 44077 2254 D1
Juna St
30900 WKLF 44092 2374 E1
Junction Rd
2100 CLEV 44102 2624 B6
June Av
- SDLK 44054 2616 B4
June St
33400 AVLK 44012 2617 C2
Juneau Ct
1700 CLEV 44109 2754 D1
Juneway Dr
400 BYVL 44140 2620 C5
Juniata Av
6500 CLEV 44103 2495 E6
Junior Pkwy
2900 BNWK 44212 3147 C6
Juniper Ct
4000 BDHT 44146 2887 C2
9500 SGVL 44136 3012 D4
9800 CcdT 44060 2253 B2
Juniper Dr
1600 WTLK 44145 2619 B7
6300 AhtT 44001 2744 B7
9400 HmbT 44024 2380 E2
Juniper Ln
- OmsT 44138 2878 D5
E Juniper Ln
10 MDHL 44022 2760 A4
W Juniper Ln
10 MDHL 44022 2759 E4
Juniper Rd
11200 CLEV 44106 2626 D1
Jupiter Dr
3100 NRYN 44133 3014 C6
Justice Dr
5100 AVON 44011 2617 E6
Just Imagine Dr
32100 AVON 44011 2618 D7
32100 AVON 44011 2619 A6
32100 AVON 44145 2619 A6
32100 WTLK 44145 2619 A6
Justin Av
14500 CLEV 44135 2752 C6
Justin St
10 BDFD 44146 2887 B6
Justin Wy
7100 MNTR 44060 2143 E7
Justo Ln
10 PRMA 44131 2883 E5
10 PRMA 44134 2883 E5
10 SVHL 44131 2883 E5
10 SVHL 44131 2884 A5

K

Kadel Av
12600 CLEV 44135 2753 A4
Kader Dr
10700 PRMA 44130 3013 A1
Kaiser Ct
100 ELYR 44035 2875 A6
35000 WLBY 44094 2250 A7
Kalene Ct
500 ETLK 44095 2142 E7
Kalvin Dr
17900 BKPK 44142 2880 E3
17900 BKPK 44142 2881 A3
Kansas Av
200 ELYR 44035 3006 E2
200 LORN 44052 2615 A5
Kapel Dr
1700 EUCL 44117 2373 E7
1900 RDHT 44117 2373 E7
1900 RDHT 44143 2373 E7
Kaplan Dr
5300 SFLD 44054 2747 A1
Karaboo Tr
10200 CcdT 44077 2253 D3
Kar A Bru Dr
400 AMHT 44001 2872 C2
Karelyn Dr
10 BERA 44017 3011 B2
Karen Ct
8600 CLEV 44106 2626 B1
Karen Dr
- SGVL 44136 3012 D3
300 CRDN 44024 2380 A7
400 BERA 44017 2880 B5
1700 EUCL 44117 2498 A2
6600 SVHL 44131 2884 B5
9500 CsTp 44026 2633 A1
9500 MsnT 44026 2633 A1
33300 AVLK 44012 2617 C2
Karen Ln
10 NCtT 44067 3153 A2
Karen Isle Dr
4800 RDHT 44143 2498 E1
5000 WLBY 44094 2250 B7
5000 WLBY 44094 2375 B1
Karen Lynne Dr
3800 BWHT 44147 3015 C4
Kares Av
18100 CLEV 44122 2757 D3
18500 CLEV 44128 2757 D3
Karl Dr
400 RDHT 44143 2498 C3
Karl St
10 BERA 44017 2879 E6
10 BERA 44017 2880 A6
Kasik Dr
100 AbnT 44023 3023 A2
Kasserine Ct
1600 TNBG 44087 3019 B4
Katey Rose Ln
300 EUCL 44143 2498 B2

Katherine Ct
9100 MNTR 44060 2038 E7
Katherine St
9100 NRDV 44039 3008 C1
Kathleen Dr
6900 MNTR 44060 2144 E6
13300 BKPK 44130 2881 D4
13300 BKPK 44142 2881 D4
13300 PMHT 44130 2881 D4
Kathryn Dr
1700 WTLK 44145 2750 D1
Kathy Dr
20200 EUCL 44117 2498 A2
Kathy Ln
7600 NCtT 44067 3153 B2
Kathy Lynn Ln
6700 INDE 44131 2884 D6
Katie Ct
4600 PryT 44081 1940 D6
Katz Rd
1800 TwbT 44087 3154 D5
Kay Av
3000 LORN 44052 2744 D3
Kay Dr
1100 AhtT 44001 2744 D7
Kaye St
700 BERA 44017 3011 A2
Kayne Dr
8000 MNTR 44060 2143 E4
Kazimier Av
6600 CHHT 44105 2755 E4
6600 CLEV 44105 2755 E4
Keats Dr
25800 NOSD 44070 2750 B5
Keemar Ct
10000 CLEV 44106 2626 B2
Keene Ct
2600 CLEV 44113 2624 C5
Keener Rd
- PryT 44081 2041 E5
Keep Ct
100 ELYR 44035 2874 E1
Keewaydin Dr
10 TMLK 44095 2250 A1
100 ETLK 44095 2250 B1
Keiper Ct
- CLEV 44113 2624 C5
Keith Dr
5900 MadT 44057 1941 D1
Keiths Close
- STBR 44241 3157 B7
Keller St
35000 AVON 44011 2748 B3
Kelley Av
3700 CLEV 44114 2625 C2
3900 CLEV 44103 2625 C2
Kelley Ln
5900 PRMA 44134 3014 A2
Kellogg Ct
5400 WLBY 44094 2374 E1
Kellogg Rd
7300 CcdT 44060 2253 D1
7300 CcdT 44077 2253 D2
Kellogg Creek Dr
7800 MNTR 44060 2253 A3
9300 MNTR 44060 2252 E3
Kelly Ct
100 ELYR 44035 3006 D3
Kelly Dr
- GFTN 44044 3141 E4
8200 MNTR 44060 2144 B6
Kelly Pl
2300 LORN 44052 2744 E2
Kelser Ct
- CrlT 44035 3006 B3
Kelsey Ct
7000 KTLD 44094 2376 A7
7000 WBHL 44094 2376 A7
Kelsey Ln
20300 SGVL 44149 3146 C5
Kelsey Rd
6100 PRMA 44129 2883 A3
Kelso Av
13400 CLEV 44110 2497 A1
Kelso St
6000 MadT 44057 1941 E1
Kelton Av
11500 CLEV 44106 2496 D7
Keltonshire Rd
6400 PRMA 44129 2882 E4
Kemper Rd
2500 CLEV 44120 2626 E4
2500 SRHT 44120 2626 E4
2600 CLEV 44120 2627 A5
Kempton Av
8900 CLEV 44108 2496 B6
Kempton Dr
100 BERA 44017 2880 A7
Ken Ct
300 BNWK 44212 3147 D7
Kenarden Dr
300 HDHT 44143 2499 E1
Kenbridge Dr
600 HDHT 44143 2499 A4
600 RDHT 44143 2499 A4
Kenbridge Rd
6500 PMHT 44130 2882 C4
Kendal Ct E
300 AMHT 44001 2872 D3
Kendal Ct W
200 AMHT 44001 2872 D3
Kendal Dr
- OBLN 44074 3138 E1
10 OBLN 44074 3003 E7
10 OBLN 44074 3004 A7
10 OBLN 44074 3139 A1
800 BWHT 44147 3150 A4
Kendall Dr
- SLN 44139 2889 B4
Kendall Ln
- AhtT 44001 2872 E6
Kendall Rd
2500 CLEV 44120 2626 E5
2500 SRHT 44120 2626 E5
Kenilworth Av
10 PnvT 44077 2040 D2
300 SDLK 44054 2616 B4
800 SFLD 44054 2616 B4
1000 CLEV 44113 2624 E6
1300 LKWD 44107 2622 A5
7300 PRMA 44129 2753 E7
Kenilworth Ln
2300 CVHT 44106 2626 E2
Kenilworth Rd
300 BYVL 44140 2620 B5

STREET Block City ZIP Map# Grid

Kenilworth Rd
2200 CVHT 44106 2626 E2
2500 CVHT 44106 2627 A2
2500 CVHT 44112 2627 A2
33500 ETLK 44095 2249 E3
Kenison Av
21400 EUCL 44123 2373 B3
Kenley Ct
26800 WTLK 44145 2620 A6
Ken Mar Industrial Pkwy
10 BWHT 44147 3015 C7
Kenmore Av
3700 PRMA 44134 2883 B1
4800 PRMA 44129 2883 A1
8600 CLEV 44106 2626 B1
Kenmore Dr
300 BYVL 44140 2620 C4
Kenmore Rd
3200 SRHT 44120 2627 D7
3200 SRHT 44120 2757 D1
3200 SRHT 44122 2627 D7
3200 SRHT 44122 2757 D1
Kenmore Wy
- NRDV 44039 3008 C1
Kennedy Av
8900 CLEV 44104 2626 B5
Kennedy Blvd
10 NHFD 44067 3018 A3
200 NHFD 44067 3017 E3
Kennedy Ct
10 ELYR 44035 2875 D5
7500 MNTR 44060 2143 D7
9300 CLEV 44104 2626 B5
Kennedy Dr
1700 WKLF 44092 2374 D2
4800 BKLN 44144 2753 C6
23800 BDHT 44146 2627 C1
Kennedy Pkwy
38600 WLBY 44094 2143 A5
Kennedy Ridge Ext
26900 NOSD 44070 2750 A7
Kennedy Ridge Rd
5300 NOSD 44070 2879 B1
24600 NOSD 44070 2750 C7
Kennelly Dr
2500 WBHL 44094 2375 E3
Kennelwood Dr
700 HDHT 44143 2499 C5
Kennerdown Av
14100 MPHT 44137 2886 A2
Kenneth Av
1800 CLEV 44109 2754 D3
5400 PRMA 44129 2883 A2
5400 PRMA 44134 2883 A2
6700 PRMA 44129 2882 E2
Kenneth Dr
100 BNWK 44212 3146 E6
1000 LKWD 44107 2622 B4
7600 CcdT 44077 2254 D2
Kenneth Ln
16500 LKWD 44107 2622 B3
Kenny Av
- CLEV 44135 2752 C4
Kenny Dr
10800 HmbT 44024 2380 D7
11000 ClrT 44024 2505 D1
11000 HmbT 44024 2505 D1
Kenny Ln
23400 NOSD 44070 2750 E6
Kenny Brook Ln
100 ELYR 44035 2874 A7
Kenshire Dr
- AVON 44011 2748 A4
Kensington Av
10 PNVL 44077 2146 B2
11200 CLEV 44111 2753 A2
11200 LNDL 44111 2753 B3
Kensington Cir
- SRSL 44022 2762 B6
100 BYVL 44140 2619 A2
Kensington Ct
10300 MDSN 44057 2044 C2
10 AURA 44202 3156 B1
100 AbnT 44023 2892 A4
19400 BHIT 44136 3146 E5
19400 BHIT 44212 3146 E5
19400 SGVL 44136 3146 E5
Kensington Dr
- EatT 44044 3141 E2
- EatT 44044 3142 A2
10 SRSL 44022 2762 B6
3300 AVON 44011 2748 B4
7100 NRDV 44039 2877 B4
25700 WTLK 44145 2620 B6
Kensington Ovl
10 RKRV 44116 2621 D4
Kensington Rd
100 VMLN 44089 2741 E4
200 RKRV 44116 2621 D5
2900 CVHT 44118 2627 B3
S Kensington Rd
500 RKRV 44116 2621 D5
Kenston Lakes Dr
17700 BbgT 44023 2890 E6
17900 BbgT 44023 2891 A6
Kent Cir
700 ELYR 44035 3006 D2
Kent Rd
2000 CVHT 44106 2627 A2
Kent St
8500 RslT 44072 2632 A5
16600 BbgT 44023 2890 B1
Kenton Av
- AURA 44202 3021 A4
- RMDV 44202 3020 E4
- RMDV 44202 3021 A4
5500 MPHT 44137 2886 D2
7500 PRMA 44129 2882 D3
Kenton Cir
1700 LNHT 44124 2629 B1
Kenton Rd
10 CNFL 44022 2760 E4
10 CNFL 44022 2761 A4
Kenton Wy
- CLEV 44105 2756 B5
Kentucky Av
200 LORN 44052 2615 A5
Kentucky Dr
- OKWD 44146 3018 D1
100 ELYR 44035 3006 B3
7200 OKWD 44146 2887 D7
Kenwick Dr
10 NCtT 44067 3153 A3
Kenwood Av
21000 RKRV 44116 2621 C5
Kenwood Ct
10 BHWD 44122 2628 E4
Kenwood Dr
400 EUCL 44123 2373 B3
700 MAYF 44040 2500 B5
700 MAYF 44143 2500 B5
4300 BWHT 44147 3015 C4
Kenwood St
100 ELYR 44035 2875 D5
100 SAHT 44001 2872 C7
15700 MDFD 44062 2767 D3
Kenwyn Blvd
2400 AVON 44011 2747 C1
Kenwyn Pl
36000 GSML 44040 2630 C2
Kenyon Av
200 BDFD 44146 2886 E3
200 ELYR 44035 2875 C6
4000 LORN 44053 2744 A4
5900 CLEV 44105 2755 D1
Kenyon Cir
31900 SLN 44139 2888 E2
Kenyon Ct
4200 LORN 44053 2744 A4
6200 MNTR 44060 2144 A4
Kenyon Dr
- HRM 44234 3161 A1
5200 PRMA 44129 2753 D7
5300 PRMA 44129 2882 D1
12700 CsTp 44026 2633 A1
12900 CsTp 44026 2632 E2
20600 MPHT 44137 2758 A7
21200 BDHT 44146 2758 B7
Kenyon Rd
100 ETLK 44095 2142 D5
16600 SRHT 44120 2757 C1
Kephart Dr
9000 MNTR 44060 2252 D2
Keppler Ct
11300 CLEV 44105 2756 D4
Kerneywood Rd
6200 PRMA 44129 2882 D4
Kerns Av
4600 CLEV 44102 2754 B2
Kerr Av
- WKLF 44092 2374 B2
10 PNVL 44077 2040 A7
100 PNVL 44077 2146 A1
Kerrwood Rd
2100 CVHT 44118 2627 B3
Kerry Ln
30500 WKLF 44092 2374 E1
E Kerry Pl
19500 SGVL 44149 3146 D4
W Kerry Pl
19800 SGVL 44149 3146 C4
Kersdale Rd
2700 PRPK 44124 2629 C5
3300 PRPK 44124 2759 B1
3400 PRPK 44122 2759 B1
3400 WDMR 44122 2759 B1
Kerwick Ct
- RMDV 44087 3020 C4
Kerwick Rd
2500 SRHT 44118 2628 B4
2500 UNHT 44118 2628 B4
Kerwin Rd
2100 SELD 44121 2628 C3
2100 UNHT 44118 2628 C3
2100 UNHT 44121 2628 C3
Keswick Ct
100 AMHT 44001 2872 D3
Keswick Dr
- BNWK 44212 3146 D7
10100 PMHT 44130 2882 C2
Keswick Rd
2900 CLEV 44120 2627 A6
2900 SRHT 44120 2627 A6
Kettering Ct
- AVON 44011 2748 B2
Kettering Ovl
10300 SGVL 44136 3012 B4
Kevin Dr
- MDBH 44130 3012 C2
Kevin Ln
12900 HmbT 44024 2380 D7
13000 ClrT 44024 2505 D1
13000 HmbT 44024 2505 D1
Kevin St
5200 SFLD 44054 2746 E3
Kew Dr
4500 NOSD 44070 2749 E6
Kew Rd
1500 CVHT 44118 2497 C7
Kewanee Av
18500 CLEV 44119 2372 E5
19300 CLEV 44119 2373 A5
19700 EUCL 44119 2373 A5
Key Plz
- CLEV 44114 2624 E1
Keyes Av
7900 CLEV 44104 2626 A4
Keynote Cir
900 BNHT 44131 2884 B1
Keys Dr
500 ELYR 44035 2875 A4
Keys Rd
11400 ManT 44255 3159 E3
Keystone Dr
800 CVHT 44121 2498 A5
900 SELD 44121 2498 A6
7600 CcdT 44077 2254 E2
Keystone Ln
12000 MsnT 44024 2634 C1
Keystone Pkwy
- BKPK 44135 2752 D6
- BKPK 44142 2752 D6
- CLEV 44135 2752 D6
Keystone Rd
1500 PRMA 44134 2883 D3
Keywest Dr
7500 PRMA 44134 3014 D1
Khouri Ct
- AVON 44011 2748 D5
Khristopher Ct
7200 CcdT 44077 2253 D1
Kidd Dr
15400 NbyT 44065 2764 D4
Kidder Av
5400 CLEV 44102 2624 B7
Kilarney Rd
35400 WLBY 44094 2250 B7
Kilbourne Dr
5300 LNHT 44124 2629 A3
Kilbridge Dr
300 HDHT 44143 2499 D2
E Kilbridge Dr
300 HDHT 44143 2499 D1
W Kilbridge Dr
300 HDHT 44143 2499 D2
Kildare Rd
3200 CVHT 44118 2627 C3
3300 UNHT 44118 2627 D3
Kildeer Av
18500 CLEV 44119 2372 E5
19300 CLEV 44119 2373 A5
19700 EUCL 44119 2373 A5
Kildeer Ct
10 CrlT 44035 3005 C3
Kildeer Ln
10 ELYR 44035 2875 D7
Kile Rd
10900 HtbT 44024 2507 A5
10900 HtbT 44064 2507 A5
10900 MtlT 44024 2507 A1
10900 MtlT 44064 2507 A1
11400 ClrT 44024 2507 A4
12100 ClrT 44046 2507 A6
Kilgour Dr
- WTLK 44145 2619 A7
Kilkenny Ct
7900 SgHT 44067 3017 B5
Killdeer Ct
300 AMHT 44001 2743 E6
Killdeer Dr
10400 KTLD 44094 2376 C6
Killians Grv
20000 SGVL 44149 3146 C4
Killingworth Ln
30000 TNBG 44087 3020 B3
Kilson Av
19300 CLEV 44135 2751 E5
Kiltie Ln
7200 SgHT 44067 3152 E3
Kim Dr
300 MDSN 44057 2044 C1
9500 CsTp 44026 2633 A2
9500 MsnT 44026 2633 A2
Kimball Dr
- MadT 44057 1843 C7
Kimberly Av
10500 CLEV 44108 2496 C5
Kimberly Cir
600 OBLN 44074 3139 B2
Kimberly Ct
500 BYVL 44140 2619 A5
1400 LORN 44053 2744 C5
32800 ETLK 44095 2249 E5
Kimberly Dr
400 AURA 44202 3156 C6
2100 WKLF 44092 2374 D3
5800 BDHT 44146 2887 D3
6400 GDHT 44125 2885 E4
10200 KTLD 44094 2376 E5
31100 BYVL 44140 2619 A5
Kimberly Ln
10 MNTR 44060 2144 E7
10 OmsT 44138 2879 A3
2500 WTLK 44145 2750 B2
7500 CsTp 44026 2501 D1
Kimberwick Ct
10 SRSL 44022 2761 E5
Kimmel Rd
3400 CLEV 44105 2755 C1
Kimmeridge Tr
11000 NbyT 44065 2634 A5
Kimrose Ln
100 BWHT 44147 3014 E3
4500 NRYN 44133 3149 B1
King Av
900 LORN 44052 2614 B7
1300 LORN 44052 2744 B1
3300 CLEV 44114 2495 B7
King Ct
9200 OmsT 44138 3009 C1
King Dr
35400 ETLK 44095 2250 B1
King St
10 ELYR 44035 2874 D3
10 EyrT 44035 2874 D3
10 OBLN 44074 3139 A3
10 PNVL 44077 2146 B1
200 FTHR 44077 2039 D4
E King St
200 CRDN 44024 2380 A7
King Arthur Ct
13800 NbyT 44065 2634 B5
14700 NRYN 44133 3148 A1
29100 WTLK 44145 2749 D3
King Coe Ln
10300 SGVL 44149 3011 D4
King Edward Ct
39200 MNTR 44060 2251 C5
39200 WLBY 44060 2251 C5
39200 WLBY 44094 2251 C5
Kingfisher Ln
8600 MCDN 44056 3018 B6
King George Blvd
100 SELD 44121 2498 C5
King James Pkwy
1700 WTLK 44145 2750 C1
Kingman Rd
14300 MDBH 44130 2881 C4
King Memorial Rd
7400 MNTR 44060 2252 E2
8000 KDHL 44060 2252 E4
8000 KDHL 44060 2253 A4
8400 CdnT 44060 2253 A5
King Mills Run
3400 FWPK 44126 2751 B2
3400 RKRV 44116 2751 B2
3400 RKRV 44126 2751 B2
King Richard Dr
2900 PRMA 44134 2883 C7
Kings Ct
9300 BKVL 44141 3150 E2
Kings Hwy
5200 FWPK 44126 2751 B5
5800 PMHT 44130 2882 B2
5800 PRMA 44130 2882 B2
19000 CLEV 44122 2757 E3
19000 WVHT 44122 2757 E3
19700 WVHT 44122 2758 A3
20400 HIHL 44122 2758 A3
Kings Wy
10500 NRYN 44133 3013 E4
Kingsborough Dr
2000 PnvT 44077 2145 C6
Kingsbrooke Ln
23100 WTLK 44145 2751 A1
Kingsbury Blvd
9700 CLEV 44104 2626 C7
Kingsbury Ct
4300 LORN 44053 2743 D4
Kingsbury Dr
- NRDV 44035 3007 B1
2700 RKRV 44116 2621 C7
Kingsbury Pt
100 MDSN 44057 2044 C1
Kingscote Pk
6600 INDE 44131 3015 E2
Kingsdale Blvd
6300 PMHT 44130 2882 B4
Kingsford Av
14000 CLEV 44105 2757 A3
14900 CLEV 44128 2757 B3
Kings Hollow Ct
9300 KDHL 44060 2252 E4
9300 MNTR 44060 2252 E4
Kingsley Dr
9100 BbgT 44023 3022 D1
Kingsley Rd
2800 SRHT 44122 2627 E7
Kings Orchard Tr
8700 BbgT 44023 2891 C3
Kings Post Pkwy
3500 RKRV 44116 2751 B2
Kingston Cir
26800 NOSD 44070 2750 A5
Kingston Ct
5300 SFLD 44054 2746 E4
7300 MNTR 44060 2251 C1
Kingston Dr
- NRDV 44039 2747 B7
10 AURA 44202 3156 E3
10 AURA 44202 3157 A3
Kingston Rd
2400 CVHT 44118 2627 D5
Kingston Tr
- OmsT 44138 3009 C2
Kingston Wy
12700 NRYN 44133 3148 A4
12800 NRYN 44133 3147 E4
Kingsview Dr
7100 SgHT 44067 3152 E3
Kingsway
1300 WTLK 44145 2620 D7
Kingsway Dr
900 LORN 44052 2744 D4
12700 CsTp 44026 2501 C7
12900 CsTp 44026 2631 C1
Kingswood Ct
15800 SGVL 44149 3146 B2
Kingswood Dr
6500 MDHT 44124 2629 E3
6500 MDHT 44124 2630 A3
6900 SLN 44139 2888 D7
17700 BbgT 44023 2890 E6
26200 OmsT 44138 2879 A7
Kingwood Dr
8200 KDHL 44060 2252 A5
Kinkel Av
2100 CLEV 44109 2624 D7
Kinsman Rd
5500 CLEV 44104 2625 D5
7000 HGVL 44022 2761 D2
7000 HGVL 44072 2761 D2
7000 RslT 44022 2761 D2
7000 RslT 44072 2761 D2
7200 CLEV 44104 2626 C7
8200 RslT 44072 2762 A2
9600 NbyT 44072 2763 A1
9600 RslT 44072 2763 A1
10100 NbyT 44065 2763 D1
10400 NbyT 44065 2764 A1
11300 CLEV 44120 2626 D7
12000 NbyT 44065 2765 A1
12100 NbyT 44021 2765 A1
12400 BtnT 44021 2765 D1
12500 CLEV 44120 2756 E1
13700 CLEV 44120 2757 A1
14000 BtnT 44021 2766 A1
14000 BURT 44021 2766 C1
14300 BtnT 44062 2766 C1
15000 BtnT 44062 2767 A2
15100 MdfT 44062 2767 B2
15400 SRHT 44120 2757 B1
16200 MDFD 44062 2767 E2
Kinsman Rd SR-8
5500 CLEV 44104 2625 D5
7200 CLEV 44104 2626 C7
11300 CLEV 44120 2626 D7
12500 CLEV 44120 2756 E1
13700 CLEV 44120 2757 A1
15400 SRHT 44120 2757 B1
Kinsman Rd SR-87
7000 HGVL 44022 2761 D2
7000 HGVL 44072 2761 D2
7000 RslT 44022 2761 D2
7000 RslT 44072 2761 D2
8200 RslT 44072 2762 A2
9600 NbyT 44072 2763 A1
9600 RslT 44072 2763 A1
10100 NbyT 44065 2763 D1
10400 NbyT 44065 2764 A1
12000 NbyT 44065 2765 A1
12100 NbyT 44021 2765 A1
12400 BtnT 44021 2765 D1
14000 BtnT 44021 2766 A1
14000 BURT 44021 2766 C1
14300 BtnT 44062 2766 C1
15000 BtnT 44062 2767 A2
15100 MdfT 44062 2767 B2
16200 MDFD 44062 2767 E2
Kinsman Rd US-422
5500 CLEV 44104 2625 D5
7200 CLEV 44104 2626 C7
11300 CLEV 44120 2626 D7
12500 CLEV 44120 2756 E1
13700 CLEV 44120 2757 A1
15400 SRHT 44120 2757 B1
Kinzel Rd
36100 AVON 44011 2747 E3
36100 AVON 44011 2748 A3
Kiowa Rd
4100 RchT 44286 3150 B6
Kipling Av
15400 CLEV 44110 2497 B3
Kipling Ct
500 RDHT 44143 2498 E4
N Kipling Pl
7100 CcdT 44077 2146 A7
S Kipling Pl
7200 CcdT 44077 2146 A6
Kipling St
100 ELYR 44035 2875 C6
Kipton East Rd
- NRsT 44074 3139 B5
- OBLN 44074 3138 A6
- PtfT 44074 3138 A6
- PtfT 44074 3139 B5
Kipton East Rd US-20
- NRsT 44074 3139 B5
- OBLN 44074 3138 A6
- PtfT 44074 3138 A6
- PtfT 44074 3139 B5
Kipton Nickle Plate Rd
43000 LrgT 44050 3139 E6
43000 LrgT 44050 3140 A6
43400 PtfT 44050 3139 E6
43400 PtfT 44074 3139 D6
45200 OBLN 44074 3138 E6
45200 PtfT 44074 3138 E6
Kirby Av
12300 CLEV 44108 2496 E3
Kirkham Av
5000 CLEV 44105 2755 D1
Kirkland Ct
2100 TwbT 44236 3155 A6
Kirkland Rd
22900 OKWD 44146 2887 C7
Kirkshire Ct
300 HDHT 44143 2499 C2
Kirkwall St
6100 MadT 44057 1941 E1
6200 MadT 44057 1942 A1
Kirkwood Av
9500 CLEV 44102 2623 D6
Kirkwood Dr
6700 MNTR 44060 2144 A6
8300 CsTp 44026 2502 B1
Kirkwood Rd
3700 CVHT 44121 2497 E6
3700 CVHT 44121 2498 A6
Kirtland Ln
1000 LKWD 44107 2622 E3
7700 TwbT 44236 3155 A6
N Kirtland Ln
7800 TwbT 44236 3155 A5
Kirtland Pl
2000 TwbT 44236 3155 A6
N Kirtland Pl
2100 TwbT 44236 3155 A5
Kirtland Rd
3800 WLBY 44094 2251 C6
39400 KTLD 44094 2251 C6
Kirtland St
13800 BURT 44021 2636 B7
Kirtland-Chardon Rd
- KDHL 44060 2251 E7
- KDHL 44094 2251 E7
6900 KTLD 44060 2251 E7
7800 KTLD 44094 2251 E7
Kirtland Chardon Rd
8100 KTLD 44094 2252 A7
8100 KTLD 44094 2377 B1
9400 KTLD 44094 2378 A4
Kirtland-Chardon Rd
9500 CdnT 44024 2378 A4
9500 CdnT 44094 2378 A4
9500 KTLD 44094 2378 A4
Kirtland Chardon Rd
9700 CdnT 44024 2378 C5
9700 CdnT 44094 2378 A4
Kirtland Lake Blvd
10800 CdnT 44024 2378 A7
10800 CdnT 44094 2378 A7
10800 KTLD 44094 2378 A7
Kirton Av
11700 BKLN 44144 2753 B5
11700 CLEV 44135 2753 A5
11700 CLEV 44144 2753 B5
13100 CLEV 44135 2752 E5
Kirtstone Ter
1700 PnvT 44077 2041 A2
Kishman Av
- VMLN 44089 2742 B5
Kitner Blvd
7500 NCtT 44067 3153 B3
Kittery Ln
7500 MNTR 44060 2251 B2
Kiwanis Dr
300 NbyT 44065 2764 C1
6700 MDBH 44130 2881 D5
Kiwanis Park Dr
400 GNVA 44041 1944 C4
400 GnvT 44041 1944 C4
Klann St
5000 PryT 44077 2041 C6
Klasen Rd
4900 MadT 44057 2044 B6
Klatka Dr
12500 MsnT 44024 2504 A7
Kleber Ct
7100 INDE 44131 2884 E2
Klein Dr
7600 MDBH 44130 3012 E2
7700 SGVL 44130 3012 E2
7700 SGVL 44136 3012 E2
Klonowski Av
7400 CLEV 44105 2756 A2
Klusner Av
2400 PRMA 44134 2883 C6
Kneale Dr
5000 LNHT 44124 2498 E6
5000 LNHT 44124 2499 A6
Kneirim Dr
3200 LORN 44053 2743 E3
Kneisel Rd
13700 VmnT 44089 2869 C1
Knickerbocker Rd
- AVLK 44012 2618 A5
4100 SDLK 44054 2616 A5
4200 SFLD 44054 2616 B5
26400 BYVL 44140 2620 A5
27800 BYVL 44140 2619 E5
Kniffen Rd
6700 LryT 44077 2256 C2
6700 LryT 44086 2256 C2
Knight Ln
4100 BNWK 44212 3146 D6
Knights Wy
9300 BKVL 44141 3150 D2
10600 NRYN 44133 3013 E5
10600 NRYN 44133 3014 A5
Knightsbridge Ln
100 AURA 44202 3021 E7
8100 CcdT 44060 2253 B4
8100 CcdT 44077 2253 B4
Knobel Dr
32100 ETLK 44095 2249 D5
32100 WLWK 44095 2249 D5
Knoll Dr
18200 MPHT 44137 2886 D1
Knolls Ln
2600 BKVL 44141 3150 B1
Knolls Wy
8100 BbgT 44023 2890 E1
Knollwood Dr
381-00 AURA 44202 3156 D3
5200 BKLN 44144 2753 C7
5200 PRMA 44129 2753 C7
5200 PRMA 44144 2753 C7
5300 PRMA 44129 2882 C1
Knollwood Rdg
9900 CcdT 44060 2145 C6
9900 CcdT 44077 2145 C6
Knollwood Tr
200 RDHT 44143 2498 D1
Knots Ln
- LORN 44052 2614 E7
Knowles Dr
3300 PRMA 44134 3014 C1
Knowles St
1800 ECLE 44112 2497 A6
Knowlton Av
11200 CLEV 44106 2496 D7
Knowlton Pkwy
19200 SGVL 44136 3146 D2
19200 SGVL 44149 3146 D2
Knox Blvd
5700 BKPK 44142 2881 C1
Knuth Av
1400 EUCL 44117 2373 E5
1400 EUCL 44132 2373 E5
Koch Ct
4800 CLEV 44102 2754 A1
Koch Dr
7600 PRMA 44134 3013 E1
7600 PRMA 44134 3014 A1
Kohout St
5200 MPHT 44137 2757 B7
5200 MPHT 44137 2886 A1
Kolar Av
9500 CLEV 44104 2626 B5
Kolbe Rd
3100 LORN 44053 2743 C3
4800 AMHT 44001 2743 D5
4800 AMHT 44053 2743 D5
4800 LORN 44001 2743 D5
Kollin Av
16200 CLEV 44128 2757 C6
16200 GDHT 44128 2757 C6
Kolthoff Dr
6300 BKPK 44142 2880 C4
6500 BERA 44017 2880 C4
6500 BERA 44142 2880 C4
Kolthoff Dr SR-237
6500 BERA 44017 2880 C4
6500 BERA 44142 2880 C4
6500 BKPK 44142 2880 C4
Kopas Dr
11100 AbnT 44255 2893 A7
Korman Av
7400 CLEV 44103 2496 A6
Kortz Cir
8600 SGVL 44136 3012 D3
Kory Ct
7100 CcdT 44077 2145 D7
Kosciuszko Av
7900 CLEV 44103 2496 A7
8500 CLEV 44108 2496 A7
Kossuth Dr
32000 AVLK 44012 2618 D4
Kouba Av
5400 CLEV 44102 2624 A7
Kourtney Ct
30400 WBHL 44092 2374 E7
Kraft St
10 BERA 44017 2880 B7
Krakow Av
6800 CLEV 44105 2755 E4
Kral Dr
7000 CyhC 44146 2886 E7
7000 WNHL 44146 2886 E7
Kramer Dr
20100 RKRV 44116 2621 D6
Krather Rd
3400 CLEV 44109 2754 C3
Krebs Rd
31600 AVLK 44012 2619 A5
31600 AVLK 44140 2619 A5
31600 BYVL 44140 2619 A5
31700 AVLK 44012 2618 E5
31700 AVON 44011 2618 E5
31700 AVON 44012 2618 E5
Krems Av
14100 MPHT 44137 2886 A2
Kresge Dr
1900 AMHT 44001 2744 A6
Krick Rd
7000 BDFD 44146 2887 A7
7000 WNHL 44146 2887 B7
W Krick Rd
20000 WNHL 44146 2887 A7
Kristen Ct
100 AMHT 44001 2872 D4
Kristin Ct
30100 WBHL 44092 2374 D6
Kristine Dr
11300 CsTp 44026 2502 B2
Kronos Ct
12200 SGVL 44149 3011 C6
Krueger Av
4300 PRMA 44134 2883 B2
4700 PRMA 44129 2883 A2
8000 CLEV 44105 2756 B2
Krueger Dr
- NRDV 44039 2877 A4
Kruse Dr
6000 SLN 44139 2888 E4
6000 SLN 44139 2889 A4
Kuenzer Dr
5700 SVHL 44131 2884 B2
Kuhlman Av
13300 CLEV 44110 2497 A2
Kurtz St
400 BERA 44017 2880 C5
Kurzemes Dr
16800 BbgT 44023 2891 B2
Kydan Ln
18100 WNHL 44146 2886 E7
Kyle Cove
38800 WLBY 44094 2143 A7
Kylemore Dr
19900 SGVL 44149 3146 C5
Kylie Ct
10 OmsT 44138 2879 B4
Kyra Ln
- LORN 44053 2743 B6

L

Labrador Ln
11300 CcdT 44077 2254 C1
Laburnum Dr
4300 PryT 44077 2041 C4
Laburnum St
4300 PryT 44077 2041 C3
Lacey Ln
- BWHT 44147 3015 D4
Laclede Rd
1400 SELD 44121 2498 B7
1400 SELD 44121 2628 B1
Lacosta Dr
7300 HDSN 44236 3155 B7
La Crosse Dr
500 MCDN 44056 3018 C6
Ladd Ln
6900 MPHT 44137 2886 A5
Ladue Tr
- AbnT 44255 2893 D7
Lady Bug Ln
- CcdT 44077 2254 D4
Lafayette Av
5500 MPHT 44137 2886 C2
Lafayette Blvd
400 SDLK 44054 2616 C4
600 SFLD 44054 2616 C4
6100 INDE 44131 2884 D4
Lafayette Dr
- ClbT 44028 3010 D2
2500 UNHT 44118 2628 C4
6400 MNTR 44060 2144 B5
10600 PMHT 44130 2882 B5
Lafayette St
100 ELYR 44035 2875 C5
Lafayette Wy
29700 WTLK 44145 2749 C4
Lafayette Villa
- MNTR 44060 2144 A4
Lafevre Rd
2200 HpfT 44041 1944 A7
Lagoon Dr
35800 ETLK 44095 2250 C1
Lagoon Ln
4600 VMLN 44089 2741 A6
La Grange Av
7500 CLEV 44103 2626 A2
Lagrange Rd
- CrlT 44050 3140 E1
10400 CrlT 44035 3005 E7
11900 CrlT 44050 3005 E6
Lagrange Rd SR-301
- CrlT 44050 3140 E1
11900 CrlT 44035 3005 E7
11900 CrlT 44050 3005 E6
N Laguardia Pkwy
15800 SGVL 44136 3012 B4
S Laguardia Pkwy
15800 SGVL 44136 3012 B5
Laing Rd
24000 BDHT 44146 2887 D4
Laird Av
9500 CLEV 44102 2623 D6
Laisy Av
8800 CLEV 44104 2626 B7
Lake Av
- AURA 44202 3021 A3
100 ELYR 44035 2875 A5
300 ELYR 44035 2874 E4
900 BbgT 44202 3021 B3
1700 EyrT 44035 2874 D3
3600 RMDV 44139 3020 E3
3600 RMDV 44202 3020 E3
3600 SLN 44139 3020 E3
3700 AURA 44139 3021 A3
3700 BbgT 44139 3021 A3
3700 RMDV 44139 3021 A3
3700 RMDV 44202 3021 A3
3700 SLN 44139 3021 A3
6000 EyrT 44035 2745 B6
6000 EyrT 44055 2745 B6
6000 ShfT 44055 2745 B6
7500 CLEV 44102 2623 D5
11500 LKWD 44102 2623 B4
11500 LKWD 44107 2623 B4
13400 LKWD 44107 2622 B3
14900 MDFD 44062 2767 C3
15300 MdfT 44062 2767 C3
S Lake Blvd
10000 PRMA 44130 3013 C2
Lake Ct
5400 CLEV 44103 2495 D6
5400 CLEV 44114 2495 D6
Lake Dr
12100 NbyT 44021 2764 E4
12100 NbyT 44021 2765 A4
12400 BtnT 44021 2765 B6
18600 AbnT 44023 3023 A2
37400 AVON 44011 2617 D7
W Lake Dr
7600 WNHL 44146 3017 E2
Lake Pl
100 LORN 44052 2614 D6
Lake Rd
- GnvT 44041 1844 D4
10 PnvT 44077 2040 C2
1800 PnvT 44077 2041 A1
6300 GOTL 44041 1844 E4
7800 GnvT 44057 1844 B4
7800 MadT 44057 1844 B4
11600 MsnT 44024 2504 D4
17800 LKWD 44107 2621 E4
17800 LKWD 44107 2622 A4
18500 RKRV 44116 2621 E5
22800 BYVL 44116 2621 B5
22800 BYVL 44140 2621 B5
23400 BYVL 44140 2620 A4
27500 BYVL 44140 2619 A2
31400 AVLK 44012 2619 A2
31400 AVLK 44140 2619 A2
31700 AVLK 44012 2618 E1
32000 AVLK 44012 2488 A7
32900 AVLK 44012 2487 E7

Cleveland Street Index

STREET Block City ZIP Map# Grid

Lake Rd
32900 AVLK 44012 2617 D1
33700 SDLK 44012 2617 A2
33700 SDLK 44054 2617 A2
Lake Rd SR-2
19200 RKRV 44116 2621 C5
Lake Rd US-6
19200 RKRV 44116 2621 B5
22800 BYVL 44116 2621 B5
22800 BYVL 44140 2621 B5
23400 BYVL 44140 2620 A4
27500 BYVL 44140 2619 A1
31400 AVLK 44012 2619 A2
31400 AVLK 44140 2619 A2
31700 AVLK 44012 2618 E1
32000 AVLK 44012 2488 A7
32900 AVLK 44012 2487 E7
32900 AVLK 44012 2617 D1
33700 SDLK 44012 2617 A2
33700 SDLK 44054 2617 A2
Lake Rd E
7100 MadT 44057 1843 D6
7500 MadT 44057 1844 A6
Lake Rd W
6000 GnvT 44041 1844 B4
6300 MadT 44057 1843 A7
6800 GnvT 44057 1844 B4
6800 MadT 44057 1844 B4
E Lake Rd
- LORN 44052 2615 D4
- LORN 44054 2615 D4
3500 SDLK 44054 2615 E4
3800 SDLK 44054 2616 A3
5300 SDLK 44054 2617 A2
5500 AVLK 44012 2617 A2
5500 SDLK 44012 2617 A2
E Lake Rd US-6
- LORN 44052 2615 D4
- LORN 44054 2615 D4
3500 SDLK 44054 2615 E4
3800 SDLK 44054 2616 A3
5300 SDLK 44054 2617 A2
5500 AVLK 44012 2617 A2
5500 SDLK 44012 2617 A2
W Lake Rd
12500 VmnT 44089 2740 B6
14200 VMLN 44089 2740 B6
W Lake Rd US-6
12500 VmnT 44089 2740 B6
14200 VMLN 44089 2740 B6
Lake St
- MadT 44057 1941 D1
5700 MONT 44060 2143 C3
5700 VMLN 44089 2740 D5
6100 MNTR 44060 2143 C3
N Lake St
10 MDSN 44057 2044 B1
100 AMHT 44001 2872 C1
100 SAHT 44001 2872 C7
200 MDSN 44057 1942 B7
600 AMHT 44001 2743 C7
800 MadT 44057 1942 B6
N Lake St SR-528
10 MDSN 44057 2044 B1
200 MDSN 44057 1942 B7
800 MadT 44057 1942 B6
S Lake St
10 MDSN 44057 2044 B1
100 AMHT 44001 2872 C2
100 SAHT 44001 2872 B7
200 SAHT 44001 3003 B1
200 SAHT 44074 3003 B1
Lake Tr
600 AURA 44202 3021 C7
600 AURA 44202 3156 C1
Lake Abram Dr
6800 MDBH 44130 2880 E5
Lake Breeze Curv
- ETLK 44095 2250 B2
Lake Breeze Dr
2600 MadT 44057 1942 A4
Lake Breeze Rd
300 SDLK 44054 2616 A6
1000 SFLD 44054 2616 A7
Lakebrook Dr
10800 KTLD 44094 2378 A7
10800 KTLD 44094 2503 A1
Lake Charles Dr
- INDE 44131 3015 C2
Lake Cir Dr
16500 SGVL 44136 3012 B3
Lake County Ln
- KTLD 44094 2377 C6
Lakecrest Blvd
10 HkyT 44133 3148 A5
10 HkyT 44233 3148 A6
10 NRYN 44133 3148 A5
Lakedge Ct
7500 HDSN 44236 3155 C7
Lakedge Ln
- HGVL 44022 2760 A1
Lake Edge Dr
10 EUCL 44123 2373 C1
Lake Edge Tr
- WLBY 44094 2142 E5
Lake Forest Ct
8600 BbgT 44023 2891 B4
Lake Forest Dr
300 BYVL 44140 2620 C5
11200 CsTp 44026 2501 E1
12200 BKVL 44141 3151 D4
16000 SGVL 44136 3012 B3
Lake Forest Tr
8600 BbgT 44023 2891 B4
Lake Forest Reserve Ln
- BHIT 44212 3145 E7
- LvpT 44212 3145 E7
- LvpT 44280 3145 E7
Lakefront Av
1200 ECLE 44108 2496 E6
1400 ECLE 44112 2496 E6
1500 ECLE 44112 2497 A6
Lake Harbour Wy
4200 AVON 44011 2748 C4
Lakehurst Dr
100 ETLK 44095 2142 C6
2300 NPRY 44081 1940 D3
N Lakehurst Dr
10 ETLK 44095 2142 C6
Lake In The Woods Tr
8500 BbgT 44023 2762 B7
8700 BbgT 44023 2891 C1
Lakeland Av
- AVLK 44012 2618 E2
1000 LKWD 44107 2622 C5

Lakeland Blvd
20000 CLEV 44119 2373 A6
20000 EUCL 44119 2373 A6
22200 EUCL 44117 2373 A6
24300 EUCL 44132 2373 C5
26500 EUCL 44132 2374 C1
27700 WKLF 44092 2374 A2
29900 WKLF 44092 2249 D7
30500 WLWK 44092 2249 D7
32800 ETLK 44095 2249 E7
33700 ETLK 44095 2250 B5
36600 WLBY 44094 2250 B5
N Lakeland Blvd
- EUCL 44132 2373 E3
20000 CLEV 44119 2373 A6
20000 EUCL 44119 2373 A6
22000 EUCL 44117 2373 B5
22000 EUCL 44123 2373 B5
Lakeland Dr
11700 NbyT 44065 2764 D1
36600 AVON 44011 2747 E2
Lakeland Frwy
- BTNH - 2496 E2
- BTNH - 2497 A1
- CLEV - 2372 C7
- CLEV - 2373 A6
- CLEV - 2496 E2
- CLEV - 2497 A1
- ETLK - 2249 C7
- ETLK - 2250 D3
- EUCL - 2373 C4
- EUCL - 2374 A2
- MNTR - 2143 D7
- MNTR - 2144 C5
- MNTR - 2145 A1
- MNTR - 2251 A3
- PNVL - 2145 B1
- PnvT - 2145 B1
- WKLF - 2249 D7
- WKLF - 2374 C1
- WLBY - 2250 D3
- WLBY - 2251 A3
- WLWK - 2249 C7
Lakeland Frwy I-90
- BTNH - 2496 E2
- BTNH - 2497 A1
- CLEV - 2372 D7
- CLEV - 2373 A6
- CLEV - 2496 E2
- CLEV - 2497 A1
- EUCL - 2373 C4
Lakeland Frwy SR-2
- BTNH - 2496 E2
- BTNH - 2497 A1
- CLEV - 2372 C7
- CLEV - 2373 A6
- CLEV - 2496 E2
- CLEV - 2497 A1
- ETLK - 2249 C7
- ETLK - 2250 D3
- EUCL - 2373 C4
- EUCL - 2374 A2
- MNTR - 2143 D7
- MNTR - 2144 C5
- MNTR - 2145 A1
- MNTR - 2251 C1
- PNVL - 2145 B1
- PnvT - 2145 B1
- WKLF - 2249 D7
- WKLF - 2374 A2
- WLBY - 2250 C4
- WLBY - 2251 A3
- WLWK - 2249 C7
Lakeland Frwy SR-44
- MNTR - 2145 B1
- PNVL - 2145 B1
- PnvT - 2145 B1
Lakemeadows Dr
10000 SGVL 44136 3012 C4
Lakemont Av
22200 EUCL 44123 2373 B3
Lake of the Falls Blvd
26600 ClbT 44028 3010 A2
26600 ClbT 44138 3010 A2
26600 ODFL 44138 3010 A2
Lake Overlook Dr
1900 MadT 44057 1941 B2
8800 MNTR 44060 2038 D5
Lake Park Dr
300 BYVL 44140 2620 E5
3400 BKVL 44141 3150 C1
Lake Point Dr
1000 LKWD 44107 2621 E4
Lake Pointe Dr
2100 AVON 44011 2617 E7
2100 AVON 44011 2747 E1
Lakeport Av
17400 CLEV 44119 2372 D5
Lakesedge Tr
17400 BbgT 44023 2890 C4
Lake Shore Blvd
- CLEV 44103 2496 A4
500 PnvT 44077 2039 C6
600 MNTR 44060 2039 A7
600 PnvT 44060 2039 B7
7000 MNTR 44060 2143 D3
7400 MadT 44057 1843 E5
7500 MadT 44057 1844 A5
7700 MONT 44060 2143 E1
8000 MNTR 44060 2144 A1
8000 MONT 44060 2144 D1
8700 CLEV 44108 2496 B4
9100 MNTR 44060 2038 E7
11800 BTNH 44108 2496 E2
13300 BTNH 44108 2497 A1
13300 BTNH 44110 2496 E1
13300 BTNH 44110 2497 A1
13300 CLEV 44110 2496 E1
13800 BTNH 44110 2372 A7
13800 CLEV 44110 2372 A7
16900 CLEV 44119 2372 D6
18400 EUCL 44119 2372 E4
19500 EUCL 44119 2373 A3
19900 EUCL 44123 2373 A3
24800 EUCL 44132 2373 C1
25700 EUCL 44132 2248 E7
27100 EUCL 44132 2249 B6
28100 WLWK 44095 2249 A7
33000 ETLK 44095 2249 D3
33500 LKLN 44095 2249 D3
34400 TMLK 44095 2249 E2
34700 ETLK 44095 2250 A2
34700 TMLK 44095 2250 A2
35900 ETLK 44095 2142 C7
37700 WLBY 44094 2142 D5

Lake Shore Blvd
37700 WLBY 44095 2142 E5
38400 WLBY 44094 2143 B4
38800 MNTR 44094 2143 B4
Lakeshore Blvd
9100 BTNH 44108 2496 B4
9100 CLEV 44108 2496 B4
19000 EUCL 44119 2372 E4
19400 EUCL 44119 2373 A3
21500 EUCL 44123 2373 B3
Lake Shore Blvd SR-283
500 PnvT 44077 2039 C6
600 MNTR 44060 2039 A7
600 PnvT 44060 2039 B7
7000 MNTR 44060 2143 D3
7700 MONT 44060 2143 E1
8000 MNTR 44060 2144 A1
8000 MONT 44060 2144 D1
9100 MNTR 44060 2038 E7
13600 BTNH 44108 2497 A1
13600 BTNH 44110 2497 A1
13800 BTNH 44110 2372 A7
13800 CLEV 44110 2372 A7
16900 CLEV 44119 2372 D6
18400 EUCL 44119 2372 E4
19500 EUCL 44119 2373 A3
19900 EUCL 44123 2373 A3
24800 EUCL 44132 2373 C1
25700 EUCL 44132 2248 E7
27100 EUCL 44132 2249 B6
28100 WLWK 44095 2249 A7
33000 ETLK 44095 2249 D3
33500 LKLN 44095 2249 D3
34400 TMLK 44095 2249 E2
34700 ETLK 44095 2250 B2
34700 TMLK 44095 2250 A2
35900 ETLK 44095 2142 C7
37700 WLBY 44094 2142 D5
37700 WLBY 44095 2142 E5
38400 WLBY 44094 2143 B4
38800 MNTR 44094 2143 B4
S Lakeshore Blvd
36400 ETLK 44095 2142 D6
N Lakeshore Ct
500 VMLN 44089 2741 B5
Lake Shore Dr
15400 NbyT 44021 2765 A4
Lakeshore Dr
8400 BbgT 44023 2891 A3
13700 BTNH 44108 2497 A1
13700 BTNH 44110 2497 A1
Lakeside Av
- NRDV 44039 2876 E7
500 LORN 44052 2614 E5
Lakeside Av E
900 CLEV 44114 2624 E2
1200 CLEV 44114 2625 A1
4000 CLEV 44114 2495 C7
E Lakeside Av
- CLEV 44113 2624 D2
200 CLEV 44114 2624 D2
W Lakeside Av
10 CLEV 44114 2624 D2
600 CLEV 44113 2624 D3
Lakeside Dr
600 AVLK 44012 2613 E5
600 AVON 44012 2618 E5
700 AVON 44011 2618 E5
1800 MadT 44057 1941 C1
8700 NRDV 44039 2876 E7
12000 NbyT 44021 2764 E4
12000 NbyT 44065 2764 E4
Lakeside Pl
10 CLEV 44110 2372 B6
Lakeside Villages Pkwy
- OmsT 44138 2878 D4
Lake Terrace Dr
900 PnvT 44077 2040 D2
Lakeview Av
- SFLD 44054 2616 E3
200 SDLK 44054 2616 E3
1100 LORN 44053 2614 A7
1200 LORN 44053 2744 B1
1400 MadT 44057 1843 B7
1400 RKRV 44116 2621 D7
Lakeview Blvd
10 PnvT 44077 2040 C2
N Lakeview Blvd
1400 LORN 44052 2614 C7
S Lakeview Blvd
1400 LORN 44052 2614 C7
Lakeview Cir
300 AURA 44202 3021 C7
8800 PRMA 44129 2882 D6
9700 SGVL 44136 3012 C4
Lakeview Ct
8000 NRYN 44133 3013 C2
20100 RKRV 44116 2621 D6
Lake View Dr
- NbyT 44065 2764 D1
Lakeview Dr
10 CrlT 44044 3006 E6
100 AVLK 44012 2618 D1
800 LORN 44052 2614 B7
4700 MNTR 44060 2038 D6
7100 PRMA 44129 2882 D7
8500 BWHT 44147 3014 D5
8800 ODFL 44138 2878 E7
8800 ODFL 44138 3009 E1
8800 OmsT 44138 2878 E7
14700 MDFD 44062 2767 B1
16100 BtnT 44021 2765 B6
16100 NbyT 44021 2765 B6
24800 BYVL 44140 2620 D4
33800 ETLK 44095 2249 E2
34100 SLN 44139 2889 A2
Lakeview Ln
- SRSL 44022 2762 C5
Lakeview Rd
600 CLEV 44108 2496 D6
1200 CLEV 44106 2496 D7
1300 CLEV 44112 2496 D7
1500 ECLE 44106 2496 E7
1500 ECLE 44112 2496 E7
1600 ECLE 44106 2626 E1
1600 ECLE 44112 2626 E1
1800 CLEV 44106 2626 E1
1800 CLEV 44112 2626 E1
11400 MsnT 44024 2504 C3
11700 NbyT 44065 2764 D1
Lakeview Ter
15700 MDBH 44130 2881 B5
Lake Vista Dr
5000 ORNG 44022 2759 C7
5000 SLN 44022 2759 C7

Lake Vista Dr
5000 SLN 44139 2759 C7
Lakeway Blvd
6000 MNTR 44060 2143 E3
6000 MONT 44060 2143 E3
Lakewood Av
300 BNWK 44212 3147 A7
1300 LKWD 44107 2623 A6
Lakewood Ct
6200 MNTR 44060 2144 D4
Lakewood Dr
100 AVLK 44012 2618 D2
13300 CsTp 44026 2632 C3
13300 CsTp 44072 2632 C3
13300 RslT 44072 2632 C3
Lakewood Beach Dr
- SFLD 44054 2615 E6
600 SDLK 44054 2615 E6
Lakewood Heights Blvd
13000 CLEV 44107 2622 D7
13000 CLEV 44107 2623 A7
13000 CLEV 44111 2622 D7
13000 CLEV 44111 2623 A7
13000 LKWD 44107 2622 D7
13000 LKWD 44107 2623 A7
Lakomis Dr
35900 ETLK 44095 2142 B7
Lakota Av
14000 CLEV 44111 2752 D3
Lalemant Dr
6800 PRMA 44129 2882 E5
6800 PRMA 44129 2883 A5
Lalemant Rd
2200 UNHT 44118 2628 B4
Lamar Ct
4400 RDHT 44143 2498 C4
Lambert Av
13200 CLEV 44105 2756 E1
13200 CLEV 44120 2756 E1
13600 CLEV 44120 2757 A1
Lambert Rd
4000 SELD 44121 2628 A1
Lambert St
13400 ECLE 44112 2497 A7
Lamberton Rd
2000 CVHT 44118 2627 B3
Lambton Ct
7500 CcdT 44060 2253 B2
Lamoille Ct
1700 CLEV 44113 2624 D6
Lamont Av
9300 CLEV 44106 2626 B2
Lamontier Av
9400 CLEV 44104 2626 C6
Lamplight Ln
2800 WBHL 44092 2374 E6
2800 WBHL 44094 2374 E6
Lamplighter Ln
15100 SGVL 44136 3147 B1
Lampson Rd
1800 CLEV 44112 2497 C3
Lamson Av
- BDFD 44146 2886 E3
500 BDFD 44146 2887 A3
Lamson Rd
7200 BDHT 44146 2887 D7
7200 OKWD 44146 2887 D7
7200 OKWD 44146 3018 D1
Lanabelle
- BKPK 44142 2751 A7
- BKPK 44142 2880 A1
Lanark Ln
600 PnvT 44077 2040 E2
3400 PRPK 44124 2759 C1
Lanbury Av
19000 CLEV 44122 2757 E2
19000 WVHT 44122 2757 E2
19700 WVHT 44122 2758 A2
Lancashire Rd
2700 CVHT 44106 2627 A2
2700 CVHT 44118 2627 A2
Lancaster Ct
- MDHL 44022 2760 A3
7100 CcdT 44077 2145 D7
7200 CcdT 44077 2253 D1
Lancaster Dr
5300 BNHT 44131 2884 B1
8200 MNTR 44060 2144 A6
11500 AbnT 44021 2893 C5
Lancaster Rd
3900 CLEV 44121 2498 A4
3900 SELD 44121 2498 A4
Lancelot Av
12400 CLEV 44108 2496 E4
Lancelot Dr
7200 PRMA 44134 2883 D7
Lancelot Ln E
14700 NRYN 44133 3148 A1
Lancelot Ln W
14700 NRYN 44133 3148 A1
Lancer Dr
1000 AMHT 44001 2872 E4
Lancewood Dr
900 MCDN 44056 3154 A4
Landchester Rd
4600 CLEV 44109 2754 E6
Lander Dr
500 HDHT 44143 2499 C3
Lander Rd
800 HDHT 44143 2499 D5
800 MAYF 44143 2499 D5
900 MDHT 44124 2499 D7
900 MAYF 44143 2499 D6
1400 MDHT 44124 2629 D2
2100 PRPK 44124 2629 D3
3700 ORNG 44022 2759 C6
3700 ORNG 44122 2759 C2
3700 ORNG 44124 2759 C2
3700 PRPK 44122 2759 C2
3700 PRPK 44124 2759 C2
4700 SLN 44022 2759 C7
4700 SLN 44139 2759 C7
Lander Rd N
2400 MDHT 44124 2629 D3
2400 PRPK 44124 2629 D4
Lander Rd S
2700 PRPK 44124 2629 C7
3600 ORNG 44022 2759 C1
3600 ORNG 44124 2759 C1
3600 PRPK 44122 2759 C1
3600 PRPK 44124 2759 C1
3700 ORNG 44022 2759 C2
Landerbrook Cir
2000 MDHT 44124 2629 C3

Landerbrook Dr
5800 MDHT 44124 2629 C3
5800 PRPK 44124 2629 C3
Lander Haven Ct
2200 MDHT 44124 2629 E3
Lander Haven Dr
- PRPK 44124 2629 E3
6000 MDHT 44124 2629 D3
Lander Rd Ext
700 HDHT 44143 2499 D5
700 MAYF 44143 2499 D5
Landerwood Dr
3300 PRPK 44124 2759 D1
Landerwood Ln
500 AVLK 44012 2618 C4
E Landerwood Rd
30800 PRPK 44124 2629 D7
30800 PRPK 44124 2759 D1
W Landerwood Rd
30400 PRPK 44124 2759 D1
Landing Ln
- RMDV 44087 3020 C4
18800 ClbT 44028 3144 B4
Landings Dr
37100 SLN 44139 2889 C3
Landings Wy
10 AVLK 44012 2618 A3
Landon Av
9600 CLEV 44102 2623 D5
Landon Ln
3800 BNWK 44212 3146 E7
Landon Rd
2600 SRHT 44122 2628 C5
Landover Ct
5500 PRMA 44131 2883 E1
5500 PRMA 44134 2883 E1
5500 SVHL 44131 2883 E1
Landsdale Cir
1500 TNBG 44087 3019 B3
Landseer Rd
17800 CLEV 44119 2372 D4
18000 EUCL 44119 2372 E5
Lands End Ln
2000 WTLK 44145 2749 A1
Lane Dr
400 BYVL 44140 2619 A4
14600 LKWD 44107 2622 D4
N Lane Dr
11800 LKWD 44107 2623 B5
S Lane Dr
11800 LKWD 44107 2623 B5
Lane Rd
3900 PryT 44077 2041 C3
3900 PryT 44081 2041 C3
Lane Rd Ext
2000 PryT 44077 2041 C1
2000 PryT 44081 2041 C1
Lanes End
1100 MCDN 44056 3154 B4
Lanes End Dr
8800 RslT 44072 2762 C5
Langale Rd
27200 WTLK 44145 2620 A6
Langdon Ln
9400 NRYN 44133 3013 C5
Langer Dr
6000 BKPK 44142 2881 A2
Langerford Dr
7200 PRMA 44129 2883 A7
Langfitt St
5000 VMLN 44089 2741 A6
5100 VMLN 44089 2740 E6
Langford Ln
2200 AVON 44011 2748 B1
Langly Av
16500 CLEV 44128 2757 C5
Langston Av
3600 CLEV 44115 2625 C4
Langston Ct
8800 MCDN 44056 3018 B5
8800 MCDN 44067 3018 B5
8800 NHFD 44067 3018 B5
Langton Av
10500 GDHT 44125 2756 C6
Langton Rd
3500 CVHT 44121 2497 E4
3500 SELD 44121 2497 E4
Lanier Av
16000 SGVL 44136 3147 B3
Lanier Dr
7300 MDBH 44130 2881 B7
7400 MDBH 44130 3012 B1
Lanken Av
18000 CLEV 44119 2372 D7
Lanmark Dr
8100 MNTR 44060 2144 A4
Lanmark Cove
500 PnvT 44077 2145 C5
Lanning Av
14900 LKWD 44107 2622 C6
Lansbury Ln
5400 LNHT 44124 2629 B2
Lansdale Rd
3800 UNHT 44118 2628 A3
Lansdowne Dr
5000 MDHL 44022 2759 E7
5000 SLN 44022 2759 E7
5000 SLN 44139 2759 E7
Lansing Av
5700 CLEV 44105 2755 D2
Lansing Dr
4300 NOSD 44070 2749 D6
4300 NOSD 44145 2749 D6
4300 WTLK 44145 2749 D6
Lansing Rd
100 VMLN 44089 2741 E4
Lansmark Ct
- BbgT 44023 2891 A4
Lansmere Rd
3200 SRHT 44120 2627 D7
3200 SRHT 44122 2627 D7
Lantern Ct
14800 MDFD 44062 2767 E2
Lantern Dr
24000 ODFL 44138 3010 D1
Lantern Ln
6800 PMHT 44130 2882 C6
Lantern Wy
500 AURA 44202 3022 B5
Lanyard Dr
7500 PRMA 44129 2882 D3
La Paz Blvd
- BERA 44017 3010 E1
- BERA 44017 3011 A1

Laramie Dr
22400 RKRV 44116 2751 A1
Larch Ct
6700 OKWD 44146 2887 E6
Larch Dr
- PRMA 44134 3014 A1
Larchmere Blvd
11700 CLEV 44120 2626 D5
12600 SRHT 44120 2626 D5
13200 CLEV 44120 2627 A5
14700 SRHT 44120 2627 A5
Larchmont Av
1400 LKWD 44107 2622 B5
Larchmont Ct
2400 WKLF 44092 2374 C4
Larchmont Dr
2100 WKLF 44092 2374 C4
5000 VMLN 44089 2741 A6
6600 MDHT 44124 2630 A1
Larchmont Rd
1300 CLEV 44110 2372 B6
1400 CLEV 44110 2497 E1
2500 BHWD 44122 2628 C5
Larchview Dr
900 PnvT 44077 2041 B3
900 PryT 44077 2041 B4
2700 PryT 44081 2041 B4
Larchwood Av
17600 CLEV 44111 2752 A3
17600 CLEV 44135 2752 A3
Larchwood Dr
10 PnvT 44077 2145 E3
400 BERA 44017 2880 A4
Lardet Av
11100 CLEV 44104 2626 D6
11100 CLEV 44120 2626 D6
Lares Ln
6500 MDBH 44130 2881 D4
Lark Ln
300 ELYR 44035 2874 E2
Lark St
2000 LKWD 44107 2623 A6
Larkfield Dr
14600 BKPK 44142 2881 C3
Larkhall Dr
6100 MadT 44057 1941 E1
Larkmont Dr
100 ELYR 44035 2875 C4
Larkmoor St
2100 LORN 44052 2615 B6
Larkspur Dr
1700 LNHT 44124 2629 B2
7300 MONT 44060 2143 C2
Larkspur Ln
4200 WVHT 44128 2757 E4
8600 MCDN 44056 3018 A7
Larkspur Rd
7800 RslT 44022 2761 D3
Larkstone Pl
100 ELYR 44035 2874 A7
Larnder Av
9500 CLEV 44102 2623 D6
La Rose Av
11000 CLEV 44105 2756 C3
La Salle Av
18200 CLEV 44119 2372 E5
Lasalle Ln
9500 MNTR 44060 2145 A4
Lascala Dr
7400 HDSN 44236 3155 B7
Laser Blvd
12800 CsTp 44026 2501 E7
12800 CsTp 44026 2631 E1
Lassiter Dr
400 HDHT 44143 2499 D2
7000 PRMA 44129 2883 A7
Lassiter Ovl
5400 PRMA 44129 2883 A6
Latimer Ct
100 SDLK 44054 2615 E4
Latimore Rd
3500 SRHT 44122 2757 E2
Latimore St
200 PNVL 44077 2040 B7
Latonia Rd
6300 INDE 44131 2884 D4
Latta Ln
6400 BosT 44141 3152 D5
6400 SgHT 44067 3152 D5
6400 SgHT 44141 3152 D5
Lattasburg Elyria Rd
- CrlT 44044 3140 E3
- CrlT 44050 3140 E7
- LrgT 44050 3140 E5
Lattasburg Elyria Rd SR-301
- CrlT 44044 3140 E3
- CrlT 44050 3140 E7
- LrgT 44050 3140 E5
Lauderdale Av
1400 LKWD 44107 2622 B5
Laughlin Ln
28500 WTLK 44145 2749 D2
Laumar Av
7600 CLEV 44105 2756 A4
Laundon St
10 ELYR 44035 2875 C6
Laura Ct
100 ELYR 44035 2874 D3
Laura Dr
1300 LORN 44053 2744 C5
38200 ETLK 44095 2250 E1
38200 WLBY 44094 2250 E1
38200 WLBY 44095 2250 E1
E Laura Dr
7300 MONT 44060 2143 C3
W Laura Dr
7200 MONT 44060 2143 C3
Laura Ln
2900 WTLK 44145 2750 B3
5500 LORN 44053 2743 C5
6400 SLN 44139 2889 D5
10200 TNBG 44087 3019 E3
Laura St
- AVON 44011 2748 E2
Laura Lee Ln
7000 SVHL 44131 2884 B7
Laurel Av
- AVLK 44012 2617 D1
19300 RKRV 44116 2621 D6
Laurel Cir
240-00 AURA 44202 3156 C2
3900 ORNG 44122 2759 C3
35800 NRDV 44039 2877 A2

Laurel Ct
10 MDHL 44022 2760 C2
300 PNVL 44077 2146 C2
7200 OmsT 44138 2878 D5
Laurel Dr
10 RKRV 44116 2621 D6
300 BERA 44017 2880 A4
1200 MCDN 44056 3019 A6
1600 TNBG 44087 3019 B6
3400 PryT 44081 1940 C7
11200 NbyT 44065 2634 B7
11200 NbyT 44065 2764 B1
19000 WNHL 44146 3018 A2
Laurel Ln
1800 AhtT 44001 2744 B7
6600 ODFL 44138 3010 B1
8100 RslT 44022 2761 E2
8900 NRYN 44133 3013 B3
10500 BKVL 44141 3016 C3
13100 VLVW 44125 2885 E5
13400 VLVW 44125 2886 A5
27000 OmsT 44138 2878 D5
29300 WKLF 44092 2374 C3
Laurel Rd
10 SRSL 44022 2761 C6
100 RslT 44022 2761 C6
3000 SRHT 44120 2627 C6
3900 LORN 44055 2745 C4
4400 SELD 44121 2498 C7
5700 INDE 44131 2884 D4
11800 CsTp 44026 2501 B4
Laurel Trc
6700 MDBH 44130 2881 B5
Laurel Wy
34400 AVON 44011 2748 B6
Laurelbrook Dr
400 SRSL 44022 2761 C6
Laureldale Rd
23900 SRHT 44122 2628 D5
24100 BHWD 44122 2628 D5
Laurel Glen Dr
3100 BWHT 44147 3015 B5
Laurel Hill Dr
1800 SELD 44121 2628 B2
2100 UNHT 44118 2628 C3
2100 UNHT 44121 2628 C3
Laurel Hill Ln
10 HGVL 44022 2630 A7
10 PRPK 44124 2630 A7
Laurelhurst Rd
2400 UNHT 44118 2628 C4
Laurell Cir
18800 SGVL 44136 3147 C5
Laurell Ln
4000 NOSD 44070 2749 E5
Laurelton Dr
26100 OKWD 44146 2887 E7
Lauren Ln
500 AMHT 44001 2872 B4
Lauren Wy
19100 SGVL 44149 3146 D3
Lauren J Dr
7200 MNTR 44060 2144 A7
7200 MNTR 44060 2252 A1
Laurent Dr
5400 PRMA 44129 2883 A5
Laurie Ln
10 NCtT 44067 3153 A2
Lavandef Payne
- WTLK 44145 2619 C6
Lavender Ct
5400 NRDV 44039 2747 B7
5400 NRDV 44039 2876 B1
Lavender Ln
100 MDSN 44057 1942 B7
Laverne Av
5400 PRMA 44129 2754 A7
5400 PRMA 44134 2754 A7
6900 PRMA 44129 2753 E7
16200 CLEV 44135 2752 B4
19900 FWPK 44126 2751 D2
19900 RKRV 44116 2751 D2
19900 RKRV 44126 2751 D2
Laverne Ln
10 HmbT 44024 2381 A3
Lawn Av
5700 MPHT 44137 2886 A2
6500 CLEV 44102 2624 A6
6800 CLEV 44102 2623 E6
Lawn Ct
6900 CLEV 44102 2623 E6
6900 CLEV 44102 2624 A6
Lawn St
200 GNVA 44041 1944 B4
Lawnbury Dr
13300 CsTp 44026 2632 C3
Lawndale Av
14800 CLEV 44128 2757 A5
Lawndale Dr
10600 PMHT 44130 2882 A6
12600 PMHT 44130 2881 E6
Lawnfield Ct
100 GNVA 44041 1944 B4
Lawnfield Dr
9300 TNBG 44087 3019 B6
Lawnfield Rd
5400 MONT 44060 2143 E1
Lawn Park Dr
6900 BKVL 44141 3151 A1
Lawnview Av
400 PNVL 44077 2040 A7
6600 CLEV 44103 2625 E1
7100 CLEV 44103 2626 A1
Lawnway Rd
1800 SELD 44121 2628 C2
Lawnwood Av
6400 PMHT 44130 2881 E5
Lawrence Av
4600 GDHT 44125 2757 A6
Lawrence Ct
41800 EyrT 44035 2874 D2
Lawrence Dr
- PRMA 44130 3013 B2
Lawrence Rd
4400 WVHT 44128 2758 C4
Lawton Av
33800 ETLK 44095 2249 E2
Lawton Dr
8600 MCDN 44056 3018 D7
Lawton Ln
3300 PRPK 44124 2629 B7
3300 PRPK 44124 2759 B1
Laydon Ln
10200 CcdT 44077 2253 D4

Cleveland Street Index

STREET
Block City ZIP Map# Grid

Layor Dr
5800 PMHT 44130 2882 B2
5800 PRMA 44130 2882 B2
Lazarro Dr
300 BWHT 44147 3014 E6
Leader Rd
10800 HmbT 44024 2380 D7
10900 HmbT 44024 2505 D1
11000 ClrT 44024 2505 D1
Leadership Ln
- PryT 44081 2042 B1
Leading Av
4300 CLEV 44109 2754 B2
Leafy Mill Ln
33000 NRDV 44039 2748 D7
Leah Ct
9100 MNTR 44060 2038 E7
Leah's Wy
10 OmsT 44138 2879 A4
Leann Ct
5200 SFLD 44054 2746 D4
Lear Rd
100 AVLK 44012 2618 D4
700 AVON 44011 2618 D5
700 AVON 44012 2618 D5
Learidge Rd
800 LNHT 44124 2498 D6
Lear Industrial Pkwy
1000 AVON 44011 2618 D6
Lear Nagle Rd
900 AVLK 44012 2618 D6
900 AVON 44011 2618 D6
900 AVON 44012 2618 D6
2000 AVON 44011 2748 D3
4800 NRDV 44011 2748 D7
4800 NRDV 44039 2748 D7
5400 NRDV 44039 2877 D2
N Lear Nagle Rd
- NRDV 44039 2877 D2
Learning Ln
10 PRRY 44081 2042 C1
Leaview Av
10 SRSL 44022 2762 C6
Leaview Ln
10 SRSL 44022 2762 B5
Leavitt Rd
1000 LORN 44052 2614 B7
1000 LORN 44053 2614 B7
1300 LORN 44052 2744 B1
1300 LORN 44053 2744 A5
5300 AMHT 44001 2744 A6
5300 AMHT 44053 2744 A6
5300 LORN 44001 2744 A6
7400 AhtT 44001 2873 A5
7400 AMHT 44001 2873 A5
9000 AhtT 44001 2872 E7
9200 AhtT 44001 3003 E2
9500 NRsT 44001 3003 E1
9800 NRsT 44074 3003 E7
12300 OBLN 44074 3003 E7
12400 NRsT 44074 3138 E1
12400 OBLN 44074 3138 E1
Leavitt Rd SR-58
1000 LORN 44052 2614 B7
1000 LORN 44053 2614 B7
1300 LORN 44052 2744 B1
1300 LORN 44053 2744 A5
5300 AMHT 44001 2744 A6
5300 AMHT 44053 2744 A6
5300 LORN 44001 2744 A6
7400 AhtT 44001 2873 A5
7400 AMHT 44001 2873 A5
9000 AhtT 44001 2872 E7
9200 AhtT 44001 3003 E2
9500 NRsT 44001 3003 E1
9800 NRsT 44074 3003 E7
12300 OBLN 44074 3003 E7
12400 NRsT 44074 3138 E1
12400 OBLN 44074 3138 E1
N Leavitt Rd
500 AMHT 44001 2744 A6
800 AMHT 44053 2744 A6
800 LORN 44001 2744 A6
800 LORN 44053 2744 A6
N Leavitt Rd SR-58
100 AMHT 44001 2744 A6
800 AMHT 44053 2744 A6
800 LORN 44001 2744 A6
800 LORN 44053 2744 A6
S Leavitt Rd
100 AhtT 44001 2873 A2
100 AMHT 44001 2873 A2
S Leavitt Rd SR-58
100 AhtT 44001 2873 A2
100 AMHT 44001 2873 A2
Leawood Ovl
10300 SGVL 44136 3012 B4
Lebern Dr
- WTLK 44070 2750 D3
- WTLK 44145 2750 D3
23700 NOSD 44070 2750 D3
Lecona Rd
800 CVHT 44121 2497 D5
Lederer Av
6500 CLEV 44127 2625 E6
Ledge Rd
10 MCDN 44056 3018 D5
10 MCDN 44067 3018 B5
10 NHFD 44067 3018 B5
10 SgHT 44067 3018 B5
1100 MCDN 44056 3019 A5
1100 TNBG 44087 3019 A5
5200 MadT 44057 2044 C7
Ledge Acres Dr
9300 MCDN 44056 3018 D4
Ledgebrook Dr
6300 BKPK 44142 2881 B4
Ledgebrook Ln
5600 SLN 44139 2889 A2
13300 CsTp 44022 2631 B3
13300 CsTp 44026 2631 B3
13300 HGVL 44022 2631 B3
13300 RslT 44022 2631 B3
Ledge Hill Dr
32700 SLN 44139 2888 E2
33300 SLN 44139 2889 A3
Ledge Lake Ct
6300 CcdT 44077 2146 D4
Ledgemont Dr
800 BWHT 44147 3015 A7
Ledgemont Ln
- NCtT 44067 3153 C4
Ledgepoint Pl
18000 SGVL 44136 3011 E6

STREET
Block City ZIP Map# Grid

Ledgeside Dr
18200 SGVL 44136 3011 E6
Ledgestone Ct
- BERA 44017 2879 E5
- BERA 44138 2879 E5
- WLBY 44094 2143 A5
Ledgeview Ct
10 MPHT 44137 2886 A4
Ledgeview Rd
1000 MCDN 44056 3018 E6
Ledgewood Av
14300 CLEV 44111 2752 D3
Ledgewood Dr
10 BDFD 44146 2886 D4
6300 INDE 44131 2884 C4
7200 KTLD 44094 2376 B6
Ledgewood Ln
1400 AVON 44011 2617 E6
Ledgewood Tr
900 LNHT 44124 2498 E6
Lee Av
10500 CLEV 44106 2496 C7
Lee Blvd
1800 ECLE 44112 2497 B6
2100 CVHT 44112 2497 B7
2100 CVHT 44118 2497 B7
2400 CVHT 44118 2627 C1
Lee Cir
300 SgHT 44067 3017 D5
Lee Ct
10 BDFD 44146 2886 E3
100 ELYR 44035 2873 E6
600 VMLN 44089 2742 A5
Lee Dr
2100 PRMA 44134 2883 E6
6300 BKPK 44142 2880 E3
Lee Rd
10 PnvT 44077 2041 A4
100 BERA 44017 2880 B7
300 BDFD 44137 2886 C4
300 BDFD 44146 2886 C4
1600 CVHT 44118 2627 C4
2700 SRHT 44118 2627 C5
2700 SRHT 44120 2627 C7
3400 SRHT 44120 2757 C1
3700 CLEV 44120 2757 C2
3700 CLEV 44128 2757 C4
5000 MPHT 44128 2757 C6
5000 MPHT 44137 2757 C7
5300 MPHT 44137 2886 C1
5800 NRDV 44039 2877 A2
Lee Rd SR-17
5300 MPHT 44137 2886 C1
Lee Rd S
5700 MPHT 44137 2886 C3
6200 BDFD 44137 2886 C3
6200 BDFD 44146 2886 C3
Leedale Av
1000 LKWD 44107 2622 C3
Leeds Av
16700 CLEV 44110 2372 C7
Leeds Rd
3500 PRPK 44122 2759 B1
3500 WDMR 44122 2759 B1
Lee Heights Blvd
3700 CLEV 44128 2757 D3
4300 WVHT 44128 2757 D5
Leeila Av
11800 CLEV 44135 2753 A4
Leenders Ln
26600 NOSD 44070 2750 A6
Lee's Ln
10 OmsT 44138 2879 B4
Lee Terrace Dr
1500 WKLF 44092 2374 D2
Leeward Ct
31700 AVLK 44012 2618 E3
31700 AVLK 44012 2619 A3
Leeward Ln
1200 WLBY 44094 2142 E5
Legacy Dr
- HDHT 44143 2499 E1
Legacy Pointe Pkwy
32300 AVLK 44012 2618 B4
Legend Ct
8400 MCDN 44056 3018 B7
E Legend Ct
300 HDHT 44143 2499 D1
W Legend Ct
300 HDHT 44143 2499 D1
Legend Dr
- HDHT 44143 2499 D1
Legend Ln
2900 WBHL 44092 2374 B7
Legend Tr
100 WLWK 44095 2249 B6
Legend Creek Dr
11600 CsTp 44026 2502 E4
11600 CsTp 44026 2503 A3
11600 MsnT 44026 2503 A3
Legends Row
- AVLK 44012 2618 C3
Legends Wy
- PRPK 44124 2629 A7
Leggett Rd
15800 MtlT 44024 2257 D6
15800 MtlT 44064 2257 D6
Lehigh Av
1300 LORN 44052 2615 B6
Lehman Dr
5800 BDHT 44146 2887 E3
Lehua Ct
10 MadT 44057 1941 B6
Leigh Ellen Av
15600 CLEV 44135 2752 C4
Leighton Ct
5100 SLN 44139 2759 C7
Leighton Rd
2600 SRHT 44120 2627 B5
Leisurewood Ln
3700 PRRY 44081 2042 C1
Lela Ln
12200 NbyT 44021 2765 A1
12200 NbyT 44065 2765 A1
Leland Tr
10500 AbnT 44023 3023 D1
Lemar Av
6700 CLEV 44114 2625 C1
Lemonwood Ct
6600 LORN 44053 2744 D7
Lemuel Bourne Ct
6900 BKVL 44141 3016 B7
Len Ct
600 AURA 44202 3022 C7

STREET
Block City ZIP Map# Grid

Lena Av
11700 BKLN 44144 2753 A5
11700 CLEV 44135 2753 A5
11700 CLEV 44144 2753 A5
Lena Dr
100 AURA 44202 3156 E5
200 AURA 44202 3157 A5
700 AURA 44255 3157 B5
Lenacrave Av
11600 CLEV 44105 2756 D2
12700 CLEV 44120 2756 E2
Lennox Av
3200 CLEV 44134 2754 C7
3300 CLEV 44109 2754 C7
Lennox Cir
3500 BNWK 44212 3147 A6
Lennox Rd
2000 CVHT 44106 2626 E3
Lenny Av
14900 MDFD 44062 2767 E2
Lenore Dr
5200 MNTR 44060 2038 E7
Lenox Ct
500 BWHT 44147 3150 A5
Lenox Dr
14700 SGVL 44136 3147 B1
Lenox Ovl
3200 AVON 44011 2748 B3
Lenwood Dr
3500 BWHT 44147 3015 B4
Leo Bullocks Pkwy
- ELYR 44035 2874 B6
Leona Dr
4100 FWPK 44116 2751 D2
4100 FWPK 44126 2751 D2
4100 RKRV 44116 2751 D2
Leona St
500 ELYR 44035 2874 E1
Leonard Av
- WKLF 44092 2374 B2
10 NCtT 44067 3152 E1
10 NCtT 44067 3153 A1
14600 LKWD 44107 2622 D6
Leonard St
10 BDFD 44146 2886 E3
100 SAHT 44001 2872 A7
300 SAHT 44001 3003 A1
400 NRsT 44001 3003 A1
1600 CLEV 44113 2624 D4
Leopold Av
3500 CLEV 44109 2754 C5
Leroy Av
9300 CLEV 44104 2626 B5
13500 CLEV 44135 2752 E3
Leroy St
800 LORN 44052 2615 C5
Leroy Center Rd
12800 LryT 44077 2147 D6
Leroy Thompson Rd
6900 LryT 44086 2256 E3
6900 LryT 44086 2257 A1
7700 LryT 44077 2256 E3
Lesbeth Ct
11300 CLEV 44108 2496 D4
Leslie Av
26100 EUCL 44132 2373 E2
34700 NRDV 44039 2877 B1
Leslie Ct
29400 WKLF 44092 2374 B1
Leslie Dr
6300 BKPK 44142 2880 E3
Leslie Ln
- AMHT 44001 2872 B1
Leslie St
10 GNVA 44041 1944 C5
Lesnick Ct
10 ELYR 44035 2875 A5
Lester Av
4400 CLEV 44127 2625 C6
Lester Dr
7700 LryT 44077 2256 C3
Letchworth Rd
23400 BHWD 44122 2628 C7
23400 BHWD 44122 2758 C1
Leuer Av
10600 CLEV 44108 2496 C4
Levan Dr
10 PNVL 44077 2146 A2
Leverett Ln
300 HDHT 44143 2499 E2
Levi Ct
8800 NRDV 44035 2876 D7
Lewis Av
- AVLK 44012 2618 B2
Lewis Dr
- VMLN 44089 2741 B6
1400 LKWD 44107 2622 E6
2100 CLEV 44107 2622 E7
2100 CLEV 44111 2622 E7
3600 PRPK 44124 2759 D1
7000 BbgT 44023 2890 A1
18200 MPHT 44137 2886 D1
Lewis Rd
5700 NOSD 44070 2879 D1
5700 NOSD 44138 2879 D1
5700 OmsT 44138 2879 D3
7500 BERA 44138 2879 D4
7500 ODFL 44138 2879 C6
7800 BERA 44017 2879 C6
7800 ODFL 44017 2879 C6
Lewis St
- AVLK 44012 2618 B1
6100 MadT 44057 1941 E1
34300 NRDV 44039 2748 C7
Lexington Av
100 ELYR 44035 2875 D6
300 PNVL 44077 2039 E7
300 PNVL 44077 2145 D1
400 PnvT 44077 2145 D1
800 LORN 44052 2614 D7
1300 LORN 44052 2744 E1
2500 LORN 44055 2744 E2
4700 CLEV 44103 2625 E1
7100 CLEV 44103 2626 A1
Lexington Blvd
10 MDSN 44057 1942 B7
Lexington Cir
200 BWHT 44147 3149 E4
200 BWHT 44147 3150 A4
Lexington Ct
3600 WTLK 44145 2749 C4
7000 NCtT 44067 3153 B4
11200 NRYN 44133 3013 D5
Lexington Dr
1400 VMLN 44089 2740 E7

STREET
Block City ZIP Map# Grid

Lexington Dr
1400 VmnT 44089 2740 E7
7500 HDSN 44236 3155 B7
Lexington Ln
3400 BNWK 44212 3147 B7
17300 SGVL 44136 3147 A4
17500 SGVL 44136 3146 E4
Lexington Sq
10 EUCL 44143 2498 A2
Lexington Wy
8000 NRDV 44039 2876 C6
Lexington Green St
7600 MDBH 44130 3012 C1
Leyton Rd
10 BDFD 44146 2886 E2
10 BDFD 44146 2887 A2
Libby Av
10900 CrlT 44035 3005 C4
Libby Rd
14400 MPHT 44137 2757 B7
19800 MPHT 44137 2758 A7
21200 BDHT 44146 2758 A7
23000 BDHT 44146 2887 C1
Libby Rd SR-17
14400 MPHT 44137 2757 B7
19800 MPHT 44137 2758 A7
21200 BDHT 44146 2758 A7
Liberio Ct
9200 MNTR 44060 2144 E1
Liberty Av
1600 LORN 44053 2742 A5
1600 VMLN 44053 2742 A5
1600 VMLN 44089 2742 A5
3900 AVON 44011 2617 E6
4500 VMLN 44089 2741 E5
4900 ShfT 44055 2746 A6
5000 VMLN 44089 2740 D5
7300 PRMA 44129 2753 E7
13000 CLEV 44135 2753 B4
14000 CLEV 44135 2752 D4
Liberty Av US-6
1600 LORN 44053 2742 A5
1600 VMLN 44053 2742 A5
1600 VMLN 44089 2742 A5
4500 VMLN 44089 2741 E5
5000 VMLN 44089 2740 D5
Liberty Blvd
- CLEV 44103 2496 A5
- CLEV 44108 2496 A5
Liberty Ct
100 ELYR 44035 2874 D1
Liberty Ln
5100 WLBY 44094 2250 A7
5100 WLBY 44094 2375 A1
38500 CrlT 44044 3141 E1
38500 EatT 44044 3141 E1
Liberty Pkwy
33000 NRDV 44039 2877 D2
Liberty Rd
4400 SELD 44121 2498 C6
4700 BTVL 44022 2889 D2
5700 BTVL 44139 2889 D3
5700 SLN 44139 2889 C7
6900 SLN 44139 3020 C3
7600 TNBG 44087 3020 C6
7600 TNBG 44139 3020 C3
7600 TwbT 44087 3020 C3
7600 TwbT 44139 3020 C3
9100 TNBG 44087 3155 C1
9900 RMDV 44087 3020 C5
Liberty St
10 BERA 44017 2880 C6
10 PNVL 44077 2146 B1
700 PnvT 44077 2146 B3
5300 MONT 44060 2038 A7
5300 MONT 44060 2144 A1
E Liberty St
10 GNVA 44041 1944 C4
W Liberty St
10 GNVA 44041 1944 B5
Liberty Bell Dr
900 AMHT 44001 2744 A6
900 AMHT 44053 2744 A6
900 LORN 44053 2744 A6
6400 BKPK 44142 2881 A4
6400 MDBH 44130 2881 A4
6400 MDBH 44142 2881 A4
Liberty Rose Dr
32000 AVLK 44012 2618 D3
Liberty St Ext
10 PNVL 44077 2040 A7
Library Av
2900 CLEV 44109 2754 C1
Library Ct
3500 CLEV 44109 2754 C1
Library Ln
5200 MPHT 44137 2757 B7
Lido Ct
6800 PRMA 44129 2882 E7
Lido Dr
8400 BWHT 44147 3014 E4
Liege Ct
- CLEV 44109 2754 C3
Liggett Dr
3700 PRMA 44134 2883 B2
Lighthouse Ct
7500 MNTR 44060 2143 D4
Lighthouse Pointe Dr
- PNVL 44077 2040 A5
Lila Pl
- TNBG 44087 3019 E4
Lilac Av
9700 GDHT 44125 2885 B1
Lilac Ct
2200 AVON 44011 2747 E2
2900 PryT 44081 2041 D3
4700 GnvT 44041 1944 E3
7100 NOSD 44070 2878 A4
7100 OmsT 44070 2878 A4
7100 OmsT 44138 2878 A4
Lilac Ln
2200 AVON 44011 2747 E2
Lilac Rd
4400 SELD 44121 2498 C7
Lillian Ct
5800 CLEV 44102 2624 A6
Lily Ln
31000 NOSD 44070 2878 A4
Lima Av
10800 CLEV 44108 2496 C5
Limberlost Ct
6600 SLN 44139 2889 D6
Lime Ln
7300 PRMA 44129 2882 E7

STREET
Block City ZIP Map# Grid

Lime Rd
- CLEV 44113 2624 D3
Limerick Ln
- GFTN 44044 3142 B4
Limeridge Rd
10200 FdmT 44255 3160 B7
10200 HrmT 44234 3160 B4
10200 HrmT 44255 3160 B4
Limestone Ct
- BERA 44138 2879 E6
Limpert Ln
27100 NOSD 44070 2750 A5
Limperts Vine Row
28100 WTLK 44145 2749 D1
Lincoln Av
- LORN 44055 2745 E5
- MPHT 44137 2757 C7
10 BERA 44017 2880 C5
1400 LKWD 44107 2622 D6
2000 PRMA 44134 2883 C1
2200 CLEV 44107 2622 D7
2200 CLEV 44111 2622 D7
4100 WLBY 44094 2250 D5
11000 GDHT 44125 2756 C7
14800 CLEV 44128 2757 A5
33800 NRDV 44039 2877 C2
Lincoln Blvd
- SDLK 44054 2616 D3
- SFLD 44054 2616 D4
10 PNVL 44077 2145 D2
600 BDFD 44146 2887 B4
1300 ShfT 44055 2745 B5
2900 CVHT 44118 2627 B2
Lincoln Dr
- ODFL 44138 2879 C7
10 CLEV 44110 2372 C6
2300 LORN 44052 2615 C5
8300 CsTp 44026 2502 A6
9200 NHFD 44067 3018 A3
9300 NHFD 44146 3018 A3
9300 WNHL 44146 3018 A3
23600 BDHT 44146 2887 C1
Lincoln Rd
1500 WKLF 44092 2374 C3
27800 BYVL 44140 2619 E5
27800 BYVL 44140 2620 A5
31000 AVON 44011 2749 A5
31000 AVON 44145 2749 A5
31000 WTLK 44145 2749 A5
N Lincoln Rd
28600 BYVL 44140 2619 D5
Lincoln St
100 AMHT 44001 2872 D1
100 ELYR 44035 2875 B6
500 AMHT 44001 2743 D7
2800 LORN 44052 2615 C5
8000 MONT 44060 2038 A7
W Lincoln St
10 OBLN 44074 3138 D4
Lincolnshire Ct
4800 BWHT 44147 3015 D4
Lincolnshire Dr
8200 SGVL 44149 3011 A3
23000 BYVL 44140 2621 A5
23100 BYVL 44140 2620 E5
Lincolnshire Ln
7400 PRMA 44134 3014 E1
Lincolnville Av
23800 OKWD 44146 2887 D7
Linda Av
14900 MDFD 44062 2767 C2
Linda Ct
19400 RKRV 44116 2621 D5
Linda Dr
4300 BhmT 44089 2741 B7
4300 VMLN 44089 2741 B7
6300 AhtT 44001 2873 D1
14500 NbyT 44065 2634 A7
20200 EUCL 44117 2498 A3
24900 NOSD 44070 2750 C6
Linda Ln
3000 SFLD 44054 2746 B2
5700 GDHT 44125 2885 D2
6900 SVHL 44131 2884 B6
7400 WNHL 44146 3017 D1
Linda St
500 RKRV 44116 2621 D5
Lindberg Dr
9200 NRYN 44133 3148 C2
Lindbergh Av
20000 CLEV 44119 2373 A5
20000 EUCL 44119 2373 A5
Lindbergh Blvd
400 BERA 44017 2880 A6
600 BERA 44017 2879 E7
600 ODFL 44017 2879 E7
600 ODFL 44138 2879 E7
9000 BERA 44138 2879 D7
9100 ODFL 44138 3010 D1
9700 ClbT 44028 3010 D2
9700 ClbT 44138 3010 D2
Linden Cir
3100 NRYN 44133 3014 C5
4100 NOSD 44070 2750 E5
Linden Dr
10 PnvT 44077 2145 D3
500 BHIT 44212 3146 B7
500 BNWK 44212 3146 B7
32800 SLN 44139 2888 E5
33400 SLN 44139 2889 A5
Linden Ln
1000 LNHT 44124 2499 A6
E Linden Ln
7600 PRMA 44130 3013 A2
7800 NRYN 44130 3013 A2
7800 NRYN 44133 3013 A2
N Linden Ln
7400 PRMA 44130 2881 E7
7400 PRMA 44130 3012 E1
S Linden Ln
7700 NRYN 44130 3013 A2
7700 NRYN 44133 3013 A2
7700 PRMA 44130 3013 A2
W Linden Ln
12800 MDBH 44130 3012 E1
12800 PRMA 44130 3012 E1
Linden Rd
3000 RKRV 44116 2621 D7
3000 RKRV 44116 2751 D1
Linden St
400 VMLN 44089 2741 A5
7800 MONT 44060 2143 E1
8000 MONT 44060 2144 A1
Linden Hill Ct
1000 SgHT 44067 3017 B5

STREET
Block City ZIP Map# Grid

Lindenwood Dr
1300 LORN 44053 2744 C5
Linden Wy Dr
11400 MsnT 44024 2504 C2
Lindford Dr
500 BYVL 44140 2619 C5
Lindholm Rd
3500 SRHT 44120 2757 C2
Lindmar Dr
10500 CcdT 44077 2145 E4
10600 CcdT 44077 2146 A4
Lindmont Dr
14900 BKPK 44142 2881 C3
Lindsay Ct
100 ELYR 44035 3006 D2
Lindsay Dr
6900 MNTR 44060 2144 B7
Lindsay Ln
7600 SLN 44139 3019 E3
10300 AbnT 44023 2892 C1
Lindsey Ln
4700 RDHT 44143 2498 E4
Lindsey Ovl
4800 RDHT 44143 2498 D4
Line Dr
- NRDV 44039 2876 D5
Line St
10500 MNTU 44255 3159 B6
Links Rd
5300 MNTR 44060 2038 D7
5300 MNTR 44060 2144 D1
Linn Av
13600 GDHT 44125 2886 A1
Linn Dr
700 CLEV 44108 2496 D6
Linn Rd
5500 AhtT 44001 2744 C6
5500 AMHT 44001 2744 C6
5500 AMHT 44053 2744 C6
5500 LORN 44053 2744 C6
Linnell Rd
4000 SELD 44121 2628 A1
Linnet Av
10300 CLEV 44111 2753 C2
Linsberry Ct
600 AVLK 44012 2618 A5
Linton Av
5400 CLEV 44105 2755 D1
Linton Ln
1400 BWHT 44147 3150 A5
Linwood Av
- VMLN 44089 2740 E5
5000 VMLN 44089 2741 A5
6500 CLEV 44103 2625 E1
7100 CLEV 44103 2626 A1
8200 CLEV 44106 2626 A1
Linwood Cir
27300 NOSD 44070 2749 E6
Linwood Ct
1300 ELYR 44035 3006 A2
Linwood Ln
100 AURA 44202 3156 C1
Lione Dr
9700 CcdT 44060 2253 B2
Lipton Av
16500 CLEV 44128 2757 C5
Lisa Dr
14000 GDHT 44125 2886 A3
14000 GDHT 44137 2886 A3
14000 MPHT 44137 2886 A3
Lisa Ln
- ClrT 44024 2506 D2
4100 NOSD 44070 2749 E5
4500 NRYN 44133 3014 A6
32500 SLN 44139 3019 E3
33400 SLN 44139 3020 A3
Lisa Wy
5200 NRDV 44039 2748 A7
Lisaview Dr
29500 BYVL 44140 2619 C5
Lisbon Rd
2600 CLEV 44104 2626 A5
Lisle Ct
35000 WLBY 44094 2375 A2
Lismore Ct
20000 SGVL 44149 3146 C5
Lismore Ln
9400 MNTR 44060 2145 A5
List Ct
4000 CLEV 44113 2624 C7
List Ln
12800 NRYN 44130 3012 E2
12800 NRYN 44133 3012 E2
12800 PRMA 44130 3012 E2
W List Ln
7800 PRMA 44130 3012 E2
Lister Ln
9400 TNBG 44087 3020 B7
Litchfield Dr
4700 RDHT 44143 2498 D1
7700 MNTR 44060 2252 A2
Litchfield Rd
2800 SRHT 44120 2627 D6
Literary Rd
300 CLEV 44113 2625 A5
800 CLEV 44113 2624 E5
Little Brook Wy
21200 SGVL 44149 3011 A4
Little Creek Pkwy
200 BNHT 44131 2884 A1
300 BNHT 44131 2755 B7
Little Flower Cir
8800 NRDV 44039 2877 B7
Little Green Ln
6100 MadT 44057 1842 E7
6100 MadT 44057 1941 E1
Little Met Pl
4500 CLEV 44135 2751 E5
Little Mountain Rd
7300 MNTR 44060 2252 C2
7700 KDHL 44060 2252 D5
9300 KDHL 44060 2253 A5
9500 CcdT 44060 2253 B5
9500 CdnT 44060 2253 B5
9700 CcdT 44077 2253 B5
Littleton Rd
12800 GDHT 44125 2885 E2
Litto Dr
7900 MDBH 44130 3012 C2
7900 SGVL 44130 3012 C3
7900 SGVL 44136 3012 C3
Live Oaks
5800 MONT 44060 2143 D2
Livermore Ln
700 ELYR 44035 2875 E2

STREET
Block City ZIP Map# Grid

Liverpool Dr
500 LvpT 44280 3145 D7
Livery Ln
13000 MsnT 44024 2634 C2
Livingston Av
1700 LORN 44052 2744 E1
3200 LORN 44055 2745 A3
3500 LORN 44052 2745 A3
Livingston Dr
35100 AVON 44011 2748 B3
Livingston Rd
3000 CLEV 44120 2626 E6
3000 CLEV 44120 2627 A7
Ljubljana Dr
700 EUCL 44119 2373 A5
Lloyd Av
800 AURA 44202 3021 A4
1100 RMDV 44202 3021 A4
Lloyd Dr
6500 BKVL 44141 3015 E4
6500 BWHT 44141 3015 E4
6500 BWHT 44147 3015 E4
Lloyd Rd
10 EUCL 44132 2249 A7
400 EUCL 44132 2374 A1
400 WKLF 44092 2374 B2
3500 CLEV 44111 2753 A2
Lloyd Rd SR-633
200 EUCL 44132 2249 A7
400 EUCL 44132 2374 A1
400 WKLF 44092 2374 B2
Lloyd Peterson Ln
3500 CLEV 44111 2752 D2
Locherie Av
18500 CLEV 44119 2372 E4
18500 EUCL 44119 2372 E4
19300 EUCL 44119 2373 A4
19300 EUCL 44123 2373 A4
Loch Lomond Ct
6100 SLN 44139 2889 E4
Lochmoor Ct
- SLN 44139 2890 A4
6200 SLN 44139 2889 E4
Lochmoor Dr
38700 SLN 44139 2889 E4
39100 SLN 44139 2890 A4
Lochness Dr
7100 CcdT 44077 2146 A7
Lochspur Ln
10 MDHL 44022 2760 A5
Locke Av
12200 CLEV 44108 2496 D4
Lockhaven Dr
6300 BKPK 44142 2881 C4
Locklie Dr
400 HDHT 44143 2499 D2
Lockridge
- CcdT 44077 2146 A7
Lockwood Av
1600 ECLE 44112 2496 E7
N Lockwood Av
1100 ECLE 44112 2496 E7
Lockwood Dr
6400 MNTR 44060 2144 A4
Lockwood Ln
400 BHIT 44212 3146 A7
Lockwood Ovl
1700 TNBG 44087 3154 B1
Lockwood Rd
4300 NPRY 44081 1940 C3
5000 MadT 44057 1941 C3
5000 MadT 44081 1941 A3
5000 NPRY 44081 1941 A3
Lockwood St
10 GNVA 44041 1944 A5
Lockyear Av
7100 CLEV 44103 2495 E7
7200 CLEV 44103 2496 A7
Locust Cir
7600 SgHT 44067 3017 C7
7600 SgHT 44067 3152 D1
Locust Ct
4200 INDE 44131 2884 C4
Locust Dr
9100 ODFL 44138 3010 A1
N Locust Dr
8200 KTLD 44094 2377 A5
S Locust Dr
8200 KTLD 44094 2377 A5
Locust Ln
10 CNFL 44022 2761 A5
22500 RKRV 44116 2621 A6
Locust St
10 OBLN 44074 3138 E3
100 ELYR 44035 2875 B6
Locust Grove Dr
- MadT 44057 1941 B5
10000 HmbT 44024 2381 A5
Lodge Dr
3000 NRYN 44133 3014 C7
Logan Ct
9700 CLEV 44106 2626 B2
16300 SGVL 44136 3012 B4
31000 WTLK 44145 2619 B7
Logan Dr
6200 SVHL 44131 2884 A4
6500 MDBH 44130 2881 D4
18000 WNHL 44146 3017 E2
Logan Ln
10200 TNBG 44087 3019 D3
Logan St
100 BDFD 44146 2887 A3
S Logan St
100 ELYR 44035 2875 D6
Loganberry Dr
26600 RDHT 44143 2373 E6
26600 RDHT 44143 2374 A6
Loganberry Ovl
800 MDSN 44057 1942 A7
Logans Wy
3900 PRRY 44081 2042 B2
Log Cabin Ct
10200 BKVL 44141 3151 D5
Lois Ln
10 HmbT 44024 2380 E3
10 HmbT 44024 2381 A3
Lola Ct
10200 CcdT 44077 2253 D1
Lola Ln
- NRYN 44133 3014 C5
Loma Ct
- CLEV 44105 2756 A1
Lombardo Ctr
5700 INDE 44131 2884 C2

STREET
Block City ZIP Map# Grid

Lombardy Dr
200 BERA 44017 2880 A5
Lombardy Ln
33600 PRPK 44124 2760 A1
Lomond Blvd
16600 SRHT 44120 2757 C1
17600 SRHT 44122 2757 C1
19600 SRHT 44122 2758 A1
London Av
15300 CLEV 44135 2752 C5
London Rd
700 CLEV 44110 2497 C2
900 CLEV 44112 2497 D2
Long Av
900 LORN 44052 2614 D7
1300 LORN 44052 2744 E1
Long Dr
400 AbnT 44023 2892 B3
Long Rd
200 MCDN 44056 3018 B5
3300 AVON 44011 2747 C4
Long St
300 AMHT 44001 2872 D1
Longano Dr
5800 INDE 44131 2885 A2
7300 INDE 44131 2884 E3
Longbeach Pkwy
300 BYVL 44140 2619 D4
Long Boat Cir
13000 NRYN 44133 3147 D4
13000 SGVL 44133 3147 D4
13000 SGVL 44136 3147 D4
Longbrook Dr
- NRDV 44039 2877 D7
8900 MCDN 44056 3018 E7
Longbrook Rd
4600 LORN 44053 2743 C5
19100 WVHT 44128 2757 E4
19800 WVHT 44128 2758 A4
Long Cove
- AVLK 44012 2618 B3
Longfellow Av
5500 CLEV 44103 2625 D3
Longfellow Dr
500 BERA 44017 2880 B5
Longfellow St
100 ELYR 44035 2875 D5
Longford Av
100 ELYR 44035 2875 D5
Long Forest Dr
8000 BKVL 44141 3015 E6
Longhorn Rd
7500 MNTR 44060 2143 D6
Longitude Ln
- AMHT 44001 2872 E3
Longleaf Rd
4400 WVHT 44128 2758 D5
Longman Ln
24500 WVHT 44128 2758 D5
Longmead Av
11700 BKLN 44144 2753 A5
11700 CLEV 44135 2753 A5
11700 CLEV 44144 2753 A5
Longmeadow Ln
10 BHWD 44122 2628 D5
10 BHWD 44122 2629 A4
Long Meadow Tr
17200 BbgT 44023 2891 C4
Long Pointe Dr
300 AVLK 44012 2618 E3
Long Ridge Dr
200 SVHL 44131 2883 E1
200 SVHL 44131 2884 A2
Longridge Rd
6300 MDHT 44124 2629 E2
6500 MDHT 44124 2630 A2
Longson Av
300 ELYR 44035 2875 D7
Long Spur Ct
13300 VLVW 44125 2885 E6
13300 VLVW 44125 2886 A6
Longspur Rd
200 HDHT 44143 2499 E2
Longton Rd
5100 LNHT 44124 2628 E1
5100 LNHT 44124 2629 A1
Longvale Rd
15300 MPHT 44137 2886 B4
15400 BDFD 44146 2886 B4
Longview Av
7200 MNTR 44060 2144 E6
7200 MNTR 44060 2252 D1
18700 MPHT 44137 2757 E7
Longview Dr
6900 SLN 44139 2888 D7
7900 BWHT 44131 3015 A2
7900 BWHT 44147 3015 A3
7900 SVHL 44131 3015 A2
10200 KTLD 44094 2376 A5
10300 WBHL 44094 2376 A5
Longview Tr
10500 AbnT 44023 2892 D5
14700 NbyT 44065 2764 D1
Longwood Av
3500 CLEV 44115 2625 C4
3700 PRMA 44134 2883 B3
3900 CLEV 44104 2625 C4
4800 PRMA 44129 2883 A3
5600 MPHT 44137 2886 C2
13000 BtnT 44021 2635 D7
Longwood Ct
- CVHT 44118 2497 E7
Longwood Dr
10 CNFL 44022 2761 B4
900 MCDN 44056 3018 E5
1500 MDHT 44124 2499 B7
1500 MDHT 44124 2629 C1
1600 LNHT 44124 2629 C2
Longwood Rd
1000 AURA 44202 3022 A6
Lonna Ct
3900 CLEV 44111 2752 C3
Lonsdale Pl
- WLBY 44094 2142 E5
Lookout Cir
18700 FWPK 44126 2752 A1
Lookout Ct
300 AVLK 44012 2618 E3
Lookout Dr
- BbgT 44023 2890 B4
- LORN 44052 2614 E7
9800 BKVL 44141 3150 C4
Loop Rd
2500 CLEV 44113 2624 C4

Lorain Av
1600 CLEV 44113 2624 D5
3100 VMLN 44089 2741 E4
3100 VMLN 44089 2742 A4
3700 LORN 44055 2745 C4
4400 CLEV 44102 2624 A6
9200 CLEV 44102 2623 D7
9900 CLEV 44111 2623 C7
10600 CLEV 44111 2753 A1
13200 CLEV 44111 2752 B2
18000 FWPK 44111 2752 A2
18000 FWPK 44126 2752 A2
Lorain Av SR-10
2000 CLEV 44113 2624 C5
4400 CLEV 44102 2624 A6
7100 CLEV 44102 2623 D7
9900 CLEV 44111 2623 C7
10600 CLEV 44111 2753 A1
13200 CLEV 44111 2752 B2
18000 FWPK 44111 2752 A2
18000 FWPK 44126 2752 A2
Lorain Blvd
- ELYR 44035 2875 A2
100 ELYR 44035 2874 E2
6000 EyrT 44035 2745 E6
6000 ShfT 44035 2745 E6
6000 ShfT 44055 2745 E6
6200 ELYR 44035 2745 E6
Lorain Blvd SR-57
- ELYR 44035 2875 A2
1700 ELYR 44035 2874 E2
6000 EyrT 44035 2745 E6
6000 ShfT 44035 2745 E6
6000 ShfT 44055 2745 E6
6200 ELYR 44035 2745 E6
Lorain Ct
- CLEV 44102 2624 B6
4100 CLEV 44113 2624 B6
12800 CLEV 44111 2753 A1
13100 CLEV 44111 2752 E1
Lorain Dr
2100 LORN 44052 2744 B1
Lorain Rd
18800 FWPK 44126 2751 A4
18800 FWPK 44126 2752 A2
22900 NOSD 44070 2751 A4
22900 NOSD 44126 2751 A4
23200 NOSD 44070 2750 A7
27300 NOSD 44070 2749 E7
28200 NOSD 44070 2878 D1
31400 NRDV 44039 2878 A3
31400 NRDV 44070 2878 A3
31600 NRDV 44039 2877 E4
34900 NRDV 44039 3008 A1
Lorain Rd SR-10
- NRDV 44039 2877 E4
18800 FWPK 44126 2751 A4
18800 FWPK 44126 2752 A2
22900 NOSD 44070 2751 A4
22900 NOSD 44126 2751 A4
23200 NOSD 44070 2750 A7
27300 NOSD 44070 2749 E7
28200 NOSD 44070 2878 D1
31400 NRDV 44039 2878 A3
31400 NRDV 44070 2878 A3
Lorain Rd SR-17
- NOSD 44070 2750 A7
27300 NOSD 44070 2749 E7
Lorain Rd SR-252
24600 NOSD 44070 2750 C6
Lorain St
16600 BbgT 44023 2890 B1
E Lorain St
10 OBLN 44074 3138 E2
200 OBLN 44074 3139 B2
600 NRsT 44074 3139 B2
E Lorain St SR-511
10 OBLN 44074 3138 E2
200 OBLN 44074 3139 B2
600 NRsT 44074 3139 B2
W Lorain St
10 OBLN 44074 3138 C2
300 NRsT 44074 3138 C2
W Lorain St SR-511
10 OBLN 44074 3138 C2
300 NRsT 44074 3138 C2
Loren Av
9100 CLEV 44105 2756 B2
Lorenzo Av
13000 CLEV 44120 2626 E7
13400 CLEV 44120 2627 A7
Loreta Dr
5300 WBHL 44094 2376 A5
Loreto Dr
2700 WBHL 44094 2376 A6
2800 WBHL 44094 2375 E6
Loreto Landing Dr
4200 PryT 44081 1940 C7
Loreto Ridge Dr
10200 KTLD 44094 2377 C5
Loretta Av
9700 CLEV 44102 2753 C1
9900 CLEV 44111 2753 C1
Loretta Ct
2900 LORN 44052 2744 C3
Lori Dr
5500 BDHT 44146 2887 C2
23000 BDFD 44146 2887 C2
Lori Ln
7700 BbgT 44202 3021 D3
33000 ETLK 44095 2249 E6
Lori Ann Dr
33400 ETLK 44095 2249 E5
Loriann Dr
1400 BERA 44017 2879 C6
1400 ODFL 44017 2879 C6
1400 ODFL 44138 2879 C6
Lorie Blvd
37500 AVON 44011 2617 C7
Lorient Dr
4600 WVHT 44128 2758 C5
Lori Jean Dr
9200 MNTR 44060 2144 E7
Lorimer Rd
1300 PRMA 44134 2883 D3
Loring Dr
10 AQLA 44024 2505 D4
Loripat Dr
5600 BWHT 44147 3015 D4
Loris Av
11000 ManT 44255 3158 A4
Lorraine Dr
8300 SGVL 44149 3010 E3
22200 SGVL 44149 3011 A2

Lorrey Pl
5300 MNTR 44060 2038 E7
5400 MNTR 44060 2144 D1
Lorrich Dr
9100 MNTR 44060 2144 E1
Lost Cr
- NCtT 44236 3153 E6
Lost Tr
17700 BbgT 44023 2891 B6
Lost Elm Rd
- CrlT 44074 3139 E2
Lost Lakes Tr
9800 AbnT 44023 2892 A1
Lost Nation Rd
1000 WLBY 44094 2143 A6
2100 WLBY 44094 2142 E7
2200 ETLK 44094 2142 E7
2200 ETLK 44095 2142 E7
2200 WLBY 44095 2142 E7
2400 ETLK 44095 2250 E2
2400 WLBY 44094 2250 E2
2400 WLBY 44095 2250 E2
Lost Pond Dr
9400 TNBG 44087 3019 D6
Lost Pond Pkwy
300 CRDN 44024 2505 A2
Lotus Dr
14800 CLEV 44128 2757 B4
18100 CLEV 44122 2757 D3
S Lotus Dr
16000 CLEV 44128 2757 C3
Lotus Ln
3200 SVHL 44131 3015 B1
7400 MNTR 44060 2143 C3
Lotusdale Dr
5800 PMHT 44130 2882 D2
5800 PRMA 44130 2882 D2
Louann Dr
6500 NOSD 44070 2878 E3
Louden Ct
100 ELYR 44035 3006 B2
Lou Groza Blvd
10 BERA 44017 2880 C5
10 BERA 44130 2880 C4
10 MDBH 44130 2880 C4
Louis Av
5300 EyrT 44035 2745 C6
5300 EyrT 44055 2745 C6
5300 ShfT 44055 2745 C6
15200 CLEV 44135 2752 C6
Louis Ct
7700 MNTR 44060 2251 D3
Louis Dr
10 MDHT 44124 2629 D3
10 PRPK 44124 2629 D3
500 BERA 44017 2880 D5
500 BERA 44130 2880 D5
500 MDBH 44130 2880 D5
5800 NOSD 44070 2879 A2
15800 NRYN 44133 3148 B2
Louis Rd
3600 BWHT 44147 3015 C4
21800 BDHT 44146 2758 B7
21800 MPHT 44137 2758 B7
Louis St
33200 ETLK 44095 2249 E5
Louisa Ct
5000 CLEV 44127 2625 D6
Louise Dr
10 SRSL 44022 2762 C6
5600 MNTR 44060 2144 B2
27700 SLN 44139 2759 A7
Louise Ln
23000 ClbT 44028 3145 E2
23000 ClbT 44149 3145 E2
23000 SGVL 44149 3145 E2
Louisiana Av
100 ELYR 44035 2875 A4
200 LORN 44052 2615 B5
300 ELYR 44035 2874 E4
3000 CLEV 44109 2754 C3
Lourdes Dr
1100 PRMA 44134 2883 E6
Loveland Ct
10 GNVA 44041 1944 C3
Loveland Rd
- MadT 44057 2043 E7
- MadT 44057 2044 A7
E Loveland Rd
- MadT 44057 2044 A7
W Loveland Rd
5300 MadT 44057 2043 D7
Lovett Pl
800 LORN 44052 2614 D7
Low St
100 CNFL 44022 2761 A5
Lowden Rd
4000 SELD 44121 2498 A4
Lowell Av
3200 LORN 44055 2745 B4
3200 ShfT 44055 2745 B4
9300 CLEV 44108 2496 B5
Lowell Dr
300 HDHT 44143 2499 D2
Lowell Ln
8900 NCtT 44067 3152 E3
8900 NCtT 44067 3153 A3
Lowell Rd
3700 CVHT 44121 2497 E5
Lowell St
100 ELYR 44035 2875 A5
200 ELYR 44035 2874 C5
1200 EyrT 44035 2874 C5
Lower Dr
- CLEV 44135 2880 E1
Lower Ter
20000 EUCL 44117 2498 A1
Lower Chelsea Dr
11500 MsnT 44024 2504 B2
Lownesdale Rd
3300 CVHT 44112 2497 D6
Low Ridge Ln
7700 MNTR 44060 2252 C3
7800 KDHL 44060 2252 C3
Lowrie Blvd
10 NHFD 44067 3018 A3
200 NHFD 44067 3017 E3
Loxley Dr
5100 RDHT 44143 2499 A3
Loya Pkwy
5200 PRMA 44129 2883 B4
5200 PRMA 44134 2883 B4
Loyola Dr
100 ELYR 44035 2746 D6
5400 PRMA 44129 2883 A4

Loyola Dr
5400 PRMA 44134 2883 A4
Loyola Rd
2200 UNHT 44118 2628 B4
Luanna Dr
1500 ETLK 44095 2249 E5
Luanne Dr
33900 NRDV 44039 2877 C1
Luary Dr
200 PNVL 44077 2146 A2
Lucas Ct
4600 ELYR 44035 2746 B7
Lucerne Av
2700 PRMA 44134 2883 C2
6600 CLEV 44103 2625 E2
Lucerne Dr
7500 MDBH 44130 3012 B1
8200 BbgT 44023 2891 A3
Lucerne Ln
20300 SGVL 44149 3146 C5
Lucia Av
7900 CLEV 44104 2626 A3
Lucille Av
300 PNVL 44077 2145 E3
300 PNVL 44077 2146 A3
4100 SELD 44121 2498 B6
5800 BKPK 44142 2880 A1
15900 CLEV 44111 2752 B2
Lucille Dr
600 ELYR 44035 2875 D3
23700 NOSD 44070 2750 D6
Lucinda Ct
- LORN 44053 2743 D3
Lucknow Av
14900 CLEV 44110 2372 B7
Lucky Bell Ln
16000 AbnT 44023 2763 A7
16000 AbnT 44065 2763 A7
16000 NbyT 44065 2763 A6
16400 AbnT 44023 2892 A2
Lucretia Ct
7600 MNTR 44060 2251 E2
Lucy Dr
9400 PMHT 44130 2882 C2
Lucy Ln
10 NCtT 44067 3017 E7
Lucydale Av
5000 NOSD 44070 2750 A7
Ludgate Rd
3500 SRHT 44120 2757 B2
Ludlow Rd
2800 CLEV 44120 2626 E5
2800 CLEV 44120 2627 A6
2900 SRHT 44120 2627 A6
Ludwin Dr
7400 SVHL 44131 3015 C1
Luelda Av
5400 PRMA 44134 2754 A7
6700 PRMA 44129 2753 E7
6700 PRMA 44129 2754 A7
Luempert Memorial Dr
900 BWHT 44147 3014 E6
Lufkin Av
5500 CLEV 44127 2625 D7
Luikart Dr
10 EUCL 44123 2373 C1
Luke Av
11600 CLEV 44104 2626 D7
11600 CLEV 44120 2626 D7
Lullaby Cir
400 AMHT 44001 2744 A7
Luman Ln
10100 TNBG 44087 3020 A4
Lunn Rd
19000 SGVL 44136 3146 D1
19000 SGVL 44149 3146 B1
Lunn Rd W
21000 SGVL 44149 3146 A2
W Lunn Rd
- ClbT 44028 3145 E2
- ClbT 44149 3145 E2
22500 SGVL 44149 3145 E2
22500 SGVL 44149 3146 A2
Luoem Tr
9100 MNTR 44060 2144 E2
Lupine Dr
7700 MNTR 44060 2143 D5
Lusandra Cir
27300 NOSD 44070 2749 E5
27300 NOSD 44070 2750 A5
Lusard St
10 PNVL 44077 2146 B1
Luther Av
4900 CLEV 44103 2625 D1
Luvison Dr
- SVHL 44131 2884 B2
Luxona Av
29300 WKLF 44092 2374 D4
Luxor Ln
100 AMHT 44001 2744 B7
Luxor Rd
1500 ECLE 44112 2497 A7
1500 ECLE 44112 2627 A1
1500 ECLE 44118 2497 A7
1500 ECLE 44118 2627 A1
Lydgate Dr
3900 NOSD 44070 2750 B5
Lydia Cir
- NRDV 44035 2876 B7
Lydia Dr
2700 BWHT 44147 3014 C6
Lydia Rd
14000 ClbT 44028 3009 B7
Lydian Av
15100 CLEV 44111 2752 C2
Lydian Ct
3500 CLEV 44111 2752 C2
Lyle Av
6800 PRMA 44134 2883 C6
Lyman Blvd
23100 SRHT 44118 2628 C5
23100 SRHT 44122 2628 C5
24100 BHWD 44122 2628 D6
Lyman Cir
- SRHT 44122 2628 C6
300 BNWK 44212 3147 A7
Lyman Rd
11600 CsTp 44026 2502 A3
Lyman's Ln
19300 SGVL 44149 3011 D7
Lyme Cir
400 BERA 44017 3010 E1
S Lyn Cir
1300 SELD 44121 2498 D7

Lynbrook Dr
7200 OKWD 44146 2887 E7
Lynch Av
10 PNVL 44077 2040 A6
Lynd Av
5000 LNHT 44124 2498 E5
5000 LNHT 44124 2499 A5
Lyndale Dr
10 CNFL 44022 2761 A5
Lyndale Rd
10 PnvT 44077 2041 B4
Lynde Dr
27200 OmsT 44138 3009 C1
Lynden Dr
400 HDHT 44143 2499 D2
Lynden Ovl
10000 PMHT 44130 2882 C4
Lyndhurst Rd
1400 LNHT 44124 2499 B7
1400 LNHT 44124 2629 B1
Lyndway Dr
12100 VLVW 44125 2885 D6
Lyndway Rd
2100 BHWD 44121 2628 C3
2100 BHWD 44122 2628 D4
2100 SELD 44121 2628 C3
Lynett Dr
6600 PRMA 44129 2882 E6
Lynford Cir
5800 HDHT 44143 2499 C5
Lynford Wy
- MNTR 44060 2252 A3
Lynhaven Dr
28400 NOSD 44070 2878 D1
Lynhurst Dr
8500 OmsT 44138 2878 D7
Lynn Dr
2900 WBHL 44092 2374 C7
9900 NRYN 44133 3013 B3
12700 CsTp 44026 2502 A7
12700 CsTp 44026 2632 A1
27100 OmsT 44138 2878 C6
Lynn Rd
400 BERA 44017 2880 A7
400 BERA 44017 3011 A1
Lynne Dr
- TwbT 44236 3154 D5
200 SDLK 44054 2617 A3
7800 TwbT 44087 3154 D5
Lynnfield Rd
3400 SRHT 44122 2757 E1
Lynnhaven Rd
8600 PMHT 44130 2882 D4
Lynn Park Dr
1300 CVHT 44121 2497 E7
Lynnview Dr
300 SgHT 44067 3017 C7
Lynton Ln
31800 SLN 44139 3019 D1
Lynton Rd
18200 SRHT 44122 2627 D7
Lynway Av
8000 ODFL 44138 2879 B6
Lyon Ln
17700 SGVL 44149 3146 D4
Lyons Av
4100 WLBY 44094 2250 D5
Lyons Gate Run
33500 AVON 44011 2748 D5
Lyonswood Dr
400 HkyT 44233 3149 B7
Lyric Av
13800 CLEV 44111 2752 E3
Lytham Cir
30800 WTLK 44145 2749 A6
Lytle Rd
3500 SRHT 44122 2758 A2
19400 NRYN 44133 3148 A5
19600 HkyT 44133 3148 A5
19600 HkyT 44233 3148 A5
Lytton Av
14700 CLEV 44110 2372 B7

M

Mabel Ct
3000 CLEV 44113 2624 C5
Macauley Av
15200 CLEV 44110 2372 B7
Macbeth Av
22000 FWPK 44126 2751 A5
22900 NOSD 44070 2750 E5
22900 NOSD 44070 2751 A5
22900 NOSD 44126 2751 A5
Macbeth Dr
2900 RKRV 44116 2621 E7
Mace Ct
1100 CLEV 44109 2624 E7
Macedonia Rd
7300 OKWD 44146 3018 D2
7500 MCDN 44056 3018 D3
7500 MCDN 44146 3018 D3
Macedonia Commons Blvd
6400 MCDN 44056 3153 C1
Machinery Av
6700 CLEV 44103 2495 E6
Macintosh Dr
3000 WTLK 44145 2749 E3
Macintosh Ln
1100 BWHT 44147 3149 E5
Mack Ct
3700 CLEV 44109 2754 C2
Mack Dr
5600 LvpT 44280 3145 D7
Mackall Rd
4400 SELD 44121 2628 C3
Mackenzie Dr
6000 INDE 44131 3015 D1
Mackert Av
- SFLD 44054 2617 A6
Macomb Av
8600 CLEV 44105 2756 B4
Macon Av
9500 CLEV 44102 2623 D7
Macon Ct
2100 WTLK 44145 2749 B1
Maddock Rd
7300 NRDV 44039 2876 D5
Maddock St
2100 ShfT 44055 2745 E6
Madison Av
- AVLK 44012 2617 C4
100 ELYR 44035 2874 E4
600 PNVL 44077 2040 C7
600 PnvT 44077 2040 D7

Madison Av
1200 PnvT 44077 2041 A7
1300 LORN 44053 2614 A7
1300 LORN 44053 2744 B1
1500 PryT 44077 2041 B7
2500 PryT 44081 2041 C7
4100 WLBY 44094 2250 D5
4800 SDLK 44054 2616 D3
5800 CLEV 44102 2624 A6
6400 NRDV 44039 2877 D3
6700 MadT 44057 1843 C7
6800 CLEV 44102 2623 C6
11600 LKWD 44102 2623 B6
11600 LKWD 44107 2623 A6
13300 LKWD 44107 2622 D6
Madison Ct
10 BHWD 44122 2629 A4
7800 CLEV 44103 2626 A3
Madison Ln
9400 NRYN 44133 3013 C5
Madison Rd
15900 MdfT 44062 2767 E7
15900 PkmT 44062 2767 E7
Madison Rd SR-528
15900 MdfT 44062 2767 E7
15900 PkmT 44062 2767 E7
Magdala Dr
10800 PRMA 44130 2882 B1
Magee Av
2000 LKWD 44107 2623 A6
Magnet Av
5300 CLEV 44127 2625 D7
Magnolia Av
10 BDFD 44146 2886 E3
10 MCDN 44056 3018 B4
10 NHFD 44067 3018 B4
Magnolia Dr
10 CLEV 44110 2372 C5
500 PNVL 44077 2146 A2
1600 CLEV 44106 2626 C1
2000 RKRV 44116 2621 D7
3300 SVHL 44131 2884 B7
3600 BNWK 44212 3147 A6
3700 BNWK 44212 3146 E6
4100 BHIT 44212 3146 D6
4300 PryT 44081 1940 C7
6000 MNTR 44060 2143 C3
6000 MONT 44060 2143 C3
6500 MadT 44057 1843 B7
7300 SVHL 44131 3015 B1
9900 ODFL 44138 3010 A1
26300 EUCL 44132 2373 E5
26300 EUCL 44143 2373 E5
28300 NOSD 44070 2878 D3
Magnolia Ln
600 AbnT 44023 2892 B4
31900 AVLK 44012 2618 D3
37800 AVON 44011 2617 C6
Magnolia Ovlk
5300 INDE 44131 2884 C6
Magnolia Pkwy
4200 WTLK 44145 2749 C5
Magnolia Wy
3300 BWHT 44147 3014 C7
Mahoning Av
100 CLEV 44113 2625 A5
Maiden Ln
8700 MNTR 44060 2038 D5
Maidstone Dr
4700 BKVL 44141 3016 D5
9700 CcdT 44060 2145 B7
Maidstone Ln
24300 BHWD 44122 2628 D4
Maile Av
1400 LKWD 44107 2622 A5
Maile Ct
10 MadT 44057 1941 B5
Main Av
1000 CLEV 44113 2624 D3
4800 AVON 44011 2748 D6
4800 NRDV 44011 2748 D6
4800 NRDV 44039 2748 D7
5400 NRDV 44039 2877 D1
W Main Ct
1000 GNVA 44041 1944 A3
1000 GnvT 44041 1944 A4
Main Dr
- AhtT 44001 2872 B2
Main St
- MDBH 44017 3011 D1
- MNTR 44060 2144 E7
10 WTLK 44145 2749 C1
100 CRDN 44024 2380 A6
100 PNVL 44077 2040 C6
200 BERA 44017 3011 C1
300 EatT 44044 3141 E3
300 GFTN 44044 3141 E3
300 GFTN 44044 3142 B6
400 VMLN 44089 2740 E5
1100 GftT 44044 3142 B6
3300 PRRY 44081 2041 E2
3300 PRRY 44081 2042 C3
3300 PryT 44081 2041 E2
4200 PryT 44081 2042 C4
5800 BosT 44141 3152 C7
7400 GSML 44040 2630 D1
7600 ODFL 44138 2879 C5
10400 MNTU 44255 3159 C6
10400 ShvT 44255 3159 C7
11700 NbyT 44065 2764 D1
17900 MDBH 44130 3012 A2
17900 SGVL 44130 3012 A2
17900 SGVL 44149 3012 A2
18000 MDBH 44130 3011 D2
18000 SGVL 44130 3011 D2
18000 SGVL 44149 3011 D2
Main St SR-44
100 CRDN 44024 2380 A6
10400 MNTU 44255 3159 C6
10400 ShvT 44255 3159 C7
Main St SR-57
300 EatT 44044 3141 E3
300 GFTN 44044 3141 E3
300 GFTN 44044 3142 B6
1100 GftT 44044 3142 B6
Main St SR-60
600 VMLN 44089 2740 E5
Main St SR-252
7900 ODFL 44138 2879 C6
Main St US-6
100 CRDN 44024 2380 A6
E Main St
10 GNVA 44041 1944 C3
10 MDSN 44057 2044 C1
100 SAHT 44001 2872 C7

E Main St
200 PNVL 44077 2040 B7
300 AhtT 44001 2872 C7
300 PNVL 44077 2146 C1
400 MadT 44057 2044 D1
500 PnvT 44077 2040 C7
900 GnvT 44041 1944 C3
E Main St SR-84
10 MDSN 44057 2044 C1
400 MadT 44057 2044 D1
E Main St SR-113
100 SAHT 44001 2872 C7
300 AhtT 44001 2872 C7
E Main St US-20
10 GNVA 44041 1944 C3
900 GnvT 44041 1944 C3
N Main St
10 CNFL 44022 2761 A5
10 OBLN 44074 3138 E2
100 AMHT 44001 2872 D1
200 CNFL 44022 2760 E4
200 NRsT 44074 3138 E2
300 CFIT 44022 2760 E4
500 AMHT 44001 2743 D5
1300 AMHT 44053 2743 D5
1300 LORN 44001 2743 D5
1300 LORN 44053 2743 D5
N Main St SR-58
10 OBLN 44074 3138 E2
200 NRsT 44074 3138 E2
S Main St
10 CNFL 44022 2761 A6
10 OBLN 44074 3138 E3
100 AMHT 44001 2872 D3
100 BbgT 44022 2761 A7
100 CyhC 44022 2761 A7
300 NRsT 44074 3138 E3
S Main St SR-58
10 OBLN 44074 3138 E3
300 NRsT 44074 3138 E3
W Main St
10 GNVA 44041 1944 A4
10 MDSN 44057 2044 A1
100 SAHT 44001 2872 B7
400 SAHT 44001 3003 A1
500 NRsT 44001 3003 A1
700 MadT 44057 2043 E2
700 MDSN 44057 2043 E2
1000 GnvT 44041 1944 A4
W Main St SR-84
10 MDSN 44057 2044 A1
700 MadT 44057 2043 E2
700 MDSN 44057 2043 E2
W Main St SR-113
100 SAHT 44001 2872 B7
400 SAHT 44001 3003 A1
500 NRsT 44001 3003 A1
W Main St SR-528
10 MDSN 44057 2044 B1
W Main St US-20
10 GNVA 44041 1944 A4
1000 GnvT 44041 1944 A4
Maine Av
200 LORN 44052 2615 B5
2800 PryT 44077 2041 C4
2800 PryT 44081 2041 D4
Main Hill Dr
4600 SVHL 44131 3015 B1
Majestic Pkwy
5300 BDHT 44146 2887 D1
Majestic Oaks Dr
16400 BbgT 44023 2761 E7
16400 BbgT 44023 2890 E1
Majestic Oaks Tr
7900 BWHT 44147 3015 B3
Majesty Ln
10500 CcdT 44077 2253 E4
Major Dr
20200 EUCL 44117 2498 A2
Malabar Ct
7200 MNTR 44060 2143 B4
Malachite Ct
- CcdT 44077 2254 D3
Malden Rd
2300 CLEV 44121 2497 E3
2400 CLEV 44121 2498 A3
Malibu Dr
7400 PRMA 44130 2882 A7
7400 PRMA 44130 3013 B1
Malin Dr
5800 BKPK 44142 2880 A1
W Mall Dr
1300 CLEV 44114 2624 C2
Mallard Av
26100 EUCL 44132 2373 E1
26800 EUCL 44132 2374 A1
Mallard Cir
4400 WTLK 44145 2749 B5
8700 NRDV 44039 2877 D7
18100 SGVL 44136 3146 E2
Mallard Ct
- MDFD 44062 2767 B1
- RMDV 44202 3020 D3
5800 MNTR 44060 2144 E2
18700 MDBH 44130 3011 E1
Mallard Dr
600 ELYR 44035 2874 D2
1500 MDHT 44124 2629 C1
6700 BKVL 44141 3150 D2
E Mallard Dr
1200 MDSN 44057 1942 A6
W Mallard Dr
1000 MDSN 44057 1942 A6
Mallard Run
- SFLD 44054 2746 C3
Mallard Bay
3900 PRRY 44081 2042 B1
Mallard Cove
1400 TNBG 44087 3019 B4
4200 AVON 44011 2748 C5
30500 WTLK 44145 2749 B5
Mallard Creek Run
100 CrlT 44050 3140 C2
6300 LORN 44053 2743 B4
Mallard Pointe
9200 BbgT 44023 3022 D2
S Mallard Pond Cir
1300 BWHT 44147 3149 E5
Mallo Pl
6300 PMHT 44130 2882 C4
Malone Av
5200 SFLD 44054 2746 D4
Malvern Av
19200 RKRV 44116 2621 E6

STREET Block	City	ZIP	Map#	Grid
Malvern Dr				
400	PNVL	44077	2146	A3
3400	BNWK	44212	3147	B6
9000	PRMA	44129	2882	D1
11100	NRYN	44133	3013	D5
Malvern Rd				
19700	SRHT	44122	2627	E6
19700	SRHT	44122	2628	A6
Manassas Ovl				
1100	PRMA	44134	2883	E7
Manatee Av				
1300	MadT	44057	1843	C6
Manchester Av				
3900	PRRY	44081	2042	B1
4300	PryT	44081	2042	D1
Manchester Ct				
100	MDSN	44057	2044	C2
200	ELYR	44035	2874	B7
300	RDHT	44143	2498	E1
Manchester Dr				
10	AURA	44202	3021	E7
12700	CsTp	44026	2501	C7
12800	CsTp	44026	2631	C1
Manchester Ln				
2300	AVON	44011	2748	B1
31000	BYVL	44140	2619	A3
Manchester Rd				
2800	SRHT	44122	2627	E6
6000	PRMA	44129	2882	E3
Manchester St				
5000	NRDV	44039	2748	A7
Mandalay Av				
15700	CLEV	44110	2497	C3
Mandalay Dr				
6200	PMHT	44130	2882	A4
6200	PRMA	44130	2882	A3
Mandell Dr				
8400	MCDN	44056	3018	B6
Manderly Ln				
10	MDHL	44022	2760	C4
Mangrove Ln				
26700	ODFL	44138	3010	A1
Manhasset Dr				
30300	BYVL	44140	2619	B3
Manhattan Av				
1400	ECLE	44112	2497	A5
7300	PRMA	44129	2753	E7
Manhattan Dr				
5500	LORN	44053	2743	C5
Manhattan Pkwy				
300	PnvT	44077	2041	B6
Mann Av				
13300	ECLE	44112	2497	A4
Mannering Dr				
600	ETLK	44095	2249	E3
Mannering Rd				
1800	CLEV	44112	2497	C3
Mannheim Ct				
7500	HDSN	44236	3154	C6
Manning Cir				
5300	NRDV	44039	2748	A7
Manning Dr				
10	BERA	44017	3011	B2
Manoa Av				
10000	BKLN	44144	2753	C4
Manor Av				
9000	CLEV	44104	2626	B6
Manor Ct				
8900	MCDN	44056	3018	B5
Manor Dr				
6800	EyrT	44035	2874	B2
7400	MONT	44060	2143	D3
13000	MsnT	44024	2635	A2
Manorbrook Dr				
100	SRSL	44022	2762	A5
500	SRSL	44022	2761	E5
Manorford Dr				
-	PMHT	44129	2882	C4
7800	PRMA	44129	2882	C4
8700	PMHT	44130	2882	C4
Manor Gate Wy				
-	MNTR	44060	2252	A2
Manor Park Av				
1200	LKWD	44107	2622	D4
Manry Ct				
7500	MNTR	44060	2143	D5
Mansfield Av				
8000	CLEV	44105	2756	A1
Mansfield Ct				
10	CcdT	44060	2145	C6
Mansfield St				
800	SDLK	44054	2616	A4
Mansion Blvd				
8400	MNTR	44060	2144	B5
Mantle Rd				
10	PnvT	44077	2040	C5
Mantle Rd Ext				
10	PnvT	44077	2040	C5
Mantua Center Rd				
10800	ManT	44255	3159	A4
10800	MNTU	44255	3159	A4
Manufacturing Rd				
4500	CLEV	44135	2752	B6
Maple Av				
-	EUCL	44132	2374	A2
-	HIHL	44128	2758	C4
-	NRDV	44039	2877	D3
-	SFLD	44054	2616	D3
-	WKLF	44092	2374	A2
-	WVHT	44128	2758	C4
10	NHFD	44067	3018	A4
100	CRDN	44024	2380	A5
300	AMHT	44001	2872	D2
300	BERA	44017	2880	C6
300	SDLK	44054	2616	D3
1000	MadT	44057	1843	E6
10600	MNTU	44255	3159	C6
12400	CLEV	44108	2496	E3
14000	GDHT	44125	2757	A7
14000	GDHT	44137	2757	A7
14000	MPHT	44137	2757	A7
14800	MDFD	44062	2767	C2
E Maple Av				
4500	GnvT	44041	1944	C1
W Maple Av				
5300	GnvT	44041	1944	B1
6300	GnvT	44041	1943	C1
6300	GnvT	44057	1943	C1
6300	MadT	44057	1943	C1
Maple Cir				
13800	SGVL	44136	3147	D4
Maple Ct				
10	OmsT	44138	2879	B4
500	MCDN	44056	3153	C2
Maple Dr				
10	OmsT	44138	2879	B4
1000	PRMA	44131	2883	E7
1000	PRMA	44134	2883	E7
1000	SVHL	44131	2883	E7
1200	LORN	44052	2615	D6
2500	TNBG	44087	3154	E1
8200	CsTp	44026	2502	A6
11100	NbyT	44065	2634	C7
17000	BbgT	44023	2891	A3
22500	FWPK	44126	2751	A6
26600	WTLK	44145	2750	A2
30400	BYVL	44140	2619	B4
33900	SLN	44139	2889	A3
36000	NRDV	44039	2876	E4
36000	NRDV	44039	2877	A4
Maple Ln				
10	AURA	44202	3156	E1
10	CNFL	44022	2761	A5
4600	NRYN	44133	3014	A6
Maple Rd				
1400	CVHT	44121	2497	E7
1500	CVHT	44118	2627	E1
1500	CVHT	44121	2527	E1
1900	SELD	44118	2627	E2
4100	LORN	44055	2745	C5
Maple St				
-	AhtT	44001	2872	B3
10	CLEV	44110	2372	C6
10	CNFL	44022	2760	E6
10	CNFL	44022	2761	A6
10	OBLN	44074	3138	E1
100	SAHT	44001	2872	A7
200	SAHT	44001	3003	A1
400	VMLN	44089	2741	A4
500	BDHT	44146	2758	D7
1500	WKLF	44092	2374	B3
4100	PRRY	44081	2042	C4
4300	PryT	44081	2042	C4
4600	WLBY	44094	2250	D6
7000	MNTR	44060	2144	B7
7200	MNTR	44060	2252	B1
7600	KTLD	44094	2251	D7
20900	SGVL	44149	3011	B3
45900	NRsT	44074	3138	E1
S Maple St				
300	ELYR	44035	3006	A2
Mapleboro Av				
16800	MPHT	44137	2886	C1
Maple Branch Tr				
10000	SGVL	44149	3011	A4
Maplebrook Dr				
10	PnvT	44077	2041	B7
Maple Brook Tr				
13100	SGVL	44136	3012	D4
Maple Cliff Dr				
1000	LKWD	44107	2622	B3
Maplecliff Dr				
10	AVLK	44012	2488	B7
5900	PMHT	44130	2882	C2
Maplecliff Rd				
17900	CLEV	44119	2372	D4
Maple Creek Dr				
500	AMHT	44001	2872	B3
Maplecrest Av				
3700	PRMA	44134	2883	B3
4800	PRMA	44129	2883	A3
6400	PMHT	44130	2882	B4
Maplecrest Rd				
3600	WDMR	44122	2759	A2
Mapledale Av				
10	BDFD	44146	2886	E4
2600	CLEV	44109	2754	C2
Mapledale Rd				
1500	WKLF	44092	2249	E7
1500	WKLF	44092	2374	E1
1500	WKLF	44094	2249	E7
1500	WLBY	44094	2249	E7
7900	MNTR	44060	2143	E4
Mapledale St				
-	RMDV	44202	3021	A5
Maple Glen Dr				
8600	CdnT	44024	2254	E6
Maplegrove Av				
4500	NRYN	44133	3014	B3
Maple Grove Dr				
7500	CsTp	44026	2631	C3
Maplegrove Dr				
1600	TNBG	44087	3019	B7
Maplegrove Ln				
100	MNTR	44060	2144	D7
Maplegrove Rd				
1400	SELD	44121	2498	B7
1400	SELD	44121	2628	B1
34600	WLBY	44094	2375	B3
35400	WBHL	44094	2375	B3
Maple Grove Marina				
-	VMLN	44089	2741	B6
Maple Heights Blvd				
15900	MPHT	44137	2886	D1
19300	MPHT	44137	2757	E7
20000	MPHT	44137	2758	A7
Maple Highlands Tr				
-	CdnT	44024	2379	D1
Maple Hill Dr				
10	SRSL	44022	2762	D6
4000	SVHL	44131	3015	B2
Maplehurst Rd				
6500	NOSD	44070	2878	D3
6700	OmsT	44070	2878	D3
6700	OmsT	44138	2878	D3
Maplelane Dr				
10	GNVA	44041	1944	C6
Maplelawn Dr				
100	BERA	44017	3011	C3
Maple Leaf Dr				
12400	GDHT	44125	2885	E2
13500	GDHT	44125	2886	A2
Maple Leaf Ln				
4800	INDE	44131	2884	C5
Maple Leap Ter				
12000	CsTp	44026	2503	A5
Maple Park Dr				
15200	MPHT	44137	2886	B3
Maple Ridge Blvd				
33600	AVON	44011	2748	C4
Mapleridge Dr				
11500	NRYN	44133	3013	D6
Maple Ridge Rd				
22900	NOSD	44070	2751	A4
23700	NOSD	44070	2750	C3
23700	NOSD	44145	2750	C3
23700	WTLK	44070	2750	C3
23700	WTLK	44145	2750	C3
Mapleridge Rd				
10	SRSL	44022	2761	C6
Maplerow Av				
12500	GDHT	44105	2756	E4
13100	GDHT	44105	2757	A4
14000	CLEV	44105	2757	A4
14000	CLEV	44128	2757	A4
14000	GDHT	44128	2757	A4
Mapleside Rd				
2300	CLEV	44104	2626	C4
Maple Springs Dr				
5200	SRSL	44022	2762	A6
Mapleton Av				
10	BDFD	44146	2886	D4
Mapleview Av				
-	SFLD	44054	2616	E3
200	SDLK	44054	2616	E3
Maple View Dr				
4400	BhmT	44089	2741	B7
4600	LrnC	44089	2741	B7
4600	VMLN	44089	2741	A7
Mapleview Dr				
10	PRMA	44131	2883	E5
10	PRMA	44134	2883	E5
10	SVHL	44131	2883	E5
10	SVHL	44131	2884	A5
Mapleview Ln				
2400	WBHL	44094	2375	C3
2800	AVON	44011	2747	E3
Mapleview Rd				
400	MCDN	44056	3018	D4
Mapleway Dr				
7500	ODFL	44138	2879	B6
7500	OmsT	44138	2879	B5
Maplewood Av				
400	SDLK	44054	2616	C4
500	BNWK	44212	3147	C7
800	PnvT	44077	2040	C2
15300	MPHT	44137	2886	B2
18500	CLEV	44135	2751	E6
21000	RKRV	44116	2621	C5
24100	EUCL	44123	2373	D2
Maplewood Cir				
32900	AVLK	44012	2617	E3
Maplewood Ct				
200	PNVL	44077	2146	A2
5300	SFLD	44054	2746	E1
16200	MPHT	44137	2886	C2
Maplewood Dr				
-	ELYR	44035	2745	E7
400	WLWK	44095	2249	B7
7500	GNWL	44139	3019	B2
14600	BtnT	44021	2766	E5
Maplewood Ln				
18800	BbgT	44023	3022	A2
Maplewood Rd				
-	ELYR	44035	2745	E7
-	ELYR	44035	2746	A7
2100	CVHT	44118	2627	B3
5900	MNTR	44060	2143	B3
5900	MONT	44060	2143	B3
6000	MDHT	44124	2499	E7
6500	MDHT	44124	2500	A7
6700	PMHT	44130	2881	E5
6900	PRMA	44130	2881	E6
11600	MsnT	44024	2504	C3
Marah Av				
9300	CLEV	44104	2626	B7
Marberry Coms				
22000	BDHT	44146	2887	B1
Marble Av				
7600	CLEV	44105	2756	A2
Marble Ct				
-	BERA	44138	2879	E6
Marble Ln				
5600	WLBY	44094	2375	A1
Marblehead Dr				
7200	HDSN	44236	3154	E7
N Marblehead Rd				
7400	HDSN	44236	3154	E7
Marbrook Ln				
500	AVLK	44012	2618	D4
Marcella Rd				
17800	CLEV	44119	2372	D5
Marcelline Ct				
7100	CHHT	44125	2755	E6
Marchmont Ct				
400	BNWK	44212	3146	E7
Marchmont Rd				
19600	SRHT	44122	2627	E7
19800	SRHT	44122	2628	A7
Marcie Dr				
800	CLEV	44109	2754	E6
4600	CLEV	44109	2755	A6
Marcie Ln				
27200	NOSD	44070	2750	A5
Marcum Blvd				
2900	WBHL	44092	2375	A7
2900	WBHL	44094	2375	A7
Marcus Dr				
4300	SFLD	44054	2616	B7
Marda Dr				
2500	PRMA	44134	2883	C6
Mardale Av				
5200	BDHT	44146	2887	B1
Marden Dr				
8400	RslT	44072	2762	A1
Mardon Ct				
10400	CcdT	44077	2145	E5
Mardon Dr				
6200	CcdT	44077	2145	E4
6200	PnvT	44077	2145	E4
Mardun Ct				
100	CrlT	44035	3006	C3
Marengo Dr				
700	BNHT	44131	2755	B7
Marewood Pl				
-	CcdT	44077	2254	C2
Margaret Av				
15900	LKWD	44107	2622	B6
Margaret Dr				
-	NRYN	44133	3013	D6
-	VMLN	44089	2741	C7
Margaretta Dr				
2800	WTLK	44145	2750	B3
Margaret Walsh Ct				
-	WLBY	44094	2251	A1
Margate Av				
15600	CLEV	44135	2752	C5
Margie Ln				
32200	AVLK	44012	2618	C4
N Marginal Dr				
-	CLEV	44102	2623	D7
-	CLEV	44111	2623	C7
-	LKWD	44107	2622	B6
31500	WLWK	44092	2249	D7
31500	WLWK	44095	2249	D7
31900	ETLK	44095	2249	D7
S Marginal Dr				
-	CLEV	44102	2623	D7
-	CLEV	44111	2622	C7
-	CLEV	44111	2623	C7
-	LKWD	44107	2622	C7
-	LKWD	44111	2622	C7
N Marginal Rd				
-	CLEV	44108	2496	A4
900	CLEV	44114	2624	E1
1300	CLEV	44114	2495	C7
1300	CLEV	44114	2625	A1
5500	CLEV	44103	2495	D5
7300	CLEV	44103	2496	A4
31200	WLWK	44092	2249	D7
31200	WLWK	44095	2249	D7
S Marginal Rd				
900	CLEV	44114	2624	E2
1100	CLEV	44114	2625	A1
2400	CLEV	44114	2495	B7
5400	CLEV	44103	2495	D6
Margot Ct				
25000	BHWD	44122	2628	E3
Marguerite Av				
12000	GDHT	44125	2756	D6
Marguerite Ct				
-	MNTR	44060	2143	E4
Maria Av				
100	BDFD	44146	2886	D3
Maria Ln				
24100	NOSD	44070	2750	D4
Marian Cir				
21800	FWPK	44126	2751	B5
Marian Dr				
5200	LNHT	44124	2499	A6
Marian Ln				
100	BERA	44017	2880	B7
20200	RKRV	44116	2621	D7
Marian Rd				
-	EatT	44028	3008	D4
Mariana Dr				
6200	PMHT	44130	2882	A4
6200	PRMA	44130	2882	A3
Marianna Blvd				
8100	BWHT	44147	3015	C4
Marie Av				
3000	LORN	44052	2744	D3
Marietta Av				
1600	PRMA	44134	2883	E1
9800	CLEV	44102	2623	C6
Marietta Dr				
900	PNVL	44077	2145	E3
Marigold Blvd				
9400	NRDV	44039	3008	D1
Marigold Rd				
4600	MNTR	44060	2038	E6
Marilyn Av				
10	MadT	44057	1844	A6
Marilyn Ln				
100	ETLK	44095	2142	C7
Marilyn Rd				
12900	CsTp	44026	2632	A2
Marina Dr				
4300	BhmT	44089	2741	B7
4300	VMLN	44089	2741	B7
W Marina Dr				
200	LORN	44052	2614	E6
E Marina Pkwy				
200	LORN	44052	2614	E6
Marine Pkwy				
5500	MONT	44060	2143	E2
6000	MNTR	44060	2143	E3
Marine St				
600	FTHR	44077	2039	C4
Mariner Dr				
13000	NRYN	44133	3147	E4
Mariner Ln				
-	LORN	44052	2614	E7
Mariners Ct				
32600	AVLK	44012	2618	A3
Mariners Wy				
200	LORN	44054	2615	D4
200	SDLK	44054	2615	D4
Marion Av				
200	PNVL	44077	2146	B2
Marion Dr				
200	BDFD	44146	2887	B3
7200	MNTR	44060	2144	C7
7200	MNTR	44060	2252	C1
Marion Pkwy				
2800	BNWK	44212	3147	D7
Marion Rd				
23000	NOSD	44070	2750	E3
23000	NOSD	44070	2751	A3
23300	NOSD	44145	2750	E3
23300	WTLK	44070	2750	E3
23300	WTLK	44145	2750	E3
Marion St				
-	SDLK	44054	2616	A4
5300	MPHT	44137	2886	B1
Marioncliff Dr				
2600	PRMA	44134	2883	C2
Maritime Ct				
31700	AVLK	44012	2619	A3
Marjory Dr				
8600	MNTR	44060	2144	C2
Mark Av				
3900	FWPK	44116	2751	D2
3900	FWPK	44126	2751	D2
3900	RKRV	44116	2751	D2
Mark Ct				
10	OmsT	44138	2879	B4
4700	NRDV	44039	2877	B2
30400	WKLF	44092	2374	E1
Mark Dr				
1900	LORN	44053	2744	B2
2000	LORN	44052	2744	B2
3400	BWHT	44147	3015	B4
6000	BDHT	44146	2887	E4
Mark Ter				
4100	CLEV	44128	2757	C3
Markal Dr				
7200	MDBH	44130	2881	A7
Markbarry Av				
27200	EUCL	44132	2374	A1
27400	EUCL	44092	2374	A1
27400	WKLF	44092	2374	A1
Markell Rd				
7200	WTHL	44094	2251	C7
7200	WTHL	44094	2376	B1
7400	WLBY	44094	2251	C7
7500	KTLD	44094	2251	D6
Market Av				
-	CLEV	44113	2624	D5
Market Dr				
100	ELYR	44035	2875	A3
Market Pl				
9100	BKVL	44141	3015	B7
9100	BKVL	44147	3015	B7
9100	BWHT	44147	3015	B7
Market Pl W				
9100	BKVL	44141	3015	B7
9100	BKVL	44147	3015	B7
9100	BWHT	44147	3015	B7
Market St				
100	WTLK	44145	2749	C1
8400	MNTR	44060	2144	B5
Market Place Dr				
7000	BbgT	44023	3021	A2
7000	BbgT	44202	3021	A3
Marko Ln				
10	BNHT	44131	2755	A7
7100	PRMA	44134	2883	C7
Marks Rd				
10	BHIT	44149	3145	E6
10	BHIT	44212	3145	E6
10	ClbT	44028	3145	E6
10	ClbT	44149	3145	E6
10	LvpT	44028	3145	E6
10	LvpT	44149	3145	E6
10	LvpT	44212	3145	E6
10	LvpT	44280	3145	E6
10	SGVL	44149	3145	E6
N Marks Rd				
8000	BERA	44017	3010	E2
8000	ClbT	44017	3010	E2
8000	ClbT	44028	3010	E4
8000	ClbT	44138	3010	E2
8000	ClbT	44149	3010	E4
8000	ODFL	44017	3010	E2
8000	ODFL	44138	3010	E2
8000	SGVL	44017	3010	E2
8000	SGVL	44149	3010	E4
S Marks Rd				
14100	ClbT	44028	3010	E7
14100	ClbT	44149	3010	E7
14100	ClbT	44149	3145	E4
14100	SGVL	44149	3010	E7
14100	SGVL	44149	3145	E3
17600	ClbT	44028	3145	E5
18700	BHIT	44149	3145	E5
18700	BHIT	44212	3145	E5
18700	LvpT	44028	3145	E5
18700	LvpT	44149	3145	E5
18700	LvpT	44212	3145	E5
18700	LvpT	44280	3145	E5
Markwood Dr				
8300	MNTR	44060	2144	B2
Marlboro Ct				
-	MAYF	44143	2500	A5
Marlboro Rd				
2400	CVHT	44118	2627	B4
Marlborough				
-	VMLN	44089	2741	E5
Marlborough Av				
7300	PRMA	44129	2753	E7
Marlborough Rd				
-	VMLN	44089	2741	E4
Marlee Ct				
100	BHIT	44212	3146	C6
Marleen Dr				
22100	FWPK	44126	2751	A5
Marlene Av				
15200	CLEV	44135	2752	C6
Marlin Dr				
13700	HmbT	44024	2381	B1
Marlindale Rd				
1900	CVHT	44118	2627	D2
Marlo Dr				
6100	CcdT	44077	2146	A3
Marloes Av				
1800	ECLE	44112	2497	B6
Marlow Av				
-	SFLD	44054	2615	E5
Marlowe Av				
1100	LKWD	44107	2622	D5
10300	CLEV	44108	2496	C4
Marlys Dr				
22400	RKRV	44116	2751	A2
Marmore Av				
2800	PRMA	44134	2754	C7
Marne Av				
11700	CLEV	44111	2753	A2
Marnell Av				
5700	MDHT	44124	2629	C1
Marnell Dr				
6100	GnvT	44041	1943	E1
Maroy Dr				
100	SAHT	44001	2872	C6
Maroy St				
100	SAHT	44001	2872	C6
Marquardt Av				
500	CLEV	44113	2625	A6
Marquette Blvd				
4200	NOSD	44070	2749	E5
Marquette Rd				
1000	CLEV	44114	2495	D6
1300	CLEV	44103	2495	D7
Marquis Av				
16200	CLEV	44111	2752	B1
Marra Dr				
5800	BDHT	44146	2887	D3
Mars Av				
1400	LKWD	44107	2622	C5
Mars Dr				
3800	BNWK	44212	3146	E7
3800	BNWK	44212	3147	A7
Marsdon Dr				
25100	EUCL	44123	2373	D2
25100	EUCL	44132	2373	D2
Marseilles Av				
100	ELYR	44035	2875	D5
Marsh Ln				
1800	PnvT	44077	2041	A3
Marsh Pl				
6000	NRDV	44039	2877	E2
Marsh Wy				
500	BHIT	44212	3146	C7
500	BNWK	44212	3146	C7
Marsha Ln				
1200	LORN	44052	2615	C6
Marshall Av				
2300	LORN	44052	2744	B2
2800	LORN	44053	2744	B2
8800	CLEV	44104	2626	B7
Marshall Dr				
800	PNVL	44077	2146	B3
Marshfield Blvd				
1900	WTLK	44145	2749	A1
Marshfield Rd				
1900	MDHT	44124	2629	E3
Marsh Harbor Ct				
17600	NRYN	44133	3148	B4
Marsh Hawk Run				
9400	CsTp	44026	2632	E3
9400	CsTp	44026	2633	A3
Marshview Ln				
-	MNTR	44060	2144	C1
Marsol Rd				
6100	MDHT	44124	2629	E1
6500	MDHT	44124	2630	A1
Marston Av				
12300	CLEV	44105	2756	E3
13400	CLEV	44105	2757	A3
Martha Av				
10	GnvT	44041	1944	E3
10	MadT	44057	1844	A6
Martha Ct				
100	ELYR	44035	2874	A7
Martha Dr				
11400	CrlT	44035	3006	C5
11400	CrlT	44044	3006	C5
Martha Rd				
16900	CLEV	44135	2752	B5
Martin Av				
4300	CLEV	44127	2625	C6
5400	VMLN	44089	2740	E6
E Martin Av				
100	AMHT	44001	2872	D1
W Martin Av				
100	AMHT	44001	2872	C1
Martin Dr				
-	LORN	44053	2743	D2
4200	NOSD	44070	2749	D6
12900	MDBH	44130	3012	E1
12900	PRMA	44130	3012	E1
13600	GDHT	44125	2886	A3
15300	NRYN	44133	3148	B1
Martin Rd				
8800	KTLD	44094	2377	D1
34900	WBHL	44094	2375	A6
Martingale Ct				
10	BTVL	44022	2889	E1
Martingale Dr				
7300	CsTp	44026	2501	B5
Martingale Ln				
8300	RslT	44072	2762	A1
Martinique Dr				
9600	CcdT	44060	2253	B1
Martin Luther King Jr Blvd				
-	CLEV	44105	2756	E4
4400	GDHT	44105	2756	E5
Martin Luther King Jr Ct				
-	HIHL	44128	2758	C4
Martin Luther King Jr Dr				
-	CLEV	44106	2496	A5
-	CLEV	44106	2626	C1
-	CVHT	44104	2626	D4
-	CVHT	44106	2626	D4
800	CLEV	44103	2496	A6
800	CLEV	44108	2496	B7
2400	CLEV	44104	2626	D5
2400	CLEV	44120	2626	D5
3300	CLEV	44104	2756	D1
3300	CLEV	44105	2756	D3
4300	GDHT	44105	2756	E4
Martins Ln				
18100	SGVL	44149	3146	D4
Martins Wy				
21600	FWPK	44126	2751	B2
21600	RKRV	44116	2751	B2
21600	RKRV	44126	2751	B2
Martins Run Dr				
-	LORN	44053	2743	D3
Martin's Run Dr				
3700	LORN	44053	2743	E3
Marview Dr				
1300	WTLK	44145	2620	B7
Marvin Av				
200	GNVA	44041	1944	B5
2500	CLEV	44109	2754	B1
4500	CLEV	44102	2754	B1
Marvin Rd				
19100	WVHT	44128	2757	E6
19800	WVHT	44128	2758	A6
Marvis Dr				
500	BYVL	44140	2619	A5
Marwell Blvd				
1700	TwbT	44236	3154	D5
Marwood Av				
19400	CLEV	44135	2751	D4
Marwyck Dr				
10	NCtT	44067	3153	A3
200	NCtT	44067	3152	E3
200	SgHT	44067	3152	E3
Marwyck Place Ln				
100	NCtT	44067	3153	A3
Mary Ct				
-	CLEV	44113	2625	A6
Mary Ln				
7600	MNTR	44060	2252	A2
N Mary Ln				
2100	SVHL	44131	2884	B6
S Mary Ln				
2100	SVHL	44131	2884	B6
Mary Ann Dr				
13800	GDHT	44125	2757	A7
Mary Clarke Dr				
38400	WLBY	44094	2251	A1
Marydale Dr				
11900	AbnT	44021	2764	E7
Mary Dale St				
35600	WLBY	44094	2375	B1
Marygate Dr				
500	BYVL	44140	2619	C5
Mary Kay Cir				
4100	NOSD	44070	2749	E5
Maryland Av				
1300	LORN	44052	2615	B6
3400	WDMR	44122	2759	B2
7600	CLEV	44105	2756	A4
10400	RMDV	44202	3020	E4
10500	RMDV	44139	3020	E4
10500	SLN	44139	3020	E4
Marymac Dr				
11800	SgHT	44067	3017	C3
11900	SgHT	44146	3017	C3
11900	WNHL	44146	3017	C3
E Mason Rd				
11300	FrnT	44089	2869	A7
11300	FrnT	44889	2869	A7
12700	VmnT	44089	2869	E5
12700	VmnT	44889	2869	B7
16300	BhmT	44089	2870	A5
16300	VmnT	44089	2870	A5
Masonic Al				
10	CNFL	44022	2761	B7
Massachusetts Av				
100	ELYR	44035	3006	B3
200	LORN	44052	2615	B5
Massie Av				
10500	CLEV	44108	2496	C6
Masters Ln				
500	AVLK	44012	2618	C4
Mastick Rd				
20000	FWPK	44126	2751	A6
22900	NOSD	44070	2751	A6
22900	NOSD	44126	2751	A6
23000	NOSD	44070	2750	D7
Mataire Ln				
10100	SGVL	44136	3012	B4
Mather Ln				
100	BTNH	44108	2496	E2
45000	HGVL	44022	2631	A7
47700	RslT	44022	2631	A7
47700	RslT	44072	2631	A7
W Mather Ln				
10	BTNH	44108	2496	D2
Mather's Wy				
2700	TNBG	44087	3020	B3
Matherson Av				
11700	CLEV	44135	2753	A4
11700	LNDL	44135	2753	B4
Mathews Av				
1200	LKWD	44107	2622	A5
Mathews St				
100	PNVL	44077	2146	A1
Matilda Av				
11200	CLEV	44105	2756	D2
Matoma Blvd				
35700	ETLK	44095	2142	B7
Mats Rd				
-	MNTU	44255	3159	C6
Matthew Ct				
9100	MNTR	44060	2144	E6
Matthews Cor				
10	OmsT	44138	2879	A4
Maud St				
800	CLEV	44103	2496	A6
Maureen Dr				
5700	SVHL	44131	2884	B2
Maurer Dr				
3300	LORN	44053	2744	C3
9600	OmsT	44138	3009	C1
9700	ClbT	44028	3009	C2
9700	ClbT	44138	3009	C2
Maurice Av				
5500	CLEV	44127	2625	D6
Maury Av				
8700	CLEV	44108	2496	B5
Mavec Av				
24300	EUCL	44123	2373	D4
Mavreen Dr				
15700	MDBH	44130	2881	B6
Maxim Ct				
8300	CLEV	44102	2623	E6
Maxwell Av				
13600	CLEV	44110	2497	A2
Maxwell Dr				
6100	MadT	44057	1941	E1
6200	MadT	44057	1942	A1
May Av				
10	NHFD	44067	3017	E4
10	NHFD	44067	3018	A4
3700	CLEV	44105	2755	C1
May Ct				
10	CNFL	44022	2761	A6
May St				
33300	NRDV	44039	2748	D7
Mayapple Cir				
6800	SLN	44139	2889	B7
Mayapple Dr				
2000	PnvT	44077	2041	A3
Mayapple Pl				
10200	BWHT	44147	3149	E4
Maybelle Dr				
23100	WTLK	44145	2620	E7
23100	WTLK	44145	2621	A7
Mayberry Av				
5900	MDHT	44124	2629	C1
Mayberry Dr				
7200	PRMA	44130	2882	C7
Maydale Av				
21500	EUCL	44123	2373	B3
Maydor Ln				
1300	SELD	44121	2498	D7
Mayfair Av				
13800	ECLE	44112	2497	A5
Mayfair Blvd				
1500	MDHT	44124	2499	B7
1500	MDHT	44124	2629	C1
Mayfair Dr				
-	BNWK	44212	3146	D7
1000	SVHL	44131	2884	A2
Mayfair Ln				
19100	WVHT	44122	2757	E4
19100	WVHT	44128	2757	E4
Mayfield Ct				
600	AMHT	44001	2872	C1
Mayfield Rd				
2500	CLEV	44106	2626	D2
2500	CVHT	44106	2626	E2
2500	CVHT	44106	2627	A2
2500	CVHT	44112	2627	A2
2700	CVHT	44118	2627	B1
3200	CVHT	44118	2497	D7
3400	CVHT	44121	2497	D7
3800	CVHT	44121	2498	A7
3900	SELD	44121	2498	E7
4600	LNHT	44121	2498	D7
4600	LNHT	44124	2498	D7
4700	SELD	44124	2498	D7
5000	LNHT	44124	2499	A7
5600	MDHT	44124	2499	D7
6500	MDHT	44124	2500	A7
6800	GSML	44040	2500	A7
7000	CsTp	44026	2501	B7
7000	GSML	44040	2501	A7
8100	CsTp	44026	2502	D7
9500	CsTp	44026	2503	A7
9700	MsnT	44026	2503	A7
9900	MsnT	44024	2503	A7
10800	MsnT	44024	2504	A7
11800	MsnT	44024	2505	A6
12400	ClrT	44024	2505	D6

Cleveland Street Index

STREET Block	City	ZIP	Map#	Grid
Mayfield Rd				
13400	ClrT	44024	2506	E6
13800	ClrT	44021	2506	B6
14400	ClrT	44046	2506	E6
14900	ClrT	44024	2507	A6
14900	ClrT	44046	2507	A6
15100	HtbT	44024	2507	B6
15100	HtbT	44046	2507	D6
15800	HtbT	44062	2507	D6
Mayfield Rd US-322				
2500	CLEV	44106	2626	D2
2500	CVHT	44106	2626	E2
2500	CVHT	44106	2627	A2
2500	CVHT	44112	2627	A2
2700	CVHT	44118	2627	B1
3200	CVHT	44118	2497	D7
3400	CVHT	44121	2497	D7
3800	CVHT	44121	2498	A7
3900	SELD	44121	2498	E7
4600	LNHT	44121	2498	D7
4600	LNHT	44124	2498	D7
4700	SELD	44124	2498	D7
5000	LNHT	44124	2499	A7
5600	MDHT	44124	2499	D7
6500	MDHT	44124	2500	A7
6800	GSML	44040	2500	A7
7000	CsTp	44026	2501	A7
7000	GSML	44040	2501	A7
8100	CsTp	44026	2502	D7
9500	CsTp	44026	2503	A7
9500	MsnT	44026	2503	A7
9900	MsnT	44024	2503	A7
10800	MsnT	44024	2504	A7
11800	MsnT	44024	2505	A6
12400	ClrT	44024	2505	D6
13400	ClrT	44024	2506	E6
13800	ClrT	44021	2506	B6
14400	ClrT	44046	2506	E6
14900	ClrT	44024	2507	A6
14900	ClrT	44046	2507	A6
15100	HtbT	44024	2507	B6
15100	HtbT	44046	2507	D6
15800	HtbT	44062	2507	D6
Mayfield St				
-	NCtT	44067	3153	B5
2100	LORN	44055	2745	E5
2100	ShfT	44055	2745	E5
2200	ShfT	44055	2746	A5
Mayfield Park Blvd				
-	MDHT	44124	2499	D7
Mayfield Ridge Rd				
1100	HDHT	44143	2499	C6
1100	MDHT	44124	2499	C7
1100	MDHT	44143	2499	C6
Mayflower Av				
5900	MDHT	44124	2629	C1
N Mayflower Dr				
5700	LORN	44053	2743	C6
S Mayflower Dr				
5700	LORN	44053	2743	C6
Mayflower Ln				
3700	SELD	44118	2627	E3
3700	SELD	44118	2628	A3
Mayfriars Dr				
37200	WBHL	44094	2375	D3
Mayland Av				
5900	MDHT	44124	2629	C1
Maynard Av				
1700	CLEV	44109	2754	D6
Maynard Rd				
3200	SRHT	44122	2627	E7
Maypine Farm Dr				
-	HDHT	44143	2499	D1
Maysday Av				
7100	PRMA	44129	2753	E7
Mayview Av				
1200	CLEV	44109	2754	D4
Mayview Ln				
7200	CsTp	44026	2501	B7
Mayview Rd				
5000	LNHT	44124	2498	E7
5000	LNHT	44124	2499	A7
Mayville Av				
5100	MPHT	44137	2757	E7
5300	MPHT	44137	2886	E1
Maywood Av				
8800	CLEV	44102	2753	D1
Maywood Rd				
1400	SELD	44121	2498	D7
1500	SELD	44121	2628	C1
Mazepa Tr				
1000	PRMA	44131	2883	E5
1000	PRMA	44134	2883	E5
1000	SVHL	44131	2883	E5
McAfee Dr				
33900	SLN	44139	2889	A1
McAlpin Ct				
1000	GFTN	44044	3141	E5
1000	GFTN	44044	3142	A5
McArthur Dr				
7300	NRDV	44039	2877	B4
McBride Av				
4900	CLEV	44127	2625	C7
McCann St				
22700	NRDL	44128	2758	C6
22700	WVHT	44128	2758	C6
McCauley Rd				
21900	SRHT	44122	2628	B6
McCausland Dr				
1500	TwbT	44236	3154	D5
McClaren Ln				
2000	BWHT	44147	3149	D5
McCleary Ct				
100	SgHT	44067	3017	E4
McCracken Blvd				
8800	GDHT	44125	2756	B7
McCracken Rd				
-	CLEV	44128	2757	C6
-	GDHT	44137	2757	A7
-	MPHT	44125	2757	A6
10800	GDHT	44125	2756	E7
13000	GDHT	44125	2757	A7
15400	GDHT	44128	2757	B6
15400	MPHT	44128	2757	B6
17000	MPHT	44137	2757	C6
18400	WVHT	44128	2757	C6
19800	MPHT	44128	2758	A6
19800	MPHT	44137	2758	A6
19800	WVHT	44128	2758	A6
McCreary Rd				
7500	SVHL	44131	3015	A2
7700	BWHT	44131	3015	B2
7700	BWHT	44147	3015	B2
McCurdy St				
2700	CLEV	44104	2626	B5
McDowell Dr				
37900	SLN	44139	2889	D7
McElhatten Av				
13600	BTNH	44110	2497	A1
13600	CLEV	44110	2497	A1
McFarland Rd				
4400	SELD	44121	2498	C5
4500	SELD	44143	2498	D5
McGhee Ln				
8000	TNBG	44087	3155	B5
8000	TwbT	44087	3155	B5
8000	TwbT	44236	3155	B5
McGowan Av				
11700	BKLN	44144	2753	A5
11700	CLEV	44144	2753	A5
12300	CLEV	44135	2753	A5
McGregor Av				
4200	NBGH	44105	2755	C3
McHadwick Dr				
-	AURA	44202	3157	A3
McIntosh Ln				
300	AMHT	44001	2743	B7
300	AMHT	44001	2872	B1
McKenzie Rd				
5400	NOSD	44070	2878	D2
6700	OmsT	44070	2878	D3
6700	OmsT	44138	2878	D3
McKinley Av				
2000	LKWD	44107	2622	B6
2000	ShfT	44055	2745	E6
2200	CLEV	44107	2622	B7
5500	NRDV	44039	2748	D7
5500	NRDV	44039	2877	D1
McKinley Dr				
9000	NHFD	44067	3017	E4
McKinley St				
600	BDFD	44146	2887	B4
2500	LORN	44052	2615	C5
5700	NRDV	44039	2877	D1
7400	MNTR	44060	2143	C7
McKinney Av				
4100	WLBY	44094	2250	D5
McLean Ct				
2500	CLEV	44113	2624	C5
McLellan Dr				
7300	WNHL	44146	3017	E2
McMackin Rd				
2000	MadT	44057	1941	B6
McMaster Ct				
400	SgHT	44067	3017	D4
McNally St				
-	RMDV	44202	3020	E4
McNeil Dr				
400	SgHT	44067	3152	D3
McPherson Cir				
500	SgHT	44067	3017	D4
McRoberts Av				
700	AURA	44202	3021	C4
McShu Ln				
7300	HDSN	44236	3155	A7
Mead Av				
4900	CLEV	44127	2625	D7
Mead Ct				
-	CLEV	44127	2625	D6
Meadow Cir				
100	BERA	44017	3011	A1
Meadow Dr				
10	BERA	44017	3011	B1
100	ELYR	44035	2875	D1
10000	CdnT	44024	2379	D4
N Meadow Dr				
6900	CcdT	44077	2145	C7
S Meadow Dr				
7000	CcdT	44077	2145	D7
7200	CcdT	44077	2253	D1
7300	CcdT	44060	2253	D1
Meadow Ln				
10	MCDN	44056	3018	A5
10	MCDN	44067	3018	A5
10	NHFD	44067	3018	A5
10	SgHT	44067	3018	A5
10	SLN	44139	2889	A1
300	CNFL	44022	2760	E7
400	PNVL	44077	2146	B1
2900	WTLK	44145	2750	C3
3100	NRYN	44133	3014	C5
3800	LORN	44055	2746	A4
5300	SFLD	44035	2746	E6
5500	BDHT	44146	2887	D2
6700	MDBH	44130	2881	B5
7100	PRMA	44134	2883	D7
7400	PRMA	44134	3014	C1
9100	BKVL	44141	3016	B4
10800	AbnT	44023	2893	A2
10900	AbnT	44023	2893	A3
13200	VmnT	44089	2869	B3
18000	SGVL	44136	3011	E6
18800	SGVL	44149	3011	E6
24400	ODFL	44138	2879	D7
24500	NOSD	44070	2750	D7
24500	WTLK	44070	2750	D3
33900	HGVL	44022	2760	A1
37000	AVON	44011	2747	D4
E Meadow Ln				
3900	ORNG	44122	2759	C3
S Meadow Ln				
4400	CLEV	44109	2754	E4
W Meadow Ln				
3900	ORNG	44122	2759	C3
Meadow St				
5300	MPHT	44137	2886	A1
29500	WKLF	44092	2374	C2
Meadow Tr				
-	ClbT	44028	3010	E4
-	ClbT	44149	3010	E4
10700	SGVL	44149	3010	E4
25500	ClbT	44028	3144	E2
Meadoway Dr				
2600	BHWD	44122	2628	E5
Meadowbrook				
600	AURA	44202	3022	B5
Meadowbrook Av				
6000	CLEV	44144	2754	A3
6300	BKLN	44144	2753	E3
6300	CLEV	44144	2753	E3
Meadowbrook Blvd				
2800	CVHT	44118	2627	B3
3500	UNHT	44118	2627	E4
3800	UNHT	44118	2628	A4
6700	INDE	44131	2884	E6
Meadowbrook Dr				
10	CrlT	44044	3006	D6
1100	AMHT	44001	2743	E6
3500	LORN	44053	2743	E6
6100	MNTR	44060	2143	D5
10600	PMHT	44130	2882	A6
12100	NbyT	44021	2765	A4
12500	PMHT	44130	2881	E6
30000	WBHL	44092	2374	D4
30000	WKLF	44092	2374	D4
Meadowbrook Pkwy				
-	PNVL	44077	2145	B2
Meadowbrook Rd				
6300	GDHT	44125	2885	E3
Meadow Brooke Wy				
7400	NCtT	44067	3153	E5
Meadow Creek Ln				
14200	CrlT	44050	3140	C5
14200	LrgT	44050	3140	C5
Meadow Creek Ovl				
32900	NRDV	44039	2748	E7
Meadow Creek Rd				
7300	SgHT	44067	3152	C2
Meadow Crest Cir				
10	HkyT	44233	3149	E6
Meadowdale Dr				
8000	MNTR	44060	2143	E4
8000	MNTR	44060	2144	A4
35600	SLN	44139	2889	C4
E Meadow Farm Ln				
-	LORN	44053	2743	B6
W Meadow Farm Ln				
-	LORN	44053	2743	B6
Meadowfield Ct				
100	ELYR	44035	2875	A1
Meadowgate Dr				
10	BDFD	44146	2887	A2
Meadow Gateway				
3000	BWHT	44147	3015	C5
Meadowgrass Rd				
10700	SGVL	44149	3011	A4
Meadowhill Ln				
10	MDHL	44022	2759	D4
22500	RKRV	44116	2621	A6
Meadowhurst Ln				
10300	MsnT	44024	2503	D1
Meadowlake Ct				
10000	CcdT	44060	2253	C2
Meadow Lakes Blvd				
-	NRDV	44039	2747	B7
-	NRDV	44039	2876	C2
Meadowlands Dr				
100	CRDN	44024	2379	D6
Meadowlane Dr				
500	RDHT	44143	2499	A3
30100	BYVL	44140	2619	C4
Meadowlane Rd				
10	PRMA	44131	3014	E2
10	PRMA	44134	3014	E2
10	SVHL	44131	3014	E2
10	SVHL	44131	3015	A2
Meadowlark Cir				
900	AURA	44202	3156	D4
Meadow Lark Dr				
-	LORN	44053	2743	D3
Meadowlark Ln				
13900	NbyT	44065	2634	B5
14800	MDFD	44062	2767	B2
19100	WVHT	44128	2757	E4
Meadowlark Rd				
600	PnvT	44077	2039	C6
Meadowlark Wy				
31600	PRPK	44124	2759	E1
Meadowlawn Blvd				
900	PRMA	44131	2883	E3
900	PRMA	44134	2883	E3
900	SVHL	44131	2883	E3
E Meadowlawn Blvd				
10	PRMA	44131	2883	D2
10	PRMA	44134	2883	D2
10	SVHL	44131	2883	D2
800	SVHL	44131	2884	A3
Meadowlawn Dr				
10	MNTR	44060	2252	D1
1300	MCDN	44056	3019	A6
7200	MNTR	44060	2144	E6
Meadow Moss Ln				
4800	NRDV	44039	2748	E7
Meadownorth Ct				
22100	SGVL	44149	3011	A4
Meadowood Blvd				
-	TNBG	44087	3020	A4
800	MDSN	44057	1942	A6
1700	TNBG	44087	3019	E3
Meadowood Dr				
600	MAYF	44040	2500	A4
600	MAYF	44143	2500	A4
N Meadowpark Dr				
7200	WNHL	44146	3017	C1
S Meadowpark Dr				
16800	WNHL	44146	3017	D2
Meadowridge Dr				
10	GNVA	44041	1944	C7
11600	CsTp	44026	2501	E4
Meadowridge Wy				
500	BSHT	44236	3153	E7
S Meadows Cir				
16900	SGVL	44136	3147	A2
Meadows Dr				
-	BKVL	44141	3016	B7
-	BKVL	44141	3151	C1
10	PnvT	44077	2040	E7
10	PnvT	44077	2146	E1
7200	INDE	44131	3015	D1
N Meadows Ln				
16900	SGVL	44136	3147	A2
Meadows Rd				
1600	MadT	44057	1842	E7
1700	MadT	44057	1941	E1
Meadows Edge Ln				
21300	SGVL	44149	3011	A5
Meadowsouth Ct				
22100	SGVL	44149	3011	A4
Meadowvale Av				
16500	CLEV	44128	2757	C5
Meadowview Dr				
200	NCtT	44067	3152	D2
200	SgHT	44067	3152	D2
407-00	AURA	44202	3156	D2
15400	MDFD	44062	2767	B1
30200	WKLF	44092	2374	D3
Meadowview Ln				
700	GSML	44040	2500	B5
700	MAYF	44040	2500	B5
1100	AMHT	44001	2743	E5
Meadow Wood Blvd				
5000	LNHT	44124	2628	E2
5100	LNHT	44124	2629	A2
Meadow Wood Dr				
6000	MadT	44057	1941	D2
11500	ClrT	44024	2505	C3
N Meadow Wood Dr				
-	MDFD	44062	2767	E1
Meadowwood Ln				
100	MDHL	44022	2759	D4
Meadow Woods Dr				
1100	MCDN	44056	3153	E1
Meadview Dr				
800	SVHL	44131	2884	A3
Meander Ln				
100	ELYR	44035	2874	A7
Meanderingwood Av				
6300	MadT	44057	1942	A2
Mechanic St				
800	GFTN	44044	3142	A6
Medfield Dr				
1000	RKRV	44116	2621	B6
Medfield Rd				
2800	PRPK	44124	2629	A5
Medford Rd				
800	CVHT	44121	2497	D5
Medhurst Av				
5000	ORNG	44022	2759	C7
5000	SLN	44022	2759	C7
5000	SLN	44139	2759	C7
Medina Av				
7900	CLEV	44103	2496	A6
Medina Frwy				
-	BKLN	-	2753	C3
-	BKPK	-	2752	B7
-	BKPK	-	2881	B1
-	BNWK	-	3147	B5
-	CLEV	-	2624	E7
-	CLEV	-	2752	D4
-	CLEV	-	2753	C3
-	CLEV	-	2754	B2
-	LNDL	-	2753	B3
-	MDBH	-	2881	B4
-	MDBH	-	3012	A1
-	SGVL	-	3012	A2
-	SGVL	-	3147	B1
Medina Frwy I-71				
-	BKLN	-	2753	C3
-	BKPK	-	2752	B7
-	BKPK	-	2881	B1
-	BNWK	-	3147	B5
-	CLEV	-	2624	E7
-	CLEV	-	2752	D4
-	CLEV	-	2753	A3
-	CLEV	-	2754	B2
-	LNDL	-	2753	B3
-	MDBH	-	2881	B4
-	MDBH	-	3012	A1
-	SGVL	-	3012	A2
-	SGVL	-	3147	B1
Medina St				
16600	BbgT	44023	2890	B1
Medusa Rd				
7500	OKWD	44146	3018	C2
Medway Rd				
300	HDHT	44143	2499	E2
Meech Av				
9300	CLEV	44105	2756	B2
Meecham St				
10	BERA	44017	2880	C7
Megan Ct				
9300	MNTR	44060	2145	A1
Mehling Ct				
4600	CLEV	44102	2624	B7
4600	CLEV	44109	2624	B7
Meigs Av				
300	GDRV	44077	2039	C6
600	PnvT	44077	2039	C6
Meigs Blvd				
15200	BKPK	44142	2881	C2
Meister Rd				
700	LORN	44052	2744	D3
700	LORN	44055	2744	D3
1100	LORN	44053	2744	A3
3600	LORN	44053	2743	E3
5500	MNTR	44060	2144	E1
Melba Av				
11100	CLEV	44104	2626	D6
11100	CLEV	44120	2626	D6
Melba St				
-	BDFD	44146	2887	C6
Melber Av				
7100	CLEV	44144	2753	E2
Melbourne Av				
3600	CLEV	44111	2752	C2
Melbourne Dr				
10	BNWK	44212	3147	A6
Melbourne Rd				
1100	ECLE	44112	2496	E7
3400	WDMR	44122	2759	B1
Melbury Av				
6300	SLN	44139	2888	E5
6300	SLN	44139	2889	A5
Meldon Blvd				
2700	BHWD	44122	2628	D6
Meldon Dr				
6100	MNTR	44060	2143	E4
Melgrave Av				
15700	CLEV	44135	2752	B3
Melgrove Av				
12600	GDHT	44105	2756	E5
Melgrove Ln				
-	AVON	44011	2747	B1
Melibee Dr				
25600	WTLK	44145	2750	B3
Melissa Ln				
22500	ClbT	44028	3010	E4
22500	ClbT	44149	3010	E4
22500	SGVL	44149	3010	E4
Mello Dr				
27600	GNWL	44139	3019	A1
Melody Ln				
3100	PRMA	44134	3014	C1
5000	WLBY	44094	2250	B7
5000	WLBY	44094	2375	B1
5800	MONT	44060	2250	B7
8200	MCDN	44056	3153	B1
8300	MCDN	44056	3018	B7
9500	BKLN	44144	2753	D6
12100	EatT	44044	3008	B7
12300	EatT	44044	3143	A1
Meloria Dr				
7900	MNTR	44060	2251	E3
Melridge Dr				
6600	CcdT	44077	2145	D6
Melrose Av				
7100	CLEV	44103	2625	E1
7600	CLEV	44103	2626	A1
Melrose Cir				
1500	WTLK	44145	2620	E7
Melrose Dr				
10	PnvT	44077	2145	C4
1000	WTLK	44145	2621	A6
E Melrose Dr				
1200	WTLK	44145	2621	A7
S Melrose Dr				
23100	WTLK	44145	2620	E7
23100	WTLK	44145	2621	A7
W Melrose Dr				
1200	WTLK	44145	2620	E7
1200	WTLK	44145	2621	A7
Melrose Ln				
-	BWHT	44147	3149	C3
Melrose Farms Dr				
-	WLBY	44094	2250	E2
-	WLBY	44094	2251	A2
Melshore Dr				
6100	MNTR	44060	2144	A5
Melville Rd				
18300	CLEV	44110	2372	E7
Melvyn Ln				
1000	ELYR	44035	3005	E1
Melzer Av				
13100	CLEV	44105	2756	E2
13100	CLEV	44120	2756	E2
13400	CLEV	44120	2757	A2
Memorial Dr				
-	BKPK	44142	2881	A3
-	BtnT	44021	2766	B2
-	BtnT	44062	2766	B2
300	CRDN	44024	2380	A5
Memory Ln				
500	BHIT	44212	3146	C7
900	VMLN	44089	2740	E6
1000	VMLN	44089	2741	A6
6500	MNTR	44060	2144	A5
9200	RslT	44072	2632	D7
24500	OmsT	44138	2879	C2
Memphis Av				
3400	CLEV	44109	2754	A4
4500	CLEV	44144	2754	A4
6500	BKLN	44144	2753	D4
6500	CLEV	44144	2753	D4
10400	LNDL	44111	2753	B3
10400	LNDL	44135	2753	B3
Memphis Villas S				
4500	BKLN	44144	2753	C5
Memphis Villas Blvd				
8600	BKLN	44144	2753	D4
Mencl Rd				
-	EatT	44044	3143	B1
Mendel Ct				
100	ELYR	44035	2875	A5
Mendelssohn Dr				
1300	WTLK	44145	2620	A7
1700	WTLK	44145	2750	B1
Mendota Av				
15500	MPHT	44137	2886	B4
15900	BDFD	44137	2886	B4
15900	BDFD	44146	2886	B4
Menlo Rd				
3400	SRHT	44120	2757	B1
Menlo Park Ln				
4000	VMLN	44089	2741	C4
Mennell Rd				
14300	GftT	44044	3142	C7
Mennonite Rd				
2600	AURA	44202	3157	E5
2600	AURA	44255	3157	E5
2600	ManT	44202	3157	E5
2600	ManT	44255	3157	E5
2600	ManT	44255	3158	E5
4000	MNTU	44255	3159	A5
5100	HrmT	44234	3160	A5
5100	HrmT	44255	3160	A5
5100	ManT	44234	3159	E5
5100	ManT	44234	3160	A5
5100	ManT	44255	3159	E5
5100	ManT	44255	3160	A5
E Mennonite Rd				
300	AURA	44202	3156	E4
300	AURA	44202	3157	D4
400	AURA	44255	3157	D4
800	ManT	44202	3157	E5
800	ManT	44255	3157	E5
W Mennonite Rd				
10	AURA	44202	3156	D4
Mentor Av				
10	PNVL	44077	2146	A1
500	PNVL	44077	2145	E2
1100	PnvT	44077	2145	D3
1200	CLEV	44113	2624	E6
2100	MNTR	44060	2145	E3
2100	PnvT	44077	2145	B6
7000	MNTR	44060	2251	E2
7000	MNTR	44094	2251	B4
7000	WLBY	44060	2251	B4
7000	WLBY	44094	2251	B4
8000	MNTR	44060	2252	A2
8700	MNTR	44060	2144	C7
38100	WLBY	44094	2250	E5
Mentor Av US-20				
100	PNVL	44077	2146	A1
500	PNVL	44077	2145	E2
1100	PnvT	44077	2145	D3
2100	MNTR	44060	2145	E3
2100	PnvT	44077	2145	B6
7000	MNTR	44060	2251	E2
7000	MNTR	44094	2251	B4
7000	WLBY	44060	2251	B4
7000	WLBY	44094	2251	B4
8000	MNTR	44060	2252	A2
8700	MNTR	44060	2144	C7
38100	WLBY	44094	2250	E5
Mentor Rd				
8500	CdnT	44060	2253	C7
8500	KDHL	44060	2253	C7
8900	CdnT	44024	2378	C1
8900	CdnT	44060	2378	C1
9300	CdnT	44024	2379	A3
10100	CRDN	44024	2379	C5
Mentor Harbor Blvd				
8100	MNTR	44060	2144	B1
8800	MNTR	44060	2038	D5
Mentor Hills Dr				
-	KDHL	44060	2252	A4
-	MNTR	44060	2252	A4
Mentor Marina				
-	MNTR	44060	2038	A7
-	MNTR	44060	2144	B1
-	MONT	44060	2038	A7
Mentor Park Blvd				
6100	MNTR	44060	2143	E4
6100	MONT	44060	2143	E4
Mentor Village Dr				
-	MNTR	44060	2251	E2
Mentorwood Dr				
8200	MNTR	44060	2144	A5
Mera Ct				
37300	SLN	44139	3020	C2
Mercantile Dr				
9200	MNTR	44060	2144	E4
9200	MNTR	44060	2145	A4
Mercantile Rd				
23000	BHWD	44122	2758	D2
Mercedes Av				
20000	RKRV	44116	2751	D1
Mercer Dr				
6000	BKPK	44142	2881	C2
Mercer Ln				
9000	BKVL	44141	3016	A4
Mercury Dr				
100	ELYR	44035	3005	C1
100	EyrT	44035	3005	C1
3100	NRYN	44133	3014	C6
Merece Dr				
18000	BKPK	44142	2881	A3
18100	BKPK	44142	2880	E3
Meredith Av				
18500	CLEV	44119	2372	E4
18500	EUCL	44119	2372	E4
19300	EUCL	44119	2373	A4
19300	EUCL	44123	2373	A4
Meredith Ln				
12200	CcdT	44077	2255	A4
Meriden Ct				
-	RMDV	44087	3020	D4
Meriden Rd				
100	PNVL	44077	2146	C2
Meridian Av				
8600	CLEV	44106	2626	B1
Meridian Ct				
400	AVLK	44012	2618	E3
Merimeade Dr				
15000	CLEV	44111	2752	C2
Merino Ln				
3000	TNBG	44087	3020	B6
Merion Ct				
7400	SLN	44139	3020	E2
Merit Dr				
10	RDHT	44143	2373	E7
10	RDHT	44143	2374	A7
Merkle Av				
5400	PRMA	44129	2754	A7
5400	PRMA	44134	2754	A7
Merl Av				
1500	CLEV	44109	2754	E6
13200	LKWD	44107	2622	E4
13200	LKWD	44107	2623	A4
Merlin Ln				
8900	MCDN	44056	3019	A7
Merlin Ovl				
14800	NRYN	44133	3148	A1
N Merlyn Pl				
7100	CcdT	44077	2146	A7
S Merlyn Pl				
7200	CcdT	44077	2146	A7
Merriam Ln				
10200	TNBG	44087	3020	B4
Merrie Ln				
8200	CsTp	44026	2502	A4
Merrill Av				
5900	CLEV	44102	2624	A7
Merrimak Dr				
400	BERA	44017	3010	E1
Merritt Rd				
12500	ClrT	44024	2635	B3
12500	MsnT	44024	2635	B3
Merrygold Blvd				
4400	WVHT	44128	2758	D5
Merrymound Rd				
3700	CVHT	44121	2497	E4
3700	SELD	44121	2497	E4
3700	SELD	44121	2498	A4
Merry Oaks Tr				
17400	BbgT	44023	2891	B4
Merryvale Dr				
8900	TNBG	44087	3154	B1
Mersey Ct				
10	CcdT	44060	2145	B7
Merwin Av				
1500	CLEV	44113	2624	D4
Messenger Rd				
15700	AbnT	44021	2764	C7
15700	NbyT	44021	2764	D7
15700	NbyT	44023	2764	C7
15700	NbyT	44065	2764	D7
16400	AbnT	44021	2893	B4
16600	AbnT	44023	2893	C2
Metcalf Av				
12800	CLEV	44120	2626	E7
Metcalf Rd				
400	ELYR	44035	2875	D3
9000	KTLD	44094	2251	C7
9000	WTHL	44094	2251	C7
9000	WTHL	44094	2376	C2
Methyl Av				
11200	CLEV	44104	2626	D5
11200	CLEV	44120	2626	D5
Metric Dr				
7700	MNTR	44060	2251	D1
Metro Ct				
6400	BDHT	44146	2887	E5
Metro Dr				
1700	EUCL	44132	2373	E5
1700	EUCL	44132	2374	A5
1700	EUCL	44143	2373	E5
Metro Health Dr				
2500	CLEV	44109	2754	D1
Metro Park Dr				
6600	MAYF	44143	2500	A3
Metro Park Tr				
-	SLN	44139	2889	A1
Metro Pks Buttermilk Flls Pkwy				
-	MAYF	44040	2500	B1
Metro Parks Ox Ln				
-	GSML	44040	2500	C1
-	GSML	44094	2500	C1
-	MAYF	44040	2500	C1
-	WBHL	44094	2500	C1
Metro Park Valley Pkwy				
-	OmsT	44138	2879	E3
-	OmsT	44142	2879	E3
Metropolitan Blvd				
8200	ODFL	44138	2879	C6
Metropolitan Dr				
4200	CLEV	44135	2752	A4
Metta Av				
6500	CLEV	44103	2495	E6
Meyer Av				
2100	CLEV	44109	2624	C7
35700	ETLK	44095	2250	B4
Miami Av				
100	ELYR	44035	2875	B7
3700	LORN	44053	2744	B4
E Miami Dr				
7700	PRMA	44134	3014	B1
N Miami Dr				
4200	PRMA	44134	3014	B2
Miami Rd				
2000	EUCL	44117	2497	E3
2000	EUCL	44117	2498	A3
7500	MONT	44060	2143	D2
Michael Av				
4300	NOSD	44070	2750	E6
Michael Ct				
100	PNVL	44077	2145	E2
Michael Dr				
10	OmsT	44138	2879	A3
5700	BKPK	44142	2881	D3
6800	MNTR	44060	2144	E6
18300	CLEV	44122	2757	D3
18300	CLEV	44128	2757	D3
35400	SLN	44139	3020	B2
Michael Ln				
900	AMHT	44001	2872	E3
42700	EyrT	44035	2745	B7
Michaels Ln				
8800	BWHT	44147	3014	D6
Michelle Dr				
-	ClbT	44028	3009	C7
-	ClbT	44028	3144	C1
Michelle Ln				
200	MDSN	44057	2043	E2
37800	ETLK	44095	2142	D5
Michigan Av				
200	ELYR	44035	3006	C1
200	LORN	44052	2615	B5
3200	PryT	44081	2041	E1
Michigan St				
500	AURA	44202	3021	B4
Middle Av				
100	ELYR	44035	2875	A7
1000	ELYR	44035	3006	A2
10500	CrlT	44035	3006	A5
11100	CrlT	44050	3006	A6
Middle Dr				
-	AhtT	44001	2872	A3
Middle St				
400	AMHT	44001	2872	D2
700	BDFD	44146	2887	B4
Middlebrook Blvd				
5700	BKPK	44142	2881	D3
6300	BKPK	44130	2881	C4
6600	MDBH	44130	2881	B6
13300	PRMA	44130	2881	E2
Middlebury Ct				
5300	SFLD	44054	2746	E5
Middledale Rd				
4800	LNHT	44124	2628	D1
Middlefield Ct				
300	PnvT	44077	2146	E2
Middlefield Rd				
2100	CVHT	44106	2627	A3
Middlehurst Rd				
1700	CVHT	44118	2627	B1
Middlepost Ln				
2900	RKRV	44116	2751	B1
Middle Post Pt				
100	CRDN	44024	2505	A2
Middle Ridge Rd				
-	AhtT	44053	2744	E7
-	LORN	44035	2744	E7
3800	PryT	44081	1940	D7
4500	MadT	44057	1941	A7
4500	MadT	44081	1941	A7
4500	PryT	44081	1941	A7
6000	LORN	44052	2745	A6
6000	LORN	44053	2745	A7
6000	MDSN	44057	1941	A7
6000	ShfT	44052	2745	A6
6000	ShfT	44053	2745	A6
6200	AhtT	44035	2745	A7
6200	EyrT	44035	2745	A7
6200	LORN	44035	2745	A7
6300	MDSN	44057	1942	D6
6400	AhtT	44035	2744	E7
6400	LORN	44053	2744	E7
6500	MadT	44057	1942	B6
7400	GnvT	44041	1943	A6
7400	GnvT	44057	1943	A6
7400	HpfT	44041	1943	A6
7400	HpfT	44057	1943	A6
7400	MadT	44057	1943	A6
43500	AhtT	44001	2744	E7
43600	AhtT	44001	2873	D1
43600	AhtT	44035	2873	D1
46000	AMHT	44001	2873	A3
46200	AMHT	44001	2872	E3
48000	AhtT	44001	2872	A4
48100	AhtT	44001	2871	D4
48100	BhmT	44001	2871	B5
Middlesex Rd				
7800	MNTR	44060	2251	D3
Middleton Dr				
-	AVON	44011	2618	B7
10	PnvT	44077	2145	D5
100	CcdT	44077	2145	D5
35400	AVON	44011	2748	B1
Middleton Rd				
1300	HDSN	44236	3154	D7
1400	CVHT	44121	2498	A7
2100	HDSN	44236	3155	D7
Midland Av				
15900	CLEV	44110	2497	C1
Midland Rd				
7400	INDE	44131	3015	E1
8000	MNTR	44060	2251	C4
26500	BYVL	44140	2620	A5
Midvale Av				
-	NOSD	44070	2878	E1
18300	CLEV	44135	2751	E6
18300	CLEV	44135	2752	B6
Midvale Dr				
11100	CrlT	44035	3005	D5
Midway Av				
3800	WVHT	44122	2757	E3
Midway Blvd				
-	PnvT	44077	2040	D2
100	ELYR	44035	2875	B2

STREET Block City ZIP Map# Grid

Midway Blvd
600 ELYR 44035 2874 E2
Midway Dr
- VMLN 44089 2741 B6
1900 TNBG 44087 3154 C1
Midway Rd
32400 AVLK 44012 2618 C1
Midway Mall
4000 ELYR 44035 2875 A2
Midwest Av
9000 GDHT 44125 2756 B7
Mika Dr
10200 BKLN 44144 2753 C6
Milan Av
100 AMHT 44001 2872 D2
1100 AhtT 44001 2872 D2
11700 CLEV 44111 2753 A2
13300 ECLE 44112 2497 A5
Milan Cres
4100 CLEV 44128 2757 C3
Milan Ct
9700 NRYN 44133 3014 C4
Milan Dr
19300 MPHT 44137 2757 E7
21000 EUCL 44119 2373 B5
Milann Dr
37500 WBHL 44094 2375 E4
Milburn Av
16800 CLEV 44135 2752 A4
Milburn Rd
26200 OKWD 44146 2887 E7
Milbury Ct
7200 OKWD 44146 2887 E7
Mildon Dr
6800 LryT 44077 2147 D7
7100 LryT 44077 2255 D1
Mildred Av
700 LORN 44052 2614 C7
1200 WTLK 44145 2619 C6
22500 FWPK 44126 2751 A5
22900 NOSD 44070 2751 A5
23200 NOSD 44070 2750 E5
Mildred Dr
30000 WLWK 44095 2249 C6
Mildred St
- NRDV 44039 2877 A2
300 PNVL 44077 2146 B2
Miles Av
9100 CLEV 44105 2756 B3
13000 CLEV 44128 2756 E3
13600 CLEV 44105 2757 A3
13600 CLEV 44128 2757 C4
17500 WVHT 44128 2757 C4
Miles Av SR-43
9100 CLEV 44105 2756 B3
13000 CLEV 44128 2756 E3
13600 CLEV 44105 2757 A3
13600 CLEV 44128 2757 C4
17500 WVHT 44128 2757 C4
Miles Ln
500 BERA 44017 3011 C2
Miles Pkwy
20500 NRDL 44128 2758 A6
20500 WVHT 44128 2758 A6
20500 WVHT 44146 2758 A6
Miles Rd
100 CNFL 44022 2760 D7
100 MDHL 44022 2760 D7
300 BTVL 44022 2760 D7
17700 WVHT 44128 2757 E5
19400 NRDL 44128 2757 E5
20000 NRDL 44128 2758 C6
20000 WVHT 44128 2758 A6
22400 BDHT 44128 2758 C6
24000 BDHT 44146 2758 D7
26300 BDHT 44022 2759 A7
26300 BDHT 44128 2759 A7
26300 BDHT 44146 2759 A7
26300 ORNG 44022 2759 D7
26300 SLN 44022 2759 D7
26300 SLN 44146 2759 A7
26300 WVHT 44022 2759 A7
26300 WVHT 44128 2759 A7
27000 SLN 44139 2759 D7
31700 MDHL 44022 2759 E7
33100 SLN 44022 2760 A7
33100 SLN 44139 2760 A7
Miles Rd SR-43
17700 WVHT 44128 2757 E5
19400 NRDL 44128 2757 E5
20000 NRDL 44128 2758 A6
20000 WVHT 44128 2758 A6
S Miles Rd
- WVHT 44146 2758 A6
16600 CLEV 44128 2757 E6
17800 WVHT 44128 2757 E6
18200 WVHT 44128 2758 A6
Miles Park Av
9100 CLEV 44105 2756 B3
Milford Dr
4600 PryT 44081 2042 B5
9000 MCDN 44056 3018 B5
9000 MCDN 44067 3018 B5
9000 NHFD 44067 3018 B4
9300 NHFD 44056 3018 B4
Milford Ln
9300 MNTR 44060 2144 E7
9300 MNTR 44060 2145 A6
Milford Pl
11200 TNBG 44087 3020 B4
Milford Rd
2500 UNHT 44118 2628 A4
3700 PRMA 44134 2883 B1
Mill Ct
- CLEV 44113 2624 C6
- GFTN 44044 3142 A6
W Mill Dr
900 HDHT 44143 2499 A6
900 LNHT 44124 2499 A6
900 LNHT 44143 2499 A6
Mill Rd
4700 BWHT 44147 3015 D4
6200 BKVL 44141 3015 D4
6200 BWHT 44141 3015 E5
6700 BKVL 44141 3016 A6
27200 NOSD 44070 2749 E7
27200 NOSD 44070 2750 A7
W Mill Rd
4700 BWHT 44147 3015 D4
Mill Run
100 AURA 44202 3022 B4
Mill St
- AVON 44011 2747 D2
10 PNVL 44077 2040 C6
300 AMHT 44001 2872 E2

Mill St
4500 MNTU 44255 3159 C6
5500 VMLN 44089 2740 E6
15900 MDFD 44062 2767 D2
25500 ODFL 44138 2879 B6
Millard Dr
600 BYVL 44140 2619 D5
Millbrook Dr
17500 BbgT 44023 2891 A5
S Millbrook Dr
17700 BbgT 44023 2891 A5
Millbrook Rd
5400 BDHT 44146 2887 C1
Millcreek Blvd
- CLEV 44105 2756 B4
22900 HIHL 44122 2758 B3
22900 HIHL 44128 2758 B3
Mill Creek Ln
10 MDHL 44022 2760 B4
Miller Av
5000 MPHT 44137 2757 B7
20000 CLEV 44119 2373 A5
20000 EUCL 44119 2373 A5
22000 EUCL 44123 2373 A5
22300 EUCL 44117 2373 A5
30000 WBHL 44092 2374 D5
30000 WKLF 44092 2374 D5
W Miller Av
29000 WBHL 44092 2374 C5
29000 WKLF 44092 2374 C5
Miller Ct
200 CrlT 44035 3006 B3
300 PNVL 44077 2145 E3
400 CLEV 44113 2625 A5
16800 SGVL 44136 3147 A3
Miller Dr
6500 NRDV 44039 2877 D4
Miller Pkwy
1400 STBR 44241 3157 A7
Miller Rd
100 AVLK 44012 2617 A6
500 AVON 44011 2617 A6
500 AVON 44012 2617 A6
5000 BKVL 44141 3150 C4
6800 BKVL 44141 3151 A4
Millers Al
- ELYR 44035 2875 A7
Millerwood Ln
7600 PRMA 44130 3012 E1
Mill Gate Dr
2800 WBHL 44094 2375 E6
2900 WBHL 44094 2376 A7
Mill Hollow Dr
10 MDHL 44022 2760 B4
Mill Hollow Ln
13900 SGVL 44136 3012 C7
14200 SGVL 44136 3147 B1
Milligan Av
11700 BKLN 44144 2753 B5
11700 CLEV 44135 2753 A5
11700 CLEV 44144 2753 B5
Millikin Ct
1500 CVHT 44118 2497 E7
Mill Morr Rd
10 PnvT 44077 2145 B5
Mill Pond Cir
4300 PryT 44081 2041 D4
Millpond Rd
10 AURA 44202 3157 A2
Millrace Ln
7400 SgHT 44067 3152 C1
Millridge Rd
800 HDHT 44143 2499 B5
Mills Av
27500 EUCL 44132 2373 E4
27500 EUCL 44132 2374 A3
Mills Cir
41100 CrlT 44050 3140 E2
Mills Dr
2500 LORN 44052 2744 B2
Mills Rd
31600 AVON 44011 2748 D6
31600 AVON 44011 2749 A6
31600 AVON 44145 2749 A6
31600 NRDV 44011 2748 D6
31600 NRDV 44011 2749 A6
31600 NRDV 44039 2748 D6
31600 NRDV 44039 2749 A6
31600 NRDV 44145 2749 A6
31600 WTLK 44145 2749 A6
36000 AVON 44011 2747 D6
36000 NRDV 44011 2747 D6
36000 NRDV 44039 2747 D6
Mills Creek Ln
4700 AVON 44011 2748 D7
4700 NRDV 44011 2748 D7
4700 NRDV 44039 2748 D7
5300 NRDV 44039 2877 E1
6300 NRDV 44039 2878 A2
Millside Ln
31700 AVLK 44012 2618 E4
Mills Industrial Pkwy
4900 AVON 44011 2748 C7
4900 NRDV 44011 2748 C7
4900 NRDV 44039 2748 C7
Millstone Dr
10 PNVL 44077 2040 C7
1100 SgHT 44067 3152 B1
13000 MsnT 44024 2634 C1
17900 BbgT 44023 2891 C6
Millstone Ln
100 AMHT 44001 2744 B6
Mill Stream Cir
100 ELYR 44035 3007 A2
Millstream Cir
9000 ODFL 44138 3009 E1
Millview Ln
12600 MsnT 44024 2503 E7
Millwood Cir
32600 NRDV 44039 2748 E6
Millwood Dr
4900 BWHT 44147 3015 D5
Millwood Ln
5400 WLBY 44094 2375 A1
Milo Av
5100 MPHT 44137 2757 A7
Milo Rd
12800 GDHT 44125 2885 E3
13500 GDHT 44125 2886 A3
13900 GDHT 44137 2886 A3
13900 MPHT 44137 2886 A3
Milton Dr
7100 MNTR 44060 2143 B7
7100 MNTR 44060 2251 B1
22300 EUCL 44123 2373 C3

Milton Rd
- SRHT 44122 2628 C5
2100 SELD 44121 2628 B3
2100 UNHT 44118 2628 B3
2100 UNHT 44121 2628 B3
2600 SRHT 44118 2628 C5
Milton St
10 BERA 44017 3011 C2
Milverton Rd
3200 CLEV 44120 2627 B7
3200 SRHT 44120 2627 A7
3300 SRHT 44120 2757 B1
Mimosa Dr
- MCDN 44056 3154 A4
Mina Av
15600 CLEV 44135 2752 C5
Miner Rd
200 HDHT 44143 2499 D4
600 MAYF 44143 2499 D5
E Miner Rd
1100 MAYF 44143 2499 D6
1100 MDHT 44124 2499 D6
1100 MDHT 44143 2499 D6
W Miner Rd
1100 MDHT 44124 2499 D6
Minerva St
700 AMHT 44001 2872 D3
Minkon Av
800 CLEV 44113 2624 E4
800 CLEV 44113 2625 A4
Minnewawa Rd
10 ETLK 44095 2250 A2
10 TMLK 44095 2250 A2
Minnie Av
2800 CLEV 44104 2626 A6
Minnie Wawa St
400 VMLN 44089 2741 A5
Minor Av
11900 CLEV 44105 2756 D3
Minor Park Rd
1800 CVHT 44118 2627 C2
Minott Ct
37000 NRDV 44035 2876 D7
Mira Ct
2400 CLEV 44109 2754 D4
Mirabeau Dr
5300 PRMA 44129 2883 A7
Mirage Av
10 AMHT 44001 2744 A7
Miramar Blvd
1500 SELD 44121 2628 A2
2100 UNHT 44118 2628 B4
2100 UNHT 44121 2628 B3
Miriam Av
1800 AVON 44011 2617 D7
1800 AVON 44011 2747 D1
Mirlo Ct
- CLEV 44102 2623 E7
Mission Rd
14500 CLEV 44135 2752 D3
Mississippi Av
200 LORN 44052 2615 B5
Missouri Av
200 LORN 44052 2615 C6
Mistletoe Av
29400 OKWD 44146 2887 D7
Mistletoe Dr
1500 CLEV 44106 2626 D1
Misty Hllw
10400 KTLD 44094 2376 C6
Misty Ln
300 PnvT 44077 2039 D7
Misty Rdg
10300 CcdT 44077 2253 D2
Misty Lake Dr
17100 SGVL 44136 3147 A4
Misty Lake Gln
16300 BbgT 44023 2762 B7
Misty Meadow Tr
38100 NRDV 44039 2747 B7
38100 NRDV 44039 2876 A1
Misty Oakes Dr
9300 BWHT 44147 3150 B1
Mitchell Av
14600 CLEV 44111 2752 D2
18900 RKRV 44116 2621 E6
Mitchell Dr
10 BDFD 44146 2887 B6
6800 NRDV 44039 2877 D4
24500 NOSD 44070 2750 C6
Mitchell Ln
10 MDHL 44022 2760 A5
Mitchell Rd
9800 ClbT 44028 3009 B3
9800 ClbT 44138 3009 B3
9800 OmsT 44138 3009 B3
Mitchells Mill Rd
9600 CdnT 44060 2378 A2
9600 CdnT 44094 2378 A2
9600 KDHL 44060 2378 A1
9600 KTLD 44060 2378 A1
9600 KTLD 44094 2378 A1
10000 CdnT 44024 2378 C2
10000 CdnT 44024 2379 A3
Mobile Ct
3500 CLEV 44109 2754 C5
Moccasin Run
9100 BbgT 44023 2891 D1
Mockingbird Ln
- MNTR 44060 2144 D2
10 ELYR 44035 2875 D7
Mock Orange Ln
500 AbnT 44023 2892 B3
Moffet Av
100 CRDN 44024 2380 A7
Mogul St
16300 BbgT 44022 2761 A7
Mohawk Av
18500 CLEV 44119 2372 E5
19300 CLEV 44119 2373 A5
19700 EUCL 44119 2373 A5
Mohawk Dr
- AURA 44202 3022 A7
1400 MadT 44057 1843 B7
4100 LORN 44055 2745 D4
8100 MDBH 44130 3012 B2
8100 SGVL 44130 3012 B2
8100 SGVL 44136 3012 B2
Mohawk Rd
7000 MNTR 44060 2143 B3
7000 MNTR 44094 2143 B3
7000 WLBY 44094 2143 B3
Mohawk Tr
400 BNWK 44212 3146 E7
13100 MDBH 44130 2881 D6

Mohegan Tr
900 WLBY 44094 2143 A5
Mohican Av
19200 CLEV 44119 2372 E6
19300 CLEV 44119 2373 A6
19700 EUCL 44119 2373 A6
Mohican Tr
16500 BbgT 44023 2891 C1
Moltke Ct
1900 CLEV 44113 2624 E7
Monaco Pl
- AVLK 44012 2618 C2
Monarch Rd
1000 SELD 44121 2498 B6
Mondamin Dr
35300 ETLK 44095 2250 B2
Moneta Av
800 AURA 44202 3021 A3
1100 RMDV 44202 3021 A3
Monica Dr
13600 NRYN 44133 3014 B7
34000 NRDV 44039 2877 C1
Monica Ln
5800 GDHT 44125 2886 A2
Monmouth Ct
100 CcdT 44060 2145 B7
Monmouth Dr
6300 PRMA 44129 2882 E4
Monmouth Rd
2900 CVHT 44118 2627 B4
E Monmouth Rd
3200 CVHT 44118 2627 C4
Monroe Av
- AVLK 44012 2617 C3
- LORN 44052 2615 C6
2500 CLEV 44113 2624 C6
6300 NRDV 44039 2877 C3
W Monroe Av
10 BDFD 44146 2887 A5
Monroe Blvd
400 PNVL 44077 2146 A3
600 PnvT 44077 2146 A3
E Monroe Cir
- GnvT 44041 1944 D5
Monroe Ct
- SDLK 44054 2616 B4
10 OBLN 44074 3138 D4
7800 MNTR 44060 2143 D7
32200 SLN 44139 3019 E1
Monroe Dr
200 NHFD 44067 3017 E3
200 NHFD 44067 3018 A3
Monroe St
10 BERA 44017 3011 C1
100 ELYR 44035 2875 A5
E Monroe St
10 BDFD 44146 2887 A4
Monroe Tr
3500 WTLK 44145 2749 C4
Mont Av
13900 CVHT 44112 2627 A1
13900 ECLE 44112 2627 A1
13900 ECLE 44118 2627 A1
Montagano Blvd
4300 SELD 44121 2498 B6
Montague Av
2300 AVON 44011 2748 B1
Montague Ct
19400 NRYN 44133 3148 B5
Montana Av
200 LORN 44052 2615 C5
5800 CLEV 44102 2624 A7
Montauk Av
4800 PRMA 44134 2883 B1
5200 PRMA 44129 2883 A1
Montauk Pt
10700 NRYN 44133 3013 C5
Montclair Av
2200 CLEV 44109 2754 C5
Montclair Cir
900 WTLK 44145 2620 A6
Montclair Dr
- HmbT 44024 2381 A6
Montclare Blvd
20900 SGVL 44149 3011 B3
Monte Dr
6400 LryT 44077 2147 B5
Montello Rd
8200 INDE 44131 3016 B2
Monterey Av
18600 CLEV 44119 2372 E4
18600 EUCL 44119 2372 E4
19300 EUCL 44119 2373 A4
Monterey Dr
6500 MDHT 44124 2500 A6
8000 KTLD 44094 2376 E7
8000 KTLD 44094 2377 A7
Monterey Bay Dr
7500 MONT 44060 2143 D2
Monterey Pine Dr
17700 SGVL 44136 3146 E5
Montevista Rd
3700 CVHT 44121 2497 E7
3700 CVHT 44121 2498 A7
Montford Rd
800 CVHT 44121 2498 A5
Montgomery Av
7100 CLEV 44104 2625 E4
7100 CLEV 44104 2626 A4
Montgomery Dr
500 BHIT 44212 3146 B7
Montgomery Pl
- BKLN 44144 2753 C4
Montgomery Rd
2800 SRHT 44122 2627 E6
2900 SRHT 44122 2628 A7
7800 SGVL 44130 3012 D2
7800 SGVL 44136 3012 D2
Monticello Blvd
10 CVHT 44118 2627 C1
2900 CVHT 44118 2497 C7
3400 CVHT 44121 2497 D6
3800 CVHT 44121 2498 A6
4000 SELD 44121 2498 B5
4300 SELD 44143 2498 D5
4800 RDHT 44143 2498 D5
Monticello Cir
100 ELYR 44035 2873 E7
100 ELYR 44035 2874 B6
Monticello Dr
10 BNWK 44212 3146 E6
10 BNWK 44212 3147 A6
200 CNFL 44022 2760 E7

Monticello Dr
500 AVLK 44012 2618 D4
7700 BKVL 44131 3016 A3
7700 BKVL 44141 3016 A3
7700 INDE 44131 3016 A3
9300 TNBG 44087 3019 C6
Monticello Place Ln
600 SELD 44143 2498 D5
Montridge Ct
8100 NRYN 44133 3013 C5
Montrose Av
14200 CLEV 44111 2622 C7
Montrose Dr
6100 MadT 44057 1941 E1
Montrose Wy
- AVON 44011 2747 D5
Montvale Dr
15000 BKPK 44142 2881 C3
Montville Ct
4400 WVHT 44128 2758 D4
Moon Ct
5000 SFLD 44054 2746 D1
Moon Rd
2800 AVON 44011 2747 A2
Moon Beam Ln
- CcdT 44077 2254 D4
Mooncrest Dr
7000 PRMA 44129 2883 A6
Moonglow Ln
4300 CLEV 44109 2755 A5
Moonstone Dr
900 AhtT 44001 2873 B2
Moore Ct
1900 CLEV 44113 2624 D5
Moore Dr
10100 PRMA 44130 2882 C7
Moore Rd
10 AVLK 44012 2617 C2
700 AVON 44011 2617 C6
700 AVON 44012 2617 C5
Mooreland Av
4000 WLBY 44094 2250 C5
Mooreland Dr
100 AVLK 44012 2617 D2
Mooreland Rd
5400 MONT 44060 2037 E7
5400 MONT 44060 2143 E1
Moorewood Av
100 AVLK 44012 2617 E3
Moorland Dr
- GftT 44044 3142 B7
2000 TNBG 44087 3019 D6
Moraine Dr
11000 TNBG 44087 3019 C4
Moran St
600 ELYR 44035 2875 A2
Morar Cir
20300 SGVL 44149 3146 C4
N Moreland Blvd
2500 SRHT 44120 2627 A5
2600 CLEV 44120 2626 E5
2600 SRHT 44120 2626 E5
S Moreland Blvd
2700 CLEV 44120 2626 E6
Moreland Ln
- AbnT 44021 2893 C2
W Moreland Rd
8300 PRMA 44129 2882 D1
Morewood Pkwy
200 RKRV 44116 2621 D4
Morgan Av
100 ELYR 44035 2874 E3
6500 CLEV 44127 2625 E7
7200 CLEV 44127 2626 A7
Morgan Ct
- SGVL 44149 3145 E3
Morgan Dr
300 PnvT 44077 2041 B6
Morgan Run
8700 ODFL 44138 2879 D7
26800 WTLK 44145 2750 A4
Morgan St
10 OBLN 44074 3138 C3
5400 MPHT 44137 2886 B1
Morgan Tr
14600 RslT 44072 2762 C1
Morison Av
10500 CLEV 44108 2496 C6
Morlee Dr
300 BNWK 44212 3146 D7
Morley Av
19500 RKRV 44116 2621 D7
Morley Dr
- RMDV 44087 3020 C4
Morley Rd
- CcdT 44077 2145 E7
2800 SRHT 44122 2628 A7
7200 CcdT 44077 2253 B5
7300 CcdT 44060 2253 B5
8300 CdnT 44060 2253 B5
Morning Dove Ln
6900 OmsT 44138 2878 D4
Morning Glory Cir
6200 SLN 44139 2889 C5
Morning Glory Ln
- OKWD 44146 2887 E5
- Okwd 44146 2888 A4
- SLN 44139 2888 A5
33800 NRDV 44039 2877 C2
Morning Glory Tr
12700 CsTp 44026 2501 B7
12700 CsTp 44026 2631 B1
Morningside Dr
10 SRSL 44022 2762 C7
4500 CLEV 44109 2754 E6
5400 PRMA 44129 2883 A2
5400 PRMA 44134 2883 A2
6600 BKVL 44141 3151 A3
6700 VLVW 44125 2885 D5
7400 WNHL 44146 3018 A1
7500 NCtT 44067 3152 E2
Morningside Rd
6700 MDBH 44130 2881 D4
Morningside Wy
- LORN 44053 2743 D3
Morning Star Av
15700 MPHT 44137 2886 B3
Morningstar Ct
2700 WBHL 44094 2375 A5
11200 NbyT 44065 2634 B5
Morning Star Dr
13000 NRYN 44133 3147 E4
16400 SGVL 44136 3147 B4
Morningstar Dr
2600 MadT 44057 1942 A4

Morning Star Tr
7000 SgHT 44067 3152 C2
Mornington Ln
1800 CVHT 44106 2627 A2
Mornington Rd
100 VMLN 44089 2741 E4
Morning View Ct
7400 BbgT 44023 2890 B4
Morningview Ter
10 BNWK 44212 3147 B6
Morrell Av
300 PnvT 44077 2039 C6
Morris Av
20100 EUCL 44119 2373 A4
21500 EUCL 44123 2373 B4
33100 ETLK 44095 2249 E5
Morris Ct
8900 CLEV 44106 2496 B7
Morris Dr
21000 SGVL 44149 3146 B1
Morris Rd
600 VMLN 44089 2741 E5
Morris Black Pl
2400 CLEV 44104 2626 C4
Morrison Av
2000 LKWD 44107 2622 C6
Morrison St
- EyrT 44035 2874 B1
200 GNVA 44041 1944 C4
Morrow Dr
6000 BKPK 44142 2881 D2
Morse Av
10 PNVL 44077 2040 A7
10 PNVL 44077 2146 A1
Morse Rd
200 BERA 44017 2880 A7
8300 BhmT 44089 2870 D5
Mortimer Av
11700 CLEV 44111 2753 A3
Mortimer Dr
300 BDFD 44146 2887 B2
Morton Av
6100 CLEV 44127 2755 D1
8500 BKLN 44144 2753 D5
22000 FWPK 44126 2751 A4
Morton Rd
200 VMLN 44089 2741 B5
Mortus Dr
1600 TNBG 44087 3019 B6
Moss Pt
18100 BbgT 44023 2890 E7
Moss Canyon Dr
800 AhtT 44001 2873 B2
Moss Glen Tr
15400 NbyT 44065 2764 E4
Moss Point Rd
12200 SGVL 44136 3012 A6
Moss Ridge Cir
12200 SGVL 44136 3012 A6
Mosswood Cir
8700 NRDV 44039 2877 E7
Mosswood Dr
2300 TNBG 44087 3155 A4
Moss Woods Dr
15000 BtnT 44062 2767 A4
15000 MdfT 44062 2767 A4
Motta Dr
39700 CrlT 44044 3006 C6
Moulton Av
12000 CLEV 44106 2496 D7
12300 CLEV 44112 2496 D7
Mound Av
5300 CLEV 44105 2755 D1
Mound St
100 ELYR 44035 2875 B6
Mountain Ash Dr
7600 CcdT 44060 2253 B3
Mountain Park Dr
7300 CcdT 44060 2253 B2
Mountain Quail Pl
7300 CcdT 44077 2254 C1
Mountainside Dr
200 PnvT 44077 2147 A1
Mountain View Dr
100 MDHL 44022 2760 C5
8800 MNTR 44060 2252 D3
Mountainview Dr
9700 WTHL 44094 2376 A3
E Mountain View Dr
9000 CdnT 44024 2253 E7
W Mountain View Dr
9000 CdnT 44024 2253 E7
Mt Auburn Av
9300 CLEV 44104 2626 B6
Mt Carmel Dr
1500 WKLF 44092 2374 D2
Mt Carmel Rd
10500 CLEV 44104 2626 C4
11500 CLEV 44120 2626 D4
Mt Herman Av
3600 CLEV 44115 2625 C4
3900 CLEV 44104 2625 C4
Mt Laurel Rd
3600 CVHT 44121 2497 E4
3600 SELD 44121 2497 E4
Mt Overlook Av
10800 CLEV 44104 2626 D4
10800 CLEV 44106 2626 C4
10900 CLEV 44120 2626 D4
12600 SRHT 44120 2626 E4
Mt Pleasant Dr
18600 AbnT 44023 3023 A1
Mt Royal Dr
8100 CcdT 44077 2253 E4
Mt Sinai Dr
10 CLEV 44106 2626 C1
Mt Union Av
1800 ECLE 44112 2497 A6
Mt Vernon Blvd
1100 CVHT 44112 2497 C6
1100 CVHT 44118 2497 C7
1100 ECLE 44112 2497 C6
Mt Vernon Ct
- CLEV 44109 2754 C2
10 CcdT 44060 2145 B7
10 ELYR 44035 2874 A7
Mountview Av
5400 GDHT 44125 2885 C1
10500 CLEV 44104 2626 C7
Mountville Dr
19600 MPHT 44137 2757 E7
20500 MPHT 44137 2758 A7
Mount Zion Cir
- OKWD 44146 3018 E1

Mourning Dove Ln
11300 CcdT 44077 2254 C1
Moving Wy
- MNTR 44060 2143 E7
- MNTR 44060 2144 A7
Mozart Dr
1300 WTLK 44145 2620 A7
Mozina Dr
1000 CLEV 44119 2372 E6
Mueller Dr
10 AVON 44011 2748 B2
Mueti Dr
- BDHT 44146 2758 B7
- MPHT 44137 2758 B7
Mueti Dr SR-43
- BDHT 44146 2758 B7
- MPHT 44137 2758 B7
Muirfield Dr
- PRPK 44124 2759 A1
300 HDHT 44143 2499 C2
Muirfield Wy
4300 WTLK 44145 2749 A5
Muirland Dr
8400 BWHT 44147 3014 E4
Muirwood Ct
7500 BbgT 44023 2890 C1
Muirwood Rd
2300 AVON 44011 2747 B1
Mulberry Av
2300 CLEV 44113 2624 C3
Mulberry Cir
12300 SGVL 44149 3011 A6
26600 EUCL 44143 2373 E5
26600 RDHT 44143 2373 E5
26600 RDHT 44143 2374 A5
Mulberry Ct
7300 OmsT 44138 2878 D5
Mulberry Dr
10 OBLN 44074 3138 C3
Mulberry Ln
300 AVLK 44012 2618 C3
1400 AVON 44011 2617 C6
5300 SFLD 44035 2746 E6
Mulberry Rd
7000 CsTp 44026 2501 D3
7000 CsTp 44040 2501 A3
7000 GSML 44040 2501 A3
8100 CsTp 44026 2502 E2
9300 CsTp 44024 2502 E2
9400 CsTp 44024 2503 A2
9400 MsnT 44024 2503 C2
Mulberry St
200 BERA 44017 2880 B6
Mulberry St SR-237
200 BERA 44017 2880 B6
Mulberry Woods
8000 CsTp 44026 2501 E3
Mull Av
100 AVLK 44012 2618 D1
Muller Rd
- BKVL 44141 3150 E4
Mulwal Dr
10 PNVL 44077 2145 E2
Mumford Av
5400 CLEV 44127 2625 D7
Mumford Rd
16300 TroT 44021 2766 E7
16300 TroT 44021 2767 A7
16300 TroT 44062 2767 A7
Munich Dr
9000 PRMA 44130 3013 C2
Municipal Dr
- HRM 44234 3161 A2
Munn Rd
14800 NbyT 44065 2763 C3
14800 NbyT 44072 2763 C3
15500 CLEV 44111 2752 B1
16300 AbnT 44023 2763 C7
16300 NbyT 44023 2763 C7
16400 AbnT 44023 2892 C5
18000 AbnT 44023 3023 C2
19100 AbnT 44022 3023 B3
19100 AbnT 44255 3023 B3
19100 ManT 44255 3023 B3
Munnberry Ovl
14700 NbyT 44065 2763 C1
14700 NbyT 44072 2763 C1
Munson Rd
7700 MNTR 44060 2143 E3
7700 MONT 44060 2143 E3
8000 MNTR 44060 2144 C4
Munson Rd SR-615
7700 MNTR 44060 2143 E3
7700 MONT 44060 2143 E3
8000 MNTR 44060 2144 A3
Munson St
400 PNVL 44077 2040 A7
Mural Dr
5700 BNHT 44131 2884 B2
5700 SVHL 44131 2884 B2
Murcott Cir
100 ORNG 44022 2759 A4
Muriel Av
3500 CLEV 44109 2754 C4
Murphy St
10 BERA 44017 2880 B6
100 GDRV 44077 2039 C6
300 PnvT 44077 2039 C6
Murray Av
4200 WLBY 44094 2250 D5
7400 MNTR 44060 2252 C2
Murray Rd
900 SELD 44121 2498 B5
8400 VLVW 44125 2885 B2
Murray St
5200 PryT 44077 2041 B7
Murray Hill Rd
2000 CLEV 44106 2626 D3
2200 CVHT 44106 2626 D3
Murray Ridge Rd
6200 EyrT 44035 2745 B7
6400 EyrT 44035 2874 B1
7800 ELYR 44035 2874 B4
9100 EyrT 44035 3005 C1
9200 ELYR 44035 3005 C2
9500 CrlT 44035 3005 D3
Murwood Dr
10 MDHL 44022 2760 B3
Music St
7900 RslT 44022 2761 E4
8200 RslT 44022 2762 A4
8300 RslT 44072 2762 A4
9300 NbyT 44072 2763 A4
9300 RslT 44072 2763 A4
10200 NbyT 44065 2763 E4

STREET
Block City ZIP Map# Grid

Music St
10800 NbyT 44065 2764 A4
11900 NbyT 44021 2764 E4
Musket Dr
9500 MNTR 44060 2253 A1
Muskingum Blvd
15200 BKPK 44142 2881 B1
Muskoka Av
18500 CLEV 44119 2372 E5
19300 CLEV 44119 2373 A5
19700 EUCL 44119 2373 A5
Mussey Av
400 ELYR 44035 3005 E1
400 ELYR 44035 3006 A1
Mustang Dr
14100 MPHT 44137 2886 A3
Mustang Pass
800 AURA 44202 3022 B4
Myra Dr
400 CRDN 44024 2380 A7
Myrick Ln
2600 TNBG 44087 3020 A5
Myrna Rd
7700 TwbT 44087 3154 E5
7700 TwbT 44236 3154 E5
Myron Av
7100 CLEV 44103 2495 E7
7100 CLEV 44103 2496 A7
Myrtle Av
16200 CLEV 44128 2757 C6
16200 GDHT 44128 2757 C6
25800 ODFL 44138 2879 B5
Myrtle Ct
40000 CrlT 44035 3005 E3
Mystic Dr
7200 HDSN 44236 3154 D7

N

Nadine Cir
2400 HkyT 44233 3148 A6
2500 HkyT 44233 3147 E6
Nagle Rd
3100 AVON 44011 2748 D6
4600 NRDV 44011 2748 D6
4600 NRDV 44039 2748 D6
Naigle Rd
30800 AVLK 44012 2619 A5
30800 AVLK 44140 2619 A5
30800 BYVL 44140 2619 A5
Naiman Pkwy
5000 ORNG 44022 2759 A7
5000 SLN 44022 2759 A7
5000 SLN 44139 2759 A7
5000 SLN 44139 2888 A1
Nanci Dr
8300 SGVL 44136 3012 D3
Nanco Dr
- ODFL 44138 2879 C7
Nancy Cir
200 BNWK 44212 3147 D6
Nancy Ct
18200 CLEV 44128 2757 D4
Nancy Dr
400 BERA 44017 2880 B5
600 AURA 44202 3021 B5
6500 NOSD 44070 2878 E3
8100 MNTR 44060 2252 A1
18000 CLEV 44121 2497 E3
Nancy Ann Dr
7300 CcdT 44077 2254 E1
Nandina Dr
28200 NOSD 44070 2749 D6
Nanford Rd
10100 CLEV 44102 2623 C5
Nan Linn Dr
4800 RDHT 44143 2498 E1
5000 WLBY 44094 2250 B7
5000 WLBY 44094 2375 B1
Nantucket Cir
- PtfT 44074 3138 D5
10 OBLN 44074 3138 D5
100 PnvT 44077 2145 B5
Nantucket Ct
- BHWD 44122 2629 A4
10 BTNH 44108 2496 E2
Nantucket Ct E
10 BHWD 44122 2629 A4
Nantucket Ct W
10 BHWD 44122 2629 A4
Nantucket Dr
10 GNVA 44041 1944 B5
300 AVLK 44012 2618 B3
2900 WLBY 44094 2250 E2
12100 MsnT 44024 2634 E2
12100 MsnT 44024 2635 A2
27200 NOSD 44070 2878 E2
27200 NOSD 44070 2879 A1
Nantucket Dr S
1800 LORN 44053 2744 B6
N Nantucket Dr
2000 LORN 44053 2744 A5
Nantucket Ln
6600 BKPK 44142 2881 A4
6600 MDBH 44130 2881 A4
6600 MDBH 44142 2881 A4
Nantucket Pl
300 VMLN 44089 2741 A4
Nantucket Row
10 RKRV 44116 2751 A1
18400 SGVL 44136 3147 A5
30800 BYVL 44140 2619 A3
Nantucket St
1000 GFTN 44044 3142 A4
Nantucket Cove
3400 BNWK 44212 3147 B7
9900 TNBG 44087 3019 D4
15500 MDFD 44062 2767 B1
Naomi Av
17600 CLEV 44111 2752 A3
17900 CLEV 44135 2752 A3
Naomi Dr
10900 PRMA 44130 2882 B1
Naomi Ln
900 AURA 44202 3022 E4
Napa Blvd
3300 AVON 44011 2748 D3
Naples Av
14800 CLEV 44128 2757 A5
Naples Dr
100 ELYR 44035 2746 D7
Naples Wy
8100 MCDN 44056 3154 A3
Narraganset Ovl
15800 MDBH 44130 2881 B4
Narragansett Av
17500 LKWD 44107 2622 A7
Narragansett Blvd
1300 LORN 44053 2744 B5
Narragansett Ln
31000 BYVL 44140 2619 A3
Narrows Rd
10 PryT 44077 2041 C3
2700 PryT 44081 2041 C3
3100 PRRY 44081 2041 E2
4400 PRRY 44081 2042 C4
4400 PryT 44081 2042 C4
Nash Av
1200 ELYR 44035 2875 D3
Nassau Dr
7600 PRMA 44130 3013 A2
Natalie Av
7000 NCtT 44067 3017 E7
7100 SgHT 44067 3017 E7
Natalie Rd
10 BDFD 44146 2886 E2
10 BDFD 44146 2887 A2
Natchez Av
2000 CLEV 44109 2754 D5
Nathan Av
5500 PRMA 44130 2882 B1
Nathaniel Ln
12000 TNBG 44087 3020 C3
Nathaniel Rd
900 CLEV 44110 2497 B2
National Av
- LORN 44055 2745 D6
- ShfT 44055 2745 D6
National Dr
12000 EatT 44044 3008 A7
12200 EatT 44044 3143 A1
National Rd
3800 AVON 44011 2617 E6
Nations Cir
- NRDV 44039 2877 E3
Natona Rd
2000 EUCL 44117 2498 A3
Nature View Ct
6000 CcdT 44077 2146 A5
Naumann Av
18600 CLEV 44119 2372 E4
18600 EUCL 44119 2372 E4
19300 EUCL 44119 2373 A4
19300 EUCL 44123 2373 A4
Nautical Dr
- LORN 44052 2614 E6
900 VMLN 44089 2741 A6
Nautical Wy
- FTHR 44077 2039 D5
Nautilus Tr
700 AURA 44202 3021 A4
800 RMDV 44202 3021 A5
3400 RMDV 44202 3020 E5
Nauvoo Rd
15800 MdfT 44062 2637 D7
Navahoe Rd
3900 CVHT 44121 2498 A6
Navajo Ln
11100 PMHT 44130 2882 B3
Navajo Tr
- MDBH 44130 2881 D6
600 MCDN 44056 3018 D5
6900 SLN 44139 2889 B7
6900 SLN 44139 3020 A1
Navarre Ct
10700 CLEV 44108 2496 C4
Naylor Dr
28600 SLN 44139 2888 B1
Naylor St
5200 PryT 44077 2041 B7
Neal Dr
10900 NbyT 44065 2764 A1
N Nearing Cir
600 GNVA 44041 1944 D4
S Nearing Cir
400 GNVA 44041 1944 D4
Nearing Cir Dr
5700 MNTR 44060 2144 C2
Nebraska Av
200 LORN 44052 2615 C5
Nebraska Dr
100 ELYR 44035 3006 E2
Nebraska St
10 PNVL 44077 2040 A7
Needlewood Cir
22300 SGVL 44149 3010 E3
22300 SGVL 44149 3011 A3
Neff Rd
16800 CLEV 44119 2372 D5
19200 CLEV 44117 2372 E6
Nehls Park Dr
29200 WKLF 44092 2374 D4
Neil Dr
7800 NRYN 44130 3012 E2
7800 NRYN 44133 3012 E2
7800 PRMA 44130 3012 E2
Nela Av
1800 ECLE 44112 2497 C4
Nela Ct
2000 ECLE 44112 2497 D4
Nela Pk
- ECLE 44112 2497 D4
Nelacrest Rd
15900 ECLE 44112 2497 C5
Neladale Rd
15900 ECLE 44112 2497 C5
Nelamere Rd
15900 ECLE 44112 2497 C5
Nela View Rd
800 CVHT 44112 2497 D5
800 ECLE 44112 2497 D5
Nelawood Rd
1900 ECLE 44112 2497 C5
Nell Av
14000 CLEV 44110 2497 A3
Nelmar Dr
10 PnvT 44077 2040 E7
10 PnvT 44077 2146 D1
Nelson Av
9300 CLEV 44105 2756 C2
Nelson Blvd
2400 PRMA 44134 3014 C2
Nelson Ct
11700 LKWD 44107 2623 B5
Nelson Dr
- PRMA 44134 3014 E2
Nelson St
10 PNVL 44077 2145 E2
600 ELYR 44035 3006 A2
1300 LKWD 44107 2622 B4
Nelson Park Dr
3300 RKRV 44116 2751 E1
Nelwood Rd
6200 PMHT 44130 2882 D4
Nemet Dr
100 PRMA 44131 2883 E6
100 PRMA 44134 2883 E6
100 SVHL 44131 2883 E6
100 SVHL 44131 2884 A6
Nemo Av
14600 CLEV 44110 2372 B7
Neo Pkwy
4600 GDHT 44128 2757 B6
Nepahwin Dr
10 ETLK 44095 2250 A2
10 TMLK 44095 2250 A1
Neptune Dr
5000 ORNG 44022 2759 C7
5000 SLN 44022 2759 C7
5000 SLN 44139 2759 C7
Neptunus Cir
37900 AVON 44011 2747 C2
Nesbitt Rd
700 SgHT 44067 3017 B6
Nethersole Dr
7300 MDBH 44130 2881 B7
Nettleton Ln
1900 BWHT 44147 3150 A5
Neufer Ct
100 ELYR 44035 2875 A5
Nevada Av
1500 LORN 44052 2615 C6
8600 CLEV 44104 2626 B4
Neville Av
7200 CLEV 44102 2753 E1
7300 CLEV 44102 2623 E7
Neville Rd
4300 SELD 44121 2628 C1
New St
200 FTHR 44077 2039 D4
New 4th St
300 FTHR 44077 2039 D3
600 PnvT 44077 2039 D3
Newark Av
3500 CLEV 44109 2624 B7
Newberry Av
900 SELD 44121 2498 C6
Newberry Dr
4300 BKLN 44144 2753 E4
4300 CLEV 44144 2753 E4
Newburg Ct
9400 CLEV 44105 2756 B4
Newbury Blvd
31600 AVLK 44012 2619 A2
Newbury Ct
1800 WTLK 44145 2750 C1
Newbury Dr
1900 WTLK 44145 2750 B1
2000 ECLE 44112 2497 B6
2200 CVHT 44112 2497 B6
2300 CVHT 44118 2497 B6
2500 CVHT 44118 2627 C1
4500 VMLN 44089 2741 B4
Newbury Ln
6600 PMHT 44130 2882 A5
Newbury Ovl
2000 HkyT 44233 3148 B6
New Castle
100 AURA 44202 3021 D7
New Castle Dr
10 CcdT 44060 2145 C6
Newcomb Dr
7600 PRMA 44129 2882 D6
Newcomb Rd
15300 MDFD 44062 2767 C5
15300 MdfT 44062 2767 C7
15400 PkmT 44062 2767 C7
Newcome St
2000 EUCL 44117 2373 D7
2000 RDHT 44117 2373 D7
2000 RDHT 44143 2373 D7
Newcomer Dr
- RslT 44072 2631 C4
New Concord Dr
10 CcdT 44060 2145 B7
Newell Rd
18300 SRHT 44122 2757 D1
Newell St
10 PNVL 44077 2145 D1
100 PnvT 44077 2145 E2
600 PNVL 44077 2039 D7
600 PnvT 44077 2039 D7
Newell Creek Dr
- MNTR 44060 2252 A3
New Hampshire Av
1300 LORN 44052 2615 C6
New Hampshire Cir
10 ELYR 44035 3006 A3
New Haven Ct
5300 SFLD 44054 2746 E4
Newhouse Ct
6500 MNTR 44060 2144 B5
New Hudson Rd
10 AURA 44202 3157 A2
New Jersey Av
1200 LORN 44052 2615 C7
New Jersey Cir
10 ELYR 44035 3006 B3
Newkirk Dr
8700 PMHT 44130 2882 C4
Newland Rd
6400 PMHT 44130 2882 C4
Newman Av
1400 LKWD 44107 2623 B6
6500 CLEV 44127 2625 E6
New Market Dr
12000 CsTp 44026 2501 A5
12000 GSML 44040 2501 A5
New Mexico Av
1200 LORN 44052 2615 C6
New Mexico Ct
1700 LORN 44052 2615 C7
Newport Av
7300 PRMA 44129 2753 E7
Newport Cir
200 BHIT 44212 3146 A6
Newport Ct
400 AVLK 44012 2619 A3
Newport Dr
100 PnvT 44077 2145 B5
1300 MCDN 44056 3019 A7
Newport Ln
3300 WLBY 44094 2250 D3
16700 MDBH 44130 2881 B5
Newport Cove
1600 TNBG 44087 3019 B5
Newton Av
9700 CLEV 44106 2626 B2
18600 EUCL 44119 2372 E4
19400 EUCL 44119 2373 A4
19700 EUCL 44123 2373 A4
Newton Cir
27000 NOSD 44070 2750 A5
Newton Dr
7600 MNTR 44060 2143 D6
Newton Rd
13300 MDBH 44130 2881 C4
Newton Pass
1500 BWHT 44147 3149 D4
New York Av
3200 PryT 44081 2041 E1
7600 CHHT 44105 2756 A4
7600 CLEV 44105 2756 A4
New York Rd
200 ELYR 44035 3006 B3
Niagara Dr
2100 LKWD 44107 2622 B6
2300 CLEV 44107 2622 B7
14000 SGVL 44136 3011 E7
Niagara Rd
200 VMLN 44089 2741 C4
Nicholas Av
9800 CLEV 44102 2623 C7
16300 SRHT 44120 2757 C2
20100 EUCL 44119 2373 A4
20100 EUCL 44123 2373 A4
Nichole Dr
300 SgHT 44067 3017 E4
Nichols Av
1300 LORN 44053 2744 A1
Nichols Rd
9800 FdmT 44231 3161 B7
9800 FdmT 44255 3161 B7
9800 HrmT 44231 3161 B7
25000 ClbT 44028 3009 D5
25000 ClbT 44028 3010 A5
Nicholson Av
400 VMLN 44089 2742 B5
1000 LKWD 44107 2622 E4
Nicki Ln
12000 CrlT 44024 2505 D1
12000 HmbT 44024 2380 D7
12000 HmbT 44024 2505 D1
Nickle Plate Diagonal Rd
12000 CrlT 44050 3005 D7
12600 CrlT 44050 3140 A7
13700 LrgT 44050 3140 A5
Nicola Dr
1200 AURA 44202 3022 E6
1200 ManT 44202 3022 E6
Nicole Cir
9400 SGVL 44136 3012 D4
Nicole Dr
600 AMHT 44001 2872 B3
Nicoles Wy
- MsnT 44024 2634 B2
Nicoll Dr
6500 NRDV 44039 2877 C4
Niessen Ct
4400 CLEV 44102 2754 B1
4400 CLEV 44109 2754 B1
Nightengale Ct
10 ELYR 44035 2875 D7
N Nightengale Pl
12000 CcdT 44077 2146 A7
Night Hawk Dr
9500 BbgT 44023 3022 E2
Nighthawk Dr
- BbgT 44023 3022 E1
Nightjar Ct
6800 VLVW 44125 2885 E6
Nightshade Ln
35300 SLN 44139 2889 B7
Night Vista Dr
5900 PRMA 44129 2883 A6
6800 PRMA 44129 2882 E6
Nikki Av
35000 NRDV 44039 2748 B7
Nimrod St E
32800 SLN 44139 2888 E7
Nimrod St W
32300 SLN 44139 2888 E7
Ninadell Av
38500 WLBY 44094 2143 A4
Nitra Av
18600 MPHT 44137 2757 E7
Niver St
- BDFD 44146 2887 A4
Nob Hl
19600 BNWK 44136 3147 A5
19600 BNWK 44212 3147 A5
19600 SGVL 44136 3147 A5
Nobb Hill Dr
7200 PRMA 44130 2882 D7
Nob Hill Dr
5000 CNFL 44022 2760 E7
5000 CNFL 44022 2889 E1
Nob Hill Ln
10500 CcdT 44077 2253 E1
Nob Hill Ovl
400 ORNG 44022 2759 C6
Noble Ct
5700 WLBY 44094 2375 A2
7400 MNTR 44060 2251 C1
Noble Rd
1700 CLEV 44110 2497 C4
1700 ECLE 44110 2497 C4
1700 ECLE 44112 2497 C4
2100 CVHT 44112 2497 D5
2200 CVHT 44121 2497 E5
2600 CVHT 44121 2498 A6
N Noble Rd
1700 CLEV 44110 2497 B4
1700 ECLE 44110 2497 B4
1700 ECLE 44112 2497 B4
S Noble Rd
1400 CVHT 44121 2498 A7
Noble Park Dr
9200 BKVL 44141 3150 E5
Nobleshire Rd
900 CVHT 44121 2497 E5
Nobottom Rd
100 BERA 44017 2880 A5
400 BERA 44017 2879 D4
400 BERA 44138 2879 E5
400 OmsT 44017 2879 E5
24600 ODFL 44138 2879 C4
24600 OmsT 44138 2879 C4
Nodding Hill Dr
- WNHL 44146 3017 A2
Nokomis Dr
10 TMLK 44095 2250 A1
Noll Dr
7100 NRDV 44039 2876 E4
Nollwood Dr
10700 MsnT 44024 2503 E2
10700 MsnT 44024 2504 A2
Noran Cir
10 BDFD 44146 2886 E2
10 BDFD 44146 2887 A2
Norbury Dr
600 BSHT 44236 3153 E7
600 HDSN 44236 3153 E7
600 HDSN 44236 3154 A7
Nordham Dr
- BDFD 44146 2887 A3
Nordica Ct
6800 CLEV 44102 2624 A6
7600 CLEV 44102 2623 E7
Nordson Dr
100 AhtT 44001 2873 A3
100 AMHT 44001 2872 E2
100 AMHT 44001 2873 A3
Nordway Rd
3400 CVHT 44118 2627 D3
3500 UNHT 44118 2627 D3
Noreen Dr
24100 NOSD 44070 2750 D3
24100 WTLK 44070 2750 D3
24100 WTLK 44145 2750 D3
Norfolk Av
3100 LORN 44055 2746 A3
Norfolk Dr
6100 PRMA 44134 2883 D3
29600 BYVL 44140 2619 C5
Norfolk Rd
2400 CVHT 44106 2626 E3
2500 CVHT 44106 2627 A2
Norma Dr
4200 SELD 44121 2498 B6
Norman Av
100 AVLK 44012 2618 D2
10500 CLEV 44106 2626 C3
28900 EUCL 44132 2374 A2
28900 WKLF 44092 2374 A2
Norman Ln
6100 MAYF 44143 2499 D6
Normandie Blvd
7600 MDBH 44130 3012 B2
7700 SGVL 44130 3012 B2
7700 SGVL 44136 3012 B2
Normandy Av
15600 CLEV 44111 2752 C1
Normandy Ct
400 AURA 44202 3156 D4
Normandy Dr
- CrlT 44035 3005 D5
10 BNWK 44212 3147 A6
10 PnvT 44077 2145 C4
5600 LORN 44053 2743 C5
7100 PRMA 44134 2883 B7
Normandy Pkwy
7700 CcdT 44077 2254 B2
Normandy Rd
3500 SRHT 44120 2757 D2
24100 ODFL 44138 3010 D1
26500 BYVL 44140 2620 A5
Norris Av
2600 PRMA 44134 2883 C3
North Av
- GNVA 44041 1944 A3
600 GnvT 44041 1944 A3
700 PnvT 44077 2039 E6
900 BNHT 44131 2754 E7
900 PRMA 44131 2754 E7
900 PRMA 44134 2754 E7
1000 GnvT 44041 1943 E2
North Av E
10 GNVA 44041 1944 B3
North Blvd
9700 AbnT 44023 3023 A1
9900 CLEV 44108 2496 B6
17800 MPHT 44137 2886 D1
North Ct
800 AMHT 44001 2743 E7
3900 CLEV 44111 2752 C3
10000 BKVL 44141 3151 D4
30800 NOSD 44070 2878 B3
North Dr
- AVLK 44012 2617 D2
- MNTR 44094 2251 B4
300 LORN 44053 2744 E6
300 LORN 44053 2745 A6
13600 GDHT 44105 2757 A4
North Ln
- AhtT 44001 2872 B2
- AMHT 44001 2872 B2
21300 OKWD 44146 3018 B1
38200 WLBY 44094 2142 E5
38200 WLBY 44094 2143 A5
North Ovl
5800 SLN 44139 2889 D3
North Rd
10 BKVL 44141 3151 A3
7600 MONT 44060 2143 D2
12500 CLEV 44111 2753 A2
31600 WLWK 44095 2249 C4
North St
100 CNFL 44022 2761 A5
100 CRDN 44024 2380 A5
300 CRDN 44024 2379 E5
400 BNHT 44131 2755 A7
500 BNHT 44131 2754 E7
500 CdnT 44024 2379 E5
500 ELYR 44035 2875 A6
600 RslT 44022 2761 B4
700 PRMA 44131 2754 E7
700 PRMA 44134 2754 E7
21900 EUCL 44117 2373 B7
North Tr
- MadT 44057 1843 C7
Northam Dr
7200 OKWD 44146 2887 D7
Northampton Rd
3700 CVHT 44121 2497 E5
3800 CVHT 44121 2498 A5
Northboro Dr
800 MAYF 44143 2500 A6
Northbridge Ct
300 BNWK 44212 3147 B7
13600 MCDN 44056 3154 A6
North Brook Tr
17100 BbgT 44023 2891 B3
Northcliff Dr
300 RKRV 44116 2621 D5
Northcliffe Av
5200 CLEV 44109 2754 B6
5200 CLEV 44144 2754 B6
5800 BKLN 44144 2754 A6
6200 BKLN 44144 2753 E6
Northcliffe Rd
3400 CVHT 44118 2627 D3
3400 UNHT 44118 2627 D3
Northcoast Point Dr
300 ETLK 44095 2250 B2
North Creek Dr
- PnvT 44077 2041 A3
Northern Av
- NOSD 44070 2878 E1
North Farm Rd
- HGVL 44022 2631 B6
Northfield Av
10 NCtT 44067 3153 A1
1700 ECLE 44112 2497 A5
Northfield Cir
- AVON 44011 2747 A6
Northfield Dr
100 ELYR 44035 2875 D1
Northfield Rd
- MPHT 44146 2758 B6
10 BDFD 44146 2887 B7
300 OKWD 44146 2887 B7
400 BDFD 44137 2887 B2
400 BDHT 44146 2887 B1
400 MPHT 44137 2887 B1
400 MPHT 44146 2887 B1
3500 HIHL 44122 2758 B5
3500 SRHT 44122 2758 A1
3600 WVHT 44122 2758 A2
4100 HIHL 44128 2758 B5
4200 WVHT 44128 2758 B4
4300 NRDL 44128 2758 B4
4900 WVHT 44146 2758 B6
5000 BDHT 44146 2758 B7
5000 MPHT 44137 2758 B7
6900 WNHL 44146 2887 B7
7100 WNHL 44146 3018 B1
7600 NHFD 44067 3018 B3
7600 NHFD 44146 3018 B3
10100 SgHT 44067 3018 A5
28800 BYVL 44140 2619 D4
Northfield Rd SR-8
- MPHT 44146 2758 B6
10 BDFD 44146 2887 B7
300 OKWD 44146 2887 B7
400 BDFD 44137 2887 B2
400 BDHT 44146 2887 B1
400 MPHT 44137 2887 B1
400 MPHT 44146 2887 B1
3500 HIHL 44122 2758 B5
3500 SRHT 44122 2758 A1
3600 WVHT 44122 2758 A2
4100 HIHL 44128 2758 B5
4300 NRDL 44128 2758 B4
4600 WVHT 44128 2758 B4
4900 WVHT 44146 2758 B6
5000 BDHT 44146 2758 B7
5000 MPHT 44137 2758 B7
6900 WNHL 44146 2887 B7
7100 WNHL 44146 3018 B1
7600 NHFD 44067 3018 B3
7600 NHFD 44146 3018 B3
10100 SgHT 44067 3018 A5
Northfield Rd SR-43
- BDHT 44146 2758 B6
- MPHT 44137 2758 B7
- MPHT 44146 2758 B6
4900 NRDL 44128 2758 B6
4900 WVHT 44128 2758 B6
4900 WVHT 44146 2758 B6
Northglen Dr
2500 WTLK 44145 2749 E2
North Hills Dr
7900 BWHT 44147 3014 D3
Northland Av
1400 LKWD 44107 2622 C5
2300 CLEV 44107 2622 B7
2300 CLEV 44111 2622 B7
Northland Rd
4800 BDHT 44128 2758 C6
4800 WVHT 44128 2758 C6
Northlane Dr
8400 BKLN 44144 2753 D5
Northline Dr
- CLEV 44119 2372 E4
- EUCL 44119 2372 E4
Northpointe Blvd
- AhtT 44001 2872 E4
- AMHT 44001 2872 E4
North Pointe Cir
9800 BKVL 44141 3150 C3
Northridge Dr
10 WLBY 44094 2375 C1
100 WLBY 44094 2250 C7
Northridge Ovl
100 BKLN 44144 2753 D6
North Ridge Rd
1600 BhmT 44001 2871 C3
1600 VMLN 44001 2871 D3
2000 VMLN 44089 2871 D3
3100 VMLN 44001 2870 E3
3100 VMLN 44089 2870 D3
3300 BhmT 44001 2870 D3
44800 AhtT 44001 2744 C6
44800 AMHT 44001 2744 C6
45800 AhtT 44001 2873 A1
45800 AMHT 44001 2873 A1
48000 AhtT 44001 2872 A2
48000 AMHT 44001 2872 A2
48200 AMHT 44001 2871 E2
52600 VmnT 44089 2870 B5
Northridge Rd
100 WLBY 44094 2250 C7
North Ridge Rd E
100 ShfT 44052 2745 A5
400 ShfT 44055 2745 A5
700 EyrT 44035 2745 A6
700 EyrT 44052 2745 A6
700 EyrT 44055 2745 A6
1800 LORN 44055 2745 D6
1900 ShfT 44035 2745 C6
2300 ShfT 44055 2746 A6
3200 SFLD 44035 2746 A6
3200 SFLD 44054 2746 A6
3200 ShfT 44035 2746 C6
3200 ShfT 44054 2746 C6
North Ridge Rd E SR-254
2200 ShfT 44035 2745 E6
2200 ShfT 44055 2745 E6
2300 ShfT 44055 2746 A6
3200 SFLD 44035 2746 A6
3200 SFLD 44054 2746 A6
3200 ShfT 44035 2746 C6
3200 ShfT 44054 2746 C6
North Ridge Rd W
100 LORN 44053 2745 A5
100 ShfT 44052 2745 A5
100 ShfT 44053 2745 A5
300 LORN 44052 2744 D5
300 LORN 44053 2744 D5
300 ShfT 44052 2744 E5
300 ShfT 44053 2744 E5
800 AhtT 44001 2744 D6
800 AhtT 44053 2744 D6
1200 AMHT 44001 2744 C6
1200 AMHT 44053 2744 C6
1200 LORN 44001 2744 C6
Northrop Ln
- WLBY 44094 2251 A6
Northrup Ln
18400 SGVL 44149 3146 C4
Northrup St
100 ELYR 44035 2875 C5
North Shore Dr
- PnvT 44077 2040 E1
North South Frwy
- CcdT - 2146 B7
- CcdT - 2253 D2
- CcdT - 2254 A1
- KDHL - 2252 E4
- KDHL - 2253 A4
- LryT - 2147 C4
- MadT - 2044 C3
- MDSN - 2044 B3
- MNTR - 2251 D5
- MNTR - 2252 B4
- MNTR - 2253 A4
North South Frwy I-90
- CcdT - 2146 B7
- CcdT - 2253 D2
- CcdT - 2254 A1
- KDHL - 2252 E4
- KDHL - 2253 A4
- LryT - 2147 C4
- MadT - 2044 C3
- MDSN - 2044 B3
- MNTR - 2251 D5
- MNTR - 2252 B4
- MNTR - 2253 A4
Northstar Ln
2300 AVON 44011 2748 E1
North Urban Cir
1700 LORN 44053 2744 B6
Northvale Blvd
3500 CVHT 44112 2497 C6
3500 ECLE 44112 2497 C6
Northview Av
14700 MDFD 44062 2767 B2
Northview Cir
34000 NRDV 44039 2877 B2
Northview Ct
4800 VMLN 44089 2741 A6
Northview Dr
- BbgT 44023 2890 E4
5900 SVHL 44131 2884 A3
16600 SGVL 44136 3147 A1
Northview Rd
1400 RKRV 44116 2621 D7
Northward Pointe Dr
12400 CsTp 44026 2502 A6
Northway Dr
100 PnvT 44077 2041 A2
5800 MadT 44057 1941 D1
Northwest Frwy
- AVON - 2619 C7
- CLEV - 2622 C7
- CLEV - 2623 A7
- CLEV - 2624 B6
- LKWD - 2622 A6
- RKRV - 2621 A6
- RKRV - 2622 A6
- WTLK - 2619 C7
- WTLK - 2620 A6
- WTLK - 2621 A6
Northwest Frwy I-90
- AVON - 2619 C7
- CLEV - 2622 C7
- CLEV - 2623 A7
- CLEV - 2624 B6
- LKWD - 2622 C7
- RKRV - 2621 A6
- RKRV - 2622 A6
- WTLK - 2619 C7
- WTLK - 2620 A6
- WTLK - 2621 A6
Northwest Frwy SR-2
- AVON - 2619 C7
- RKRV - 2621 A6
- WTLK - 2619 C7
- WTLK - 2620 A6
- WTLK - 2621 A6
North Winds Dr
5700 MONT 44060 2143 E1
Northwood Av
12800 SRHT 44120 2626 E4
15300 MPHT 44137 2886 B2
17400 LKWD 44107 2622 A4
20700 FWPK 44126 2751 C2
Northwood Cir
33100 AVLK 44012 2617 D3
Northwood Ct
32500 NRDV 44039 2748 E7
Northwood Dr
3100 PRPK 44124 2629 D7
4800 SDLK 44054 2616 D3
8500 BWHT 44147 3014 D5
E Northwood Dr
9700 ClbT 44028 3010 C1
9700 ClbT 44138 3010 C1
9700 ODFL 44138 3010 C2
W Northwood Dr
- ClbT 44028 3010 C2
- ClbT 44138 3010 C2
- ODFL 44138 3010 C2
Northwood Ln
3100 WTLK 44145 2749 B3
Northwood Rd
3700 UNHT 44118 2627 E3
13500 RslT 44072 2632 C4
Northwood St
41300 EyrT 44035 2745 D6

Cleveland Street Index

STREET Block	City	ZIP	Map#	Grid
Northwood Tr				
22100	SGVL	44149	3011	A5
Northwood Hollow Ct				
100	AMHT	44001	2872	B3
Northwood Lakes Dr				
17800	BbgT	44023	2890	C5
Northwoods Cir				
10500	CdnT	44024	2378	E7
Northwoods Ct				
7500	CcdT	44077	2254	C1
Norton Av				
17400	LKWD	44107	2622	B4
Norton Dr				
7600	MadT	44057	1844	A5
12100	CsTp	44026	2502	A5
Norton Pkwy				
-	MNTR	44060	2251	E3
-	MNTR	44060	2252	A4
Norton Rd				
3500	CLEV	44111	2752	D2
21800	BDHT	44146	2758	B7
21800	MPHT	44137	2758	B7
Norvale Cir E				
-	GSML	44040	2630	C2
Norvale Cir W				
6700	GSML	44040	2630	B2
Norway Av				
15500	CLEV	44111	2752	C1
Norway St				
2500	PryT	44077	2041	C3
Norwell Av				
18000	CLEV	44135	2752	A4
Norwich Dr				
200	BWHT	44147	3149	E4
200	BWHT	44147	3150	A5
Norwich Pl				
-	NRDV	44035	3007	B1
Norwood Dr				
2700	MadT	44057	1942	B4
5700	BKPK	44142	2879	E1
6000	MNTR	44060	2144	D3
Norwood Rd				
1000	CLEV	44103	2495	E7
3200	SRHT	44122	2627	E7
3400	SRHT	44122	2757	E1
3500	SRHT	44122	2758	A1
Notabene Dr				
10300	PMHT	44130	2882	B3
Notingham Ct				
29200	WTLK	44145	2749	D2
Notle St				
2600	ShvT	44255	3157	E7
2600	STBR	44255	3157	E7
Notre Dame Av				
10800	CLEV	44104	2626	C4
Notre Dame Cir				
100	ELYR	44035	3006	D1
Nottingham				
10	AURA	44202	3021	E7
Nottingham Ct				
100	CcdT	44060	2145	C6
13100	MsnT	44024	2635	A2
Nottingham Dr				
100	ELYR	44035	2875	C1
2400	PRMA	44134	2883	C7
21100	FWPK	44126	2751	B5
32300	AVLK	44012	2618	C3
Nottingham Ln				
2900	HGVL	44022	2630	C6
Nottingham Pkwy				
2000	AVON	44011	2618	B7
2000	AVON	44011	2748	B1
11800	NRYN	44133	3148	A4
Nottingham Pl				
500	PNVL	44077	2040	C6
Nottingham Rd				
17100	CLEV	44119	2372	D6
18500	CLEV	44110	2372	E7
18600	CLEV	44117	2372	E7
19400	CLEV	44110	2373	A7
19400	EUCL	44110	2373	A7
19400	EUCL	44117	2373	A7
Nottinghill Ln				
2500	CVHT	44106	2626	D4
2500	CVHT	44106	2627	A3
Novak Rd				
1000	GFTN	44044	3142	A4
Nowlen St				
8200	MNTR	44060	2252	A1
8400	MNTR	44060	2144	B7
Noyes Ct				
1100	CLEV	44109	2624	E7
Nursery Av				
2900	CLEV	44127	2625	C6
Nutmeg Ct				
12100	NRYN	44133	3013	B5
Nutmeg Ln				
12100	NRYN	44133	3013	B5
Nutwood Ln				
28400	WKLF	44092	2374	B4
Nyack Ct				
19400	CLEV	44110	2372	E7
Nye Rd				
10	PnvT	44077	2145	B4
900	CLEV	44110	2497	B2
O				
Oak Av				
-	HIHL	44128	2758	C4
-	NRDV	44039	2877	D3
-	SFLD	44054	2746	C4
7100	CHHT	44105	2755	E4
7100	CLEV	44105	2755	E4
Oak Cir				
4400	NOSD	44070	2750	E6
Oak Ct				
27300	EUCL	44132	2374	A1
Oak Dr				
10	OmsT	44138	2879	B4
11100	NbyT	44065	2634	C7
Oak Ln				
4400	NOSD	44070	2750	D6
7000	SVHL	44131	2884	B7
Oak Rd				
-	CrlT	44044	3141	D3
10	RKRV	44116	2621	D4
3100	CVHT	44118	2627	C1
Oak St				
-	AhtT	44001	2872	B3
100	ELYR	44035	2874	D4
200	OBLN	44074	3138	D3
300	SDLK	44054	2616	D3
400	BDHT	44146	2758	D7
700	PNVL	44077	2040	B6
Oak St				
900	GFTN	44044	3142	A5
1200	WLBY	44094	2142	E5
2700	WBHL	44092	2374	E5
2700	WBHL	44094	2374	E5
7000	BbgT	44022	2761	A7
7000	CNFL	44022	2761	A7
7800	MNTR	44060	2143	E5
10700	MNTU	44255	3159	B5
12900	GDHT	44125	2756	E7
35100	NRDV	44039	2877	B1
Oak Bark Tr				
21300	SGVL	44149	3011	B5
Oak Branch Tr				
10000	SGVL	44149	3011	A4
Oak Brook Cir				
8800	TNBG	44087	3154	B1
Oakbrook Dr				
4300	PryT	44081	2041	E4
13600	NRYN	44133	3013	C7
Oakbrook Ovl				
7900	PRMA	44129	3013	D2
Oak Cliff Dr				
300	BYVL	44140	2620	E5
Oakcrest Dr				
4200	LORN	44053	2743	C4
Oakdale Av				
1700	LORN	44052	2744	E1
2500	LORN	44055	2744	E1
4800	WLBY	44094	2250	E7
15300	CLEV	44128	2757	B4
Oakdale Cir				
10	ELYR	44035	3006	E2
Oakdale Dr				
-	NOSD	44070	2878	D3
-	PMHT	44130	2882	A6
100	SAHT	44001	2872	C6
Oakdale Rd				
200	BERA	44017	2880	B6
2100	CVHT	44118	2627	C3
6600	MNTR	44060	2144	A6
9100	PRMA	44129	2882	C1
30000	WLWK	44095	2249	C7
Oakdale St				
-	NCtT	44067	3153	B5
15600	MDFD	44062	2767	C1
Oakes Rd				
100	BWHT	44147	3149	E1
100	BWHT	44147	3150	B1
2100	BKVL	44141	3150	B1
2100	BWHT	44141	3150	B1
6700	BKVL	44141	3151	A1
Oakfield Av				
11800	CLEV	44105	2756	D1
12900	CLEV	44120	2756	E1
Oak Glen Dr				
8800	CdnT	44024	2254	E6
Oakham Rd				
1600	EUCL	44117	2373	C7
Oakhill Blvd				
4500	LORN	44053	2743	C4
Oak Hill Cir				
38300	WLBY	44094	2251	A3
Oak Hill Dr				
400	RDHT	44143	2498	C3
7500	CsTp	44026	2501	C4
Oakhill Dr				
24200	EUCL	44117	2373	D7
Oak Hill Ln				
38300	WLBY	44094	2250	E2
38300	WLBY	44094	2251	A2
Oakhill Rd				
7300	OKWD	44146	3018	E1
7700	NRYN	44133	3013	D7
15400	ECLE	44112	2497	C5
16100	CVHT	44112	2497	C5
Oakhill Ter				
300	MCDN	44056	3018	B6
Oak Hollow Dr				
400	MDSN	44057	2044	A2
11400	CdnT	44024	2254	C6
Oak Hollow Ln				
15200	SGVL	44149	3146	B2
Oak Hollow Rd				
400	AURA	44202	3156	C4
Oakhurst Av				
11700	CcdT	44077	2254	E5
Oakhurst Cir				
7600	BKVL	44131	3016	C3
7600	BKVL	44141	3016	C3
7600	INDE	44131	3016	C3
7600	INDE	44141	3016	C3
Oakhurst Ct				
600	AMHT	44001	2743	D7
Oakhurst Dr				
500	BHIT	44212	3146	A7
7800	BKVL	44141	3016	C3
32500	NRDV	44039	2748	E7
Oakhurst Ln				
21100	SGVL	44149	3146	B2
Oakhurst St				
700	AMHT	44001	2743	D7
Oak Knoll Ct				
8300	NRYN	44133	3014	A3
Oak Knoll Dr				
3200	PRPK	44124	2629	D7
Oak Knoll St				
34000	ETLK	44095	2249	E2
34000	ETLK	44095	2250	A2
34000	LKLN	44095	2249	E2
Oakland Av				
12000	CLEV	44106	2496	D7
Oakland Dr				
1200	LNHT	44124	2498	E7
E Oakland Rd				
23700	BYVL	44140	2620	D5
W Oakland Rd				
27800	BYVL	44140	2620	A5
28100	BYVL	44140	2619	D5
Oakland St				
-	RMDV	44202	3020	E4
Oakland Park Dr				
14000	SGVL	44136	3012	C3
Oaklawn Ct				
-	AURA	44202	3156	D1
Oaklawn Dr				
1700	PRMA	44134	2883	D2
Oak Leaf Dr				
8600	SGVL	44136	3012	C3
Oak Leaf Ovl				
-	AURA	44202	3021	B5
100	OKWD	44146	3018	B1
Oakleaf Rd				
-	BDFD	44146	2887	C7
7300	OKWD	44146	2887	C7
Oakleaf Rd				
7300	OKWD	44146	3018	C1
Oakleaf Rd SR-14				
-	OKWD	44146	2887	C7
S Oakleaf Rd				
7400	OKWD	44146	3018	C2
Oakleigh Dr				
10	BNWK	44136	3147	C6
10	BNWK	44212	3147	C6
10	SGVL	44136	3147	C6
Oakley Av				
4600	CLEV	44102	2624	B7
4600	CLEV	44109	2624	B7
Oakley Green Dr				
100	ELYR	44035	3006	D2
Oak Meadow Dr				
7600	TwbT	44236	3154	D6
7700	TwbT	44087	3154	D6
Oakmont Dr				
700	AVLK	44012	2618	C5
5000	LNHT	44124	2628	E1
5000	LNHT	44124	2629	A1
N Oakmont Dr				
10	NCtT	44067	3153	C3
S Oakmont Dr				
10	NCtT	44067	3153	B4
Oakmont Ln				
500	AURA	44202	3021	D5
Oakmont Rd				
-	NCtT	44067	3153	B4
Oakmont Wy				
10500	CcdT	44077	2253	E3
E Oakmont Wy				
10	NCtT	44067	3153	C4
Oakmoor Rd				
300	BYVL	44140	2620	C5
600	WTLK	44140	2620	C5
600	WTLK	44145	2620	C5
Oakmount Rd				
1400	SELD	44121	2498	D7
1400	SELD	44121	2628	C1
Oaknoll Dr				
400	AhtT	44001	2873	B1
Oak Park Av				
2100	CLEV	44109	2754	B6
4500	CLEV	44144	2754	B6
Oakpark Blvd				
12000	GDHT	44125	2885	E1
13500	GDHT	44125	2886	A1
Oak Park Dr				
9500	BKVL	44141	3016	C3
Oak Point Ests				
6200	LORN	44053	2743	B5
Oak Point Rd				
3700	LORN	44053	2743	C5
5900	AMHT	44001	2743	C7
5900	AMHT	44053	2743	C7
5900	LORN	44001	2743	C7
Oak Ridge Dr				
5400	WLBY	44094	2374	E1
5400	WLBY	44094	2375	A1
Oakridge Dr				
10	GNVA	44041	1944	C6
1200	CVHT	44121	2497	E7
4100	NRYN	44133	3014	B3
5100	WLBY	44094	2249	E7
5100	WLBY	44094	2374	E1
7600	CcdT	44060	2253	C2
8500	OmsT	44138	2878	E7
8500	OmsT	44138	2879	A7
Oakshire Ct				
15400	MDBH	44130	2881	A5
Oak Shore Grn				
10	BTNH	44108	2496	E1
Oakstone Tr				
8000	CdnT	44024	2254	C7
9100	CdnT	44024	2379	C1
Oakton Cir				
400	MAYF	44143	2500	B3
Oak Trail Ct				
20700	SGVL	44149	3011	B4
Oak Tree Blvd N				
-	INDE	44131	2884	C3
Oak Tree Blvd S				
6000	INDE	44131	2884	C3
Oak Tree Ct				
-	MDBH	44130	2881	B4
Oaktree Dr				
8400	MCDN	44056	3153	E2
34600	WLBY	44094	2375	A1
Oak Tree Dr N				
6200	LORN	44053	2743	B5
Oak Tree Dr S				
6300	LORN	44053	2743	C5
Oak Tree Tr				
-	NbyT	44024	2634	C5
-	NbyT	44065	2634	C5
Oakview Av				
11700	CLEV	44108	2496	D4
Oakview Blvd				
12300	GDHT	44125	2885	E2
13500	GDHT	44125	2886	A2
Oak View Cir				
300	HkyT	44233	3147	E7
2600	BWHT	44147	3014	C4
Oakview Ct				
9100	TNBG	44087	3019	B7
Oak View Dr				
4900	VMLN	44089	2741	A7
Oakview Dr				
900	HDHT	44143	2499	A6
900	LNHT	44124	2499	A6
900	LNHT	44143	2499	A6
3000	WBHL	44092	2374	B7
Oakview Ln				
36200	AVON	44011	2747	E3
Oakview Rd				
500	MCDN	44056	3018	D5
Oakview St				
23200	ODFL	44138	2879	D7
Oakville Rd				
5700	MDHT	44124	2499	C7
Oakwood Av				
-	CrlT	44035	3006	B3
-	ELYR	44035	3006	B3
-	SVHL	44131	3015	A2
10	BDFD	44146	2886	E4
500	SDLK	44054	2616	C4
2800	LORN	44055	2745	E3
5300	MPHT	44137	2886	E1
Oakwood Blvd				
-	ShfT	44035	2745	E6
10	PnvT	44077	2040	D2
5000	LORN	44055	2745	E5
5000	ShfT	44055	2745	E6
Oakwood Cir				
6000	NRDV	44039	2877	E2
6000	NRDV	44039	2878	A2
27000	OmsT	44138	2878	D3
30300	NOSD	44070	2878	A1
Oakwood Ct				
2000	AVON	44011	2747	D1
Oakwood Dr				
100	AVLK	44012	2618	E2
700	MAYF	44040	2500	B5
700	MAYF	44143	2500	B5
900	ELYR	44035	2874	D4
1000	VMLN	44089	2740	D6
2800	WBHL	44094	2374	E6
5300	SFLD	44054	2746	E1
5300	SFLD	44054	2747	A1
6500	INDE	44131	2884	C5
6500	SVHL	44131	3015	A1
8000	KTLD	44094	2376	E7
9600	TNBG	44087	3019	C5
27000	NOSD	44070	2878	C3
27000	NOSD	44138	2878	C3
27000	OmsT	44138	2878	C3
29400	WKLF	44092	2374	B1
Oakwood Ln				
1100	HkyT	44133	3149	A6
1100	HkyT	44233	3149	A6
1100	NRYN	44133	3149	A6
1200	HkyT	44133	3148	E5
1200	HkyT	44233	3148	E5
1200	NRYN	44133	3148	E5
3000	WTLK	44145	2750	A3
8500	NRYN	44133	3014	B3
11900	CsTp	44026	2502	B4
Oakwood Pkwy				
-	OKWD	44146	3018	D1
Oakwood Pl				
21400	SGVL	44149	3146	A1
Oakwood Rd				
-	CVHT	44121	2498	A7
-	SELD	44121	2498	A7
6700	PMHT	44130	2881	E6
6900	PRMA	44130	2881	E7
Oakwood St				
200	CrlT	44035	3006	B3
200	ELYR	44035	3006	B3
Oakwood Tr				
3100	BWHT	44147	3014	C7
Oakwood Commons Dr				
21200	OKWD	44146	2887	C7
Oasis Blvd				
10	MadT	44057	1941	B6
Ober Ln				
7100	BbgT	44023	2761	B7
Oberlin Av				
100	LORN	44052	2614	D7
1200	LORN	44052	2744	C5
3100	LORN	44053	2744	C5
6000	AhtT	44001	2744	C6
6000	AhtT	44053	2744	C6
6000	LORN	44001	2744	C6
Oberlin Mnr				
-	LORN	44053	2744	C3
Oberlin Rd				
10	OBLN	44074	3139	B3
100	ELYR	44035	3006	A2
100	NRsT	44074	3139	B2
5500	AhtT	44001	2744	C7
5500	AMHT	44001	2744	C6
6300	AhtT	44001	2873	D1
7100	AhtT	44035	2873	B5
8500	AhtT	44001	3004	B1
8500	AhtT	44035	3004	B1
8500	NRsT	44001	3004	B1
8500	NRsT	44035	3004	B1
9400	NRsT	44074	3004	B5
Oberlin Elyria Rd				
400	CrlT	44035	3005	B7
400	ELYR	44035	3005	E2
42200	CrlT	44074	3005	B7
42500	CrlT	44074	3139	E2
42500	CrlT	44074	3140	A1
42500	NRsT	44074	3139	D3
44000	OBLN	44074	3139	C3
Ocala Dr				
4400	PRMA	44134	3014	B2
Ocean Pt				
6600	MNTR	44060	2145	A5
Ocean Reef				
37300	WLBY	44094	2250	D3
Octavia Rd				
1600	CLEV	44112	2497	C3
October Ln				
5800	MadT	44057	1941	D1
Offshore Dr				
-	LORN	44052	2614	E6
Ogontz Av				
2200	CLEV	44107	2622	B7
2200	CLEV	44111	2622	B7
2200	LKWD	44107	2622	B7
2200	LKWD	44111	2622	B7
O'Henry Cir				
6500	NRDV	44039	2877	C3
Ohio Av				
1500	LORN	44052	2615	D6
14200	CLEV	44128	2757	A5
14200	GDHT	44125	2757	A5
14200	GDHT	44128	2757	A5
Ohio St				
200	ELYR	44035	2875	B5
800	AURA	44202	3021	B4
3200	PryT	44081	2041	E2
5200	VMLN	44089	2740	E5
6900	MNTR	44060	2143	D7
Ohio Tpk				
-	AhtT	-	2871	E5
-	AhtT	-	2872	B5
-	AhtT	-	2873	C4
-	AMHT	-	2872	E4
-	BERA	-	3010	D1
-	BERA	-	3011	A2
-	BhmT	-	2871	A7
-	BKVL	-	3150	B4
-	BWHT	-	3149	E3
-	BWHT	-	3150	A4
-	ELYR	-	2874	E3
-	ELYR	-	2875	E4
-	EyrT	-	2873	D3
-	EyrT	-	2874	E3
-	NRDV	-	2875	E4
-	NRDV	-	2876	A5
-	NRDV	-	2877	A5
-	NRDV	-	2878	B6
-	NRYN	-	3012	E6
-	NRYN	-	3013	A7
Ohio Tpk				
-	NRYN	-	3148	C1
-	NRYN	-	3149	E3
-	ODFL	-	3010	B1
-	OmsT	-	2878	B6
-	OmsT	-	2879	A7
-	OmsT	-	3010	B1
-	RchT	-	3150	E6
-	RchT	-	3151	A6
-	RHFD	-	3150	E6
-	RHFD	-	3151	A6
-	SGVL	-	3011	A2
-	SGVL	-	3012	A4
Ohio Tpk I-80				
-	AhtT	-	2871	E5
-	AhtT	-	2872	B5
-	AhtT	-	2873	C4
-	AMHT	-	2872	E4
-	BERA	-	3010	D1
-	BERA	-	3011	C3
-	BhmT	-	2871	B7
-	BKVL	-	3150	A4
-	BWHT	-	3149	E3
-	BWHT	-	3150	A4
-	ELYR	-	2874	E3
-	ELYR	-	2875	E4
-	EyrT	-	2873	D3
-	EyrT	-	2874	E3
-	NRDV	-	2875	E4
-	NRDV	-	2876	A5
-	NRDV	-	2877	A5
-	NRDV	-	2878	B6
-	NRYN	-	3012	E6
-	NRYN	-	3013	A7
-	NRYN	-	3148	C1
-	NRYN	-	3149	E3
-	ODFL	-	3010	E1
-	OmsT	-	2878	B6
-	OmsT	-	2879	A7
-	OmsT	-	3010	B1
-	RchT	-	3150	E6
-	RchT	-	3151	A6
-	RHFD	-	3150	E6
-	RHFD	-	3151	A6
-	SGVL	-	3011	A2
-	SGVL	-	3012	A4
Ohio Tpk I-90				
-	AhtT	-	2871	E5
-	AhtT	-	2872	B5
-	AhtT	-	2873	C4
-	AMHT	-	2872	E4
-	BhmT	-	2871	B7
Ohlman Av				
11300	CLEV	44108	2496	D5
Okalona Rd				
4000	SELD	44118	2628	A3
4000	SELD	44121	2628	A3
Old Rd				
-	NbyT	44065	2764	D2
Old Abbe Rd				
3700	SFLD	44054	2746	E3
Old Alexander Rd				
-	VLVW	44125	3016	E1
Old Barn Dr				
900	AURA	44202	3156	C4
Old Brainard Rd				
2900	PRPK	44124	2629	B7
3200	PRPK	44124	2759	A1
Old Brecksville Rd				
5400	INDE	44131	2884	E1
Old Brookpark Rd				
-	CLEV	44131	2755	A7
500	BNHT	44109	2755	A7
500	BNHT	44131	2755	A7
500	CLEV	44109	2755	A7
Old Colorado Av				
-	SFLD	44054	2615	E7
3900	SFLD	44054	2616	C7
Old Cord Ln				
-	GSML	44040	2500	E7
Old Detroit Rd				
19000	RKRV	44116	2621	E5
Olde Bennett Rd				
19400	NRYN	44133	3147	E5
Olde Egbert Rd E				
10	BDFD	44146	2887	A5
Olde Egbert Rd W				
100	BDFD	44146	2887	A6
Olde Eight Rd				
-	NHFD	44067	3018	A6
-	SgHT	44067	3018	A6
7400	BSHT	44236	3153	C7
7800	BSHT	44067	3153	C6
7800	NCtT	44067	3153	B4
7800	NCtT	44236	3153	C6
9100	NCtT	44067	3152	E1
9300	NCtT	44067	3017	E7
9500	SgHT	44067	3017	E7
9700	NCtT	44067	3018	A6
Olde Farm Ln				
7200	MNTR	44060	2143	B5
Olde Field Ct				
6600	MNTR	44060	2143	C5
Olde Meadows Ct				
6800	MNTR	44060	2143	C5
Olde Orchard Rd				
13200	SGVL	44136	3147	D5
Olde Pond Ln				
9500	TNBG	44087	3019	C6
Olde Stone Ct				
11500	CcdT	44077	2254	D2
Olde Surrey Ct				
17300	SGVL	44136	3147	A4
Olde Towne Tr				
100	BERA	44017	3011	C1
19800	BNWK	44136	3147	C5
19800	BNWK	44212	3147	C5
19800	SGVL	44136	3147	C5
Olde York Rd				
6300	PMHT	44130	2882	B4
Old Farm Rd				
10	MDHL	44022	2759	D5
Old Granger Rd				
7800	GDHT	44125	2756	A7
7800	VLVW	44125	2756	A7
Old Grayton Rd				
4900	CLEV	44135	2751	C6
Old Green Rd				
3400	BHWD	44122	2758	C1
Old Harper Rd				
5800	SLN	44139	2888	C3
Old Heisley Rd				
6900	MNTR	44060	2145	A6
Old Hickory				
-	AURA	44202	3021	C5
Old Highland Dr				
8900	BKVL	44141	3016	B7
Old Hogsback Rd				
-	CLEV	44107	2622	A7
-	LKWD	44107	2622	A7
Old Johnnycake				
9600	CcdT	44060	2145	A6
9600	MNTR	44060	2145	A6
9700	CcdT	44077	2145	A6
Old Kinsman Rd				
33600	HGVL	44022	2760	A1
33600	PRPK	44022	2760	A1
33600	PRPK	44124	2760	A1
Old Lake Rd				
-	VMLN	44089	2740	D5
300	LORN	44053	2743	B4
Old Lorain Rd				
-	CLEV	44126	2752	A2
-	FWPK	44126	2752	A2
17800	CLEV	44111	2752	A2
17800	CLEV	44135	2752	A2
Old Meadow Dr				
8900	BbgT	44023	2891	C6
Old Middle Ridge Rd				
6000	EyrT	44053	2745	A6
6000	LORN	44052	2745	A6
6000	LORN	44053	2745	A6
45200	AhtT	44001	2873	B3
Old Mill Pth				
1300	BWHT	44147	3149	E5
Old Mill Rd				
700	AURA	44202	3156	A5
1200	AURA	44087	3156	A5
1200	AURA	44236	3156	A5
1200	TwbT	44087	3156	A5
1200	TwbT	44236	3156	A5
2000	MadT	44057	1941	D2
2100	TNBG	44087	3155	A5
2100	TNBG	44236	3155	A5
2100	TwbT	44087	3155	E5
2100	TwbT	44236	3155	D5
7000	CsTp	44026	2501	B7
7000	GSML	44040	2500	C7
7200	GSML	44040	2630	D1
7700	CsTp	44026	2631	A1
7700	GSML	44040	2631	A1
Old Mill Rd SR-174				
-	GSML	44040	2630	E1
Old Munson Rd				
8400	MNTR	44060	2144	B4
Old North Dr				
10	NCtT	44067	3152	E1
10	SgHT	44067	3152	E1
Old Oak Blvd				
7200	MDBH	44130	2880	E7
7200	MDBH	44130	3011	E1
Old Oak Dr				
14800	SGVL	44149	3146	B1
Old Oak Rd				
1200	AMHT	44001	2744	A7
Old Orchard				
22900	FWPK	44126	2751	A6
Old Orchard Dr				
10100	BKVL	44141	3151	D5
Old Plank Ln				
10	MDHL	44022	2760	D6
Old Pleasant Valley Rd				
13000	MDBH	44130	2881	D6
13000	PRMA	44130	2881	E7
Old Post Rd				
8200	ODFL	44138	2879	A6
Old Quarry Ln				
7300	BKVL	44141	3016	A5
Old Reservoir Rd				
400	BERA	44017	3011	C1
Old Rider Rd				
15000	BtnT	44021	2765	C3
Old River Rd				
1000	CLEV	44113	2624	C3
Old Rockside Rd				
100	PRMA	44131	2883	E2
100	PRMA	44134	2883	E2
100	SVHL	44131	2883	E2
100	SVHL	44131	2884	A2
7400	INDE	44131	2884	E3
7600	INDE	44131	2885	A3
7900	INDE	44125	2885	A3
7900	VLVW	44125	2885	A3
18000	BDFD	44146	2886	D3
Old Royalton Rd				
6200	BKVL	44141	3015	E6
6200	BWHT	44141	3015	E7
6200	BWHT	44147	3015	E7
6800	BKVL	44141	3016	A6
Old Royalwood Rd				
900	BWHT	44147	3014	E6
Old Salem Tr				
-	HDHT	44143	2499	E1
Old Schady Rd				
26800	OmsT	44138	2879	A7
Old Shore Dr				
30700	NOSD	44070	2878	A2
Oldsmar Av				
1300	MadT	44057	1843	C7
Old Som Ln				
-	HGVL	44022	2760	A2
10	MDHL	44022	2760	A2
10	PRPK	44022	2760	A2
Old South Miles Rd				
32100	SLN	44139	2888	E4
Old State Rd				
-	HtbT	44046	2637	B3
8400	CcdT	44024	2255	D5
8400	CcdT	44077	2255	D5
8400	HmbT	44024	2255	D7
8400	HmbT	44077	2255	D5
8800	HmbT	44024	2380	E1
8800	HmbT	44024	2381	A2
10900	ClrT	44024	2506	D4
10900	HmbT	44024	2506	D4
12100	ClrT	44021	2506	E6
12100	ClrT	44046	2506	E6
12600	ClrT	44021	2636	E1
12600	ClrT	44046	2636	E1
12800	ClrT	44021	2637	A2
12800	ClrT	44046	2637	A2
13400	HtbT	44021	2637	A3
13500	MdfT	44021	2637	B4
13500	MdfT	44046	2637	B4
13600	MdfT	44062	2637	C6
14300	MdfT	44062	2767	D1
15000	MDFD	44062	2767	D4
Old State Rd SR-608				
8400	CcdT	44024	2255	D5
8400	CcdT	44077	2255	D5
Old State Rd SR-608				
8400	HmbT	44024	2255	D7
8400	HmbT	44077	2255	D5
8800	HmbT	44024	2380	E1
8800	HmbT	44024	2381	A2
10900	ClrT	44024	2506	D4
10900	HmbT	44024	2506	D4
12100	ClrT	44021	2506	E6
12100	ClrT	44046	2506	E6
12600	ClrT	44021	2636	E1
12600	ClrT	44046	2636	E1
12800	ClrT	44021	2637	A2
12800	ClrT	44046	2637	A2
13400	HtbT	44021	2637	A3
13400	HtbT	44046	2637	A3
13500	MdfT	44021	2637	B4
13500	MdfT	44046	2637	B4
13600	MdfT	44062	2637	C6
14300	MdfT	44062	2767	D1
15000	MDFD	44062	2767	D4
Old Tannery Tr				
17300	BbgT	44023	2890	D4
Old Village Ln				
8600	MNTR	44060	2144	C7
Old Virginia Ln				
6200	PMHT	44130	2882	A3
Old West Ridge Rd				
-	AhtT	44035	2745	A7
-	EyrT	44035	2745	A7
-	LORN	44035	2745	A7
-	LORN	44053	2745	A7
8100	ELYR	44035	2873	E5
8100	EyrT	44035	2873	E5
Old Willoughby Dr				
38400	WLBY	44094	2251	A1
Oleander Ovl				
400	MDSN	44057	1942	B7
Olive Av				
2000	LKWD	44107	2622	C6
5100	NRDV	44039	2748	C7
5100	NRDV	44039	2877	C1
Olive Ct				
6000	CLEV	44103	2625	D2
Olive St				
10	CNFL	44022	2760	E7
10	CNFL	44022	2761	A7
100	ELYR	44035	2875	D5
100	GDRV	44077	2039	B5
Oliver Ct				
8800	NRDV	44035	2876	C7
Oliver Dr				
18100	SGVL	44149	3146	D4
Oliver Rd				
10800	CLEV	44111	2753	B2
Oliver St				
700	SDLK	44054	2616	A4
Olivet Av				
-	EyrT	44035	2745	E6
-	ShfT	44035	2745	E6
-	ShfT	44055	2745	E6
9900	CLEV	44108	2496	B7
Olivet Ct				
-	CLEV	44108	2496	C7
Olivet Dr				
400	ELYR	44035	2875	D3
Olivewood Av				
1400	LKWD	44107	2622	D5
Olmar Dr				
10900	CdnT	44024	2378	E7
10900	CdnT	44024	2503	E1
10900	MsnT	44024	2503	E1
Olmsted Ct				
27200	NOSD	44070	2749	E7
27200	NOSD	44070	2750	A7
Olmsted Dr				
3100	NOSD	44070	2750	E3
Olmway Av				
8000	ODFL	44138	2879	B6
Olney Ct				
11300	CLEV	44105	2756	D4
Olympia Rd				
17800	CLEV	44112	2497	D2
Olympus Ct				
12500	SGVL	44149	3011	D6
Olympus Wy				
12400	SGVL	44149	3011	D6
Omaha Av				
3000	LORN	44055	2745	B3
O'Malley Dr				
100	PRMA	44134	2883	E1
Omega Av				
5400	BDHT	44146	2887	D1
Omega Ct				
9500	MNTR	44060	2145	A5
Onaway Ovl				
5600	PRMA	44130	2882	C2
Onaway Rd				
3100	SRHT	44120	2627	A7
O'Neil Blvd				
4400	ShfT	44055	2745	B6
4900	EyrT	44035	2745	B6
4900	EyrT	44055	2745	B6
O'Neill Dr				
37100	SLN	44139	2889	C3
Onoko Dr				
19800	FWPK	44126	2751	D1
19800	RKRV	44116	2751	D1
19800	RKRV	44126	2751	D1
Onondaga Av				
1500	LKWD	44107	2622	D6
Ontario St				
700	GFTN	44044	3142	A5
1200	CLEV	44113	2624	E3
1200	CLEV	44114	2624	D2
1900	CLEV	44115	2624	E3
Ontario St SR-8				
1900	CLEV	44114	2624	E3
1900	CLEV	44115	2624	E3
2000	CLEV	44113	2624	E3
Ontario St SR-14				
1900	CLEV	44114	2624	E3
1900	CLEV	44115	2624	E3
2000	CLEV	44113	2624	E3
Ontario St SR-87				
1900	CLEV	44114	2624	E3
1900	CLEV	44115	2624	E3
2000	CLEV	44113	2624	E3
Ontario St US-422				
1900	CLEV	44114	2624	E3
1900	CLEV	44115	2624	E3
2000	CLEV	44113	2624	E3
Opal St				
5500	NRDV	44039	2877	C2
Opalocka Dr				
12600	CsTp	44026	2502	B7

STREET Block City ZIP Map# Grid

Opalocka Dr
12700 CsTp 44026 2632 B1
Opportunity Av
- PRRY 44081 2042 C1
E Oralee Ln
7400 TwbT 44236 3154 C6
N Oralee Ln
1300 TwbT 44236 3154 C5
S Oralee Ln
1300 TwbT 44236 3154 C6
W Oralee Ln
7400 TwbT 44236 3154 C5
Orange Av
1400 CLEV 44115 2625 B4
Orange Av SR-8
1400 CLEV 44115 2625 B4
Orange Av SR-87
1400 CLEV 44115 2625 B4
Orange Av US-422
1400 CLEV 44115 2625 B4
Orange Grv
10 BKPK 44142 2752 B7
Orange Ln
16600 AbnT 44021 2893 D2
Orange Pl
- ORNG 44022 2759 A3
3600 ORNG 44122 2759 A2
3600 WDMR 44122 2759 A1
E Orange St
10 CNFL 44022 2761 A5
W Orange St
10 CNFL 44022 2760 E6
10 CNFL 44022 2761 A6
Orangedale Rd
4200 ORNG 44022 2759 C4
E Orange Hill Cir
100 ORNG 44022 2759 C6
W Orange Hill Cir
- SLN 44022 2759 C6
- SLN 44139 2759 C6
10 ORNG 44022 2759 C6
Orange Meadow Ln
4100 ORNG 44022 2759 B4
Orange Tree Dr
100 ORNG 44022 2759 A5
Orangewood Dr
3900 ORNG 44122 2759 B3
4000 ORNG 44022 2759 B3
Orchard Av
800 AURA 44202 3021 A4
1200 RMDV 44202 3021 A4
4100 CLEV 44113 2624 B6
4200 WLBY 44094 2250 D5
5000 ShfT 44055 2745 C6
5300 EyrT 44035 2745 C6
5300 EyrT 44055 2745 C6
5400 PRMA 44129 2883 A1
5400 PRMA 44134 2883 A1
6700 PRMA 44129 2882 E1
8500 BKLN 44144 2753 D4
14800 MDFD 44062 2767 C2
Orchard Bch
- VmnT 44089 2740 A7
Orchard Blvd
6600 PMHT 44130 2882 A5
Orchard Cir
10 ORNG 44022 2759 B6
Orchard Ct
2000 SFLD 44054 2616 C7
41600 EyrT 44035 2874 D2
Orchard Dr
- CcdT 44077 2254 C4
- MNTR 44060 2251 B4
- MNTR 44094 2251 B4
2800 WBHL 44092 2374 C5
31500 WLWK 44095 2249 C4
Orchard Ext
2000 WBHL 44092 2374 C5
2000 WKLF 44092 2374 C5
Orchard Grv
10 OmsT 44138 2879 B4
10 PNVL 44077 2145 E2
300 BERA 44017 2880 C6
300 SgHT 44067 3017 C7
Orchard Ln
- NRYN 44133 3013 A5
1000 BWHT 44147 3149 D4
5100 NRDV 44039 2748 D7
Orchard Pl
2100 CLEV 44113 2624 C6
Orchard Rd
500 WLBY 44094 2143 A4
3900 CVHT 44121 2498 A6
4500 FWPK 44126 2751 A4
4600 MNTR 44060 2038 D5
4700 CLEV 44128 2757 B6
4700 GDHT 44128 2757 B6
8100 CcdT 44077 2254 C4
11400 MsnT 44024 2504 C3
35000 SLN 44139 2888 E6
Orchard St
- SAHT 44001 3003 C1
10 OBLN 44074 3139 A2
100 GNVA 44041 1944 C4
200 CNFL 44022 2760 E7
200 FTHR 44077 2039 D4
4400 MNTU 44255 3159 B6
5400 MPHT 44137 2886 B1
8100 ODFL 44138 2879 C6
36900 AVON 44011 2747 D2
Orchard Wy
2200 BHWD 44122 2628 E3
3100 WTLK 44145 2749 E3
Orchard Glen Dr
1200 AMHT 44001 2743 B7
Orchard Grove Av
1400 LKWD 44107 2622 C5
6000 CLEV 44144 2754 A3
6300 BKLN 44144 2753 E3
6300 CLEV 44144 2753 E3
20200 RKRV 44116 2621 D7
Orchard Grove Dr
16600 MDBH 44130 2881 B5
75000 RDHT 44143 2498 E5
Orchard Heights Dr
1100 MAYF 44143 2499 E6
1100 MDHT 44124 2499 E7
1100 MDHT 44143 2499 E6
Orchard Hill Blvd
6000 LORN 44053 2744 D7
Orchard Hill Dr
100 AMHT 44001 2872 E1
100 AMHT 44001 2873 A1
18000 WNHL 44146 3017 E2
18500 WNHL 44146 3018 A2

Orchard Hill Ln
10200 TNBG 44087 3020 A4
Orchard Park Av
14400 CLEV 44111 2752 D1
Orchard Park Dr
700 RKRV 44116 2621 A6
4000 PRMA 44134 2883 B5
4800 PRMA 44129 2883 A5
32200 AVLK 44012 2618 C2
Orchardview Rd
100 PRMA 44131 3014 E2
100 PRMA 44134 3014 E2
100 SVHL 44131 3014 E2
100 SVHL 44131 3015 A2
Orchid Av
5500 MNTR 44060 2144 A1
Ordner Dr
13900 SGVL 44136 3011 E7
13900 SGVL 44136 3146 E1
Oregon Av
4200 PryT 44081 2041 D4
Oregon Tr
10 ClrT 44024 2505 C6
Orey Av
5500 CLEV 44105 2755 D2
Orianna St
7900 BKVL 44141 3016 B3
Orin Wy
2800 TNBG 44087 3020 B4
Oring Rd
29600 NOSD 44070 2749 D6
Orinoco Av
13800 ECLE 44112 2497 A5
Oriole Av
26000 EUCL 44132 2373 E1
26800 EUCL 44132 2374 A1
Oriole Ct
10 ELYR 44035 2875 E7
5700 MNTR 44060 2144 E2
Oriole Dr
600 ETLK 44095 2250 D1
Oriole Pl
11500 MsnT 44024 2504 B3
Orkney Rd
1600 MadT 44057 1842 E7
1700 MadT 44057 1941 E1
Orlando Dr
7500 PRMA 44134 3014 D1
Orleans Av
9300 CLEV 44105 2756 B1
Orme Rd
12600 GDHT 44125 2885 E2
Ormiston Av
19300 EUCL 44119 2372 E5
19300 EUCL 44119 2373 A5
Ormond Av
1300 MadT 44057 1843 C6
Ormond Rd
3200 CVHT 44118 2627 C4
Ornelda Av
7100 MadT 44057 1843 D7
Oroszy Av
4800 ShfT 44052 2745 A5
4800 ShfT 44055 2745 A5
Orton Ct
6300 CLEV 44103 2495 E7
Orton Rd
10 PnvT 44077 2147 B2
Orville Av
11200 CLEV 44106 2496 D7
Orvos Ct
9100 MNTR 44060 2144 E1
Osage Av
7400 CLEV 44105 2756 A2
Osage Dr
7900 MDBH 44130 3011 E2
7900 SGVL 44130 3011 E2
7900 SGVL 44149 3011 E2
52100 BhmT 44001 2870 C7
Osage Wy
3000 BWHT 44147 3014 C7
Osborn Ln
2900 TNBG 44087 3020 C4
Osborn Rd
4600 CLEV 44105 2757 A5
4600 CLEV 44128 2757 A5
4600 GDHT 44105 2757 A5
4600 GDHT 44125 2757 A6
4900 GDHT 44128 2757 A6
27800 BYVL 44140 2619 E5
27800 BYVL 44140 2620 A5
Osborn St
5000 GDHT 44128 2757 B7
5000 MPHT 44128 2757 B7
Osborne Av
700 LORN 44052 2614 C7
Osborne Dr
8900 MNTR 44060 2144 D6
Osborne Rd
24900 ClbT 44028 3010 A3
26000 ClbT 44028 3009 D3
27600 ClbT 44028 3008 E4
27600 EatT 44028 3008 E4
Osbourne Rd
26500 ClbT 44028 3009 B4
Osceola Av
11700 CLEV 44108 2496 D6
12400 CLEV 44112 2496 E6
12400 ECLE 44112 2496 E6
Osmond Ct
6500 CLEV 44105 2755 E1
Osmond Rd
13400 BtnT 44021 2635 D5
13400 BtnT 44024 2635 D5
13400 ClrT 44021 2635 E4
13400 ClrT 44024 2635 E4
Ostend Av
9900 CLEV 44108 2496 B6
Oster Rd
4700 SDLK 44054 2616 D4
4700 SFLD 44054 2616 D4
Otani Ct
7700 SGVL 44136 3012 A7
Othello Av
13500 CLEV 44110 2497 A1
Otis Ct
400 SgHT 44067 3017 D4
7100 CLEV 44104 2625 E5
7300 CLEV 44104 2626 A5
Otis Pl
15700 MPHT 44137 2757 B7
Otokar Av
3000 CLEV 44127 2625 D6
Ottawa Av
6700 MadT 44057 1843 B7

Ottawa Dr
8500 BKVL 44141 3016 D6
Ottawa Rd
7100 CLEV 44105 2755 E3
7400 CLEV 44105 2756 A3
Otten Rd
- NRDV 44039 2747 C7
5600 NRDV 44039 2876 B2
Otter Av
8100 CLEV 44104 2626 A6
Otto Ct
5600 CLEV 44102 2624 A7
Outerbelt East Frwy
- BDFD - 2887 C4
- BDHT - 2758 D7
- BDHT - 2887 D1
- BHWD - 2629 B3
- BHWD - 2758 E3
- BHWD - 2759 A1
- HDHT - 2499 E2
- LNHT - 2629 C2
- MCDN - 3018 C3
- MDHT - 2499 E5
- MDHT - 2500 A6
- MDHT - 2629 D2
- OKWD - 2887 C7
- OKWD - 3018 C1
- ORNG - 2758 E4
- ORNG - 2759 A3
- PRPK - 2629 A4
- PRPK - 2759 A1
- WBHL - 2374 E7
- WVHT - 2758 D7
Outerbelt East Frwy I-271
- BDFD - 2887 C4
- BDHT - 2758 D7
- BDHT - 2887 D1
- BHWD - 2629 B3
- BHWD - 2758 E3
- BHWD - 2759 A1
- HDHT - 2499 E3
- LNHT - 2629 C2
- MCDN - 3018 C3
- MDHT - 2499 E5
- MDHT - 2500 A6
- MDHT - 2629 D2
- OKWD - 2887 C7
- OKWD - 3018 C2
- ORNG - 2758 E4
- ORNG - 2759 A3
- PRPK - 2629 A4
- PRPK - 2759 A1
- WBHL - 2374 E7
- WVHT - 2758 E4
Outerbelt East Frwy I-480
- BDFD - 2887 C4
- BDHT - 2887 C4
- OKWD - 2887 C7
- OKWD - 3018 C1
Outerbelt East Frwy SR-14
- OKWD - 2887 C7
- OKWD - 3018 C1
Outerbelt East Frwy US-422
- BHWD - 2758 E3
- BHWD - 2759 A2
- ORNG - 2758 E4
- ORNG - 2759 A3
- WVHT - 2758 E5
Outerbelt South Frwy
- BKLN - 2753 A6
- BNHT - 2755 A7
- BNHT - 2884 B1
- CLEV - 2751 D6
- CLEV - 2752 B7
- CLEV - 2753 B6
- CLEV - 2754 A6
- CLEV - 2755 A7
- CLEV - 2757 A7
- FWPK - 2751 C6
- GDHT - 2756 E7
- GDHT - 2757 A7
- GDHT - 2885 A1
- INDE - 2884 D1
- INDE - 2885 A1
- MPHT - 2757 A7
- NOSD - 2750 C7
- NOSD - 2751 A6
- NOSD - 2878 E2
- NOSD - 2879 A1
- NRDV - 2878 A4
- OmsT - 2878 E2
- VLVW - 2885 B1
- WVHT - 2757 D6
- WVHT - 2758 A6
Outerbelt South Frwy I-480
- BKLN - 2753 A6
- BNHT - 2755 A7
- BNHT - 2884 A1
- CLEV - 2751 D6
- CLEV - 2752 B7
- CLEV - 2753 B6
- CLEV - 2754 A6
- CLEV - 2755 A7
- CLEV - 2757 A7
- FWPK - 2751 A6
- GDHT - 2756 E7
- GDHT - 2757 A7
- GDHT - 2885 A1
- INDE - 2884 D1
- INDE - 2885 A1
- MPHT - 2757 A7
- NOSD - 2750 C7
- NOSD - 2751 A6
- NOSD - 2878 E2
- NOSD - 2879 A1
- NRDV - 2878 A4
- OmsT - 2878 E2
- VLVW - 2885 B1
- WVHT - 2757 D6
- WVHT - 2758 A6
Outerbelt West Frwy
- OKWD - 3018 C2
Outerbelt West Frwy I-271
- OKWD - 3018 C2
Outerbelt West Frwy I-480
- OKWD - 3018 C2

Outerbelt West Frwy SR-14
- OKWD - 3018 C2
Outhwaite Av
4000 CLEV 44104 2625 C4
4000 CLEV 44115 2625 C4
Outley Park Dr
33100 SLN 44139 2889 A7
33100 SLN 44139 3019 E1
33100 SLN 44139 3020 A1
Outlook Av
7400 BKLN 44144 2753 E4
Outlook Dr
4400 BKLN 44144 2753 D5
Outrigger Curv
- PnvT 44077 2040 D3
Outrigger Ln
100 NCtT 44067 3153 C5
Outrigger Cove
700 PnvT 44077 2040 D2
Outriggers Cove
10100 RMDV 44202 3020 D5
Oval Dr
- AQLA 44024 2505 D4
- SRHT 44120 2627 B5
7400 INDE 44131 3015 E1
Overbrook Av
2100 LKWD 44107 2622 A6
Overbrook Dr
4000 BKVL 44141 3015 E6
Overbrook Rd
10 ELYR 44035 2875 B4
1500 LNHT 44124 2629 A1
Overland Dr
10 OmsT 44138 2879 A3
Overland Ln
33300 SLN 44139 2889 A4
Overland Park Dr
19400 SGVL 44149 3146 D1
Overlook Av
8100 BWHT 44147 3015 A4
Overlook Ct
400 PNVL 44077 2146 A3
24800 ODFL 44138 2879 C7
38200 NRDV 44039 2747 B7
Overlook Dr
462-00 AURA 44202 3156 D3
2600 TNBG 44087 3020 A6
8700 KTLD 44094 2251 D6
11400 NbyT 44065 2764 D2
17000 BbgT 44023 2891 A3
21700 FWPK 44126 2751 B5
22700 EUCL 44117 2373 B7
30100 WKLF 44092 2374 E2
38600 CrlT 44044 3006 E5
E Overlook Dr
100 ETLK 44095 2142 D6
W Overlook Dr
100 ETLK 44095 2142 C6
Overlook Ln
- WNHL 44146 2886 C7
2000 CVHT 44106 2627 A3
Overlook Pl
10 BDFD 44146 2887 C3
Overlook Rd
- AVLK 44012 2618 D2
10 BTVL 44022 2889 D1
10 PnvT 44077 2146 D1
200 VMLN 44089 2741 D4
400 GSML 44040 2500 D2
1100 LKWD 44107 2622 A4
2100 CLEV 44106 2626 E2
2100 CVHT 44106 2626 E2
2500 CVHT 44106 2627 A2
4900 GDHT 44125 2756 E6
5500 PRMA 44129 2882 D1
11600 MsnT 44024 2504 C3
12000 NbyT 44021 2764 E4
12000 NbyT 44065 2764 E4
E Overlook Rd
2600 CVHT 44106 2627 A2
2700 CVHT 44118 2627 B2
S Overlook Rd
2100 CVHT 44106 2626 E3
Overlook St
- RMDV 44202 3020 E4
Overlook Wy
5700 NRDV 44039 2876 C1
Overlook Brook Ct
300 AbnT 44023 2892 A3
Overlook Brook Dr
200 AbnT 44023 2892 A3
Overlook Park Dr
200 CLEV 44110 2372 B7
Overlook Ridge Dr
800 CLEV 44109 2755 A4
Overture Dr
15100 NbyT 44065 2763 E4
15100 NbyT 44065 2764 A3
Oviatt Dr
10 NCtT 44067 3153 B3
Oviatt Ln
10300 TNBG 44087 3020 B3
E Oviatt Rd
26100 BYVL 44140 2620 B5
W Oviatt Rd
27200 BYVL 44140 2620 A5
27900 BYVL 44140 2619 E5
Ovington Av
6500 CLEV 44127 2755 E1
Owaissa Dr
10 ETLK 44095 2250 A2
10 TMLK 44095 2250 A2
Owego Av
1400 LKWD 44107 2622 A5
Owego St
300 PNVL 44077 2040 A7
900 PNVL 44077 2039 E5
Owens Rd
14600 NbyT 44065 2764 D1
Owls Hollow Ln
17300 BbgT 44023 2890 D3
Owls Roost Cove
- AURA 44202 3021 B5
Owosso Av
6700 CLEV 44105 2755 E3
Oxford Av
200 ELYR 44035 2875 C6
17200 CLEV 44111 2752 B2
Oxford Cir
- WTLK 44145 2749 A4
2000 HkyT 44233 3148 B6
Oxford Ct
- ORNG 44022 2759 C3
- ORNG 44122 2759 C3

Oxford Ct
6200 BDHT 44146 2887 E4
35200 NRDV 44039 2877 B1
Oxford Dr
200 AURA 44202 3021 B7
600 BWHT 44147 3150 A5
600 RchT 44286 3150 A5
1200 MadT 44057 1843 D6
3400 LORN 44053 2744 A3
7900 MDBH 44130 3011 E2
7900 SGVL 44130 3011 E2
7900 SGVL 44149 3011 E3
8100 PRMA 44129 2882 D4
Oxford Ln
7900 CsTp 44026 2501 E3
Oxford Ovl
17600 SGVL 44136 3147 A3
E Oxford Ovl
3300 NOSD 44070 2750 D4
N Oxford Ovl
24200 NOSD 44070 2750 D4
S Oxford Ovl
24200 NOSD 44070 2750 D4
W Oxford Ovl
3300 NOSD 44070 2750 D4
Oxford Rd
- CVHT 44121 2497 E5
18800 SRHT 44122 2627 E6
37200 ETLK 44095 2142 D6
Oxford St
1900 TNBG 44087 3154 C2
1900 TwbT 44087 3154 C2
Oxford Tr
9200 BKVL 44141 3015 A7
9200 BKVL 44141 3150 B1
9200 BKVL 44147 3015 A7
9200 BWHT 44147 3015 A7
Oxford Glen Dr
9600 MNTR 44060 2145 A1
Oxford Park Ln
26900 OmsT 44138 2878 E3
26900 OmsT 44138 2879 A3
Oxgate Ct
7500 HDSN 44236 3155 C7
Oxgate Ln
32000 HGVL 44022 2630 A7
Ox Ridge Tr
- HDHT 44143 2499 E1
N Oxshire Pl
7100 CcdT 44077 2146 A7
Oynes Ct
4200 CLEV 44128 2757 C4
Ozark Av
16700 CLEV 44110 2372 C6
16900 CLEV 44119 2372 C6

P

Pabin Ct
8500 MCDN 44056 3153 E2
Pacific Av
5600 CLEV 44102 2754 A1
Packard Av
7200 MDBH 44130 2881 B7
Packard Cir
7100 MDBH 44130 2881 B6
Packard Ct
6500 MNTR 44060 2144 C5
7000 BKVL 44141 3016 A7
Packard Dr
2300 LORN 44055 2746 A5
Padanarum Rd
2800 GnvT 44041 1943 E3
4000 GnvT 44041 1844 E7
4600 GOTL 44041 1844 E5
Paddock Cir
600 BERA 44017 3010 E2
12300 SGVL 44149 3011 A6
Paddock Ct
8300 MNTR 44060 2251 C5
Paddock Dr
7400 CsTp 44026 2501 C5
13100 MsnT 44024 2634 A2
Padua Dr E
12000 NRYN 44133 3014 A6
Padua Dr N
6000 NRYN 44133 3013 E6
6000 NRYN 44133 3014 A6
Page Av
1700 ECLE 44112 2497 B5
Page Ct
- SDLK 44054 2616 B4
5900 CLEV 44103 2625 D1
Page Dr
10100 CcdT 44060 2253 D3
10100 CcdT 44077 2253 D3
Page Rd
400 AURA 44202 3157 B4
400 AURA 44255 3157 B4
1000 AURA 44241 3157 B6
1300 STBR 44202 3157 B6
1300 STBR 44241 3157 B6
Pagent Ln
10 OmsT 44138 2879 A3
Paige Pl
10 PNVL 44077 2146 A1
Paine Av
5200 MPHT 44137 2757 C7
Paine St
1500 LORN 44052 2615 B6
Painesville Ravenna Rd
10300 MNTU 44255 3159 B7
10300 ShvT 44255 3159 B7
10900 ManT 44255 3159 C3
Painesville Ravenna Rd SR-44
10300 MNTU 44255 3159 B7
10300 ShvT 44255 3159 B7
10900 ManT 44255 3159 C3
Painesville Warren Rd
6100 CcdT 44077 2146 C4
6100 PnvT 44077 2146 C3
12000 CcdT 44077 2147 A5
12400 LryT 44077 2147 B5
13000 LryT 44077 2255 E1
13000 LryT 44077 2256 B2
14000 LryT 44086 2256 D3
14500 LryT 44086 2257 A3
14800 TpnT 44024 2257 A3
14800 TpnT 44086 2257 A3
Painesville Warren Rd SR-86
6100 CcdT 44077 2146 C4
6100 PnvT 44077 2146 C3
12000 CcdT 44077 2147 A5

Painesville Warren Rd SR-86
12400 LryT 44077 2147 B5
13000 LryT 44077 2255 E1
13000 LryT 44077 2256 B2
14000 LryT 44086 2256 D3
14500 LryT 44086 2257 A3
14800 TpnT 44024 2257 A3
14800 TpnT 44086 2257 A3
Painter Rd
7400 OKWD 44146 3018 C2
Paisley Dr
5900 NOSD 44070 2879 A2
Paisley Rd
1800 MadT 44057 1941 E1
Palamino Tr
300 AURA 44202 3022 B4
Palda Dr
16700 CLEV 44128 2757 C4
Palisades Dr
4700 MadT 44057 2044 A5
Palisades Pkwy
7300 MNTR 44060 2251 B2
30300 WKLF 44092 2374 D1
Pallister Dr
4000 CLEV 44105 2755 C2
Palm Av
2800 LORN 44055 2746 A5
Palm Blvd
10 MadT 44057 1941 B6
Palm Cir
18800 FWPK 44126 2752 A1
Palm Dr
24000 NOSD 44070 2750 D6
Palmer Av
10 PnvT 44077 2145 C4
Palmer Dr
2400 WBHL 44094 2375 B3
3300 RKRV 44116 2751 A2
Palmer Ln
11200 TNBG 44087 3020 B3
Palmer Rd
11200 CcdT 44077 2146 C4
Palmerston Dr
6700 MNTR 44060 2143 D6
N Palmerston Dr
6600 MNTR 44060 2143 D5
Palmerston Rd
3400 SRHT 44122 2757 D2
Palmetto St
10 BDFD 44146 2886 E3
Palm Springs Dr
3500 LORN 44053 2744 C3
Palomino Tr
8500 KTLD 44094 2377 B7
8500 KTLD 44094 2502 B1
Palo Verde Ct
800 ETLK 44095 2250 B3
Palo Verde Dr
- ETLK 44095 2250 B3
Pam Ct
23300 EUCL 44123 2373 C2
Pamela Ct
6100 BKPK 44142 2881 B3
Pamela Dr
7200 NRYN 44133 3013 D2
10100 SGVL 44149 3011 C4
13500 GDHT 44125 2885 E4
Pamela Ln
- BHIT 44212 3146 A7
Pamilla Cir
- AVLK 44012 2618 D2
Pamona Av
7900 NCtT 44067 3153 A1
Panama Dr
3300 PRMA 44134 3014 C2
Panna Ln
900 CLEV 44109 2754 E5
Panorama Dr
10 PRMA 44131 2883 E4
10 PRMA 44134 2883 E4
10 SVHL 44131 2883 E4
10 SVHL 44131 2884 A4
Panorama Pkwy
- SGVL 44136 3147 C4
Par Ln
2200 WBHL 44094 2375 A3
2200 WLBY 44094 2375 A3
Parade St
10 OmsT 44138 2879 A3
Paradise Al
400 FTHR 44077 2039 D4
Paradise Blvd
10 MadT 44057 1941 B6
Paradise Ct
10 FTHR 44077 2039 D4
Paradise Dr
- ELYR 44035 2874 B6
Paradise Ln
24300 EUCL 44123 2373 D1
Paradise Rd
10 PnvT 44077 2147 A2
300 PryT 44077 2147 B2
Paradise Wy
6800 NRDV 44039 2876 E3
Parafine Av
- CLEV 44113 2624 E6
Paris Av
3100 CLEV 44109 2624 C7
Park Av
- RDHT 44143 2499 A3
100 AMHT 44001 2872 E1
100 CRDN 44024 2379 E7
100 CRDN 44024 2380 A7
100 ELYR 44035 2875 C7
1100 AMHT 44001 2873 A2
1200 AhtT 44001 2873 A2
1200 ELYR 44035 3006 C1
1300 MadT 44057 1843 B7
7100 CLEV 44105 2755 E3
7400 CLEV 44105 2756 A3
8400 MCDN 44056 3153 D1
37200 WLBY 44094 2250 D5
S Park Av
10 BDFD 44146 2887 B4
Park Blvd
100 PNVL 44077 2146 A2
800 EUCL 44117 2498 B4
800 SELD 44117 2498 B4
800 SELD 44121 2498 C5
N Park Blvd
- CVHT 44104 2626 D4
- SRHT 44122 2628 A5
1600 CVHT 44106 2626 E4
2500 CVHT 44106 2627 B5

N Park Blvd
2600 CVHT 44118 2627 B5
18200 CVHT 44120 2627 D5
18200 SRHT 44118 2627 E5
18200 SRHT 44120 2627 D5
19600 SRHT 44122 2627 E5
20600 SRHT 44118 2628 A5
20600 UNHT 44118 2628 A5
26500 ODFL 44138 3010 A1
28900 SLN 44139 2759 C7
S Park Blvd
2600 CVHT 44118 2627 B5
2600 SRHT 44118 2627 B5
5600 PRMA 44134 2883 D1
13800 SRHT 44120 2627 A5
17500 SRHT 44122 2627 E6
19900 SRHT 44122 2628 A6
W Park Blvd
2600 SRHT 44120 2627 B6
Park Cir
16600 BbgT 44023 2890 E1
16600 BbgT 44023 2891 A1
N Park Cir
10 BKPK 44142 2881 C3
Park Ct
1700 EUCL 44117 2498 A2
2400 WTLK 44145 2750 B2
Park Dr
- AVLK 44012 2618 B2
- CrlT 44035 3006 C1
- ELYR 44035 2875 A5
- ELYR 44035 3006 C1
- MDHT 44124 2500 A7
- SLN 44139 2889 B1
- SRHT 44120 2627 D5
10 CLEV 44134 2754 C7
200 BNHT 44131 2755 A7
200 CRDN 44024 2379 D5
400 BYVL 44140 2620 E5
2400 PRMA 44134 2883 C5
2700 CVHT 44118 2627 D5
2700 LORN 44052 2744 E2
2700 SRHT 44118 2627 D5
4700 CLEV 44109 2754 B3
4700 CLEV 44144 2754 B3
4700 SDLK 44054 2616 C3
5000 VMLN 44089 2740 E5
5000 VMLN 44089 2741 A5
13300 BKPK 44130 2881 E3
13300 BKPK 44142 2881 D3
13300 PMHT 44130 2881 E3
17000 BbgT 44023 2891 A3
Park Dr W
- NOSD 44070 2750 A7
E Park Dr
4800 NOSD 44070 2749 E7
16800 CLEV 44119 2372 D5
N Park Dr
10 AURA 44202 3156 E4
10 BDFD 44146 2887 B3
21000 FWPK 44126 2751 B4
27800 NOSD 44070 2749 E6
36100 AVON 44011 2747 E4
S Park Dr
- CrlT 44035 3006 B1
- ELYR 44035 3006 B1
200 AURA 44202 3156 E4
4800 FWPK 44126 2751 B4
5200 LORN 44053 2743 C5
36200 AVON 44011 2747 E5
36200 AVON 44011 2748 A5
W Park Dr
2100 LORN 44053 2744 A2
4600 FWPK 44126 2751 B4
4800 NOSD 44070 2749 D7
Park Ln
- BYVL 44140 2619 D4
10 CLEV 44110 2372 C6
10 MDHL 44022 2760 B6
3800 NBGH 44105 2755 B2
5100 NOSD 44070 2750 D7
10500 CLEV 44106 2626 C2
30800 PRPK 44124 2629 D6
Park Ovl
600 MDSN 44057 2044 A2
Park Pl
10 BDFD 44146 2887 C4
100 SRSL 44022 2761 C6
400 BERA 44017 2880 A5
500 ELYR 44035 2875 C6
2400 WTLK 44145 2750 B2
3700 CLEV 44109 2754 E2
15800 LKWD 44107 2622 C6
26300 NOSD 44070 2750 B5
N Park Pl
10 PNVL 44077 2040 C7
S Park Pl
10 PNVL 44077 2040 C7
10 PNVL 44077 2146 C1
Park Pt
11700 SGVL 44136 3012 C5
Park Rd
- CLEV 44119 2372 C5
- CyhC 44119 2372 D5
- ELYR 44035 2875 A5
- PnvT 44077 2147 B1
10 PnvT 44077 2041 B4
5300 CLEV 44135 2880 E1
E Park Rd
8700 TwbT 44087 3154 D2
N Park Rd
2100 TwbT 44087 3154 D2
S Park Rd
2100 TwbT 44087 3154 D2
W Park Rd
2700 AVON 44011 2748 A2
3600 CLEV 44111 2752 C2
Park Sq
5800 LORN 44053 2743 C6
Park St
10 BERA 44017 2880 C7
10 GNVA 44041 1944 B4
10 MDSN 44057 2044 B1
5500 MONT 44060 2143 E1
10700 MNTU 44255 3159 C5
29300 WKLF 44092 2374 C3
E Park St
100 CRDN 44024 2380 A6
14500 BURT 44021 2766 B1
E Park St SR-44
100 CRDN 44024 2380 A6
E Park St SR-87
14500 BURT 44021 2766 B1
E Park St US-6
100 CRDN 44024 2380 A6

STREET
Block City ZIP Map# Grid

N Park St
10 OBLN 44074 3138 E2
13800 BURT 44021 2636 B7
N Park St SR-87
13800 BURT 44021 2636 A7
S Park St
10 OBLN 44074 3138 E3
W Park St
14500 BURT 44021 2766 A1
W Park St SR-87
14500 BURT 44021 2766 A1
Park Tr
5000 NRDV 44039 2747 B7
Park Wy
- BtnT 44021 2635 E7
W Park Circle Dr
16600 BbgT 44023 2890 E1
Parkcliff Ct
20700 FWPK 44126 2751 C4
Parkcliff Dr
20600 FWPK 44126 2751 C4
Park Cliff Rd
12100 SGVL 44136 3011 E5
Parkdale Av
14000 CLEV 44111 2752 D2
21700 FWPK 44126 2751 B4
Parkdale Dr
8300 NRYN 44133 3013 D3
Parkdale Rd
3700 CVHT 44121 2497 E7
3700 CVHT 44121 2498 A7
Park East Dr
3500 BHWD 44122 2758 E2
34300 SLN 44139 2889 A6
Parkedge Cir
22300 FWPK 44126 2751 B4
Parkedge Dr
4500 FWPK 44126 2751 B4
10900 CLEV 44104 2626 C7
Parker Ct
100 CdnT 44024 2379 C6
100 CRDN 44024 2379 C6
Parker Dr
1500 MDHT 44124 2500 A7
1500 MDHT 44124 2630 A1
7300 MNTR 44060 2252 C1
12000 CsTp 44026 2502 C5
Parker Rd
400 AURA 44202 3022 C6
1000 AURA 44023 3022 D4
1000 BbgT 44023 3022 D4
Park Fulton Ovl
4000 CLEV 44144 2754 B3
Parkgate Av
- CLEV 44103 2496 B6
9000 CLEV 44108 2496 B6
Parkgate Dr
- WLBY 44094 2250 C7
Parkgate Ovl
6600 SVHL 44131 2884 B5
Parkgrove Av
15200 CLEV 44110 2372 B7
Parkhall Dr
10 PnvT 44077 2041 A6
E Parkhaven Dr
100 PRMA 44131 2883 E6
100 PRMA 44134 2883 E6
100 SVHL 44131 2883 E6
500 SVHL 44131 2884 A6
Parkhaven Row
1400 LKWD 44107 2622 E5
Park Heights Av
10700 GDHT 44125 2756 C7
Park Heights Rd
10200 CLEV 44104 2626 C7
Parkhill Av
11600 CLEV 44104 2626 D6
11600 CLEV 44120 2626 D6
Parkhill Dr
5800 PMHT 44130 2882 C2
5800 PRMA 44130 2882 C2
Parkhill Rd
1400 CVHT 44121 2497 E7
Parkhurst Dr
5200 SFLD 44054 2746 D5
10500 CLEV 44111 2753 B1
Parkknoll Dr
12300 GDHT 44125 2756 D6
Parkland Av
6400 BKPK 44142 2880 B3
6500 BERA 44017 2880 B4
6500 BERA 44142 2880 B4
Parkland Blvd
200 VMLN 44089 2741 D4
6000 MDHT 44124 2629 D2
6500 SLN 44139 2888 D7
Parkland Dr
- PMHT 44130 2882 C1
10 AVLK 44012 2617 D1
5700 PRMA 44130 2882 C1
6000 SRSL 44022 2762 A6
9700 TNBG 44087 3019 B4
15600 SRHT 44120 2627 E7
17700 SRHT 44122 2627 E7
18600 SRHT 44122 2757 D1
33100 ETLK 44095 2249 E3
Parkland Ovl
200 BNWK 44212 3147 A7
Parkland Rd
7000 INDE 44131 3015 E1
32200 WLWK 44095 2249 D4
33000 ETLK 44095 2249 D4
Parklane Av
19600 RKRV 44116 2751 D1
Parklane Dr
2800 PRMA 44134 2883 C3
19900 RKRV 44116 2751 D1
20900 FWPK 44126 2751 C3
26200 EUCL 44132 2373 E2
Parklawn Av
16200 MDBH 44130 2881 B7
Parklawn Dr
300 RKRV 44116 2621 B5
4200 WLBY 44094 2251 B5
11200 CLEV 44108 2496 D5
Park Ledge Dr
1000 MCDN 44056 3018 E6
Parkleigh Dr
900 PRMA 44131 2883 E3
900 PRMA 44134 2883 E3
900 SVHL 44131 2883 E3
E Parkleigh Dr
10 PRMA 44131 2883 D2
10 PRMA 44134 2883 D2
10 SVHL 44131 2883 D2
800 SVHL 44131 2884 A2
Park Ln Dr
16400 SGVL 44136 3147 A3
Park Ln Rd
11300 NbyT 44065 2764 C1
Parkman Blvd
14100 BKPK 44142 2881 D2
Park Meadow Dr
100 ELYR 44035 3006 D1
Park Moss Av
11500 SGVL 44136 3012 C6
Parkmount Av
4500 CLEV 44135 2752 A5
18200 CLEV 44135 2751 E5
Park North Dr
6500 SLN 44139 2889 A6
Park Place Dr
- EatT 44044 3142 E2
9500 BKVL 44141 3016 D3
Parkridge Av
5900 CLEV 44144 2754 A3
N Park Ridge Av
- TwbT 44087 3154 C5
Park Ridge Dr
5600 NOSD 44070 2878 D1
Parkridge Dr
2400 HkyT 44233 3148 A6
Park Ridge Ln
8500 MCDN 44056 3154 A2
Park Row Av
1300 LKWD 44107 2622 A5
Parkside
200 BSHT 44236 3153 B7
Parkside Av
- AVLK 44012 2617 B2
Parkside Blvd
500 SELD 44143 2498 B4
Parkside Cir
1500 LNHT 44121 2498 D7
1500 LNHT 44124 2498 D7
1500 SELD 44121 2498 D7
1500 SELD 44124 2498 D7
Park Side Dr
- PNVL 44077 2145 B2
Parkside Dr
200 BYVL 44140 2620 B4
500 AVLK 44012 2618 E4
1000 LKWD 44107 2622 D3
2600 HDSN 44236 3155 C7
4000 BKLN 44144 2753 E3
7500 PRMA 44130 3013 C1
8500 CsTp 44026 2502 B7
8600 SgHT 44067 3018 A5
17300 NRYN 44133 3148 A3
20100 RKRV 44116 2621 D4
33600 EatT 44028 3143 D3
S Parkside Dr
4300 BKLN 44144 2753 E4
Parkside Pl
1000 CLEV 44108 2496 B6
Parkside Rd
1000 CLEV 44108 2496 B6
11300 MsnT 44024 2504 C3
Parkside Tr
5000 SLN 44139 2759 B7
5100 SLN 44139 2888 B1
Parkton Dr
4300 CLEV 44122 2757 D5
4300 WVHT 44122 2757 D5
4300 WVHT 44128 2757 D5
Parkview Av
700 LORN 44052 2614 C7
1200 LORN 44052 2744 C1
1400 MadT 44057 1843 B6
6800 PRMA 44134 2883 D6
9400 CLEV 44104 2626 C6
9700 GDHT 44125 2756 C5
11600 CLEV 44120 2626 D6
19900 RKRV 44116 2751 D1
Park View Cir
9700 SGVL 44136 3012 C4
Parkview Ct
100 ELYR 44035 2875 A6
Parkview Dr
- MAYF 44143 2500 A1
10 BERA 44017 3011 B1
10 OmsT 44138 2879 A3
10 PNVL 44077 2040 B6
200 AVLK 44012 2618 A2
300 SDLK 44054 2616 D4
300 SVHL 44131 2884 A6
1300 LNHT 44124 2499 A7
2000 TNBG 44087 3019 D4
3300 AVON 44011 2748 C4
12500 CsTp 44026 2502 B7
15400 NbyT 44065 2764 D4
27700 EUCL 44132 2249 A7
E Parkview Dr
6900 PRMA 44134 2883 E6
N Parkview Dr
100 AURA 44202 3156 E3
S Parkview Dr
600 AURA 44202 3156 E4
W Parkview Dr
6900 PRMA 44134 2883 D6
Parkview Ln
1100 BWHT 44147 3149 E3
5800 FWPK 44126 2751 B6
34500 WLBY 44094 2375 A2
Parkview Rd
- WBHL 44094 2375 A7
7300 BKVL 44141 3151 C3
33800 WBHL 44092 2375 A7
Parkway E
- NOSD 44070 2750 B7
Parkway Blvd
- AURA 44202 3156 D1
10 MDSN 44057 2044 A2
38000 WLBY 44094 2250 E1
E Parkway Blvd
600 AURA 44202 3156 C1
W Parkway Blvd
600 AURA 44202 3156 B1
Parkway Ct
38700 WLBY 44094 2143 A3
Parkway Dr
- BWHT 44147 3014 E6
- ODFL 44138 2879 C4
900 VmnT 44089 2740 A7
10 OmsT 44138 2879 A4
100 ETLK 44095 2142 C7
200 BERA 44017 2880 B6
1200 LORN 44053 2744 C5
1400 LKWD 44107 2622 E5
1800 CVHT 44118 2627 C2
4800 GDHT 44125 2756 D6
11400 MsnT 44024 2504 C3
14400 BtnT 44021 2635 E7
E Parkway Dr
900 ELYR 44035 2875 C3
100 MDSN 44057 2044 A2
N Parkway Dr
10 ETLK 44095 2142 C6
6800 MDBH 44130 2881 D5
12500 CLEV 44105 2756 E4
12500 GDHT 44105 2756 E4
S Parkway Dr
6800 MDBH 44130 2881 D5
12700 GDHT 44105 2756 E4
13100 GDHT 44105 2757 A4
W Parkway Dr
100 MDSN 44057 2043 E2
Parkway Rd
800 CLEV 44108 2496 D5
W Parkway Rd
13700 CLEV 44135 2752 D5
Parkway Shops
10 BERA 44017 2880 C7
Park West Ovl
4300 CLEV 44135 2751 E4
Parkwood Av
100 AVLK 44012 2617 E2
4000 ManT 44255 3159 A3
21000 FWPK 44126 2751 C4
Park Wood Cir
5600 BTVL 44022 2889 C2
Parkwood Dr
100 BERA 44017 2880 A6
600 CLEV 44108 2496 C5
1200 CLEV 44106 2496 C7
3500 WTLK 44145 2749 E4
8100 KTLD 44094 2376 E6
8100 KTLD 44094 2377 A6
11700 CdnT 44024 2379 D1
23500 ClbT 44028 3010 C2
27100 EUCL 44132 2248 E7
27100 EUCL 44132 2249 A7
27700 WKLF 44092 2249 A7
28300 WLWK 44095 2249 A6
28300 WLWK 44132 2249 A6
Parkwood Ln
10500 CdnT 44024 2379 A6
15000 SGVL 44136 3146 C3
Parkwood Rd
1400 LKWD 44107 2622 E5
6100 MNTR 44060 2143 E3
Parkwood St
10 OBLN 44074 3138 C2
Park Wy Dr
32700 SLN 44139 2888 E5
Parliament Dr
10700 NRYN 44133 3014 A5
Parma Heights Blvd
5800 PMHT 44130 2882 C2
5800 PRMA 44130 2882 C2
Parmalee Dr
2100 SVHL 44131 2884 B6
6900 MNTR 44060 2144 C7
10000 TNBG 44087 3020 B4
Parma Park Blvd
6600 PMHT 44130 2882 A7
7000 PRMA 44130 2882 A7
Parmaview Ln
7700 NRYN 44133 3014 C2
7700 NRYN 44134 3014 C2
7700 PRMA 44134 3014 C2
Parmelee Av
8900 CLEV 44108 2496 B5
Parmelee Dr
- AQLA 44024 2505 D4
- ClrT 44024 2505 D5
Parmely Av
100 ELYR 44035 2874 E3
Parmenter Dr
7900 PRMA 44129 2882 D4
Parmly Pl
200 PNVL 44077 2040 B7
Parmly Rd
3100 NPRY 44081 1940 B6
3700 PryT 44081 1940 A5
Parnell Rd
21700 SRHT 44122 2628 B5
Parsons Ct
1200 RKRV 44116 2621 E5
Parsons Dr
100 AVLK 44012 2618 C1
2400 WBHL 44094 2375 B3
Parsons Rd
1000 GFTN 44044 3141 D5
1000 GFTN 44044 3142 A5
38500 CrlT 44044 3141 A5
38500 LrgT 44044 3141 A5
38800 LrgT 44050 3141 A5
38900 CrlT 44050 3141 A5
40000 CrlT 44050 3140 A5
40000 LrgT 44050 3140 A5
43200 CrlT 44050 3139 E4
43200 LrgT 44074 3139 E4
43200 LrgT 44050 3139 E5
43400 NRsT 44074 3139 A3
44200 OBLN 44074 3139 C4
Parsons Pond Cir
3600 WTLK 44145 2749 A4
Partridge Ct
400 MCDN 44056 3018 B6
7800 MNTR 44060 2143 E5
Partridge Dr
17000 SGVL 44136 3146 E2
N Partridge Dr
12700 VLVW 44125 2885 E5
13100 VLVW 44125 2886 A5
S Partridge Dr
12700 VLVW 44125 2885 E6
12700 VLVW 44125 2886 A6
Partridge Ln
100 HGVL 44022 2631 B5
100 RslT 44072 2631 B6
100 SLN 44139 2889 B3
Partridge Tr
9800 KTLD 44094 2377 B3
10500 BKVL 44141 3016 C4
Partridge Meadows Ct
2000 HDSN 44236 3155 A6
Partridge Meadows Dr E
7500 HDSN 44236 3155 A7
Partridge Meadows Dr N
2000 HDSN 44236 3154 E6
2000 HDSN 44236 3155 A6
Pasadena Av
100 ELYR 44035 2875 C5
500 SDLK 44054 2616 B4
10500 CLEV 44108 2496 C6
N Pasadena Av
900 ELYR 44035 2875 C3
Pasadena Dr
2400 SVHL 44131 2884 B6
Pasnow Av
18600 CLEV 44119 2372 E4
18600 EUCL 44119 2372 E4
18600 EUCL 44119 2373 A4
18600 EUCL 44123 2373 A4
Patio Ln
10 OmsT 44138 2879 B4
Patricia Av
9600 NRDV 44039 3007 E1
Patricia Ct
9500 CrlT 44035 3005 A1
9500 ELYR 44035 3005 A1
Patricia Dr
12600 NRYN 44133 3012 E3
12600 SGVL 44133 3012 E3
12600 SGVL 44136 3012 E3
Patriot Ct
- PNVL 44077 2146 A3
- PnvT 44077 2146 A3
Patriot Dr
13900 BtnT 44021 2635 C5
Patriots' Wy
- INDE 44131 2884 C2
Patt Ct
- WLBY 44094 2250 D4
Patterson Dr
6800 MNTR 44060 2144 C6
Patterson Ln
9200 OmsT 44138 3009 C1
39400 SLN 44139 2889 E6
Patterson Pkwy
20400 HIHL 44122 2758 A3
20400 WVHT 44122 2758 A3
Patti Pk
1300 WTLK 44145 2619 C7
Pattie Dr
300 BERA 44017 3010 E1
300 BERA 44017 3011 A1
Patton Ct
1200 TNBG 44087 3019 A4
Patton Dr
- BKVL 44141 3016 A6
33800 NRDV 44039 2877 C4
Patton Rd
4100 CLEV 44109 2754 E4
Patton St
9800 TNBG 44087 3019 A4
Paul Av
12000 CLEV 44106 2626 E2
Paul St
10 BDFD 44146 2887 B6
300 OKWD 44146 2887 B7
Paula Blvd
5600 NRDV 44039 2877 B2
Paula Dr
6700 MDBH 44130 2881 C5
Paulding Blvd
15500 BKPK 44142 2881 B2
Paulette Dr
16200 BtnT 44021 2765 B7
Pauline Dr
400 LvpT 44280 3145 D7
Paul Pine Rd
7800 SgHT 44067 3017 C7
Pau Pau Ct
6500 BDHT 44146 2887 D6
Pawnee Av
18500 CLEV 44119 2372 E5
19300 CLEV 44119 2373 A5
19700 EUCL 44119 2373 A5
Pawnee Tr
13100 MDBH 44130 3012 D1
13100 PRMA 44130 3012 E1
Paw Paw Lake Dr
10 SRSL 44022 2762 C5
Pawtucket Ln
100 PnvT 44077 2145 C4
Paxton Rd
100 ETLK 44095 2142 D5
800 CLEV 44108 2496 E5
2800 SRHT 44120 2627 C6
Payne Av
400 PNVL 44077 2040 B6
1300 CLEV 44114 2625 C1
3900 CLEV 44103 2625 C1
Peach Blvd
800 WLBY 44094 2143 A4
Peach Dr
- AVON 44011 2618 E7
Peach St
- VMLN 44089 2740 E4
10 OmsT 44138 2879 A4
Peach Tree Dr
11400 CsTp 44026 2502 C3
Peachtree Dr
10000 SGVL 44149 3011 C4
Peachtree Ln
10 PnvT 44077 2145 C3
22500 RKRV 44116 2621 A6
Pear Av
5800 CLEV 44102 2624 A6
6800 CLEV 44102 2623 E6
Pear St
33400 AVON 44011 2748 D2
Pearl Av
2800 LORN 44055 2745 D3
4700 EyrT 44035 2745 D6
4700 EyrT 44055 2745 D6
Pearl Ct
- CLEV 44113 2624 D6
Pearl Rd
10 BHIT 44212 3146 D7
10 BNWK 44136 3146 D5
10 BNWK 44149 3146 D5
10 BNWK 44212 3146 D7
10 SGVL 44136 3146 D5
10 SGVL 44149 3146 D5
3600 CLEV 44109 2754 C5
4500 CLEV 44144 2754 C5
5000 CLEV 44129 2754 A7
5000 PRMA 44109 2754 A7
5000 PRMA 44129 2754 A7
5300 PRMA 44129 2753 E7
5300 PRMA 44129 2882 E1
5700 PRMA 44130 2882 D2
5800 PMHT 44129 2882 D2
5800 PMHT 44130 2882 A5
6600 MDBH 44130 2881 C6
6600 PMHT 44130 2881 D5
7400 MDBH 44130 3012 A2
7700 SGVL 44130 3012 A2
7700 SGVL 44136 3012 A2
7700 SGVL 44149 3012 A2
9000 SGVL 44136 3011 D5
9000 SGVL 44149 3011 D5
12200 CdnT 44024 2255 A7
12400 HmbT 44024 2255 C7
Pearl Rd SR-3
3600 CLEV 44109 2754 C5
4500 CLEV 44144 2754 C5
5000 CLEV 44129 2754 A7
5000 PRMA 44109 2754 A7
5000 PRMA 44129 2754 A7
5300 PRMA 44129 2753 E7
5300 PRMA 44129 2882 E1
Pearl Rd US-42
10 BHIT 44212 3146 D7
10 BNWK 44136 3146 D5
10 BNWK 44149 3146 D5
10 BNWK 44212 3146 D7
10 SGVL 44136 3146 D5
10 SGVL 44149 3146 D5
3600 CLEV 44109 2754 C5
4500 CLEV 44144 2754 C5
5000 CLEV 44129 2754 A7
5000 PRMA 44109 2754 A7
5000 PRMA 44129 2754 A7
5300 PRMA 44129 2753 E7
5300 PRMA 44129 2882 E1
5700 PRMA 44130 2882 D2
5800 PMHT 44129 2882 D2
5800 PMHT 44130 2882 A5
6600 MDBH 44130 2881 C6
6600 PMHT 44130 2881 D5
7400 MDBH 44130 3012 A2
7700 SGVL 44130 3012 A2
7700 SGVL 44136 3012 A2
7700 SGVL 44149 3012 A2
9000 SGVL 44136 3011 D5
9000 SGVL 44149 3011 D5
Pearl St
10 PNVL 44077 2146 B1
100 AMHT 44001 2872 E2
400 BERA 44017 2880 C5
34100 NRDV 44039 2877 C2
S Pearl St
6000 EyrT 44035 2745 D6
6000 EyrT 44055 2745 D6
6000 ShfT 44055 2745 D6
Pearldale Av
16200 CLEV 44135 2752 B4
Pearlview Dr
13800 SGVL 44136 3011 E7
14300 SGVL 44136 3146 E1
Pearse Av
4400 NBGH 44105 2755 C3
Pear Tree Dr
7800 CsTp 44026 2501 D4
Peartree Ln
6500 MNTR 44060 2143 E5
Pease Dr
2700 FWPK 44116 2751 C1
2700 FWPK 44126 2751 C1
2700 RKRV 44116 2751 C1
Pease Rd
14100 MPHT 44137 2886 A1
Peasley Rd
9000 BhmT 44001 2870 E7
Pebble Ct
- WLBY 44094 2143 A5
6200 NRDV 44039 2876 D2
Pebble Beach Ovl
30800 WTLK 44145 2749 A2
Pebble Beach Cove
800 PnvT 44077 2040 E2
9800 RMDV 44202 3020 E6
9800 RMDV 44202 3021 A6
Pebblebrook Ct
- AVLK 44012 2617 D3
Pebble Brook Dr
- NRDV 44039 2877 D7
- NRDV 44039 3008 D1
Pebblebrook Dr
300 WBHL 44094 2374 E5
Pebble Brook Ln
6000 NOSD 44070 2879 B2
9500 SGVL 44149 3011 A4
Pebblebrook Ln
10 MDHL 44022 2759 E5
10 MDHL 44022 2760 A6
Pebblebrook Ovl
2000 WTLK 44145 2750 E2
Pebblebrook Tr
12600 NRYN 44133 3012 E2
Pebble Brooke Ct
7500 NCtT 44067 3153 E5
Pebble Cove
2200 WTLK 44145 2750 E2
11300 CcdT 44077 2146 B6
Pebble Creek Ct
8200 BbgT 44023 2890 E6
8200 BbgT 44023 2891 A6
Pebble Creek Dr
2100 TNBG 44087 3019 D6
Pebblecreek Dr
6300 INDE 44131 2884 C5
Pebble Creek Ln
5300 PryT 44077 2041 B7
5400 PryT 44077 2147 B1
Pebble Creek Pass
4600 BHIT 44212 3146 B7
Pebblehurst Ct
2100 PnvT 44077 2145 B6
Pebble Lake Tr
37800 NRDV 44039 2747 B7
Pebblestone Ct
14400 SGVL 44136 3147 C4
Pecan Ct
3800 ORNG 44022 2759 D3
Pecan Dr
400 BERA 44017 2880 A5
7300 PRMA 44129 2882 D7
Pecan Ovl
15500 MDBH 44130 2881 C5
Peck Av
6900 CLEV 44103 2495 E6
Peck Rd
10100 ManT 44255 3159 E6
10100 ShvT 44255 3159 E7
10300 MNTU 44255 3159 E6
10600 ManT 44234 3159 E6
10700 MNTU 44234 3159 E5
Peckham Av
11600 HRM 44234 3161 A2
Peckham Rd
14400 BtnT 44021 2636 B7
14400 BtnT 44021 2766 C1
14400 BtnT 44062 2636 B7
14400 BURT 44021 2636 B7
14400 BURT 44021 2766 C1
Peeble Creek Ln
- ELYR 44035 2746 A7
Peg Dr
- LORN 44052 2744 D5
Pekin Ct
9100 MNTR 44060 2144 E1
Pekin Rd
8500 RslT 44072 2632 B6
9300 NbyT 44065 2633 E6
9300 NbyT 44072 2633 A6
9300 RslT 44072 2633 A6
10500 NbyT 44065 2634 A6
11800 NbyT 44021 2635 A6
11800 NbyT 44065 2635 A6
Pelham Dr
4600 BKLN 44144 2754 A6
5400 PRMA 44129 2883 A3
5400 PRMA 44134 2883 A3
6600 PRMA 44129 2882 D3
7500 CsTp 44026 2501 C5
Pelham Pl
3300 AVON 44011 2747 E3
Pelican Ln
- LORN 44052 2614 E7
Pelican Cove
11300 CcdT 44077 2146 B6
11300 CcdT 44077 2254 C1
Pelican Lake Dr
38000 NRDV 44039 2747 B7
Pellett Dr
300 BYVL 44140 2619 B4
Pelley Dr
700 CLEV 44109 2754 E6
700 CLEV 44109 2755 A6
Pelret Pkwy
10 BERA 44017 2879 D6
Pelton Ct
1000 CLEV 44113 2624 E5
Pelton Rd
38100 WLBY 44094 2250 E4
38100 WLBY 44094 2251 A4
Pemberton Dr
100 ELYR 44035 3006 D3
14100 BKPK 44142 2881 D2
Pembridge Ct
100 SDLK 44054 2615 E4
Pembroke Cove
400 BNWK 44212 3147 B7
Pembrook Rd
900 CVHT 44121 2497 D6
Pembrooke Ln
1900 AVON 44011 2618 B7
Pembrooke Ovl
20500 SGVL 44149 3146 B5
Pendley Rd
600 WLWK 44095 2249 D5
Penfield Av
300 ELYR 44035 2874 D5
10500 GDHT 44125 2756 C7
Penfield Dr
8500 SgHT 44067 3017 E5
Penfield Ln
6000 SLN 44139 2889 D4
Penhurst Rd
1300 CLEV 44110 2372 E7
Penn Ct
1000 GFTN 44044 3142 B5
3100 CLEV 44113 2624 B5
Penn Pl
900 CcdT 44077 2145 E3
900 PNVL 44077 2145 E3
Pennant Ct
8300 CLEV 44102 2623 E6
Penney Pines Cir
17100 SGVL 44136 3147 A4
Pennfield Rd
900 CVHT 44121 2497 E6
Penniman Dr
10200 HmbT 44024 2380 E5
Pennington Dr
10 PnvT 44077 2145 D5
Pennington Rd
3500 SRHT 44120 2757 B2
Pennsylvania Av
100 ELYR 44035 3006 A3
1200 LORN 44052 2615 D6
5800 MPHT 44137 2886 C3
6600 CLEV 44103 2625 E1
Pennsylvania Ct
1700 LORN 44052 2615 C7
Pennsylvania Dr
- NRDV 44039 2877 D5
Pennsylvania St
1200 AURA 44202 3021 A4
1200 BbgT 44202 3021 A4
Penny Ln
17100 BbgT 44023 2890 B3
39500 CrlT 44035 3006 C2
Pennywhistle Cir
6900 CcdT 44077 2145 C7
Penrose Av
1800 CLEV 44112 2626 E1
1800 ECLE 44112 2626 E1
Penrose Ct
10 ELYR 44035 2746 A7
Pensacola Av
3900 CLEV 44109 2754 C4
Penshurst Dr
7000 CcdT 44060 2145 B7
24500 BHWD 44122 2628 D4
Penton Ct
- RMDV 44087 3020 C4
Peony Av
10700 CLEV 44111 2753 B2
Pepper Av
14600 CLEV 44110 2497 B2
Pepper Ct
10800 CcdT 44077 2146 A7
Pepper Dr
35900 SLN 44139 2889 C3
Peppercorn Ct
1400 BWHT 44147 3149 D5
Peppercorn Dr
25700 WTLK 44145 2620 B6
Peppercorn Ln
1200 BWHT 44147 3149 E5
Peppercorn Ter
1400 BWHT 44147 3149 E5
Peppercreek Dr
10 PRPK 44124 2629 E6
13700 SGVL 44136 3012 D5
Pepperdine Dr
100 ELYR 44035 2746 D6
Peppergrass Cir
16500 SGVL 44136 3147 A4
Pepper Hollow Ln
6500 MDHT 44124 2500 A6
Pepperidge Dr
10 GNVA 44041 1944 C6
Peppermill Ct
30600 NOSD 44070 2878 A4
Peppermill Run
8400 BbgT 44023 3022 A1
Peppermint Pl
11200 NRYN 44133 3013 B5
Pepper Ridge Dr
8900 BKLN 44144 2753 D3
Pepper Ridge Rd
10 HGVL 44022 2630 A5
10 HGVL 44124 2630 A5
10 PRPK 44124 2629 E5
10 PRPK 44124 2630 A5
Pepper Tree Ln
100 PnvT 44077 2145 C3
Pepperwood Ct
6100 MNTR 44060 2144 D3
Pepperwood Dr
500 BHIT 44212 3146 C7
500 BNWK 44212 3146 C7
16200 SGVL 44136 3147 B4
Pepperwood Ln
10 PRPK 44124 2629 C5
Percy Av
6500 CLEV 44127 2625 E6
Peregrine Dr
2200 AVON 44011 2747 E2
Peregrine Pl
700 AMHT 44001 2872 B3
Perennial Ln
6700 MNTR 44060 2145 A6
Pergl Rd
27200 GNWL 44139 2888 A7
27200 GNWL 44139 3019 A1
27200 Okwd 44146 2888 A7
Perham Dr
500 BERA 44017 3010 E1
Periwinkle Dr
10 OmsT 44138 2879 A4
Periwinkle Ln
4400 RDHT 44143 2498 C3
Periwinkle Wy
2200 AVON 44011 2747 E2
Perkins Av
3000 CLEV 44114 2625 C2
3800 CLEV 44103 2625 C2
S Perkins Ct
6300 BDHT 44146 2887 E5
Perkins Dr
8800 MNTR 44060 2252 D2
Perkins Rd
5400 BDHT 44146 2887 E2
S Perkins Rd
6000 BDHT 44146 2887 E4
Perkins St
- ELYR 44035 2874 E2
Perl Ct
3100 BWHT 44147 3014 C2
3100 NRYN 44133 3014 C3
3100 NRYN 44147 3014 C2
7900 BWHT 44133 3014 C2
7900 PRMA 44134 3014 C2
Perry Cir
4400 SVHL 44131 3015 C1
27100 OmsT 44138 3009 C1
Perry Ct
- CLEV 44114 2625 B1
100 ELYR 44035 2875 C6
3500 LORN 44053 2743 D3
Perry Dr
8500 RslT 44072 2632 B4
30800 BYVL 44140 2619 B5
35200 ETLK 44095 2142 B7
Perry St
400 VMLN 44089 2740 D5
Perry Park Rd
3300 PryT 44081 2041 E1
Pershing Av
3700 PRMA 44134 2883 B1
4200 CLEV 44105 2625 C7
4200 CLEV 44127 2625 C7
4800 PRMA 44129 2883 A1
Pershing Dr
8000 BKVL 44141 3015 E4
Persimmon Dr
29900 WTLK 44145 2749 C6
Persimmon Ln
3200 AVON 44011 2748 C3
4800 NRYN 44133 3014 B4
Persons Ct
10 ELYR 44035 2874 D4
Perth Dr
300 HDHT 44143 2499 C1
Perth Rd
1700 MadT 44057 1842 D7
1700 MadT 44057 1941 D1
Peterson Ln
- WTLK 44145 2620 E7
Petrarca Rd
2200 CLEV 44106 2626 C3
Pettibone Rd
7000 BbgT 44023 3021 B1
7000 SLN 44023 3021 B1
7000 SLN 44139 3021 B1
8200 BbgT 44023 3022 A1
26000 OKWD 44146 3018 E2
26200 GNWL 44139 3019 D2
26200 Okwd 44146 3019 D2
30700 SLN 44139 3019 D2
32800 SLN 44139 3020 A2
Pheasant Ct
1600 MDSN 44057 1942 A6
12000 MsnT 44024 2504 D5
35400 BTVL 44139 2889 B3
Pheasant Dr
4800 LORN 44053 2743 B5
Pheasant Ln
100 HGVL 44022 2631 B6
8600 KTLD 44094 2377 B4
23200 WTLK 44145 2750 E1

Cleveland Street Index

STREET
Block City ZIP Map# Grid

Pheasant Ln
23200 WTLK 44145 2751 A1
Pheasant Run
- SFLD 44054 2746 C3
100 MDHT 44124 2629 E2
Pheasant Tr
16700 SGVL 44136 3147 A2
Pheasant Run Cir
12000 NRYN 44133 3148 A1
Pheasant Run Dr
10 CNFL 44022 2761 B6
Pheasant Run Ln
8700 KDHL 44060 2252 C6
Pheasant Run Pl
9300 SGVL 44149 3011 C3
Pheasants Walk Dr
5400 NOSD 44070 2878 C1
Phelps Av
1300 LKWD 44107 2622 A5
Phelps St
100 PNVL 44077 2040 C6
Philena Av
3800 CLEV 44109 2754 C3
Philetus Av
6500 CLEV 44127 2625 E6
Philip Av
5000 MPHT 44137 2757 D7
Philip Pkwy
10200 STBR 44241 3156 B7
Phillip Ct
10 ELYR 44035 2875 A5
Phillips Av
11700 CLEV 44108 2496 D6
12400 CLEV 44112 2496 E6
12400 ECLE 44112 2496 D6
29900 WKLF 44092 2249 C7
29900 WKLF 44092 2374 C1
Philomethian St
10 CNFL 44022 2761 B7
Phyllis Av
- LORN 44053 2743 D3
Piccadilly Sq
38300 WLBY 44094 2250 E1
Piccolo Pl
10 OmsT 44138 2879 A4
Pickett Rd
3200 LORN 44053 2744 A3
3500 LORN 44053 2743 E3
Pickway Dr
6000 BKPK 44142 2881 C2
Pickwick Dr
100 NCtT 44067 3153 A3
Picone Ln
24600 BDHT 44146 2887 D2
Piedmont Ct
2500 WTLK 44145 2749 C2
Pierce Dr
19000 SGVL 44136 3146 D1
19000 SGVL 44149 3146 D1
Pierce St
15900 MDFD 44062 2767 D2
Piercefield Dr
6300 MDHT 44143 2499 E6
Piermont Rd
1000 SELD 44121 2498 B6
Pierpont Av
9200 CLEV 44108 2496 B6
Pierson Dr
400 RDHT 44143 2498 E3
Pike Av
- LORN 44055 2745 C4
Pike Blvd
15300 BKPK 44142 2881 B1
Pike Dr
28100 ORNG 44022 2759 B5
Pilgrim Av
16500 CLEV 44111 2622 B7
Pilgrim Dr
8800 BbgT 44023 2891 B6
9500 MNTR 44060 2253 A3
Pilgrim Rd
8500 BbgT 44023 2891 A6
Pilsen Av
5800 CLEV 44102 2624 A7
Pinckneya Dr
5100 NRYN 44133 3014 B4
Pine Av
- LORN 44055 2745 C4
Pine Cir
3800 NOSD 44070 2749 E5
Pine Ct
1700 AVON 44011 2748 E1
2800 PryT 44081 2041 D3
N Pine Ct
200 AURA 44202 3156 D1
S Pine Ct
200 AURA 44202 3156 D2
Pine Dr
- MNTR 44094 2251 B4
1600 AVON 44011 2618 E7
1600 AVON 44011 2748 E1
Pine Ln
5400 SLN 44139 2888 D2
S Pine Ln
4700 PryT 44081 2042 E3
Pine Ovl
4400 PRMA 44134 3014 B1
Pine Pt
7200 CcdT 44077 2146 C7
Pine St
10 GNVA 44041 1944 B4
100 ELYR 44035 2875 B6
300 BDHT 44146 2758 D7
7000 BbgT 44022 2761 A7
7000 CNFL 44022 2761 A7
Pine Vw
- MadT 44057 1941 E6
- MDSN 44057 1941 E6
Pine Acres Ln
11300 CsTp 44026 2502 D2
Pinebark Pl
1600 TNBG 44087 3019 B7
Pine Branch Cir
33000 NRDV 44039 2877 D1
Pinebrook Cir
3200 PryT 44081 2041 E4
Pinebrook Dr
12500 NRYN 44133 3012 E3
12500 NRYN 44133 3013 A3
Pinebrook Ln
32300 PRPK 44124 2759 E2
Pine Cone Dr
7500 PRMA 44134 3014 B1
Pinecone Dr
5900 MNTR 44060 2145 A3

Pinecone Dr
9200 MNTR 44060 2144 E3
Pine Cone Ovl
800 SgHT 44067 3152 B2
Pine Creek Ct
8200 BbgT 44023 2890 E7
8200 BbgT 44023 2891 A7
Pine Creek Ln
8500 SgHT 44067 3018 A5
8600 SgHT 44067 3017 E5
Pine Crest Dr
10 BTVL 44022 2889 E1
10 BTVL 44022 2890 A1
Pinecrest Dr
10 BDFD 44146 2887 B5
3800 ORNG 44122 2759 A3
Pinecrest Ln
7500 GNWL 44139 3019 A2
Pinecrest Pl
1200 WLBY 44094 2142 E5
Pinecrest Rd
9900 CcdT 44060 2253 B4
9900 CcdT 44077 2253 C4
Pine Forest Dr
3900 PRMA 44134 3014 B1
14000 NRYN 44133 3013 E7
14000 NRYN 44133 3148 E1
14000 NRYN 44133 3149 A1
Pinegate Dr
10300 CdnT 44024 2378 D7
10300 CdnT 44024 2503 D1
Pinegrove Av
7800 PRMA 44129 2882 D1
Pine Hill Ct
4000 NRYN 44133 3014 B3
Pinehill Dr
5300 MONT 44060 2037 E7
5300 MONT 44060 2038 A7
5300 MONT 44060 2143 E1
Pine Hill Rd
1100 SgHT 44067 3017 A7
Pinehill Rd
7000 CcdT 44077 2145 E7
7100 CcdT 44077 2146 A7
7100 CcdT 44077 2254 A1
Pine Hill Tr
15100 MDBH 44130 2881 C7
Pine Hollow Cir
100 CRDN 44024 2505 A2
Pine Hollow Dr
8500 RslT 44072 2632 B4
Pine Hollow Pl
3300 PryT 44081 1940 D7
Pinehurst Av
200 CrlT 44035 3006 D3
200 ELYR 44035 3006 D3
Pinehurst Blvd
10 ETLK 44095 2142 C6
Pine Hurst Ct
7300 MDBH 44130 2881 C7
Pinehurst Ct
5700 HDHT 44143 2499 C3
Pinehurst Dr
10 AURA 44202 3156 B1
1700 EUCL 44117 2498 A2
7900 KTLD 44094 2376 E2
8000 PRMA 44129 2882 D7
8300 PRMA 44130 2882 D7
11600 MsnT 44024 2504 D1
30800 WTLK 44145 2749 B2
32200 AVLK 44012 2618 C4
Pinehurst Rd
500 HDHT 44143 2499 C3
7400 MONT 44060 2143 D2
Pine Lakes Dr
13900 SGVL 44136 3012 C4
Pine Manor Dr
9600 CdnT 44024 2379 D3
Pine Meadow Pl
100 PnvT 44077 2040 D6
Pineneedle Dr
9200 MNTR 44060 2144 E4
9200 MNTR 44060 2145 A4
Pine Needle Tr
10100 SGVL 44149 3011 B4
Pineo Ct
300 SgHT 44067 3017 E5
Pine Ridge Ct
7300 MDBH 44130 2881 C7
Pine Ridge Dr
- TNBG 44087 3154 B1
Pineridge Dr
2100 WKLF 44092 2374 E3
Pine Ridge Ovl
4800 INDE 44131 2884 C7
Pine River Ct
7400 MDBH 44130 2881 C7
Pine River Dr
10 BTVL 44022 2889 D1
Pine Spring Dr
1200 MCDN 44056 3153 E2
1200 MCDN 44056 3154 A2
Pine Trails Cir
2900 HDSN 44236 3155 D6
Pine Trails Ln
2800 HDSN 44236 3155 D6
2800 TwbT 44236 3155 D6
Pine Tree Ct
7400 MDBH 44130 2881 C7
Pine Tree Dr
8800 MCDN 44056 3018 C6
Pinetree Dr
6600 MNTR 44060 2144 A5
Pine Tree Ln
2200 TNBG 44087 3019 C6
Pine Tree Pl
11500 SGVL 44136 3012 C5
Pinetree Rd
30400 PRPK 44124 2759 D1
32900 PRPK 44124 2760 A1
33400 PRPK 44022 2760 A1
Pinetree Rd SR-87
30400 PRPK 44124 2759 D1
Pine Valley Cir
10700 CcdT 44077 2253 E4
10700 CcdT 44077 2254 A4
Pine Valley Tr
14900 MDBH 44130 2881 C7
Pineview Cir
300 BERA 44017 2880 A6
20600 SGVL 44149 3146 B2
32900 NRDV 44039 2877 D7
Pineview Ct
6500 BSHT 44236 3153 B7
13400 MDBH 44130 2881 D5

Pine View Dr
4800 VMLN 44089 2741 A7
Pineview Dr
- MadT 44057 1941 E5
10 PnvT 44077 2040 E7
200 BERA 44017 2880 A6
6100 MDSN 44057 1941 E5
27200 WTLK 44145 2749 E4
27200 WTLK 44145 2750 A4
Pineview Ln
5800 WLBY 44094 2375 A1
Pineview Ovl
9200 BKVL 44141 3150 C1
Pine Ville Tr
10 AURA 44202 3156 E3
Pineway Dr
8200 ODFL 44138 2879 B6
Pinewood Av
- NRDV 44039 2877 D3
Pinewood Cir
1000 LNHT 44124 2499 A6
Pinewood Ct
- PRMA 44134 2883 E2
8700 MNTR 44060 2144 C4
Pinewood Dr
300 BYVL 44140 2619 D4
700 BSHT 44236 3153 B7
4800 SDLK 44054 2616 D3
7300 MDBH 44130 2881 C7
7300 MDBH 44130 3012 C1
15200 SGVL 44149 3146 C2
Pinewood Mnr
- ELYR 44035 2874 E2
Pinewood St
100 ELYR 44035 3006 B1
Pinewood Tr
11600 CsTp 44026 2501 E3
Pine Woods Wy
7200 OmsT 44138 2878 E4
Pinewood View Rd
700 SgHT 44067 3152 B2
Pinnacle Dr
100 BNWK 44212 3146 E6
Pinnacle Pkwy
2100 TNBG 44087 3155 A4
Pinnacle Park Dr
5500 SVHL 44131 2884 A2
Pin Oak Cir
10 NCtT 44067 3153 A2
100 ELYR 44035 3005 A1
5300 SFLD 44054 2616 E7
5300 SFLD 44054 2746 E1
5300 SFLD 44054 2747 A1
Pin Oak Ct
5500 INDE 44131 2884 D4
Pin Oak Dr
3500 LORN 44052 2615 D5
3500 LORN 44054 2615 D5
3500 SDLK 44054 2615 D5
3500 SFLD 44054 2615 D5
4700 VMLN 44089 2741 A5
8200 PRMA 44130 3013 D1
14300 SGVL 44136 3012 C4
Pinoak Dr
9000 ODFL 44138 3010 A1
Pin Oak Pkwy
32800 AVLK 44012 2617 D5
32800 AVLK 44012 2618 A4
Pinta St
17300 CLEV 44110 2497 D1
Pin Tail Dr
6700 BKVL 44141 3150 D2
N Pintail Dr
100 AbnT 44023 2892 A3
S Pintail Dr
100 AbnT 44023 2892 A4
Pinyon Ln
4400 WTLK 44145 2749 C5
Pioneer Rd
15600 HtbT 44046 2637 E1
15600 HtbT 44062 2637 E1
Pioneer Tr
2700 HDSN 44236 3155 D7
2800 ManT 44255 3158 E4
3700 ManT 44255 3159 E3
5200 ManT 44234 3159 E3
5400 HrmT 44234 3160 A3
5400 ManT 44234 3160 A3
5700 HrmT 44255 3160 E4
6600 HrmT 44234 3161 A4
6600 HrmT 44255 3161 A4
E Pioneer Tr
10 AURA 44202 3157 E3
100 AURA 44202 3156 E1
1100 AURA 44255 3157 E3
1100 ManT 44255 3157 E3
2400 ManT 44255 3158 A3
W Pioneer Tr
10 AURA 44202 3156 E1
Pioneers Creek Cir
17300 SGVL 44136 3147 A5
Pioneers Point Ln
6100 BKVL 44141 3016 C5
Pioneer Trail Dr
12600 NRYN 44133 3013 C6
Pipers Ct
5500 PRMA 44134 2883 E1
Pipes Ct
700 SgHT 44067 3152 C1
Pippen Cir
1400 BWHT 44147 3149 D4
Pirates Tr
1600 PnvT 44077 2040 E1
10000 RMDV 44202 3020 D5
10000 TNBG 44202 3020 D5
Pirates Cove
2900 RMDV 44202 3020 D5
Pirates Cove Dr
18000 SGVL 44136 3147 D4
Pitts Blvd
6400 NRDV 44039 2877 C4
Pittsburgh Av
2200 CLEV 44115 2625 B4
Pittsburgh Av SR-14
2200 CLEV 44115 2625 B4
Pittsburgh Av SR-43
2200 CLEV 44115 2625 B4
Pixley Ct
2100 CLEV 44109 2754 D3
Placid Cove
13900 SGVL 44136 3146 E1
13900 SGVL 44136 3147 A1
Plainfield Av
6300 BKLN 44144 2753 E4
6300 CLEV 44144 2753 E4

Plainfield Av
6300 CLEV 44144 2754 A4
Plainfield Rd
1000 CVHT 44121 2498 A6
1000 SELD 44121 2498 A7
Plains Ct
38500 WLBY 44094 2143 A4
Plains Rd
7700 MONT 44060 2143 E3
7800 MNTR 44060 2143 E3
8000 MNTR 44060 2144 A2
Plainview Ct
25200 ClbT 44028 3010 A4
Plane Av
17200 CLEV 44110 2497 D1
Plank Rd
7800 LryT 44086 2257 B4
7800 TpnT 44024 2257 B4
7800 TpnT 44086 2257 D5
8200 TpnT 44064 2257 D5
8300 MtlT 44064 2257 E7
Plank Rd SR-86
7800 LryT 44086 2257 B4
7800 TpnT 44024 2257 C5
7800 TpnT 44086 2257 B4
8200 TpnT 44064 2257 D5
8300 MtlT 44064 2257 E7
Plant Ln
19400 BKPK 44142 2880 E3
Plant St
1200 LORN 44055 2745 B3
Plantation Dr
7700 BKVL 44131 3016 A2
7700 BKVL 44141 3016 A3
Plantation Pl
- NRDV 44039 3008 C1
34600 NRDV 44039 2877 B7
Planters Grove Ln
31000 WTLK 44145 2749 A1
Plas Dr
100 CrlT 44035 3006 C3
Plato Av
15200 CLEV 44110 2497 B2
Platt Av
7100 CLEV 44104 2625 E4
7300 CLEV 44104 2626 A4
Platten Av
8500 CLEV 44102 2623 D6
Players Club Dr
7200 CcdT 44077 2254 B1
Plaza Blvd
7600 MNTR 44060 2251 D3
Plaza Dr
- WBHL 44092 2374 B5
10 CNFL 44022 2761 B7
1000 AMHT 44001 2872 E4
12200 BKPK 44130 2881 E2
12200 BKPK 44142 2881 E2
12200 PRMA 44130 2881 E2
12200 PRMA 44130 2882 A3
N Plaza Dr
9000 NHFD 44067 3018 B4
Pleasant Av
10 GNVA 44041 1944 B3
500 PNVL 44077 2040 B6
5200 NRDV 44039 2748 D7
5400 NRDV 44039 2877 D1
7200 BERA 44017 2880 D6
7200 BERA 44130 2880 D6
7200 MDBH 44017 2880 D6
7200 MDBH 44130 2880 D6
Pleasant Dr
10 CNFL 44022 2761 A6
Pleasant Pl
2300 MadT 44057 1941 C3
Pleasant Run
2400 SVHL 44131 3015 B1
N Pleasant St
10 OBLN 44074 3138 E1
S Pleasant St
10 OBLN 44074 3138 E3
Pleasant Tr
24800 RDHT 44143 2498 C2
Pleasantdale Rd
1600 CLEV 44109 2754 D6
Pleasant Hill Dr
7400 PRMA 44130 3013 A1
Pleasant Lake Blvd
10300 PRMA 44130 3013 C1
Pleasant Ridge Pl
11500 SGVL 44136 3012 C6
Pleasantvale Ct
9100 MNTR 44060 2252 E3
Pleasant Valley Rd
37000 WBHL 44094 2375 D5
38000 WBHL 44094 2376 A5
E Pleasant Valley Rd
- INDE 44125 3016 C1
- VLVW 44125 3016 A1
100 PRMA 44131 3014 E1
100 PRMA 44134 3014 E1
100 SVHL 44131 3014 E1
100 SVHL 44131 3015 A1
5600 INDE 44131 3015 C1
7100 INDE 44131 3016 C1
W Pleasant Valley Rd
900 PRMA 44131 3014 E1
900 PRMA 44134 3014 D1
900 SVHL 44131 3014 E1
3400 PRMA 44134 2883 B7
3600 PRMA 44129 2883 B7
4700 PRMA 44129 2882 D7
4700 PRMA 44134 2882 E7
7300 PRMA 44130 2882 D7
12800 PRMA 44130 2881 E7
12900 MDBH 44130 2881 E7
Pleasantview Av
200 SDLK 44054 2616 E3
Pleasant View Blvd
2300 SVHL 44131 3015 A1
Pleasantview Dr
- SDLK 44054 2616 E3
7500 PRMA 44134 3014 C1
9000 NCtT 44067 3153 A3
Pleasantview Tr
7800 CcdT 44060 2253 A3
Pleasantwood Dr
7200 INDE 44131 2884 C7
Plover Dr
- GnvT 44041 1944 D1
Plover St
12200 LKWD 44107 2623 A6
Plum Pth
21400 RKRV 44116 2621 C6

Plum St
100 FTHR 44077 2039 D4
Plumbrook Ct
32200 AVLK 44012 2618 C4
Plum Brook Ln
9600 SGVL 44149 3011 A4
Plum Creek Dr
14000 ClbT 44028 3009 C7
14400 ClbT 44028 3144 C1
Plum Creek Tr
17500 BbgT 44023 2891 C5
Plum Ridge Dr
11700 HRM 44234 3161 A1
Plumwood Dr
4200 NOSD 44070 2750 E5
Plumwood Ln
7600 SVHL 44131 3015 A2
Plymouth Av
2800 PRPK 44124 2629 D6
2900 FWPK 44126 2751 C1
2900 RKRV 44116 2751 C1
10700 GDHT 44125 2756 C6
Plymouth Ct
300 BNWK 44212 3147 B7
Plymouth Dr
100 BYVL 44140 2619 A3
1000 GFTN 44044 3142 A4
4200 SELD 44121 2498 B5
5800 LORN 44053 2743 C6
Plymouth Ovl
1900 HkyT 44233 3148 B6
Plymouth Pl
10 AURA 44202 3157 A3
15300 ECLE 44112 2497 B5
Plymouth Rd
100 ETLK 44095 2142 D5
1300 CLEV 44109 2754 E4
Plymouth Row
17400 SGVL 44136 3146 E4
Pocono Dr
22800 RKRV 44116 2751 A1
Poe Av
3900 CLEV 44109 2754 B2
Poertner Dr
800 BERA 44017 2879 E6
N Point Dr
10 AVLK 44012 2618 D1
10 LrnC 44012 2618 D1
S Point Dr
100 AVLK 44012 2618 E1
W Point Dr
4500 FWPK 44126 2751 C4
7300 NRDV 44039 2877 C4
N Pointe Ct
7200 CcdT 44077 2253 E1
Pointe Dr
8700 BWHT 44147 3015 C6
Pointe Pkwy
4900 BDHT 44128 2758 D6
4900 BDHT 44146 2758 D6
4900 WVHT 44128 2758 D6
N Pointe Pkwy
- AMHT 44001 2743 E6
- AMHT 44053 2743 E6
- LORN 44053 2743 E6
Pointe Breeze
200 AbnT 44023 2892 A3
Point Overlook Pl
11600 SGVL 44136 3012 B6
Poland Ct
6600 CLEV 44105 2755 E3
Pole Av
1700 LORN 44052 2744 C2
3200 LORN 44053 2744 C3
Police Al
- PNVL 44077 2040 C6
Polk Ct
7000 MNTR 44060 2143 D6
Polo Club Dr
14200 SGVL 44136 3147 B1
E Polo Club Dr
- SGVL 44136 3147 B1
Pololei Dr
10 MadT 44057 1941 B5
Polonia Av
6800 CLEV 44105 2755 E3
Polo Park Dr
4100 MNTR 44060 2251 B5
4100 MNTR 44094 2251 B5
4100 WLBY 44060 2251 B5
4100 WLBY 44094 2251 B5
Pomeroy Av
16300 CLEV 44110 2497 C2
Pomeroy Blvd
15500 SGVL 44136 3147 B1
Pomona Dr
5900 PRMA 44130 2882 A3
Pomona Rd
1100 CVHT 44121 2498 A6
Pompano Ct
7700 PRMA 44134 3014 C2
Pompton Dr
27100 NOSD 44070 2879 A1
Ponciana Av
17400 CLEV 44135 2752 A5
18300 CLEV 44135 2751 E5
E Pond Ct
7500 CcdT 44077 2254 C2
W Pond Ct
7500 CcdT 44077 2254 C2
Pond Dr
10 RKRV 44116 2621 A5
N Pond Ln
10300 TNBG 44087 3020 A3
Pond Rd
12000 NbyT 44021 2764 E4
12000 NbyT 44065 2764 E4
12100 NbyT 44021 2765 A4
12300 BtnT 44021 2765 B5
Pond Run
433-00 AURA 44202 3156 D2
Pond Brook Ln
7600 MCDN 44056 3154 A5
Ponderosa Dr
12600 NRYN 44133 3013 C6
Ponderosa Ln
9400 ODFL 44138 3010 A1
Pondhaven Ct
1300 PnvT 44077 2041 A7
Pondside Dr
31800 AVLK 44012 2618 E5
Pondside Pt
27000 OmsT 44138 2878 D5
Pond View Ct
3400 AVON 44011 2748 D4

Pondview Ct
- MadT 44057 1843 C7
Pontiac Av
800 PnvT 44077 2040 D2
Pontiac Dr
1700 EUCL 44117 2498 A2
Pontiac St
1500 ECLE 44112 2496 E6
1600 ECLE 44112 2497 A6
Popham Ln
32800 SLN 44139 3019 E2
Popham Pl
7200 SLN 44139 3019 E2
Poplar Av
- EUCL 44132 2374 A2
10 CLEV 44110 2372 C6
Poplar Ct
200 AURA 44202 3156 D1
Poplar Dr
1500 LORN 44053 2744 C4
6300 INDE 44131 2884 C4
38000 WLBY 44094 2250 E1
Poplar Ln
1500 PNVL 44077 2145 B3
4500 NRYN 44133 3014 B6
7600 MNTR 44060 2251 D4
Poplar St
- VMLN 44089 2740 E4
800 ELYR 44035 2875 E4
35000 NRDV 44039 2877 B1
Port Av
7100 CLEV 44104 2625 E6
7300 CLEV 44104 2626 A6
Port Dr
36400 ETLK 44095 2142 D7
Portage Av
5700 CLEV 44127 2625 D7
Portage Dr
4900 VMLN 44089 2741 A5
5200 VMLN 44089 2740 E5
36000 ETLK 44095 2142 C7
N Portage Dr
- VMLN 44089 2740 E4
S Portage Dr
- VMLN 44089 2740 E4
Portage Rd
1600 LNHT 44124 2629 B1
Portage St
7300 SLN 44139 3020 E2
Port Cove
31800 AVLK 44012 2618 E2
Porter Rd
3900 WTLK 44145 2749 D5
4000 NOSD 44070 2749 D5
4000 NOSD 44145 2749 D5
4000 WTLK 44070 2749 D5
5300 NOSD 44070 2878 E1
Porter Creek Dr
300 BYVL 44140 2619 D4
Porter's Ln
19500 SGVL 44149 3146 D1
Portia Ct
100 ELYR 44035 3006 B3
Portland Av
- MPHT 44128 2757 E7
- MPHT 44137 2757 E7
- WVHT 44128 2757 E7
Portland Ct
- VmnT 44089 2740 B6
Portland Dr
200 VMLN 44089 2741 B4
Portland Rd
- WVHT 44128 2757 E6
Portlew Rd
11600 NbyT 44065 2764 C2
Portman Av
2100 CLEV 44109 2754 C6
Portman Rd
50600 BhmT 44001 2871 A7
51200 HetT 44001 2870 C7
51200 HetT 44889 2870 C7
Port Royal Ct
7200 MNTR 44060 2143 C5
Portsmouth Dr
3000 BNWK 44212 3147 C7
Portsmouth Cove
3700 PRRY 44081 2042 B2
Portz Pkwy
34100 SLN 44139 2889 A6
Post Rd
100 PnvT 44077 2040 C3
2500 TNBG 44087 3020 A5
Postal Dr
9100 BWHT 44147 3015 B7
Postal Rd
5700 BKPK 44135 2880 D2
5700 BKPK 44142 2880 D2
5700 CLEV 44135 2880 D2
Potomac Av
13800 ECLE 44112 2497 A5
Potomac Dr
10 SRSL 44022 2762 B6
100 ELYR 44035 2873 E6
5300 BKVL 44141 3150 C3
9100 NRYN 44133 3013 C3
17700 SGVL 44136 3146 E1
Potomac Ln
10 ELYR 44035 2875 A3
Potter Ct
1900 CLEV 44113 2624 D6
Potterstone Wy
- AVON 44011 2748 E3
Powell Av
1800 CVHT 44118 2627 D2
Powell Dr
300 BYVL 44140 2619 B4
Powell Rd
30100 WLWK 44095 2249 C6
Powers Blvd
- PRMA 44134 2883 A5
5500 PRMA 44129 2883 A5
6200 PRMA 44129 2882 E5
Powers Rd
10 BDFD 44146 2886 E4
10 BDFD 44146 2887 A3
Praha Av
4900 CLEV 44127 2625 C6
Prairie Cross
7900 MCDN 44056 3154 B4
Prairie Mdws
20400 SGVL 44149 3011 C4
Prairie Dunes Ct
7400 SLN 44139 3020 E2
Prairie Grass Ln
- MNTR 44060 2144 C1

Prame Av
2100 CLEV 44109 2624 D7
Prasse Rd
4200 SELD 44121 2498 B7
Pratt Av
9300 CLEV 44105 2756 B3
Pratt Blvd
100 CrlT 44035 3006 B3
100 ELYR 44035 3006 B3
Pratt Ln
10200 TNBG 44087 3020 B4
Prayner Av
5100 MPHT 44137 2758 A7
5100 MPHT 44146 2758 A7
Preakness Dr
9400 NHFD 44067 3018 A3
9400 NHFD 44146 3018 A3
9400 WNHL 44146 3018 A3
Preble Av
8000 CLEV 44104 2626 A6
Prell Dr
9500 BWHT 44147 3149 D3
Prelog Ln
9000 KTLD 44094 2377 D7
Prentice Rd
10 PnvT 44077 2145 B4
Prescott Dr
8500 CsTp 44026 2632 B2
Preservation Blvd
- SFLD 44054 2746 C3
Preserve Dr
10 WLBY 44094 2375 B2
Preserve Ln
100 NCtT 44056 3018 B7
100 NCtT 44067 3018 B7
300 MCDN 44056 3018 B7
Preserve Tr
7500 CcdT 44077 2254 B2
Presidential Dr
2000 AVON 44011 2617 E6
Presidential Pkwy
1900 TNBG 44087 3019 C6
Presler Ct
28000 WTLK 44145 2749 E3
Presley Av
7300 MNTR 44060 2252 B1
Prestige Woods Blvd
- AURA 44202 3157 B3
Preston Av
9500 CLEV 44102 2623 D5
Preston Pl
28000 WTLK 44145 2749 D2
W Preston Pl
28300 WTLK 44145 2749 D2
Preston Rd
18400 WVHT 44128 2757 E6
19800 WVHT 44128 2758 A6
Preston St
100 ELYR 44035 2875 C5
Preston Hill Ct
7800 MNTR 44060 2253 A3
Preston Valley Dr
9200 BKVL 44141 3016 D5
Prestwick Cross
4300 WTLK 44145 2749 A5
Prestwick Dr
- BWHT 44147 3149 C3
Prestwick Ln
5400 HDHT 44143 2499 B3
Preyer Av
1600 CVHT 44118 2627 B1
Price Rd
24600 BDHT 44146 2887 D2
Priday Av
20100 EUCL 44119 2373 A3
20100 EUCL 44123 2373 A3
Priebe Av
16600 CLEV 44128 2757 C6
Priem Rd
- BERA 44017 3011 A2
- SGVL 44017 3011 A2
8000 SGVL 44149 3011 A4
Primary Rd
19100 CLEV 44135 2751 E7
19200 CLEV 44135 2880 E1
Primavera Dr
5400 MNTR 44060 2144 E1
5500 MNTR 44060 2145 A1
Primrose Av
11000 CLEV 44108 2496 D6
Primrose Cir
10000 TNBG 44087 3019 B4
15900 MDBH 44130 2881 B5
Primrose Ct
18900 AbnT 44023 3023 B3
Primrose Dr
800 SVHL 44131 2884 A4
7300 MONT 44060 2143 C3
Primrose Ln
2200 AVON 44011 2747 E2
8500 MCDN 44056 3018 B6
15000 MDFD 44062 2767 B2
26300 WTLK 44145 2750 A4
Prince Av
9300 CLEV 44105 2756 C2
Prince Charles Dr
1200 WTLK 44145 2620 D7
13600 NRYN 44133 3014 B7
Princess Ct
3400 BKVL 44141 3016 D5
Princess Anne Av
4200 LORN 44052 2744 D4
Princeton Av
500 ELYR 44035 2875 C7
800 AMHT 44001 2743 E6
11600 CLEV 44105 2756 D3
Princeton Blvd
3700 CVHT 44121 2497 E4
3700 SELD 44121 2497 E4
3800 SELD 44121 2498 A5
Princeton Cir
17700 SGVL 44149 3146 B3
Princeton Ct
6300 PMHT 44130 2882 C4
7400 MNTR 44060 2251 C1
Princeton Dr
- MsnT 44024 2504 E4
- MsnT 44024 2505 A4
- NRDV 44035 3007 B1
4800 NRYN 44133 3014 A4
Princeton Pl
3600 WTLK 44145 2749 C4
7600 MDBH 44130 3012 D2
Princeton Rd
2400 CVHT 44118 2627 D5

Cleveland Street Index

STREET
Block City ZIP Map# Grid

Princeton Rd
2400 UNHT 44118 2627 D4
11400 HtbT 44024 2507 B7
11400 HtbT 44046 2507 B7
11400 HtbT 44064 2507 B5
12300 HtbT 44046 2637 C3
Princeton St
3000 MDSN 44057 1941 E6
Princewood Dr
7900 HDSN 44236 3155 C6
Princton Cir
- AVON 44011 2747 A3
Prior Ct
2100 CLEV 44106 2626 E2
Priorway Dr
15500 NbyT 44072 2763 B4
Priscilla Av
2700 PRMA 44134 2883 C4
Privacy Ln
- CsTp 44026 2502 A5
Private Dr
5900 PMHT 44130 2882 C2
14700 ECLE 44112 2497 B6
Privet Ln
10 NCtT 44067 3153 B4
Proctor Ct
11300 CLEV 44105 2756 D4
Proctor Rd
7700 HmbT 44024 2256 C3
7700 HmbT 44077 2256 C3
7700 LryT 44024 2256 C3
7700 LryT 44077 2256 C3
Production Dr
7300 MNTR 44060 2251 D1
Professor Av
2100 CLEV 44113 2624 E5
2300 CLEV 44113 2625 A5
Professor Rd
400 SELD 44121 2498 D7
900 LNHT 44124 2498 D6
900 SELD 44124 2498 D6
900 SELD 44143 2498 D6
N Professor St
10 OBLN 44074 3138 D1
200 NRsT 44074 3138 D1
12300 NRsT 44074 3003 D7
S Professor St
10 OBLN 44074 3138 D4
Pro Gram Pkwy
600 GNVA 44041 1944 B3
Progress Dr
19300 SGVL 44136 3011 C5
19300 SGVL 44149 3011 C5
Progress Pkwy
9200 MNTR 44060 2144 E2
9200 MNTR 44060 2145 A2
13700 NRYN 44133 3013 A7
Progressive Dr
- HDHT 44143 2499 E5
- MAYF 44143 2499 E5
Project Av
3000 CLEV 44115 2625 C3
Promenade Plz
- WTLK 44145 2619 B7
Promontory Plz
300 ETLK 44095 2142 C7
300 ETLK 44095 2250 C1
Prospect Av
1400 RKRV 44116 2621 E5
4000 CLEV 44103 2625 D2
4000 CLEV 44115 2625 C2
Prospect Av E
10 CLEV 44113 2624 E3
10 CLEV 44115 2624 E3
1000 CLEV 44115 2625 C3
3600 CLEV 44103 2625 C2
W Prospect Av
10 CLEV 44113 2624 E3
10 CLEV 44115 2624 E3
Prospect Ct
- CLEV 44115 2625 B3
Prospect Rd
4200 CLEV 44103 2625 D2
8500 BERA 44017 3011 B2
8500 SGVL 44017 3011 B2
8500 SGVL 44149 3011 B7
14000 SGVL 44149 3146 B3
18900 BHIT 44149 3146 B5
18900 BHIT 44212 3146 B5
Prospect Rd SR-237
8500 BERA 44017 3011 B2
8500 SGVL 44017 3011 B2
8500 SGVL 44149 3011 B7
Prospect St
10 BERA 44017 2880 B7
10 CrlT 44044 3006 E5
100 AMHT 44001 2872 D2
200 BERA 44017 3011 B1
200 ELYR 44035 2875 C7
200 GNVA 44041 1944 C5
500 FTHR 44077 2039 D3
600 LkeC 44077 2039 E3
700 SGVL 44017 3011 B2
700 SGVL 44149 3011 B2
1100 ELYR 44035 3006 C1
1500 CrlT 44035 3006 C1
8300 MNTR 44060 2252 B1
38200 WLBY 44094 2250 E5
Prospect St SR-237
10 BERA 44017 2880 B7
200 BERA 44017 3011 B1
700 SGVL 44017 3011 B2
700 SGVL 44149 3011 B2
E Prospect St
10 PNVL 44077 2040 A7
4600 MNTU 44255 3159 C6
N Prospect St
10 OBLN 44074 3138 D2
S Prospect St
10 OBLN 44074 3138 C3
W Prospect St
200 PNVL 44077 2040 A7
200 PNVL 44077 2145 E1
200 PNVL 44077 2146 A1
4400 MNTU 44255 3159 B6
Prosser Av
5500 CLEV 44103 2495 D7
Prossor St
10 OBLN 44074 3138 E2
Prouty Rd
10100 CcdT 44077 2145 D7
10500 CcdT 44077 2146 A7
Providence Ct
100 BTNH 44108 2496 E2
Providence Dr
2000 HkyT 44233 3148 B6
30400 PRPK 44124 2629 D6
Province Ct
5700 LORN 44053 2743 C6
Province Ln
9200 BKVL 44141 3016 D5
Provincetown Ct
1000 GFTN 44044 3142 A4
Provincetown Ln
30300 BYVL 44140 2619 B5
Ptarmigan Ct
8500 KTLD 44094 2377 B4
Public Sq
10 CLEV 44113 2624 E3
10 CLEV 44114 2624 E3
10 CLEV 44115 2624 E3
Public Sq US-20
10 CLEV 44113 2624 E3
10 CLEV 44114 2624 E3
10 CLEV 44115 2624 E3
Public Sq E
6600 INDE 44131 2884 E5
Public Sq W
6600 INDE 44131 2884 E5
Puddingstone Dr
7600 CsTp 44026 2501 D1
Pueblo Dr
3900 LORN 44053 2743 E1
Pugwash Cir
400 SgHT 44067 3017 D4
Pulaski Av
7900 CLEV 44103 2496 A6
8200 CLEV 44108 2496 B6
Pulaski St
100 BERA 44017 2880 B6
Pumpkin Ln
4400 BWHT 44147 3015 C5
Punderson Rd
15300 NbyT 44021 2764 E4
15300 NbyT 44021 2765 A4
15300 NbyT 44065 2765 A4
15500 NbyT 44065 2764 E4
Pupule Cir
100 MadT 44057 1941 B6
Purdue Av
500 ELYR 44035 3006 C1
Purdue Ct
1300 PnvT 44077 2147 A1
Puritan Av
11600 CLEV 44105 2756 D4
11600 GDHT 44105 2756 D4
23700 EUCL 44123 2373 D3
Puritan Dr
7900 MNTR 44060 2143 E6
8000 MNTR 44060 2144 A6
Puritas Av
13900 CLEV 44135 2752 D5
19300 CLEV 44135 2751 E5
19900 FWPK 44126 2751 D4
19900 FWPK 44135 2751 D4
Puritas Park Dr
4500 CLEV 44135 2751 E5
Purnell Av
19300 RKRV 44116 2621 D6
Puth Dr
34300 AVON 44011 2748 C2
Putnam Av
11600 CLEV 44105 2756 D3
Putnam Ct
9600 TNBG 44087 3020 A6
Putney Dr
700 BERA 44017 3010 E1
Pyle South Amherst Rd
10 OBLN 44074 3138 B4
200 NRsT 44074 3138 B4
1700 AhtT 44001 2872 C5
1700 SAHT 44001 2872 C6
7500 AMHT 44001 2872 C3
10600 NRsT 44074 3003 B5
10600 SAHT 44074 3003 B5
Pythias Av
15600 CLEV 44110 2372 C6

Q

Quail Cir
8600 KTLD 44094 2377 B3
Quail Ct
300 AMHT 44001 2743 E6
Quail Dr
300 ELYR 44035 2874 E2
10000 BKVL 44141 3151 D4
Quail Hllw
2400 AVON 44011 2747 C1
Quail Ln
10 HGVL 44022 2631 A5
Quail Ovl
13900 NRYN 44133 3014 C7
Quail Run
5400 NOSD 44070 2878 C1
Quail St
2000 LKWD 44107 2623 A6
Quail Hollow Av
37700 AVON 44011 2747 C1
Quail Hollow Cir
800 AVLK 44012 2618 C4
Quail Hollow Ct
45200 AhtT 44001 2873 B2
Quail Hollow Dr
7600 SVHL 44131 3015 B1
11000 CcdT 44077 2254 E2
19000 SGVL 44136 3147 A3
23200 WTLK 44145 2750 E2
Quail Hollow Ln
10 MDHL 44022 2760 C3
Quail Point Ln
8200 MNTR 44060 2144 B3
Quailridge Ct
8700 MCDN 44056 3018 A7
Quail Ridge Dr
10 BTVL 44022 2890 A1
14000 NRYN 44133 3148 A1
Quail Roost
200 MDHT 44124 2629 E2
Quail Run Dr
300 BWHT 44147 3014 D4
Quails Nest Ln
7300 NRDV 44039 2876 B4
Quail Woods Dr
14700 CdnT 44024 2254 E5
12000 CdnT 44024 2255 A5
Quarry Dr
800 CVHT 44121 2498 A5
900 SELD 44121 2498 B5
Quarry Ln
600 RDHT 44143 2498 D4
6000 INDE 44131 2884 D3
N Quarry Ln
10 BERA 44017 2880 C7
S Quarry Ln
10 BERA 44017 3011 B2
10 MDBH 44017 3011 B2
Quarry Rd
- ClbT 44028 3010 B4
7000 AhtT 44001 2872 A5
7000 AMHT 44001 2872 B2
8800 SAHT 44001 2872 A5
9500 NRsT 44001 3003 A2
9500 NRsT 44074 3003 A3
14600 PttT 44074 3138 A7
N Quarry Rd
1000 AhtT 44001 2872 B1
1000 AMHT 44001 2872 A1
1300 AMHT 44001 2743 A7
1300 AMHT 44053 2743 A7
Quarry Ridge Rd
25600 ClbT 44028 3009 E3
Quarry Stone Ln
200 BERA 44017 3011 C1
Quarrystone Ln
6700 MDBH 44130 2881 B5
Quartermane Cir
12000 MsnT 44024 2504 C5
35000 BTVL 44139 2889 B2
35000 SLN 44139 2889 B2
Quartz Ct
- WLBY 44094 2143 A5
Quebec Av
9300 CLEV 44106 2626 B4
10500 CLEV 44104 2626 C4
Queen Av
2500 CLEV 44113 2624 D6
Queen Ann Ct
4500 SELD 44121 2498 C5
Queen Ann Wy
- PryT 44081 2041 C7
5200 PryT 44077 2041 C7
Queen Anne Av
4100 LORN 44052 2744 D4
Queen Anne Cir
100 ELYR 44035 3006 D1
Queen Annes Gate
1200 WTLK 44145 2620 D7
Queen Anns Wy
21300 FWPK 44126 2751 B5
35200 AVON 44011 2748 B4
Queen Mary Dr
4500 SELD 44121 2498 C5
4500 SELD 44143 2498 C5
Queens Ct
10 ELYR 44035 2875 D5
100 SDLK 44054 2615 E4
1500 PnvT 44077 2041 B6
1500 WTLK 44145 2620 C7
Queens Hwy
5200 PRMA 44130 2753 B7
5400 PRMA 44130 2882 B1
5700 PMHT 44130 2882 B1
Queens Wy
6200 BKVL 44141 3150 D2
6500 NRYN 44133 3013 E4
6500 NRYN 44133 3014 A4
10000 AbnT 44023 2892 B3
Queensboro Dr
5100 RDHT 44143 2498 E3
5100 RDHT 44143 2499 A3
Queensbridge Ln
11700 NRYN 44133 3148 A5
20900 HkyT 44133 3148 A5
20900 HkyT 44233 3148 A5
N Queensferry Pl
7100 CcdT 44077 2146 A7
Queens Gate
4200 AVON 44011 2748 D5
Queens Park Av
6500 MDHT 44124 2500 A7
Queenston Rd
2300 CVHT 44118 2627 D4
Queenswood Dr
400 BYVL 44140 2620 E5
500 BYVL 44140 2621 A5
Quentin Rd
300 ETLK 44095 2249 E3
16700 CLEV 44112 2497 C4
Querulous St
- CLEV 44111 2752 B3
Quigley Rd
2800 CLEV 44113 2625 A7
3000 CLEV 44109 2625 A7
Quill Ct
- GnvT 44041 1944 C2
Quilliams Rd
500 CLEV 44121 2497 E4
500 CVHT 44121 2497 E5
500 SELD 44121 2497 E4
Quimby Av
5500 CLEV 44103 2625 D1
Quincy Av
4000 CLEV 44104 2625 D4
4000 CLEV 44115 2625 C4
7100 CLEV 44104 2626 A4
8400 CLEV 44106 2626 B4
Quincy St
10 ELYR 44035 2875 B6
Quincy Adams Ct
- LORN 44053 2743 E5
Quinebaugh Ct
- MDBH 44130 2881 A5
Quinn Ct
- CLEV 44103 2496 A6
7000 CLEV 44103 2495 E6
Quinn Rd
18100 AbnT 44023 2892 A7
18100 AbnT 44023 3023 A2

R

Rabbit Run Dr
4000 BKLN 44144 2753 D3
16800 SGVL 44136 3146 E3
Rabun Ln
4400 RDHT 44143 2498 C4
Raccoon Tr
17000 SGVL 44136 3146 E2
17000 SGVL 44136 3147 A2
Raccoon Hill Dr
- KTLD 44094 2376 B5
Race Rd
7200 NRDV 44039 2876 C5
Race St
100 BERA 44017 2880 A7
100 BERA 44017 3011 A1
300 BERA 44017 2879 E7
Racebrook Rd
600 GSML 44040 2500 D4
Rachael Dr
41500 LrgT 44050 3140 C7
Rachel Ln
400 AVLK 44012 2617 C3
4700 RDHT 44143 2498 D4
8200 NRDV 44039 2877 C6
Racoon Hill Dr
7200 KTLD 44094 2376 B4
Radcliff Rd
3500 CVHT 44121 2497 D6
Radcliffe Dr
1900 WTLK 44145 2750 B1
Radcliffe Rd
12900 CcdT 44024 2255 D5
12900 CcdT 44077 2255 D5
12900 HmbT 44024 2255 D5
12900 HmbT 44077 2255 C5
12900 LryT 44024 2255 D5
12900 LryT 44077 2255 D5
13100 HmbT 44024 2256 A5
13100 LryT 44024 2256 A5
13100 LryT 44077 2256 A5
13700 HmbT 44077 2256 B5
14400 LryT 44086 2256 C5
Rademaker Blvd
15200 BKPK 44142 2881 B2
Rader Ln
- CrlT 44044 3141 E2
- EatT 44044 3141 E2
Radford Dr
600 HDHT 44143 2499 A4
600 RDHT 44143 2499 A4
Radio Ln
10 CLEV 44114 2625 B1
Radio Pl
10 PNVL 44077 2040 C5
Radley Dr
100 PnvT 44077 2147 A1
Radnor Rd
1700 CVHT 44118 2627 B1
5700 MDHT 44124 2629 C1
Rae Rd
1200 LNHT 44124 2499 B7
Ragall Pkwy
7500 MDBH 44130 3012 B1
Rail King Ct
- BbgT 44023 3022 D2
Railroad Pl
16700 BbgT 44023 2890 A2
Railroad St
300 PNVL 44077 2040 B6
900 GFTN 44044 3142 A5
E Railroad St
100 ELYR 44035 2874 E5
Railway Av
- CLEV 44113 2624 E5
- CLEV 44113 2625 A5
Rainbow Dr
- CcdT 44077 2254 D4
10 PnvT 44077 2040 D2
100 AMHT 44001 2743 D7
14000 CLEV 44111 2752 D1
24000 NOSD 44138 2879 C1
24000 OmsT 44138 2879 C1
Rainbow Ln
9300 NRYN 44133 3013 C2
Rainbow Rd
4400 SELD 44121 2628 C1
Rainbow End
300 AURA 44202 3156 D5
Rainier Ct
5500 PRMA 44134 2883 E1
Raintree Blvd
- ClbT 44028 3010 A2
- ClbT 44138 3010 A2
26100 ODFL 44138 3010 A2
Rain Tree Cir
38300 NRDV 44039 2747 B7
Raintree Dr
11700 MsnT 44024 2503 B4
Raleigh Ct
100 AURA 44202 3021 E7
Raleigh Dr
- MAYF 44143 2500 A5
100 ELYR 44035 2874 B7
Ralph Av
2100 CLEV 44109 2754 D6
Ralston Dr
5500 PRMA 44129 2883 A5
Ramage Av
15200 MPHT 44137 2886 B3
Rambler Av
41500 EyrT 44035 2874 D2
Rambler Dr
4500 MNTR 44060 2039 A4
Ramblewood Ct
5100 SLN 44139 2759 E7
Ramblewood Dr
3800 RchT 44286 3150 B7
6200 MNTR 44060 2144 C4
Ramblewood Tr
1200 SELD 44121 2498 C7
Rambling Creek Tr
17400 BbgT 44023 2890 C4
Ramona Av
1200 LKWD 44107 2622 D4
Ramona Blvd
9300 CLEV 44104 2626 B7
Ramona Dr
15800 MDBH 44130 2881 B6
Ramona St
4100 WLBY 44094 2251 B5
Ramsay Rd
2600 BHWD 44122 2628 E5
Ramsey Av
15400 CLEV 44128 2757 B4
N Ramsgate Pl
7100 CcdT 44077 2146 A7
Ranch Dr
- WLBY 44094 2375 C1
Ranch Rd
10 WLBY 44094 2250 C7
10 WLBY 44094 2375 C1
8600 CsTp 44026 2632 C1
23100 BHWD 44122 2628 C4
23100 UNHT 44118 2628 C4
Ranchland Dr
1100 HDHT 44143 2499 C7
1100 MDHT 44124 2499 C7
1100 MDHT 44143 2499 C7
Ranchview Av
4300 NOSD 44070 2750 B6
W Ranchview Av
4300 NOSD 44070 2750 B6
Ranchview Dr
6100 INDE 44131 3015 D2
Ranchwood Dr
15000 SGVL 44149 3146 D1
Randall Ct
10 CRDN 44024 2380 A7
Randall Dr
4000 BNWK 44212 3146 D6
24600 NOSD 44070 2750 C6
N Randall Dr
4800 NRDL 44128 2758 B6
4800 WVHT 44128 2758 C6
Randall Rd
400 ELYR 44035 2875 D3
1700 CLEV 44113 2624 B5
Randall St
- LORN 44052 2615 B6
Rand Creek Ct
- MDSN 44057 1942 A6
10 MDSN 44057 1941 E6
Randolph Dr
- LORN 44053 2743 E4
6900 PRMA 44129 2882 E6
Randolph Ln
- AhtT 44001 2872 E6
Randolph Pkwy
20300 HIHL 44122 2758 A3
20300 WVHT 44122 2758 A3
Randolph Rd
3400 CVHT 44121 2497 D5
6000 BDHT 44146 2887 D4
6200 BDFD 44146 2887 C5
Random Rd
2000 CLEV 44106 2626 D2
Randy Rd
5800 BDHT 44146 2887 D3
Ranett Av
7600 HDSN 44236 3155 B7
Rangeview Dr
5600 SVHL 44131 2884 A2
Rankin Rd
22500 BDHT 44146 2887 C1
Ranney Pkwy
27100 WTLK 44145 2619 D6
Ransome Rd
400 HDHT 44143 2499 B3
Rapids Rd
14600 BtnT 44021 2766 A2
14600 BURT 44021 2766 A2
14900 BtnT 44021 2765 E4
15700 TroT 44021 2765 E7
Rashell Dr
18900 WNHL 44146 3018 A2
Rathbun Av
7100 CLEV 44105 2755 E4
Rauland Dr
16700 WNHL 44146 3017 D2
Rauscher Ct
100 ELYR 44035 3006 E1
Raven Cir
100 ELYR 44035 3006 E3
Ravencrest Dr
- HGVL 44022 2631 B7
- RslT 44022 2631 B7
- RslT 44072 2631 B7
Ravenglass Blvd
100 AMHT 44001 2872 D3
Ravenhill Dr
700 SgHT 44067 3152 C2
Ravenna Rd
900 CcdT 44077 2146 C5
900 PnvT 44077 2146 B3
7200 CcdT 44077 2254 D1
7600 HDSN 44236 3155 E7
7600 STBR 44236 3155 E7
7700 TwbT 44236 3155 E6
8000 TwbT 44087 3155 D5
8300 CcdT 44024 2254 D5
8300 CdnT 44024 2254 D7
8800 TNBG 44087 3155 D5
9000 CdnT 44024 2379 D1
9800 TNBG 44087 3154 E1
10000 CRDN 44024 2379 E5
10000 TNBG 44087 3019 D7
11200 GNWL 44139 3019 D7
11200 MCDN 44056 3019 D7
11200 MCDN 44146 3019 D7
11200 Okwd 44146 3019 D7
11200 TNBG 44056 3019 D7
11200 TNBG 44139 3019 D7
11600 CRDN 44024 2505 A3
11600 MsnT 44024 2505 B7
12600 MsnT 44024 2635 B4
13400 NbyT 44021 2635 B4
13400 NbyT 44024 2635 B4
13400 NbyT 44065 2635 B4
14200 NbyT 44021 2765 A3
14200 NbyT 44065 2765 A1
15400 NbyT 44021 2764 E6
15400 NbyT 44065 2764 E6
16200 AbnT 44021 2764 E7
16400 AbnT 44021 2893 D5
16400 AbnT 44255 2893 D5
18200 AbnT 44234 2893 C7
Ravenna Rd SR-44
11600 CRDN 44024 2505 A3
11600 MsnT 44024 2505 B7
12600 MsnT 44024 2635 B4
13400 NbyT 44021 2635 B4
13400 NbyT 44024 2635 B4
13400 NbyT 44065 2635 B4
14200 NbyT 44021 2765 A3
14200 NbyT 44065 2765 A1
15400 NbyT 44021 2764 E6
15400 NbyT 44065 2764 E6
16200 AbnT 44021 2764 E7
16400 AbnT 44021 2893 D5
16400 AbnT 44255 2893 D5
18200 AbnT 44234 2893 C7
Ravenna Rd SR-82
9100 TNBG 44087 3155 A1
Ravenswood Dr
6900 PRMA 44129 2882 D6
Ravenswood Ln
8500 MCDN 44056 3018 B6
Ravenway Dr
5000 NRDV 44039 2747 B7
Ravenwood Dr
12400 ClrT 44024 2635 B2
12400 MsnT 44024 2635 B3
Ravenwood Ln
10400 CcdT 44077 2253 D1
Ravine Blvd
5900 PRMA 44134 2883 D3
Ravine Dr
- MNTR 44094 2251 B4
300 AURA 44202 3156 C2
800 CVHT 44112 2497 C5
800 ECLE 44112 2497 C5
6700 MAYF 44040 2500 B4
Ravines Edge Wy
41000 CrlT 44050 3140 D1
E Ravine View Ct
10400 NRYN 44133 3148 B3
W Ravine View Ct
10400 NRYN 44133 3148 B3
Rawlings Av
7500 CLEV 44104 2626 A5
Rawnsdale Rd
3600 SRHT 44122 2757 E2
Rawson St
- GftT 44044 3142 B6
Ray Ct
8700 TwbT 44087 3154 D2
Raya Ovl
15500 NRYN 44133 3148 B2
Raymond Av
9300 CLEV 44104 2756 B1
10600 GDHT 44125 2756 C7
Raymond Dr
10 GNVA 44041 1944 C5
7600 MNTR 44060 2143 D4
12300 MsnT 44024 2503 E6
Raymond St
- BDHT 44146 2758 A7
15400 MPHT 44137 2757 C7
19800 MPHT 44137 2758 A7
Raymont Blvd
3400 UNHT 44118 2627 D3
Raynham Dr
7200 BDHT 44146 2887 E7
7200 OKWD 44146 2887 E7
Raynor Dr
100 BDFD 44146 2887 A3
Rays Ln
100 MCDN 44056 3018 B7
Reading Av
36100 WLBY 44094 2250 B6
Reading Wy
- NRDV 44039 2877 D6
Reamer Pl
300 OBLN 44074 3138 C3
Reaser Ct
100 ELYR 44035 2875 E6
Rebecca Dr
- MNTR 44094 2251 B4
Rebecca Ln
10 BHIT 44212 3146 A6
Recher Av
20700 EUCL 44119 2373 A5
Rechner Dr
26300 WTLK 44145 2750 B3
Reckman Ct
3200 NRYN 44133 3014 C3
Recreational Pk
- PNVL 44077 2040 B7
Redbay Ln
4900 NRYN 44133 3014 B4
Red Bird Rd
1500 LkeC 44057 1843 A7
1500 MadT 44057 1843 A7
1600 MadT 44057 1942 A1
Red Bird Beach Dr
6200 MadT 44057 1842 E7
6200 MadT 44057 1843 A7
Redbridge Ln
33600 SLN 44139 2889 A2
Redbud Pl
1300 LORN 44053 2744 C4
Red Bush Ln
1200 MCDN 44056 3153 E1
Red Delicious Ln
10 AMHT 44001 2872 B1
Redding Rd
4300 CLEV 44109 2754 E4
Reddington Av
14100 MPHT 44137 2886 A2
Red Doe Cir
2800 RHFD 44286 3150 D7
Redell Av
7400 CLEV 44103 2626 A1
Red Fawn Pth
432-00 AURA 44202 3156 C2
Redfern Rd
3700 PRMA 44134 2883 B3
4800 PRMA 44129 2883 A3
23000 ClbT 44028 3010 C3
23000 ClbT 44149 3010 E3
23000 SGVL 44149 3010 E3
Red Fox Tr
- OKWD 44146 2887 E5
7500 HDSN 44236 3155 D7
17200 BbgT 44023 2890 C3
Red Fox Pass
2400 WBHL 44094 2375 D3
Red Hill Dr
700 LORN 44052 2744 D4
Redington Dr
- NRDV 44035 3007 C1
Redman Av
- CLEV 44109 2754 E2
Red Maple Dr
1300 PnvT 44077 2041 A7
Red Mill Cove
3900 PRRY 44081 2042 B1
Red Mill Valley Rd
4200 NPRY 44081 1940 C6
4200 PryT 44081 1940 C6
N Red Oak
10200 NRYN 44133 3014 C5
S Red Oak
10200 NRYN 44133 3014 C5
Red Oak Av
32700 AVON 44011 2748 D6
Red Oak Dr
2800 PryT 44081 2041 D3
6600 MNTR 44060 2144 E5
N Red Oak Dr
16800 SGVL 44136 3147 A5
S Red Oak Dr
16800 SGVL 44136 3147 A5
Red Oak Ln
500 BYVL 44140 2620 C5
700 GNVA 44041 1944 D5
Red Oaks Dr
- BKVL 44141 3016 B4
8500 CsTp 44026 2502 B5
Red Pine Dr
10 PnvT 44077 2041 A7
Red Pine Wy
4800 NRDV 44039 2748 D7
Red Raven Rd
27900 PRPK 44124 2629 B4
N Redrock Dr
16400 SGVL 44136 3147 A4
S Redrock Dr
16400 SGVL 44136 3147 A4
Redtail Ct
2500 TNBG 44087 3019 E7
8600 MCDN 44056 3018 A6
Red Tail Ln
8900 KTLD 44094 2252 B7
Red Tailed Ln
800 AMHT 44001 2872 B4
Redwick Ct
- AVON 44011 2748 B2
Redwood Blvd
32500 AVLK 44012 2618 A2
32800 AVLK 44012 2617 D2
Redwood Ct
- AhtT 44001 2872 E6
- NRDV 44039 2877 C7
5700 MONT 44060 2143 E2
8400 MCDN 44056 3153 E2
Redwood Dr
400 BERA 44017 2880 A4
4400 PryT 44077 2041 C4
4800 SDLK 44054 2616 D3
5400 WLBY 44094 2375 A1
25900 ODFL 44138 3010 A1
Redwood Rd
3100 CVHT 44118 2627 C2
19200 CLEV 44110 2372 E7
19200 CLEV 44110 2373 A7
Reed Av
400 PNVL 44077 2145 D1
400 PnvT 44077 2145 D1
8400 GDHT 44125 2756 B6
Reed Rd
- NOSD 44070 2750 E6
9000 NRDV 44039 2877 C7
9000 NRDV 44039 3008 C1
9200 EatT 44039 3008 C2
12000 EatT 44028 3008 C7
12000 EatT 44044 3008 C7
12200 EatT 44028 3143 C2
12200 EatT 44044 3143 C2
N Reed Rd
9500 EatT 44028 3008 C3
Reedhurst Ln
- MNTR 44060 2253 A1
9400 MNTR 44060 2145 A7
Reeds Court Tr
1800 WTLK 44145 2749 D1
Reef Rd
5500 MONT 44060 2143 E1
5500 MONT 44060 2144 A1
Reese Rd
18300 CLEV 44119 2372 E6
Reeve Rd
900 ELYR 44035 2875 C3
Reeves Av
1800 LORN 44052 2744 B2
2900 LORN 44053 2744 B2
3400 CLEV 44105 2755 C1
Reeves Rd
2800 ETLK 44095 2250 D1
2800 WLBY 44094 2250 D1
2800 WLBY 44095 2250 D1
Regal Dr
6900 PRMA 44129 2882 E7
Regal Pl
- AbnT 44021 2765 A7
Regal Wy
24500 WTLK 44145 2620 D7
Regalia Av
11100 CLEV 44104 2626 D7
11400 CLEV 44120 2626 D7
Regal Oaks Cir
- AURA 44202 3157 B3
Regal Ridge Cir
7900 MCDN 44056 3154 B5
Regan Ct
1900 HDSN 44236 3154 E7
Regan St
4400 MNTU 44255 3159 B6
Regatta Dr
200 AVLK 44012 2619 A2
Regatta Tr
9800 RMDV 44202 3020 E5
Regency Cir
29200 WTLK 44145 2749 C3
Regency Ct
100 ELYR 44035 2875 B1
32300 AVLK 44012 2618 C3
Regency Dr
5200 PRMA 44129 2883 A6
5200 PRMA 44134 2883 A5
6600 PRMA 44129 2882 E6
7600 WNHL 44146 3018 A2
14400 SGVL 44149 3146 C1
Regency Pl
- WTLK 44145 2749 C2
Regency Woods Dr
9000 KTLD 44094 2252 A7
9000 KTLD 44094 2377 B1
Regent Ct
100 BWHT 44147 3149 D3
Regent Dr
5300 SFLD 44054 2746 E1
Regent Rd
3200 CLEV 44127 2625 E7
3400 CLEV 44127 2755 E1
29900 WKLF 44092 2249 C7
Regent Park Dr
11500 MsnT 44024 2634 D1
Regina Av
3000 LORN 44052 2744 D3
Regina Ct
4600 PryT 44081 1940 D7
Regina Dr
200 BDFD 44146 2886 D3
600 VMLN 44089 2742 A5
Regina Ln
7100 ODFL 44138 2879 B6
7100 OmsT 44138 2879 B6

Cleveland Street Index

STREET
Block City ZIP Map# Grid
Rehwinkle Rd
400 SgHT 44067 3152 D2
Reichert Rd
9000 PRMA 44130 2882 C7
Reid Av
400 LORN 44052 2614 E7
1400 LORN 44052 2744 E1
2500 LORN 44055 2744 E2
Reid Dr
6700 PMHT 44130 2882 C5
Reindeer Av
12300 GDHT 44125 2756 D6
Reinwald Rd
3500 LORN 44053 2743 E3
3500 LORN 44053 2744 A3
Remington Av
10500 CLEV 44108 2496 C4
Remington Cir
27500 WTLK 44145 2619 E7
Remington Dr
1500 WTLK 44145 2619 E7
9500 MNTR 44060 2253 A1
Remington Pt
2800 ManT 44202 3023 A6
2900 ManT 44255 3023 B6
Remora Blvd
15300 BKPK 44142 2881 B2
Rena Ct
25200 EUCL 44132 2373 D2
Renaissance Ct
100 AbnT 44023 2892 B4
Renaissance Pkwy
10 OmsT 44138 2879 A3
700 PNVL 44077 2145 D2
700 PnvT 44077 2145 D2
4300 WVHT 44022 2758 E5
4300 WVHT 44128 2758 E5
26500 WVHT 44022 2759 A4
Renee Dr
5400 HDHT 44143 2499 B4
5900 BKPK 44142 2881 C2
Renfield Rd
900 CVHT 44121 2498 A5
900 SELD 44121 2498 A5
Reno Av
9300 CLEV 44105 2756 C2
Reno Dr
11900 PRMA 44130 2882 A3
Renrock Rd
2000 CVHT 44118 2627 B3
Renwood Av
18600 CLEV 44119 2372 E4
18600 EUCL 44119 2372 E4
19300 EUCL 44119 2373 A4
19300 EUCL 44123 2373 A4
38400 AVON 44011 2747 B1
Renwood Dr
5400 PRMA 44129 2883 A3
5400 PRMA 44134 2883 A3
8200 PRMA 44129 2882 D3
Renwood Rd
4400 SELD 44121 2628 C1
6600 INDE 44131 3015 D1
N Renwood Rd
6900 INDE 44131 2884 E7
6900 INDE 44131 3015 E1
Republic Dr
400 SgHT 44067 3017 D4
Research Dr
- ETLK 44094 2250 C3
- ETLK 44095 2250 C3
- WLBY 44094 2250 C3
Reserve Av
- PtfT 44074 3138 E5
10 OBLN 44074 3138 D5
Reserve Cir N
2000 LORN 44053 2744 A5
Reserve Cir S
2000 LORN 44053 2744 A5
E Reserve Cir
1900 AVON 44011 2617 E7
N Reserve Cir
36300 AVON 44011 2617 E7
S Reserve Cir
36400 AVON 44011 2617 E7
W Reserve Cir
1900 AVON 44011 2617 E7
Reserve Ct
- AVON 44011 2617 E7
10500 CLEV 44106 2626 C2
21000 FWPK 44126 2751 C1
Reserve Dr
7200 WTHL 44094 2376 B3
Reserve Ln
8600 MCDN 44056 3153 E1
12100 CsTp 44026 2502 A5
14200 MDBH 44130 2881 D7
Reserve Run
9100 BKVL 44141 3150 C5
Reserve Tr
400 SRSL 44022 2761 E5
Reserve Wy
- SFLD 44035 2747 A4
- SFLD 44054 2747 A4
4200 AVON 44011 2748 C5
5300 SFLD 44035 2746 E5
5300 SFLD 44054 2746 E4
Reservoir Dr
- PMHT 44130 2882 D3
10700 MNTU 44255 3159 C5
Resource Dr
700 BNHT 44131 2884 C1
W Resource Dr
700 BNHT 44131 2884 B1
Resting Mdw
17800 SGVL 44136 3146 E1
Restivo Cir
- AVON 44011 2748 E5
Restor Av
18600 CLEV 44122 2757 E4
Retford Pkwy
700 PnvT 44077 2040 E3
Retriever Run
- RslT 44072 2632 E7
Reublin Ct
600 ELYR 44035 2875 A4
Revely Av
2000 LKWD 44107 2622 C6
Revere Av
10900 CLEV 44105 2756 C2
Revere Cir
14000 MDBH 44130 3012 C2
Revere Ct
100 ELYR 44035 2873 E6
3600 CLEV 44109 2754 C3

STREET
Block City ZIP Map# Grid
Revere Ct
10300 CcdT 44077 2145 D4
Revere Dr
- NRDV 44035 3007 B1
500 BYVL 44140 2619 D5
5400 NOSD 44070 2879 A1
6800 PMHT 44130 2882 C6
Revere Ln
10 ELYR 44035 2875 A3
Revere Pl
1800 LORN 44053 2744 B5
Revere Rd
1800 CVHT 44118 2627 E2
Rex St
16300 CLEV 44128 2757 C6
16300 MPHT 44128 2757 C6
Rexford Av
11800 CLEV 44105 2756 D1
27800 BYVL 44140 2619 E5
27800 BYVL 44140 2620 A5
Rexway Av
3400 BHWD 44122 2758 C1
3400 HIHL 44122 2758 C1
Rexwood Av
12600 GDHT 44105 2756 E5
13600 GDHT 44105 2757 A5
13900 CLEV 44105 2757 A5
14000 CLEV 44128 2757 A5
Rexwood Rd
2100 CVHT 44118 2627 C3
Reyburn Rd
1800 CLEV 44112 2497 D3
1900 ECLE 44112 2497 D3
2000 CVHT 44112 2497 D4
Reynolds Rd
5800 MONT 44060 2143 C3
6000 MNTR 44060 2143 C7
7300 MNTR 44060 2251 C2
Reynolds Rd SR-306
6200 MNTR 44060 2143 C7
7300 MNTR 44060 2251 C2
Reynosa Ct
600 BERA 44017 3011 A1
Rhine Cir
33000 AVON 44011 2748 D3
Rhode Island Dr
200 ELYR 44035 3006 A3
Rhodes Ct
3200 CLEV 44109 2754 C1
Rhonda Dr
5900 NRDV 44039 2877 A2
Rhonda Ln
15100 LrgT 44050 3140 C7
Ribbonwood Ovl
600 MDSN 44057 1942 A7
Rice Ct
100 AhtT 44001 2872 A4
Rice Dr
7700 MNTR 44060 2143 D3
Rice Rd
7500 BhmT 44001 2871 D3
48000 AhtT 44001 2872 A4
48100 AhtT 44001 2871 D3
Rice Industrial Pkwy
300 AMHT 44001 2873 A2
Rice Park Dr
10 AVLK 44012 2488 B7
Richard Ct
1000 WKLF 44092 2374 B1
Richard Dr
9800 BKLN 44144 2753 C6
11200 PRMA 44130 2882 B1
15300 BKPK 44142 2881 B3
Richard Rd
6600 BSHT 44236 3153 B7
7900 BWHT 44134 3014 D3
7900 BWHT 44147 3014 D3
7900 PRMA 44134 3014 D3
Richard St
10 GNVA 44041 1944 B6
Richards Av
25100 EUCL 44123 2373 D2
25100 EUCL 44132 2373 D2
Richards Dr
5300 MNTR 44060 2038 D7
13000 SGVL 44149 3011 C7
Richelieu Av
4300 SDLK 44054 2616 C3
Rich Hills Dr
8300 BWHT 44147 3015 B5
Richie Dr
500 BNWK 44212 3147 A7
Richland Av
2000 LKWD 44107 2622 E6
2100 CLEV 44107 2622 E7
2100 CLEV 44111 2622 E7
10100 GDHT 44125 2756 C6
Richland Dr
100 AVLK 44012 2617 E1
Richland Rd
- BHWD 44122 2628 E5
Richmar Dr
800 WTLK 44145 2620 A6
Richmond Av
9300 CLEV 44105 2756 B3
Richmond Pl
- ECLE 44112 2497 B5
Richmond Rd
- EUCL 44132 2373 E5
100 EUCL 44117 2373 E5
100 EUCL 44143 2373 E5
100 RDHT 44117 2373 E6
100 RDHT 44143 2373 E6
200 RDHT 44143 2498 E2
700 LNHT 44124 2498 E3
700 LNHT 44143 2498 E5
800 PNVL 44077 2039 E7
800 PnvT 44077 2039 D6
1000 GDRV 44077 2039 D6
1500 LNHT 44124 2628 E2
2000 BHWD 44122 2628 E7
2000 BHWD 44124 2628 E3
3000 BHWD 44122 2758 E2
3700 HIHL 44122 2758 E3
3700 WVHT 44122 2758 E3
4300 WVHT 44022 2758 E4
4400 WVHT 44128 2758 E6
4800 BDHT 44128 2758 E7
4800 BDHT 44146 2758 E7
5500 SLN 44139 2888 A2
5700 Okwd 44146 2888 A3
6500 GNWL 44139 2888 A3
6800 GNWL 44146 2888 A3
7000 GNWL 44139 3019 A3
7000 Okwd 44146 3019 A3

STREET
Block City ZIP Map# Grid
Richmond Rd
25700 BDHT 44146 2887 E1
26000 BDHT 44146 2888 A1
26000 SLN 44146 2888 A1
Richmond Rd SR-87
2900 BHWD 44122 2628 E7
3000 BHWD 44122 2758 E1
Richmond Rd SR-175
- EUCL 44132 2373 E5
100 EUCL 44117 2373 E5
100 EUCL 44143 2373 E5
100 RDHT 44117 2373 E6
100 RDHT 44143 2373 E6
200 RDHT 44143 2498 E2
700 LNHT 44124 2498 E3
700 LNHT 44143 2498 E5
1500 LNHT 44124 2628 E2
2000 BHWD 44122 2628 E7
2000 BHWD 44124 2628 E3
3000 BHWD 44122 2758 E2
3700 HIHL 44122 2758 E3
4200 WVHT 44122 2758 E4
4300 WVHT 44022 2758 E4
4400 WVHT 44128 2758 E6
4800 BDHT 44128 2758 E7
4800 BDHT 44146 2758 E7
5500 SLN 44139 2888 A2
25700 BDHT 44146 2887 E1
26000 BDHT 44146 2888 A1
26000 SLN 44146 2888 A1
Richmond Rd SR-283
800 PNVL 44077 2039 E7
800 PnvT 44077 2039 D6
1000 GDRV 44077 2039 D6
Richmond Sq
10 EUCL 44143 2498 B2
Richmond St
- PNVL 44077 2039 D6
10 PNVL 44077 2040 A7
10 PNVL 44077 2146 B1
600 PnvT 44077 2039 E7
900 FTHR 44077 2039 D6
Richmond St SR-283
- PNVL 44077 2039 D6
10 PNVL 44077 2040 A7
600 PnvT 44077 2039 E7
Richmond St SR-535
600 PNVL 44077 2039 E7
600 PnvT 44077 2039 E7
900 FTHR 44077 2039 D6
Richmond Bluffs Dr
4800 RDHT 44143 2498 E1
Richmond Park East Dr
400 RDHT 44143 2499 A3
Richmond Park West Dr
400 RDHT 44143 2499 A2
Richner Av
3900 CLEV 44113 2624 C7
Richner Ct
2600 TNBG 44087 3154 E1
2700 TNBG 44087 3155 B1
Richwood Av
5700 BKPK 44142 2881 D1
Richwood Dr
- MNTR 44060 2143 E1
7800 MONT 44060 2143 E1
Rickey Ln
30000 WKLF 44092 2374 D2
Riddell
- ELYR 44035 2875 E7
Riddle Rd
15400 RslT 44022 2761 D4
Rider Rd
- BtnT 44021 2765 C3
N Rider Rd
14400 BtnT 44021 2635 C7
14400 BtnT 44021 2765 C1
S Rider Rd
14600 BtnT 44021 2765 C1
Ridge Cir
100 ELYR 44035 2874 A6
Ridge Ct
9500 TNBG 44087 3019 C5
N Ridge Dr
15500 RslT 44072 2762 D5
S Ridge Dr
37100 AVON 44011 2747 D3
W Ridge Dr
7900 BWHT 44147 3014 C3
14400 RslT 44072 2631 E7
Ridge Ln
5400 SLN 44139 2888 D2
Ridge Rd
10 HkyT 44133 3148 D5
10 HkyT 44233 3148 D7
10 NRYN 44133 3148 D3
3400 BKLN 44102 2753 E1
3400 BKLN 44144 2753 E1
3400 CLEV 44102 2753 E1
3400 CLEV 44144 2753 E1
5100 BKLN 44129 2753 E7
5100 CLEV 44129 2753 E7
5100 PRMA 44129 2753 E5
5100 PRMA 44144 2753 E7
5400 PRMA 44129 2882 E7
7300 PRMA 44134 2882 E7
7400 PRMA 44129 3013 E1
7400 PRMA 44134 3013 E1
7800 NRYN 44129 3013 E2
7800 NRYN 44133 3013 E4
7800 NRYN 44134 3013 E2
28700 WKLF 44092 2374 D3
33300 WKLF 44092 2375 A3
33300 WLBY 44094 2375 B2
36800 WLBY 44094 2250 D7
Ridge Rd SR-3
10 HkyT 44133 3148 D5
10 HkyT 44233 3148 D7
10 NRYN 44133 3148 D3
5400 PRMA 44129 2882 E7
7300 PRMA 44134 2882 E7
7400 PRMA 44129 3013 E1
7400 PRMA 44134 3013 E1
7800 NRYN 44129 3013 E2
7800 NRYN 44133 3013 E4
7800 NRYN 44134 3013 E2
Ridge Rd SR-84
28700 WKLF 44092 2374 D3
33300 WKLF 44092 2375 A3
33300 WLBY 44094 2375 B2
36800 WLBY 44094 2250 D7
Ridge Rd SR-174
37700 WLBY 44094 2250 D7
N Ridge Rd
1200 PnvT 44077 2040 D5

STREET
Block City ZIP Map# Grid
N Ridge Rd
1700 PnvT 44077 2041 B3
2400 PryT 44077 2041 B3
2400 PryT 44081 2041 B3
3400 PryT 44081 1940 E6
3400 PryT 44081 2042 A1
3700 NPRY 44081 1940 E6
4700 MadT 44057 1941 A5
4700 MadT 44081 1941 A5
4700 NPRY 44081 1941 A5
4700 PryT 44081 1941 A5
6200 MadT 44057 1942 E4
7500 GnvT 44041 1943 A5
7500 GnvT 44057 1943 A5
7500 MadT 44057 1943 A5
N Ridge Rd US-20
1200 PnvT 44077 2040 D5
1700 PnvT 44077 2041 B3
2400 PryT 44077 2041 B3
2400 PryT 44081 2041 B3
3400 PryT 44081 1940 E6
3400 PryT 44081 2042 A1
3700 NPRY 44081 1940 E6
4700 MadT 44057 1941 A5
4700 MadT 44081 1941 A5
4700 NPRY 44081 1941 A5
4700 PryT 44081 1941 A5
6200 MadT 44057 1942 D4
7500 GnvT 44041 1943 A5
7500 GnvT 44057 1943 A5
7500 MadT 44057 1943 A5
N Ridge Rd E
4500 GnvT 44041 1944 E3
N Ridge Rd E US-20
4500 GnvT 44041 1944 E3
N Ridge Rd W
5900 GnvT 44041 1943 C4
6700 GnvT 44057 1943 B4
N Ridge Rd W US-20
5900 GnvT 44041 1943 C4
6700 GnvT 44057 1943 B4
S Ridge Rd
2600 PryT 44077 2041 D6
2600 PryT 44081 2041 D6
2800 PryT 44081 2042 A5
4400 PRRY 44081 2042 D4
4500 PryT 44057 2042 D4
5000 MadT 44057 2043 C2
5000 MadT 44081 2043 A3
5000 PryT 44057 2043 A3
5000 PryT 44081 2043 A3
5900 MDSN 44057 2043 E2
7100 MadT 44057 2044 D1
7100 MDSN 44057 2044 D1
7300 MadT 44057 1942 E7
7400 MadT 44057 1943 A7
7800 HpfT 44041 1943 A7
7800 HpfT 44057 1943 A7
S Ridge Rd SR-84
2600 PryT 44077 2041 D6
2600 PryT 44081 2041 D6
2800 PryT 44081 2042 A5
4400 PRRY 44081 2042 D4
4500 PryT 44057 2042 D4
5000 MadT 44057 2043 C2
5000 MadT 44081 2043 A3
5000 PryT 44057 2043 A3
5000 PryT 44081 2043 A3
5900 MDSN 44057 2043 E2
7100 MadT 44057 2044 D1
7100 MDSN 44057 2044 D1
7300 MadT 44057 1942 E7
7400 MadT 44057 1943 A7
7800 HpfT 44041 1943 A7
7800 HpfT 44057 1943 A7
S Ridge Rd E
10 GNVA 44041 1944 C6
500 GnvT 44041 1944 C6
S Ridge Rd E SR-84
10 GNVA 44041 1944 C6
500 GnvT 44041 1944 C6
S Ridge Rd W
10 GNVA 44041 1944 B6
200 HpfT 44041 1944 B6
5800 HpfT 44041 1943 C7
6800 HpfT 44057 1943 B7
6800 MadT 44057 1943 B7
S Ridge Rd W SR-84
10 GNVA 44041 1944 B6
200 HpfT 44041 1944 B6
5800 HpfT 44041 1943 C7
6800 HpfT 44057 1943 B7
6800 MadT 44057 1943 B7
W Ridge Rd
1100 AhtT 44001 2744 E7
6400 AhtT 44035 2744 E7
6400 AhtT 44035 2745 A7
6400 AhtT 44035 2874 A1
6400 EyrT 44035 2745 A7
6700 AhtT 44035 2873 E2
6700 EyrT 44035 2873 E2
7800 ELYR 44035 2873 E4
8100 EyrT 44035 2874 A6
8700 ELYR 44035 2874 A7
8900 CrlT 44035 3005 B4
8900 ELYR 44035 3005 A1
8900 EyrT 44035 3005 A2
12100 CrlT 44074 3005 B7
Ridge St
100 ELYR 44035 2875 B5
Ridgebrook Cir
1800 LNHT 44122 2628 D3
Ridgebury Blvd
4800 LNHT 44124 2498 D6
4800 SELD 44121 2498 D6
4800 SELD 44124 2498 D6
5000 LNHT 44124 2499 A6
5300 HDHT 44143 2499 A6
5300 LNHT 44143 2499 A6
5600 MDHT 44124 2499 A6
5600 MDHT 44143 2499 A6
5900 MAYF 44143 2499 D6
6300 MDHT 44124 2500 A6
6300 MDHT 44143 2500 A6
Ridgebury Dr
2000 PnvT 44077 2145 B6
Ridgecliff Cir
11800 SGVL 44136 3011 E5
Ridgecliff Dr
6700 SLN 44139 2889 B6
Ridge Creek Rd
12900 SGVL 44136 3012 A7
Ridgecreek Tr
10 MDHL 44022 2760 A6

STREET
Block City ZIP Map# Grid
Ridgecrest Dr
10 PnvT 44077 2146 E2
10 PnvT 44077 2147 A2
10 SRSL 44022 2762 C6
Ridgedale Rd
7900 NRYN 44133 3013 E3
Ridgefield Av
7400 PRMA 44129 2882 E1
Ridgefield Rd
1500 CVHT 44118 2627 B1
Ridgehill Rd
1900 CLEV 44121 2497 E3
Ridgehills Dr
28500 WBHL 44092 2374 B5
28500 WKLF 44092 2374 B5
Ridgehurst Dr
1900 WKLF 44092 2374 E2
Ridgeland Av
19400 CLEV 44135 2751 D4
Ridgeland Cir
4200 CLEV 44135 2751 D4
Ridgeland Dr
100 AhtT 44001 2873 A1
100 AMHT 44001 2873 A1
1900 AVON 44011 2617 E7
1900 AVON 44011 2747 E1
Ridgeland St
4800 LORN 44055 2745 E6
4800 ShfT 44055 2745 E6
Ridgelawn Av
100 PNVL 44077 2039 E7
100 PNVL 44077 2040 A6
Ridgeline Av
18000 CLEV 44135 2752 A4
Ridgeline Ct
19100 SGVL 44136 3146 E5
Ridge Line Dr
9800 NRYN 44133 3014 A4
Ridgeline Dr
24300 BDHT 44146 2887 D6
Ridge Meadow Ct
1900 TNBG 44087 3019 C5
Ridgemore Av
7100 CLEV 44144 2753 E3
Ridge Park Dr
3300 BWHT 44147 3015 B5
Ridge Peak Ct
10 GDHT 44137 2886 A4
10 MPHT 44137 2886 A4
Ridge Plaza Dr
6200 NRDV 44039 2877 A2
Ridge Point Cir
17000 SGVL 44136 3012 A6
Ridgeside Dr
9300 MNTR 44060 2252 E1
9300 MNTR 44060 2253 A1
Ridgeton Dr
16700 CLEV 44128 2757 C4
Ridgeton Rd
17600 WVHT 44128 2757 D4
N Ridgetop Dr
- TwbT 44087 3154 C5
- TwbT 44236 3154 C5
Ridgeview Blvd
5500 NRDV 44039 2877 A3
Ridgeview Dr
100 PRMA 44131 3014 E1
100 PRMA 44134 3014 E1
100 SVHL 44131 3014 E1
100 SVHL 44131 3015 A1
1600 WKLF 44092 2374 D2
4000 VMLN 44089 2741 C5
9300 MCDN 44056 3018 E5
Ridgeview Ln
5700 WLBY 44094 2375 A1
Ridgeview Rd
4000 CLEV 44144 2754 A4
6500 MDHT 44124 2630 A1
Ridgeview Tr
9600 CcdT 44060 2253 B3
19000 BbgT 44023 3022 A3
Ridgewater Dr
10500 CcdT 44077 2145 E5
Ridgeway Dr
530-00 AURA 44202 3156 D3
6000 BDHT 44146 2887 D4
7700 MNTR 44060 2252 A2
Ridgeway Ln
35400 WLBY 44094 2375 B2
Ridgewick Dr
1500 WKLF 44092 2374 D2
Ridgewood Av
1400 LKWD 44107 2623 A6
5400 PRMA 44129 2883 A1
5400 PRMA 44134 2883 A1
6700 PRMA 44129 2882 E1
19000 CLEV 44122 2757 E3
19000 WVHT 44122 2757 E3
19700 WVHT 44122 2758 A3
20400 HIHL 44122 2758 A3
Ridgewood Ct
1500 TNBG 44087 3019 B4
Ridgewood Dr
300 ETLK 44095 2142 D7
9700 TNBG 44087 3019 C4
15800 MDFD 44062 2767 D2
E Ridgewood Dr
10 PRMA 44131 2883 E4
10 PRMA 44134 2883 E4
10 SVHL 44131 2883 E4
10 SVHL 44131 2884 A4
W Ridgewood Dr
900 PRMA 44131 2883 E4
900 PRMA 44134 2883 C4
900 SVHL 44131 2883 E4
3900 PRMA 44129 2883 A5
6300 PRMA 44129 2882 C5
8500 PMHT 44129 2882 D5
8500 PMHT 44130 2882 C5
8500 PRMA 44130 2882 C5
Ridgewood Ln
5500 BKVL 44141 3150 C4
8300 RslT 44072 2762 A2
Ridgewood Rd
10 CNFL 44022 2761 B6
Ridgewood St
- LORN 44055 2745 E6
4900 ShfT 44055 2745 E6
Ridgewood Lakes Dr
6400 PRMA 44129 2882 E4
Riding Tr
11500 CcdT 44077 2254 D1
Ridpath Av
15000 CLEV 44110 2372 B7

STREET
Block City ZIP Map# Grid
Riedham Rd
3500 SRHT 44120 2757 C2
Riegelsberger Rd
35000 AVON 44011 2748 A4
Riester Av
6600 PRMA 44134 2883 B5
Rife Ct
15600 SRHT 44120 2757 B1
Riley Av
- ELYR 44035 2874 D3
- EyrT 44035 2874 D3
Riley Ct
12000 TNBG 44087 3020 B3
Riley Rd
1000 AURA 44202 3021 A7
1000 AURA 44202 3156 A1
W Rim Dr
23900 ClbT 44028 3010 A5
Rinard Rd
2300 CVHT 44118 2627 D4
Rindlewood Ln
14600 RslT 44072 2761 B1
Ringneck Cir
16900 SGVL 44136 3147 A3
Rio Av
1400 LKWD 44107 2622 A5
Rio Grande Tr
- ClrT 44024 2505 C6
Rio Nero Dr
- INDE 44131 3016 B1
Rio Vista Dr
6300 CcdT 44077 2146 D4
Ripley Rd
- CLEV 44120 2627 A6
2900 CLEV 44120 2626 E6
8100 NRYN 44133 3013 C3
Rippling Brook Ln
7100 CcdT 44060 2145 C7
Rita Dr
400 LvpT 44280 3145 C7
2700 LORN 44053 2744 A3
7200 INDE 44131 2884 D7
7200 INDE 44131 3015 D1
Rivendell Rd
600 SgHT 44067 3152 C2
River Dr
- ETLK 44095 2250 C1
10 ETLK 44095 2142 B7
W River Dr
7900 RslT 44072 2631 E6
7900 RslT 44072 2632 A6
River Ln
3600 RKRV 44116 2751 B2
3900 FWPK 44116 2751 B2
3900 FWPK 44126 2751 B2
River Pl
- RKRV 44116 2621 D7
River Pt
- LKWD 44126 2621 E7
- RKRV 44116 2621 E7
- RKRV 44126 2621 E7
River Rd
10 HkyT 44133 3149 A6
10 HkyT 44233 3149 A6
10 NRYN 44133 3149 A6
1100 CLEV 44113 2624 C3
2100 WBHL 44094 2250 D7
2100 WBHL 44094 2375 D1
2100 WLBY 44094 2250 D7
2800 PryT 44077 2041 E7
2800 PryT 44081 2041 E7
2800 PryT 44081 2042 A7
2900 GSML 44040 2500 C1
2900 GSML 44094 2500 C1
2900 WBHL 44094 2500 C1
4000 PryT 44057 2042 E6
5000 PryT 44057 2043 A5
5700 MadT 44057 2043 C5
6000 MadT 44057 2044 B5
7300 ODFL 44138 2879 C5
7300 OmsT 44138 2879 C5
11000 MsnT 44024 2504 B5
17300 BbgT 44023 2890 A4
17300 BbgT 44139 2890 A3
17300 SLN 44139 2890 A3
River Rd SR-94
10 HkyT 44133 3149 A6
10 HkyT 44233 3149 A6
10 NRYN 44133 3149 A6
River Rd SR-174
2100 WBHL 44094 2250 D7
2100 WBHL 44094 2375 D1
2100 WLBY 44094 2250 D7
2900 GSML 44040 2500 C1
2900 GSML 44094 2500 C1
2900 WBHL 44094 2500 C1
E River Rd
2200 SFLD 44054 2616 B7
2200 SFLD 44054 2746 B1
4800 SFLD 44035 2746 C6
9500 CrlT 44035 3006 C3
9500 ELYR 44035 3006 B1
9800 ClbT 44028 3010 B4
9800 ClbT 44138 3010 C2
9800 ODFL 44138 3010 C2
14000 ClbT 44028 3145 A3
17700 LvpT 44028 3145 A5
17700 LvpT 44280 3145 A5
38500 EatT 44035 3006 E4
E River Rd SR-252
9800 ClbT 44028 3010 B4
9800 ClbT 44138 3010 C2
9800 ODFL 44138 3010 C2
14000 ClbT 44028 3145 A3
17700 LvpT 44028 3145 A5
17700 LvpT 44280 3145 A5
E River Rd N
9500 ClbT 44028 3010 C2
9500 ClbT 44138 3010 C2
9500 ODFL 44138 3010 C2
W River Rd
10 ClbT 44028 3144 E5
10 ClbT 44280 3144 E5
10 LvpT 44280 3144 D7
600 VMLN 44089 2740 E5
700 VMLN 44089 2741 A5
5100 LORN 44055 2746 B6
5100 ShfT 44055 2746 B6
6400 LrnC 44089 2741 B6
6500 BhmT 44089 2741 B7
6700 BhmT 44089 2870 B1
W River Rd N
100 ELYR 44035 2874 E6
500 ELYR 44035 2875 A5
2500 ELYR 44035 2746 A7

STREET
Block City ZIP Map# Grid
W River Rd N
3100 ShfT 44035 2746 A6
3100 ShfT 44055 2746 A6
W River Rd S
1900 CrlT 44035 3005 E3
1900 ELYR 44035 3005 E1
6100 ELYR 44035 2874 E7
River Run
3000 AVON 44011 2748 B2
River Run S
- CcdT 44077 2253 E2
River Smt
5400 NRYN 44133 3149 A3
River St
10 CNFL 44022 2761 B6
10 MDSN 44057 2044 B3
100 GDRV 44077 2039 C5
700 PnvT 44077 2039 C6
4100 WLBY 44094 2250 E5
River St SR-174
4100 WLBY 44094 2250 E5
River St SR-283
600 GDRV 44077 2039 C6
700 PnvT 44077 2039 C6
River St SR-528
10 MDSN 44057 2044 B3
River St US-20
4100 WLBY 44094 2250 E5
E River St
400 ELYR 44035 2875 B6
1000 ELYR 44035 3006 B1
1100 CrlT 44035 3006 B1
River Tr
- LNHT 44124 2628 E2
Riverbank Dr
4000 PryT 44057 2042 B7
4200 PryT 44081 2042 C6
River Beach Rd
11500 ManT 44234 3160 A2
Riverbed St
1200 CLEV 44113 2624 D3
River Bend Dr
38300 WLBY 44094 2250 E7
Riverbend Dr
- LORN 44052 2614 E7
Rivercliff Dr
18500 FWPK 44126 2752 A2
River Creek Rd Rd
- LNHT 44124 2628 E2
Rivercrest Dr
6700 BKVL 44141 3016 A3
Riverdale Ct
100 ELYR 44035 2875 B7
Riverdale Dr
300 RKRV 44116 2621 E4
400 ETLK 44095 2142 D7
6200 MadT 44057 2044 A5
River Edge Dr
5500 ELYR 44035 2746 B6
5500 ShfT 44035 2746 B6
5500 ShfT 44055 2746 B6
Riveredge Dr
10400 PRMA 44130 2753 C7
Riveredge Pkwy
10 BERA 44017 2880 B4
Riveredge Rd
3800 CLEV 44111 2752 A3
3800 CLEV 44135 2752 A3
Rivergate Dr
22100 RKRV 44116 2751 A2
River Glen Dr
14500 RslT 44072 2631 E7
14500 RslT 44072 2761 E1
14800 RslT 44022 2761 E1
24800 ClbT 44028 3010 B4
River Glen Rd
300 AURA 44202 3022 B6
River Industrial Rd
3400 LORN 44052 2615 C7
River Moss Rd
11500 SGVL 44136 3012 A6
River Mountain Dr
10 MDHL 44022 2760 D5
River Oaks Dr
- RKRV 44116 2621 B7
2600 RKRV 44116 2751 B1
9600 NRYN 44133 3013 A3
River Oaks Tr
7400 GSML 44040 2500 D4
River Ridge Ct
38400 CrlT 44044 3141 D2
38400 EatT 44044 3141 D2
River Ridge Dr
4100 CLEV 44109 2755 A4
River Ridge Rd
11600 SGVL 44136 3011 E5
River Rock Ln
10300 NRYN 44133 3148 B4
River Run Dr
900 MCDN 44056 3154 B5
N River Run Dr
- CcdT 44077 2253 E1
River Run Ln
10200 NRYN 44133 3148 B4
Rivers Edge
- WBHL 44094 2375 D2
River's Edge Dr
200 AMHT 44001 2872 C3
Rivers Edge Dr E
18700 BbgT 44023 3021 E2
Rivers Edge Dr W
18700 BbgT 44023 3021 D2
Rivers Edge Ln
700 PNVL 44077 2146 C2
700 PnvT 44077 2146 C2
Riverside Av
4300 CLEV 44102 2754 B2
4300 CLEV 44109 2754 B2
Riverside Blvd
400 ETLK 44095 2250 C1
Riverside Ct
100 ELYR 44035 2875 B6
Riverside Dr
10 BERA 44017 2880 C7
10 PnvT 44077 2040 D7
10 PnvT 44077 2146 D2
200 PNVL 44077 2146 D2
700 VMLN 44089 2741 A6
800 ELYR 44035 2875 A7
800 PnvT 44077 2147 A1
1000 ELYR 44035 3006 A1
1300 LKWD 44107 2622 A6
1400 PryT 44077 2147 B1
2300 CLEV 44107 2622 A7
2500 PryT 44077 2041 C7

Cleveland Street Index

STREET Block City ZIP Map# Grid

Riverside Dr
2500 PryT 44081 2041 C7
2600 LORN 44055 2746 B4
4900 WLBY 44094 2250 E7
5300 BKPK 44142 2880 C3
8300 RslT 44072 2632 A6
8900 BbgT 44023 3022 C3
17100 CLEV 44111 2622 B7
17100 LKWD 44111 2622 B7
Riverside Dr SR-84
400 PnvT 44077 2146 D2
800 PnvT 44077 2147 A1
1400 PryT 44077 2147 B1
2500 PryT 44077 2041 C7
2500 PryT 44081 2041 C7
Riverside Dr SR-237
1500 LKWD 44107 2622 A6
2300 CLEV 44107 2622 A7
17100 CLEV 44111 2622 B7
17100 LKWD 44111 2622 B7
S Riverside Dr
7700 BbgT 44202 3021 D3
Riverside Commons Dr
- WLBY 44094 2250 E3
- WLBY 44094 2251 A3
Riverstone Dr
10 MDHL 44022 2760 C4
River Valley Blvd
17600 NRYN 44133 3148 B4
River Valley Tr
1100 HkyT 44233 3149 A7
Riverview Av
19200 RKRV 44116 2621 D6
Riverview Ct
- GnvT 44041 1944 C1
10 BTVL 44022 2760 D7
Riverview Dr
900 MCDN 44056 3018 D7
5300 NRYN 44133 3149 A4
18700 BbgT 44023 3022 B2
24700 ClbT 44028 3010 B2
N Riverview Dr
36200 ETLK 44095 2250 C2
S Riverview Dr
36200 ETLK 44095 2250 C3
Riverview Ln
2800 LORN 44055 2746 B4
Riverview Rd
- INDE 44125 2885 C7
- INDE 44131 2885 C7
- VLVW 44125 2885 C7
400 GSML 44040 2500 D2
6900 BosT 44141 3152 B5
7200 INDE 44131 3016 C1
7200 INDE 44141 3016 C1
7500 BKVL 44141 3152 A2
7700 BKVL 44141 3016 E7
9000 BKVL 44141 3151 E1
River Walk Cir
17100 NRYN 44133 3149 B3
River Walk Ct
22200 RKRV 44116 2751 A1
River Walk Dr
22200 RKRV 44116 2751 B1
Riverway Dr
17300 LKWD 44107 2622 B6
Riverwood Av
19300 RKRV 44116 2621 D6
Riverwood Dr
4600 PryT 44057 2042 E5
8800 NRDV 44039 2877 D7
11000 CrlT 44044 3006 C6
11600 MsnT 44024 2503 C3
Riverwood Ln
9600 AbnT 44023 2763 A7
Riverwood Wy
8800 KTLD 44094 2251 E7
8800 KTLD 44094 2252 A7
Riviera Av
10 AMHT 44001 2744 B7
Riviera Dr
21400 FWPK 44126 2751 B6
Riviera Ln
2800 WTLK 44145 2749 A3
Riviera Wy
1000 MCDN 44056 3154 A3
Riviera Ridge Rd
36800 WBHL 44094 2375 D3
Roadoan Rd
4300 BKLN 44144 2753 D6
Road to Happiness
700 VMLN 44089 2740 C5
Roanoke Av
2200 CLEV 44109 2754 C4
Roanoke Cir
6100 PRMA 44134 2883 E3
Roanoke Ct
9200 NRYN 44133 3013 D4
27600 WTLK 44145 2619 E7
Roanoke Dr
1300 PRMA 44134 2883 E3
3000 VMLN 44089 2742 A5
Roanoke Rd
700 SELD 44121 2497 E5
800 CVHT 44121 2497 E6
Roanoke Wy
600 WTLK 44145 2619 E7
Robens Ct
100 CNFL 44022 2760 E7
Robert Av
3600 CLEV 44109 2624 B7
Robert Cir
4200 SELD 44121 2498 B6
Robert Ct
5500 NRDV 44039 2877 B1
Robert Dr
5700 BKPK 44142 2881 B2
14300 MDBH 44130 2881 C6
21900 RKRV 44116 2751 B2
Robert Ln
10600 AbnT 44023 2892 E4
39500 CrlT 44035 3006 C2
Robert Pkwy
2800 BNWK 44212 3147 D6
Robert St
- ELYR 44035 2874 C3
- EyrT 44035 2874 C3
7700 PRMA 44134 3014 E2
29900 WKLF 44092 2249 C7
29900 WKLF 44092 2374 C1
Roberta Dr
31100 BYVL 44140 2619 A5
Robert Bishop Dr
- WVHT 44122 2758 E4
4300 BHWD 44122 2758 D3

Robert Bishop Dr
4300 HIHL 44122 2758 D4
Robertdale Rd
5800 BDHT 44146 2887 E3
5800 OKWD 44146 2887 E3
Robert Donaldson Ct
6900 BKVL 44141 3016 B7
Robert Lockwood Jr Dr
1400 CLEV 44113 2624 D3
Roberts Av
21500 EUCL 44123 2373 B3
Roberts Ct
8700 ODFL 44138 2879 D7
Roberts Rd
33800 ETLK 44095 2249 E2
33800 LKLN 44095 2249 E2
33900 ETLK 44095 2250 A2
Roberts Run
300 BYVL 44140 2621 A5
Roberts St
600 SDLK 44054 2616 A4
Roberts Wy
3400 PryT 44081 1940 C7
Robertson Av
11600 CLEV 44105 2756 D4
Robin Cir
6100 MAYF 44143 2499 D5
Robin Dr
200 BERA 44017 2880 D6
300 BERA 44130 2880 D6
300 MDBH 44130 2880 D6
600 ETLK 44095 2250 D1
Robin Ln
- LORN 44053 2743 D3
400 MCDN 44056 3153 C2
8000 BKVL 44141 3016 C3
8800 KTLD 44094 2252 C7
Robin Rd
300 ELYR 44035 2874 E2
Robin St
2000 LKWD 44107 2623 A6
Robindale Dr
16000 SGVL 44136 3147 B2
Robindale St
1500 WKLF 44092 2374 C2
Robinhood Av
800 PnvT 44077 2040 D2
21000 FWPK 44126 2751 B5
Robinhood Dr
400 AURA 44202 3021 C6
2400 PRMA 44134 2883 C7
2600 LORN 44053 2743 E2
4800 WLBY 44094 2250 C7
5000 WLBY 44094 2375 C1
13500 GDHT 44125 2885 E3
Robinia Dr
24300 BDHT 44146 2887 D3
Robin Park Blvd
10 OBLN 44074 3138 C2
Robinson Av
9600 GDHT 44125 2756 C5
Robinson Rd
8700 CdnT 44024 2254 E6
8700 CdnT 44024 2255 A7
9000 CdnT 44024 2380 A2
Robinwood Av
- AVLK 44012 2617 D2
- SFLD 44054 2615 E5
700 SDLK 44054 2616 C4
1400 LKWD 44107 2622 D5
Robinwood Dr
4600 MNTR 44060 2038 E5
Robin Wood Ln
11400 AbnT 44021 2893 C2
11400 AbnT 44023 2893 C2
Robinwood Ln
7100 GSML 44040 2630 C2
Robinwood Ter
8200 MCDN 44056 3018 B6
Robley Ln
600 MAYF 44040 2500 B4
Robson Rd
11100 CrlT 44044 3006 D6
12400 CrlT 44044 3141 D1
35800 EatT 44044 3141 D1
Roc Ln
22800 OKWD 44146 2887 C7
Rochelle Av
14700 CLEV 44135 2752 C4
Rochelle Blvd
6600 PMHT 44130 2882 B5
Rochelle Dr
14000 MPHT 44137 2886 A3
Rochester Rd
2600 SRHT 44122 2628 D6
Rock Ct
1800 CVHT 44118 2627 B2
Rock & Roll Blvd
800 CLEV 44114 2624 E2
2000 CLEV 44115 2624 E3
2000 CLEV 44115 2625 A3
Rockcliff Dr
- LKWD 44107 2622 A7
18900 LKWD 44116 2621 E6
18900 LKWD 44126 2621 E7
18900 LKWD 44126 2622 A7
18900 RKRV 44116 2621 E6
18900 RKRV 44126 2621 E6
Rockcliffe Rd
- GDHT 44125 2885 B1
Rock Creek Cir
- NRDV 44039 2877 D7
22200 SGVL 44149 3011 A4
Rock Creek Dr
600 AURA 44202 3021 B6
Rock Creek Rd
13900 HmbT 44024 2381 B2
14300 HmbT 44024 2256 D7
14800 HmbT 44024 2257 A6
14800 MtlT 44024 2257 B5
14800 TpnT 44024 2257 B5
15500 TpnT 44086 2257 B5
Rock Creek Rd SR-166
13900 HmbT 44024 2381 B2
14300 HmbT 44024 2256 D7
14800 HmbT 44024 2257 A6
14800 MtlT 44024 2257 B5
14800 TpnT 44024 2257 B5
15500 TpnT 44086 2257 B5
Rock Creek Run
200 AMHT 44001 2744 A7
Rockdove Ln
7700 CcdT 44077 2254 C3
Rockefeller Av
2400 CLEV 44115 2625 B5

Rockefeller Ln
8400 SgHT 44067 3017 C4
Rockefeller Rd
1300 WKLF 44092 2374 D5
2700 WBHL 44092 2374 D5
2700 WBHL 44094 2374 D5
3000 HDHT 44092 2374 D7
3000 HDHT 44143 2374 D7
Rocker St
- BbgT 44022 2890 A1
- CNFL 44022 2890 A1
7000 BbgT 44023 2890 A1
Rockfern Av
300 ELYR 44035 2874 D5
14300 CLEV 44111 2752 D3
Rockford Dr
32800 SLN 44139 2888 E2
32800 SLN 44139 2889 A2
Rockhaven Dr
5700 SVHL 44131 2884 A2
Rockhaven Rd
12200 MsnT 44024 2503 B7
12200 MsnT 44026 2503 B7
12800 MsnT 44026 2633 C1
13100 NbyT 44026 2633 C3
13100 NbyT 44065 2633 C3
Rockingham Rd
7300 MNTR 44060 2252 C1
Rocking Horse Tr
10400 KTLD 44094 2377 C6
Rockland Av
1400 RKRV 44116 2621 E6
18200 CLEV 44135 2751 E5
18200 CLEV 44135 2752 A5
Rockland Dr
4300 BKLN 44144 2753 E4
4300 CLEV 44144 2753 E4
Rockledge Dr
300 BYVL 44140 2620 D4
6300 BKVL 44141 3016 A5
Rockledge Ln
400 BHIT 44212 3146 B7
24800 RDHT 44143 2498 D1
Rock Ledge Wy
10300 NRYN 44133 3148 B4
Rocklyn Rd
2600 BHWD 44122 2628 C5
2600 SRHT 44122 2628 C5
Rock Point Cir
5600 NRDV 44039 2877 E1
Rockport Av
3600 CLEV 44111 2752 C2
Rockport Ln
5800 FWPK 44126 2751 B6
6700 MNTR 44060 2145 A5
Rock Ridge Ct
6700 MDBH 44130 2881 B4
Rockridge Ct
8600 MCDN 44056 3018 B6
Rockside Pl
6000 INDE 44131 2884 D3
Rockside Rd
200 PRMA 44131 2883 E2
200 PRMA 44134 2883 E2
200 SVHL 44131 2883 E2
200 SVHL 44134 2884 A2
3700 INDE 44131 2884 A2
7300 INDE 44125 2885 B4
7300 INDE 44131 2885 A3
8000 VLVW 44125 2885 B4
10500 GDHT 44125 2885 E3
11500 MsnT 44024 2504 C3
13700 GDHT 44125 2886 A2
13800 GDHT 44137 2886 A2
13800 MPHT 44137 2886 C3
17500 BDFD 44146 2886 D2
17500 MPHT 44146 2886 D2
20000 BDFD 44137 2887 A1
20000 BDFD 44146 2887 A2
20000 MPHT 44137 2887 A1
22800 BDHT 44146 2887 A2
Rockside Woods Blvd
5800 INDE 44131 2884 D3
Rockspring Dr
8300 BbgT 44023 2891 A2
Rockway Av
1400 LKWD 44107 2622 B5
Rockwell Av
900 CLEV 44114 2624 E2
1200 CLEV 44114 2625 A2
Rockwell Ct
7400 MNTR 44060 2251 E1
Rockwood Ct
500 AVLK 44012 2618 B4
8700 MNTR 44060 2144 C4
Rockwood Dr
200 PNVL 44077 2040 B7
10500 KTLD 44094 2376 C6
Rockwood Ln
11900 CcdT 44077 2254 E3
Rockwood Rd
4600 CLEV 44105 2756 A5
4600 GDHT 44105 2756 A5
4600 GDHT 44125 2756 A6
Rocky Pointe
29200 WTLK 44145 2749 C2
Rocky Ridge Dr
- WTLK 44145 2749 A2
Rocky River Dr
3100 CLEV 44107 2622 B7
3100 CLEV 44111 2622 B7
3100 LKWD 44107 2622 B7
3100 LKWD 44111 2622 B7
3200 CLEV 44111 2752 B2
3900 CLEV 44135 2752 A5
4800 CLEV 44135 2751 E6
4900 BKPK 44135 2751 E6
4900 BKPK 44142 2751 E6
4900 CLEV 44142 2751 E6
Rocky River Dr SR-237
3100 CLEV 44107 2622 B7
3100 CLEV 44111 2622 B7
3100 LKWD 44107 2622 B7
3100 LKWD 44111 2622 B7
3200 CLEV 44111 2752 B2
3900 CLEV 44135 2752 A5
4800 CLEV 44135 2751 E6
4900 BKPK 44135 2751 E6
4900 BKPK 44142 2751 E6
4900 CLEV 44142 2751 E6
N Rocky River Dr
10 BERA 44017 2880 B6
800 BERA 44142 2880 C4
800 BKPK 44142 2880 C4

N Rocky River Dr SR-237
800 BERA 44017 2880 C4
800 BERA 44142 2880 C4
800 BKPK 44142 2880 C4
S Rocky River Dr
10 BERA 44017 2880 C7
10 BERA 44017 3011 C1
400 MDBH 44017 3011 C1
20000 MDBH 44130 3011 D1
Rocky River Ovl
2300 RKRV 44116 2621 E6
2300 RKRV 44116 2622 A6
Rocky Top Cir
1100 MCDN 44056 3154 B4
Rocky Top Ct
10 MPHT 44137 2886 A4
Rodgers Dr
30000 WKLF 44092 2374 D2
Rodman Ct
900 CLEV 44110 2497 A3
Roe Blvd
6800 MadT 44057 1843 C6
Roedean Dr
9000 PRMA 44129 2753 D7
Roehl Av
3300 CLEV 44109 2624 C7
Roeper Rd
7600 PRMA 44134 3014 A1
Roger Dr
23300 EUCL 44123 2373 C2
Rogers Av
6500 CLEV 44127 2625 E6
Rogers Rd
- WBHL 44094 2500 D1
6400 CcdT 44077 2147 A5
7400 GSML 44040 2500 D1
7400 GSML 44094 2500 D1
36600 WBHL 44094 2375 D7
38200 WBHL 44094 2376 A7
38500 KTLD 44094 2376 A7
Roig St
- EyrT 44035 2874 B1
Rokeby Rd
600 ETLK 44095 2249 E3
Roland Av
6100 CLEV 44127 2625 D7
Roland Dr
5300 GDHT 44125 2885 E1
5300 GDHT 44125 2886 A1
Roland Rd
800 LNHT 44124 2499 A6
Roll & Hold Pkwy
8100 MCDN 44056 3153 D2
Rollin Dr
9600 WTHL 44094 2376 C2
Rolling Av
5000 ShfT 44055 2745 C5
5300 EyrT 44035 2745 C6
5300 EyrT 44055 2745 C6
Rolling Acres Ct
6700 CcdT 44077 2145 D6
Rollingbrook Cir
9300 ODFL 44138 3009 D1
Rolling Brook Dr
18100 BbgT 44023 2891 A7
Rolling Brook Rd
8000 SgHT 44067 3017 D6
Rollingbrook Rd
18900 ClbT 44028 3144 C5
18900 ClbT 44280 3144 C5
18900 LvpT 44280 3144 C5
Rollingbrook Tr
7200 SLN 44139 3020 D2
Rolling Brooke Wy
500 NCtT 44067 3153 D5
Rolling Hills Dr
1700 TNBG 44087 3019 B5
3400 PRPK 44124 2759 D1
Rolling Meadow Ln
11800 NRYN 44133 3014 A6
Rolling Meadows Dr
1200 VMLN 44089 2741 B7
11200 HrmT 44234 3161 B4
11200 HrmT 44255 3161 B4
Rollingview Dr
4000 SVHL 44131 3015 B2
Rolliston Rd
3600 SRHT 44120 2757 C2
Roman Rd
- WTLK 44145 2620 E7
- WTLK 44145 2750 E1
Romane Dr
1200 SgHT 44067 3017 A5
Rome Cir
1200 BWHT 44147 3149 E4
Rome Beauty Dr
800 AMHT 44001 2872 B1
1000 AMHT 44001 2743 A7
Romeo Rd
5900 GnvT 44041 1943 E4
5900 GnvT 44041 1944 A4
Romford Rd
- HDHT 44143 2499 C5
Romilly Ovl
7100 PRMA 44129 2882 E6
Ronald Ct
4700 NRDV 44039 2877 B2
Ronald Dr
10700 PRMA 44130 3013 B1
30500 WLWK 44095 2249 D6
Ronan Rd
24200 BDHT 44146 2887 D3
Rondel Rd
800 CLEV 44110 2497 C2
Rook Cir
17600 CLEV 44112 2497 D3
Rookhill Cir
17700 CLEV 44112 2497 D3
Rookwood Cir
17700 CLEV 44112 2497 D3
Rookwood Rd
1900 CLEV 44112 2497 D3
Roosevelt Av
- AVON 44011 2748 D6
- NRDV 44011 2748 D6
- NRDV 44039 2748 D7
- NRDV 44039 2877 D1
100 ELYR 44035 2875 C5
1600 LKWD 44107 2622 D6
2000 ShfT 44055 2745 E6
6800 MNTR 44060 2144 D7
Roosevelt Ct
10 OBLN 44074 3138 D4
Roosevelt Dr
- ODFL 44138 2879 C6

Roosevelt Dr
10 GnvT 44041 1944 B2
10 PNVL 44077 2145 D2
400 GNVA 44041 1944 B2
9000 NHFD 44067 3018 A4
Roosevelt Rd
30800 WKLF 44092 2374 E1
30800 WKLF 44092 2375 A1
Roosting Ln
- NRDV 44039 2876 D2
Root Rd
200 LORN 44052 2615 D7
3800 NOSD 44070 2750 C5
6800 NRDV 44039 2877 B5
8900 NRDV 44039 3008 D1
9400 EatT 44028 3008 D1
9400 EatT 44039 3008 D1
10000 ClbT 44028 3008 E3
10600 ClbT 44028 3009 C6
18400 BbgT 44023 2890 A7
18400 BbgT 44023 3021 A1
Roryanna Dr
9300 CdnT 44024 2379 C2
Rosalee Av
900 ELYR 44035 2875 D3
Rosalie Av
1000 LKWD 44107 2622 C3
Rosalie Dr
13800 GDHT 44125 2757 A7
Rosalind Av
1800 ECLE 44112 2496 E7
1800 ECLE 44112 2497 A7
9200 CLEV 44106 2626 B1
Rosa Parks Dr
1300 CLEV 44106 2496 D7
1300 CLEV 44108 2496 D7
Rosbough Dr
17500 MDBH 44130 2881 A6
Rose Av
- VmnT 44089 2740 C5
Rose Blvd
800 HDHT 44143 2499 C5
900 MDHT 44124 2499 C5
900 MDHT 44143 2499 C6
Rose Ct
10 GnvT 44041 1944 E3
3000 CLEV 44115 2625 C3
Rose Dr
400 BERA 44017 3011 A1
4000 BNWK 44212 3146 D7
Rose Ln
- AhtT 44001 2872 B2
- AMHT 44001 2872 B2
10 LKWD 44107 2622 D4
Rose Rd
25600 NOSD 44070 2750 C4
25600 WTLK 44070 2750 C4
25600 WTLK 44145 2750 B4
Rose St
33300 NRDV 44039 2877 D1
Rosebelle Av
5800 NRDV 44039 2877 A2
Rosebud Dr
8600 MNTR 44060 2252 C1
Rosebury Ct
100 MDHT 44124 2630 A1
Rosecliff Dr
5300 LORN 44053 2743 C6
Rosecliff Rd
17800 CLEV 44119 2372 E4
18000 EUCL 44119 2372 E4
Rosecrest Dr
1600 LORN 44053 2744 C5
Rosedale Av
1700 ECLE 44112 2497 B4
6500 AhtT 44001 2873 C1
6600 AhtT 44035 2873 C1
6700 PMHT 44130 2882 B6
Rosedale Dr
7200 CcdT 44060 2145 B7
7200 CcdT 44060 2253 B1
Rosedale Rd
3300 CVHT 44112 2497 D6
Rosehill Av
- AVLK 44012 2617 B3
9800 CLEV 44104 2626 C5
Rose Hill Ln
27500 BYVL 44140 2619 E4
Roseland Av
19200 EUCL 44117 2497 E1
19600 EUCL 44117 2498 A1
20500 EUCL 44117 2373 A7
Roseland Dr
1300 MCDN 44056 3019 A6
1500 TNBG 44087 3019 B6
Roseland Rd
17800 CLEV 44112 2497 D2
Roseland Wy
1500 WTLK 44145 2620 C7
Roselawn Av
38200 WLBY 44094 2250 E7
Roselawn Dr
7500 MNTR 44060 2252 E2
16200 BtnT 44021 2765 B7
Roselawn Rd
1100 LNHT 44124 2498 D6
1500 MDHT 44124 2499 D7
1500 MDHT 44124 2629 D1
3600 WDMR 44122 2759 B2
Rosemarie Ct
10900 CcdT 44077 2146 B6
Rosemary Av
15000 CLEV 44111 2752 C1
Rosemary Ln
9100 MNTR 44060 2038 E5
Rosemere St
- ELYR 44035 3006 C2
9900 CrlT 44035 3006 C2
Rosemond Rd
3900 CVHT 44121 2498 A6
Rosemont Ct
4300 LORN 44053 2743 D4
Rosemont Dr
6800 BKVL 44141 3150 E1
6800 BKVL 44141 3151 A1
Rosemont Rd
1800 ECLE 44112 2497 B6
Rosena Av
1400 MadT 44057 1843 B7
Roseside Dr
5200 CLEV 44109 2754 B7
5200 PRMA 44109 2754 B7
5200 PRMA 44134 2754 B7
Rosetta Dr
12700 MsnT 44026 2503 B7

Rosetta Dr
12700 MsnT 44026 2633 B1
Roseville Ct
4400 CLEV 44127 2625 C6
Rosewood Av
- AVLK 44012 2617 E1
10 NHFD 44067 3018 A4
100 NHFD 44067 3017 E4
1400 LKWD 44107 2622 C5
7500 GDHT 44105 2756 A5
9500 CLEV 44105 2756 B5
9700 CLEV 44125 2756 C5
32900 AVLK 44012 2618 A1
Rosewood Blvd
1500 AVON 44011 2617 D6
Rosewood Cir
6800 INDE 44131 2884 E6
Rosewood Ct
- AhtT 44001 2872 E6
4500 CLEV 44105 2756 C5
5300 SFLD 44054 2746 E1
6700 MDBH 44130 2881 A4
Rosewood Dr
10 AVLK 44012 2617 D1
10 LmC 44012 2617 D1
800 ELYR 44035 2875 E1
4800 SDLK 44054 2616 D4
9800 CdnT 44024 2380 A3
9900 CdnT 44024 2379 E4
Rosewood Ln
8500 MNTR 44060 2144 B4
13000 SGVL 44136 3012 D3
Rosewood Ovl
3100 NRYN 44133 3014 C5
Rosewood Pl
- ELYR 44035 2875 E1
Rosewood St
41300 EyrT 44035 2745 D6
Rosewood Tr
33500 WBHL 44094 2375 A6
Rosita Ln
24100 NOSD 44070 2750 D4
Roslyn Dr
19600 RKRV 44116 2621 D4
Ross Av
2700 NBGH 44105 2755 B3
14400 CLEV 44128 2757 B3
Ross Cir
26700 NOSD 44070 2750 A6
Ross Rd
6900 MadT 44057 2044 D7
Rosslyn Rd
11800 PMHT 44130 2882 A4
12800 PMHT 44130 2881 E4
12900 BKPK 44130 2881 E4
12900 BKPK 44142 2881 E4
Rossmoor Rd
2000 CVHT 44118 2627 D3
Rotary Dr
7100 WNHL 44146 2886 E7
Rothwood Av
- NCtT 44067 3153 A2
N Roundhead Dr
31700 SLN 44139 3019 E1
S Roundhead Dr
31700 SLN 44139 3019 E2
Roundhead Pl
32900 SLN 44139 3019 E1
Roundwood Rd
3000 HGVL 44022 2630 B7
3300 HGVL 44022 2760 B2
3400 MDHL 44022 2760 B2
Rouse Av
7300 CLEV 44104 2625 E6
7300 CLEV 44104 2626 A6
Rousseau Dr
5600 PRMA 44129 2883 A7
6600 PRMA 44129 2882 E7
Rowan Dr
200 BERA 44017 2880 A5
Rowelyn Av
600 SDLK 44054 2616 B4
Rowena Av
15100 MPHT 44137 2886 B4
15700 BDFD 44137 2886 B4
15700 BDFD 44146 2886 B4
Rowland Rd
100 VMLN 44089 2741 C4
Rowley Av
1100 CLEV 44109 2624 E7
Roxanne Ln
5100 BHIT 44212 3145 E6
5100 BHIT 44212 3146 A6
Roxboro Av
14400 CLEV 44111 2622 D7
Roxboro Dr
15400 MDBH 44130 2881 B4
Roxboro Rd
200 VMLN 44089 2741 D4
2300 CVHT 44106 2627 A4
2400 CVHT 44106 2626 E4
Roxburghe Dr
4300 BKVL 44141 3150 D3
Roxbury Ct
10 BHWD 44122 2628 E5
Roxbury Rd
1800 ECLE 44112 2496 E7
1800 ECLE 44112 2626 E1
2300 AVON 44011 2748 B1
9100 PMHT 44130 2882 C3
Roxbury Park Dr
31100 BYVL 44140 2619 A2
Roxford Rd
1800 ECLE 44112 2497 B6
Roy Av
7000 CLEV 44104 2625 E6
21900 BDHT 44146 2887 B1
Roy Dr
1000 LKWD 44107 2622 D3
Roy Rd
5400 HDHT 44143 2499 B4
Royal Blvd
13600 GDHT 44125 2756 E7
13600 GDHT 44125 2757 A7
13600 GDHT 44125 2885 E1
13600 GDHT 44125 2886 A1
Royal Ct
5700 WLBY 44094 2375 A2
Royal Dr
1000 AMHT 44001 2872 E4
Royal Pkwy
5800 PMHT 44130 2882 B2
5800 PRMA 44130 2882 C2
Royal Rd
800 CLEV 44110 2497 C2

Royal St
5300 MPHT 44137 2886 B1
Royale Oak Ct
8600 MNTR 44060 2252 C2
Royal Forest Dr
27600 WTLK 44145 2749 E1
27600 WTLK 44145 2750 A1
Royal Haven Dr
8300 NRYN 44133 3013 D3
Royal Oak Blvd
300 RDHT 44143 2498 D1
Royal Oak Ct
3100 WTLK 44145 2749 B3
Royal Oak Dr
10 AURA 44202 3022 A7
1000 SRSL 44022 2762 A6
1800 PnvT 44077 2041 A3
10400 SGVL 44136 3012 B4
15400 MDFD 44062 2767 B3
Royal Oaks Cir
1700 HDSN 44236 3154 E6
Royal Portrush Dr
7200 SLN 44139 3020 E3
Royal Ridge Dr
7600 PRMA 44129 2882 D6
Royal Ridge Ln
14900 NRYN 44133 3148 E1
Royal St. George Dr
4300 AVON 44011 2748 C6
Royalton Rd
- CrlT 44044 3006 E6
3000 BWHT 44147 3014 C7
3000 NRYN 44133 3014 A7
3000 NRYN 44147 3014 C7
6200 NRYN 44133 3013 C7
11700 NRYN 44133 3012 E7
12700 SGVL 44133 3012 E7
12700 SGVL 44136 3012 C7
17800 SGVL 44136 3011 E7
18600 SGVL 44149 3011 C7
22300 ClbT 44028 3010 D7
22300 ClbT 44149 3010 E7
22300 SGVL 44149 3010 E7
25100 ClbT 44028 3009 D7
27400 ClbT 44028 3008 E7
27400 EatT 44028 3008 E7
34500 EatT 44044 3008 C7
35700 EatT 44044 3007 C7
38100 EatT 44044 3006 E6
Royalton Rd SR-82
- CrlT 44044 3006 E6
3000 BWHT 44147 3014 C7
3000 NRYN 44133 3014 A7
3000 NRYN 44147 3014 C7
6200 NRYN 44133 3013 C7
11700 NRYN 44133 3012 E7
12700 SGVL 44133 3012 E7
12700 SGVL 44136 3012 C7
17800 SGVL 44136 3011 E7
18600 SGVL 44149 3011 C7
22300 ClbT 44028 3010 D7
22300 ClbT 44149 3010 E7
22300 SGVL 44149 3010 E7
25100 ClbT 44028 3009 D7
27400 ClbT 44028 3008 E7
27400 EatT 44028 3008 E7
34500 EatT 44044 3008 C7
35700 EatT 44044 3007 C7
38100 EatT 44044 3006 E6
E Royalton Rd
- BKVL 44141 3015 E7
- BWHT 44141 3015 E7
100 BWHT 44147 3014 E7
2400 BKVL 44147 3015 B7
4800 BWHT 44147 3015 D7
6900 BKVL 44141 3016 A7
E Royalton Rd SR-82
- BWHT 44141 3015 E7
100 BWHT 44147 3014 E7
100 BWHT 44147 3015 A7
2400 BKVL 44141 3015 B7
2400 BKVL 44147 3015 B7
6900 BKVL 44141 3016 A7
W Royalton Rd
1000 BWHT 44147 3014 D7
2900 NRYN 44133 3014 C7
2900 NRYN 44147 3014 C7
W Royalton Rd SR-82
1000 BWHT 44147 3014 D7
2900 NRYN 44133 3014 C7
2900 NRYN 44147 3014 C7
Royal Valley Dr
9200 NRYN 44133 3014 B4
Royalview Dr
7300 PRMA 44129 2882 D7
8300 PRMA 44130 2882 D7
30100 WLWK 44095 2249 C6
Royalview Ln
- SGVL 44136 3147 C1
Royalwood Rd
1100 BWHT 44147 3014 B6
2700 NRYN 44133 3014 C6
2700 NRYN 44147 3014 C6
5700 NRYN 44133 3013 E6
Royal Woods Pl
30500 WTLK 44145 2749 B3
Roycroft Av
1400 LKWD 44107 2622 B5
Roycroft Dr
6500 PRMA 44129 2882 E4
Rozelle Av
1100 ECLE 44112 2496 E6
Ruble Ct
5000 CLEV 44104 2625 D4
Ruby Av
3000 CLEV 44109 2754 C5
Ruby Ln
4600 BHIT 44212 3146 B7
Rubyvale Rd
2400 UNHT 44118 2628 C4
Rudolph Av
9400 GDHT 44125 2885 B1
Rudwick Rd
1800 CLEV 44112 2497 D3
Rudy Dr
20600 SGVL 44149 3011 B5
Rudyard Rd
700 CLEV 44110 2497 C2
Rue Saint-Ann Ct
26700 WVHT 44122 2759 A5
Rue Saint-Gabriel Ct
4400 WVHT 44022 2759 A5
Rue St Georges
1200 WTLK 44145 2620 D6

Cleveland Street Index

STREET	Block	City	ZIP	Map#	Grid
Rugby Ct	24000	BDHT	44146	2887	D4
Rugby Rd	-	LNHT	44124	2629	C2
	-	MDHT	44124	2629	C2
	13400	CLEV	44110	2497	A3
Rugby St	1800	TwbT	44087	3154	C2
Ruggiero Cir	-	MDBH	44130	3012	C2
Ruhr Dr	-	PRMA	44130	3013	C2
Rumson Rd	3100	CVHT	44118	2497	C7
	3400	CVHT	44121	2497	C7
Runn St	200	BERA	44017	2880	B6
Running Brook Dr	9000	PRMA	44130	3013	C1
Runny Meade Tr	-	RslT	44022	2761	C2
Runnymede Av	10200	GDHT	44125	2756	C6
Runnymede Blvd	3500	CVHT	44121	2497	E4
	3600	SELD	44121	2497	E4
Ruple Pkwy	-	BKPK	44142	2880	A3
	-	CLEV	44142	2880	A3
	5800	BKPK	44142	2879	E3
Ruple Rd	800	CLEV	44110	2497	C2
	4100	SELD	44121	2498	B5
Rural Rd	600	ETLK	44095	2250	D2
Rush Rd	1500	WKLF	44092	2374	E2
	1500	WLWK	44092	2374	E1
Rush St	200	ELYR	44035	2874	E5
Rushleigh Rd	900	CVHT	44121	2497	E6
Rushmore Ct	25000	RDHT	44143	2498	C3
Rushmore Dr	400	RDHT	44143	2498	C2
Rushmore Wy	7000	CcdT	44077	2146	B7
Rushton Dr	8100	MNTR	44060	2144	A1
	8100	MONT	44060	2144	A1
Rushton Rd	1600	SELD	44121	2628	C1
	4400	SELD	44121	2498	C7
Rushwood Ln	7900	SgHT	44067	3017	C6
Rusnak Tr	1300	BWHT	44147	3015	A4
Russell Av	2000	PRMA	44134	2754	C7
	3900	LORN	44055	2745	B4
	3900	ShfT	44055	2745	B4
	10000	GDHT	44125	2756	C6
	24000	EUCL	44123	2373	D3
	24700	EUCL	44132	2373	D3
Russell Ct	7000	CLEV	44103	2625	E1
Russell Dr	34000	SLN	44139	3020	A2
Russell Ln	-	BKVL	44141	3016	D2
	-	INDE	44131	3016	D2
	-	INDE	44141	3016	D2
	8000	CLEV	44144	2753	E2
	14500	RslT	44072	2631	E7
	14500	RslT	44072	2632	A7
	14500	RslT	44072	2762	A1
Russell Rd	1300	CLEV	44103	2495	E7
	1300	CLEV	44103	2625	E1
	15000	RslT	44022	2761	B3
	15000	RslT	44072	2761	B3
	15500	CNFL	44022	2761	B4
	26500	BYVL	44140	2620	A4
Russell St	4100	LORN	44055	2745	B4
	4100	ShfT	44055	2745	B4
Russellhurst Dr	7800	KTLD	44094	2376	D1
Russet Dr	3400	BWHT	44147	3015	C5
Russett Woods Ct	606-00	AURA	44202	3156	C3
Russett Woods Ln	500-00	AURA	44202	3156	C3
Russia Rd	5800	NRsT	44001	3003	D3
	5800	NRsT	44074	3003	D3
	5800	SAHT	44001	3003	D3
	5800	SAHT	44074	3003	D3
	41200	CrlT	44035	3005	A3
	42600	CrlT	44035	3004	E3
	42600	CrlT	44074	3004	E3
	42600	CrlT	44074	3005	A3
	42600	NRsT	44035	3004	A3
	42600	NRsT	44074	3004	A3
	44600	NRsT	44001	3004	B3
Rust Dr	11400	CsTp	44026	2502	B2
Rustic Dr	3000	NRYN	44133	3014	C7
Rustic Hllw	18000	SGVL	44136	3146	E4
Rustic Ln	8200	HmbT	44024	2256	B5
	8200	LryT	44024	2256	C4
	25600	WTLK	44145	2750	B3
Rustic Ovl	7000	SVHL	44131	2884	B7
Rustic Rd	-	CLEV	44135	2752	A3
Rustic Tr	900	PRMA	44131	2883	E5
	900	PRMA	44134	2883	E5
	900	SVHL	44131	2883	E5
Rustic Hill Ln	200	AhtT	44001	2873	C1
Rutgers Ct	300	ELYR	44035	3006	C2
	1000	PnvT	44077	2146	E1
Ruth Dr	6100	SVHL	44131	2884	B4
	13400	SGVL	44136	3012	D6
Ruth St	10	GNVA	44041	1944	B5
	200	BYVL	44140	2619	C3
	7500	MNTR	44060	2252	B2
Ruth Ellen Dr	100	RDHT	44143	2374	A5
Rutherford Rd	1000	CVHT	44112	2497	C6
	1000	CVHT	44118	2497	C6
Rutland Av	11400	CLEV	44108	2496	D3
Rutland Dr	500	HDHT	44143	2499	C3
	7700	MNTR	44060	2143	D5
Rutledge Av	7400	CLEV	44102	2623	E5
Ryan Ct	-	CrlT	44035	3006	B3
Ryan Dr	9600	MNTR	44060	2039	B7
	9600	PnvT	44060	2039	B7
	9600	PnvT	44077	2039	B7
	16200	WNHL	44146	2886	A5
Rybak Av	13600	GDHT	44125	2885	E3
	13600	GDHT	44125	2886	A3
Rybarcyk Ln	7600	EyrT	44035	2874	B3
Rydalmount Rd	1400	CVHT	44118	2497	D7
	1400	CVHT	44118	2627	D1
Rydalwood Ln	10	HGVL	44022	2760	B2
	10	MDHL	44022	2760	B2
Ryder Rd	11200	HRM	44234	3160	E3
	11200	HrmT	44234	3160	E3
	11200	HrmT	44255	3160	E3
Rye Rd	21800	SRHT	44122	2628	B6
Ryeberry Ln	600	AVLK	44012	2618	A5
Rye Gate Dr	19300	NRYN	44133	3148	A4
Rye Gate St	300	BYVL	44140	2619	C4
Ryeland Dr	4100	BWHT	44147	3015	C5
S River Run	-	CcdT	44077	2253	E1
S					
Sable Ct	5200	MNTR	44060	2039	B7
Sable Rd	800	CLEV	44119	2372	D5
Sablewood Dr	10100	AbnT	44023	3023	B3
Sabol Ct	37500	EatT	44044	3007	B5
Sackett Av	2700	CLEV	44109	2754	C1
	4400	CLEV	44102	2754	B1
Sacramento Av	13800	CLEV	44111	2752	E2
Saddle Cr	2800	AVON	44011	2748	B2
Saddle Ln	5500	SLN	44139	2888	B2
	7500	MNTR	44060	2251	C4
Saddleback Ln	7400	GSML	44040	2500	D1
Saddle Brook Ln	1500	WTLK	44145	2619	D7
Saddle Horn Cir	12400	SGVL	44149	3011	A6
Saddlehorn Cir	24900	ClbT	44028	3010	C4
Saddler Rd	200	BYVL	44140	2619	C3
Saddlewood Dr	4800	SDLK	44054	2616	C3
Saddlewood Ln	11300	CcdT	44077	2254	C2
Safeguard Plz	600	BNHT	44131	2884	B1
Safford St	10	MDSN	44057	2044	C1
Sagamore Av	7500	CLEV	44103	2626	A2
Sagamore Dr	1600	EUCL	44117	2497	E2
	1600	EUCL	44117	2498	A2
Sagamore Rd	-	SgHT	44067	3016	E3
	-	SgHT	44125	3016	E3
	-	VLVW	44125	3016	E3
	-	VLVW	44125	3017	D3
	10	NHFD	44067	3018	A3
	10	NHFD	44146	3018	A3
	10	WNHL	44146	3018	A3
	200	SgHT	44067	3017	E3
	200	SgHT	44067	3018	A3
	200	SgHT	44146	3017	E3
	200	SgHT	44146	3018	A3
	200	WNHL	44146	3017	D3
	1100	PRMA	44134	2883	E7
N Sagamore Rd	19200	FWPK	44126	2751	E1
S Sagamore Rd	19100	FWPK	44126	2751	E2
Sagamore Hills Blvd	7600	SgHT	44067	3017	D7
	7600	SgHT	44067	3152	D1
Sagewood Ln	700	AbnT	44023	2892	B3
Sagramore Dr N	1000	STBR	44241	3156	E7
	1000	STBR	44241	3157	A7
Sailor Cir	12600	NRYN	44133	3147	E4
Sailors Cove	31700	AVLK	44012	2619	A3
Sailorway Dr	5300	VMLN	44089	2741	A7
	5400	VMLN	44089	2740	E7
	5500	VmnT	44089	2740	E7
St. Albans Rd	3400	CVHT	44121	2497	D6
St. Andrews	100	ELYR	44035	3006	D3
	31300	WTLK	44145	2749	A6
St. Andrews Dr	300	HDHT	44143	2499	D2
	3200	PRMA	44134	3014	C2
E St. Andrews Dr	300	HDHT	44143	2499	D1
W St. Andrews Dr	300	HDHT	44143	2499	D1
St. Andrews Ln	100	AURA	44202	3021	E6
	400	BWHT	44147	3149	C4
St. Andrews Wy	11300	CcdT	44077	2146	C7
St. Anne's Ct	-	AVON	44011	2748	D5
St. Anthony Ln	16300	CLEV	44111	2752	B1
St. Catherine Av	9300	CLEV	44104	2756	B1
St. Charles Av	1100	LKWD	44107	2622	D5
St. Charles Pl	5400	MNTR	44060	2144	E1
St. Clair Av	-	CLEV	44110	2496	E4
	-	CLEV	44112	2496	E4
	-	ECLE	44110	2496	E4
	-	ECLE	44112	2496	E4
	4000	CLEV	44103	2495	C7
	4000	CLEV	44114	2495	C7
	4000	WLBY	44094	2250	C5
	7300	CLEV	44103	2496	B5
	7500	MNTR	44060	2251	D2
	8400	CLEV	44108	2496	D4
	13200	CLEV	44110	2497	D1
	17600	CLEV	44110	2372	D7
	18900	CLEV	44117	2372	E7
	19400	CLEV	44117	2373	A6
	22100	EUCL	44117	2373	C5
	22200	EUCL	44132	2373	C5
St. Clair Av NE	100	CLEV	44114	2624	E2
	1300	CLEV	44114	2625	A2
	3900	CLEV	44103	2625	C1
W St. Clair Av	10	CLEV	44113	2624	D3
	10	CLEV	44114	2624	E3
St. Clair St	-	WLBY	44094	2250	D4
	100	ELYR	44035	2875	B5
N St. Clair St	10	PNVL	44077	2040	B7
	900	PNVL	44077	2039	E5
	1100	FTHR	44077	2039	E5
S St. Clair St	10	PNVL	44077	2040	B7
	10	PNVL	44077	2146	B1
St. Francis Ct	4200	AVON	44011	2748	D5
St. Francis Dr	6000	SVHL	44131	2884	A3
	33600	AVON	44011	2748	C5
St. Germain Blvd	4400	WVHT	44022	2759	A5
St. Ives	30100	WTLK	44145	2749	B3
St. James Av	14000	CLEV	44135	2752	D4
St. James Blvd	5100	LORN	44053	2744	B5
St. James Ct	26800	ODFL	44138	3009	E1
St. James Dr	7600	MNTR	44060	2143	D5
	12700	ManT	44255	3023	C5
W St. James Pkwy	2400	CVHT	44106	2626	E4
St. James Pl	17900	AbnT	44023	2892	E6
	17900	AbnT	44023	2893	A6
	17900	AbnT	44255	2892	E6
St. James St	2100	MadT	44057	1942	C2
	13000	CLEV	44135	2752	E4
	13000	CLEV	44135	2753	B4
N St. James St	2100	CVHT	44106	2627	A3
W St. James St	2500	CVHT	44106	2627	A4
St. John Av	11800	CLEV	44111	2753	A3
St. John Ct	7400	MNTR	44060	2143	C6
St. John Dr	1500	MadT	44057	1843	A7
St. John's Wy	-	WLBY	44094	2251	A6
St. Joseph Blvd	11000	ManT	44255	3159	C4
St. Joseph Dr	100	AMHT	44001	2743	E7
	100	AMHT	44001	2872	E1
	6000	SVHL	44131	2884	A3
St. Lawrence Blvd	10	ETLK	44095	2142	D7
	500	ETLK	44094	2142	D7
	500	WLBY	44094	2142	D7
	500	WLBY	44095	2142	D7
St. Lawrence Cir	300	SgHT	44067	3017	E4
St. Mark Av	10500	CLEV	44111	2753	B1
St. Maron Blvd	34400	AVON	44011	2748	B6
St. Maron Dr	-	SVHL	44131	2884	A4
St. Michaels Wy	1000	MadT	44057	1941	C2
St. Olga Av	2500	CLEV	44113	2625	A6
St. Peters Wy	5300	MNTR	44060	2038	E7
	5300	MNTR	44060	2144	E1
	5400	MNTR	44060	2145	A1
St. Petersburg Dr	3700	PRMA	44134	3014	B2
St. Roccos Ct	3300	CLEV	44109	2624	C7
St. Sharbel Ct	33600	AVON	44011	2748	C5
St. Thomas Ln	5500	MadT	44057	1941	C2
St. Tikhon Av	2500	CLEV	44113	2625	A6
Salberry St	8500	BWHT	44147	3015	B5
Salem Av	800	ELYR	44035	2875	E2
	6900	CLEV	44127	2755	E1
Salem Cir	7700	HDSN	44236	3155	B6
Salem Ct	10	AVLK	44012	2619	A2
	10	BHWD	44122	2629	A4
	10	HkyT	44133	3148	B5
	10	HkyT	44233	3148	B6
	10	NRYN	44133	3148	B5
Salem Dr	-	VMLN	44089	2741	A4
	7600	HDSN	44236	3155	B7
	30300	BYVL	44140	2619	B3
Salem Ln	500	BNWK	44212	3147	D7
Salem Pkwy	1700	WTLK	44145	2750	B1
Salem Rd	1900	PnvT	44077	2041	A4
N Salem Row	18200	SGVL	44136	3146	E4
S Salem Row	18400	SGVL	44136	3146	E4
Salida Rd	7300	MONT	44060	2143	C2
Salient Pl	300	ETLK	44095	2142	C7
Salisbury Dr	7800	PRMA	44129	2882	D4
Salisbury Rd	3700	CVHT	44121	2497	E5
	3700	SELD	44121	2497	E5
	3800	SELD	44121	2498	A5
	20800	WVHT	44146	2758	A6
Sally Av	-	CLEV	44135	2751	E6
	-	CLEV	44135	2752	A6
Salt Lick Ct	5100	MNTR	44060	2039	A7
Samara Ct	13100	HmbT	44024	2380	D2
Samuel Dr	12700	ManT	44255	3023	C5
	23600	EUCL	44143	2498	C1
Samuel St	10	MDSN	44057	2044	B1
	100	ELYR	44035	2874	D3
	200	EyrT	44035	2874	D3
Samuel Lord Dr	7300	BbgT	44023	2761	B7
Sanctuary Cir	7500	BKVL	44141	3150	D3
Sanctuary Dr	-	AbnT	44023	3023	E3
	-	AbnT	44255	3023	E3
	8800	KDHL	44060	2252	B5
Sanctuary Ln	27000	OmsT	44138	2878	D5
Sand Ct	5500	PRMA	44134	2883	E1
Sandalhaven Dr	15100	MDBH	44130	2881	B5
Sandalwood Ct	2300	TNBG	44087	3019	E3
Sandalwood Dr	400	BYVL	44140	2621	A5
	700	ELYR	44035	2875	E1
	700	MAYF	44040	2500	A5
	1700	AVON	44011	2617	D7
	2200	TNBG	44087	3019	E3
	2300	TNBG	44087	3020	A4
	6600	MAYF	44143	2500	A5
Sandalwood Ln	700	AbnT	44023	2892	B3
	10200	TNBG	44087	3020	A4
	20100	SGVL	44149	3146	C3
Sandalwood Rd	22000	BDHT	44146	2887	B1
Sandbridge Ct	7000	MNTR	44060	2145	A7
Sand Creek Cir	10900	SGVL	44149	3011	A5
Sand Dune Ct	-	MNTR	44060	2144	C1
Sandelwood Av	5900	NRDV	44039	2877	A1
Sanders Av	500	PNVL	44077	2040	A6
Sanders Ln	27700	NOSD	44070	2749	E5
Sandfield Dr	6300	BKPK	44142	2881	B4
Sandfordshire Ln	-	AVON	44011	2747	E5
Sandgate Dr	12000	CsTp	44026	2502	E4
Sandgate Rd	1700	MadT	44057	1941	D1
	11800	CsTp	44026	2502	E4
Sandhurst Dr	300	HDHT	44143	2499	C2
	6300	BKPK	44142	2881	A3
Sandhurst Rd	25000	BDHT	44146	2887	D4
San Diego Av	13400	CLEV	44111	2752	D2
Sandpiper Av	300	ELYR	44035	3006	E3
	500	CrlT	44035	3006	E3
Sandpiper Ct	7000	CcdT	44077	2145	D7
	33100	NRDV	44039	2877	D7
Sandpiper Dr	5500	PRMA	44134	2883	E1
Sandpiper Ln	5900	NOSD	44070	2879	B2
Sandra Dr	500	BNWK	44212	3146	D7
Sandridge Dr	500	AMHT	44001	2872	C1
Sandridge Ln	10	WLBY	44094	2375	A2
Sands Av	10	AMHT	44001	2744	B7
Sands Blvd	10	MadT	44057	1941	A5
Sandstone Blvd	100	AMHT	44001	2744	B6
	100	AMHT	44053	2744	B6
	100	LORN	44053	2744	B6
Sandstone Ct	-	CLEV	44105	2756	C4
Sandstone Dr	100	PnvT	44077	2041	A7
	8000	SgHT	44067	3017	B5
Sandstone Ln	32800	NRDV	44039	2877	E1
Sandstone Tr	10100	ClbT	44028	3009	D2
Sandstone Ridge Wy	-	BERA	44138	2879	D4
	-	OmsT	44138	2879	D4
Sandtrap Cir	300	PnvT	44077	2040	E4
Sandtree Ln	7100	MNTR	44060	2144	E7
Sandusky Av	9300	CLEV	44105	2756	C2
Sandusky St	600	VMLN	44089	2740	E5
Sandy Ln	3300	AVON	44011	2748	C4
	22000	FWPK	44126	2751	A5
N Sandy Ln	3200	AVON	44011	2748	D3
Sandy Hill Dr	26600	EUCL	44143	2373	E6
	26600	RDHT	44143	2373	E6
	26600	RDHT	44143	2374	A5
Sandy Hill Rd	10	SgHT	44067	3017	E6
Sandy Hook Dr	4800	PRMA	44134	3014	A1
	6600	PRMA	44134	3013	E1
Sandy Knoll Dr	35900	ETLK	44095	2250	B3
Sandy Oaks Tr	9000	CdnT	44024	2254	D7
Sandy Ridge Dr	-	NRDV	44039	2876	C2
Sandy Springs Dr	16900	NRYN	44133	3149	B4
Sandy Wy Dr	10	CrlT	44035	3006	C2
San Fernando Cir	4300	INDE	44131	3015	C1
Sanford Av	16200	CLEV	44110	2497	C2
Sanford Dr	3700	PRMA	44134	3014	B2
Sanford St	10	PNVL	44077	2039	E6
	10	PnvT	44077	2039	E6
	100	PNVL	44077	2040	A6
	900	VMLN	44089	2741	A7
San Remo Ct	8100	MCDN	44056	3154	A3
Sansdan Ct	1700	PnvT	44077	2041	A3
Santa Clara Dr	27200	WTLK	44145	2620	A6
Santa Fe Ct	100	ELYR	44035	3006	D2
	1000	GFTN	44044	3142	B5
Santa Fe Tr	-	ClrT	44024	2505	C6
Santin Cir	10	BDFD	44146	2886	C5
Santina Wy	4100	LORN	44053	2743	D4
Sapphire Ct	9000	PRMA	44130	3013	C1
Sarah Ct	9100	MNTR	44060	2038	E7
Sarah Lee Dr	7500	CcdT	44077	2254	E2
Saranac Dr	19800	FWPK	44126	2751	D2
	19800	RKRV	44116	2751	D2
	19800	RKRV	44126	2751	D2
Saranac Rd	17000	CLEV	44110	2497	D1
Sarasota Dr	3800	PRMA	44134	3014	B1
N Sarasota Dr	7400	PRMA	44134	3014	C1
Saratoga Av	1700	CLEV	44109	2754	D5
Saratoga Ct	10	BHWD	44122	2628	E2
Saratoga Dr	20700	FWPK	44126	2751	C4
Saratoga Rd	7400	MDBH	44130	3012	C1
Saratoga Tr	17700	SGVL	44136	3147	A5
	19400	BNWK	44136	3147	A5
	19400	BNWK	44212	3147	A5
Sassafras Cir	8900	NRYN	44133	3013	B3
Sassafras Dr	100	VmnT	44089	2869	D1
	4600	PRMA	44129	2883	B7
	4600	PRMA	44134	2883	B7
	15000	SGVL	44136	3012	C3
Sassafras Ln	30900	WTLK	44145	2749	A6
Saturn Dr	12300	NRYN	44133	3014	C6
Sauer Av	8600	CLEV	44102	2623	D6
Savage Rd	16600	BbgT	44023	2761	D7
	16600	BbgT	44023	2890	D2
Savage St	300	BERA	44017	2880	A5
Savannah Av	13800	ECLE	44112	2497	A5
Savannah Ct	14300	SGVL	44136	3147	C4
Savannah Dr	6400	MNTR	44060	2143	C4
	6800	NRDV	44039	2876	E3
Savannah Pkwy	1800	WTLK	44145	2619	A7
	1800	WTLK	44145	2749	B1
Savannah Tr	-	AVON	44011	2748	D5
Savoy Dr	3800	FWPK	44126	2752	A1
Sawgrass Cir	-	AVLK	44012	2618	A4
	17300	NRYN	44133	3149	A3
Saw Grass Ct	-	MNTR	44060	2144	C1
Sawgrass Ln	15100	MDFD	44062	2767	B3
Sawmill Bnd	100	CRDN	44024	2505	B2
	23600	ODFL	44138	3010	D1
Saw Mill Cir	4000	NOSD	44070	2750	D5
Sawmill Ct	7100	CcdT	44077	2145	D7
Saw Mill Dr	-	NRDV	44035	3007	B1
Sawmill Dr	700	AVLK	44012	2618	D5
	10000	HmbT	44024	2380	E5
	10000	HmbT	44024	2381	A4
Saw Mill Trc	-	NRDV	44035	3007	B1
Sawtell Rd	3000	CLEV	44127	2625	D6
Saxe Av	9100	CLEV	44105	2756	B2
Saxon Dr	5500	GDHT	44125	2885	C1
	8800	KTLD	44094	2251	D6
Saxton St	10	MDSN	44057	2044	B2
Saybrook Av	13100	GDHT	44105	2756	E5
	13600	GDHT	44105	2757	A5
	14000	CLEV	44105	2757	A5
	14100	CLEV	44128	2757	A5
Saybrook Dr	1100	MCDN	44056	3018	E7
	8400	BKLN	44144	2753	D6
	9300	NRDV	44035	3007	C1
	11000	CcdT	44077	2146	B6
Saybrook Ln	11300	AbnT	44021	2893	B1
	11300	AbnT	44023	2893	B1
Saybrook Rd	2200	UNHT	44118	2628	A4
Sayle Dr	29400	WBHL	44092	2374	D5
	29400	WBHL	44094	2374	D5
Saylor Dr	6200	BKPK	44142	2881	D4
Saywell Av	11300	CLEV	44108	2496	D6
	12300	CLEV	44112	2496	D6
	12300	ECLE	44112	2496	D6
Scarborough Ln	400	PnvT	44077	2145	B6
Scarborough Rd	2600	CVHT	44106	2627	B4
	2600	CVHT	44118	2627	B4
E Scarborugh Rd	3200	CVHT	44118	2627	C4
	3500	UNHT	44118	2627	D4
Scarlet Oak Dr	5800	BDHT	44146	2887	D3
Scarlet Oak Ln	8600	PRMA	44130	3013	D2
Scarlet Oak Tr	14900	SGVL	44149	3146	B1
Scarsdale Ln	600	RslT	44022	2761	A3
Scenic Dr	10	OmsT	44138	2879	A4
Scenic Ln	300	PRMA	44131	2883	E5
	300	PRMA	44134	2883	E5
	300	SVHL	44131	2883	E5
	300	SVHL	44131	2884	A5
Scenic Rd	19100	RKRV	44116	2621	E5
Scenic St	1400	LKWD	44107	2622	A5
Scenic Park Dr	1500	LKWD	44107	2621	E5
Scenic Park Ovl	6500	MDBH	44130	2881	E4
Scenic Point Rd	1100	SgHT	44067	3017	A7
Scenic Pointe	21700	SGVL	44149	3011	A5
Scenicview Dr	7500	INDE	44131	3015	D2
	8500	BWHT	44147	3014	D5
Schaaf Dr	6200	BKPK	44142	2881	C4
	6200	MDBH	44130	2881	C4
	6200	MDBH	44142	2881	C4
Schaaf Ln	-	BNHT	44131	2755	A7
E Schaaf Rd	10	BNHT	44131	2755	B7
	1000	BNHT	44131	2884	C1
	1200	INDE	44131	2884	D1
W Schaaf Rd	10	BNHT	44109	2755	A7
	10	BNHT	44131	2755	A6
	10	CLEV	44109	2755	A7
	10	CLEV	44131	2755	A7
	400	CLEV	44109	2754	E6
Schadden Rd	-	EyrT	44035	2874	D1
Schade Av	6100	CLEV	44103	2495	E7
Schaden Rd	100	ELYR	44035	2875	A1
	41000	ELYR	44035	2874	D1
Schady Rd	-	ODFL	44138	3010	B1
	-	OmsT	44138	3010	B1
	26800	ODFL	44138	2878	E7
	26800	ODFL	44138	2879	A7
	26800	OmsT	44138	2878	D7
	26800	OmsT	44138	2879	A7
Schaefer Av	6500	CLEV	44103	2495	E7
Schaefer St	8800	MNTR	44060	2144	C7
Schaffer Dr	36400	NRDV	44039	2876	D3
Schell Av	2100	CLEV	44109	2754	D6
Schenely Av	17800	CLEV	44119	2372	D5
Schiller Av	3500	CLEV	44109	2754	C5
	4100	CLEV	44144	2754	C5
Schlather Ln	18900	RKRV	44116	2621	E6
Schneider Av	7100	CLEV	44102	2623	E7
Schneider Ct	35200	AVON	44011	2618	A6
Schoepf Rd	6800	NCtT	44067	3153	A5
Scholl Rd	2200	UNHT	44118	2627	E4
School Av	15200	CLEV	44110	2497	B2
School Dr	7400	BKLN	44144	2753	E5
School Ln	10	ManT	44255	3159	A2
School St	10	BERA	44017	2880	C6
	100	ELYR	44035	2874	E5
	1600	ShfT	44055	2745	C5
Schoolhouse Av	-	NRDV	44039	2748	B7
Schooner Ct	32500	AVLK	44012	2618	B3
Schooner Ln	400	NCtT	44067	3153	C5
Schooners Cove	7200	CcdT	44077	2146	B6
Schreiber Rd	11400	VLVW	44125	2885	E5
	13500	GDHT	44125	2886	A5
	13500	VLVW	44125	2886	A5
	13700	GDHT	44137	2886	A5
	13700	MPHT	44137	2886	A5
Schuberts Al	10	OmsT	44138	2879	B4
Schueller Blvd	-	SFLD	44054	2617	A6
Schustrich Rd	5500	HrmT	44234	3160	D6
	5500	HrmT	44255	3160	D6
	5500	ManT	44255	3160	D6
Schuyler Av	15000	CLEV	44111	2752	C3
Schwab Dr	10700	PRMA	44130	3013	B1
Schwartz Rd	28900	WTLK	44145	2749	C4
	31500	AVON	44011	2749	A3
	31500	AVON	44145	2749	A3
	31600	AVON	44011	2748	C3
Science Pkwy	-	ETLK	44095	2250	C3
Science Park Dr	25700	BHWD	44122	2628	E7
	25700	BHWD	44122	2629	A7
Scioto Av	13800	ECLE	44112	2497	A5
Scioto Ct	7400	SLN	44139	3020	E2
Scituate Ct	1000	EatT	44044	3142	A4
	1000	GFTN	44044	3142	A4
Scotch Pine Ct	4100	PryT	44081	2042	E3
Scotch Pine Wy	4700	NRDV	44039	2748	D6
	20400	SGVL	44149	3011	C5
Scothan Av	200	CLEV	44113	2625	A5
Scotland Dr	7800	BbgT	44023	2890	D6
Scotland St	6200	MadT	44057	1843	A7
Scott Blvd	24400	ODFL	44138	3010	C2
Scott Ct	2000	ELYR	44035	3006	B2
Scott Dr	6400	BKPK	44142	2880	E3
	20200	SGVL	44149	3146	C1
Scott St	-	PnvT	44077	2039	D7
Scottsdale Blvd	15500	CLEV	44120	2757	B2
	15500	CLEV	44128	2757	B2
	15500	SRHT	44120	2757	B2
	17500	SRHT	44122	2757	D2
	20000	SRHT	44122	2758	A2
Scottsdale Cir	7200	MNTR	44060	2144	D7
	7300	MNTR	44060	2252	D1
Scottsdale Dr	4800	NRYN	44133	3014	A4
	9200	BWHT	44147	3014	D7
	9500	BWHT	44147	3149	D1
	10400	SGVL	44136	3012	B5
Scottsmour Ct	36400	AVON	44011	2747	D4
Scottwood Av	11300	CLEV	44108	2496	D6
Scovill Av	5500	CLEV	44104	2625	D4
Scranton Ct	1800	CLEV	44109	2624	D7
Scranton Rd	1800	CLEV	44113	2624	E5
	3000	CLEV	44109	2624	D7
	3200	CLEV	44109	2754	D1
Scranton Woods Tr	10700	NbyT	44065	2634	A7
Scupper Ln	10	NCtT	44067	3153	C4
Sea Pns	6000	MNTR	44060	2144	B3
Seabrooke Av	22300	EUCL	44123	2373	B2
Seabury Av	21000	FWPK	44126	2751	B5
Searay Curv	-	PnvT	44077	2040	D3
Sea Ray Cove	3600	RMDV	44202	3020	E6
Searsdale Av	2200	CLEV	44109	2754	C4
Seaton Ct	500	AMHT	44001	2872	E3
Seaton Pl	8400	MNTR	44060	2252	B2
Seaton Rd	3300	CVHT	44118	2497	D7
Seaward Wy	100	AVLK	44012	2618	E2
Seaworld Dr	900	AURA	44202	3021	C3
Sebastian Ct	5300	HDHT	44143	2499	A3
Sebert Av	6500	CLEV	44105	2755	E2
Sebor Rd	3100	SRHT	44120	2627	A7
Sebring Av	1300	MadT	44057	1843	C6

STREET
Block City ZIP Map# Grid

Seco Blvd
13500 BtnT 44021 2766 A1
13500 BURT 44021 2766 A1
Second St
- HmbT 44024 2380 C3
- LORN 44052 2744 E4
- MNTR 44060 2144 D7
Secretariat Ct
4500 AVON 44011 2747 B6
Sector Av
11700 CLEV 44111 2623 A7
Sector Dr
10 BDFD 44146 2886 D2
Sedalia Av
16200 CLEV 44135 2752 B3
Sederis Ln
500 ELYR 44035 2875 A7
Sedge Cir
35500 SLN 44139 3020 B1
Sedge Ct
- AbnT 44255 2893 D7
Sedgefield Ovl
31500 SLN 44139 3019 D1
Sedgewick Ct
100 BNWK 44212 3147 B6
1100 NRYN 44133 3013 C5
Sedgewick Rd
- LNHT 44124 2498 E6
2800 SRHT 44120 2627 C6
N Sedgewick Rd
- LNHT 44124 2498 D6
S Sedgewick Rd
4700 SELD 44121 2498 D6
5000 LNHT 44124 2498 E6
Sedley Rd
24300 RDHT 44143 2373 C7
Seeley Rd
13100 LryT 44077 2041 C7
13100 LryT 44077 2147 D1
13100 LryT 44081 2147 D1
Seeley St
300 AMHT 44001 2872 C1
Seiberling Dr
100 SgHT 44067 3017 E5
100 SgHT 44067 3018 A5
Selby Cir
16200 SGVL 44136 3147 A3
Selfridge Pkwy
- WVHT 44122 2758 A3
4000 HIHL 44122 2758 A3
Selhurst Rd
4300 NOSD 44070 2750 B6
Selig Dr
6300 INDE 44131 2884 D6
Selkirk Dr
6100 MadT 44057 1941 E1
Selkirk Rd
2700 BHWD 44122 2628 E5
2800 BHWD 44122 2629 A5
Sellers Av
11200 CLEV 44108 2496 D4
Selma Av
6500 CLEV 44127 2625 E6
Seltzer Wy
900 CLEV 44114 2624 E2
Selwick Dr
7400 PRMA 44129 2882 D6
Selworthy Ln
7100 SLN 44139 3019 D1
Selwyn Rd
800 CVHT 44112 2497 D5
1100 CVHT 44121 2497 D5
Selzer Av
2100 CLEV 44109 2754 D3
Selzer Ct
- CLEV 44109 2754 D3
Seminary Ln
8500 CsTp 44026 2502 B6
Seminary St
10 BERA 44017 2880 C7
Seminole Av
9500 CLEV 44108 2496 B5
Seminole Ln
9000 MCDN 44056 3018 D6
Seminole Rd
19500 EUCL 44117 2497 E2
19500 EUCL 44117 2498 A2
Seminole St
6000 MNTR 44060 2143 B4
6000 MONT 44060 2143 B3
Seminole Wy
34100 SLN 44139 2889 A7
Semra Cir
7500 PRMA 44130 3013 D1
Seneca Av
100 ELYR 44035 2874 D5
2800 LORN 44055 2745 D3
16600 LKWD 44107 2622 B7
Seneca Blvd
1200 BWHT 44147 3014 E7
Seneca Ct
300 AVLK 44012 2618 D3
9800 BKVL 44141 3150 C3
14000 CLEV 44111 2752 D1
Seneca Dr
1400 MadT 44057 1843 B7
27200 WTLK 44145 2749 E2
27200 WTLK 44145 2750 A2
32300 SLN 44139 3019 E3
33300 SLN 44139 3020 A3
Seneca Pl
5600 WLBY 44094 2375 A1
Seneca Rd
1900 EUCL 44117 2498 A2
6100 MNTR 44060 2143 B4
6600 MAYF 44040 2500 A5
6600 MAYF 44143 2500 A5
Seneca Tr
6300 MNTR 44060 2143 B5
14400 MDBH 44130 2881 C7
Senlac Hills Dr
10 CNFL 44022 2761 B6
Sentinel Dr
4700 BKVL 44141 3150 C3
Sentry Ln
26800 WTLK 44145 2620 A6
Sequoia Ct
5800 MONT 44060 2143 E2
Sequoia Dr
5100 PRMA 44134 3014 A1
Sequoia Tr
29800 WTLK 44145 2749 C6
Serene Ct
9900 TNBG 44087 3019 C4

Serenity Ln
28800 WKLF 44092 2374 B4
E Serenity Ln
2000 LORN 44053 2744 B4
N Serenity Ln
4200 LORN 44053 2744 B4
W Serenity Ln
2100 LORN 44053 2744 A4
Serio Dr
7400 INDE 44131 3015 C1
Service Ct
1700 EUCL 44117 2498 A1
Service Dr
10 ELYR 44035 3006 A1
Service Ln
3500 PryT 44081 1940 B7
Service Center Dr
6300 INDE 44131 2884 D6
Sesquicentennial Dr
- PRMA 44130 2882 A7
Sesquicentennial Park Rd
- PMHT 44130 2882 A7
- PRMA 44130 2882 A7
Seth Paine Ct
7900 BKVL 44141 3016 A7
Seth Payne St
7900 BKVL 44141 3016 B3
Seton Dr
- AVON 44011 2748 B2
- ClbT 44028 3009 C2
- ClbT 44138 3009 C2
9500 OmsT 44138 3009 C2
Settlement Acres Dr
13300 BKPK 44130 2881 D3
13300 BKPK 44142 2881 D3
13300 PMHT 44130 2881 D3
Settlers Ct
7600 MNTR 44060 2253 A2
Settlers Ln
28500 PRPK 44124 2629 B3
Settlers Psg
8100 BKVL 44141 3016 C5
Settlers Run
14400 SGVL 44136 3147 A1
14500 SGVL 44136 3146 E1
Settlers Tr
17700 AbnT 44023 2893 B5
Settlers Wy
100 AVON 44011 2617 E6
Settler's Wy
14300 SGVL 44149 3146 D1
14400 SGVL 44149 3011 D7
Settlers Reserve Ovl
1700 WTLK 44145 2749 D1
Settlers Reserve Wy
1600 WTLK 44145 2619 D7
1700 WTLK 44145 2749 D1
Settlers Ridge Rd
7100 GSML 44040 2500 C7
Seven Hills Blvd
6900 SVHL 44131 2884 B7
Seven Oaks Dr
1600 LNHT 44124 2628 E1
19000 SGVL 44136 3147 A5
Seven Pines Dr
5100 LORN 44053 2744 B5
Seventh St
- LORN 44052 2744 E4
- ShfT 44052 2744 E4
Severance Cir
10 CVHT 44118 2497 D7
10 CVHT 44118 2627 E1
Severn Ln
1500 WKLF 44092 2374 E1
1500 WLWK 44092 2374 E1
Severn Rd
3400 CVHT 44118 2627 D1
3700 CVHT 44121 2627 D1
Seville Av
15300 CLEV 44128 2757 B5
Seville Dr
26200 BHWD 44122 2628 E3
26200 BHWD 44122 2629 A4
Sexton Ct
2700 BWHT 44147 3149 D5
Sexton Rd
4200 CLEV 44105 2756 B4
Seymour Av
2000 CLEV 44113 2624 C6
Shadeland Av
11500 CLEV 44108 2496 D3
Shadeland St
- RMDV 44202 3020 E5
Shadetree Ct
7000 OmsT 44138 2878 D5
Shade Tree Tr
36100 AVON 44011 2617 D6
Shadley St
2700 ShvT 44255 3158 A7
Shadowbrook Cir
- AURA 44202 3156 D1
Shadowbrook Dr
7200 KTLD 44094 2376 B5
32200 SLN 44139 2759 E7
Shadow Creek Dr
- WTLK 44145 2749 B5
Shadow Creek Tr
700 AMHT 44001 2872 C2
Shadow Hill Tr
9400 CsTp 44026 2502 E5
9500 CsTp 44026 2503 A5
9600 CsTp 44024 2503 A5
9600 MsnT 44024 2503 A5
Shadowood Dr
10800 NbyT 44065 2764 A2
Shadowrow Rd
800 WLBY 44094 2143 A4
Shadow Wood Cir
9800 AbnT 44023 2763 A7
Shady Dr
300 AMHT 44001 2872 D1
37000 NRDV 44039 2876 D6
Shady Ln
100 PnvT 44077 2040 D2
400 ETLK 44095 2250 C1
2100 SVHL 44131 2884 B6
7100 MNTR 44060 2144 D7
7600 NCtT 44067 3153 E2
9900 BKLN 44144 2753 C6
13200 CsTp 44026 2502 E3
13200 CsTp 44026 2632 A3
Shady Lake Dr
2700 VMLN 44089 2742 A5
Shadylawn Av
100 AMHT 44001 2743 D7

Shady Ln Dr
8200 BWHT 44147 3014 E4
Shady Moss Ln
4800 NRDV 44039 2748 E7
Shadyoak Blvd
11900 GDHT 44125 2885 E1
13500 GDHT 44125 2886 A1
Shady Pine Pl
3300 PryT 44081 1940 D7
Shady Ridge Ln
5000 BNHT 44131 2755 B7
Shadyside Av
4700 CLEV 44109 2754 B3
4700 CLEV 44144 2754 B4
Shadyside Dr
- ETLK 44095 2250 C1
6100 VMLN 44089 2740 C5
Shadyway Rd
12800 GDHT 44125 2885 E3
Shadywood Ln
4000 WVHT 44122 2757 E3
9500 TNBG 44087 3019 B6
Shaffer Dr
1200 LORN 44053 2744 C6
Shagbark Tr
10 AURA 44202 3157 C1
11200 SGVL 44149 3011 B5
Shaker Blvd
10000 CLEV 44104 2626 C5
11000 CLEV 44120 2626 E5
13300 CLEV 44120 2627 A5
13400 SRHT 44120 2627 C6
18400 SRHT 44122 2627 E6
19500 SRHT 44122 2628 A6
23100 BHWD 44122 2628 E6
25600 BHWD 44122 2629 A6
26100 PRPK 44124 2629 A6
32700 HGVL 44022 2630 D6
32700 PRPK 44124 2630 A6
36100 NRDV 44039 2876 E7
Shaker Blvd SR-87
10000 CLEV 44104 2626 C5
11000 CLEV 44120 2626 E5
13300 CLEV 44120 2627 A5
13400 SRHT 44120 2627 C6
18400 SRHT 44122 2627 E6
19500 SRHT 44122 2628 A6
23100 BHWD 44122 2628 C6
Shaker Ct
9500 OmsT 44138 3009 C1
Shaker Dr
- NRDV 44039 2876 E7
10900 NRYN 44133 3013 B4
29300 WKLF 44092 2374 B1
Shaker Rd
2500 CVHT 44118 2627 D5
Shaker Sq
13100 CLEV 44120 2626 E5
Shakercrest Blvd
2700 BHWD 44122 2628 D6
Shaker Glen Ln
10 SRHT 44122 2628 A7
Shakerwood Rd
19000 CLEV 44122 2757 E2
19000 WVHT 44122 2757 E2
19700 WVHT 44122 2758 A2
Shakespeare Dr
600 BERA 44017 2880 B4
Shakespeare Ln
100 AVON 44011 2748 B2
Shakespeare Pkwy
1000 CLEV 44108 2496 B6
Shale Av
9900 CLEV 44104 2626 C5
Shale Ct
- BERA 44017 2879 E5
Shale Brook Ct
10000 SGVL 44149 3011 A4
Shale Brook Wy
10100 SGVL 44149 3011 A4
Shaleside Ct
15400 MDBH 44130 2881 A5
Shallow Creek Cir
400 NCtT 44067 3153 E5
400 NCtT 44236 3153 E5
Shamrock Av
11600 CLEV 44111 2753 B3
11600 LNDL 44111 2753 B3
11600 LNDL 44135 2753 B3
Shamrock Dr
7300 MONT 44060 2143 C2
Shandle Blvd
5600 MNTR 44060 2144 C2
S Shandle Blvd
5700 MNTR 44060 2144 C2
Shandon Ct
20900 SGVL 44149 3146 B4
Shaner Dr
6900 WNHL 44146 2886 E6
6900 WNHL 44146 2887 A7
Shankland Rd
4700 WLBY 44094 2250 C7
Shannon Ct
14700 BURT 44021 2766 A1
Shannon Ln
6600 MNTR 44060 2145 A5
Shannon Rd
3400 CVHT 44118 2627 E1
3700 CVHT 44121 2627 E1
Sharon Ct
2800 TNBG 44087 3020 A6
Sharon Dr
700 WTLK 44145 2620 D6
7600 MONT 44060 2143 D2
10400 PRMA 44130 2882 B1
18700 BbgT 44023 3021 D2
23200 NOSD 44070 2750 E4
Sharon Ln
22100 FWPK 44126 2751 A5
Sharonbrook Dr
100 TNBG 44087 3019 A4
Sharondale Dr
900 AMHT 44001 2744 A6
1000 LORN 44001 2744 A6
1000 LORN 44053 2744 A6
6200 SLN 44139 2889 B5
W Sharondale Dr
33300 SLN 44139 2889 A4
Sharonlee Dr
7300 MNTR 44060 2252 A1
Sharon Ln Dr
9300 NRYN 44133 3014 C4
Sharp Ln
8200 CsTp 44026 2502 A1

Sharp Rd
8800 OmsT 44138 2878 B7
8800 OmsT 44138 3009 B1
9100 ClbT 44028 3009 B2
9100 ClbT 44138 3009 B2
Sharpe Av
37200 WLBY 44094 2250 D5
Shasta Ct
15600 CLEV 44110 2372 C7
Shasta Dr
10500 CdnT 44024 2379 A6
Shaw Av
- KTLD 44094 2376 E1
1700 ECLE 44112 2497 B5
9100 KTLD 44094 2377 A1
12500 CLEV 44108 2496 E4
13000 CLEV 44112 2496 E4
13000 ECLE 44112 2496 E4
17400 LKWD 44107 2622 B4
Shaw Dr
36000 NRDV 44039 2876 E7
Shaw Ln
- LKWD 44107 2622 A4
Shawn Dr
34800 NRDV 44039 2877 B1
Shawnee Av
18500 CLEV 44119 2372 E6
19700 CLEV 44119 2373 A6
19700 EUCL 44119 2373 A6
Shawnee Ct
1000 VMLN 44089 2741 B6
Shawnee Dr
4000 LORN 44055 2745 D4
5600 LNHT 44124 2629 B1
5600 MDHT 44124 2629 B1
Shawnee Ln
500 BDFD 44146 2886 C5
Shawnee Rd
19000 EUCL 44117 2497 E2
Shawnee Tr
- MNTR 44094 2143 A4
- WLBY 44094 2143 A4
10 AURA 44202 3157 A1
7000 MNTR 44060 2143 A4
7800 GTVL 44231 3161 E4
13600 MDBH 44130 2881 D6
Shawondassee Dr
10 TMLK 44095 2250 A1
Shaw View Av
1300 ECLE 44112 2497 B5
Shear St
10 ELYR 44035 2874 E5
Shearer Rd
7300 SgHT 44067 3152 D2
Shedd Rd
15000 BtnT 44021 2767 A7
15000 BtnT 44062 2767 A7
15000 MdfT 44062 2767 A7
15000 PkmT 44062 2767 A7
15000 TroT 44021 2767 A7
15000 TroT 44062 2767 A7
Sheerbrook Dr
1000 SRSL 44022 2761 E7
1000 SRSL 44022 2762 A7
Sheerwater Ln
38300 WLBY 44094 2142 E5
Sheffield Dr
- SDLK 44054 2616 E3
- SFLD 44054 2616 E3
Sheffield Rd
500 SDLK 44054 2616 B4
1300 SELD 44121 2498 B7
1400 SELD 44121 2628 B1
Sheffield Ter
100 BNWK 44212 3147 B6
1600 PnvT 44077 2040 E2
1700 PnvT 44077 2041 A2
Shelbourne Ct
8700 CLEV 44106 2626 B4
Shelburne Dr
7600 MDBH 44130 3012 D2
Shelburne Rd
17400 CVHT 44118 2627 D5
17400 SRHT 44118 2627 D5
19500 SRHT 44118 2628 A5
20200 SRHT 44122 2628 A5
Shelby Av
500 PNVL 44077 2040 A6
Shelby Ct
10 GFTN 44044 3142 A4
Shelby Dr
16200 BKPK 44142 2881 B1
Sheldon Av
1800 ECLE 44112 2497 B5
Sheldon Blvd
13300 BKPK 44142 2881 D4
13300 MDBH 44130 2881 D4
13300 MDBH 44142 2881 D4
14500 BKPK 44130 2881 C4
Sheldon Rd
10 BERA 44017 2880 B4
10 BERA 44142 2880 B4
10 BKPK 44142 2880 B4
100 BERA 44130 2880 B4
5500 LNHT 44124 2499 B6
11300 ManT 44234 3159 D2
11300 ManT 44255 3159 D3
15100 BKPK 44142 2881 A4
15100 MDBH 44130 2881 A4
15100 MDBH 44142 2881 A4
18000 MDBH 44130 2880 E4
18000 MDBH 44142 2880 E4
Shelford Dr
7300 SLN 44139 3020 C2
Shelia Av
17900 CLEV 44111 2752 A3
17900 CLEV 44135 2752 A3
Shelley Dr
3900 NOSD 44070 2750 B5
Shelley Pkwy
700 BERA 44017 2880 B4
Shelley Rd
2700 SRHT 44122 2628 B6
Shelly Av
33900 NRDV 44039 3008 C1
Shelly Ct
33400 AVLK 44012 2617 C3
Shelly Dr
- LORN 44053 2744 B4
2900 SVHL 44131 3015 B2
6700 MadT 44057 1942 B2
Shelly Wy
6900 MadT 44057 1942 C2
Sheltered Cove
8200 MNTR 44060 2144 A3

Shelton Blvd
100 ETLK 44095 2142 D6
Shelton Ct
- BWHT 44147 3150 A5
2700 MadT 44057 1942 E4
Shelton Dr
19500 CLEV 44110 2373 A7
Shenandoah Ct
7200 MNTR 44060 2143 B4
Shenandoah Dr
9100 NRYN 44133 3013 C4
9600 BKVL 44141 3150 D3
Shenandoah Ovl
1300 PRMA 44134 2883 E7
Shenandoah Rdg
19800 SGVL 44149 3146 C1
Shepard Ln
- NOSD 44070 2750 E7
- NOSD 44070 2879 E1
Shepard Rd
2800 PryT 44077 2041 E4
2800 PryT 44081 2041 D4
2800 PryT 44081 2042 A4
8200 MCDN 44056 3153 E2
8800 MCDN 44056 3018 E7
9000 MCDN 44056 3019 A4
9200 MCDN 44087 3019 A6
9200 TNBG 44087 3019 A4
9700 TNBG 44056 3019 A4
9900 GNWL 44139 3019 A4
9900 MCDN 44146 3019 A4
9900 Okwd 44146 3019 A4
9900 TNBG 44139 3019 A4
Shepard Tr
9600 MCDN 44056 3019 A4
9600 TNBG 44056 3019 A4
9600 TNBG 44087 3019 A4
Shepard Hills Blvd
900 MCDN 44056 3018 D6
Shepherds Gln
5000 WLBY 44094 2250 A7
5000 WLBY 44094 2375 A1
Sheppards Pt
- BYVL 44140 2621 A5
Sheraton Dr
- PRMA 44129 2883 A2
3700 PRMA 44134 2883 B2
Sherborn Rd
6300 PMHT 44130 2882 A5
Sherborne Rd
24000 BDHT 44146 2887 D4
Sherbrook Dr
28900 WKLF 44092 2374 C4
Sherbrook Rd
1400 SELD 44121 2498 A7
1400 SELD 44121 2628 A1
Sherbrooke Av
- WTLK 44145 2620 C7
Sherbrooke Ovl
3800 BNWK 44212 3146 E7
18100 SGVL 44136 3146 E4
Sherbrooke Rd
- SRHT 44118 2628 A6
2700 SRHT 44122 2628 A6
Sherbrooke Valley Ct
2900 WBHL 44094 2376 A7
Sherbrook Park Dr
33800 SLN 44139 2889 A3
Sheri Dr
200 BNWK 44212 3146 D7
Sheridan Dr
1200 PRMA 44134 2883 E7
Sheridan Rd
1400 SELD 44121 2498 D7
1400 SELD 44121 2628 C1
1500 LNHT 44121 2628 D2
1500 LNHT 44122 2628 D2
Sheriff St
100 ELYR 44035 2874 D3
100 EyrT 44035 2874 D3
Sherman Av
7500 CLEV 44104 2626 A4
Sherman Dr
1200 PRMA 44134 2883 E7
Sherman Ln
9300 NRYN 44133 3013 C5
Sherman Rd
7000 CsTp 44026 2501 B5
7000 GSML 44040 2501 A5
7400 GSML 44040 2500 E5
8100 CsTp 44026 2502 E6
9200 CsTp 44024 2503 A5
9200 CsTp 44026 2503 A5
9200 MsnT 44024 2503 C5
9200 MsnT 44026 2503 C5
10700 MsnT 44024 2504 A5
Sherman St
400 ELYR 44035 2875 B7
400 GNVA 44041 1944 C5
1200 ELYR 44035 3006 B1
1500 HpfT 44041 1944 D7
Sherri Dr
8700 MCDN 44056 3018 E7
W Sherri Dr
6800 MCDN 44056 3018 E7
Sherrie Dr
600 LORN 44053 2744 E6
Sherrington Rd
17900 SRHT 44122 2757 D1
Sherry Av
13700 CLEV 44135 2752 E4
Sherry Ln
300 BERA 44017 2880 A4
Sherwin Dr
2100 TNBG 44087 3019 E4
2400 TNBG 44087 3020 A4
Sherwin Rd
4300 WLBY 44094 2251 B6
Sherwood Av
800 ELYR 44035 2875 E2
Sherwood Blvd
1600 EUCL 44117 2373 C7
1700 EUCL 44117 2498 C1
Sherwood Cir
13400 GDHT 44125 2885 E4
Sherwood Ct
10 BHWD 44122 2628 E4
400 PNVL 44077 2146 A3
Sherwood Dr
400 AURA 44202 3021 C6
400 BYVL 44140 2619 C5
700 MDSN 44057 2043 E3
700 MDSN 44057 2044 A3
800 MCDN 44056 3018 D7
2400 PRMA 44134 2883 C7

Sherwood Dr
2500 LORN 44053 2743 E2
5200 FWPK 44126 2751 B5
5700 NOSD 44070 2878 D2
7400 MNTR 44060 2252 E1
14800 SGVL 44149 3146 C2
27400 WTLK 44145 2749 E3
34300 SLN 44139 2889 B2
Sherwood Ln
35700 WBHL 44094 2375 B3
Sherwood Rd
3700 CVHT 44121 2497 E4
3700 SELD 44121 2497 E4
3700 SELD 44121 2498 A4
9300 CLEV 44104 2626 B5
Sherwood Tr
6600 NRYN 44133 3013 E5
9300 BKVL 44141 3150 D2
11600 CsTp 44026 2501 B3
Sheryl Dr
800 CLEV 44109 2754 E6
Shetland Cir
700 BERA 44017 3010 E2
700 BERA 44017 3011 B2
Shetland Ct
300 HDHT 44143 2499 C1
8800 KTLD 44094 2377 C6
Shields Av
- AVLK 44012 2617 B2
Shilling Dr
- ELYR 44035 2874 B5
Shillingham Wy
100 PnvT 44077 2145 C6
Shiloh Cir
1700 PRMA 44134 2883 E6
Shiloh Dr
12100 CsTp 44026 2502 C6
E Shiloh Dr
12200 CsTp 44026 2502 C5
N Shiloh Dr
8800 CsTp 44026 2502 C5
W Shiloh Dr
12100 CsTp 44026 2502 B5
Shiloh Pk
2500 WTLK 44145 2750 C2
Shiloh Rd
15200 CLEV 44110 2372 B7
Shinnecock Dr
7300 SLN 44139 3020 E2
Shipherd Av
9100 CLEV 44106 2496 B7
Shipherd Cir
10 OBLN 44074 3139 A3
Ships Channel
2400 CLEV 44113 2624 B3
Shire Ct
14500 RsIT 44072 2632 C7
14500 RsIT 44072 2762 C1
Shireen Dr
14300 SGVL 44149 3146 C1
Shirley Av
15200 MPHT 44137 2886 B4
15700 BDFD 44137 2886 B4
15700 BDFD 44146 2886 B4
26200 EUCL 44132 2373 E2
26800 EUCL 44132 2374 A2
Shirley Dr
4400 SELD 44121 2628 C1
Sholle Dr
10 BSHT 44236 3153 B6
Shopping Plz
10 CNFL 44022 2761 A6
E Shore Blvd
- ETLK 44095 2249 E2
- LKLN 44095 2249 E2
- TMLK 44095 2249 E2
10 TMLK 44095 2250 A1
35300 ETLK 44095 2250 B1
W Shore Blvd
400 SDLK 44054 2616 C4
800 SFLD 44054 2616 C4
W Shore Ct
15700 LKWD 44107 2622 C3
Shore Dr
200 ETLK 44095 2142 D6
4000 LORN 44053 2743 E2
5800 MadT 44057 1941 D1
6100 MadT 44057 1842 E7
11400 NbyT 44065 2764 C1
14500 NbyT 44065 2634 C7
W Shore Rd
10 AVLK 44012 2617 C1
Shoreacre Dr
1100 MadT 44057 1843 E6
Shore Acres Dr
14800 CLEV 44110 2372 B7
Shoreby Dr
10 BTNH 44108 2496 D2
Shore Center Dr
22400 EUCL 44123 2373 B2
Shoreham Dr
32500 WLWK 44095 2249 D3
36900 ETLK 44095 2142 D6
Shoreland Av
19200 RKRV 44116 2621 D6
E Shoreland Av
18400 RKRV 44116 2622 A6
18500 RKRV 44116 2621 E6
Shoreline Dr
4800 VMLN 44089 2741 A4
Shoreline Wy
4700 VMLN 44089 2741 A4
5200 VMLN 44089 2740 E4
Shoreview Av
24600 EUCL 44123 2373 D1
24800 EUCL 44132 2373 D1
26800 EUCL 44132 2374 A1
Short St
700 VMLN 44089 2740 E5
Short Court St
100 CRDN 44024 2380 A6
Shorthorn Dr
8300 SgHT 44067 3017 D5
Shortline Dr
10 OmsT 44138 2879 A4
Shoshone Tr
900 MCDN 44056 3018 D6
Shubert Dr
26700 WTLK 44145 2620 A7
Shupe Av
400 AMHT 44001 2872 D3
Shurmer Dr
23000 WVHT 44128 2758 C4
Shurmer Rd
16000 SGVL 44136 3147 A2

Shurmer Rd
17000 SGVL 44136 3146 E2
18300 SGVL 44149 3146 D1
Siam Av
3500 CLEV 44113 2624 C6
Sicily Ct
33700 NRDV 44039 3008 D1
Sidaway Av
6500 CLEV 44127 2625 E6
6900 CLEV 44104 2625 E6
Side Av
5700 CLEV 44102 2624 A6
Sidney Dr
26900 EUCL 44132 2373 E4
26900 EUCL 44132 2374 A4
Siegler Dr
6100 BKPK 44142 2880 E3
6100 BKPK 44142 2881 A3
26000 BHWD 44122 2628 E7
26000 BHWD 44122 2629 A7
Sierra Dr
5400 WLBY 44094 2375 A1
Sierra Ovl
8300 PRMA 44130 3013 D1
Signal Hl
10 AbnT 44023 2892 A4
Signature Dr
39000 SLN 44139 3020 E2
Signet Av
12300 CLEV 44120 2626 E7
Sikes Ln
2800 TNBG 44087 3020 B5
Silk Av
9500 CLEV 44102 2623 D5
Silktree Ln
30800 WTLK 44145 2749 B6
Silkwood Ln
6800 SLN 44139 2889 B7
Silmore
11800 CLEV 44108 2496 D3
Silsby Ct
3800 AVON 44011 2747 E4
Silsby Rd
3200 CVHT 44118 2627 C3
3300 UNHT 44118 2627 C3
3800 CLEV 44111 2752 C2
3800 UNHT 44118 2628 A3
4300 BHWD 44122 2628 C3
E Silsby Rd
23300 BHWD 44122 2628 D3
Silver Cr
4500 BKVL 44141 3150 E3
4500 BKVL 44141 3151 A2
Silver Ct
5900 MNTR 44060 2144 A3
Silver Dr
10 PNVL 44077 2145 E2
Silver Rd
12600 GDHT 44125 2756 E7
13600 GDHT 44125 2757 A7
Silver St
1300 WKLF 44092 2374 C2
Silver Beech Ln
7500 MNTR 44060 2251 D4
Silverberry Ln
700 HDSN 44236 3154 A6
Silverbrook Ct
800 BWHT 44147 3015 A7
Silvercreek Dr
8400 RsIT 44072 2632 A7
8400 RsIT 44072 2762 B1
Silverdale Av
2100 CLEV 44109 2754 D6
Silverdale Cir
1300 TNBG 44087 3019 B3
Silverdale Rd
4300 NOSD 44070 2750 A6
Silveridge Tr
2100 WTLK 44145 2749 B1
Silverleaf Dr
9700 NRYN 44133 3014 B3
Silvermound Dr
6600 MNTR 44060 2143 D5
Silver Oak Cir
1500 TNBG 44087 3019 B7
Silver Oak Dr
4400 AVON 44011 2748 C6
Silver Springs Tr
10 SRSL 44022 2762 D6
Silverton Av
8700 CLEV 44102 2753 D1
Silverton St
3000 AVON 44011 2747 C2
Silvertree Ct
5700 MadT 44057 1941 D2
Silver Tree Tr
10700 NRYN 44133 3148 B2
Simecek Dr
9200 TNBG 44087 3155 B1
Simich Dr
300 SVHL 44131 2884 A5
Simmons Pl
2000 MadT 44057 1941 D2
Simon Av
7900 CLEV 44103 2496 A6
Simon St
- NRDV 44039 2876 A4
Simons Dr
500 BNWK 44212 3147 A7
Simsbury Ct
9600 TNBG 44087 3020 B6
Singer Av
100 GDRV 44077 2039 C6
300 PnvT 44077 2039 C6
Singer Av SR-283
100 GDRV 44077 2039 C6
300 PnvT 44077 2039 C6
Singer Dr
10000 STBR 44241 3157 A7
Singlefoot Tr
8600 KTLD 44094 2377 C3
Sinton Pl
2700 PRPK 44124 2629 C5
Sioux Ln
800 MCDN 44056 3018 D6
Sipple Av
100 AMHT 44001 2872 D1
Sir John Av
4200 NRYN 44133 3014 B7
Sir Richard Av
4200 NRYN 44133 3014 B7
Sir Robert Av
4200 NRYN 44133 3014 B7
Sir Roberts Ct
7400 MNTR 44060 2143 C6

STREET
Block City ZIP Map# Grid

Sisson Rd
14300 HmbT 44024 2381 D7
Sites Rd
27900 BYVL 44140 2619 E4
Sittingbourne Dr
7000 CcdT 44060 2145 B7
Sittingbourne Ln
2400 BHWD 44122 2628 D4
Sivon Dr
10 PnvT 44077 2041 A4
Sixth St
- LORN 44052 2744 E4
- ShfT 44052 2744 E4
Skeel Ct
- CLEV 44109 2754 B2
Skiff St
4000 WLBY 44094 2250 D5
Skinner Av
700 PNVL 44077 2039 E5
700 PnvT 44077 2039 E7
Skinner Rd
4700 ManT 44234 3159 D1
4700 ManT 44255 3159 D1
Skippers Cove
3700 RMDV 44202 3020 E5
Skye Rd
- HDHT 44143 2499 C1
Skyhaven Rd
7400 NCtT 44067 3153 C4
Skyland Dr
700 MCDN 44056 3018 E4
1000 MCDN 44056 3019 A4
9500 TNBG 44087 3019 A4
S Skyland Dr
9400 MCDN 44056 3018 E5
Skylane Dr
200 NCtT 44067 3153 A3
300 NCtT 44067 3152 E3
4200 CLEV 44109 2755 A5
Skylark Ct
500 ELYR 44035 2875 D2
Skylark Dr
7400 PRMA 44130 2882 A7
7400 PRMA 44130 3013 A1
Skyline Dr
10 MDHL 44022 2760 D6
200 ELYR 44035 3005 B1
1700 RDHT 44143 2373 E7
5700 SVHL 44131 2884 A2
7900 BWHT 44131 3015 C3
7900 BWHT 44147 3015 C3
7900 INDE 44131 3015 C3
26700 OmsT 44138 2878 E6
26700 OmsT 44138 2879 A6
36800 WBHL 44094 2375 D5
E Skyline Dr
1700 LORN 44053 2744 B3
N Skyline Dr
200 SVHL 44131 2883 E1
200 SVHL 44131 2884 A1
W Skyline Dr
2400 LORN 44053 2744 A3
Skyline Ln
8100 RslT 44022 2761 E2
8100 RslT 44072 2761 E2
Skylineview Dr
7700 CcdT 44060 2253 B2
Skytop Ln
35400 WLBY 44094 2375 B1
Skyview Dr
10 BNWK 44136 3147 A5
10 BNWK 44212 3147 A6
10 PRMA 44131 2883 E4
10 PRMA 44134 2883 E4
10 SGVL 44136 3147 A5
10 SVHL 44131 2883 E4
10 SVHL 44131 2884 A4
3800 BNWK 44212 3146 D6
4100 BHIT 44212 3146 D6
5700 SLN 44139 2889 A3
Skyview Rd
300 CLEV 44109 2755 B5
Sladden Av
9400 GDHT 44105 2756 B5
9400 GDHT 44125 2756 B5
Slate Dr
- BERA 44138 2879 E5
Slater Dr
6000 BKPK 44142 2881 A2
Sleepy Hollow Dr
- WBHL 44094 2375 D7
100 AMHT 44001 2872 D4
7500 PRMA 44130 3013 A1
14600 RslT 44072 2762 E1
26700 WTLK 44145 2750 A1
Slife Rd
39500 CrlT 44044 3141 B1
40200 CrlT 44044 3140 E1
40800 CrlT 44050 3140 E1
Sloane Av
1300 LKWD 44107 2622 A5
Sloane Av SR-254
1300 LKWD 44107 2622 A5
Sloane Av US-20
1300 LKWD 44107 2622 A5
Smith Av
- BKPK 44142 2752 C7
3900 CLEV 44109 2754 C2
4700 ShfT 44052 2745 A5
23700 WTLK 44145 2750 D2
Smith Ct
10 ELYR 44035 2875 B6
600 RKRV 44116 2621 D5
1800 CLEV 44113 2624 D5
5100 SFLD 44054 2746 E1
Smith Rd
5000 BKPK 44135 2752 C7
5000 BKPK 44142 2752 C7
5000 CLEV 44135 2752 C7
5200 BKPK 44142 2881 C4
6500 MDBH 44130 2881 D6
6500 MDBH 44142 2881 C4
9300 WTHL 44094 2376 A2
9400 WTHL 44094 2375 E3
13100 PMHT 44130 2881 E6
Smith St
10 OBLN 44074 3138 E4
Smithfield Dr
800 SgHT 44067 3152 B1
Smithfield Rd
29800 ORNG 44022 2759 C4
Smokerise Dr
8700 MCDN 44056 3018 D7
Smugglers Cove
3400 WLBY 44094 2250 D3
10200 RMDV 44202 3020 E5
Snavely Rd
400 RDHT 44143 2498 D3
Snell Dr
5300 MNTR 44060 2039 A7
5300 MNTR 44060 2145 A1
Snell Rd
23000 ClbT 44028 3010 E5
23000 ClbT 44149 3010 D5
23000 SGVL 44149 3010 D5
Snow Rd
900 PRMA 44131 2883 E2
900 PRMA 44134 2883 B2
900 SVHL 44131 2883 E2
4600 PRMA 44129 2883 A2
6700 PRMA 44129 2882 E2
8400 PRMA 44130 2882 C2
8500 PMHT 44130 2882 C2
12000 NbyT 44021 2764 E6
12000 NbyT 44021 2765 A6
12000 NbyT 44065 2764 E6
12300 BtnT 44021 2765 B6
12400 BKPK 44130 2881 E2
12400 BKPK 44142 2881 B2
12400 PRMA 44130 2881 E2
16300 AbnT 44021 2765 B7
16300 TroT 44021 2765 B7
18000 BKPK 44142 2880 E2
Snowberry Ct
7600 MNTR 44060 2253 A2
Snowberry Ln
2400 PRPK 44124 2629 E4
Snowbird Cir
6400 MadT 44057 1942 A4
Snow Blossom Ln
4800 BKVL 44141 3150 B5
Snowflower Dr
21300 RKRV 44116 2621 C7
Snowshoe Tr
16400 BbgT 44023 2891 C1
Snowville Rd
- BKVL 44141 3152 A5
7300 BKVL 44141 3151 D5
W Snowville Rd
5000 BKVL 44141 3150 D5
6700 BKVL 44141 3151 A5
Snyder Av
2200 CLEV 44109 2754 D4
Snyder Rd
16100 SRSL 44022 2762 D7
16200 BbgT 44022 2762 E7
16200 BbgT 44023 2762 E7
16300 BbgT 44023 2891 D5
18400 BbgT 44023 3022 D1
18800 AURA 44023 3022 D3
18800 AURA 44202 3022 D3
Sobieski Av
12100 CLEV 44135 2753 A4
Soika Av
11600 CLEV 44104 2626 D7
11600 CLEV 44120 2626 D7
Solether Ln
10 CNFL 44022 2760 E5
10 MDHL 44022 2760 E5
Solon Blvd
6400 SLN 44139 2888 E6
Solon Rd
10 BDFD 44146 2887 B4
10 CNFL 44022 2760 E7
300 BDHT 44146 2887 C5
400 BTVL 44022 2889 C2
400 CNFL 44022 2889 D1
25800 OKWD 44146 2887 E5
26100 Okwd 44146 2888 A5
26100 SLN 44139 2888 B5
33400 SLN 44139 2889 C2
35600 BTVL 44139 2889 C2
Solon Industrial Pkwy
29800 SLN 44139 2888 C7
Som Ct
- MAYF 44143 2500 A4
Som Center Rd
- WLBY 44094 2250 A6
- WLBY 44095 2250 A6
200 MAYF 44040 2500 A1
200 MAYF 44092 2500 A1
200 MAYF 44094 2500 A1
200 WBHL 44092 2500 A1
200 WBHL 44094 2500 A1
400 ETLK 44095 2250 B6
400 TMLK 44095 2250 A2
500 MAYF 44143 2500 A5
900 MDHT 44124 2500 A6
900 MDHT 44143 2500 A6
1500 MDHT 44124 2630 A2
1600 GSML 44124 2630 A1
1900 GSML 44040 2630 A4
2000 HGVL 44022 2630 A7
2000 HGVL 44040 2630 A3
2000 PRPK 44124 2630 A7
2300 PRPK 44022 2630 A4
2500 WBHL 44094 2375 A4
2600 HGVL 44124 2630 A7
2900 WBHL 44092 2375 A7
3300 HGVL 44022 2760 A1
3300 PRPK 44124 2760 A1
3400 PRPK 44022 2760 A1
3600 MDHL 44022 2760 A3
3600 MDHL 44124 2760 A2
4200 MDHL 44022 2759 E6
4900 SLN 44022 2759 E7
4900 SLN 44139 2759 E7
5100 SLN 44139 2760 A7
5200 SLN 44139 2889 A7
5200 WLBY 44094 2375 A2
7000 SLN 44139 3020 A3
7600 TNBG 44087 3020 A3
7600 TNBG 44139 3020 A3
Som Center Rd SR-91
- WLBY 44094 2250 A6
- WLBY 44095 2250 A6
200 MAYF 44040 2500 A1
200 MAYF 44092 2500 A1
200 MAYF 44094 2500 A1
200 WBHL 44092 2500 A1
200 WBHL 44094 2500 A1
400 ETLK 44095 2250 A6
400 TMLK 44095 2250 A2
500 MAYF 44143 2500 A5
900 MDHT 44124 2500 A6
900 MDHT 44143 2500 A6
1600 GSML 44124 2630 A1
1900 GSML 44040 2630 A4
1900 MDHT 44124 2630 A4
2000 HGVL 44022 2630 A7
2000 HGVL 44040 2630 A3
2000 PRPK 44124 2630 A7
2300 PRPK 44022 2630 A4
2500 WBHL 44094 2375 A4
2600 HGVL 44124 2630 A7
2900 WBHL 44092 2375 A7
3300 HGVL 44022 2760 A1
3300 PRPK 44124 2760 A1
3400 PRPK 44022 2760 A1
3600 MDHL 44022 2760 A3
3600 MDHL 44124 2760 A2
4200 MDHL 44022 2759 E6
4900 SLN 44022 2759 E7
4900 SLN 44139 2759 E7
5100 SLN 44139 2760 A7
5200 SLN 44139 2889 A7
5200 WLBY 44094 2375 A2
7000 SLN 44139 3020 A3
7600 TNBG 44087 3020 A3
7600 TNBG 44139 3020 A3
Somerdale Av
5700 BKPK 44142 2881 D1
Somers Cir
- GSML 44040 2630 B3
Somerset Av
9900 CLEV 44108 2496 B6
Somerset Ct
4900 AVON 44011 2747 B6
4900 NRDV 44011 2747 B6
4900 NRDV 44039 2747 B6
7200 NCtT 44067 3153 B4
Somerset Dr
10 HkyT 44233 3148 B6
400 CNFL 44022 2889 E1
3100 BHWD 44122 2628 A7
3100 SRHT 44122 2628 A7
6000 NOSD 44070 2878 C2
6600 BKVL 44141 3015 E3
8500 BWHT 44147 3014 D5
10500 HmbT 44024 2380 C6
11100 NRYN 44133 3013 A5
Somerset Ln
6600 SVHL 44131 2884 B5
Somerset Ovl
6800 BKVL 44141 3015 E3
Somerset Tr
11200 CcdT 44077 2146 C7
Somerton Rd
3000 CVHT 44118 2627 C1
Somerville Dr
7200 OKWD 44146 2887 E7
Somia Dr
2600 PRMA 44134 2883 C3
Sommer Wy
- ELYR 44035 2875 A7
Somrack Dr
2300 WBHL 44094 2375 C3
Sonesta Av
300 ELYR 44035 3006 D2
Sonesta Ct
100 ELYR 44035 3006 D1
Songbird Ln
7100 NRDV 44039 2876 B4
Song Bird St
400 ELYR 44035 3006 D3
Sonny Dr
7700 WNHL 44146 3017 D2
7800 SgHT 44067 3017 D3
7800 SgHT 44146 3017 D3
Sonoma Ct
27800 WTLK 44145 2749 E1
Sonoma Wy
- AVON 44011 2748 D4
Sonora Av
3200 CLEV 44114 2625 B1
Sonora Ct
600 BERA 44017 3011 A1
Sontag Ln
4700 MNTU 44255 3159 D5
Sophia Av
9200 CLEV 44104 2626 B6
Sorrel Ct
- GnvT 44041 1944 C1
Sorrelwood Ln
100 SRSL 44022 2761 D5
Sorrento Av
16000 CLEV 44128 2757 C4
Sorrento Ln
32800 AVLK 44012 2617 E3
32800 AVLK 44012 2618 A4
Sotogrande Ct
7400 SLN 44139 3020 E2
Sourbrook Ln
32400 NRDV 44039 2748 E7
South Av
- SDLK 44054 2615 E5
- SDLK 44054 2616 A5
South Blvd
5200 MPHT 44137 2757 C7
5200 MPHT 44137 2886 D2
9700 AbnT 44023 3023 A2
9800 CLEV 44108 2496 B6
South Cir
10 BDFD 44146 2886 C5
South Ct
10100 BKVL 44141 3151 D4
30800 NOSD 44070 2878 B3
South Dr
- AVLK 44012 2617 B2
- AVLK 44012 2618 E1
- MNTR 44094 2251 B4
- VMLN 44089 2741 E4
- VMLN 44089 2742 A4
18000 SGVL 44136 3011 E3
18000 SGVL 44136 3012 A3
18000 SGVL 44149 3011 E3
18000 SGVL 44149 3012 A3
South Ln
- AhtT 44001 2872 B2
10 MDHL 44022 2760 C4
6800 WTHL 44094 2376 B2
23900 BDHT 44146 2887 C2
South Ovl
200 CRDN 44024 2505 A1
37600 SLN 44139 2889 D4
South Rd
10 BKVL 44141 3151 A4
South St
10 BbgT 44022 2761 A7
10 BNHT 44131 2884 A1
10 CNFL 44022 2761 A7
10 CyhC 44022 2761 A7
10 OBLN 44074 3138 D3
100 CRDN 44024 2380 A7
300 CRDN 44024 2505 A1
400 FTHR 44077 2039 D4
600 BNHT 44131 2883 E1
600 MsnT 44024 2505 A2
5100 VMLN 44089 2740 D5
5100 VMLN 44089 2741 A5
38200 WLBY 44094 2250 E6
South St SR-44
100 CRDN 44024 2380 A7
300 CRDN 44024 2505 A1
600 MsnT 44024 2505 A2
South St SR-60
5500 VMLN 44089 2740 E5
E South St
10 PNVL 44077 2146 B1
W South St
10 PNVL 44077 2146 B1
South Wy
7100 HDSN 44236 3154 A7
Southampton Dr
300 AURA 44202 3021 D7
7500 NRYN 44133 3013 D5
Southampton Ln
2100 AVON 44011 2748 B1
Southbend Cir
21000 RKRV 44116 2621 C6
South Bend Dr
1600 RKRV 44116 2621 C6
Southbridge Blvd
500 BNWK 44212 3147 C7
Southbridge Cir
27600 WTLK 44145 2749 E4
Southbridge Ln
100 PnvT 44077 2145 B6
South Brook Tr
8800 BbgT 44023 2891 C4
Southern Av
12300 GDHT 44125 2756 D6
27700 NOSD 44070 2878 E2
Southern St
7800 HpfT 44041 1943 B7
7800 HpfT 44057 1943 B7
7800 MadT 44057 1943 B7
Southfield Av
6300 BKLN 44144 2753 E4
6300 CLEV 44144 2753 E4
6300 CLEV 44144 2754 A4
Southgate Park Blvd
20500 MPHT 44137 2887 A1
20600 BDHT 44146 2887 B1
Southgrove Rd
6300 MNTR 44060 2143 B4
Southham Cir
400 BERA 44017 3010 D1
South Hills Blvd
9000 BWHT 44147 3015 D7
Southington Blvd
300 PNVL 44077 2146 A3
Southington Ct
36200 AVON 44011 2747 E5
Southington Dr
5400 PRMA 44129 2883 A4
5400 PRMA 44134 2883 A4
6900 PRMA 44129 2882 D4
Southington Rd
2600 SRHT 44120 2627 B5
13500 CLEV 44120 2627 A6
Southland Av
16000 CLEV 44111 2752 B1
Southland Dr
6800 MDBH 44130 2881 E5
7400 MONT 44060 2143 D2
Southlane Dr
8400 BKLN 44144 2753 D5
Southpark Ctr
100 SGVL 44136 3012 A7
100 SGVL 44136 3147 A1
Southpoint Dr
1700 CLEV 44109 2754 D1
South Point Tr
600 BERA 44017 3011 B2
Southpointe Pkwy
6700 BKVL 44141 3150 E5
Southporte
18500 SGVL 44136 3146 E1
Southridge Ct
8900 SgHT 44067 3017 D3
Southridge Dr
300 CLEV 44109 2755 A5
Southridge Rd
700 SgHT 44067 3017 C3
Southside Park Dr
7100 SLN 44139 3020 A1
Southview Av
13100 CLEV 44105 2756 E2
13100 CLEV 44120 2756 E2
13100 CLEV 44120 2757 A2
Southview Ct
9600 SGVL 44136 3012 B4
Southview Dr
10 BDFD 44146 2887 A2
4900 VMLN 44089 2741 A7
Southview Ln
16500 SGVL 44136 3012 A3
Southway Ct
6500 BKPK 44142 2881 B4
Southway Dr
15400 BKPK 44142 2881 B4
Southwick Dr
10 BDFD 44146 2886 E3
Southwick Ln
200 AURA 44202 3021 E7
Southwick Pl
31800 SLN 44139 2759 D7
Southwind Ct
11000 SGVL 44149 3011 A5
South Winds Dr
5700 MONT 44060 2143 E2
Southwood Av
13500 CLEV 44111 2752 E3
Southwood Dr
200 CrlT 44035 3006 B3
200 ELYR 44035 3006 B3
2700 WTLK 44145 2750 A3
4600 BKLN 44144 2753 D5
4800 SDLK 44054 2616 D4
21100 FWPK 44126 2751 C1
Southwood Ln
26900 OmsT 44138 2878 E3
26900 OmsT 44138 2879 A3
Southwood Rd
10 PnvT 44077 2041 B3
1600 PryT 44077 2041 B3
7400 MNTR 44060 2252 C1
Southwyck Dr
100 SRSL 44022 2761 E6
Sowinski Av
7900 CLEV 44103 2496 A7
8200 CLEV 44108 2496 B7
Sowul Dr
7100 CcdT 44077 2145 D7
7100 CcdT 44077 2253 D1
Spafford Ovl
700 SgHT 44067 3152 C1
Spafford Pl
7300 CLEV 44105 2755 E2
Spafford Rd
6800 BKPK 44142 2879 E2
6800 OmsT 44138 2879 E2
6800 OmsT 44142 2879 E2
7400 CLEV 44105 2755 E2
7400 CLEV 44105 2756 A2
Spanghurst Dr
7200 WNHL 44146 3017 D1
Spangler Ct
7200 CLEV 44103 2625 D2
Spangler Rd
3300 CVHT 44112 2497 D6
Sparky Ln
- NOSD 44070 2750 A6
Sparrow Flight Dr
3000 SVHL 44131 3015 B2
Sparrowhawk Wy
- OKWD 44146 2887 E4
- Okwd 44146 2888 A5
- SLN 44139 2888 A5
Spatterdock Ln
34900 SLN 44139 3020 B1
35600 SLN 44139 2889 B7
Spaulding Ct
5000 LORN 44053 2743 C4
E Spaulding St
38200 WLBY 44094 2250 E5
W Spaulding St
38000 WLBY 44094 2250 D5
Spear Av
14300 CLEV 44120 2757 A1
Spear Rd
10900 CcdT 44077 2146 B7
10900 CcdT 44077 2254 A1
Spearhead Dr
9800 BKVL 44141 3150 C4
Spectrum Pkwy
- BHWD 44122 2758 E2
Speedway Ovlk
12600 ECLE 44112 2496 E6
Speidel Av
19900 FWPK 44126 2751 D2
Spencer Av
5300 CLEV 44103 2495 D7
Spencer Cir
2900 GnvT 44041 1944 E4
Spencer Cir W
3000 GnvT 44041 1944 E3
Spencer Ct
8500 NRDV 44039 2877 C7
Spencer Dr
1100 HRM 44234 3161 A2
2900 GnvT 44041 1944 E3
Spencer Ln
22200 FWPK 44126 2751 A5
Spencer Rd
3100 RKRV 44116 2751 B1
3900 FWPK 44116 2751 B1
3900 FWPK 44126 2751 B1
5000 LNHT 44124 2498 E6
5000 LNHT 44124 2499 A6
Spencer St
12300 ClrT 44024 2505 C5
Spencer Park Dr
11700 ManT 44234 3160 A2
Sperry Cir
700 WTLK 44145 2620 D6
Sperry Dr
23700 WTLK 44145 2620 C6
Sperry Ln
15700 MDFD 44062 2767 C2
Sperry Rd
9100 KDHL 44060 2252 D7
9200 KDHL 44060 2377 E1
9200 KDHL 44060 2378 A1
9200 KTLD 44060 2378 A1
9200 KTLD 44094 2378 A3
9600 KTLD 44094 2377 E4
10900 CsTp 44026 2502 D5
10900 CsTp 44094 2502 E3
10900 KTLD 44094 2502 E3
12700 CsTp 44026 2632 E3
13300 CsTp 44072 2632 E3
13300 RslT 44072 2632 E3
13600 NbyT 44072 2633 A5
13600 RslT 44072 2633 A4
13700 NbyT 44065 2633 A5
14200 NbyT 44065 2763 B1
14200 NbyT 44072 2763 B1
15000 BhmT 44089 2870 B6
15000 VmnT 44089 2869 E6
15000 VmnT 44089 2870 B6
Sperrys Forge Ct
2000 WTLK 44145 2749 D1
Sperrys Forge Tr
1600 WTLK 44145 2619 D7
1800 WTLK 44145 2749 D1
Spiceberry Cir
11100 AbnT 44255 2893 A6
Spicebush Ln
500 AbnT 44023 2892 B3
35300 SLN 44139 2889 B7
Spicers Ln
800 SgHT 44067 3152 B2
Spilker Av
6400 CLEV 44103 2495 E6
Spillgate Trc
1100 BWHT 44147 3149 E5
Spinach Dr
6900 MNTR 44060 2144 A6
Spindlewood Ct
19500 NRYN 44133 3148 A5
Spindrift Dr
36500 ETLK 44095 2142 C7
Spinnaker Cir
19200 SGVL 44136 3146 E5
Spinnaker Ct
4600 MNTR 44060 2039 A5
Spinnaker Dr
32500 AVLK 44012 2618 B3
Spinnaker Run
10100 RMDV 44202 3020 D5
Spino Dr
1700 EUCL 44117 2373 C7
1700 EUCL 44117 2498 C1
Spokane Av
3500 CLEV 44109 2754 B4
4500 CLEV 44144 2754 B4
Spotswood Dr
5600 LNHT 44124 2629 B3
Sprague Av
10700 CLEV 44108 2496 C4
Sprague Rd
10 BERA 44017 3011 B2
23000 BERA 44017 3010 E2
23000 ClbT 44017 3010 E2
23000 ClbT 44138 3010 A2
23000 ODFL 44017 3010 E2
23000 ODFL 44138 3010 C2
23000 SGVL 44017 3010 E2
24400 ClbT 44028 3010 A2
25400 ClbT 44028 3009 C2
25400 ClbT 44138 3009 C2
26000 ODFL 44138 3009 D2
26100 OmsT 44138 3009 C2
31500 ClbT 44028 3008 E2
31500 ClbT 44138 3008 E2
31500 EatT 44028 3008 E2
31500 EatT 44039 3008 E2
31500 EatT 44138 3008 E2
31500 NRDV 44039 3008 E2
31500 NRDV 44138 3008 E2
31500 OmsT 44138 3008 E2
Sprague Rd SR-252
24400 ClbT 44028 3010 C2
24400 ClbT 44138 3010 C2
24400 ODFL 44138 3010 C2
E Sprague Rd
- BKVL 44131 3016 A2
- BKVL 44141 3016 A2
- INDE 44131 3016 A2
10 BWHT 44131 3014 E2
10 BWHT 44131 3015 A2
10 BWHT 44134 3014 E2
10 BWHT 44147 3014 E2
10 BWHT 44147 3015 A2
10 PRMA 44131 3014 E2
10 PRMA 44134 3014 E2
10 SVHL 44131 3014 E2
10 SVHL 44131 3015 A2
2600 INDE 44131 3015 D2
4500 BKVL 44131 3015 E2
4500 BKVL 44141 3015 E2
4500 BWHT 44141 3015 E2
W Sprague Rd
200 BERA 44017 3011 A2
200 SGVL 44017 3011 A2
400 BERA 44017 3010 E2
400 SGVL 44017 3010 E2
500 ClbT 44017 3010 E2
500 ClbT 44028 3010 E2
500 ClbT 44138 3010 E2
500 ODFL 44017 3010 E2
500 ODFL 44138 3010 E2
900 BWHT 44131 3014 E2
900 BWHT 44134 3014 C2
900 BWHT 44147 3014 C2
900 PRMA 44131 3014 E2
900 PRMA 44134 3014 C2
900 SVHL 44131 3014 E2
3000 NRYN 44133 3014 C2
3000 NRYN 44134 3014 C2
3000 NRYN 44147 3014 C2
5100 PRMA 44129 3013 E2
5100 PRMA 44134 3013 E2
9000 NRYN 44130 3013 E2
9000 NRYN 44133 3013 E2
9000 PRMA 44130 3013 E2
12000 NRYN 44130 3012 E2
12000 NRYN 44133 3012 E2
12000 PRMA 44130 3012 E2
12700 MDBH 44130 3012 D2
12700 SGVL 44130 3012 D2
12700 SGVL 44133 3012 E2
12700 SGVL 44136 3012 D2
16800 SGVL 44149 3012 A2
Sprecher Av
12100 CLEV 44135 2753 A6
13000 CLEV 44135 2752 E6
Sprengel Av
14300 CLEV 44135 2752 D4
Spring Ct
13800 LryT 44024 2256 B5
Spring Dr
100 SRSL 44022 2761 D5
Spring Rd
400 BNHT 44109 2755 A5
400 BNHT 44131 2755 A5
400 CLEV 44109 2755 A5
900 CLEV 44109 2754 D5
11400 CsTp 44026 2501 D2
Spring St
10 BERA 44017 2880 C6
10 ELYR 44035 2874 D3
10 EyrT 44035 2874 D3
10 OBLN 44074 3139 A3
100 AMHT 44001 2872 E2
W Spring St
13500 BURT 44021 2636 A7
Spring Blossom Dr
7400 MNTR 44060 2143 C6
Springblossom Tr
13000 CsTp 44026 2631 B2
Springbrook Cir
- ELYR 44035 2874 B6
Springbrook Ct
10200 CcdT 44077 2253 D2
Springbrook Dr
300 BNHT 44131 2755 A7
Springbrook Rd
- RslT 44022 2761 E2
Spring Creek Rd
10 NCtT 44067 3017 D7
100 SgHT 44067 3017 D7
Spring Crest Dr
4100 BKLN 44144 2753 D4
Springdale Av
7900 PRMA 44129 2882 E1
14700 MDFD 44062 2767 C2
18500 CLEV 44135 2751 E6
S Springdale Av
15000 MDFD 44062 2767 C2
Springdale Dr
38200 NRDV 44039 2747 B7
Springdale Ln
200 MDHL 44022 2759 E4
Springdale Rd
6600 BKPK 44130 2881 C4
6600 BKPK 44142 2881 C4
6600 MDBH 44130 2881 C4
6600 MDBH 44142 2881 C4
Springer Dr
8000 KTLD 44094 2376 E5
8000 KTLD 44094 2377 A5
N Springer Dr
10400 KTLD 44094 2376 E5
Springfield Cir
- ClbT 44028 3009 C3
20700 SGVL 44149 3146 B3
Springfield Dr
- AVON 44011 2747 A2
- LvpT 44280 3144 A6
8000 NRYN 44133 3013 D7
Springfield Rd
4800 BDHT 44128 2758 E7
4800 BDHT 44146 2758 E7
4800 WVHT 44128 2758 E6
Spring Garden Av
1400 LKWD 44107 2622 B5
Spring Garden Rd
7400 PRMA 44129 2882 E2
Spring Grove Dr
1900 MadT 44057 1941 B2
5500 SLN 44139 2888 D2
Springhill Dr
8600 MCDN 44056 3018 B6
10300 BKVL 44141 3151 B3
N Springhill Dr
300 MCDN 44056 3018 B5
Springhouse Ln E
9700 CcdT 44060 2145 B7
Springhouse Ln W
9700 CcdT 44060 2145 B7
Spring Lake Blvd
10 PnvT 44077 2041 B3
2400 PryT 44077 2041 B3
Springledge Rd
6900 SgHT 44067 3017 D7
Springmont Rd
200 SgHT 44067 3017 D7
Spring Pond Rd
300 SgHT 44067 3017 D6
Spring Run Blvd
- PnvT 44077 2040 E2
Springside Ln
26900 ODFL 44138 3009 D1
32100 SLN 44139 2888 E2
32600 SLN 44139 2889 A2
Springside Ovl
2300 BKVL 44141 3150 B5
Springtree Dr
- LvpT 44280 3144 A7
Springvale Cir
34300 AVON 44011 2748 C5
Springvale Dr
4100 AVON 44011 2748 B5
4400 WVHT 44128 2758 D5
Spring Valley Dr
8700 MNTR 44060 2144 C7
8800 BWHT 44147 3015 A6
14300 RslT 44072 2632 D7
N Spring Valley Park Dr
8500 BbgT 44023 3022 B2
S Spring Valley Park Dr
8400 BbgT 44023 3022 B2
Springview Dr
6700 INDE 44131 3015 E2
12100 NbyT 44021 2764 E4
12100 NbyT 44021 2765 A4
Springview Rd
8100 SgHT 44067 3017 D6
Springway Rd
11200 MsnT 44024 2504 B3
Springwood Cir
- TNBG 44087 3019 B4
Springwood Ct
5700 MONT 44060 2143 E2
38000 NRDV 44039 2747 C7
Springwood Dr
4700 BKLN 44144 2753 D6
5800 MONT 44060 2143 E2
Springwood Rd
10 NCtT 44067 3017 E7
100 SgHT 44067 3017 E7
6200 PMHT 44130 2882 D4
Spruce Av
- AVLK 44012 2618 A5
- NRDV 44039 2877 D3
1200 CLEV 44113 2624 C3
4300 BHIT 44212 3146 D7
4300 BNWK 44212 3146 C7
Spruce Ct
2900 LORN 44052 2744 C3
3300 AVON 44011 2748 C3
Spruce Dr
200 BERA 44017 2880 A5
500 OBLN 44074 3138 B2
11200 CsTp 44026 2502 B1
20500 SGVL 44149 3146 B2
28300 NOSD 44070 2878 D3
Spruce Ln
10 MNTR 44060 2144 E7
3000 HDSN 44236 3155 D6
3000 TwbT 44236 3155 D6
Spruce St
100 ELYR 44035 2874 D4
35100 NRDV 44039 2877 B1
Sprucedale Rd
900 BWHT 44147 3015 A3
Spruce Hill Dr
8900 MCDN 44056 3018 B5
8900 MCDN 44067 3018 B5
8900 NHFD 44067 3018 B5
Spruce Pine Wy
4800 NRDV 44039 2748 D6
Spruce Pointe
12100 SGVL 44149 3011 A6
Spruce Pointe Ln
- BHIT 44212 3145 E7
Spruce Run Dr
13200 NRYN 44133 3012 E6
Spruce Tree Ln
1200 AMHT 44001 2744 A7
Sprucewood St
4700 AVON 44011 2748 E6
Spyglass Dr
200 ELYR 44035 3006 D3
Spyglass Hill Dr
17700 SGVL 44136 3147 D4

Cleveland Street Index

STREET Block	City	ZIP	Map#	Grid
Square Dr				
10	MDSN	44057	1942	B6
Square Cir Dr				
10	MDSN	44057	1942	B6
Squire Dr				
4600	SgHT	44067	3017	E4
Squire Ln				
7000	RslT	44072	2631	C7
Squire Pl				
10	BDFD	44146	2887	B4
Squire Rd				
24000	ClbT	44028	3145	B1
Squire St				
-	LORN	44055	2745	C5
100	CrlT	44035	3005	E3
1500	ShfT	44055	2745	C5
Squires Ct				
100	SAHT	44001	3003	D1
10300	CcdT	44077	2145	D4
Squires Ln				
100	CRDN	44024	2505	A1
Squires Rd				
900	AURA	44202	3021	C4
900	BbgT	44202	3021	C3
Squirrel Hollow Ln				
16000	SGVL	44136	3146	E3
Squirrel Nest Dr				
6300	LORN	44053	2743	B5
Squirrel Run Dr				
18300	MDBH	44130	2880	E5
SR-2				
-	AhtT	-	2744	E7
-	AhtT	-	2745	A7
-	AMHT	-	2743	D7
-	AMHT	-	2744	B6
-	AMHT	-	2871	E1
-	AMHT	-	2872	A1
-	AVON	-	2617	B7
-	AVON	-	2618	D7
-	AVON	-	2619	A6
-	AVON	-	2747	A1
-	BhmT	-	2870	D1
-	BhmT	-	2871	E1
-	CLEV	-	2372	E6
-	CLEV	-	2373	A6
-	CLEV	-	2497	A1
-	ELYR	-	2746	B7
-	ELYR	-	2874	E1
-	ELYR	-	2875	A1
-	EUCL	-	2373	D4
-	EyrT	-	2745	A7
-	EyrT	-	2874	B1
-	LORN	-	2744	E7
-	PNVL	-	2039	E6
-	PNVL	-	2040	D5
-	PNVL	-	2145	B1
-	PnvT	-	2039	E7
-	PnvT	-	2040	A6
-	PnvT	-	2041	A3
-	PnvT	-	2145	C1
-	SFLD	-	2746	D5
-	SFLD	-	2747	A1
-	VMLN	-	2870	E1
-	VMLN	-	2871	C1
-	VmnT	-	2869	C1
-	VmnT	-	2870	A1
-	WTLK	-	2619	A6
SR-2 Cleveland Mem Shoreway				
-	BTNH	-	2496	E3
-	CLEV	-	2495	C6
-	CLEV	-	2496	A4
-	CLEV	-	2624	E1
-	CLEV	-	2625	A1
-	CLEV	44102	2623	E4
-	CLEV	44102	2624	A4
-	CyhC	-	2495	D5
SR-2 Cleveland Mem Shrwy Frwy				
-	BTNH	-	2496	D3
-	CLEV	-	2495	E5
-	CLEV	-	2496	B4
SR-2 Clifton Blvd				
-	LKWD	44107	2621	E4
-	RKRV	44107	2621	E4
-	RKRV	44116	2621	E4
9200	CLEV	44102	2623	D5
11600	LKWD	44102	2623	B4
11600	LKWD	44107	2623	A4
12900	LKWD	44107	2622	A4
SR-2 Detroit Rd				
19500	RKRV	44116	2621	C6
SR-2 Lake Rd				
19200	RKRV	44116	2621	E5
SR-2 Lakeland Frwy				
-	BTNH	-	2496	E1
-	BTNH	-	2497	A1
-	CLEV	-	2372	C7
-	CLEV	-	2373	A6
-	CLEV	-	2496	E1
-	CLEV	-	2497	B1
-	ETLK	-	2249	E7
-	ETLK	-	2250	B5
-	EUCL	-	2373	B5
-	EUCL	-	2374	A2
-	MNTR	-	2143	E6
-	MNTR	-	2144	A6
-	MNTR	-	2145	A1
-	MNTR	-	2251	C1
-	PNVL	-	2145	B1
-	PnvT	-	2145	B1
-	WKLF	-	2249	E7
-	WKLF	-	2374	B2
-	WLBY	-	2250	E3
-	WLBY	-	2251	B2
-	WLWK	-	2249	E7
SR-2 Northwest Frwy				
-	AVON	-	2619	A6
-	RKRV	-	2621	A6
-	WTLK	-	2619	E7
-	WTLK	-	2620	A7
-	WTLK	-	2621	A6
SR-3 W 25th St				
1400	CLEV	44113	2624	D6
3000	CLEV	44109	2624	D7
3200	CLEV	44109	2754	D1
SR-3 Pearl Rd				
3600	CLEV	44109	2754	A7
4500	CLEV	44144	2754	C5
5000	CLEV	44129	2754	A7
5000	PRMA	44109	2754	A7
5000	PRMA	44129	2754	A7
5300	PRMA	44129	2753	E7
5300	PRMA	44129	2882	E1
SR-3 Ridge Rd				
10	HkyT	44133	3148	D5
10	HkyT	44233	3148	D6
10	NRYN	44133	3148	D5
5400	PRMA	44129	2882	E6
7300	PRMA	44134	2882	E7
7400	PRMA	44129	3013	E1
7400	PRMA	44134	3013	E1
7800	NRYN	44129	3013	E2
7800	NRYN	44133	3013	E7
7800	NRYN	44134	3013	E2
SR-8				
-	BSHT	44067	3153	D6
-	BSHT	44236	3153	D6
-	CLEV	44115	2625	B4
-	MCDN	44056	3018	A6
-	MCDN	44056	3153	B1
-	MCDN	44067	3018	A6
-	NCtT	44056	3018	B7
-	NCtT	44056	3153	C3
-	NCtT	44067	3018	B7
-	NCtT	44067	3153	C3
-	NCtT	44236	3153	D6
-	NHFD	44067	3018	B7
-	SgHT	44067	3018	B7
SR-8 Broadway Av				
800	CLEV	44115	2625	A4
SR-8 Chagrin Blvd				
15600	CLEV	44120	2757	B1
15600	SRHT	44120	2757	B1
17600	SRHT	44122	2757	E1
19400	SRHT	44122	2758	A1
SR-8 Kinsman Rd				
5500	CLEV	44104	2625	E5
7200	CLEV	44104	2626	A6
11300	CLEV	44120	2626	D7
12300	CLEV	44120	2756	E1
13700	CLEV	44120	2757	A1
15400	SRHT	44120	2757	B1
SR-8 Northfield Rd				
-	MPHT	44146	2758	B6
10	BDFD	44146	2887	B4
300	OKWD	44146	2887	B7
400	BDFD	44137	2887	B2
400	BDHT	44146	2887	B2
400	MPHT	44137	2887	B2
400	MPHT	44146	2887	B2
3500	HIHL	44122	2758	A2
3500	SRHT	44122	2758	B4
3600	WVHT	44122	2758	A2
4100	HIHL	44128	2758	A4
4300	NRDL	44128	2758	B4
4600	WVHT	44128	2758	B5
4900	WVHT	44146	2758	B6
5000	BDHT	44146	2758	B7
5000	MPHT	44137	2758	B7
6900	WNHL	44146	2887	B7
7100	WNHL	44146	3018	B2
7600	NHFD	44067	3018	B3
7600	NHFD	44146	3018	B3
10100	SgHT	44067	3018	A5
SR-8 Ontario St				
1900	CLEV	44114	2624	E4
1900	CLEV	44115	2624	E4
2000	CLEV	44113	2624	E4
SR-8 Orange Av				
1400	CLEV	44115	2625	A4
SR-8 Woodland Av				
2500	CLEV	44115	2625	C4
3800	CLEV	44104	2625	C4
SR-10				
-	EatT	-	3006	E4
-	EatT	-	3007	A4
-	NRDV	-	2877	E4
-	NRDV	-	3007	E1
-	NRDV	-	3008	A1
SR-10 Carnegie Av				
10	CLEV	44113	2624	E4
10	CLEV	44115	2624	E4
SR-10 Lorain Av				
2000	CLEV	44113	2624	D5
4400	CLEV	44102	2624	E4
7100	CLEV	44102	2623	E7
9900	CLEV	44111	2623	C7
10600	CLEV	44111	2753	A1
13200	CLEV	44111	2752	C2
18000	FWPK	44111	2752	A2
18000	FWPK	44126	2752	A2
SR-10 Lorain Rd				
-	NRDV	44039	2877	E4
18800	FWPK	44126	2752	A2
18900	FWPK	44126	2751	E2
22900	NOSD	44070	2751	B4
22900	NOSD	44126	2751	A4
23200	NOSD	44070	2750	A7
27300	NOSD	44070	2749	E7
28200	NOSD	44070	2878	D1
31400	NRDV	44039	2878	B2
31400	NRDV	44070	2878	A3
SR-14				
-	HDSN	-	3155	D7
-	MCDN	-	3018	E4
-	MCDN	-	3019	A5
-	OKWD	-	3018	E4
-	TNBG	-	3019	A5
-	TNBG	-	3154	E2
-	TNBG	-	3155	A2
-	TwbT	-	3155	B3
SR-14 E 34th St				
2700	CLEV	44115	2625	B5
SR-14 Broadway Av				
10	BDFD	44137	2886	D2
10	BDFD	44146	2886	D2
10	MPHT	44137	2886	C1
10	MPHT	44146	2886	D2
500	BDFD	44146	2887	B5
1400	OKWD	44146	2887	C7
3900	CLEV	44115	2625	C6
3900	CLEV	44127	2625	C6
5800	CLEV	44127	2755	E1
6200	CLEV	44105	2755	D1
7400	CLEV	44105	2756	A3
9300	CLEV	44125	2756	C5
9300	GDHT	44105	2756	C5
9300	GDHT	44125	2756	C5
13500	GDHT	44125	2757	A6
14100	GDHT	44128	2757	A6
14100	MPHT	44125	2757	A6
14100	MPHT	44128	2757	A6
14100	MPHT	44137	2757	B7
SR-14 Oakleaf Rd				
-	OKWD	44146	2887	C7
SR-14 Ontario St				
1900	CLEV	44114	2624	E4
1900	CLEV	44115	2624	E4
2000	CLEV	44113	2624	E4
SR-14 Outerbelt East Frwy				
-	OKWD	-	2887	C7
-	OKWD	-	3018	C1
SR-14 Outerbelt West Frwy				
-	OKWD	-	3018	C1
SR-14 Pittsburgh Av				
2200	CLEV	44115	2625	D7
SR-14 Warner Rd				
-	CLEV	44105	2756	B3
SR-17 Brookpark Rd				
700	BNHT	44109	2754	E7
700	BNHT	44131	2754	E7
700	CLEV	44109	2754	D7
700	PRMA	44109	2754	D7
700	PRMA	44131	2754	E7
700	PRMA	44134	2754	D7
1500	CLEV	44134	2754	D7
5200	PRMA	44129	2754	A7
6000	CLEV	44129	2754	A7
6700	BKLN	44129	2753	E7
6700	BKLN	44144	2753	E7
6700	CLEV	44129	2753	E7
6700	PRMA	44129	2753	E7
6700	PRMA	44144	2753	E7
10100	PRMA	44130	2753	E7
11700	CLEV	44135	2753	E7
11700	CLEV	44144	2753	E7
11700	PRMA	44135	2753	E7
13000	BKPK	44130	2752	E7
13000	BKPK	44135	2752	C7
13000	BKPK	44142	2752	C7
13000	CLEV	44135	2752	C7
13000	PRMA	44130	2752	E7
13000	PRMA	44135	2752	E7
18200	BKPK	44135	2751	E7
18200	BKPK	44142	2751	E7
18200	CLEV	44135	2751	E7
18200	CLEV	44142	2751	E7
22400	FWPK	44126	2751	B6
22500	NOSD	44070	2751	B6
22500	NOSD	44126	2751	B6
23000	NOSD	44070	2750	B6
SR-17 Granger Rd				
-	INDE	44125	2884	E1
5500	BNHT	44131	2884	D1
5500	INDE	44131	2884	D1
6900	VLVW	44131	2884	E1
7500	VLVW	44125	2884	E1
7500	VLVW	44125	2885	A1
7700	GDHT	44125	2885	A1
8900	GDHT	44125	2756	C7
13600	GDHT	44125	2757	A7
13600	GDHT	44137	2757	A7
13600	MPHT	44137	2757	A7
SR-17 E Granger Rd				
10	BNHT	44131	2755	A7
900	BNHT	44131	2884	D1
1200	INDE	44131	2884	D1
SR-17 W Granger Rd				
300	BNHT	44131	2755	B7
SR-17 Lee Rd				
5300	MPHT	44137	2886	C1
SR-17 Libby Rd				
14400	MPHT	44137	2757	C7
19800	MPHT	44137	2758	C7
21200	BDHT	44146	2758	C7
SR-17 Lorain Rd				
-	NOSD	44070	2750	A6
27300	NOSD	44070	2749	E7
SR-20				
-	CrlT	-	3006	E4
-	EatT	-	3006	E4
SR-21				
-	CHHT	-	2755	D3
-	CLEV	-	2625	C6
-	NBGH	-	2755	D3
SR-21 Brecksville Rd				
-	CHHT	44125	2755	E7
-	CHHT	44131	2755	E7
-	INDE	44125	2755	E7
-	INDE	44131	2755	E7
-	VLVW	44125	2755	E7
-	VLVW	44131	2755	E7
4700	RHFD	44286	3151	A7
5200	RHFD	44141	3151	A6
5400	INDE	44125	2884	E1
5400	INDE	44131	2884	E4
5400	VLVW	44125	2884	E1
5400	VLVW	44131	2884	E1
7100	INDE	44131	3015	E1
7600	INDE	44131	3016	A3
7700	BKVL	44131	3016	A2
8600	BKVL	44141	3016	A7
9000	BKVL	44141	3151	A2
SR-21 Willow Frwy				
-	CHHT	-	2755	D5
-	CLEV	-	2625	B4
-	CLEV	-	2755	C1
-	NBGH	-	2755	C2
SR-43				
-	CLEV	44105	2756	B3
SR-43 E 34th St				
2700	CLEV	44115	2625	B5
SR-43 Aurora Rd				
21700	BDHT	44146	2758	B7
21700	MPHT	44146	2758	B7
23100	BDHT	44146	2887	C1
26700	BDHT	44146	2888	A2
26700	SLN	44139	2888	A2
33200	SLN	44139	2889	C7
37800	SLN	44139	3020	D1
39700	SLN	44139	3021	A2
40000	BbgT	44023	3021	A2
40000	BbgT	44139	3021	A2
40000	BbgT	44202	3021	A2
SR-43 N Aurora Rd				
10	AURA	44202	3021	C5
10	BbgT	44023	3021	A2
10	BbgT	44139	3021	A2
10	BbgT	44202	3021	A2
10	SLN	44139	3021	A2
SR-43 S Aurora Rd				
10	AURA	44202	3156	E1
SR-43 Bartlett Rd				
-	BDHT	44146	2758	C7
SR-43 Broadway Av				
800	CLEV	44115	2625	A4
3900	CLEV	44127	2625	C6
5800	CLEV	44127	2755	E1
6200	CLEV	44105	2755	D1
7400	CLEV	44105	2756	A3
SR-43 S Chillicothe Rd				
100	AURA	44202	3156	E7
1200	STBR	44202	3156	E6
10100	STBR	44241	3156	E7
SR-43 Miles Av				
9100	CLEV	44105	2756	B3
13000	CLEV	44128	2756	E3
13500	CLEV	44105	2757	B4
13500	CLEV	44128	2757	B4
17500	WVHT	44128	2757	D5
SR-43 Miles Rd				
17700	WVHT	44128	2757	D5
19400	NRDL	44128	2757	E5
20000	NRDL	44128	2758	A6
20000	WVHT	44128	2758	A6
SR-43 Mueti Dr				
-	BDHT	44146	2758	B7
-	MPHT	44137	2758	B7
SR-43 Northfield Rd				
-	BDHT	44146	2758	B6
-	MPHT	44137	2758	B6
-	MPHT	44146	2758	B6
4900	NRDL	44128	2758	B6
4900	WVHT	44128	2758	B6
4900	WVHT	44146	2758	B6
SR-43 Pittsburgh Av				
2200	CLEV	44115	2625	D7
SR-44				
-	CcdT	-	2145	E4
-	CcdT	-	2146	A5
-	CcdT	44024	2254	B5
-	CcdT	44077	2254	A1
-	CdnT	44024	2254	B5
-	CdnT	44024	2379	B1
-	CRDN	44024	2379	C5
-	PNVL	-	2145	C1
-	PnvT	-	2145	D3
SR-44 Center St				
100	CRDN	44024	2379	E6
100	CRDN	44024	2380	A6
SR-44 N Hambden St				
100	CRDN	44024	2380	A6
SR-44 S Hambden St				
100	CRDN	44024	2380	A6
SR-44 Heisley Rd				
-	GDRV	44077	2039	B4
-	MNTR	44060	2039	B4
-	MNTR	44060	2145	A1
-	PnvT	44060	2039	B6
-	PnvT	44077	2039	B6
SR-44 Lakeland Frwy				
-	MNTR	-	2145	B1
-	PNVL	-	2145	B1
-	PnvT	-	2145	B1
SR-44 Main St				
100	CRDN	44024	2380	A6
10400	MNTU	44255	3159	C7
10400	ShvT	44255	3159	C7
SR-44 Painesville Ravenna Rd				
10300	MNTU	44255	3159	C7
10300	ShvT	44255	3159	B7
10900	ManT	44255	3159	C5
SR-44 E Park St				
100	CRDN	44024	2380	A6
SR-44 Ravenna Rd				
11600	CRDN	44024	2505	A3
11600	MsnT	44024	2505	B7
12600	MsnT	44024	2635	B1
13400	NbyT	44021	2635	B4
13400	NbyT	44024	2635	B4
13400	NbyT	44065	2635	B4
14200	NbyT	44021	2765	A2
14200	NbyT	44065	2765	A2
15400	NbyT	44021	2764	E7
15400	NbyT	44065	2764	E7
16200	AbnT	44021	2764	E7
16400	AbnT	44021	2893	E1
16400	AbnT	44255	2893	E1
18200	AbnT	44234	2893	C7
SR-44 South St				
100	CRDN	44024	2380	A7
300	CRDN	44024	2505	A1
600	MsnT	44024	2505	A2
SR-44 Water St				
100	CRDN	44024	2380	A6
SR-57 E 28th St				
100	LORN	44055	2745	A2
SR-57 Avon Belden Rd				
15500	GftT	44044	3142	E7
SR-57 Broadway				
300	LORN	44052	2614	E7
1500	LORN	44052	2744	E1
2000	LORN	44052	2745	A1
2600	LORN	44055	2745	A2
SR-57 S East Byp				
-	CrlT	44044	3006	E5
-	EatT	44035	3006	E3
-	EatT	44044	3006	E4
-	EatT	44044	3007	A4
-	ELYR	44035	2875	E7
-	ELYR	44035	3006	E1
SR-57 Grafton Rd				
2400	CrlT	44044	3006	E6
2400	EatT	44044	3006	E6
3000	CrlT	44044	3141	E1
3000	EatT	44044	3141	E2
13300	GFTN	44044	3141	E3
SR-57 Grafton Eastern Rd				
36000	GftT	44044	3142	C7
36700	GFTN	44044	3142	C7
SR-57 Grove Av				
-	ShfT	44035	2745	E6
2700	LORN	44055	2745	E5
4800	ShfT	44055	2745	E5
SR-57 John F Kennedy Mem Pkwy				
-	ELYR	44035	2874	E4
-	ELYR	44035	2875	E4
SR-57 Lorain Blvd				
6000	EyrT	44035	2745	E7
6000	ShfT	44035	2745	E6
6000	ShfT	44055	2745	E6
6200	ELYR	44035	2745	E7
6500	ELYR	44035	2874	E1
SR-57 Main St				
300	EatT	44044	3141	E3
300	GFTN	44044	3141	E3
300	GFTN	44044	3142	A4
1100	GftT	44044	3142	B6
SR-58 Ashland Oberlin Rd				
-	NRsT	44074	3138	E5
-	OBLN	44074	3138	E5
-	PtfT	44074	3138	E5
SR-58 Leavitt Rd				
1000	LORN	44052	2614	B7
1000	LORN	44053	2614	B7
1300	LORN	44052	2744	B1
1300	LORN	44053	2744	B1
5300	AMHT	44001	2744	A6
5300	AMHT	44053	2744	A6
5300	LORN	44001	2744	A6
7400	AhtT	44001	2873	A6
7400	AMHT	44001	2873	A3
9200	AhtT	44001	2872	E7
9200	AhtT	44001	3003	E1
9500	NRsT	44001	3003	E1
9800	NRsT	44074	3003	E6
12300	OBLN	44074	3003	E7
12400	NRsT	44074	3138	E1
12400	OBLN	44074	3138	E1
SR-58 N Leavitt Rd				
100	AMHT	44001	2744	B4
800	AMHT	44053	2744	A6
800	LORN	44001	2744	A6
800	LORN	44053	2744	A6
SR-58 S Leavitt Rd				
100	AhtT	44001	2873	A1
100	AMHT	44001	2873	A1
SR-58 N Main St				
10	OBLN	44074	3138	E2
200	NRsT	44074	3138	E1
SR-58 S Main St				
10	OBLN	44074	3138	E7
300	NRsT	44074	3138	E4
SR-60 Main St				
600	VMLN	44089	2740	E5
SR-60 South St				
5500	VMLN	44089	2740	E5
SR-60 State Rd				
1400	VmnT	44089	2740	E7
1400	VmnT	44089	2869	E3
4700	FrnT	44889	2869	E7
4700	VmnT	44889	2869	E7
SR-60 State St				
800	VMLN	44089	2740	E6
1200	VmnT	44089	2740	E7
SR-82				
-	HrmT	44234	3161	E4
-	HrmT	44255	3161	E4
SR-82 Aurora Rd				
3600	TNBG	44087	3155	D2
3600	TwbT	44087	3155	E2
SR-82 E Aurora Rd				
10	NCtT	44067	3152	E1
10	NCtT	44067	3153	A1
300	MCDN	44056	3153	B1
1400	MCDN	44056	3154	B1
1500	TNBG	44087	3154	B1
2800	TNBG	44087	3155	B2
3400	TwbT	44087	3155	C2
SR-82 W Aurora Rd				
10	NCtT	44067	3152	E1
100	SgHT	44067	3152	C1
900	SgHT	44067	3017	B7
1300	BKVL	44141	3016	E7
1300	SgHT	44067	3016	E7
1300	SgHT	44141	3016	E7
SR-82 Chippewa Rd				
7300	BKVL	44141	3016	E6
13000	SgHT	44067	3016	E7
13000	SgHT	44141	3016	E7
SR-82 Garfield Rd				
11400	HRM	44234	3161	A2
SR-82 E Garfield Rd				
10	AURA	44202	3157	D1
1200	ManT	44202	3157	E1
SR-82 Ravenna Rd				
9100	TNBG	44087	3155	C2
SR-82 Royalton Rd				
-	CrlT	44044	3006	E6
3000	BWHT	44147	3014	C7
3000	NRYN	44133	3014	A7
3000	NRYN	44147	3014	C7
6200	NRYN	44133	3013	D7
11700	NRYN	44133	3012	E7
12700	SGVL	44133	3012	E7
12700	SGVL	44136	3012	B7
17800	SGVL	44136	3011	E7
18600	SGVL	44149	3011	D7
22300	ClbT	44028	3010	D7
22300	ClbT	44149	3010	E7
22300	SGVL	44149	3010	E7
25100	ClbT	44028	3009	C7
27400	ClbT	44028	3008	E7
27400	EatT	44028	3008	D7
34500	EatT	44044	3008	C7
35700	EatT	44044	3007	B7
38100	EatT	44044	3006	E6
SR-82 E Royalton Rd				
-	BKVL	44141	3015	E7
100	BWHT	44147	3014	E7
2400	BKVL	44147	3015	B7
2400	BWHT	44141	3015	B7
4800	BWHT	44147	3015	E7
6900	BKVL	44141	3016	A7
SR-82 W Royalton Rd				
1000	BWHT	44147	3014	E7
2900	NRYN	44133	3014	C7
2900	NRYN	44147	3014	C7
SR-82 State St				
7800	GTVL	44231	3161	E5
7800	HrmT	44231	3161	E5
SR-82 Twinsburg-Warren Rd				
500	AURA	44202	3021	D7
500	AURA	44202	3156	B1
1100	AURA	44087	3156	A2
1100	TwbT	44087	3156	A2
2600	AURA	44202	3157	E1
2600	ManT	44202	3157	E1
2600	ManT	44202	3158	A1
3000	ManT	44255	3158	B2
3700	ManT	44255	3159	B2
4700	ManT	44234	3159	B2
5300	ManT	44234	3160	C2
5500	HrmT	44234	3160	A2
7100	GTVL	44231	3161	E5
7100	HrmT	44231	3161	D4
7100	HrmT	44234	3161	B4
7100	HrmT	44255	3161	B4
SR-82 W Wakefield Rd				
5700	HrmT	44234	3160	B2
5700	ManT	44234	3160	A2
6500	HRM	44234	3160	E2
6600	HRM	44234	3161	A2
SR-82 Welshfield Limavle Rd S				
11300	HRM	44234	3161	A3
SR-82 Welshfield Limavle Rd S				
11300	HrmT	44234	3161	A3
SR-83 Avon Belden Rd				
100	AVLK	44012	2488	A7
100	AVLK	44012	2618	A6
700	AVON	44011	2618	A5
700	AVON	44012	2618	A5
1600	EatT	44044	3142	E2
1600	GFTN	44044	3142	E6
4900	AVON	44011	2748	A6
4900	NRDV	44011	2748	A6
4900	NRDV	44039	2748	A6
5000	NRDV	44039	2877	A2
9000	NRDV	44039	3007	E7
9000	NRDV	44039	3008	A1
9400	EatT	44039	3007	E7
9400	EatT	44044	3007	E7
14700	GftT	44044	3142	E6
SR-83 Center Rd				
-	AVON	44011	2618	A7
800	AVLK	44012	2618	A5
800	AVON	44012	2618	A5
2000	AVON	44011	2748	A6
4200	NRDV	44011	2748	A6
4200	NRDV	44039	2748	A6
SR-83 Chester Rd				
36000	AVON	44011	2618	A7
SR-83C				
-	EatT	44035	3007	E1
-	EatT	44039	3007	E1
-	EatT	44044	3007	E2
-	NRDV	44039	3007	E1
SR-83C Butternut Ridge Rd				
10800	EatT	44035	3007	E2
10800	EatT	44039	3007	E2
10800	EatT	44044	3007	E2
10800	NRDV	44039	3007	E2
SR-84 Bank St				
800	PNVL	44077	2146	C2
800	PnvT	44077	2146	C2
SR-84 Bishop Rd				
2400	WKLF	44092	2374	B4
2700	WBHL	44092	2374	B5
SR-84 Chardon Rd				
21000	EUCL	44117	2498	B1
23500	EUCL	44143	2498	C1
23800	RDHT	44143	2498	C1
24400	RDHT	44143	2373	D7
26500	RDHT	44143	2374	B6
27200	WBHL	44092	2374	B6
SR-84 Johnnycake Ridge Rd				
10	PnvT	44077	2146	B3
7300	MNTR	44060	2251	B5
8000	MNTR	44060	2252	B2
8400	KDHL	44060	2252	B2
9300	MNTR	44060	2253	A2
9600	CcdT	44060	2253	A1
9800	CcdT	44060	2145	C6
9800	CcdT	44077	2145	C6
9800	CcdT	44077	2253	C1
10600	CcdT	44077	2146	C2
38200	WLBY	44094	2250	E7
38500	WLBY	44094	2251	C4
38900	MNTR	44094	2251	B5
SR-84 E Main St				
10	MDSN	44057	2044	D1
400	MadT	44057	2044	D1
SR-84 W Main St				
10	MDSN	44057	2044	B1
700	MadT	44057	2043	E2
700	MDSN	44057	2043	E2
SR-84 Ridge Rd				
28700	WKLF	44092	2374	B4
30600	WKLF	44092	2375	A3
30600	WLBY	44094	2375	A3
36800	WLBY	44094	2250	C7
SR-84 S Ridge Rd				
2600	PryT	44077	2041	C7
2600	PryT	44081	2041	C7
2800	PryT	44081	2042	B5
4400	PRRY	44081	2042	D4
4500	PryT	44057	2042	D4
5000	MadT	44057	2043	A3
5000	MadT	44081	2043	A3
5000	PryT	44057	2043	A3
5000	PryT	44081	2043	A3
5900	MDSN	44057	2043	E2
7100	MadT	44057	2044	D1
7100	MDSN	44057	2044	D1
7300	MadT	44057	1942	E7
7400	MadT	44057	1943	A7
7800	HpfT	44041	1943	B7
7800	HpfT	44057	1943	B7
SR-84 S Ridge Rd E				
10	GNVA	44041	1944	B6
500	GnvT	44041	1944	B6
SR-84 S Ridge Rd W				
10	GNVA	44041	1944	B6
200	HpfT	44041	1944	B6
5800	HpfT	44041	1943	C7
6800	HpfT	44057	1943	B7
6800	MadT	44057	1943	B7
SR-84 Riverside Dr				
400	PnvT	44077	2146	E2
800	PnvT	44077	2147	A1
1400	PryT	44077	2147	B1
2500	PryT	44077	2041	C7
2500	PryT	44081	2041	C7
SR-84 S State St				
400	PNVL	44077	2146	C2
700	PnvT	44077	2146	C2
SR-84 E Walnut Av				
200	PNVL	44077	2146	C1
400	PnvT	44077	2146	D2
SR-86 Painesville Warren Rd				
6100	CcdT	44077	2146	C3
6100	PnvT	44077	2146	C3
12000	CcdT	44077	2147	A5
12400	LryT	44077	2147	B5
13000	LryT	44077	2255	E1
13000	LryT	44077	2256	A1
14000	LryT	44086	2256	C3
14700	LryT	44086	2257	A3
14800	TpnT	44024	2257	A3
14800	TpnT	44086	2257	A3
SR-86 Plank Rd				
7800	LryT	44086	2257	B4
7800	TpnT	44024	2257	B4
7800	TpnT	44086	2257	B4
8200	TpnT	44064	2257	E6
8300	MtlT	44064	2257	E6
SR-86 N State St				
10	PNVL	44077	2040	B6
SR-86 S State St				
10	PNVL	44077	2040	B7
10	PNVL	44077	2146	C2
700	PnvT	44077	2146	C2
SR-87				
-	CLEV	44115	2625	B4
SR-87 Broadway Av				
800	CLEV	44115	2625	A4
SR-87 Buckeye Rd				
8400	CLEV	44104	2626	A5
SR-87 E Center St				
13800	BURT	44021	2766	D2
14000	BtnT	44021	2766	B1
SR-87 W Center St				
13500	BtnT	44021	2766	A1
13500	BURT	44021	2766	A1
SR-87 Chagrin Blvd				
25600	BHWD	44122	2758	E1
26900	BHWD	44122	2759	A1
26900	ORNG	44122	2759	A1
26900	WDMR	44122	2759	A1
28900	ORNG	44124	2759	B1
28900	PRPK	44124	2759	B1
29800	PRPK	44122	2759	C1
SR-87 E High St				
15900	MDFD	44062	2767	D2
SR-87 W High St				
15300	MDFD	44062	2767	B2
15400	MdfT	44062	2767	B2
SR-87 Kinsman Rd				
7000	HGVL	44022	2761	A2
7000	HGVL	44072	2761	A2
7000	RslT	44022	2761	A2
7000	RslT	44072	2761	A2
8200	RslT	44072	2762	A1
9600	NbyT	44072	2763	A1
9600	RslT	44072	2763	A1
10100	NbyT	44065	2763	C1
10400	NbyT	44065	2764	B2
12000	NbyT	44065	2765	A1
12100	NbyT	44021	2765	A1
12400	BtnT	44021	2765	E1
14000	BtnT	44021	2766	C1
14000	BURT	44021	2766	C1
14300	BtnT	44062	2766	D2
15000	BtnT	44062	2767	A2
15100	MDFD	44062	2767	B2
15100	MdfT	44062	2767	B2
SR-87 Ontario St				
1900	CLEV	44114	2624	E3
1900	CLEV	44115	2624	E3
2000	CLEV	44113	2624	E3
SR-87 Orange Av				
1400	CLEV	44115	2625	A4
SR-87 E Park St				
14500	BURT	44021	2766	B1
SR-87 N Park St				
13800	BURT	44021	2636	B7
SR-87 W Park St				
-	BURT	44021	2766	A1
SR-87 Pinetree Rd				
30400	PRPK	44124	2759	D1
SR-87 Richmond Rd				
2900	BHWD	44122	2628	E7
3000	BHWD	44122	2758	E1
SR-87 Shaker Blvd				
10000	CLEV	44104	2626	D5
11000	CLEV	44120	2626	D5
13300	CLEV	44120	2627	C6
13400	SRHT	44120	2627	A5
18400	SRHT	44122	2627	E6
19500	SRHT	44122	2628	C6
23100	BHWD	44122	2628	D6
SR-87 Woodland Av				
2500	CLEV	44115	2625	C4
3800	CLEV	44104	2625	E4
7500	CLEV	44104	2626	B5
SR-87 S Woodland Rd				
32900	PRPK	44124	2759	E1
32900	PRPK	44124	2760	B2
33200	PRPK	44022	2760	B2
33700	HGVL	44022	2760	A2
33700	MDHL	44022	2760	A2
45800	HGVL	44022	2761	A2
45800	HGVL	44072	2761	A2
SR-91 Darrow Rd				
7300	HDSN	44236	3154	E7
7700	TwbT	44236	3154	E6
7900	TNBG	44087	3154	E7
7900	TNBG	44236	3154	E5
7900	TwbT	44087	3154	E5
8700	TNBG	44087	3155	A2
9200	TNBG	44087	3020	A6
9700	TNBG	44087	3019	E5
10300	SLN	44139	3020	A3
10300	TNBG	44139	3020	A3
SR-91 Som Center Rd				
-	WLBY	44094	2250	B5
-	WLBY	44095	2250	B5
200	MAYF	44092	2500	A1
200	MAYF	44094	2500	A1
200	MAYF	44143	2500	A2
200	WBHL	44092	2500	A1
200	WBHL	44094	2500	A1
400	ETLK	44095	2250	B5
400	TMLK	44095	2250	A2
700	MAYF	44040	2500	A4
900	MDHT	44124	2500	A6
900	MDHT	44143	2500	A6
1500	MDHT	44124	2630	A1
1600	GSML	44124	2630	A1
1900	GSML	44040	2630	A7
2000	HGVL	44022	2630	A3
2000	HGVL	44040	2630	A3
2000	PRPK	44124	2630	A3
2300	PRPK	44022	2630	A4
2500	WBHL	44094	2375	A6
2600	HGVL	44124	2630	A4
2900	WBHL	44092	2375	A7
3300	HGVL	44022	2760	A1
3300	PRPK	44124	2760	A2
3400	PRPK	44022	2760	A2
3600	MDHL	44022	2760	A2
3600	MDHL	44124	2760	A2
4200	MDHL	44022	2759	E6
4900	SLN	44022	2759	E7
4900	SLN	44139	2759	E7
5100	SLN	44139	2760	A7
5200	SLN	44139	2889	A6
5200	WLBY	44094	2375	A1
7000	SLN	44139	3020	A1
7600	TNBG	44087	3020	A3
7600	TNBG	44139	3020	A3

Cleveland Street Index

STREET Block City ZIP Map# Grid

SR-94 River Rd
10 HkyT 44133 3149 A5
10 HkyT 44233 3149 A5
10 NRYN 44133 3149 A5
SR-94 State Rd
4200 CLEV 44109 2754 C4
4900 CLEV 44134 2754 C7
4900 PRMA 44109 2754 C7
4900 PRMA 44134 2754 C7
5400 PRMA 44134 2883 C3
7000 PRMA 44129 2883 B6
7400 PRMA 44134 3014 B1
7800 NRYN 44134 3014 A4
7800 NRYN 44134 3014 A2
14200 NRYN 44133 3149 A2
20000 HkyT 44133 3149 B5
20000 HkyT 44233 3149 B5
SR-113
- ELYR 44035 2874 C4
- EyrT 44035 2874 B4
SR-113 Center Ridge Rd
19400 RKRV 44116 2621 D7
20600 FWPK 44116 2751 C1
20600 FWPK 44126 2751 C1
20600 RKRV 44116 2751 C1
22800 WTLK 44116 2751 A1
22800 WTLK 44145 2751 A1
23100 WTLK 44145 2750 B2
27200 WTLK 44145 2749 A6
31400 NRDV 44039 2749 A7
31400 NRDV 44145 2749 A7
31600 NRDV 44039 2748 E7
31600 NRDV 44039 2877 B3
36100 NRDV 44039 2876 D4
SR-113 Cleveland St
700 ELYR 44035 2875 E5
900 ELYR 44039 2875 E5
900 NRDV 44039 2875 E5
SR-113 John F Kennedy Mem Pkwy
- ELYR 44035 2874 C4
- ELYR 44035 2875 E4
- EyrT 44035 2874 C4
SR-113 E Main St
100 SAHT 44001 2872 C7
300 AhtT 44001 2872 D7
SR-113 W Main St
100 SAHT 44001 2872 B7
400 SAHT 44001 3003 A1
500 NRsT 44001 3003 A1
SR-113 Telegraph Rd
43100 ELYR 44035 2874 B4
43300 ELYR 44035 2873 E5
43300 EyrT 44035 2873 E5
43300 EyrT 44035 2874 A5
43400 AhtT 44035 2873 C6
44000 AhtT 44001 2873 C6
46100 AhtT 44001 2872 E6
SR-113 Wooster Rd
1500 RKRV 44116 2621 E5
2500 LKWD 44126 2621 E7
2500 RKRV 44126 2621 E7
SR-166 Rock Creek Rd
13900 HmbT 44024 2381 C2
14300 HmbT 44024 2256 E7
14800 HmbT 44024 2257 A6
14800 MdT 44024 2257 B5
14800 TpnT 44024 2257 B5
15500 TpnT 44086 2257 D3
SR-168 S Cheshire Rd
- BtnT 44021 2766 B2
- BtnT 44062 2766 B2
- BURT 44021 2766 B2
SR-168 S Cheshire St
- BURT 44021 2766 B1
14700 BtnT 44021 2766 B2
14700 BtnT 44062 2766 B2
SR-168 Tavern Rd
14800 BtnT 44021 2766 E5
14800 BtnT 44062 2766 E5
14800 BURT 44021 2766 E5
16300 BtnT 44021 2767 A7
16300 BtnT 44062 2767 A7
16300 TroT 44021 2767 A7
16300 TroT 44062 2767 A7
SR-174 Chagrin River Rd
10 GSML 44094 2500 C1
- WBHL 44094 2500 C1
400 GSML 44040 2500 D6
1500 GSML 44040 2630 E2
2000 HGVL 44022 2630 E3
2000 HGVL 44040 2630 E3
SR-174 Old Mill Rd
- GSML 44040 2630 E1
SR-174 Ridge Rd
37700 WLBY 44094 2250 E7
SR-174 River Rd
- WBHL 44094 2250 D7
- WLBY 44094 2250 D7
2100 WBHL 44094 2375 D6
2900 GSML 44040 2500 C1
2900 GSML 44094 2500 C1
2900 WBHL 44094 2500 C1
SR-174 River St
4100 WLBY 44094 2250 E5
SR-175 E 260th St
200 EUCL 44132 2373 E4
1500 EUCL 44117 2373 E5
1500 EUCL 44143 2373 E5
SR-175 Cannon Rd
27200 BDHT 44146 2888 A2
27200 SLN 44139 2888 A2
27300 SLN 44146 2888 A2
SR-175 Richmond Rd
- EUCL 44132 2373 E7
100 EUCL 44117 2373 E7
100 EUCL 44143 2373 E7
100 RDHT 44117 2373 E6
100 RDHT 44143 2373 E6
300 RDHT 44143 2498 E1
700 LNHT 44124 2498 E7
700 LNHT 44143 2498 E5
1500 LNHT 44124 2628 E1
2000 BHWD 44122 2628 E7
2000 BHWD 44124 2628 E3
3000 BHWD 44122 2758 E3
3700 HIHL 44122 2758 E1
3700 WVHT 44122 2758 E1
4300 WVHT 44022 2758 E5
4400 WVHT 44128 2758 E5
4800 BDHT 44128 2758 E7
4800 BDHT 44146 2758 E7
5500 BDHT 44146 2888 A1
5500 SLN 44139 2888 A1
25700 BDHT 44146 2887 E1

SR-175 Richmond Rd
26000 SLN 44146 2888 A1
SR-176 Broadview Rd
4800 RchT 44286 3149 E6
4800 RchT 44286 3150 A7
4900 CLEV 44109 2754 D7
4900 CLEV 44134 2754 D7
5000 PRMA 44134 2754 D7
5300 BWHT 44147 3149 E6
5300 PRMA 44134 2883 E6
5300 RchT 44147 3149 E5
5300 RchT 44233 3149 E6
6300 PRMA 44131 2883 E4
6300 SVHL 44131 2883 E4
7400 PRMA 44131 3014 E3
7400 PRMA 44134 3014 E3
7400 SVHL 44131 3014 E3
7800 BWHT 44131 3014 E3
7800 BWHT 44134 3014 E3
7800 BWHT 44147 3014 E7
SR-176 Brookpark Rd
1500 CLEV 44109 2754 D7
1500 CLEV 44134 2754 D7
1500 PRMA 44109 2754 D7
1500 PRMA 44134 2754 D7
SR-176 Jennings Frwy
- CLEV - 2754 E3
- CLEV - 2755 A5
SR-237 W Bagley Rd
10 BERA 44017 2880 C6
SR-237 Berea Frwy
- BKPK - 2751 E7
- BKPK - 2880 E1
- CLEV - 2880 E1
- CLEV 44142 2880 D3
SR-237 Brookpark Rd
18200 BKPK 44135 2751 E7
18200 BKPK 44135 2752 A7
18200 BKPK 44142 2751 E7
18200 BKPK 44142 2752 A7
18200 CLEV 44135 2751 E7
18200 CLEV 44135 2752 A7
18200 CLEV 44142 2751 E7
SR-237 W Clifton Blvd
1100 LKWD 44107 2622 A4
SR-237 Front St
200 BERA 44017 2880 C6
SR-237 Henry St
10 BERA 44017 2880 B7
SR-237 Kolthoff Dr
6500 BERA 44017 2880 C4
6500 BERA 44142 2880 C4
6500 BKPK 44142 2880 C4
SR-237 Mulberry St
200 BERA 44017 2880 C6
SR-237 Prospect Rd
8500 BERA 44017 3011 B2
8500 SGVL 44017 3011 B2
8500 SGVL 44149 3011 B3
SR-237 Prospect St
10 BERA 44017 2880 C5
200 BERA 44017 3011 B7
700 SGVL 44017 3011 B2
700 SGVL 44149 3011 B2
SR-237 Riverside Dr
1500 LKWD 44107 2622 A6
2300 CLEV 44107 2622 A7
17100 CLEV 44111 2622 B7
17100 LKWD 44111 2622 B7
SR-237 Rocky River Dr
3100 CLEV 44107 2622 B7
3100 CLEV 44111 2622 B7
3100 LKWD 44107 2622 B7
3100 LKWD 44111 2622 B7
3200 CLEV 44111 2752 B1
3900 CLEV 44135 2752 A5
4800 CLEV 44135 2751 E6
4900 BKPK 44135 2751 E7
4900 BKPK 44142 2751 E7
4900 CLEV 44142 2751 E7
SR-237 N Rocky River Dr
800 BERA 44017 2880 C3
800 BKPK 44017 2880 C3
800 BKPK 44142 2880 C4
SR-252 Columbia Rd
10 ClbT 44028 3145 A5
10 LvpT 44028 3145 A5
10 LvpT 44280 3144 E7
10 LvpT 44280 3145 A5
300 BYVL 44140 2620 C5
600 WTLK 44140 2620 C5
600 WTLK 44145 2620 C7
1700 WTLK 44145 2750 D6
3200 NOSD 44070 2750 D6
3200 NOSD 44145 2750 C3
3200 WTLK 44070 2750 D6
5900 NOSD 44070 2879 C2
6200 OmsT 44070 2879 C2
6200 OmsT 44138 2879 C2
8000 ODFL 44138 2879 B7
9000 ODFL 44138 3010 B1
9700 ClbT 44028 3010 B2
9700 ODFL 44028 3010 B2
SR-252 Great Northern Blvd
4500 NOSD 44070 2750 C7
5000 NOSD 44070 2879 C1
SR-252 Lorain Rd
24600 NOSD 44070 2750 C6
SR-252 Main St
7900 ODFL 44138 2879 C5
SR-252 E River Rd
9800 ClbT 44028 3010 A7
9800 ClbT 44138 3010 C2
9800 ODFL 44138 3010 C2
14000 ClbT 44028 3145 A5
17700 LvpT 44028 3145 A5
17700 LvpT 44280 3145 A5
SR-252 Sprague Rd
24400 ClbT 44028 3010 B3
24400 ClbT 44138 3010 B3
24400 ODFL 44138 3010 B3
SR-254 Detroit Rd
- LKWD 44107 2621 E5
- RKRV 44116 2621 E5
4700 SFLD 44035 2746 E5
4700 SFLD 44054 2746 E5
5400 AVON 44011 2747 A5
5400 SFLD 44011 2747 A5
5400 SFLD 44035 2747 A5
5400 SFLD 44054 2747 A5
19000 RKRV 44116 2621 E6
22800 WTLK 44116 2621 A6
22800 WTLK 44145 2621 A1
23300 WTLK 44145 2620 A7

SR-254 Detroit Rd
27300 WTLK 44145 2619 C7
30400 WTLK 44145 2749 B1
31400 AVON 44145 2749 A1
32000 AVON 44011 2749 B1
32200 AVON 44011 2748 E1
SR-254 North Ridge Rd E
2200 ShfT 44035 2745 E6
2200 ShfT 44055 2745 E6
2300 ShfT 44055 2746 A6
3200 SFLD 44035 2746 C6
3200 SFLD 44054 2746 C6
3200 ShfT 44035 2746 C6
3200 ShfT 44054 2746 C6
SR-254 Sloane Av
1300 LKWD 44107 2622 A4
SR-283 Andrews Rd
5500 MONT 44060 2143 E1
6100 MNTR 44060 2143 E3
SR-283 Lake Shore Blvd
500 PnvT 44077 2039 C6
600 MNTR 44060 2039 C6
600 PnvT 44060 2039 B7
7000 MNTR 44060 2143 B4
7700 MONT 44060 2143 E2
8000 MNTR 44060 2144 A1
8000 MONT 44060 2144 E1
9100 MNTR 44060 2038 E7
13600 BTNH 44108 2497 A1
13600 BTNH 44110 2497 A1
13700 BTNH 44108 2372 A7
13700 BTNH 44110 2372 A7
13700 CLEV 44110 2372 A7
16900 CLEV 44119 2372 D6
18400 EUCL 44119 2372 E4
19500 EUCL 44119 2373 A3
19900 EUCL 44123 2373 C1
24800 EUCL 44123 2373 D1
25700 EUCL 44132 2248 E7
27200 EUCL 44132 2249 A7
28100 WLWK 44095 2249 C5
33000 ETLK 44095 2249 D3
33500 LKLN 44095 2249 D3
34400 TMLK 44095 2249 E2
34700 ETLK 44095 2250 C1
34700 TMLK 44095 2250 A2
35900 ETLK 44095 2142 C7
37700 WLBY 44094 2142 E5
37700 WLBY 44095 2142 E5
38400 WLBY 44094 2143 E1
38800 MNTR 44094 2143 B4
SR-283 Richmond Rd
800 PNVL 44077 2039 E7
800 PnvT 44077 2039 E7
1000 GDRV 44077 2039 D6
SR-283 Richmond St
- PNVL 44077 2039 E7
10 PNVL 44077 2040 A7
600 PnvT 44077 2039 E7
SR-283 River St
600 GDRV 44077 2039 C6
700 PnvT 44077 2039 C6
SR-283 Singer Av
100 GDRV 44077 2039 C6
300 PnvT 44077 2039 C6
SR-291 Engle Rd
5000 BKPK 44135 2752 B7
5000 BKPK 44142 2752 A7
5000 BKPK 44142 2881 A1
5000 CLEV 44135 2752 A7
6400 MDBH 44130 2881 A6
6400 MDBH 44142 2881 A4
7500 MDBH 44130 3012 A1
SR-291 Fowles Rd
16600 MDBH 44130 3012 A1
SR-301
- CrIT - 3006 A6
- EatT - 3006 E4
SR-301 Abbe Rd
100 SDLK 44054 2616 E2
500 SFLD 44054 2616 E7
2300 SFLD 44054 2746 E2
4400 SFLD 44035 2746 E5
SR-301 N Abbe Rd
10 ELYR 44035 2875 E2
800 ELYR 44035 2746 E6
1200 SFLD 44035 2746 E6
5000 SFLD 44054 2746 E5
SR-301 S East Byp
- EatT 44035 3006 E3
- EatT 44044 3006 E4
- ELYR 44035 2875 E7
- ELYR 44035 3006 E1
SR-301 John F Kennedy Mem Pkwy
- ELYR 44035 2875 E4
SR-301 Lagrange Rd
- CrIT 44050 3140 E6
11900 CrIT 44035 3005 E7
11900 CrIT 44050 3005 E6
SR-301 Lattasburg Elyria Rd
- CrIT 44044 3140 E3
- CrIT 44050 3140 E1
- LrgT 44050 3140 E5
SR-305 E Wakefield Rd
6900 HRM 44234 3161 B2
6900 HrmT 44234 3161 B2
7100 HrmT 44231 3161 E2
SR-306
- KTLD 44094 2251 C5
- WLBY 44094 2251 C5
SR-306 Broadmoor Rd
- WLBY 44060 2251 D7
- WLBY 44094 2251 D7
8000 MNTR 44060 2251 D7
SR-306 Chillicothe Rd
5000 SRSL 44022 2762 A5
5200 BbgT 44022 2762 A7
5200 BbgT 44023 2762 A7
8800 KTLD 44094 2251 D6
9100 KTLD 44094 2376 E2
9700 KTLD 44094 2377 A7
11000 CsTp 44026 2502 B7
11000 CsTp 44094 2502 A2
11000 KTLD 44094 2502 A2
12700 CsTp 44026 2632 B1
13400 CsTp 44072 2632 A3
13400 RslT 44072 2632 A6
14600 RslT 44072 2762 A7
15000 RslT 44072 2762 A3
16400 BbgT 44023 2891 A6
18400 BbgT 44023 3022 A3
18900 AURA 44023 3022 A3
18900 AURA 44202 3022 A3

SR-306 N Chillicothe Rd
10 AURA 44202 3021 E7
10 AURA 44202 3156 E1
500 AURA 44202 3022 A5
1000 AURA 44023 3022 A3
1000 BbgT 44023 3022 A3
SR-306 S Chillicothe Rd
10 AURA 44202 3156 E1
SR-306 Reynolds Rd
6200 MNTR 44060 2143 C7
7300 MNTR 44060 2251 C1
SR-307 Warner Rd
6700 MadT 44057 2044 E3
6700 MDSN 44057 2044 E3
SR-511
- NRsT 44074 3138 A2
- OBLN 44074 3138 B2
SR-511 Cleveland Oberlin Rd
- OBLN 44074 3139 C2
43700 NRsT 44074 3139 D2
SR-511 E Lorain St
10 OBLN 44074 3138 E2
200 OBLN 44074 3139 A2
600 NRsT 44074 3139 B2
SR-511 W Lorain St
10 OBLN 44074 3138 E2
300 NRsT 44074 3138 C2
SR-528 Chardon-Madison Rd
4300 MadT 44057 2044 B1
4300 MDSN 44057 2044 B3
SR-528 Hubbard Rd
2700 MadT 44057 1942 B7
2700 MDSN 44057 1942 B7
SR-528 N Lake St
10 MDSN 44057 2044 B1
200 MDSN 44057 1942 B7
800 MadT 44057 1942 B6
SR-528 Madison Rd
15900 MdfT 44062 2767 E7
15900 PkmT 44062 2767 E7
SR-528 W Main St
10 MDSN 44057 2044 B1
SR-528 River St
10 MDSN 44057 2044 B1
SR-534 N Broadway
10 GNVA 44041 1944 C4
500 GnvT 44041 1944 C2
SR-534 S Broadway
10 GNVA 44041 1944 B4
SR-534 N Broadway St
700 GNVA 44041 1944 C2
700 GnvT 44041 1944 C2
SR-534 S Broadway St
1200 GNVA 44041 1944 C6
SR-535 East St
600 FTHR 44077 2039 D5
SR-535 Fairport Nursery Rd
10 PnvT 44077 2040 B3
500 FTHR 44077 2039 D4
500 PnvT 44077 2039 E3
SR-535 Richmond St
600 PNVL 44077 2039 E7
600 PnvT 44077 2039 E7
900 FTHR 44077 2039 D6
SR-608 Concord-Hambden Rd
11500 CcdT 44077 2146 D7
11500 CcdT 44077 2254 E1
11900 CcdT 44077 2255 B4
12700 CcdT 44024 2255 C5
12700 HmbT 44024 2255 C5
12700 HmbT 44077 2255 C5
SR-608 Old State Rd
8400 CcdT 44024 2255 C5
8400 CcdT 44077 2255 C5
8400 HmbT 44024 2255 D6
8400 HmbT 44077 2255 C5
8800 HmbT 44024 2380 E1
8800 HmbT 44024 2381 C6
10900 ClrT 44024 2506 C2
10900 HmbT 44024 2506 C2
12100 ClrT 44021 2506 E6
12100 ClrT 44046 2506 E6
12600 ClrT 44021 2636 E1
12600 ClrT 44046 2636 E1
12800 ClrT 44021 2637 A2
12800 ClrT 44046 2637 A2
13400 HtbT 44021 2637 A3
13400 HtbT 44046 2637 A3
13500 MdfT 44021 2637 B5
13500 MdfT 44046 2637 B5
13600 MdfT 44062 2637 B5
14300 MdfT 44062 2767 D1
15000 MDFD 44062 2767 D4
SR-608 N State Av
14700 MDFD 44062 2767 D1
14700 MdfT 44062 2767 D1
SR-608 S State Av
14900 MDFD 44062 2767 D3
15300 MdfT 44062 2767 D4
SR-611
- LORN 44053 2743 D2
SR-611 E 21st St
100 LORN 44052 2745 A1
SR-611 W 21st St
100 LORN 44052 2744 D1
2300 LORN 44053 2744 A1
3300 LORN 44053 2743 E2
SR-611 Colorado Av
- LORN 44054 2615 D7
1400 LORN 44052 2615 D7
3500 SFLD 44054 2615 E7
3900 SFLD 44054 2616 C7
5300 AVON 44011 2617 B7
5300 SFLD 44011 2617 B7
5300 SFLD 44054 2617 B7
37000 AVON 44011 2747 D1
SR-611 Henderson Dr
1700 LORN 44052 2615 B7
1900 LORN 44052 2745 A1
SR-615 Center St
6300 MNTR 44060 2144 B7
7300 MNTR 44060 2252 B1
8200 KDHL 44060 2252 B4
SR-615 Chillicothe Rd
- KDHL 44060 2251 E6
- KDHL 44060 2251 E6
- KTLD 44060 2251 E6
8400 KDHL 44060 2252 A5
8400 KDHL 44094 2252 A5
8400 KTLD 44060 2252 A5
8400 KTLD 44094 2252 A5

SR-615 Chillicothe Rd
8800 KTLD 44094 2251 E6
SR-615 Munson Rd
7700 MNTR 44060 2143 E3
7700 MONT 44060 2143 E3
8000 MNTR 44060 2144 A3
SR-633 Lloyd Rd
200 EUCL 44132 2249 A7
400 EUCL 44132 2374 B2
400 WKLF 44092 2374 B2
SR-640 Vine St
31000 WLWK 44095 2249 E5
32500 ETLK 44095 2249 E4
33700 ETLK 44095 2250 A5
36300 ETLK 44094 2250 B5
36300 WLBY 44094 2250 B5
SR-700 Burton Limaville Rd S
10000 FdmT 44255 3161 A7
10000 HrmT 44231 3161 A7
10000 HrmT 44255 3161 A7
SR-700 S Cheshire Rd
- BtnT 44021 2766 B2
- BtnT 44062 2766 B2
- BURT 44021 2766 B2
SR-700 S Cheshire St
- BURT 44021 2766 B1
14700 BtnT 44021 2766 B2
14700 BtnT 44062 2766 B2
SR-700 Claridon Troy Rd
14400 BtnT 44021 2766 B5
14400 BtnT 44062 2766 B2
16000 TroT 44021 2766 A7
SR-700 Garfield Rd
11400 HRM 44234 3161 A2
11900 HrmT 44234 3161 A1
SR-700 Tavern Rd
14800 BtnT 44021 2766 B2
14800 BtnT 44062 2766 B2
14800 BURT 44021 2766 B2
SR-700 Welshfield Limavle Rd S
10400 FdmT 44255 3161 A7
10400 HrmT 44231 3161 A6
10400 HrmT 44255 3161 A7
11300 HRM 44234 3161 A3
11900 HrmT 44234 3161 A1
Stacey Ct
100 MDSN 44057 2043 E2
Stacy Ct
4800 RDHT 44143 2498 D4
Stacy Ln
7000 CsTp 44026 2501 A5
7000 GSML 44040 2501 A5
Stadium Dr
6900 BKVL 44141 3016 A6
Stafford Av
19200 MPHT 44137 2886 E1
19800 MPHT 44137 2887 A1
Stafford Dr
400 ELYR 44035 2875 D2
6000 NOSD 44070 2878 C2
6700 MDHT 44124 2630 A1
8400 SGVL 44149 3011 E3
Stafford Rd
8800 BbgT 44023 2891 C2
9400 AbnT 44023 2892 B2
9400 BbgT 44023 2892 A2
10600 AbnT 44023 2893 A2
11800 AbnT 44021 2893 E1
11800 AbnT 44255 2893 E1
Staffordshire Ct
16700 AbnT 44021 2893 B1
16700 AbnT 44023 2893 B1
Stage Av
10 PNVL 44077 2039 E7
Stage One Rd
26700 RDHT 44143 2498 E1
26700 RDHT 44143 2499 A1
Staghorn Dr
24300 BDHT 44146 2887 D3
Stag Thicket Ln
16900 SGVL 44136 3146 E3
Stallion Ct
39000 AVON 44011 2747 B6
Stamford Av
7500 MNTR 44060 2251 C3
Stamford Ct
10100 SGVL 44136 3012 C4
Stamm Rd
9800 FdmT 44231 3160 E7
9800 FdmT 44255 3160 E7
9800 HrmT 44231 3160 E7
Stanard Av
5300 CLEV 44103 2495 D7
Stanbury Rd
6000 PRMA 44129 2882 E4
Standish Av
5300 PRMA 44134 2883 C4
14800 MDFD 44062 2767 C2
Stanfield Dr
2400 PRMA 44134 2883 C6
12900 MsnT 44024 2634 E2
Stanford Av
500 ELYR 44035 2875 C7
3500 CLEV 44109 2754 C4
4000 LORN 44053 2744 A4
20400 FWPK 44126 2751 C2
Stanford Dr
2200 WKLF 44092 2374 C4
Stanford Pl
300 BWHT 44147 3149 C3
Stanford Rd
100 BERA 44017 2880 B7
5700 BosT 44067 3152 C6
5700 BosT 44141 3152 D6
5700 SgHT 44141 3152 D6
6500 NCtT 44141 3152 D6
6800 NCtT 44067 3152 E6
6800 SgHT 44067 3152 E6
23300 SRHT 44122 2628 C6
Stanford St
1800 TNBG 44087 3154 C2
1800 TwbT 44087 3154 C2
Stang Rd
43500 AhtT 44001 2873 C3
43500 AhtT 44035 2873 C3
43500 EyrT 44035 2873 C3
Stanhope Rd
3700 SELD 44118 2628 A3
3700 SELD 44121 2628 A3
Stanley Av
5000 MPHT 44128 2757 B7
5000 MPHT 44137 2757 B7

Stanley Dr
13900 BtnT 44021 2635 C5
Stanley Ln
11200 TNBG 44087 3020 B4
Stanmary Dr
200 BERA 44017 3011 C1
Stanridge Rd
10 CNFL 44022 2760 E5
10 CNFL 44022 2761 A5
Stansbury Dr
5000 MDHL 44022 2759 D7
5000 ORNG 44022 2759 D7
5000 SLN 44022 2759 D7
5000 SLN 44139 2759 D7
St Anthonys Wy
- AVON 44011 2748 D4
Stanwell Dr
800 HDHT 44143 2499 C6
900 MDHT 44124 2499 C6
900 MDHT 44143 2499 C6
Stanwich St
2700 ShvT 44255 3158 A7
Stanwood Rd
1800 ECLE 44112 2497 B5
Stapleton Dr
10500 SGVL 44136 3012 B4
Star Av
7400 CLEV 44103 2495 E7
7400 CLEV 44103 2496 A7
N Star Dr
12600 NRYN 44133 3147 E4
12800 SGVL 44133 3147 E4
12800 SGVL 44136 3147 E4
N Star Rd
9200 KTLD 44094 2376 E1
Starboard Dr
36400 ETLK 44095 2142 D7
Starboard Cove
31800 AVLK 44012 2618 E1
Starburst Rd
8100 MNTR 44060 2144 A3
Starbush Ct
- AbnT 44255 2893 D6
Stardust Tr
10 AMHT 44001 2744 B7
Stargate Dr
100 ELYR 44035 3006 D2
Stark Dr
2700 WBHL 44094 2375 A6
6000 BKPK 44142 2881 C2
Stark St
700 SDLK 44054 2616 A4
Starkweather Av
7000 CLEV 44113 2625 A6
800 CLEV 44113 2624 E6
Starlight Dr
10 PRMA 44131 2883 E6
10 PRMA 44134 2883 E6
10 SVHL 44131 2883 E6
100 SVHL 44131 2884 A6
4300 CLEV 44109 2755 A5
8800 MCDN 44056 3018 C6
Starling Ct
10 ELYR 44035 2875 D7
Starlite Dr
700 BERA 44017 3011 A2
700 SGVL 44017 3011 A2
13300 BKPK 44142 2881 D3
Starr Cir
1300 BWHT 44147 3149 D4
Starview Dr
300 BNWK 44212 3146 E7
Stary Dr
3800 PRMA 44134 3014 B1
N State Av
14700 MDFD 44062 2767 D1
14700 MdfT 44062 2767 D1
N State Av SR-608
14700 MDFD 44062 2767 D1
14700 MdfT 44062 2767 D1
S State Av
14900 MDFD 44062 2767 D3
15300 MdfT 44062 2767 D4
S State Av SR-608
14900 MDFD 44062 2767 D3
15300 MdfT 44062 2767 D4
State Rd
10 HkyT 44133 3149 B5
10 HkyT 44233 3149 B7
10 NRYN 44133 3149 A5
1400 VmnT 44089 2740 E7
1400 VmnT 44089 2869 E4
4200 CLEV 44109 2754 C7
4700 FrnT 44889 2869 E7
4700 VmnT 44889 2869 E7
4900 CLEV 44134 2754 C7
4900 PRMA 44109 2754 C7
4900 PRMA 44134 2754 C7
5400 PRMA 44134 2883 C2
7000 PRMA 44129 2883 B6
7400 PRMA 44134 3014 B2
7800 NRYN 44133 3014 A6
7800 NRYN 44134 3014 A2
State Rd SR-60
1400 VmnT 44089 2740 E7
1400 VmnT 44089 2869 E4
4700 FrnT 44889 2869 E7
4700 VmnT 44889 2869 E7
State Rd SR-94
4200 CLEV 44109 2754 C7
4900 CLEV 44134 2754 C7
4900 PRMA 44109 2754 C7
4900 PRMA 44134 2754 C7
5400 PRMA 44134 2883 C2
7000 PRMA 44129 2883 B6
7400 PRMA 44134 3014 B2
7800 NRYN 44133 3014 A6
7800 NRYN 44134 3014 A2
14200 NRYN 44133 3149 A5
20000 HkyT 44133 3149 B5
20000 HkyT 44233 3149 B5
State St
500 ELYR 44035 3006 A2
800 VMLN 44089 2740 E6
1100 GFTN 44044 3142 B5
1200 VmnT 44089 2740 E7
7800 GTVL 44231 3161 E5
7800 HrmT 44231 3161 E5
State St SR-60
800 VMLN 44089 2740 E6
1200 VmnT 44089 2740 E7
State St SR-82
7800 GTVL 44231 3161 E5
7800 HrmT 44231 3161 E5

N State St
300 PNVL 44077 2040 B7
900 PNVL 44077 2039 E5
N State St SR-86
10 PNVL 44077 2040 B7
S State St
10 PNVL 44077 2040 B7
10 PNVL 44077 2146 C2
700 PnvT 44077 2146 C2
S State St SR-84
400 PNVL 44077 2146 C2
700 PnvT 44077 2146 C2
S State St SR-86
10 PNVL 44077 2040 B7
10 PNVL 44077 2146 C2
700 PnvT 44077 2146 C2
Station Rd
10 ClbT 44280 3144 B7
10 LvpT 44280 3144 B7
9800 ClbT 44028 3009 C7
9800 ClbT 44138 3009 C2
9800 OmsT 44138 3009 C2
13000 BKVL 44141 3016 E7
13700 MdfT 44021 2637 A5
13700 MdfT 44062 2637 A5
14200 ClbT 44028 3144 B4
Station St
8400 MNTR 44060 2144 B7
32900 SLN 44139 2888 E5
32900 SLN 44139 2889 A5
Statten Ct
1500 PnvT 44077 2041 B5
Staunton Dr
1200 PRMA 44134 2883 E3
Staunton Rd
1700 CVHT 44118 2627 E2
2000 UNHT 44118 2627 E2
Stearns Rd
- CLEV 44106 2626 D3
5700 NOSD 44070 2878 D2
6500 NOSD 44138 2878 C3
6500 OmsT 44070 2878 C3
6500 OmsT 44138 2878 C7
Steel Av
- LORN 44055 2745 D6
- ShfT 44055 2745 D6
Steele Av
100 PNVL 44077 2146 C1
Steelton St
100 CrIT 44035 3005 E3
Steelwood Ln
7200 CsTp 44026 2631 B1
Steeple Chase
100 WBHL 44092 2374 B5
39000 AVON 44011 2747 A6
Steeplechase Dr
- MDFD 44062 2767 E1
8200 MNTR 44060 2251 C4
Steeplechase Ln
12200 SGVL 44149 3011 A6
Steeple Chase Run
100 NHFD 44067 3018 A3
Steep Rock Dr
400 SgHT 44067 3017 D5
Steinbeck Ct
6600 NRDV 44039 2877 D4
Steinway Av
9400 CLEV 44104 2626 B5
Steinway Blvd
15200 MPHT 44137 2886 B3
Stella Ln
10800 AbnT 44255 2892 E7
10800 AbnT 44255 2893 A7
Stephanie Dr
8600 NRYN 44133 3014 A3
Stephanie Ln
5900 SLN 44139 2888 D3
Stephen Av
24300 EUCL 44123 2373 C3
24800 EUCL 44132 2373 D3
Stephen Rd
25000 OKWD 44146 3018 D2
Stephens Wy
- MsnT 44024 2503 E3
Steris Wy
5900 MNTR 44060 2144 E2
Sterling Av
10 PNVL 44077 2146 C1
5600 MPHT 44137 2886 C2
Sterling Cir
300 BERA 44017 2879 E7
300 BERA 44017 2880 A7
Sterling Ct
9600 TNBG 44087 3020 B6
Sterling Dr
- PRPK 44124 2629 A7
- PRPK 44124 2759 A1
Sterling Rd
600 WKLF 44092 2249 A7
2800 LORN 44052 2615 C5
Sterling Wy
20300 SGVL 44149 3146 B1
Sterling Glen Ln
17700 AbnT 44023 2892 B5
Sterncrest Dr
10 MDHL 44022 2759 D5
10 ORNG 44022 2759 D5
Sterns St
300 OBLN 44074 3139 A1
Steven Blvd
300 RDHT 44143 2498 D2
Steven Dr
3600 SVHL 44131 2884 B4
Steven David Dr
7900 BERA 44017 3011 A2
7900 SGVL 44017 3011 A2
7900 SGVL 44149 3011 A2
Stevens Blvd
100 ETLK 44095 2249 E3
100 LKLN 44095 2249 E2
34000 ETLK 44095 2250 C4
36200 WLBY 44094 2250 B4
Stevens St
4600 LORN 44053 2743 D2
Stevenson Rd
800 CLEV 44110 2497 C2
Stevenson St
5100 RDHT 44143 2498 E3
5100 RDHT 44143 2499 A3
Stewart Av
9000 CLEV 44108 2496 B5
Stewart Ct
- OBLN 44074 3139 A3
25400 OKWD 44146 2887 D7

STREET
Block City ZIP Map# Grid

Stewart Dr
29300 NOSD 44070 2878 C2
Stick Rd
48600 BhmT 44001 2871 D7
Stickney Av
3500 CLEV 44109 2754 C5
4100 CLEV 44144 2754 B6
Stillbrooke Dr
14600 SGVL 44136 3146 E1
Stillman Rd
2000 CVHT 44118 2627 B3
Stillson Av
2900 CLEV 44105 2755 B1
Still Water Blvd
400 ELYR 44035 3007 A2
400 NRDV 44035 3007 A1
500 EatT 44035 3007 A2
Still Water Ct
- CcdT 44077 2255 A3
Stillwater Ct
1400 BWHT 44147 3015 A6
Stillwater Dr
14900 RslT 44022 2761 D2
14900 RslT 44072 2761 D2
Stillwater Ln
30100 SLN 44139 2759 C7
30100 SLN 44139 2888 C1
Stillwell Rd
14500 ClrT 44024 2506 E5
14500 ClrT 44024 2507 A5
15200 HtbT 44024 2507 B5
15200 HtbT 44046 2507 B5
Stillwood Av
15700 CLEV 44111 2752 C1
Stilmore Rd
4000 SELD 44118 2628 A2
4000 SELD 44121 2628 A2
Stimson Ct
3100 CLEV 44109 2754 C4
Stirling Ct
3600 CLEV 44115 2625 C3
Stirling Dr
400 HDHT 44143 2499 C3
Stirling Rd
1600 MadT 44057 1843 A7
1600 MadT 44057 1942 A1
Stirrup Ct
8300 MNTR 44060 2251 D4
St James Tr
- AVON 44011 2748 D5
Stock Av
6400 CLEV 44102 2624 A7
Stockbridge Av
15500 CLEV 44128 2757 B3
Stockbridge Dr
12300 CsTp 44026 2501 C6
Stockbridge Rd
7900 MNTR 44060 2251 C4
Stockholm Rd
3200 SRHT 44120 2627 C7
Stockton Av
19100 MPHT 44137 2886 E1
19800 MPHT 44137 2887 A1
Stockton Cir
200 MCDN 44056 3018 A6
Stockton Dr
- NbyT 44065 2634 A5
Stockton Ln
17500 BbgT 44023 2891 D4
Stockwell St
10 PNVL 44077 2146 B2
Stockwood Dr
- SLN 44139 3020 C1
Stoer Rd
3500 SRHT 44122 2757 E2
Stokes Blvd
- CLEV 44120 2626 D4
1900 CLEV 44106 2626 C3
2100 CLEV 44104 2626 D3
Stone Av
5400 CLEV 44102 2624 A4
Stone Cr
- MDHT 44143 2500 A6
100 MDHT 44124 2500 A6
Stone Ct
1300 WTLK 44145 2620 B7
2600 CLEV 44113 2624 C5
Stone Rd
7100 INDE 44131 2884 E5
7300 INDE 44131 2885 A5
9600 VLVW 44125 2885 C4
14400 NbyT 44065 2634 D7
14400 NbyT 44065 2764 D1
Stone Arbor Ln
- BHIT 44212 3145 E7
Stonebriar Ln
- NRDV 44039 2877 B7
- NRDV 44039 3008 B1
Stonebridge Ct
5200 SLN 44139 2759 C7
Stone Bridge Dr
200 SgHT 44067 3017 D5
Stonebridge Dr
- WLBY 44094 2143 A5
400 AMHT 44001 2872 C1
E Stonebrooke Ct
300 ORNG 44022 2759 B6
W Stonebrooke Dr
- SLN 44022 2759 B7
- SLN 44139 2759 B7
10 ORNG 44022 2759 B7
Stonebrooke Ovl
100 ORNG 44022 2759 B6
Stone Canyon Ct
200 HkyT 44233 3149 D6
Stone Creek Dr
37100 NRDV 44039 2876 D2
Stonecreek Dr
10 CFIT 44022 2761 A4
Stone Creek Ln
1600 TNBG 44087 3019 B5
11600 CcdT 44077 2254 D4
Stone Creek Ovl
14700 SGVL 44149 3146 D1
Stonecrest Dr
6300 BKPK 44142 2881 B4
Stonefield Dr
2400 AVON 44011 2747 A2
Stonefield Pl
39300 AVON 44011 2747 A1
Stonegate Cir
- NRDV 44035 3007 C1
27900 WTLK 44145 2749 E4
Stonegate Dr
11500 MsnT 44024 2503 C4
Stoneham Rd
7300 GSML 44040 2630 D2
10900 PMHT 44130 2882 B3
Stonehaven Cir
700 HDSN 44236 3154 A6
Stonehaven Ct
100 BWHT 44147 3149 C3
Stonehaven Dr
200 PNVL 44077 2146 C2
N Stonehaven Dr
300 HDHT 44143 2499 C2
S Stonehaven Dr
300 HDHT 44143 2499 C2
Stonehaven Rd
1600 MadT 44057 1842 E7
1600 MadT 44057 1941 E1
4000 SELD 44118 2628 A2
4000 SELD 44121 2628 A2
Stonehedge Dr
100 ELYR 44035 3006 D3
10100 CcdT 44077 2145 D7
14700 RslT 44072 2761 D1
23800 WTLK 44145 2750 D2
24100 NOSD 44070 2750 D2
24100 NOSD 44145 2750 D2
24100 WTLK 44070 2750 D2
Stonehedge Wy
10 AMHT 44001 2872 C3
Stonehill Ln
10 MDHL 44022 2760 A2
Stone Hill Ovl
800 AURA 44202 3021 B6
Stonehinge Cir
10600 NRYN 44133 3014 A5
Stone Hollow Rd
9900 CcdT 44060 2253 B3
10000 CcdT 44077 2253 C3
Stonelake Dr
1800 BHWD 44122 2628 D3
1800 LNHT 44122 2628 D3
Stoneledge Dr
11100 ClrT 44024 2506 E1
Stoneleigh Rd
3600 CVHT 44121 2497 E4
3600 SELD 44121 2497 E4
Stone Loch Ct
6700 MDBH 44130 2881 A5
Stone Mill Dr
9400 MNTR 44060 2253 A2
Stonepath St
2200 LORN 44052 2744 B1
2200 LORN 44053 2744 B1
Stonepointe Dr
- BERA 44138 2879 E4
Stone Ridge Dr
- KTLD 44094 2376 C5
Stoneridge Rd
7800 MCDN 44056 3154 B5
16300 BbgT 44022 2761 B7
16300 BbgT 44023 2761 B7
16300 CNFL 44022 2761 B7
16300 CyhC 44022 2761 B7
Stoneridge Tr
13400 SGVL 44136 3147 D5
Stone Ridge Wy
- BERA 44017 2879 E5
- BERA 44138 2879 E5
Stones Levee
400 CLEV 44113 2624 E4
Stone's Throw
- WTLK 44145 2750 C1
Stonesthrow Dr
- BERA 44138 2879 E5
Stone Valley Dr
500 AhtT 44001 2873 B2
Stonewood Ct
1000 WTLK 44145 2621 A7
1200 PnvT 44077 2041 A7
7300 MNTR 44060 2252 E1
Stonewood Dr
10 MDHL 44022 2760 A2
Stonewood Ln
6200 SLN 44139 2889 C5
Stonewood Pt
2300 AVON 44011 2747 C1
Stonewycke Dr
10800 CcdT 44077 2146 A5
Stoney Ln
5400 PryT 44077 2041 B7
5400 PryT 44077 2147 B1
Stoney Brook Cir
1100 MCDN 44056 3154 B4
Stoney Brook Ct
18000 BbgT 44023 2890 E6
Stoney Brook Dr
- ELYR 44035 2746 A7
8100 BbgT 44023 2890 E7
8100 BbgT 44023 2891 A6
32200 AVLK 44012 2618 C1
Stoneybrook Dr
8900 BWHT 44147 3015 A6
Stoneybrook Ln
7900 MNTR 44060 2251 E3
Stoney Brook Rd
600 SgHT 44067 3152 C1
Stoneybrook Rd
22900 NOSD 44070 2750 E3
22900 NOSD 44070 2751 A3
Stoney Creek Dr
3000 NRYN 44133 3014 B7
Stoney Creek Ln
9100 PMHT 44130 2882 C5
Stoney Lake Dr
37500 NRDV 44039 2747 C7
37500 NRDV 44039 2876 D1
Stoney Meadow Dr
- NRDV 44039 2747 C6
Stoneyridge Dr
2600 MadT 44057 1942 A4
Stoney Ridge Ln
600 RDHT 44143 2498 E4
Stoney Ridge Rd
2500 AVON 44011 2747 C6
4000 NRDV 44011 2747 C6
4000 NRDV 44039 2747 C6
4800 NRDV 44039 2876 D1
Stoney Run Cir
1700 BWHT 44147 3015 A7
Stoney Run Tr
10 BWHT 44147 3014 E7
10 BWHT 44147 3015 A7
Stoney Springs Dr
12700 ClrT 44024 2635 D1
13400 ClrT 44024 2636 A1
Stonington Ct
800 MCDN 44056 3154 A5
Stonington Dr
1500 HDSN 44236 3154 D7
Stonington Rd
9100 PMHT 44130 2882 C3
Stonybrook Dr
7300 MDBH 44130 2881 C7
7300 MDBH 44130 3012 C1
Stony Brook Ln
32500 SLN 44139 2888 E2
Stony Point Dr
17900 SGVL 44136 3147 C5
Storer Av
3300 CLEV 44109 2754 C1
4500 CLEV 44102 2754 A1
Stormes Dr
11400 PRMA 44130 3013 A2
Storrington Ovl
5500 PRMA 44134 2883 E1
Storrs St
400 PNVL 44077 2040 B6
Story Rd
3900 FWPK 44126 2752 A2
4100 FWPK 44126 2751 E2
18800 FWPK 44116 2751 E1
18800 RKRV 44116 2751 E1
18800 RKRV 44126 2751 E1
Storybook Ln
11800 CsTp 44026 2501 E4
Stoughton Av
9600 CLEV 44104 2626 B6
Stoughton Dr
19400 SGVL 44149 3146 C2
Stover Ln
8800 BKVL 44141 3016 B6
Stow Rd
7600 HDSN 44236 3155 D7
7900 TwbT 44236 3155 D6
8000 TwbT 44087 3155 D6
Stowaway Cove
400 AVLK 44012 2618 E3
Stradford Ct
- AVON 44011 2748 E6
- NRDV 44011 2748 E6
- NRDV 44039 2748 E6
Strandhill Rd
3500 SRHT 44122 2757 D2
3700 CLEV 44122 2757 D3
3700 CLEV 44128 2757 D3
Stratford Av
20500 RKRV 44116 2621 C5
Stratford Cir
6800 MNTR 44060 2143 E6
20600 SGVL 44149 3146 B1
Stratford Ct
10 BHWD 44122 2628 E4
300 AURA 44202 3021 E6
900 MAYF 44143 2500 A5
900 STBR 44241 3156 D7
Stratford Dr
200 BWHT 44147 3150 A4
200 NHFD 44067 3018 B5
6100 PMHT 44130 2882 C3
7800 PRMA 44129 2882 D4
7900 NRYN 44133 3013 D7
30500 SLN 44139 2888 D2
Stratford Rd
10 PnvT 44077 2145 C5
200 CcdT 44077 2145 D6
2300 CVHT 44118 2627 B4
Stratford Tr
12900 CsTp 44026 2631 C1
Stratford Wy
- WBHL 44092 2374 B6
Stratford Ridge Dr
11100 CdnT 44024 2379 B5
Strathalan Dr
6200 BDHT 44146 2887 D5
Strathaven Dr
5400 HDHT 44143 2499 B2
Strathavon Rd
3500 SRHT 44120 2757 C2
Strathmore Av
1700 ECLE 44112 2497 A5
Strathmore Dr
6500 VLVW 44125 2885 E5
6500 VLVW 44125 2886 A6
Stratton Ct
9800 CcdT 44060 2145 B7
Stratton Rd
3400 BHWD 44122 2758 C1
3400 HIHL 44122 2758 C1
Strauss Dr
1800 WTLK 44145 2750 A1
Strawberry Ln
- MAYF 44040 2500 B1
- MAYF 44094 2500 B1
- WBHL 44094 2375 B6
- WBHL 44094 2500 B1
5000 WLBY 44094 2250 C7
5000 WLBY 44094 2375 C1
9800 MsnT 44026 2503 A6
26300 WTLK 44145 2750 A4
N Strawberry Ln
10 MDHL 44022 2760 A3
S Strawberry Ln
100 MDHL 44022 2760 A3
Strawbridge Cir
8600 MCDN 44056 3018 A7
Strawbridge Ct
10 BHWD 44122 2629 A4
Streamside Dr
- NRYN 44133 3012 E3
- SGVL 44133 3012 E3
- SGVL 44136 3012 E3
Stream View Dr
- AVON 44011 2748 D4
Streamview Dr
33400 AVON 44011 2748 D4
Streator Pl
1000 LORN 44052 2614 E7
Strongsville Blvd
7900 MDBH 44130 3011 E2
7900 SGVL 44130 3011 E2
7900 SGVL 44149 3011 E2
17800 SGVL 44136 3012 A2
17800 SGVL 44149 3012 A2
Strother Av
- PnvT 44077 2039 C6
Stroud Rd
6700 MDBH 44130 2881 C5
Struhar Dr
2400 RKRV 44116 2621 E7
Strumbly Dr
500 HDHT 44143 2499 A3
Strumbly Pl
38100 WLBY 44094 2250 E2
St Theresa Blvd
- AVON 44011 2748 E5
Stuart Ct
3100 NRYN 44133 3014 C3
Stuart Dr
800 SELD 44121 2498 C5
10400 CcdT 44077 2145 E6
Stuart Ln
8700 SgHT 44067 3017 E4
Stuart Rd
3600 CVHT 44112 2497 C6
Stubbins Rd
2600 RchT 44141 3151 B7
Stuble Ln
7200 WNHL 44146 3017 D1
Stuckey Ln
9700 CdnT 44024 2378 B6
Stumph Rd
5800 PMHT 44130 2882 B4
5800 PRMA 44130 2882 B4
Stump Hollow Ln
7300 HGVL 44022 2631 B7
7300 RslT 44022 2631 B7
7300 RslT 44072 2631 B7
Sturbridge Ct
5300 SFLD 44054 2746 E4
Sturbridge Dr
500 HDHT 44143 2499 C3
6900 CcdT 44077 2146 C7
Sturbridge Ln
3400 BNWK 44212 3147 B6
27200 WTLK 44145 2620 A6
37300 WLBY 44094 2250 D3
Substation Rd
10 BHIT 44149 3146 B5
10 BHIT 44212 3146 B6
10 SGVL 44149 3146 B5
Success Blvd
- PryT 44081 1940 B7
- PryT 44081 2042 B1
10 PRRY 44081 2042 C1
Sudbury Dr
26400 NOSD 44070 2750 A5
Sudbury Rd
1700 GSML 44040 2630 D1
3600 SRHT 44120 2757 C2
Suffield Rd
6600 MDHT 44124 2630 A3
Suffolk Ln
2400 MDHT 44124 2629 C3
2400 PRPK 44124 2629 C3
3000 BNWK 44212 3147 D7
15300 RslT 44022 2761 D4
Suffolk Rd
3900 SELD 44121 2498 A4
Sugar Ct
11100 NRYN 44133 3013 B4
Sugar Ln
600 ELYR 44035 2875 E7
600 ELYR 44035 3006 E1
Sugarbush Cir
400 BHIT 44212 3146 A7
9700 ODFL 44138 3010 E2
Sugarbush Dr
9100 MNTR 44060 2144 E5
Sugarbush Gln
100 CRDN 44024 2505 B2
Sugar Bush Ln
10 SRSL 44022 2762 A6
Sugarbush Ln
7100 RslT 44022 2761 B3
7700 CsTp 44026 2501 A1
7700 CsTp 44040 2501 A1
7700 GSML 44040 2500 E1
7700 GSML 44040 2501 A1
Sugarbush Tr
7500 HDSN 44236 3155 D7
Sugar Creek Ln
- NRDV 44039 2876 D1
Sugar Hill Tr
17300 BbgT 44023 2891 B3
Sugarhouse Hill Ct
- KTLD 44094 2376 C5
Sugar Ridge Rd
36100 NRDV 44039 2876 A6
38500 NRDV 44039 2875 E7
39400 ELYR 44035 2875 E7
39400 ELYR 44039 2875 E7
Sugar Sand Ln
7100 NOSD 44070 2878 B4
Sugar Tree Dr
8500 RslT 44022 2762 B3
8500 RslT 44072 2762 A3
Sugarwood Tr
10100 MsnT 44024 2503 C7
10100 MsnT 44026 2503 C7
E Sulgrave Ovl
2900 BHWD 44122 2628 D6
2900 SRHT 44122 2628 D6
W Sulgrave Ovl
2800 BHWD 44122 2628 D6
2800 SRHT 44122 2628 D6
Sulgrave Rd
2600 BHWD 44122 2628 D6
3000 SRHT 44122 2628 D7
Sullivan Dr
35000 NRDV 44039 2748 B7
Sulphur Springs Dr
- BTVL 44022 2760 C7
- BTVL 44022 2889 C1
Sulzer Av
1400 EUCL 44132 2373 D5
Summer Ln
4600 BKLN 44144 2753 C6
Summer Rd
8300 MCDN 44056 3153 C1
8400 MCDN 44056 3018 C7
Summerdale Av
10300 GDHT 44125 2756 C6
Summerfield Rd
14400 BHWD 44122 2628 C4
14400 UNHT 44118 2628 C4
Summer Hill Dr
7100 CcdT 44077 2145 E7
7100 CcdT 44077 2253 E1
Summerhill Dr
200 AURA 44202 3156 D4
34300 AVON 44011 2748 C5
Summerland Av
11800 CLEV 44111 2753 A3
22900 NOSD 44070 2750 E5
Summerland Av
22900 NOSD 44070 2751 A5
Summer Place Dr
19600 SGVL 44149 3146 D2
Summers Rd
11700 CsTp 44026 2501 E4
Summerset Dr
7700 WNHL 44146 3017 C2
11100 CrlT 44035 3005 D5
33900 SLN 44139 3020 A3
Summerset Ln
8800 ODFL 44138 3010 B1
Summersweet Tr
7900 SgHT 44067 3017 B5
Summer Wind Dr
6500 BKVL 44141 3150 B5
Summerwood Dr
- CcdT 44077 2254 E3
- CcdT 44077 2255 A3
1400 BWHT 44147 3015 B7
Summerwood Ln
5400 WLBY 44094 2375 A1
Summit
- CLEV 44113 2624 D2
- CLEV 44114 2624 D2
Summit Av
10 MCDN 44056 3018 B3
10 NHFD 44056 3018 B3
10 NHFD 44067 3018 B3
1000 LKWD 44107 2622 C4
13900 GDHT 44125 2886 A3
13900 GDHT 44137 2886 A3
13900 MPHT 44137 2886 A3
Summit Blvd
1200 BWHT 44147 3014 E7
Summit Cir
5500 BKVL 44141 3015 E6
Summit Dr
- BtnT 44021 2635 E7
- MNTR 44060 2143 B7
1100 HDHT 44143 2499 C7
1100 MDHT 44124 2499 C7
1100 MDHT 44143 2499 C7
8200 BbgT 44023 2890 E2
8200 BbgT 44023 2891 A2
14700 NbyT 44065 2764 C1
Summit Ln
30500 PRPK 44124 2759 D1
Summit Ovl
5500 PRMA 44134 2883 D1
Summit Rd
5300 LNHT 44124 2629 A1
7300 BbgT 44023 3021 A2
7300 BbgT 44139 3021 A2
7300 BbgT 44202 3021 A2
7300 SLN 44139 3021 A2
Summit St
4400 WLBY 44094 2250 E6
E Summit St
10 CNFL 44022 2761 A5
W Summit St
10 CNFL 44022 2760 E6
10 CNFL 44022 2761 A5
Summit Commerce Pk
1800 TNBG 44087 3154 E5
Summit Park Dr
10 INDE 44131 2884 C3
Summit Park Rd
3800 CVHT 44121 2497 E6
3800 CVHT 44121 2498 A6
Summitview Dr
7200 SVHL 44131 2884 A7
Sumner Av
900 CLEV 44115 2625 A3
Sumner Rd
7800 HmbT 44024 2256 E6
7800 LryT 44024 2256 E6
7800 LryT 44086 2256 E6
Sumner St
100 NRsT 44074 3139 A3
100 OBLN 44074 3138 E3
100 OBLN 44074 3139 A3
200 ELYR 44035 2875 C6
4500 SFLD 44054 2746 B2
Sumpter Ct
3700 CLEV 44115 2625 C3
Sumpter Rd
18700 WVHT 44128 2757 E6
19800 WVHT 44128 2758 A6
Sun Av
- WKLF 44092 2374 A4
Sunbury Ovl
800 PNVL 44077 2040 A5
Suncliff Pl
17800 SGVL 44136 3011 E6
Sun Crest Ct
13400 SGVL 44136 3012 A7
Suncrest Ct
5500 PRMA 44134 2883 E1
Sunderland Dr
5500 PRMA 44129 2883 A3
6600 PRMA 44129 2882 E3
Sundew Ln
100 SRSL 44022 2761 E5
Sundown Tr
10000 NRYN 44133 3148 B5
Sunfish Cove
4200 AVON 44011 2748 C4
Sunflower Ct
7600 MNTR 44060 2143 D5
Sunflower Dr
100 BNWK 44212 3146 E6
Sunflower Ln
33800 NRDV 44039 2877 C2
Sunflower Ovl
1200 BWHT 44147 3149 D5
Sunhaven Ovl
3200 PRMA 44134 3014 C1
Sun Meadow Ct
38600 NRDV 44039 2747 A7
Sun Meadow Tr
17200 SGVL 44149 3146 B3
Sunningdale Rd
1600 MDHT 44124 2629 D1
Sunning Hill Dr
- KTLD 44094 2251 C7
- WTHL 44094 2251 C7
Sunny Ln
4700 BKLN 44144 2753 C6
Sunnycliff Av
9600 GDHT 44125 2885 B2
Sunnydale Dr
8200 BKVL 44141 3015 E5
Sunny Glen Av
16200 CLEV 44128 2757 C6
Sunny Glen Av
16200 GDHT 44128 2757 C6
Sunny Hill Cir
4300 CLEV 44109 2754 E4
Sunnyhill Dr
22200 RKRV 44116 2751 A1
Sunny Ln Rd
5500 MPHT 44137 2886 B2
Sunnyside Av
14100 MDBH 44130 2881 D5
Sunnyside Dr
18200 CLEV 44110 2372 E7
Sunnyside Rd
400 VMLN 44089 2742 A6
1200 VMLN 44089 2871 A2
2500 VMLN 44001 2871 A3
Sunnyslope Rd
5300 MPHT 44137 2887 A1
Sunnyvale Ct
9300 MNTR 44060 2252 E3
Sunnywood Dr
6200 SLN 44139 2889 B5
Sunnywood Ln
100 PnvT 44077 2146 D1
Sun Ray Dr
6100 PRMA 44134 2883 E3
Sunray Dr
9600 OmsT 44138 3009 B2
Sun Ridge Cir
11700 MsnT 44024 2504 A3
Sunridge Cir
12300 SGVL 44136 3011 E6
Sun Ridge Ln
800 SRSL 44022 2762 C6
Sunrise Blvd
10 OmsT 44138 2879 B4
9500 NRYN 44133 3013 B5
Sunrise Ct
9300 MNTR 44060 2252 E1
Sunrise Dr
10 CLEV 44134 2754 C7
100 AMHT 44001 2743 D7
Sunrise Ln
7800 RslT 44072 2631 D4
Sunrise Ovl
7400 MDBH 44130 3012 D1
7500 PRMA 44134 3014 C1
Sunrise Tr
10900 BKVL 44141 3016 C4
Sunrise Ridge Ln
- AbnT 44023 2892 A5
Sunset Av
- CLEV 44135 2751 E4
- CLEV 44135 2752 A4
- LORN 44052 2614 E6
- LORN 44052 2615 A6
300 SDLK 44054 2616 B4
6000 INDE 44131 2884 D5
Sunset Blvd
2300 LORN 44052 2744 B2
Sunset Ct
10 PnvT 44077 2040 D1
8000 CLEV 44103 2626 A1
Sunset Dr
- NbyT 44065 2764 C1
10 BERA 44017 2880 A7
10 CLEV 44134 2754 C7
10 SRSL 44022 2762 D6
400 AMHT 44001 2872 D2
600 MDSN 44057 2044 A2
700 MDSN 44057 2043 E3
1700 EUCL 44117 2373 E7
1700 EUCL 44143 2373 E7
1700 RDHT 44143 2373 E7
2100 WKLF 44092 2374 C3
5800 BDHT 44146 2887 E3
7000 MONT 44060 2143 B3
7000 MONT 44094 2143 B3
7000 WLBY 44094 2143 B3
9900 AbnT 44023 3023 B1
15100 SGVL 44136 3147 A2
17000 BbgT 44023 2890 E3
19000 CLEV 44122 2757 E3
19000 WVHT 44122 2757 E3
19700 WVHT 44122 2758 A3
20400 HIHL 44122 2758 A3
24800 BYVL 44140 2620 D4
29200 WTLK 44145 2749 C1
36300 ETLK 44095 2142 C6
Sunset Ln
3000 MAYF 44040 2500 A1
3000 MAYF 44092 2500 A1
3000 MAYF 44094 2500 A1
3000 WBHL 44092 2500 A1
3000 WBHL 44094 2500 A1
5500 PRMA 44134 2883 E1
Sunset Ovl
4500 BKLN 44144 2753 C5
12300 NRYN 44133 3014 C6
24800 NOSD 44070 2879 C1
Sunset Rd
- MDSN 44057 2043 E3
100 AVLK 44012 2488 C7
100 AVLK 44012 2618 C1
1100 MAYF 44143 2499 D6
1100 MDHT 44124 2499 D6
1100 MDHT 44143 2499 D6
6300 GDHT 44125 2885 D3
Sunset St
200 NHFD 44067 3017 E4
Sunset Tr
4500 BKLN 44144 2753 C5
Sunset Cove Cir
10 ETLK 44095 2142 C6
Sunshine Ct
1000 GFTN 44044 3142 B6
Sunshine Dr
- CcdT 44077 2254 D3
10900 CdnT 44024 2254 A7
Sunstone Dr
7700 BKVL 44141 3016 D6
Sunview Av
14800 CLEV 44128 2757 B5
Sunview Dr
1700 TNBG 44087 3019 C4
8500 BWHT 44147 3014 D5
Sunview Rd
1300 LNHT 44124 2499 B7
1400 LNHT 44124 2629 B1
Sun Vista Dr
7000 PRMA 44129 2882 E6
Sunwood Ovl
16400 BNWK 44136 3147 A5
16400 BNWK 44212 3147 A5
16400 SGVL 44136 3147 A5
Superior Av
- CLEV 44113 2624 D4
- LORN 44055 2745 D6
- ShfT 44055 2745 D6
4000 CLEV 44103 2625 C1
4000 CLEV 44114 2625 C1
5100 CLEV 44103 2495 E7
7400 CLEV 44103 2496 A7
8300 CLEV 44106 2496 A7
8300 CLEV 44108 2496 A7
12400 CLEV 44112 2496 E7
12400 ECLE 44112 2496 E7
Superior Av US-6
- CLEV 44113 2624 D4
4000 CLEV 44103 2625 C1
4000 CLEV 44114 2625 C1
5100 CLEV 44103 2495 E7
7400 CLEV 44103 2496 A7
8300 CLEV 44106 2496 A7
8300 CLEV 44108 2496 A7
12400 CLEV 44112 2496 E7
12400 ECLE 44112 2496 E7
Superior Av US-20
- CLEV 44113 2624 D4
Superior Av US-322
- CLEV 44113 2624 D4
Superior Av E
10 CLEV 44114 2624 E3
1200 CLEV 44114 2625 A2
3800 CLEV 44103 2625 C1
Superior Av E US-6
10 CLEV 44114 2624 E3
1200 CLEV 44114 2625 A2
3800 CLEV 44103 2625 C1
Superior Av E US-20
10 CLEV 44114 2624 E3
Superior Av E US-322
10 CLEV 44114 2624 E3
1200 CLEV 44114 2625 A2
W Superior Av
100 CLEV 44113 2624 D3
100 CLEV 44114 2624 D3
100 CLEV 44115 2624 D3
W Superior Av US-6
100 CLEV 44113 2624 D3
100 CLEV 44114 2624 D3
100 CLEV 44115 2624 D3
W Superior Av US-20
100 CLEV 44113 2624 D3
100 CLEV 44114 2624 D3
100 CLEV 44115 2624 D3
W Superior Av US-322
100 CLEV 44113 2624 D3
100 CLEV 44114 2624 D3
100 CLEV 44115 2624 D3
Superior Rd
13500 ECLE 44112 2497 A7
13800 ECLE 44118 2497 A7
14100 CVHT 44118 2627 B1
14100 ECLE 44112 2627 B1
14100 ECLE 44118 2627 B1
14700 UNHT 44118 2627 D3
Superior Park Dr
3300 CVHT 44118 2627 D2
Superior Via
2200 CLEV 44113 2624 C4
Surf Av
2700 LORN 44053 2743 D2
Surfside Cir
1100 AURA 44202 3021 A5
1200 RMDV 44202 3021 A5
3700 RMDV 44202 3020 E6
N Surfside Cir
10000 AURA 44202 3021 A5
10000 RMDV 44202 3020 E5
10000 RMDV 44202 3021 A5
Surfside Ct
1200 AURA 44202 3021 A6
Surrey Cir
700 BERA 44017 3011 A2
24500 WTLK 44145 2750 C3
Surrey Ct
10 CcdT 44060 2145 B7
E Surrey Ct
3700 RKRV 44116 2751 E1
W Surrey Ct
3700 RKRV 44116 2751 E1
Surrey Dr
- AURA 44202 3157 A4
10 BNWK 44212 3146 E6
6200 NOSD 44070 2878 C2
Surrey Ln
10 CLEV 44110 2372 C6
10 GNVA 44041 1944 C7
7200 CsTp 44026 2501 B5
32500 AVLK 44012 2618 A2
Surrey Pl
1800 GSML 44040 2630 C2
Surrey Rd
2000 CVHT 44106 2626 E3
Surrey Downs Dr
14900 RslT 44072 2762 B2
Surry Dr
200 NCtT 44067 3152 E2
200 SgHT 44067 3152 E2
Susan Av
17700 CLEV 44111 2752 A3
Susan Ct
500 ETLK 44095 2142 E7
Susan Dr
15300 BKPK 44142 2881 B3
Susan Ln
10 HmbT 44024 2381 A3
S Sussex Ct
600 AURA 44202 3021 C7
Sussex Dr
200 AURA 44202 3021 C6
9200 ODFL 44138 3010 A1
Sussex Ln
100 ELYR 44035 2874 B6
Sussex Pl
2200 MadT 44057 1942 B2
Sussex Rd
19600 SRHT 44122 2757 E1
19600 SRHT 44122 2758 A1
Sutcliffe Dr
400 BYVL 44140 2619 E5
Sutherland Av
6700 PMHT 44130 2882 B6
Sutherland Ct
6800 MNTR 44060 2143 D6
Sutherland Dr
300 HDHT 44143 2499 D2
Sutherland Rd
3500 SRHT 44122 2757 E2

Cleveland Street Index

STREET
Block City ZIP Map# Grid

Sutton Dr
6500 NOSD 44070 2878 C3
Sutton Ln
5500 WLBY 44094 2375 A1
Sutton Pl
- SRHT 44120 2627 B7
10 CLEV 44120 2757 B1
10 SRHT 44120 2757 B1
6800 MDBH 44130 2881 B5
Sutton Rd
3200 SRHT 44120 2627 B7
3500 PRPK 44122 2759 B1
3500 WDMR 44122 2759 B1
Suwanee Av
24900 OKWD 44146 2887 D7
Suwanee Dr
5800 MONT 44060 2143 C2
Suzanne Ln
6400 SLN 44139 2889 D5
Svec Av
13100 CLEV 44105 2756 E2
13100 CLEV 44120 2756 E2
13600 CLEV 44120 2757 A2
Swaffield Rd
4200 SELD 44121 2498 B6
Swallow Dr
7900 MCDN 44056 3153 C2
Swan St
10 GNVA 44041 1944 B4
Swan Lake Blvd
14000 NRYN 44133 3014 A7
14000 NRYN 44133 3149 A1
Swanson Ct
10300 CcdT 44077 2145 D5
Sweeney Av
5100 CLEV 44127 2625 D6
Sweet Bay Ct
2500 BWHT 44147 3149 D5
Sweetbay Dr
6000 NRYN 44133 3014 B4
Sweet Bay Ln
- CLEV 44105 2756 B4
Sweet Birch Dr
5800 BDHT 44146 2887 D3
Sweetbriar Ct
32500 NRDV 44039 2748 E7
Sweetbriar Dr
1000 VMLN 44089 2740 E6
1000 VMLN 44089 2741 A6
26300 NOSD 44070 2750 A5
Sweetbriar Ln
13800 RsIT 44072 2631 C6
Sweetgum Tr
7900 CcdT 44060 2253 A3
Sweet Hollow Dr
7500 MNTR 44060 2253 A2
Sweetleaf Ln
10000 NRYN 44133 3014 B4
Sweet Spice Ovl
12100 NRYN 44133 3013 B5
Sweet Valley Dr
8000 VLVW 44125 2885 A3
Sweetwater Dr
2500 BKVL 44141 3150 B3
Swetland Blvd
4800 RDHT 44143 2373 E7
4800 RDHT 44143 2498 E1
Swetland Ct
5000 RDHT 44143 2498 E1
5000 RDHT 44143 2499 A1
Swetland Rd
6500 MadT 44057 1843 B6
Swift St
- CLEV 44113 2624 D6
Swingos Ct
1800 CLEV 44115 2625 A3
Swinton Cir
- AVON 44011 2747 A4
Switzer Rd
23000 BKPK 44142 2879 E1
Sycamore Cir
300 AVLK 44012 2618 C3
14000 SGVL 44136 3012 D4
Sycamore Ct
900 ETLK 44095 2250 B3
6300 INDE 44131 2884 C4
Sycamore Dr
10 OmsT 44138 2879 B4
10 PnvT 44077 2040 C2
400 AURA 44202 3021 C6
700 EUCL 44132 2374 A2
2000 BDFD 44146 2887 C3
2000 BDHT 44146 2887 C3
4600 LORN 44053 2744 C5
22200 FWPK 44126 2751 A6
Sycamore Ln
500 AURA 44202 3021 C6
39100 CrlT 44044 3006 D7
Sycamore Ovl
29900 WTLK 44145 2749 C6
Sycamore Rd
3100 CVHT 44118 2627 C1
6400 MNTR 44060 2143 E5
11600 MsnT 44024 2504 B3
Sycamore St
- ELYR 44035 2875 D4
10 CLEV 44110 2372 C6
10 OBLN 44074 3138 B3
2000 CLEV 44113 2624 D3
35500 NRDV 44039 2877 A2
Sydenham Rd
20600 SRHT 44122 2628 A6
Sykora Rd
3500 CLEV 44105 2755 C1
Sylmar Dr
5700 BWHT 44147 3015 D4
Sylvan Av
1000 LKWD 44107 2622 C3
Sylvan Dr
29500 WLWK 44095 2249 B6
Sylvan Ln
9700 CcdT 44060 2145 B7
Sylvan Rd
2700 GNVA 44041 1944 E5
2700 GnvT 44041 1944 E5
15800 RsIT 44022 2761 D5
15900 SRSL 44022 2761 D5
Sylvanhurst Ln
9700 MsnT 44026 2503 A6
Sylvanhurst Rd
3300 CVHT 44112 2497 D6
Sylvania Rd
1100 CVHT 44121 2498 A6
Sylvia Av
14000 BTNH 44110 2497 A1
Sylvia Av
14000 CLEV 44110 2497 A1
Sylvia Ct
6200 BKPK 44142 2880 E3
Sylvia Dr
300 CRDN 44024 2380 B7
6100 BKPK 44142 2880 E3
6100 BKPK 44142 2881 A2
8600 MNTR 44060 2144 C7
34000 ETLK 44095 2249 E2
34000 ETLK 44095 2250 A2
Symphony Ln
- PRPK 44124 2629 A7
Symphony St
10 OmsT 44138 2879 A4
Syracuse Av
18000 CLEV 44110 2372 D7
18000 CLEV 44119 2372 D7
Syracuse Ct
200 ELYR 44035 3006 D2

T

Taberna Ln
9500 OmsT 44138 3009 B1
Tabernacle St
400 VMLN 44089 2741 A5
Tabor Av
14100 MPHT 44137 2886 A2
Tacoma Av
- ShfT 44055 2746 A5
2800 LORN 44055 2746 A5
11100 CLEV 44108 2496 D6
Taft Av
100 ELYR 44035 2875 A5
300 BDFD 44146 2887 B3
2000 ShfT 44055 2745 E6
12200 CLEV 44108 2496 E3
Taft St
7100 MNTR 44060 2143 C7
7300 MNTR 44060 2251 C1
Tager Dr
- HmbT 44024 2380 C3
Tail Feather Dr
- NRDV 44039 2876 C2
Tait St
1400 LORN 44053 2744 A1
Talbot Av
- WLBY 44094 2250 C5
9300 CLEV 44106 2626 B1
Talbot Cir
- MNTR 44060 2252 A3
Talbot Dr
10 BDFD 44146 2887 A3
6800 PRMA 44129 2882 E5
6800 PRMA 44129 2883 A6
Talbot Ln
4100 LORN 44055 2746 B4
Talford Av
15500 CLEV 44128 2757 B2
Talford Dr
800 SVHL 44131 2884 A3
Tall Oaks Dr
6000 MNTR 44060 2143 C3
6000 MONT 44060 2143 C3
Tall Oaks Tr
26900 OmsT 44138 2878 E4
Tallow Tree Dr
12800 MsnT 44024 2634 D1
Tall Pines Dr
11600 MsnT 44024 2504 D2
Tall Timber Cir
12600 NRYN 44133 3013 D6
Tall Timbers Dr
5000 RchT 44286 3150 C6
Tall Tree Tr
2900 WBHL 44092 2374 B7
17300 BbgT 44023 2890 C3
Tallwood Ct
4200 NOSD 44070 2750 B5
10500 CcdT 44077 2145 E7
Tallwood Dr
25700 NOSD 44070 2750 B5
Tallyho Ct
33500 SLN 44139 3020 A1
Tallyho Dr
33100 SLN 44139 3019 E1
33100 SLN 44139 3020 A1
Tally Ho Ln
400 RDHT 44143 2498 E3
Talmadge Av
800 WKLF 44092 2249 B7
800 WKLF 44092 2374 B1
Tamalga Dr
4200 SELD 44121 2498 B6
Tamarac Blvd
1100 WLBY 44094 2142 E5
38000 WLBY 44094 2143 A5
Tamarack Dr
100 BERA 44017 2880 A7
3800 PRMA 44134 3014 B1
S Tamarack Dr
7500 PRMA 44134 3014 B2
Tamarack Tr
8500 BbgT 44023 3022 A1
9800 BKVL 44141 3150 B3
29800 WTLK 44145 2749 C6
Tamarin Ct
9500 MNTR 44060 2145 A7
Tamarind Dr
6500 BDHT 44146 2887 D6
Tamiami Dr
7500 PRMA 44134 3014 E1
Tamiami Tr
100 ClrT 44024 2505 C6
Tammany Ct
100 CcdT 44060 2145 B7
Tampa Av
1200 CLEV 44109 2754 D5
Tampico Ct
600 BERA 44017 3010 E1
Tanager Ct
5700 MNTR 44060 2144 E2
33100 NRDV 44039 3008 D1
Tanager Dr
9500 HmbT 44024 2380 B2
Tanager Ovl
8000 BKVL 44141 3016 C4
Tanager Tr
10300 BKVL 44141 3016 C4
Tanbark Ln
19500 SGVL 44149 3011 D4
Tanbark Tr
9800 CcdT 44060 2253 B2
Tandem Ct
33300 SLN 44139 2889 A3
Tanglewood
1100 ManT 44255 3159 A3
Tanglewood Ct
17400 BbgT 44023 2891 A4
32800 AVLK 44012 2618 A2
Tanglewood Dr
4600 LORN 44053 2744 C5
7100 INDE 44131 2884 E4
19100 NRYN 44133 3147 E5
Tanglewood Ln
300 BYVL 44140 2619 B4
6300 SVHL 44131 2884 B4
8000 PRMA 44129 3013 D2
Tanglewood Rd
9100 MCDN 44056 3018 E6
Tanglewood Sq
8500 BbgT 44023 2891 A4
Tanglewood Tr
8400 BbgT 44023 2891 A4
10700 CcdT 44077 2146 A4
Tanhollow Tr
1700 BWHT 44147 3149 D4
Tanner Av
9900 CLEV 44108 2496 B7
Tanners Farm Dr
- PnvT 44077 2041 B7
- PryT 44077 2041 B7
Tannery St
100 ELYR 44035 2875 B6
Tannery Wy
9700 ClbT 44028 3010 D1
9700 ClbT 44138 3010 D1
9700 ODFL 44138 3010 D1
Tappan Cir
800 VMLN 44089 2740 D5
Tappan Ovl
400 MDSN 44057 2044 A3
Tara-Lynn Dr
24600 NOSD 44070 2750 C4
Taras Dr
11300 NRYN 44133 3012 E5
11300 SGVL 44133 3012 E5
11300 SGVL 44136 3012 E5
Tarbell Av
10 BDFD 44146 2887 A4
6500 MadT 44057 1843 B7
Tare Creek Pkwy
- MDFD 44062 2767 B1
Tarkington Av
16200 CLEV 44128 2757 C5
17800 WVHT 44128 2757 C5
Tarlton Av
1500 CLEV 44109 2754 D4
Tarry Ln
700 AMHT 44001 2872 B2
Tarrymore Rd
17200 CLEV 44119 2372 D5
Tartan Ct
10 CNFL 44022 2761 B6
Tate Av
2000 CLEV 44109 2754 C5
Tatra Av
5000 MPHT 44128 2757 D6
5000 MPHT 44137 2757 D7
5000 WVHT 44128 2757 D6
Tattersall Ct
10 ELYR 44035 2874 E5
Tattersall Dr
7300 CsTp 44026 2501 C5
Tattler Ct
7700 CcdT 44077 2254 C3
Taunton Av
7400 BKLN 44144 2753 E4
Tauton Dr
600 BERA 44017 3010 E1
Tavern Rd
14800 BtnT 44021 2766 D4
14800 BtnT 44062 2766 D4
14800 BURT 44021 2766 B2
16000 BtnT 44021 2767 A7
16000 BtnT 44062 2767 A7
16000 TroT 44021 2767 A7
16300 TroT 44062 2767 A7
Tavern Rd SR-168
14800 BtnT 44021 2766 D4
14800 BtnT 44062 2766 D4
14800 BURT 44021 2766 B2
16000 BtnT 44021 2767 A7
16000 BtnT 44062 2767 A7
16000 TroT 44021 2767 A7
16300 TroT 44062 2767 A7
Tavern Rd SR-700
14800 BtnT 44021 2766 B2
14800 BtnT 44062 2766 B2
14800 BURT 44021 2766 B2
Tawny Brook Ln
19400 SGVL 44149 3011 D5
Taylor Av
- AVLK 44012 2617 C3
3900 BKVL 44141 3015 C7
3900 BKVL 44147 3015 C7
3900 BWHT 44147 3015 C7
Taylor Ct
4500 CLEV 44102 2624 B5
4500 CLEV 44113 2624 B5
5200 SFLD 44054 2746 D4
Taylor Ln
2500 TNBG 44087 3020 B4
4500 WVHT 44022 2758 E5
4500 WVHT 44128 2758 E5
Taylor Pkwy
38600 NRDV 44039 2875 E6
38600 NRDV 44039 2876 A6
Taylor Pl
500 PNVL 44077 2040 A6
Taylor Rd
- CLEV 44135 2751 B7
- CLEV 44135 2880 B1
10 BDFD 44146 2887 A5
1700 ECLE 44112 2497 B4
5000 BDHT 44128 2758 C7
5000 WVHT 44128 2758 C7
E Taylor Rd
100 BDFD 44146 2887 B5
N Taylor Rd
1800 ECLE 44112 2497 B5
1900 CVHT 44112 2497 D6
2300 CVHT 44118 2497 D6
2300 CVHT 44121 2497 D6
S Taylor Rd
1400 CVHT 44118 2497 D7
1400 CVHT 44118 2627 D4
1400 CVHT 44121 2497 D7
S Taylor Rd
2000 UNHT 44118 2627 D3
Taylor St
100 AhtT 44001 2872 E2
100 AMHT 44001 2872 E2
400 ELYR 44035 2875 D6
1300 ELYR 44039 2875 E6
1300 NRDV 44039 2875 E6
25000 ODFL 44138 2879 B6
Taylor Industrial Pkwy
37800 NRDV 44039 2876 B5
Taylor May Rd
8500 BbgT 44023 2891 B7
9300 AbnT 44023 2891 E7
9300 AbnT 44023 2892 B6
10200 AbnT 44255 2892 E6
10900 AbnT 44023 2893 A6
10900 AbnT 44255 2893 B6
Taylors Mill Turn
1700 WTLK 44145 2749 E1
Taylor Wells Rd
11000 ClrT 44024 2506 A2
11000 HmbT 44024 2381 A7
11000 HmbT 44024 2506 A2
12400 ClrT 44024 2505 E6
12600 ClrT 44024 2635 E1
13100 BtnT 44021 2636 A2
13100 BtnT 44024 2636 A2
13100 ClrT 44024 2636 A2
Tayport Dr
5400 SLN 44139 2888 E2
Teaberry Cir
100 SRSL 44022 2761 D5
Teal Ct
3400 RMDV 44202 3020 D4
3700 PRRY 44081 2042 B1
4400 WTLK 44145 2749 B6
Teal Dr
- HmbT 44024 2381 E2
Teal St
100 CrlT 44035 3006 D3
100 ELYR 44035 3006 D3
Teal Trc
10 MDHT 44124 2629 E2
Teal Cove
7000 CcdT 44077 2145 D7
Tea Rose Dr
7700 MNTR 44060 2252 E2
Teasel Ct
6800 SLN 44139 2889 B6
32000 AVLK 44012 2618 D4
Tecumseh Ct
10500 CLEV 44108 2496 C7
Tedman Ct
100 ELYR 44035 3006 B2
Tegam Wy
10 GNVA 44041 1944 B4
Telbir Av
19200 RKRV 44116 2621 D6
Telegraph Ln
4100 VMLN 44089 2741 C4
Telegraph Rd
43000 ELYR 44035 2874 A5
43300 ELYR 44035 2873 D6
43300 EyrT 44035 2873 D6
43300 EyrT 44035 2874 A5
43400 AhtT 44035 2873 D6
44000 AhtT 44001 2873 A6
46000 AhtT 44001 2872 D7
Telegraph Rd SR-113
43300 ELYR 44035 2873 D6
43300 ELYR 44035 2874 A5
43300 EyrT 44035 2873 D6
43300 EyrT 44035 2874 A5
43400 AhtT 44035 2873 D6
44000 AhtT 44001 2873 A6
46000 AhtT 44001 2872 D7
Telfair Av
16200 CLEV 44128 2757 C6
Telhurst Rd
4400 SELD 44121 2498 C7
Telling Dr
10 GNVA 44041 1944 D7
10 HpfT 44041 1944 D7
Temblethurst Rd
1800 SELD 44121 2628 B2
Temblett Av
11300 CLEV 44108 2496 D5
Temblett Ter
4400 SELD 44121 2628 B3
Temple Av
200 PnvT 44077 2039 B6
1500 MDHT 44124 2499 B7
1500 MDHT 44124 2629 C1
3500 LORN 44053 2744 B4
6800 CLEV 44127 2625 E7
Temple Ct
200 ELYR 44035 2875 B6
Temple Dr
19100 SGVL 44136 3146 D1
19100 SGVL 44149 3146 D1
Tennessee Dr
100 ELYR 44035 3006 E2
Tenney Av
100 AMHT 44001 2872 D2
900 AhtT 44001 2872 E2
Tennyson Av
3800 SDLK 44054 2615 E4
4600 SDLK 44054 2616 C3
Tennyson Ln
3900 NOSD 44070 2750 C5
Tennyson Rd
2600 CLEV 44104 2626 B5
Teresa Ct
3200 PryT 44081 1940 D7
Terminal Av
13000 CLEV 44135 2753 B4
14300 CLEV 44135 2752 C4
Terminal Dr
7400 LORN 44053 2742 C6
Ternes Ln
500 ELYR 44035 2875 E6
Terra Ln
100 AMHT 44001 2743 E7
100 AMHT 44001 2872 E1
1000 AMHT 44053 2743 E6
1000 LORN 44053 2743 E6
Terrace Ct
10100 PRMA 44130 2882 C7
Terrace Dr
100 BDFD 44146 2887 A2
9800 TNBG 44087 3019 E4
27900 NOSD 44070 2878 E3
27900 NOSD 44138 2878 D3
27900 OmsT 44138 2878 D3
Terrace Ln
100 BKLN 44144 2753 D5
Terrace Plz
500 WLWK 44095 2249 D6
Terrace Rd
13500 ECLE 44112 2497 B6
Terrace Park Dr
9000 MNTR 44060 2252 D1
Terre Dr
6300 BKPK 44142 2881 E4
6400 MDBH 44130 2881 E4
6400 MDBH 44142 2881 E4
Terrell Ct
400 RDHT 44143 2498 C3
Terrell Dr
- NRDV 44035 3007 B1
- NRDV 44039 2876 B7
37100 NRDV 44035 2876 B7
Terrell Ln
5000 SFLD 44054 2746 D1
Terrett Av
3800 CLEV 44113 2624 B5
Territory Rd
- AVON 44011 2617 E7
Terry Ct
17800 CLEV 44119 2372 D6
Tewksbury Ln
8100 CcdT 44077 2253 C5
12900 ClrT 44024 2505 C2
Texas Av
3700 LORN 44055 2745 B4
3700 ShfT 44055 2745 B4
7300 MNTR 44060 2143 C6
Thacker St
700 BERA 44017 2880 C4
700 BERA 44142 2880 C4
700 BKPK 44142 2880 C4
Thackeray Av
5500 CLEV 44103 2625 D3
Thackeray Ct
8100 BWHT 44147 3015 B4
Thackeray Tr
400 RDHT 44143 2499 A4
Thames Av
10 BDFD 44137 2886 D2
10 BDFD 44146 2886 D2
10 MPHT 44137 2886 D2
14500 CLEV 44110 2497 B1
Thames Dr
4600 NRYN 44133 3014 B3
Thatcher Dr
1300 PnvT 44077 2041 A6
Thatcher's Ln
14200 SGVL 44149 3146 D1
Thatchum Ln
7400 CcdT 44060 2253 D1
7400 CcdT 44077 2253 D1
Thayne Rd
1900 CVHT 44118 2627 D2
1900 UNHT 44118 2627 D3
The Bluffs
11600 SGVL 44136 3012 A6
The Burns
500 BERA 44017 2880 B5
The Capes Blvd
1000 PnvT 44077 2145 C4
Thelma Dr
200 SDLK 44054 2617 A3
Thelma St
- NRDV 44039 2877 D1
The Mall
100 BERA 44017 2880 B4
Theodore St
5100 MPHT 44137 2757 C7
Theota Av
- PRMA 44129 2882 D1
3700 PRMA 44134 2883 B1
5200 PRMA 44129 2883 A1
Theresa Ln
10 MNTR 44060 2144 E7
24500 NOSD 44070 2750 D5
Theresa St
- NRDV 44039 2748 D7
Thicket Ln
24400 ODFL 44138 2879 D7
Third St
- HmbT 44024 2380 C2
- LORN 44052 2744 E4
- MNTR 44060 2144 D7
Thistle Ct
10200 BWHT 44147 3149 E4
Thistle Dr
7100 SLN 44139 3020 A1
Thistle Ln
7500 RsIT 44072 2631 C7
7500 RsIT 44072 2761 C1
Thistle Tr
300 MDHT 44124 2629 E2
Thistleridge Dr
900 MCDN 44056 3154 B5
Thistlewood Dr
6100 MNTR 44060 2143 D3
6100 MONT 44060 2143 D3
Thomas Ct
9100 MNTR 44060 2144 E1
Thomas St
10 OBLN 44074 3139 B2
5000 MPHT 44137 2757 D7
5300 MPHT 44137 2886 D1
15700 NbyT 44065 2763 B5
30000 WLWK 44095 2249 C6
Thomas Alva Dr
300 VMLN 44089 2741 C5
Thompson Av
14700 MDFD 44062 2767 D2
Thompson Blvd
14100 BKPK 44142 2881 D2
Thompson Dr
- SAHT 44001 2872 C6
Thompson Rd
12200 VMLN 44089 2869 A3
Thompson St
4100 PRRY 44081 2042 C3
Thompson-Rye Cir
10300 TNBG 44087 3020 A4
Thomson Cir
3200 RKRV 44116 2751 B2
Thor Ct
2500 PryT 44077 2041 B3
Thoreau Av
- SFLD 44054 2615 E6
Thoreau Dr
5000 PRMA 44129 2883 A7
6300 PRMA 44129 2882 E7
Thoreau Rd
1200 LKWD 44107 2623 A5
Thorn Av
9600 CLEV 44108 2496 B6
Thornapple Dr
6600 MAYF 44040 2500 B4
6600 MAYF 44143 2500 A4
Thornapple Ln
3200 PRPK 44124 2760 A1
7200 SLN 44139 3020 A1
7800 RsIT 44072 2631 D7
Thornberry Ln
500 BHIT 44212 3146 D7
Thornbrook Av
6600 OmsT 44138 2879 B3
Thornbury Rd
5000 LNHT 44124 2498 E7
5000 LNHT 44124 2499 A7
Thorncliffe Blvd
7100 PRMA 44134 2883 D7
Thorne Av
8000 KTLD 44094 2376 E1
8000 KTLD 44094 2377 A1
Thorne Rd
3300 CVHT 44112 2497 D6
3300 CVHT 44121 2497 D6
Thornfield Dr
39300 AVON 44011 2747 A2
Thorn Hill Dr
- ManT 44255 3159 A4
Thornhill Dr
700 CLEV 44108 2496 E5
1000 ECLE 44108 2496 E5
1000 ECLE 44112 2496 E6
Thornhill Ln
500 AURA 44202 3022 C7
Thornhope Rd
13200 CLEV 44135 2752 E5
Thornhurst Av
12500 GDHT 44105 2756 E4
13100 GDHT 44105 2757 A4
Thornhurst Dr
8000 NRYN 44133 3014 B3
8000 NRYN 44134 3014 B3
8000 PRMA 44134 3014 B3
Thornridge Av
19400 CLEV 44135 2751 D4
Thornridge Cir
4300 CLEV 44135 2751 D4
Thornsway Tr
- MAYF 44143 2500 B3
Thorntail Ct
- CcdT 44077 2254 D2
Thornton Av
- CLEV 44102 2623 B5
10900 GDHT 44125 2756 C7
Thornton Ct
1000 MCDN 44056 3153 D1
Thornton Dr
5400 PRMA 44129 2883 A3
5400 PRMA 44134 2883 A3
7300 PRMA 44129 2882 E2
14700 NRYN 44133 3147 E1
Thornton Ln
- AVON 44011 2747 B1
Thorn Tree Dr
3100 NRYN 44133 3014 B5
Thorntree Dr
- BKVL 44141 3016 B5
Thornwood
1100 ManT 44255 3159 A3
Thornwood Av
11400 CLEV 44108 2496 D6
Thornwood Blvd
700 ELYR 44035 2875 E1
Thornwood Rd
- VMLN 44089 2741 D5
Thorpe Rd
18000 AbnT 44023 2892 D7
18000 AbnT 44023 3023 D3
18000 AbnT 44255 2892 D7
18400 AbnT 44255 3023 D1
18900 ManT 44255 3023 D3
Thraves Rd
12400 GDHT 44125 2885 E2
13600 GDHT 44125 2886 A2
13900 GDHT 44137 2886 A2
13900 MPHT 44137 2886 A2
Three Village Dr
5100 LNHT 44124 2628 E2
Throckley Av
15600 CLEV 44128 2757 B2
Thrush Av
10100 CLEV 44102 2753 C2
10100 CLEV 44111 2753 C2
Thrush St
12200 LKWD 44107 2623 A6
Thunderbird Dr
5800 MONT 44060 2143 B3
6000 MNTR 44060 2143 B3
6000 MPHT 44137 2886 A3
Thurgood Av
3700 CLEV 44115 2625 C3
Thurman Av
2000 CLEV 44113 2624 E5
2200 CLEV 44113 2625 A5
Thut Rd
- BtnT 44062 2767 A1
- MdfT 44062 2767 A1
Thwing Rd
10 CdnT 44024 2504 A1
10 CRDN 44024 2504 C1
10 MsnT 44024 2504 A1
9600 CdnT 44024 2378 B7
9600 CdnT 44094 2378 B7
9600 KTLD 44094 2378 B7
10000 CdnT 44024 2503 D1
10300 MsnT 44024 2503 D1
Tibbetts Rd
10500 KTLD 44094 2376 D6
10500 KTLD 44094 2501 D1
11100 CsTp 44026 2501 D1
11100 CsTp 44094 2501 D1
E Tibbitts St
10 GNVA 44041 1944 C5
W Tibbitts St
10 GNVA 44041 1944 B5
Tiber Ct
7500 MCDN 44056 3153 E5
7500 MCDN 44056 3154 A5
Tiber Dr
100 PNVL 44077 2146 B1
Tiber Pl
100 PNVL 44077 2146 B1
Tidewater Dr
37000 SLN 44139 3020 C2
Tiedeman Rd
4200 BKLN 44144 2753 B6
5000 PRMA 44130 2753 C7
5000 PRMA 44144 2753 C7
Tiffany Ct
5800 LNHT 44124 2629 C3
35400 AVON 44011 2748 B3
Tiffany Dr
8600 NRYN 44133 3014 B3
10400 CcdT 44077 2145 D7
10400 CcdT 44077 2253 D1
Tiffany Ln
10600 PMHT 44130 2882 B5
Tiffany Rdg
22500 RKRV 44116 2751 A1
Tiffin Ct
6100 MNTR 44060 2144 B3
Tilby Rd
7100 NRYN 44133 3013 D3
Tilden Av
100 CRDN 44024 2379 E7
Tilden St
- VMLN 44089 2740 E5
Tiller Dr
9100 OmsT 44138 3009 B1
Tillerman Ct
27300 OmsT 44138 3009 B1
Tillman Av
4600 CLEV 44102 2624 B4
Tillotson St
600 ELYR 44035 2875 A2
Timber Av
7700 TwbT 44087 3154 D5
7700 TwbT 44236 3154 D5
Timber Ct
1700 TNBG 44087 3019 C3
Timber Ln
10 AURA 44202 3156 E3
600 GNVA 44041 1944 D4
7100 OmsT 44138 2878 E4
8100 CcdT 44024 2254 C5
8100 CcdT 44077 2254 C5
8100 CdnT 44024 2254 C5
10800 AbnT 44023 2892 E3
14700 MDBH 44130 2881 C7
14700 MDBH 44130 3012 C1
18800 FWPK 44126 2752 A1
30400 BYVL 44140 2619 B3
Timber Tr
1000 EatT 44044 3142 A3
1000 GFTN 44044 3142 A3
1300 TwbT 44236 3154 C6
5900 NOSD 44070 2878 B2
8000 BKVL 44141 3016 A5
8200 BbgT 44023 3021 E3
8200 BbgT 44023 3022 A2
Timber Cove
25600 NOSD 44070 2750 B6
Timber Creek Cir
19100 SGVL 44136 3147 A5
Timbercreek Dr
10300 KTLD 44094 2376 B5
Timbercreek Rd
600 SgHT 44067 3152 C2
Timber Edge Dr
4700 RchT 44286 3150 C6
8700 NRDV 44039 2877 D7
Timber Edge Pl
11500 SGVL 44136 3012 C5
Timberhill Dr
600 MCDN 44056 3018 B6
Timberidge Ct
9400 MNTR 44060 2145 A7
Timberidge Tr
300 GSML 44040 2500 E2
Timber Lake Dr
13900 SGVL 44136 3012 C4
Timberland Ln
1400 TNBG 44087 3019 B4
Timberlane Dr
10 NCtT 44067 3018 A7
100 ELYR 44035 2746 C7
300 AVLK 44012 2618 A2
6100 INDE 44131 3015 D2
23100 BHWD 44122 2628 C4
23100 UNHT 44118 2628 C4
35400 SLN 44139 2889 C3
Timberlane Rd
23800 WVHT 44128 2758 D5
Timberlane Tr
8900 NRYN 44133 3013 B3
Timber Lea Ct
1300 WTLK 44145 2620 D7
Timberline Dr
2500 WBHL 44094 2375 A4
16400 SGVL 44136 3147 A4
Timberline Tr
500 MAYF 44143 2500 B3
700 SgHT 44067 3152 C2
Timber Oak Ct
21300 SGVL 44149 3011 B5
Timber Pointe Tr
11700 ManT 44255 3159 C2
Timber Ridge Dr
10 CNFL 44022 2760 E5
10 CNFL 44022 2761 A5
100 CrlT 44035 3006 E4
1200 MCDN 44056 3153 E1
1200 MCDN 44056 3154 A1
4400 INDE 44131 3015 C1
7900 NRYN 44130 3013 C2
7900 NRYN 44133 3013 C2
7900 PRMA 44130 3013 C2
15000 MDFD 44062 2767 B2
Timber Ridge Ln
35500 WLBY 44094 2375 B2
Timber Ridge Rd
- GFTN 44044 3142 A6
Timber View Dr
4600 VMLN 44089 2741 A7
Timberview Dr
800 AMHT 44001 2743 E7
800 AMHT 44001 2744 A7
4600 LORN 44053 2744 B5
34700 AVON 44011 2748 B4
Timberwood Dr
2700 BWHT 44147 3014 C5
Timeless Ln
6400 MadT 44057 1942 A3
Timothy Cir
32500 SLN 44139 2888 E2
Timothy Dr
7300 NRDV 44039 2877 C4

STREET Block City ZIP Map# Grid

Timothy Ln
600 CLEV 44109 2755 A5
700 CLEV 44109 2754 E5
9100 KTLD 44094 2251 D7
10000 TNBG 44087 3020 B4
12200 BKVL 44141 3151 D4
Tina Dr
- MNTR 44060 2143 E4
Tina Ln
48200 AhtT 44001 2872 A2
48200 AMHT 44001 2872 A2
Tinker Av
100 PNVL 44077 2146 A1
Tinkers Ct
27200 GNWL 44139 2888 B7
Tinkers Ln
700 SgHT 44067 3152 C1
2700 TNBG 44087 3155 A1
Tinkers Tr
100 CRDN 44024 2505 B2
200 AURA 44202 3156 D4
Tinkers Creek Dr
10 AURA 44202 3156 D4
Tinkers Creek Rd
10900 VLVW 44125 2885 D7
10900 VLVW 44125 2886 A6
10900 WNHL 44146 2886 A6
Tinkers Valley Dr
27000 GNWL 44139 2888 A7
27000 Okwd 44146 2888 A7
Tinkers View Dr
1600 TNBG 44087 3019 C3
Tinman Rd
6200 MNTR 44060 2144 E4
Tiny Ln
- VLVW 44125 2885 B2
Tioga Av
8300 CLEV 44105 2756 B4
Tioga Tr
500 WLBY 44094 2143 A4
Tiolki Ln
- GTVL 44231 3161 E5
- HrmT 44231 3161 E5
Tipperary Ln
9500 MNTR 44060 2145 A5
Titan Dr
3100 NRYN 44133 3014 C6
Titus Av
2200 CLEV 44109 2754 D1
Titus Hill Ln
32700 AVLK 44012 2617 E4
32700 AVLK 44012 2618 A4
Tiverton Rd
- CLEV 44110 2372 E7
- CLEV 44110 2373 A7
Tobik Tr
6700 PMHT 44130 2882 C6
Toby Dr
- AbnT 44023 2892 C3
Todd Dr
5200 MadT 44057 1941 A4
5200 MadT 44081 1941 A4
5200 NPRY 44081 1941 A4
Tokay Av
14100 MPHT 44137 2886 A2
Toledo Av
2700 LORN 44055 2745 A3
4100 ShfT 44055 2745 A4
4700 ShfT 44052 2745 A5
Toledo St
- VMLN 44089 2740 E5
Tolland Dr
- RMDV 44087 3020 D4
Tolland Rd
3500 SRHT 44122 2757 E2
Tollis Pkwy
400 BWHT 44147 3014 D5
Tom Ln
4500 CLEV 44109 2754 E5
Tomahawk Dr
10 AVLK 44012 2618 E2
Tomahawk Ln
4200 VMLN 44089 2741 B6
Tompkins Av
8500 CLEV 44102 2623 D6
Tomson Dr
13100 SGVL 44149 3011 C7
Tonawanda Dr
2600 RKRV 44116 2621 A7
2600 RKRV 44116 2751 A1
Tonbridge Ct
6200 BDHT 44146 2887 D5
Tonsing Dr
11400 GDHT 44125 2885 D1
12200 GDHT 44125 2756 D7
Topaz Ct
34100 NRDV 44039 2748 C7
Topaz Ln
300 BHIT 44212 3146 B7
Topeka Av
13800 CLEV 44110 2497 A2
Topping Ln
3000 HGVL 44022 2630 B6
Topps Industrial Pk
4700 WLBY 44094 2250 B6
Top Rail Ln
8300 RslT 44072 2762 A1
Torbenson Dr
1800 CLEV 44112 2497 E3
1900 CLEV 44121 2497 E3
Torrance Av
8600 BKLN 44144 2753 D4
Torrington Av
2400 PRMA 44134 2883 B1
4800 PRMA 44129 2883 A1
Torrington Rd
2800 SRHT 44120 2627 E6
2800 SRHT 44122 2627 E6
Tortugas Ln
9100 MNTR 44060 2144 E2
Torwood Ct
4300 CLEV 44109 2754 B2
Toscana Dr
- NRYN 44133 3014 C4
Toth Dr
- NCtT 44067 3017 E7
- NCtT 44067 3018 A7
Tourelle Dr
6100 HDHT 44143 2499 D2
Tournament Dr
600 AVLK 44012 2618 C4
Tower Blvd
600 LORN 44052 2744 E3
1100 LORN 44053 2744 C4
Tower Dr
20300 WNHL 44146 3018 A1
Tower Ln
300 AMHT 44001 2872 B4
Tower Park Dr
8400 TwbT 44087 3154 C3
Town Center Blvd
- PNVL 44077 2145 B2
Town Centre Dr
7000 BWHT 44147 3015 A7
7000 BWHT 44147 3149 E1
7000 BWHT 44147 3150 A1
Townley Ct
- RMDV 44087 3020 C3
Townley Rd
3500 SRHT 44122 2757 E2
Townline Rd
- MadT 44057 1941 A2
- NPRY 44081 1941 A2
10 AURA 44202 3022 E6
10 AURA 44202 3157 E1
10 ManT 44202 3022 E6
10 ManT 44202 3157 E1
2100 MadT 44081 1941 A4
2500 PryT 44081 1941 A5
3400 MadT 44057 2043 A1
3400 MadT 44081 2043 A1
Townmill Ct
300 PNVL 44077 2146 A2
Townpath Dr
- VLVW 44125 2885 B3
Towns Ln
500 RDHT 44143 2498 C3
Townsend Av
7900 CLEV 44104 2626 A4
Townsend Ct
100 CcdT 44060 2145 B7
Townsend Rd
4300 RchT 44286 3150 D6
4300 RHFD 44286 3150 E7
5200 BKVL 44141 3150 D6
5200 RchT 44141 3150 D6
Towpath Dr
6000 VLVW 44125 2885 B3
Towpath Rd
600 BWHT 44147 3150 A4
900 BWHT 44147 3149 E4
Trabar Dr
2700 WBHL 44092 2374 C5
Track Av
4500 CLEV 44127 2625 C6
Track Rd
11700 NbyT 44065 2764 D1
Tracy Av
20100 EUCL 44119 2373 A4
20100 EUCL 44123 2373 A4
Tracy Ln
15100 SGVL 44136 3147 B1
31900 SLN 44139 2888 E2
Tracy Tr
9000 PRMA 44129 2882 D7
9000 PRMA 44130 2882 C7
Tradewinds Cir
- PRPK 44124 2629 A7
Tradewinds Dr
12700 NRYN 44133 3147 E4
12700 SGVL 44133 3147 E4
12700 SGVL 44136 3147 D4
31600 AVLK 44012 2619 A2
31700 AVLK 44012 2618 E2
Tradewinds Cove
900 PNVL 44077 2040 E2
3400 RMDV 44202 3020 D5
Trafalgar Av
15600 CLEV 44110 2372 C7
Trafalgar Sq
2600 WLBY 44094 2250 E1
N Trail Ln
- CLEV 44105 2756 B4
S Trail Ln
- CLEV 44105 2756 B4
Trail Run
8900 BKLN 44144 2753 D4
Trailard Dr
2300 WBHL 44094 2375 D2
Trail End Dr
700 AhtT 44001 2873 C2
Trails Lndg
15000 BNWK 44136 3147 C5
15000 BNWK 44212 3147 C5
15000 SGVL 44136 3147 C5
Trails Edge Ct
13400 SGVL 44136 3012 A7
Trails End
10 AURA 44202 3157 B1
7500 BbgT 44023 2890 C4
Trails End Ct
4800 WTLK 44145 2749 A6
5200 SFLD 44054 2746 E3
Trails End Dr
28600 SLN 44139 2888 B1
Trailside Dr
7300 SgHT 44067 3152 A1
Trailside Pl
18100 SGVL 44136 3011 E6
Trailwood Ct
8800 MNTR 44060 2144 D4
32500 SLN 44139 2759 E7
Trailwood Dr
300 PNVL 44077 2146 A2
1900 TNBG 44087 3019 D4
Train Av
1700 CLEV 44113 2624 D5
4300 CLEV 44102 2624 A7
Train Ct
- CLEV 44102 2624 A7
Tranquility Ln
4400 LORN 44053 2744 A4
Transit St
100 PNVL 44077 2039 E6
Transport Rd
2600 CLEV 44115 2625 B5
Transportation Blvd
5300 GDHT 44125 2756 C7
5300 GDHT 44125 2885 C1
Transportation Dr
4800 SFLD 44035 2746 D5
4800 SFLD 44054 2746 D5
Trapper Tr
19800 SGVL 44149 3146 C1
Trappers Tr
14800 RslT 44072 2761 C1
14900 RslT 44022 2761 C2
Traveler's Pt
- AVON 44011 2617 E7
Traver Rd
3500 SRHT 44122 2758 A2
Travers Rd
1600 MadT 44057 1842 E7
Travis Dr
1100 MadT 44057 1844 A5
6100 HDHT 44143 2499 D4
Traymore Av
5800 BKLN 44144 2754 A5
5800 CLEV 44144 2754 A5
6200 BKLN 44144 2753 E6
Traymore Blvd
100 ETLK 44095 2142 D5
Traymore Ct
6800 MNTR 44060 2143 D6
Traymore Dr
17400 BbgT 44023 2891 A4
Traymore Rd
2200 UNHT 44118 2628 A4
2600 SRHT 44118 2627 E5
2600 UNHT 44118 2627 E5
Traynham Rd
3600 SRHT 44122 2758 A2
Treadway Av
1400 CLEV 44109 2754 D4
Treadway Blvd
- SFLD 44054 2616 C4
400 SDLK 44054 2616 C4
Treadway Dr
13000 MsnT 44024 2635 A2
Treadwell Av
24900 EUCL 44117 2373 D6
Treasure Isle Dr
17800 SGVL 44136 3147 D4
Treat Rd
10 AURA 44202 3021 D4
19200 WNHL 44146 2887 A7
Trebec Av
20100 EUCL 44119 2373 A5
Trebisky Rd
400 RDHT 44143 2498 D5
500 SELD 44143 2498 D5
600 SELD 44121 2498 D5
Tree Ln
3300 NOSD 44070 2750 E4
Tree Fern Ct
1500 TNBG 44087 3019 C3
Treelawn Dr
7600 INDE 44131 3016 C2
Treeline Dr
6900 BKVL 44141 3150 E5
6900 BKVL 44141 3151 A5
Tree Moss Ln
5600 NRDV 44039 2877 E2
Treeside Ln
500 AVLK 44012 2618 E4
Treetop Ct
- AURA 44202 3156 D1
5500 PRMA 44134 2883 E1
Treetops Ct
7600 NRYN 44133 3013 D7
Treetop Trail Dr
8600 BWHT 44147 3015 A6
Treetower Dr
8300 BbgT 44023 2891 A4
Treeworth Blvd
200 BWHT 44147 3015 C7
Tremaine Dr
27000 EUCL 44132 2374 A4
28000 EUCL 44092 2374 A4
28000 WKLF 44092 2374 A4
Tremont Av
2300 CLEV 44113 2624 E5
2400 CLEV 44113 2625 B5
Tremont Rd
3800 CVHT 44121 2497 E6
Tremont St
400 ELYR 44035 2875 A6
Trent Av
3500 CLEV 44109 2624 C7
Trent Ct
- GnvT 44041 1944 C1
Trenton Av
7700 CLEV 44104 2626 A6
13900 SGVL 44136 3147 C5
Trenton Ct
3700 WTLK 44145 2749 C4
Trenton Ovl
13700 SGVL 44136 3147 D5
Trenton Pl
- WLBY 44094 2250 A7
- WLBY 44094 2375 A1
Trenton Sq
10 EUCL 44143 2498 A2
Trenton Tr
3900 BNWK 44212 3146 E7
7600 MDBH 44130 3012 D1
Tressa Av
3000 LORN 44052 2744 D3
Tressel St
100 BERA 44017 2880 C7
Trevitt Cir N
600 EUCL 44143 2498 B2
Trevitt Cir S
700 EUCL 44143 2498 B3
Trevitt Cir W
500 EUCL 44143 2498 B2
Trevor Ln
7000 PRMA 44129 2882 E6
Trian Ct
7400 MNTR 44060 2253 A1
Tricia Dr
24500 WTLK 44145 2750 C3
Triedstone St
2400 CLEV 44115 2625 C4
Trillium Dr
17400 BbgT 44023 2891 A4
Trillium Ln
9200 MNTR 44060 2144 E2
9300 MNTR 44060 2145 A1
Trillium Tr
19200 SGVL 44149 3011 D5
31300 PRPK 44124 2629 D7
Trillum Gln
300 AURA 44202 3156 C1
Trimble Ct
8400 MNTR 44060 2144 B3
Trimble Pl
900 SgHT 44067 3152 B1
Trinity Ct
2700 AVON 44011 2748 D2
Trinity Rd
1600 MadT 44057 1842 E7
1700 MadT 44057 1941 E1
Trinter Rd
15200 BhmT 44089 2870 B5
15200 VmnT 44089 2869 E4
15200 VmnT 44089 2870 B5
Trisch Cir
2800 TwbT 44087 3154 E5
Trish Ln
9100 HmbT 44024 2381 A1
Triskett Rd
11500 CLEV 44111 2753 A1
12300 CLEV 44111 2623 A7
13000 CLEV 44111 2622 E7
13900 CLEV 44111 2752 C2
Trivue Cir
9400 TNBG 44087 3019 D6
Troika Cir
400 SgHT 44067 3017 D5
Trolley Tr
10 MDHL 44022 2760 B5
Trolley Vw
10 OmsT 44138 2879 A3
Tropicana Av
100 AMHT 44001 2744 B7
Trotter Ct
25100 ClbT 44028 3010 D3
Trotter Ln
600 BERA 44017 3010 E2
700 SGVL 44017 3010 E2
1500 PnvT 44077 2041 B6
7500 MNTR 44060 2252 D1
9200 NHFD 44067 3018 A3
Trotters Ridge Ln
1400 WTLK 44145 2619 D7
Trotwood Dr
7300 CcdT 44077 2253 C1
7400 CcdT 44060 2253 C1
Trotwood Park Dr
19300 SGVL 44149 3146 D1
Troubadour Dr
200 SgHT 44067 3017 D5
Trouper St
- HmbT 44024 2380 C2
Trowbridge Av
2500 CLEV 44109 2754 C1
Troy Ct
9600 MNTR 44060 2253 A3
Troy Ovl
6400 PRMA 44129 2882 E7
6400 PRMA 44129 2883 A7
Truax Av
16700 CLEV 44111 2752 B3
Truman Av
29900 WKLF 44092 2249 C7
29900 WKLF 44092 2374 C1
Truman Ct
7300 MNTR 44060 2143 C7
Trumbull Av
3600 CLEV 44115 2625 C5
Trumpeter Blvd
5300 NRYN 44133 3149 A1
Truscon Av
5600 CLEV 44127 2625 D6
Truxton Pl
3200 AVON 44011 2747 E5
Tryon Rd
24300 OKWD 44146 3018 D1
26200 GNWL 44139 3019 A1
26200 Okwd 44146 3019 A1
Tuckahoe Av
14000 CLEV 44111 2752 D1
Tucker Ct
2900 TNBG 44087 3020 B5
Tuckmere Dr
10 PnvT 44077 2146 B3
Tucson Dr
11800 PMHT 44130 2882 A2
11800 PRMA 44130 2882 A2
Tudor Av
10 BDFD 44137 2886 D2
10 BDFD 44146 2886 D2
10 MPHT 44137 2886 D2
14800 CLEV 44111 2752 C2
Tudor Cir
6000 NRYN 44133 3014 A5
6400 BKVL 44141 3150 D2
6600 NRYN 44133 3013 E5
Tudor Ct
6200 MAYF 44143 2500 A5
Tudor Dr
2200 CVHT 44106 2627 A4
28700 NOSD 44070 2749 D7
Tudor Pl
9700 HmbT 44024 2381 E3
Tuland Av
13600 CLEV 44111 2622 E7
Tulane Ct
100 ELYR 44035 2746 D7
Tulip Ln
10 MNTR 44060 2144 E7
8100 BbgT 44023 2890 E2
8400 BbgT 44023 2891 A2
16100 WNHL 44146 2886 C7
Tulip Tr
6400 INDE 44131 2884 E4
6500 INDE 44131 2885 A5
Tulip Wy
6300 CcdT 44077 2146 C5
Tullamore Rd
3100 CVHT 44118 2627 C3
3300 UNHT 44118 2627 D3
Tullis Dr
33400 AVON 44011 2748 D4
Tunbridge Dr
7000 CcdT 44060 2145 B7
Tunbridge Ln
24200 BHWD 44122 2628 D5
Tungsten Rd
24100 EUCL 44117 2373 C5
25200 EUCL 44132 2373 C5
26900 EUCL 44132 2374 A4
Tupelo Dr
6600 BDHT 44146 2887 D6
6700 OKWD 44146 2887 D6
Turkey Meadow Ln
17100 SGVL 44136 3147 A3
Turn Av
- CLEV 44102 2624 B6
- CLEV 44113 2624 B6
Turnberry Cross
100 BWHT 44147 3149 D3
Turnberry Ln
500 RDHT 44143 2498 C3
5400 HDHT 44143 2499 B3
Turnbridge Rd
28800 BYVL 44140 2619 D4
Turnburry Ct
31400 WTLK 44145 2749 A6
Turnburry Dr
5000 PryT 44057 2042 E4
5000 PryT 44057 2043 A4
Turnburry Rd
3500 PRPK 44122 2759 B1
3500 WDMR 44122 2759 B1
Turner Blvd
1800 ELYR 44035 2874 A6
Turner Dr
10 AQLA 44024 2505 C4
200 ClrT 44024 2505 D4
Turner St
500 ELYR 44035 2874 E6
500 ELYR 44035 2875 A6
Turney Ct
100 PNVL 44077 2040 B7
Turney Rd
300 BDFD 44146 2886 C4
600 BDFD 44137 2886 C4
600 MPHT 44137 2886 C4
4200 CLEV 44105 2756 B4
4200 PryT 44057 2042 E5
4200 PryT 44081 2042 E3
4500 GDHT 44105 2756 B5
4600 GDHT 44125 2756 C6
5300 GDHT 44125 2885 E2
6200 GDHT 44125 2886 A4
6300 GDHT 44137 2886 A3
Turning Leaf Tr
9800 BKVL 44141 3150 C5
Turnpike Plz
46400 AMHT 44001 2872 D4
Turnstone Ln
- CcdT 44077 2254 D2
Turtle Cr
2600 WTLK 44145 2749 A2
Turtle Tr
- WLBY 44094 2250 A7
N Turtle Tr
34800 WLBY 44094 2250 B7
S Turtle Tr
34800 WLBY 44094 2375 A1
35100 WLBY 44094 2250 B7
Turtleback Cove
- AVON 44011 2748 B4
Tuscany Cir
- AVON 44011 2748 E4
Tuscany Dr
600 MCDN 44056 3153 E6
600 MCDN 44056 3154 A6
600 NCtT 44236 3153 E6
Tuscarawas St
200 ELYR 44035 2874 E5
Tuscora Av
11000 CLEV 44108 2496 D6
12400 CLEV 44112 2496 E6
12400 ECLE 44108 2496 E6
12400 ECLE 44112 2496 E6
Tuttle Av
3400 CLEV 44111 2752 C1
Tuttle Ct
10 GNVA 44041 1944 B4
Tuttle Dr
31300 BYVL 44140 2619 A4
Tuttle Rd
9700 OmsT 44138 3009 C2
E Tuttle Park Rd
1800 MadT 44057 1941 D1
W Tuttle Park Rd
1800 MadT 44057 1941 D1
Tuxedo Av
200 BNHT 44109 2755 A7
200 BNHT 44131 2755 B7
200 CLEV 44109 2755 A7
600 BNHT 44131 2754 B7
800 PRMA 44131 2754 E7
800 PRMA 44134 2754 E7
5200 PRMA 44129 2754 A7
Tweed Ln
5900 MadT 44057 1941 D1
Twelve Oaks Dr
- SGVL 44136 3012 B4
Twickenham Dr
2300 BHWD 44122 2628 D4
Twilight Dr
100 SVHL 44131 2883 E6
100 SVHL 44131 2884 A6
7700 LkeC 44060 2143 D1
7700 MONT 44060 2143 D1
Twin Cir
3200 NOSD 44070 2750 D3
24400 WTLK 44070 2750 D3
24400 WTLK 44145 2750 D3
Twin Acre Ct
10 MDHL 44022 2760 A2
Twinbrook Rd
8600 MNTR 44060 2144 C6
Twin Cir Dr
2100 TNBG 44087 3019 D6
Twin Creek Ct
8300 MNTR 44060 2144 B3
Twin Creeks Dr
200 AbnT 44023 2892 A3
Twin Hills Dr
8800 TNBG 44087 3154 E1
Twinky Ln
3000 CLEV 44109 2624 D7
3000 CLEV 44113 2624 D7
Twin Lakes Dr
100 ELYR 44035 3005 B1
5800 PMHT 44129 2882 D2
5800 PMHT 44130 2882 D2
5800 PRMA 44129 2882 D2
30100 WKLF 44092 2374 D2
Twin Lakes Tr
7400 RslT 44022 2761 C5
Twin Mills Ln
11400 MsnT 44024 2503 E2
Twin Oaks Dr
7900 BWHT 44136 3014 C3
7900 BWHT 44147 3014 C3
7900 PRMA 44134 3014 C3
Twin Oaks Tr
11500 CdnT 44024 2254 C7
Twinsburg Rd
1200 MCDN 44056 3154 E5
1200 MCDN 44087 3154 E5
1200 MCDN 44236 3154 E5
1200 TwbT 44087 3154 E5
1200 TwbT 44236 3154 E5
E Twinsburg Rd
10 NCtT 44067 3153 D5
600 NCtT 44236 3153 D5
700 MCDN 44056 3153 D5
800 MCDN 44056 3154 B5
W Twinsburg Rd
10 NCtT 44067 3153 A6
10 NCtT 44236 3153 B6
500 NCtT 44141 3153 A6
Twinsburg-Warren Rd
10 AURA 44202 3156 D1
400 AURA 44202 3021 D7
1100 AURA 44087 3156 A2
1100 TwbT 44087 3156 A2
2600 AURA 44202 3157 E1
2600 ManT 44202 3157 E1
2600 ManT 44202 3158 A1
3000 ManT 44255 3158 A1
3700 ManT 44255 3159 A2
4700 ManT 44234 3159 A2
5300 ManT 44234 3160 A2
5500 HrmT 44234 3160 A2
7100 GTVL 44231 3161 E5
7100 HrmT 44231 3161 D4
7100 HrmT 44234 3161 C4
7100 HrmT 44255 3161 C4
Twinsburg-Warren Rd SR-82
10 AURA 44202 3156 D1
400 AURA 44202 3021 D7
1100 AURA 44087 3156 A2
1100 TwbT 44087 3156 A2
2600 AURA 44202 3157 E1
2600 ManT 44202 3157 E1
2600 ManT 44202 3158 A1
3000 ManT 44255 3158 A1
3700 ManT 44255 3159 A2
4700 ManT 44234 3159 A2
5300 ManT 44234 3160 A2
5500 HrmT 44234 3160 A2
7100 GTVL 44231 3161 E5
7100 HrmT 44231 3161 D4
7100 HrmT 44234 3161 C4
7100 HrmT 44255 3161 C4
Tyler Av
13000 CLEV 44111 2753 A3
13400 CLEV 44111 2752 E3
Tyler Blvd
- WLBY 44094 2375 A1
7400 MNTR 44060 2251 C2
7500 MNTR 44060 2143 D7
7900 MNTR 44060 2144 A6
Tyler Ct
- CLEV 44109 2754 C1
Tyler St
600 ELYR 44035 2874 E4
Tympani Tr
10 OmsT 44138 2879 A4
Tyndall Rd
3800 UNHT 44118 2628 A5
Tyndall Falls Dr
25300 ODFL 44138 3010 C1
Tyronne Av
19300 EUCL 44119 2372 E5
19300 EUCL 44119 2373 A5

U

Udall Rd
11700 HrmT 44231 3161 D1
11700 HrmT 44234 3161 D1
Uhlin Dr
7100 MDBH 44130 2881 C6
Underpass Rd
- CLEV 44135 2751 C7
Underwood Av
18500 CLEV 44119 2372 E6
Union Av
6400 CLEV 44105 2755 E1
6400 CLEV 44127 2755 E1
7200 CLEV 44105 2756 C1
7200 CLEV 44127 2756 A1
7900 CLEV 44104 2756 C1
11400 CLEV 44120 2756 E1
13500 CLEV 44120 2757 A1
Union Cir
24300 BHWD 44122 2628 D3
Union St
10 BDFD 44146 2887 A5
10 MDSN 44057 2044 B1
10 WTLK 44145 2749 C1
200 OBLN 44074 3138 C1
7700 MNTR 44060 2143 D3
38200 WLBY 44094 2250 E5
E Union St
10 GNVA 44041 1944 C5
W Union St
10 GNVA 44041 1944 B5
Unionville Dr
- NRDV 44035 3007 B1
United Ct
- CLEV 44113 2624 C5
Unity Av
10000 CLEV 44102 2753 C1
10000 CLEV 44111 2753 C1
University Av
100 ELYR 44035 3006 D1
200 CcdT 44077 2145 E3
200 PNVL 44077 2145 E3
University Blvd
2500 UNHT 44118 2628 A4
2600 SRHT 44118 2628 A5
20600 SRHT 44122 2628 A5
University Ct
700 CLEV 44113 2625 B5
University Pkwy
4200 UNHT 44118 2628 B4
4400 BHWD 44122 2628 C4
4400 UNHT 44122 2628 C4
University Rd
1000 CLEV 44113 2624 E5
University St
- MDBH 44017 2880 D6
- MDBH 44130 2880 D6
200 BERA 44017 2880 D6
200 BERA 44130 2880 D6
University Hospital Dr
2000 CLEV 44106 2626 D2
Unwin Rd
2300 CLEV 44103 2625 D3
2300 CLEV 44104 2625 D3
Upland Ct
- CLEV 44109 2754 B3
Upland Rd
400 BYVL 44140 2620 D5
Upper Dr
- CLEV 44135 2880 D1
Upper Chelsea Dr
11400 MsnT 44024 2504 B2
Upper Forty Dr
- MAYF 44040 2500 C3
Upper Terrace Dr
19700 EUCL 44117 2498 A2
Upper Valley Dr
19000 EUCL 44117 2497 E2
19200 EUCL 44117 2498 A2
Uppingham Rd
24200 BDHT 44146 2887 D4
Upson Ct
10100 TNBG 44087 3020 B4
Upton Av
14900 CLEV 44110 2372 B7
Urban Cir S
1700 LORN 44053 2744 B6
Urban Dr
4300 SELD 44121 2498 B6
Urban St
10 PnvT 44077 2145 D3
Urbana Rd
1600 CLEV 44112 2497 C3
Ursula Ct
30000 NOSD 44070 2878 C3
US-6 W 25th St
- CLEV 44113 2624 C4
US-6 Buckley Blvd
- CLEV 44113 2624 C4
US-6 Center St
100 CRDN 44024 2380 A6
US-6 Chardon Rd
7000 KTLD 44094 2376 B6
7000 WBHL 44094 2376 A5
8200 KTLD 44094 2377 A6
9600 CdnT 44024 2378 A7
9600 CdnT 44094 2378 A7
9600 KTLD 44094 2378 B6
10800 CdnT 44024 2379 B6
11100 CRDN 44024 2379 B6
21000 EUCL 44117 2498 C1
23500 EUCL 44143 2498 C1
23800 RDHT 44143 2498 C1
24400 RDHT 44143 2373 D7
26500 RDHT 44143 2374 A6
27200 WBHL 44092 2374 D6
29300 WBHL 44094 2374 D6
31900 WBHL 44094 2375 A5
US-6 Cleveland Mem Shoreway
- CLEV 44102 2623 E4
- CLEV 44102 2624 A4
- CLEV 44113 2624 C4
US-6 Clifton Blvd
- LKWD 44107 2621 E4
- RKRV 44107 2621 E4
- RKRV 44116 2621 E4
9200 CLEV 44102 2623 C5
11600 LKWD 44102 2623 B4
11600 LKWD 44107 2623 B4
12900 LKWD 44107 2622 E4
US-6 Detroit Av
2400 CLEV 44113 2624 C4
US-6 E Erie Av
100 LORN 44052 2614 E6
800 LORN 44052 2615 A5
3500 LORN 44054 2615 D4
3500 SDLK 44054 2615 D4
US-6 W Erie Av
100 LORN 44052 2614 C7
2300 LORN 44053 2614 B7
2700 LORN 44053 2744 A1
3100 LORN 44053 2743 B3
6100 LORN 44053 2742 E4
8000 VMLN 44053 2742 C4
8000 VMLN 44089 2742 C4
US-6 E Erie Br
100 LORN 44052 2614 D6
US-6 Euclid Av
13500 ECLE 44112 2497 C4
16300 CLEV 44112 2497 C4
18000 CLEV 44121 2497 D2
18400 CLEV 44117 2497 E2
18400 EUCL 44117 2497 E2
19600 EUCL 44117 2498 A1
20400 EUCL 44143 2498 A1
US-6 Gar Hwy
12500 CRDN 44024 2380 B6
US-6 GAR Hwy
12700 HmbT 44024 2380 E4
13500 HmbT 44024 2381 A4
US-6 N Hambden St
100 CRDN 44024 2380 A6
400 HmbT 44024 2380 B6
US-6 S Hambden St
100 CRDN 44024 2380 A6
US-6 Lake Rd
19200 RKRV 44116 2621 E5
22800 BYVL 44116 2621 A5
22800 BYVL 44140 2621 A5
23400 BYVL 44140 2620 A4
27500 BYVL 44140 2619 E4
31400 AVLK 44012 2619 B2
31400 AVLK 44140 2619 B2
31700 AVLK 44012 2618 D1
32000 AVLK 44012 2488 B7
32800 AVLK 44012 2487 E7
32900 AVLK 44012 2617 B2
33700 SDLK 44012 2617 B2
33700 AVLK 44054 2617 A2
US-6 E Lake Rd
- LORN 44052 2615 D4
- LORN 44054 2615 D4
3500 SDLK 44054 2615 C4
3800 SDLK 44054 2616 A3
5400 SDLK 44054 2617 A2
5500 AVLK 44012 2617 A2
5500 SDLK 44012 2617 A2
US-6 W Lake Rd
12500 VmnT 44089 2740 A7
14200 VMLN 44089 2740 C6
US-6 Liberty Av
1600 LORN 44053 2742 C4
1600 VMLN 44053 2742 C4
1600 VMLN 44089 2742 A5
4500 VMLN 44089 2741 B5
5100 VMLN 44089 2740 E5
US-6 Main St
100 CRDN 44024 2380 A6
US-6 E Park St
100 CRDN 44024 2380 A6
US-6 Superior Av
- CLEV 44113 2624 D3
4000 CLEV 44103 2625 C1
4000 CLEV 44114 2625 C1

STREET
Block City ZIP Map# Grid

US-6 Superior Av
5100 CLEV 44103 2495 D7
7100 CLEV 44103 2496 A7
8300 CLEV 44106 2496 A7
8300 CLEV 44108 2496 A7
12400 CLEV 44112 2496 E7
12400 ECLE 44112 2496 E7
US-6 Superior Av E
10 CLEV 44114 2624 E2
1200 CLEV 44114 2625 D1
3800 CLEV 44103 2625 C1
US-6 W Superior Av
100 CLEV 44113 2624 E3
100 CLEV 44114 2624 E3
100 CLEV 44115 2624 E3
US-6 Water St
100 CRDN 44024 2380 A6
200 CRDN 44024 2379 E6
600 CdnT 44024 2379 C6
US-20
- CrlT - 3005 D6
- CrlT - 3006 E4
- CrlT - 3139 E2
- CrlT - 3140 A1
- EatT - 3006 E4
- NRsT - 3139 E2
US-20 W 25th St
- CLEV 44113 2624 C4
US-20 Buckley Blvd
- CLEV 44113 2624 C4
US-20 Casement Av
400 PnvT 44077 2040 C6
US-20 Center Ridge Rd
19400 RKRV 44116 2621 D7
20600 FWPK 44116 2751 C1
20600 FWPK 44126 2751 C1
20600 RKRV 44116 2751 B1
22800 WTLK 44116 2751 A1
22800 WTLK 44145 2751 A1
23100 WTLK 44145 2750 A2
27200 WTLK 44145 2749 A6
31400 NRDV 44039 2749 A7
31400 NRDV 44145 2749 A7
31600 NRDV 44039 2748 E7
31600 NRDV 44039 2877 B3
36100 NRDV 44039 2876 E3
US-20 Cleveland St
700 ELYR 44035 2875 E5
900 ELYR 44039 2875 E4
900 NRDV 44035 2875 E4
US-20 Cleveland Mem Shoreway
- CLEV 44102 2623 E4
- CLEV 44102 2624 A4
- CLEV 44113 2624 C4
US-20 Clifton Blvd
9200 CLEV 44102 2623 C5
11600 LKWD 44102 2623 B4
11600 LKWD 44107 2623 B4
12900 LKWD 44107 2622 E4
US-20 W Clifton Blvd
1100 LKWD 44107 2622 A4
US-20 Detroit Av
2400 CLEV 44113 2624 C4
US-20 Detroit Rd
- LKWD 44107 2621 E5
- RKRV 44107 2621 E5
- RKRV 44116 2621 E5
US-20 S East Byp
- EatT 44035 3006 E3
- EatT 44044 3006 E4
- ELYR 44035 2875 E7
- ELYR 44035 3006 E1
US-20 Erie St
4000 WLBY 44094 2250 E5
US-20 E Erie St
10 PNVL 44077 2040 E4
800 PnvT 44077 2040 C6
US-20 W Erie St
10 PNVL 44077 2146 A1
US-20 Euclid Av
100 CLEV 44114 2624 E3
100 CLEV 44115 2624 E3
900 CLEV 44114 2625 E2
1200 CLEV 44115 2625 A3
3600 CLEV 44103 2625 C2
7300 CLEV 44103 2626 A2
8400 CLEV 44106 2626 C2
12200 ECLE 44106 2626 E1
12400 ECLE 44112 2626 E1
12500 ECLE 44112 2496 E7
13500 ECLE 44112 2497 C4
16300 CLEV 44112 2497 C4
18000 CLEV 44121 2497 D2
18400 CLEV 44117 2497 E2
18400 EUCL 44117 2497 E2
19600 EUCL 44117 2498 A1
20400 EUCL 44143 2498 A1
20700 EUCL 44117 2373 B7
25400 EUCL 44132 2373 E4
26000 EUCL 44143 2373 E4
27000 EUCL 44132 2374 D1
28300 WKLF 44092 2374 A4
30300 WLWK 44092 2374 D1
30500 WKLF 44092 2249 E7
30500 WLWK 44092 2249 E7
30700 WKLF 44094 2249 E7
30700 WLBY 44094 2249 E7
34000 WLBY 44094 2250 A7
US-20 Kipton East Rd
- NRsT 44074 3139 A6
- OBLN 44074 3138 B6
- PttT 44074 3138 B6
- PttT 44074 3139 A6
US-20 E Main St
10 GNVA 44041 1944 C4
900 GnvT 44041 1944 D3
US-20 W Main St
10 GNVA 44041 1944 E3
1000 GnvT 44041 1944 A4
US-20 Mentor Av
100 PNVL 44077 2146 A1
500 PNVL 44077 2145 E2
1100 PnvT 44077 2145 D3
2100 MNTR 44060 2145 D3
2100 PnvT 44060 2145 B6
7000 MNTR 44060 2251 C3
7000 MNTR 44094 2251 B4
7000 WLBY 44060 2251 B4
7000 WLBY 44094 2251 B4
8000 MNTR 44060 2252 A1
8700 MNTR 44060 2144 D7
38100 WLBY 44094 2250 E5
US-20 Public Sq
10 CLEV 44113 2624 E3
10 CLEV 44114 2624 E3
10 CLEV 44115 2624 E3
US-20 N Ridge Rd
1200 PnvT 44077 2040 D5
1700 PnvT 44077 2041 C2
2400 PryT 44077 2041 B3
2400 PryT 44081 2041 B3
3400 PryT 44081 1940 A7
3700 NPRY 44081 1940 E6
4700 MadT 44057 1941 C5
4700 MadT 44081 1941 C5
4700 NPRY 44081 1941 C5
4700 PryT 44081 1941 C5
6200 MadT 44057 1942 B4
7500 GnvT 44041 1943 B4
7500 GnvT 44057 1943 B4
7500 MadT 44057 1943 A5
US-20 N Ridge Rd E
4500 GnvT 44041 1944 E3
US-20 N Ridge Rd W
5900 GnvT 44041 1943 B4
6700 GnvT 44057 1943 B4
US-20 River St
4100 WLBY 44094 2250 E5
US-20 Sloane Av
1300 LKWD 44107 2622 A5
US-20 Superior Av
- CLEV 44113 2624 D3
US-20 Superior Av E
10 CLEV 44114 2624 E3
US-20 W Superior Av
100 CLEV 44113 2624 E3
100 CLEV 44114 2624 E3
100 CLEV 44115 2624 E3
US-20 Wooster Rd
1500 RKRV 44116 2621 E5
2500 LKWD 44126 2621 E7
2500 RKRV 44126 2621 E7
US-42 W 25th St
1400 CLEV 44113 2624 D7
3000 CLEV 44109 2624 D7
3200 CLEV 44109 2754 D1
US-42 Pearl Rd
10 BHIT 44212 3146 D7
10 BNWK 44136 3146 D5
10 BNWK 44149 3146 D5
10 BNWK 44212 3146 D7
10 SGVL 44136 3146 D5
10 SGVL 44149 3146 D5
3600 CLEV 44109 2754 A7
4500 CLEV 44144 2754 C5
5000 CLEV 44129 2754 A7
5000 PRMA 44109 2754 A7
5000 PRMA 44129 2754 A7
5300 PRMA 44129 2753 E7
5300 PRMA 44129 2882 E1
5700 PRMA 44130 2882 D2
5800 PMHT 44129 2882 D2
5800 PMHT 44130 2882 B4
6600 MDBH 44130 2881 D6
6600 PMHT 44130 2881 E5
7400 MDBH 44130 3012 B1
7700 SGVL 44130 3012 A2
7700 SGVL 44136 3012 A2
7700 SGVL 44149 3012 A2
9100 SGVL 44136 3011 D7
9100 SGVL 44149 3011 D7
US-322 E 13th St
1700 CLEV 44114 2625 A2
US-322 Chester Av
2200 CLEV 44114 2625 C2
3600 CLEV 44103 2625 C2
7300 CLEV 44103 2626 A2
8400 CLEV 44106 2626 A2
US-322 Detroit Av
2400 CLEV 44113 2624 C4
US-322 Euclid Av
10900 CLEV 44106 2626 C2
US-322 Mayfield Rd
2500 CLEV 44106 2626 E2
2500 CVHT 44106 2626 E2
2500 CVHT 44106 2627 B1
2500 CVHT 44118 2627 B1
2700 CVHT 44118 2627 A1
3200 CVHT 44118 2497 C7
3400 CVHT 44121 2497 D7
3800 CVHT 44121 2498 B7
3900 SELD 44121 2498 D7
4600 LNHT 44121 2498 D7
4600 LNHT 44124 2498 E7
4700 SELD 44124 2498 D7
5000 LNHT 44124 2499 D7
5600 MDHT 44124 2499 B7
6800 GSML 44040 2500 E6
6800 MDHT 44124 2500 B7
7000 GSML 44040 2501 A7
7300 CsTp 44026 2501 C7
8100 CsTp 44026 2502 C7
9400 CsTp 44026 2503 A6
9500 MsnT 44026 2503 A7
9900 MsnT 44026 2503 B7
10800 MsnT 44024 2504 B7
12100 MsnT 44024 2505 A6
12400 ClrT 44024 2505 C6
13400 ClrT 44024 2506 C6
13800 ClrT 44021 2506 C6
14400 ClrT 44046 2506 E6
14900 ClrT 44024 2507 A6
14900 ClrT 44046 2507 A6
15100 HtbT 44024 2507 C6
15100 HtbT 44046 2507 C6
15800 HtbT 44062 2507 D6
US-322 Superior Av
- CLEV 44113 2624 D3
US-322 Superior Av E
10 CLEV 44114 2624 E2
1200 CLEV 44114 2625 A2
US-322 W Superior Av
100 CLEV 44113 2624 E3
100 CLEV 44114 2624 E3
100 CLEV 44115 2624 E3
US-422
- AbnT - 2892 E6
- AbnT - 2893 C5
- BbgT - 2890 A5
- BbgT - 2891 D5
- BbgT - 2892 A6
- BDHT - 2758 B6
- BHWD - 2759 A2
- CLEV 44115 2625 B4
- MPHT - 2758 A6
- NRDL - 2758 B6
- ORNG - 2758 E4
- ORNG - 2759 A2
- SLN - 2759 A7
- SLN - 2888 B1
- SLN - 2889 B4
- SLN - 2890 A5
- WVHT - 2758 B7
- WVHT - 2759 A6
US-422 Broadway Av
800 CLEV 44115 2625 A4
US-422 Chagrin Blvd
15600 CLEV 44120 2757 B1
15600 SRHT 44120 2757 B1
17600 SRHT 44120 2757 E1
19400 SRHT 44122 2757 D1
20800 BHWD 44122 2758 E1
20800 HIHL 44122 2758 A1
26900 BHWD 44122 2759 A1
US-422 Kinsman Rd
5500 CLEV 44104 2625 E6
7200 CLEV 44104 2626 D7
11300 CLEV 44120 2626 D7
12300 CLEV 44120 2756 E1
13700 CLEV 44120 2757 A1
15400 SRHT 44120 2757 B1
US-422 Ontario St
1900 CLEV 44114 2624 E3
1900 CLEV 44115 2624 E3
2000 CLEV 44113 2624 E3
US-422 Orange Av
1400 CLEV 44115 2625 A4
US-422 Outerbelt East Frwy
- BHWD - 2758 E3
- BHWD - 2759 A2
- ORNG - 2758 E4
- ORNG - 2759 A2
- WVHT - 2758 E5
US-422 Woodland Av
2500 CLEV 44115 2625 C4
3800 CLEV 44104 2625 C4
Usher Rd
8200 ODFL 44138 2879 B6
8400 OmsT 44138 2879 B7
9000 ODFL 44138 3010 A1
9000 OmsT 44138 3010 A1
9200 ClbT 44138 3009 E2
9200 ClbT 44138 3010 A1
9200 ODFL 44138 3009 E1
9400 ClbT 44028 3009 E2
Usufruct Av
17000 CLEV 44111 2752 B2
Utah Ct
4300 PryT 44081 2041 D3
Utica Av
1700 LORN 44052 2744 C1
5500 CLEV 44103 2625 D1
Utopia Av
- CLEV 44110 2497 B2
Uxbridge Dr
28500 WLWK 44095 2249 B6

V

Vahalla Dr
7300 SLN 44139 3020 E2
Vail Dr
9900 TNBG 44087 3020 A4
Vale Dr
200 BDFD 44146 2887 B4
4800 NRYN 44133 3014 A4
Valencia Cir
100 ORNG 44022 2759 A5
Valentine Av
1700 CLEV 44109 2754 D1
Valentine Rd
14500 LryT 44086 2256 E2
14500 LryT 44086 2257 B2
14500 TpnT 44086 2257 B2
Valerie Ct
800 ETLK 44095 2250 B3
Valerie Ln
7400 HDSN 44236 3155 B7
Valeside Ln
7300 OmsT 44138 2878 D5
Valewood Dr
1800 PRMA 44134 2883 D2
Valkyries Cir
- CrlT 44044 3141 B4
Vallevista Dr
6500 MDHT 44124 2500 A6
Valley Blvd
900 ELYR 44035 2875 C3
Valley Dr
700 AMHT 44001 2872 B3
8200 BbgT 44023 2890 E3
8200 BbgT 44023 2891 A3
N Valley Dr
3800 FWPK 44126 2751 E1
18700 FWPK 44126 2622 A7
18800 FWPK 44126 2752 A1
S Valley Dr
4000 FWPK 44126 2751 E2
W Valley Dr
3800 FWPK 44126 2752 A1
Valley Ln
3000 NRYN 44133 3014 C3
5500 BDHT 44146 2888 A2
5500 SLN 44139 2888 A2
8200 PRMA 44130 3013 D1
8800 BbgT 44023 3022 B3
12000 GDHT 44125 2885 D3
W Valley Ln
18500 FWPK 44126 2622 A7
Valley Pkwy
- BERA 44017 2879 E4
- BERA 44017 2880 B6
- BERA 44017 3011 B1
- BERA 44142 2879 E4
- BERA 44142 2880 A4
- BKPK 44017 2880 A3
- BKPK 44070 2879 E1
- BKPK 44126 2751 B6
- BKPK 44138 2879 E2
- BKPK 44142 2879 E3
- BKPK 44142 2880 A4
- BKVL 44141 3016 D7
- CLEV 44107 2621 E7
- CLEV 44107 2622 A7
- CLEV 44111 2622 B7
- CLEV 44126 2621 E7
- CLEV 44142 2622 A7
- FWPK 44107 2622 A7
- FWPK 44126 2622 A7
- LKWD 44107 2621 E6
- LKWD 44107 2622 A7
- LKWD 44116 2622 A6
- LKWD 44126 2621 E7
- LKWD 44126 2622 A7
- MDBH 44017 3011 C2
- MDBH 44130 3011 D2
- NOSD 44070 2879 E1
- NOSD 44142 2879 E1
- OmsT 44070 2879 E2
- OmsT 44138 2879 E2
- OmsT 44142 2879 E3
- RKRV 44107 2622 A6
- RKRV 44116 2622 A6
- SGVL 44136 3011 E4
- SGVL 44136 3012 B6
- SGVL 44149 3011 D3
- WBHL 44094 2375 B5
2500 BKVL 44141 3150 E2
2500 BWHT 44141 3150 B2
2500 BWHT 44147 3150 B2
3300 BWHT 44147 3149 C2
3300 NRYN 44133 3149 D2
3300 NRYN 44147 3149 B2
4400 CLEV 44111 2752 A1
4400 CLEV 44126 2752 A1
4400 FWPK 44111 2752 A1
4400 FWPK 44126 2752 A2
4600 FWPK 44126 2751 B6
5600 BKVL 44141 3151 A2
6300 NRYN 44133 3148 A2
11500 NRYN 44133 3147 E1
11500 SGVL 44133 3147 E1
11500 SGVL 44136 3147 E1
24000 BKPK 44142 2751 B6
24000 NOSD 44070 2750 E7
24000 NOSD 44070 2751 B6
24000 NOSD 44142 2751 B6
Valley Rd
3600 CLEV 44109 2754 D4
16100 NbyT 44021 2765 A7
16300 AbnT 44021 2765 A7
16700 AbnT 44255 2893 E5
Valley Belt Rd
900 BNHT 44131 2755 C7
900 INDE 44131 2755 C7
5400 INDE 44131 2884 D1
Valley Brook Blvd
10 HkyT 44233 3148 B6
Valley Brook Cir
700 SgHT 44067 3152 C1
Valley Brook Dr
37900 WBHL 44094 2375 E7
Valleybrook Dr
4700 BKVL 44141 3150 B4
Valley Brook Ovl
200 HkyT 44233 3148 B7
Valley Creek Dr
900 ETLK 44095 2250 B4
16900 SGVL 44136 3012 A7
Valley Forge Cir
100 ELYR 44035 2873 E7
100 ELYR 44035 2874 A7
Valley Forge Dr
4300 FWPK 44126 2751 C4
9800 PMHT 44130 2882 C6
36700 SLN 44139 2889 C4
Valley Forge Ln
10 ELYR 44035 2875 B3
Valleypark Cir
2000 BWHT 44147 3014 E4
Valley Park Dr
900 BWHT 44147 3014 E4
Valley Parkway Dr
900 BKVL 44141 3150 B2
900 BWHT 44141 3150 B2
900 BWHT 44147 3149 E2
900 BWHT 44147 3150 A2
1100 NRYN 44133 3149 D2
1100 NRYN 44147 3149 D2
Valley Ranch Dr
6300 GDHT 44137 2885 E4
6300 GDHT 44137 2886 A4
6300 MPHT 44137 2886 A4
Valley Ridge Dr
36200 ETLK 44095 2250 C4
Valley Ridge Farm
10 HGVL 44022 2630 D4
Valleyside Rd
4300 CLEV 44135 2751 E4
Valleyview
1200 BWHT 44147 3149 E5
Valleyview Av
15600 CLEV 44135 2752 B4
Valley View Cir
700 AURA 44202 3021 B5
Valleyview Ct
8000 NRYN 44133 3013 C2
E Valley View Ct
6000 MNTR 44060 2144 C3
W Valley View Ct
6000 MNTR 44060 2144 C3
Valley View Dr
2100 RKRV 44116 2622 A6
2100 WKLF 44092 2374 D3
5800 BKPK 44142 2879 E1
12300 CsTp 44026 2501 E6
12300 CsTp 44026 2502 A7
Valleyview Dr
300 PNVL 44077 2146 C1
3700 LORN 44053 2743 E2
9800 ClbT 44028 3010 C2
9800 ClbT 44138 3010 D2
9800 ODFL 44138 3010 D2
12100 NbyT 44021 2765 A4
36300 ETLK 44095 2142 D7
Valley View Ln
- AVON 44011 2748 C5
Valley View Ovl
8800 KTLD 44094 2377 C3
Valley View Rd
7500 HDSN 44236 3154 D7
8100 MCDN 44056 3154 C7
8800 MCDN 44056 3153 D1
10000 MCDN 44056 3018 B6
10400 NCtT 44067 3018 A6
10700 NCtT 44067 3017 E6
10700 SgHT 44067 3017 D5
12000 SgHT 44067 3016 E3
12000 SgHT 44125 3016 E3
12000 VLVW 44125 3016 E3
Valleyview Tr
8200 NRYN 44133 3013 D3
Valley Villas Dr
7400 PRMA 44129 2882 C7
7400 PRMA 44130 2882 C7
7400 PRMA 44130 3013 D1
Valley Vista Dr
7600 INDE 44131 3016 A2
12200 MsnT 44024 2503 B6
12200 MsnT 44026 2503 A6
36100 ETLK 44095 2250 B3
Valley Woods Dr
4300 INDE 44131 2884 C7
Valplast St
15900 MDFD 44062 2767 D3
Van Aken Blvd
2700 CLEV 44120 2627 A6
2800 SRHT 44120 2627 A6
15500 SRHT 44120 2757 C1
17700 SRHT 44122 2757 D1
18900 SRHT 44122 2758 A1
Van Buren Av
- ELYR 44035 2875 A4
Vanburen Ct
7100 MNTR 44060 2143 D7
Van Buren Rd
1900 ECLE 44112 2497 A6
E Vancey Dr
6400 BERA 44017 2880 C4
6400 BERA 44142 2880 C4
6400 BKPK 44142 2880 C4
N Vancey Dr
21000 BKPK 44142 2880 C3
W Vancey Dr
6400 BERA 44017 2880 C3
6400 BERA 44142 2880 B3
6400 BKPK 44142 2880 B3
Vanda Av
100 AVLK 44012 2618 D2
Vandalia Av
4700 CLEV 44109 2754 B6
4700 CLEV 44144 2754 A6
5800 BKLN 44144 2754 A6
6200 BKLN 44144 2753 E6
Vandemar St
1300 CVHT 44121 2498 A7
Vanderbilt Ct
100 ELYR 44035 3006 D2
Van Epps Av
10 GNVA 44041 1944 C4
Van Epps Rd
4900 BNHT 44109 2755 B6
4900 BNHT 44131 2755 B6
4900 CLEV 44109 2755 B6
4900 CLEV 44131 2755 B6
Van Ess Dr
10 OmsT 44138 2879 A4
Van Oaks Dr
600 AMHT 44001 2872 C2
2000 TNBG 44087 3019 D3
Van Pelt Rd
1900 HpfT 44041 1943 D7
Vantage Pt
- RKRV 44116 2621 B7
Van Wert Av
5700 BKPK 44142 2881 D2
Vardon Dr
2400 LORN 44053 2743 E2
Varian Av
6400 CLEV 44103 2495 E7
Vashti Av
12400 CLEV 44108 2496 E4
Vas J Championship Dr
- CLEV 44119 2372 E4
- EUCL 44119 2372 E4
Vassar Av
200 ELYR 44035 3006 B1
2600 LORN 44053 2744 A4
Vassar Dr
- PnvT 44077 2147 A1
Vassar St
1800 ECLE 44112 2497 A6
Vaughn Rd
10200 FdmT 44255 3160 A7
10200 HrmT 44234 3160 A4
10200 HrmT 44255 3160 A6
10200 ManT 44255 3160 A6
10200 ShvT 44255 3160 A7
10600 ManT 44234 3160 A4
15600 BKVL 44141 3152 B4
15700 SgHT 44067 3152 B4
Vega Av
2500 CLEV 44113 2624 C6
Vegas Dr
500 ETLK 44095 2250 A2
Velma Av
5400 PRMA 44129 2754 A7
5400 PRMA 44134 2754 A7
6700 PRMA 44129 2753 E7
14300 CLEV 44128 2757 A4
Velour Av
14600 CLEV 44110 2497 B3
Venice Ct
1000 MCDN 44056 3154 A3
Venning Ct
5700 CLEV 44104 2625 D5
Ventanas Cir
- AVLK 44012 2618 D2
Ventnor Av
15600 CLEV 44135 2752 C5
Ventura Cir
100 BNHT 44131 2755 B7
Venture Dr
5500 PRMA 44130 2881 E1
Venture Ln
- HmbT 44024 2380 D7
Venus Dr
3900 BNWK 44212 3146 E7
9500 HmbT 44024 2381 C3
Vera Dr
8200 BKVL 44141 3015 E5
8200 BWHT 44141 3015 E5
8200 BWHT 44147 3015 E5
Vera St
22400 NRDL 44128 2758 C6
22400 WVHT 44128 2758 C6
Vermilion Dr
- VMLN 44089 2741 E4
- VMLN 44089 2742 A4
Vermilion Rd
500 VMLN 44089 2741 C7
2800 BhmT 44001 2870 E4
2800 BhmT 44089 2870 E4
2800 VMLN 44001 2870 E4
2800 VMLN 44089 2870 E4
8000 BhmT 44089 2871 A5
9300 BhmT 44889 2871 A7
9400 BhmT 44001 2871 B7
Vermilion Shrs
- VMLN 44089 2742 A5
Vermont Av
2400 CLEV 44113 2624 C4
2800 PryT 44077 2041 C4
2800 PryT 44081 2041 C4
Vermont Dr
600 LORN 44052 2615 D5
Vermont Rd
500 ELYR 44035 2875 D4
Vernon Av
10600 GDHT 44125 2756 C6
Vernon Dr
4500 NOSD 44070 2750 D6
Vernon Ln
400 MCDN 44056 3018 B7
Vernon Rd
2100 SELD 44118 2628 A3
2100 UNHT 44118 2628 A3
Vernondale Dr
6100 PMHT 44130 2882 C3
Veron Ln
2800 TNBG 44087 3020 A6
Verona Rd
4000 SELD 44118 2628 A2
4000 SELD 44121 2628 A2
Versailles Dr
10100 SGVL 44136 3012 C4
Versailles Pl
8100 MCDN 44056 3154 A3
Vesely Ct
500 ETLK 44095 2142 E7
Vesling Dr
- CrlT 44044 3006 D5
Vesta Av
7900 NCtT 44067 3153 A1
Vestry Av
2500 CLEV 44113 2624 C5
Veterans Memorial Pkwy
- AVON 44011 2747 B5
Vezber Dr
2300 SVHL 44131 3015 B2
Via San Angelo Dr
33700 AVON 44011 2748 C6
Viceroy St
- CcdT 44077 2254 C3
Vickie Ln
5500 BDHT 44146 2887 D2
Vicksburg Dr
1000 PRMA 44131 2883 E7
1000 PRMA 44134 2883 E7
1000 SVHL 44131 2883 E7
10600 PMHT 44130 2882 B2
Victor Av
3000 CLEV 44127 2625 D6
Victor Dr
34000 ETLK 44095 2249 E2
34100 ETLK 44095 2250 A2
Victoria Av
1400 LKWD 44107 2622 C6
Victoria Cir
7700 INDE 44131 2884 E5
7700 INDE 44131 2885 A5
Victoria Ct
100 ELYR 44035 3006 D2
14800 LKWD 44107 2622 C5
Victoria Dr
5400 LORN 44053 2744 C5
7000 MNTR 44060 2144 D7
8400 BWHT 44147 3014 E4
16600 AbnT 44021 2893 C1
Victoria Ln
- EatT 44035 3007 D1
5100 NOSD 44070 2750 B7
8900 NRDV 44035 2876 C7
9100 NRDV 44035 3007 C1
Victoria Rd
1700 CLEV 44112 2497 C3
Victoria Lake Cir
400 BHIT 44212 3146 A7
Victory Av
3000 LORN 44055 2745 B3
Victory Blvd
3900 CLEV 44111 2752 E3
4100 CLEV 44135 2752 E4
10400 NHFD 44067 3018 A4
Victory Dr
1300 SELD 44121 2498 C7
Victory Ln
13500 MsnT 44024 2634 D3
Vienna Dr
9000 PRMA 44130 3013 C2
Vienna Pl
8600 CLEV 44106 2626 B3
View Dr
14200 NbyT 44065 2634 C7
14400 NbyT 44065 2764 B1
22600 EUCL 44143 2498 B3
22600 RDHT 44143 2498 B3
View Rd
2200 CLEV 44109 2754 D1
Viewcrest Ct
4600 LORN 44053 2743 D4
Viewmount Dr
7700 CcdT 44077 2253 D3
View Point Dr
33600 EatT 44028 3143 D4
Viking Ct
9200 CLEV 44102 2623 D5
37900 AVON 44011 2747 C2
Viking Pkwy
30800 WTLK 44145 2619 A6
Vilamoura Dr
4200 AVON 44011 2748 C6
Villa Dr
1300 SELD 44121 2498 B7
Villa Pl
- PryT 44081 1940 C7
Villa Angela Dr
- CLEV 44110 2372 C5
- CLEV 44119 2372 C5
Villa Beach Dr
10 CLEV 44110 2372 B6
Villa East Dr
200 FTHR 44077 2039 D5
Village Cir
700 MAYF 44040 2500 C4
Village Ct
8900 ODFL 44138 3009 E1
Village Dr
- PRMA 44129 3014 E1
- PRMA 44134 3014 E1
100 SVHL 44131 3014 E1
100 SVHL 44131 3015 A1
200 BWHT 44147 3014 E5
1200 WLBY 44094 2143 A5
7000 CcdT 44060 2145 B7
10400 GTVL 44231 3161 E6
Village Dr E
300 SVHL 44131 3015 A1
Village Dr N
100 SVHL 44131 3014 E1
Village Dr W
200 SVHL 44131 3015 E1
200 SVHL 44131 3015 A1
Village Ln
- BHWD 44122 2628 E4
- BHWD 44122 2629 A4
26600 ODFL 44138 2879 A7
26600 ODFL 44138 3010 A1
N Village Ln
- BHWD 44122 2628 E4
W Village Ln
- BHWD 44122 2628 E4
Village Pkwy
700 SgHT 44067 3152 B1
Village Pl
10 BHWD 44122 2628 E4
Village Tr
700 GSML 44040 2500 C4
700 MAYF 44040 2500 C4
Village Cir Dr
100 CNFL 44022 2761 A6
Village Club Dr
600 SgHT 44067 3152 C1
Village Green Dr
3000 WTLK 44145 2749 E3
20300 SGVL 44149 3011 C3
Village Park Dr
10 OmsT 44138 2879 A4
Villa Grande Dr
11200 NRYN 44133 3014 B6
Villa Lago Dr
1000 MCDN 44056 3154 A3
Villa Marina Ct
8300 MNTR 44060 2144 B2
Villanova Cir
100 ELYR 44035 2746 D7
Villaview Rd
1000 CLEV 44119 2372 D7
16700 CLEV 44110 2372 C7
19300 CLEV 44119 2373 A6
19500 EUCL 44119 2373 A6
Ville Ct
7300 PRMA 44129 2883 A7
Vincent Av
10 NHFD 44067 3018 A3
600 CLEV 44114 2624 E3
4800 LORN 44055 2746 A6
4800 ShfT 44055 2746 A6
Vincent Dr
2500 SVHL 44131 3015 B2
12700 CsTp 44026 2502 D7
12700 CsTp 44026 2632 D1
12700 ManT 44255 3023 C5
23700 NOSD 44070 2750 D3
Vincent St
100 CNFL 44022 2761 A6
Vine Av
2800 LORN 44055 2745 C3
N Vine Av
20600 EUCL 44119 2373 A5
Vine Ct
2900 CLEV 44113 2624 B5
3800 CLEV 44102 2624 B5
22500 RKRV 44116 2751 A2
Vine St
- AVON 44011 2748 A2
10 WTLK 44145 2749 C1
100 FTHR 44077 2039 D4
100 GNVA 44041 1944 B4
5300 MPHT 44137 2757 C7
5300 MPHT 44137 2886 C1
31000 WLWK 44095 2249 C4
32500 ETLK 44095 2249 E4
33700 ETLK 44095 2250 D5
36300 ETLK 44094 2250 B5
36300 WLBY 44094 2250 B5
Vine St SR-640
30100 WLWK 44095 2249 D4
32500 ETLK 44095 2249 E4
33700 ETLK 44095 2250 D5
36300 ETLK 44094 2250 B5
36300 WLBY 44094 2250 B5
E Vine St
10 OBLN 44074 3138 E3
W Vine St
10 OBLN 44074 3138 D3
Vineland Rd
400 BYVL 44140 2620 D5
N Vinemont Ct
7500 HDSN 44236 3154 C6
S Vinemont Ct
7500 HDSN 44236 3154 D6
Vineshire Rd
900 CVHT 44121 2497 E5
Vinewood Dr
100 AVLK 44012 2617 E2
2000 PRMA 44134 2883 D2
29300 WKLF 44092 2374 B1
Vinewood Ovl
300 AVLK 44012 2617 D2
Vineyard Av
7600 GDHT 44105 2756 A5
8200 CLEV 44105 2756 A5
Vineyard Ct
600 WTLK 44145 2620 A6
Vineyard Dr
10 BNWK 44212 3146 E6
100 BWHT 44147 3014 E5
Vineyard Pk
3300 AVON 44011 2748 D3
Vineyard Rd
100 AVLK 44012 2488 C7
100 AVLK 44012 2618 C1
6900 INDE 44131 2884 D6
30000 WLWK 44095 2249 C7
Vintage Cir
33300 AVON 44011 2748 D3
Vintage Ct
9300 MNTR 44060 2252 E2
Vintage Ln
8400 MCDN 44056 3018 B7
Viola Av
10 CLEV 44110 2372 C6
14000 CLEV 44111 2752 D3
Violet Av
15000 CLEV 44135 2752 C5

STREET Block City ZIP Map# Grid

Violet Ct
2200 AVON 44011 2747 E2
Virginia Av
10 CLEV 44110 2372 C5
100 ELYR 44035 3006 B3
1100 LKWD 44107 2622 C4
3300 CLEV 44109 2754 C2
5400 PRMA 44129 2883 A1
5400 PRMA 44134 2883 A1
6700 PRMA 44129 2882 E1
22900 NOSD 44070 2750 E5
22900 NOSD 44070 2751 A5
Virginia Ct
5500 AMHT 44001 2744 C6
Virginia Dr
10 PnvT 44077 2040 C7
4200 FWPK 44126 2751 E2
Virginia Rd
3200 VMLN 44089 2741 E5
3200 VMLN 44089 2742 A5
3400 WDMR 44122 2759 B1
Vista Av
8100 GDHT 44125 2756 A6
Vista Cir
10 NOSD 44070 2879 B1
5600 WLBY 44094 2375 A2
Vista Ct
100 ELYR 44035 2875 C2
100 NOSD 44070 2879 B1
Vista Dr
- NOSD 44070 2879 B1
7500 PRMA 44134 3014 B1
8900 NRYN 44133 3014 C4
11100 HrmT 44234 3161 A4
11100 HrmT 44255 3161 A4
Vista Ln
10 AURA 44202 3021 C7
8300 PRMA 44130 3013 D1
Vista Lake Wy
38000 NRDV 44039 2747 B7
Vista Pointe Dr
11300 ClrT 44024 2505 C2
Vista Ridge Cir
10 BWHT 44147 3149 E5
10 HkyT 44147 3149 E5
10 HkyT 44233 3149 E6
Vita Ln
29200 NOSD 44070 2878 B4
Vivian Av
4700 CLEV 44127 2625 C7
Vivian Dr
200 BERA 44017 3011 A2
1000 GFTN 44044 3142 A4
Vivian St
100 SAHT 44001 2872 C7
Voelker Av
600 EUCL 44123 2373 C3
Vokes Dr
33900 ETLK 44095 2250 A5
Vondracek Dr
- SLN 44139 2888 E5
Vorderman Av
100 NHFD 44067 3018 A4
Vrooman Rd
5000 LryT 44077 2041 C7
5000 PryT 44077 2041 C7
5000 PryT 44081 2041 C7
5300 LryT 44077 2147 D4
7600 GnvT 44041 1844 A6
7600 GnvT 44057 1844 A6
7600 MadT 44057 1844 A6
Vulcan Ct
9300 CLEV 44102 2623 D6

W

Waban Rd
10 ETLK 44095 2250 B2
10 TMLK 44095 2250 B1
Wabash Av
1000 GFTN 44044 3142 B5
Waco Ct
2700 CLEV 44113 2624 C5
Wacoka Dr
10 ETLK 44095 2142 B6
Wade Av
- ELYR 44035 3006 B2
1900 CLEV 44113 2624 D6
Wade Ovl
10 CLEV 44106 2626 C2
Wadena St
1800 ECLE 44112 2496 E7
1800 ECLE 44112 2626 E1
Wade Park Av
5800 CLEV 44103 2625 D1
5800 CLEV 44103 2626 A1
8200 CLEV 44106 2626 C1
12200 CLEV 44106 2496 E7
12200 CLEV 44112 2496 E7
Wadsworth Av
10500 GDHT 44125 2756 C6
Wadsworth Rd
2600 SRHT 44122 2628 C6
Wagar Av
1400 LKWD 44107 2622 B5
W Wagar Cir
21000 RKRV 44116 2621 C6
Wagar Rd
300 RKRV 44116 2621 C7
2600 FWPK 44126 2751 C1
2600 RKRV 44116 2751 C1
Wagner Av
7300 CLEV 44104 2625 C5
7300 CLEV 44104 2626 A5
Wagner Ct
10100 TNBG 44087 3019 D3
Wagon Wheel Dr
33000 SLN 44139 2888 E3
33000 SLN 44139 2889 A3
Waikiki Dr
10 MadT 44057 1941 B5
Wailele Dr
10 MadT 44057 1941 B6
Wainfleet Av
13100 CLEV 44135 2752 E5
Wainstead Av
13400 CLEV 44111 2752 E3
Wainstead Dr
7500 PRMA 44129 2882 D3
Wainwright Dr
7300 NRDV 44039 2877 C4
Wainwright Ter
9700 ClbT 44028 3010 E2
9700 ClbT 44138 3010 E2
9700 ODFL 44138 3010 E2

Waite Hill Rd
6600 WTHL 44094 2375 E1
6600 WTHL 44094 2376 A1
9100 WLBY 44094 2250 E7
9100 WTHL 44094 2250 E7
Wakefield Av
5800 CLEV 44102 2624 A6
6900 CLEV 44102 2623 E6
Wakefield Cir
20600 SGVL 44149 3146 B4
Wakefield Ct
10 PNVL 44077 2146 B2
Wakefield Ln
2500 WTLK 44145 2749 E2
E Wakefield Rd
6900 HRM 44234 3161 B2
6900 HrmT 44234 3161 B2
7100 HrmT 44231 3161 D2
E Wakefield Rd SR-305
6900 HRM 44234 3161 B2
6900 HrmT 44234 3161 B2
7100 HrmT 44231 3161 D2
W Wakefield Rd
5700 HrmT 44234 3160 B2
5700 ManT 44234 3160 B2
6500 HRM 44234 3160 E2
6600 HRM 44234 3161 A2
W Wakefield Rd SR-82
5700 HrmT 44234 3160 B2
5700 ManT 44234 3160 B2
6500 HRM 44234 3160 E2
6600 HRM 44234 3161 A2
Wakefield Run
- NRDV 44035 2876 C6
- NRDV 44039 2876 C6
Wakefield Run Blvd
10 BWHT 44147 3149 D5
10 HkyT 44147 3149 D5
10 HkyT 44233 3149 D6
100 RchT 44233 3149 E6
100 RchT 44286 3149 E6
Wake Robin Dr
7400 HDSN 44236 3155 A7
7400 PRMA 44130 2882 C7
7400 PRMA 44130 3013 D1
16000 NbyT 44065 2763 B6
Wake Robin Rd
4600 MNTR 44060 2038 D6
Walbrook Av
2500 CLEV 44109 2754 C6
Walcott Rd
- CLEV 44135 2751 B7
- CLEV 44135 2880 A1
Waldamere Av
4500 WLBY 44094 2250 D6
Walden Av
15400 CLEV 44128 2757 B2
Walden Ct
6000 MNTR 44060 2144 C3
Walden Dr
700 AURA 44202 3156 C3
30900 WTLK 44145 2619 B7
31100 WTLK 44145 2749 B1
Walden Rd
2200 CVHT 44112 2497 C6
2200 CVHT 44118 2497 C6
2200 ECLE 44112 2497 C6
Walden Oaks Dr
12800 MsnT 44024 2634 C1
Walden Pond Cir
- HkyT 44233 3149 B6
Walden Reserve Blvd
- HkyT 44233 3149 B6
Walden Ridge Dr
- HkyT 44233 3149 C6
Waldensa Av
29200 WKLF 44092 2374 D4
Waldmer Dr
33900 ETLK 44095 2249 E2
33900 ETLK 44095 2250 A2
Waldo Wy
1000 TNBG 44087 3019 A4
Waldorf Dr
10 PnvT 44077 2145 C4
Waldorf Pl
6300 INDE 44131 2884 E4
Wales Av
2700 PRMA 44134 2883 C3
Wales Ct
4500 CLEV 44102 2624 B5
4500 CLEV 44113 2624 B5
Walford Av
9700 CLEV 44102 2753 C2
9900 CLEV 44111 2753 C2
Walford Rd
4600 WVHT 44128 2758 D5
Walker Av
8700 CLEV 44105 2756 B3
Walker Ln
- PNVL 44077 2145 C2
Walker Ovl
- INDE 44131 2885 A3
Walker Rd
5100 SDLK 44054 2616 E3
5400 AVLK 44012 2617 C3
5400 SDLK 44012 2617 A3
5400 SDLK 44054 2617 A3
30800 BYVL 44140 2619 A3
31500 AVLK 44012 2619 A3
31500 AVLK 44140 2619 A3
31700 AVLK 44012 2618 D3
Walkers Ln
8800 KTLD 44094 2377 C6
Walking Stick Wy
13800 SGVL 44136 3147 C4
Wall St
7000 INDE 44125 2885 A2
7000 INDE 44131 2885 A2
7000 VLVW 44125 2885 A2
Wallace Blvd
5200 NRDV 44039 2748 C7
5200 NRDV 44039 2877 C2
Wallace Ct
- EatT 44044 3142 A3
Wallace Dr
100 BERA 44017 3011 A1
100 BERA 44017 3010 E1
Wallace Ln
1500 LORN 44053 2744 A1
Walleyford Dr
400 BERA 44017 3010 E1
Wallingford Av
11000 GDHT 44125 2756 D7
Wallingford Dr
9200 TNBG 44087 3020 A6

Wallingford Gln
300 RDHT 44143 2498 E1
Wallingford Rd
3700 CVHT 44121 2497 E5
3700 SELD 44121 2497 E4
3800 SELD 44121 2498 A5
Wallings Rd
3000 BWHT 44147 3014 C4
3000 NRYN 44133 3014 B5
3000 NRYN 44147 3014 C4
5900 NRYN 44133 3013 E6
6500 BKVL 44141 3015 E3
6500 BWHT 44141 3015 E3
6500 BWHT 44147 3015 E3
6800 BKVL 44141 3016 A3
E Wallings Rd
100 BWHT 44147 3014 E3
600 BWHT 44147 3015 D3
5000 BKVL 44141 3015 E3
5000 BWHT 44141 3015 E3
W Wallings Rd
900 BWHT 44147 3014 D4
2900 NRYN 44133 3014 C4
2900 NRYN 44147 3014 C4
Wallu Dr
100 SAHT 44001 3003 A1
Walmar Dr
200 BYVL 44140 2619 A4
Walnut Av
- SFLD 44054 2746 C5
900 CLEV 44114 2624 E2
1600 CLEV 44114 2625 A2
E Walnut Av
10 PNVL 44077 2146 C1
400 PnvT 44077 2146 C1
E Walnut Av SR-84
200 PNVL 44077 2146 C1
400 PnvT 44077 2146 C1
W Walnut Av
10 PNVL 44077 2146 A2
600 PNVL 44077 2145 E2
Walnut Ct
3500 LORN 44053 2744 C3
3700 ORNG 44022 2759 D2
9000 NRDV 44039 2877 C7
32200 AVLK 44012 2618 C3
Walnut Dr
100 AMHT 44001 2873 A1
300 BERA 44017 2880 A5
500 EUCL 44132 2374 A2
6700 MAYF 44040 2500 B4
17600 SGVL 44149 3146 C4
32800 AVON 44011 2748 E1
Walnut Ln
1600 RKRV 44116 2621 C6
26100 NOSD 44070 2879 B2
Walnut St
- SAHT 44001 2872 C7
- SAHT 44001 3003 C1
10 CNFL 44022 2761 A6
10 GNVA 44041 1944 C4
10 OBLN 44074 3138 E2
400 VMLN 44089 2741 A5
800 ELYR 44035 2874 D4
4600 MNTU 44255 3159 C5
5500 MONT 44060 2143 E1
Walnut Tr
17500 BbgT 44023 2891 B5
Walnut Trc
13400 MsnT 44024 2634 C4
13400 NbyT 44024 2634 C4
Walnut Creek Dr
15200 SGVL 44149 3146 C2
Walnut Hill Dr
12600 NRYN 44133 3012 E7
Walnut Hills Av
3600 ORNG 44122 2759 A2
3600 WDMR 44122 2759 A2
Walnut Point Dr
- WTLK 44145 2749 A2
W Walnut Ridge Dr
10900 CsTp 44026 2501 B1
Walnutridge Rd
10900 CsTp 44026 2501 C2
Walnut Ridge Tr
300 AURA 44202 3021 C5
Walnutwood Dr
7600 SVHL 44131 3015 A2
Walt Ct
3600 CLEV 44111 2752 C2
Walter Av
3700 PRMA 44134 2883 B1
Walter Rd
2000 WTLK 44145 2750 D4
2700 NOSD 44070 2750 D4
2700 NOSD 44145 2750 D2
2700 WTLK 44070 2750 D4
Walter Main Rd
2100 GnvT 44041 1943 D6
2100 HpfT 44041 1943 D6
Walters Rd
300 CNFL 44022 2761 B6
400 RslT 44022 2761 B6
400 SRSL 44022 2761 B6
6900 BSHT 44236 3153 E7
6900 HDSN 44236 3153 E7
7300 MCDN 44056 3153 E7
7300 MCDN 44236 3153 E7
7300 NCtT 44236 3153 E7
7500 NCtT 44067 3153 E5
Walter Waite Ct N
6700 BKVL 44141 3016 B7
Walter Waite Ct S
6700 BKVL 44141 3016 B7
Walton Av
1800 CLEV 44113 2624 C7
Walton Blvd
2400 TNBG 44087 3020 A5
Walton Rd
6900 CyhC 44146 2886 E6
6900 WNHL 44146 2886 E7
7100 WNHL 44146 3017 E2
7800 SgHT 44067 3017 E3
7800 SgHT 44146 3017 E3
Walvern Blvd
15200 MPHT 44137 2886 B4
15700 BDFD 44146 2886 B4
Walwick Ct
700 BERA 44017 3011 B2
Walworth Av
300 EUCL 44132 2373 D1
4500 CLEV 44102 2624 B6
4500 CLEV 44113 2624 B6
Wamelink Av
9500 CLEV 44104 2626 B5

Wanaka Blvd
35700 ETLK 44095 2142 B7
Wanda Av
12000 CLEV 44135 2753 A4
Wanda Dr
5400 LORN 44053 2744 C5
Wanda St
100 CrlT 44035 3005 E3
Wandle Av
10 BDFD 44146 2886 E3
10 BDFD 44146 2887 A3
Wandsworth Rd
4000 CVHT 44121 2628 A1
4000 SELD 44121 2628 A1
War Av
6900 CLEV 44105 2755 E4
Warblers Ln
- NRDV 44039 2876 B4
Warblers Roost
6000 BKVL 44141 3016 C5
Ward Dr
12400 CsTp 44026 2502 A7
Ward Rd
7100 PRMA 44134 2883 C7
Warden Av
100 ELYR 44035 2874 E3
100 EyrT 44035 2874 D3
Wareham Rd
5900 PRMA 44129 2882 E3
5900 PRMA 44129 2883 A3
Warner Rd
10 HkyT 44233 3147 E6
2600 BNWK 44212 3147 E6
2600 BNWK 44233 3147 E6
4200 CLEV 44105 2756 A5
4500 GDHT 44105 2756 A5
4500 GDHT 44125 2756 A7
4800 GDHT 44125 2755 E7
4800 VLVW 44125 2755 E7
5200 VLVW 44125 2884 E1
6700 MadT 44057 2044 C3
6700 MDSN 44057 2044 C3
Warner Rd SR-14
- CLEV 44105 2756 B3
Warner Rd SR-307
6700 MadT 44057 2044 C3
6700 MDSN 44057 2044 C3
Warner St
- ELYR 44035 2874 E3
- EyrT 44035 2874 E3
300 PNVL 44077 2040 A7
Warren Av
100 ELYR 44035 2875 D6
1100 ELYR 44035 3006 D1
Warren Pkwy
2400 TNBG 44087 3020 A4
9800 TNBG 44087 3019 D5
Warren Rd
1100 LKWD 44107 2622 D6
2200 CLEV 44107 2622 D7
2200 CLEV 44111 2622 D7
3200 CLEV 44111 2752 C1
29900 WKLF 44092 2249 C7
Warrendale Rd
3700 SELD 44118 2627 E2
3700 SELD 44118 2628 A2
3800 SELD 44121 2628 A2
8700 MNTR 44060 2144 C2
Warren Point Ln
7500 HDSN 44236 3154 D6
Warrensville Center Rd
10 BDFD 44146 2887 A3
500 BDFD 44137 2887 A2
500 MPHT 44137 2887 A2
1300 CVHT 44121 2498 A7
1300 SELD 44121 2498 A7
1500 CVHT 44121 2628 A1
1500 SELD 44121 2628 A2
1700 SELD 44118 2628 A2
2100 UNHT 44118 2628 A4
2100 UNHT 44121 2628 A3
2500 SRHT 44118 2628 A6
2600 SRHT 44122 2628 A7
3600 SRHT 44122 2758 A2
3700 WVHT 44122 2758 A2
3900 HIHL 44122 2758 A3
4100 HIHL 44128 2758 A4
4200 WVHT 44128 2758 A3
4300 NRDL 44128 2758 A4
4800 WVHT 44146 2758 A3
5000 MPHT 44128 2758 A6
5000 MPHT 44137 2758 A7
5000 MPHT 44146 2758 A6
Warrington Dr
6700 NOSD 44070 2878 C3
Warrington Ln
10 CcdT 44060 2145 C6
Warrington Rd
2800 SRHT 44120 2627 B6
Warsaw Av
6400 CLEV 44105 2755 E3
Warwick Ct
100 ELYR 44035 2874 B6
200 AURA 44202 3021 E6
Warwick Dr
700 SDLK 44054 2615 E5
5400 PRMA 44129 2883 A3
5400 PRMA 44134 2883 A3
Warwick Ln
10 RKRV 44116 2621 B6
7400 CsTp 44026 2631 C1
Warwick Rd
2500 CLEV 44120 2627 A5
2500 SRHT 44120 2627 A5
Warwickshire Ln
33100 SLN 44139 2888 E7
33100 SLN 44139 2889 A7
Wasatka Dr
- MNTR 44060 2143 B3
- MNTR 44094 2143 B3
- WLBY 44094 2143 A3
Wasatka St
7000 MNTR 44060 2143 B3
7000 MNTR 44094 2143 B3
7800 WLBY 44094 2143 B3
Wascana Av
2000 LKWD 44107 2622 E6
2100 CLEV 44107 2622 E7
2100 CLEV 44111 2622 E7
Washburne Rd
5300 BDHT 44146 2887 C1
Washington Av
100 LORN 44052 2615 D6
600 ELYR 44035 2875 A6
1100 CLEV 44113 2624 C4

Washington Av
1100 LORN 44052 2744 D2
4700 LORN 44053 2744 D5
5500 MNTR 44060 2144 A1
5500 MONT 44060 2144 A1
8000 NRYN 44133 3013 C5
16600 MPHT 44137 2886 C2
Washington Blvd
- SRHT 44122 2628 C5
10 CLEV 44110 2372 C5
1100 MAYF 44143 2499 D6
1100 MDHT 44124 2499 D6
1100 MDHT 44143 2499 D6
2800 CVHT 44118 2627 B2
3400 UNHT 44118 2627 D3
3600 SELD 44118 2627 E3
3800 UNHT 44118 2628 A3
13800 SRHT 44118 2628 C5
14400 SRHT 44118 2628 C5
33600 NRDV 44039 2877 C2
Washington Cir
300 OBLN 44074 3138 D4
Washington Ct
700 BDFD 44146 2887 A4
3800 NBGH 44105 2755 B2
32700 SLN 44139 3019 E1
Washington Dr
200 NHFD 44067 3017 E3
200 NHFD 44067 3018 A3
1000 EatT 44044 3142 A3
1000 GFTN 44044 3142 A3
Washington Sq
10 EUCL 44143 2498 B2
Washington St
- OBLN 44074 3138 D5
- PtfT 44074 3138 D5
100 AMHT 44001 2872 E1
100 CRDN 44024 2379 E6
400 AMHT 44001 2743 E7
400 VMLN 44089 2740 E6
600 BDFD 44146 2887 A4
11800 AbnT 44021 2893 D5
11800 AbnT 44255 2893 D5
E Washington St
10 CNFL 44022 2761 D7
10 PNVL 44077 2146 B1
400 SRSL 44022 2761 D7
7600 BbgT 44022 2761 C7
7600 BbgT 44023 2761 C7
7900 BbgT 44023 2890 E1
8200 BbgT 44023 2891 E3
9600 AbnT 44023 2892 D5
9600 BbgT 44023 2892 A4
10700 AbnT 44023 2893 B5
11300 AbnT 44021 2893 B5
11400 AbnT 44255 2893 D5
W Washington St
10 CNFL 44022 2760 E6
10 CNFL 44022 2761 A6
10 PNVL 44077 2146 A1
Washington Wy
29600 WTLK 44145 2749 B4
Washington Park Blvd
- CLEV 44105 2755 C2
3600 CHHT 44105 2755 C3
3600 NBGH 44105 2755 C3
Wasil Rd
- NbyT 44065 2764 D1
W Wason Dr
1400 STBR 44241 3157 A7
Water St
10 CNFL 44022 2761 A6
10 ELYR 44035 2875 A6
10 FTHR 44077 2039 C3
10 GNVA 44041 1944 C3
100 CRDN 44024 2379 B6
100 CRDN 44024 2380 A6
600 CdnT 44024 2379 C6
24600 ODFL 44138 2879 B5
Water St SR-44
100 CRDN 44024 2380 A6
Water St US-6
100 CRDN 44024 2379 B6
100 CRDN 44024 2380 A6
600 CdnT 44024 2379 C6
Waterberry Ct
700 AVLK 44012 2618 A5
Waterbridge Dr
5100 NRYN 44133 3149 B4
Waterbury Av
- AVLK 44012 2617 B2
5300 MPHT 44137 2886 D2
Waterbury Cir
26400 NOSD 44070 2750 A5
Waterbury Dr
300 ETLK 44095 2142 D7
400 BERA 44017 3010 E1
Waterbury Rd
- CLEV 44107 2622 E6
- CLEV 44111 2622 E6
1400 LKWD 44107 2622 E6
Watercress Rd
10800 SGVL 44149 3011 A5
Watercrest Av
- MPHT 44137 2887 B2
19000 MPHT 44137 2886 E1
Watercrest Dr
16800 NRYN 44133 3149 B3
Waterfall Dr
10 CrlT 44044 3006 E6
10 EatT 44044 3006 E6
Waterfall Rd
10700 SGVL 44149 3010 E4
10700 SGVL 44149 3011 A4
Waterfall Tr
7400 RslT 44022 2761 C4
Waterfall Wy
2900 WTLK 44145 2749 A3
Waterford Cir
5300 SFLD 44035 2746 E5
5300 SFLD 44035 2747 A6
Waterford Ct
500 AVLK 44012 2617 C3
3800 ORNG 44122 2759 A3
Waterford Dr
- WLBY 44094 2142 E5
10 SRSL 44022 2762 B6
2900 TNBG 44087 3020 A4
5000 SFLD 44035 2746 E6
5000 SFLD 44054 2746 E6
15000 NRYN 44133 3147 E5
Waterford Ln
10 BHWD 44122 2628 E4
10 MNTR 44060 2145 B5
10 PnvT 44060 2145 B6
10 PnvT 44077 2145 B6

Waterford Pkwy
- BHIT 44149 3146 C5
- BHIT 44212 3146 C5
18800 SGVL 44149 3146 C5
Waterford Tr
9900 AbnT 44023 3023 B2
Waterford Wy
3200 AVON 44011 2748 B3
Waterfowl Ln
12100 MsnT 44024 2505 A7
Waterfowl Wy
7200 CcdT 44077 2254 C1
Waterfront Pl
- PnvT 44077 2040 E1
Waterloo Rd
- CLEV 44110 2497 B1
15200 CLEV 44110 2372 B7
16100 CLEV 44119 2372 C7
S Waterloo Rd
15700 CLEV 44110 2372 C7
15700 CLEV 44110 2497 A1
15700 CLEV 44119 2372 D7
19000 CLEV 44119 2373 A6
19800 EUCL 44119 2373 A6
Waterman Av
6100 CLEV 44127 2625 D6
Watermark Ln
1200 FTHR 44077 2039 D6
Water Oaks Blvd
- CcdT 44077 2146 C6
Waterpepper Cir
6800 SLN 44139 2889 B7
Water Pointe Ln
- BHIT 44212 3146 A7
Waters Dr
8200 MCDN 44056 3018 B7
8200 MCDN 44056 3153 B1
Waters Edge Dr
100 ELYR 44035 3006 D2
1900 AVON 44011 2749 A1
1900 AVON 44145 2749 A1
1900 WTLK 44145 2749 A1
Waterside Dr
300 AVLK 44012 2617 D2
8400 SgHT 44067 3017 D5
26900 ODFL 44138 3009 D1
Waters Wy Dr
100 WLWK 44095 2249 D7
Water Tower Dr
200 MDSN 44057 2044 B3
200 MadT 44057 2044 C3
Waterview Ct
- AVLK 44012 2617 D3
Watkin Rd
27100 OmsT 44138 3009 C1
N Watling Wy
6100 MadT 44057 1842 E7
6200 MadT 44057 1941 E1
6200 MadT 44057 1942 A1
S Watling Wy
6100 MadT 44057 1941 E1
6200 MadT 44057 1942 A1
Watson Av
38800 NRDV 44039 2876 A4
Watson Ct
3500 LORN 44053 2743 E3
Watson Dr
- CrlT 44035 3006 A4
Watson Rd
20400 MPHT 44137 2758 A7
Watson St
10 PNVL 44077 2146 A1
Watt Rd
13800 RslT 44072 2632 D6
14400 RslT 44072 2762 D1
Watterson Av
12300 CLEV 44105 2756 E3
Waverly Av
100 ELYR 44035 2874 E5
Waverly Ct
5800 CLEV 44102 2624 A5
Waverly Ln
10 SRSL 44022 2761 E6
Waverly Pl
100 LORN 44052 2614 B7
3900 SELD 44121 2498 A4
Waverly Rd
200 ETLK 44095 2249 E4
Waverly St
100 BERA 44017 2880 C7
200 BERA 44130 2880 D7
200 MDBH 44130 2880 D7
Wa Wa Taysee St
4800 VMLN 44089 2741 A4
Waxberry Dr
6400 SVHL 44131 2884 A4
Way Av
9100 CLEV 44105 2756 C2
Wayland Av
11700 CLEV 44111 2753 A2
Wayne Av
1400 LKWD 44107 2622 A5
Wayne Ct
10100 CLEV 44106 2626 C3
24600 EUCL 44123 2373 D3
Wayne Dr
200 BERA 44017 2880 A7
16700 CLEV 44128 2757 C4
Wayne Ln
10 HmbT 44024 2381 A3
Wayne Rd
4100 ManT 44255 3159 A1
Wayne St
500 ELYR 44035 3006 A2
Wayne Tr
1000 VMLN 44089 2741 B6
Waynesboro Dr
1400 TwbT 44087 3154 C6
1400 TwbT 44236 3154 C6
Waynoka Rd
2100 EUCL 44117 2498 A3
Wayside Av
- NCtT 44067 3153 B5
Wayside Dr
7000 MNTR 44060 2145 A6
Wayside Ln
28900 BYVL 44140 2619 D4
Wayside Rd
700 CLEV 44110 2497 C2
900 CLEV 44112 2497 C2
Waywood Dr
11900 TNBG 44087 3019 D3
Weatherby Dr
6700 MNTR 44060 2143 D6

N Weatherby Dr
6600 MNTR 44060 2143 E5
Weathersfield Dr
9800 CcdT 44060 2253 C2
10000 CcdT 44077 2253 D2
Weatherstone Dr
- BERA 44138 2879 D5
5000 NRDV 44039 2747 B6
Weathertop Ln
9700 AbnT 44023 2892 A1
Weathervane Ct
7600 CcdT 44060 2253 C2
Weathervane Dr
- MDFD 44062 2767 E1
9400 BbgT 44023 2891 E6
Weathervane Ln
10 BNWK 44136 3147 B5
10 BNWK 44212 3147 B6
10 SGVL 44136 3147 B5
Weatherwood Ln
2100 BWHT 44147 3149 D5
Weaver Dr
1500 AMHT 44001 2744 C6
Webb Rd
1000 LKWD 44107 2622 B4
4500 PryT 44081 2042 C5
4700 PryT 44057 2042 C6
Webb Cliff Dr
17800 LKWD 44107 2622 A4
Webber Rd
32700 AVLK 44012 2618 A4
32800 AVLK 44012 2617 C4
Weber Av
28900 EUCL 44132 2374 A2
28900 WKLF 44092 2374 A2
Weber Rd
7600 MONT 44060 2143 D2
Weber Park Dr
22000 BDFD 44146 2887 C7
22000 OKWD 44146 2887 C7
Webster Av
900 CLEV 44115 2625 B4
Webster Cir
2500 HDSN 44236 3155 C6
Webster Ct
200 PNVL 44077 2146 B1
3300 CLEV 44114 2625 C2
Webster Rd
7500 MDBH 44130 3012 B1
7900 SGVL 44130 3012 C2
7900 SGVL 44136 3012 B1
16300 MDBH 44130 2881 A7
30500 BYVL 44140 2619 B3
Wedgefield Ln
12200 CsTp 44026 2501 E6
Wedgewood Av
100 ELYR 44035 2875 E3
Wedgewood Cir
300 BWHT 44147 3149 C4
Wedgewood Ct
8500 OmsT 44138 2879 A7
Wedgewood Dr
500 AVLK 44012 2618 C4
2100 SFLD 44054 2615 E7
5900 MONT 44060 2143 C3
6000 MNTR 44060 2143 C3
6400 BKPK 44142 2880 D4
6400 MDBH 44130 2880 D4
6400 MDBH 44142 2880 D4
6500 NOSD 44070 2878 B3
7900 CsTp 44026 2501 E5
30100 SLN 44139 2888 C1
Wedgewood Ln
15800 SGVL 44149 3146 B3
Wefel Av
7400 BKLN 44144 2753 E4
Welch Rd
1400 PnvT 44077 2041 A7
Welk Ct
- AMHT 44001 2872 E4
9100 MNTR 44060 2144 E1
Welk Rd
9800 CdnT 44024 2378 B5
Welland Dr
7100 MNTR 44060 2143 B7
Weller Rd
600 ELYR 44035 2875 A4
Wellesley Av
1800 ECLE 44112 2497 A6
5200 NOSD 44070 2749 C7
5400 NOSD 44070 2878 C1
Wellesley Blvd
10 CcdT 44077 2145 B6
10 PnvT 44077 2145 B6
Wellesley Cir
600 AVLK 44012 2618 D4
Wellesley Ln
11700 MsnT 44024 2503 E4
Wellfleet Dr
500 BYVL 44140 2619 B5
1000 GFTN 44044 3142 A4
7200 HDSN 44236 3154 E7
Wellingford Ct
33500 SLN 44139 2889 A2
Wellington Av
2400 PRMA 44134 2883 D3
4800 PRMA 44129 2883 A3
Wellington Ct
200 MDSN 44057 2044 C2
7100 BSHT 44236 3153 E6
18100 SGVL 44136 3146 E4
Wellington Dr
4500 PryT 44081 2042 C5
11100 CdnT 44024 2379 B3
29500 NOSD 44070 2878 C3
Wellington Rd
2400 CVHT 44118 2627 C5
5600 LNHT 44124 2629 B1
5600 MDHT 44124 2629 B1
10100 ShvT 44255 3158 A7
Wellington St
10 BERA 44017 2880 B5
Wellman Rd
10200 STBR 44236 3156 A7
Wellmon St
600 BDFD 44146 2887 C4
Wellner Rd
31000 WLWK 44095 2249 C5
Wells Pl
200 EUCL 44132 2249 A7
Wells Fleet Cir
3000 WLBY 44094 2250 E2
Wellsley Pl
10 BNWK 44212 3147 B6

STREET Block City ZIP Map# Grid

Wellswood Tr
12700 CsTp 44026 2501 B7
12700 CsTp 44026 2631 B1
Welshfield Limaville Rd S
10400 FdmT 44255 3161 A7
10400 HrmT 44231 3161 A6
10400 HrmT 44255 3161 A7
11300 HRM 44234 3161 A6
11900 HrmT 44234 3161 A1
Welshfield Limavle Rd S SR-82
11300 HRM 44234 3161 A6
11300 HrmT 44234 3161 A6
Welshfield Limavle Rd S SR-700
10400 FdmT 44255 3161 A7
10400 HrmT 44231 3161 A6
10400 HrmT 44255 3161 A7
11300 HRM 44234 3161 A6
11900 HrmT 44234 3161 A1
Welshire Dr
500 BYVL 44140 2619 C5
Welton Dr
15300 ECLE 44112 2497 B5
Wembley Ct
8400 BbgT 44023 2761 E7
8400 BbgT 44023 2762 A7
Wemple Rd
14700 CLEV 44110 2497 B3
14700 ECLE 44110 2497 B3
14700 ECLE 44112 2497 B3
Wendell Av
4800 CLEV 44127 2625 C6
Wendell St
- AVON 44011 2747 E5
Wenden Ct
10 BTNH 44108 2496 E1
10 BTNH 44108 2497 A1
Wendover Dr
23100 BHWD 44122 2628 C4
23100 UNHT 44118 2628 C4
23100 UNHT 44122 2628 C4
Wendy Dr
3700 CLEV 44122 2757 D3
3900 CLEV 44128 2757 D3
12100 PRMA 44130 3013 A1
19600 MDBH 44130 2880 D5
19800 BERA 44017 2880 D5
19800 BERA 44130 2880 D5
Wendy Ln
600 ELYR 44035 2875 A7
Wengatz Dr
13100 MDBH 44130 3012 D1
13100 PRMA 44130 3012 D1
Wengler Dr
5700 BKPK 44142 2881 B2
Wenhaven Dr
15400 RslT 44022 2761 E4
Wenso Rd
900 BDFD 44146 2887 B5
Wentworth Av
6400 BKPK 44142 2880 B3
7400 CLEV 44102 2623 D7
Wentworth Ln
7500 CcdT 44060 2253 B2
Wentworth Rd
10200 ShvT 44255 3158 A7
10400 ManT 44255 3158 A6
Werner Ct
2900 LORN 44052 2744 C3
Wescott Wy
- NRDV 44035 3007 B1
Wesley Av
400 ELYR 44035 2875 E3
13000 CLEV 44111 2753 A2
13200 CLEV 44111 2752 E2
Wesley Dr
600 BERA 44017 2880 B4
7900 MDBH 44130 3012 D2
7900 SGVL 44130 3012 D2
7900 SGVL 44136 3012 E2
8400 PMHT 44129 2882 D2
8400 PMHT 44130 2882 D2
8400 PRMA 44129 2882 D2
8400 PRMA 44130 2882 D2
Wesleyan Ct
100 ELYR 44035 3006 B1
West Av
10 ELYR 44035 2875 A7
900 CLEV 44113 2624 D3
1000 ELYR 44035 3006 A1
13000 CLEV 44111 2752 E3
13000 CLEV 44111 2753 A2
West Blvd
1900 CLEV 44102 2623 C6
2000 CLEV 44111 2623 C7
3200 CLEV 44111 2753 C1
3500 CLEV 44102 2753 C1
4000 BKLN 44144 2753 E3
5300 MPHT 44137 2886 C1
West Dr
- MNTR 44094 2251 B4
- SDLK 44054 2615 E4
10 CLEV 44134 2754 C7
10 OmsT 44138 2879 A4
500 BNWK 44212 3146 E7
700 SDLK 44054 2616 A4
West Pl
200 PNVL 44077 2146 A2
West Rd
5700 MONT 44060 2143 D2
13400 NRsT 44074 3139 D3
13800 PtfT 44074 3139 D5
22900 BERA 44017 2879 E7
22900 ODFL 44017 2879 E7
24300 ODFL 44138 2879 D7
35300 EatT 44044 3008 A7
West St
- MadT 44057 1943 A7
10 BERA 44017 2880 A7
10 CNFL 44022 2761 B6
10 GNVA 44041 1944 A6
300 AMHT 44001 2872 D2
400 BERA 44017 2879 E7
400 ODFL 44017 2879 E7
400 ODFL 44138 2879 E7
2200 HpfT 44041 1944 A6
13600 BtnT 44021 2636 A7
13600 BtnT 44021 2766 A2
13600 BURT 44021 2636 A7
13600 BURT 44021 2766 A2
West Area Rd
- BKPK 44135 2751 A7
- BKPK 44142 2751 A7
- BKPK 44142 2880 A1
- CLEV 44135 2751 A7
Westborough Rd
10900 PMHT 44130 2882 B4
Westbourne Rd
4700 LNHT 44124 2498 D7
4700 SELD 44121 2498 D7
Westbridge Dr
200 BERA 44017 2880 B6
Westbrook Dr
100 EUCL 44132 2249 A6
4200 BKLN 44144 2753 D4
5800 BKPK 44142 2881 D2
Westbrook Wy
600 BSHT 44236 3153 E7
600 HDSN 44236 3153 E7
600 HDSN 44236 3154 A7
Westbrooke Ln
19100 SGVL 44149 3146 D4
Westburn Av
1900 CLEV 44112 2497 D4
1900 ECLE 44112 2497 D4
Westbury Dr
500 PnvT 44077 2145 C5
Westbury Rd
3300 CLEV 44120 2757 B1
3300 SRHT 44120 2627 B7
3300 SRHT 44120 2757 B1
Westchester Av
9800 CLEV 44108 2496 B6
Westchester Ct
1500 PnvT 44077 2041 B5
Westchester Dr
10 BNWK 44212 3147 A6
100 AhtT 44001 2872 D4
100 AMHT 44001 2872 D3
23200 NOSD 44070 2750 E3
Westchester Pkwy
27600 WTLK 44145 2619 E6
27600 WTLK 44145 2620 A6
Westchester Rd
21800 SRHT 44122 2628 B6
Westchester Tr
12700 CsTp 44026 2501 B7
12700 CsTp 44026 2631 B2
West Creek Ct
- AVLK 44012 2617 D2
Westdale Av
15700 CLEV 44135 2752 B4
Westdale Dr
- PRMA 44130 2881 E7
- PRMA 44130 2882 A7
Westdale Rd
1400 SELD 44121 2498 B7
1400 SELD 44121 2628 B1
Westerham Rd
6000 MDHT 44124 2629 D2
Western Av
- OBLN 44074 3138 C1
10000 CLEV 44102 2623 C7
10000 CLEV 44111 2623 C7
Western Pkwy
38100 WLBY 44094 2142 E6
Westfield Av
16600 CLEV 44110 2497 C2
Westfield Cir
1000 PnvT 44077 2146 E2
Westfield Dr
- AVON 44011 2747 A2
8300 NRDV 44039 2876 E6
14600 NbyT 44065 2764 C1
Westfield Ln
10 RKRV 44116 2621 C7
18900 SGVL 44136 3147 A5
Westfield Park Dr
8400 OmsT 44138 2878 D7
Westford Cir
- WTLK 44145 2619 C7
Westgate Mall
3000 FWPK 44116 2751 D1
3000 RKRV 44116 2751 D1
20800 FWPK 44126 2751 C1
West Geauga Plaza Dr
- CsTp 44026 2502 A7
West Hampton Dr
9000 NRYN 44133 3013 C5
Westhaven Ln
19900 FWPK 44126 2751 D1
19900 RKRV 44116 2751 D1
19900 RKRV 44126 2751 D1
West Hemlock
2300 NPRY 44081 1940 D3
Westhill Blvd
1400 WTLK 44145 2620 D6
Westhill Dr
8000 BbgT 44023 2890 E3
8000 BbgT 44023 2891 A3
Westin Wy
500 ELYR 44035 3007 A1
500 NRDV 44035 3007 A1
Westlake Av
1100 LKWD 44107 2622 B4
5400 PRMA 44129 2883 A1
5400 PRMA 44134 2883 A1
5400 PRMA 44129 2882 E1
Westlake Dr
500 AMHT 44001 2872 C1
Westlake Gdns
- LORN 44053 2743 D2
Westlake Village Ct
28600 WTLK 44145 2749 D3
Westlake Village Dr
28600 WTLK 44145 2749 D4
Westland Av
14500 CLEV 44111 2752 D1
14600 CLEV 44111 2622 C7
Westlawn Blvd
8700 ODFL 44138 2879 E7
Westlawn Dr
28200 NOSD 44070 2878 D3
29900 BYVL 44140 2619 C4
Westlawn Rd
5000 BDHT 44128 2758 D7
5000 WRVL 44128 2758 D7
Westminster Av
35400 AVON 44011 2748 A6
35400 NRDV 44011 2748 A6
35400 NRDV 44039 2748 A6
Westminster Dr
- LORN 44053 2744 A4
5600 SLN 44139 2888 C2
5900 PRMA 44129 2882 D3
20500 SGVL 44149 3146 B4
29400 NOSD 44070 2878 C3
Westminster Ln
2600 WLBY 44094 2250 E1
4700 BWHT 44147 3015 C5
Westminster Rd
2100 CVHT 44118 2627 B3
Westminster Wy
- EatT 44035 3007 B1
Westmont Dr
4300 SFLD 44054 2746 D4
Westmoor Ln
20100 BERA 44017 2880 D5
20100 BERA 44130 2880 D5
20100 MDBH 44130 2880 D5
Westmoor Rd
2200 RKRV 44116 2621 D7
8100 MNTR 44060 2251 C4
Weston Av
- WTLK 44145 2750 C2
Weston Ct
5500 WLBY 44094 2375 A1
Weston Rd
18000 CLEV 44112 2497 E3
18000 CLEV 44121 2497 E3
Weston Pointe
11700 SGVL 44149 3011 A5
Westover Av
19200 FWPK 44126 2751 D1
19200 RKRV 44116 2751 D1
19200 RKRV 44126 2751 D1
Westover Dr
10 SRSL 44022 2762 B6
Westover Rd
1300 CVHT 44118 2497 C7
Westown Blvd
27200 WTLK 44145 2749 E3
27200 WTLK 44145 2750 A3
Westpoint Pkwy
800 WTLK 44145 2620 D6
West Pointe Cir
100 CRDN 44024 2505 B1
Westpointe Dr
- AhtT 44001 2873 A3
- AMHT 44001 2872 E3
- AMHT 44001 2873 A3
Westport Av
20100 EUCL 44119 2373 A4
23100 EUCL 44123 2373 C4
Westport Dr
8400 MNTR 44060 2144 B5
Westporte Pl
- AVLK 44012 2617 C3
Westridge Cir
11400 MsnT 44024 2634 B3
West Ridge Dr
- RslT 44072 2631 E7
Westropp Av
14000 BTNH 44110 2497 A1
14000 CLEV 44110 2497 A1
14200 CLEV 44110 2372 A7
Westview Av
15500 CLEV 44128 2757 B3
22100 BKPK 44142 2880 A3
Westview Ct
2300 LORN 44052 2744 B2
West View Dr
17600 BbgT 44023 2890 E5
Westview Dr
400 BDFD 44146 2887 A2
4400 NOSD 44070 2750 C6
6600 BKVL 44141 3150 E3
6600 BKVL 44141 3151 A3
9700 PRMA 44129 2753 C7
Westway Dr
19700 RKRV 44116 2621 D6
Westwind Ct
11000 SGVL 44149 3011 A5
Westwind Dr
100 AVLK 44012 2618 E2
Westwood Av
400 BNWK 44212 3147 A7
1400 LKWD 44107 2622 C5
1900 ELYR 44035 3006 B3
Westwood Dr
- GnvT 44041 1944 C1
700 PNVL 44077 2146 B2
900 WLBY 44094 2142 E5
1400 LORN 44053 2744 C5
1600 TNBG 44087 3019 C4
6700 BKVL 44141 3150 E1
6700 BKVL 44141 3151 A1
9000 KTLD 44094 2252 A7
9300 MCDN 44056 3018 E5
14600 NbyT 44072 2763 A1
18700 SGVL 44136 3011 E7
18700 SGVL 44149 3011 A6
22300 ClbT 44028 3010 E6
22300 ClbT 44149 3010 E6
22300 SGVL 44149 3010 E6
36000 NRDV 44039 2876 E5
36000 NRDV 44039 2877 A4
Westwood Ln
26900 OmsT 44138 2878 E3
26900 OmsT 44138 2879 A3
Westwood Rd
3700 UNHT 44118 2627 E3
10200 ClbT 44028 3010 D3
20800 FWPK 44126 2751 A2
22900 WTLK 44126 2751 A2
22900 WTLK 44145 2750 A2
22900 WTLK 44145 2751 A2
29800 BYVL 44140 2619 D4
Westwood Park Blvd
20200 SGVL 44149 3011 C7
Wetherburn Wy
7400 HDSN 44236 3154 E7
Wetherill Ct
3600 AVON 44011 2747 E4
Wethersfield Ct
4700 RDHT 44143 2498 D1
Wethersfield Dr
7200 HDSN 44236 3154 D7
Wetmore St
100 GDRV 44077 2039 C6
100 PnvT 44077 2039 C6
Wetzel Av
3600 CLEV 44109 2754 B6
3600 CLEV 44144 2754 A6
Wexford Av
900 BKNT 44131 2754 E7
900 PRMA 44131 2754 E7
900 PRMA 44134 2754 E7
Wexford Dr
- MsnT 44024 2504 B2
36800 SLN 44139 3020 C1
Wexford Ln
- MDBH 44130 2881 B5
Weybridge Dr
28700 WTLK 44145 2749 D3
Weybridge Rd
2800 SRHT 44120 2627 C6
Weyburne Av
19300 CLEV 44135 2751 D5
Weymouth Cir
1500 WTLK 44145 2619 D7
Weymouth Dr
1900 HDSN 44236 3154 E7
6000 MNTR 44060 2144 B3
Weymouth Ln
16400 SGVL 44136 3147 A4
Weymouth Pl
10 AURA 44202 3157 A3
Weymouth Rd
2800 SRHT 44120 2627 A6
Whalers Cove
9300 MNTR 44060 2145 A5
Wharton Dr
7300 HGVL 44022 2631 B5
7300 RslT 44072 2631 B5
Wheat Ct
3300 CLEV 44113 2624 B5
3800 CLEV 44102 2624 B5
Wheatfield Dr
400 AURA 44202 3156 C4
Wheatfield Ln
9700 CcdT 44060 2145 C7
Wheatley Av
- LORN 44053 2743 D2
Wheaton Ct
9300 OmsT 44138 3009 C1
Wheaton Dr
- AVON 44011 2747 A3
4300 SFLD 44054 2746 E5
Wheaton Pl
27300 OmsT 44138 3009 C1
Wheeler Ct
8700 MNTR 44060 2144 C2
Wheeler Rd
10900 GTVL 44231 3161 E4
11000 HrmT 44231 3161 E3
14000 GDHT 44125 2886 A3
14000 GDHT 44137 2886 A3
14000 MPHT 44137 2886 A3
14500 CrlT 44050 3141 B6
14500 LrgT 44050 3141 B6
Wheeler Creek Rd
2800 GnvT 44041 1943 D4
3900 GnvT 44041 1844 D6
Wheelers Ln
19100 SGVL 44149 3011 D7
Wheelock Dr
10 BDFD 44146 2887 A4
Wheelock Rd
800 CLEV 44103 2496 A6
Whetstone Cir
4900 BHIT 44212 3146 A7
Whippoorwill Av
1100 LKWD 44107 2622 E4
Whippoorwill Ln
8600 PRMA 44130 3013 D1
Whiskey Ln
11800 BKVL 44141 3151 D3
Whiskey Island Dr
2800 CLEV 44113 2624 A4
4600 CLEV 44102 2624 A4
Whispering Pt
3200 AVON 44011 2748 A3
Whispering Shrs
2700 VMLN 44089 2742 A4
Whispering Cove Cir
2200 WTLK 44145 2749 A2
Whispering Oaks Blvd
5100 PRMA 44129 2883 A5
Whispering Pines Cir
19300 SGVL 44136 3146 E5
Whispering Pines Dr
8200 RslT 44072 2631 E7
8200 RslT 44072 2632 A7
Whispering Pines Pl
5700 LORN 44053 2744 E6
Whispering Sand Dr
6600 MadT 44057 1942 B1
Whisperwood Ln
10 HGVL 44022 2631 A7
700 ManT 44202 3022 E5
1000 AURA 44202 3022 E4
9700 AbnT 44023 2763 A7
14900 HGVL 44022 2761 A1
14900 RslT 44022 2761 A1
Whistler Ct
5200 NRYN 44133 3149 A1
Whistlewood Wy
3700 PRRY 44081 2042 B2
Whitacre Cir
2500 BKVL 44141 3150 B3
Whitacre Ct
10 BDFD 44146 2887 B4
Whitaker Dr
7200 PRMA 44130 2882 C7
Whitaker Cove
10 AVLK 44012 2617 C4
Whitby Av
7600 MNTR 44060 2251 D3
Whitby Rd
900 CVHT 44112 2497 D5
Whitcomb Rd
15900 CLEV 44110 2497 C2
White Av
5500 CLEV 44103 2625 D1
11000 CrlT 44035 3005 C5
White Ct
100 ELYR 44035 3006 B2
White Rd
- WBHL 44094 2500 A1
2400 UNHT 44118 2628 C4
6400 MAYF 44092 2500 A1
6400 MAYF 44143 2500 A1
6400 WBHL 44092 2500 A1
8700 KDHL 44060 2252 C7
8700 KDHL 44094 2252 C7
8700 KTLD 44094 2252 C7
14900 BtnT 44062 2766 E3
26200 RDHT 44143 2374 A7
26200 WBHL 44092 2374 D7
White St
10 BERA 44017 2880 A5
White Angel Dr
4500 PryT 44081 1940 D7
White Ash Dr
1400 PnvT 44077 2041 A7
White Ash Tr
10300 TNBG 44087 3020 A3
White Bark Cir
4500 NRYN 44133 3014 B6
White Bark Dr
20200 SGVL 44149 3146 B2
White Cedar Pl
4100 PryT 44081 2041 D3
E Whitedove Ln
7000 MDBH 44130 2880 E6
N Whitedove Ln
18300 MDBH 44130 2880 D6
W Whitedove Ln
6900 MDBH 44130 2880 E6
White Fir Ln
17700 SGVL 44136 3146 E5
17700 SGVL 44136 3147 A5
Whiteford Dr
5900 HDHT 44143 2499 D3
Whitehall Dr
10 BERA 44017 3011 B2
4400 SELD 44121 2498 C6
Whitehaven Av
5200 NOSD 44070 2749 C7
5200 NOSD 44070 2878 C1
Whitehaven Dr
7700 PRMA 44129 2882 D4
Whitehead Av
8100 CLEV 44105 2756 C3
Whitehead Rd
13200 CrlT 44050 3140 C4
14500 LrgT 44050 3140 C6
Whitehill Dr
27600 WTLK 44145 2619 E6
White Marsh Dr
2000 TNBG 44087 3019 E3
2300 TNBG 44087 3020 A4
Whitemarsh Ln
18400 SGVL 44149 3146 D4
Whitemarsh Wy
7400 HDSN 44236 3154 D6
White Oak Cir
15200 MDBH 44130 2881 C5
White Oak Ct
200 AURA 44202 3156 D1
4100 PryT 44081 2041 D3
White Oak Dr
200 ELYR 44035 2875 E4
5800 MNTR 44060 2144 C3
7500 SLN 44139 3019 E2
8800 TNBG 44087 3154 D1
18600 AbnT 44023 3023 C2
White Oak Ln
- NOSD 44070 2749 B7
- NOSD 44145 2749 B7
- WTLK 44070 2749 B7
- WTLK 44145 2749 B7
White Oak Rd
9000 KTLD 44094 2252 B7
White Oak Tr
3900 ORNG 44122 2759 C3
White Oak Wy
5600 NRDV 44039 2877 E1
White Oaks Cir
9100 BKVL 44141 3016 B4
N White Oaks Dr
16500 SGVL 44136 3147 A4
S White Oaks Dr
16500 SGVL 44136 3147 A4
Whitepine Ct
7600 MNTR 44060 2252 C2
White Pine Dr
5800 BDHT 44146 2887 D3
7500 CsTp 44026 2501 C5
White Pine Wy
4800 NRDV 44039 2748 D7
White Pines St
4000 AVON 44011 2748 C5
White Sands Blvd
7000 MadT 44057 1843 C6
White Spruce Dr
300 MCDN 44056 3018 B5
Whitestone Ct
11800 NRYN 44133 3148 A5
White Swan Ct
5200 NRYN 44133 3149 A1
Whitetail Av
300 ELYR 44035 2874 D5
Whitetail Ct
3800 RHFD 44286 3150 D7
White Tail Dr
430-00 AURA 44202 3156 C2
Whitetail Dr
300 SRSL 44022 2762 A5
White Tail Ln
- LORN 44053 2743 B6
Whitetail Ln
10 BTVL 44022 2889 E2
White Tail Run
- BhmT 44001 2870 C7
- HetT 44001 2870 C7
Whitetail Run Ln
8600 KDHL 44060 2252 C6
White Tail Run Pl
7400 CcdT 44077 2254 C1
Whitethorn Av
5000 NOSD 44070 2750 A7
7800 CLEV 44103 2626 A1
Whitethorn Dr
5600 MONT 44060 2143 D2
Whitethorn Rd
3100 CVHT 44118 2627 C1
Whiteway Dr
26600 RDHT 44143 2373 E6
26600 RDHT 44143 2374 A6
Whitewood Dr
1800 MadT 44057 1942 A1
11100 NbyT 44065 2634 B4
Whitewood Pkwy
9400 TNBG 44087 3019 D6
Whitewood Rd
8200 BKVL 44141 3015 E5
8200 BKVL 44141 3016 A5
Whitfield Ln
1000 RDHT 44143 2498 C3
Whiting Dr
8300 CsTp 44026 2502 A5
Whitman Av
3100 CLEV 44113 2624 C5
Whitman Blvd
100 ELYR 44035 2875 D2
Whitman Ct
- CLEV 44113 2624 C5
Whitmore Av
11200 CLEV 44108 2496 D5
Whitmore Ct
10 PnvT 44077 2040 E7
Whitney Av
6600 CLEV 44103 2495 E7
6600 CLEV 44103 2625 E1
Whitney Ln
8200 CcdT 44077 2253 D4
Whitney Rd
13000 NRYN 44133 3012 E3
13000 SGVL 44133 3012 E3
13000 SGVL 44136 3012 B3
18200 SGVL 44136 3011 E3
18200 SGVL 44149 3011 D3
Whiton Rd
2600 UNHT 44118 2628 C5
Whittier Av
5500 CLEV 44103 2625 D1
Whittington Dr
7300 PRMA 44129 2882 D3
8600 PMHT 44129 2882 D3
8600 PMHT 44130 2882 D3
Whittlesay Ln
1000 RKRV 44116 2621 B6
Whittlesey Rd
48900 BhmT 44001 2871 D1
48900 VMLN 44001 2871 D1
48900 VMLN 44089 2871 D1
WH Marlin Ct
- CLEV 44110 2497 B3
Whooper Ct
5200 NRYN 44133 3149 A1
Wichita Av
4000 CLEV 44109 2754 B5
4200 CLEV 44144 2754 B5
5900 BKLN 44144 2754 A5
Wickens Pl
- LORN 44052 2614 E6
Wickfield Av
19000 CLEV 44122 2757 E2
19000 WVHT 44122 2757 E2
19700 WVHT 44122 2758 A2
Wickfield Dr
5800 PMHT 44130 2882 D2
5800 PRMA 44130 2882 D2
Wickford Ct
17700 CLEV 44112 2497 D2
Wickford Rd
1600 CLEV 44112 2497 D2
Wickham Pl
1600 PnvT 44077 2040 E2
Wickland St
200 PNVL 44077 2146 A1
Wickley Ln
5500 BDHT 44146 2887 E2
Wicklow Ct
1000 EatT 44044 3142 A3
Wicklow Dr
10 ETLK 44095 2142 B6
Wicklow Rd
2600 SRHT 44120 2627 A5
Widgeon Ct
1300 MDSN 44057 1942 A6
Widgeon Dr
10000 AbnT 44023 2892 B6
Wiese Rd
8200 BKVL 44141 3016 C5
Wight Oaks Dr
7000 WNHL 44146 2886 C7
Wilber Av
5400 PRMA 44129 2883 A2
5400 PRMA 44134 2883 A2
6700 PRMA 44129 2882 E2
Wilbert Dr
10200 KTLD 44094 2377 B5
Wilbert Rd
1000 LKWD 44107 2622 E4
11300 MsnT 44024 2504 B2
Wilbur Av
10000 CLEV 44106 2626 C3
41100 EyrT 44035 2745 C6
Wilburn Dr
4500 SELD 44121 2498 C6
Wilcox Dr
8900 TNBG 44087 3154 D1
Wildberry Cir
700 AVLK 44012 2618 A5
Wildbrook Dr
500 BYVL 44140 2619 C5
Wild Cherry Ovl
3800 ORNG 44122 2759 B2
Wild Cherry Tr
3800 ORNG 44122 2759 B2
Wildel Dr
7800 TwbT 44087 3154 E5
7800 TwbT 44236 3154 E5
Wilder Av
800 ELYR 44035 2875 E2
Wilder Rd
9800 CdnT 44024 2379 A4
Wilderness Dr
7700 MNTR 44060 2253 A3
Wilderness Ln
5900 PMHT 44130 2882 B3
Wilderness Psg
9100 BbgT 44023 2891 D1
Wilderness Tr
24100 ODFL 44138 2879 D7
31000 WTLK 44145 2749 A2
Wildflower Cir
13500 RslT 44072 2631 D3
Wildflower Dr
2700 RKRV 44116 2621 C7
Wildflower Ln
- NRDV 44039 2877 C2
Wild Flower Wy
- MNTR 44060 2144 C1
Wildflower Wy
10200 BWHT 44147 3149 D5
Wilding Chase
10 CNFL 44022 2761 B4
Wildlife Wy
3600 CLEV 44109 2754 B3
4000 CLEV 44144 2754 C3
Wild Oak Dr
5900 NOSD 44070 2878 A2
Wild Oak Pl
17400 BbgT 44023 2890 C4
Wildwood Av
6400 BKPK 44142 2880 B3
6500 BERA 44017 2880 B3
6500 BERA 44142 2880 B3
Wildwood Cir
1500 WTLK 44145 2619 B7
Wildwood Ct
5500 WLBY 44094 2375 A1
Wildwood Dr
1100 AMHT 44001 2743 D6
1100 LrnC 44089 2741 B6
1100 VMLN 44089 2741 A6
7800 MNTR 44060 2252 D3
8800 NRYN 44133 3013 A3
9400 HmbT 44024 2380 D2
24100 EUCL 44123 2373 D2
24400 WTLK 44145 2750 C2
Wildwood Ln
17600 CLEV 44119 2372 D5
19500 SGVL 44149 3146 C3
Wildwood Pl
100 ELYR 44035 2746 D7
Wildwood Tr
6600 MAYF 44143 2500 A3
10100 MsnT 44024 2503 C2
Wilkenson Cir
5400 MNTR 44060 2145 B1
Wilkes Ln
500 RDHT 44143 2498 C3
Wilks Ln
2700 WTLK 44145 2749 C2
Willard Av
10 BDFD 44146 2887 A2
8500 CLEV 44102 2623 D7
11600 GDHT 44125 2885 E1
Willard Ct
10 OBLN 44074 3138 E2
Willard Rd
10 AURA 44202 3157 A1
E Willard Rd
13900 RslT 44072 2631 E5
W Willard Rd
13900 RslT 44072 2631 D5
Willet Cir
5200 NOSD 44070 2749 D7
Willey Av
1600 CLEV 44113 2624 D5
William Cir
1500 PRMA 44134 2883 E5
William Dr
- VMLN 44089 2741 B5
William St
10 BDFD 44146 2887 B6
7600 MNTR 44060 2143 D4
Williams Av
11600 CLEV 44120 2626 E5
23200 EUCL 44123 2373 C2
Williams Ct
- AVLK 44012 2617 E4
3000 AVON 44011 2748 E4
5000 SFLD 44054 2746 D1
Williams Dr
6200 BKVL 44141 3015 E5
6200 BWHT 44141 3015 D5
6200 BWHT 44147 3015 D5
25900 WTLK 44145 2750 B1
Williams Rd
6500 CcdT 44077 2147 A7
7200 CcdT 44077 2254 E1
7200 CcdT 44077 2255 A1
8400 HmbT 44024 2256 C7
8400 HmbT 44024 2381 C1
8400 HmbT 44077 2256 C7
8400 LryT 44024 2256 C7
8400 LryT 44077 2256 C7
Williams St
10 CNFL 44022 2761 B6
10 ELYR 44035 2875 C6
10 GDRV 44077 2039 C4
10 PnvT 44077 2039 C4
500 PNVL 44077 2040 A6
14500 MPHT 44137 2757 A7
Williamsburg
5800 AMHT 44001 2744 B6
5800 AMHT 44053 2744 B6
5800 LORN 44053 2744 B6
Williamsburg Ct
10 MDSN 44057 1942 B7
100 AbnT 44023 2892 B4
20300 BERA 44017 2880 C5
20300 BERA 44130 2880 C5
20300 MDBH 44130 2880 C5
Williamsburg Dr
100 AVLK 44012 2618 D1
500 HDHT 44143 2499 C3
2000 PRMA 44134 2883 D4
5500 LORN 44053 2744 B6
Williamsburg Ovl
18000 SGVL 44136 3146 E4
Williamson Av
11800 LKWD 44107 2623 A4
Williamston Av
4300 BKLN 44144 2753 D5
Williamstown Dr
4400 NOSD 44070 2750 A6
Willis St
10 BDFD 44146 2887 A4
Williston Dr
5500 PRMA 44129 2883 A6
Willman Av
15100 CLEV 44135 2752 C5
Willo St
33400 AVON 44011 2748 D2
Wil Lou Ln
6700 NRDV 44039 2877 C4
Willoughby Pkwy
38100 WLBY 44094 2142 E7
Willoughcroft Dr
4600 WLBY 44094 2250 D6
Willow Av
4200 LORN 44055 2746 A4
29600 WKLF 44092 2374 D2
Willow Bnd
1100 BWHT 44147 3149 E5
Willow Cir
410-00 AURA 44202 3156 D2
14400 SGVL 44136 3012 C4
32000 AVLK 44012 2618 D3
Willow Ct
10000 BKVL 44141 3151 D4
Willow Dr
- TNBG 44087 3019 D3
300 PNVL 44077 2146 B1
500 EUCL 44132 2374 A2
6400 INDE 44131 2884 C5
37100 ETLK 44095 2142 D5
Willow Frwy
- BKVL - 3015 D7
- BKVL - 3150 E6
- BWHT - 3015 D2
- CHHT - 2755 D4
- CLEV - 2625 B4
- CLEV - 2755 C1

STREET Block	City	ZIP	Map#	Grid
Willow Frwy				
-	INDE	-	2755	E7
-	INDE	-	2884	D2
-	INDE	-	3015	D1
-	NBGH	-	2755	C3
-	RHFD	-	3150	E6
Willow Frwy I-77				
-	BKVL	-	3015	D7
-	BKVL	-	3150	E6
-	BWHT	-	3015	D2
-	CHHT	-	2755	D4
-	CLEV	-	2625	B4
-	CLEV	-	2755	D4
-	INDE	-	2755	E7
-	INDE	-	2884	D2
-	INDE	-	3015	D1
-	NBGH	-	2755	C3
-	RHFD	-	3150	E6
Willow Frwy SR-21				
-	CHHT	-	2755	D4
-	CLEV	-	2625	C7
-	CLEV	-	2755	C1
-	NBGH	-	2755	C2
Willow Ln				
100	CNFL	44022	2761	A5
200	BERA	44017	2880	A5
3100	BHWD	44122	2628	E7
5200	SDLK	44054	2616	E2
5300	VMLN	44089	2740	E5
8400	HmbT	44024	2256	A5
8400	LryT	44024	2256	A6
8400	LryT	44077	2256	A6
9200	ODFL	44138	3010	A1
9700	CcdT	44060	2145	B7
21000	SGVL	44149	3011	B3
29200	WBHL	44092	2374	C7
30500	WLWK	44095	2249	C6
Willow Pkwy				
4400	CHHT	44125	2755	D4
Willow St				
400	BHIT	44212	3146	C7
500	BNWK	44212	3146	C7
1100	GFTN	44044	3142	B6
7200	SLN	44139	3020	E3
N Willow St				
1000	GFTN	44044	3142	B6
Willow Wy				
7200	OmsT	44138	2878	A4
30500	BYVL	44140	2619	B5
Willowbend Dr				
100	MDSN	44057	1942	B6
Willowbrook Ct				
9100	ODFL	44138	3009	E1
Willowbrook Dr				
-	RMDV	44087	3020	C4
-	TNBG	44087	3020	C4
10	NRsT	44074	3139	B2
10	OBLN	44074	3139	B2
3200	PRPK	44124	2629	E7
3200	PRPK	44124	2759	E1
4500	MNTR	44060	2038	E5
4900	CHHT	44125	2755	E6
7900	CsTp	44026	2501	D2
Willow Brook Ln				
2000	HkyT	44233	3148	B6
32600	NRDV	44039	2877	E1
Willow Brook Ovl				
2200	HkyT	44233	3148	A6
Willowbrook Rd				
-	OBLN	44074	3139	B2
Willowbrook Cove				
10	AURA	44202	3021	B7
Willow Creek Ct				
-	EatT	44028	3143	E4
Willow Creek Dr				
-	EatT	44028	3143	E4
700	AMHT	44001	2872	B3
Willow Creek Ln				
-	EatT	44028	3143	E4
Willow Creek Pl				
11400	ClbT	44028	3008	E6
11400	EatT	44028	3008	E6
Willowdale Av				
1800	CLEV	44109	2754	D2
Willowdale Dr				
38800	WLBY	44094	2251	B5
Willow Hill Dr				
11300	CsTp	44026	2501	D2
Willow Hollow Ct				
800	AMHT	44001	2872	B2
Willowhurst Rd				
1800	CLEV	44112	2497	D3
Willowick Dr				
30500	WLWK	44095	2249	E4
33000	ETLK	44095	2249	E2
33900	LKLN	44095	2249	E2
Willow Lake Dr				
700	SgHT	44067	3017	C4
6500	NRYN	44133	3148	E2
Willowmere Av				
11100	CLEV	44108	2496	C5
Willowood Ct				
1400	PnvT	44077	2041	A7
Willow Park Rd				
500	ELYR	44035	2875	A4
Willow Run Dr				
3600	WTLK	44145	2750	B4
7300	MNTR	44060	2143	C4
Willow Tree Ln				
6600	GNWL	44139	2888	A7
Willow Wood Dr				
16700	SGVL	44136	3147	A5
Willow Wood Ln				
10	MDHL	44022	2760	C3
Willow Woods Dr				
7300	OmsT	44138	2878	A5
Willshire Ln				
12300	MsnT	44024	2503	C6
Willshire Rd				
1300	LNHT	44124	2499	A7
Willson Dr				
9000	BbgT	44023	3022	D1
Wilma Dr				
14000	SGVL	44136	3012	D3
Wilmar Ct				
3800	CVHT	44121	2498	A7
Wilmar Rd				
1400	CVHT	44121	2498	A7
1400	CVHT	44121	2628	A1
Wilmington Dr				
10	PnvT	44077	2145	C4
300	BWHT	44147	3150	A5
500	RchT	44286	3150	A5
14700	SGVL	44136	3146	E1
Wilmington Rd				
4000	SELD	44118	2628	A2
4000	SELD	44121	2628	A2
Wilmore Av				
20100	EUCL	44119	2373	A4
21500	EUCL	44123	2373	B4
Wilmot St				
100	GDRV	44077	2039	C5
Wilshire Ct				
100	ELYR	44035	2875	E3
Wilshire Dr				
800	AMHT	44001	2743	E6
1000	AMHT	44001	2744	A6
Wilson Av				
2200	ShfT	44055	2745	E6
2300	ShfT	44055	2746	A6
38000	WLBY	44094	2250	E5
Wilson Ct				
400	SgHT	44067	3017	D4
Wilson Dr				
5400	MNTR	44060	2038	C7
5400	MNTR	44060	2144	C1
25400	ODFL	44138	2879	C6
Wilson Ln				
2900	TNBG	44087	3020	B5
Wilson St				
-	ShfT	44055	2746	A6
2200	LORN	44052	2615	C5
Wilson Mills Rd				
100	CRDN	44024	2379	D7
300	CRDN	44024	2504	C2
5100	RDHT	44143	2498	E5
5100	RDHT	44143	2499	A5
5200	HDHT	44143	2499	D5
5900	MAYF	44143	2499	D5
6400	MAYF	44143	2500	A5
6600	MAYF	44040	2500	B5
7000	CsTp	44026	2501	B4
7000	GSML	44040	2501	A4
7100	GSML	44040	2500	C4
8100	CsTp	44026	2502	D4
9500	CsTp	44024	2502	E4
9500	CsTp	44024	2503	A4
9500	CsTp	44026	2503	A4
9600	MsnT	44024	2503	D3
10800	MsnT	44024	2504	A3
Wilton Av				
13000	CLEV	44135	2752	E5
Wilton Ln				
7500	NRYN	44133	3013	D5
Wilton Rd				
1700	CVHT	44118	2627	B2
Wiltshire Dr				
8600	MCDN	44056	3018	E7
8600	MCDN	44056	3153	E1
Wiltshire Rd				
2800	BWHT	44147	3149	A5
2800	NRYN	44133	3149	A5
2800	NRYN	44147	3149	A5
3700	MDHL	44022	2760	B3
5400	HkyT	44133	3148	E5
5400	HkyT	44233	3148	E5
5400	NRYN	44133	3148	E5
Wimbledon Rd				
23200	SRHT	44122	2628	C6
24400	BHWD	44122	2628	D6
Win Dr				
100	WLWK	44095	2249	D7
Winchell Rd				
900	AURA	44202	3022	D5
1000	ManT	44202	3022	E5
2600	ManT	44202	3023	A5
2600	ManT	44255	3023	E5
3500	SRHT	44122	2757	E2
12300	CcdT	44024	2255	A5
12300	CcdT	44077	2255	B4
12300	CdnT	44024	2255	A5
Winchester Av				
10	CLEV	44110	2372	C6
1400	LKWD	44107	2623	A6
Winchester Ct				
200	AURA	44202	3021	E7
1600	WTLK	44145	2619	E7
10400	NRYN	44133	3013	E4
18000	SGVL	44136	3147	A4
Winchester Dr				
1100	PRMA	44134	2883	E3
1500	WTLK	44145	2619	E7
6100	SVHL	44131	2884	A3
7200	SLN	44139	3020	A2
11500	MsnT	44024	2504	C1
Winchester Ln				
300	BNWK	44212	3147	D7
Winchester Ovl				
900	SVHL	44131	2884	A3
Winchester Pl				
7200	CcdT	44077	2253	D1
Winchester Rd				
1400	LNHT	44124	2499	B7
1400	LNHT	44124	2629	A2
Winchester Vly				
9200	CsTp	44026	2632	D2
9200	CsTp	44026	2633	A2
Winckles St				
100	ELYR	44035	2875	C5
N Wind Dr				
27600	EUCL	44132	2249	A6
Windbrook Ct				
100	ELYR	44035	2746	C7
Windcliff Rd				
12100	SGVL	44136	3011	E5
Windermere Dr				
900	WLBY	44094	2142	E4
1100	WLBY	44094	2143	A5
Windermere St				
1800	ECLE	44112	2497	A6
Windgate Dr				
100	ELYR	44035	3006	D2
Windham Ct				
100	BWHT	44147	3149	E5
Windham Dr				
8200	MNTR	44060	2252	A2
10400	PRMA	44130	2882	B2
Winding Tr				
19300	SGVL	44149	3146	D1
Winding Wy				
7300	BKVL	44141	3016	B6
7500	HDSN	44236	3155	B7
14700	NRYN	44133	3147	E1
Windingbrook Ln				
11100	CsTp	44026	2502	C2
Winding Creek Ln				
5900	NOSD	44070	2878	A2
Windingcreek Ln				
1000	LNHT	44124	2498	E6
Winding Oak Dr				
18300	MDBH	44130	2880	E5
E Winding Oak Dr				
6900	MDBH	44130	2880	E5
N Winding Oak Dr				
18100	MDBH	44130	2880	E5
Winding River Tr				
10	BTVL	44022	2760	D7
10	MDHL	44022	2760	D7
Winding Trail Pl				
7400	CcdT	44077	2254	C1
Windjammer Ct				
10	PNVL	44077	2039	E6
10	PnvT	44077	2039	E6
5700	MadT	44057	1941	C1
Windjammer Tr				
9900	RMDV	44202	3020	E5
Windjammer Cove				
3600	RMDV	44202	3020	E5
N Windmill Ct				
1100	AVON	44011	2617	C7
S Windmill Ct				
1200	AVON	44011	2617	B7
Windmill Ln				
1300	BWHT	44147	3149	E5
7000	CcdT	44060	2145	B7
Windmill Wy E				
1100	AVON	44011	2617	C7
Windmill Wy N				
1100	AVON	44011	2617	C7
Windmill Wy S				
1200	AVON	44011	2617	C7
Windmill Point Rd				
15500	HtbT	44024	2507	C4
15500	HtbT	44046	2507	C4
Windridge Dr				
7900	BWHT	44147	3015	A5
Windrow Ln				
1400	BWHT	44147	3149	D5
Windrunner Tr				
-	PnvT	44077	2040	D2
Windrush Ct				
5500	PRMA	44134	2883	D1
Windrush Dr				
10	HGVL	44022	2760	B2
10	MDHL	44022	2760	B2
600	WTLK	44145	2621	A6
Windrush Ln				
10	BHWD	44122	2628	E3
Windsford Cir				
4900	AVON	44011	2747	B6
4900	NRDV	44011	2747	B6
4900	NRDV	44039	2747	B6
Windsong Ct				
3500	WTLK	44145	2750	A4
Windsong Tr				
8300	CcdT	44077	2255	A5
Windsor Cir				
1500	MDHT	44124	2630	B1
Windsor Ct				
10	RKRV	44116	2621	B6
3800	LORN	44053	2743	E2
Windsor Ct N				
34200	ETLK	44095	2250	A2
Windsor Ct S				
34200	ETLK	44095	2250	A2
N Windsor Ct				
3000	WTLK	44145	2749	C3
S Windsor Ct				
3100	WTLK	44145	2749	C3
Windsor Dr				
200	ELYR	44035	2875	D2
1600	MDHT	44124	2630	B1
5000	NRDV	44039	2747	B7
8100	NRYN	44133	3013	D7
16000	SGVL	44136	3147	B2
28300	NOSD	44070	2878	D2
E Windsor Dr				
9000	ODFL	44138	3009	E1
W Windsor Dr				
9000	ODFL	44138	3009	E1
Windsor Ln				
600	SgHT	44067	3152	C1
7100	MNTR	44060	2144	C7
Windsor Pl				
200	NHFD	44067	3018	B4
Windsor Rd				
3800	CVHT	44121	2497	E5
3800	CVHT	44121	2498	A5
Windsor St				
4200	WLBY	44094	2250	D5
Windsor Wy				
8200	BWHT	44147	3014	C5
9500	TNBG	44087	3020	B6
Windsor Castle Dr				
14400	SGVL	44149	3146	B1
Windstream Ln				
4500	BKVL	44141	3150	E3
Windswept Cir				
18100	BbgT	44023	2891	E6
Windswept Dr				
9100	BKVL	44141	3150	C1
Windward Cir				
320-00	AURA	44202	3156	C2
Windward Dr				
-	AVLK	44012	2618	B3
200	ELYR	44035	2875	D1
670-00	AURA	44202	3156	C2
2200	WTLK	44145	2749	D2
36200	ETLK	44095	2142	C6
Windward Ln				
10	AbnT	44023	2892	A4
380-00	AURA	44202	3156	C2
Windward Rd				
17700	CLEV	44119	2372	D4
18000	EUCL	44119	2372	E5
Windward Wy				
10	AbnT	44023	2892	A4
300	AVLK	44012	2618	E2
300	AVLK	44012	2619	A3
18400	SGVL	44136	3146	E4
Windward Hills Dr				
6700	BKVL	44141	3016	A7
Windwood Wy				
7100	OmsT	44138	2878	E4
Windy Hill Dr				
10	WBHL	44094	2375	E7
2400	LNHT	44124	2629	C3
2400	MDHT	44124	2629	C3
2400	PRPK	44124	2629	C4
11700	MsnT	44024	2504	D7
Windy Hill Ln				
37100	SLN	44139	2889	D5
Windy Hollow Ln				
30700	NOSD	44070	2878	A2
Windy Lakes Cir				
-	BbgT	44023	2891	E6
Windy Willow Dr				
6400	SLN	44139	2889	D5
Winesap Ct				
2200	BWHT	44147	3149	D4
Winesap Dr				
2200	BWHT	44147	3149	D4
Winesap Rd				
600	AMHT	44001	2743	B7
Winfield Av				
2200	RKRV	44116	2622	A6
Winfield Dr				
5400	MNTR	44060	2038	D7
5400	MNTR	44060	2144	D1
Winfield Park Dr				
14600	NbyT	44072	2763	A1
Wing Rd				
17000	AbnT	44023	2892	D4
Wingate Dr				
11000	AbnT	44023	2893	A5
Wingate Rd				
15300	MPHT	44137	2886	B2
Wingedfoot Dr				
2300	WTLK	44145	2750	E2
23300	WTLK	44145	2751	A2
Winger Dr				
3700	LORN	44053	2744	A4
Winners Cir				
-	AVLK	44012	2618	E5
31500	AVLK	44012	2619	A5
Winona Cir				
6700	MDBH	44130	2881	C4
Winona Rd				
2000	EUCL	44117	2497	E2
Winrock Dr				
-	HRM	44234	3161	B1
Winsford Rd				
3200	CVHT	44112	2497	D5
Winslow Av				
1100	CLEV	44113	2624	C3
Winslow Ct				
-	SRHT	44120	2757	C1
Winslow Dr				
-	AURA	44202	3157	A4
Winslow Rd				
17300	SRHT	44120	2757	D1
17700	SRHT	44122	2757	E1
Winson Cir				
37800	NRDV	44035	2876	B7
Winsor Dr				
29900	BYVL	44140	2619	B4
Winsor Ter				
10	CLEV	44103	2625	D2
Winsted Rd				
7300	HDSN	44236	3154	D7
Winston Dr				
30300	BYVL	44140	2619	B3
Winston Ln				
6600	SLN	44139	2889	E6
Winston Rd				
1000	CVHT	44121	2498	A6
1000	SELD	44121	2498	A7
Winter Ln				
4500	BKLN	44144	2753	C5
Winterberry Dr				
7600	HDSN	44236	3155	C7
Winterberry Ln				
10	MDHL	44022	2760	A5
9400	KDHL	44060	2253	A4
11400	MsnT	44024	2503	B2
30900	WTLK	44145	2749	A6
Winterbrook Dr				
-	AVON	44011	2748	C5
Wintergreen Dr				
10000	CdnT	44024	2379	E4
12000	CdnT	44024	2380	A4
32200	SLN	44139	2759	E7
Wintergreen Hl				
10	PnvT	44077	2146	D3
Wintergreen Ln				
10	MNTR	44060	2144	E7
Winterhaven Dr				
6400	MadT	44057	1942	A3
Winterpark Dr				
1600	PRMA	44134	3014	D2
Winthrop Ct				
8200	MNTR	44060	2252	A2
Winthrop Dr				
100	ELYR	44035	2746	C7
2900	PRMA	44134	2883	C4
Winthrop Rd				
2800	SRHT	44120	2627	C6
10100	ShvT	44255	3157	E7
10400	ManT	44255	3157	E7
Winton Av				
1400	LKWD	44107	2622	B5
Winton Park Dr				
3800	NOSD	44070	2750	A5
Winward Ln				
-	BHIT	44212	3145	E7
Wire Av				
7800	CLEV	44105	2756	A2
Wisconsin Cir				
100	ELYR	44035	3006	D1
Wisner Rd				
9100	CdnT	44060	2378	C1
9600	CdnT	44094	2378	A4
10100	CdnT	44024	2378	A5
10100	KTLD	44094	2378	A5
Wisteria Dr				
8000	BbgT	44023	2890	E7
27900	NOSD	44070	2749	E6
Wisteria Wy				
2200	AVON	44011	2747	E2
Witch Hazel Ln				
7100	SLN	44139	3020	B1
Wittenburg Av				
-	ELYR	44035	3006	D2
Wixford Ln				
5300	MNTR	44060	2039	A7
5300	MNTR	44060	2145	A1
Woburn Av				
-	CLEV	44144	2753	E4
3700	CLEV	44109	2754	B4
4700	CLEV	44144	2754	B5
6700	BKLN	44144	2753	E4
Woda Av				
18200	CLEV	44122	2757	D2
Wolcott Dr				
10	BSHT	44236	3153	C6
Wolf Av				
7000	PRMA	44129	2882	E1
13500	GDHT	44125	2885	E1
13500	GDHT	44125	2886	A1
Wolf Av				
13500	GDHT	44137	2886	A1
13500	MPHT	44137	2886	A1
Wolf Ct				
200	ELYR	44035	2875	B7
Wolf Dr				
300	BWHT	44147	3014	E4
300	BWHT	44147	3015	A4
13200	SGVL	44136	3012	D3
Wolf Rd				
6300	BKPK	44130	2881	C4
6300	BKPK	44142	2881	C4
6400	MDBH	44130	2881	C4
6400	MDBH	44142	2881	C4
23700	BYVL	44140	2620	E5
27400	BYVL	44140	2619	B4
Wolf Creek Ln				
-	GDHT	44125	2756	C6
Wolfpen Dr				
10	SRSL	44022	2762	B7
Wolf Run Cir				
16800	SGVL	44136	3146	E3
Wolverton Dr				
4600	WVHT	44128	2758	C5
Wolzhaven Av				
20700	SGVL	44149	3011	B4
Wondergrove Dr				
100	EUCL	44132	2249	A7
Wonderlust Ct				
10	PnvT	44077	2040	E7
Wonneta Pkwy				
23700	WTLK	44145	2620	E7
Wood Av				
2800	LORN	44055	2745	B2
3600	ShfT	44055	2745	B4
3700	PRMA	44134	2883	B1
4800	PRMA	44129	2883	A1
6500	INDE	44131	2884	D5
Wood Ovl				
12000	NRYN	44133	3013	A5
Wood Rd				
1500	CVHT	44118	2627	E1
1500	CVHT	44121	2627	E1
3300	MadT	44057	1941	B7
3300	MadT	44057	2043	C3
38300	WLBY	44094	2250	E2
38300	WLBY	44094	2251	A2
Wood St				
-	CrlT	44035	3006	A3
10	PNVL	44077	2146	A1
500	ELYR	44035	3006	A3
4400	WLBY	44094	2250	E6
23600	BDHT	44146	2887	C1
29500	WKLF	44092	2374	C2
35200	NRDV	44039	2877	A1
Woodacre Dr				
2300	HDSN	44236	3155	B7
Wood Acre Tr				
17100	AbnT	44023	2892	A3
17100	BbgT	44023	2891	E4
17100	BbgT	44023	2892	A3
Woodall Rd				
30100	SLN	44139	2759	C7
W Woodall Rd				
29100	SLN	44139	2759	C7
Woodberry Blvd				
8100	BbgT	44023	2761	E7
8200	BbgT	44023	2762	A7
Woodberry Ln				
12500	SGVL	44149	3011	A6
Woodbine Av				
3000	CLEV	44113	2624	C5
Woodbine Cir				
400	MAYF	44143	2500	B3
Woodbine Ovl				
100	MDSN	44057	1942	B7
Woodbine St				
35200	NRDV	44039	2877	A1
Woodbriar Cir				
12300	SGVL	44136	3011	E6
Woodbridge Av				
2500	CLEV	44109	2754	B1
Woodbridge Cir				
100	CRDN	44024	2505	A2
Woodbridge Ct				
800	AMHT	44001	2872	C1
8500	NRDV	44039	2877	D6
Woodbridge Gln				
300	RDHT	44143	2498	E1
Woodbridge Ln				
200	CRDN	44024	2505	A2
4500	BKVL	44141	3150	E3
Woodbridge Tr				
700	SgHT	44067	3152	C2
Woodbridge Wy				
-	AVLK	44012	2619	A4
31800	AVLK	44012	2618	E5
Woodbridge Condominiums				
1200	WLBY	44094	2143	A5
Woodbrook Av				
15100	BDFD	44146	2886	B4
15100	MPHT	44137	2886	B4
Woodburn Dr				
10	HGVL	44022	2760	B2
10	MDHL	44022	2760	B2
Woodbury Av				
17700	CLEV	44135	2752	A4
Woodbury Ct				
9100	MNTR	44060	2252	E3
Woodbury Dr				
6300	SLN	44139	2889	B5
14600	NbyT	44065	2764	C1
Woodbury Ln				
10	NCtT	44067	3153	B4
1100	NRYN	44133	3013	C5
Woodbury Rd				
2800	SRHT	44120	2627	B6
Woodbury St				
100	ELYR	44035	2875	D5
Woodbury Hills Dr				
4700	PRMA	44134	3014	A1
Woodchip Ln				
9400	BWHT	44147	3149	D1
Wood Chuck Cir				
10	AhtT	44001	2744	C7
Woodchuck Ct				
10400	TNBG	44087	3019	C3
Woodchuck Hllw				
12100	CsTp	44026	2502	E5
Woodcreek Cir				
3200	WTLK	44145	2749	E3
Wood Creek Dr				
6700	MDBH	44130	2881	C5
15500	TpnT	44024	2257	C5
Woodcreek Dr				
9700	CcdT	44060	2145	C6
Woodcrest Ct				
100	ELYR	44035	2875	C1
4400	LORN	44053	2743	D4
Woodcrest Dr				
-	SAHT	44001	2872	C6
300	MCDN	44056	3018	B6
9000	BKVL	44141	3016	A7
30800	ORNG	44022	2759	D6
E Woodcrest Dr				
4800	ORNG	44022	2759	D6
4800	SLN	44022	2759	D6
4800	SLN	44139	2759	D6
W Woodcrest Dr				
4800	ORNG	44022	2759	D6
4800	SLN	44022	2759	D6
4800	SLN	44139	2759	D6
Woodcrest Ln				
13000	CsTp	44026	2631	C2
Woodcroft Ct				
9500	KTLD	44094	2376	E2
Wood Duck Av				
11200	CcdT	44077	2146	B7
Wood Duck Ct				
-	RMDV	44202	3020	E3
7000	SLN	44139	3020	B1
Wooded Vw				
6400	BSHT	44236	3153	B7
Woodfield Ct				
2600	AVON	44011	2747	B2
Woodfield Dr				
32100	AVLK	44012	2618	C1
Woodfield Tr				
21700	SGVL	44149	3011	A6
Woodford Av				
-	ELYR	44035	2874	D7
17400	LKWD	44107	2622	B4
Woodford St				
4600	MNTU	44255	3159	C5
Woodgate Cir				
4100	WTLK	44145	2749	E5
Woodhaven Av				
6300	BKLN	44144	2753	E4
6300	CLEV	44144	2753	E4
6300	CLEV	44144	2754	A4
Woodhaven Cir				
32000	NRDV	44039	2877	D7
Woodhaven Ct				
100	AURA	44202	3021	D7
Woodhaven Dr				
-	AVLK	44012	2618	A1
-	TpnT	44024	2257	C5
700	AMHT	44001	2872	E3
8800	OmsT	44138	2879	A7
18200	SGVL	44149	3146	D4
Woodhaven Pl				
100	OBLN	44074	3138	C3
Woodhawk Dr				
6300	MDHT	44124	2629	E2
6300	MDHT	44124	2630	A2
Woodhawk Ln				
8600	KTLD	44094	2252	B7
Woodhill Ct				
9400	CLEV	44104	2626	B6
Woodhill Dr				
100	AMHT	44001	2872	E1
8200	TpnT	44024	2257	C5
8300	MtlT	44024	2257	C5
9100	KTLD	44094	2252	A7
23500	BKPK	44142	2879	E2
42800	EyrT	44035	2874	A2
N Woodhill Dr				
100	AMHT	44001	2872	E1
200	AMHT	44001	2743	E7
Woodhill Rd				
2300	CLEV	44104	2626	B6
2300	CLEV	44106	2626	C4
Woodhill St				
5800	PryT	44077	2147	B2
Woodhill St Ext				
5800	PryT	44077	2147	B2
Wood Hollow Dr				
10800	MsnT	44024	2504	A3
Woodhollow Dr				
10	BNWK	44212	3146	E6
4000	ManT	44255	3159	A1
Wood Hollow Rd				
8500	SgHT	44067	3017	E6
Woodhurst Av				
1500	MDHT	44124	2499	D7
1500	MDHT	44124	2629	E1
Woodhurst Dr				
9300	SGVL	44149	3011	C4
Woodie Gln				
11200	CdnT	44024	2379	B4
Woodiebrook Rd				
100	CRDN	44024	2505	A2
100	MsnT	44024	2505	A2
200	CRDN	44024	2504	E2
11300	MsnT	44024	2504	C2
Woodin Rd				
11800	CdnT	44024	2379	E3
12000	CdnT	44024	2380	E3
12400	HmbT	44024	2380	B3
13300	HmbT	44024	2381	A3
Woodlake Dr				
600	AURA	44202	3021	C6
7400	WNHL	44146	3017	D1
10800	KTLD	44094	2378	A7
10800	KTLD	44094	2503	A1
Woodland Av				
10	PnvT	44077	2145	D3
300	ELYR	44035	2874	D5
2100	CLEV	44115	2625	C4
3800	CLEV	44104	2625	E4
7000	BbgT	44022	2890	A1
7000	BbgT	44023	2890	A1
7000	BTVL	44022	2890	A1
7500	CLEV	44104	2626	C4
11500	CLEV	44120	2626	D4
Woodland Av SR-8				
2500	CLEV	44115	2625	C4
3800	CLEV	44104	2625	C4
Woodland Av SR-87				
2500	CLEV	44115	2625	C4
3800	CLEV	44104	2625	E4
7500	CLEV	44104	2626	A4
Woodland Av US-422				
2500	CLEV	44115	2625	C4
3800	CLEV	44104	2625	C4
Woodland Ct				
500	SRSL	44022	2761	E5
1500	TNBG	44087	3019	B3
Woodland Dr				
400	ETLK	44095	2250	C2
5600	NRDV	44039	2877	E1
Woodland Pl				
8800	MNTR	44060	2252	C2
N Woodland Rd				
-	CVHT	44118	2627	B5
-	SRHT	44118	2627	B5
-	SRHT	44120	2627	B5
25900	BHWD	44122	2628	E5
26100	BHWD	44122	2629	A5
27300	PRPK	44124	2629	B4
S Woodland Rd				
13200	CLEV	44120	2626	E6
13300	CLEV	44120	2627	D7
13800	SRHT	44120	2627	D7
18400	SRHT	44122	2627	D7
19800	SRHT	44122	2628	A7
23100	BHWD	44122	2628	E7
26000	BHWD	44122	2629	A7
26000	PRPK	44124	2629	A7
29000	PRPK	44124	2759	D1
32900	PRPK	44124	2760	A2
33200	PRPK	44022	2760	A2
33700	HGVL	44022	2760	E2
33700	MDHL	44022	2760	E2
45800	HGVL	44022	2761	A2
45800	HGVL	44072	2761	A2
S Woodland Rd SR-87				
32900	PRPK	44124	2759	E1
32900	PRPK	44124	2760	A2
33200	PRPK	44022	2760	A2
33700	HGVL	44022	2760	E2
33700	MDHL	44022	2760	E2
45800	HGVL	44022	2761	A2
45800	HGVL	44072	2761	A2
Woodland St				
100	OBLN	44074	3138	D2
Woodland Tr				
-	AVON	44011	2747	A2
Woodland Trc				
10	AURA	44202	3156	C1
Woodland Wy				
36000	NRDV	44039	2876	E7
36000	NRDV	44039	3007	E1
Woodland Chase				
1000	EatT	44044	3142	A3
1000	GFTN	44044	3142	A3
Woodland Glade Dr				
2000	TwbT	44236	3155	A6
Woodlands Dr				
3900	VMLN	44089	2741	C5
Woodlands Ln				
6900	SLN	44139	2889	C7
Woodlands Tr				
7700	CsTp	44026	2631	C1
Woodlane Dr				
500	BYVL	44140	2620	C5
900	MAYF	44143	2499	D6
N Woodlane Dr				
6100	MAYF	44143	2499	D5
S Woodlane Dr				
6100	MAYF	44143	2499	D6
6200	MDHT	44143	2499	D6
Woodlark Cir				
11300	CcdT	44077	2254	C2
Woodlawn Av				
1800	CLEV	44112	2626	E1
1800	ECLE	44112	2626	E1
33900	NRDV	44039	2877	C3
Woodlawn Cir				
400	BERA	44017	2880	D5
Woodlawn Ct				
17000	SGVL	44149	3146	C3
Woodlawn Dr				
1000	MCDN	44056	3018	E5
2900	PRMA	44134	2883	C3
14400	NbyT	44065	2634	C7
Woodlawn St				
10	GNVA	44041	1944	C3
Woodleaf Rd				
16700	SGVL	44136	3012	A6
Woodleigh Rd				
33000	HGVL	44022	2630	A7
33000	PRPK	44124	2630	A7
33000	PRPK	44124	2760	A1
Woodline Rd				
24700	BDHT	44146	2887	D6
Woodmere Dr				
200	WLWK	44095	2249	B7
400	BERA	44017	2880	A7
500	BERA	44017	3011	A1
600	BWHT	44147	3014	E4
600	BWHT	44147	3015	A3
2200	CVHT	44106	2627	A4
17000	BbgT	44023	2890	E3
17000	BbgT	44023	2891	A2
24100	NOSD	44070	2750	D4
Woodmill Cir				
5500	BKVL	44141	3016	B5
Woodmill Dr				
2200	WTLK	44145	2749	D1
Wood Oak Cir				
30300	WTLK	44145	2749	B3
Woodpark Dr				
400	BYVL	44140	2619	E5
Woodpark Ln				
3800	NOSD	44070	2749	E5
Woodpath Ct				
1400	TwbT	44236	3154	D5
Wood Path Dr				
29200	NOSD	44070	2878	C1
Woodpath Dr				
7600	TwbT	44236	3154	C6
Woodpath Tr				
3800	WTLK	44145	2750	B4
25600	NOSD	44070	2750	C4
25600	NOSD	44145	2750	C4
Woodridge Cir				
400	BERA	44017	3010	E1
12100	SGVL	44136	3011	E6
Woodridge Ct				
32600	NRDV	44039	2748	E7
Woodridge Dr				
100	ELYR	44035	2875	D1
12000	NRYN	44133	3013	A5
12100	NRYN	44133	3012	E5
Woodridge Ln				
8800	MNTR	44060	2038	D6
Wood Ridge Rd				
299-00	AURA	44202	3156	D2
500	GNVA	44041	1944	D4
600	GnvT	44041	1944	D5
Woodridge Rd				
100	VMLN	44089	2741	D4

STREET Block City ZIP Map# Grid

Woodridge Rd
3400 CVHT 44112 2497 D6
3400 CVHT 44118 2497 D6
3400 CVHT 44121 2497 D6
3800 CVHT 44121 2498 A6
Woodrow Av
10 BDFD 44146 2887 A4
600 WKLF 44092 2249 B7
1500 MDHT 44124 2499 D7
1500 MDHT 44124 2629 E1
3700 PRMA 44134 2883 B3
4800 PRMA 44129 2883 A3
Woodruff Av
- AVLK 44012 2617 C2
Woodruff Ct
2500 WTLK 44145 2749 C2
6700 MDBH 44130 2881 B4
Woodruff Dr
- SFLD 44054 2616 E3
400 SDLK 44054 2616 E3
1900 PnvT 44077 2145 B5
Woodruff Ln
9800 NbyT 44065 2763 B7
Woodrun Dr
- NRYN 44133 3149 A4
10600 SGVL 44136 3012 D5
Woodrush Cir
100 SRSL 44022 2761 D5
N Woods Ln
5400 SLN 44139 2888 B1
Woodsdale Ln
31700 SLN 44139 2759 E7
31700 SLN 44139 2888 E1
Woods Edge Ct
7900 CcdT 44060 2253 C3
Woodshire Dr
16600 SGVL 44149 3146 D3
Woods Hole
13100 MsnT 44024 2634 E2
Woodside Av
200 VMLN 44089 2741 E5
12300 CLEV 44108 2496 E5
38200 WLBY 44094 2250 E6
Woodside Cir
31800 AVLK 44012 2618 D4
Woodside Cross N
18000 SGVL 44149 3146 D4
Woodside Cross S
18200 SGVL 44149 3146 D4
Woodside Ct
12200 SGVL 44136 3011 E6
Woodside Dr
100 CrlT 44035 3005 D5
300 SgHT 44067 3017 D4
1100 AMHT 44001 2873 A1
1100 RKRV 44116 2621 C5
3800 NOSD 44070 2750 D5
4000 NRYN 44133 3014 B3
12500 CsTp 44026 2502 A7
S Woodside Dr
12800 CsTp 44026 2502 A7
12800 CsTp 44026 2632 A1
Woodside Ln
24100 BHWD 44122 2628 D7
Woodside Rd
10 SRSL 44022 2761 C6
5400 MONT 44060 2037 E7
5400 MONT 44060 2143 E1
5900 HDHT 44143 2499 C4
Woodslee Ct
13500 CLEV 44111 2622 E7
Woodsmore Dr
5600 SLN 44139 2888 E2
Woodsong Dr
15000 MDFD 44062 2767 B3
Woodsong Wy
100 AbnT 44023 2892 A4
Woodspring Cir
32800 NRDV 44039 2877 D6
Woodstar Ln
- CcdT 44077 2254 C2
Woodstock Av
100 AVLK 44012 2488 A7
100 AVLK 44012 2618 A1
10800 CLEV 44104 2626 D4
10800 CLEV 44120 2626 D4
20400 FWPK 44126 2751 C2
Woodstock Dr
3700 LORN 44053 2743 E2
Woodstock Rd
300 ETLK 44095 2249 E3
1600 GSML 44040 2630 C2
1900 HGVL 44022 2630 C3
1900 HGVL 44040 2630 C3
Woodstock Run
17200 SGVL 44149 3146 C3
Woodstone Cir
32800 NRDV 44039 2877 D7
Woodstone Dr
8900 BKVL 44141 3016 D6
Woods Way Dr
9100 KTLD 44094 2377 A1
Woodsway Ln
7800 RslT 44072 2631 D7
Wood Thrush Av
6900 CcdT 44077 2146 C7
Wood Thrush Dr
4300 PRMA 44134 2883 B5
Woodvale Ct
9200 MNTR 44060 2252 E3
Woodview Blvd
10600 PMHT 44130 2882 A6
Woodview Cir
21200 SGVL 44149 3011 B5
Wood View Dr
4900 VMLN 44089 2741 A7
Woodview Dr
100 ELYR 44035 2875 D1
2500 BWHT 44147 3015 B4
3300 NOSD 44070 2750 E4
9400 MCDN 44056 3018 D5
10000 CdnT 44024 2379 E4
10000 CdnT 44024 2380 A4
Woodview Rd
700 CVHT 44121 2497 D6
Woodview Tr
400 AURA 44202 3021 C7
Woodwalk Dr
6900 BKVL 44141 3016 B7
Woodward Av
1400 LKWD 44107 2622 B6
1800 CVHT 44118 2627 B2
2300 CLEV 44107 2622 B7
2300 CLEV 44111 2622 B7
3700 LORN 44055 2745 C4
9700 CLEV 44106 2626 B2
Woodward Blvd
12000 GDHT 44125 2885 D1
13500 GDHT 44125 2886 A1
Woodway Av
3600 PRMA 44134 2754 B7
Woodway Dr
29300 WKLF 44092 2374 B1
Woodway Rd
23600 BHWD 44122 2628 D4
Woodwind Ct
8700 BWHT 44147 3015 A5
Woodworth Av
10 PnvT 44077 2040 C7
Woodworth Dr
4000 LORN 44053 2743 E3
Woodworth Rd
13200 CLEV 44110 2496 E3
13200 ECLE 44110 2496 E3
13200 ECLE 44112 2496 E3
13300 CLEV 44110 2497 A4
13300 ECLE 44110 2497 A4
13300 ECLE 44112 2497 A4
Woodyard Rd
7700 HDSN 44236 3155 A7
Woolman Ct
8500 PRMA 44130 2882 A2
Wooster Cir
500 SgHT 44067 3017 D4
Wooster Ct
7300 MNTR 44060 2251 C1
Wooster Pkwy
7400 PRMA 44129 2882 E1
Wooster Rd
1500 RKRV 44116 2621 E7
2500 LKWD 44107 2621 E7
2500 RKRV 44126 2621 E7
3000 LKWD 44116 2621 E7
3100 RKRV 44116 2751 D2
3900 FWPK 44126 2751 D1
3900 FWPK 44126 2751 D1
3900 RKRV 44126 2751 D1
Wooster Rd SR-113
1500 RKRV 44116 2621 E7
2500 LKWD 44126 2621 E7
2500 RKRV 44126 2621 E7
Wooster Rd US-20
1500 RKRV 44116 2621 E7
2500 LKWD 44126 2621 E7
2500 RKRV 44126 2621 E7
Wooster St
200 ELYR 44035 3006 A1
Wooster Park Wy
19500 LKWD 44126 2621 C6
19500 RKRV 44116 2621 C6
19500 RKRV 44126 2621 C6
Worden Rd
- WKLF 44095 2249 B7
800 WKLF 44092 2249 B7
800 WLWK 44095 2249 B7
900 WKLF 44092 2374 C1
Wordsworth Ct
400 RDHT 44143 2499 A3
Worley Av
6600 CLEV 44105 2755 E2
7400 CLEV 44105 2756 A2
Worlington Dr
7400 SLN 44139 3020 C2
Worrell Rd
2700 KTLD 44094 2376 A7
2700 WBHL 44094 2376 A7
3000 CsTp 44026 2501 A1
3000 CsTp 44040 2501 A1
3000 CsTp 44094 2501 A1
3000 GSML 44040 2501 A1
3000 GSML 44094 2501 A1
3000 KTLD 44094 2501 A1
3000 WBHL 44094 2501 A1
Worthington Av
12900 CLEV 44111 2753 A3
Worthington Ct
700 MCDN 44056 3154 A6
6100 MNTR 44060 2144 B3
Worthington Ln
27200 OmsT 44138 3009 C1
Worthington Pl
2400 AVON 44011 2748 B1
Worthington Park Dr
7900 MDBH 44130 3011 E2
7900 SGVL 44130 3011 E2
7900 SGVL 44149 3011 E2
Worton Blvd
1100 MAYF 44143 2499 E7
1100 MDHT 44124 2499 E7
1100 MDHT 44143 2499 E7
Worton Park Dr
800 HDHT 44143 2499 E5
800 MAYF 44143 2499 E6
Wren Av
6500 CLEV 44127 2625 E6
Wren Cir
100 ELYR 44035 2874 E2
Wren Ct
10 RKRV 44116 2621 B6
9000 MNTR 44060 2144 D1
Wren Dr
8000 MCDN 44056 3153 C2
Wren Rd
16600 BbgT 44023 2891 A1
Wrenford Ct
8500 MCDN 44056 3018 B6
Wrenford Rd
1500 SELD 44121 2628 B3
2100 UNHT 44118 2628 B3
2100 UNHT 44121 2628 B3
2600 SRHT 44118 2628 B5
2600 SRHT 44122 2628 B5
Wren Haven Cir
- NRDV 44039 3008 D1
Wren Haven Dr
2000 HDSN 44236 3154 E6
2000 HDSN 44236 3155 A6
Wrens Ln
5500 WLBY 44094 2375 A1
Wrenwood Dr
10 ETLK 44095 2142 C6
7600 HrmT 44231 3161 E2
9600 KTLD 44094 2377 A3
11800 HRM 44234 3161 A1
Wright Av
1600 RKRV 44116 2621 E5
7200 BDFD 44146 2887 B7
7200 OKWD 44146 2887 B7
7200 OKWD 44146 3018 B1
Wright Ct
9300 CLEV 44108 2496 B5
Wright Rd
7900 BWHT 44131 3015 C3
7900 BWHT 44147 3015 C4
7900 INDE 44131 3015 C3
Wright St
37900 WLBY 44094 2250 D6
Wright Way Dr
- AhtT 44001 2872 E6
Wurst Ct
100 ELYR 44035 2875 B6
Wyandot Rd
8900 CsTp 44026 2632 C1
Wyandotte Av
1400 LKWD 44107 2622 E7
2100 CLEV 44107 2622 E7
2100 CLEV 44111 2622 E7
Wyandotte Rd
1900 EUCL 44117 2498 A2
Wyant Dr
9200 MNTR 44060 2252 E2
Wyatt Rd
4300 CLEV 44128 2757 C4
8100 BWHT 44147 3015 B5
15500 ECLE 44112 2497 B6
Wychwood Dr
10 MDHL 44022 2760 B2
Wye Rd
10200 MsnT 44024 2633 D1
10200 MsnT 44026 2633 D1
Wyleswood Dr
100 BERA 44017 3011 A1
500 BERA 44017 3010 E1
700 BERA 44017 2879 D7
700 ODFL 44138 2879 D7
Wymore Av
1800 ECLE 44112 2497 B5
Wyncote Rd
4000 SELD 44118 2628 A2
4000 SELD 44121 2628 A2
Wyndemere Wy
35700 AVON 44011 2748 A3
Wynde Tree Dr
2300 SVHL 44131 3015 B2
Wyndgate Ct
2500 WTLK 44145 2749 C2
Wyndham Ln
100 AURA 44202 3021 D6
Wyndtree Dr
10500 CcdT 44077 2145 E7
Wynewood Pl
100 CRDN 44024 2504 E1
Wynford Ln
9000 OmsT 44138 2878 C7
Wynn Av
100 ELYR 44035 3006 E3
Wynn Rd
2000 CVHT 44118 2627 D3
2000 UNHT 44118 2627 D3
Wynnewood Pl
20100 SGVL 44149 3146 C4
Wynwood Dr
1700 RKRV 44116 2621 A7

X

Xavier Ct
7300 NRDV 44039 2877 B4
Xavier St
100 ELYR 44035 3006 D2
Xenia Ct
5600 CLEV 44102 2624 A7

Y

Yacht Club Dr
10 LKWD 44107 2621 E4
10 RKRV 44107 2621 E4
10 RKRV 44116 2621 E4
Yager Dr
13100 SGVL 44149 3011 C7
Yale Av
100 ELYR 44035 3006 B1
1500 MadT 44057 1843 B7
8800 CLEV 44108 2496 B5
Yale Dr
- MsnT 44024 2504 E4
- MsnT 44024 2505 A4
3900 LORN 44055 2745 E4
Yale Pl
1300 PnvT 44077 2147 A1
Yale St
8500 TwbT 44087 3154 D2
Yarish Rd
- GftT 44044 3141 E7
Yarmouth Ct
8500 SgHT 44067 3017 E5
Yarmouth Ln
500 BYVL 44140 2619 C5
Yarmouth Ovl
10000 MDBH 44130 2881 B4
Yarmouth Rd
1000 GFTN 44044 3142 A3
Yarrow Pl
11400 SGVL 44149 3011 A5
Yarrow Tr
22100 SGVL 44149 3011 A5
22500 SGVL 44149 3010 E5
Yatchsmans Cove Dr
- ETLK 44095 2250 C3
Yeakel Av
9300 CLEV 44104 2626 B5
Yearling Dr
400 BERA 44017 3010 E2
400 BERA 44017 3011 A2
Yellowbrick Rd
8200 MNTR 44060 2144 A6
Yellow Springs Dr
6400 MadT 44057 1942 A3
Yellowstone Pkwy
8700 OmsT 44138 2879 A7
Yellowstone Rd
800 CVHT 44121 2497 E5
1300 CVHT 44118 2497 E7
Yellowwood Dr
9500 MNTR 44060 2253 A3
9600 CcdT 44060 2253 A3
Yennicook Wy
7500 HDSN 44236 3154 E6
Yeoman Dr
25600 WTLK 44145 2750 B3
Yeshiva Ln
28500 WKLF 44092 2374 B4
Yoder Blvd
100 AVLK 44012 2618 C1
Yorick Av
15200 CLEV 44110 2497 B3
York Av
2800 CLEV 44113 2624 D6
York Blvd
12400 GDHT 44125 2885 E2
13600 GDHT 44125 2886 A2
York Cres
7100 NRDV 44039 2877 B4
York Ct
900 VMLN 44089 2740 D6
5700 WLBY 44094 2375 A2
York Dr
2900 LORN 44053 2743 E2
5700 LNHT 44124 2629 C3
York Rd
6300 PMHT 44130 2882 B4
7000 PRMA 44130 2882 C5
7500 PRMA 44130 3013 C4
7800 NRYN 44130 3013 B2
7800 NRYN 44133 3013 C7
14300 NRYN 44133 3148 C1
York St
- CrlT 44035 3005 C5
600 FTHR 44077 2039 D3
600 PnvT 44077 2039 D3
33400 AVLK 44012 2617 C2
York-Alpha Dr
9500 NRYN 44133 3013 B7
York-Delta Dr
12700 NRYN 44133 3013 B6
York Harbor Ln
1000 PnvT 44077 2145 C4
York Imperial Dr
10 AMHT 44001 2872 B1
Yorkshire Av
3700 PRMA 44134 2883 B3
4800 PRMA 44129 2883 A3
Yorkshire Ct
100 ELYR 44035 2875 D5
Yorkshire Dr
8100 MNTR 44060 2144 A5
8200 BbgT 44023 3022 A2
N Yorkshire Dr
1100 BWHT 44147 3150 A5
S Yorkshire Dr
1200 BWHT 44147 3150 A5
Yorkshire Rd
2900 CVHT 44118 2627 C2
York Theta Dr
9700 NRYN 44133 3013 B6
Yorktown Ct
4400 LORN 44053 2743 D4
7300 MNTR 44060 2251 C1
Yorktown Dr
6100 PRMA 44134 2883 D3
29800 WTLK 44145 2749 B4
Yorktown Ln
10 ELYR 44035 2875 A3
7500 MDBH 44130 3012 D2
Yorktown Ovl
18300 SGVL 44136 3146 E4
Yorktown Pl
200 VMLN 44089 2741 B4
Yorktown Rd
5600 LORN 44053 2743 C5
Yorkview Dr
8500 NRYN 44133 3013 C3
Yorkview Dr E
8500 NRYN 44133 3013 C3
Yorkview Dr W
8500 NRYN 44133 3013 C3
Yorkwood Ct
8800 MNTR 44060 2144 C4
Yosemite Dr
2000 EUCL 44117 2373 D7
2000 RDHT 44117 2373 D7
2000 RDHT 44143 2373 D7
Young Dr
7300 WNHL 44146 3018 A1
Yunker Ct
100 CrlT 44035 3006 E4
Yvonne Dr
9300 NRYN 44133 3013 C3

Z

Zachary Tr
4600 BHIT 44212 3146 B6
Zackary Ct
- PryT 44081 1940 E6
Zanes Trc
100 ClrT 44024 2505 C6
Zaremba Dr
13300 BKPK 44130 2881 E4
13300 BKPK 44142 2881 D4
13300 PMHT 44130 2881 E4
Zehman Ct
6200 BKPK 44142 2880 E3
6200 BKPK 44142 2881 A3
Zehman Dr
6100 BKPK 44142 2881 A3
6200 BKPK 44142 2880 E3
Zelis Rd
11900 LNDL 44135 2753 B4
Zeller Ct
10 BERA 44017 2880 C5
Zeman Av
24500 EUCL 44123 2373 D2
26800 EUCL 44132 2373 E2
26800 EUCL 44132 2374 A2
Zenas Ct
2900 TNBG 44087 3020 B5
Zenith Dr
14600 NbyT 44065 2764 C1
Zimmer Av
9800 CLEV 44102 2623 C6
Zingales Rd
300 BDFD 44146 2886 D3
Zinnia Ct
6600 MNTR 44060 2143 D5
Zoar Ct
5600 CLEV 44102 2624 A7
Zoeter Av
6600 CLEV 44103 2625 E1
Zona Ln
7400 PRMA 44130 3013 A1
Zorn Ln
400 MAYF 44143 2500 B3
Zverina Ln
- SGVL 44136 3011 E7
- SGVL 44149 3011 E7

#

1st Av
13300 ECLE 44112 2496 E6
13300 ECLE 44112 2497 A6
20000 BERA 44017 2880 C4
20000 BERA 44130 2880 C4
20000 MDBH 44130 2880 C4
1st Pl
400 ELYR 44035 2875 A6
7300 OKWD 44146 2887 C6
1st St
- BDHT 44146 2887 D1
10 BDFD 44146 2887 A5
10 CLEV 44134 2754 C7
10 MadT 44057 1941 A5
10 ManT 44255 3158 B2
100 PNVL 44077 2146 A1
400 GNVA 44041 1944 C3
800 LORN 44052 2614 D6
5000 VMLN 44089 2741 A4
7200 MNTR 44060 2143 C3
8200 BKLN 44144 2753 D2
8200 CLEV 44144 2753 D2
10700 MNTU 44255 3159 C6
26600 WTLK 44145 2620 A6
E 1st St
2000 CLEV 44115 2624 C2
W 1st St
1000 LORN 44052 2614 D6
2nd Av
10 BERA 44017 2880 C5
6500 INDE 44131 2884 E5
13300 ECLE 44112 2496 E6
13300 ECLE 44112 2497 A6
2nd St
- BDHT 44146 2887 D1
- VMLN 44089 2741 A5
10 CLEV 44134 2754 D7
10 ELYR 44035 2875 B6
10 MadT 44057 1941 A5
10 ManT 44255 3158 C2
100 FTHR 44077 2039 D3
100 PNVL 44077 2146 A1
300 GNVA 44041 1944 B3
600 ELYR 44035 2874 E6
8200 BKLN 44144 2753 D2
8200 CLEV 44144 2753 D2
10600 MNTU 44255 3159 C6
27200 WTLK 44145 2620 A5
37200 WLBY 44094 2250 D5
E 2nd St
2100 CLEV 44115 2624 C2
W 2nd St
1000 LORN 44052 2614 D6
1600 CLEV 44113 2624 C2
1600 CLEV 44115 2624 C2
3rd Av
10 BERA 44017 2880 C5
13300 ECLE 44112 2496 E5
13300 ECLE 44112 2497 A5
3rd St
- BDHT 44146 2887 D1
10 CLEV 44134 2754 D7
10 MadT 44057 1941 A5
10 ManT 44255 3158 C2
100 FTHR 44077 2039 D3
100 PNVL 44077 2040 A7
200 ELYR 44035 2875 A6
300 GDRV 44077 2039 C6
400 GNVA 44041 1944 B3
600 ELYR 44035 2874 E6
600 PnvT 44077 2039 C6
8200 CLEV 44144 2753 D2
37700 WLBY 44094 2250 D5
E 3rd St
- CLEV 44115 2624 E3
1300 CLEV 44114 2624 C2
W 3rd St
- CLEV 44109 2625 A7
1000 CLEV 44114 2624 D2
1500 CLEV 44113 2624 C2
1500 CLEV 44115 2624 C2
2200 CLEV 44113 2625 A5
4th Av
10 BERA 44017 2880 C5
13300 ECLE 44112 2497 A5
4th St
- BDHT 44146 2887 D1
10 CLEV 44134 2754 D7
10 MadT 44057 1941 A5
10 ManT 44255 3158 C2
100 ELYR 44035 2875 A7
100 FTHR 44077 2039 C3
400 GNVA 44041 1944 B3
8200 BKLN 44144 2753 D2
8200 CLEV 44144 2753 D2
E 4th St
2000 CLEV 44114 2624 E3
2000 CLEV 44115 2624 E3
W 4th St
100 LORN 44052 2614 D6
1200 CLEV 44113 2624 D3
2500 CLEV 44113 2625 A6
4400 CLEV 44109 2755 A5
5100 BNHT 44131 2755 A7
5th Av
- CRDN 44024 2379 D6
100 CRDN 44024 2380 A5
13300 ECLE 44112 2497 A5
E 5th Av
10 BERA 44017 2880 C5
W 5th Av
10 BERA 44017 2880 C5
5th St
- BDHT 44146 2887 D1
10 CLEV 44134 2754 D7
10 MadT 44057 1941 A5
100 ManT 44255 3158 C2
200 ELYR 44035 2875 A7
200 FTHR 44077 2039 C4
5100 VMLN 44089 2740 E4
5100 VMLN 44089 2741 A4
W 5th St
100 LORN 44052 2614 C6
2100 CLEV 44113 2625 A5
5000 BNHT 44131 2755 A7
5100 BNHT 44131 2884 A1
6th Av
- CRDN 44024 2379 E6
13200 CLEV 44108 2496 E5
13200 CLEV 44112 2496 E5
13200 ECLE 44112 2496 E5
13300 ECLE 44112 2497 A5
W 6th Ct
400 LORN 44052 2614 D7
6th St
- BDHT 44146 2887 E1
10 CLEV 44134 2754 D7
200 FTHR 44077 2039 D4
200 ManT 44255 3158 C2
400 ELYR 44035 2875 A7
5100 VMLN 44089 2740 E4
5100 VMLN 44089 2741 A5
E 6th St
100 LORN 44052 2614 E6
1200 CLEV 44114 2624 E2
2200 CLEV 44115 2624 E3
W 6th St
- CLEV 44115 2624 C2
100 LORN 44052 2614 D7
1100 CLEV 44113 2624 D3
2100 CLEV 44113 2625 A5
4500 CLEV 44109 2755 A5
5000 BNHT 44131 2755 A7
5100 BNHT 44131 2884 A1
7th Av
100 CRDN 44024 2379 D5
W 7th Ct
900 LORN 44052 2614 D7
7th St
- BDHT 44146 2887 E1
200 ELYR 44035 2875 A7
200 FTHR 44077 2039 C4
200 ManT 44255 3158 B2
5100 VMLN 44089 2740 E4
5100 VMLN 44089 2741 A5
E 7th St
2200 CLEV 44115 2624 E3
W 7th St
100 LORN 44052 2614 E7
2000 CLEV 44113 2624 E5
2200 CLEV 44113 2625 A6
5000 BNHT 44131 2754 E7
5100 BNHT 44131 2883 E1
8th Pl
400 ELYR 44035 2875 A7
E 8th Pl
- CLEV 44115 2624 E3
- CLEV 44115 2625 A3
8th St
100 ManT 44255 3158 B2
200 BDHT 44146 2887 E1
200 ELYR 44035 2875 A7
E 8th St
100 LORN 44052 2614 E7
W 8th St
100 LORN 44052 2614 D7
2400 CLEV 44113 2625 A6
5000 BNHT 44131 2754 E7
5100 BNHT 44131 2883 E1
E 9th Pl
- CLEV 44115 2624 E3
- CLEV 44115 2625 A3
9th St
100 BDHT 44146 2887 D1
200 ELYR 44035 2875 A7
200 ManT 44255 3158 B2
E 9th St
- CLEV 44115 2625 A4
100 LORN 44052 2614 E7
2600 CLEV 44113 2625 A4
W 9th St
- PRMA 44131 2883 E2
- PRMA 44134 2883 E2
- SVHL 44131 2883 E2
100 LORN 44052 2614 D7
1100 CLEV 44113 2624 D3
9th St Al
300 ELYR 44035 2875 A7
10th St
300 BDHT 44146 2887 D1
300 ELYR 44035 2875 A7
E 10th St
- CLEV 44115 2625 A3
100 LORN 44052 2614 E7
W 10th St
100 LORN 44052 2614 E7
1200 CLEV 44113 2624 D3
4300 CLEV 44109 2754 E5
5200 PRMA 44109 2754 E7
5200 PRMA 44134 2754 E7
10th St Al
300 ELYR 44035 3006 A1
W 11th Ct
1000 CLEV 44109 2624 E7
W 11th Pl
2000 CLEV 44113 2624 E5
3100 CLEV 44109 2624 E7
11th St
400 ELYR 44035 3006 A1
W 11th St
100 LORN 44052 2614 D7
2000 CLEV 44113 2624 E5
2900 CLEV 44109 2624 E7
4100 CLEV 44109 2754 E4
11th Street Al
300 ELYR 44035 3006 A1
W 12th Pl
4000 CLEV 44109 2754 E4
12th St
300 ELYR 44035 3006 A1
1000 LORN 44052 2614 D7
E 12th St
1200 CLEV 44114 2624 E2
1700 CLEV 44114 2625 A3
2400 CLEV 44115 2625 A3
W 12th St
2800 CLEV 44113 2624 E6
2900 CLEV 44109 2624 E7
4200 CLEV 44109 2754 E4
12th Street Al
- ELYR 44035 3006 A1
W 13th Pl
- CLEV 44109 2624 E7
2000 CLEV 44113 2624 E5
13th St
400 ELYR 44035 3006 A1
E 13th St
1100 CLEV 44114 2624 E2
1300 CLEV 44114 2625 A2
1800 CLEV 44115 2625 A2
E 13th St US-322
1700 CLEV 44114 2625 A2
W 13th St
100 LORN 44052 2614 E7
1100 LORN 44052 2744 C1
2300 LORN 44053 2614 B7
3700 CLEV 44109 2754 E2
14th St
200 ELYR 44035 3006 A1
E 14th St
- CLEV 44115 2625 A4
- LORN 44052 2614 E7
W 14th St
100 LORN 44052 2614 E7
300 LORN 44052 2744 D1
2000 CLEV 44113 2624 E5
2300 LORN 44053 2744 B1
2900 CLEV 44109 2624 E7
3700 CLEV 44109 2754 E2
15th St
200 ELYR 44035 3006 A1
E 15th St
1800 CLEV 44114 2625 A2
W 15th St
100 LORN 44052 2744 E1
2000 CLEV 44113 2624 E5
3600 CLEV 44109 2754 E2
E 16th Pl
- CLEV 44115 2625 A3
W 16th Pl
2300 CLEV 44113 2624 E6
16th St
200 CrlT 44035 3006 A1
200 ELYR 44035 3006 A1
E 16th St
1100 CLEV 44114 2625 A1
W 16th St
100 LORN 44052 2744 E1
500 ELYR 44035 3005 E1
2900 CLEV 44109 2624 E7
2900 CLEV 44113 2624 E7
3800 CLEV 44109 2754 E2
5200 PRMA 44134 2754 E7
5300 PRMA 44134 2883 E1
W 17th Pl
3100 CLEV 44109 2624 E7
3800 CLEV 44109 2754 E3
17th St
300 ELYR 44035 3006 A1
500 ELYR 44035 3005 E1
E 17th St
1200 CLEV 44114 2625 A2
1800 CLEV 44115 2625 A3
W 17th St
100 LORN 44052 2744 E1
2000 CLEV 44113 2624 D5
3100 CLEV 44109 2624 E7
3200 CLEV 44109 2754 D1
W 18th Pl
2400 CLEV 44113 2624 D6
3100 CLEV 44109 2624 D7
18th St
300 ELYR 44035 3006 A2
700 ELYR 44035 3005 E2
E 18th St
100 LORN 44052 2744 E1
100 LORN 44052 2745 A1
1200 CLEV 44114 2625 A2
1800 CLEV 44115 2625 A3
W 18th St
100 LORN 44052 2744 E1
2000 CLEV 44113 2624 D5
3800 CLEV 44109 2754 E3
19th Ct
2000 LORN 44052 2744 B1
W 19th Pl
- CLEV 44109 2624 D7
2500 CLEV 44113 2624 D6
3200 CLEV 44109 2754 D1
19th St
700 ELYR 44035 3005 E2
E 19th St
100 LORN 44052 2744 E1
100 LORN 44052 2745 A1
1500 CLEV 44114 2625 A2
2000 CLEV 44115 2625 A3
W 19th St
1200 LORN 44052 2744 C1
2000 CLEV 44113 2624 D5
3800 CLEV 44109 2754 D3
W 20th Pl
2000 CLEV 44113 2624 D5
E 20th St
100 LORN 44052 2745 A1
1100 CLEV 44114 2625 A1
W 20th St
100 LORN 44052 2744 E1
100 LORN 44052 2745 A1
1900 CLEV 44113 2624 D5
2300 LORN 44053 2744 B1
3800 CLEV 44109 2754 D3
W 21st Pl
- CLEV 44109 2754 D2
- CLEV 44113 2624 D5
E 21st St
100 LORN 44052 2745 A1
1300 CLEV 44114 2625 A2
2000 CLEV 44115 2625 B3
E 21st St SR-611
100 LORN 44052 2745 A1
W 21st St
100 LORN 44052 2744 A1
1800 CLEV 44113 2624 D5
2300 LORN 44053 2744 B1
3300 LORN 44053 2743 E2
3800 CLEV 44109 2754 D3
W 21st St SR-611
100 LORN 44052 2744 A1
2300 LORN 44053 2744 B1
3300 LORN 44053 2743 E2
W 22nd Av
3900 CLEV 44109 2754 D3
W 22nd Pl
3700 CLEV 44109 2754 D2
E 22nd St
100 LORN 44052 2745 A2
1100 CLEV 44114 2625 A1
1800 CLEV 44115 2625 B3
W 22nd St
100 LORN 44052 2744 D2
1800 CLEV 44113 2624 D4
3900 CLEV 44109 2754 D3
W 23rd Pl
3200 CLEV 44109 2624 D7
3200 CLEV 44109 2754 D1
E 23rd St
100 LORN 44052 2745 A2
300 LORN 44055 2745 A2
1200 CLEV 44114 2625 A1
W 23rd St
100 LORN 44052 2744 D2
1800 CLEV 44113 2624 D5

STREET Block	City	ZIP	Map#	Grid
W 23rd St				
2100	LORN	44053	2744	B2
3800	CLEV	44109	2754	D3
W 24th Pl				
-	CLEV	44113	2624	D5
E 24th St				
1300	CLEV	44114	2625	B2
1900	CLEV	44115	2625	B2
W 24th St				
1200	LORN	44052	2744	C2
1800	CLEV	44113	2624	D5
2100	LORN	44053	2744	B2
3800	CLEV	44109	2754	D3
5200	CLEV	44134	2754	D7
5200	PRMA	44134	2754	D7
5300	PRMA	44134	2883	D1
W 25th Pl				
-	CLEV	44113	2624	C5
1200	LORN	44052	2744	C2
E 25th St				
300	LORN	44052	2745	A2
300	LORN	44055	2745	A2
1300	CLEV	44114	2625	B1
W 25th St				
100	LORN	44052	2744	E2
100	LORN	44052	2745	A2
1200	CLEV	44113	2624	C4
3000	CLEV	44109	2624	D7
3200	CLEV	44109	2754	D1
5200	CLEV	44134	2754	D7
5200	PRMA	44134	2754	D7
W 25th St SR-3				
1400	CLEV	44113	2624	C4
3000	CLEV	44109	2624	D7
3200	CLEV	44109	2754	D1
W 25th St US-6				
-	CLEV	44113	2624	C4
W 25th St US-20				
-	CLEV	44113	2624	C4
W 25th St US-42				
1400	CLEV	44113	2624	C4
3000	CLEV	44109	2624	D7
3200	CLEV	44109	2754	D1
W 26th Pl				
-	CLEV	44113	2624	D6
E 26th St				
100	LORN	44052	2745	A2
100	LORN	44055	2745	A2
1100	CLEV	44114	2625	B1
3900	CHHT	44105	2755	B3
3900	NBGH	44105	2755	B3
W 26th St				
100	LORN	44052	2744	E2
100	LORN	44052	2745	A2
100	LORN	44055	2744	E2
1400	CLEV	44113	2624	C4
4600	CLEV	44109	2754	D6
5200	CLEV	44134	2754	D7
5200	PRMA	44134	2754	D7
W 27th Pl				
1500	CLEV	44113	2624	C4
E 27th St				
200	LORN	44055	2745	A2
1500	CLEV	44114	2625	B2
4000	CHHT	44105	2755	B3
4000	NBGH	44105	2755	B3
W 27th St				
100	LORN	44052	2745	A2
100	LORN	44055	2744	E2
100	LORN	44055	2745	A2
1900	LORN	44052	2744	B2
2500	CLEV	44113	2624	D6
4800	CLEV	44109	2754	D6
W 28th Pl				
2500	CLEV	44113	2624	D6
E 28th St				
100	LORN	44055	2745	D2
2100	CLEV	44115	2625	B3
2200	LORN	44055	2746	A2
E 28th St SR-57				
100	LORN	44055	2745	D2
W 28th St				
-	PRMA	44134	2883	D1
100	LORN	44055	2744	E2
100	LORN	44055	2745	A2
1200	LORN	44052	2744	C2
1300	CLEV	44113	2624	C4
4200	CLEV	44109	2754	D4
5200	CLEV	44134	2754	D7
5200	PRMA	44134	2754	D7
W 29th Pl				
1700	CLEV	44113	2624	C5
E 29th St				
1600	LORN	44055	2745	E2
2200	LORN	44055	2746	A2
3900	NBGH	44105	2755	B3
W 29th St				
-	CLEV	44109	2754	D1
100	LORN	44055	2744	E2
100	LORN	44055	2745	A2
1200	LORN	44052	2744	C2
1300	CLEV	44113	2624	C4
1800	LORN	44053	2744	B2
5600	PRMA	44134	2883	C2
E 30th St				
1300	CLEV	44114	2625	B2
1400	LORN	44055	2745	E3
2200	LORN	44055	2746	A3
2600	CLEV	44115	2625	B4
W 30th St				
100	LORN	44055	2744	E3
100	LORN	44055	2745	A3
1900	LORN	44052	2744	B2
1900	LORN	44053	2744	B2
2800	CLEV	44113	2624	D7
3100	CLEV	44113	2624	D7
3200	CLEV	44109	2754	D1
W 31st Pl				
-	CLEV	44109	2754	D2
1600	CLEV	44113	2624	C5
E 31st St				
1300	CLEV	44114	2625	B1
1500	LORN	44055	2745	C3
2100	CLEV	44115	2625	C3
2200	LORN	44055	2746	A3
3000	SFLD	44054	2746	B3
3000	SFLD	44055	2746	B3
W 31st St				
100	LORN	44055	2744	E3
100	LORN	44055	2745	A3
3100	CLEV	44109	2624	D7
3100	CLEV	44113	2624	D7
3200	CLEV	44109	2754	D1
W 32nd Pl				
2600	CLEV	44113	2624	D6
3700	CLEV	44109	2754	C2
E 32nd St				
1300	CLEV	44114	2625	B1
2000	CLEV	44115	2625	C2
2200	LORN	44055	2745	E3
2200	LORN	44055	2746	A3
W 32nd St				
100	LORN	44055	2744	E3
200	LORN	44055	2744	E3
600	LORN	44052	2744	E3
2800	CLEV	44113	2624	D7
3100	CLEV	44109	2624	C7
3200	CLEV	44109	2754	C1
6200	PRMA	44134	2883	C4
W 33rd Pl				
1800	CLEV	44113	2624	C5
3600	CLEV	44109	2754	C2
E 33rd St				
1200	CLEV	44114	2495	B7
1200	CLEV	44114	2625	B1
2100	CLEV	44115	2625	C3
2200	LORN	44055	2745	E3
2200	LORN	44055	2746	A3
W 33rd St				
-	CLEV	44134	2754	C7
100	LORN	44055	2745	A3
300	LORN	44055	2744	E3
1200	LORN	44052	2744	C3
1200	LORN	44053	2744	C3
1400	CLEV	44113	2624	C4
3100	CLEV	44109	2624	C7
3200	CLEV	44109	2754	C1
5200	PRMA	44134	2754	C7
5300	PRMA	44134	2883	C1
W 34th Pl				
2000	CLEV	44113	2624	C5
3100	CLEV	44109	2624	C7
E 34th St				
1300	CLEV	44114	2625	C1
2200	LORN	44055	2745	E3
2300	CLEV	44115	2625	C3
2600	LORN	44055	2746	A3
E 34th St SR-14				
2700	CLEV	44115	2625	C5
E 34th St SR-43				
2700	CLEV	44115	2625	C5
W 34th St				
100	LORN	44055	2745	A3
200	LORN	44055	2744	E3
1200	LORN	44052	2744	C3
1200	LORN	44053	2744	C3
3200	CLEV	44109	2624	C7
3300	CLEV	44109	2754	C1
E 35th Pl				
2300	CLEV	44115	2625	C4
E 35th St				
2100	CLEV	44115	2625	C3
2200	LORN	44055	2745	E3
2200	LORN	44055	2746	A3
W 35th St				
100	LORN	44055	2745	A3
200	LORN	44055	2744	E3
1200	LORN	44052	2744	C3
1200	LORN	44053	2744	C3
3200	CLEV	44109	2624	C7
3200	CLEV	44109	2754	C1
E 36th St				
-	LORN	44055	2746	A3
100	LORN	44055	2745	A3
1000	ShfT	44055	2745	B3
1300	CLEV	44114	2625	C1
1900	CLEV	44115	2625	C2
W 36th St				
-	CLEV	44109	2624	C7
100	LORN	44055	2744	E3
100	LORN	44055	2745	A3
300	LORN	44052	2744	E3
300	LORN	44055	2744	E3
1700	LORN	44053	2744	B3
2100	CLEV	44113	2624	C6
3700	CLEV	44109	2754	C2
E 37th Ct				
-	LORN	44055	2745	C4
E 37th St				
1700	CLEV	44114	2625	C2
1800	LORN	44055	2745	D3
2100	CLEV	44115	2625	C3
2300	LORN	44055	2746	A3
W 37th St				
100	LORN	44052	2745	A4
100	LORN	44055	2745	A4
1000	LORN	44052	2744	D3
1200	LORN	44053	2744	C3
2100	CLEV	44113	2624	C6
3700	CLEV	44109	2754	C3
E 37th St Ovl				
2400	LORN	44055	2746	A4
E 38th St				
1100	CLEV	44114	2495	B7
1200	CLEV	44114	2625	B1
1300	LORN	44055	2745	C4
2100	CLEV	44115	2625	C3
2400	LORN	44055	2746	A4
3800	NBGH	44105	2755	C2
W 38th St				
100	LORN	44052	2745	A4
1000	LORN	44052	2744	D3
1200	LORN	44053	2744	B3
2800	CLEV	44113	2624	C7
3100	CLEV	44109	2624	C7
3200	CLEV	44109	2754	C1
39th Ct				
-	LORN	44055	2745	C4
E 39th Ct				
1800	LORN	44055	2745	D4
W 39th Pl				
3500	CLEV	44109	2754	C1
E 39th St				
-	LORN	44052	2745	A4
-	ShfT	44052	2745	A4
400	ShfT	44055	2745	A4
1300	CLEV	44103	2625	C1
1300	CLEV	44114	2625	C1
2100	CLEV	44115	2625	C3
2100	LORN	44055	2745	E4
2400	LORN	44055	2746	A4
W 39th St				
100	LORN	44052	2745	A4
100	LORN	44055	2745	A4
100	ShfT	44052	2745	A4
100	ShfT	44055	2745	A4
1200	LORN	44052	2744	C4
1200	LORN	44053	2744	C4
3600	CLEV	44109	2754	C2
E 40th Ct				
-	LORN	44055	2745	C4
W 40th Pl				
2000	CLEV	44113	2624	C6
E 40th St				
1000	CLEV	44114	2495	C7
1300	CLEV	44103	2625	C2
1300	CLEV	44114	2625	C2
1900	CLEV	44115	2625	C5
2100	CLEV	44104	2625	C5
2100	LORN	44055	2745	E4
2500	LORN	44055	2746	A4
3800	NBGH	44105	2755	C2
W 40th St				
1200	LORN	44052	2744	C4
1200	LORN	44053	2744	A4
2300	CLEV	44113	2624	C6
3100	CLEV	44109	2624	C7
3800	CLEV	44109	2754	C3
7600	PRMA	44134	3014	B1
W 41st Pl				
2200	CLEV	44113	2624	C6
E 41st St				
300	ShfT	44052	2745	A4
300	ShfT	44055	2745	A4
1300	CLEV	44103	2495	C7
1300	CLEV	44103	2625	C1
1300	CLEV	44114	2495	C7
2200	LORN	44055	2745	E4
2200	LORN	44055	2746	A4
3900	NBGH	44105	2755	C3
W 41st St				
1400	LORN	44053	2744	C4
2000	CLEV	44113	2624	C5
2700	CLEV	44109	2624	C7
3700	CLEV	44109	2754	C2
W 42nd Pl				
1100	LORN	44052	2744	D4
1900	CLEV	44113	2624	B5
1900	LORN	44053	2744	B4
E 42nd St				
200	ShfT	44052	2745	A4
200	ShfT	44055	2745	A4
1800	LORN	44055	2745	E4
2300	LORN	44055	2746	A4
3800	NBGH	44105	2755	C3
4000	CHHT	44105	2755	C3
W 42nd St				
1700	LORN	44053	2744	B4
2000	CLEV	44113	2624	C6
3700	CLEV	44109	2754	C2
W 43rd Pl				
-	CLEV	44109	2754	B1
-	CLEV	44113	2624	B6
E 43rd St				
-	LORN	44055	2745	C5
100	ShfT	44052	2745	A4
100	ShfT	44055	2745	A4
1300	CLEV	44103	2495	C7
1300	CLEV	44103	2625	C1
1300	CLEV	44114	2495	C7
2100	CLEV	44104	2625	D3
3800	NBGH	44105	2755	C2
W 43rd St				
-	CLEV	44113	2624	B6
1400	LORN	44053	2744	C4
3100	CLEV	44109	2624	B7
3200	CLEV	44109	2754	B1
5700	PRMA	44134	2883	B2
E 44th Pl				
3200	CLEV	44105	2625	C7
3200	CLEV	44127	2625	C7
W 44th Pl				
-	CLEV	44109	2754	B2
E 44th St				
200	ShfT	44052	2745	A4
200	ShfT	44055	2745	A4
3500	CLEV	44105	2755	C1
4000	CHHT	44105	2755	C3
4000	NBGH	44105	2755	C3
W 44th St				
1200	LORN	44052	2744	C4
1200	LORN	44053	2744	C4
1700	CLEV	44113	2624	B5
3000	CLEV	44109	2624	B7
3200	CLEV	44109	2754	B1
5200	PRMA	44109	2754	B7
5200	PRMA	44134	2754	B7
5500	PRMA	44134	2883	B1
W 45th Pl				
-	CLEV	44113	2624	B6
E 45th St				
-	LORN	44055	2745	D5
100	ShfT	44052	2745	A5
100	ShfT	44055	2745	A5
1200	CLEV	44114	2495	C7
1300	CLEV	44103	2495	C7
1300	CLEV	44103	2625	D1
2600	CLEV	44104	2625	C4
2600	CLEV	44115	2625	C5
3100	CLEV	44105	2625	C6
3100	CLEV	44127	2625	C6
W 45th St				
1000	LORN	44052	2744	D4
1200	CLEV	44102	2624	B4
1400	CLEV	44113	2624	B6
3300	CLEV	44109	2754	B1
3500	CLEV	44102	2754	B1
4400	CLEV	44144	2754	B5
5200	PRMA	44109	2754	B7
5200	PRMA	44134	2754	B7
5700	PRMA	44134	2883	B2
E 46th Pl				
-	CLEV	44105	2755	C2
W 46th Pl				
-	CLEV	44102	2624	B5
E 46th St				
100	ShfT	44052	2745	A5
100	ShfT	44055	2745	A5
2000	CLEV	44103	2625	D3
2400	CLEV	44104	2625	D4
3400	CLEV	44105	2755	C1
W 46th St				
-	CLEV	44102	2624	B6
3100	CLEV	44109	2624	B7
3200	CLEV	44102	2754	B1
5200	CLEV	44109	2754	B7
5200	PRMA	44109	2754	B7
5200	PRMA	44134	2754	B7
5700	PRMA	44134	2883	B2
E 47th Pl				
-	CLEV	44104	2625	C5
W 47th Pl				
3600	CLEV	44102	2754	B2
E 47th St				
300	ShfT	44052	2745	A5
400	ShfT	44055	2745	A5
1300	CLEV	44103	2495	C7
1300	CLEV	44103	2625	D1
1300	CLEV	44114	2495	C7
2700	CLEV	44104	2625	D5
3100	CLEV	44127	2625	C7
3500	CLEV	44105	2755	C1
W 47th St				
1700	CLEV	44102	2624	B5
3100	CLEV	44102	2754	B1
4300	CLEV	44109	2754	B4
4300	CLEV	44144	2754	B4
E 48th Pl				
1500	CLEV	44103	2625	D1
W 48th Pl				
-	CLEV	44102	2624	B5
E 48th St				
100	ShfT	44052	2745	A5
300	ShfT	44055	2745	A5
3200	CLEV	44127	2625	C7
3600	CLEV	44105	2755	C2
W 48th St				
1400	CLEV	44102	2624	B6
3200	CLEV	44102	2754	B1
4000	CLEV	44144	2754	B3
5200	CLEV	44109	2754	B7
5200	PRMA	44109	2754	B7
5200	PRMA	44134	2754	B7
5500	PRMA	44134	2883	B1
E 49th Pl				
3100	CLEV	44127	2625	C7
49th St				
100	ELYR	44035	2875	A2
600	ELYR	44035	2874	E2
E 49th St				
-	NBGH	44105	2755	C3
1000	CLEV	44114	2495	C7
1300	CLEV	44103	2495	C7
1500	CLEV	44103	2625	D1
2100	CLEV	44104	2625	D3
2900	CLEV	44127	2625	C6
3300	CLEV	44127	2755	C1
3500	CLEV	44105	2755	C1
4000	CHHT	44105	2755	C3
4000	CHHT	44125	2755	C3
W 49th St				
1300	CLEV	44102	2624	B4
3300	CLEV	44102	2754	B1
4000	CLEV	44144	2754	B3
5200	CLEV	44109	2754	B7
5200	PRMA	44109	2754	B7
5200	PRMA	44134	2754	B7
49th Street Br				
-	ELYR	44035	2875	A2
E 50th Pl				
1600	CLEV	44103	2625	D1
W 50th Pl				
-	CLEV	44102	2624	B5
50th St				
-	ELYR	44035	2874	D2
-	EyrT	44035	2874	D2
E 50th St				
2500	CLEV	44104	2625	D4
2900	CLEV	44127	2625	D6
3400	CLEV	44127	2755	C1
3600	CLEV	44105	2755	D2
3700	NBGH	44105	2755	D2
W 50th St				
1400	CLEV	44102	2624	B5
3200	CLEV	44102	2754	B1
4000	CLEV	44144	2754	B3
5200	CLEV	44109	2754	B7
5200	PRMA	44109	2754	B7
5200	PRMA	44134	2754	B7
E 51st Pl				
2900	CLEV	44127	2625	D6
W 51st Pl				
-	CLEV	44102	2624	B7
-	CLEV	44102	2754	B1
51st St				
-	ELYR	44035	2874	D2
41500	EyrT	44035	2874	D2
E 51st St				
1300	CLEV	44103	2495	D7
1300	CLEV	44114	2495	D7
2500	CLEV	44104	2625	D5
2900	CLEV	44127	2625	D6
3400	CLEV	44127	2755	D1
W 51st St				
3000	CLEV	44102	2624	B7
4400	CLEV	44144	2754	B5
5300	PRMA	44134	2754	B7
5300	PRMA	44134	2883	B1
E 52nd Pl				
3400	CLEV	44127	2755	D1
52nd St				
-	ELYR	44035	2874	E2
-	EyrT	44035	2874	D2
E 52nd St				
1300	CLEV	44103	2495	D7
1300	CLEV	44114	2495	D7
3300	CLEV	44127	2625	D7
3300	CLEV	44127	2755	D1
3600	CLEV	44105	2755	D2
3900	CHHT	44105	2755	D3
3900	NBGH	44105	2755	D3
W 52nd St				
1400	CLEV	44102	2624	B5
3200	CLEV	44102	2754	B1
4300	CLEV	44144	2754	B4
5200	CLEV	44109	2754	B7
5200	PRMA	44109	2754	B7
5200	PRMA	44134	2754	B7
E 53rd St				
1200	CLEV	44114	2495	C7
1300	CLEV	44103	2495	D7
3300	CLEV	44127	2625	D7
3300	CLEV	44127	2755	D1
3500	CLEV	44105	2755	D2
3900	CHHT	44105	2755	D3
3900	NBGH	44105	2755	D3
W 53rd St				
1200	CLEV	44102	2624	B4
4400	CLEV	44144	2754	B5
E 54th Pl				
1500	CLEV	44103	2625	D1
E 54th St				
2900	CLEV	44127	2625	D6
3500	CLEV	44105	2755	D2
3900	CHHT	44105	2755	D3
3900	NBGH	44105	2755	D3
W 54th St				
1300	CLEV	44102	2624	A4
3200	CLEV	44102	2754	A1
4500	CLEV	44144	2754	B5
5200	CLEV	44109	2754	A7
5200	PRMA	44109	2754	A7
5200	PRMA	44129	2754	A7
5200	PRMA	44134	2754	A7
5400	PRMA	44129	2883	A2
5400	PRMA	44134	2883	A3
E 55th St				
1000	CLEV	44103	2495	D6
1000	CLEV	44114	2495	D6
1600	CLEV	44103	2625	D1
2200	CLEV	44104	2625	D3
2800	CLEV	44127	2625	D6
3400	CLEV	44127	2755	D1
3500	CLEV	44105	2755	D2
3900	NBGH	44105	2755	D2
4000	CHHT	44105	2755	D2
W 55th St				
1400	CLEV	44102	2624	A5
E 56th Pl				
1600	CLEV	44103	2625	D1
3200	CLEV	44127	2625	D7
E 56th St				
4000	CLEV	44105	2755	D3
W 56th St				
3000	CLEV	44102	2624	A7
3200	CLEV	44102	2754	A1
4000	CLEV	44144	2754	A4
E 57th St				
1800	CLEV	44103	2625	D2
2300	CLEV	44104	2625	D4
2900	CLEV	44127	2625	D6
3500	CLEV	44105	2755	D2
W 57th St				
1400	CLEV	44102	2624	A5
4000	CLEV	44144	2754	A4
E 58th St				
1100	CLEV	44103	2495	D7
3900	CLEV	44105	2755	D3
W 58th St				
1200	CLEV	44102	2624	A6
3300	CLEV	44102	2754	A1
3500	CLEV	44144	2753	E2
3500	CLEV	44144	2754	A2
W 59th Pl				
3300	CLEV	44102	2754	A1
E 59th St				
1200	CLEV	44103	2495	D7
1300	CLEV	44103	2625	D1
2300	CLEV	44104	2625	D4
2900	CLEV	44127	2625	D6
3500	CLEV	44105	2755	D2
W 59th St				
1300	CLEV	44102	2624	A5
3300	CLEV	44102	2754	A1
4100	CLEV	44144	2754	A4
E 60th St				
-	CLEV	44103	2625	D1
1100	CLEV	44103	2495	D7
W 60th St				
3300	CLEV	44102	2754	A1
4300	CLEV	44144	2754	A4
5200	CLEV	44109	2754	A7
5200	PRMA	44109	2754	A7
5200	PRMA	44129	2754	A7
5300	PRMA	44129	2883	A1
E 61st Pl				
2000	CLEV	44103	2625	D2
E 61st St				
1000	CLEV	44103	2495	E7
1400	CLEV	44103	2625	D1
2300	CLEV	44104	2625	D4
2800	CLEV	44127	2625	D6
3500	CLEV	44105	2755	D2
W 61st St				
1300	CLEV	44102	2624	A5
3200	CLEV	44102	2754	A1
4300	CLEV	44144	2754	A4
E 62nd St				
1000	CLEV	44103	2495	D6
2600	CLEV	44104	2625	D5
W 62nd St				
3400	CLEV	44102	2754	A1
4100	CLEV	44144	2754	A4
4400	BKLN	44144	2754	A4
E 63rd St				
800	CLEV	44103	2495	D6
1400	CLEV	44103	2625	E1
2300	CLEV	44104	2625	E4
2900	CLEV	44127	2625	D6
3500	CLEV	44105	2755	D2
W 63rd St				
3100	CLEV	44102	2624	A7
3100	CLEV	44102	2754	A1
3900	CLEV	44144	2754	A3
W 64th Pl				
1800	CLEV	44102	2624	A5
E 64th St				
900	CLEV	44103	2495	E6
2400	CLEV	44104	2625	E4
2800	CLEV	44127	2625	E6
3900	CLEV	44105	2755	E3
W 64th St				
1300	CLEV	44102	2624	A5
E 65th St				
1300	CLEV	44103	2495	E7
1300	CLEV	44103	2625	E1
2300	CLEV	44104	2625	E4
2900	CLEV	44127	2625	E6
3300	CLEV	44127	2755	E1
3500	CLEV	44105	2755	E2
W 65th St				
1200	CLEV	44102	2624	A5
3200	CLEV	44102	2754	A1
3500	CLEV	44102	2753	E2
E 66th Pl				
1000	CLEV	44103	2495	E6
E 66th St				
1000	CLEV	44103	2495	E6
1300	CLEV	44103	2625	E1
2400	CLEV	44104	2625	E4
2900	CLEV	44127	2625	E6
3300	CLEV	44127	2755	E1
3800	CLEV	44105	2755	E3
W 66th St				
3500	CLEV	44102	2753	E1
3500	CLEV	44102	2754	A1
4300	CLEV	44144	2754	A4
4400	BKLN	44144	2753	E5
4400	BKLN	44144	2754	A4
W 67th Pl				
4400	BKLN	44144	2753	E4
E 67th St				
800	CLEV	44103	2495	E6
2300	CLEV	44103	2625	E4
2300	CLEV	44104	2625	E4
2900	CLEV	44127	2625	E6
3600	CLEV	44105	2755	E2
W 67th St				
1200	CLEV	44102	2624	A4
3200	CLEV	44102	2623	E7
3200	CLEV	44102	2754	A1
3500	CLEV	44102	2753	E1
5200	PRMA	44129	2754	A7
5300	PRMA	44129	2883	A1
E 68th Pl				
1700	CLEV	44103	2625	E1
W 68th Pl				
2100	CLEV	44102	2624	A6
E 68th St				
1000	CLEV	44103	2495	E6
1700	CLEV	44103	2625	E2
2600	CLEV	44104	2625	E5
3100	CLEV	44127	2625	E7
4000	CLEV	44105	2755	E3
W 68th St				
-	CLEV	44102	2624	A6
E 69th Pl				
900	CLEV	44103	2495	E6
1700	CLEV	44103	2625	E2
W 69th Pl				
4400	BKLN	44144	2753	E5
E 69th St				
900	CLEV	44103	2495	E6
1800	CLEV	44103	2625	E2
2100	CLEV	44104	2625	E3
3400	CLEV	44105	2755	E1
3400	CLEV	44127	2755	E1
W 69th St				
1200	CLEV	44102	2624	A4
2100	CLEV	44102	2623	D6
3500	CLEV	44102	2753	E1
E 70th Pl				
-	CLEV	44105	2755	E2
E 70th St				
800	CLEV	44103	2495	E6
1500	CLEV	44103	2625	E2
2200	CLEV	44104	2625	E3
3300	CLEV	44127	2625	E7
3300	CLEV	44127	2755	E1
3400	CLEV	44105	2755	E1
W 70th St				
1200	CLEV	44102	2624	A5
3100	CLEV	44102	2623	E7
E 71st Pl				
2700	CLEV	44104	2625	E5
W 71st Pl				
4400	BKLN	44144	2753	E5
E 71st St				
1000	CLEV	44103	2495	E7
1400	CLEV	44103	2625	E2
2200	CLEV	44104	2625	E4
3400	CLEV	44127	2625	E7
3500	CLEV	44105	2755	E1
3500	CLEV	44127	2755	E1
4300	CHHT	44105	2755	E4
4400	CHHT	44125	2755	E4
W 71st St				
1800	CLEV	44102	2623	E5
E 72nd Pl				
900	CLEV	44103	2495	E6
2000	CLEV	44103	2625	E2
4900	CHHT	44125	2755	E6
E 72nd St				
600	CLEV	44103	2495	E5
600	CLEV	44103	2496	A4
1400	CLEV	44103	2625	E1
2800	CLEV	44104	2625	E6
3300	CLEV	44127	2625	E7
3300	CLEV	44127	2755	E1
3800	CLEV	44105	2755	E2
E 73rd Pl				
1200	CLEV	44103	2496	A7
3600	CLEV	44105	2755	E2
E 73rd St				
700	CLEV	44103	2496	A5
1600	CLEV	44103	2626	A1
1800	CLEV	44103	2625	E2
2100	CLEV	44104	2625	E3
3400	CLEV	44127	2626	A7
3400	CLEV	44127	2756	A1
4200	CLEV	44105	2755	E4
W 73rd St				
1200	CLEV	44102	2623	E5
3200	CLEV	44102	2753	E1
E 74th St				
900	CLEV	44103	2496	A6
2100	CLEV	44103	2626	A3
2300	CLEV	44104	2626	A3
3500	CLEV	44105	2756	A1
3500	CLEV	44127	2756	A1
3600	CLEV	44105	2755	E2
W 74th St				
1200	CLEV	44102	2623	E5
E 75th Pl				
-	CLEV	44104	2626	A6
1300	CLEV	44103	2496	A7
E 75th St				
800	CLEV	44103	2496	A6
1800	CLEV	44103	2626	A2
2400	CLEV	44104	2626	A4
3300	CLEV	44127	2756	A1
3800	CLEV	44105	2756	A2
W 75th St				
1400	CLEV	44102	2623	E5
E 76th Pl				
1300	CLEV	44103	2496	A7
E 76th St				
800	CLEV	44103	2496	A6
2300	CLEV	44103	2626	A3
2300	CLEV	44104	2626	A3
3400	CLEV	44105	2756	A1
3400	CLEV	44127	2756	A1
W 76th St				
1100	CLEV	44102	2623	E5
E 77th Pl				
-	CLEV	44105	2756	A1
-	CLEV	44127	2756	A1
E 77th St				
800	CLEV	44103	2496	A6
1600	CLEV	44103	2626	A1
2200	CLEV	44104	2626	A3
3600	CLEV	44105	2756	A2
W 77th St				
1400	CLEV	44102	2623	E5
E 78th Pl				
1300	CLEV	44103	2496	A7
E 78th St				
900	CLEV	44103	2496	A6
1500	CLEV	44103	2626	A1
2800	CLEV	44104	2626	A5
3400	CLEV	44105	2756	A1
3400	CLEV	44127	2756	A1
W 78th St				
-	NRYN	44129	3013	E2
-	NRYN	44133	3013	E2
-	PRMA	44129	3013	E2
1200	CLEV	44102	2623	E5
5200	BKLN	44144	2753	E7
5200	PRMA	44129	2753	E7
5200	PRMA	44144	2753	E7
5400	PRMA	44129	2882	E1
E 79th St				
700	CLEV	44103	2496	A5
1400	CLEV	44103	2626	A1
2200	CLEV	44104	2626	A7
3000	CLEV	44127	2626	A7
4000	CLEV	44105	2756	A3
W 79th St				
1300	CLEV	44102	2623	E5
5800	PRMA	44129	2882	E2
E 80th Pl				
-	CLEV	44104	2626	A5
W 80th Pl				
1400	CLEV	44102	2623	E5
E 80th St				
1300	CLEV	44103	2496	A7
1300	CLEV	44103	2626	A1
2500	CLEV	44104	2626	A4
3200	CLEV	44127	2626	A7
3500	CLEV	44105	2756	A1
3500	CLEV	44127	2756	A1
W 80th St				
1300	CLEV	44102	2623	E5
E 81st Pl				
2100	CLEV	44103	2626	A3
E 81st St				
1100	CLEV	44103	2496	A7
1300	CLEV	44103	2626	A1
2500	CLEV	44104	2626	A4
3500	CLEV	44105	2756	A1
4800	GDHT	44125	2756	A6
W 81st St				
1400	CLEV	44102	2623	E5
E 82nd Pl				
-	CLEV	44103	2626	A2
E 82nd St				
600	CLEV	44103	2496	A5
1300	CLEV	44103	2626	A1
2300	CLEV	44104	2626	A4
3500	CLEV	44105	2756	A1
W 82nd St				
3100	CLEV	44102	2623	E7
3200	CLEV	44102	2753	E1
E 83rd Pl				
-	CLEV	44103	2626	A2
-	CLEV	44105	2756	A4
E 83rd St				
1100	CLEV	44103	2496	A7
1900	CLEV	44103	2626	A2
2000	CLEV	44106	2626	A3
2200	CLEV	44104	2626	A3
W 83rd St				
1200	CLEV	44102	2623	E5
5200	BKLN	44144	2753	D7
5200	PRMA	44129	2753	D7
5200	PRMA	44144	2753	D7
E 84th St				
1100	CLEV	44103	2496	A7
1100	CLEV	44108	2496	A7
1300	CLEV	44103	2626	A1
1300	CLEV	44106	2496	A7
2100	CLEV	44106	2626	A3
2400	CLEV	44104	2626	A4
4700	GDHT	44125	2756	A6
W 84th St				
-	NRYN	44129	3013	D2
-	NRYN	44133	3013	D2
-	PRMA	44129	3013	D2
1400	CLEV	44102	2623	E5
3200	CLEV	44102	2753	E1
5300	PRMA	44129	2753	D7
5400	PRMA	44129	2882	D1
E 85th St				
1100	CLEV	44103	2496	A7
1100	CLEV	44108	2496	A7
1300	CLEV	44106	2496	A7
1800	CLEV	44103	2626	B2
1800	CLEV	44106	2626	B2
2200	CLEV	44104	2626	A3
4300	CLEV	44105	2756	B4
4600	GDHT	44105	2756	B5
4600	GDHT	44125	2756	B6
W 85th St				
1400	CLEV	44102	2623	D5
E 86th St				
1100	CLEV	44103	2496	B7
1100	CLEV	44106	2496	B7
1100	CLEV	44108	2496	B7
1600	CLEV	44103	2626	B2
2100	CLEV	44106	2626	B4
2400	CLEV	44104	2626	B4
3900	CLEV	44105	2756	A3
4500	GDHT	44105	2756	B5
4600	GDHT	44125	2756	B5
W 86th St				
3100	CLEV	44102	2623	D7
3200	CLEV	44102	2753	D1
E 87th St				
1100	CLEV	44103	2496	B7
1100	CLEV	44106	2496	B7
1100	CLEV	44108	2496	B7
2100	CLEV	44106	2626	B3
2600	CLEV	44104	2626	B5
3300	CLEV	44127	2626	B7
W 87th St				
1200	CLEV	44102	2623	D5
E 88th Pl				
1700	CLEV	44106	2626	B2
E 88th St				
-	CLEV	44103	2496	A5
800	CLEV	44108	2496	B5
1300	CLEV	44106	2496	B7
2300	CLEV	44106	2626	B4
3000	CLEV	44104	2626	B7
3400	CLEV	44104	2756	B1
3500	CLEV	44105	2756	B1
4600	GDHT	44105	2756	B5
4600	GDHT	44125	2756	B6
W 88th St				
3100	CLEV	44102	2623	D7
3200	CLEV	44102	2753	D1

Cleveland Street Index

STREET Block	City	ZIP	Map#	Grid
E 89th Pl				
700	CLEV	44108	2496	B5
E 89th St				
1200	CLEV	44106	2496	B7
1200	CLEV	44108	2496	B7
1600	CLEV	44106	2626	B1
2100	CLEV	44104	2626	B5
3400	CLEV	44104	2756	B1
3400	CLEV	44105	2756	B1
W 89th St				
1200	CLEV	44102	2623	D5
E 90th Pl				
1500	CLEV	44106	2626	B1
E 90th St				
1200	CLEV	44106	2496	B7
1200	CLEV	44108	2496	B7
2100	CLEV	44104	2626	B3
2100	CLEV	44106	2626	B3
4600	CLEV	44105	2756	B5
4600	GDHT	44105	2756	B5
4600	GDHT	44125	2756	B6
W 90th St				
1900	CLEV	44102	2623	D6
3100	CLEV	44102	2753	D1
E 91st St				
600	CLEV	44108	2496	B5
1300	CLEV	44106	2496	B7
1600	CLEV	44106	2626	B1
2800	CLEV	44104	2626	B6
3500	CLEV	44104	2756	B1
3500	CLEV	44105	2756	B3
W 91st St				
1200	CLEV	44102	2623	D5
3200	CLEV	44102	2753	D1
E 92nd St				
-	CLEV	44105	2756	B3
600	CLEV	44108	2496	B5
1300	CLEV	44106	2496	B7
1400	CLEV	44106	2626	B1
2700	CLEV	44104	2626	B5
W 92nd St				
3100	CLEV	44102	2623	D7
E 93rd Pl				
1600	CLEV	44106	2626	B1
E 93rd St				
600	CLEV	44108	2496	B5
1300	CLEV	44106	2496	B7
1400	CLEV	44106	2626	B1
2300	CLEV	44104	2626	B3
3400	CLEV	44104	2756	B1
3400	CLEV	44105	2756	B3
4600	GDHT	44105	2756	B5
4600	GDHT	44125	2756	B6
W 93rd St				
1200	CLEV	44102	2623	D5
E 94th St				
600	CLEV	44108	2496	B4
1300	CLEV	44106	2496	B7
1300	CLEV	44106	2626	B1
3100	CLEV	44104	2626	B7
4100	CLEV	44105	2756	B3
4600	GDHT	44105	2756	B5
4600	GDHT	44125	2756	B5
5400	GDHT	44125	2885	B1
W 94th St				
3100	CLEV	44102	2623	D7
3200	CLEV	44102	2753	D1
5500	PRMA	44129	2882	D1
E 95th St				
600	CLEV	44108	2496	B5
1300	CLEV	44106	2496	B7
2100	CLEV	44106	2626	B3
3700	CLEV	44105	2756	B2
4800	GDHT	44125	2756	B6
W 95th St				
-	CLEV	44102	2623	D5
3200	CLEV	44102	2753	D1
W 96th Pl				
-	CLEV	44102	2623	D5
E 96th St				
600	CLEV	44108	2496	B4
1500	CLEV	44106	2626	B1
2600	CLEV	44104	2626	B5
3700	CLEV	44105	2756	B2
4800	GDHT	44125	2756	B6
5300	GDHT	44125	2885	B1
W 96th St				
1900	CLEV	44102	2623	D6
E 97th St				
500	BTNH	44108	2496	B4
1000	CLEV	44108	2496	B6
1800	CLEV	44106	2626	B2
2800	CLEV	44104	2626	B5
3600	CLEV	44105	2756	C2
4800	GDHT	44125	2756	B6
W 97th St				
3100	CLEV	44102	2623	D7
3200	CLEV	44102	2753	D1
E 98th Pl				
-	CLEV	44108	2496	B6
4100	CLEV	44105	2756	C3
E 98th St				
1000	CLEV	44108	2496	B6
2800	CLEV	44104	2626	C5
3400	CLEV	44104	2756	C1
3500	CLEV	44105	2756	C1
5000	GDHT	44125	2756	C7
W 98th St				
1400	CLEV	44102	2623	D7
3200	CLEV	44102	2753	D1
E 99th Pl				
-	CLEV	44108	2496	B7
2700	CLEV	44104	2626	C5
E 99th St				
-	CLEV	44105	2756	C2
500	BTNH	44108	2496	B4
500	CLEV	44108	2496	B4
1200	CLEV	44106	2496	B7
2800	CLEV	44104	2626	C5
3400	CLEV	44104	2756	C1
4600	GDHT	44105	2756	C5
4600	GDHT	44125	2756	C5
W 99th St				
1900	CLEV	44102	2623	D6
3200	CLEV	44102	2753	C1
E 100th Pl				
-	CLEV	44105	2756	C3
E 100th St				
700	CLEV	44108	2496	B5
2000	CLEV	44106	2626	B3
2800	CLEV	44104	2626	C6
3700	CLEV	44105	2756	C2
5200	GDHT	44125	2756	C7
W 100th St				
3000	CLEV	44102	2623	C7
3200	CLEV	44102	2753	C1
3200	CLEV	44111	2623	C7
3200	CLEV	44111	2753	C1
E 101st St				
500	CLEV	44108	2496	B5
1800	CLEV	44106	2626	C2
W 101st St				
1400	CLEV	44102	2623	C6
3000	CLEV	44111	2623	C7
E 102nd St				
800	CLEV	44108	2496	C5
1200	CLEV	44106	2496	C7
2000	CLEV	44106	2626	C3
2800	CLEV	44104	2626	C7
3300	CLEV	44104	2756	C1
3800	CLEV	44105	2756	C2
5200	GDHT	44125	2756	C7
W 102nd St				
1200	CLEV	44102	2623	C5
3500	CLEV	44111	2753	C2
E 103rd St				
1200	CLEV	44106	2496	C7
1200	CLEV	44108	2496	C7
2100	CLEV	44106	2626	C3
2700	CLEV	44104	2626	C5
3300	CLEV	44104	2756	C1
3300	CLEV	44105	2756	C1
W 103rd St				
1200	CLEV	44102	2623	C5
2000	CLEV	44111	2623	C6
3500	CLEV	44111	2753	C2
E 104th Pl				
1100	CLEV	44108	2496	C7
E 104th St				
2800	CLEV	44104	2626	C6
3300	CLEV	44104	2756	C1
3500	CLEV	44105	2756	C2
4500	GDHT	44125	2756	C5
W 104th St				
1100	CLEV	44102	2623	C5
2000	CLEV	44111	2623	C6
3500	CLEV	44111	2753	C2
E 105th Pl				
-	CLEV	44105	2756	C3
E 105th St				
400	BTNH	44108	2496	C4
400	CLEV	44108	2496	C5
1200	CLEV	44106	2496	C7
1400	CLEV	44106	2626	C3
3200	CLEV	44104	2626	C7
3300	CLEV	44104	2756	C1
3300	CLEV	44105	2756	C1
5200	GDHT	44125	2756	C7
W 105th St				
1200	CLEV	44102	2623	C5
2000	CLEV	44111	2623	C6
3200	CLEV	44111	2753	C2
E 106th Pl				
1100	CLEV	44108	2496	C7
E 106th St				
-	CLEV	44108	2496	C4
1400	CLEV	44106	2496	C7
1400	CLEV	44106	2626	C1
2800	CLEV	44104	2626	C5
3300	CLEV	44104	2756	C1
3500	CLEV	44105	2756	C1
4800	GDHT	44125	2756	C6
W 106th St				
1200	CLEV	44102	2623	C5
2000	CLEV	44111	2623	C7
3700	CLEV	44111	2753	C2
E 107th Pl				
-	CLEV	44108	2496	C4
E 107th St				
600	CLEV	44108	2496	C4
1300	CLEV	44106	2496	C7
1400	CLEV	44106	2626	C1
4800	GDHT	44125	2756	C6
W 107th St				
1400	CLEV	44102	2623	C5
3500	CLEV	44111	2753	C2
E 108th St				
400	CLEV	44108	2496	C4
1400	CLEV	44106	2496	C7
1400	CLEV	44106	2626	C1
2800	CLEV	44104	2626	C5
3300	CLEV	44104	2756	C1
3500	CLEV	44105	2756	C1
4800	GDHT	44125	2756	C6
W 108th St				
1200	CLEV	44102	2623	C5
E 109th St				
400	CLEV	44108	2496	C4
1300	CLEV	44106	2496	C7
2000	CLEV	44106	2626	C3
2500	CLEV	44104	2626	C4
3700	CLEV	44105	2756	C2
4800	GDHT	44125	2756	C6
E 110th Ct				
2500	CLEV	44104	2626	C4
E 110th St				
400	CLEV	44108	2496	D4
1300	CLEV	44106	2496	C7
2400	CLEV	44104	2626	C5
3300	CLEV	44104	2756	C1
3300	CLEV	44105	2756	C1
4900	GDHT	44125	2756	C6
W 110th St				
1100	CLEV	44102	2623	B5
2000	CLEV	44111	2623	B6
3200	CLEV	44111	2753	B1
E 111th St				
1000	CLEV	44108	2496	D7
1200	CLEV	44106	2496	D7
1500	CLEV	44106	2626	D1
2500	CLEV	44104	2626	D4
4100	CLEV	44105	2756	C3
4900	GDHT	44125	2756	D6
5300	GDHT	44125	2885	C1
W 111th St				
1200	CLEV	44102	2623	B5
3000	CLEV	44111	2623	B7
3200	CLEV	44111	2753	B1
E 112th St				
1000	CLEV	44108	2496	D6
1100	CLEV	44106	2496	D6
1400	CLEV	44106	2626	D1
2600	CLEV	44104	2626	D5
3500	CLEV	44104	2756	D1
3500	CLEV	44105	2756	D1
5100	GDHT	44125	2756	D7
W 112th St				
1200	CLEV	44102	2623	B5
3000	CLEV	44111	2623	B7
3200	CLEV	44111	2753	B1
E 113th St				
600	CLEV	44108	2496	D5
1100	CLEV	44106	2496	D6
3300	CLEV	44104	2626	D7
3300	CLEV	44104	2756	D1
3500	CLEV	44105	2756	D1
5000	GDHT	44125	2756	D7
E 114th St				
1300	CLEV	44108	2496	D7
1400	CLEV	44106	2496	D7
1400	CLEV	44106	2626	D1
2600	CLEV	44104	2626	D5
3300	CLEV	44104	2756	D1
3300	CLEV	44105	2756	D1
5000	GDHT	44125	2756	D7
W 114th St				
1200	CLEV	44102	2623	B5
2000	CLEV	44111	2623	B7
3200	CLEV	44111	2753	B1
E 115th St				
400	CLEV	44108	2496	D4
1200	CLEV	44106	2496	D7
1400	CLEV	44106	2626	D1
2600	CLEV	44104	2626	D5
5000	GDHT	44125	2756	D7
W 115th St				
1000	CLEV	44102	2623	B4
3000	CLEV	44111	2623	B7
3200	CLEV	44111	2753	B1
E 116th Pl				
1700	CLEV	44106	2626	D1
E 116th St				
1300	CLEV	44106	2496	D7
1400	CLEV	44106	2626	D1
2700	CLEV	44120	2626	D7
2800	CLEV	44104	2626	D7
3300	CLEV	44104	2756	D1
3300	CLEV	44120	2756	D1
3400	CLEV	44105	2756	D1
4300	GDHT	44105	2756	D4
W 116th St				
1200	CLEV	44102	2623	B5
3000	CLEV	44111	2623	B7
3200	CLEV	44111	2753	B1
3700	LNDL	44111	2753	B2
E 117th St				
400	CLEV	44108	2496	D4
1300	CLEV	44106	2496	D7
1900	CLEV	44106	2626	D1
2800	CLEV	44120	2626	D6
3300	CLEV	44105	2756	D1
3300	CLEV	44120	2756	D1
5000	GDHT	44125	2756	D7
W 117th St				
-	BKLN	44144	2753	B3
1100	CLEV	44102	2623	B4
1100	LKWD	44102	2623	B4
1100	LKWD	44107	2623	B4
2000	CLEV	44111	2623	B5
3200	CLEV	44111	2753	B2
3800	LNDL	44111	2753	B3
3800	LNDL	44135	2753	B3
W 118th Pl				
-	CLEV	44111	2623	B7
E 118th St				
400	CLEV	44108	2496	D4
1400	CLEV	44106	2496	D7
1500	CLEV	44106	2626	D1
2700	CLEV	44120	2626	D5
3300	CLEV	44105	2756	D1
3300	CLEV	44120	2756	D1
W 118th St				
3300	CLEV	44111	2753	B1
4400	CLEV	44135	2753	B5
E 119th St				
1800	CLEV	44106	2626	D1
2700	CLEV	44120	2626	D5
3300	CLEV	44105	2756	D1
3300	CLEV	44120	2756	D1
4300	GDHT	44105	2756	D4
5100	GDHT	44125	2756	D7
W 119th St				
3100	CLEV	44111	2623	B7
3200	CLEV	44111	2753	B1
3900	LNDL	44135	2753	B3
E 120th St				
1300	CLEV	44106	2496	D7
1300	CLEV	44108	2496	D7
1500	CLEV	44106	2626	D1
2700	CLEV	44120	2626	D5
3500	CLEV	44105	2756	D2
3500	CLEV	44120	2756	D1
5400	GDHT	44125	2885	D1
W 120th St				
3000	CLEV	44111	2623	A7
3300	CLEV	44111	2753	A1
4000	CLEV	44135	2753	B3
4000	LNDL	44135	2753	B3
E 121st St				
2600	CLEV	44120	2626	E5
3300	CLEV	44105	2756	D1
3300	CLEV	44120	2756	D1
W 121st St				
3000	CLEV	44111	2623	A7
3100	CLEV	44111	2753	A1
4200	CLEV	44135	2753	A4
E 122nd St				
1500	CLEV	44106	2626	D1
2600	CLEV	44120	2626	E5
5400	GDHT	44125	2885	D1
W 122nd St				
3200	CLEV	44111	2753	A1
4200	CLEV	44135	2753	A4
E 123rd St				
800	CLEV	44108	2496	D6
1300	CLEV	44106	2496	D7
1500	CLEV	44106	2626	E1
2900	CLEV	44120	2626	E7
3300	CLEV	44105	2756	E1
3300	CLEV	44120	2756	E1
W 123rd St				
3200	CLEV	44111	2753	A1
4200	CLEV	44135	2753	A4
E 124th Pl				
1900	CLEV	44106	2626	E2
E 124th St				
1100	CLEV	44108	2496	D7
1300	CLEV	44106	2496	E7
1300	CLEV	44112	2496	E7
2400	CLEV	44120	2626	E4
3500	CLEV	44105	2756	E1
3500	CLEV	44120	2756	E1
5300	GDHT	44125	2756	D7
5400	GDHT	44125	2885	E1
W 124th St				
4600	CLEV	44135	2753	A6
E 125th St				
400	CLEV	44108	2496	E4
1000	CLEV	44112	2496	E6
1000	ECLE	44108	2496	E6
1000	ECLE	44112	2496	E6
1200	CLEV	44106	2496	E7
2000	CLEV	44106	2626	E2
2700	CLEV	44120	2626	E6
3400	CLEV	44105	2756	E1
3400	CLEV	44120	2756	E1
W 125th St				
-	CLEV	44135	2753	A3
3200	CLEV	44111	2753	A1
E 126th St				
400	CLEV	44108	2496	E4
1900	CLEV	44106	2626	E2
2400	CLEV	44120	2626	E4
3400	CLEV	44105	2756	E1
3400	CLEV	44120	2756	E1
4400	GDHT	44105	2756	E5
5100	GDHT	44125	2756	E7
W 126th St				
3200	CLEV	44111	2623	A7
3200	CLEV	44111	2753	A1
4700	CLEV	44135	2753	A6
E 127th Pl				
-	CLEV	44108	2496	E3
E 127th St				
400	CLEV	44108	2496	E4
2400	CLEV	44120	2626	E4
2400	SRHT	44120	2626	E4
3500	CLEV	44105	2756	E2
3500	CLEV	44120	2756	E1
W 127th St				
3200	CLEV	44111	2623	A7
3200	CLEV	44111	2753	A1
4600	CLEV	44135	2753	A6
E 128th St				
400	CLEV	44108	2496	E4
2600	CLEV	44120	2626	E5
2600	SRHT	44120	2626	E5
3400	CLEV	44120	2756	E1
4200	CLEV	44105	2756	E4
5100	GDHT	44125	2756	E7
5400	GDHT	44125	2885	E1
W 128th St				
3200	CLEV	44111	2623	A7
3200	CLEV	44111	2753	A1
4400	CLEV	44135	2753	A5
E 129th St				
400	CLEV	44108	2496	E4
800	ECLE	44108	2496	E6
3500	CLEV	44105	2756	E1
3500	CLEV	44120	2756	E1
5300	GDHT	44125	2756	D7
5300	GDHT	44125	2885	E1
W 129th St				
3200	CLEV	44111	2623	A7
3200	CLEV	44111	2753	A1
E 130th St				
600	CLEV	44108	2496	E4
800	ECLE	44108	2496	E6
2600	SRHT	44120	2626	E5
2700	CLEV	44120	2626	E6
3300	CLEV	44120	2756	E1
3800	CLEV	44105	2756	E2
5700	GDHT	44125	2885	E2
W 130th St				
10	BNWK	44133	3147	E5
10	BNWK	44136	3147	E5
10	BNWK	44212	3147	E6
10	BNWK	44233	3147	E6
10	HkyT	44133	3147	E5
10	HkyT	44233	3147	E6
10	NRYN	44133	3147	E5
10	SGVL	44133	3147	E2
10	SGVL	44136	3147	E5
3200	CLEV	44111	2622	E7
3200	CLEV	44111	2752	E1
3500	CLEV	44111	2753	A2
4000	CLEV	44135	2753	A6
4700	CLEV	44135	2752	E6
4800	PRMA	44130	2752	E7
4800	PRMA	44135	2752	E7
5200	BKPK	44130	2752	E7
5200	BKPK	44142	2752	E7
5300	BKPK	44130	2881	E1
5300	BKPK	44142	2881	E1
5300	PRMA	44130	2881	E1
6000	PMHT	44130	2881	E3
6400	MDBH	44130	2881	E3
6400	MDBH	44142	2881	E4
7300	MDBH	44130	3012	E1
7300	PRMA	44130	3012	E1
7600	NRYN	44130	3012	E2
7600	NRYN	44133	3012	E7
7600	SGVL	44130	3012	E2
7600	SGVL	44133	3012	E7
7600	SGVL	44136	3012	E7
E 131st St				
100	CLEV	44108	2496	E3
800	ECLE	44108	2496	E6
1000	ECLE	44112	2496	E6
3500	CLEV	44105	2756	E3
3500	CLEV	44120	2756	E1
4100	CLEV	44128	2756	E3
4300	GDHT	44105	2756	E5
4500	GDHT	44125	2756	E5
5300	GDHT	44125	2885	E1
W 131st St				
3200	CLEV	44111	2752	E1
3300	CLEV	44111	2753	A1
4300	CLEV	44135	2752	E5
E 132nd St				
-	CLEV	44120	2756	E1
3200	CLEV	44120	2626	E7
5200	GDHT	44125	2756	E7
5300	GDHT	44125	2885	E1
W 132nd St				
3300	CLEV	44111	2752	E1
3500	CLEV	44111	2753	A2
4300	CLEV	44135	2752	E4
E 133rd St				
700	BTNH	44108	2496	E2
700	BTNH	44110	2496	E2
700	CLEV	44110	2496	E2
1200	ECLE	44110	2496	E4
1200	ECLE	44112	2496	E4
1300	ECLE	44112	2497	A4
3500	CLEV	44120	2756	E1
4200	CLEV	44105	2756	E4
5200	GDHT	44125	2756	E7
5400	GDHT	44125	2885	E1
W 133rd St				
3400	CLEV	44111	2752	E1
4400	CLEV	44135	2752	E5
E 134th St				
900	CLEV	44110	2497	A3
1200	ECLE	44110	2497	A4
1200	ECLE	44112	2497	A4
3200	CLEV	44120	2626	E7
3300	CLEV	44120	2756	E1
4200	CLEV	44105	2756	E4
5300	GDHT	44125	2756	E7
5300	GDHT	44125	2885	E1
W 134th St				
3500	CLEV	44111	2752	E2
4100	CLEV	44135	2752	E4
E 135th St				
1200	CLEV	44110	2497	A4
1200	ECLE	44110	2497	A4
1200	ECLE	44112	2497	A4
3200	CLEV	44120	2626	E7
3200	CLEV	44120	2627	A7
3300	CLEV	44120	2756	E1
4100	CLEV	44105	2756	E3
4100	CLEV	44128	2756	E3
4800	GDHT	44125	2756	E6
5300	GDHT	44125	2885	E1
W 135th St				
3300	CLEV	44111	2752	E1
4600	CLEV	44135	2752	E5
E 136th St				
600	CLEV	44110	2497	A1
3900	CLEV	44120	2757	A3
4100	CLEV	44128	2757	A3
4200	CLEV	44105	2757	A4
4200	GDHT	44105	2757	A4
4500	GDHT	44105	2756	E5
4500	GDHT	44125	2756	E5
W 136th St				
3000	CLEV	44107	2622	E7
3000	CLEV	44111	2622	E7
3000	LKWD	44107	2622	E7
3300	CLEV	44111	2752	E1
4400	CLEV	44135	2752	E5
E 137th St				
800	CLEV	44110	2497	A2
1200	ECLE	44110	2497	A4
1200	ECLE	44112	2497	A4
3100	CLEV	44120	2627	A7
3300	CLEV	44120	2757	A1
4200	CLEV	44105	2757	A4
W 137th St				
3000	CLEV	44107	2622	E7
3000	CLEV	44111	2622	E7
3000	LKWD	44107	2622	E7
3300	CLEV	44111	2752	E1
3900	CLEV	44135	2752	E2
5000	BKPK	44135	2752	E7
5000	BKPK	44142	2752	E7
E 138th Pl				
800	CLEV	44110	2497	A3
E 138th St				
700	CLEV	44110	2497	A2
3500	CLEV	44120	2757	A1
4000	CLEV	44105	2757	A3
4000	CLEV	44128	2757	A3
5200	GDHT	44125	2757	A7
W 138th St				
3000	CLEV	44107	2622	E7
3000	CLEV	44111	2622	E7
3000	LKWD	44107	2622	E7
3600	CLEV	44111	2752	E2
4300	CLEV	44135	2752	E4
E 139th St				
-	CLEV	44110	2497	A2
1300	ECLE	44112	2497	A4
3200	CLEV	44120	2627	A7
3300	CLEV	44120	2757	A1
4000	CLEV	44128	2757	A3
4200	CLEV	44105	2757	A4
4300	GDHT	44105	2757	A4
5300	GDHT	44125	2886	A1
W 139th St				
3000	CLEV	44107	2622	E7
3000	CLEV	44111	2622	E7
3000	LKWD	44107	2622	E7
3500	CLEV	44111	2752	E2
4300	CLEV	44135	2752	E4
5000	BKPK	44135	2752	D7
5000	BKPK	44142	2752	D7
E 140th St				
-	GDHT	44125	2886	A3
-	GDHT	44137	2886	A3
-	MPHT	44137	2886	A3
400	CLEV	44110	2372	A7
500	BTNH	44110	2497	A1
500	CLEV	44110	2497	A3
3200	CLEV	44120	2627	A7
3200	SRHT	44120	2627	A7
3300	CLEV	44120	2757	A1
3800	CLEV	44128	2757	A2
3900	CLEV	44105	2757	A1
W 140th St				
3000	CLEV	44107	2622	E7
3000	CLEV	44111	2622	E7
3000	LKWD	44107	2622	E7
3200	CLEV	44111	2752	D3
3900	CLEV	44135	2752	D4
5000	BKPK	44135	2752	D7
5000	BKPK	44142	2752	D7
E 141st St				
800	CLEV	44110	2497	A2
1200	ECLE	44112	2497	A4
3900	CLEV	44105	2757	A3
4200	CLEV	44128	2757	A4
4800	GDHT	44125	2757	A6
4800	GDHT	44128	2757	A6
5300	MPHT	44137	2757	B7
5300	MPHT	44137	2886	A1
W 141st St				
3200	CLEV	44111	2622	D7
3200	CLEV	44111	2752	D1
E 142nd St				
400	CLEV	44110	2372	A7
400	CLEV	44110	2497	A1
1200	ECLE	44110	2497	A4
1200	ECLE	44112	2497	A4
3200	CLEV	44120	2627	A7
3300	CLEV	44120	2757	A1
3700	CLEV	44128	2757	A2
4300	CLEV	44105	2757	A4
4600	GDHT	44125	2757	A5
W 142nd St				
3100	CLEV	44111	2622	D7
3200	CLEV	44111	2752	D1
E 143rd St				
400	CLEV	44110	2372	A7
500	CLEV	44110	2497	A1
1200	ECLE	44110	2497	A4
1200	ECLE	44112	2497	A4
3200	CLEV	44120	2627	A7
3200	CLEV	44120	2757	A1
4300	CLEV	44105	2757	A4
4300	CLEV	44128	2757	A4
4500	GDHT	44105	2757	A5
4500	GDHT	44125	2757	A5
4500	GDHT	44128	2757	A5
W 143rd St				
3600	CLEV	44111	2752	D2
3900	CLEV	44135	2752	D4
E 144th St				
800	CLEV	44110	2497	A3
1200	ECLE	44110	2497	A4
1200	ECLE	44112	2497	A4
3500	CLEV	44120	2757	A2
3500	CLEV	44128	2757	A1
4500	GDHT	44128	2757	A5
W 144th St				
3100	CLEV	44111	2622	D7
3200	CLEV	44111	2752	D1
4000	CLEV	44135	2752	D3
E 145th St				
1000	CLEV	44110	2497	B3
1200	ECLE	44110	2497	B4
1200	ECLE	44112	2497	B4
3200	CLEV	44120	2627	A7
3200	CLEV	44120	2757	A1
W 145th St				
3400	CLEV	44111	2752	D1
4100	CLEV	44135	2752	D4
E 146th St				
300	CLEV	44110	2372	B7
600	CLEV	44110	2497	B1
1100	ECLE	44112	2497	A3
1200	ECLE	44110	2497	B4
3200	CLEV	44120	2627	A7
3200	SRHT	44120	2627	A7
3500	CLEV	44120	2757	A2
3600	CLEV	44128	2757	A2
5500	MPHT	44137	2886	A2
W 146th St				
3000	CLEV	44111	2622	D7
3400	CLEV	44111	2752	D2
4200	CLEV	44135	2752	D4
E 147th St				
300	CLEV	44110	2372	B7
500	CLEV	44110	2497	B1
3200	CLEV	44120	2627	B7
3400	CLEV	44120	2757	B1
3600	CLEV	44128	2757	A3
W 147th St				
-	BKPK	44135	2752	D7
3500	CLEV	44111	2752	D2
4300	CLEV	44135	2752	D5
5000	BKPK	44142	2752	D7
5200	BKPK	44142	2881	D1
E 148th St				
300	CLEV	44110	2372	B7
900	CLEV	44110	2497	B3
3900	CLEV	44128	2757	B3
W 148th St				
3300	CLEV	44111	2752	D1
4200	CLEV	44135	2752	D4
5000	BKPK	44142	2752	C7
5200	BKPK	44142	2881	C1
E 149th St				
200	CLEV	44110	2372	B7
800	CLEV	44110	2497	B3
3200	CLEV	44120	2627	B7
3200	CLEV	44120	2757	B1
3500	CLEV	44128	2757	B2
W 149th St				
4400	CLEV	44135	2752	C5
5000	BKPK	44142	2752	C7
5200	BKPK	44142	2881	C1
E 150th St				
200	CLEV	44110	2372	B7
800	CLEV	44110	2497	B2
3400	CLEV	44120	2757	B1
3400	SRHT	44120	2757	B1
3900	CLEV	44128	2757	B3
W 150th St				
3700	CLEV	44111	2752	C3
3900	CLEV	44135	2752	C4
4900	BKPK	44135	2752	C7
5000	BKPK	44142	2752	C7
5200	BKPK	44142	2881	C1
E 151st St				
200	CLEV	44110	2372	B7
3500	CLEV	44120	2757	B2
3900	CLEV	44128	2757	B3
W 151st St				
3300	CLEV	44111	2752	C1
3900	CLEV	44135	2752	C3
5000	BKPK	44142	2752	C7
5200	BKPK	44142	2881	C1
E 152nd St				
300	CLEV	44110	2372	B7
500	CLEV	44110	2497	B3
1000	ECLE	44110	2497	B4
1000	ECLE	44112	2497	B4
3400	CLEV	44120	2757	B1
3400	SRHT	44120	2757	B1
W 152nd St				
3400	CLEV	44111	2752	C1
4200	CLEV	44135	2752	C4
E 153rd Pl				
-	CLEV	44110	2497	B2
E 153rd St				
800	CLEV	44110	2497	B3
3400	CLEV	44120	2757	B1
3400	SRHT	44120	2757	B1
3600	CLEV	44128	2757	B3
W 153rd St				
3000	CLEV	44111	2622	C7
4200	CLEV	44135	2752	C4
E 154th Pl				
600	CLEV	44110	2497	B2
E 154th St				
700	CLEV	44110	2497	B2
3400	CLEV	44120	2757	B1
3400	SRHT	44120	2757	B1
3600	CLEV	44128	2757	B3
W 154th St				
4200	CLEV	44135	2752	C4
E 155th St				
700	CLEV	44110	2497	B2
3700	CLEV	44128	2757	B3
W 155th St				
3000	CLEV	44111	2622	C7
3200	CLEV	44111	2752	C1
4200	CLEV	44135	2752	C4
E 156th St				
10	CLEV	44110	2372	B7
600	CLEV	44110	2497	B1
4300	CLEV	44128	2757	B4
W 156th St				
4400	CLEV	44135	2752	C5
E 157th Pl				
700	CLEV	44110	2497	B2
E 157th St				
400	CLEV	44110	2372	C7
600	CLEV	44110	2497	C1
W 157th St				
3100	CLEV	44111	2622	C7
3200	CLEV	44111	2752	C1
4400	CLEV	44135	2752	C5
E 158th Pl				
-	CLEV	44110	2497	C2
E 158th St				
400	CLEV	44110	2372	C7
4300	CLEV	44128	2757	B4
W 158th St				
3300	CLEV	44111	2752	C1
3900	CLEV	44135	2752	C2
E 159th St				
-	CLEV	44110	2372	C6
600	CLEV	44110	2497	C1
W 159th St				
3000	CLEV	44107	2622	C7
3000	CLEV	44111	2622	C7
3000	LKWD	44107	2622	C7
3200	CLEV	44111	2752	C1
E 160th St				
300	CLEV	44110	2372	C7
600	CLEV	44110	2497	C1
4000	CLEV	44128	2757	B4
W 160th St				
3000	CLEV	44111	2622	C7
3800	CLEV	44111	2752	B2
4000	CLEV	44135	2752	C3
E 161st St				
-	CLEV	44120	2757	C2
-	SRHT	44120	2757	C2
200	CLEV	44110	2372	C6
3700	CLEV	44128	2757	C2
W 161st St				
4000	CLEV	44111	2752	B3
4000	CLEV	44135	2752	B3
5000	BKPK	44135	2752	B7
5000	BKPK	44142	2752	B7
E 162nd St				
-	CLEV	44119	2372	C7
300	CLEV	44110	2372	C7
600	CLEV	44110	2497	C1
4200	CLEV	44128	2757	C4
W 162nd St				
3100	CLEV	44107	2622	B7
3100	CLEV	44111	2622	B7
3100	LKWD	44107	2622	B7
3200	CLEV	44111	2752	B1
3900	CLEV	44135	2752	B2
E 163rd St				
300	CLEV	44110	2372	C7
300	CLEV	44119	2372	C7
600	CLEV	44110	2497	C2
4200	CLEV	44128	2757	C4
W 163rd St				
4000	CLEV	44111	2752	B3
4000	CLEV	44135	2752	B3
E 164th St				
200	CLEV	44110	2372	C7
4200	CLEV	44128	2757	C4
W 164th St				
5000	BKPK	44135	2752	B7
5000	BKPK	44142	2752	B7
5000	BKPK	44142	2881	B1
5000	CLEV	44135	2752	B7
E 165th St				
300	CLEV	44110	2372	C7
300	CLEV	44119	2372	C7
700	CLEV	44110	2497	C1
W 165th St				
3100	CLEV	44107	2622	B7
3100	CLEV	44111	2622	B7
3100	LKWD	44107	2622	B7
3200	CLEV	44111	2752	B1
3900	CLEV	44135	2752	B3
E 166th St				
700	CLEV	44110	2497	C2
W 166th St				
4000	CLEV	44111	2752	B3
4000	CLEV	44135	2752	B3
167th Pl				
16600	CLEV	44128	2757	C4
E 167th St				
1000	CLEV	44110	2372	C6
1200	CLEV	44119	2372	C7
4200	CLEV	44128	2757	C4
W 167th St				
4400	CLEV	44135	2752	B5
E 168th Pl				
4200	CLEV	44128	2757	C4
E 168th St				
1000	CLEV	44110	2372	C7
1200	CLEV	44119	2372	C7
1300	CLEV	44110	2497	C1
W 168th St				
3800	CLEV	44111	2752	B2
4100	CLEV	44135	2752	B4
E 169th St				
1000	CLEV	44110	2372	D6
1200	CLEV	44119	2372	C7
3700	CLEV	44128	2757	C2
W 169th St				
3600	CLEV	44111	2752	B2
E 170th Pl				
4200	CLEV	44128	2757	C4
E 170th St				
1100	CLEV	44110	2372	D7
1100	CLEV	44119	2372	D7
1300	CLEV	44110	2497	D1
W 170th St				
4400	CLEV	44135	2752	B5
E 171st St				
1000	CLEV	44110	2372	D6
1000	CLEV	44119	2372	D6
1300	CLEV	44110	2497	D1
W 171st St				
4300	CLEV	44135	2752	B5

STREET Block	City	ZIP	Map#	Grid
E 172nd Pl				
4200	CLEV	44128	2757	C4
E 172nd St				
1100	CLEV	44110	2372	D7
1100	CLEV	44119	2372	D7
1400	CLEV	44110	2497	D1
W 172nd St				
4400	CLEV	44135	2752	B5
E 173rd St				
1100	CLEV	44119	2372	D7
1400	CLEV	44110	2497	D1
3700	CLEV	44120	2757	D3
3700	CLEV	44128	2757	D3
3700	SRHT	44120	2757	D3
W 173rd St				
4300	CLEV	44135	2752	B4
E 174th Pl				
4200	CLEV	44128	2757	D4
E 174th St				
1000	CLEV	44119	2372	D6
1400	CLEV	44110	2497	D1
4500	CLEV	44128	2757	D5
W 174th St				
4400	CLEV	44135	2752	B5
E 175th St				
1100	CLEV	44119	2372	D7
1400	CLEV	44110	2497	D1
4200	CLEV	44128	2757	D4
E 176th St				
1000	CLEV	44119	2372	D6
1400	CLEV	44110	2497	D1
3800	CLEV	44128	2757	D3
4200	WVHT	44128	2757	D4
W 176th St				
3700	CLEV	44111	2752	B2
4300	CLEV	44135	2752	B5
E 177th Pl				
4200	CLEV	44128	2757	D4
E 177th St				
1000	CLEV	44119	2372	D6
3700	CLEV	44120	2757	D3
3700	CLEV	44122	2757	D3
3700	CLEV	44128	2757	D3
3700	SRHT	44120	2757	D3
3700	SRHT	44122	2757	D3
W 177th St				
4400	CLEV	44135	2752	A5
E 178th St				
900	CLEV	44119	2372	D6
4100	CLEV	44128	2757	D4
4200	WVHT	44128	2757	D4
W 178th St				
3700	CLEV	44111	2752	A2
E 179th St				
900	CLEV	44119	2372	D6
1300	CLEV	44110	2372	D7
W 179th St				
3700	CLEV	44111	2752	A2
W 180th St				
4200	CLEV	44135	2752	A4
E 181st St				
4100	CLEV	44122	2757	D4
4100	CLEV	44128	2757	D4
4200	WVHT	44122	2757	D4
4200	WVHT	44128	2757	D4
W 181st St				
4200	CLEV	44135	2752	A4
W 182nd St				
4200	CLEV	44135	2752	A4
E 183rd St				
3700	CLEV	44122	2757	D2
3900	CLEV	44128	2757	D3
W 183rd St				
4400	CLEV	44135	2752	A5
E 185th St				
100	CLEV	44119	2372	E3
100	EUCL	44119	2372	E3
1300	CLEV	44110	2372	E7
1300	CLEV	44110	2497	E1
W 185th St				
4400	CLEV	44135	2751	E5
4400	CLEV	44135	2752	A4
E 186th St				
1200	CLEV	44110	2372	E7
3700	CLEV	44122	2757	E3
E 187th St				
1200	CLEV	44110	2372	E7
4000	CLEV	44122	2757	E3
W 187th St				
4200	CLEV	44135	2751	E4
E 188th St				
-	CLEV	44122	2757	E2
-	SRHT	44122	2757	E2
700	CLEV	44119	2372	E5
1200	CLEV	44110	2372	E7
W 188th St				
4700	CLEV	44135	2751	E6
E 189th St				
-	EUCL	44119	2372	E3
3800	CLEV	44122	2757	E3
4200	WVHT	44122	2757	E4
4200	WVHT	44128	2757	E4
W 189th St				
4200	CLEV	44135	2751	E4
E 190th St				
100	EUCL	44119	2372	E3
W 190th St				
4500	CLEV	44135	2751	E5
E 191st St				
100	EUCL	44119	2372	E3
1400	EUCL	44117	2497	E2
W 191st St				
4200	CLEV	44135	2751	E4
E 192nd St				
10	EUCL	44119	2372	E3
W 192nd St				
1300	RKRV	44116	2621	E5
4200	FWPK	44126	2751	E2
4400	CLEV	44135	2751	E5
E 193rd St				
500	EUCL	44119	2372	E5
900	CLEV	44119	2372	E6
1400	EUCL	44117	2497	E1
W 193rd St				
4400	CLEV	44135	2751	E5
E 194th St				
10	EUCL	44119	2372	E3
W 194th St				
4300	CLEV	44135	2751	E4
E 195th St				
200	EUCL	44119	2372	E3
200	EUCL	44119	2373	A4
1400	EUCL	44117	2497	E1
E 196th St				
10	EUCL	44119	2372	E3
10	EUCL	44119	2373	A3
1400	EUCL	44117	2497	E1
W 196th St				
-	FWPK	44116	2751	E2
-	RKRV	44116	2751	E2
3900	FWPK	44126	2751	E2
4600	CLEV	44135	2751	D5
E 197th St				
10	EUCL	44119	2372	E3
10	EUCL	44119	2373	A3
700	CLEV	44119	2373	A5
W 197th St				
4200	CLEV	44135	2751	D4
W 198th St				
4700	CLEV	44135	2751	D6
E 199th St				
10	EUCL	44119	2372	E3
10	EUCL	44119	2373	A3
E 200th St				
10	EUCL	44119	2373	A5
10	EUCL	44123	2373	A3
600	CLEV	44119	2373	A5
1000	CLEV	44117	2373	A6
1000	EUCL	44117	2373	A6
E 201st St				
10	EUCL	44123	2373	A3
E 202nd St				
10	EUCL	44123	2373	A3
W 202nd St				
4200	FWPK	44116	2751	D2
4200	FWPK	44126	2751	D2
4200	RKRV	44116	2751	D2
E 203rd Pl				
-	EUCL	44119	2373	A5
E 203rd St				
10	EUCL	44123	2373	A3
E 204th St				
10	EUCL	44123	2373	A3
1400	EUCL	44117	2498	A1
W 204th St				
3900	FWPK	44126	2751	D2
E 205th St				
-	EUCL	44119	2373	A5
10	EUCL	44123	2373	A3
E 206th St				
10	EUCL	44123	2373	A2
E 207th St				
10	EUCL	44123	2373	A2
800	EUCL	44119	2373	A5
E 208th St				
10	EUCL	44123	2373	A3
500	EUCL	44119	2373	A5
W 208th St				
4100	FWPK	44126	2751	C3
E 209th St				
10	EUCL	44123	2373	A2
800	EUCL	44119	2373	A5
E 210th St				
200	EUCL	44123	2373	B3
800	EUCL	44119	2373	A5
W 210th St				
3100	FWPK	44126	2751	C4
3100	RKRV	44116	2751	C1
E 211th St				
-	EUCL	44119	2373	A5
10	EUCL	44123	2373	A2
W 211th St				
4100	FWPK	44126	2751	C3
E 212th St				
10	EUCL	44123	2373	A2
700	EUCL	44119	2373	B5
1500	EUCL	44117	2373	B7
W 212th St				
3400	FWPK	44126	2751	C2
E 213th St				
500	EUCL	44119	2373	B5
900	EUCL	44123	2373	B4
W 213th St				
3400	FWPK	44126	2751	C2
E 214th St				
10	EUCL	44123	2373	B2
900	EUCL	44119	2373	B5
1500	EUCL	44117	2373	B7
W 214th St				
3400	FWPK	44126	2751	C2
E 215th St				
300	EUCL	44123	2373	B3
W 215th St				
4000	FWPK	44126	2751	B3
E 216th St				
10	EUCL	44123	2373	B2
800	EUCL	44119	2373	B5
E 217th St				
10	EUCL	44123	2373	B2
W 217th St				
4000	FWPK	44126	2751	B3
E 218th St				
200	EUCL	44123	2373	B3
800	EUCL	44119	2373	B5
E 219th St				
10	EUCL	44123	2373	B2
1300	EUCL	44117	2373	B7
W 219th St				
4000	FWPK	44126	2751	B3
E 220th St				
10	EUCL	44123	2373	B2
800	EUCL	44119	2373	B5
W 220th St				
3900	FWPK	44126	2751	B6
E 221st St				
10	EUCL	44123	2373	B1
1300	EUCL	44117	2373	B7
1900	EUCL	44117	2498	B1
W 221st St				
4400	FWPK	44126	2751	B4
E 222nd St				
200	EUCL	44123	2373	B4
700	EUCL	44119	2373	B4
900	EUCL	44117	2373	B6
W 222nd St				
3900	FWPK	44126	2751	B3
E 223rd St				
800	EUCL	44123	2373	B5
1800	EUCL	44117	2373	B7
1800	EUCL	44117	2498	B1
W 223rd St				
3900	FWPK	44126	2751	B3
E 224th St				
10	EUCL	44123	2373	B1
900	EUCL	44117	2373	B5
1900	EUCL	44117	2498	B1
W 224th St				
3800	FWPK	44126	2751	A3
E 225th St				
900	EUCL	44117	2373	C5
900	EUCL	44123	2373	C5
1800	EUCL	44117	2498	B1
W 225th St				
4400	FWPK	44126	2751	A4
E 226th St				
10	EUCL	44123	2373	B1
1900	EUCL	44117	2498	B1
W 226th St				
3800	FWPK	44126	2751	A3
E 227th St				
1700	EUCL	44117	2373	B7
1700	EUCL	44117	2498	B1
W 227th St				
3800	FWPK	44126	2751	A3
E 228th St				
700	EUCL	44123	2373	C4
1500	EUCL	44117	2373	C7
1900	EUCL	44117	2498	C1
W 228th St				
4400	FWPK	44126	2751	A5
W 229th St				
3800	FWPK	44126	2751	A3
E 230th St				
800	EUCL	44117	2373	C4
800	EUCL	44123	2373	C4
1500	EUCL	44117	2498	C1
W 230th St				
2700	NOSD	44070	2751	A3
2700	NOSD	44145	2751	A3
2700	WTLK	44145	2751	A3
W 231st St				
3000	NOSD	44070	2751	A4
E 232nd St				
200	EUCL	44123	2373	C2
1700	EUCL	44117	2498	C1
W 232nd St				
3600	NOSD	44070	2750	E4
3600	NOSD	44070	2751	A4
E 233rd St				
10	EUCL	44123	2373	C1
1900	EUCL	44117	2498	C1
W 233rd St				
-	NOSD	44145	2750	E3
-	WTLK	44145	2750	E3
2700	NOSD	44070	2750	E3
E 234th St				
1700	EUCL	44117	2498	C1
E 235th St				
100	EUCL	44123	2373	C1
E 236th St				
700	EUCL	44123	2373	C4
800	EUCL	44117	2373	C4
1600	EUCL	44117	2498	C1
E 237th St				
800	EUCL	44123	2373	C4
900	EUCL	44117	2373	C4
E 238th St				
10	EUCL	44123	2373	C1
1700	EUCL	44117	2373	C7
1700	EUCL	44117	2498	C1
1700	EUCL	44143	2498	C1
E 239th St				
800	EUCL	44123	2373	C4
900	EUCL	44117	2373	C4
E 240th St				
500	EUCL	44123	2373	D3
1700	EUCL	44117	2373	D7
1700	RDHT	44117	2373	C7
1700	RDHT	44143	2373	C7
E 241st St				
300	EUCL	44123	2373	C2
E 242nd St				
10	EUCL	44123	2373	D1
E 243rd St				
200	EUCL	44123	2373	D1
1600	EUCL	44117	2373	D6
E 244th St				
200	EUCL	44123	2373	D1
E 245th St				
400	EUCL	44123	2373	D2
900	EUCL	44132	2373	D3
E 246th St				
200	EUCL	44123	2373	D1
E 248th St				
200	EUCL	44123	2373	D1
800	EUCL	44132	2373	D3
1400	EUCL	44117	2373	D5
E 249th St				
700	EUCL	44123	2373	D3
E 250th St				
200	EUCL	44123	2373	D3
200	EUCL	44132	2373	D3
1400	EUCL	44117	2373	D5
E 252nd St				
10	EUCL	44132	2373	D1
1400	EUCL	44117	2373	D5
E 253rd St				
400	EUCL	44132	2373	D2
E 254th St				
500	EUCL	44132	2373	D3
1500	EUCL	44117	2373	D5
E 255th St				
200	EUCL	44132	2373	D1
E 256th St				
700	EUCL	44132	2373	D3
1500	EUCL	44117	2373	D5
E 257th St				
200	EUCL	44132	2373	E1
E 258th St				
600	EUCL	44132	2373	E3
E 260th St				
100	EUCL	44132	2248	E7
200	EUCL	44132	2373	E4
1500	EUCL	44117	2373	E5
1500	EUCL	44143	2373	E5
E 260th St SR-175				
200	EUCL	44132	2373	E4
1500	EUCL	44117	2373	E5
1500	EUCL	44143	2373	E5
E 261st St				
600	EUCL	44132	2373	E2
1500	EUCL	44143	2373	E5
E 262nd St				
200	EUCL	44132	2248	E7
200	EUCL	44132	2373	E1
E 263rd St				
700	EUCL	44132	2373	E2
E 264th St				
100	EUCL	44132	2248	E7
200	EUCL	44132	2373	E1
E 265th St				
100	EUCL	44132	2248	E7
E 266th St				
200	EUCL	44132	2248	E7
200	EUCL	44132	2373	E1
E 267th St				
10	EUCL	44132	2248	E7
E 270th St				
10	EUCL	44132	2248	E7
200	EUCL	44132	2373	E1
E 271st St				
200	EUCL	44132	2248	E7
300	EUCL	44132	2373	E1
300	EUCL	44132	2374	A1
E 272nd St				
100	EUCL	44132	2248	E7
100	EUCL	44132	2249	A7
300	EUCL	44132	2374	A1
E 273rd St				
300	EUCL	44132	2249	A7
E 274th St				
400	EUCL	44132	2374	A1
E 275th St				
400	EUCL	44132	2374	A1
E 276th St				
200	EUCL	44132	2249	A7
1200	EUCL	44132	2374	A4
E 279th St				
1200	EUCL	44132	2374	A3
E 280th St				
10	EUCL	44132	2249	A6
E 284th St				
100	WLWK	44095	2249	A6
E 285th St				
200	WLWK	44095	2249	A7
E 286th St				
100	WLWK	44095	2249	A6
1300	EUCL	44132	2374	A3
1300	WKLF	44092	2374	A3
E 288th St				
200	WLWK	44095	2249	B7
500	WKLF	44092	2249	B7
500	WKLF	44095	2249	B7
E 289th St				
100	WLWK	44095	2249	B6
1000	WKLF	44092	2374	B3
E 290th St				
1500	WKLF	44092	2374	B3
E 291st St				
100	WLWK	44095	2249	B6
1500	WKLF	44092	2374	B3
E 293rd St				
100	WLWK	44095	2249	B6
1400	WKLF	44092	2374	C2
E 294th St				
100	WLWK	44095	2249	B6
1400	WKLF	44092	2374	C2
E 296th St				
1500	WKLF	44092	2374	C2
E 298th St				
1500	WKLF	44092	2374	D2
E 300th St				
400	WLWK	44095	2249	C6
700	WKLF	44092	2249	C7
1300	WKLF	44092	2374	D1
E 302nd St				
700	WLWK	44095	2249	D7
E 305th St				
200	WLWK	44095	2249	D6
800	WLWK	44092	2249	D7
1000	WKLF	44092	2249	D7
1000	WKLF	44092	2374	D1
1000	WLWK	44092	2374	D1
E 307th St				
200	WLWK	44095	2249	C5
E 308th St				
200	WLWK	44095	2249	C5
E 309th St				
300	WLWK	44095	2249	C5
E 310th St				
200	WLWK	44095	2249	D5
E 312th St				
200	WLWK	44095	2249	C5
E 314th St				
100	WLWK	44095	2249	C4
E 315th St				
100	WLWK	44095	2249	C4
E 316th St				
100	WLWK	44095	2249	C4
E 317th St				
100	WLWK	44095	2249	C4
E 319th St				
300	WLWK	44095	2249	D5
E 320th St				
200	WLWK	44095	2249	D4
E 321st St				
400	WLWK	44095	2249	D5
E 322nd St				
200	WLWK	44095	2249	D4
E 323rd St				
200	WLWK	44095	2249	D4
E 324th St				
100	WLWK	44095	2249	D4
E 325th St				
-	WLWK	44095	2249	D3
E 326th St				
200	WLWK	44095	2249	D4
E 327th St				
200	WLWK	44095	2249	D4
E 328th St				
200	WLWK	44095	2249	D4
1400	ETLK	44095	2249	E5
E 329th St				
200	WLWK	44095	2249	D4
E 330th St				
200	WLWK	44095	2249	D4
1400	ETLK	44095	2249	E5
E 331st St				
200	ETLK	44095	2249	E4
E 332nd St				
300	ETLK	44095	2249	D3
E 337th St				
1100	ETLK	44095	2249	E4
E 340th St				
1100	ETLK	44095	2250	A4
E 341st St				
700	ETLK	44095	2250	A2
E 342nd St				
700	ETLK	44095	2250	A2
E 343rd St				
700	ETLK	44095	2250	A2
E 344th St				
700	ETLK	44095	2250	A2
E 345th St				
700	ETLK	44095	2250	A2
4800	WLBY	44094	2250	A7
E 346th St				
800	ETLK	44095	2250	A3
E 347th St				
700	ETLK	44095	2250	A2
E 348th St				
700	ETLK	44095	2250	A2
E 349th St				
600	ETLK	44095	2250	A2
E 351st St				
1100	ETLK	44095	2250	A4
E 353rd St				
700	ETLK	44095	2250	B2
E 354th St				
1100	ETLK	44095	2250	B4
E 355th St				
1400	ETLK	44095	2250	B5
4600	WLBY	44094	2250	B6
E 357th St				
1100	ETLK	44095	2250	B4
E 359th St				
1100	ETLK	44095	2250	B4
E 360th St				
1100	ETLK	44095	2250	B4
E 361st St				
-	WLBY	44094	2250	B5
-	WLBY	44095	2250	B5
1400	ETLK	44095	2250	B5
E 362nd St				
1100	ETLK	44095	2250	B4
E 363rd St				
1400	ETLK	44095	2250	B5
E 364th St				
3700	ETLK	44094	2250	B4
3700	ETLK	44095	2250	B4
3700	WLBY	44094	2250	B4
E 365th St				
-	ETLK	44094	2250	C5
1500	ETLK	44095	2250	C5
3700	WLBY	44094	2250	C4
E 367th St				
1400	ETLK	44095	2250	C5

Cleveland Points of Interest Index

Airports

Feature Name	Address, City, ZIP Code	Map#	Grid
Burke Lakefront, CLEV		2495	B6
Cleveland-Hopkins International, CLEV		2880	D1
Columbia, ClbT		3009	A6
Concord Airpark, CcdT		2255	A1
Cuyahoga County, RDHT		2498	E2
Elyria, CrlT		3006	B4
Far View, HrmT		3160	E3
Lorain County Regional, NRsT		3004	C3
Willoughby Lost Nation Municipal, WLBY		2143	A6

Beaches, Harbors & Water Rec

Feature Name	Address, City, ZIP Code	Map#	Grid
Bass Lake Club, MsnT		2504	C4
Beaver Park Marina, LORN		2743	A3
Chagrin Lagoon Yacht Club, ETLK		2142	A7
Channel Park Marina, CLEV		2624	B4
Cleveland Yachting Club, RKRV		2621	E4
Columbia Park Beach, BYVL		2620	C4
Commodore's Club, CLEV		2624	C4
East 55th Street Marina, CLEV		2495	C5
East Bank Marina, ETLK		2250	C1
Edgewater Marina, CLEV		2624	A4
Emerald Necklace Marina, LKWD		2621	E5
Fairport Harbor, FTHR		2039	C3
Fishing Pier, RKRV		2621	B5
Forest City Yacht Club, CLEV		2495	C6
Gordon Shore Boat Club, CLEV		2495	C6
Hidden Harbor Marina, NOSD		2879	C2
Huntington Beach, BYVL		2619	E4
Maple Grove Marina, VMLN		2741	B6
Mentor Harbor Yachting Club, MONT		2037	E7
Northeast Yacht Club, CLEV		2372	A7
Olde River Yacht Club, CLEV		2624	B3
Perkins Beach, CLEV		2623	E4
Punderson Marina, NbyT		2764	C2
Riverbend Marina, FTHR		2039	C5
Riverside Marina, VMLN		2741	B6
Spitzer Lake Marina, LORN		2614	D5
Whiskey Island Marina, CLEV		2624	B3

Buildings

Feature Name	Address, City, ZIP Code	Map#	Grid
Alcoa	1600 Harvard Av, CHHT, 44125	2755	A3
Avery Dennison	250 Chester St, PNVL, 44077	2040	A7
BF Goodrich Headquarters	BKVL, 44141	3151	B4
Coca-Cola Bottling	25000 Miles Rd, BDHT, 44146	2758	D7
Ford	650 Miller Rd, AVLK, 44012	2617	A4
Ford Assembly Plant	LORN, 44053	2742	D5
Ford Motor Company	5600 Engle Rd, BKPK, 44142	2881	A1
General Motors Powertrain Division	5520 Chevrolet Blvd, PRMA, 44130	2882	A1
GE Tungsten Products Plant	21800 Tungsten Rd, EUCL, 44117	2373	A6
Goodrich Landing Gear	8000 Krueger Av, CLEV, 44105	2756	A2
Loreal USA	30601 Carter St, SLN, 44139	2888	D5
LTV Steel	5800 Lombardo Ctr, INDE, 44131	2884	C2
Lubrizol	29400 Lakeland Blvd, WKLF, 44092	2374	B2
Nestle's	30003 Bainbridge Rd, SLN, 44139	2888	C2
Nestle USA	5750 Harper Rd, SLN, 44139	2888	C2
Northern Ohio Industrial Park	ELYR, 44035	2874	C5
Northrop Grumman	1900 Richmond Rd, LNHT, 44124	2628	D2
Noveon	9911 Brecksville Rd, BKVL, 44141	3151	A4
Office Industrial Park	ECLE, 44112	2497	C4
Perry Nuclear Power Plant	10 Center Rd, NPRY, 44081	1940	C4
Radiometer America	810 Sharon Dr, WTLK, 44145	2620	D6
Rockefeller Building	614 W Superior Av, CLEV, 44113	2624	D3
Rockwell	1 Allen Bradley Dr, MDHT, 44124	2629	D2
Stoneco	900 Clark Av, CLEV, 44113	2625	A7
Terminal Tower	50 Public Sq, CLEV, 44115	2624	E3
US Steel	2199 E 28th St, LORN, 44055	2745	E2

Buildings - Governmental

Feature Name	Address, City, ZIP Code	Map#	Grid
Amherst City Hall	206 S Main St, AMHT, 44001	2872	D2
Amherst Twp Hall	7530 Oberlin Rd, AhtT, 44001	2873	C3
Anthony J Celebrezze Federal Building	1240 Rock & Roll Blvd, CLEV, 44114	2624	E2
Aquilla Village Hall	65 Turner Dr, AQLA, 44024	2505	C4
Ashtabula County Court West	117 W Main St, GNVA, 44041	1944	B4
Auburn Twp Hall	11010 E Washington St, AbnT, 44023	2893	A5
Aurora City Hall	130 S Chillicothe Rd, AURA, 44202	3156	E1
Avon City Hall	36080 Chester Rd, AVON, 44011	2618	A7
Avon Lake City Hall	150 Avon Belden Rd, AVLK, 44012	2618	A1
Avon Lake Civic Center	150 Avon Belden Rd, AVLK, 44012	2488	A7
Bainbridge Twp Town Hall	17826 Chillicothe Rd, BbgT, 44023	2891	A6
Bay Village City Hall	350 Dover Center Rd, BYVL, 44140	2620	A4
Beachwood City Hall	2700 Richmond Rd, BHWD, 44122	2628	E5
Bedford City Hall	165 Warrensville Center Rd, BDFD, 44146	2887	A3
Bedford Heights City Hall	5661 Perkins Rd, BDHT, 44146	2887	E2
Bentleyville Village Hall	6253 Chagrin River Rd, BTVL, 44022	2889	D1
Berea City Hall	11 Berea Coms, BERA, 44017	2880	C7
Berea Municipal Court	11 Berea Coms, BERA, 44017	2880	C7
Bratenahl Village Hall	411 Bratenahl Rd, BTNH, 44108	2496	C4
Brecksville City Hall	9069 Brecksville Rd, BKVL, 44141	3016	A7
Broadview Heights City Hall	9543 Broadview Rd, BWHT, 44147	3149	E2
Brooklyn City Hall	7619 Memphis Av, BKLN, 44144	2753	E4
Brooklyn Heights Village Hall	345 Tuxedo Av, BNHT, 44131	2755	A7
Brook Park City Hall	6161 Engle Rd, BKPK, 44142	2881	A3
Brownhelm Twp Hall	1940 North Ridge Rd, VMLN, 44001	2871	C3
Burton Twp Hall	14821 Rapids Rd, BURT, 44021	2766	A1
Burton Village Hall	14588 W Park St, BURT, 44021	2636	A7
Carl B Stokes United States Court House	801 W Superior Av, CLEV, 44113	2624	D3
Carlisle Twp Town Hall	11969 Lagrange Rd, CrlT, 44050	3005	E6
Chagrin Falls Town Hall	83 N Main St, CNFL, 44022	2761	A6
Chagrin Falls Village Hall	21 W Washington St, CNFL, 44022	2761	A6
Chardon Twp Hall	9949 Mentor Rd, CdnT, 44024	2379	B4
Chardon Village Hall	111 Water St, CRDN, 44024	2380	A6
Chester Twp Hall	12701 Chillicothe Rd, CsTp, 44026	2502	B7
Claridon Town Hall	13930 Mayfield Rd, ClrT, 44024	2506	B6
Cleveland City Hall	601 E Lakeside Av, CLEV, 44114	2624	E2
Cleveland Heights City Hall	40 Severance Cir, CVHT, 44118	2497	D7
Cleveland Heights Municipal Court	40 Severance Cir, CVHT, 44118	2497	D7
Cleveland Municipal Court	1200 Ontario St, CLEV, 44113	2624	D2
Columbia Town Hall	25496 Royalton Rd, ClbT, 44028	3009	E7
Concord Town Hall	7229 Ravenna Rd, CcdT, 44077	2254	D1
Cuyahoga County Administration Building	1219 Ontario St, CLEV, 44114	2624	D2
Cuyahoga County Court House	1 W Lakeside Av, CLEV, 44113	2624	D2
Cuyahoga County Health District	1375 Euclid Av, CLEV, 44114	2625	A3
Cuyahoga County Jail	1215 W 3rd St, CLEV, 44113	2624	D3
Cuyahoga Heights Village Hall	4863 E 71st St, CHHT, 44125	2755	E6
East Cleveland City Hall	14340 Euclid Av, ECLE, 44112	2497	A6
East Cleveland Municipal Court	14340 Euclid Av, ECLE, 44112	2497	A6
Eastlake City Hall	35150 Lake Shore Blvd, ETLK, 44095	2250	B2
Eaton Twp Town Hall	12043 Avon Belden Rd, EatT, 44044	3007	E7
Elyria City Hall	131 Court St, ELYR, 44035	2875	A6
Elyria Municipal Court	328 Broad St, ELYR, 44035	2875	B6
Elyria Twp Hall	41416 Griswold Rd, EyrT, 44035	2874	E1
Euclid City Hall	585 E 222nd St, EUCL, 44123	2373	B3
Euclid Municipal Court	555 E 222nd St, EUCL, 44123	2373	B3
Fairport Harbor Village Hall	220 3rd St, FTHR, 44077	2039	C3
Fairview Park City Hall	20777 Lorain Rd, FWPK, 44126	2751	C3
Federal Bureau of Investigation	1501 Lakeside Av E, CLEV, 44114	2624	E2
Federal Reserve Bank of Cleveland	1455 E 6th St, CLEV, 44114	2624	E2
Frank J Lausche State Office Building	615 W Superior Av, CLEV, 44113	2624	D3
Garfield Heights City Hall	5407 Turney Rd, GDHT, 44125	2885	D1
Garfield Heights Civic Center	5407 Turney Rd, GDHT, 44125	2756	D7
Garfield Heights Justice Center	5555 Turney Rd, GDHT, 44125	2885	D1
Gates Mills Town Hall	1470 Chagrin River Rd, GSML, 44040	2500	E7
Geauga County Administration Building	231 Main St, CRDN, 44024	2380	A6
Geauga County General Health District	470 Center St, CRDN, 44024	2379	D5
Geauga County Jail	13205 Ravenna Rd, MsnT, 44024	2635	A3
Geauga County Municipal Court	108 S Hambden St, CRDN, 44024	2380	A6
Geneva City Hall	44 N Forest St, GNVA, 44041	1944	C3
Glenwillow Village Hall	29555 Pettibone Rd, GNWL, 44139	3019	C2
Grafton Correctional Institution	2500 Avon Belden Rd, GFTN, 44044	3142	E4
Grafton Village Hall	960 Main St, GFTN, 44044	3142	A5
Grand River Village Hall	205 Singer Av, GDRV, 44077	2039	C6
Hambden Twp Town Hall	13887 GAR Hwy, HmbT, 44024	2381	B3
Highland Heights City Hall	5827 Highland Rd, HDHT, 44143	2499	C3
Highland Heights Village Hall	3700 Northfield Rd, SRHT, 44122	2758	A2
Hiram Twp Hall	11616 Garfield Rd, HRM, 44234	3161	A2
Hiram Village Hall	11617 Garfield Rd, HRM, 44234	3161	A2
Howard M Metzenbaum US Courthouse	201 Superior Av E, CLEV, 44114	2624	E3
Hunting Valley Village Hall	38252 Fairmount Blvd, HGVL, 44022	2630	D5
Independence City Hall	6800 Brecksville Rd, INDE, 44131	2884	E6
Kirtland City Hall	9301 Chillicothe Rd, KTLD, 44094	2376	E1
Kirtland Hills Village Hall	8026 Chillicothe Rd, KDHL, 44060	2252	C3
Lake County Administration Building	105 Main St, PNVL, 44077	2040	B7
Lake County Court House	47 N Park Pl, PNVL, 44077	2040	B7
Lake County General Health District	33 Mill St, PNVL, 44077	2040	B7
Lake County Jail	104 E Erie St, PNVL, 44077	2040	A7
Lakeline Village Hall	33801 Lake Shore Blvd, LKLN, 44095	2249	E2
Lakewood City Hall	12650 Detroit Av, LKWD, 44107	2623	A5
Lakewood City Hall Annex	12805 Detroit Av, LKWD, 44107	2623	A5
Lakewood Municipal Court	12650 Detroit Av, LKWD, 44107	2623	A5
Linndale Village Hall	4016 W 119th St, LNDL, 44135	2753	B3
Lorain City Hall	200 W Erie Av, LORN, 44052	2614	D6
Lorain Civic Center	617 Broadway, LORN, 44052	2614	E6
Lorain Correctional Institution	2075 Avon Belden Rd, GFTN, 44044	3142	E3
Lorain County Administration Building	226 Middle Av, ELYR, 44035	2875	A6
Lorain County Common Pleas Court	308 2nd St, ELYR, 44035	2875	A6
Lorain County Domestic Relations Court	226 Middle Av, ELYR, 44035	2875	B6
Lorain County General Health District	9880 Murray Ridge Rd, ELYR, 44035	3005	C2
Lorain County Jail	9896 Murray Ridge Rd, ELYR, 44035	3005	C2
Lorain County Probate Court	226 Middle Av, ELYR, 44035	2875	A6
Lyndhurst City Hall	5301 Mayfield Rd, LNHT, 44124	2499	A7
Lyndhurst Municipal Court	5301 Mayfield Rd, LNHT, 44124	2499	A7
Macedonia City Hall	9691 Valley View Rd, MCDN, 44056	3153	D1
Madison Twp Municipal Offices	2065 Hubbard Rd, MadT, 44057	1942	B2
Madison Village Hall	126 W Main St, MDSN, 44057	2044	B1
Mantua Twp Hall	4122 Twinsburg-Warren Rd, ManT, 44255	3159	A2
Mantua Village Hall	W High St, MNTU, 44255	3159	C5
Maple Heights City Hall	5353 Lee Rd, MPHT, 44137	2886	C1
Mayfield Heights City Hall	6154 Mayfield Rd, MDHT, 44124	2499	D7
Mayfield Town Hall	Wilson Mills Rd, MAYF, 44143	2500	A5
Mentor City Hall	8500 Civic Center Blvd, MNTR, 44060	2144	B4
Mentor Civic Center	8500 Civic Center Blvd, MNTR, 44060	2144	C4
Mentor Municipal Court	8500 Civic Center Blvd, MNTR, 44060	2144	B4
Mentor On The Lake Village Hall	5860 Andrews Rd, MONT, 44060	2143	E2
Middleburg Heights City Hall	15700 E Bagley Rd, MDBH, 44130	2881	B6
Middleburg Heights Mayor s Court	15700 E Bagley Rd, MDBH, 44130	2881	B6
Middlefield Village Hall	14860 N State Av, MDFD, 44062	2767	D2
Moreland Hills Village Hall	4350 Som Center Rd, MDHL, 44022	2759	E5
Munson Twp Hall	12210 Auburn Rd, MsnT, 44024	2504	A5
Newburgh Heights Village Hall	4000 Washington Park Blvd, NBGH, 44105	2755	C3
Newbury Town Hall	14899 Auburn Rd, NbyT, 44065	2764	A2
New Russia Twp Hall	46268 Butternut Ridge Rd, NRsT, 44074	3003	D7
Northeast Pre-Release Center	2675 E 30th St, CLEV, 44115	2625	B4
Northfield Center Town Hall	9546 Brandywine Rd, NCtT, 44067	3152	E1
Northfield Village Hall	10455 Northfield Rd, NHFD, 44067	3018	B4
North Olmsted City Hall	5200 Dover Center Rd, NOSD, 44070	2750	A7
North Perry Village Hall	4449 Lockwood Rd, NPRY, 44081	1940	D3
North Randall City Hall	21937 Miles Rd, NRDL, 44128	2758	B6
North Ridgeville City Hall	7307 Avon Belden Rd, NRDV, 44039	2877	A4
North Royalton City Hall	13834 Ridge Rd, NRYN, 44133	3013	E7
Oakwood Municipal Court	24800 Broadway Av, OKWD, 44146	3018	D1
Oakwood Village Hall	24800 Broadway Av, OKWD, 44146	3018	D1
Oberlin City Hall	85 S Main St, OBLN, 44074	3138	E3
Oberlin Municipal Court	85 S Main St, OBLN, 44074	3138	E3
Olmsted Falls City Hall	26100 Bagley Rd, ODFL, 44138	2879	B6
Olmsted Town Hall	26900 Cook Rd, OmsT, 44138	2879	A4
Orange Village Hall	4600 Lander Rd, ORNG, 44022	2759	C5
Painesville City Hall	7 Richmond St, PNVL, 44077	2146	B1

FEATURE NAME Address City ZIP Code	MAP#	GRID
Painesville Twp Hall 55 Nye Rd, PnvT, 44077	2145	C4
Parma City Hall 6611 Ridge Rd, PRMA, 44129	2882	E5
Parma Heights City Hall 6281 Pearl Rd, PMHT, 44130	2882	B4
Parma Municipal Court 5555 Powers Blvd, PRMA, 44129	2883	A5
Pepper Pike City Hall 28000 Shaker Blvd, PRPK, 44124	2629	B6
Perry Twp Hall 3740 Center Rd, PRRY, 44081	2042	B1
Probate Court of Cuyahoga County 1 W Lakeside Av, CLEV, 44113	2624	D3
Reminderville City Hall 3602 Glenwood Dr, RMDV, 44202	3020	E4
Richmond Heights City Hall 457 Richmond Rd, RDHT, 44143	2498	E3
Rocky River City Hall 21012 Hilliard Blvd, RKRV, 44116	2621	C7
Rocky River Municipal Court 21012 Hilliard Blvd, RKRV, 44116	2621	C7
Russell Town Hall 8501 Kinsman Rd, RslT, 44072	2762	B2
Sagamore Hills Town Hall 11551 Valley View Rd, SgHT, 44067	3017	C4
Seven Hills City Hall 7325 Summitview Dr, SVHL, 44131	2884	A7
Shaker Heights City Hall 3400 Lee Rd, SRHT, 44120	2627	C7
Shaker Heights Municipal Court 3355 Lee Rd, SRHT, 44120	2627	C7
Sheffield City Hall 4340 Colorado Av, SFLD, 44054	2616	B7
Sheffield Lake City Hall 609 Harris Rd, SDLK, 44054	2616	C3
Sheffield Lake Civic Center 4575 Edgewater Dr, SDLK, 44054	2616	B3
Sheffield Twp Hall 5200 Clinton Av, ShfT, 44055	2745	D5
Solon City Hall 34200 Bainbridge Rd, SLN, 44139	2889	A5
South Amherst Village Hall 103 W Main St, SAHT, 44001	2872	B7
South Euclid City Hall 1349 S Green Rd, SELD, 44121	2498	C7
South Euclid Municipal Court 1349 S Green Rd, SELD, 44121	2498	C7
South Russell Village Hall 5205 Chillicothe Rd, SRSL, 44022	2762	A6
Strongsville City Hall 18688 Royalton Rd, SGVL, 44136	3011	E7
Strongsville Mayors Court 18688 Royalton Rd, SGVL, 44136	3011	E7
Timberlake Village Hall 11 E Shore Blvd, TMLK, 44095	2249	E1
Twinsburg City Hall 10075 Ravenna Rd, TNBG, 44087	3019	E7
Twinsburg Twp Hall 9833 Ravenna Rd, TNBG, 44087	3154	E1
United States Bankruptcy Court 201 Superior Av E, CLEV, 44114	2624	E3
United States Court of Appeals 201 Superior Av E, CLEV, 44114	2624	E3
University Heights City Hall 2300 Warrensville Center Rd, UNHT, 44118	2628	A3
Valley View Town Hall 6848 Hathaway Rd, VLVW, 44125	2885	C5
Vermilion City Hall 5511 Liberty Av, VMLN, 44089	2740	E5
Vermilion Municipal Building 687 Decatur St, VMLN, 44089	2740	D5
Waite Hill Village Hall 7215 Eagle Mills Rd, WTHL, 44094	2376	B3
Walton Hills Village Hall 7595 Walton Rd, WNHL, 44146	3017	E2
Warrensville Heights City Hall 4301 Warrensville Center Rd, WVHT, 44128	2758	A4
Warrenville Heights Civic Center 4567 Green Rd, WVHT, 44128	2758	C5
Westlake City Hall 27700 Hilliard Blvd, WTLK, 44145	2749	E1
Wickliffe City Hall 28730 Ridge Rd, WKLF, 44092	2374	B4
Willoughby City Hall 1 E Spaulding St, WLBY, 44094	2250	E5
Willoughby Hills City Hall 35405 Chardon Rd, WBHL, 44094	2375	B5
Willoughby Hills Mayor's Court 35405 Chardon Rd, WBHL, 44094	2375	B5
Willoughby Municipal Court 38000 Vine St, WLBY, 44094	2250	E4
Willowick City Hall 30435 Lake Shore Blvd, WLWK, 44095	2249	C5
Woodmere Village Hall 27899 Chagrin Blvd, WDMR, 44122	2759	A1

Cemeteries

FEATURE NAME	MAP#	GRID
Acacia Memorial Park Cem, MDHT	2630	A1
Alger Cem, CLEV	2752	B3
All Saints Cem, NCtT	3153	A4
All Souls Cem, CdnT	2378	D4
Aurora City Cem, AURA	3156	E1
Avon Cem, AVON	2748	A1
Bedford Cem, BDFD	2887	B5
Beebetown Cem, LvpT	3145	D6
B'Nai Jeshurun Cem, CLEV	2496	E4
Brakeman-Peters Cem, LryT	2256	C2
Brecksville Cem, BKVL	3015	E7
Brooklyn Heights Cem, CLEV	2754	C5
Brown Cem, KTLD	2377	D7
Brownhelm Cem, VMLN	2871	A3
Butternut Ridge Cem, EatT	3007	B3
Butternut Ridge Cem, NOSD	2879	B1
Calvary Cem, GDHT	2756	D4
Calvary Cem, LORN	2744	E5
Center Chardon Cem, CdnT	2378	E1
Center Woodside Cem, CsTp	2502	A7
Chardon Municipal Cem, CRDN	2379	E7
Chardon Road Cem, WBHL	2374	C5
Chesed Shel Emeth Cem, BKLN	2753	E2
Chester Twp Cem, CsTp	2502	A5
Chestnut Grove Cem, BERA	2879	C5
City of Elyria Cem, CrlT	3005	D4
Claridon Cem, ClrT	2505	C6
Claridon Center Cem, ClrT	2506	B6
Cleveland Cem, AMHT	2872	E1
Coe Ridge Cem, NOSD	2750	D5
Concord Twp Cem, CcdT	2146	D7
Crownhill Cem, AMHT	2872	C2
Crown Hill Cem, TNBG	3154	E2
East Claridon Cem, ClrT	2506	E6
East Cleveland Cem, CLEV	2626	D1
Eastlawn Memorial Gardens Cem, BNWK	3147	D7
Elyria Cem, AhtT	2873	C6
Erie St Cem, CLEV	2625	A3
Euclid Cem, EUCL	2498	A1
Evergreen Cem, PNVL	2040	C7
Evergreen Cem, SAHT	2872	B7
Evergreen Cem, WTLK	2749	C5
Evergreen Hill Cem, CNFL	2761	A7
Evergreen Memorial Park, BDHT	2887	B1
Fairview Cem, HRM	3161	A2
Fairview Memorial Park, MDSN	2044	B2
Fairview Park Cem, FWPK	2751	E2
Fields Cem, NRDV	2877	C6
Fowler Cem, BbgT	3022	C1
Fowlers Mill Cem, MsnT	2503	E6
Garfield Cem, SFLD	2746	C6
Geauga County Home Cem, ClrT	2635	C2
Hambden Twp Cem, HmbT	2381	B3
Harvard Grove Cem, CLEV	2755	D2
Hemlock Cem, INDE	2884	E6
Highland Hills Cem, HIHL	2758	B1
Hillcrest Memorial Park Cem, BDHT	2887	E2
Hillside Cem, MNTU	3159	B6
Holy Cross Cem, BKPK	2881	D1
Holy Ghost Cem, PRMA	2883	A1
Holy Trinity Cem, AVON	2748	D2
Huntoon Cem, CcdT	2146	D4
Kirtland South Cem, KTLD	2376	E5
Lakeside Cem, BYVL	2619	D3
Lakeview Cem, CVHT	2627	A1
Lakewood Park Cem, RKRV	2621	B7
Laporte Cem, CrlT	3006	D5
Leroy Cem, LryT	2147	D5
Locust Grove Cem, TNBG	3154	E1
Lorain Jewish Cem, ShfT	2745	B6
Lower Cem, BtnT	2766	A2
Lutheran Cem, CLEV	2754	B5
Madison Memorial Cem, MadT	1942	E5
Maple Grove Cem, VmnT	2869	C5
Maple Grove Cem, WBHL	2375	C3
Maple Shade Cem, INDE	2884	E3
Maple Street Cem, KTLD	2251	D7
Mayfield Cem, CVHT	2627	A1
Memorial Park, BKLN	2753	E4
Mentor Avenue Cem, PnvT	2145	C4
Mentor Municipal Cem, MNTR	2144	D6
Middlefield Cem, MDFD	2767	E2
Middle Ridge Cem, AhtT	2873	C2
Middle Ridge Cem, MadT	1942	C5
Monroe Cem, CLEV	2624	C6
Morton Cem, NbyT	2763	D5
Mount Olive Cem, SLN	2888	A2
Mount Pleasant Cem, GnvT	1944	D5
Munn Cem, NbyT	2763	C4
Murray South Ridge Cem, CrlT	3005	D3
Newbury Cem, NbyT	2764	A2
North Chardon Cem, CdnT	2254	D7
Northfield Macedonia Cem, NCtT	3018	A6
North Madison Cem, MadT	1942	B4
North Murray Ridge Cem, ELYR	2874	B5
North Ridge Cem, MadT	1942	A4
North Royalton Cem, NRYN	3013	E7
Old Settlers Cem, CsTp	2502	E7
Orange Hill Cem, HGVL	2630	A4
Park Synagogue Cem, BHWD	2758	E1
Perry Cem, PryT	1940	B7
Pitkin Cem, CRDN	2380	A5
Plains Road Cem, WLBY	2143	A4
Plainview Cem, AURA	3156	E4
Pleasant Hill Cem, BtnT	2635	C4
Polish Cem, PRMA	2883	A1
Resthaven Memory Gardens, AVON	2748	A4
Restland Cem, BbgT	2891	A5
Ridge Hill Memorial Park, AhtT	2744	C6
Ridgelawn Cem, ELYR	2875	B5
Ridge Road Cem No 1, BKLN	2753	E2
Ridgeview Cem, NRDV	2876	E3
Riverside Cem, CLEV	2754	D2
Riverside Cem, PNVL	2146	D1
Roselawn Cem, SLN	2888	E4
Royalton Cem, NRYN	3148	C2
Rugby Cem, BhmT	2870	D5
Russell Twp Cem, RslT	2632	A4
St. Adalbert Cem, MDBH	2880	E6
St. Andrews Cem, PRMA	3014	C1
St. John Cem, SELD	2628	C1
St. John's Cem, CLEV	2625	E5
St. Joseph's Cem, AVON	2748	E2
St. Joseph's Cem, CLEV	2626	A5
St. Mary Cem, EyrT	2874	D3
St. Mary of Falls Cem, BERA	2879	D6
St. Mary's Cem, BERA	2880	B5
St. Mary's Cem, CHHT	2755	E5
St. Mary's Cem, CLEV	2624	C7
St. Mary's Cem, CrlT	3141	E2
St. Paul Cem, EUCL	2373	A6
St. Peters Cem, NRDV	2877	A3
St. Teresa Cem, SFLD	2616	E6
St. Theodosius Orthodox Cem, BKLN	2753	E5
Scranton Cem, CLEV	2624	D6
South Ridge Cem, MadT	2043	C2
South Russell Cem, SRSL	2761	E6
Sugar Ridge Cem, NRDV	2876	B6
Sunset Memorial Cem, OmsT	2879	C3
Waite Hill Cem, WTHL	2376	A1
Welton Cem, BURT	2636	B7
Western Reserve Memorial Gardens, CsTp	2502	A2
Westlawn Cem, ManT	3159	A2
West Park Cem, CLEV	2753	D3
Westwood Cem, OBLN	3138	C3
Whitehaven Memorial Cem, MAYF	2500	A3
Williams Cem, BtnT	2636	A4
Williams Cem, KTLD	2376	C6
Willoughby Cem, WLBY	2250	D5
Woodland Cem, CLEV	2625	E4
Woodvale Cem, MDBH	3012	A1
Workmans Cem, PRMA	2883	B1
Zion Memorial Park, BDHT	2887	B1

Colleges & Universities

FEATURE NAME Address City ZIP Code	MAP#	GRID
Ashland University-Elyria 1005 N Abbe Rd, ELYR, 44035	2746	E7
ATS Institute of Technology 230 Alpha Pk, HDHT, 44143	2499	E3
Baldwin Wallace College 275 Eastland Rd, BERA, 44017	2880	D6
Bryant & Stratton Cleveland Downtown Campus 1700 E 13th St, CLEV, 44114	2625	A2
Bryant & Stratton College 27557 Chardon Rd, WBHL, 44092	2374	A5
Bryant & Stratton Parma Campus 12955 Snow Rd, PRMA, 44130	2881	E2
Capital University-Cleveland 1468 W 9th St, CLEV, 44113	2624	D3
Case Western Reserve University-Cleveland 10900 Euclid Av, CLEV, 44106	2626	C2
Case Western Reserve Univ-Hunting Valley 37125 Fairmount Blvd, HGVL, 44022	2630	D4
Cleveland Institute of Art 11411 East Blvd, CLEV, 44106	2626	C2
Cleveland Institute of Music 11021 East Blvd, CLEV, 44106	2626	D1
Cleveland State University 2121 Euclid Av, CLEV, 44114	2625	B2
Cuyahoga Community College-Eastern Campus 4250 Richmond Rd, HIHL, 44122	2758	D3
Cuyahoga Community College-Metro 2900 Community College Av, CLEV, 44115	2625	B3
Cuyahoga Comm Coll-Unified Technologies Ct 2415 Woodland Av, CLEV, 44115	2625	B4
Cuyahoga Community College-Western Campus 11000 W Pleasant Valley Rd, PRMA, 44130	2882	B7
Cuyahoga Valley Joint Vocational 8001 Brecksville Rd, BKVL, 44141	3016	A3
English Nanny & Governess School 37 S Franklin St, CNFL, 44022	2761	A6
Hiram College 11715 Garfield Rd, HRM, 44234	3161	B2
Hondros College 7350 Industrial Park Blvd, MNTR, 44060	2251	B2
Hondros College Cleveland South 4100 Rockside Rd, INDE, 44131	2884	C3
ITT Technical Institute 14955 W Sprague Rd, SGVL, 44136	3012	B2
John Carroll University 20700 N Park Blvd, UNHT, 44118	2628	B4
Kent State University-Geauga 14111 Claridon Troy Rd, BtnT, 44021	2636	B5
Lake Erie College 391 W Washington St, PNVL, 44077	2146	A1
Lakeland Community College 7700 Clocktower Dr, KTLD, 44094	2251	D5
Lakeland Community College-East 201 Water Tower Dr, MDSN, 44057	2044	B3
Lorain County Community College 1005 N Abbe Rd, ELYR, 44035	2746	E7
MTI Business College 1140 Euclid Av, CLEV, 44115	2625	A3
Myers College 112 Prospect Av E, CLEV, 44115	2624	E3
Myers University-Cleveland Heights 2490 Lee Blvd, CVHT, 44118	2627	B1
Myers University-Eastlake 35353 Curtis Blvd, ETLK, 44095	2250	A5
Myers University-Rocky River 20525 Center Ridge Rd, RKRV, 44116	2621	C7
Notre Dame College 4545 College Rd, SELD, 44121	2628	C2
Oberlin College 173 W Lorain St, OBLN, 44074	3138	D2
Ohio Business College 1907 North Ridge Rd E, LORN, 44055	2745	D6
Ohio College of Podiatric Medicine 10515 Carnegie Av, CLEV, 44106	2626	C2
Ohio Technical College 1374 E 51st St, CLEV, 44103	2495	C7
Parma School of Practical Nursing 8001 Brecksville Rd, BKVL, 44141	3016	A3
Rabbinical College of Telshe 28400 Euclid Av, WKLF, 44092	2374	A4
Remington College 14445 Broadway Av, MPHT, 44137	2757	A7
Sawyer College of Business-Cleveland 13027 Lorain Av, CLEV, 44111	2753	A1
Siegal College of Judaic Studies 26500 Shaker Blvd, BHWD, 44122	2629	A6
Stautzenberger College-Strongsville 12925 Pearl Rd, SGVL, 44136	3011	D6
University of Phoenix-Cleveland Campus 5005 Rockside Rd, INDE, 44131	2884	C3
Ursuline College 2550 Lander Rd N, PRPK, 44124	2629	C4
Vatterott College 5025 E Royalton Rd, BWHT, 44147	3015	C7
Virginia Marti College 11724 Detroit Av, LKWD, 44107	2623	B5
West Side Institute of Technology 9801 Walford Av, CLEV, 44102	2753	C2
Yavne College for Women 1970 S Taylor Rd, CVHT, 44118	2627	D2

Entertainment & Sports

FEATURE NAME Address City ZIP Code	MAP#	GRID
Alpine Valley 10620 Mayfield Rd, MsnT, 44024	2503	D7
Beck Center for the Arts 17801 Detroit Av, LKWD, 44107	2622	B5
Berea Summer Theatre 95 E Bagley Rd, BERA, 44017	2880	C6
Boston Mills Ski Resort 7100 Riverview Rd, BosT, 44141	3152	B7
Brandywine Ski Resort 1146 W Highland Rd, SgHT, 44067	3152	C4
Cassidy Theatre 6200 Pearl Rd, PMHT, 44130	2882	B3
Chagrin Valley Little Theater 40 River St, CNFL, 44022	2761	A6
Cleveland Botanical Garden 11030 Juniper Rd, CLEV, 44106	2626	C1
Cleveland Browns Stadium 1085 W 3rd St, CLEV, 44114	2624	D2
Cleveland Convention Center 500 E Lakeside Av, CLEV, 44114	2624	E2

Cleveland Points of Interest Index

FEATURE NAME Address City ZIP Code	MAP#	GRID
Cleveland Metroparks Zoo & Rainforest 3900 Wildlife Wy, CLEV, 44109	2754	B3
Cleveland Play House 8500 Euclid Av, CLEV, 44106	2626	A2
Cleveland Public Theatre 6415 Detroit Av, CLEV, 44102	2624	A5
Cuyahoga County Fairground 164 Eastland Rd, BERA, 44017	2880	D7
Dance Theatre of Ohio 9258 Mentor Av, MNTR, 44060	2144	E7
Dobama Theatre 1846 Coventry Rd, CVHT, 44106	2627	B2
Dover Lake Waterpark 1150 W Highland Rd, SgHT, 44067	3152	C4
East Cleveland Community Theater 14108 Euclid Av, ECLE, 44112	2497	A6
Eastlake Stadium 35300 Vine St, ETLK, 44095	2250	B5
Ely Stadium West Av, ELYR, 44035	3006	A2
Evans Amphitheatre 3350 Superior Park Dr, CVHT, 44118	2627	C2
Foulke Cultural Arts Center 3615 Euclid Av, CLEV, 44114	2625	C2
Geauga County Fairgrounds 14373 N Cheshire St, BURT, 44021	2636	B6
Geauga Lake & Wildwater Kingdom 1060 N Aurora Rd, BbgT, 44202	3021	B3
Geauga Lyric Theatre Guild 101 Water St, CRDN, 44024	2380	A6
Holden Arboretum KDHL, 44060	2253	A6
Holden Arboretum 9500 Sperry Rd, KTLD, 44094	2378	A2
Huntington Playhouse 28601 Lake Rd, BYVL, 44140	2619	D3
Inlet Dance Theatre 3921 Mayfield Rd, CVHT, 44121	2498	A7
International Exposition Center 1 I-X Center Dr, BKPK, 44142	2880	C2
Jacobs Field 2401 Ontario St, CLEV, 44115	2624	E3
Karamu House 2355 E 89th St, CLEV, 44106	2626	B3
Lake County Fairgrounds 1301 Mentor Av, PnvT, 44077	2145	D4
Loews Yorktown Theatre 6208 Brookpark Rd, CLEV, 44129	2754	A7
Lorain County Speedway 9100 Leavitt Rd, AhtT, 44001	2872	E7
Mayfield Village Performance Arts Center Wilson Mills Rd, MAYF, 44143	2500	A5
Near West 36119 Center Ridge Rd, NRDV, 44039	2877	A3
Near West Theatre 2012 W 25th St, CLEV, 44113	2624	D5
Northfield Park NHFD, 44067	3018	B3
Northfield Park Race Track 10705 Northfield Rd, NHFD, 44067	3018	B3
Ohio Dance Theater 39 S Main St, OBLN, 44074	3138	E2
Painesville Speedway 500 Fairport Nursery Rd, PnvT, 44077	2040	C4
Playhouse Square Center 1501 Euclid Av, CLEV, 44114	2625	A2
Quicken Loans Arena 1 Center Ct, CLEV, 44115	2624	E3
Rabbit Run Theatre 5648 Chapel Rd, MadT, 44057	1941	C2
Severance Hall 11001 Euclid Av, CLEV, 44106	2626	C2
Thistledown NRDL, 44128	2758	A5
Thistledown Race Track 21501 Emery Rd, NRDL, 44128	2758	A5
Tower City Ampitheater 1887 W 3rd St, CLEV, 44113	2624	E4
Wolstein Center 2000 Prospect Av E, CLEV, 44115	2625	A3
Workshop Players 44820 Middle Ridge Rd, AhtT, 44001	2873	C2

Golf Courses

FEATURE NAME	MAP#	GRID
Acacia CC, LNHT	2629	A3
Airport Greens GC, WBHL	2374	C7
Amherst Golf Links, NRsT	3003	E1
Astorhurst CC, WNHL	2886	A7
Auburn Springs CC, AbnT	2892	B2
Aurora Golf & CC, AURA	3157	B1
Avondale GC, AVON	2747	B3
Avon Oaks CC, AVON	2748	E1
Barrington GC, AURA	3021	D6
Beechmont CC, ORNG	2759	C1
Berkshire Hills GC, MsnT	2503	A7
Big Met GC, FWPK	2751	E3
Black Brook CC, MNTR	2144	D1
Bob-O-Link GC, AVON	2748	A5
Boston Hills CC, BSHT	3153	C7
Brentwood GC, EatT	3142	A1
Briardale Greens GC, EUCL	2373	C2
Briarwood GC, BWHT	3149	C3
Canterbury GC, SRHT	2628	B7
Carlisle GC, CrlT	3141	C2
Casement Club GC, PnvT	2040	C6
Chagrin Valley CC, MDHL	2759	E6
Chardon Lakes GC, CRDN	2505	A1
Cherry Ridge GC, ELYR	2875	B3
Columbia Hills CC, ClbT	3145	A2
Country Club, The, PRPK	2629	D5
Country Club of Hudson, HDSN	3155	A7
Creekwood GC, EatT	3008	D2
Deer Lake GC, GnvT	1844	D4
Dorlon GC, ClbT	3144	B3
Elyria CC, CrlT	3005	D4
Emerald Valley GC, LORN	2744	B5
Emerald Woods GC, ClbT	3010	D5
Erie Shores GC, MadT	1843	E6
Forest Hills GC, CrlT	3005	C5
Fowler's Mill GC, MsnT	2633	C2
Fox Creek Golf & Racquet Club, LORN	2743	C4
Gleneagles GC, TNBG	3020	A4
Grandview GC, HtbT	2637	A3
Grantwood GC, SLN	3020	E1
Green Ridge GC, WKLF	2374	C3
Hawthorne Valley CC, SLN	2888	A3
Hickory Nut GC, ClbT	3010	D7
Highland Park GC, HIHL	2758	C1
Hilliard Lakes GC, AVON	2749	A5
Hinckley Hills GC, HkyT	3149	B7
Ironwood GC, HkyT	3149	B7
Johnny Cake Ridge GC, MNTR	2251	B6
Kirtland CC, WLBY	2251	C6
Lakewood CC, WTLK	2749	B2
Legend Lake GC, MsnT	2504	B1
Links GC, The, OmsT	2879	A3
Little Met GC, CLEV	2752	A2
Little Mountain CC, CcdT	2253	E2
Lost Nation Municipal GC, WLBY	2143	A7
Madison CC, MadT	1941	E2
Mallard Creek GC, EatT	3008	D7
Manakiki GC, WBHL	2375	B4
Mastick Woods GC, CLEV	2751	D4
Mayfield Sand Ridge Club, SELD	2628	D1
North Olmsted GC, NOSD	2879	B1
Oakwood Club, CVHT	2628	A1
Oberlin CC, OBLN	3138	B3
Orchard Hills GC, CsTp	2501	D2
Painesville CC, PnvT	2146	D3
Pepperidge Tree GC, MadT	1942	C4
Pepper Pike CC, PRPK	2630	A5
Pine Brook GC, EatT	3007	B4
Pine Hills GC, HkyT	3147	E7
Pine Ridge CC, WKLF	2374	E2
Pleasant Hill GC, ClrT	2635	C3
Powderhorn GC, MadT	2044	D2
Punderson GC, NbyT	2764	D3
Quail Hollow Resort & CC, CcdT	2254	B1
Red Tail GC, AVON	2748	D6
Ridgewood GC, PRMA	2882	E4
Riverside GC, ClbT	3010	C2
Rolling Green GC, HtbT	2507	D6
Royal Crest GC, ClbT	3010	D7
Royal Oaks GC, GFTN	3141	E5
St. Denis GC, CdnT	2378	E6
Sand Ridge GC, MsnT	2505	A6
Seneca GC, BWHT	3150	A2
Shaker Heights CC, SRHT	2627	E7
Shawnee Hills GC, BDFD	2887	A6
Signature of Solon, SLN	3020	E2
Sleepy Hollow GC, BKVL	3151	A2
Springvale GC, NOSD	2879	B1
Spring Valley CC, ELYR	2875	C2
Stonewater GC, HDHT	2499	C1
Sweetbriar GC, AVLK	2618	C5
Tanglewood CC, BbgT	2891	B3
Thunder Hill GC, MadT	2044	C6
Valleaire GC, HkyT	3148	E6
Walden Golf & CC, AURA	3156	C3
Westlake Meadowood GC, WTLK	2749	C5
Westwood CC, RKRV	2621	A7
Wicked Woods GC, NbyT	2635	B6
Willow Creek GC, VmnT	2870	A2

Historic Sites

FEATURE NAME Address City ZIP Code	MAP#	GRID
Burton Log Cabin 14590 E Park St, BURT, 44021	2766	B1
James A Garfield National Historic Site 8095 Mentor Av, MNTR, 44060	2252	A1
Mentor Avenue District W Washington St, PNVL, 44077	2146	A1
Nicholson House 13335 Detroit Av, LKWD, 44107	2622	E5
Peace Memorial W 119th St, LNDL, 44135	2753	B3

Hospitals

FEATURE NAME Address City ZIP Code	MAP#	GRID
Allen Med Ctr 200 W Lorain St, OBLN, 44074	3138	D2
Campus Hosp of Cleveland 18120 Puritas Av, CLEV, 44135	2752	A4
CHP Regional Med Ctr 3700 Kolbe Rd, LORN, 44053	2743	C3
Cleveland Clinic Children's Hosp for Rehab 2801 Martin Luther King Jr Dr, CLEV, 44104	2626	D5
Cleveland Clinic Foundation 9500 Euclid Av, CLEV, 44106	2626	B3
Cleveland Clinic Solon Family Health Center 29800 Bainbridge Rd, SLN, 44139	2888	C3
Deaconess Hosp 4229 Pearl Rd, CLEV, 44109	2754	C4
EMH Amherst Hosp 254 Cleveland Av, AMHT, 44001	2872	D1
EMH Regional Med Ctr 630 E River St, ELYR, 44035	2875	B6
Euclid Hosp 18901 Lake Shore Blvd, EUCL, 44119	2372	E3
Fairview Hosp 18101 Lorain Av, CLEV, 44111	2752	A3
Grace Hosp 2307 W 14th St, CLEV, 44113	2624	E5
Hillcrest Hosp 6780 Mayfield Rd, MDHT, 44124	2500	B7
Huron Hosp 13951 Terrace Rd, ECLE, 44112	2497	A7
Kaiser Permanente 5105 Som Center Rd, WLBY, 44094	2250	A7
Kaiser Permanente-Parma Med Ctr 12301 Snow Rd, PRMA, 44130	2882	A2
Lake Hosp System 10 E Washington St, PNVL, 44077	2146	B1
Lakewest Hosp 36000 Euclid Av, WLBY, 44094	2250	B7
Lakewood Hosp 14519 Detroit Av, LKWD, 44107	2622	D5
Lutheran Hosp 1730 W 25th St, CLEV, 44113	2624	C4
Manor Care Health Services 37603 Euclid Av, WLBY, 44094	2250	D6
Marymount Hosp 12300 McCracken Rd, GDHT, 44125	2756	D7
Metrohealth Med Ctr 2500 Metro Health Dr, CLEV, 44109	2754	D1
Northcoast Behav Hlthcr Sys Cleveland Camp 1708 Southpoint Dr, CLEV, 44109	2754	E1
Northcoast Behav Hlthcr Sys Northfield Camp 1756 Sagamore Rd, SgHT, 44067	3017	A3
Parma Community General Hosp 7007 Powers Blvd, PRMA, 44129	2882	E5
Sagamore Hills Med Ctr 863 W Aurora Rd, SgHT, 44067	3017	B7
St. John West Shore Hosp 29000 Center Ridge Rd, WTLK, 44145	2749	D4
St. Vincent Charity Hosp 2351 E 22nd St, CLEV, 44115	2625	B3
St. Vincent Solon Medical Campus 33001 Solon Rd, SLN, 44139	2888	E4
South Pointe Hosp 20000 Harvard Av, WVHT, 44122	2758	A3
Southwest General Health Center 18697 E Bagley Rd, MDBH, 44130	2880	E7
UHHS Bedford Med Ctr 44 Blaine Av, BDFD, 44146	2887	A3
UHHS Geauga Regional Hosp 13207 Ravenna Rd, ClrT, 44024	2635	B2
UHHS Heather Hill Hosp 12340 Bass Lake Rd, MsnT, 44024	2504	D6
UHHS Laurelwood Hosp 35900 Euclid Av, WLBY, 44094	2250	B7
UHHS Memorial Hosp of Geneva 870 W Main St, GNVA, 44041	1944	A4
UHHS Richmond Heights Hosp 27100 Chardon Rd, RDHT, 44143	2374	A6
University Hosps of Cleveland 11100 University Hospital Dr, CLEV, 44106	2626	D2
Veterans Affairs Med Ctr 10701 East Blvd, CLEV, 44106	2626	C1
Windsor Hosp 115 E Summit St, CNFL, 44022	2761	A5

Law Enforcement

FEATURE NAME Address City ZIP Code	MAP#	GRID
Amherst Police Dept 911 N Lake St, AMHT, 44001	2872	C1
Aquilla Police Dept 65 Turner Dr, AQLA, 44024	2505	C4
Aurora Police Dept 100 S Aurora Rd, AURA, 44202	3156	E1
Avon Lake Police Dept 32855 Walker Rd, AVLK, 44012	2617	E3
Avon Police Dept 36774 Detroit Rd, AVON, 44011	2747	D1
Beachwood Police Dept 2700 Richmond Rd, BHWD, 44122	2628	E5
Bentleyville Village Police 6253 Chagrin River Rd, BTVL, 44022	2889	D1
Berea Police Dept 11 Berea Coms, BERA, 44017	2880	C7
Bratenahl Police Dept 411 Bratenahl Rd, BTNH, 44108	2496	C3
Brecksville Police Dept 9069 Brecksville Rd, BKVL, 44141	3016	A7
Brooklyn Police Dept 7619 Memphis Av, BKLN, 44144	2753	E4
Brunswick Hills Police Dept 505 Substation Rd, BHIT, 44212	3146	B7
Chagrin Falls Police 21 W Washington St, CNFL, 44022	2761	A6
Chester Police Dept 12696 Opalocka Dr, CsTp, 44026	2502	B7
Cleveland Heights Police Dept 40 Severance Cir, CVHT, 44118	2497	D7
Cleveland Mounted Police 1150 E 58th St, CLEV, 44103	2495	D7
Cleveland Police 1300 Ontario St, CLEV, 44113	2624	D2
Cleveland Police Dept 9333 Kinsman Rd, CLEV, 44104	2626	B7
Cleveland Police Dept 3481 Fulton Rd, CLEV, 44109	2754	C1
Cleveland Police Dept 881 E 152nd St, CLEV, 44110	2497	B2
Cuyahoga Heights Police Dept 5480 Grant Av, CHHT, 44125	2755	D4
East Cleveland Police Dept 14340 Euclid Av, ECLE, 44112	2497	A6
Eastlake Police Dept 35150 Lake Shore Blvd, ETLK, 44095	2250	B2
Elyria Patrol Post 38000 Cletus Dr, EatT, 44035	3007	B3
Elyria Police Dept 18 West Av, ELYR, 44035	2875	A6
Euclid Police Dept 545 E 222nd St, EUCL, 44123	2373	B3
Fairview Park Police 20777 Lorain Rd, FWPK, 44126	2751	C3
Garfield Heights Police Dept 5555 Turney Rd, GDHT, 44125	2885	D1
Gates Mills Police Dept 1470 Chagrin River Rd, GSML, 44040	2500	E7
Geauga County Sheriff 13281 Ravenna Rd, MsnT, 44024	2635	B3
Geneva Police Dept 44 N Forest St, GNVA, 44041	1944	C4
Glenwillow Village Police Dept 29555 Pettibone Rd, GNWL, 44139	3019	C2
Grafton Police Dept 1009 Chestnut St, GFTN, 44044	3142	B6
Highland Heights Police Dept 5827 Highland Rd, HDHT, 44143	2499	C3
Highland Hills Police Dept 3700 Northfield Rd, SRHT, 44122	2758	A2
Hiram Police Dept 11617 Garfield Rd, HRM, 44234	3161	A2
Hunting Valley Police Dept Fairmount Blvd, HGVL, 44022	2630	D4
Independence Police 6800 Brecksville Rd, INDE, 44131	2884	E6
Kirtland Hills Police Dept 8026 Chillicothe Rd, KDHL, 44060	2252	C3
Kirtland Police Dept 9301 Chillicothe Rd, KTLD, 44094	2376	E1
Lake County Sheriff 104 E Erie St, PNVL, 44077	2040	B7
Lakewood Police Dept 12650 Detroit Av, LKWD, 44107	2623	A5
Lorain County Sheriff's Office 9896 Murray Ridge Rd, ELYR, 44035	3005	C2
Lorain Police Dept 100 W Erie Av, LORN, 44052	2614	D6
Lyndhurst City Police Dept 5301 Mayfield Rd, LNHT, 44124	2499	A7
Macedonia Police Dept 9683 Valley View Rd, MCDN, 44056	3153	D1

Cleveland Points of Interest Index

FEATURE NAME Address City ZIP Code	MAP#	GRID
Madison Twp Police Dept 2065 Hubbard Rd, MadT, 44057	1942	B2
Mantua Police Dept W High St, MNTU, 44255	3159	C5
Maple Heights Police Dept 5353 Lee Rd, MPHT, 44137	2886	C1
Mayfield Police Dept 6621 Wilson Mills Rd, MAYF, 44143	2500	A5
Mentor On The Lake Police Dept 5860 Andrews Rd, MONT, 44060	2143	E2
Mentor Police Dept 8500 Civic Center Blvd, MNTR, 44060	2144	B4
Middleburg Heights Police Dept 15850 E Bagley Rd, MDBH, 44130	2881	B6
Middlefield Village Police Dept 14860 S State Av, MDFD, 44062	2767	D2
Moreland Hills Police Dept 4350 Som Center Rd, MDHL, 44022	2759	E5
Newburgh Heights Police Dept 4071 Washington Park Blvd, NBGH, 44105	2755	C3
Northfield Center Police Station 9546 Brandywine Rd, SgHT, 44067	3152	E1
North Ridgeville Police Dept 7307 Avon Belden Rd, NRDV, 44039	2877	A4
North Royalton Police Dept 14000 Bennett Rd, NRYN, 44133	3013	E7
Oberlin Police Dept 85 S Main St, OBLN, 44074	3138	E3
Ohio State Highway Patrol-Chardon 530 Center St, CRDN, 44024	2379	C5
Orange Village Police Dept 4600 Lander Rd, ORNG, 44022	2759	C5
Painesville Police Dept 28 Mentor Av, PNVL, 44077	2146	A1
Parma Heights Police Dept 6184 Pearl Rd, PMHT, 44130	2882	C3
Parma Police Dept 5555 Powers Blvd, PRMA, 44129	2883	A5
Reminderville Police Dept 3602 Glenwood Dr, RMDV, 44202	3020	E4
Richmond Heights Police Dept 457 Richmond Rd, RDHT, 44143	2498	E3
Rocky River Police Dept 21012 Hilliard Blvd, RKRV, 44116	2621	C7
Sagamore Hills Police Dept 11551 Valley View Rd, SgHT, 44067	3017	C4
Seven Hills Police Dept 7325 Summitview Dr, SVHL, 44131	2884	A7
Shaker Heights Police Dept 3355 Lee Rd, SRHT, 44120	2627	C7
Sheffield Lake Police Dept 609 Harris Rd, SDLK, 44054	2616	C3
Sheffield Village Police Dept 4340 Colorado Av, SFLD, 44054	2616	B7
Solon Police 34200 Bainbridge Rd, SLN, 44139	2889	A5
Solon Police Dept 33000 Solon Rd, SLN, 44139	2888	E5
South Amherst Police Dept 128 E Main St, SAHT, 44001	2872	C7
South Russell Village Police Dept 5205 Chillicothe Rd, SRSL, 44022	2762	A6
Strongsville Police Dept 18688 Royalton Rd, SGVL, 44136	3011	E7
University Circle Police Dept 12100 Euclid Av, CLEV, 44106	2626	D1
University Heights Police 2304 Warrensville Center Rd, UNHT, 44118	2628	A3
Valley View Police Dept 6848 Hathaway Rd, VLVW, 44125	2885	C5
Vermilion Police Dept 5791 Liberty Av, VMLN, 44089	2740	D5
Waite Hill Police Dept 7215 Eagle Mills Rd, WTHL, 44094	2376	B3
Walton Hills Polis Dept 7595 Walton Rd, WNHL, 44146	3017	E1
Westlake Police 27300 Hilliard Blvd, WTLK, 44145	2750	A1
Wickliffe Police Dept 28730 Ridge Rd, WKLF, 44092	2374	B4
Willoughby City Police Dept 36700 Euclid Av, WLBY, 44094	2250	C7
Willoughby Hills Police Dept 35405 Chardon Rd, WBHL, 44094	2375	B5
Woodmere Village Police 27899 Chagrin Blvd, WDMR, 44122	2759	B1

Libraries

FEATURE NAME Address City ZIP Code	MAP#	GRID
Amherst Public 221 Spring St, AMHT, 44001	2872	E2
Ashtabula County District-Geneva Branch 860 Sherman St, GNVA, 44041	1944	C5
Avon Lake Public 32649 Electric Blvd, AVLK, 44012	2618	B1
Beachwood Branch 25501 Shaker Blvd, BHWD, 44122	2628	E6
Berea Branch 7 Berea Coms, BERA, 44017	2880	C7
Brooklyn Branch 3706 Pearl Rd, CLEV, 44109	2754	D2
Brook Park Branch 6155 Engle Rd, BKPK, 44142	2881	A3
Burton Public 14588 W Park St, BURT, 44021	2766	A1
Cleveland Heights Public 2345 Lee Rd, CVHT, 44118	2627	C4
Cleveland Public 5806 Woodland Av, CLEV, 44104	2625	D5
Cleveland Public 1566 Crawford Rd, CLEV, 44106	2626	B1
Cleveland Public 11602 Lorain Av, CLEV, 44111	2753	B1
Cleveland Public 1900 Fulton Rd, CLEV, 44113	2624	C5
Cleveland Public-Addison 6901 Superior Av, CLEV, 44103	2495	E7
Cleveland Public-Broadway 5417 Broadway Av, CLEV, 44127	2625	D7
Cleveland Public-Collinwood 856 E 152nd St, CLEV, 44110	2497	B2
Cleveland Public- E 131st St 3830 E 131st St, CLEV, 44105	2756	E2
Cleveland Public-Fleet 7224 Broadway Av, CLEV, 44105	2755	E2
Cleveland Public-Garden Valley 7100 Kinsman Rd, CLEV, 44104	2625	E6
Cleveland Public-Glenville 11900 St. Clair Av, CLEV, 44108	2496	D4
Cleveland Public-Harvard-Lee 16918 Harvard Av, CLEV, 44128	2757	C3
Cleveland Public-Langston Hughes 10200 Superior Av, CLEV, 44106	2496	C7
Cleveland Public-Lorain 8216 Lorain Av, CLEV, 44102	2623	E7
Cleveland Public-Main 325 Superior Av E, CLEV, 44114	2624	E3
Cleveland Public-Martin Luther King Jr 1962 Stokes Blvd, CLEV, 44106	2626	C2
Cleveland Public-Mt Pleasant 14000 Kinsman Rd, CLEV, 44120	2757	A1
Cleveland Public-Rice 2820 E 116th St, CLEV, 44104	2626	D5
Cleveland Public-South Brooklyn 4303 Pearl Rd, CLEV, 44109	2754	C4
Cleveland Public-Sterling 2200 E 30th St, CLEV, 44115	2625	B3
Cleveland Public-West Park 15637 Lorain Av, CLEV, 44111	2752	C2
Columbia Branch 13824 Columbia West River Rd, ClbT, 44028	3009	E7
Coventry Village 1925 Coventry Rd, CVHT, 44118	2627	B2
Cuyahoga County-Garfield Heights 5409 Turney Rd, GDHT, 44125	2885	D1
Cuyahoga County-Parma Ridge 5850 Ridge Rd, PRMA, 44129	2882	E2
Cuyahoga County Public 6206 Pearl Rd, PMHT, 44130	2882	B3
Cuyahoga County Public-Breksville Branch 9089 Brecksville Rd, BKVL, 44141	3016	A7
Cuyahoga County Public-Brooklyn 4480 Ridge Rd, BKLN, 44144	2753	E5
Cuyahoga County Public-Chagrin Falls 100 E Orange St, CNFL, 44022	2761	A6
Cuyahoga Co Public-Fairview Park Regional 21255 Lorain Rd, FWPK, 44126	2751	C3
Cuyahoga County Public-Independence 6361 Service Center Dr, INDE, 44131	2884	D6
Cuyahoga County Public-Lyndhurst 4645 Mayfield Rd, SELD, 44121	2498	C7
Cuyahoga Co Public-Maple Heights Regional 5225 Library Ln, MPHT, 44137	2757	B7
Cuyahoga County Public-North Olmsted 27403 Lorain Rd, NOSD, 44070	2749	E7
Cuyahoga County Public-North Royalton 14600 State Rd, NRYN, 44133	3149	A1
Cuyahoga County Public-Olmsted Falls 7850 Main St, ODFL, 44138	2879	C5
Cuyahoga County Public-Orange 31300 Chagrin Blvd, PRPK, 44124	2759	D2
Cuyahoga County Public-Parma Snow 2121 Snow Rd, PRMA, 44134	2883	D2
Cuyahoga County Public-Solon 33800 Inwood Rd, SLN, 44139	2889	A6
Cuyahoga County Public-Strongsville 18700 Westwood Dr, SGVL, 44136	3011	E7
Cuyahoga County Public-Warrensville 4383 Clarkwood Pkwy, WVHT, 44128	2758	C4
Cuyahoga County-Southeast Branch 70 Columbus St, BDFD, 44146	2887	A4
Cuyahohaga Public 502 Cahoon Rd, BYVL, 44140	2620	A4
East Cleveland Public 14101 Euclid Av, ECLE, 44112	2497	A6
East Cleveland Public-Caledonia 960 Caledonia Av, CVHT, 44112	2497	C5
East Cleveland Public-North 1425 Hayden Av, ECLE, 44112	2497	A5
Eastlake Public 36706 Lake Shore Blvd, ETLK, 44095	2142	C6
Elyria-Neighborhood Center Branch 107 Oberlin Rd, ELYR, 44035	3006	A1
Elyria Public 320 Washington Av, ELYR, 44035	2875	A5
Euclid Public 631 E 222nd St, EUCL, 44123	2373	B4
Fairport Public 335 Vine St, FTHR, 44077	2039	D3
Fulton Branch 3545 Fulton Rd, CLEV, 44109	2754	C2
Geauga County Public 17222 Snyder Rd, BbgT, 44023	2891	D3
Geauga County Public-Chardon 110 E Park St, CRDN, 44024	2380	A6
Geauga County Public-Geauga West 13455 Chillicothe Rd, CsTp, 44026	2632	A3
Geauga County Public-Middlefield 16167 E High St, MDFD, 44062	2767	E2
Grafton-Midview Public 983 Main St, GFTN, 44044	3142	A5
Jefferson Branch 850 Jefferson Av, CLEV, 44113	2624	E6
Kelvin Smith 11055 Euclid Av, CLEV, 44106	2626	D2
Kirtland Public 9267 Chillicothe Rd, KTLD, 44094	2376	E1
Lake Branch 5842 Andrews Rd, MONT, 44060	2143	E2
Lakewood Public 15425 Detroit Av, LKWD, 44107	2622	C5
Lakewood Public-Madison 13229 Madison Av, LKWD, 44107	2623	A6
Lorain Public 351 W 6th St, LORN, 44052	2614	D7
Lorain Public-Avon Branch 37485 Harvest Av, AVON, 44011	2747	D1
Lorain Public-Columbia Branch 13824 E River Rd, ClbT, 44028	3010	A6
Lorain Public-North Ridgeville Branch 6401 Jaycox Rd, NRDV, 44039	2877	B2
Lorain Public-North Ridgeville Branch 4125 E Lake Rd, SDLK, 44054	2616	A3
Madison Public 6111 Middle Ridge Rd, MadT, 44057	1941	E6
Mayfield Regional 6080 Wilson Mills Rd, MAYF, 44143	2499	D5
Memorial Nottingham Branch 17109 Lake Shore Blvd, CLEV, 44110	2372	D6
Mentor Public 4669 Corduroy Rd, MNTR, 44060	2038	E5
Mentor Public-Lake Branch 5642 Andrews Rd, MONT, 44060	2143	E1
Middleburg Heights Public 15600 E Bagley Rd, MDBH, 44130	2881	B6
Morley 184 Phelps St, PNVL, 44077	2040	B7
Newbury Public 14779 Auburn Rd, NbyT, 44065	2764	A1
Noble Neighborhood 2800 Noble Rd, CVHT, 44121	2498	A6
Nordonia Hills Public 9458 Olde Eight Rd, NCtT, 44067	3017	E7
North Ridgeville Branch 35700 Bainbridge Rd, NRDV, 44039	2877	A4
Oberlin Public 65 S Main St, OBLN, 44074	3138	E2
Padraic Pearse Center 22770 Lake Shore Blvd, EUCL, 44123	2373	C2
Parma Regional 7335 Ridge Rd, PRMA, 44129	2882	E7
Perry Public 3753 Main St, PRRY, 44081	2042	A2
Portage Co District-Aurora Memorial Branch 115 E Pioneer Tr, AURA, 44202	3157	A1
Richmond County-Richmond Town Square 691 Richmond Rd, RDHT, 44143	2498	E4
Ritter 57 E Bagley Rd, BERA, 44017	2880	C6
Ritter Public 5680 Liberty Av, VMLN, 44089	2740	E5
Rockport Branch 4421 W 140th St, CLEV, 44135	2752	E5
Rocky River Public 1600 Hampton Rd, RKRV, 44116	2621	D6
Shaker Heights Public 16500 Van Aken Blvd, SRHT, 44120	2757	C1
Shaker Heights Public 20600 Fayette Rd, SRHT, 44122	2628	A6
South Branch 2121 Homewood Dr, LORN, 44055	2745	E4
Technical Processing 11000 W Pleasant Valley Rd, PRMA, 44130	2882	B7
Twinsburg Public 10050 Ravenna Rd, TNBG, 44087	3019	E7
Union Branch 3463 E 93rd St, CLEV, 44104	2756	B1
University Heights Public 13866 Cedar Rd, UNHT, 44118	2628	A3
Walz Branch 7910 Detroit Av, CLEV, 44102	2623	E5
West Lake Porter Public 27333 Center Ridge Rd, WTLK, 44145	2750	A2
Wickliffe Public, The 1713 Lincoln Rd, WKLF, 44092	2374	C3
Willoughby Public 30 River St, WLBY, 44094	2250	E5
Willowick Public 263 E 305th St, WLWK, 44095	2249	C5

Military Installations

FEATURE NAME Address City ZIP Code	MAP#	GRID
Armory Bell St, CNFL, 44022	2761	B6
Armory Grove Av, LORN, 44055	2745	E3
Brook Park Armory 6225 Engle Rd, BKPK, 44142	2881	A3
US Coast Guard Station N Marginal Rd, CLEV, 44114	2624	E1
US Coast Guard Station 110 Alabama Av, LORN, 44052	2614	D6
US Coast Guard Station PnvT, 44077	2039	C2
Willoughby Armory 4180 Grove Av, WLBY, 44094	2250	C5

Museums

FEATURE NAME Address City ZIP Code	MAP#	GRID
103rd Ohio Volunteer Infantry Civil War Mus 5501 E Lake Rd, SDLK, 44054	2617	A2
African American Mus 1765 Crawford Rd, CLEV, 44106	2626	A2
Allen Memorial Art Mus 87 N Main St, OBLN, 44074	3138	D2
American Slovenian Polka Foundation 19400 Arrowhead Av, CLEV, 44119	2372	E5
Art House 3119 Denison Av, CLEV, 44109	2754	C3
Bain Park Cabin Historical Mus 21077 N Park Dr, FWPK, 44126	2751	B4
Brooklyn Historical Mus 4442 Ridge Rd, BKLN, 44144	2753	E5
Century Village Mus 14641 E Park St, BURT, 44021	2766	B1
Children's Mus of Cleveland, The 10730 Euclid Av, CLEV, 44106	2626	C2
Clague House Mus 1371 Clague Rd, WTLK, 44145	2620	E7
Cleveland Hungarian Heritage Mus 1301 Rock & Roll Blvd, CLEV, 44114	2624	E2
Cleveland Mus of Art 11150 East Blvd, CLEV, 44106	2626	C2
Cleveland Mus of Contemporary Art 8501 Carnegie Av, CLEV, 44103	2626	B2
Cleveland Mus of Natural History 1 Wade Ovl, CLEV, 44106	2626	C1
Cleveland State University Art Mus Euclid Av, CLEV, 44114	2625	A2
Dunham Tavern Mus 6709 Euclid Av, CLEV, 44103	2625	E2
Euclid Historical Mus 21129 North St, EUCL, 44117	2373	A7
Great Lakes Science Center 601 Erieside Av, CLEV, 44114	2624	D2
Hickories Mus 509 Washington Av, ELYR, 44035	2875	A5
Indian Mus of Lake County 391 W Washington St, PNVL, 44077	2146	A1
Inland Seas Maritime Mus 480 Main St, VMLN, 44089	2740	E5
International Women's Air & Space Mus 1501 N Marginal Rd, CLEV, 44114	2624	E1
Little Italy Mus, The 12026 Mayfield Rd, CLEV, 44106	2626	D2
Mahler Mus 118 E Bridge St, BERA, 44017	2880	C7

Cleveland Points of Interest Index

FEATURE NAME / Address City ZIP Code	MAP#	GRID
Maltz Mus of Jewish Heritage 2929 Richmond Rd, BHWD, 44122	2628	E6
Marine Mus 129 2nd St, FTHR, 44077	2039	C3
National Cleveland-Style Polka Hall of Fame 605 E 222nd St, EUCL, 44123	2373	B3
Oberlin Heritage Center 74 S Professor St, OBLN, 44074	3138	D3
Palmer House Mus 9390 Olde Eight Rd, NCtT, 44067	3017	E7
Patrons of Arts in Vatican Mus 32125 Solon Rd, SLN, 44139	2888	D5
Peter Miller House Mus 33740 Lake Rd, AVLK, 44012	2617	A2
Rock & Roll Hall of Fame and Mus 1 Erieside Av, CLEV, 44114	2624	D1
Rose Hill Mus 27715 Rose Hill Ln, BYVL, 44140	2619	E4
Sculpture Center 1834 E 123rd St, CLEV, 44106	2626	E1
Shaker Historical Mus 16740 S Park Blvd, SRHT, 44120	2627	C5
Shandy Hall 6333 S Ridge Rd W, HpfT, 44041	1943	D7
Simoni Glassworks Gallery 12828 W Geauga Tr, CsTp, 44026	2631	B1
Soldiers & Sailors Monument 3 Public Sq, CLEV, 44113	2624	E3
Steamship William G Mather Mus 1001 Rock & Roll Blvd, CLEV, 44114	2624	E1
USS Cod Submarine Memorial 661 Lee Ct, VMLN, 44089	2742	A5
USS Cod WWII Submarine Mus 1089 N Marginal Rd, CLEV, 44114	2624	E1
Western Reserve Fire Mus 310 Carnegie Av, CLEV, 44115	2624	E4
Western Reserve Historical Society 10825 East Blvd, CLEV, 44106	2626	C1

Open Space

FEATURE NAME / Address City ZIP Code	MAP#	GRID
Amherst Beaver Creek Reservation, AMHT	2872	C2
Aquilla Wildlife Area, ClrT	2505	D3
Auburn Marsh Wildlife Area, AbnT	2893	A3
Audubon Society, AURA	3157	B4
Bedford Reservation, WNHL	2886	C5
Big Creek Reservation, BKLN	2753	C4
Big Creek Reservation, MDBH	3011	E1
Blanche Novak Audubon Preserve, AURA	3022	D6
Bradley Woods Reservation, WTLK	2749	C6
Brecksville Reservation, NRYN	3148	B2
Burton Wetlands Nature Preserve, BtnT	2765	D4
Columbia Reservation, ClbT	3010	A7
Geauga Pk Wildlife Perserve, MsnT	2505	A3
Girdled Road Reservation, CcdT	2255	C3
Hach-Otis State Nature Preserve, WBHL	2375	D4
Hambden Orchard Wildlife Area, HmbT	2381	D6
Indian Hollow Reservation, GftT	3141	E7
Lakeshore Reservation Coastal Park, NPRY	1940	D2
Mentor Lagoons Nature Preserve & Marina, - MNTR	2038	B6
Mentor Marsh State Nature Preserve, MNTR	2038	D7
Mill Stream Run Reservation, SGVL	3147	D2
Pioneer Trail Audubon Sanctuary, AURA	3157	D2
South Chagrin Reservation, BTVL	2889	C1
Vermilion River Reservation, BhmT	2870	C4
West Creek Reserve, PRMA	2883	D4
Whitesburg Nature Preserve, CNFL	2761	B4

Other

FEATURE NAME / Address City ZIP Code	MAP#	GRID
Cuyahoga Valley Scenic Railroad Rockside Rd, INDE, 44131	2885	A3
Healthspace Cleveland 8911 Euclid Av, CLEV, 44106	2626	B2
Kirtland Temple 9020 Chillicothe Rd, KTLD, 44094	2251	D7
Lake Erie Nature & Science Center 28728 Wolf Rd, BYVL, 44140	2619	E4
Lorain Lighthouse LrnC, 44052	2614	C5
NASA Glenn Research Center 21000 Brookpark Rd, CLEV, 44135	2751	B7
National Shrine Of Our Lady Of Lourdes 21281 Chardon Rd, EUCL, 44117	2498	B1
Old South Church 9802 Chillicothe Rd, KTLD, 44094	2377	A3
St. Paul Shrine 4120 Euclid Av, CLEV, 44103	2625	D2

Park & Ride

FEATURE NAME / Address City ZIP Code	MAP#	GRID
RTA Park & Ride-Ashby, SRHT	2627	B7
RTA Park & Ride-Avalon, SRHT	2757	D1
RTA Park & Ride-Brecksville, BKVL	3016	A7
RTA Park & Ride-Brookpark, CLEV	2752	A7
RTA Park & Ride-Clague Rd, WTLK	2620	E6
RTA Park & Ride-Drexmore, CLEV	2627	A5
RTA Park & Ride-East 55th, CLEV	2625	D5
RTA Park & Ride-Farnsleigh, SRHT	2758	A1
RTA Park & Ride-Great Northern Mall, NOSD	2750	B7
RTA Park & Ride-Kenmore, SRHT	2757	D1
RTA Park & Ride-Lynnfield, SRHT	2757	E1
RTA Park & Ride-Onaway, SRHT	2627	A6
RTA Park & Ride-Pearl Rd, SGVL	3011	E4
RTA Park & Ride-St. Clair, CLEV	2496	E4
RTA Park & Ride-St. Clair, EUCL	2373	D4
RTA Park & Ride-South Woodland, CLEV	2627	A6
RTA Park & Ride-Sperry Dr, WTLK	2620	C6
RTA Park & Ride-Sprague Rd, BERA	3011	B2
RTA Park & Ride-Superior, ECLE	2496	E7
RTA Park & Ride-Triskett, CLEV	2622	E7
RTA Park & Ride-W 117th-Madison, CLEV	2623	B6
RTA Park & Ride-W 150th-Puritas, CLEV	2752	C4
RTA Park & Ride-West Blvd-Cudell, CLEV	2623	D5
RTA Park & Ride-West Park, CLEV	2752	D2
RTA Park & Ride-Windermere, ECLE	2497	A6
RTA Park & Ride-Woodhill, CLEV	2626	B5

Parks & Recreation

FEATURE NAME / Address City ZIP Code	MAP#	GRID
Abbe Road Pk, ELYR	2875	E2
Abbey Pk, CLEV	2624	D5
Academy Court Pk, ELYR	2874	B7
Adams Pk, TNBG	3019	A4
Alex F Nason Pk, WLBY	2250	C4
All American Sports Center, NRDV	2876	C4
Amherst Beaver Creek Pk, AMHT	2743	C7
Amherst Twp Pk, AhtT	2873	C1
Anna Woods Pk, CLEV	2626	D4
Archmere Pk, CLEV	2754	B6
Arcola Creek Pk, MadT	1844	B5
Avon Isle Pk, AVON	2747	D2
AW Robertson Pk, TwbT	3154	D5
Bain Pk, FWPK	2751	C3
Baltic Pk, CLEV	2623	C5
Bartish Pk, LORN	2744	A3
Beachwood City Pk, BHWD	2628	D6
Beachwood Pk, CLEV	2372	D4
Belle Pk, AVLK	2618	B3
Bellflower Pk, MNTR	2143	B5
Belmont Pk, CLEV	2623	B7
Benhoff Pk, MPHT	2886	B2
Bentleyville Pk, BTVL	2889	C1
Bessie Benner Metzenbaum Pk, CsTp	2631	E2
Bexley Pk, SELD	2628	B1
Bicentennial Pk, AURA	3157	A1
Bicentennial Pk, AVLK	2617	D1
Big Creek Pk, CdnT	2380	A1
Bill Stanton Community Pk, MadT	1941	C1
Birchwood Pk, TNBG	3154	D1
Black River Reservation, ELYR	2746	B5
Bleser Pk, AVLK	2618	A1
Bohlken Pk, FWPK	2751	C2
Bonnie Banks Pk, PRMA	3013	B2
Bradley Pk, BYVL	2619	B4
Bradley Road Nature Pk, WTLK	2749	B4
Brainard Pk, LNHT	2629	B2
Bratenahl Village Pk, BTNH	2496	C3
Brecksville Reservation, BKVL	3151	C2
Breezy Point Pk, AURA	3021	E7
Bridgeport City Pk, BNWK	3147	C7
Broadview Heights Recreation Pk, BWHT	3014	E6
Brooklyn Heights Village Pk, BNHT	2884	A1
Brook Pk, BKPK	2881	E1
Brownhelm Twp Pk, VMLN	2871	C2
Brucye Pk, ETLK	2250	C1
Buchert Memorial Pk, MNTU	3159	C5
Butternut Pk, CrlT	3005	D6
Cahoon Memorial Pk, BYVL	2619	E4
Cain Pk, CVHT	2627	C2
Caledonia Pk, CVHT	2497	C5
Calgary Pk, CLEV	2754	D3
Calvin Pk, SVHL	2884	B3
Campbell Pk, WBHL	2375	B5
Carlisle Equestrian Center, CrlT	3140	B2
Carlisle Reservation, CrlT	3140	C1
Carlisle Twp Community Pk, CrlT	3005	E7
Carrie Cain Pk, CLEV	2496	D5
Cascade Pk, ELYR	2875	B4
Cavanaugh Pk, BKPK	2752	E6
Cedarbrook Pk, PNVL	2146	A2
Center Pk, PRMA	2883	D5
Center Valley Pk, TNBG	3019	D5
Central Pk, ETLK	2250	A2
Central Pk, LORN	2744	E2
Chagrin River Pk, ETLK	2250	D2
Chapin Forest Reservation, KTLD	2376	E4
Chardon Pk, CRDN	2380	A5
Chesterland City Pk, CsTp	2502	B7
Chestnut Trails Pk, TNBG	3019	D4
Children's Schoolhouse Nature Pk, KDHL	2252	D5
City Hall Pk, PRMA	2882	E5
City Pk, SGVL	3011	E6
City Pk, SRHT	2628	D6
City Pk, TNBG	3019	E7
City Side Forest Pk, CLEV	2757	B4
Civic League Pk, WKLF	2374	C3
Clague Pk, WTLK	2620	E7
Cleveland Lakefront State Pk, CLEV	2495	D5
Cleveland Metro Pk, BYVL	2619	E4
Cleveland Metro Pk, CLEV	2754	B3
Coit Pk, CLEV	2497	A5
Columbia Pk, ClbT	3009	E7
Community Pk, SDLK	2616	A3
Concord Twp Pk, CcdT	2254	D1
Concord Woods Nature Pk, CcdT	2146	B7
Coulby Pk, WKLF	2374	B4
Cranwood Pk, GDHT	2756	E5
Creek Pk, CdnT	2379	E3
Crodele Pk, GDHT	2756	B6
Crossburn Pk, CLEV	2752	E6
Cudell Commons Pk, CLEV	2623	C5
Cumberland Pk, CVHT	2627	B1
Cuyahoga Valley National Pk, BSHT	3153	A7
Cuyahoga Valley National Pk, SgHT	3152	D5
Cuyahoga Valley National Pk, VLVW	2885	C7
Daniels Pk, WLBY	2250	E2
David R Wiley Memorial Pk, MAYF	2500	A3
Dennison Pk, CVHT	2498	A5
Desan Pk, RDHT	2498	D3
Detroit W 25th Pk, CLEV	2624	C4
Donald E Krueger Pk, MNTR	2252	E2
Drakefield Pk, CLEV	2752	C3
Drake Pk, CLEV	2753	A3
Duck Pond Picnic Area, CrlT	3140	D1
Dudley Pk, WLWK	2249	D5
Dunham Pk, MPHT	2886	A4
Eastlake Garden Pk, ETLK	2142	E7
Eastlake Port Authority, ETLK	2250	B1
Eaton Twp Community Pk, EatT	3008	A7
Edgewater Pk, CLEV	2623	E4
Edison Village Pk, VMLN	2741	C4
Edwards Pk, LKWD	2622	B4
Eldon Russell Pk, TroT	2765	E7
Eleanor B Garfield Pk, MNTR	2251	E1
Elmwood Pk, INDE	2884	D5
Elmwood Pk, LORN	2744	D4
Elmwood Pk, RKRV	2621	B5
El Rey Grotto Pk, AhtT	2873	A7
Ely Pk, ELYR	2875	A6
Elyria Community Recreation Center, ELYR	3006	C1
Elyria South Pk, ELYR	3006	B2
Elywood Pk, ELYR	2875	B5
Emery Pk, CLEV	2752	E3
Endora Pk, CLEV	2497	D3
Erie Shores Pk, SDLK	2616	D2
Euclid Creek Pk, CLEV	2372	E7
Euclid Heritage Pk, EUCL	2373	A7
Euclid Memorial Pk, EUCL	2373	B3
Euclid Pk, EUCL	2373	B2
Fairless Pk, LORN	2746	A5
Fairport Harbor Lakefront Pk, FTHR	2039	C3
Fairview Pk, CLEV	2624	C5
Fairview Pk, FWPK	2751	B4
Falbo Pk, LORN	2744	D3
Falconwood Square Pk, WLBY	2250	D7
Featherston Pk, WKLF	2374	D2
Ferndale Pk, SDLK	2616	B4
Finger Pk, CLEV	2626	A6
Flora Pk, CLEV	2496	C5
Forest Hill Pk, ECLE	2497	B7
Forest Hills Pk, CLEV	2496	D5
Frank Novak Pk, CLEV	2624	C5
Freedom Pk, SDLK	2615	E5
French Creek Reservation, SFLD	2746	C1
Frontier Pk, NRDV	2877	E1
Fulton Pk, LORN	2745	B3
Fulton Pk South, LORN	2745	C3
Furnace Run Metro Pk, RHFD	3150	E7
Gardina Pk, CLEV	2495	D6
Garfield Pk, CLEV	2756	B4
Garfield Pk, LORN	2615	C5
Gateway Pk, ELYR	2874	E5
Geneva State Pk, GnvT	1844	E4
George Daniel Pk, LORN	2744	D2
Gerard Pk, PRMA	2883	A2
Gillie Pk, TNBG	3020	A6
Gilmore Pk, CLEV	2752	E5
Gilson Pk, WLBY	2250	E3
Glamer Pk, PRMA	3013	B1
Glen Chamberlin Pk, TNBG	3019	C7
Glendale Pk, CLEV	2757	B2
Glenmeadow Pk, TNBG	3019	D4
Glenview Pk, CLEV	2496	C3
Glenwillow Community Pk, GNWL	3019	A2
Gordon Pk, CLEV	2496	A5
Goudreau Pk, CLEV	2754	E6
Grannis Pk, FWPK	2751	D2
Green of Kensington Green, The, SRSL	2762	B6
Greencroft Pk, BDFD	2886	D2
Green Valley Pk, PRMA	3014	B1
Greenwood Pk, CLEV	2624	C6
Groton Pk, CLEV	2497	E3
G Street Pk, LORN	2615	D5
Guenther Pk, SDLK	2617	A3
Gunning Pk, CLEV	2752	B4
Halloran Pk, CLEV	2753	A2
Harmody Pk, CLEV	2754	E4
Harmon Pk, LORN	2744	E3
Headlands Beach State Pk, PnvT	2039	B3
Headwaters Pk, ClrT	2637	A2
Headwaters Pk, HtbT	2507	A6
Headwaters Pk, MdfT	2637	B4
Helen Hazen Wyman Pk, PnvT	2146	D4
Helen Simpson Pk, CLEV	2626	E6
Heritage Pk, CLEV	2624	D4
Herman Pk, CLEV	2624	A4
Hetzel Pk, PRMA	2883	B6
Hidden Valley Pk, MadT	2044	A6
Highland Heights Community Pk, HDHT	2499	C4
Highview Pk, LORN	2615	B6
Hillandale Pk, EUCL	2374	A5
Hilltop Pk, ELYR	2875	D1
Hodgson Pk, MNTR	2143	B7
Hogback Ridge Pk, MadT	2044	D5
Hollywood Pk, PRMA	2883	A4
Homewood Pk, LORN	2746	A4
Horseshoe Lake Pk, SRHT	2627	B5
Houston Fisher Pk, ETLK	2249	E4
Humphrey Pk, CLEV	2372	C6
Hyacinth Pk, CLEV	2625	D6
Idalia Pk, CLEV	2757	D3
Impett Pk, CLEV	2622	C7
Indian Hollow Reservation Pk, CrlT	3141	D5
Indian Point Pk, LryT	2147	D1
Interstate Pk, BDFD	2887	B6
Intihar Pk, WKLF	2374	B1
Inwood Pk, AVLK	2617	E2
Jackson Pk, PNVL	2145	D2
James A Garfield National Historical Site, - MNTR	2252	A2
James Day Pk, SFLD	2616	B7
James Hanna Pk, PRMA	2882	B1
Jaquay Lake Pk, ClbT	3009	D3
Jefferson Pk, CLEV	2752	E2
Jindra Pk, WKLF	2374	B1
John Muir Pk, PRMA	2883	D1
John R McMinn Memorial Pk, MONT	2143	E2
Kauffman Pk, LKWD	2622	C4
Kawalec Recreational Fields, MsnT	2504	A5
Kennedy Pk, LORN	2743	D5
Kenneth J Sims Pk, EUCL	2373	C1
Kerruish Pk, CLEV	2757	C6
Kingsbury Run Pk, CLEV	2626	B7
Kirtland Pk, CLEV	2495	C7
Kirtland Recreation Pk, KTLD	2376	D1
Kiwanis-Moore Pk, AURA	3156	E1
Klein Pk, MDBH	3012	E2
Kossuth Pk, CLEV	2626	D5
Kowalski Pk, CLEV	2755	E1
Kurtz Pk, PMHT	2881	E3
Lake Farm Pk, KTLD	2377	C7
Lake In the Woods Pk, BbgT	2762	C7
Lake Pk, CLEV	2623	E5
Lakeside Landing Pk, LORN	2614	D6
Lakeview Pk, LORN	2614	B7
Lakewood Beach Pk, SDLK	2615	E3
Lakewood Pk, LKWD	2622	D3
Lawn Madison Pk, CLEV	2623	E6
League Pk, CLEV	2625	E1
Ledges Pk, TNBG	3020	A6
Leroy Pk, LryT	2147	D6
Lexington Green Pk, PMHT	2882	D4
Lincolncowles Pk, BDFD	2887	A4
Lincoln Pk, CLEV	2624	E6
Lincoln Pk, SDLK	2616	D3
Lincoln Pk, WLBY	2250	D5
Lincoln Pk East, LORN	2745	B3
Linden Pk, RKRV	2751	D1
List Lane Pk, PRMA	3012	E2
Liz Strahan Pk, AURA	3021	A4
Lombardo Pk, VLVW	2885	C5
Longfellow Pk, LORN	2615	B5
Longwood Pk, MCDN	3154	A1
Lorain County Metropark North Ridgeville, - NRDV	2876	B3
Lou Groza Pk, BERA	3011	A1

Cleveland Points of Interest Index

Parks & Recreation

FEATURE NAME Address City ZIP Code	MAP#	GRID
Louis J Bacci Recreational Pk, CHHT	2755	E7
Lowe Pk, CLEV	2754	C6
Lucille M Heasley Fields, NRYN	3014	A5
Luke Easter Pk, CLEV	2626	D7
Lyndhurst Pk, LNHT	2499	A7
Macedonia Memorial Pk, MCDN	3153	C1
Madison Pk, LKWD	2623	A6
Madison Twp Pk, MadT	1843	B6
Manry Pk, WLWK	2249	C6
Maple Heights Pk, LORN	2615	D6
Maplewood Pk, CLEV	2751	D6
Marine Pk, PNVL	2146	C2
Marion Motley Playfield, CLEV	2625	E6
Marlborough Pk, PRMA	2753	D7
Martin Bradley Field, NOSD	2878	A2
Martin Luther King Jr Pk, CLEV	2496	C4
Martin Luther King Jr Pk, OBLN	3138	E3
Martin Pk, RKRV	2751	B2
Mason's Landing Pk, PryT	2147	C1
Maude Neiding Memorial Pk, AMHT	2872	E1
Mayfield Heights Recreation Pk, MDHT	2629	E1
McGowan Pk, CLEV	2753	A5
Medina County Parks, BHIT	3146	C7
Mel Harder Pk, HmbT	2380	B7
Memorial Pk, SDLK	2616	A3
Mentor Beach Pk, MONT	2143	D1
Mercedes Cotner Pk, CLEV	2753	D2
Merl Pk, LKWD	2622	E4
Michael A Riles Youth Complex, PRMA	2883	B2
Middleton Pk, HDSN	3154	D7
Miller Pk, PRMA	2882	B1
Miller Road Pk, AVLK	2617	B2
Mill Hollow Bacon Woods Pk, BhmT	2870	D3
Mineral Lake Pk, MDFD	2767	C2
Mohican Pk, CLEV	2752	E1
Morley Pk, RKRV	2621	D7
Morse Pk, PNVL	2040	A7
Morton Pk, FWPK	2751	B4
Morton Pk, MNTR	2039	A5
Mortus Pk, TNBG	3019	B6
M Trombra Pk, CLEV	2497	C3
Munn Pk, CLEV	2752	B1
Nathan Hale Pk, PMHT	2882	A6
Neff Pk, CLEV	2372	E6
Nehls Pk, WKLF	2374	C4
Nelson Russ Pk, FWPK	2751	A5
Nike Pk, PRMA	2882	A7
North Chagrin Metropolitan Pk, WBHL	2375	B7
Northgate Pk, AVON	2747	C1
North Olmsted Community Pk, NOSD	2749	E7
North Perry Pk, NPRY	1940	C3
North Pk, BNWK	3147	A6
North Pk, GFTN	3142	B4
North Pk, SVHL	2884	A2
North Pk Sports Complex, ELYR	2875	E4
North Royalton Memorial Pk, NRYN	3149	A1
North Townline Pk, MadT	1941	B2
Oakwood Community Pk, OKWD	3018	E1
Oakwood Pk, LORN	2745	E3
Oberlin Recreational Complex, OBLN	3138	D4
Old Field, MDHL	2760	D4
Olmsted Falls East River Pk, ODFL	2879	C5
Olmsted Falls Picnic Area, ODFL	2879	C5
Orchard Hill Pk, LORN	2744	E7
Orlando Pk, WKLF	2374	D2
Orr Pk, CLEV	2626	C2
Overlook Beach Pk, MONT	2143	C2
Paine Falls Pk, LryT	2147	E2
Painesville City Kiwanis Recreation Pk, PNVL	2040	B6
Painesville Twp Pk, PnvT	2040	C2
Palmer Ball Field, NRDV	2877	C3
Parma Heights Pk, PMHT	2882	B3
Parsons Gardens, WLBY	2250	D4
Patsie C Campagna Pk, LORN	2744	A2
Pattison Pk, ECLE	2496	E6
Pawlak Pk, LORN	2744	D1
Penitentiary Glen Reservation, KTLD	2377	A2
Pepperwood Pk, BNWK	3146	B7
Picnic Lake Pk, AURA	3021	A4
Pioneer Field Pk, ELYR	2875	D3
PJ Taylor Pk, CLEV	2372	E7
Polo Field, MDHL	2760	D2
Porath Pk, LORN	2745	D4
Portage Pk, SLN	3021	A2
Port Pk, CLEV	2625	E6
Presidents Pk, MNTR	2143	D7
Public Square, CLEV	2624	E3
Pulaski Pk, LORN	2744	E1
Punderson State Pk, NbyT	2764	D2
Purvis Pk, UNHT	2628	B3
Quarry Pk North, SELD	2498	A5
Quarry Pk South, SELD	2498	B5
Rainbow Pk, CLEV	2752	D1
Ray Harmon Pk, AURA	3157	C6
Reed Pk, BDHT	2887	D4
Reese Pk, BYVL	2620	E5
Regency Pk, PRMA	2883	A5
Repko Pk, LORN	2745	A3
Resatar Pk, AVLK	2619	A2
Reservoir Pk, GFTN	3142	B6
Resources Center Pk, MadT	2044	A5
Richmond Heights Community Pk, RDHT	2499	A2
Ridgewood Lake Pk, PRMA	2882	E4
River Road Pk, BbgT	2890	A4
River Road Pk, MadT	2043	C5
Riverside Pk, CLEV	2752	A5
Riverview Pk, MadT	2044	B6
Riverview Pk, RslT	2632	A5
Roadside Pk, ClrT	2506	B6
Roadside Pk, HmbT	2381	B3
Roberto Clemente Pk, CLEV	2624	C6
Rockefeller Pk, CLEV	2496	A5
Rocky River Pk, RKRV	2621	D4
Rocky River Reservation, SGVL	3011	D3
Roemisch Fields Pk, WBHL	2375	B5
Roland Pk, LNHT	2499	A6
Roman Pk, WTLK	2619	D6
Rookery Pk, The, MsnT	2633	C3
Rotary Pk, PNVL	2040	A6
Royalview Pk, PRMA	2882	D7
Ryan Pk at Ridge Acres, WLBY	2250	B7
Sagamore Hills Twp Pk, SgHT	3017	B4
St. Clair Pk, WLBY	2250	C5
Sam Miller Pk, CLEV	2496	B5
Sandy Hook Pk, PRMA	3013	E1
Schaefer Pk, LNHT	2498	D6
Schwartz Pk, AVON	2748	C4
Selwick Pk, PRMA	2882	D6
Settlers Pk of Bainbridge, BbgT	2891	B5
Shady Drive Baseball Complex, NRDV	2876	D6
Shaker Lakes Pk, SRHT	2627	A5
Shaw Rink Pk, ECLE	2497	B4
Sheldon Pk, AURA	3156	D3
Shell Cove Pk, SDLK	2616	D2
Sherod Pk, VmnT	2740	B6
Shiloh Pk, PRMA	2883	D3
Showse Pk, VMLN	2741	E4
Soccer Complex, NRDV	2877	C7
Solon Community Pk, SLN	2889	A6
South Central Pk, NRDV	2877	A4
Southerly Pk, SRHT	2627	B6
Southgate USA Pk, MPHT	2886	B2
South Pk, PRMA	2883	D2
Sports Pk, WTLK	2749	D5
Stafford Pk, MPHT	2886	E1
State Road Pk, PRMA	2883	B4
Stearns Homestead Pk, PRMA	2883	A6
Streator Pk, LORN	2614	E7
Stroud Pk, PMHT	2882	C5
Sugarbush Pk, MCDN	3018	E5
Sunny Acres Pk, LORN	2744	B2
Sunny Lake Pk, AURA	3157	C3
Sunset Pk, AVLK	2618	B1
Sunset Pk, WLBY	2142	E4
Surfside Pk, ETLK	2142	D7
Surrarrer Pk, SGVL	3012	C3
Taft Pk, BDFD	2887	B3
Tappan Square, OBLN	3138	D2
Tate Pk, GNVA	1944	D4
Terminal Pk, CLEV	2752	D4
Thornton Pk, SRHT	2628	A7
Thrush Pk, CLEV	2753	C2
Thurgood Marshall Recreation Center, CLEV	2626	A1
Tinker's Creek State Pk, AURA	3156	B6
Tinkers Wood Pk, TNBG	3019	B3
Todd Field, WLBY	2250	E5
Tony Brush Pk, CLEV	2626	D2
Topeka Pk, CLEV	2497	A2
Towpath Trails Pk, VLVW	2885	B7
Tremont Pk, CLEV	2624	E6
Trent Pk, CLEV	2624	C7
Tri-City Pk, RKRV	2751	A2
Trumbull Woods Pk, HDSN	3155	E7
Tulard Pk, CLEV	2622	D7
Tuttle Pk, MadT	1941	D1
Twinsburg Twp Square, TNBG	3154	E1
Valleyview Woods, VLVW	2885	E4
Valleywood Pk, SVHL	3015	A2
Venus Pk, BNWK	3146	E6
Veterans Memorial Pk, AVLK	2488	A7
Veterans Memorial Pk, MNTR	2144	A2
Veterans Memorial Pk, PNVL	2040	B7
Veteran's Memorial Pk, FTHR	2039	C3
Veterans Pk, AVON	2747	B5
Vic Janowicz Memorial Pk, ELYR	3006	D2
Victory Pk, SELD	2498	B7
Village of Cuyahoga Heights Pk, CHHT	2755	C4
Village Square, CRDN	2380	A6
Voinovich Pk, CLEV	2624	D1
Volunteer Field, SFLD	2616	C5
Volunteer Pk, SGVL	3146	A2
Wade Pk, CLEV	2626	C1
Wagar Pk, RKRV	2621	C7
Walker Road Pk, AVLK	2619	A4
Walter A Burks Pk, CLEV	2496	C6
Walters Grove Pk, PRMA	2883	B1
Warsaw Pk, CLEV	2755	E3
Washington Pk, CLEV	2755	B2
Washington Pk, LORN	2614	D6
WC Reed Playfield, CLEV	2754	D2
Weiss Field, AVLK	2617	C4
Western Heights Pk, ELYR	2874	E7
West Geauga Commons Rec Area, RslT	2632	A5
Westlake Pk, WTLK	2749	D3
West Pk, ELYR	2874	C5
Westshore Pk, SDLK	2616	C3
Westwood Pk, LORN	2744	C5
Westwoods Pk, RslT	2762	E2
White City Pk, BTNH	2372	A7
Whitlam Woods Pk, HmbT	2255	B7
Wiegands Lake Pk, RslT	2762	D1
Wildwood Cultural Center, MNTR	2252	C2
Wildwood Pk, CLEV	2372	C5
Willard Pk, CLEV	2624	E2
Williams Pk, PNVL	2040	A6
Willoughby Municipal Pk, WLBY	2143	A4
Willowick Lakefront Lodge, WLWK	2249	B5
Willow Pk, EUCL	2374	A2
Willow Pk, GFTN	3142	B6
Willow Pk, LORN	2744	B3
Winterhurst Ice Rink, LKWD	2622	D7
York Road Recreation Field, NRYN	3148	C1
Yorktown Greek Pk, PMHT	2882	B4
Young Pk, WNHL	3018	A1

Post Offices

FEATURE NAME Address City ZIP Code	MAP#	GRID
Amherst 350 N Leavitt Rd, AMHT, 44001	2744	A7
Aurora 400 Aurora Commons Cir, AURA, 44202	3156	D1
Avon 36545 Detroit Rd, AVON, 44011	2747	E1
Avon Lake 33501 Lake Rd, AVLK, 44012	2617	C1
Bay Village 27106 E Oviatt Rd, BYVL, 44140	2620	A5
Bay Village Retail Store 630 Dover Center Rd, BYVL, 44140	2620	A5
Beachland 891 E 185th St, CLEV, 44119	2372	E5
Beachwood Branch 3695 Green Rd, BHWD, 44122	2758	C2
Bedford Branch 89 Willis St, BDFD, 44146	2887	A4
Berea 24 Seminary St, BERA, 44017	2880	C7
Briggs Branch 5611 State Rd, PRMA, 44134	2883	C1
Broadview Heights 2525 E Royalton Rd, BWHT, 44147	3015	B7
Brooklyn Branch 6200 Biddulph Rd, BKLN, 44144	2754	A5
Brook Park Branch 14770 Snow Rd, BKPK, 44142	2881	D2
Burton 14525 W Park St, BURT, 44021	2636	A7
Chagrin Falls 160 E Washington St, CNFL, 44022	2761	A6
Chardon 150 Center St, CRDN, 44024	2379	E6
Cleveland 2400 Orange Av, CLEV, 44115	2625	B4
Cleveland Heights Branch 3 Severance Cir, CVHT, 44118	2627	E1
Collinwood Station 890 E 152nd St, CLEV, 44110	2497	B2
Cranwood Station 16828 Harvard Av, CLEV, 44128	2757	C3
East Cleveland Branch 1700 Shaw Av, ECLE, 44112	2497	B5
Edgewater Branch 1380 W 117th St, LKWD, 44107	2623	B5
Elyria 345 E Bridge St, ELYR, 44035	2875	C6
Erieview Station 1240 Rock & Roll Blvd, CLEV, 44114	2624	E2
Euclid Branch 21551 Euclid Av, EUCL, 44117	2373	B7
Fairview Park Branch 4435 W 220th St, FWPK, 44126	2751	B3
Garfield Heights Branch 12401 Rockside Rd, VLVW, 44125	2885	D3
Gates Mills 1500 Chagrin River Rd, GSML, 44040	2630	E1
Geneva 1041 S Broadway, GNVA, 44041	1944	B6
Glenville Bratenahl Branch 630 E 105th St, CLEV, 44108	2496	C4
Grafton 926 Main St, GFTN, 44044	3142	A5
Grand River 340 Wetmore St, GDRV, 44077	2039	C6
Hiram 11676 Hayden St, HRM, 44234	3161	A2
Independence Branch 6509 Brecksville Rd, INDE, 44131	2884	E5
Jesse C Owens Station 5600 Woodland Av, CLEV, 44104	2625	D5
Kamms Station 3762 Rocky River Dr, CLEV, 44111	2752	B2
Lakewood Branch 1475 Warren Rd, LKWD, 44107	2622	D5
Lorain Broadway Retail 439 Reid Av, LORN, 44052	2614	D6
Lorain Carrier Annex 3190 Colorado Av, LORN, 44052	2615	D7
Lyndhurst Mayfield Branch 5815 Landerbrook Dr, MDHT, 44124	2629	C3
Madison 375 N Lake St, MDSN, 44057	1942	B7
Mantua 10748 Main St, MNTU, 44255	3159	C5
Maple Heights Branch 16300 Broadway Av, MPHT, 44137	2886	C1
Mentor 8600 Tyler Blvd, MNTR, 44060	2144	C6
Middlefield 15993 E High St, MDFD, 44062	2767	D2
Midpark Branch 13301 Smith Rd, MDBH, 44130	2881	D6
Newburg Station 8745 Broadway Av, CLEV, 44105	2756	B3
Noble 25101 N Lakeland Blvd, EUCL, 44132	2373	D3
Northfield 10377 Valley View Rd, MCDN, 44056	3018	B6
North Olmsted 28475 Lorain Rd, NOSD, 44070	2878	D1
North Ridgeville Branch 34760 Center Ridge Rd, NRDV, 44039	2877	C2
North Royalton Branch 13901 State Rd, NRYN, 44133	3014	A7
Oberlin 68 S Main St, OBLN, 44074	3138	E3
Olmsted Falls Branch 8000 Brookside Dr, ODFL, 44138	2879	B5
Painesville 215 E Jackson St, PNVL, 44077	2040	B7
Parma Branch 7801 Day Dr, PRMA, 44129	2882	E5
Pearlbrook Station 4160 Pearl Rd, CLEV, 44109	2754	C4
Perry 3754 Center Rd, PRRY, 44081	2042	B1
Public Square Station 410 Superior Av E, CLEV, 44114	2624	E3
Puritas Park Station 14039 Puritas Av, CLEV, 44135	2752	D5
Richmond Heights Branch 454 Richmond Rd, RDHT, 44143	2498	E3
Rocky River Branch 19525 Hilliard Blvd, RKRV, 44116	2621	E6
Shaker Finance Station 2855 E 130th St, CLEV, 44120	2626	E6
Shaker Heights Station 3675 Warrensville Center Rd, SRHT, 44122	2758	A1
Sheffield Lake Branch 4214 Ivanhoe Av, SDLK, 44054	2616	B4
Shore Branch 22751 Shore Center Dr, EUCL, 44123	2373	C2
Solon Branch 33333 Station St, SLN, 44139	2889	A5
Solon Retail Store 33533 Aurora Rd, SLN, 44139	2889	A5
South Euclid Branch 1568 S Green Rd, SELD, 44121	2628	C1
South Lorain Station 1680 E 28th St, LORN, 44055	2745	B2
Station A 6600 Lorain Av, CLEV, 44102	2624	A6
Station B/C 1650 E 55th St, CLEV, 44103	2625	D1
Strongsville Branch 15500 Pearl Rd, SGVL, 44149	3146	D2
Tower City Retail 50 Public Sq, CLEV, 44115	2624	E3

Cleveland Points of Interest Index

Post Offices

FEATURE NAME / Address City ZIP Code	MAP#	GRID
Twinsburg Main Office 8935 Darrow Rd, TNBG, 44087	3155	A2
University Center 1950 E 101st St, CLEV, 44106	2626	C2
Westlake Branch 27300 Center Ridge Rd, WTLK, 44145	2750	A2
West Park Station 14500 Lorain Av, CLEV, 44111	2752	D2
Wickliffe 1400 Lloyd Rd, WKLF, 44092	2374	B2
Willoughby 4040 Erie St, WLBY, 44094	2250	E5
Willoughby Retail Store 37812 Vine St, WLBY, 44094	2250	D5
Willowick 260 E 312th St, WLWK, 44095	2249	C5
Willow Station 5725 Portage Av, CLEV, 44127	2625	D7

Schools

FEATURE NAME / Address City ZIP Code	MAP#	GRID
Academy of St Bartholomew 14875 Bagley Rd, MDBH, 44130	2881	C7
Adlai Stevenson Elementary School 3938 Jo Ann Dr, CLEV, 44122	2757	D2
Adrian Elementary School 1071 Homestead Rd, SELD, 44121	2498	B6
Agnon School 26500 Shaker Blvd, BHWD, 44122	2629	A6
Albert Hart Middle School 3901 E 74th St, CLEV, 44105	2756	A2
Albion Elementary School 9360 Albion Rd, NRYN, 44133	3013	C4
Albion Middle School 11109 Webster Rd, SGVL, 44136	3012	C5
Alexander Bell K-8 School 11815 Larchmere Blvd, CLEV, 44120	2626	D4
Allen Elementary School 16400 Park Lane Dr, SGVL, 44136	3147	A2
All Saints of St John Vianney 28702 Euclid Av, WKLF, 44092	2374	B3
Almira K-8 Academy 3380 W 98th St, CLEV, 44102	2753	D1
Amherst Junior High School 548 Milan Av, AMHT, 44001	2872	C2
Amherst Steele High School 450 Washington St, AMHT, 44001	2872	D1
Andrew Rickoff Elementary School 3500 E 147th St, CLEV, 44120	2757	A1
Andrews School 38588 Mentor Av, WLBY, 44094	2251	A5
Anton Grdina Elementary School 3050 E 77th St, CLEV, 44104	2626	A6
Archbishop Lyke-St. Henry 18230 Harvard Av, CLEV, 44128	2757	D3
Archbishop Lyke-St. Timothy 4351 E 131st St, GDHT, 44105	2756	E4
Artemus Ward Halle 7901 Halle Av, CLEV, 44102	2623	E7
Arthur Road Elementary School 33425 Arthur Rd, SLN, 44139	2889	A7
Ascension School 4400 W 140th St, CLEV, 44135	2752	D5
Assumption Academy 9183 Broadview Rd, BWHT, 44147	3014	E7
Assumption School 30 Lockwood St, GNVA, 44041	1944	A4
Audubon K-8 School 3055 Martin Luther King Junior, CLEV, 44104	2626	C6
Aurora High School 109 W Pioneer Trl, AURA, 44202	3156	D1
Aurora Upper Intermediate School 24200 Aurora Rd, BDHT, 44146	2887	D1
Avon East Elementary School 3100 Nagel Rd, AVON, 44011	2748	D3
Avon Heritage Elementary School 35575 Detroit Rd, AVON, 44011	2748	B1
Avon High School 37545 Detroit Rd, AVON, 44011	2747	D2
Avon Lake High School 175 Avon Belden Rd, AVLK, 44012	2618	A1
Avon Middle School 3075 Stoney Ridge Rd, AVON, 44011	2747	E3
Ballard Brady Middle School 32000 Chagrin Blvd, PRPK, 44124	2759	E2
Bassett Elementary School 2155 Bassett Rd, WTLK, 44145	2749	D1
Bay High School 29230 Wolf Rd, BYVL, 44140	2619	D4
Bay Middle School 27725 Wolf Rd, BYVL, 44140	2619	E4
Beachwood High School 25100 Fairmount Blvd, BHWD, 44122	2628	D5
Beachwood Middle School 2860 Richmond Rd, BHWD, 44122	2628	E6
Beaumont School 3301 N Park Blvd, CVHT, 44118	2627	C5
Bedford Senior High School 481 Northfield Rd, BDFD, 44146	2887	B2
Bellflower Elementary School 6655 Reynolds Rd, MNTR, 44060	2143	C5
Benedictine High School 2900 Martin Luther King Junior, CLEV, 44104	2626	C6
Benjamin Franklin School 1905 Spring Rd, CLEV, 44109	2754	D5
Berea Senior High School 165 E Bagley Rd, BERA, 44017	2880	D6
Bethany Christian School 6195 Broadview Rd, PRMA, 44134	2883	E3
Bethany Lutheran School 6041 Ridge Rd, PRMA, 44129	2882	E3
Bethel Christian Academy 12901 W Pleasant Valley Rd, PRMA, 44130	2881	E7
Bethlehem Christian School 27250 Emery Rd, ORNG, 44022	2759	A5
Big Creek Elementary School 7247 Big Creek Pkwy, MDBH, 44130	2881	B7
Birch Primary School 24100 Palm Dr, NOSD, 44070	2750	D6
Birchwood School 16210 Lorain Av, CLEV, 44111	2752	B2
Bolton K-8 School 9803 Quebec Av, CLEV, 44106	2626	B4
Boulevard Elementary School 1749 Lee Rd, CVHT, 44118	2627	C1
Boulevard Elementary School 14900 Drexmore Rd, SRHT, 44120	2627	B5
Brecksville-Broadview Heights High School 6380 Mill Rd, BWHT, 44147	3015	E5
Brentmoor Elementary School 7671 Johnnycake Ridge Rd, MNTR, 44060	2251	D4
Brooklawn Elementary School 11801 Worthington Av, CLEV, 44111	2753	B3
Brooklyn High School 9200 Biddulph Rd, BKLN, 44144	2753	D5
Brooklyn Middle School 9200 Biddulph Rd, BKLN, 44144	2753	D5
Brookpark Memorial Elementary School 16900 Holland Rd, BKPK, 44142	2881	A3
Brookridge Elementary School 4500 Ridge Rd, BKLN, 44144	2753	E5
Brookside High School 1812 Harris Rd, SFLD, 44054	2616	C6
Brookview Elementary School 14105 Snow Rd, BKPK, 44142	2881	D2
Brunswick Memorial Elementary School 3845 Magnolia Dr, BNWK, 44212	3146	E6
Brush High School 4875 Glenlyn Rd, LNHT, 44124	2498	D7
Bryden Elementary School 25501 Bryden Rd, BHWD, 44122	2628	E7
Buckeye Elementary School 175 Buckeye Rd, PnvT, 44077	2145	E4
Buckeye-Woodland K-8 School 9511 Buckeye Rd, CLEV, 44104	2626	B5
Buhrer Elementary School 1600 Buhrer Av, CLEV, 44109	2624	E7
Burton Elementary School 13724 Carlton St, BURT, 44021	2766	A1
Butternut Primary School 26669 Butternut Ridge Rd, NOSD, 44070	2879	A1
Caledonia Elementary School 914 Caledonia Av, CVHT, 44112	2497	C5
Canterbury Elementary School 2530 Canterbury Rd, CVHT, 44118	2627	E4
Captain Arthur Roth Elementary School 12523 Woodside Av, CLEV, 44108	2496	E5
Cardinal High School 14785 Thompson Av, MDFD, 44062	2767	E1
Cardinal Middle School 14717 Thompson Av, MDFD, 44062	2767	D1
Carl F Shuler School 13501 Terminal Av, CLEV, 44135	2752	E4
Carl-Louis Stokes Academy 2225 E 40th St, CLEV, 44103	2625	D3
Carylwood Intermediate School 1387 Caryl Dr, BDFD, 44146	2887	C6
Cascade Elementary School 233 Bond St, ELYR, 44035	2875	A4
Case Elementary School 4050 Superior Av, CLEV, 44103	2625	C1
Cedarbrook Elementary School 350 Cedarbrook Dr, PNVL, 44077	2146	A2
Cedar Hill Christian School 12601 Cedar Rd, CVHT, 44106	2627	A3
Center Middle School 13200 Pearl Rd, SGVL, 44149	3011	D7
Central Elementary School 27 Public Sq, BKVL, 44141	3016	A7
Central Primary School 799 Washington St, BDFD, 44146	2887	A4
Chagrin Falls High School 400 E Washington St, CNFL, 44022	2761	B6
Chagrin Falls Intermediate School 77 E Washington St, CNFL, 44022	2761	A6
Chagrin Falls Middle School 342 E Washington St, CNFL, 44022	2761	B6
Chambers Elementary School 14305 Shaw Av, ECLE, 44112	2497	A4
Chapman Elementary School 13883 Drake Rd, SGVL, 44136	3147	D3
Chardon High School 151 Chardon Av, CRDN, 44024	2380	A5
Chardon Middle School 424 North St, CRDN, 44024	2380	A5
Charles A Mooney K-8 School 3213 Montclair Av, CLEV, 44109	2754	C5
Charles Dickens Elementary School 3552 E 131st St, CLEV, 44105	2756	E1
Charles Eliot Middle School 15700 Lotus Dr, CLEV, 44128	2757	B3
Charles Lake K-8 School 9201 Hillock Av, CLEV, 44108	2496	B4
Chestnut Intermediate School 30395 Lorain Rd, NOSD, 44070	2878	B2
Chippewa Elementary School 8611 Wiese Rd, BKVL, 44141	3016	C6
Clara Westropp K-8 Fund School 19101 Puritas Av, CLEV, 44135	2751	E5
Clark Elementary School 5550 Clark Av, CLEV, 44102	2624	A7
Clearview High School 4700 Broadway, ShfT, 44052	2745	A5
Cleveland Central Catholic High School 6550 Baxter Av, CLEV, 44105	2755	D1
Cleveland Heights High School 13263 Cedar Rd, CVHT, 44118	2627	C3
Cleveland School of the Arts 2064 Stearns Rd, CLEV, 44106	2626	C3
Cleveland School of the Arts-Dike 2501 E 61st St, CLEV, 44104	2625	D4
Col John Glenn Elementary School 1300 E Dartmoor Av, SVHL, 44131	2884	B3
Collinwood High School 15210 St. Clair Av, CLEV, 44110	2497	B3
Columbia High School 14168 W River Rd, ClbT, 44028	3009	E7
Columbia Middle School 13646 W River Rd, ClbT, 44028	3009	E7
Columbus Intermediate School 23600 Columbus Rd, BDHT, 44146	2887	C3
Copopa Elementary School 14168 W River Rd, ClbT, 44028	3009	E7
Cornerstone Christian Academy 2846 Som Center Rd, WBHL, 44094	2375	A6
Coventry Elementary School 2843 Washington Blvd, CVHT, 44118	2627	B2
Craddock Elementary School 105 Hurd Rd, AURA, 44202	3157	A1
Crestview Elementary School 300 W 130th St, BNWK, 44212	3147	E6
Crestwood Elementary School 42331 Griswold Rd, EyrT, 44035	2874	C1
Crestwood High School 10919 Main St, MNTU, 44255	3159	C5
Crestwood Intermediate School 11260 Bowen Rd, ManT, 44255	3159	B3
Crestwood Middle School 10880 John Edward Dr, MNTU, 44255	3159	B5
Crestwood Primary School 11256 Bowen Rd, ManT, 44255	3159	B3
Cuyahoga Heights Elementary School 4880 E 71st St, CHHT, 44125	2755	E6
Cuyahoga Heights High School 4820 E 71st St, CHHT, 44125	2755	E6
Cuyahoga Heights Middle School 4840 E 71st St, CHHT, 44125	2755	E6
Dag Hammarskjold Elementary School 4040 Tamarack Dr, PRMA, 44134	3014	B1
Daniel Morgan Elementary School 1440 E 92nd St, CLEV, 44106	2626	B1
Denison School 3799 W 33rd St, CLEV, 44109	2754	C2
Dentzler Elementary School 3600 Dentzler Rd, PRMA, 44134	2883	C6
Dodge Intermediate School 10225 Ravenna Rd, TNBG, 44087	3019	D7
Dorothy E Lewis Elementary School 32345 Cannon Rd, SLN, 44139	2888	E2
Dover Elementary School 2300 Dover Center Rd, WTLK, 44145	2750	A1
Drake Elementary School 20566 Albion Rd, SGVL, 44149	3011	C5
Dunham Elementary School 5965 Dunham Rd, MPHT, 44137	2886	B3
Durling Elementary School 100 N Ridge Rd W, ShfT, 44052	2745	A5
Early College Program High School 1935 Euclid Av, CLEV, 44114	2625	A2
East Clark Elementary School 885 E 146th St, CLEV, 44110	2497	B2
Eastern Heights Junior High School 528 Garford Av, ELYR, 44035	2875	C7
Eastgate Elementary School 336 S Logan St, ELYR, 44035	2875	D7
East High School 1349 E 79th St, CLEV, 44103	2496	A7
East HS School for Creative Expression 1379 E 79th St, CLEV, 44103	2496	A7
Eastlake Middle School 35972 Lake Shore Blvd, ETLK, 44095	2142	C7
Eastview Elementary School 230 Lear Rd, AVLK, 44012	2618	D2
Eastwood Elementary School 198 E College St, OBLN, 44074	3138	E2
Eastwood Elementary School 4050 Eastwood Ln, WVHT, 44122	2757	E3
Edison Elementary School 5288 Karen Isle Dr, WLBY, 44094	2375	B1
Edith Whitney Elementary School 13548 Whitney Rd, SGVL, 44136	3012	D3
Elmwood Elementary School 5275 Turney Rd, GDHT, 44125	2756	D7
Ely Elementary School 312 Gulf Rd, ELYR, 44035	2875	C5
Elyria Catholic High School 725 Gulf Rd, ELYR, 44035	2875	C4
Elyria High School 311 6th St, ELYR, 44035	2875	A7
Emerson Middle School 13439 Clifton Blvd, LKWD, 44107	2622	E4
Emile de Sauze Elementary School 4747 E 176th St, CLEV, 44128	2757	D6
Empire Computech K-8 School 9113 Parmelee Av, CLEV, 44108	2496	B5
Erie Elementary School 333 Naples Dr, ELYR, 44035	2746	D7
Erieview Elementary School 32630 Electric Blvd, AVLK, 44012	2618	B1
Euclid High School 711 E 222nd St, EUCL, 44123	2373	B4
Euclid Park Elementary School 17914 Euclid Av, CLEV, 44112	2497	D3
Fairfax Elementary School 3150 Fairfax Rd, CVHT, 44118	2627	C4
Fairfax Elementary School 6465 Curtiss Ct, MNTR, 44060	2144	A4
Fairport Harding High School 329 Vine St, FTHR, 44077	2039	D3
Fairview High School 4507 W 213th St, FWPK, 44126	2751	C3
Fairwood Elementary School 191 Race St, BERA, 44017	3011	A1
Falls-Lenox Primary School 26450 Bagley Rd, ODFL, 44138	2879	A6
Fernway Elementary School 17420 Fernway Rd, SRHT, 44120	2627	D7
First Baptist Christian School 11400 Lagrange Rd, CrlT, 44035	3005	E5
Fitch Intermediate School 7105 Fitch Rd, OmsT, 44138	2879	A4
F Jacinto Elementary School 2515 Marshall Av, LORN, 44052	2744	B2
Ford Middle School 17001 Holland Rd, BKPK, 44142	2881	A3
Forest Elementary School 28963 Tudor Dr, NOSD, 44070	2749	D7
Forest Hill Parkway K-8 School 450 E 112th St, CLEV, 44108	2496	D4
Forestlawn Elementary School 3975 Forestlawn Av, SDLK, 44054	2616	A4
Forest Park Middle School 27000 Elinore Av, EUCL, 44132	2373	E2
Franklin Elementary School 446 11th St, ELYR, 44035	3006	A1
Franklin Elementary School 13465 Franklin Blvd, LKWD, 44107	2622	E5
Franklin Roosevelt Middle School 800 Linn Dr, CLEV, 44108	2496	C5
Frederick Roehm Middle School 7220 Pleasant Av, BERA, 44017	2880	D6
Fuchs Mizrachi School 2301 Fenwick Rd, UNHT, 44118	2628	A3
Fullerton Elementary School 5920 Fullerton Av, CLEV, 44105	2755	D2
Garfield Elementary School 13114 Detroit Av, LKWD, 44107	2623	A5

Cleveland Points of Interest Index

FEATURE NAME Address City ZIP Code	MAP#	GRID
Garfield Elementary School 200 W 31st St, LORN, 44055	2745	A3
Garfield Elementary School 7090 Hopkins Rd, MNTR, 44060	2144	D7
Garfield Heights High School 4900 Turney Rd, GDHT, 44125	2756	C6
Garfield Heights Middle School 12000 Maple Leaf Dr, GDHT, 44125	2885	D2
Garnett Primary School 4275 W 208th St, FWPK, 44126	2751	C3
Garrett Morgan School of Science 4016 Woodbine Av, CLEV, 44113	2624	B5
Gates Mills Elementary School 7639 Colvin Rd, GSML, 44040	2500	E7
Gearity Professional Development Elem-School 2323 Wrenford Rd, UNHT, 44118	2628	B4
Geneva Area Junior High School 839 Sherman St, GNVA, 44041	1944	C5
Geneva Elementary School 119 S Eagle St, GNVA, 44041	1944	B4
George W Carver K-8 School 2201 E 49th St, CLEV, 44103	2625	D3
Gesu School 2450 Miramar Blvd, UNHT, 44118	2628	A4
Giddings Elementary School 2250 E 71st St, CLEV, 44103	2625	E3
Gilmour Academy High School 34001 Cedar Rd, GSML, 44040	2630	A3
Glenbrook Elementary School 23500 Glenbrook Blvd, EUCL, 44117	2373	C7
Glendale Primary School 400 W Glendale St, BDFD, 44146	2886	D4
Glenville High School 650 E 113th St, CLEV, 44108	2496	D4
Goldwood Primary School 21600 Center Ridge Rd, RKRV, 44116	2751	B1
Gracemount Elementary School 16200 Glendale Av, CLEV, 44128	2757	C2
Grant Elementary School 1470 Victoria Av, LKWD, 44107	2622	C5
Grant Elementary School 38281 Hurricane Dr, WLBY, 44094	2250	E2
Greater Heights Charter Academy 112 Prospect Av E, CLEV, 44115	2624	E3
Greenbriar Middle School 11810 Huffman Rd, PRMA, 44130	2882	A3
Green Valley Elementary School 2401 W Pleasant Valley Rd, PRMA, 44134	3014	D1
Greenview Upper Elementary School 1825 S Green Rd, SELD, 44121	2628	C2
Gross Schechter Day School 27601 Fairmount Blvd, PRPK, 44124	2629	A5
Gurney Elementary School 1155 Bell Rd, SRSL, 44022	2762	A6
Hadden Elementary School 1800 Mentor Av, PnvT, 44077	2145	C5
Hale Road Elementary School 56 Hale Rd, PnvT, 44077	2041	A4
Hambden Elementary School 13871 Gar Hwy, HmbT, 44024	2381	B3
Hannah Gibbons K-8 School 1200 E 200th St, EUCL, 44117	2373	A6
Harding Middle School 16600 Hilliard Rd, LKWD, 44107	2622	B6
Harmon Middle School 130 Aurora Hudson Rd, AURA, 44202	3156	E2
Harrison Elementary School 12911 Madison Av, LKWD, 44107	2623	A6
Harvey High School 167 W Washington St, PNVL, 44077	2146	B1
Hathaway Brown School 19600 N Park Blvd, SRHT, 44122	2627	E5
Hawken School-Lyndhurst Campus 5000 Clubside Rd, LNHT, 44124	2628	E1
Hayes Elementary School 16511 Hilliard Rd, LKWD, 44107	2622	B7
H Barbara Booker School 2121 W 67th St, CLEV, 44102	2624	A6
Headlands Elementary School 5028 Forest Rd, MNTR, 44060	2038	D6
Hebrew Academy of Cleveland 1860 S Taylor Rd, CVHT, 44118	2627	D2
Heritage Christian School 4403 Tiedeman Rd, BKLN, 44144	2753	C4
Heritage Middle School Moduler 1850 Garfield Rd, ECLE, 44112	2497	A7
Hershey Montessori School 10229 Prouty Rd, CcdT, 44077	2145	D7
Heskett Middle School 5771 Perkins Rd, BDHT, 44146	2887	E2
Hilliard Elementary School 24365 Hilliard Blvd, WTLK, 44145	2750	D1
Hillside Middle School 1 Educational Park Dr, SVHL, 44131	2884	A7
Hilltop Elementary School 24524 Hilltop Dr, BHWD, 44122	2628	D3
Hilton Elementary School 6812 Mill Rd, BKVL, 44141	3016	A6
Hobart Middle School 200 W Walnut Av, PNVL, 44077	2146	A2
Holly Lane Elementary School 3057 Holly Ln, WTLK, 44145	2750	B3
Holy Cross School 175 E 200th St, EUCL, 44123	2373	A3
Holy Family School 7367 York Rd, PRMA, 44130	2882	B7
Holy Name Elementary School 8328 Broadway Av, CLEV, 44105	2756	A3
Holy Name High School 6000 Queens Hwy, PMHT, 44130	2882	B2
Holy Spirit Academy 370 Center Rd, BDFD, 44146	2887	A2
Holy Trinity School 2610 Nagel Rd, AVON, 44011	2748	D2
Homer Nash Kimball Elementary School 94 River St, MDSN, 44057	2044	B2
Homewood Elementary School 2500 Goble Dr, LORN, 44055	2746	A5
Hopkins Elementary School 7565 Hopkins Rd, MNTR, 44060	2252	D2
Horace Mann Middle School 1215 W Clifton Blvd, LKWD, 44107	2622	A4
Hudson Montessori School 7545 Darrow Rd, HDSN, 44236	3155	A7

FEATURE NAME Address City ZIP Code	MAP#	GRID
Huntington Elementary School 979 N St. Clair St, PNVL, 44077	2039	E5
Immaculate Conception School 4129 Superior Av, CLEV, 44103	2625	C1
Immaculate Conception School 37940 Euclid Av, WLBY, 44094	2250	D6
Incarnate Word Academy 6618 Pearl Rd, PMHT, 44130	2882	A5
Independence High School 6001 Archwood Rd, INDE, 44131	2884	D6
Independence Middle School 6111 Archwood Rd, INDE, 44131	2884	D6
Independence Primary School 7600 Hillside Rd, INDE, 44131	2885	A7
Indian Hills Elementary School 1941 Sagamore Dr, EUCL, 44117	2498	A2
Iowa-Maple Elementary School 12510 Maple Av, CLEV, 44108	2496	E3
Irving Elementary School 1110 W 4th St, LORN, 44052	2614	D6
James E Hanna Elementary School 11212 Snow Rd, PRMA, 44130	2882	B2
James Ford Rhodes Ed Campus 5100 Biddulph Av, CLEV, 44144	2754	B5
Jamison K-8 Computech School 13905 Harvard Av, CLEV, 44105	2757	A3
JD Rockefeller School 5901 Whittier Av, CLEV, 44103	2625	D1
Jefferson Elementary School 35980 Lake Shore Blvd, ETLK, 44095	2142	C7
John Dewey Elementary School 23401 Emery Rd, WVHT, 44128	2758	C5
John F Kennedy High School 17100 Harvard Av, CLEV, 44128	2757	C3
John Marshall High School 3952 W 140th St, CLEV, 44111	2752	D3
John Muir Elementary School 5531 W 24th St, PRMA, 44134	2883	D1
Johnnie Wilson Middle School 2700 Washington Av, LORN, 44052	2744	D2
John R Williams Junior High School 625 Riverside Dr, PnvT, 44077	2146	D2
John W Raper Elementary School 1601 E 85th St, CLEV, 44106	2626	B1
Jordak Elementary School 16000 E High St, MDFD, 44062	2767	D2
Joseph F Landis Elementary School 10118 Hampden Av, CLEV, 44108	2496	B7
Joseph Gallagher Middle School 6601 Franklin Blvd, CLEV, 44102	2624	A5
Josiah Harris Elementary School 393 S Lake St, AMHT, 44001	2872	C2
Kensington Intermediate School 20140 Lake Rd, RKRV, 44116	2621	D5
Kenston High School 17425 Snyder Rd, BbgT, 44023	2891	E4
Kenston Intermediate School 17419 Snyder Rd, BbgT, 44023	2891	E4
Kenston Middle School 17425 Snyder Rd, BbgT, 44023	2891	E4
Kentucky Elementary School 3805 Terrett Av, CLEV, 44113	2624	C5
Kinsner Elementary School 19091 Waterford Pkwy, SGVL, 44149	3146	C5
Kirtland Elementary School 9140 Chillicothe Rd, KTLD, 44094	2251	D7
Kirtland High School 9150 Chillicothe Rd, KTLD, 44094	2376	D1
Kirtland Middle School 9152 Chillicothe Rd, KTLD, 44094	2376	E1
Knollwood Elementary School 4975 Oster Rd, SDLK, 44054	2616	D4
Lake Catholic High School 6733 Reynolds Rd, MNTR, 44060	2143	C5
Lake Elementary School 7625 Pinehurst Dr, MONT, 44060	2143	D2
Lake Ridge Academy 37501 Center Ridge Rd, NRDV, 44039	2876	C4
Lakeview Elementary School 1953 W 11th St, LORN, 44052	2614	B7
Lakewood Digital Charter Academy 1470 Warren Rd, LKWD, 44107	2622	C5
Lakewood High School 14100 Franklin Blvd, LKWD, 44107	2622	D5
Lakewood Lutheran School 1419 Lakeland Av, LKWD, 44107	2622	C5
Lamuth Middle School 6700 Auburn Rd, CcdT, 44077	2146	B5
Lander Elementary School 1714 Lander Rd, MDHT, 44124	2629	D1
Langston Middle School 150 N Pleasant St, OBLN, 44074	3138	E2
Larkmoor Elementary School 1201 Nebraska Av, LORN, 44052	2615	C6
Lathrop Elementary School 61 Roosevelt Dr, PNVL, 44077	2145	D2
Lear North Elementary School 5580 Lear Nagle Rd, NRDV, 44039	2877	D1
Learwood Middle School 340 Lear Rd, AVLK, 44012	2618	D2
Ledgemont Elementary Middle School 16200 Burrows Rd, TpnT, 44086	2257	E5
Ledgeview Elementary School 9130 Shepard Rd, MCDN, 44056	3018	E6
Lee Burneson Middle School 2240 Dover Center Rd, WTLK, 44145	2750	A1
Lee Eaton Elementary School 115 Ledge Rd, NHFD, 44067	3018	B5
Leighton Elementary School 121 Aurora Hudson Rd, AURA, 44202	3156	E2
Leroy Elementary School 13613 Painesville Warren Rd, LryT, 44077	2256	A2
Lewis S Mayer Middle School 21200 Campus Dr, FWPK, 44126	2751	C3
Liberty Elementary School 5700 Jaycox Rd, NRDV, 44039	2877	B1
Lincoln Elementary School 280 E 206th St, EUCL, 44123	2373	A3
Lincoln Elementary School 15615 Clifton Blvd, LKWD, 44107	2622	C4
Lincoln Elementary School 1600 E 31st St, LORN, 44055	2745	C3
Lincoln-West High School 3202 W 30th St, CLEV, 44109	2624	D7
Lomond Elementary School 17917 Lomond Blvd, SRHT, 44122	2757	D1

FEATURE NAME Address City ZIP Code	MAP#	GRID
Longfellow Accelerated Learning School 650 E 140th St, CLEV, 44110	2497	A1
Longfellow Elementary School 35200 Stevens Blvd, ETLK, 44095	2250	A4
Longfellow Elementary School 1100 Leroy St, LORN, 44052	2615	C5
Longfellow Middle School 305 Louisiana Av, LORN, 44052	2615	B5
Lorain Admiral King High School 2600 Ashland Av, LORN, 44052	2744	C2
Lorain High School Digital Charter 2350 Pole Av, LORN, 44052	2744	B2
Lorain Middle School Digital Charter 2350 Pole Av, LORN, 44052	2744	C2
Lorain Southview High School 2270 E 42nd St, LORN, 44055	2745	E4
Louis Agassiz Elementary School 3595 Bosworth Rd, CLEV, 44111	2753	B2
Louisa May Alcott Elementary School 10308 Baltic Rd, CLEV, 44102	2623	C5
Louis Pasteur Pk-8 Academy 815 Linn Dr, CLEV, 44108	2496	D5
Lowden Elementary School 4106 Lowden Rd, SELD, 44121	2498	A4
Lowell Elementary School 3200 Clinton Av, LORN, 44055	2745	D3
Luis Munoz Marin School 1701 Castle Av, CLEV, 44113	2624	D7
Lutheran High School East 3565 Mayfield Rd, CVHT, 44121	2497	D7
Lutheran High School West 3850 Linden Rd, RKRV, 44116	2751	D1
Madison Avenue Elementary School 845 Madison Av, PnvT, 44077	2040	D7
Madison Elementary School 16601 Madison Av, LKWD, 44107	2622	B6
Madison High School 3100 Burns Rd, MadT, 44057	1941	E6
Madison Middle School 1941 Red Bird Rd, MadT, 44057	1942	A1
Magnificat High School 20770 Hilliard Blvd, RKRV, 44116	2621	C7
Maple Elementary School 308 Maple Av, CRDN, 44024	2380	A5
Maple Heights Senior High School 5500 Clement Av, MPHT, 44137	2886	C1
Maple Intermediate School 24101 Maple Ridge Rd, NOSD, 44070	2750	D4
Maple Leaf Intermediate School 5764 Turney Rd, GDHT, 44125	2885	D2
Margaret Spellacy Middle School 655 E 162nd St, CLEV, 44110	2497	C1
Marion Seltzer Elementary School 1468 W 98th St, CLEV, 44102	2623	D6
Marion-Sterling Elementary School 3033 Central Av, CLEV, 44115	2625	C3
Mary Bethune Elementary School 11815 Moulton Av, CLEV, 44106	2496	D7
Mary Bethune K-8 School Wadpark 10700 Churchill Av, CLEV, 44106	2496	C7
Masson Elementary School 1800 W 40th St, LORN, 44053	2744	B4
Mayfield Center Elementary School 6625 Wilson Mills Rd, MAYF, 44143	2500	A5
Mayfield High School 6116 Wilson Mills Rd, MAYF, 44143	2499	D5
Mayfield Middle School 1123 Som Center Rd, MDHT, 44124	2500	A6
McKinley Elementary School 3349 W 125th St, CLEV, 44111	2753	A1
McKinley Elementary School 602 Plum St, FTHR, 44077	2039	D4
McKinley Elementary School 1351 W Clifton Blvd, LKWD, 44107	2622	A4
McKinley Elementary School 1200 Lost Nation Rd, WLBY, 44094	2143	A5
Meister Road Elementary School 3301 Meister Rd, LORN, 44053	2743	E3
Melridge Elementary School 6689 Melridge Dr, CcdT, 44077	2145	E5
Memorial Junior High School 8979 Mentor Av, MNTR, 44060	2144	D7
Memorial Junior High School 1250 Professor Rd, SELD, 44121	2498	D7
Memorial K-8 School 410 E 152nd St, CLEV, 44110	2372	B7
Memorial Park Elementary School 22800 Fox Av, EUCL, 44123	2373	C3
Mentor Christian School 8600 Lake Shore Blvd, MNTR, 44060	2144	C1
Mentor High School 6477 Center St, MNTR, 44060	2144	B4
Mercer Elementary School 23325 Wimbledon Rd, SRHT, 44122	2628	C6
Messiah Lutheran School 4401 W 215th St, FWPK, 44126	2751	B3
Metro Catholic Parish School 1910 W 54th St, CLEV, 44102	2624	A6
Michael R White Elementary School 1000 E 92nd St, CLEV, 44108	2496	B6
Midpark Senior High School 7000 Paula Dr, MDBH, 44130	2881	C5
Midview East Elementary School 13070 Durkee Rd, EatT, 44044	3142	B2
Midview High School 38199 Capel Rd, EatT, 44044	3141	E1
Midview Middle School 37999 Capel Rd, EatT, 44044	3142	A1
Midview North Elementary School 13070 Durkee Rd, EatT, 44044	3142	B2
Midview West Elementary School 13070 Durkee Rd, EatT, 44044	3142	B2
Miles K-8 School 11918 Miles Av, CLEV, 44105	2756	D3
Miles Park Elementary School 4092 E 146th St, CLEV, 44128	2757	A3
Milkovich Middle School 5500 Clement Av, MPHT, 44137	2886	C1
Millridge Elementary School 962 Millridge Rd, HDHT, 44143	2499	B5
ML King Junior Law-Career High School 1651 E 71st St, CLEV, 44103	2625	E1
Montessori Children's School 28370 Bassett Rd, WTLK, 44145	2749	D2
Monticello Middle School 3665 Monticello Blvd, CVHT, 44121	2497	E6

Schools

Cleveland Points of Interest Index

Schools

FEATURE NAME Address City ZIP Code	MAP#	GRID
Mosdos Ohr Hatorah School 1508 Warrensville Center Rd, CVHT, 44121	2498	A7
Mosdos Ohr Hatra School 1700 S Taylor Rd, CVHT, 44118	2627	D1
Mound Elementary School 5405 Mound Av, CLEV, 44105	2755	D1
Munson Elementary School 12687 Bass Lake Rd, MsnT, 44024	2504	D7
Muraski Elementary School 20270 Royalton Rd, SGVL, 44149	3011	C7
Nathan Hale Middle School 3588 Martin Luther King Junior, CLEV, 44105	2756	C1
Newbury Elementary School 14775 Auburn Rd, NbyT, 44065	2764	A1
Newbury Junior Senior High School 14775 Auburn Rd, NbyT, 44065	2764	A1
New Day Academy 291 E 222nd St Ste 205, EUCL, 44123	2373	B2
Newton D Baker School of Arts 3690 W 159th St, CLEV, 44111	2752	B2
Noble Elementary School 1293 Ardoon St, CVHT, 44121	2498	A7
Nordonia High School 8006 S Bedford Rd, MCDN, 44056	3153	C2
Nordonia Middle School 73 Leonard Av, NCtT, 44067	3017	E7
Normandy Elementary School 26920 Normandy Rd, BYVL, 44140	2620	A5
Normandy Senior High School 2500 W Pleasant Valley Rd, PRMA, 44134	3014	D1
Northfield Baptist Christian School 311 W Aurora Rd, SgHT, 44067	3152	D1
Northfield Elementary School 9374 Olde 8 Rd, NCtT, 44067	3017	E7
North High School 34041 Stevens Blvd, ETLK, 44095	2250	A3
North Madison Elementary School 6735 N Ridge Rd, MadT, 44057	1942	B4
North Olmsted High School 5755 Burns Rd, NOSD, 44070	2878	E1
North Olmsted Middle School 27351 Butternut Ridge Rd, NOSD, 44070	2749	E7
North Ridgeville High School 34600 Bainbridge Rd, NRDV, 44039	2877	B4
North Ridgeville Middle School 35895 Center Ridge Rd, NRDV, 44039	2877	A3
North Royalton High School 14713 Ridge Rd, NRYN, 44133	3148	E1
North Royalton Middle School 14709 Ridge Rd, NRYN, 44133	3148	E1
Northwood Junior High School 700 Gulf Rd, ELYR, 44035	2875	C4
Notre Dame-Cathedral Latin School 13000 Auburn Rd, MsnT, 44024	2634	A1
Notre Dame Elementary School 13000 Auburn Rd, MsnT, 44024	2634	A1
Oakwood Elementary School 925 Spruce St, ELYR, 44035	2874	D4
Oberlin High School 281 N Pleasant St, OBLN, 44074	3138	E1
Oliver Perry Elementary School 18400 Schenely Av, CLEV, 44119	2372	E5
Olmsted Falls High School 26939 Bagley Rd, OmsT, 44138	2878	E6
Olmsted Falls Middle School 27045 Bagley Rd, OmsT, 44138	2878	D6
Onaway Elementary School 3115 Woodbury Rd, SRHT, 44120	2627	B6
Open Door Christian School 8287 W Ridge Rd, ELYR, 44035	2874	A5
Orange High School 32000 Chagrin Blvd, PRPK, 44124	2759	D2
Orchard Hollow Elementary School 8700 Hendricks Rd, MNTR, 44060	2144	C3
Orchard Middle School 6800 Som Center Rd, SLN, 44139	2889	A7
Orchard School of Science 4200 Bailey Av, CLEV, 44113	2624	B6
Our Lady of Angels School 3644 Rocky River Dr, CLEV, 44111	2752	B2
Our Lady of Good Counsel School 4419 Pearl Rd, CLEV, 44109	2754	C5
Our Lady of Mt Carmel 1355 W 70th St, CLEV, 44102	2624	A5
Our Lady of Mt Carmel School 29840 Euclid Av, WKLF, 44092	2374	C2
Our Lady of Peace School 12406 Buckingham Av, CLEV, 44120	2626	E5
Our Shepherd Lutheran School 508 Mentor Av, PNVL, 44077	2146	A1
Oxford Elementary School 939 Quilliams Rd, CVHT, 44121	2497	E5
Padua Franciscan High School 6740 State Rd, PRMA, 44134	2883	B5
Park Elementary School 111 Goodrich Ct, CRDN, 44024	2380	A6
Parknoll Elementary School 499 Nobottom Rd, BERA, 44017	2879	E5
Park Side Elementary School 6845 Som Center Rd, SLN, 44139	2889	A7
Parkside Intermediate School 24525 Hilliard Blvd, WTLK, 44145	2750	D1
Parkview Intermediate School 21620 Mastick Rd, FWPK, 44126	2751	B5
Parma Heights Christian Academy 8971 W Ridgewood Dr, PMHT, 44130	2882	D5
Parma Park Elementary School 6800 Commonwealth Blvd, PMHT, 44130	2882	A5
Parma Senior High School 6285 W 54th St, PRMA, 44134	2883	A3
Patrick Henry Middle School 1000 Lakeview Rd, CLEV, 44108	2496	D5
Paul L Dunbar Elementary School 2200 W 28th St, CLEV, 44113	2624	D5
Paul Revere K-8 School 10706 Sandusky Av, CLEV, 44105	2756	C2
Paul S Gardiner Elementary School 9421 Bainbridge Rd, BbgT, 44023	2891	E5
Pearl Road Elementary School 6125 Pearl Rd, PMHT, 44130	2882	C3
Perry Elementary School 1 Learning Ln, PRRY, 44081	2042	C1
Perry High School 1 Success Blvd, PryT, 44081	2042	C1
Perry Middle School 2 Learning Ln, PRRY, 44081	2042	C1

FEATURE NAME Address City ZIP Code	MAP#	GRID
Phillips-Osborne School 150 Gillett St, PNVL, 44077	2146	A1
Pine Intermediate School 4267 Dover Center Rd, NOSD, 44070	2750	A5
Pinnacle Charter Academy 860 E 222nd St, EUCL, 44119	2373	B4
Pleasant Valley Elementary School 9906 W Pleasant Valley Rd, PRMA, 44130	2882	C7
Pleasantview Elementary School 7700 Malibu Dr, PRMA, 44130	3013	A1
Powers Elementary School 401 Washington St, AMHT, 44001	2872	E1
Preparing Academic Leaders Academy 21100 Southgate Park Blvd, MPHT, 44137	2887	A1
Prospect Elementary School 1843 Stanwood Rd, ECLE, 44112	2497	B5
Prospect Elementary School 1410 Prospect St, ELYR, 44035	3006	C1
Prospect Elementary School 36 S Prospect St, OBLN, 44074	3138	C2
Puritas Community Charter School 15204 Puritas Av, CLEV, 44135	2752	C5
Raintree Academy 3150 Mayfield Rd, CVHT, 44118	2627	C1
Ramah Academy 4770 Lee Rd, CLEV, 44128	2757	C6
Randallwood Elementary School 21865 Clarkwood Pkwy, HIHL, 44128	2758	B4
Ratner School 4900 Anderson Rd, LNHT, 44124	2498	E5
Raymond Elementary School 18500 Raymond St, MPHT, 44137	2757	D7
RB Chamberlin Middle School 10270 Ravenna Rd, TNBG, 44087	3019	D7
Red Bird Elementary School 1956 Red Bird Rd, MadT, 44057	1942	A1
Redwood Elementary School 32967 Redwood Blvd, AVLK, 44012	2617	E2
Regina High School 1857 S Green Rd, SELD, 44121	2628	C2
Renwood Elementary School 8020 Deerfield Dr, PRMA, 44129	2882	E3
Reynolds Elementary School 6176 Reynolds Rd, MNTR, 44060	2143	C3
RG Jones International School 3575 W 130th St, CLEV, 44111	2753	A1
Rice Elementary School 7640 Lake Shore Blvd, MNTR, 44060	2143	D3
Richmond Heights Christian School 25595 Chardon Rd, RDHT, 44143	2373	E7
Richmond Heights Elementary School 447 Richmond Rd, RDHT, 44143	2498	E3
Richmond Heights High School 447 Richmond Rd, RDHT, 44143	2498	E2
Richmond Heights Middle School 447 Richmond Rd, RDHT, 44143	2498	E3
Ridge-Brook Elementary School 7915 Manhattan Av, PRMA, 44129	2753	E7
Ridgebury Elementary School 1111 Alvey Rd, LNHT, 44124	2499	A6
Ridge Junior High School 7860 Johnnycake Ridge Rd, MNTR, 44060	2251	E3
Riveredge Elementary School 224 Emerson Av, BERA, 44017	2880	B4
Riverside High School 585 Riverside Dr, PnvT, 44077	2146	D2
Riverside School 14601 Montrose Av, CLEV, 44111	2622	D7
Roadoan Elementary School 4525 Roadoan Rd, BKLN, 44144	2753	D5
Robert C Lindsey Elementary School 11844 Caves Rd, CsTp, 44026	2501	D4
Robert Fulton Elementary School 3291 E 140th St, CLEV, 44120	2627	A7
Rockside Elementary School 5740 Lawn Av, MPHT, 44137	2886	A2
Rocky River High School 20951 Detroit Rd, RKRV, 44116	2621	C6
Rocky River Middle School 1631 Lakeview Av, RKRV, 44116	2621	D6
Roosevelt Elementary School 6121 W River Rd S, ELYR, 44035	2874	E7
Roosevelt Elementary School 551 E 200th St, EUCL, 44119	2373	A4
Roosevelt Elementary School 14237 Athens Av, LKWD, 44107	2622	D6
Rose Education Center 5515 Ira Av, CLEV, 44144	2754	A6
Rowland Elementary School 4300 Bayard Rd, SELD, 44121	2628	B2
Roxboro Elementary School 2405 Roxboro Rd, CVHT, 44106	2626	E4
Roxboro Middle School 2400 Roxboro Rd, CVHT, 44106	2626	E4
Roxbury Elementary School 6795 Solon Blvd, SLN, 44139	2888	E7
Royal View Elementary School 13220 Ridge Rd, NRYN, 44133	3013	E7
Royalview Elementary School 31500 Royalview Dr, WLWK, 44095	2249	D6
Rozelle Elementary School 12917 Phillips Av, ECLE, 44112	2496	E6
Ruffing Montessori School East 3380 Fairmount Blvd, CVHT, 44118	2627	C5
Ruffing Mont Rocky River School 1285 Orchard Park Dr, RKRV, 44116	2621	A6
Rushwood Elementary School 8200 Rushwood Ln, SgHT, 44067	3017	C6
Sailorway Middle School 5355 Sailorway Dr, VMLN, 44089	2741	A7
St. Adalbert School 56 Adelbert St, BERA, 44017	2880	C6
St. Adalbert School 2345 E 83rd St, CLEV, 44104	2626	A4
St. Agatha-St. Aloysius School 640 Lakeview Rd, CLEV, 44108	2496	D4
St. Albert-The Great School 6667 Wallings Rd, NRYN, 44133	3013	E6
St. Angela Merici School 20830 Lorain Rd, FWPK, 44126	2751	C3
St. Ann School 2160 Stillman Rd, CVHT, 44118	2627	B3
St. Anselm School 13013 Chillicothe Rd, CsTp, 44026	2632	B1
St. Anthony of Padua School 1339 E Erie Av, LORN, 44052	2615	A5

FEATURE NAME Address City ZIP Code	MAP#	GRID
St. Anthony of Padua School 6800 State Rd, PRMA, 44134	2883	B5
St. Augustine Academy 14808 Lake Av, LKWD, 44107	2622	D4
St. Barnabas School 9200 Olde 8 Rd, NCtT, 44067	3153	A1
St. Bernadette School 2300 Clague Rd, WTLK, 44145	2750	E2
St. Brendan School 4242 Brendan Ln, NOSD, 44070	2750	E5
St. Bridget School 5620 Hauserman Rd, PRMA, 44130	2882	C1
St. Charles Borromeo School 7107 Wilber Av, PRMA, 44129	2882	E2
St. Christopher School 1610 Lakeview Av, RKRV, 44116	2621	D6
St. Clair Elementary School 280 N St. Clair St, PNVL, 44077	2040	B7
St. Clare School 5655 Mayfield Rd, LNHT, 44124	2499	B7
St. Columbkille School 6740 Broadview Rd, PRMA, 44134	2883	E5
St. Dominic School 3455 Norwood Rd, SRHT, 44122	2757	E1
St. Edward High School 13500 Detroit Av, LKWD, 44107	2622	E4
St. Felicitas School 140 Richmond Rd, EUCL, 44117	2373	E5
St. Francis de Sales School 3421 Snow Rd, PRMA, 44134	2883	C2
St. Francis of Assisi School 6850 Mayfield Rd, GSML, 44040	2500	B7
St. Francis School 7206 Myron Av, CLEV, 44103	2495	E7
St. Gabriel School 9935 Johnnycake Ridge Rd, CcdT, 44060	2145	C7
St. Gregory-The Great School 4478 Rushton Rd, SELD, 44121	2498	C7
St. Helen School 12060 Kinsman Rd, NbyT, 44065	2764	E1
St. Ignatius High School 1911 W 30th St, CLEV, 44113	2624	C5
St. Ignatius of Antioch Elementary School 10205 Lorain Av, CLEV, 44111	2623	C7
St. Jerome Elementary School 15100 Lake Shore Blvd, CLEV, 44110	2372	B7
St. Joan of Arc School 498 E Washington St, CNFL, 44022	2761	C6
St. John Bosco School 6460 Pearl Rd, PMHT, 44130	2882	A4
St. John Lutheran School 1027 E 176th St, CLEV, 44119	2372	D6
St. John Lutheran School 11333 Granger Rd, GDHT, 44125	2756	D7
St. John Lutheran School 4386 Mayfield Rd, SELD, 44121	2498	C7
St. John Nepomucene School 3777 Independence Rd, CLEV, 44105	2755	C2
St. Josaphat Ukrainian School 5720 State Rd, PRMA, 44134	2883	C2
St. Joseph Academy 3430 Rocky River Dr, CLEV, 44111	2752	B1
St. Joseph Catholic School 11045 Saint Joseph Blvd, ManT, 44255	3159	C4
St. Joseph Collinwood School 14405 St. Clair Av, CLEV, 44110	2497	A3
St. Joseph School 175 St. Joseph Dr, AMHT, 44001	2872	E1
St. Joseph School 32929 Lake Rd, AVLK, 44012	2617	E1
St. Jude School 594 Poplar St, ELYR, 44035	2875	D4
St. Justin Martyr School 35741 Stevens Blvd, ETLK, 44095	2250	B4
St. Leo-The Great School 4900 Broadview Rd, CLEV, 44109	2754	D6
St. Louis School 2463 N Taylor Rd, CVHT, 44121	2497	D7
St. Luke School 13889 Clifton Blvd, LKWD, 44107	2622	E4
St. Mark Lutheran School 4464 Pearl Rd, CLEV, 44109	2754	C5
St. Mark School 15724 Montrose Av, CLEV, 44111	2622	C7
St. Martin De-Porres High School 6111 Lausche Av, CLEV, 44103	2495	D7
St. Martin of Tours School 14600 Turney Rd, MPHT, 44137	2886	A4
St. Mary Byzantine School 4600 State Rd, CLEV, 44109	2754	C5
St. Mary of the Falls School 8262 Columbia Rd, ODFL, 44138	2879	C6
St. Mary School 2680 Stoney Ridge Rd, AVON, 44011	2747	D2
St. Mary School 265 Baker St, BERA, 44017	2880	A6
St. Mary School 716 E 156th St, CLEV, 44110	2497	B2
St. Mary School 401 North St, CRDN, 44024	2379	E5
St. Mary School 237 4th St, ELYR, 44035	2875	B7
St. Mary School 8540 Mentor Av, MNTR, 44060	2252	B1
St. Mary School 268 N State St, PNVL, 44077	2040	B7
St. Mary School 5450 Ohio St, VMLN, 44089	2740	E5
St. Mel School 14440 Triskett Rd, CLEV, 44111	2752	D1
St. Michael School 6906 Chestnut Rd, INDE, 44131	2884	E5
St. Monica School 13633 Rockside Rd, GDHT, 44125	2885	E2
St. Paschal Baylon School 5360 Wilson Mills Rd, HDHT, 44143	2499	A5
St. Patrick West Park School 17720 Puritas Av, CLEV, 44135	2752	A5
St. Paul Lutheran School 27981 Detroit Rd, WTLK, 44145	2619	E7
St. Peter Chanel High School 480 Northfield Rd, BDFD, 44146	2887	A2
St. Peter-Lorain School 3601 Oberlin Av, LORN, 44052	2744	D3
St. Peter-North Ridgeville School 35749 Center Ridge Rd, NRDV, 44039	2877	A3

Cleveland Points of Interest Index

Schools

FEATURE NAME Address City ZIP Code	MAP#	GRID
St. Raphael School 525 Dover Center Rd, BYVL, 44140	2620	A5
St. Richard School 26855 Lorain Rd, NOSD, 44070	2750	A7
St. Rita School 33200 Baldwin Rd, SLN, 44139	2888	E5
St. Robert Bellarmine School 23802 Lake Shore Blvd, EUCL, 44123	2373	C1
St. Rocco School 3205 Fulton Rd, CLEV, 44109	2624	C7
St. Stanislaus School 6615 Forman Av, CLEV, 44105	2755	E1
St. Therese School 10608 Penfield Av, GDHT, 44125	2756	C7
St. Thomas Lutheran School 21165 Detroit Rd, RKRV, 44116	2621	C6
St. Thomas More School 4180 N Amber Dr, BKLN, 44144	2753	E4
St. Vincent de Paul School 13442 Lorain Av, CLEV, 44111	2752	E1
St. Vincent de Paul School 41315 N Ridge Rd, EyrT, 44035	2745	E6
St. William School 351 E 260th St, EUCL, 44132	2373	E1
Samuel Bissell Elementary School 1811 Glenwood Dr, TNBG, 44087	3019	C4
Scranton Elementary School 1991 Barber Av, CLEV, 44113	2624	D6
Second New Hope Christian Academy 2917 E 116th St, CLEV, 44120	2626	D5
Shaker Heights High School 15911 Aldersyde Dr, SRHT, 44120	2627	B7
Shaker Heights Middle School 20600 Shaker Blvd, SRHT, 44122	2628	A6
Shaw High School 15320 Euclid Av, ECLE, 44112	2497	B5
Sheffield Middle School 1919 Harris Rd, SFLD, 44054	2616	C7
Shiloh Middle School 2303 Grantwood Dr, PRMA, 44134	2883	D3
Shore Junior High School 5670 Hopkins Rd, MNTR, 44060	2144	B1
Shupe Elementary School 600 Shupe Av, AMHT, 44001	2872	D3
Smith Elementary School 535 Wyleswood Dr, BERA, 44017	3010	E1
Solon High School 33600 Inwood Dr, SLN, 44139	2889	A6
Solon Middle School 6835 Som Center Rd, SLN, 44139	2889	A7
South Amherst Middle School 152 W Main St, SAHT, 44001	2872	B7
South High School 7415 Broadway Av, CLEV, 44105	2756	A2
South High School 5000 Shankland Rd, WLBY, 44094	2250	C7
Southlyn Elementary School 1340 Professor Rd, SELD, 44121	2498	D7
South Street Elementary School 5735 South St, VMLN, 44089	2740	E5
Spencer Elementary School 4641 N Ridge Rd E, GnvT, 44041	1944	E3
Spruce Primary School 28590 Windsor Dr, NOSD, 44070	2878	D2
SS Cosmas & Damian School 10429 Ravenna Rd, TNBG, 44087	3019	D6
SS Cyril-Methodius School 1639 Alameda Av, LKWD, 44107	2623	A6
SS Joseph-John School 12580 Pearl Rd, SGVL, 44149	3011	D6
SS Peter-Paul School 4740 Turney Rd, GDHT, 44125	2756	B5
SS Thomas Aquinas-Philip School 9101 Superior Av, CLEV, 44108	2496	B7
Stafford Elementary School 19800 Stafford Av, MPHT, 44137	2886	E1
State Road Elementary School 6121 State Rd, PRMA, 44134	2883	C3
State Street Elementary School 348 S State St, PNVL, 44077	2146	B1
Sterling Morton Elementary School 9292 Jordan Dr, MNTR, 44060	2038	E5
Strongsville High School 20025 Lunn Rd, SGVL, 44149	3146	C1
Sunbeam K-8 School 11731 Mt Overlook Av, CLEV, 44120	2626	D4
Sunview Elementary School 5520 Meadow Wood Blvd, LNHT, 44124	2629	B2
Superior Elementary School 1865 Garfield Rd, ECLE, 44112	2497	A7
Surrarrer Elementary School 9306 Priem Rd, SGVL, 44149	3011	A3
Taft Elementary School 13701 Lake Av, LKWD, 44107	2622	E4
Telshe High School 28400 Euclid Av, WKLF, 44092	2374	A4
Temple Emmanuel Religious School 2200 S Green Rd, UNHT, 44118	2628	B3
Tennyson Elementary School 555 Kenilworth Av, SDLK, 44054	2616	B3
Thomas Jefferson Magnet School 1455 E 260th St, EUCL, 44132	2373	E5
Thomas Jefferson Middle School 3145 W 46th St, CLEV, 44109	2624	B7
Thoreau Park Elementary School 5401 W 54th St, PRMA, 44134	2883	A1
Timmons Elementary School 9595 E Washington St, BbgT, 44023	2891	E4
Tremont Montessori School 2409 W 10th St, CLEV, 44113	2624	E6
Trinity High School 12425 Granger Rd, GDHT, 44125	2756	D7
Troy Intermediate School 237 Belmar Blvd, AVLK, 44012	2617	D2
Twinsburg High School 10084 Ravenna Rd, TNBG, 44087	3019	D7
Union K-8 School 6701 Union Av, CLEV, 44127	2755	E1
University Lower School 20701 Brantley Rd, SRHT, 44122	2628	A6
University Upper School 2785 Som Center Rd, HGVL, 44022	2630	A5
Upson Elementary School 490 E 260th St, EUCL, 44132	2373	E1
Urban Community School 4909 Lorain Av, CLEV, 44102	2624	B6
Valley Christian Academy 1037 East Blvd, AURA, 44202	3021	A4
Valley Forge High School 9999 Independence Blvd, PMHT, 44130	2882	C6
Valley Vista Elementary School 4049 Wallings Rd, NRYN, 44133	3014	B5
Vermilion High School 1250 Sanford St, VMLN, 44089	2741	A6
Vermilion Intermediate School 935 Decatur St, VMLN, 44089	2740	D6
Villa Angela-St. Joseph High School 18491 Lake Shore Blvd, CLEV, 44119	2372	E4
Vincent Elementary School 2303 N Ridge Rd E, ShfT, 44055	2746	A6
Wade Park Elementary School 7600 Wade Park Av, CLEV, 44103	2626	A1
Walter G Nord Middle School 501 Lincoln St, AMHT, 44001	2872	D1
Walter Kidder Elementary School 3650 Grafton Rd, BNWK, 44212	3147	A7
Walton Elementary School 3409 Walton Av, CLEV, 44113	2624	C7
Warrensville Heights High School 4270 Northfield Rd, WVHT, 44128	2758	A4
Warrensville Heights Middle School 4285 Warrensville Center Rd, WVHT, 44128	2758	A4
Washington Elementary School 503 Vegas Dr, ETLK, 44095	2250	A2
Washington Elementary School 1025 W 23rd St, LORN, 44052	2744	D2
Watterson-Lake Elementary School 1422 W 74th St, CLEV, 44102	2623	E5
Waverly School 1810 W 54th St, CLEV, 44102	2624	A5
Westerly Elementary School 30301 Wolf Rd, BYVL, 44140	2619	C4
West Geauga High School 13401 Chillicothe Rd, CsTp, 44026	2632	B3
West Geauga Middle School 8611 Cedar Rd, CsTp, 44026	2632	B2
West Lake High School 27830 Hilliard Blvd, WTLK, 44145	2749	E1
West Park Lutheran School 4260 Rocky River Dr, CLEV, 44135	2752	A4
Westview Elementary School 155 Moore Rd, AVLK, 44012	2617	C2
Westwood Elementary School 13738 Caves Rd, RslT, 44072	2631	D4
Westwood Elementary School 19000 Garden Blvd, WVHT, 44128	2757	E4
Westwood Junior High School 42350 Adelbert St, EyrT, 44035	2874	C2
Whitney Young Middle School 17900 Harvard Av, CLEV, 44128	2757	D3
Whittier Middle School 3201 Seneca Av, LORN, 44055	2745	D3
Wickliffe Elementary School 1821 Lincoln Rd, WKLF, 44092	2374	C3
Wickliffe High School 2255 Rockefeller Rd, WKLF, 44092	2374	D3
Wickliffe Middle School 29240 Euclid Av, WKLF, 44092	2374	C3
Wilbur Wright School 11005 Parkhurst Dr, CLEV, 44111	2753	B1
Wilcox Elementary School 34580 Bainbridge Rd, NRDV, 44039	2877	B4
Wilcox Primary School 9198 Darrow Rd, TNBG, 44087	3155	A1
Wiley Middle School 2181 Miramar Blvd, UNHT, 44121	2628	B3
William Barr Elementary School 2180 Lake Breeze Rd, SFLD, 44054	2616	A7
William C Bryant Elementary School 3121 Oak Park Av, CLEV, 44109	2754	C6
William Foster Elementary School 12801 Bangor Av, GDHT, 44125	2885	E1
Willo-Hill Christian School 4200 State Route 306, KTLD, 44094	2251	D6
Willoughby Middle School 36901 Ridge Rd, WLBY, 44094	2250	C7
Willow Elementary School 5004 Glazier Av, CLEV, 44127	2625	C6
Willowick Middle School 31500 Royalview Dr, WLWK, 44095	2249	D6
Windsor Elementary School 264 Windsor Dr, ELYR, 44035	2875	D2
Woodbury Elementary School 15400 S Woodland Rd, SRHT, 44120	2627	B6
Woodland Hills Elementary School 9201 Crane Av, CLEV, 44105	2756	B1
Yavne Girls High School 2475 S Green Rd, BHWD, 44122	2628	C4
Zellers Elementary School 18199 Cook Av, SGVL, 44136	3146	E1

Shopping Centers

FEATURE NAME Address City ZIP Code	MAP#	GRID
Avon Commons Shopping Senter Detroit Rd, AVON, 44011	2618	A7
Beachwood Place Mall 26300 Cedar Rd, BHWD, 44122	2628	E3
City View Center Transportation Blvd, GDHT, 44125	2885	C1
Crocker Park 25 Main St, WTLK, 44145	2749	C1
Eastgate Shopping Center Eastgate Dr, MDHT, 44124	2500	A7
Euclid Square Mall 100 Euclid Square Mall, EUCL, 44132	2373	D4
Great Lakes Mall 7850 Mentor Av, MNTR, 44060	2251	E2
Legacy Village 25001 Cedar Rd, LNHT, 44124	2628	D3
Macedonia Commons 8210 Macedonia Commons Blvd, MCDN, 44056	3153	B1
Marketplace at Four Corners, The N Aurora Rd, BbgT, 44023	3021	A2
Meadowbrook Market Square Northfield Rd, BDFD, 44146	2887	A2
Meadowland Town Center Center St, CRDN, 44024	2379	C5
Midway Mall 3343 Midway Blvd, ELYR, 44035	2875	A2
Painesville Commons & Plaza Mentor Av, PnvT, 44077	2145	D4
Parmatown Mall 7899 W Ridgewood Dr, PRMA, 44129	2882	D5
Parmatown Plaza 7899 Ridge Rd, PRMA, 44129	2882	E5
Plazas at Great Northern, The Lorain Rd, NOSD, 44070	2750	A6
Randall Park Mall 20801 Miles Rd, NRDL, 44128	2758	A5
Richmond Town Square 691 Richmond Rd, RDHT, 44143	2498	E4
Severance Town Center 3640 Mayfield Rd, CVHT, 44118	2497	D7
Southgate USA 20950 Libby Rd, MPHT, 44137	2887	A1
Southland Shopping Center 6871 Pearl Rd, MDBH, 44130	2881	D5
University Square Cedar Rd, SELD, 44118	2628	A3
Vineyards, The 34670 Vine St, ETLK, 44095	2250	A5
Westfield Shoppingtown Great Northern 4954 Great Northern Blvd, NOSD, 44070	2750	B7
Westfield Shoppingtown SouthPark 500 Southpark Ctr, SGVL, 44136	3012	A7
Westgate Mall 3211 Westgate Mall, FWPK, 44126	2751	C1

Subdivisions & Neighborhoods

FEATURE NAME	MAP#	GRID
Alexanders, INDE	3016	A2
Beaver Park, LORN	2743	B3
Brownhelm, VMLN	2871	C3
Collinwood, CyhC	2496	D2
Elberta Beach, VMLN	2741	B4
Geauga Lake, AURA	3021	B4
Mentor Headlands, MNTR	2038	E5
Midpark, PMHT	2881	E5
Parkview, FWPK	2751	A5
Shawville, SFLD	2746	B6
Shore, EUCL	2373	B2
South Lorain, LORN	2745	C3
South Park, INDE	2884	D6
Vermilion-on-the-Lake, VMLN	2741	D4
West Fairport, MNTR	2038	E5
West View, ODFL	3010	B1

Transportation

FEATURE NAME	MAP#	GRID
Amtrak-Cleveland Station, CLEV	2624	D2
Amtrak-Elyria Station, ELYR	2875	C6
Greyhound Bus Lines, ELYR	2875	A6
Greyhound-Cleveland, CLEV	2625	A2
Greyhound-Maple Heights, MPHT	2887	A1
RTA-Ashby Station, SRHT	2627	B7
RTA-Attleboro Station, SRHT	2627	D6
RTA-Avalon Station, SRHT	2757	D1
RTA-Belvoir Station, SRHT	2628	B6
RTA-Brookpark Station, CLEV	2752	A7
RTA-Cleveland Hopkins International Airport, - CLEV	2880	E1
RTA-Courtland Station, SRHT	2627	E6
RTA-Coventry Station, SRHT	2627	A5
RTA-Drexmore Station, CLEV	2627	A6
RTA-E 79th Station, CLEV	2626	A5
RTA-E 105th-Quincy Station, CLEV	2626	B4
RTA-E 116th Station, CLEV	2626	D5
RTA-East 34th-Campus Station, CLEV	2625	B4
RTA-East 55th Station, CLEV	2625	D5
RTA-Eaton Station, SRHT	2627	E6
RTA-Euclid Station, CLEV	2626	D1
RTA-Farnsleigh Station, SRHT	2758	A1
RTA-Flats East Bank Station, CLEV	2624	D3
RTA-Green Station, SRHT	2628	C6
RTA-Kenmore Station, SRHT	2757	D1
RTA-Lee Station, SRHT	2757	C1
RTA-Lynnfield Station, SRHT	2757	D1
RTA-North Coast Station, CLEV	2624	E2
RTA-Onaway Station, SRHT	2627	A6
RTA-Settlers Landing Station, CLEV	2624	D3
RTA-Shaker Square Station, CLEV	2626	E5
RTA-South Harbor Station, CLEV	2624	E1
RTA-Southington Station, SRHT	2627	B5
RTA-South Park Station, SRHT	2627	B5
RTA-South Woodland Station, CLEV	2627	A6
RTA-Superior Station, ECLE	2496	E7
RTA-Tower City-Public Square Station, CLEV	2624	E3
RTA-Triskett Station, CLEV	2622	E7
RTA-University Circle Station, CLEV	2626	D3
RTA-W 3rd Street Station, CLEV	2624	C2
RTA-Warrensville Station, SRHT	2628	A6
RTA-West 25th-Ohio City Station, CLEV	2624	D5
RTA-West 65th-Madison Station, CLEV	2624	A6
RTA-West 117th-Madison Station, CLEV	2623	B6
RTA-West 150th-Puritas Station, CLEV	2752	C3
RTA-West Blvd-Cudell Station, CLEV	2623	C5
RTA-West Green Station, SRHT	2628	B6
RTA-West Park Station, CLEV	2752	D2
RTA-Windermere Station, ECLE	2497	A6
RTA-Woodhill Station, CLEV	2626	B5

Visitor Information

FEATURE NAME Address City ZIP Code	MAP#	GRID
Canal Visitors Center Hillside Rd, VLVW, 44125	2885	C6
Carlisle Visitor Center 12882 Nickle Plate Diagonal Rd, CrlT, 44050	3140	C2
Lake County Visitors Bureau 1610 Mentor Av, PnvT, 44077	2145	C4
Lorain County Visitors Bureau 8025 Leavitt Rd, AhtT, 44001	2873	A4
Lorain County Visitors Bureau 611 Broadway, LORN, 44052	2614	E6
Northern Summit County Tourist Information 453 E Aurora Rd, MCDN, 44056	3153	B1
North Ridgeville Visitors Bureau 34845 Lorain Rd, NRDV, 44039	2877	B7
Visitor Center 1170 Old River Rd, CLEV, 44113	2624	C3
Visitor Center 50 Public Sq, CLEV, 44115	2624	E3
Visitor Center Chillicothe Rd, KTLD, 44094	2251	D6

CUT ALONG DOTTED LINE

RAND McNALLY

Thank you for purchasing this Rand McNally Street Guide!
We value your comments and suggestions.

Please help us serve you better by completing this postage-paid reply card.
This information is for internal use ONLY and will not be distributed or sold to any external third party.

Missing pages? Maybe not... Please refer to the "Using Your Street Guide" page for further explanation.

Street Guide Title: Cleveland **ISBN-13# 978-0-5288-6673-9** **MKT: CLE**

Today's Date: __________ Gender: ☐M ☐F Age Group: ☐18-24 ☐25-31 ☐32-40 ☐41-50 ☐51-64 ☐65+

1. What type of industry do you work in?
   ☐Real Estate ☐Trucking ☐Delivery ☐Construction ☐Utilities ☐Government
   ☐Retail ☐Sales ☐Transportation ☐Landscape ☐Service & Repair
   ☐Courier ☐Automotive ☐Insurance ☐Medical ☐Police/Fire/First Response
   ☐Other, please specify: __________
2. What type of job do you have in this industry? __________
3. Where did you purchase this Street Guide? (store name & city) __________
4. Why did you purchase this Street Guide? __________
5. How often do you purchase an updated Street Guide? ☐Annually ☐2 yrs. ☐3-5 yrs. ☐Other: __________
6. Where do you use it? ☐Primarily in the car ☐Primarily in the office ☐Primarily at home ☐Other: __________
7. How do you use it? ☐Exclusively for business ☐Primarily for business but also for personal or leisure use
   ☐Both work and personal evenly ☐Primarily for personal use ☐Exclusively for personal use
8. What do you use your Street Guide for?
   ☐Find Addresses ☐In-route navigation ☐Planning routes ☐Other: __________
   Find points of interest: ☐Schools ☐Parks ☐Buildings ☐Shopping Centers ☐Other: __________
9. How often do you use it? ☐Daily ☐Weekly ☐Monthly ☐Other: __________
10. Do you use the internet for maps and/or directions? ☐Yes ☐No
11. How often do you use the internet for directions? ☐Daily ☐Weekly ☐Monthly ☐Other: __________
12. Do you use any of the following mapping products in addition to your Street Guide?
    ☐Folded paper maps ☐Folded laminated maps ☐Wall maps ☐GPS ☐PDA ☐In-car navigation ☐Phone maps
13. What features, if any, would you like to see added to your Street Guide? __________
14. What features or information do you find most useful in your Rand McNally Street Guide? (please specify)
    ____
15. Please provide any additional comments or suggestions you have. __________

We strive to provide you with the most current updated information available if you know of a map correction, please notify us here.

Where is the correction? Map Page #: __________ Grid #: __________ Index Page #: __________

Nature of the correction: ☐Street name missing ☐Street name misspelled ☐Street information incorrect
☐Incorrect location for point of interest ☐Index error ☐Other: __________

Detail: __________

I would like to receive information about updated editions and special offers from Rand McNally
☐via e-mail E-mail address: __________
☐via postal mail
Your Name: __________ Company (if used for work): __________
Address: __________ City/State/ZIP: __________

Thank you for your time and help. We are working to serve you better.
This information is for internal use ONLY and will not be distributed or sold to any external third party.

CUT ALONG DOTTED LINE

TAPE SHUT TAPE SHUT

get directions at
randmcnally.com

2ND FOLD LINE

CUT ALONG DOTTED LINE

NO POSTAGE
NECESSARY
IF MAILED
IN THE
UNITED STATES

BUSINESS REPLY MAIL

FIRST-CLASS MAIL PERMIT NO. 388 CHICAGO IL

POSTAGE WILL BE PAID BY ADDRESSEE

RAND MCNALLY
CONSUMER AFFAIRS
PO BOX 7600
CHICAGO IL 60680-9915

1ST FOLD LINE

RAND McNALLY

The most trusted name on the map.

You'll never need to ask for directions again with these Rand McNally products!

- EasyFinder® Laminated Maps
- Folded Maps
- Street Guides
- Wall Maps
- CustomView Wall Maps
- Road Atlases
- Motor Carriers' Road Atlases

CUT ALONG DOTTED LINE

SGTG_07